INTRODUCTORY
SCOTS LAW

THEORY AND PRACTICE

SECOND EDITION

SEÁN J CROSSAN

ALISTAIR B WYLIE

HODDER
GIBSON
AN HACHETTE UK COMPANY

The Publishers would like to thank the following for permission to reproduce copyright material:

Acknowledgements

Every effort has been made to trace all copyright holders, but if any have been inadvertently overlooked the Publishers will be pleased to make the necessary arrangements at the first opportunity.

Although every effort has been made to ensure that website addresses are correct at time of going to press, Hodder Gibson cannot be held responsible for the content of any website mentioned in this book. It is sometimes possible to find a relocated web page by typing in the address of the home page for a website in the URL window of your browser.

Hachette's policy is to use papers that are natural, renewable and recyclable products and made from wood grown in sustainable forests. The logging and manufacturing processes are expected to conform to the environmental regulations of the country of origin.

Orders: please contact Bookpoint Ltd, 130 Milton Park, Abingdon, Oxon OX14 4SB. Telephone: (44) 01235 827720. Fax: (44) 01235 400454. Lines are open 9.00 – 5.00, Monday to Saturday, with a 24-hour message answering service. Visit our website at www.hoddereducation.co.uk. Hodder Gibson can be contacted direct on: Tel: 0141 848 1609; Fax: 0141 889 6315; email: hoddergibson@hodder.co.uk

Cover photo © Ciaran Donnelly/Faculty of Advocates
Illustrations by Phoenix Photosetting, Chatham, Kent
Typeset in 10/13pt ITC Century Light by Phoenix Photosetting, Chatham, Kent
Printed and bound in Great Britain by CPI Group (UK) Ltd, Croydon, CR0 4YY

A catalogue record for this title is available from the British Library

ISBN-13: 978 0340 99174 9

CONTENTS

INTRODUCTION

Welcome to Introductory Scots Law: Theory and Practice 2nd Edition. This new version includes updated cases as well as comprehensive coverage of the latest legislation. It builds on the success of the first edition and also includes expanded chapters on criminal law, consumer law and employment law.

We have also included a range of legal documents (e.g. Sheriff Civil Court forms, Initial Writs and Applications to the Office of Employment Tribunals) which can be accessed online at **www.hoddereducation.co.uk/introscotslaw**. These resources are signposted throughout the book and will, hopefully, enhance the learning experience for students and general readers of the text.

This book is intended as a general introduction to the laws of Scotland (with an emphasis on business law). It has been written in accessible language wherever possible and is particularly suitable for students who are studying SQA units in law at National and Higher National Qualification levels. It will also be of use to students who are studying Scots law as part of a university course or a professional level course and also to those individuals with a general interest in Scots law.

The authors are experienced educators with over 20 years of teaching experience between them gained in the secondary, further and higher education sectors. They are graduates of both Scottish and English universities and, consequently, have experience of both Scots and English law.

Each chapter is structured in the same way for ease of use and comprises:

◆ Chapter introduction
◆ Main content
  • Key points
  • Online resources
  • Highlighted cases
  • Highlighted legislation
◆ Summary
◆ Revision questions comprising
  • Short answer questions
  • Case studies
  • Essay-type questions

Readers can also access suggested answers to questions at **www.hoddereducation.co.uk/introscotslaw**.

We hope that readers will find this second edition both useful and rewarding.

The authors have attempted to state the law as accurately as possible until 1 February 2010. From time to time, we offer an updates service for the book at **www.hoddereducation.co.uk/introscotslaw**.

We would remind readers that this book is a general legal textbook and it is no substitute for expert legal advice. The authors cannot possibly set out every single possible legal scenario which might be relevant to a particular dispute or case. Anyone thinking of contemplating legal action in Scotland should, therefore, consult a suitably qualified Scottish solicitor before embarking on such a course. It is worth reminding readers that laws can change very quickly and it is always sensible to take advice as to the current legal position.

Seán J Crossan
Alistair B Wylie
February 2010

SCOTTISH LEGAL FRAMEWORK AND SOURCES OF SCOTS LAW

Introduction

This introductory chapter to the book looks at the framework of the Scottish legal system. The impact of the creation of a Scottish Parliament and continuing European legislation cannot be underestimated and this has an influence on the laws of Scotland and the UK as a whole. The sources of Scots law are also identified and considered along with a detailed look at the civil and criminal justice systems.

This chapter covers the following areas:

- The Scottish Parliament •
- Sources of Scots law •
- The legal profession in Scotland •
- The civil justice system •
- The criminal justice system •
- Alternative methods of resolving legal disputes •
- The influence of European Courts •

The Scottish Parliament

Devolution is the process by which a national body (the Westminster Parliament) delegates or distributes powers to a local or regional body (the Scottish Parliament). In theory, devolution should mean that laws and decisions are made at a level closer to the point at which they will have an impact. The devolution settlement means that Scotland has a Parliament with devolved powers within the United Kingdom. Any powers that remain with the UK Parliament are reserved.

Since the introduction of the Scotland Act 1998, Scotland now has two parliaments which make laws that have a direct impact on Scottish society. These two parliaments are the Westminster or United Kingdom Parliament and the Scottish or Holyrood Parliament.

Key point: There are now two Parliaments which make laws for Scotland – Westminster (London) and Holyrood (Edinburgh)

In a referendum on 11 September 1997, the people of Scotland voted overwhelmingly for the creation of a Scottish Parliament which would have tax varying powers. This would be the first time in almost 300 years that a Parliament making laws for Scotland would sit in Edinburgh. However, unlike the previous Scottish Parliament which was abolished by the Act of Union in 1707, the new Scottish Parliament is not a completely independent body. The Scottish Parliament is an inferior body in comparison to Westminster. True, Westminster has given many powers and responsibilities to the Scottish Parliament, but it is worth bearing in mind that a simple Act of the Westminster Parliament is all that would be required to abolish Scotland's new Parliament. Indeed, Westminster has already abolished a local assembly or parliament.

During the 1970s, Westminster abolished the Stormont Parliament or Assembly which made laws for Northern Ireland. Stormont had been in existence for approximately 50 years, but this did not prevent Westminster from reimposing direct rule on Northern Ireland from London. Admittedly, the abolition of Stormont was carried out against a background of increasing Irish Republican and Loyalist violence in Northern Ireland. Power was devolved to Stormont again in 1999 following the Good Friday Agreement. However, the lesson to draw from Stormont is that Westminster will remain the supreme law making authority in the United Kingdom despite devolution.

The creation of the Scottish Parliament

On 6 May 1999, the Scottish electorate voted in the first election for the Scottish Parliament. No political party secured a majority and this situation led to the formation of a coalition government (the Scottish Executive) supported by the Scottish Labour Party and the Scottish Liberal Democrat Party. Labour's Donald Dewar would become Scotland's First Minister (Prime Minister in all but name). The first session of the Scottish Parliament would begin in July 1999. However, the first few months of the Parliament were seen as an introductory session with Members of the Scottish Parliament (MSPs) being given a chance to settle in to their new positions.

 Key point: The First Minister is effectively the Scottish Prime Minister in all but name.

The organisation of the Scottish Parliament

Currently, the Scottish Parliament has 129 members – 73 are directly elected from local areas or constituencies and the other 56 members are elected using a system which achieves an element of proportional representation (the Additional Member System).

Drawn from these 129 Members of Parliament is the group of Ministers who will form the Scottish Executive (now referred to as the Scottish Government since the Scottish National Party formed a government in May 2007). The political party or parties with a majority of seats will usually form the Scottish Government. The First Minister heads the Scottish Government with the assistance of the Deputy First Minister. The First Minister is nominated by the Parliament and his appointment is confirmed by the British Monarch. The First Minister will advise the Monarch when it comes to the appointment of other Scottish Government Ministers and the appointment of the Lord Advocate and the Solicitor-General for Scotland. Legal advice is provided to the Scottish Government by the Lord Advocate and the Solicitor-General for Scotland.

The Scottish Parliament elects one of its members to serve as the Presiding Officer (this individual would be referred to as the Speaker at Westminster) and two other members to serve as his deputies. The Presiding Officer and his deputies chair sessions of the Parliament, convene and chair meetings of the Parliamentary Bureau, interpret the rules in relation to parliamentary procedure and, generally, represent the parliament at meetings with other parliamentary and government bodies.

 Key point: 129 Members of Parliament (MSPs) sit at Holyrood who elect a Presiding Officer (speaker) from their number to chair sessions of the parliament.

Devolved powers

Clearly, the Scottish people had expressed their desire for the creation of such a body in the referendum of September 1997. This was the easy part. It took specialist government lawyers a considerable amount of time and effort to draw up the detailed plans for the Scottish Parliament. Subsequently, these plans were introduced in the shape of the Scotland Bill in January 1998 to Westminster where they had to pass through both the House of Commons and the House of Lords before being given the Royal Assent. As a result of the Scotland Act 1998, the Scottish Parliament was given powers to make laws for Scotland.

Before the first session of the Scottish Parliament 1999–2003 (each Scottish Parliament sits for a four-year fixed period), all statute law for Scotland was dealt with by Westminster. Many Scots felt that Westminster's role in the law-making process for Scotland was unsatisfactory because it made laws for the United Kingdom as a whole and these laws were not always suited to Scottish local conditions.

 Key point: Devolution allows the Scottish Parliament to create its own laws in certain predetermined (devolved) areas of policy.

With devolution, the Scottish Parliament can now pass laws in the following areas:

- ◆ Agriculture, forestry and fishing
- ◆ Arts, culture and sport
- ◆ Education and training
- ◆ Environment
- ◆ Health
- ◆ Housing
- ◆ Local government
- ◆ Planning
- ◆ Scottish legal system (including criminal and civil justice)
- ◆ Social work
- ◆ Statistics, public registers and the Scottish records
- ◆ Tourism, economic development and financial assistance to industry

◆ Transport
◆ Police and Fire Services

By March 2007, the Scottish Parliament had already passed some 127 Acts (with another nine awaiting Royal Assent) as a result of its devolved powers since 1999. This quickly led to some major differences in the law between Scotland and the rest of the United Kingdom. Examples include the abolition of tuition fees for students courtesy of the Education (Graduate Endowment and Student Support) (Scotland) Act 2001 and the provision of free care for the elderly in the Community Care and Health (Scotland) Act 2002. The rest of the United Kingdom has not followed Scotland's lead in these areas.

Session 1 Bills by type and outcome (as at 26 March 2007)

Type of bill	Introduced	Passed	Withdrawn	Fallen
Executive	51	50	1	Nil
Committee	3	3	Nil	Nil
Member's	16	8	2	6
Private	3	1	Nil	2
Total	**73**	**62**	**3**	**8**

Session 2 Bills by type and outcome (as at 26 March 2007)

Type of bill	Introduced	Passed		Total passed	With-drawn	Fallen	In progress at 26 March
		Received Royal Assent	Awaiting Royal Assent				
Executive	53	46	7	53	Nil	Nil	Nil
Committee	1	1	Nil	1	Nil	Nil	Nil
Member's	18	2	1	3	5	6	4
Private	9	7	1	8	Nil	Nil	1
Totals	**81**	**56**	**9**	**65**	**5**	**6**	**5**

Source: The Scottish Parliament (www.scottish.parliament.uk)

The Calman Commission on Scottish Devolution

This body commenced a review of the process of devolution which had been established under the provisions of the Scotland Act 1998. The Commission commenced its work in April 2008 and it was headed by Sir Kenneth Calman, Chancellor of the University of Glasgow. If the Commission's proposals are ever implemented, it will mean that the Scottish Parliament will receive significant, additional powers from Westminster. The creation of the Commission was officially approved by the UK Prime Minister, Gordon Brown in January 2008.

The specific remit of the Commission (taken from its website: www.commissiononscottishdevolution.org.uk) was:

"To review the provisions of the Scotland Act 1998 in the light of experience and to recommend any changes to the present constitutional arrangements that would enable the Scottish Parliament to serve the people of Scotland better, improve the financial accountability of the Scottish Parliament, and continue to secure the position of Scotland within the United Kingdom."

The Commission published its full report on 15 June 2009 and amongst other things, it proposed that the Scottish Parliament be allowed to set its own rate of income tax for the country as the way in which Scotland is funded from the public purse should be radically reformed. It also suggested that the Scottish Parliament should have responsibility for some aspects of road traffic legislation (the speed and drink driving limits) which, currently, are an area reserved to Westminster. Whether the proposals of the Calman Commission will be implemented remain to be seen and are to be the subject of debate for those individuals interested in the continuing development of the Scottish Parliament.

The full report of the Commission and its potential implications for the future governance of Scotland can be viewed at the official website referred to above.

Reserved matters

Despite the introduction of devolved government, Westminster will continue to make laws for Scotland in many important areas. In fact, Acts of the Scottish Parliament are considered to have the status of secondary legislation which has an inferior status to primary legislation which Westminster deals with. The areas of policy that Westminster will continue to have responsibility for are known as reserved matters. These include:

- Abortion, human fertilisation, embryology, genetics, xeno-transplantation and vivisection
- Common markets
- Constitutional matters
- Data protection
- Employment law
- Energy
- Equal opportunities
- Foreign policy, defence and national security matters
- Gambling and the National Lottery
- Immigration and nationality
- Social security
- Taxation, economic and monetary matters
- Trade and industry (including competition policy and consumer protection)
- Transport

 Key point: Acts of the Scottish Parliament are regarded as secondary legislation and therefore have a lower status than Acts of the Westminster Parliament.

If, for example, the Scottish Parliament wished to introduce a new law which had the effect of closing down the Faslane nuclear submarine base on the River Clyde, this would not be permissible. The Scottish Parliament has no right to legislate in defence matters. If the Scottish Parliament did go ahead and pass an Act which attempted to close down Faslane, this would be at best an example of gesture politics and, at worst, would leave the Parliament open to a serious legal challenge in the courts. Put simply, such an Act of the Scottish Parliament would have no legal effect.

The distinction between devolved and reserved matters is in theory a simple one, but practically speaking, there may be areas of policy where both parliaments could potentially legislate. In the future, this may lead to conflicts between Holyrood and Westminster. Immigration issues, for example, are a reserved matter, but as the row over the Dungavel Detention Centre during 2003 has shown, the division of responsibilities between Holyrood and Westminster is not always clear-cut. Controversy had arisen concerning the practice of forcing the children of detainees to be educated in Dungavel itself thus denying them the opportunity to be taught in local schools. At first glance, it would appear that the UK Home Secretary has responsibility for Dungavel, but the education of children is a matter for the Scottish Parliament.

Although the Scotland Act 1998 appears to make a clear distinction between areas of policy which are reserved to the Westminster Parliament and those powers which are devolved to the Scottish Parliament, in practice problems have inevitably arisen where areas of policy can merge and boundaries can become very blurred.

The UK Energy Bill was introduced to the Westminster Parliament in 2008, but its provisions did not extend to Scotland. Although energy is a reserved issue, the current Nationalist-led Scottish Government has consistently opposed the UK Government's proposals to concentrate on nuclear power stations in order to meet the nation's energy needs. The Scottish Government has been very successful because it publicly stated that it would not grant planning permission for the building of additional nuclear power facilities in Scotland. The planning system in Scotland is, ultimately, under the control of the Scottish Parliament.

In September 2009, the Scottish Government had to decide whether or not to release Mr Al Megrahi, the Libyan convicted of the bombing of the Pan Am passenger jet over Lockerbie in 1988, on compassionate grounds. Although the decision to release Mr Al Megrahi was of critical importance to the UK Government's foreign policy and its relationship with the American Government, it was Kenny McAskill MSP, the Scottish Justice Secretary, and not the UK Justice Secretary who decided to release Mr Al Megrahi.

 Key point: The Scottish Parliament cannot legislate in policy areas, for example, defence that are regarded as being reserved matters.

The Sewel Motion

There will be occasions when Westminster will introduce a law to Scotland which, strictly speaking, could have been dealt with by the Scottish Parliament. Under what is known as the Sewel Motion, the Scottish Parliament can ask Westminster to pass laws for Scotland. In September 2003, the Scottish Parliament passed the issue of same-sex relationships being given similar status to marriage to Westminster. This means that Westminster will introduce a Bill which covers the whole of the United Kingdom, not just for Scotland. The use of the Sewel Motion can save valuable Scottish parliamentary time. However, this procedure has been criticised because it gives the Scottish Parliament an opportunity to avoid legislating on awkward social issues like same-sex marriage.

There is no legal requirement in the Scotland Act 1998 that the Scottish Parliament should be forced to ask the Westminster Parliament to legislate on its behalf in relation to a devolved issue and is merely an example of a non-binding constitutional convention or practice.

By October 2008, Sewel Motions had been invoked no fewer than 99 times by the Scottish Parliament, with four more proposals to use the convention under consideration in 2009. The willingness of the Scottish Parliament to use the Sewel Motion has been criticised by more nationalist minded individuals who see its widespread application as undermining the importance of Holyrood as a legislative body.

 Key point: The Sewel Motion allows the Scottish Parliament to ask the Westminster Parliament to pass laws for Scotland.

How a Bill becomes law in Scotland

In common with Westminster, a draft law or Bill introduced in the Scottish Parliament must complete various procedures in order to become part of Scots law. The three main types of Bill are:

◆ Executive Bills
◆ Committee Bills
◆ Member's Bills

Executive Bills are promoted and supported by the Scottish Government. If the Scottish Government wishes to introduce a Bill it must also be accompanied by extensive notes detailing what impact the Bill will have on a range of issues such as, for example, human rights and equal opportunities.

Committee Bills are introduced into parliament by one or more of the various parliamentary committees whose membership consists of different MSPs from the different political parties.

Member's Bills are the result of an individual MSP taking it upon himself or herself to introduce a Bill with or without the support of the Executive or a committee.

 Key point: There are three types of Bills that may be introduced in the Scottish Parliament – Executive Bills, Members' Bills and Committee Bills.

There are, however, a number of important differences between Westminster and the Scottish Parliament. It should be remembered that Westminster has two Houses of Parliament – the Commons and the Lords – with a Bill having to pass through each House in order to receive the Royal Assent. The Scottish Parliament by comparison has one chamber only through which a Bill must pass.

The committee system in the Scottish Parliament is much more powerful than its Westminster counterparts. Unlike the committees at Westminster, a Holyrood committee can take the initiative and introduce a new Bill to parliament. As there is only one chamber in the parliament, it was always intended that the committees would play a powerful role. A Scottish parliamentary committee is the place where MSPs can really scrutinise the contents of a Bill and propose all sorts of changes or amendments to it. Currently, there are 16 parliamentary committees operating, each one chaired by a Convener. In order to coordinate the work of the committees, the Conveners regularly meet with one another as the Conveners' Group.

Finally, individual MSPs have more of a chance of introducing Bills to parliament and achieving success. Tommy Sheridan, the colourful former MSP, was able to introduce a Bill to outlaw the practice of warrant sales which later became law as the Abolition of Poindings and Warrant Sales (Scotland) Act 2001. Considering the stranglehold that the British Government has over Westminster, it is very unlikely that an ordinary Member of Parliament could have achieved similar results as Tommy Sheridan. Perhaps emboldened by this success, Mr Sheridan introduced a Bill in October 2003 which proposed to abolish the Council Tax and replace it with a local income tax. This time, however, his attempt to change the law was unsuccessful.

 Key point: A Bill is a proposal which may or may not become law at a later date.

When a Bill is introduced to the Scottish Parliament the stages it must undergo depend on whether it is classified as public or private.

Public Bills
Stages of Public Bills

The procedure for a Public Bill introduced in the Parliament is as follows:

(a) consideration of the Bill's general principles and a decision on whether to agree to these principles (**Stage 1**);

(b) consideration of the details of the Bill (**Stage 2**); and

(c) final consideration of the Bill and a decision whether to pass or reject it (**Stage 3**).

Private Bills
Stages of Private Bills

The procedure for a Private Bill introduced in the Parliament is as follows:

(a) consideration of the general principles of the Bill and whether it should proceed as a Private Bill, preliminary consideration of objections and a decision whether to agree to those general principles and whether the Bill should proceed as a Private Bill (**Preliminary Stage**);

(b) consideration of the details of the Private Bill (**Consideration Stage**); and

(c) final consideration of the Private Bill and a decision whether to pass or reject it (**Final Stage**).

If the Scottish Parliament votes in favour of the Bill, it will then be presented to the monarch to receive Royal Assent, thus becoming an Act of the Scottish Parliament.

 Key point: A Bill (whether Public or Private in nature) undergoes three stages as it passes through the Scottish Parliament.

Overview

Although the Scotland Act 1998 gives extensive law-making powers to the Scottish Parliament which will have a direct impact on many areas of Scottish life, it should not be forgotten that the Westminster Parliament remains the supreme law-making authority in the United Kingdom. Unlike the old Scottish Parliament before 1707, Holyrood is not an independent body. It is an inferior and a subordinate body to

Westminster and this will remain the case if and when the people of Scotland ever decide to vote for Scottish independence. Westminster has not given up its right to legislate for Scotland completely. Holyrood will have to be particularly careful that it passes laws in the areas of policy which have been devolved to it by Westminster. Failure to do so may incur Westminster's displeasure and, more seriously, a challenge before the courts.

Sources of Scots Law

The laws of Scotland simply do not appear out of thin air. When we talk about the sources of Scots law, we mean where does a law come from and how is it made? The Scottish legal system has developed over hundreds of years and has been influenced in all sorts of ways by Scotland's history and culture. The feudal system, for example, which was introduced into Scotland from England during the reign of King David I (1124–53), directly influenced how land was owned in Scotland for nearly a thousand years. The remains of this system of landownership are only now being phased out.

 Key point: The Scottish legal system has evolved and developed over hundreds of years.

Scots law is a mixed or hybrid system of law drawing upon many different influences, for example, Roman law and common law. Other hybrid systems of law include systems in Quebec, Louisana and South Africa. England and other Commonwealth countries like English-speaking Canada, New Zealand and Australia are common law jurisdictions where judges have had a great deal of influence in the development of the law. The United States of America is also a common law jurisdiction.

The most important sources of Scots law today are Acts of Parliament, common law, delegated legislation and European Union law. Some sources of law such as feudal law and canon law are of historical interest only. Many of our laws in modern times are deliberately written down for the benefit of future generations. However,

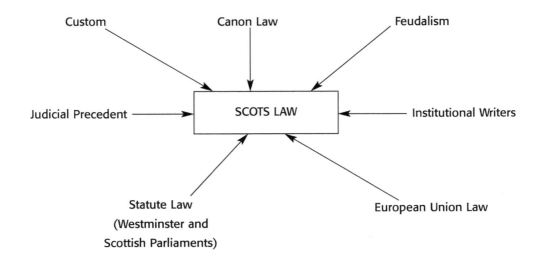

there are numerous legal rules that are unwritten which have been handed down to us as customs and practices. Furthermore, judges very often make laws when they sit in court and these judicial decisions are followed by other courts so that they in turn become binding legal rules.

 Key point: The most important sources of modern Scots law are statute (parliamentary) law, common law and European law.

Acts of Parliament

Acts of Parliament are often referred to as legislation or statute law. Before the introduction of the Scotland Act 1998, the Westminster Parliament (the national parliament of the United Kingdom) alone made laws for Scotland. However, Westminster has given the Scottish Parliament authority in many different areas of policy to make law. This does not mean that Westminster has become irrelevant. Far from it. The Scottish Parliament is an inferior body to Westminster and all it would take is the passing of a simple Act by Westminster to abolish the Scottish Parliament. Westminster is still the supreme law-making body in the United Kingdom despite the introduction of devolution. When we talk about parliament we mean the Houses of Commons and the Lords and the Monarch. To become law, a Bill must pass through the House of Commons and the House of Lords before being sent to Her Majesty, the Queen who will sign the Bill into law.

 Key point: Acts of Parliament are often referred to as legislation or statute law.

Westminster is the supreme law-making institution and no other court or body can question the validity of an Act of Parliament. Courts must apply an Act of Parliament and cannot declare it illegal. Before Westminster can make a new law, certain procedures must be followed. Proposed laws are presented to parliament in the form of a Bill. The Bill does not simply become law there and then, it must be debated and eventually voted upon before it can be said to form part of the law of the land. A Bill may be introduced by either the House of Commons or the House of Lords.

Public and Private Bills

Most Bills will be Public Bills in that they apply to society as a whole. Public Bills are sponsored by Government Ministers or individual members of the Commons or the Lords. Private Bills, on the other hand, are usually very restrictive in that they apply to a very small group of people or a particular organisation or body. They do not apply to society or to the public across the board. Examples of Private Bills which became Acts include the London Development Agency Act 2003 and the Nottingham City Council Act 2003. Clearly these Acts apply only to the London Development Agency and to Nottingham City Council.

 Key point: Public Bills are much more common than Private Bills and affect society as a whole.

Parliamentary Procedure

The way in which a Bill becomes law at Westminster is outlined below.

First Reading

The Bill is introduced to the House of Commons. A vote does not take place, but the Second Reading of the Bill is arranged. The contents of the Bill will then be published.

Second Reading

The Bill will face its first test in that it will have to face a vote. If the Bill is defeated in the vote, it can go no further. The Bill would have to be reintroduced in the next parliamentary year at the earliest. If the House approves the Bill then it can proceed to the next stage. The debate is not usually lengthy as most of the detailed work on the Bill is yet to come.

Committee Stage

A small group of members of the House of Commons from both the Government and the opposition will form a committee to discuss the Bill in detail. There is nothing to stop larger groups of MPs or even the whole House sitting as a committee. The Committee stage is where the Bill will be most likely to face major changes to its original content. The meaning of words and phrases will be picked over by the members and even entire sections of the Bill could be rewritten or taken out completely. The Bill may now be completely different from the version that was first introduced to the House. If the Bill relates to Scotland only, it will be referred to either the Scottish Standing Committee or the Scottish Grand Committee. In practice, referrals to these Scottish Committees will tend to be less common these days because the Scottish Parliament now deals with the bulk of new laws for Scotland. The Scottish Grand Committee is a committee of the House of Commons. It is not a select committee (as opposed to the Scottish Affairs Select Committee), but rather a grand committee composed of all 59 Scottish MPs.

Report Stage

The Committee will have to give a progress report about the Bill to the House of Commons. The Commons will want to know what changes have been made to the Bill and these will have to be considered in detail. The Report Stage is also an opportunity for more changes to be made to the Bill.

Third Reading

This will be the crunch time for the Bill. The House will debate the final version of the Bill and a vote will be taken. If the Bill is defeated, then it will have to be reintroduced during the next parliamentary year – provided of course that the Government has the stomach for a fight. If the Bill is supported by a majority of MPs, then it will go to the House of Lords.

 Key point: Bills passing through the Westminster Parliament go through the following stages: First Reading, Second Reading, Committee Stage, Report Stage and Third Reading before they can become Acts of Parliament.

The House of Lords

The House of Lords has very similar legislative procedures to the House of Commons, but there are some differences. The Chancellor of the Exchequer does not have to submit his Budget to the Lords (a Finance Bill) because since 1911 the

Lords have had no right to deal with such a Bill. During the Committee Stage of a Bill, the entire House sits as a Committee in order to propose changes to the Bill's contents. Once the Bill has successfully passed through the Lords, it receives the Royal Assent and thus the Bill becomes an Act.

The new Act may now come into force immediately or there could be a delay. The Companies Act 2006 received the Royal Assent on 18 November 2006. However, important provisions of the Act were not made effective until 1 October 2009 and many of the new rules were phased in gradually from 2006 onwards. Copies of the new legislation will be made publicly available in print or on the Internet by Her Majesty's Stationery Office.

The powers of the House of Lords

It should be noted, however, that the Lords can only delay the passage of a Bill. Certainly, the Lords can make its own changes to a Bill, but these changes can ultimately be rejected by the Commons. If the Lords decides to block the passage of a Bill twice in one parliamentary session, the Commons can use its powers under the Parliament Acts of 1911 and 1949 to force the Bill through despite the Lords' hostility. The Bill would then go the Queen in any case and receive the Royal Assent. The Bill would, therefore, become law. It is worth pointing out that the days are long gone when a King or a Queen could refuse to give the Royal Assent. In modern times, this stage is purely a formality.

Since 1949, the House of Commons has overridden opposition by the House of Lords by using its powers contained in the Parliament Act to introduce the following legislation:

◆ War Crimes Act 1991
◆ European Parliamentary Elections Act 1999
◆ Sexual Offences (Amendment) Act 2000
◆ Hunting Act 2004

The Salisbury Convention

In the past, the House of Lords followed the Salisbury Convention which meant that it would not attempt to block a Bill which had been proposed by the Government in its election manifesto which had passed its second or third reading in the House of Commons. This constitutional convention, formulated by Lord Salisbury, the then Conservative Leader of the House of Lords between 1942 and 1957, acknowledged the fact that the House of Commons enjoyed a democratic mandate from the electorate which the unelected peers did not. Amendments could be made to Government Bills, but any attempt by members of the House of Lords to destroy or wreck a legislative proposal which enjoyed majority support in the Commons (and by implication amongst the voters) would not be tolerated or allowed. In recent years, however, Conservative and Liberal Democrat members of the House of Lords have publicly stated that the Salisbury Convention is not an absolute concept and they are free to oppose legislative proposals put forward by the current Labour Government with which they strongly disagree.

 Key point: The House of Lords is the weaker of the two Houses of Parliament because, unlike the Commons, it has no power to deal with Finance Bills and it only has the power to delay Bills.

Where do Bills come from?

The vast majority of new legal proposals will be introduced in the House of Commons. The Commons is the more important House of Parliament. The government of the day, headed by the Prime Minister and their supporters, sit in the House of Commons. When a general election is held for Westminster, the voters are being asked to vote for members of the House of Commons who are called Members of Parliament (MPs). The political party that secures the largest number of seats in the House of Commons will usually form the next government. The purpose of a general election is, therefore, to elect a parliament which, in turn, will make laws for the United Kingdom. The members of the House of Lords do not face the British voters and, therefore, they cannot be said to enjoy the same authority as MPs who regularly have to stand for re-election. In any case, in 1911 the Commons emerged as the winner in a power struggle with the Lords and since then the Lords have accepted that they are not as powerful as the Commons.

 Key point: The House of Commons as the democratically elected chamber will introduce many more Bills than the House of Lords.

It should be appreciated that a government will come to power with clear ideas about the kinds of laws that it wishes to see introduced. These ideas are contained in a manifesto which contains all sorts of proposals for running the country. In this way, a political party is advertising its policies and telling the voters what it would do if elected to form the next British government.

When the present Labour Government was first elected in 1997, it had already made clear that it wished to introduce devolved parliaments or assemblies for Scotland, Northern Ireland and Wales. Legislation to set up these three bodies soon followed the Government's election victory. However, governments will often consider legislation to cope with particular problems that arise from time to time, for example, tougher laws to combat illegal immigrants or the introduction of identity cards to crack down on terrorism.

A government will often wish to see whether it has enough public support before introducing a Bill to parliament on a particular subject. A Green Paper will be published outlining the government's proposals. If public opinion is broadly favourable to the government's proposals, then a White Paper will be published which provides much more detail. When the government minister has prepared his Bill, he will approach the government's business manager in the Commons (the Leader of the House) and ask for parliamentary time to be allocated.

 Key point: Governments will often give advance warning of their legislative proposals by publishing a Green Paper. Once confident that support exists for its legislative proposals, the government will then publish a White Paper.

Getting a Bill through Parliament

In 1997, Donald Dewar, the then Scottish Secretary, had spent a considerable amount of time with his team of civil servants and other experts preparing the Scotland Bill. The Scotland Bill proposed to establish a Scottish Parliament. The Bill was given a slot in the parliamentary timetable in January 1998 and, after having passed through both Houses of Parliament, it was sent to the Queen in order to receive the Royal Assent in November 1998. Upon receiving the Royal Assent, the Bill became law as the Scotland Act 1998. From January to November may seem like a relatively short period, but it is worth pointing out that ten months of parliamentary time was required and this Bill was considered to be a priority.

It is perfectly possible for an ordinary Member of Parliament to introduce a Bill to Parliament. This is known as a Private Member's Bill. These types of Bills, however, do not have a very high success rate. The government controls the parliamentary timetable and naturally it will give priority to its own Bills. If there is not enough time for a Private Member's Bill to be debated and voted upon, then that is simply too bad. Admittedly, some significant changes to the law have been made as a result of Private Member's Bills. The Abortion Act 1967 was originally introduced as a Bill by David Steel, the Liberal MP. Steel's Bill later received support from the then Labour Government and went on to become an Act. If the government had not supported Steel's Bill it would have probably failed.

The UK Parliament is elected for a maximum period of five years and the government will want to use as much of this time as possible to promote its own Bills. Theoretically, if the government controls a majority of seats in the House of Commons it should face few problems getting its Bills through. However, governments can upset their own supporters who may then choose to rebel by voting against their own government's proposals. Even if the government manages to get a Bill through the Commons, as we have seen, the House of Lords will still have the right to examine the Bill and make all sorts of changes to it.

 Key point: Most Public Bills will be promoted by government ministers, but it is possible for ordinary MPs to introduce their own Bills (Private Member's Bills).

Secondary or delegated legislation

As we have seen, there are various parliamentary procedures which have to be followed before a Bill can become an Act. These procedures can be very time consuming and Bills can fall victim to all sorts of delays. There are ways in which laws can be introduced very quickly without having to introduce a Bill to parliament and get it through the legislative process.

Statutory Instruments

Very often, an Act of Parliament may contain powers which allow a government minister to make new laws without the minister first having to consult parliament. Such Acts are known as Parent Acts. Statutory Instrument No. 20 of the Justice of the Peace Courts (Sheriffdem of Tayside, Central and Fife) Amendment Order 2009 allows the Scottish Ministers at Holyrood to exercise powers conferred on them by virtue of the Criminal Proceedings etc. (Scotland) Act 2007. This Statutory Instrument permits the Scottish Ministers to reorganise the Justice of the Peace Courts in Tayside, Central and Fife without first having to seek permission from the Scottish Parliament. In this way, Parliament can focus on more important matters and leave relatively minor matters to the appropriate Minister or Ministers.

In this way, time can be saved and all the First Minister will have to do is to provide the Scottish Parliament with a report (usually at a later stage) about the operation of the new rules. However, the First Minister must stay within the powers that the Parent Act gives him or the new rules could be subject to a legal challenge.

In an emergency situation, for example, during times of war, Orders in Council can be used by the British government to introduce new legislation. This type of legislation can be rushed through both Houses of Parliament very quickly

Acts of Sederunt

This allows the Court of Session to make laws which regulate the conduct of business in all the Scottish civil courts. An example of this type of law is the Act of Sederunt (Ordinary Cause Rules Amendment) (Personal Injuries Actions) 2009 Scottish Statutory Instrument No. 285 of 2009.

Acts of Adjournal

The High Court of Justiciary can introduce these Acts to organise the business and procedures of the High Court of Justiciary and the lower Scottish criminal courts. An example of this type of law is the Act of Adjournal (Criminal Procedure Rules Amendment No. 5) (Miscellaneous) 2009 (Scottish Statutory Instrument No. 345 of 2009).

By-laws

The Westminster or the Scottish Parliament will often use a Parent Act to give law-making powers to an inferior body such as a local council. An example of this is the Licensing (Scotland) Act 1976 (soon to be amended) which deals with the licensing of public houses, bars, nightclubs and restaurants in Scotland. Under this Act, local councils have been given powers to make rules or by-laws which regulate the opening of such establishments. This is not a matter which should take up the Scottish Parliament's valuable time. Local councils are best placed to understand local conditions and what may be appropriate for the City of Edinburgh may not be right for a rural area like Argyll and Bute. It is vital, of course, that councils do not act beyond the powers granted to them otherwise there is every possibility of a legal challenge being mounted.

 Key point: Secondary legislation allows new laws to be brought in very speedily and effectively without the need to seek parliamentary approval – which can be very time consuming and which is not always granted.

The unwritten laws of Scotland

So far, we have examined written sources of Scots law, but not every legal rule in Scotland will be in written form. The unwritten laws of Scotland fall into two categories:

◆ Custom
◆ Judicial precedent or case law

 Key point: Unwritten laws arise from custom and judicial precedent (case law).

Custom

Customs are practices which have been handed down over many generations. In order to have the force of law, customs must be well established and they must continue to be in force. If a custom has fallen into disuse, it is highly unlikely that it will continue to be enforceable. Furthermore, customs can be overruled by superior forms of law such as Acts of Parliament or other legislation. It is worth pointing out that custom as a source of law is not as important as it once was.

 Key point: Customs develop over a period of time and are commonly accepted practices.

The use of customs in relation to landownership and use is particularly common. *Udal tenure* is one such example. This is a curious system of land tenure and is found only in Orkney and Shetland. *Udal tenure* was imposed on the islands by the Viking conquerors who originally came from Norway and is a type of freeholding. Unlike the feudal system, the Scottish (later the British) Crown was not acknowledged as superior – this is due to the Vikings' hearty dislike of authority and the fact that they did not acknowledge the Scottish Crown as the relevant authority. In fact, the Vikings were more likely to be loyal to the Norwegian Crown!

The Vikings took the land by force and, very often, held on to it by violent means. The Vikings regarded it almost as a sacred duty to fight off all comers who might have designs on their land. Under the Udal system, an individual's tenure of the land was, therefore, as strong as he was. The Udal system is not as common in the islands now and, in modern times, there has been an increasing trend towards the introduction of feudalism.

In certain trades or professions, customs or business practices were given explicit recognition by the courts. In international trade, strange initials or phrases such as FOB, CIF, ex-factory or ex-ship would often feature in contracts. To an outsider, these initials or phrases are completely baffling. However, to someone who works in a particular trade or business, the initials FOB would make perfect sense. In an FOB (free on board) contract, a buyer of goods will become responsible for any loss, damage or theft to the property when the goods have passed over the ship's rail. If the goods are damaged, lost or stolen before they pass over the ship's rail, then the seller would be responsible.

In criminal law, certain types of behaviour will be automatically regarded as reprehensible and as such will be regarded as threatening the security of society or the community as a whole. Those individuals who commit crimes will run the risk of being imprisoned or fined. Not every rule of criminal behaviour, however, will be contained in an Act of Parliament. Some crimes have always been forbidden by society. The crime of murder is one example. There is no written rule in Scots law which says that murder is a crime, but society has always regarded the taking of innocent, human life without justification as an evil or wicked act.

Judicial precedent (case law)

Legal rules are not always as clear as we would like them to be and this will mean that the courts have an opportunity to clarify the law. Test cases will often be brought before the courts which raise a very important point of law and judges will have to make a decision. When a judge makes a decision at the end of a court case, he is often not just making a decision which applies to the immediate facts of the case before him. The decision which the judge has made may actually become a legal rule in its own right which future judges and courts will be under a duty to follow if they encounter a similar legal problem. The practice of following previous judicial decisions is known as judicial precedent or *stare decisis* (standing by previous decisions).

 Key point: Judicial precedent develops from case law and the 'testing' of laws in court. The rulings of a higher court decision must be followed.

How do judges make rules of law?

Not every judge can make a new rule. The authority of the judge or the court will be a major factor to consider here. If the judge holds a relatively junior position, for example, a Sheriff or a Justice of the Peace, it is very unlikely that they will be able to create a new rule of law. If, on the other hand, the ruling came from superior courts, for example, the Court of Session or the House of Lords, this decision would have to be followed by the lower or inferior courts. Therefore, the position of the court is very important. As we shall see when we come to an examination of the legal system, the Scottish courts are ranked in order of importance from the highest in the land to the lowest. If a lawyer wishes to use a previous judicial decision in order to argue their case, the decision must be in point. When a lawyer talks about a previously decided case being in point, they mean that the legal rule which it established is relevant to the case that the judges are currently considering. In order to follow a previously decided case, a court must be absolutely certain that the case presently before it raises exactly the same legal issues as an older decision. The facts of the older case and the facts of the current case do not have to be the same. Two examples of criminal decisions of the Appeal Court of the High Court of Justiciary, which were decided on the same day, demonstrate the doctrine of judicial precedent in action:

 Procurator Fiscal, Dunoon *v* Dominick (22 July 2003) the accused had allegedly displayed material of a pornographic nature in a manner that two girls aged nine and ten-years old could not avoid seeing it. It was also alleged that the accused had conducted himself in a disorderly manner and that he had followed the two girls in an attempt to force them to view the pornographic material. This caused the girls to experience a state of fear and alarm. The accused was charged, amongst other things, with the common law crime of shameless indecency.

 MacLean *v* Procurator Fiscal, Inverness (22 July 2003) it was alleged that the accused, a female teacher, had conducted a relationship of a sexual nature with a 15-year-old boy while he was a pupil at the school at which she taught English. This alleged relationship continued after the boy was no longer a pupil. The accused also allegedly indulged in communications (telephone calls and letters) with the boy which were inappropriate and of an indecent nature. The accused was charged with the common law crime of shameless indecency.

In **Harris v Her Majesty's Advocate (2009)** the High Court of Justiciary clarified the law on what type of behaviour could constitute a breach of the peace. Conduct committed in private (where the accused voiced threats against police officers during an interview) does not constitute a breach of the peace. Again, their Lordships clarified the law on breach of the peace without reference to the Scottish Parliament.

The question before the judges in both cases was whether the charge of shameless indecency was unspecific and unclear and, therefore, a breach of the European Convention on Human Rights which demands that the accused must be charged with a crime that is reasonably clear and certain. The main criticism of the common law crime of shameless indecency that it is used to cover all sorts of behaviour. A problematic area was whether it covered indecent acts committed in public or whether an accused who committed similar acts in private could also be charged with shameless indecency. In **Procurator Fiscal, Dunoon v Dominick** it was held that the crime of shameless indecency as it now exists has no satisfactory basis in the law of Scotland and these types of behaviour should be treated as falling within the scope of the crime of public indecency. Whether a particular act is indecent will depend on the circumstances of the case judged by social standards that will change from age to age and these will be the standards that would be applied by the average citizen in contemporary society. Where indecent acts are committed in private, the option of charging the accused with lewd and libidinous behaviour is still very much open. The precedent laid down in **Dominick** was followed in the related case of **MacLean v Procurator Fiscal, Inverness**.

These two cases effectively reformed an area of Scottish criminal law without the consent and the participation of either the democratically elected Scottish and Westminster Parliaments. Unless the politicians decide to intervene and pass a law overruling the High Court of Justiciary, the lower Scottish criminal courts must follow these rulings in **Dominick** and **MacLean**. It is now no longer competent to charge an accused with the common law crime of shameless indecency.

 Key point: Somewhat controversially, senior judges can make a new rule of law without either the participation or prior approval of democratically elected politicians.

Persuasive precedents

Many previous court cases are merely regarded as persuasive in the sense that a lawyer could choose to use legal arguments from them, but it is by no means certain that a court will follow the decision. English cases, unless previously accepted by the Scottish courts, may raise some interesting issues but they will not be automatically accepted as authority in Scotland. Similarly, decisions of the lower Scottish courts such as the Justice of the Peace Court, the Sheriff Court and the Outer House of the Court of Session may be regarded as persuasive, but not binding. A case will be regarded as having binding authority in Scotland if it is a decision of the High Court of Justiciary, the Inner House of the Court of Session or the UK Supreme Court (in a Scottish appeal). Generally speaking, judges or courts are bound to follow the decisions of superior courts.

Key point: Some previous judicial decisions will merely be persuasive in that they are not regarded as binding precedents.

A previous judicial decision consists of two parts:

◆ The *ratio decidendi*
◆ *Obiter dicta*

The *ratio decidendi* or simply, the ratio, is the actual legal rule which is established by the court case. This rule can often be simply expressed in one or two sentences. However, the report of the actual judgement could run to many pages. It is very common for judges to go on at length when they deliver the judgement. Statements or examples which the judges provide when they make their decisions are of interest to academics and lawyers, but they do not actually form part of the judgement. Such statements or examples are known as *obiter dicta* (or things said by the way). It is very important to be able to distinguish between the *ratio decidendi* and *obiter dicta*.

Many important areas of Scots law are made up of rules which judges and not parliament have made. Contract law is only one example where many of the legal rules governing the creation of contracts and the rights of the parties are contained in previously decided court cases. Judges have to be careful that they are not seen to be overruling laws which either the Westminster or Scottish Parliament have made. Both parliaments are very jealous of their powers and will often express disapproval if they believe that judges have gone too far by making a new law. Judges, after all, exist to interpret and to give effect to the will of parliament as expressed in various Acts and secondary legislation.

Judicial approaches to statutory interpretation

When a Scottish judge attempts to interpret a statutory provision in an Act of Parliament or a piece of secondary legislation, he or she can apply one of three possible rules:

The literal rule – means that the words used in the legislation are given their everyday, ordinary or literal meaning. Such an approach will be taken by judges who are firmly of the opinion that they have been appointed merely to apply the law and it is not their place to become legislators or law-makers. The literal rule is obviously an example of judges erring on the side of caution, but it can lead to absurdities or injustices. This will be especially the case when Parliament has drafted legislation poorly. The application of the literal rule can be seen in an example involving the Sex Discrimination Act 1975. The Act makes it very clear that central to the success of any claim is the complainant's ability to compare his or her allegedly less favourable treatment to an actual or hypothetical male/female comparator. If he or she cannot do this, the claim will fail. A woman claiming that she has suffered discrimination on the grounds of her sex must be able to carry out a like with like comparison. The woman's circumstances and those of her male comparator must be the same (they should not be materially different) otherwise a meaningful comparison cannot be made. When the Act of 1975 was first introduced, cases involving alleged discrimination connected to a woman's pregnancy encountered an unexpected problem which the Parliamentary draftsmen had not taken into account: how you can compare a pregnant woman's situation with that of a man. This is not a valid comparison and, therefore, many of the earliest sex discrimination claims failed because some judges applied the literal approach to the Act even if this made the law something of an ass and, more seriously, led to a blatant injustice.

The golden rule – this an attempt by some judges to get round the problem caused by the application of the literal rule. The judge will apply the law literally, but he or she will do so in a way that avoids the creation of absurdities or injustices. This approach is sometimes referred to as the gloss on the literal rule.

The mischief rule – in this situation the judge will ignore the wording in the legislation and instead will examine what mischief the statute was supposed to cure. There are dangers here because the judge is obviously second guessing the will of Parliament and using his or her own interpretation in order to decide the legal issue at hand. This approach is often referred to as the purposive approach.

 Key point: A judicial precedent consists of two parts – the *ratio decidendi* and the *obiter dicta*.

The European Union or Community

The European Union is an organisation or a club of 27 member states. Like most organisations or clubs, the members have to obey the rules or laws in order to reap the benefits of membership. Britain has been a member of the European Union since 1 January 1973 as a result of the European Communities Act 1972.

The development of the European Union can be traced back to the Treaty of Paris 1951 when the original six member states – Belgium, France, Germany, Italy, Luxembourg and the Netherlands – established a single market in coal and steel by creating the European Coal and Steel Community. The Community was formed some six years after the end of the Second World War (1939–45) and was a deliberate attempt to heal the tremendous damage that had been inflicted on Europe as a result of that War. A Coal and Steel Community had tremendous symbolism, not just because former enemies made a commitment never to go war with one another again, but the fact that coal and steel were used to make weapons. In 1957, this cooperation between the six states was deepened with the signing of the Treaty of Rome and the Euratom Treaty. It was the Treaty of Rome that particularly captured the imagination with its dream of creating a single European market where the free movement of people, goods, services and capital could be promoted. It was hoped by promoting deeper economic cooperation between the member states, that the desire to go to war would be a thing of the past. The single market was eventually established on 1 January 1993.

Although the three Treaties laid down a blueprint for the single European market, it would take many years of planning and the introduction of a huge range of laws in each of the member states to make this dream a reality. In order to make the single market a reality, the member states would all have to introduce laws which brought their very different legal systems closer together. This process was known as harmonising the laws in the different member states. Regrettably, Britain chose not to be involved in the European project until much later and, arguably, missed its opportunity to be a major influence on the development of the European

Union. By the time Britain became a member of the European Union in 1973, many of the key laws were already in place and Britain had to accept these as the price of membership. On 1 January 2007, Romania and Bulgaria entered the European Union as its newest members. Consequently, the membership of the European Union increased from the previous 25 member states to 27. This meant that some changes to the institutional framework of the European Union were necessary.

 Key point: The European Union is an organisation or a club of 27 member states and, as with most organisations or clubs, the members have to obey the rules or laws in order to reap the benefits of membership.

Sources of European Law

The laws of the European Union can be used in any of the national courts by member states, by private individuals and by organisations. There are two sources of law:

- Primary legislation
- Secondary legislation

 Key point: Sources of European legislation can be found in primary and secondary legislation.

Primary legislation or law is contained in the original three Treaties – Paris 1951, Rome 1957 and Euratom 1957. These Treaties lay down broad goals which the member states will attempt to achieve. They can often be sketchy where details are concerned. However, it is possible to use Treaty Articles to enforce a variety of rights if the Article in question is sufficiently clear and precise. Other Treaties such as the Treaty on European Union 1992, the Treaty of Amsterdam 1997, the Treaty of Nice 2000 and the Treaty of Lisbon 2007 have also added to the primary law of the European Union.

 Key point: Primary legislation or law is contained in the original three Treaties – Paris 1951, Rome 1957 and Euratom 1957 and any other subsequent Treaties, for example, Maastricht, Amsterdam, Nice and Lisbon.

The Lisbon Treaty (Treaty on the functioning of the EU)

The Lisbon Treaty which was signed by European Heads of Government in 2007 was finally ratified in November 2009 when Vaclav Klaus, the Czech President signed the Treaty into law. The Czech Republic was the last Member State to ratify the Treaty. The Treaty subsequently became law across the 27 European member states on 1 December 2009. The Lisbon Treaty has had a troubled history – the Republic of Ireland initially rejected it in a referendum held in June 2008. Irish voters, however, voted in favour of the Treaty in a second referendum held in October 2009. The last remaining obstacle to ratification of the Treaty was the opposition of President Klaus of the Czech Republic who had refused to sign it into law, despite the fact that the Czech Parliament had voted in favour of its provisions. Eventually, the Czech Constitutional Court ruled in favour of the Treaty and President Klaus was forced to capitulate.

In order for a European Treaty to become legally binding, all existing member states must ratify or approve it either by means of a parliamentary vote or in a referendum, depending upon each country's constitutional arrangements. Supporters of the Treaty claimed that it was necessary in order to overhaul the constitutional machinery of the European Union. The original European Treaties envisaged arrangements for six Member States not the current membership of 27 countries. Admittedly, the Treaty will reform the qualified majority voting system which should theoretically mean that European decision making will be easier. The right of member states to use their national veto will be reduced. Unanimous decision making will still be required in the areas of defence, foreign policy, social security and taxation.

One of the biggest changes which the introduction of the Lisbon Treaty entailed was the appointment of a President of the European Council (the body of which represents the national governments). The President is appointed for two and a half years initially with an option to be reappointed to the post for a further two and a half years. The President will be assisted by a High Representative for Foreign Affairs and a permanent diplomatic service. One of the main tasks of the new President will be to prepare for summits of European Heads of Government as he will be responsible for chairing these meetings. From 2014, the number of European Commissioners will be reduced and the system of qualified majority voting will be reformed.

Despite these institutional reforms, each Government of the member states will continue to hold the rotating presidency of the Council of Ministers for six months at a time and there is speculation that this arrangement could be a source of tension between President Van Rompuy and the European Governments.

The Treaty also commits member states to be bound by the European Union's Charter of Fundamental Rights which includes areas such as bioethics, data protection and employment rights. The United Kingdom negotiated a protocol to the Lisbon Treaty which should, in theory, minimise the influence of the Charter and prevent the European Court of Justice deciding that British laws are inconsistent with fundamental rights. The Charter gives workers the right to strike – the introduction of which past and present UK Governments are bitterly opposed.

The first European Council President is Herman Van Rompuy, a former Belgian Prime Minister, and the first High Representative for Foreign Affairs is Baroness Cathy Ashton of Upholland from the United Kingdom. Both Mr Van Rompuy and Baroness Ashton were appointed to their respective positions in December 2009 with the consent of the 27 governments of the member states. The posts are not directly elected – a fact which critics of the Treaty have not been slow to highlight.

This appointment of a President for Europe is not as radical as many have suggested. The powers of the new President have not been properly laid out and there is considerable doubt as to how he will interact with the two other existing European Presidents – José Manuel Barroso (Commission President) and Jerzy Buzek (President of the European Parliament). The suspicion is that the new European Council President will be little more than a symbolic Mr Europe.

Key point: The provisions of the Treaty of Lisbon will significantly reform the institutional structures of the European Union and streamline decision making processes which are more suited to a group of 27 plus member states operating in the 21st Century.

Sources of European Union Law

Article 288 of the Treaty on the Functioning of the EU lists the five sources of European law which are known as secondary legislation. The Treaties list broad aims or objectives, but they often do not provide the details. Secondary legislation is, therefore, necessary to flesh out the Treaties of the European Union. Secondary legislation includes:

◆ Regulations
◆ Directives
◆ Decisions
◆ Recommendations
◆ Opinions

Key point: Secondary legislation is made up of Regulations, Directives, Decisions, Recommendations and Opinions.

As soon as Regulations are published in the Official Journal of the European Union, they are legally binding. They do not need to be implemented by the Westminster Parliament or the Scottish Parliament. They can be enforced in all the national courts. In this way, Regulations are said to be directly applicable and have direct effect.

Key point: Regulations are legally binding as soon as they are published in the Official Journal of the European Union.

In order to have legal force, the Westminster Parliament must pass legislation to make Directives effective. The Sale and Supply of Goods to Consumers Regulations 2002 began life as the European Directive 1999/44/EC on Certain Aspects of the Sale of Consumer Goods and Associated Guarantees. It was only when the Regulations were passed into law on 31 March 2003 that the Directive became effective. However, member states will have to obey a strict time period for implementing directives because failure to introduce legislation could result in legal action being taken against the country's government.

Decisions include judgements of the European Court of Justice and the courts of the member states will have to obey these and follow them. The Council and the Commission can also issue decisions but these are usually addressed to particular member states, individuals or bodies who will have to abide by them.

Recommendations and opinions are generally held to have no binding force, but in **Grimaldi v Fonds des Maladies Professionelles (1990)** it was held that they may have some indirect legal effect. The European Court of Justice stated that domestic courts are bound to take recommendations into consideration in order to decide disputes submitted to them, in particular where they are capable of clarifying the interpretation of other provisions of national or Community law.

We also have what is known as 'soft law' i.e. resolutions, programmes, notices or guidelines. This is an imprecise term, but it can still be quite useful as a general category. Other sources of law include international Treaties which the European Union has made, for example, the Lomé and Yaoundé Conventions giving trade rights to African, Caribbean and Pacific nations.

The Institutions of the European Union

Article 9 of the Treaty on the Functioning of the EU lists some of the main institutions of the European Union:

- Parliament (Articles 189 to 201)
- Commission (Articles 211 to 219)
- European Court of Justice (Articles 220 to 245)
- Council of Ministers (Articles 246 to 248)
- Court of Auditors (Articles 310–325)

The Council of Ministers (www.consilium.europa.eu)

The Council was, and probably still is, the most powerful institution of the European Union. All 27 member states are represented on this body. At the regular meetings of the Council, it is normal practice for a country's foreign minister to attend. Often, however, the minister with a responsibilty for a particular policy area e.g. finance, transport or the environment will attend the meetings depending upon the topic to be discussed. At the European Council meetings, the Head of Government e.g. the Prime Minister or the President will represent the relevant member state. Since the introduction of the Lisbon Treaty the new European Union President, Herman Van Rompuy, will chair European Council meetings.

Qualified Majority Voting

The various European Treaties stipulate areas of policy in which proposed changes to the law must be achieved by a simple majority, qualified majority or unanimity.

Qualified majority voting is a system of weighted voting whereby each member state is allocated a number of votes under the European Treaties with the bigger countries (in terms of population size) being given a larger number of votes. Such a system will be used in the following circumstances:

- if a majority of member states approve (in some cases a two-thirds majority);
- a minimum of 255 votes is cast in favour of the proposal, out of a total of 345 votes.

A member state can ask to have it officially verified that the votes in favour are representative of at least 62 per cent of the total population of the European Union. If this figure has not been achieved, it is highly unlikely that the proposed legislative change will be put into effect.

The main advantage associated with qualified majority voting is that the larger member states e.g. Germany cannot dominate proceedings and will very often be forced to build coalitions of interest with the smaller member states in order to make changes to European law.

Distribution of votes for each member state	
Germany, France, Italy, United Kingdom	29
Spain, Poland	27
Romania	14
Netherlands	13
Belgium, Czech Republic, Greece, Hungary, Portugal	12
Austria, Bulgaria, Sweden	10
Denmark, Ireland, Lithuania, Slovakia, Finland	7
Cyprus, Estonia, Latvia, Luxembourg, Slovenia	4
Malta	3
TOTAL	**345**
Source: europa.eu (the official website of the European Union)	

The European Parliament (www.europarl.europa.eu)

Parliament was first known as the Assembly, but since 1962, it has been referred to as the European Parliament. When the European Union consisted of 15 member states (until 30 April 2004), the Parliament had 626 members or MEPs. The 1997 Treaty of Amsterdam set a limit of 700 members. This limit was soon viewed as unrealistic given the fact that, on 1 May 2004, 10 new member states joined the European Union. From 2004–2007, the Parliament will have 732 members in total and, if Bulgaria and Romania become member states in 2007, the number of MEPs will increase to 786. The word 'Parliament' can be very misleading – it in no way resembles the Westminster Parliament and it is often restricted in all sorts of ways. Additionally, it cannot pass laws in its own right, but a failure to consult Parliament might lead to any subsequent legislation being cancelled. In **Roquette Frères *v* Council (1980)** rules for regulating the use of isuglucose were challenged and annulled because Parliament had not been given a reasonable opportunity to scrutinise the proposals. Parliament's role is now more than just an advisory one.

The Single European Act 1986 and the Treaty of European Union 1992 introduced a cooperation procedure and a co-decision procedure respectively in relation to Parliament. These had the effect of giving Parliament much more power in the area of legislative proposals. In many situations, the Council will not be able to pass laws without the cooperation and consent of Parliament.

Over the years, the Parliament has acquired more powers and it was instrumental in getting rid of the European Commission led by its former President Jacques Santer in 1999 in the wake of serious allegations of corruption and maladministration. The Lisbon Treaty now gives Parliament an equal status with the Council of Ministers.

The European Commission (www.europa.eu)

The European Commission is effectively the civil service of the European Union. In June 2006, the Commission employed a staff of approximately 34,335 (which includes external staff). The Commission has no formal power to make laws. It can propose new laws, but the Council and Parliament may have other ideas. The Commission's main task is to ensure that member states, business organisations and individuals follow the laws of the European Union. The Commission will not be slow in taking parties to a court if it considers that laws have been broken or ignored.

The Commission will have a membership of 30 Commissioners from 1 May 2004 (this will include 10 new appointees from each one of the new member states). Each Commissioner will take responsibility for a particular area of policy, for example, the Single Market or external relations with third countries. Previously, the "Big Five" member states: France, Germany, Italy, Spain and the United Kingdom each appointed two Commissioners, with the other 20 states appointing one Commissioner each. However, in 2005, the "Big Five" lost one of their Commissioners. There are now 27 European Commissioners (including the current President, José Manuel Barroso) as a result of the most recent wave of enlargement. In theory, the first loyalty of each Commissioner is to the European Union rather than to the member state that appointed him or her. The Lisbon Treaty contains provisions which will see the overall number of Commissioners reduced by 2014 onwards.

The Court of Justice (curia.europa.eu)

The Court of Justice (CJ) consists of 27 judges (each appointed by a member state) who are assisted by eight Advocates-General (who will themselves have been lawyers or judges of extremely high standing). The Advocates-General are appointed by common agreement of the member states.

The number of judges has increased to 27 from the previous 25 in order to represent each member state of the European Union. Eight Advocates-General will continue to assist the judges.

The Court of Justice may choose to sit in any of the following arrangements:

◆ Plenary (full) session with all 27 judges in attendance;
◆ A Grand Chamber of 13 judges; or
◆ Chambers consisting of 3–5 judges

A plenary session of the court is likely to be necessary in situations where proceedings to dismiss the European Ombudsman or a European Commissioner have been initiated. Furthermore, a plenary session may take place where a legal matter of special significance or great difficulty has been brought before the court for a resolution.

Grand Chamber proceedings are more likely to take place when a member state or one of the European institutions e.g. the Commission or Parliament is appearing before the court as a party to legal proceedings. In more mundane matters, however, the court operates better in chambers of 3–5 judges.

The Court of Justice is represented by a President of the Court and the various Chambers will elect a President from amongst their membership to represent them. A President of a Chamber of five judges will normally elected for three years and, in comparison, a President of a Chamber of three judges will be elected for just one year. The court also appoints a Registrar who acts as its secretary general and who has responsibility for administrative matters i.e. will manage the various departments with the authority of the President of the court.

The Single European Act 1986 also established a Court of First Instance in order to ease the pressure in relation to the Court of Justice's workload. The Court of First Instance (now renamed the General Court since the ratification of the Lisbon

Treaty) deals primarily with issues such as agriculture, state subsidies, competition, commercial policy, regional policy, trade-mark law, transport and disputes between the European Union and its staff. The General Court has a membership of 27 judges each appointed by agreement of the member states. A President of this court will be elected by the judges to serve for a term of three years and a Registrar is also appointed to serve a term of six years. The Judges are appointed by mutual agreement of all the governments of the member states for a renewable term of six years. There are no permanent Advocates General attached to this court.

The Court of Auditors

This body was established in 1977. It has primary responsibility for the scrutiny of the European Union's finances i.e. that the budget is being spent correctly. The Court will attempt to expose any financial irregularities in the European Union's budget and this is a highly politically-sensitive role given the huge amounts of money involved and the perception (rightly or wrongly) that the money is not being spent correctly. The Court will submit an annual report to the Council and the Parliament which contains detailed information about the European Union's finances for the previous financial year. This institution is becoming much more important as time passes and it played a major role in forcing the European Commission to resign en masse in 1999 after allegations of maladministration were widely exposed.

The Court has 27 full-time members appointed for a renewable term of six years from each one of the member states. These members will have been professional auditors or will have special experience as accountancy practitioners. In order to have more efficient procedures, the Court can organise its members into units called "chambers" who will be allocated particular areas of responsibility. A President of the Court is elected by the members to serve for a term of three years. The members of the Court are supported by a staff of approximately 550 – about half of whom are professional auditors. The Court can send these staff members out on inspections throughout the European Union to investigate the different ways in which money is being spent. As one would expect, the Court is a completely autonomous institution and its members enjoy complete independence. However, the Court of Auditors has no legal powers of its own, and when it uncovers fraud or improper practices, these should be reported to the appropriate European Union institution which must take the necessary action to rectify the situation.

 Key point: The five main institutions of the European Union are the Council, the Commission, the Parliament, the European Court of Justice and the Court of Auditors.

Why is European law so unique?

It cannot be altered unilaterally by the governments of the member states and all are collectively bound by it. Fundamentally more important is the fact that European law confers rights and duties without the further participation of the member states. Unlike other international treaties, the citizens of the member states can enforce Treaty provisions against one another, their governments and the European institutions. The view that the European Union is a different and autonomous (independent) legal order has been consistently promoted by the Court of Justice.

Key point: European law cannot be altered by any one member state and all are bound by it.

In **Van Gend en Loos (1963)** the Court stated most clearly that the member states have limited their sovereign rights. Again, in **Costa v ENEL (1964)**, the Court of Justice stated that member states had experienced a 'permanent limitation of their sovereign rights' when they joined the European Community. European Community obligations would not be unconditional, merely contingent, if they could be called into question by the member states. In the view of the European Court of Justice, European law always prevails over national law. In **Internationale Handelsgesselschaft (1970)** the Court of Justice stated that even constitutional provisions of the Member States can be struck down. In **Simmenthal SPA v Commission (1979)** it was stated that national courts must set aside national law which may conflict with European law, and it did not matter whether the national law had been passed before the state become a member of the European Union. In **Francovich and Bonifaci v Italy (1992)** it was held that an individual may sue a member state (the government) for damages for loss suffered as a result of a Member State's failure to implement a European Union Directive.

Hutter v Technische Universität Graz (2009) is a very recent case which demonstrates the supremacy of European Union law over domestic law. Although this case was originally brought before the Austrian courts, it is a very good example of the fact that all member states of the European Union have limited their rights of national sovereignty over a range of policy areas (in this case, education policy). Very often in the United Kingdom, we are quick to complain about having to obey European rules and regulations, but it is the same story for all other member states. By becoming a signatory to the various European Treaties, a country has to limit its national sovereignty – this is the price of membership.

In the **Hutter** case, the Court of Justice decided that an Austrian national law which permitted employers to treat employees differently according to age was in breach of the European Union's Equal Treatment Directive 2000/78. The Austrian Government argued unsuccessfully that the reason for this difference in treatment between age groups was to promote a legitimate and proportionate aim i.e. to ease the entry of younger apprentices into the workforce and to ensure that general education was not treated unfavourably in comparison with vocational education. The Austrian national law was discriminatory and would have to be overruled in order to make it comply with European Union law.

This case has relevance well beyond the borders of Austria and, as shall see in our study of age discrimination in Chapter 7, employment lawyers across the European Union will be studying the decision of the European Court of Justice with great interest.

However, the idea that European Union law is superior to the law of each member state has caused serious problems for Britain and this argument has not always been easily accepted. The British courts appear to have reached a compromise which amounts to the following: as long as Britain remains a member of the European Union, European law will be regarded as superior to British law. Should Britain choose to leave the European Union at any point in the future or if the Westminster Parliament passes an Act that expressly contradicts the idea of the supremacy of European law, then the position will most definitely change.

 Key point: The British courts appear to have reached a compromise which amounts to the following – as long as Britain remains a member of the European Union, European law will be regarded as superior to British law.

The supremacy of European law undermined?

On 30 June 2009, the German Federal Constitutional Court in Karlsruhe made a statement that could potentially undermine the doctrine of the supremacy of European law. The court had been asked by Peter Gauweiler, a Christian Social Union member of the Bundestag (the German Federal Parliament), to consider whether the Treaty of Lisbon, signed by the Heads of State or Government of the 27 member states on 13 December 2007, was compatible with German law. Apparently, the Treaty complies with German law, but this was not the source of the controversy.

The judges went on to state that national courts (presumably not the Court of Justice) should be the final arbiters when dealing with the interpretation and implementation of European law.

In a statement released by the Constitutional Court, the following assertion is made:

"The authorisation to transfer sovereign powers to the European Union ... is ... granted under the condition that the sovereign statehood of a constitutional state is maintained on the basis of a responsible integration programme according to the principle of conferral and respecting the Member States' constitutional identity, and that at the same time the Federal Republic of Germany does not lose its ability to politically and socially shape the living conditions on its own responsibility".

Such a suggestion by the German Constitutional Court (the highest court in the land) is completely at odds with the orthodox position which emphasises the supremacy of European law at the expense of national law. It is little wonder that that José Manuel Barroso, the European Commission President, reacted so negatively to the opinion of the German Court. It remains to be seen whether the actions of the German Constitutional Court represent a real challenge to the doctrine of the supremacy of European law or whether it is a position from which the German judges will be forced to retreat by the Court of Justice.

The Role of the Court of Justice (CJ)

The CJ (http://curia.europa.eu) sits in Luxembourg and its task is to ensure that the laws of the European Union are properly observed when the member states implement their treaty obligations via their domestic legal systems. Admittedly, the vast bulk of cases coming before the CJ will be firmly rooted in the civil system. Criminal courts, however, should be aware that certain decisions by them may infringe European law. In such a case, the court may choose to approach the CJ for clarification of European law. In the English criminal case of **R v Marlborough Street Stipendiary Magistrates *ex parte* Bouchereau (1977)** the magistrate in question made a recommendation for the deportation of Bouchereau, but it was claimed that the magistrate had no power to do this as Bouchereau was a migrant worker as defined under the Treaty of Rome. The Magistrate referred the case to the CJ in Luxembourg for a preliminary ruling.

The decisions of the CJ must be accepted by the courts of the member states. It is important to note that the decisions of the CJ cannot be appealed. Matters brought to the court are disposed of before all the judges, although some preliminary (interlocutory) matters can be dealt with by a division of three judges. The CJ consists of professional judges, academic lawyers and public servants. A judge may only be removed by the unanimous decision of the other judges.

 Key point: The Court of Justice sits in Luxembourg and its task is to ensure that the laws of the European Union are properly observed when the member states implement their Treaty obligations via their domestic legal systems.

Procedure

At the CJ, more emphasis is placed on written submissions (pleadings) rather than on oral arguments. The proceedings are more inquisitorial in nature and the judges play a far more active role in asking questions during the proceedings. Eight Advocates-General assist the court and provide the CJ with independent opinions before it publishes its decision. The opinions of the Advocates-General, however, are not always followed by the CJ; but they can be extremely interesting in their own right.

The CJ gives a single decision – dissenting views are not revealed. The enforcement of the Court's decisions will be carried out by the national courts of the member states. The language spoken at the hearing before the Court will normally be that of the pursuer, unless the pursuer is suing a member state which means that the language spoken will be that member state's.

 Key point: The CJ gives a single decision – dissenting views are not revealed and the enforcement of the Court's decisions will be carried out by the national courts of the member states.

A particularly important role for the CJ is its power to give preliminary rulings under Article 267 of the Treaty of Rome. A preliminary ruling concerns an application to the ECJ from any court or tribunal of a member state requesting that an area of EU law be clarified. Article 267 references were particularly important in the early days of the Community when European law was being built from the ground up.

The CJ may also deal with the following types of actions:

- ◆ Actions against a member state by the Commission for failure to fulfil Treaty obligations (Article 226)
- ◆ Actions by one member state against another for failure to fulfil Treaty obligations (Article 227)
- ◆ Actions by a member state, an individual or a company/business association against the Council or the Commission for acting in breach of the Treaties (Article 263)
- ◆ Actions by a member state against the Council or the Commission for failure to act (Article 232)

The role of the Court of Justice at Luxembourg

The English Court of Appeal in **Bulmer *v* Bollinger (1974)** stated that the English High Court and the Court of Appeal had a right to interpret European law without referring the matter to the CJ. If the case went before the House of Lords (now the UK Supreme Court), however, that court is **bound** to refer the case to the ECJ if either or both parties wish it. Any court or tribunal of a member state (under Article 267) may request a preliminary ruling but only the Supreme Court is bound to do this if one of the parties before it requests this procedure.

In **Bulmer** (the so called 'Champagne' case), Lord Denning MR laid down certain guidelines on whether a judge should refer the matter to the CJ:

1 The time involved to obtain a ruling – Article 267 references can take a long time to be heard. Would this lead to undue protraction of the case, delays and expense for both parties?

2 The CJ must not be swamped with Article 267 references – all the judges of the CJ must deliberate on a reference from a national court and they are not allowed to split into divisions to consider the matter.

3 The question must concern a matter of interpretation of the Treaty only. The manner in which a national court/tribunal interpreted the Treaty (wrongly or incompletely) can provide grounds for an Article 267 reference.

4 The difficulty surrounding the question of European law raised i.e. the complexity of the point of law. Is it entirely appropriate that a Scottish or English judge should decide the matter?

5 The national court will have to consider the wishes of the parties and this will be especially so when one of the parties does not wish the case to be referred to the CJ for a preliminary ruling.

6 A national court should not refer a case to the CJ for a preliminary ruling if the principal of law has already been sufficiently clarified by previous decisions.

If the area of European law is sufficiently clear then the judge will have no need to refer the case to the CJ under Article 267. This is known as the doctrine of *Acte Claire*.

 Key point: The preliminary ruling procedure under Article 267 is used by national courts as a means of clarifying EU law.

The Human Rights Act 1998

This Act came into force on 2 October 2000 and it implements the European Convention on Human Rights directly into United Kingdom law. The European Convention aims to protect basic human and democratic rights. It was partly incorporated into Scots law a year before the rest of the United Kingdom by means of the Scotland Act 1998.

In 1950, the United Kingdom signed the European Convention on Human Rights and Fundamental Freedoms which was inspired by the Universal Declaration of

This, of course, leads us to the fundamental question: do we promote human rights for everyone in society or only those whom we regard as deserving of the protection of the law? Supporters of the Human Rights Act 1998 argue that, as the United Kingdom lacks a written constitution (like the USA and Germany) guaranteeing full democratic rights and freedoms, anything which protects the individual from the abuse of state power in this country can only be viewed as a positive development. In 2005, for example, the House of Lords came out strongly against the notion that the use of intelligence as evidence in British courts obtained from the torture of terror suspects was a clear breach of the United Kingdom's human rights obligations under European and international laws.

One thing is certain: there has been a huge rise in human rights cases being brought before the Scottish courts (and before the other UK courts and, indeed, the European Court of Human Rights) as a result of the Human Rights Act. The Act, of course, permits individuals to pursue claims against public authorities in either the UK courts or before the European Court of Human Rights.

 Key point: The Human Rights Act 1998 permits individuals to raise actions against the State in the British courts or before the European Court of Human Rights.

 Pretty *v* United Kingdom (2002) Diane Pretty was suffering from a serious degenerative disease. She wished to end her life and due to the seriousness of her condition (in the latter stages of the disease) she was confined to a wheelchair and her husband was her primary carer. Pretty had asked her husband to help her to commit suicide, but she was concerned that he would face criminal prosecution for helping her to kill herself. She took legal action to clarify the law as to whether she had the right under Article 2 of the European Convention to choose the time and the means of her death (by involving a third party). Normally, Article 2 is about the right to life not the right to die.

Held: by the European Court of Human Rights that Article 2 was about the protection of a person's right to life and it did not give a person the right to die whether assisted by a third party or a public body.

 Peck *v* UK (2003) Peck suffered from a serious depressive illness. He tried to commit suicide by slitting his wrists while in a public street. The street had CCTV cameras and Peck's attempted suicide was captured on film. The film and still images were later released publicly without Peck consenting to this and no attempt was made to safeguard his identity. He later took legal action against the local authority which controlled the CCTV cameras alleging that his right to a private life (protected by Article 8 of the Convention) had been abused.

Held: by the European Court of Human Rights that the filming of the incident did not necessarily breach Peck's human rights under Article 8 of the Convention. However, the local authority had failed to justify why it had released images of the incident in the first place and why it had failed to safeguard Peck's identity. These actions, therefore, represented an unwarranted and disproportionate interference in Peck's private life.

Connors *v* UK (2004) a family of gypsies had used a local authority run camping site for 13 years. Members of the family were later accused of being involved in anti-social behaviour and the local authority had the family removed from the site using a summary eviction procedure. The family took legal action against the local authority claiming that the decision to evict them from the site had effectively made them homeless and this was a breach of the right to respect of the home under Article 8.

Held: by the European Court of Human Rights that the local authority's summary eviction procedure did not give the family proper protection and, therefore, the decision to make them homeless was a breach of Article 8. The family was allegedly evicted on the grounds of protecting the public interest, but the local authority had failed to bring sufficient evidence to prove that the eviction was valid on these grounds.

 Napier *v* Scottish Ministers [2005] Robert Napier, a prisoner in HMP Barlinnie, was awarded £2,000 in compensation when he took the Scottish prison service to court in relation to the practice of inmates at Scottish prisons having to slop out. Many Scottish prisons were built in the Victorian era and many of the cells lack modern toilet facilities. Inmates are, therefore, provided with a bucket which they have to empty every morning. Napier argued that this practice was breach of Article 3 of the European Convention which prohibits cruel and degrading treatment or punishment. Napier also claimed that a skin condition from which he suffered had also worsened as a result of this practice.

Held: by Lord Bonomy in the Outer House of the Court of Session that the Scottish Prison Service was in breach of Article 3 and that Napier's human rights had been abused. The Scottish Ministers subsequently admitted that they were retaining £58 million in order to meet compensation claims brought by 1,400 inmates of Scotland's prisons taking legal action against the practice of slopping out.

 Hirst *v* United Kingdom [2004]; Hirst *v* United Kingdom (No. 2) [2006] John Hirst, a British convict serving a discretionary life sentence for manslaughter, took a case to the European Court of Human Rights in Strasbourg to protest against the practice first established under the UK Forfeiture Act of 1878 which prevents prisoners from having the right to vote in elections. The current law is contained in Section 3 of the Representation of the People Act 1983. Hirst, with two other individuals, had initially brought a case to the English High Court in 2001 in order to argue that the continuing ban on prisoners being able to vote was incompatible with Article 3 of the European Convention on Human Rights. Hirst and his fellow litigants lost the case and decided to take the matter to Strasbourg in March 2004. Lord Filkin, the Parliamentary Under-Secretary of State at the Department for Constitutional Affairs, remarked of the case that:

> *"It has been the view of successive governments, including this government, that persons who have committed crimes serious enough to warrant a custodial sentence should forfeit the right to have a say in how the country is governed while they are detained … For many*

years it has been part of our society's tradition that, when people are imprisoned, they lose a range of rights, one of which is the right to participate in elections."

The European Court of Human Rights ruled against the blanket ban on prisoners exercising the vote in elections (the British Government subsequently lost the appeal to the Grand Chamber of the court) on the grounds that it was incompatible with the Convention. Consequently, the British Government conceded that it would have to make changes to the law banning all prisoners from exercising the vote in an election. Practically speaking, it appears as if those prisoners serving a sentence of less than four years will be permitted to exercise the vote in future. Those prisoners serving longer sentences for more serious crimes will not have this right extended to them.

The British Government has failed to implement fully the **Hirst** decision. In October 2008, William Beggs, the notorious Scottish murderer who is currently serving a life sentence at HMP Peterhead, organised a campaign to include prisoners on the electoral register. Sheriff Colin Harris, sitting at Aberdeen Sheriff Court, dismissed this attempt and Beggs subsequently appealed to the Court of Session. In July 2009, the Press and Journal newspaper revealed that 224 inmates at Peterhead had been in touch with the body which supervises the electoral register in the North-East of Scotland in an attempt to be given the right to vote in elections.

 A (and others) *v* Secretary of State for the Home Department [2005] the House of Lords made the landmark ruling that evidence obtained from terrorist suspects who may have been subjected to torture by foreign intelligence operatives could not be used in British courts. Eight men were being held indefinitely in British prisons without charge on the mere suspicion of participating in terrorist activities. The men brought the case before the House of Lords arguing that their detention was illegal under the European Convention. The British Government argued that the intelligence obtained about the men was compelling and, therefore, their continued detention without charge was justified as a matter of national security. The Government had won an earlier appeal in the English Court of Appeal which had ruled that information against the men which had been obtained from agents of foreign intelligence services, who may or may not have used torture in order to acquire this intelligence, could be admissible in British courts. The Court of Appeal stated that there was no obligation on the British Government to inquire about the methods surrounding the way in which foreign intelligence services gathered information about terrorist suspects. The House of Lords said that this was completely unacceptable and was clear breach of the United Kingdom's obligations under domestic and international human rights laws.

 R (Williamson and others) *v* Secretary of State for Education and Employment (and others) (2005) a school sought to challenge the ban on corporal punishment of children by using Article 9 of the European Convention. Article 9 promotes freedom of thought and religion and was used (rather bizarrely) by the school to argue that its teachers were acting *in loco parentis* (in the place of the parents) in respect of the pupils in its care and it should have discretion (as parents do), in the setting of a Christian education, about how to punish children who misbehave. Such discretion may, ultimately, involve the use of corporal punishment.

Held: by the House of Lords that the continuing statutory prohibition on the corporal punishment of children was a legitimate and proportionate aim in that it protected children from being subjected to violence. The school's attempt to have the ban overturned was, therefore, unsuccessful.

The Influence of the European Court of Human Rights

This court sits in Strasbourg and was established by the Convention for the Protection of Human Rights and Fundamental Freedoms.

The European Court of Human Rights (www.echr.coe.int/echr/) is a single, full-time court which deals with the enforcement of human rights and democratic freedoms which are protected by the European Convention on Human Rights (see the Human Rights Act 1998). It sits at Strasbourg in France and it should not be confused with the European Court of Justice – it is a completely separate institution. The Court of Human Rights is the court of the Council of Europe, an organisation of more than 40 European member states. All the member states of the European Union are members of this body. The Council of Europe is a body which aims to promote culture, the rule of law and respect for democratic freedoms.

The court heard its first case in 1960 – **Lawless *v* Ireland (1961)** – in which Lawless, a member of the Irish Republican Army, took legal action against the authorities of the Irish Republic whereby he alleged that he had been illegally detained and held in a military camp whilst attempting to travel to the United Kingdom. Lawless alleged that the actions of the Irish Republic in detaining him constituted breaches of Article 5 (the right to liberty and security), Article 6 (the right to a fair trial) and Article 7 (the general prohibition of the enactment of retrospective criminal offences) of the European Convention. Lawless ultimately lost his case because the Irish Government was able to rely on the argument that its need to promote national security was of greater importance than a person's individual human rights given the very real threat of terrorism with which it had to deal.

The Lawless case is of great importance since it is regarded as the first decision of its type which saw the application of international human rights laws and the first case which was tried by an international court or tribunal where a private citizen took legal action against a state.

In **Lawless**, Rene Cassin, the then President of the European Court of Human Rights made the following, robust declaration:

"The court exists only to serve the cause of justice."

Until 2 October 2000, British citizens who were alleging that their human rights had been violated by the State were forced to take their cases to this court. Very often, it could take up to five years or longer to have the case heard and decided. As a result of the introduction of the Human Rights Act 1998 and the Scotland Act 1998, British citizens can now directly enforce the rights given to them by the European Convention in British courts.

property damage. The three individuals were shot and killed by members of the elite SAS regiment before the bomb could be detonated. The SAS did not give the three IRA members an opportunity to surrender first. It was this shoot-to-kill policy which fell foul of the Strasbourg judges. The right to life is guaranteed by Article 2 of the European Convention and is considered to be one of its most important provisions – contracting states are not permitted to ignore or abuse this right. As will be appreciated, the judgment in **McCann** caused considerable controversy and outrage in the United Kingdom. In fact, over many years, the United Kingdom has found itself dragged before the European Court in relation to its handling of the political situation in Northern Ireland (which was at its worst phase from the early 1970s until the first IRA ceasefire in 1994). The United Kingdom argued that it was taking legitimate measures to safeguard the lives and security of its citizens in its effort to combat terrorism. However, the European Court did not always see eye to eye with the United Kingdom.

 Key point: The European Court of Human Rights recognises that member states have a measure of discretion in the way that they give effect to general standards set out in the Convention.

 Key point: The Human Rights Act 1998 has led to a huge increase in these types of cases going to court.

Historical sources of law

These sources of law are now very much on the margins and play little importance in the development of Scots law. The historical sources of law include:

◆ The institutional writers
◆ Canon law
◆ Feudal law

 Key point: Historical source of law include the institutional writers, Canon law and Feudal law.

The institutional writers

In the past, various Scottish lawyers have contributed in an outstanding way to our understanding of the development of the Scots law. The ideas that these individuals promoted are still debated in Scottish universities to this day and may even be used in court cases to illustrate important legal points. These individuals include:

◆ Sir Thomas Craig who published *Jus Feudale* in 1655
◆ John Dalrymple, Viscount Stair, who published *Institutions of the Law of Scotland* in 1681
◆ Lord Bankton who published *An Institute of the Laws of Scotland* in 1751
◆ Professor John Erskine who published *Institute of the Law of Scotland* in 1772
◆ Baron Hume who published his *Lectures* between 1786 and 1822
◆ Professor George Bell who published *Commentaries on the Law of Scotland and the Principles of Mercantile Jurisprudence* in 1810, followed by the *Principles of the Law of Scotland* in 1829

As should be somewhat obvious, the institutional writers have not published anything since 1829!

In **McDyer *v* Celtic Football and Athletic Company Ltd and Others** (3 March 2000) the Court of Session heard arguments from both lawyers that drew heavily on the work of Bankton and Hume (see Chapter 3).

 Key point: The institutional writers are historical individuals who have recorded the development and contributed to our understanding of Scots law.

Canon law

This is the law of the Christian Church which is based on the biblical books of the Old and New Testaments. It is worth remembering that this source played a very important role in the development of Scots law. When the Court of Session was created in 1532, the first Lord President was the Roman Catholic Abbot of Cambuskenneth. Furthermore, half the judges of the court were either Roman Catholic priests or monks who arrived at their decisions based on their training in Canon law. After the period known as the Reformation from 1560 onwards, the influence of the Roman Catholic Church was swept away and the new Calvinist (Protestant) religion promoted by John Knox and the other Reformers held sway. However, Scotland remained a remarkably religious country until the 1960s.

 Key point: Canon law is the law of the Christian church.

Today, we obviously live in a less religious age, but the influences of Canon law can still be felt. The Scots law of Incest is based almost in its entirety on the Old Testament Book of Leviticus. The Book of Leviticus also forbids marriages between same sex partners and Scots law, despite recent proposals, has not yet recognised such unions. The fact that murder is also a crime could be said to be directly influenced by the Old Testament Book of Exodus which tells the story of the Jewish Prophet Moses who received the Ten Commandments directly from God. These Ten Commandments were a set of legal and moral rules for the Jewish people which were later adopted by Christians. Whether the vast majority of us like it or not, the influence of Canon law is still felt in modern Scottish society.

Feudal law

The feudal system is described as a multi-tiered system of land ownership and, consequently, it can be very complex. It was introduced to Scotland during the reign of King David I (1124–53). From the earliest days of the system, it operated, however, on very simple principles. The King (the Superior) would grant parcels of land to his supporters (vassals) who, in return, would administer the land (very often in the role of Sheriff – another English practice) and, more importantly, they would provide the King with soldiers in times of war or civil unrest.

In other words, the feudal system was all about maintaining royal power in Scotland (i.e. land for loyalty). The land was *never* granted absolutely – if a vassal (i.e. the person who held the land) failed to keep his side of the bargain, the King would remove all his rights to the land and appoint someone in his place. These supporters would in turn distribute parts of the land to their followers in order to retain their loyalty. Property is divided into two categories:

◆ Heritable property
◆ Moveable property

The fundamental principle of the feudal system always centred around tenure. This means that the land was granted according to certain conditions which the vassal had to carry out dutifully. It may be rather hard to believe, but the feudal system survived into the twenty-first century before it was abolished on 28 November 2004 when the provisions of the Abolition of Feudal Tenure etc. (Scotland) Act 2000 took effect.

 Key point: Feudal law is an ancient system of land ownership which was abolished in November 2004.

The Legal Profession in Scotland

In Scotland, as in England, practising lawyers are divided into two groups:

◆ Solicitors and solicitor-advocates
◆ Advocates

Solicitors

This term has been in use in Scotland since 1922 and originated in England. Before 1922, solicitors in Scotland were referred to as notaries and writers.

Most practising Scottish lawyers will be solicitors. A solicitor can be hired directly by members of the public and solicitors' firms can be found in the high streets of most towns and cities in Scotland. Solicitors are trained to deal with all sorts of legal matters from the beginning of a case to its end. All solicitors must hold a current practising certificate and be members of the Law Society of Scotland. The Law Society is the recognised professional body which regulates solicitors and which disciplines those members who break the rules.

Solicitors will appear before both the criminal and the civil courts. Before the introduction of the Law Reform (Miscellaneous Provisions) Scotland Act 1990, solicitors were confined to the lower Scottish courts, namely, the Justice of the Peace and Sheriff Courts. It is now possible for a solicitor to take further examinations in order to gain a qualification which makes it possible for him to appear before the higher Scottish courts such as the High Court of Justiciary, the Court of Session and the UK Supreme Court. This now means that a solicitor-advocate can appear before all the Scottish courts.

To become a solicitor, there are two possible paths:

By Law Society Examinations – a trainee must first register as a pre-diploma trainee with a firm of solicitors. The Law Society stipulates what exams the trainee must pass in order to complete this course. Trainees must become familiar with the three compulsory areas of conveyancing, court work and either trusts and executries or the work of a local authority. This initial training period will last for three years.

By university degree – a student will register for a Bachelor of Laws degree (LLB) in Scots Law at one of the nine Scottish universities offering this course. It will take a student three years to gain a Pass degree and four years to gain an Honours degree. Many students will now complete an Honours degree owing to the very stiff competition for jobs with law firms.

Passing Law Society or university exams is only part of the training process. Budding solicitors will have to register for a Diploma in Legal Practice at one of the Scottish universities which provide this training. Entrance to the Diploma is by no means automatic and universities can afford to pick and choose the best students. Students are expected to attend the Diploma course for a period of 26 weeks. The Diploma course is highly practical in content and nature and students will often be taught by practising solicitors.

After completion of the Diploma in Legal Practice, the trainee will have to complete a period of further training of two years with a qualified solicitor. However, trainee solicitors can apply for a restricted practising certificate after one year which means that it is possible for them to appear in court as long they are supervised by a qualified solicitor. When trainees have finished their training, they can apply to the Law Society of Scotland for a full practising certificate. This will allow them to set up in business on their own, set up in partnership with other solicitors or become an employee of a firm, then an associate, then perhaps a partner. In 2009, the Law Society was looking at proposals to make the training of solicitors more flexible.

Advocates

There are just under 500 practising advocates in Scotland today. These lawyers are specialists in pleadings in court. The pleading in court is concerned with the preparation and presentation of a case. Some advocates have the reputation of being experts in a particular field of law and, as a result, they provide opinions on complex legal questions. They are a completely separate branch of the legal profession from solicitors. They are self-employed and do not form partnerships with other advocates. Advocates, unlike solicitors, are not members of a law firm. Advocates tend to be organised into units called stables with a clerk who will be responsible for administrative matters. Members of the profession will either be referred to as Junior Counsel or Senior Counsel. Senior Counsels are referred to as Queen's Counsels and have the initials QC after their names. Practising advocates of ten years' standing can apply to the Dean of the Faculty of Advocates to be admitted to the ranks of QCs.

As previously mentioned, the Law of Society of Scotland is the professional organisation which represents the interests of solicitors. The body which represents the interests of advocates is the Faculty of Advocates in Edinburgh. This a democratic organisation headed by a Dean who is elected by the membership. The Faculty of Advocates is self-regulating and it determines who can become an advocate.

In order to become an advocate, an individual will usually have gained at least a lower second class LLB Honours degree from one of the nine Scottish universities which offer this course or have passed the Law Society exams. There are other recognised degrees which would be acceptable to the Faculty of Advocates. Upon admission, the candidate (known as an Intrant) will have to pass Faculty exams and obtain a Diploma in Legal Practice from a Scottish university. The Intrant will have to complete a training period of 21 months with a qualified solicitor and serve an apprenticeship of nine months with a recognised advocate. The apprenticeship with an advocate is known as 'devilling'. Finally, the Intrant must pass the Faculty examination in Evidence, Practice and Procedure. An Intrant will then be admitted to membership of the Faculty of Advocates.

Advocates can appear in all the Scottish courts whether criminal or civil. Before the introduction of the Law Reform (Miscellaneous Provisions) Scotland Act 1990, only advocates could appear before the most senior Scottish courts – the High Court of Justiciary, the Court of Session and the UK Supreme Court. Solicitors were, therefore forced to instruct an advocate to appear on behalf of one of their clients before these courts. Now, of course, the small number of solicitor-advocates will be able to represent clients. However, ordinary solicitors will continue to instruct advocates or solicitor-advocates.

Advocates will be instructed by solicitors to appear in a case. They do not deal with members of the public directly. Advocates will attend consultations with a client, but this meeting will almost always take place in the presence of the client's solicitor. It should be appreciated that the solicitor will have done most of the work when it comes to preparing the case such as taking precognitions (witness statements) and keeping on top of the vast amounts of paperwork that the case will no doubt generate.

When appearing in court, a QC or Senior Counsel will be assisted by a Junior Counsel. Advocates have a distinctive appearance in that they wear a wig and a gown. This marks them out from a solicitor who will wear a simple black gown when appearing in court.

Association of Commercial Attorneys (ACA)

The Association has been approved by the Lord President of the Court of Session, the Office of Fair Trading and the Scottish Government. Such individuals must complete a four-day Sheriff Court practice training course and hold a Master of Laws (LLM) in construction law or a construction related qualification. This Masters degree permits them to appear on behalf of their clients before the Sheriff Court in small claims and summary claims in cases which involve construction and building. Members of the Association will have to instruct a solicitor or an advocate to appear on their client's behalf in ordinary claims in the Sheriff Court. The first Commercial Attorneys had the right of appearance in the Sheriff Court from April 2009.

 Key points: In order to be regarded as a qualified lawyer in Scotland, an individual must either be a solicitor, a solicitor-advocate or an advocate.

Paralegals

For many years, clerks have been employed in law firms to undertake particular types of legal work in the areas of conveyancing, executries and trusts. An increasing number of law firms are also employing paralegals. Paralegals will often have a professional or vocational qualification, such as a Higher National Certificate or Diploma in Legal Services, often gained at a Further Education College. These types of employees, although not solicitors nor advocates, will have a background in the law and have a good working knowledge of legal procedures.

The Scottish Paralegals Association has been in existence since 1993 and is the only professional body representing the interests and the views of paralegals which is recognised by the Law of Society of Scotland. There are now moves afoot to introduce registered paralegals to Scotland, which will ensure a uniformity and consistency in the training of such individuals.

Law Reform (Miscellaneous Provisions) Scotland Act 1990

Under this Act, there exist provisions which would allow certain suitable persons to represent members of the public before the Scottish courts. These legal representatives would not need to be solicitors or advocates. Safeguards, however, would have to be in place to allow these individuals to practise law in Scotland. The people most likely to benefit from these provisions would be those individuals who possess a law degree, but who are not practising lawyers. The provisions in the Act of 1990 were never brought into force. In 2003, the Scottish Executive was considering proposals to open up the provision of legal services in Scotland in an attempt to increase competition by bringing the 1990 Act fully into force. This development is partly in response to events in England where it looks as if the Law Society and the Bar Council will lose their monopoly on legal services. The Scottish Government introduced a Bill to increase competition in the legal services market in 2009 and we shall now turn our attention to this development.

The Legal Profession (Scotland) Bill

The proposals contained in this Bill were published by the Scottish Government on 7 January 2009. The main purpose of the Bill is to open up the Scottish legal services market to greater competition.

In essence the Bill, if passed into law by the Scottish Parliament, would allow lawyers in Scotland to set up alternative business structures thus allowing them to enter into commercial relationships with other professionals who are not lawyers. Presently, the traditional way in which lawyers have carried out business is by way of a partnership regulated by the Partnership Act 1890 or as limited liability partnership regulated by the Limited Liability Partnership Act 2000. Both of these business structures are firmly based on the idea of a commercial organisation where its members (practising lawyers regulated by their own professional bodies e.g. the Law Society of Scotland) deliver legal services to the public.

If the Bill is implemented, it will be much easier for lawyers in Scotland to enter into relationships with non-lawyers in order to deliver a range of legal services to the public. It will also be easier for individuals (subject to a fit to own test) who are not lawyers to be the proprietors of legal practices. The new system of alternative business structures will also necessitate a thorough overhaul of the current system of regulation for those providing legal services to the public.

The reforms were considered necessary after *Which?*, the consumer organisation, submitted a complaint to the Office of Fair Trading about the perceived lack of competition in the Scottish legal services market. Whether the Bill will actually achieve this objective is a subject for future discussion.

Key point: Many individuals who are not qualified lawyers also provide legal services, for example, paralegals and those individuals who hold a law degree.

The Law Officers of the Crown

Since the introduction of the Scotland Act in 1998, there are now three Scottish law officers. These individuals are:

◆ The Lord Advocate
◆ The Solicitor-General for Scotland
◆ The Advocate-General for Scotland

Before the creation of the Scottish Parliament, Scotland had just two law officers – the Lord Advocate and the Solicitor-General. The Lord Advocate and the Solicitor-General are legal advisors of the Scottish Government in Edinburgh whereas the Advocate-General is both a member of the United Kingdom government in London and its legal advisor on Scottish matters.

These appointments are political in nature in the sense that the First Minister for Scotland will appoint the Lord Advocate and the Solicitor-General and the British Prime Minister will appoint the Advocate-General. Previous holders of the two most established law officer posts were often active politicians in either the Conservative or Labour Parties although a party political background is probably of much less importance these days. It will be appreciated that these individuals may have to leave their posts if there was a change of Scottish or British governments.

Elish Angiolini, the Lord Advocate is the most senior Scottish law officer. Mrs Angiolini is the first woman and the first solicitor to hold this post. Despite being a solicitor, she holds the rank of Senior Counsel (Queen's Counsel). Mrs Angiolini is entitled to use the initials QC because she acts as counsel to the Crown despite the fact that she is not, and never has been, a member of the Faculty of Advocates. Mrs Angiolini had previously been the Solicitor-General for Scotland and she succeeded Colin Boyd QC, the former Lord Advocate in 2006. The Lord Advocate has a number of important functions:

1   They are the principal state prosecutor with responsibility for the Scottish public prosecution system.

2   They will appear as the prosecutor in major criminal trials, for example, the Lockerbie and the Moira Jones murder trial before the High Court of Justiciary.

3   They are the head of the Crown Office and Procurator Fiscal Service, the Scottish Government department with responsibility for all crimes committed in Scotland.

4   They are the legal adviser to the Scottish Government.

5   They represent the Scottish Government in the Scottish Courts, the European Court of Justice and the European Court of Human Rights.

Frank Mulholland QC is the current Solicitor-General for Scotland. The Solicitor-General is the Lord Advocate's assistant. He was appointed to the post in May 2007, replacing John Beckett. The Solicitor-General can use the title Queen's Counsel and the initials QC will appear after his name despite the fact that he is a solicitor because by reason of his appointment he is a legal adviser to the Crown in Scotland.

The Lord Advocate and the Solicitor-General are assisted in their duties by Advocate Deputes. Advocate Deputes are usually experienced, practising members of the Faculty of Advocates and they usually hold these positions for three years. Advocates Depute appear as prosecutors before the criminal courts in jury trials. The two law officers of the Crown Office and the Advocate Deputes are referred to as Crown Counsel.

The post of Advocate-General for Scotland was introduced as a result of the Scotland Act 1998. Dr Lynda Clark QC (as she was then) was the first holder of the post and she was an advocate. Dr Clark, who had also served as a Labour MP, was subsequently raised to the peerage by the then Prime Minister Tony Blair and, in January 2006, she was appointed as a Senator of the College of Justice. This appointment to the Scottish judiciary meant that Baroness Clark had to tender her resignation as Advocate-General. Neil Davidson QC (who would later become Lord Glen Cova) replaced Baroness Clark and is the current Advocate-General for Scotland. Interestingly, Lord Glen Cova previously served as Solicitor-General for Scotland.

The Advocate-General is a member of the United Kingdom Government Department for Constitutional Affairs. The Advocate-General has a number of important functions:

1   They are a legal adviser to the British government on matters of Scots law.

2   They can represent the British government in legal proceedings before the Scottish courts and the Judicial Committee of the Privy Council where the case involves devolution or human rights issues.

3   They have the right to refer Scottish Parliament Bills to the Judicial Committee of the Privy Council in order to ensure that the Scottish Parliament is acting within its powers.

4   They serve on a number of British Cabinet committees.

The Advocate-General is also referred to as Crown Counsel.

 Key point: There are three Scottish Law Officers who provide legal advice to the Crown on matters of Scots law – the Lord Advocate, the Solicitor-General and the Advocate-General.

Judicial appointments

All appointments of Judges and Sheriffs in Scotland are, theoretically, within the gift of the Queen acting on the recommendation of the First Minister for Scotland. The First Minister, in turn, seeks the advice of the independent Judicial Appointments Board which was established in 2002. The Board is regulated by the Judiciary and Courts (Scotland) Act 2008 and its current Chair is Sir Muir Russell. The Board now advertises judicial posts, as and when appropriate, and will interview candidates and provide a shortlist of people suitable for appointment as judges. An example of an advertisement from the Board's website can be seen below:

The Civil Justice System

The civil justice system, unlike criminal law, primarily exists to resolve legal disputes between private individuals in areas as diverse as family law, company law, partnership law, banking and finance law, sale of goods and services, consumer law, personal injury claims, trusts, defamation actions, succession issues and divorce.

 Key point: The civil justice system exists to resolve legal disputes between private individuals.

In many situations, the main function of the civil justice system will be to compensate the victim who has suffered a loss as a result of someone's wrongful behaviour. Surprisingly, most legal disputes are firmly in the realm of the civil jurisdiction. However, amongst members of the Scottish public, there still remains a surprisingly high degree of ignorance about the importance of the civil justice system. Crime, of course, grabs the headlines and takes hold of the public's imagination in a way that civil law never could.

Criminal law, on the other hand, is an attempt by the state to maintain law and order by punishing certain individuals who indulge in behaviour which is regarded as criminal and anti-social. The state uses the criminal law, therefore, to punish criminals on behalf of the community or society.

 Key point: Criminal law is an attempt by the state to maintain law and order through the punishment of criminal and anti-social behaviour.

Unlike criminal law, the parties to a civil action are not required to demonstrate that their version of the story has been proved beyond a reasonable doubt. Civil trials have a much lower standard of proof or evidence. A judge in a civil action will decide the outcome of a case by weighing up the balance of probabilities. This means that a Sheriff, for example, will decide to favour one party over the other by favouring the version of the facts which he considers to be more accurate or more believable.

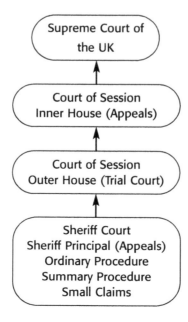

Technically, it is possible for the Sheriff to decide the case on the testimony of one witness and that witness could be one of the parties. Corroboration or the ability to back up all the evidence is not strictly required as in criminal law. Obviously, the more reliable witnesses and evidence that a party in a civil action can rely upon will strengthen the case in their favour.

The parties to a civil action are referred to as *litigants*. The *pursuer* is the person who brings the dispute to the attention of the court by lodging a legal action. The *defender* is the party against whom the legal action is being brought. At this point, it is important to stress that the civil courts are a facility or a resource which the state provides in order to resolve civil disputes in a peaceful fashion.

People cannot be forced to use the civil courts if they have no desire to do so. If, for example, someone owes you money for work that you have performed for them and you do not receive the money, it is entirely up to you whether you decide to pursue the matter before the courts if persuasion fails. A judge will not come to your door and issue you with a personal invitation to attend your local court and have your case heard. If you do nothing, you have no one to blame but yourself for your predicament. The state merely provides court facilities which the parties to a private or civil dispute are free to use if they wish.

 Key point: The pursuer and the defender are the parties to a civil action and together they are referred to as litigants.

Burden of proof in civil cases

In the cases of **Mullan *v* Anderson 1993** and **Napier *v* Scottish Ministers [2005]**, the Inner House of the Court of Session expressly rejected the notion that, in some civil cases, there can be an intermediate standard of proof sitting somewhere between the balance of probabilities (the normal civil standard) and beyond reasonable doubt (the normal criminal standard). Civil cases which departed from the normal standard of proof i.e. the balance of probabilities would represent a radical break from established Scottish tradition and should be strenuously discouraged.

The civil justice system in Scotland consists of three major courts:

◆ The Supreme Court of the UK
◆ The Court of Session
◆ The Sheriff Court

The Sheriff Court and the Court of Session

The Sheriff Court and the Court of Session are both courts of trial and courts of appeal. The Supreme Court of the UK, by comparison, hears Scottish civil appeals only.

Civil cases are allocated to the various courts for trial by reference to the value of the case. The Court of Session can hear cases which have a monetary value of more than £5,000. If the case is valued at below £5,000, it must be heard in the Sheriff

Court – although the Sheriff Court can also deal with actions which have a value greater than £5,000. It is possible, therefore, for a case which has a value greater than £5,000 to be heard by either the Sheriff Court or the Court of Session. This is known as concurrent jurisdiction.

 Key point: The value of a case does not include any claim for expenses or interest. These matters are dealt with after the court has made its decision.

Where the pursuer has a choice of whether to raise a claim before the Sheriff Court or the Court of Session, he will often choose the Sheriff Court for very sensible reasons. The Sheriff Court is a local court and if the pursuer lives outside Edinburgh he may not want to go to the bother of travelling to and from Edinburgh (not to mention the travelling costs). There are 49 Sheriff Courts located throughout Scotland, whereas there is only a single Court of Session with 32 judges. It is likely that the Sheriff Court will be able to deal with the case more quickly than the Court of Session. A pursuer attending the Sheriff Court will normally make use of the services of a single lawyer (his solicitor). If the action is before the Court of Session, the pursuer will have to hire a solicitor who will then have to instruct an advocate to appear before the Court of Session. Some solicitors have qualified as solicitor-advocates and consequently they will have the right to appear in the Court of Session.

 Key point: the shared jurisdiction of the Sheriff Court and the Court of Session is known as concurrent jurisdiction and this applies to cases valued at £5,000 or more.

A pursuer will only really prefer the Court of Session if the cases involves very large amounts of money or if it is likely that the defender will eventually appeal to the Court of Session if the pursuer wins the case. However, as already discussed, the Sheriff Court is not restricted in any way to the value of cases that it can deal with. The choice of court will often be dictated by the pursuer's particular needs and personal circumstances.

The Sheriff Court

The Sheriff Court is the lowest civil court in Scotland. However, it is also the busiest civil court in Scotland. The Sheriff Court is organised into geographical units called sheriffdoms. There are six sheriffdoms in Scotland:

- Glasgow and Strathkelvin
- North Strathclyde
- South Strathclyde, Dumfries and Galloway
- Tayside, Central and Fife
- Lothian and Borders
- Grampian, Highland and Islands

The six sheriffdoms are further divided into 49 Sheriff Court districts. These districts are, however, not divided equally between the sheriffdoms. The sheriffdoms which are located in the central belt of Scotland i.e. the geographical area roughly between the Rivers Clyde and Forth, has the largest concentration of Sheriff Courts. This arrangement clearly makes sense because most of the Scottish population lives in this area and there is a much higher demand for Sheriff Court services.

Key point: There are six Sheriffdoms and 49 Sheriff Court Districts in Scotland.

In each Sheriff Court district, there will be one or more Sheriffs who will act as judges and administer justice in the various civil disputes that are brought before the court. Each sheriffdom has a senior Sheriff known as the Sheriff Principal whose responsibility it is to hear civil appeals from the Sheriff Court.

The jurisdiction or powers of the Sheriff Court in civil cases

The Sheriff Court can hear all sorts of civil disputes and it is most definitely not limited to dealing with cases which involve small amounts of money or are of little importance. There is nothing, in principle, to prevent the Sheriff Court from giving judgement in a multi-million pound legal action. The jurisdiction or powers of the Sheriff Court are very extensive as to the types of cases that it can hear. In fact, the Sheriff Court has privative or exclusive power to judge cases which are valued below the sum of £5,000. This means that all cases valued below this figure must be dealt with by the Sheriff Court. As for cases which have a value exceeding £5,000, the Sheriff Court shares jurisdiction with the Court of Session in Edinburgh. Unlike England, Scotland does not have an institution like the Coroner's Court which deals with fatal accidents and suspicious deaths. In Scotland, therefore, the Sheriff usually deals with fatal accident enquiries and suspicious deaths.

 Key point: Cases valued below the sum of £5,000 must be dealt with by the Sheriff Court.

If a pursuer is determined to begin a legal action against a defender in the Sheriff Court, a key question must be asked:

'Which Sheriff Court has jurisdiction or the right to hear the case?'

It will be remembered that there are six sheriffdoms and 49 Sheriff Court districts in Scotland. However, there are rules of jurisdiction which can help the pursuer to choose the correct Sheriff Court. The jurisdiction of the Sheriff Court is extremely broad and will be based on a number of factors. These grounds of jurisdiction can then be used to decide which Court will hear the case:

1   In which Sheriff Court district does the defender live?

    This is usually the most common way in which a particular Sheriff Court can be said to have jurisdiction over the defender. The pursuer will quite simply find out where the defender lives. If the defender lived in Greenock, then the pursuer would lodge his claim at Greenock Sheriff Court.

2   Does the defender carry on a business within a particular Sheriff Court district?

    This is particularly useful if the defender is a business or carries on a business. The pursuer would make enquiries as to where the defender has his physical place of business. If the defender carried on a business in Paisley, then the action could be commenced at Paisley Sheriff Court.

3   Does the legal action centre around the performance of a contract (a legally enforceable agreement) and, if so, in which Sheriff Court district was the contract to be performed or carried out?

What if the defender, a builder, had agreed to build a garden wall for a pursuer who lived in Aberdeen and, subsequently, the defender failed to carry out his side of the bargain? The pursuer could argue that as the contract was to be carried out or performed in Aberdeen, then Aberdeen Sheriff Court should have jurisdiction to hear the case.

4   Does the legal action involve heritable property (i.e. land, buildings and things which form part of the land) and, if so, in which Sheriff Court district is the heritable property physically situated or located?

What if, for example, a tenant wished to force a landlord to comply with his contractual duty under the terms of lease to carry out repairs to the leaking roof of a property? If the property was situated in Edinburgh, then Edinburgh Sheriff Court could have jurisdiction over the dispute.

5   Does the legal action relate to a delictual action (an action for damages for loss or injury wrongfully caused) and, if so, in which Sheriff Court district did the loss or injury occur?

What if the defender, as a result of his dangerous or careless driving, knocked down and seriously injured the pursuer? The question to ask here is where did the accident occur? If the answer is somewhere in Glasgow, then Glasgow Sheriff Court could have jurisdiction if the pursuer or his family decide to raise a personal injury claim against the defender.

 Key point: The Sheriff Court is said to have geographical jurisdiction, jurisdiction over certain people and jurisdiction over certain property.

Civil Procedures in the Sheriff Court

There are three civil procedures in the Sheriff Court:

◆ Small claims
◆ Summary procedure
◆ Ordinary procedure

Technically, small claims are part of the summary procedure, but it is often more sensible to separate small claims from summary procedure. We shall look at each procedure in turn.

An important feature of civil justice in the Sheriff Court is that the Sheriff sits alone to hear the case. There is no jury and it is very rare in Scotland for a jury to participate in a civil trial.

 Key point: For practical purposes, there are three procedures in the Sheriff Court: small claims, summary procedures and ordinary procedures.

New limits for Sheriff Court civil claims from 14 January 2008:

◆ Claims under £3,000 are small claims
◆ Claims valued between £3,000 and £5,000 are summary cause actions
◆ Claims valued in excess of £5,000 are ordinary cause actions

Although, probably less relevant now, any Sheriff Court civil actions raised in Scotland prior to 14 January 2008, will have to be dealt with under the older rules and financial limits.

It should also be appreciated that any ordinary cause action i.e. claims valued at over £5,000 can be pursued in either the Sheriff Court or the Court of Session.

The previous limits for civil claims in the Sheriff Court prior to 14 January 2008 were as follows:

◆ Claims under £750 were small claims
◆ Claims valued between £750 and £1,500 were summary cause actions
◆ Claims valued in excess of £1,500 were ordinary cause actions

Under the previous rules for initiating civil claims in Scotland, an ordinary cause action for sums in excess of £1,500 could be raised in either the Sheriff Court or the Court of Session.

Serving a summons in a Sheriff Court Action

A pursuer, who is an ordinary member of the public, cannot take it upon himself to issue a summons to the defender personally. There are certain procedures which must be followed. Before serving the summons, the pursuer or his representatives must secure the permission or authority of the Sheriff Court that will hear the case. It is also important to bear in mind that, in the interests of fairness, the defender must be given a reasonable opportunity to weigh up his options when he is served with a summons.

The court forms or summons will contain all the essential information of the case i.e. the names and addresses of the pursuer and the defender; what action the pursuer wishes the court to take; the amount claimed by the pursuer plus expenses and interest; the name of the pursuer's solicitor or authorised lay representative; and the pursuer's statement of claim i.e. an account of why he is raising the claim in the first place.

The summons that the defender receives is similar to the pursuer's copy. However, there are important differences. The defender's copy will spell out the various options open to the defender. These options include admitting the claim and paying the pursuer. The defender may be able to make payment to the pursuer by instalments if he is not a business. The defender may choose to object to the claim and he can give the pursuer notice of his intention to defend the claim. Finally, the defender could choose to do nothing at all. This is not a very wise course of action because the pursuer could ultimately ask the court to award a court order or decree against the defender – even if the defender failed to turn up in court.

There are two different types of form which can be completed by the pursuer depending on whether the defender is an individual i.e. a member of the public or a company or an organisation. Form 1a must be used if the pursuer intends to sue an individual and Form 1b must be used if the defender is a company or an organisation. Both forms are very similar in that they are copies of the pursuer's summons. An example of these forms can be seen on the Introductory Scots Law website.

There are three possible ways in which a summons can be served on the defender:

◆ Service of the summons by the Sheriff Clerk (available to members of the public, but not companies and partnerships, in small claims only).
◆ Postal service by a solicitor or a Sheriff Officer where Royal Mail recorded delivery will be used.
◆ Personal service by a Sheriff Officer accompanied by a witness where the summons will physically be handed to the defender or his representative. Failing this, the Sheriff Officer can pin a copy of the summons to the door of the defender's property and, as a back-up procedure, a copy of the summons will be sent to the defender by recorded delivery.

Key point: There are three ways in which a summons can be served – service by the Sheriff Clerk, postal service and service by Sheriff Officers.

The pursuer must make sure that the defender is given a period of 21 days to respond to the summons. If the defender lives or carries on a business outside Europe, 42 days is the period of notice which must be given.

In small claims and summary actions, there are pre-printed forms which are available from the Sheriff Court. The pursuer or his solicitor will have to complete the various forms which make up the summons. In ordinary actions, however, the pursuer's solicitor will have to draft a summons as the Sheriff Court does not provide a form. This type of summons is referred to as an initial writ and they tend to follow a particular pattern.

Small claims procedure

The small claims procedure was introduced to the Sheriff Court on 30 November 1988 by the Law Reform (Miscellaneous Provisions) (Scotland) Act 1988. This procedure was implemented as the result of the recommendations made by the Royal Commission on Legal Services in Scotland (The Hughes Commission).

The Royal Commission's main recommendation was that:

There should be a small claims procedure within the Sheriff Court which is sufficiently simple, cheap, quick and informal to encourage individual litigants to use it themselves without legal representation. ... Small claims justice should not be seen as second-hand justice.

It is arguable whether the aims of the Commission have been met. The small claims procedure in the Sheriff Court is now little better than a debt collection agency used mainly by banks, credit card companies and finance companies to pursue feckless debtors. In point of fact, the number of ordinary members of the public making use of the system has decreased dramatically over the last few years. (See the Introductory Scots Law website for statistics on small claims in Scotland.) The high expectations which greeted the introduction of the small claims procedure in 1988 have almost certainly not been realised.

A great deal has also been made about the simplicity of the system. However, ordinary members of the public who have attempted to take a case to the small claims court have often been baffled by the complexity of the procedure. This means that, at some point, legal advice will have to be sought in order for the claim to proceed – something that the architects of the system were keen to avoid.

 Key point: The small claims should be sufficiently simple, cheap, quick and informal in order to encourage individual litigants to use it themselves without legal representation.

Reform of the small claims system

As previously discussed, on 14 January 2008, the ceiling for small claims actions in the Sheriff Court rose from £750 to £3,000.

Until the introduction of this reform, the previous small claims ceiling of £750 had remained unchanged since the introduction of the Small Claims Procedure in November 1988. This development has been broadly welcomed by such bodies as the Scottish Consumer Council which had lobbied strongly for the Scottish small claims system to be brought more into line with the procedure operated in the English County Court where such claims may be lodged up to a limit of £5,000.

Mike Dailly, Principal Solicitor at Govan Law Centre had previously expressed strong reservations about raising the small claims' ceiling in Scotland. Mr Dailly's main objection seemed to centre around the fact that, as Legal Aid for representation by solicitors in small claims hearings is not available, many people with limited financial means would be denied a legal representative if the ceiling was raised to cover claims of greater value. Under the old system, such individuals with limited financial means who wished to lodge claims valued at more than £750 were entitled to have a solicitor represent them in the Sheriff Court provided they met certain criteria under Scottish Legal Aid Board rules.

A further change to the small claims system means that it will no longer be competent to hear personal injury claims in this court. From 14 January 2008, it is necessary for a pursuer to be legally represented in these types of claims.

As a result of the changes to the Small Claims Procedure, solicitors may now feel that it is worth their while to offer representation to clients on a 'No Win No Fee' basis if their claim is close to the upper limit of £3,000. In past years, the previous limit of £750 doubtless deterred many solicitors from representing ordinary members of the public at small claims hearings on economic grounds. Put simply, many solicitors were of the view that attending a small claims hearing was not worth the bother unless the client was prepared to put up hard cash to cover the costs of preparation of the case and legal representation.

Small Claims Actions

There are three types of small claims action:

An action for payment of money

This is the most straightforward type of claim. Here, the pursuer will be raising a court action to recover a sum of money (which must not exceed £3,000) that he alleges is owed to him by the defender. This type of action usually involves the failure to repay private debts, business debts or loans from banks, building societies or finance companies. An example of this action can be seen on the Introductory Scots Law website.

An action for an implement of an obligation

The pursuer is asking the court to force the defender to carry out some duty which he has undertaken to complete usually under the terms of a contract. If, for example, the pursuer had entered into a contract with an antiques dealer (the defender) to buy a valuable painting and the dealer later refused to hand over the item, the pursuer could raise this type of action in order to get possession of the goods. The item which is the centre of the dispute must be valued at less than £3,000 because the pursuer must also state that he would be prepared to accept an alternative sum of money as compensation if the item was no longer in the hands of the defender. An example of this action can be seen on the Introductory Scots Law website.

An action for the recovery of moveable property

This type of action allows the pursuer to recover property which the defender is refusing to return to him. If you had put your television into a repair shop and the shop later refused to return your property to you, you could raise an action at the Sheriff Court to have the item returned to you. Again, you would have to state that you would be prepared to accept an alternative sum of money which must not exceed £3,000 if the defender could not return your property to you. An example of this action can be seen on the Introductory Scots Law website.

 Key point: There are three types of actions in small claims – payment of money, implement of an obligation and recovery of moveable property.

Starting a small claims action

The pursuer must first complete the appropriate pre-printed forms and return these to the correct Sheriff Court which has jurisdiction to hear the case.

Once authority has been granted from the Sheriff Court, the pursuer will have to serve a copy of the summons on the defender. The summons contains two important dates – the Return Day and the Hearing Date. The Return Day is the date by which the defender must return his copy of the summons to the Sheriff Clerk's Department. The Return Day will normally be exactly one week before the case is first to be heard in court.

The second date on the summons is known as the Hearing Date. The Hearing Date is the date when the case will first be heard (or called) in court. Both parties and their solicitors (if any) must attend court on this date.

Both copies of the summons, must be returned to the Sheriff Court by the parties before the Return Day.

In a defended small claim, the parties will first meet formally on the Hearing Date when a Hearing will take place. At the Hearing, the Sheriff will attempt to establish the broad facts of the case and to discover if there is any common ground between the parties. The parties will be asked if there is a possibility that the dispute could be resolved there and then. If this is not possible, the Sheriff will continue the Hearing to a later date when the parties will have to attend court in order for a trial to take place. At the trial, the parties will come to court with their respective witnesses and evidence. A trial or proof will usually take place some six weeks after the Hearing Date.

 Key point: In a defended small claim, the parties will first meet formally on the Hearing Day when a Hearing will take place. The dispute could be settled at this Hearing but, if this is not possible, the Sheriff will continue the Hearing to another date.

The conduct of the Hearing in the small claims court is very informal. The Sheriff usually chooses not to wear his wig and gown in order to put the parties at ease. Furthermore, the Sheriff will often come down from the bench and conduct the Hearing by sitting with the parties at a table in the courtroom. The parties usually address the Sheriff simply as 'Sheriff' and not by the more formal title of 'my Lord' or 'my Lady'. The Sheriff will hear the parties, their witnesses and scrutinise the evidence presented. At the end of the Hearing, the Sheriff will make a decision or, failing this, a written decision will be issued within 28 days.

The parties in a small claims dispute are not required to hire the services of a solicitor. It is perfectly possible for a party to represent themselves from beginning to end. If, however, a party lacks the confidence to do this, they can appoint a suitable person to act for them. The Sheriff must give his approval before such a person can act for one of the parties. Suitable lay representatives might include Citizens Advice Bureau Workers, Trading Standards Officers, community workers, individuals who hold a law degree but are not practising solicitors or any decent and articulate members of the community.

Very often, a party will be forced to represent themselves or ask a suitable person to conduct the case on their behalf because Legal Aid is not available to ordinary people to help them pay the costs of legal representation in the Sheriff Court under the small claims system. However, Legal Aid advice and assistance might be available to offset the costs of an interview with a solicitor when a party is first seeking advice in respect of the small claims system. The fact that a party does not need a solicitor to conduct the case for him has been hailed as an advantage of the system whereby ordinary people can take a case to court and do the whole thing themselves without running up huge legal bills. Cynics might see this as a distinct disadvantage as people might lack the necessary confidence to pursue or defend a claim without the help of a solicitor, especially if you happen to come from a poorer or less well-educated background.

 Key point: The procedure at the small claims Hearing is very informal and the parties need not be legally represented.

The amount of expenses claimable

The rules relating to expenses which can be claimed by the winning party in small claims have been overhauled since 14 January 2008, and are detailed below:

Small Claims Expenses from 14 January 2008	
1 Claims valued at up to £200:	No expenses are payable
2 Claims valued between £200 and £1,500:	Up to £150 can be claimed
3 Claims valued between £1,500 and £3,000:	Up to 10% of the claim's value

However, the Sheriff can continue to disregard the rules relating to expenses if they feel that a party has behaved outrageously or unreasonably by pursuing or defending the action and, in such situations, the normal rules for expenses will apply.

Small Claims expenses prior to 14 January 2008	
1 Claims valued at up to £200:	No expenses were payable
2 Claims valued between £200 and £750:	Up to £75 could be claimed

The limits on the amount of expenses which can be claimed by the winning party is regarded as another advantage of the Small Claims procedure. This feature is regarded as a huge incentive for parties to use the system because a characteristic of other civil claims is that the loser has to pay the winner's legal fees in addition to their own legal expenses – which could be a very substantial sum of money. Restricting the amount of legal expenses payable to a maximum of £300 i.e. 10% of the value of a claim for £3,000 should, in theory, encourage people to use the procedure. However, £300 might be viewed as a very large sum of money by an unemployed single parent on state benefits. This figure must, of course, be contrasted with the previous maximum limit for expenses which was £75 and it is, therefore, highly debatable whether the new rules will actually encourage members of the public to use the system.

Appeals

It is possible to appeal against the decision of the Sheriff, but the party wishing to do so must lodge an appeal on a point of law. Appeals are made to the Sheriff Principal, the senior Sheriff in each Sheriffdom. In practice, appeals from a small claims case tend to be rare.

Quite simply, the party making the appeal (the appellant) must demonstrate that the Sheriff got the law wrong. The person making an appeal cannot do so simply because they happen to dislike the Sheriff's decision. The appeal must raise an important point of law and, therefore, any doubt or confusion regarding the law can be removed.

In an appeal, the procedure is much more formal and the parties will have to hire solicitors to appear for them. The normal rules of expenses apply in an appeal and this is something the parties will have to bear in mind i.e. the loser will usually have to pay the costs of the winner, which could amount to quite a substantial sum of money. However, Legal Aid is often granted to a party who cannot afford to pay the services of a solicitor from his own pocket.

Key point: An appeal on a point of law regarding the decision of the Sheriff can be made to the Sheriff Principal.

Summary procedure

This procedure was first introduced to the Sheriff Court in 1976 and was supposedly aimed at making the Sheriff Court much more efficient and more accessible to members of the public. Claims which are dealt with by summary procedure are valued at between £3,000 and £5,000.

The Sheriff Court under summary procedure can deal with a variety of actions:

- Payment
- Specific implement
- Recovery of heritage or moveables
- Multiplepoinding
- Furthcoming

Payment
These types of action are similar to a small claims action. The main difference here is that such actions are for sums of money from £3,000 to £5,000.

Specific implement
Again, as with small claims, the pursuer is asking the court to force the defender to carry out his contractual duties. If, as an alternative, the pursuer is seeking compensation, this sum of money must fall between £3,000 and £5,000.

Recovery of heritage or moveables
This involves situations where the pursuer wants the court to order the defender to return the pursuer's property. Theoretically, the value of the property is not important, but if the pursuer wishes to claim a sum of money as an alternative to the property this amount must fall between £3,000 and £5,000. Unlike small claims where the pursuer can only recover moveable property, this action allows the pursuer to recover heritable property (land and buildings) which the defender is preventing him from using, for example, where the defender refuses to leave a house that he is renting from the pursuer when the lease runs out.

Multiplepoinding
This is useful where two or more people claim ownership of the same property, for example, when a car has been stolen and the ownership of the item is in question, the court can decide who is the legal owner of the goods. Such an action is also useful where businesses come to an end and questions will arise concerning who owns certain property such as money in a partnership bank account or office equipment.

Furthcoming
The pursuer will always be concerned that the defender will empty bank accounts or get rid of assets before the court has made its decision in a payment action. Furthcoming allows the pursuer to apply to the court, pending its decision on the main action, for an order to freeze the defender's bank accounts or property which

may be held by third parties for the defender. If the defender is prevented from getting access to his bank or property, he has real incentive for paying what he owes to the pursuer. It should be noted that furthcoming applies only to the defender's assets which are held by third parties and not to assets which the defender controls personally.

 Key point: Summary procedure in the Sheriff Court deals with a variety of actions valued over £3,000 but less than £5,000.

Starting a summary procedure action

 As with a small claims action, the pursuer must first complete the appropriate pre-printed forms and return these to the correct Sheriff Court which has jurisdiction to hear the case. These pre-printed forms are very similar to the ones used in a small claims action – an example can be seen on the Introductory Scots Law website.

The pursuer will have to have the court's authority before the summons can be served on the defender who, again, will have to be given the appropriate notice period. The summons will alert the defender to two dates, the Return Day and the Calling Day. The defender must return the summons to the court by the Return Date. If the parties are unwilling to settle the case on the Calling Date, the Sheriff will have to arrange a civil trial or a proof.

 Key point: The pursuer can commence a summary cause by filling in a pre-printed form which must be served on the defender using either postal or personal service.

In summary procedure, however, the parties should be legally represented by solicitors. The normal rules of expenses also apply to summary procedure in that the costs that the losing party may have to pay are not restricted to between £150–£300. It is highly likely that the loser will have to pay his opponent's legal fees (which could be substantial) as well as his own.

At the proof (trial), the parties will come to court with witnesses and evidence. The parties' solicitors will lead their clients and their witnesses through the evidence. Both solicitors will have the right to cross-examine the other party and their witnesses. At the end of the Hearing, the Sheriff can make a decision or he can reserve judgement for 28 days and then issue a written decision.

 Key point: A summary cause Hearing is more formal than a small claims action and the parties need to be legally represented.

Appeals from a judgement of the Sheriff in a summary procedure action go to the Sheriff Principal and the appeal hearing is very similar to a small claims appeal hearing. Appeals must be made on a point of law i.e. one of the parties must claim that the Sheriff got the law wrong. There may even be the possibility of a further right of appeal from the Sheriff Principal to the Inner House of the Court of Session.

 Key point: Appeals on a point of law from the judgement of the Sheriff in summary causes go to the Sheriff Principal – there may even be a further appeal to the Court of Session.

Ordinary procedure

This type of action must be used by a pursuer where the sum claimed exceeds £5,000 in value.

Ordinary procedure covers a wide range of cases:

- Payment actions (such as debt recovery)
- Delict (such as personal injury and property damage claims)
- Family law (such as divorce, custody, separation, paternity and adoption)
- Recovery of heritable and moveable property
- Specific implement
- Multiplepoinding
- Interdict (a decree preventing the defender from doing something or requiring the defender to do something)
- Furthcoming
- Declarator (a decree which sets out the rights of the parties to the dispute)

Many of these actions can be found in small claims and summary procedure. However, they will have to be dealt with under ordinary procedure because the value of the case is over £5,000. Since 2 November 2009, the Sheriff Court now has a simplified personal injury procedure for ordinary causes which is very similar to the Court of Session's procedure for such claims. The Sheriff can also chair fatal accident enquiries and hear applications from social work authorities. Examples of initial writs and other documents commencing ordinary Sheriff Court activities can be seen on the Introductory Scots Law website.

 Key point: Ordinary cause actions deal with a variety of cases that have a value of £5,000 or more.

The ordinary procedure is the most complex type of case in the Sheriff Court and individual litigants would be very unwise to represent themselves. Generally speaking, a solicitor will represent a party in an ordinary procedure action, although it is perfectly possible that an advocate may appear for one of the litigants at the trial.

There is a great deal of preparation that will have to be carried out before a trial or a proof can be set. Once the parties have prepared their evidence and identified their witnesses, the Sheriff will set a date for the trial or proof.

As with the other Sheriff Court actions, the parties or their solicitors will be given every opportunity to cross-examine the other party and witnesses at the trial or proof. The Sheriff can usually decide the case after the Hearing has been completed. Sometimes, the Sheriff will delay judgement and issue a written decision at a later date, but there must be no unreasonable delays on the Sheriff's part.

 Key point: Ordinary cause actions are the most complex type of Sheriff court case and the parties will need to be legally represented at the Hearing.

Appeals in ordinary procedure are more complicated. A party has the choice of appealing to the Sheriff Principal or directly to the Inner House of the Court of Session. It may be cheaper and more practical in the long run to appeal to the Inner House because decisions of the Sheriff Principal can be challenged by an appeal to the Court of Session. There may even be a further appeal from the Court of Session to the Supreme Court of the UK.

Appeals are, again, made on a point of law whereby one of the parties is claiming that the judge or judges got the law wrong.

 Key point: In Ordinary Causes, appeals can go the Sheriff Principal and then go further to the Inner House of the Court of Session. Alternatively, appeals could go to the Inner House directly, thus, cutting out the Sheriff Principal altogether. An appeal may even end up going to the Supreme Court of the UK.

The Court of Session

The Court of Session is Scotland's supreme civil court and it has its permanent headquarters in Parliament House in Edinburgh. It is both a court of first instance (where cases will be heard for the first time) and a court of appeal. The court was founded in 1532 by the College of Justice Act. The first Lord President of the court was the Abbot of Cambuskenneth. The background to the creation of this court is an interesting one as Pope Clement VII provided the financial assistance which led to its establishment. This papal handout was granted on the condition that half the judges on the new court were clerics i.e. Roman Catholic priests or brothers with a strong background in canon law. This arrangement remained in place until the Reformation, led by John Knox, established the Protestant faith as the new state religion of Scotland later in the sixteenth century.

The present membership of court numbers 34 permanent judges who are given the formal title of 'Senators of the College of Justice'. Alternatively, they may be referred to as 'Lords of Council and Session'. The two most important members of the court are the Lord President (currently Lord Hamilton) and his deputy, the Lord Justice Clerk (currently Lord Gill). These two individuals, of course, also hold the most senior positions in the High Court of Justiciary. As a result of the Court of Session Act 1810, the Court is split into an Outer House (which mainly deals with cases at first instance) and an Inner House (which is mainly an appeal court).

 Key point: The Court of Session is Scotland's supreme civil court.

Unlike the Sheriff Court which is restricted to hearing cases from a particular local area in Scotland (from the appropriate Sheriffdom or Sheriff Court District), the jurisdiction of the Court of Session covers the whole of Scotland. The Court of Session will only be excluded from hearing cases by an Act of Parliament or where the Sheriff Court has exclusive jurisdiction to hear a case i.e. summary actions with a monetary value of less than £3,000. In turn, the Court of Session has the sole right to hear the following types of cases:

◆ Reduction (cancellation) of a contract
◆ Tenor of a lost document where its authenticity has to be proved
◆ Actions of adjudication where rights of ownership of heritable property are granted to a pursuer
◆ Liquidation of limited companies where the share capital has a value of more than £120,000

 An example of a summons and response in a Court of Session case can be seen on the Introductory Scots Law website.

Previously, the Court of Session had exclusive jurisdiction in actions for declarator of marriage, but these types of cases can now be dealt with by the Sheriff Court.

However, it should be remembered that the Outer House of the Court of Session and the Sheriff Court will potentially share jurisdiction where the case is valued at £5,000 or more. In such situations, it will be up to the litigants whether they decide to use the services of the Sheriff Court or the Court of Session. Obviously, matters of cost, time and convenience will play a large part in deciding which court is chosen to hear the case.

The court is organised into an Outer House and an Inner House. Cases in the Outer House are either commenced by way of an action or a petition. An action involves the pursuer serving a summons on the defender. A petition, on the other hand, seeks the assistance of the Court of Session in some matter and is a less formal procedure than a summons. The petitioner is asking the court to do something which is right and proper and which he has no authority to do himself.

The Outer House has a membership of 24 judges who are known as Lords Ordinary. The Lords Ordinary will usually sit alone to hear cases, although on extremely rare occasions a civil jury of 12 may be present. The services of a civil jury may be called upon in a defamation action or even certain personal injury claims. Jury trials also take place where the case involves essential error and allegations of force and fear in relation to contract (see Chapter 2). The Lords Ordinary will hear cases for the first time which involve delict, contract, commercial cases, trusts, succession, family actions and judicial review. Until the 1970s, the Court of Session was the only court in Scotland which had exclusive jurisdiction over divorce actions. The Sheriff Court can now hear divorce cases.

As can be seen, the Outer House of the Court of Session deals with a very broad range of legal work. Certain judges are regarded as experts in a particular field of law. Currently, Lords Clark, MacKay of Drumadoon and Drummond Young are regarded as the leading commercial judges in the Court of Session. Commercial actions cover cases involving sales of goods and services, banking and insurance transactions and issues relating to contracts generally. There are now five female Senators of the College of Justice: Lady Paton, Lady Smith, Lady Dorrian, Lady Clark of Calton and Lady Stacey.

 Key point: The Outer House is primarily a trial court.

It is rare for the Inner House to hear cases at first instance. To all intents and purposes, the Inner House is really an appeal court – although it does sometimes sit as a trial court. The Inner House is organised into two units known as the First and Second Divisions. It is wrong to assume that the First Division is superior in any way to the Second Division as both have equal authority. The Lord President heads the First Division and the Lord Justice Clerk is responsible for the work of the Second Division. Until 1933, a litigant had a choice as to which Division heard a case, but this right was abolished and, given the fact that a lot of emphasis is placed on the equality of both Divisions, this would appear to have been a sensible reform.

Sometimes in a particularly difficult case, both Divisions will come together to form a court of seven judges as in the case of **Scottish Discount Company v Blin (1986)**. However, in **Wright v Bell (1905)**, the entire court of 13 judges heard the case. The members of both Divisions will be appointed by the First Minister of Scotland, on behalf of the Queen, after consultations have been held with the Lord President and Lord Justice Clerk.

Each Division has a membership of five judges, but in order for the court to sit and make judgements, three judges must be present. In more recent times, the increasing numbers of cases being brought before the Inner House has meant that it will be common for an additional or Extra Division of three judges to be formed to hear cases. This arrangement is a convenient way in which pressure can be taken off the other two Divisions. The main task of the various Divisions is to deal with cases on appeal from the Outer House, the Sheriff Court and certain tribunals and other bodies, for example, the Employment Appeal Tribunal and the Lands Tribunal for Scotland to name but two. Sometimes if a case is particularly important or it involves a particularly complex point of law, or if it is necessary to overrule a previous binding decision of the Court of Session, five or more judges may sit together to hear the appeal. As previously mentioned, it has not been unknown for both Divisions to sit together to form a court of seven judges as in **Scottish Discount Company v Blin (1986)**. However, in **Wright v Bell (1905)**, the entire court of 13 judges heard the case.

 Key point: The Inner House is primarily an appeal court.

There is nothing to prevent people from representing themselves in the Court of Session. However, this is not recommended as procedures of the Court of Session can be very complex. More usually, a litigant will be represented by an advocate, who is also referred to as 'counsel'. Companies and partnerships must always be legally represented. Since the introduction of the Law Reform (Miscellanous Provisions) (Scotland) Act 1990, solicitor-advocates – solicitors who have completed additional, professional examinations – have the right to appear before the Court of Session and plead cases on behalf of their clients. Solicitor-advocates are members of the Law Society of Scotland while Advocates will be members of the Faculty of Advocates (in England such lawyers are known as barristers). Lawyers from one of the other 26 member states of the European Union also may have a right to appear on behalf of a client in the Court of Session.

 Key point: The parties to a case heard by the Court of Session will be legally represented by either a solicitor-advocate or an Advocate.

From 1 October 2009, an appeal on a point of law against a decision of the Inner House will proceed to the new UK Supreme Court sitting at the Guildhall, London. Previously, the vast majority of appeals were dealt with by the House of Lords (sitting in its judicial capacity) and other cases which involved devolution or human rights issues were heard by Judicial Committee of the Privy Council sitting in Downing Street, London.

Constitutional reform and the Supreme Court of the UK

As previously discussed, a very significant set of reforms came into force on 1 October 2009 when the Constitutional Reform Act 2005 became law. Judicial powers in Scottish civil appeals, which were previously the preserve of the House of

Lords, were abolished and a completely independent Supreme Court for the United Kingdom came into existence. This constitutional reform was viewed as necessary in terms of recent legislation which introduced devolved government throughout parts of the United Kingdom and because of the growing importance of human rights legislation i.e. it is absolutely essential for the highest court in the land to be seen to be completely separate and independent from the legislature (the UK Parliament) and the executive (the UK Government).

The new Supreme Court will hear criminal and civil appeals from England, Wales and Northern Ireland. It will also hear civil appeals from the Inner House of the Court of Session and it will assume responsibility for devolution and human rights cases from Scotland which were previously heard by the Privy Council. Thus, the Privy Council ceased to have any jurisdiction over Scottish criminal matters from 1 October 2009 onwards.

The Supreme Court of the United Kingdom formally commenced its right to hear certain types of criminal appeals (devolution and human rights) from Scotland's High Court of Justiciary during the week beginning 7 December 2009. The appeals were:

1   **Allison *v* Her Majesty's Advocate**

2   **McInnes *v* Her Majesty's Advocate**

3   **Martin *v* Her Majesty's Advocate**

4   **Miller *v* Her Majesty's Advocate.**

Appeals 1 and 2 involve the failure of the Crown to disclose evidence to the defence during the trial of the accused persons and whether this was a breach of human rights legislation in the sense that it prejudiced their right to a fair trial guaranteed by Article 6 of the European Convention on Human Rights. The appeals also deal with establishing the parameters of the test which is to be applied by the High Court of Justiciary in future cases when assessing whether a miscarriage of justice has occurred.

Appeals 3 and 4, on the other hand, are concerned with the Scottish Parliament's decision to increase the sentencing powers for Sheriffs which affect road traffic offences. The argument is that the Scottish Parliament has no right to increase the sentencing power of Sheriff in relation to these types of offences when responsibility for road traffic legislation is a reserved matter i.e. it is a matter for the Westminster Parliament alone to amend or make laws in this area.

The Supreme Court also dealt with the case of **Duncan MacLean *v* Her Majesty's Advocate (2009)** which, again is a human rights appeal from the High Court of Justiciary. This case is discussed later in the chapter in relation to the right of an accused to have a solicitor present when questioned by police officers.

The Supreme Court is located at Middlesex Guildhall in London. From 1 October 2009, the Law Lords will be known as Justices of the Supreme Court and they no longer have the right to be members of the House of Lords. The new court will have Lord Phillips of Worth Matravers as its first President and Lord Hope of Craighead will be the first Deputy President of the Supreme Court. A large number of the other judges who sat in the House of Lords will become the first members to sit in the new Supreme Court. Lord Scott of Foscote, one of the former Law Lords, retired from office on 30 September 2009 and did not take up an appointment as a Justice of the Supreme Court. Sir Anthony Clarke, the former Master of the Rolls (Head of the Civil Division of the English Court of Appeal) was Lord Scott's successor.

The Lord Chancellor will, however, remain an important office of the British State in that the holder will continue to be a Minister of the Crown.

When a vacancy arises amongst the Justices of the Supreme Court, a selection commission will appoint a new member to the Court. This commission will consist of the President and the Deputy President of the Supreme Court sitting together with members of the various judicial appointments bodies for England, Wales, Northern Ireland and Scotland.

The creation of a Supreme Court was necessitated by the introduction of devolved government in the United Kingdom and the steadily increasing importance of human rights. In other countries, for example, the United States, there is a very clear separation of powers as regards the different branches of government i.e. the Executive, the Legislature and the Judiciary – something which has been quite obviously lacking in the British parliamentary system.

Until 2009, the House of Lords was both part of the Legislature and the highest court in the land for civil appeals from Scotland. Clearly, it is absolutely critical that the Judiciary is seen to be completely independent from political interference and considerations. Consequently, the creation of a Supreme Court is an attempt by the British State to be seen to be guaranteeing and underpinning judicial independence.

The House of Lords

Until 1 October 2009, the House of Lords was the highest civil appeal court in Scotland and the United Kingdom.

This court sat in Westminster, London. Originally, the House of Lords was not to have any right to hear appeals from the Court of Session. In fact, the Treaty of Union of 1707, whereby Scotland and England became the United Kingdom, appeared to rule out any role for the House of Lords in the affairs of the Court of Session. The case of **Greenshields v Magistrates of Edinburgh** in 1711 shattered this belief and, since this date, it was the practice of the House of Lords to hear Scottish civil appeals.

 Key point: The House of Lords heard Scottish civil appeals from 1711 until 1 October 2009.

From which civil courts did the House of Lords hear appeals?

The House of Lords heard criminal and civil appeals from the English Court of Appeal, the English High Court and the Divisional Courts of the English High Court. Additionally, the Lords heard appeals from the Court of Session in Edinburgh and the Supreme Court of Northern Ireland in civil cases only. In Scottish appeals, one or two Scottish law lords normally participated and, if the appeal came from Northern Ireland, one Northern Irish law lord would usually be part of that court. However, there was nothing to prevent a Scottish appeal being heard by a court of English and Northern Irish judges. The procedure in the House of Lords was informal in the sense that judges did not sit in a courtroom to hear appeals. Appeals were usually heard in one of the committee rooms of the Houses of Parliament and the judges customarily wore business suits rather than the more formal dress of wigs and gowns. Appeals to the House of Lords were heard by at least three Law Lords – although it was more likely for five or even seven judges to sit in order to hear a case.

The Judicial Committee of the Privy Council

This court is a direct descendant of the ancient English King's Council which was a type of Cabinet which advised the Crown. The court's jurisdiction is derived from the Judicial Committee Act 1833. The Judicial Committee is not part of the English Supreme Court. The Privy Council is the final court of appeal in civil and criminal matters from the courts of some Commonwealth countries and British territories. The Privy Council is still the final court of appeal for civil and criminal appeals from the Channel Islands, the Isle of Man and Gibraltar. Strictly speaking, there is no right of appeal. It is traditional to petition the Crown for leave to appeal. The Privy Council sits to hear cases in Downing Street, London.

 Key point: The Privy Council was originally an English Court that had no jurisdiction to hear Scottish cases.

Constitutional developments and the changing role of the Privy Council

As a result of the Scotland Act 1998 and the Human Rights Act 1998, the Privy Council was given a new lease of life. Under the Scotland Act 1998 and the Human Rights Act 1998, the Privy Council was given jurisdiction in devolution matters and human rights issues. This meant that even the decisions of the supreme Scottish criminal court, the High Court of Justiciary, could be challenged if they appeared to breach the Scotland Act or the Human Rights Act.

This development was surprising given the fact that the supremacy of the High Court of Justiciary appeared to be guaranteed from the nineteenth century onwards with the decision of the **Mackintosh v Lord Advocate (1876)**. It was thought that this case ruled out any further right of appeal in criminal matters to an English court i.e. the House of Lords. Devolution and the direct incorporation of the European Convention on Human Rights and Fundamental Freedoms into British law significantly undermined this belief.

To be fair, however, the Privy Council probably had little impact on Scottish legal affairs despite its ten year involvement with the Scottish courts. The court ceased to have any jurisdiction in Scottish legal matters after 1st October 2009 when the new Supreme Court for the United Kingdom assumed responsibility for these types of appeals.

 One notable example of a decision of the High Court of Justiciary being overturned by the Privy Council was that of **Brown v Stott (2000)** in which the owner of a vehicle was compelled under the Road Traffic Act 1988 to give information as to the identity of the driver at the time when the relevant offence was committed. The offence was one of drunk driving. The accused argued that the very fact that she had to admit to the police that she had driven the car in response to their questioning of her amounted to

71

self-incrimination. Her response would, of course, be used against her at the trial and she claimed, therefore, that her right to a fair trial had been breached under Article 6 of the European Convention on Human Rights because she had self-incriminated herself (remember, it is up to the Prosecution to prove the guilt of the accused and the accused is under no duty to help the prosecution convict him or her). The accused was convicted in the Sheriff Court. The High Court of Justiciary held that the Crown had no power to rely on evidence of the admission which the accused had been compelled to make under the Road Traffic Act. The appeal was allowed. However, the Privy Council had other ideas and decided to overturn this ruling. The Privy Council confirmed the rule that an accused had to answer truthfully when the police questioned him or her in relation to a suspected offence under the Road Traffic Act.

 Key point: As a result of the Scotland Act 1998 and the Human Rights Act 1998, the Privy Council was given the right to hear appeals from the Court of Session and the High Court of Justiciary where the case involves human rights or devolution issues. This jurisdiction was abolished on 1 October 2009 when the UK Supreme Court assumed responsibility for Scottish appeals involving human rights and devolution issues.

Civil justice reform in Scotland (Lord Gill's Review)

For a number of years, concerns have been raised about the quality of Scottish civil justice and, in particular, whether it effectively meets the needs of those individuals it supposedly serves. One perception that many members of the public hold, rightly or wrongly, is that Scottish lawyers have a strangle-hold over the legal system and this almost monopolistic position represents a formidable barrier to innovation and more competition in the legal services market.

With these concerns in mind, Cathy Jamieson MSP, the previous Scottish Labour Justice Minister, gave Lord Gill, the Lord Justice Clerk (Scotland's second most senior judge), the task of overhauling the civil justice system by asking him to chair a wide-ranging review.

The work of Lord Gill and the members of his Project Board began on 2 April 2007 and they were charged with the following tasks:

◆ to assess the costs of civil legal proceedings from the position of litigants using the system and the taxpayer funding the system
◆ to assess whether alternative methods of dispute resolution e.g. mediation and conciliation could be used much more effectively in relation to civil disputes and thus encourage the parties to resolve disputes without having to resort to court proceedings.
◆ to assess the impact and efficacy of modern communication methods in court proceedings
◆ to assess the impact of better case management systems e.g. earlier intervention by judges in court proceedings and the issuing of directions relating to witnesses and productions and the exchange of information between the parties to a dispute

◆ to assess the jurisdiction of the different Scottish civil courts and procedures and this could result in any of the following developments:
   ◇ reforms to the jurisdiction of the Sheriff Court and the Court of Session
   ◇ certain types of cases would not be permitted to be heard in the Court of Session
   ◇ reform of the current civil appeals system
   ◇ abolition of the current Sheriffdoms and replacement with a single Sheriff Court covering the whole of Scotland

The Review also looked at aspects of the Legal Aid scheme and consider how parties to a civil dispute might benefit from improved legal services and whether these should be provided in the main by solicitors or by other individuals or organisations e.g. the Citizens' Advice Bureau.

Members of the public and other interested bodies were invited to participate in the work of the Review by ensuring that their views and opinions reached Lord Gill and his Project Board no later than 31 March 2008.

Lord Gill's Review of the Scottish Civil Courts was finally published on 30 September 2009. The main recommendations of the Gill Review are:

◆ the creation of a national Sheriff Appeal Court which would hear summary criminal and civil appeals
◆ the creation of a new type of judge known as a District Judge who would sit in the Sheriff Court to hear summary criminal cases and small claims (less than £5,000). These judges would also have responsibility for referrals from the Children's Hearing, cases involving housing disputes between tenants and landlords and certain types of family law actions
◆ all civil cases valued at below £150,000 should be heard in the Sheriff Court or by a District Judge
◆ a drastic reduction in the number of temporary Sheriffs who should be appointed to deal with emergencies only and such appointments should be made from the ranks of retired lawyers or judges (not lawyers who are currently practising)
◆ more specialist Sheriffs (e.g. experts in commercial law) in each Sheriffdom should be encouraged to deal with cases which fall into their area of expertise
◆ Edinburgh Sheriff Court should be given the right to deal with personal injury claims from across Scotland and civil juries could be used in this court. Lord Gill is keen to see the Sheriff Court deal with more personal injury claims in order to reduce pressure on the Court of Session
◆ the Court of Session should only be able to deal with civil cases worth more than £150,000
◆ the Court of Session will remain the principal court for more complex matters such as devolution matters, patents and taxation
◆ a single procedure for the Court of Session to replace ordinary and summary application
◆ greater use of class actions should be encouraged whereby groups of litigants can pursue claims together and thus reduce significantly the costs of raising a civil action
◆ greater use of mediation and conciliation should be promoted in civil disputes as an alternative to court action

◆ At national level, the Lord Advocate who is assisted by the Solicitor General and together both of whom oversee the work of the Crown Office in Edinburgh; and
◆ At the local level, the Procurator Fiscal Service and the various Scottish police forces.

The day-to day investigation of criminal acts in Scotland is carried out by the police service which, at first instance, reports to the Procurator Fiscal, the local state prosecutor (rather like the District Attorney in the United States of America). The Procurator Fiscal, in turn, reports to and is responsible to the Lord Advocate and the **Solicitor General**. The prosecution of a crime and the whole system of public prosecution in Scotland is the responsibility of the Lord Advocate (currently Elish Angiolini QC). The Lord Advocate is, of course, the Crown's chief law officer in Scotland and the person who is in charge of the Crown Office, a Department which is answerable to the Scottish Government in Edinburgh. When carrying out their enquires into the commission of any crime, the police follow the instructions of a fiscal when carrying out the investigation but, practically speaking, the police will be left to run things as they see fit.

 Key point: The Lord Advocate and Solicitor General oversee the Scottish prosecution service.

What is the role of the police in criminal investigations?

The police clearly have a very important role when it comes to the investigation of crime as they are responsible for gathering the evidence which will determine whether a prosecution will proceed against an accused person. It is important to note, however, that although the police can charge an individual with a crime they do not make the decision as to whether that person will face trial in a criminal court. The State prosecution service i.e. the Procurator Fiscal Service or the Crown Office shall have the responsibility of making such a decision. After the conclusion of their investigation, the police must submit a report of their findings to the fiscal who will ultimately determine whether any potential prosecution of the accused should proceed.

To begin with, the police will gather evidence against a person suspected of committing a criminal offence by questioning potential witnesses who may have been present at the scene of the crime or may be able to provide important information which could assist the police in their enquiries.

Under the Criminal Procedure (Scotland) Act 1995, the police have the power to do any of the following:

1   Detain a suspect for questioning

2   Charge the suspect if there is sufficient evidence after the period of detention

3   Arrest the suspect

The powers of the police to arrest, detain and search suspects can be exercised by both uniformed officers and those officers who are in plain clothes. Obviously, the latter category of officer should clearly identify themselves to suspects e.g. by producing a warrant card at the time they wish to exercise the relevant power – as long as it is practicable to do so.

The police also have a general power to disperse individuals who may be preventing other people from going about their lawful business. Similarly, the police can disperse individuals who are acting in a riotous fashion or may be committing a breach of the peace, but police officers must generally justify such actions on their part. Failure to comply with a police instruction to disperse may result in arrest and detention.

Potential witnesses should be prepared to give the police their full assistance and the police are entitled to approach and question anyone they believe may be able to progress the investigation. Generally speaking, however, members of the public are not legally obliged to provide answers to questions posed to them by police officers and there is a heavy reliance placed by officers on public goodwill. The only piece of information that a member of the public must provide to police officers during questioning is his or her name and address.

Admittedly, many decent and law abiding members of the community will be only too happy to help the police with their enquiries. There is no legal requirement for a police officer to caution a member of the public when carrying out questioning. A caution is a warning that anything the interviewee says in response to police questions may be relied upon at a later date – usually as evidence in a criminal court.

 Key point: In the course of a criminal investigation, the police can detain a suspect for questioning, charge a suspect or arrest a suspect.

In certain circumstances, however, a member of the public is legally obliged to provide answers in response to police questioning. Such occasions shall arise when the police conduct investigations under the Terrorism Act 2000, Prevention of Terrorism Act 2005 and the Road Traffic Acts. Under Section 172 of the Road Traffic Act 1988, an individual suspected of committing a road traffic offence must answer police questions (see **Brown v Stott (2000)** discussed earlier).

The police must conduct their questioning of a member of the public in accordance with strict rules. It is important to remember that the intelligence gained by police officers in the course of their investigation of a crime must be able to withstand the scrutiny of a defence lawyer should a criminal trial later go ahead. Obviously, the prosecutor will base his or her case on the intelligence or information gathered by the police during the initial stages of the investigation. It is not hard to understand that, if the police evidence is basically unsound, this could have severe repercussions for a successful prosecution at any subsequent criminal trial. At the very least, the evidence gathered by the police during questioning of the public or suspected offenders must be admissible. What does this mean? Very simply, it means whether the police evidence will be allowed to be used in a court.

It has often been said that the police evidence against an accused person must be reliable and credible and capable of corroboration.

 Key point: In certain circumstances, an individual must provide answers to police questioning.

What powers do the police have to detain suspects?

Section 14 of the Criminal Procedure (Scotland) Act 1995 gives the police the right to detain an individual whom they believe, at this stage of their enquiries, may have committed the offence currently under investigation. The euphemism often used at this stage of the investigation is that an individual is helping the police with their enquiries. Alternatively, the police can always question an individual who is suspected of committing the offence and then simply let them go without the need for detention. Whatever course of action the police decide to exercise in such situations, all answers obtained from the suspect must be acquired fairly in order to permit such information to be used in later legal proceedings. Police officers should, therefore, be very aware of the (common law) rules laid down by the Scottish courts which govern the acquisition of information from suspects. Most information obtained in a fair manner by police officers will be admissible i.e. can be used in court as evidence. The same would not be true if any evidence had been obtained from officers in a way that involved bullying and harassment of the suspect, taking unfair advantage of the suspect's age, diminished mental capacity or in situations where inducements were offered to the suspect in return for co-operation with the investigation. Furthermore, any answers which were obtained by officers conducting what amounted to a cross-examination of the suspect are not likely to satisfy the requirement of admissibility. A suspect who has been detained for a number of hours at the police station may also place themselves under pressure to provide answers to police questions in an attempt to obtain early release and such a course of action may not always be in their best interests.

Police officers should, therefore, err on the side of caution when it comes to obtaining information from suspects as any competent defence lawyer will be able to expose and challenge any shortcomings as to how the evidence from the suspect was obtained. Ultimately, it will be up to the Scottish criminal court dealing with the matter to determine the reliability and credibility of the police evidence.

 Key point: Section 14 of the Criminal Procedure (Scotland) Act 1995 gives the police the right to detain a suspect.

When can the power of detention be exercised by the police?

Section 14 of the Criminal Procedure (Scotland) Act 1995 states that a police officer can detain a suspect in situations where they have 'reasonable grounds for suspecting that a person has committed or is committing an offence punishable by imprisonment'.

The police officer exercising the power of detention must inform the suspect of the nature of his/her suspicion, the general nature of the offence committed and the reason(s) for the detention.

After the officer has decided to detain a suspect, they must escort the detainee to a police station as soon as this is reasonably practicable. The suspect or detainee need not be taken to the nearest police station.

There are strict time limits regulating the period of detention and, in normal circumstances, a suspect can be held by the police for a maximum of six hours. In theory, this period should give the police enough time to decide what they intend to do with the detainee i.e. arrest the suspect, detain the suspect under some other criminal legislation or even release the suspect.

Under the Terrorism Act 2000 and the Prevention of Terrorism Act 2005, a suspect could be detained for questioning for a maximum period of 28 days.

The police must inform the suspect when the detention period is at an end. It is important to note that, should a detainee be held for more than six hours, it will not necessarily invalidate anything done by the police during the initial detention period.

Should the police exhaust the full period of detention, they will not be able to detain the suspect at a later date if their suspicions relate to the same grounds or circumstances of a criminal offence.

 Key point: The power of detention can be exercised by the police where a reasonable suspicion exists that a suspect has committing a crime punishable by imprisonment.

What information should be recorded by the police if detention is exercised?

There are certain details which police officers must record if they exercise the right to detain a suspect under Section 14 of the 1995 Act. These details include:

1   the place or locus where the suspect was originally detained and the police station or other premises to which the suspect is taken

2   any other place to which the person is taken *during* the detention

3   the time when detention begins and the time of arrival at the police station or other premises

4   the general nature of the suspected criminal offence

5   the time when the detainee is informed of the right to refuse to answer any questions and to request that information about the detention should be communicated to a solicitor (under section 15(1)(b) of the 1995 Act) and to another person e.g. a relative

6   the time when such a request to inform the suspect's solicitor and another person is

   (a) made and **(b)** complied with

7   the time of the suspect's release from detention or, if applicable, the time of the suspect's arrest.

Generally, most Scottish police forces will have their own standard forms or paperwork for recording details of a suspect's detention, but it seems to be the case that if the detaining officer(s) record the details in a notebook this will be sufficient to comply with the provisions of the Criminal Procedure (Scotland) Act 1995.

 Key point: If the power of detention is exercised by the police, certain details **must** be recorded for future reference.

Is it necessary for the detainee's interview to be tape recorded or by recorded by other electronic means?

If the detainee is suspected of committing a sufficiently serious crime, the police officers may decide to record the interview on a tape machine or on a digital recorder. The older tape recording machines produce two copies of the interview – one copy which is retained by the detainee and one which is retained by the police.

These tapes were extremely difficult to tamper with and forensic experts could carry out tests to determine whether a tape had indeed been tampered with. Many interviews may actually be visually recorded by police forces in order to ensure maximum accuracy.

The purpose of recording an interview is so that any information obtained from the detainee during questioning by police officers can be used in future criminal proceedings. It is normal practice for the recording of the interview to be transcribed for use in a subsequent trial if the detainee is charged with an offence. If the prosecution decides to use the transcript in a criminal trial, a copy, which has been officially certified by the transcriber, must be served on the accused at least 14 days before the trial. The accused has the right to challenge the accuracy of the transcript during the trial and, ultimately, if such objections prove to have foundation, this evidence may be inadmissible in court. It may, therefore, be useful for both the prosecution and the defence to call the transcriber as a witness to verify or undermine the accuracy of the the interview transcript.

The transcriber's testimony is usually sufficient to validate the transcript's production and its accuracy. The transcriber's evidence does not need to be corroborated. However, it does not take a leap of imagination to realise that the accuracy of the transcript could still be challenged by a good defence lawyer. A defence lawyer may even wish to have the tape played in court in order to discredit the police in order to demonstrate the manner in which the questions were put to the accused and how these were answered.

If no transcript is provided, the court cannot insist that one be provided. In summary trials, however, the judge may adjourn the proceedings in order to request a transcript. The defence solicitor may on request receive a copy of the transcript from the fiscal (and there is usually a payment of a small fee for this).

 Key point: Where sufficiently serious crimes are concerned, the police may wish to record any interview with a detainee.

Do the police have a right to question a detainee?

Yes, the police do have such a right, but the detainee may choose not to cooperate by refusing to answer questions posed by officers. The only information which the detainee is legally obliged to provide to the police is their name and address. The diligent and careful police officer will caution the detainee that they are not under any legal obligation to answer questions (the common law caution), but if a response to police questions is forthcoming this information may be noted down and used at a future criminal trial. The detainee must be informed of his/her right not to respond to police questions at the time when the detention begins and upon arrival at the police station.

Can the police search a detainee?

Yes, the police do have the power to search a detainee's person but **not** premises owned by the detainee.

 Key point: The police have the right to search a detainee; get the detainee to participate in an ID parade; and obtain prints and impressions from the detainee.

Can the police force a detainee to participate in an identity parade?

If an identity parade is to be held, the suspect – whether a detainee under Section 14 or not – is entitled to have a solicitor in attendance. This solicitor could be the suspect's own or a legal aid duty solicitor.

What if the police subsequently decide that a suspect should have to take part in an identity parade after a period of detention has ended? A Sheriff could, at a later time, grant a warrant to the police to detain the suspect further for the purpose of an identity parade. This period of detention should be strictly limited to the amount of time required to conduct the identity parade.

Can the police obtain prints and impressions from a detainee?

The police may be of the opinion that it is advisable to obtain fingerprints and palmprints from the detainee. Additionally, the police may wish to obtain other prints and impressions from an external part of the body provided it is reasonable to do given the specific circumstances of the crime under investigation.

If criminal proceedings do not go ahead or if the accused is acquitted after undergoing a trial, all prints and impressions obtained by the police must be destroyed. As we shall see, however, there are different rules governing DNA samples which have been taken from a detainee and this matter is discussed below.

Police officers of the rank of Inspector and above can authorise an officer to take samples such as hair, nails, blood (by means of a swab only) and saliva from the detainee. Certain police forces may also be in the habit of photographing detainees – a practice which is covered by Section 18 of the Criminal Procedure (Scotland) Act 1995

If the detainee decides to put up a struggle against a police officer attempting to obtain prints, impressions or samples, the Criminal Procedure (Scotland) Act 1995 permits the officer to use reasonable force in order to achieve this objective.

Does the detainee have any special rights during the detention period?

Section 15 of the Criminal Procedure (Scotland) Act 1995 provides protection to those suspects who undergo a period of police detention. Adult detainees i.e. someone older than sixteen years of age is entitled to inform two people that he has been detained and the location of the detention. These individuals will often be the detainee's solicitor and a close relative or friend. The detainee should be allowed to contact these individuals without delay, but the detainee must not be unreasonable in the choice of the two named individuals. If it turned out to be the case that one or both individuals could not be not contacted because they were not sufficiently close to the police station, the police may feel disinclined to contact them. The police may also delay contacting certain individuals to communicate the fact of the detention if, for example, it may hamper the conclusion of the criminal investigation or in terrorist cases where intelligence operations against terror suspects are still ongoing. It is often assumed that the detainee has the right to contact personally the two people nominated by him i.e. by telephone. This is, in fact, not the case and the police officers may choose to contact the individuals nominated by the detainee.

Other statutes such as the Terrorism Act 2000 and the Prevention of Terrorism Act 2005, the Misuse of Drugs Act 1971 (detention of a person for the purpose of searching him for possession of drugs) and the Criminal Law (Consolidation)

(Scotland) Act 1995 (detention in connection with drug smuggling offences) can be used to detain suspects.

 Key point: Adult detainees have the right to inform two other people that they are being held by the police.

Do the police have any other rights to detain a suspect?

The police are also entitled to detain a suspect under Section 13 of the Criminal Procedure (Scotland) Act 1995. This power, however, is a more limited right of detention and is primarily geared towards helping the police to identify a suspect or a potential witness to a crime. Any individual detained under Section 13 (whether as a suspect or a witness) is obliged to provide to a police officer the details of their name and address. If the officer is detaining a suspect, they must have reasonable grounds for suspecting that an individual is in the process of committing or has committed a crime. When detaining the suspect, the officer may simply be seeking an explanation which could actually allay any suspicions previously aroused.

Potential witnesses can also be detained under Section 13 and, in such circumstances, they must also provide details of their name and address to the officer. In turn, the officer must provide an explanation to the suspect or witness why the detention is deemed necessary i.e. the general nature of the crime under investigation. A Section 13 detention may be carried out at the locus of the crime or at any other location where an officer is entitled to be present. The detention may last until such time as the officer can verify the details provided by the suspect or the witness. This may mean that the detainee can be held at the locus by the police officer, but this should be exercised speedily. The officer may have to use reasonable force in certain situations to force a suspect to comply with the exercise of detention. Failure to comply with the conditions of detention may result in the commission of a criminal offence by a suspect.

An officer cannot forcibly detain a potential witness, but if such an individual failed to provide details of their name and address they may be guilty of a criminal offence.

Unlike detention under Section 14 of the Criminal Procedure (Scotland) Act 1995, a Section 13 detention does not have to involve the commission of a crime which is punishable by imprisonment.

 Key point: The police can also detain a suspect under Section 13 of the Criminal Procedure (Scotland) Act 1995.

Can the police charge a suspect?

Following on from their initial investigation of a criminal offence, the police may be of the opinion that they now have enough evidence to charge a suspect. If the police decide to proceed with this course of action, the suspect must be properly cautioned which means they should be informed that they are not obliged to say anything in answer to the charge, but that anything they do say may be used in evidence against him or her. The suspect has now become the accused.

This is the type of caution that most people are readily familiar with and known as a 'common law caution'. Should the suspect choose to make a statement or a voluntary confession after being cautioned, this information would be regarded as admissible evidence in any future criminal proceedings.

When a suspect has been charged, they should not be subjected to further police questioning as answers given after this the caution will be treated as inadmissible in evidence. If the accused wishes to make a voluntary statement or confession, a police officer completely unconnected with the ongoing investigation should be brought in to note this development. The statement given by the accused should then be read to the accused to verify its accuracy. If the statement is accurate, the accused and the police office who noted its contents should both sign it.

In the vast majority of circumstances, the accused will not wish to make any statement or declaration until such time as they have been able to consult with a solicitor.

 Key point: If the police are of the opinion that they have enough evidence against the suspect, they may decide to press criminal charges.

What are the police powers of arrest?

Arrest can be defined as the forcible detention of the suspect – possibly by police officers physically restraining the suspect – and is an extremely serious development in the investigation of a criminal offence. In situations where the police have decided to arrest the suspect, they do not have to worry about detaining the suspect for more than six hours.

Police officers should, however, be aware of the provisions of Section 17(1) of the Police (Scotland) Act 1967 (as amended) which makes it clear that it is the duty of any police officer to take every precaution that any person charged with an offence is not unreasonably and unnecessarily detained in custody.

Additionally, Section 135(3) and (4) of the Criminal Procedure (Scotland) Act 1995 makes it quite clear that a person arrested under a summary warrant (whether in relation to a common law or other statutory offence), must where reasonably practicable, be brought before a competent criminal court not later than the first day after the arrest. Obviously, if the suspect was arrested on a normal Friday, Saturday or Sunday, they should appear in court on the following Monday (provided of course that the Monday is not a public holiday).

With these statutory guidelines in mind, however, it would not appear to be absolutely fatal to a future criminal trial if the suspect did not appear in court on the first available date after being arrested by the police. It should go without saying that it is sensible not to delay unduly the appearance of the suspect in court on the first available court date after his or her arrest.

 Key point: Arrest is the forcible detention of the suspect by the police.

Do police officers need a warrant to arrest a suspect?

Generally speaking, police officers will only seek a warrant to arrest a suspect if the criminal offence is of a type which would normally be tried under solemn procedure i.e. a trial where a judge sits with a jury of fifteen members of the public (in the Sheriff Court and the High Court of Justiciary).

It is normal practice for the police to lodge a writ called a petition to a Sheriff which is a request for a warrant to arrest a suspect. The petition is issued in the name of the local procurator fiscal and will contain details of the alleged offence and requests that the court approve the application to arrest the suspect. It has been argued that a magistrate could also grant the petition, but Section 34(2) of the Criminal Procedure (Scotland) Act 1995 seems to envisage that a sheriff is the proper authority for the granting of an arrest warrant. It appears to be the case that a sheriff will not ask many questions about the nature of the petition because there is a presumption that the procurator is acting lawfully and with authority when the application for the arrest warrant is submitted.

There will, of course, be situations when a suspect is arrested by police officers who have not yet obtained a warrant. It is then imperative for the procurator fiscal to submit a petition to the Sheriff as soon as reasonably practicable after the arrest has been carried out. The submission of the petition in such circumstances will normally take place when the suspect appears in court for the first time before the sheriff and usually the procurator fiscal's request is granted in such circumstances.

In theory, the procurator fiscal will not usually seek an arrest warrant if an individual is suspected of committing a summary offence i.e. the prosecution of the crime would be dealt with by a judge sitting alone in the Justice of the Peace Court or the Sheriff Court). It may be sensible for the procurator fiscal to seek an arrest warrant (by submitting a writ called a citation) from a judge of the relevant trial court) in the following circumstances:

1   the suspect's whereabouts are unknown

2   the suspect has failed to respond to a citation

3   it is necessary to have the suspect fingerprinted

4   it is necessary to have the suspect participate in an identity parade

5   the suspect is a flight risk

6   the case would be time-barred if citation proceeded normally

7   the accused is in custody in another criminal jurisdiction e.g. England

 Key point: Police will only seek an arrest warrant if the crime is to be tried under solemn procedure.

How common is it for police officers to arrest suspects without a warrant?

Arresting a suspect without a warrant is actually a very common practice under Scots common law. As previously remarked, the act of carrying out an arrest is a fairly serious development in the investigation of a crime and it might be presumed that the police have thought very carefully before deciding to arrest someone with or without having first obtained a warrant.

There is always the possibility that a suspect who has been arrested by the police could later bring a legal challenge in the civil courts against the relevant Chief Constable for the actions of his or her officers. In a civil action before the Outer House of the Court of Session, **Henderson v Chief Constable, Fife Police 1988**, it was held that the person claiming unlawful arrest **must** prove that the arrest was unreasonable and unnecessary.

 In the **Henderson** case, four employees barricaded themselves into their employer's laboratory. The police were called to the premises to remove the workers under the Trespass (Scotland) Act 1865. The four workers were

arrested and imprisoned in the police cells. The workers alleged that their arrest was unreasonable and unnecessary for the following reasons:

1 the arrests were completely unjustified

2 if the arrests were justified, there was no need to detain the employees in the cells

3 the police were unjustified in demanding that the female worker remove her bra when she was taken into custody

4 the police were unjustified in handcuffing one of the employees

The employees' civil action failed on the first two counts but was successful on the last two counts. Although the employees were admittedly intelligent and articulate, the police had exercised the power of arrest under the Trespass (Scotland) Act 1865 reasonably. Asking the female worker to remove an item of clothing and handcuffing another worker did, however, constitute an invasion of personal liberty.

 Key point: Arrest without a warrant is a very common occurrence.

When can a constable arrest someone without a warrant?

This may occur in the following circumstances:

1 if the constable has seen a crime committed or where the suspect is identified and is running away from the locus

2 the seriousness of the offence has been duly considered

3 the suspect may have gone into hiding with the intention of fleeing

4 the suspect has no fixed abode (permanent residence)

It is not normal practice for a police officer to arrest a suspect without a warrant in circumstances where the individual is going to be charged and then released to appear at a criminal trial at a later date. In such a situation, the suspect can then be cited to appear at the subsequent trial.

A police officer may arrest a suspect without a warrant under the Road Traffic Act 1988 to obtain a breath test (Section 6) or to obtain a sample (Section 7). Clearly, in such circumstances, it is absolutely imperative that a police officer acts swiftly to arrest and detain a suspect, but this power must be exercised reasonably and the officer in question must have an honest belief that his or actions were justified. The Terrorism Act 2000 also permits police officers to arrest a suspect without a warrant in order to prevent the commission of a terrorist attack.

 Key point: The Road Traffic Act 1988 gives the police the right to arrest suspects without a warrant.

Can members of the public arrest a suspect?

Yes, a private citizen can make an arrest without a warrant if they witness a serious crime, but the arrested person must be handed over to the police as soon possible. This situation is commonly known as a citizen's arrest.

Key point: Private citizens can make an arrest without a warrant i.e. a citizen's arrest.

What procedures are carried out by the police after arrest?

The police may feel that it is now imperative to obtain prints and samples from the suspect.

As discussed earlier, every reasonable effort should be made to bring the suspect before the courts as soon as reasonably practicable. Before any court appearance, the suspect may be detained in the cells at a police station, or wherever is practicable in more remote locations where a police cell is not readily available.

The suspect should be permitted to inform a solicitor about the arrest and should be allowed to have a private interview with the solicitor before making a court appearance. Someone over the age of 16 who has been arrested generally has a right to inform one other person of the arrest, but the police may be understandably reluctant to divulge this information to another person whom they had good reason to believe was also involved in the commission of the crime or if they had strong grounds for believing that the progress of their investigation would be seriously hampered or undermined.

The time when the suspect makes the request to inform the solicitor and one other person regarding the circumstances of the arrest and when the request was actioned should be recorded by police officers.

Any failure by the police to inform the relevant persons about the suspect's arrest could be viewed very negatively at a subsequent trial in the sense that any evidence obtained could be regarded as tainted and, therefore, inadmissible. A judge or a jury may well draw the conclusion that any such evidence was obtained from the suspect under duress by the police officers. It should be noted that the police officers may actually communicate the fact that the suspect has been arrested to a solicitor and one other nominated person rather than the suspect being permitted to do this personally.

A suspect who has been arrested on the grounds of murder, attempted murder or culpable homicide has a right to the services of the legal aid duty solicitor. The duty solicitor must act for the suspect until he is released on bail or fully committed. A suspect who has been arrested on other grounds is **not** entitled to the assistance of the Legal Aid duty solicitor unless:

1 he is to be placed on an identity parade

2 he is to appear in court on petition or it is his first appearance in court from custody

3 if he is to appear in court under summary procedure

If the suspect decides to accept the services of a solicitor he may, of course, be eligible for Legal Aid in any case throughout the duration of the ciminal investigation and any subsequent prosecution.

 Key point: A suspect who has been arrested for murder or attempted murder or culpable homicide has a right to the services of the legal aid duty solicitor.

Can a suspect who has been arrested be searched by police officers?

If the offence is of a common law nature e.g. theft, the police may search the suspect. It is not sensible for the police to carry out a search prior to the arrest of the suspect unless this course of action can be justified by the officers in question i.e. they can demonstrate that such a search was fair and reasonable in the circumstances. It would probably only be advisable for officers to contemplate carrying out a search of a suspect in an emergency situation.

If the police have arrested a suspect after having first obtained a warrant, they will possess the necessary authority to carry out a strip search. This authority, however, does not extend to an invasive search of the suspect's person e.g. searching for drugs which may be stored in a person's rectum. In order to carry out such a search of a suspect, officers would require the authority of a special warrant.

Can the police question a suspect who has been arrested?

Yes, police officers can do this – within limits – and as long as the questions put to the suspect are regarded as fair. The problem for officers will be that, if they overstep the mark and engage in an interrogation which is later viewed as highly unfair to the suspect's interests, any evidence gained from this exchange may be regarded by a court as tainted and inadmissible.

A suspect is at liberty to make a confession or a statement to police officers following on from the arrest and the suspect's solicitor may have advised the client that it is in his or her best interests to do this. In these circumstances, the confession or the statement will be admissible as evidence at the subsequent trial. Clearly, if the statement or confession was obtained by officers placing the suspect under duress, its value as evidence would be extremely questionable.

It should be remembered that the suspect will probably have exercised the right to have a solicitor present and any questioning by the police officers will have been tape recorded.

In any event, the police may have reason to continue to question a suspect who has been arrested because there may well be a sound belief concerning this individual's involvement in other alleged criminal offences which the officers are anxious to investigate.

 Key point: The police, within certain limits, are entitled to question a person who has been arrested.

Will a suspect be detained by the police until the trial?

A suspect may continue to be held in custody by the police until the first available court date if the alleged offence is to be prosecuted under solemn procedure. If, however, the offence is to be tried under summary procedure, the police have discretion to release the suspect with the proviso that the suspect will attend the first available court hearing (normally within the next 14 days). In order to be released from custody, the suspect must sign an undertaking that they will attend the court hearing. This is normal procedure for road traffic offences which involve the suspect being charged with drinking and driving. It is highly unusual for a suspect to be released after having given a verbal undertaking to police officers that they will attend the first available court hearing, but it is not entirely unknown for this option to be exercised. In any event, the procurator fiscal has the power to order a suspect to be released from police custody.

If the suspect fails to attend court on the date of the hearing, they have committed a criminal offence in terms of the Criminal Procedure (Scotland) Act 1995. In such circumstances, the hearing will be suspended and an arrest warrant will be issued by the court. Such an offence of failing to attend court can be dealt with at the subsequent trial or may itself be the subject of additional criminal charges or a further trial.

 Key point: A suspect may be detained by the police until trial if the offence is to be prosecuted under solemn procedure.

Can the police carry out a personal search of a suspect?

The general rule is that a person may not be searched personally by police officers unless such individual has been detained or arrested.

In Scotland, the police can exercise their powers of stop and search if an individual is suspected of being in possession of any of the following items:

- ◆ Illegal drugs
- ◆ Offensive weapons
- ◆ Stolen property
- ◆ Alcohol (this relates to attendance at major football or rugby events and also if you are using public transport to travel to such events)
- ◆ Money or the money equivalent of more than £1,000 if such sums are suspected of being the acquired from the proceeds of crime
- ◆ Fireworks that may be used in a way that breaches anti-social behaviour legislation.

A suspect could also be searched if the Police believe that they possess evidence of a breach of the Protection of Wild Mammals (Scotland) Act 2002.

It is important to note that the Police do not need to have gone to the bother of obtaining a search warrant in all of the situations outlined above, but officers **must** have a reasonable suspicion that a crime has been committed by the suspect. If any of the items outlined above are found on the suspect's person, Police Officers have the right to confiscate them and they may be used in evidence at a future criminal trial.

In a search without a warrant, the Police officers have limited powers in that they cannot carry out a strip search of the suspect. The officers can, however, ask a suspect to remove coats, jackets, gloves, hats or to empty pockets during a search without a warrant.

A Police officer with the rank of assistant Chief Constable or above has the power to order searches of people or vehicles in relation to anti-terrorism operations.

Can the police carry out a search of premises?

Premises can only normally be searched by the police if a court has issued a search warrant. It will not be necessary for the police to obtain a warrant if a person agrees that the officers can carry out a search of the relevant premises.

Stopping and searching vehicles

Under Sections 165 and 166 of the Road Traffic Act 1988, the police have the power to stop the driver of a vehicle (who is suspected of an offence under the Act) and ask the driver to produce the following documents:

◆ a valid driving licence
◆ a valid insurance certificate
◆ a valid MOT certificate.

Under Section 165, the driver **must** also provide their name and address when requested to do so by police officers.

Section 44 of the Terrorism Act 2000

This legislative provision gives the police extended powers to stop and search individuals. Immediately after the terrorist attack at Glasgow Airport on 30 June 2007, all Scottish Police forces had the right to use Section 44 as a means of combating terrorism. Admittedly, this power was in force for 28 days only after the terrorist incident at Glasgow.

Currently, however, the only force in Scotland permitted to use Section 44 is the British Transport Police. Basically, Police officers can stop and search any individual who happens to be in a designated area e.g. Waverley and Glasgow Central Railway Stations. The Police do not need to justify why they have stopped someone under Section 44 and critics of the legislation (such as the human rights organisation Liberty) have argued that the Police have been permitted to use their powers indiscriminately. Liberty has produced evidence which tends to show that Black and Asian people are four times more likely to be stopped and searched under Section 44 in comparison with white people.

The Police are not permitted to carry out an invasive body search of a suspect under Section 44 and they are limited to carrying out what is popularly known as a "pat down search" which should be conducted by an officer of the same gender as the suspect. The suspect should only be asked to remove outer clothing and bags can be searched. A suspect cannot object to being searched by officers and there is always the danger that a person who gets into a vehement argument with the Police could be charged with a breach of the peace. Failure by suspects to co-operate with officers who wish to carry out a search could lead to them being arrested.

A suspect is **not** required to provide any of the following to the police during the search:

◆ name and address
◆ an explanation why you happen to be present at the locus
◆ a DNA sample

Furthermore, a suspect is not obliged to cooperate with attempts by officers to take their photograph.

After the search has been conducted, the officers should provide the suspect with a paper record of the incident irrespective of whether they have provided their name and address.

Members of the public (whether suspects or not) are under a duty to provide answers to questions posed by the Police under anti-terrorism legislation. The public should be aware of these Police powers in the following circumstances:

An individual is legally obliged to provide information to Police officers which may prevent the carrying out of a terrorist offence (Section 38B: Terrorism Act 2000).

At an airport, harbour or other port, an individual must answer police questions so that they can verify whether or not they are a terrorist. Failure to answer such questions could result in the commission of an imprisonable offence (Schedule 7: Terrorism Act 2000).

What is the legal position if the police fail to obtain a warrant?

Any evidence obtained by the police in such a situation may well be tainted and regarded as inadmissible at the suspect's trial. There are situations, however, where it will not be absolutely necessary for police officers to obtain a warrant before a search is carried out.

The Misuse of Drugs Act 1971 (illegal drugs), Civic Government (Scotland) Act 1982 (stolen property) and the Criminal Law (Consolidation) (Scotland) Act 1995 (offensive weapons) allow a search without a warrant to be conducted by officers. The police must have reasonable grounds for suspecting that such an offence which the statute addresses is or has been committed. It is not necessary for the police to obtain the consent of the person whom they wish to search.

 Key point: Failure by police to obtain a warrant before a search is carried out could make any evidence obtained inadmissable.

What about a search with a warrant?

The procurator fiscal will apply for a search warrant, usually after having received information from the police officers investigating the commission of the crime.

If the offence is a common law crime, the warrant can be issued by any justice (this includes a Sheriff) and is enforceable anywhere in Scotland. Some Acts of Parliament do, however, stipulate that a Sheriff must issue a search warrant. The Misuse of Drugs Act 1971 has a fairly stringent requirement that the relevant magistrate must take evidence on oath from police officers before issuing a search warrant.

The police do not need to disclose to the suspect the fact that the warrant has been issued unless the relevant legislation stipulates such a course of action.

The fact that a warrant has been granted to the police need not be communicated to an alleged offender unless the statute demands this. In practice, the police will normally inform a suspect that a search warrant has been issued if the offence is a common law crime, but if the officers were of the opinion that there is a real danger that the suspect might go ahead and destroy any potential evidence following on from such a disclosure they would probably not impart this information.

It may well be the case that no one has actually been detained or arrested when an application for a search warrant is made, but the police must have a reasonable suspicion that a crime has been committed. The purpose of the search in such a situation will be, of course, to obtain evidence in order to assist the prosecution of the suspect. Some Acts of Parliament may, however, contain a condition to the effect that the procurator fiscal is prevented from obtaining a search warrant until a suspect has been charged.

In a situation, where the interests of justice are deemed to be paramount, a very limited warrant may be issued to the police in order for them to obtain a blood sample from a suspect who has not yet been charged with the commission of an offence. This type of warrant is issued for one purpose amd one purpose only and cannot be used to effect a wider search of a suspect's person or premises. Clearly, the justice who issues such a warrant will have to balance the rights of the suspect against the wider interest of protecting and safeguarding the public.

Under the common law, the procurator fiscal has the right to apply for a warrant to carry out a search of banking records for the purpose of making copies of the information contained there.

 Key point: Some statutes, contrary to the usual practice e.g. the Public Order Act 1936, stipulate that a Sheriff must issue a search warrant.

What details must search warrants contain?

The warrant should contain the following information:

1 it must be dated

2 it must be signed by the person granting it (i.e. the justice).

Can a suspect challenge the validity of a search warrant?

A suspect has such a right to challenge a warrant by making an application to the High Court of Justiciary. It does not matter if the warrant relates to summary or solemn criminal offences.

When can a search no longer be carried out?

When the suspect has been committed for trial under solemn procedure or, in summary proceedings when a trial diet has been set down, it is no longer competent for the procurator fiscal to apply for a search warrant in connection with suspected crimes.

 In **Her Majesty's Advocate v Milford (1973)** this general rule was departed from when a search warrant was granted after the full committal of the accused in order that a blood sample could be obtained where the offence in question involved an alleged rape.

Theoretically, a search warrant could be issued after the accused has been served with an indictment. If this occurred, the suspect should be given a reasonable opportunity to make known any objections to this development.

 Key point: A suspect can challenge a search warrant by raising proceedings in the High Court of Justiciary.

What about evidence obtained by an irregular search?

This issue may arise in circumstances where the police failed to obtain a warrant and then carried out the search or if they exceeded the authority given to them by the warrant. The danger for the prosecution authorities will, of course, be that any evidence obtained as a result of an irregular search may be regarded as tainted or inadmissible. The relevant court will have to consider this issue and such

or weakness of the police suspicions can be assessed. The solicitor may be of the opinion that the case against the suspect is very strong and that it be would in the best interests of the client to disclose fully all that they know about the circumstances of the alleged offence. This may involve the suspect making a statement or a full confession to the police. Any statement or confession should be recorded by the police.

It may be the case, however, that the solicitor is of the view that the evidence which the police have against the suspect is very flimsy and that the suspect would be better advised to make no disclosure at this time – other than to confirm the details of his or name and address.

 Key point: When the solicitor acting for the accused arrives at the police station, they should liaise with the investigating police officers to determine the strength of the case.

What should the solicitor do if the suspect has been charged?

Again, the solicitor should liaise with the lead investigating officer upon arrival at the police station to determine what has already happened. As previously discussed, the suspect is not compelled to answer any further police questions after the police have issued a caution and charged him or her with a criminal offence. If the suspect wishes to make a statement or a full confession to the police, the solicitor should make the officers aware of this intention. The statement or the confession should be recorded by the police and the solicitor should be in attendance. Does a defence solicitor have to be present when the police question the accused?

The accused, while in police custody, has a right to have a private interview with a solicitor at least once before they make an appearance in court. If, however, the accused makes statements or admissions to police officers while being interviewed without the presence of a defence solicitor, such information may be used against them by the prosecution at a subsequent trial.

In November 2009, the High Court of Justiciary, sitting as the Scottish court of Criminal Appeal in Edinburgh, ruled in **Duncan MacLean v Her Majesty's Advocate** that evidence obtained during a Police interview with a suspect was not rendered invalid merely because his solicitor was absent at the relevant time. During the interview, the suspect made a number of damning statements which the Crown intended to rely upon at his subsequent trial. The suspect later attempted to bring an action against the Police on the grounds that his human rights had been breached. Their Lordships ruled that this had not been the case and any evidence obtained during the interview could be used at MacLean's upcoming criminal trial. At the time of writing, MacLean had appealed to the Supreme Court in London in an attempt to have the decision of the High Court overturned.

 Key point: The defence solicitor is present at the police station to safeguard the interests of the accused.

What is the role of the solicitor if the police decide to hold an identity parade?

The police may have a witness who can identify the suspect and they may be anxious to hold an identity parade to strengthen the case against the suspect. The suspect will be asked to stand in line with a number of other individuals and the witness will be asked to view the line-up through a one way mirror. The suspect cannot refuse to take part in the parade and any such refusal would no doubt strengthen the suspicions of the police that they had apprehended the correct person. Participation in the parade should not necessarily be viewed as a negative experience for the suspect because the witness could fail to identify him or her thus considerably weakening the police case.

The solicitor attends the parade as an observer in order to make sure that it is carried out properly so that the witness cannot be directed by the police to pinpoint a particular individual i.e. the suspect. The police are also under a duty to ensure that the other participants in the parade are of a similar age, gender, build or height to the suspect. It is equally important that police officers who have not participated in the criminal investigation involving the suspect are given responsibility for organising and carrying out the parade.

If the solicitor feels that the police have not carried out the parade fairly, they can give evidence to this effect at the suspect's trial and, again, the issue of the fairness or admissibility of the prosecution's evidence will be firmly placed in the spotlight.

 Key point: The defence solicitor will attend an identity parade to ensure that it is properly conducted by the police.

What rules govern the treatment of children who are being investigated by the police?

The police will have to tread very carefully when dealing with children who are suspected of committing a criminal offence. Currently, a child under the age of eight cannot be guilty of a criminal offence. In other words, a criminal prosecution cannot be brought against a child under the age of eight. Criminal responsibility in Scotland, therefore, begins at the age of eight.

However, Kenny McAskill MSP, the Scottish Justice Secretary announced proposals (contained in the Criminal Justice and Licensing Bill) in March 2009 to increase the age of criminal responsibility to twelve in order to bring Scots criminal law into line with most of Europe. In England and Wales, by comparison, the age of criminal responsibility will continue to be ten. Elish Angiolini QC, the current Lord Advocate, has supported this change to the law because previously she criticised the current age of criminal responsibility as too low.

 Key point: The age of criminal responsibility is to be raised from eight years of age to twelve years of age.

What rules govern the arrest and detention children?

Section 15 of the Criminal Procedure (Scotland) Act 1995 governs the detention of children i.e. persons below the age of 16 by police officers.

If the police decide to exercise their powers of detention in relation to a child under Section 14 of the Act of 1995, that child's parents or guardians have a right to be informed of this development without any undue delay on the part of the officers. The parents or guardians should be allowed access to the child unless the officers have a reasonable suspicion that the adults are also involved in the commission of the offence. Access to the child may be denied if this would hamper or hinder the police investigation or it if was simply harmful to the child.

Key point: Section 15 of the Criminal Procedure (Scotland) Act 1995 governs the detention of children.

After a child has been arrested, it is normal procedure to release the child into the custody of his parents or guardians as long as the responsible adult has given a commitment to the officers that the child will attend court on the first available date. The decision to release the child will be the responsibility of at least an Inspector or the senior officer in charge of the police station.

If a child has been arrested, the police will normally release them on an undertaking having been given by them, their parent or guardian that they will attend his court case. A decision to release the child will be taken by an officer of the rank of Inspector or above or by the officer in charge of the police station to which the child has been brought. In the following circumstances, the police will decline to release the child:

1   if the charge is homicide or another serious (grave) crime

2   it is in the interest of the child in order to remove him or her from the influence of a reputed criminal or prostitute

3   if the officer is of the opinion that by releasing the child the ends of justice would not be served.

If the decision is made that the child should continue to be held in custody, the police station is not usually deemed as an appropriate place of detention and an alternative location will be sought be the police e.g. the child may be placed in the care of the local social work authorities. Again, a police officer of at least the rank of Inspector would normally take this decision to continue to hold the child in custody. There will, however, be situations where it will be completely impractical to remove the child from the police station where they are being detained. This may arise for the following reasons:

1   it is not practical to remove the child to a place of safety

2   that the child is of such an unruly character that detention in the police station is the only practical option

3   that the child's state of health or mental or bodily condition may make detention inadvisable.

During any period of detention by police officers, it is normal procedure for a child not to have contact with or be held with an adult also accused of a crime at the police station and the police may have to hold the child in a separate cell. This practice of separating a child from adults accused of committing a crime is reinforced at the trial stage. After a child has been released from custody and cited to appear for trial on the first available court date, the child will not be allowed to mix or associate with an accused adult and may be directed to a separate or specially designated waiting room at the court in order to achieve this purpose.

If the child is detained by the police, but no criminal charges follow, the Principal Reporter must be informed. The child may then be dealt with under the Children's Hearing system.

Key point: When a child has been arrested or detained, it is normal practice for the police to release them into the custody of a parent/guardian or other responsible adult.

What are the judicial procedures in respect of children?

Normally, it is not competent for a child below 16 years of age to be prosecuted in a criminal court without the permission of the Lord Advocate and private prosecutions of children would definitely not be permitted. It is the practice of the Lord Advocate to issue guidelines to the procurator fiscal service from time to time about best practice when it comes to dealing with children who are involved as suspects in a criminal investigation.

If a child is to be prosecuted in Scotland, the trial shall take place in either the Sheriff Court or the High Court of Justiciary.

It is the duty of the child's parent or guardian to be in attendance at the trial and the police officer who exercised the power of arrest should have made this very clear to the person responsible for the child. It may, in fact, be the case that the child has been removed from his or her parent by social work authorities and, in such situations, a social worker will attend the court hearing. Furthermore, in situations, where the parent or guardian is a co-accused of the child's or may be suspected of involvement in the commission of the criminal offence, it would not reasonable for this person to attend court.

In situations where a child is being brought to trial in either the Sheriff Court or the High Court of Justiciary, the relevant Chief Constable of police for the area in which the crime took place has a duty to inform the social work authority which has responsibility for the area in which the court has jurisdiction. The nature of the alleged criminal offence committed by the child and the date and time of any scheduled court appearance will be communicated to the social work authorities so that a background report about the child can be provided to the court.

 Key point: A child under the age of 16 should not be prosecuted in a criminal court without the express permission of the Lord Advocate.

What safeguards exist to protect a child who is to appear in a criminal court?

Under both summary and solemn procedure, the media is restricted as to what it can report regarding a criminal prosecution of a child under the age of 16.

What is the media prevented from disclosing to the public?

The publishing or broadcasting of the child's:

- name
- address
- school

The media is also not permitted to disclose any details which would help to identify the child.

Interestingly, the restrictions placed on the media do not just apply to a child accused of committing a crime, but any child involved in criminal proceedings (i.e.

Justice of the Peace Courts by early 2010. These changes to the Scottish legal system were introduced as a result of the introduction of the provisions of the Judiciary and Courts (Scotland) Act 2008.

The judges of the Justice of the Peace Court mainly deal with less serious types of crime in comparison with the Sheriff Court and the High Court of Justiciary. The Justice of the Peace Court will tend to deal with matters such as breach of the peace, assault, vandalism, theft (excluding housebreaking), speeding, vehicle excise, TV licensing, electricity fraud and various other road traffic offences.

Under a major shake-up of criminal jurisdiction, Justices of the Peace have been given powers that Sheriffs have such as issuing a driving ban or endorsing the driving licences of motorists convicted of various offences e.g. careless driving, driving without insurance and driving while serving a motoring ban. The aim of this reform is to reduce the workload of Sheriffs so that they can concentrate on dealing with more serious types of crime. The Justice of the Peace Court cannot deal with assaults where the victim suffers a wound, for example, where the skin is broken or where bones are broken.

 Key point: The Justice of the Peace Court is the most junior of the Scottish criminal courts and it deals with relatively minor crimes.

All trials in the Justice of the Peace Court are conducted under summary procedure meaning that the judges sit alone. In other words, there is no jury. The Justice of the Peace Court judges are masters of the facts in that they alone will decide whether the accused is guilty or not. If the judges should find the accused guilty after the trial, then they will also impose the appropriate sentence.

There are two types of judge who sit in the Justice of the Peace Court – a Justice of the Peace and a Stipendiary Magistrate.

Justices of the Peace

Justices of the Peace are most likely to be found in the Justice of the Peace Court. Generally, these individuals are not legally qualified. Justices of the Peace have been in existence since 1609 and currently there are approximately 700 of them dispensing justice in Scotland. In other words, they are not qualified to act as solicitors or advocates. The Justice of the Peace Court Association, a voluntary body representing all Justice of the Peace Courts in Scotland, does provide regular training programmes for Justices to ensure that minimum standards are maintained. Justices do not receive a salary for their services, but they may be reimbursed for travelling expenses. Many Justices will be recruited from the ranks of Scotland's councillors – although being a member of a local council is not an essential qualification to become one of these judges. The Scottish Executive will make appointments to the ranks of Justices of Peace as and when required.

 Key point: Two types of judge can sit in the Justice of the Peace Court – a lay Justice of the Peace and a legally qualified Stipendiary Magistrate.

A legally qualified clerk of the court will be present to advise the Justices regarding matters of law and procedure. The clerk is a practising lawyer (usually a solicitor)

who is employed by the Scottish Courts Service. The Justices merely rely upon the clerk's legal advice. The clerk does not have a say in the magistrates' actual verdict. It should be noted that Justices have complete independence when it comes to making a verdict. Justices can sit alone or a bench of three Justices can often sit.

A Justice of the Peace can impose a maximum prison sentence of 60 days and impose a maximum fine of £2500 (known as a level 4 fine).

Section 46 of the Criminal Proceedings etc. (Reform) (Scotland) Act 2007 permits the powers of a Justice of the Peace to be increased by order of the Scottish Ministers at Holyrood.

Stipendiary Magistrates

A Stipendiary Magistrate, on the other hand, will be legally qualified. Such individuals will have been practising lawyers for at least five years i.e. a solicitor or an advocate. These judges sit alone without the assistance of a legally qualified clerk. These judges are professional magistrates and, consequently, they receive a salary for their services. A Stipendiary Magistrate can impose a maximum prison sentence of one year if the crime involves violence or dishonesty and the accused has relevant previous convictions. A maximum fine of £10,000 can also be imposed on a guilty person. Interestingly, as we shall see, a Stipendiary Magistrate has exactly the same powers as a Sheriff under summary procedure in the Sheriff Court. It is worth pointing out that the City of Glasgow Council is the only Scottish local authority which uses Stipendiary Magistrates in its Justice of the Peace Court.

 Key point: A lay Justice of the Peace can impose a 60-day term of imprisonment and/or a £2500 fine whereas a legally qualified Stipendiary Magistrate can impose a prison sentence of one year and/or a £10,000 fine.

An accused on trial before the Justice of the Peace Court will usually be represented by a solicitor. And the prosecutor will be from the Procurator Fiscal Service. The Fiscal is a civil servant who is employed by the Scottish Executive and who has responsibility at the local level for the investigation and prosecution of crimes. The accused will be given a document known as a complaint which will detail the charges that he or she is facing.

An appeal from a decision of the Justice of the Peace Court is made to the High Court of Justiciary in Edinburgh.

Summary justice reform – the McInnes Report

In November 2001, Sheriff Principal John McInnes QC was commissioned by the then Scottish Executive (now Government) to produce a report on summary criminal justice. This was a highly significant exercise since 96% of all crimes dealt with by the justice system in Scotland are under summary procedure. After conducting his review of the operation of summary criminal justice, Sheriff Principal McInnes reported back with various recommendations in January 2004.

One of Sheriff Principal McInnes' most controversial recommendations was the abolition of lay justices (Justices of the Peace) in the District Court. If the recommendations by Sheriff McInne had been followed to their logical conclusion, such justices would have been replaced by professional judges.

The Scottish Executive/Government, however, decided to retain lay justices operating within their existing powers (significantly, the two lay members of the McInnes Committee had been opposed to any abolition).

The appointment of lay justices will now be similar to that of part-time sheriffs. A lay justice would be appointed for a fixed period of five years. At the end of this period, the justice should be eligible for reappointment to the bench until they reached the compulsory retirement age of 70. There will also be a greater commitment to the training and education of lay justices in order to promote greater consistency in the way that summary criminal justice is delivered.

Following on from the work of Sheriff McInnes, the Scottish Executive or Government undertook a consultation exercise to determine whether the term lay justice should continue to be used. A suggested alternative had been the title 'community justice' in order to emphasise the fact that these justices come from the local communities which they are meant to serve, although the older title of Justice of the Peace was eventually retained.

One concrete result of the McInnes' recommendations is that a greater distinction is now made between those justices who can hear trials and those with more limited functions such as signing justices i.e. those who mainly sign police warrants.

 Key point: The McInnes Report paved the way for a major shake-up of summary criminal justice in Scotland.

The Criminal Proceedings etc. (Reform)(Scotland) Act 2007

Following on from the McInnes Report, the above legislation has made a number of important changes to summary criminal proceedings which paved the way for the replacement of the old District Courts with the new Justice of the Peace Courts and the Sheriff Court.

It should be recalled that summary prosecutions account for 96% of criminal court actions in Scotland, so any reforms are bound to be significant.

Justice of the Peace Courts

The new Justice of the Peace Courts, which replace the older District Courts, were introduced to different areas of Scotland during 2008. The first reforms took effect in the Sheriffdom of Lothian and Borders in March 2008. These reforms mean that the Scottish Court Service took over responsibility for the new courts leading to a unified court system in Scotland for the first time. Previously, local authorities had been responsible for running the District Courts.

The following Sheriffdoms now have Justice of the Peace Courts operating:

◆ Lothian & Borders
◆ Grampian, Highlands and Islands
◆ Glasgow & Strathkelvin

Justice of the Peace Courts were introduced to the following Sheriffdoms during 2009/2010:

◆ Tayside Central & Fife
◆ South Strathclyde, Dumfries & Galloway
◆ North Strathclyde

As discussed, Sheriff John McInnes, who had been given responsibility by the Scottish Executive (now the Scottish Government) to review the operation of summary criminal justice, had recommended that Justices of the Peace should be abolished and replaced with legally qualified Stipendiary Magistrates – who, of course, would have to be paid. This recommendation was not followed and lay Justices of the Peace will continue to serve local communities as part of the new court structure and, thus, the State will save quite a considerable amount of money in the process.

Under a major shake-up of the summary criminal justice system, the new courts will take over responsibility for many motoring offences which previously had been the preserve of the Sheriff Court.

New legislation had to be introduced in the UK Parliament to permit this change to Scottish criminal jurisdiction as motoring and traffic law remains an area of responsibility reserved to Westminster.

Changes to sentencing powers

Under the Criminal Proceedings etc. (Reform) (Scotland) Act 2007, the sentencing powers of Sheriffs and Stipendiary Magistrates have increased. The judges will now be able to sentence someone who has been found guilty of a common law crime by imposing a prison term up to one year. Previously, the judges could impose prison terms of between three to six months depending on the circumstances e.g. if the guilty party had relevant previous convictions.

The amount which Sheriffs and Stipendiary Magistrates can impose as fines will also rise from the previous limit of £5,000 to £10,000.

Other reforms to criminal law

The Criminal Proceedings etc. (Reform) (Scotland) Act 2007 introduced the following changes:

1   Sheriffs and Stipendiary Magistrates sitting in summary criminal trials (i.e. non-jury hearings) have had their powers of sentencing increased from 3-6 months to 12 months and the current level of fine will be increased from £5000 to a maximum fine of £10,000.

2   The introduction of orders whereby a minor offender could be forced to pay up to £5000 in compensation to a victim as an alternative to facing a criminal trial and possible conviction.

3   Fiscal fines have been increased from the present maximum of £100 to £500.

4   A new post of Fines Enforcement Officer has been created to ensure greater efficiency in the collection of fines. This Officer will be able to arrest an individual's wages or earnings.

5   Prosecutors will now be allowed to apply for all outstanding charges against an accused to be rolled up into one case – even if these charges were initiated in different Sheriffdoms.

 Key point: The Criminal Proceedings etc. (Scotland) Act 2007 makes major changes to the Scottish Criminal Justice system.

Changes to bail conditions

On 10 December 2007, Kenny MacAskill, Justice Secretary in the Scottish Government announced changes to the way in which the bail conditions operate. Anyone breaching bail conditions could now face a prison sentence of up to one year. Previously, the maximum sentence had been three months for breach of bail conditions. For those individuals who commit more serious breaches of their bail conditions, this could mean facing between two to five years in prison.

The Sheriff Court

In terms of work load, the Sheriff Court is the busiest criminal court in Scotland. Glasgow Sheriff Court, for instance, is the busiest criminal court in Europe dealing with approximately 330 criminal cases per day. The present Sheriff Court was established by the Sheriff Courts Act 1971.

The Sheriff Court, it will be remembered, can also hear civil cases. The organisation of the Sheriff Court in civil matters (Sheriffdoms and Sheriff Court districts) is exactly the same for the criminal court. A Sheriff Court can deal with all crimes committed within the boundaries of the Sheriffdom. In practice, however, there will be many crimes which the Sheriff Court cannot deal with. Crimes such as murder, rape, treason, incest and piracy will be tried by Scotland's supreme criminal court, the High Court of Justiciary. Furthermore, particularly serious crimes such as trafficking in drugs and armed robbery will come under the jurisdiction of the High Court.

Sheriffs will have been practising lawyers for at least ten years. They can be appointed from the ranks of solicitors or advocates.

 Key point: The Sheriff Court is the busiest criminal court in Scotland.

There are two criminal procedures in the Sheriff Court:

◆ A summary procedure
◆ A solemn procedure

Summary procedure

A trial of an accused under summary procedure means that the Sheriff will sit alone to try the case. There is no jury present and the Sheriff will decide the guilt or the innocence of the accused. The Sheriff will be the master of the facts. If the prosecution proves beyond a reasonable doubt that the accused is guilty, then the Sheriff will decide the appropriate punishment. Less serious crimes are dealt with under summary procedure. The accused will receive a document known as a complaint which details the charges that he or she is accused of. Here is an example of a complaint document:

Under the Criminal Procedure (Scotland) Act 1995

IN THE SHERIFF COURT OF LOTHIAN AND BORDERS AT EDINBURGH

THE COMPLAINT OF THE PROCURATOR FISCAL AGAINST

**Ref No: PS 40 101109
John Young
23 Glebe Street**   **Date of Birth: 1.4.79**
Edinburgh

The charge against you is that on 31 October, 2009 in Colinton Road, Edinburgh you did drive motorcycle registration number ABC 123 in a dangerous manner and you did collide with motor vehicle registration number SO52 BBX contrary to Section 2 of the Road Traffic Act 1988.

Munro McDonald
Procurator-Fiscal Depute

The powers of a Sheriff under summary procedure are exactly the same as that of a stipendiary magistrate sitting in the Justice of the Peace Court. A Sheriff can impose a maximum prison sentence of one year and/or a fine of up to £10,000. When dealing with the most serious types of offences and, possibly where the guilty party has relevant previous convictions, the Sheriff will often make full use of these powers. However, a Sheriff's sentencing powers can be affected by Acts of Parliament which will stipulate the maximum sentence or punishment that can be imposed in relation to particular offences.

Admittedly, the last majority Conservative Government (1992–97) introduced legislation to increase the power of summary Sheriffs, but these provisions were not brought into force. The Crime and Punishment (Scotland) Act 1997 would have given Sheriffs the power to impose a maximum prison sentence of six months and, where the guilty party had relevant previous convictions for certain offences, a maximum prison sentence of one year could have been a possibility.

 Key point: A Sheriff under summary procedure has exactly the same powers as a stipendiary magistrate in the Justice of the Peace courts.

Appeals from a decision of a Sheriff under summary procedure are made to the High Court of Justiciary in Edinburgh.

Solemn procedure

More serious types of crimes are dealt with under solemn procedure. The Sheriff sits with a jury of 15 men and women. This time, the jury will be the 'master of the facts' in that it will decide the innocence or guilt of the accused. Should the jury return a guilty verdict, then it is for the Sheriff to impose the appropriate punishment.

A Sheriff under solemn procedure can impose a maximum prison sentence of up to five years and/or an unlimited fine. If the Sheriff is of the opinion that his sentencing powers are not adequate enough to punish an offender, he can send the accused to be sentenced in the High Court of Justiciary. The High Court has unlimited powers of imprisonment and fine.

On 1 May 2004, section 13(1) of the Crime and Punishment (Scotland) Act 1997 relating to Sheriff's sentencing powers under solemn procedure, was finally brought into force. This meant that a Sheriff's powers of imprisonment were increased from three to five years. This change aimed to remove cases from the High Court that could just as easily be dealt with by Sheriffs. The result of these reforms is that certain categories of accused (e.g. sex or violent) may face a prison sentence of up to five years in the Sheriff Court.

In a solemn trial, the accused will receive a document detailing the charges that he or she is facing. This document is known as an indictment.

 Key point: The Sheriff Court has two types of criminal procedure – summary (the Sheriff sits alone) and solemn (the Sheriff and a jury of 15).

An accused will usually be represented by a solicitor when the Sheriff Court is sitting under solemn procedure. However, it is not unusual for the accused to be represented by an advocate. The prosecution of the accused is normally conducted by the Procurator Fiscal, but an Advocate Depute may appear for the prosecution.

Appeals from a decision of a Sheriff under solemn procedure are made to the High Court of Justiciary in Edinburgh.

 Key point: A Sheriff under summary procedure can impose a prison sentence of three to six months and/or a £5000 fine whereas under solemn procedure he can impose a prison sentence of up to five years and/or an unlimited fine.

The High Court of Justiciary

The High Court of Justiciary is the most senior and most powerful of Scotland's criminal courts. The High Court was founded by the Courts Act 1672, but it can trace its roots back much further to the medieval practice of sending judges (known as justiciars) out on circuit or ayre to various parts of Scotland to dispense criminal justice. These judges originally heard both civil and criminal cases, but eventually they became responsible for criminal trials.

As a result of the decision in the case of the **Mackintosh v Lord Advocate (1876)**, the right of any further appeal in criminal matters to an English court i.e. the House of Lords was ruled out. As shall be seen later in this chapter, the Scotland Act 1998 originally gave the English court known as the Privy Council the right to hear appeals from the High Court where the case involves issues relating to devolved government or human rights issues. From 1 October 2009, the Supreme Court of the United Kingdom has taken over the Privy Council's former responsibility for devolution and human rights appeals from the High Court.

 Key point: The High Court of Justiciary is Scotland's supreme criminal court.

The High Court of Justiciary is often simply referred to as the High Court, but it should not be confused with the English High Court which is a completely different body altogether. The Lord Justice General (currently Lord Hamilton) is the president of the High Court and his deputy is the Lord Justice Clerk (currently Lord Gill). In addition to the Lord Justice General and Lord Justice Clerk, the remaining 34 judges of the Court of Session also sit on the High Court. These 34 judges who, when sitting in the High Court, are referred to as Lords Commissioners of Justiciary. The judges of the High Court are overwhelmingly male and, in 2009, there were just five female members of this court, namely, Lady Paton, Lady Smith, Lady Dorrian, Lady Clark of Calton and Lady Stacey.

The High Court's permanent base and headquarters is in Edinburgh. The High Court, however, is not confined to holding trials in Edinburgh and one of its distinctive features is that it can sit as a trial court in the cities and the larger towns throughout Scotland. This is known as 'going on circuit' when the High Court sits outside Edinburgh and often the local Sheriff Court will play host to the High Court. Glasgow is the exception, with the city having its own permanent building for the use of the High Court near Glasgow Green. Furthermore, the High Court sits in Glasgow for 11 months of the year, unlike any other circuit location in Scotland. The four circuits are Home, West, North and South.

 Key point: The High Court has its permanent base in Edinburgh, but it also sits throughout the towns and cities of Scotland – this practice is known as 'going on circuit'.

The High Court's jurisdiction extends over the whole of Scotland and over all crimes committed in Scotland. In practice, the High Court tends to deal only with the most serious types of crime such as the so-called 'pleas of the Crown' which includes murder, rape, treason and incest. Armed robbery, and serious drug crimes will also come under the jurisdiction of the High Court. Where many less serious types of crime are concerned, the High Court is often prevented from exercising its jurisdiction as a result of various Acts of Parliament which stipulate that these less serious offences should be dealt with under summary procedure. The High Court has unlimited powers of imprisonment and fine.

The procedure in the High Court is almost always solemn where one Lord Commissioner of Justiciary can sit with a jury of 15 men and women. Here is an example of an indictment document:

INDICTMENT

ALEXANDER SAWNEY BEAN, Prisoner in Her Majesty's Prison of the Tolbooth, EDINBURGH

You are indicted at the instance of The Right Honourable EILISH ANGIOLINI, Queen 's Counsel, Her Majesty's Advocate, and the charge against you is that:

On 24 DECEMBER 2008 you ALEXANDER SAWNEY BEAN, in the house then occupied by you, at 101, Killmermont Street Edinburgh, did assault John McInarlin, strike him on the head repeatedly with a hammer, kick him repeatedly on the body and strike him on the body with a knife or similar instrument and you did, thus, murder him.

 Key point: The High Court deals with the most serious types of crime and the procedure is almost always solemn i.e. one Lord Commissioner of Justiciary can sit with a jury of 15. The High Court has unlimited powers of imprisonment and fine.

It should be noted that, at the trial of the two Libyans accused of planning the terrorist attack on the American passenger jet, PanAM flight 103 over the Scottish town of Lockerbie in December 1988, the services of a jury were not required and three Lords Commissioners of Justiciary formed the trial court. Lockerbie was, of course, the worst mass murder in Scottish criminal legal history and the arrangements for the trial were exceptional to say the least. The trial itself did not take place physically in Scotland, but at a former United States Air Force base called Camp Zeist in the Netherlands which was turned over to the jurisdiction of the High Court.

When dealing with appeals, the High Court sits only in Parliament House in Edinburgh. However, in 2001, the appeal of one of the Libyans involved in the Lockerbie bombing was conducted at Camp Zeist in the Netherlands before five High Court judges. The normal practice is for at least three judges to sit to hear appeals by an individual against his conviction and two judges will sit when the appeal is against the length of the sentence imposed on a guilty person. The High Court hears appeals from the High Court when it sits as a trial court, the Sheriff Court (both summary and solemn cases) and from the Justice of the Peace Court.

 Key point: The High Court sits in Edinburgh to hear appeals from the other Scottish criminal courts.

Cases in the High Court are prosecuted by certain advocates or solicitor-advocates (advocate deputes) who are chosen to represent the Lord Advocate, in whose name all prosecutions are brought in the public interest. It is possible, although extremely rare, for a private prosecution to be brought. The defence will usually be conducted by an advocate or solicitor-advocate. In addition a practitioner from another member state of the European Union may appear for a client in the circumstances prescribed by the European Communities (Services of Lawyers) Order 1978. An accused may conduct his own defence.

Differences between Summary and Solemn Procedure

Summary Criminal Procedure	Solemn Criminal Procedure
Judge sits alone (no jury present)	Judge sits with a jury of 15
Trial is on complaint i.e. the document outlining the charges faced by the accused	Trial is on indictment i.e. the document outlining the charges faced by the accused
Trial takes place in District/Justice of the Peace Court or Sheriff Court	Trial takes place in the Sheriff Court or the High Court of Justiciary
Procurator Fiscal normally prosecutes the accused	Procurator Fiscal can prosecute the accused in the Sheriff Court and an Advocate Depute will normally prosecute in the High Court
Accused is normally represented by a solicitor or a solicitor advocate	Accused can be represented by a solicitor, a solicitor advocate or an advocate
Procedure is used to deal with more minor crimes e.g. breach of the peace, traffic offences, minor assaults and theft	Procedure is used to deal with more serious crimes e.g. serious assault, murder, rape and drug trafficking
Summary courts have lesser powers of imprisonment and fine	Solemn courts have far greater powers of imprisonment and fine e.g. High Court has unlimited powers of imprisonment and fine
e.g. Sheriff Court can impose up to 1 year' imprisonment and £10,000 maximum fine	
Appeal to the Justiciary Roll Court of the High Court of Justiciary in Edinburgh	Appeal to the High Court sitting as the Scottish Court of Criminal Appeal in Edinburgh

Punishment

A judge may be of the opinion that imposing a fine or a period of imprisonment is not the most appropriate or effective way in which to punish an offender and it may be better to consider some alternatives.

What alternatives does the judge have at his or her disposal?

Probation orders

A local authority officer could supervise the offender for a period between six months and three years. The offender must agree to the terms of the probation order and an action plan must be in place which sets out how the offender will reform their behaviour. Commonly, all sorts of conditions are imposed on the offender e.g. where they will live; they may be subject to a curfew; they may have to compensate the victim; or they may have to attend a programme dealing with drug and alcohol addiction.

Community Service

This type of punishment can be used if the offender is over the age of 16. This entails the offender having to carry out some sort of unpaid work which benefits the community at large. Typically, the offender will be sentenced to community service lasting for a period between 80 to 240 hours and this must be carried out within 12 months.

A number of conditions have to be met if the judge decides to impose this kind of punishment:

◆ the offender must agree to this sentence
◆ the offender must be suitable for community service
◆ provision of suitable community service must be available in the area where the offender is usually resident

The judge will have access to community service reports before deciding that this is the most appropriate way of dealing with the offender.

Caution

The judge demands a surety or a sum of money from the offender which is a guarantee of future good behaviour. Normally, if the offender behaves and does not break the law for a period of anything up to 12 months, the sum will be returned. This option, however, is seldom used by the Scottish Courts.

Reparation

Section 249 of the Criminal Procedure (Scotland) Act 1995 does recognise situations where the offender can be forced to pay compensation or damages to the victim for any injuries or property damage arising out of the criminal act. The compensation sum is paid to the clerk of court by the offender.

As a result of the Criminal Proceedings etc. (Reform) (Scotland) Act 2007, it is now possible for a Sheriff to impose an order whereby a minor offender could be forced to pay up to £5000 in compensation to a victim as an alternative to facing a criminal trial and possible conviction.

Restriction of liberty orders

This involves the practice of the offender being "tagged" whereby an electronic device is fitted to the person's ankle or wrist. The offender will face severe restrictions as to their moments and may actually be subject to a curfew in the sense that they are not permitted to leave their home at night. The offender's movements can then be tracked by a central computer meaning that any breach of the curfew become obvious. Breach of the curfew by the offender is likely to lead to automatic imprisonment. This may seem like a soft option, but it is estimated that these types of arrangements are much more cost effective than sending a person to prison to be lodged at taxpayers' expense. The practice of "tagging" is best used for people who would normally face a prison sentence of up to six months. Generally, a person will be subject to "tagging" for a period which is twice as long as any prison sentence which could have been imposed.

Additional criminal punishments

In addition to a judge imposing non-custodial sentences, the procurator fiscal has the option of imposing a fine on an offender. As a result of the Criminal Proceedings etc (Scotland) Act 2007, the maximum amount that the fiscal can impose on an offender is now £500 (previously the maximum fine was £100).

 Key point: Imprisonment and fines are not the only punishments available to a Scottish criminal judge. There are a variety of alternative punishments: probation orders, community service, caution, reparation and restriction of liberty orders.

The Lord Advocate's Reference to the High Court

Under the Criminal Procedure (Scotland) Act 1995, the Lord Advocate, the most senior Scottish Law Officer, may ask the High Court to comment upon a legal point which has arisen as a result of a particular case. This procedure permits the High Court to give an opinion which will hopefully clarify the law and provide guidance to judges in future cases where the same point of law is at issue. A reference from the Lord Advocate to the High Court will not affect the outcome of the particular case for which the opinion is sought.

 A particularly interesting example of a reference from the Lord Advocate to the High Court occurred in **Lord Advocate's Reference Number 1 of 2000**. In this case, three peace protesters were accused of illegal entry to a ship which was anchored on Loch Goil in June 1999. The ship had a role in relation to submarines carrying Trident missiles. The protesters faced criminal damage and theft charges in relation to equipment which was on the ship. In their defence, the protesters claimed that their actions were justified because they were attempting to draw attention to the British Government's continued possession of nuclear weapons – a situation which the protesters argued was a crime under international law. At the trial at Greenock Sheriff Court, the Sheriff, Margaret Gimblet, directed the jury to return a not guilty verdict in relation to several of the charges. As for the remainder of the charges, the jury found the protesters not guilty. The Sheriff Gimblet was extensively criticised for the way in she had directed the jury to return not guilty verdicts. It was felt that this judgement would give the green light to other peace protesters to carry out similar acts as part of their ongoing anti-nuclear weapons campaign. The Lord Advocate, therefore, felt it necessary to refer the case to the High Court for clarification where it was held that the protesters were not justified in their actions.

 Key point: the Lord Advocate may ask the High Court to comment upon a legal point which has arisen as a result of a particular case, thus, permitting the High Court to give an opinion which will hopefully clarify the law and provide guidance to judges in future cases where the same point of law is at issue.

The Scottish Criminal Cases Review Commission

This is a statutory body established by section 194A of the Criminal Procedure (Scotland) Act 1995. The Commission (www.sccrc.org.uk) consists of seven members and one of these acts as Chairman. The role of the Commission is to investigate cases where a miscarriage of justice may have taken place. If the Commission is of the opinion that a conviction in a criminal case may be unsafe, it can take steps to refer the matter to the High Court of Justiciary. Furthermore, the Commission can also investigate sentences which were handed down by the courts. Any person can make an application to the Commission in order to request that it investigate a particular case. The Commission has been given robust powers of investigation and it can force individuals and organisations to hand over documents and provide testimony.

There is no point contacting the Commission until an appeal has been heard by the High Court. The Appeals system, of course, exists to correct earlier mistakes and it would be completely inappropriate for the Commission to pre-judge the High Court's final decision in the matter. The Commission does not provide legal services to an applicant. The Commission merely investigates the circumstances of a conviction or a sentence and then makes a recommendation to the High Court. Applicants are advised to secure the services of a lawyer if it is likely that the case will be revisited by the High Court.

In September 2003, one of the most high profile referrals to be referred to the Commission so far was the conviction of Abdelbaset Ali Mohmed Al Megrahi. Megrahi was convicted of the murder of 270 people as a result of the Lockerbie Bombing in January 2001. He unsuccessfully appealed against his conviction later in 2001. Megrahi's solicitors made the application to the Commission in order for it to review their client's conviction.

The Commission is answerable to Scottish Ministers and the Scottish Parliament. It is a non-departmental body which is sponsored by the Scottish Government's Justice Department. The Commission has its headquarters in Glasgow.

 Key point: The role of the Scottish Criminal Cases Review Commission is to investigate cases where a miscarriage of justice may have taken place.

Criminal Court Procedure

As we are already aware, criminal trials in Scotland are conducted under two types of procedure:

◆ Summary
◆ Solemn

Less serious crimes are dealt with under summary procedure where a judge sits alone i.e. the presiding judge is therefore 'master of the facts' and will determine the appropriate sentence to be handed down if the accused is found guilty. On the other hand, more serious crimes are conducted under solemn procedure where usually one judge sits with a jury of fifteen. In this type of trial, the jury is said to be 'master of the facts' and the judge's role is merely to impose the penalty if the guilt of the accused is established beyond reasonable doubt.

We shall look at the workings of both types of criminal procedure in turn.

Summary procedure – preliminary plea

As the name suggests, summary procedure is supposed to deal with minor crimes relatively quickly and efficiently and is used in the Justice of the Peace Court and the Sheriff Court. A judge presides and no jury is present.

The accused person is prosecuted on complaint. A complaint is the document which outlines the specific nature of the criminal offence which the accused will have to answer at the trial.

 Key point: Summary procedure is supposed to deal with minor crimes relatively quickly and efficiently and is used in the Justice of the Peace Courts and the Sheriff Court.

The First Calling

The first time that the prosecution and the defence lawyers appear in court will be at the First Calling. This is not a trial as members of the public would understand matters and largely deals with technical and operational matters surrounding the proposed trial of the accused.

It is not usually necessary for the judge to be present in court at the First Calling. The Criminal Proceedings etc (Reform)(Scotland) Act 2007 permits the clerk of the court to deal with a number of administrative issues without the judge having to be present. Normally, the defence and the prosecution would be in attendance at the First Calling, but it is also possible for the clerk to deal with matters in their absence. The clerk may already be in possession of all the necessary information in writing. The clerk can deal with matters competently if they have already received a written or verbal plea of not guilty from the accused or if there is going to be a continuation of the plea to date in the future. Theoretically, this should permit matters to be dealt with speedily and efficiently and also to ease the financial burden on the tax-payer.

At this stage of proceedings, it is very common indeed for the defence lawyer to raise an objection to some aspect of the prosecution case against the accused e.g. the validity of the prosecution case may be challenged on the grounds that the alleged offence does not, in fact, represent a breach of the criminal law. In such circumstances, the defence lawyer will be strongly arguing that the accused has not committed any crime and, therefore, in such a situation it is clearly incompetent and unjust to proceed to a criminal trial.

If the defence lawyer were to raise such an objection to the continuation of the criminal process in such circumstances, it would be normal practice for the judge to arrange a separate diet or sitting of the court in order to deal with this kind of objection. At this diet, the judge will hear legal arguments or submissions from the prosecution and the defence in order to determine whether a trial is actually necessary. If the defence lawyer was able to persuade the judge that the charges against the accused were incompetent, the prosecution would be forced to abandon its case. On the other hand, the prosecution may well prove to the judge that there is a case to answer against the accused which means that criminal proceedings can now begin in earnest.

If there is a case to answer, a plea (guilty or not guilty) must be entered by the accused. It is a possibility that the defence lawyer may consider an appeal to the High Court of Justiciary in Edinburgh challenging the judge's decision.

At the First Calling, it is highly possible (and very probable) that no plea will be entered on behalf of the accused. There could be several reasons for this failure to enter a plea. In a large number of cases, the accused has simply failed to submit a response to the complaint meaning that the trial may not proceed. In this situation, the accused will be issued with a formal warning advising them to submit a response to the complaint.

The prosecution could proceed with the case if so minded. A defence lawyer may also appear before the court on behalf of the accused where no plea has been entered – it could be that the accused has not yet firmly communicated the plea which they wish to enter. Summary procedure can deal with such eventualities fairly comfortably as the judge can arrange a further diet or sitting in order to accommodate these types of situation.

In order for courts to operate more efficiently in Scotland, a criminal justice model was introduced as a result of the Criminal Proceedings etc. (Reform) (Scotland) Act 2007. This legislation allows a continuation of a hearing to proceed where no plea has been entered by the accused. It is hoped that, in many cases, this will promote early resolution of the matter and will increase efficiency.

In theory, this system of case management means that the prosecution and the defence can iron out any problems well in advance of a trial by identifying evidence which is agreed upon by the parties and by pinpointing any potential areas of dispute. Hopefully, a much clearer understanding of the evidential and legal issues surrounding the case can be established well before the case proceeds to trial. Previously, many criminal cases were bedevilled by a lack of preparation on the part of both the prosecution and the defence which led to delays, inconvenience and cost to the tax-payer.

 Key point: The first time that the prosecution and the defence lawyers appear in court will be at the First Calling and largely deals with technical and operational matters surrounding the proposed trial of the accused.

What if the accused decides to enter a guilty plea?

The judge should be present at the First Calling in order to impose the relevant punishment.

An accused can enter a plea of guilty at any stage of criminal proceedings in Scotland. It should be noted that in terms of Section 196 of the Criminal Procedure (Scotland) Act 1995, an accused who pleads guilty to a charge may be entitled to have any sentence imposed on him by a judge discounted or reduced. The sentencing judge should direct the clerk of the court to minute the discount or reduction as a permanent entry in the court records. The minute should merely state that the sentence imposed on the accused was discounted in terms of Section 196 of the Criminal Procedure (Scotland) Act 1995 and the sentence would otherwise have been X (i.e. the undiscounted sentence).

There is no need for the sentencing judge to provide reasons for the amount of the discount, but they will have to justify the discount should the case proceed to an appeal before the Justiciary Roll Court.

What if the accused decides to enter a not guilty plea?

The case will obviously have to proceed to a full trial under summary procedure. There are two important stages of the procedure which must be considered and these are:

◆ the intermediate diet

◆ the trial diet

 Key point: Summary procedure consists of two stages: the intermediate diet and the trial diet.

What is the intermediate diet?

This sitting of the court will normally take place two weeks prior to the trial diet. The purpose of the intermediate diet is to check that both defence and prosecution are ready to proceed to trial.

The parties are obliged to state at the intermediate diet that their witnesses and evidence are in a state of readiness for the trial. It will be necessary, for example, to find out how many witnesses are going to appear at the trial. Both parties will be asked at this stage whether they are ready to proceed to trial as originally planned. If they both answer positively, then the trial diet will take place within the next fourteen days. If, however, one or both of the parties cannot give a firm undertaking that they are ready for the trial, a further intermediate diet will have to be set down meaning that the trial diet will be postponed. A new trial diet will therefore be arranged and, fourteen days prior to this, a second intermediate diet will take place. At the second intermediate diet, the parties will again be quizzed about the stage of their preparations and, hopefully, they will both be ready to proceed to trial.

Proposed sittings of the court and will then be scheduled to take place some three or four months after the First Calling. The clerk of the court will notify these dates to the prosecution and defence by calling them out in court and both lawyers will take note of these.

Currently, there are proposals on the table to have the intermediate diet take place four weeks before the trial diet. Such proposals are strongly supported by the prosecution service which argues that it would force the parties to ensure that their preparations were well in hand before any trial can take place.

The Criminal Proceedings etc (Reform)(Scotland) Act 2007 places a clear duty on judges to ensure that the parties are properly prepared. As part and parcel of any efficient case management system, judges should be asking if the parties are prepared for trial and what steps they are taking to make sure that they reach the necessary state of preparation.

 Key point: The purpose of the intermediate diet is to check that both defence and prosecution are ready to proceed to trial.

The trial diet

What if the accused intends to enter a plea of guilty at the trial?

His or her name will be called out at the beginning of the trial, their identity will be confirmed and they will be asked to respond to the charge. The defence solicitor will also identify themselves and will verify to the court that they represent the accused. The guilty plea will then be communicated to the court.

Procedure at a summary trial is very much dependent upon whether the accused decides to plead guilty or not guilty. If the accused has entered into a plea bargain with the Crown by pleading guilty to a lesser charge than the one originally framed by the prosecution, the fiscal should alert the judge to this development. Generally, the prosecution and defence lawyers will have entered into prior discussions with one another before the trial commences about the possibility of a plea bargain. It may be the case, for example, that the accused will admit to causing a breach of the peace in return for the more serious charge of assault being dropped by the prosecution. Obviously, the defence lawyer should fully advise his client about the implications of entering into such an arrangement with the prosecution. Most of the time, a plea bargain will result in the accused having a less severe punishment imposed by the judge.

In spite of this arrangement between the lawyers, the judge still has a duty to question the accused in order to ensure that they are happy with this outcome and that they fully understand the nature of the charge to which they are now pleading guilty.

The procurator fiscal will then inform the judge whether the accused has any relevant, previous convictions – a fact which will be crucial to the type of punishment which the judge ultimately decides to impose. Usually, the procurator fiscal will have a list of these convictions prepared in advance to hand to the judge when sentencing is about to take place. It may be the case, however, that the accused does not have any previous convictions i.e. it may be the first time that they have ever appeared in a criminal court or, if they have been the accused in a previous trial, they escaped conviction.

The procurator fiscal will then go on to give a brief description of the nature and circumstances of the crime. This account of the offence will have been agreed in advance with the defence lawyer. The defence lawyer, in turn, will respond to the narrative just delivered by the fiscal and will then proffer a plea in mitigation i.e. some sort of excuse for the behaviour of the accused which will, hopefully, reduce the punishment which the judge will subsequently impose. A plea in mitigation will almost certainly highlight the personal circumstances of the accused or other relevant factors in order to lessen or reduce the seriousness of the offence. The defence lawyer could also put forward a suggestion as to the type of punishment which the court might impose in this particular situation, but it should be remembered that it is basically the judge's decision alone to decide the type of punishment. If the defence suggests that a fine might be the most appropriate punishment in this case, it should be made very clear how much the accused can afford to pay each week.

It should, of course, be appreciated that, as the accused has decided to plead guilty, there is no need for witnesses and other evidence to be brought in.

 Key point: The Trial diet is where the Crown's evidence against the accused will be fully tested in court.

After hearing the lawyers' submissions, the judge will then impose the sentence, but it should be remembered that, in many cases, sentencing may actually be postponed in order for the court to obtain more information about the accused. The judge may be keen to obtain a social enquiry report from the relevant social work authorities before deciding on a sentence. In a case where the judge is strongly of the opinion that a custodial sentence should be handed down, it is very likely that a social enquiry report would be sought before doing this. Almost certainly, this would happen if the accused was being sent to prison for the first time or if the accused was under the age of 21.

In these types of circumstances, the judge would have no hesitation in postponing the case for a further three or four weeks while awaiting the preparation of the social enquiry report. The case will then call again in court and, following the social enquiry report, the judge should be in a position to impose the sentence.

During the period in which the trial has been postponed, the accused may be remanded in custody for very good reasons (e.g. there is a very high risk of flight), but there is a duty to ensure that the case calls again in court within three weeks of the postponement.

 Key point: Procedure at a summary trial is very much dependent upon whether the accused decides to plead guilty or not guilty.

What if the accused enters a plea of not guilty?

When the accused decides to enter a plea of not guilty, it will be necessary to hold a trial where the prosecution's evidence can be heard and tested.

Before the trial, it is very important for the procurator fiscal to ensure that all the witnesses appearing for the Crown are present. It should be appreciated that if a witness fails to turn up for either the Crown or the defence then this may cause the trial to be delayed or even postponed to a later date.

There may be a variety of reasons for the failure of the witness to turn up at court on the day of the trial. When faced with this news, the judge will doubtless wish to make enquiries to establish that that the witness was properly cited to appear. The failure to put in an appearance by the witness could be a genuine mistake e.g. the people responsible for issuing the citation may have got the address of the witness wrong. If, on the other hand, the witness has made a decision not to attend proceedings, the judge could issue an arrest warrant meaning that the individual in question could be forcibly brought before the court. It is more usual to issue a warning to a witness about a failure to attend court before resorting to the fairly drastic step of issuing an arrest warrant.

If the failure of the witness to attend court can be explained by sloppy paperwork (on either the part of the defence or prosecution), the judge may refuse to grant an adjournment or postponement of the trial and matters will proceed as normal without that witness being available to give testimony. In extreme situations, the absence of a witness could have devastating consequences for the prosecution and may lead to desertion of the charges or abandonment of the case. Desertion of the charges means that the procurator fiscal applies for the diet or the sitting of the court to be abandoned (possibly for the time being). This is normally achieved by way of a motion being submitted to the court (known as *pro loco et tempore*) which allows the prosecution to issue a new complaint against the accused dealing with the specific criminal offence. This allows the prosecution to keep its options open because there is always the possibility that a case may be brought against the accused sometime in the near future. *Pro loco et tempore* is a Latin phrase meaning "for the time being" and relates to the fact that criminal proceedings are postponed against the accused temporarily.

The judge may agree to such a motion or, alternatively, a decision could be made to abandon proceedings altogether (*desert simpliciter*) which means that no further action will be taken against the accused. In such situations, the defence lawyer will argue that the case should be abandoned (or deserted) since the accused has already been subjected to a considerable degree of inconvenience and that the prosecution has had plenty of time to put together a credible case. In applying for a postponement, the defence will almost certainly argue that the prosecution is wasting time and this tactic ought not to be tolerated by the court.

In any event, it is within the power of the prosecution to abandon proceedings against the accused at any point. This will often occur when it becomes apparent that the evidence aginst the accused is very flimsy and it will be very difficult for the prosecution to obtain a conviction. If proceedings are abandoned in such circumstances, the prosecution will not be able to initiate a fresh complaint against the accused in the future.

 Key point: When the accused decides to enter a plea of not guilty, it will be necessary to hold a trial where the prosecution's evidence can be heard and tested.

The Trial Diet

If the accused has decided to enter a plea of not guilty, it will be necessary to hold a trial. As the prosecution has decided to pursue charges against the accused, the fiscal will open proceedings. The fiscal has to prove the charges against the accused.

The first witness will be brought into the court and the judge will administer the oath. This is normal oath which most people are familiar with i.e. "I promise to tell the truth, the whole truth and nothing but the truth…". The witness can swear by Almighty God if they so wish and can swear on the Bible or some other holy book or scriptures. Alternatively, if the witness is not particularly religious, they may wish to affirm that they will tell the whole truth and nothing but the truth.

The case for the prosecution

It is then the task of the fiscal to question the witness about the evidence which they are offering to the court. It is very important to understand that the fiscal cannot lead the witness through the evidence because the defence lawyer would lodge all sorts of objections to this. The witness is being subjected to an examination by the fiscal and this process is often referred to as the examination-in-chief. At the end of the testimony, the witness will simply be asked if they can identify the accused and this is done by the witness pointing to the accused who will be sitting in the dock.

At the end of the examination of the witness, the defence will have the right of cross-examination which allows the account just given to the court to be challenged. An effective defence lawyer will wish to undermine the witness testimony (and the prosecution's case) by highlighting all sorts of irregularities or inconsistencies. In this way, the defence will be attempting to establish that there is reasonable doubt as to whether the accused committed the offence for which they are now being tried. The job of any good defence lawyer is to discredit the validity of any statement by a prosecution witness in order to secure an acquittal of the accused.

After the cross-examination by the defence, the fiscal can re-examine the witness in an attempt (possibly a futile attempt some might say) to clear up any misunderstandings or problems arising from the testimony.

 Key point: In a summary trial, the Prosecution proceeds with its case first by calling its witnesses and producing its evidence. The defence can then produce its own witnesses and evidence. Both sides have the right to cross-examine each other's witnesses.

It should be noted, that the prosecution and the defence do not have to alert one another to the nature of the testimony to be given by their respective witnesses at the trial, but they do so in any case as a matter of professional courtesy. From a tactical viewpoint, this may be a shrewd move because it could force the other side to recognise that their case is weak.

In many trials, the testimony of a witness may not be an issue at all and the parties can agree before the trial that such evidence is not in dispute and will not be challenged. If the parties can agree on the evidence, a document referred to as a Minute of Admissions can be drawn up to reflect this fact. It may well be the case, that there is absolutely no dispute between the parties that the victim of a crime sustained injuries and had to receive treatment at a local hospital. The potential testimony of the doctor and other medical personnel who treated the victim is not in any doubt whatsoever, but what will be hotly disputed is whether the accused is responsible for those injuries.

Productions should be submitted to the court by the prosecution to aid its case against the accused. Productions would include photographic evidence, film footage from CCTV cameras or mobile phones, weapons retrieved, finger-print and DNA evidence and incriminating documents. There is no obligation for the prosecution to lodge such evidence with the court before the trial, but it probably a good idea to do this. Failure by the prosecution to lodge productions before the trial will simply mean that the defence will request an adjournment of proceedings in order to formulate a response.

Once the witnesses and productions for the prosecution have been deployed, the Crown will close its case.

The case for the defence

The defence will then take centre stage in order to make the appropriate response to the prosecution case. It is important to realise that the accused is under no obligation whatsoever to give evidence in his or her defence. For very sound tactical reasons, the defence may be of the opinion that this is not necessary e.g. it has now become apparent that the prosecution case is so weak that any competent defence lawyer will be able to undermine it and plant reasonable doubt in the mind of the judge so that the outcome of the trial is the acquittal of the accused. It is of critical importance that we remember that the burden of proof is placed on the prosecution which means that the fiscal has to prove that there is a case to answer against the accused. It is essential that the fiscal can corroborate or back-up the evidence which s/he is bringing against the accused. Failure to do this will almost certainly mean that the case for the prosecution will collapse.

121

In situations, where the prosecution against the accused is flimsy to say the least (more cruel critics may use the word ramshackle), the defence can submit a motion that there is no case to answer. It may not even be necessary for the defence to introduce evidence in support of the accused given the poor state of the evidence for the prosecution. The judge may very well agree and dismiss the charges, thus acquitting the accused in the process.

If, however, the defence does decide to introduce evidence to the court, the clear purpose is to weaken the case for the prosecution and, hopefully, discredit the charges against the accused.

If the accused is to give evidence, they should appear on the stand and be sworn in before any other witnesses for the defence appear. The accused will be examined by the defence solicitor (the examination-in-chief). The prosecution will then be permitted to cross-examine the accused in the hope that something might emerge that will lead the judge to conclude that accused is indeed guilty of the offence. The defence solicitor can then re-examine the accused to clarify any points which may have arisen as a result of the prosecution's questions.

The same procedure will be repeated for any witnesses that the defence wishes to appear on behalf of the accused.

The defence does not have to give advance warning to the prosecution about the witnesses it intends to call or the productions upon which it intends to rely. In practice, however, the defence will probably do this as a matter of professional courtesy because the prosecution will request an adjournment to consider such evidence and possibly challenge it.

As can be appreciated, both parties do set out quite deliberately to undermine the credibility of the other's evidence, but the stakes are probably higher for the prosecution which must establish beyond reasonable doubt that the accused actually committed the crime.

At the conclusion of the trial, the fiscal will go first and address the court asking the judge to convict the accused. The defence has a right of reply and will ask the judge to favour its evidence by acquitting the accused. The judge must be satisfied that the accused is guilty beyond reasonable doubt and, in such situations, the judge must acquit.

If the accused is acquitted of the charges, they are said to have 'tholed their assize' and the prosecution cannot attempt to have a retrial unless the fiscal is able to mount a successful conviction.

In Scotland, as we have seen, there are two acquittal verdicts: not guilty and not proven. This is unusual as most western criminal legal systems only have the not guilty verdict. The not proven verdict is a statement by the judge (or the jury in solemn cases) that there is some doubt as to the complete innocence of the accused, but that the prosecution had been unable to demonstrate beyond a reasonable doubt that the person on trial committed the offence(s). If the prosecution evidence does not show that a person is guilty beyond a reasonable doubt a judge sitting in a summary trial must acquit.

The not proven verdict allows a judge to comment, perhaps unfavourably, on the behaviour of the accused without actually imposing a punishment. Although a not proven verdict results in the accused being acquitted, it carries a stigma and it is often remarked by members of the public that the accused did commit the offence, but that the prosecution was incompetent or unlucky in the way that it handled its case.

Summary appeals

All appeals from summary criminal trials in Scotland must be heard by the Justiciary Roll Court (which is part of the High Court of Justiciary) in Edinburgh.

 Key point: All appeals from summary criminal trials in Scotland must be heard by the Justiciary Roll Court (which is part of the High Court of Justiciary) in Edinburgh.

Generally, three judges will sit to hear an appeal against conviction and only two judges are required to hear an appeal against sentence.

In order to appeal either against conviction or sentence, the offender must make an application for a draft stated case within one week of having been convicted by the court. A draft stated case will be prepared by the trial judge and will set out the reasons why the offender was convicted of a crime or why it was necessary to impose the particular sentence which was handed down. If the convicted person is facing a prison sentence, they can apply for bail which allows them to remain at liberty pending the outcome of the appeal.

Section 175 of the Criminal Procedure (Scotland) Act 1995 permits an appeal against the conviction of the offender. Such an appeal will often be founded either on the premise that there has been a miscarriage of justice or there is legal technicality which may call into question the conviction of the offender. Normally three judges sit to hear an appeal against a person's conviction.

Section 175 of the 1995 Act also allows an offender to appeal against the sentence imposed by the court. A sentence may be deemed to be unduly excessive for the type of crime committed or a legal error may have been made by the judge and it is, therefore, necessary for the accused to lodge an appeal. In appeals by the convicted person against sentence, it is customary practice for two judges to sit.

An alternative route of appeal to Section 175 for an offender is to introduce a Bill of Suspension to the High Court. Such an appeal is based on the notion that the treatment of the offender at the trial has breached the rules of natural justice e.g. there was a serious procedural irregularity that was allowed to go unchecked at the trial. There is no time limit for the submission of this type of appeal.

The High Court may also exercise its appellate jurisdiction in terms of the legal principle known as *Nobile Officium* which gives it the power to intervene in criminal cases in circumstances which are regarded as absolutely exceptional and the offender has no other route for challenging the sentence of the trial court. This power may be exercised by the High Court where there is evidence of clear injustice or oppression.

The convicted person making the appeal must convince the appeal judges of the High Court that the case has merit, otherwise leave or permission to appeal will be refused.

Appeals by the prosecution in summary cases

It may be the case that the Crown considers the punishment imposed by the judge on the convicted person to be unduly lenient. In these circumstances, an appeal can be submitted by the Crown. This may mean that the High Court can impose a harsher sentence on a person who was convicted of a crime at the original trial.

Key point: In situations where the Crown considers the punishment imposed by the judge on the convicted person to be unduly lenient, an appeal can be submitted to the High Court and this may lead to the imposition of a harsher sentence.

The prosecution can also appeal on a point of law to the High Court in situations where the trial court acquitted the accused. If the appeal is successful it has absolutely no bearing on the fate of the accused who will remain completely at liberty and cannot face a retrial. The purpose of this type of appeal is to set a benchmark for the future so that the law is effectively clarified for trial judges.

The prosecution has four weeks running from the decision of the trial court in which to submit an appeal. The right of the prosecution to bring an appeal is not subject to the scrutiny of a judge in the way that appeals by a convicted person would be handled i.e. does the appeal have any merits?

Decisions of appeal hearings

There are several possible outcomes in an appeal hearing which are:

◆ The High Court could allow the appeal in its entirety thus overturning the original verdict of the trial court. This may mean that the convicted person is now acquitted of all crimes or it may mean that a retrial will have to take place.
◆ The High Court could allow part of the appeal which means that some aspects of the original decision of the trial court will need to be altered e.g. if the convicted person appealed against their sentence, then a lower sentence will be imposed or if the prosecution appealed against sentence, then a higher sentence will be imposed.
◆ The High Court could reject the appeal e.g. the conviction will still stand or the attempt by the convicted person to have the sentence reduced has failed and perhaps an even longer sentence will be imposed than the one originally handed down by the trial court.

Can decisions of the High Court in summary appeals be challenged?

In theory, there is a right of further appeal and, it is possible to lodge an appeal challenging the decision of the High Court with the UK Supreme Court in London. Presently, however, such appeals, are only competent if they involve human rights and devolution issues as envisaged by the Scotland Act 1998. The UK Supreme Court's jurisdiction in this area stems from the Constitutional Reform Act 2005.

Solemn trials

If the offence is much more serious in nature e.g. assault with a weapon or murder, the accused will be tried under solemn procedure. Solemn procedure involves a trial where there is a presiding judge and a jury of fifteen. This type of trial can take place in either the Sheriff Court or the High Court of Justiciary. If convicted of an offence under solemn procedure, the accused will probably face a much tougher sentence.

The role of the judge in these types of trial is very different from the role played in a summary trial. The jury looks at the factual evidence which will determine the innocence or the guilt of the accused. In this way, the jury is often referred to as "master of the facts" and it is the task of the judge to impose the punishment should the accused be found guilty.

 Key point: Solemn criminal procedure deals with much more serious offences and such trials take place in the Sheriff Court and the High Court of Justiciary.

Appearance on petition: the first hearing

A solemn trial commences with the accused appearing on petition before a Sheriff. There are a number of things to note about this hearing:

1 The initial court appearance takes place before a Sheriff even if the offence e.g. murder is not one which can be tried in the Sheriff Court.

2 The petition is the document which sets out the charges against the accused.

3 The accused appears in private before the Sheriff accompanied by a defence lawyer (the fiscal will also be present and other court officials), but members of the public will not be granted access to this hearing. The hearing often takes place in the Sheriff's private chambers or in a locked court room.

4 It is normal practice for the accused not to enter a plea to the charges at this stage and the defence lawyer will state that the accused intends to make no plea or declaration at this point in proceedings.

5 The Sheriff must be satisfied at this point that the prosecution has evidence against the accused. It is normal practice for the prosecution to present at least two pieces of evidence to the Sheriff to demonstrate that there may be a case to answer against the accused. Theoretically, the prosecution could present just one piece of evidence against the accused.

6 If the Sheriff is satisfied that the charge(s) against the accused constitute a crime or crimes known to law, they will sign the petition.

7 The Sheriff will then deal with such matters as applications for legal aid and bail by the accused.

8 The legal aid application is usually straightforward, but the application for bail may be refused.

9 In the vast majority of cases, the procurator fiscal will ask the Sheriff to commit the accused for further examination. The reason for this is to give the prosecution an opportunity to investigate the alleged offences in order to make a final decision on whether to proceed against the accused.

10 If the accused has been remanded in custody, they must be released within eight days if a decision is made not to commit him or her for trial. The decision to commit an accused for trial may be made at the first court appearance if it is deemed that there is enough evidence for the prosecution to proceed, but usually there will be a second, subsequent hearing where such a decision will be taken.

 Key point: A solemn trial commences with the accused appearing on petition before a Sheriff.

Appearance on petition: the second hearing

At this second hearing, the prosecution must inform the Sheriff whether it now has enough evidence to prosecute the accused. If there is a lack of clear evidence, the accused must be released, but if there is sufficient evidence the prosecution will ask the judge to fully commit the accused to trial.

If the accused is fully committed for trial, certain time limits begin to run which the prosecution must strictly adhere to, as failure to do so may mean that proceedings against the accused will have to be abandoned.

 Key point: If the accused appears on petition for a second time, the Crown must convince the Sheriff that there is enough evidence to prosecute the accused.

What are these time limits?

Basically, they depend very much on whether the accused has been granted bail or not pending the start of the trial.

If the accused has been fortunate enough to obtain bail, they must be tried under solemn procedure within one year of being committed for trial.

If, however, the accused has been refused bail, they must be brought to trial in the Sheriff Court within **110 days** of being fully committed. In a High Court case e.g. a murder trial, the prosecution has **140 days** from the date of committal to bring the accused to trial.

If the prosecution finds that it is unable to comply with the time limits, an application can always be made to a judge to have them extended as long as there is good reason to do so.

Furthermore, the accused must also have the indictment served on him/her within **80 days** of being fully committed for trial if they have been refused bail.

An indictment must be served on the accused in a High Court trial 29 clear days before the preliminary hearing.

In a Sheriff Court trial, the indictment must be served on the accused at least 15 clear days before the first diet.

 Key point: If the accused has been refused bail, they must be brought to trial in the Sheriff Court within 110 days of being fully committed. In a High Court case, the prosecution has 140 days from the date of committal to bring the accused to trial.

The indictment

The indictment can be served on either the accused or the defence lawyer. As previously explained, it is the document which sets out the charge(s) or the principal accusation(s) of criminal behaviour allegedly committed by the accused.

 Key point: The indictment can be served on either the accused or the defence lawyer.

Section 69(1) of the Criminal Procedure (Scotland) Act 1995 makes it very clear that the prosecution is not permitted to attach any notice of the accused's previous convictions (if they exist) to the indictment or to any of the productions which will in due course be submitted to the court.

The indictment will be accompanied by a list of witnesses for the prosecution and, on a separate sheet, a list of relevant, previous convictions.

The relevant court of trial, will receive a copy of the indictment (which includes details of witnesses, previous convictions and the transcript of any judicial examination) either before the document is served on the accused or on the actual day of service.

In relation to a Sheriff Court trial, Section 68 of the Criminal Procedure (Scotland) Act 1995 gives the accused or the defence lawyer the right to inspect any productions lodged by the prosecution. Such an inspection will take place at the Sheriff Clerk's office where the productions have been lodged.

The prosecution may wish to bring in new evidence at a later stage of proceedings but, in terms of Section 67 of the 1995 Act, the court must be informed in writing of this intention at least two days before the jury is sworn in. There is no guarantee that such evidence will actually be sanctioned by the court.

The prosecution can call any of the witnesses or use any of the productions which are listed with the indictment. This is clearly a decision for the prosecutor to make as the trial progresses.

In High Court cases if the accused wishes to challenge the indictment, the competency of proceedings or the admissibility of evidence, seven days' clear notice must be given to the court and also to the prosecution before the preliminary hearing has taken place.

When the prosecution gives the accused details of the witnesses that it intends to call at the trial, this gives the defence the opportunity to precognosce these individuals i.e. obtain statements from them.

If the defence intends to call witnesses in order to appear at the trial and give evidence on behalf of the accused, such individuals must receive an official citation in order to compel their appearance. The full names and addresses of any witnesses together with details of any productions upon which the defence intends to rely at the trial should be communicated in writing to the prosecution shortly before the First Diet.

In a High Court trial, such details must be provided to the Crown Agent at least seven clear days before the preliminary hearing. Failure to comply with such time limits may mean that certain witnesses or production items cannot be used at the trial unless the court agrees to admit this as evidence (Section 68 of the 1995 Act).

Conducting a judicial examination of the accused

The rules governing judicial examinations can be found in Sections 35–39 of the Criminal Procedure (Scotland) Act 1995.

When an accused has been fully committed for trial, an opportunity exists for the prosecution to put questions to him/her. The prosecution will often wish to use this facility in situations where the accused has appeared on petition privately before a Sheriff.

 Key point: When an accused has been fully committed for trial under solemn procedure, an opportunity exists for the prosecution to put questions to them by way of a judicial examination.

This stage of solemn procedure is by no means compulsory, but it is very commonly used by the prosecution. Such a procedure, in theory, affords the accused person an opportunity to sketch the outlines of the case for his/her defence.

In the presence of the accused, the fiscal will read out the charge(s) contained in the indictment and the accused will have a right to respond. It should be emphasised that the fiscal does not have the right to cross-examine the accused as this not a trial. The accused is free to respond to the charge(s) if they so wish and they will have a defence lawyer present to advise them in this regard. The defence lawyer will clearly be anxious that the case for the accused is not prejudiced at an early stage of proceedings, but there is really nothing that can be done to prevent the accused from volunteering information if they are so minded.

It is extremely common for an accused to be advised by their solicitor to say nothing in response to questions from the fiscal. The danger for the accused is that the prosecution may try to put a negative inference on the fact that the accused refused to answer certain questions i.e. the inference being that the accused has something to hide. After all, surely some who is completely innocent has nothing to hide and will only be too happy to cooperate in order to have the matter cleared up as quickly as possible? What is the accused hiding?

At the end of the examination, the defence lawyer can, with the Sheriff's permission, ask the accused to clarify various issues which arose from the questions put by the prosecution in order to clear up any possible misunderstandings or confusion. The defence lawyer can also highlight the fact that the accused failed to answer certain questions and that it may be advisable to provide the information sought by the fiscal.

The questions put to the accused by the prosecution are tape recorded and, critically, the answers or statements obtained during this process are admissible as evidence by either party at the subsequent trial.

First diets

This is a compulsory stage of solemn proceedings in the Sheriff Court and the accused is legally obliged to attend. Such diets usually take place, at the earliest, fifteen clear days after the service of the indictment and not less than ten clear days before the trial itself.

A first diet is a device used by the judge to determine whether the parties are prepared to proceed to trial and to establish the evidence which has been agreed upon by the parties.

When the first diet has been concluded, the accused is expected to enter a plea of not guilty or guilty.

Under Section 77 of the 1995 Act, if the accused enters a guilty plea, they will have to sign a copy of the plea (which is also signed by the Sheriff).

 Key point: A first diet is a device used by the judge to determine whether the parties are prepared to proceed to trial and to establish the evidence which has been agreed upon by the parties.

Preliminary hearings

Since April 2005, an important procedural reform has been introduced to the High Court. Parties in a criminal case (the Crown and the accused) will now have to submit themselves to a preliminary hearing in order for a High Court judge to determine their readiness (or not as the case may be) for trial. Once it has been determined that both sides are ready to proceed, a trial diet (hearing) will be set. This important reform should prevent delays which often plagued trials under the previous system and it should minimise the disruption and inconvenience often experienced by witnesses.

This type of hearing is compulsory i.e. the accused will have to attend. Such a hearing will normally take place within 110 days of the accused being fully committed for trial in situations where bail was refused. If the accused has been at liberty (i.e. on bail), such a hearing will normally take place within eleven months of full committal.

 Key point: Parties in a criminal case before the High Court (the Crown and the accused) will now have to submit themselves to a preliminary hearing in order for a judge to determine their readiness (or not as the case may be) for trial.

The purpose of this hearing is for the judge to deal with a number of matters, it will:

♦ verify that the accused has a solicitor present
♦ handle any preliminary pleas that have been submitted e.g. the admissibility of certain prosecution evidence (seven days notice to the court must be given by the defence)
♦ establish the witnesses for the prosecution
♦ determine how well prepared or otherwise the parties are for trial and identify the evidence agreed upon
♦ ensure that the accused enters a plea i.e. not guilty or guilty.

An accused being tried under solemn procedure who pleads guilty to the indictment may have the sentence discounted or reduced in terms of Section 196 of the Criminal Procedure (Scotland) Act 1995. As with summary procedure, the clerk of the court should make a permanent record of this development and also the sentence that the accused would have received had they been subsequently convicted by the jury despite maintaining a plea of not guilty throughout the trial. Again, the sentencing judge does not have to justify the discount in the court records, but the Scottish Court of Criminal Appeal will doubtless demand an explanation in the event of an appeal. The minute of the trial court records should merely state that the sentence imposed on the accused was discounted in terms of Section 196 of the Criminal Procedure (Scotland) Act 1995 and the sentence would otherwise have been X (i.e. the undiscounted sentence).

Section 76 of the Criminal Procedure (Scotland) Act 1995

This section allows an accused to send a letter to the prosecution stating that they are prepared to consider the possibility of pleading guilty to a lesser charge than the one originally framed in the indictment. It is, therefore, an opportunity for the accused to attempt to plea bargain with the prosecution. It should be noted that such a course of action does not commit the accused to pleading guilty at the trial – the accused may change his/her mind for a variety of reasons.

The purpose of a plea bargain arrangement is, of course, the opportunity for both parties to conclude matters much more swiftly without the need for a jury trial which can be very time consuming and costly.

Commencing a solemn trial

In both the High Court and the Sheriff Court, the clerk will read out the indictment and the accused, who is already present in the dock, will be asked to plead guilty or not guilty.

Should the accused decide to plead guilty, s/he will have to sign a copy of the plea which the judge will also sign. Sentence can now be imposed on the accused by the judge.

What if the accused decides to maintain a plea of not guilty?

The trial will have to begin in earnest and the fifteen members of the jury will have to be picked and sworn in. The court will already be in possession of a list of potential jurors and membership of the jury is carried out by drawing lots i.e. all the names of the potential jurors are placed in a bowl and they are selected at random. The juror's name is read out and the individual in question will have to take a seat in the jury box. The prosecution and defence can both object to the presence of certain individuals on the jury.

After being selected, the jurors will then be sworn in and they should not discuss the case with anyone other than their colleagues on the jury.

Trial under solemn procedure

The prosecution's case

The prosecutor (whether a fiscal or an Advocate Depute) will commence proceedings against the accused by calling the first prosecution witness. The witness will take an oath to tell the whole truth and nothing but the truth.

The examination-in-chief for the prosecution

Procedure is quite similar to a summary trial in that an examination-in-chief of the witnesses for the prosecution will follow. As we are aware, the prosecutor will take (not lead) the witnesses through their evidence. During this process, any productions will be referred to by the prosecutor in order to strengthen the case against the accused.

During the testimony by the witnesses, the prosecution will ask them to identify the accused by pointing to the person sitting in the dock. Clearly, if the witness cannot positively identify the accused, the prosecution case has been seriously undermined to say the least.

The defence will be allowed the opportunity to conduct a cross-examination of the prosecution witnesses in the hope that any or all testimony given to the court can be undermined or called into question.

After this, the prosecution has the right to re-examine any of its witnesses in order to address any issues raised by the defence – although it may be too late to undo serious damage to the credibility and reliability of the witness during the defence's cross-examination.

Key point: In a solemn trial, the Prosecution proceeds with its case first by calling its witnesses and producing its evidence. The defence can then produce its own witnesses and evidence. Both sides have the right to cross-examine each other's witnesses.

The prosecution has then concluded its case and it is now the turn of the defence to commence its case.

The case for the defence

The defence can respond to the prosecution in a number of ways:

1 By making a calculation that the prosecution evidence is so weak that there is no case to answer. If the defence reaches such a conclusion, a submission can be made to the judge requesting that the charges against the accused be dismissed. If so, the jurors must be sent out and both lawyers will present legal arguments to the judge who, alone, will decide the matter as the 'master of the law'. The judge has absolute discretion in legal matters during the trial and it will up to him/her to decide whether the prosecution has actually corroborated the evidence against the accused and, if not, to dismiss the charges.

 In **Angus Robertson Sinclair *v* Her Majesty's Advocate (2007)** Angus Sinclair, the accused, had been charged with the murders of two girls (Christine Eadie and Helen Scott) both aged 17. It was alleged that Sinclair had murdered the girls in 1977 and then dumped the bodies in East Lothian. Both victims had last been seen alive while frequenting the World's End public house in Edinburgh. Sinclair was eventually brought to trial in 2007 with the media inevitably dubbing proceedings "The World's End Trial". In September 2007, the defence lawyers acting for Angus Sinclair, a convicted killer and sex offender, successfully moved to have the charges against the accused dismissed on the grounds that there was no case to answer. Lord Clarke, the trial judge, eventually decided that there was no case to answer and the prosecution case collapsed. In any case, Sinclair is currently serving a life sentence for the murder of Mary Gallagher in 1978.

2 It may be decided that, for a number of reasons, the accused will not give evidence at the trial and, indeed, there is no requirement for the accused to take the oath and give testimony. This does not mean that the defence harbours any doubts about the accused and it may simply be a tactical decision not to call the accused to the stand to give evidence.

3 If, however, the accused decides to give evidence, they will go before the other witnesses for the defence.

The examination-in-chief for the defence

The accused will then be subjected to an examination-in-chief by their lawyer. The prosecution will then be given an opportunity to cross-examine and the defence can then re-examine the witness in relation to any matters raised by the prosecution if necessary. When the prosecutor embarks on a cross-examination of the defence witnesses, they are attempting to undermine the reliability and credibility of these individuals just as the defence lawyer did some time earlier in the trial. Productions may also be used to help the accused convince the jurors that they have committed no crime.

A similar process is conducted with the other witnesses for the defence. After the witnesses for the accused have given testimony, the case for the defence has been concluded.

Submissions to the jury

Both lawyers – the prosecutor going first – address the jury at the end of the trial in an attempt to convince the jurors to favour their respective positions. The prosecution is asking for a conviction of the accused, whereas the defence is asking for an acquittal verdict.

The function of the jury

Once the lawyers have concluded their submissions, the judge will address the jury in order to emphasise that they are the 'masters of the facts' in that they have complete discretion when it comes to the task of deciding the verdict of the court. The judge will tell the jurors that they have a choice of three possible verdicts and they will provide any necessary explanations relating to legal matters e.g. the difference between murder and culpable homicide in Scotland. The jury should be reminded of the need for the prosecution to corroborate the case against the accused and that, if they are entertaining reasonable doubts about the strength of the evidence against the accused, they must acquit.

One problematic area for a judge is if they decide to sum up the evidence presented by both parties during the trial, but this could later open him/her to the accusation that the jury was led towards a particular verdict. After all, it is not for the judge to tell the jury whether they believe that the accused is guilty or not.

The prosecution case against the accused must be proved beyond reasonable doubt in order to convince the jury to hand down a guilty verdict. If the prosecution has been unable to persuade the jury of the case against the accused, then one of the two acquittal verdicts must be decided upon.

Does the jury have to reach a unanimous verdict?

In Scotland, a jury can select one of the three available verdicts by a bare majority (eight jurors) and there is no requirement that the jurors' decision be unanimous.

Trials will have to be stopped if the number of jurors falls below 13 in situations where individuals have been forced to retire from jury service due to illness or where they have died during the trial's duration. It is perfectly possible for a trial to continue with at least 13 jurors, but a majority of eight must favour one of the three possible verdicts.

 Key point: The jury is the master of the facts in a criminal trial and its decision can be by majority verdict.

Once these matters have been dealt with, the jury will be sent out to consider its verdict and this could be achieved fairly quickly or it may be a longer process depending upon the complexity of the trial. When the jury returns with a verdict, the clerk of the court will ask the foreman (the jurors' representative) if they have managed to arrive at a verdict. The foreman will read out the verdict and confirm whether this decision was arrived at by majority or by unanimity.

If the jury has selected one of the acquittal verdicts, the accused is free to leave the court (they have tholed the assize), but if a guilty verdict has been decided upon the offender (as they now are) will have to be sentenced by the judge. The prosecution will then submit a motion to the judge asking for the offender to be sentenced. Normally, at this time, the prosecution shall make the judge fully aware of any previous convictions the offender may have, which should be taken into consideration before sentence is passed.

The Contempt of Court Act 1981

One thing that should be appreciated by anyone who has to undertake jury service is that they are prevented by law from discussing the nature of the deliberations in the jury room at the end of the trial. In other words, what was said in the jury room, stays in there. The verdict which jurors reach is obviously in the public domain, but the reasons why a decision was arrived at are often shrouded in complete secrecy. Section 8 of the Contempt of Court Act 1981 makes it a criminal offence to discuss what went in the jury room during deliberations about the guilt or innocence of the accused. Some academics who are very interested in the role of the jury often find this to be a very frustrating restriction which prevents them from undertaking meaningful research about the dynamics of those who serve as jurors.

Appeals

All appeals from solemn criminal trials in Scotland must be heard by the High Court of Justiciary sitting as the Scottish Court of Criminal Appeal which always sits in Edinburgh. In an appeal against conviction, at least three judges must sit to hear the case and it is not essential for a unanimous decision to be reached (although at the Lockerbie appeal of Abdelbaset Ali Mohmed Al Megrahi in 2002, five appeal judges sat and the hearing took place in the Netherlands for political reasons). In appeals against sentence, it is more normal to have just two judges sitting on the bench.

A person who has been convicted under solemn procedure has 14 days to appeal against the sentence running from the day on which the court made its decision.

If, however, the convicted person wishes to appeal against both sentence and conviction, they must give the High Court written notice of this intention within 14 days of the trial court's decision. The actual appeal must be lodged six weeks on from the written notification being submitted to the High Court.

 Key point: All appeals from solemn criminal trials in Scotland must be heard by the High Court of Justicary sitting as the Scottish Court of Criminal Appeal which always sits in Edinburgh.

During the appeal process, a convicted person who is facing imprisonment can apply for bail which will allow them to remain at liberty pending the decision of the appeal judges.

Under Section 104 of the Criminal Procedure (Scotland) Act 1995, the judges of the Scottish Court of Criminal Appeal have a great deal of discretion in the way in which the appeal is conducted. It is important to note the following factors:

Submission of evidence to the court

Very often, the parties can submit evidence e.g. a witness statement to be used in the case seven days before the intermediate diet. Failure by the other side to dispute this evidence before the intermediate diet could mean that it is accepted as fact and cannot be questioned at a later date.

Criminal special defences

Traditionally, in Scotland, there were four special defences available to an accused:

◆ Alibi
◆ Incrimination
◆ Insanity
◆ Self-defence

 Key point: Special defences in Scottish Criminal law include alibi, automatism, coercion, incrimination, insanity and self-defence.

If the accused intended to plead any of these special defences, they must notify the court and prosecution formally of this development.

Two other defences are nowadays treated as special defences and, again, formal notification of the intention of the accused to make use of these at his/her trial is required. These defences are:

◆ Automatism
◆ Coercion or necessity

 Key point: Nowadays, automatism and coercion or necessity are treated as special defences.

Alibi

When the accused puts forward the special defence of alibi, they are claiming that they have a witness or evidence which can prove that they could not have committed the criminal act because they were present at another location when the offence is alleged to have taken place.

 Her Majesty's Advocate *v* Tobin (2008) Peter Tobin, the notorious Scottish serial killer, was on trial for the abduction and murder of 15 year old Vicky Hamilton in 1991. Tobin attempted to use the defence of alibi to demonstrate that he had not been present in Scotland when the abduction and murder of his victim was thought to have taken place. Tobin claimed that he had been present in Portsmouth when the schoolgirl had disappeared. His reliance on this defence failed and Tobin was convicted of the murder of Vicky Hamilton.

Incrimination

When the accused attempts to rely on the special defence of incrimination, s/he is attempting to deny any liability for the crime and they are effectively pointing the finger of blame towards another individual.

Angus Robertson Sinclair v Her Majesty's Advocate (2007) Angus Robertson, who was accused of committing the murder and rape of two teenage girls in 1977, attempted to incriminate Gordon Hamilton, his long deceased brother-in-law, of involvement in the murders.

Insanity

In situations where the defence of insanity is relied upon, the accused is claiming that they suffered from some sort of recognised mental or psychiatric disorder which led to a complete alienation of reason at the time the offence was committed.

In **Her Majesty's Advocate v Kidd (1960)** Lord Strachan issued the following directions to the jury about the test for insanity in Scotland:

"First, in order to excuse a person from responsibility for his acts on the grounds of insanity, there must have been an alienation of reason in relation to the act committed. There must have been some mental defect, to use a broad neutral word, a mental defect by which his reason was overpowered and was thereby rendered incapable of exerting his reason to control his conduct and reactions. If his reason was alienated in relation to the act committed, he was not responsible for that act, even though otherwise he may have been apparently quite rational."

The accused is asking the court to return a plea of not guilty by reason of insanity in terms of Section 54(6) of the Criminal Procedure (Scotland) Act 1995. The use of the defence of insanity in Scotland is actually quite rare in practice and two doctors must independently verify the mental state of the accused i.e. that they suffered from insanity at the time the offence was committed. When the accused has committed a very serious crime such as murder and manages to convince the High Court of Justiciary that they were insane when the offence was committed, this will mean detention in the State Hospital for an indefinite period of time.

It should be noted that it is the responsibility of the defence lawyers acting for the accused to prove that they were insane at the time the offence was committed.

It should be appreciated that any attempt by an accused person to argue that a mental defect caused by their own (admittedly reckless) actions should be treated in an equivalent way to insanity will fail.

 In **Brennan v Her Majesty's Advocate (1977)** an attempt by the accused to use the defence of insanity failed. The argument put forward by the accused was that he was so intoxicated after consuming a large amount of alcohol and a quantity of LSD on the day that he murdered his father and that this disordered mental state rendered him effectively insane. The accused had, of course, consumed the alcohol and the drugs voluntarily and he should, therefore, be held fully responsible for the consequences of his actions.

According to the High Court of Justiciary in **Carraher v Her Majesty's Advocate (1946)** and **Kennedy v Her Majesty's Advocate (1944)**, a psychopathic personality disorder suffered by the accused does not provide grounds for pleading the defence of insanity.

 Key point: In situations where the accused attempts to rely on the defence of insanity, they must be suffering from a recognised psychiatric disorder which leads to a complete breakdown in reason at the time the offence was committed.

Insanity at the time of the trial

Sometimes lawyers acting for the accused will use the defence of insanity to argue that they are not fit to stand trial because they would not understand proceedings at the subsequent hearing. This particular argument would be used in situations where the accused has subsequently become insane i.e. after the commission of the criminal offence. The lawyers acting for the accused are not necessarily claiming that they were insane at the time the offence was committed. Under Section 54(1) of the Criminal Procedure (Scotland) Act 1995, two doctors will have to verify independently that the accused is not fit to stand trial by reason of insanity.

Diminished responsibility

This is an area of law which is closely related to insanity, but the definition of diminished responsibility is actually broader than insanity and relates to an abnormality of the mind which is not as serious a mental condition as insanity. A successful plea of diminished responsibility may reduce the severity of the charge faced by the accused, for example, from one of homicide to culpable homicide or the accused may be found guilty of homicide but they suffered from some sort of mental aberration at the time the offence was committed.

 Galbraith v Her Majesty's Advocate (2002) the accused was found guilty of murdering her husband (who was a police officer) by shooting him in the head at their cottage in Furnace in Argyll in 1999. She was sentenced to life imprisonment. It was originally claimed by the accused that intruders had broken into the couple's cottage and committed the murder, but she later confessed to having carried out the killing. The accused had argued, however, that she should have been convicted of the lesser offence of culpable homicide (which equates to manslaughter in England and Wales) by reason of her diminished responsibility when she committed the offence. The reason for the diminished responsibility of the accused was the alleged physical and mental abuse suffered by her at the hands of her husband over many years. The alleged abuse suffered by the accused led to a situation where she was no longer able to think rationally about the consequences of her actions. The jury at Galbraith's trial rejected this argument whereupon she duly appealed to the High Court sitting as the Scottish Court of Criminal Appeal. At the appeal, important guidelines were established in relation to the concept of diminished responsibility. The Court of Criminal Appeal concluded that:

"In essence, the judge must decide whether there is evidence that, at the relevant time, the accused was suffering from an abnormality of mind which substantially impaired the ability of the accused, as compared with a normal person, to determine or control his acts."

In any event, the Scottish Court of Criminal Appeal rejected Galbraith's argument that she had not been fully responsible for her husband's death and she was ordered to face a retrial.

 Key point: Diminished responsibility is closely related to insanity, but relates to an abnormality of the mind which is not as serious as insanity.

Self-defence

An accused will put forward this defence to justify a breach of the criminal law which arose as a result of an attempt to defend himself, another individual or to protect property. The defence will not be available in the following circumstances:

1   If the use of force was disproportionate or unreasonable.

2   If the accused was able to preserve his personal safety or the safety of others, without having to rely on the use of physical force, for example, by fleeing the scene and thus guaranteeing his and the security of others by doing so.

 Her Majesty's Advocate *v* Doherty (1954) Doherty attempted (unsuccessfully as it turned out) to rely on the defence of self-defence at his trial for murder. Doherty had become involved in an altercation with another individual which had become very violent and had degenerated into something resembling a duel where both parties were armed (Doherty had used a bayonet style weapon during the fight). Doherty's plea of self-defence fell down at a crucial hurdle: he could have escaped down a back stair of the tenement building in which the fight took place and avoided further violence. Self-defence involves the use of reasonable force to protect life and limb and such force should be used with the intention of making good an escape once an assailant has been disabled. Doherty returned to the scene of the fight and took up a weapon with the intention of injuring his opponent and it was with total disregard as to whether his actions ended in the death of this individual.

 Key point: A person relying on the defence of self-defence must show that they used reasonable force and that there was no choice but to use force.

Automatism

Automatism is a condition whereby an individual unconsciously loses control of the body through no fault of his own, for example, due to the involuntary ingestion of mind altering drugs or a condition such as epilepsy. Crucially, the accused did not make a conscious decision to ingest the harmful substances and the fault lies with other individuals. It is during the unconscious episode that the accused commits a crime, but does not know what is happening and has little (if any) recollection of this event having taken place.

 Her Majesty's Advocate *v* Ross (1991) the accused had been drinking in a public house and, while present there, he subjected several of his fellow drinkers to a violent assault with a knife. It later emerged that someone in the public house had placed temazepam and LSD tablets in the lager can from which the accused had been drinking. The combination of temazepam and LSD had caused the accused to suffer an extremely violent reaction and this was the reason for him carrying out the attack on the other customers in the public house. The accused relied on the defence of automatism and was subsequently acquitted because he was able to convince the court that he had lost control of his body. It should, of course, be appreciated that the accused had no knowledge that he had ingested the temazepam and LSD tablets and could not be held responsible for what later happened.

Key point: Automatism occurs when a person unconsciously loses control of the body through no fault of their own.

External and internal automatism

Often the type of automatism found in **Her Majesty's Advocate v Ross** (above) is referred to as **external automatism**, because the reason for the loss of control by the accused is caused by an external factor, for example, ingesting drugs without his knowledge.

In the past, the Scottish courts have permitted attempts by an accused to use a defence of **internal automatism**. Internal automatism is caused by some physical condition from which the accused suffers, for example, epilepsy, diabetes or sleep-walking. It could be argued, however, that the concept of internal automatism was limited by the decision of the High Court of Justiciary in **Her Majesty's Advocate v Cunningham (1963)** where the accused failed to convince the court that his epilepsy should be used as a defence to the charge that he had committed a number of road traffic offences. Previously, however, the Scottish courts had recognised the concept of internal automatism as a defence (as in **His Majesty's Advocate v Ritchie (1926)**). Admittedly the decision in **Cunningham**, is now viewed by many lawyers and academics as a blatant attempt by the High Court of Justiciary to narrow the range of possible defences available to the accused in Scots criminal law.

 Key point: Automatism can be classified as either external or internal automatism.

Coercion and necessity

This special defence amounts to a plea by the accused that they were subjected to threats of violence or intimidation by a co-accused and the nature of the threats or intimidation was so serious that they had the effect of overcoming an ordinary person's strength of will with the result that they felt forced to participate in a criminal enterprise. In Scots law, the defence of coercion would only be successful if there was a very real possibility that the accused would be killed or subjected to very serious bodily harm by their co-accused if they refused to take part in the commission of the crime.

 Cochrane v Her Majesty's Advocate (2001) Cochrane was a 17 year old who had a very low IQ. Cochrane was encouraged to take part in a criminal act by his co-accused who had resorted to threatening him that explosives would be planted near to his house to blow it up and that he would be physically attacked. As a result of these threats, Cochrane participated in the crime. He attempted to rely on the defence of coercion at his trial, but he was successfully convicted of his participation in the criminal act. Cochrane appealed to the High Court of Justiciary against his conviction and his lawyers claimed that the Sheriff should have taken steps to notify the jury about his low IQ and the likelihood that the threats he had received would be more potent to someone like him. The High Court disagreed and said that the test for coercion should be applied objectively and was not dependent upon the personal characteristics of an individual.

The defence of necessity is also closely associated with coercion in Scots law. An accused would attempt to use the defence of necessity in situations where they had quite clearly broken the criminal law, but this breach can be justified in that it was carried out to avoid death or extremely serious physical harm to the accused or other individuals. The defences of coercion or necessity in Scotland are not available to an accused who has broken the law in order to prevent physical destruction or damage to property.

 Key point: Coercion can be used as a defence when the accused has been threatened or intimidated and the nature of these threats is so serious that they overcome an ordinary person's strength of will, with the result that they take part in a crime.

 In **Moss v Howdle (1997)** the accused had driven a motor vehicle at excessive speed to reach the nearest service station. His actions constituted a breach of the Road Traffic Act 1988, but he claimed that he had acted out of necessity. A passenger in the vehicle had suddenly cried out when he experienced unexpected pain. The accused was convinced that the passenger was suffering from a serious illness which required immediate medical treatment. This assumption later turned out to be wrong, but by then the accused had broken the law. In the Sheriff Court, the accused was convicted of a breach of the criminal law whereupon he appealed to the High Court of Justiciary. Although the High Court recognised the existence of the defence of necessity in Scotland, it was not available to the accused in this case because he could have stopped the vehicle on the hard shoulder of the motorway to assist the passenger whose well-being he thought was endangered.

 In **Lord Advocate's Reference Number 1 of 2000**, the High Court of Justiciary refused to allow the defence of necessity to succeed which had been put forward by three co-accused peace campaigners who had entered the Faslane Naval Base and carried out a number of acts of malicious damage. Critically, the three individuals could not be said to have faced an immediate threat which meant that they were forced to break the criminal law. The three individuals were, of course, acquitted by the jury at their trial at Greenock Sheriff Court on the direction of Sheriff Margaret Gimblet. The Lord Advocate submitted the case to the High Court in order for guidelines to be established for future cases.

 Key point: Necessity can be used as a defence in situations where the accused had committed a crime in order to prevent death or serious injury being suffered by the accused or other person.

Coercion and necessity distinguished

In order to distinguish between coercion and necessity, it is necessary to enquire about the immediacy of the danger or threat which faces the accused or some other person. If the danger is of an immediate or imminent nature, the accused would rely on a defence of necessity to justify his or her breach of the criminal law. On the other hand, a less imminent danger which led to the accused breaking the law would entail a reliance on the defence of coercion.

 Key point: The difference between necessity and coercion is the immediacy of the relevant danger or threat.

Alternative methods of resolving legal disputes

There has been a great increase in administrative justice which is dispensed through special courts or tribunals during the twentieth century. Many legal and constitutional writers have viewed this trend as alarming because, rightly or wrongly, they feel that it undermines the jurisdiction of the longer established courts such as the Sheriff Court or the Court of Session.

These courts of special jurisdiction operate outside what we would recognise as the traditional legal system of Scotland. The increasing role which these administrative courts and tribunals have taken on is largely due to the government's greatly expanded powers in relation to important issues like pensions, social security, taxation, industrial relations, immigration, planning and compulsory purchase orders. As a result of the government's expanded responsibilities it is hardly surprising that disputes often arise between individuals and the state.

However, it would be a mistake to assume that these special courts and tribunals deal solely with disputes between private citizens and the state. The Scottish Land Court, for example, deals with disputes between landlord and tenant in crofting and agricultural matters.

Another point to note is that courts or tribunals of special jurisdiction do not always sit on a permanent basis. Some are very temporary in nature. Obviously, we cannot cover every type of special court or tribunal exhaustively so we will concentrate our efforts on the most prominent.

 Key point: Not all legal disputes are dealt with by the Scottish criminal and civil courts. There are special courts and tribunals that exist to hear certain types of dispute, for example, the Employment Tribunal.

Administrative Justice and Tribunals Council (www.ajtc.gov.uk)

From 1 November 2007, the Administrative Justice and Tribunals Council replaced the Council on Tribunals which previously had responsibility for regulating the work of many of the statutory Tribunals now operating in Scotland and across the United Kingdom. The Tribunals, Courts and Enforcement Act 2007 brought these changes into effect.

The Children's Hearing or Panel (www.chscotland.gov.uk)

In Scotland, a child under the age of eight cannot be guilty of a criminal offence. In other words, a criminal prosecution cannot be brought against a child under the age of eight. Criminal responsibility in Scotland, therefore, begins at the age of eight.

The age of criminal responsibility for children will soon to be raised from eight years of age to 12 in a move which will bring Scotland into line with other European countries. Until this reform, Scotland had one of the lowest ages for criminal responsibilty in the Western World. A child under the age of 16 cannot be prosecuted in a criminal court without the permission of the Lord Advocate. Children will only appear in the Sheriff Court and the High Court of Justiciary if they are accused of murder, assault which endangers life or driving offences which are punishable by disqualification. Private prosecutions of children would definitely not be allowed. The Lord Advocate will occasionally issue instructions to procurator fiscals which address the treatment of children in criminal matters.

The Children's Hearing was established by the Social Work (Scotland) Act 1968 and is now regulated by the Children (Scotland) Act 1995. It is an alternative to sending children to trial in an adult court. The aim of the Children's Hearing is to prevent young people from being exposed to the criminal justice system in the hope that they will be given a chance to reform before their behaviour has more serious consequences. The Children's Hearing is, therefore, deliberately not part of the Scottish criminal justice system.

Individuals who sit on the Children's Panel come from a wide range of different backgrounds. They are members of the public and volunteers aged between the ages of 18 and 60. They will have been selected by Scottish Government Ministers on the recommendations of the Children's Panel Advisory Committee for the local council area and they will have received training to help them in their role. A panel of three members will sit (at least one of them being a female). Cases are referred to the Hearing by the Reporter to the Children's Hearing.

 Key point: The Children's Hearing is an alternative way of dealing with children accused of committing crimes.

In May 2009, the Scottish Government announced proposals to overhaul the current system of Children's Hearings or Panels. Presently, the 32 Hearings or Panels in Scotland are run by volunteers with training and support provided by local authorities. Under the Government's proposals, a national body called the Scottish Children's Hearing Tribunal would take over responsibility for the running of all Hearings or Panels in the country. These proposals, however, have been universally attacked and greeted with dismay by those individuals involved in administering the system. In late August 2009, the Scottish Government announced that it had decided to delay pressing ahead with the proposed reforms to the system until 2010 at the earliest. This led to accusations from the opposition parties in the Scottish Parliament that the Government had effectively abandoned its plans to change the system in the face of overwhelming opposition. It now remains to be seen whether the Government will risk the introduction of reforms to the system.

Employment Tribunals (www.employmenttribunals.gov.uk)

The huge increase in employment law in the United Kingdom generally has led to a much more prominent role for Employment Tribunals in areas like sexual, racial and disability discrimination, equal pay cases, unfair and wrongful dismissal actions. Employment Tribunals (previously known as Industrial Tribunals) are governed by Part I of the Employment Tribunals Act 1996 (www.employmenttribunals.gov.uk).

Some of the legislation which confers jurisdiction on Employment Tribunals includes:

- The Equal Pay Act 1970
- The Sex Discrimination Acts 1975 and 1986
- Part-time Workers (Prevention of Less Favourable Treatment) Regulations 2000
- Employment Equality (Religion or Belief) Regulations 2003
- Employment Equality (Sexual Orientation) Regulations 2003
- Employment Equality (Age) Regulations 2006
- The Race Relations Act 1976
- The Disability Discrimination Act 1995
- The Employment Rights Act 1996
- The Working Time Regulations 1998
- The Employment Act 2002

www

An example of paperwork submitted by parties to an Employment Tribunal claim (The ET1 and ET3) can be seen on the Introductory Scots Law website.

In Scotland, the Employment Judge of a Tribunal is appointed by the UK Ministry of Justice on the recommendation of the Judicial Appointments Commission for England and Wales. The Employment Judge sits with two other individuals appointed by the Ministry of Justice. These lay members have been selected from a panel on the strength of them possessing detailed knowledge or extensive ability in relation to commercial or industrial matters. In some situations, the Employment Judge may sit alone to decide cases. This eventuality occurs if both parties agree to this or the case is undefended.

The Employment Tribunal sits at suitable locations throughout Scotland (Edinburgh, Glasgow, Dundee and Aberdeen) in order to determine the varied issues which come before them. The hearings are very informal in style and the parties are not required to be represented by a lawyer – although this will often be the case. Since 15 January 2000, Legal Aid has been available to parties who otherwise would not be in a position to hire the services of a lawyer. The hearing before a Tribunal will normally be held in public, unless there are compelling reasons for this not to be the case, for example, where allegations of sexual harassment will be discussed. Decisions of the Tribunal are reached by majority and it is possible for the two lay members of the panel to outvote the Employment Judge. An appeal is made to the Employment Appeal Tribunal in Edinburgh on a point of law.

Many Employment Tribunals claims are resolved by the parties themselves prior to the hearing or with the Assistance of Conciliation and Arbitration Service (ACAS). An example of an ACAS COT3 agreement negotiated by the parties to an Employment Tribunal hearing can be seen on the Introductory Scots Law website.

www

Key point: Employment Tribunals sit with a legally qualified Employment Judge and two lay members and they have jurisdiction to deal with employment law disputes.

The Employment Appeal Tribunal (EAT) (www.employment appeals.gov.uk)

If an individual is dissatisfied with the decision of an Employment Tribunal, it can be challenged by appealing to the EAT on a point of law only. It is absolutely vital, for the appellant's sake, that the facts are properly presented to the Tribunal at the original hearing. The EAT (www.employmentappeals.gov.uk) will only look at the version of events presented at the Tribunal – it is extremely rare for new evidence to be introduced.

The EAT is a superior court and has its headquarters in Edinburgh. It is regulated by Part II of the Employment Tribunals Act 1996.

Appeals to the EAT are commenced by serving the Employment Tribunal with a notice of appeal within 42 days of the original Tribunal decision being issued to the parties. Legal Aid is available to individuals for appeals to the EAT and the parties are expected to be legally represented.

Appeals before the EAT are usually heard before a judge of the Court of Session who acts as President and between two and four appointed members. The President of the EAT is appointed by the Lord President of the Court of Session. As for the lay members, they are appointed by the Queen on the joint recommendation of the Lord Chancellor and the Secretary of State for Trade and Industry. These appointed members of the EAT are not part of the judiciary, but they will have specialist knowledge or experience of industrial relations as representatives of either employers or workers. The hearing normally proceeds in public but it can be held in private for reasons of national security or trade secrets, for example.

It is vitally important that in each appeal, equal numbers of persons representing employers and workers participate. In cases of major importance, the presiding judge and four lay members (an equal balance between employers and workers) will sit. There may be one or three lay members present if the parties agree to this.

The EAT need not reach a unanimous decision and majority decisions are just as binding. Each member of the EAT has a vote and it is possible that the judge could be outvoted. This outcome, however, is extremely rare. Exceptionally, providing that the parties agree, the case could be heard by the judge and one or three members. The EAT may review or change any of its previous decisions, for example, on the grounds of new evidence.

An appeal is made to the Inner House of the Court of Session with the possibility of a further appeal to the House of Lords.

 Key point: The EAT is a superior court and has its headquarters in Edinburgh and it hears appeals from the Employment Tribunal. There is a further right of appeal on a point of law to the Court of Session and, possibly, the House of Lords.

The Health and Safety Executive (www.hse.gov.uk)

As we shall see in our discussion in Chapter 6, employers owe a number of legal duties to their employees generally to provide a safe workplace, safe equipment, safe working systems, competent supervisors and fellow employees. These duties are underpinned by both the civil and criminal law.

Individuals who are concerned about the undesirable and lax health and safety procedures in their workplace may not wish to initiate legal action personally against their employer, but they can complain to a body known as the Health and Safety Executive which may then initiate an investigation. Employers who breach health and safety rules could be civilly liable to anyone who suffers an injury as a result of dangerous working practices and then could face fines imposed by the criminal courts under health and safety legislation. It should be noted that health and safety does not just cover employees, but anyone who comes into contact with an employer's operations, for example, customers entering a retail premises or a factory.

The Health and Safety Executive (HSE) is a non-departmental public organisation which is supervised by the UK Government Department for Work and Pensions. It is a UK wide organisation, but it has a Scottish section with offices in Edinburgh, Glasgow, Aberdeen and Inverness. Health and safety remains the responsibility of the Westminster Parliament and it will make laws in this area **not** the Scottish Parliament. The HSE and the Scottish Government and Parliament do, however, enjoy a close working relationship as the devolved Scottish administration makes laws which affect many work-places in Scotland, for example, the ban on smoking in public places which was introduced in March 2006. The Scottish section of the HSE has its own Director who is Head of the Field Operations Directorate in Scotland.

In late 2009, the HSE employed approximately 270 staff in Scotland. Of these employees, some 170 work as frontline inspectors (this includes about 80 general and construction inspectors, as well as chemicals industry and offshore inspectors and specialists who are involved in cross-border activities). The inspectors are supported in their work by Scottish based policy and administrative staff.

Lobbying political or trade union representatives

Individuals who wish to express concern about a potential legal issue, again, may not wish to instruct lawyers to act for them in this regard. If they are members of Trade Unions, they could contact their officials to ask for support (which could include legal advice and representation).

It is also possible to approach elected politicians to ask for their help in dealing with an issue which has legal ramifications. Elected politicians in Scotland include the following individuals:

◆ Local Councillors
◆ Members of the Scottish Parliament (MSPs)
◆ Members of the Westminster Parliament (MPs)
◆ Members of the European Parliament (MEPs)

An example of a successful lobbying campaign is outlined below:

In June 2002, James O'Donovan, the local Branch Secretary of the Educational Institute of Scotland (a Trade Union which represents the majority of Scottish teachers and lecturers) at Glasgow's Central College of Commerce was dismissed by the Board of Management for alleged gross misconduct. Many EIS members at the College and across Scotland suspected that the dismissal was motivated by anti-Trade Union policies being promoted by the College's former management. In any case, EIS members ran a very effective lobbying campaign to gather support from Members of the Scottish Parliament in order to have Mr O'Donovan reinstated to his lecturing post at the College. The EIS nationally provided legal support and Mr O'Donovan won his Employment Tribunal case in December 2003. The College was ordered to reinstate Mr O'Donovan, but it decided to appeal against this aspect of the Tribunal's decision. Eventually, following further campaigning by EIS members and supporters (from across the political spectrum), the College Board of Management finally gave in and reinstated Mr O'Donovan in 2005. During the long campaign to have Mr O'Donovan reinstated, a number of articles appeared on television and in the local and national press which undoubtedly put the College Board of Management under a great deal of pressure. An account of Mr O'Donovan's Employment Tribunal action is provided in Chapter 6.

The Lands Tribunal for Scotland (www.lands-tribunal-scotland.org.uk)

This body considers whether burdensome title conditions should be removed from heritable property. The Lands Tribunal is organised under the following statutes and rules:

(a) Lands Tribunal Act 1949

(b) Tribunal and Inquiries Act 1992

(c) Title Conditions (Scotland) Act 2003

(d) Tribunals, Courts and Enforcement Act 2007

(e) Lands Tribunals for Scotland Rules 1971 (as amended) and the Lands Tribunals for Scotland Rules 2003

Other statutes also confer jurisdiction upon the Tribunal:

(a) Housing Scotland Act 1987

(a) Land Compensation (Scotland) Acts 1963 and 1973

(c) Coal Mining (Subsidence) Act 1957 and Coal Mining Subsidence Act 1991

(d) Abolition of Feudal Tenure etc. (Scotland) Act 2000

(e)   Land Reform (Scotland) Act 2003

(f)   Agricultural Holdings (Scotland) Act 2003

According to the Tribunal's website (www.lands-tribunal-scotland.org.uk), it deals mainly with the following types of cases:

◆ the discharge or variation of title conditions
◆ tenants' rights to purchase their public sector houses
◆ disputed compensation for compulsory purchase of land or loss in value of land caused by public works
◆ valuations for rating on non-domestic premises
◆ appeals against the Keeper of the Registers of Scotland
◆ appeals about valuation of land on pre-emptive purchase
◆ voluntary or joint references in which the Tribunal acts as arbiter

Membership of the Tribunal

The membership of the Tribunal consists of suitably qualified legal members and others who have experience in the valuation of land. Currently (in 2010) the Tribunal consists of a President, Lord McGhie, and three other members – one legal member and two members experienced in valuation matters.

Any one or more of its members may exercise the jurisdiction of the Tribunal. Where two or more members deal with a case, the senior legal member will normally preside. Any disagreements between members about a decision will be resolved by majority vote. In the event of an equal number of members sitting at the hearing, the member presiding will have a casting vote. The Tribunal will follow similar procedures to those operating in the Court of Session and the Sheriff Court. The Tribunal will try to be as flexible as possible in its organisation. There is a right of appeal on a point of law to the Court of Session. Further appeal to the Supreme Court of the United Kingdom may be allowed with the permission of the Court of Session.

An example of correspondence from the Lands Tribunal can be seen on the Introductory Scots Law website.

Other tribunals which are discussed in this book are:

◆ the Consumer Credit Appeals Tribunal (see Chapter 4);
◆ and the Company Names Tribunal (see Chapter 5)

 Key point: The Lands Tribunal for Scotland considers whether unnecessary or oppressive conditions imposed on land should be removed, it considers cases where the value of land is in dispute and it can make decisions in certain disputes in relation to council house purchases by tenants. The Tribunal also has the authority to hear appeals against decisions of the Keeper of the Registers of Scotland.

The Scottish Land Court (www.scottish-land-court.org.uk)

This body was created in 1912 as a result of the Small Landholders (Scotland) Act 1911. It is now regulated under the terms of the Scottish Land Court Act 1993. The court exists to determine the outcome of disputes between tenants and landlords in agricultural and crofting matters. Its jurisdiction comes from two statutes, namely, the Agricultural Holdings (Scotland) Act 1991 and the Crofters (Scotland) Act 1993.

However, the Court's jurisdiction is limited in the sense that it cannot decide questions of land ownership which are within the jurisdiction of the Sheriff Court and the Court of Session. The title of the court is slightly misleading in that it is not authorised to deal with all legal disputes which are concerned with land. The court most certainly is not authorised to deal with land issues in a town or urban setting.

The Court consists of a Chairman and three members who will have a background in crofting and farming matters. Its Chairman, Lord McGhie, is also the President of the Lands Tribunal for Scotland and they share the same offices, although both bodies are completely separate as far as their functions are concerned. The Scottish Land Court has jurisdiction in the areas of agricultural disputes between landlords and tenants. The Court may sit as a Divisional Court where cases are heard by a Court member and a legal assessor. Alternatively, a Full Court can be convened where a minimum or quorum of two members is required and the Chairman. Parties have a right of appeal to the Court of Session but only on a point of law. The Chairman of the Scottish Land Court enjoys the same status and benefits as a judge of the Court of Session.

 Key point: The Scottish Land Court exists to determine the outcome of disputes between tenants and landlords in agricultural and crofting matters.

The Court of The Lord Lyon (www.lyon-court.com/lordlyon)

This Court is presided over by Lord Lyon who is a Minister of the Crown and a judge of the realm. Scotland, together with Spain, is one of the few countries to have retained the services of this type of court up until the present day. The Court deals with matters relating to heraldry and the right to use certain ancient titles. A person who wishes to claim the right to use an ancient Scottish title will, of course, have to produce evidence to substantiate the claim and the Lord Lyon will have to be satisfied before he grants such a right. Heraldic symbols and coats of arms were very important in societies where most people did not possess the skills of reading and writing – this also included the landed aristocracy. Many powerful individuals adopted symbols or coats of arms which over the years became associated with these individuals or their families. As time went on, the possession of a coat of arms marked a person out as being someone of importance and wealth. Such persons were obviously very keen to have exclusive control over these symbols and the Court of the Lord Lyon was established to deal with disputes in relation to these matters. It was common practice for these symbols to be copied and used by other individuals who had no right to use them. Amazingly, even to this day, disputes can arise regarding the rights of individuals to use certain symbols or titles. A school will have to be very careful when it decides to redesign its crest or motto that it does not infringe someone else's right to use a symbol or a coat of arms. The Lord Lyon also protects the rights of the Crown to use certain symbols and coats of arms.

The Court of the Lord Lyon has its headquarters in Her Majesty's New Register House in Edinburgh. The Court has both criminal and civil jurisdiction. It is an offence for anyone to use a coat of arms or a heraldic symbol belonging to another person. To this end, the Court can impose fines on offenders and even terms of imprisonment. The Court has a prosecutor known as a Procurator Fiscal.

 Key point: The Court of the Lord Lyon is a court of special jurisdiction which has responsibility for determining who has the right to use certain heraldic symbols, coats of arms and ancient Scottish titles.

Courts Martial

The British armed services have their own tribunals or courts where members of the military who breach the services' disciplinary codes and/or commit other offences may face trial. Now, as a result of the Armed Forces Act 2006, a permanent court martial is to be created and this body will begin functioning from 31 October 2009. The constitution and the procedure of this body will be governed by the Armed Forces (Court Martial) Rules 2009. The accused is entitled to be legally represented at the hearing. The accused is permitted to rely on witnesses and evidence in order to support his defence and his legal representative will be permitted to cross-examine the prosecution's witnesses. In fact, procedures at the court martial will be similar to those of a civilian court and are closely modelled on the procedure operated in the English Crown Court. On occasion, however, courts martial are not open to members of the public for reasons of national security. Courts martial must ensure that the accused enjoys a right to a fair trial which is protected by the European Convention on Human Rights. In peacetime, it is more likely that members of the military who commit serious crimes or who commit crimes outside military quarters would face trial in the ordinary Scottish criminal courts.

There had been concerns for some time that the way in which courts martial had been operated amounted to a breach of human rights laws. In December 2003, the European Court of Human Rights decided in the case of **Grieves v the United Kingdom**, that British law was incompatible with the European Convention on Human Rights in relation to the operation of courts martial. Article 6 of the European Convention guarantees a right to a fair trial and under the then current naval disciplinary rules this standard was not being achieved. The main problem was the fact that the Judge Advocate who presides over such cases was appointed by the Chief Judge Advocate, a serving naval officer and therefore the Judge Advocate's independence could not be guaranteed. In many respects, this situation bore a striking resemblance to the decision of the High Court of Justiciary in **Starrs v Ruxton (2000)** where the widespread use of temporary Sheriffs was successfully challenged on the ground that such appointees were not sufficiently independent from the control of Scottish Ministers – a situation itself which was felt to be a breach of Article 6 of the European Convention.

To its credit, however, the Government of the United Kingdom accepted the criticisms of the European Court in **Grieves** and speedily brought in reforms to the court martial system by first implementing the Naval Discipline Act 1957 Remedial Order 2004 and subsequently by introducing the Armed Forces Act 2006.

 Key point: A court martial deals with members of the armed forces who have committed crimes or who are guilty of breaches of discipline.

Ombudsman schemes

The establishment of ombudsman schemes is a very popular route which provides citizens with a safeguard against maladministration by public authorities. This is an alternative to the more traditional route of beginning a legal action for judicial review in the Court of Session. Ombudsman schemes are modelled upon the Scandinavian office of the Ombudsman.

The Scottish Public Services Ombudsman (www.spso.org.uk)

The Scottish Public Services Ombudsman Act 2002 established a single Ombudsman to deal with complaints by the public which involve the Scottish Executive and Parliament, the National Health Service in Scotland, Scottish local authorities and Scottish Housing Associations. The Ombudsman scheme is all about the prevention of abuses of power by a wide range of Scottish and even British public bodies, for example, the Scottish Legal Aid Board. Professor Alice Brown is the first Scottish Ombudsman to be appointed. The Scottish Public Services Ombudsman and her three assistant Ombudsmen are appointed by the Queen on the recommendation of the Scottish Parliament.

United Kingdom Parliamentary Ombudsman or the Parliamentary Commissioner for Administration

This scheme provides a further check on abuses of power by British government departments under the provisions of the Parliamentary Commissioner Act 1967. This jurisdiction of the Ombudsman was extended by the Parliamentary Commissioner Act 1994. The current post-holder, Ann Abraham, was appointed in 2002 by the Crown and has the same security of tenure as a senior judge. The Ombudsman is also a member of the Council on Tribunals. The main function of the Ombudsman is to investigate complaints relating to the exercise of administrative functions. Complaints from the public about the behaviour of individual Westminster MPs can be investigated by the Office of the Parliamentary Commissioner for Standards (www.parliament.uk/pcs/). The Parliamentary & Health Service Ombudsman (www.ombudsman.org.uk) deals with abuses by British government departments.

The Scottish Parliamentary Standards Commissioner (www.spsc.co.uk) investigates allegations of misconduct committed by Members of the Scottish Parliament. This post was established by the Scottish Parliamentary Standards Commissioner Act 2002.

Unfortunately, the Ombudsman is undoubtedly less effective than her counterparts in other countries. Britain is alone in preventing its national

Ombudsman initiate her own investigations. The Ombudsman cannot investigate complaints against the police, judges or local authorities.

 Key point: The Ombudsman scheme allows members of the public to make complaints about alleged maladministration in relation to the provision of public services.

Other Ombudsman and regulatory authorities

In the areas of banking, insurance and building societies, Ombudsmen have been appointed to deal, on a limited basis, with disputes in those industries.

The Council of the London Stock Exchange has appointed such a person to mediate in disputes between investors and stockbrokers.

Sections 150 to 160 of the Pensions Act 1995 established a Pensions Ombudsman to deal with disputes between an individual and a pension scheme or provider regarding the way in which pensions schemes are run. Complaints about the sales and marketing of pension schemes are dealt with by the Financial Ombudsman Service.

There is also a Financial Services Authority (FSA, www.fsa.gov.uk) which was set up as a result of the Financial Services and Markets Act 2000 and deals with deals with complaints concerning the United Kingdom's financial services industry such as the mis-selling of endowment mortgages in the 1980s and 1990s.

Many of the utilities industries e.g. gas, water, electricity and telecommunications have a regulator who ensures that they are acting fairly. Members of the public who are dissatisfied with, for example, an electricity provider can complain to Ofgem, the Office of Gas and Electricity Markets (www.ofgem.gov.uk).

 Key point: In the areas of banking, insurance and building societies, Ombudsmen have been appointed to deal, on a limited basis, with disputes in those industries.

The Standards Commission for Scotland (www.standardscommission scotland.org.uk)

The Standards Commission for Scotland was set up as a result of the Ethical Standards in Public Life etc. (Scotland) Act 2000. This regulatory authority ensures that the individual members of various public bodies e.g. boards of management of Further Education colleges, boards of NHS Trusts and councillors carry out their functions in accordance with strict Codes of Conduct approved by the Scottish Parliament.

If members of the public feel or suspect that a member of a public body or a councillor has breached these Codes of Conduct (which promote the highest standards of ethical behaviour in public life), they are entitled to raise a complaint with the Standards Commission which will then investigate the matter. If the complaint or the allegation is well-founded, the Commission can then take action against the individual who has breached the relevant Code of Conduct. In extreme cases, an individual who has fallen well below the ethical standard of behaviour expected of him or her may be removed from his or her post. The Commission promotes and enforces ethical standards across the 32 local authorities in Scotland

and 129 Scottish public bodies. The Commission, although publicly funded, is completely independent of the Scottish Government. It does, however, produce an annual report of its activities which it lays before the Scottish Parliament. The Commission does not deal with issues of maladministration in the public bodies for which it has responsibility. It is more concerned with how the individual members of these bodies conduct themselves.

If, for example, a councillor had behaved in a disrespectful way towards his or her colleagues or the employees of the council, this would be potentially a matter for the Standards Commission to investigate. Alternatively, a member of a board of management of the local Further Education college may not have disclosed a personal interest in a contract which the college is proposing to enter with a business. The board member, as things turn out, is a shareholder in that business. This could well represent a breach of ethical standards by the Board member and may lead to an investigation being carried out by the Standards Commission. If, however, a council, as an organisation, was in breach of auditing or financial rules, this would be a matter for the Scottish Public Services Ombudsman.

Professional bodies

Certain professions such as accountants and lawyers are regulated by their own professional bodies. If a member of the public wishes to make a complaint against a solicitor or a solicitor-advocate that they have previously instructed to act on their behalf, they can approach the Law Society of Scotland, the relevant professional body, which will investigate the complaint and take any necessary disciplinary action against the member in breach of professional standards. The Faculty of Advocates in Edinburgh is the relevant professional body for those lawyers practising as advocates before the Scottish courts.

In extreme cases, a lawyer who has committed a serious breach of professional rules may be struck off by the Law Society or the Faculty of Advocates and this will mean that such an individual is no longer permitted to practise in the short term or longer term.

If a member of the public is still unhappy with the outcome of an investigation against a lawyer by the relevant professional body, they have the right to make a further complaint to the Scottish Legal Complaints Commission which will then ask the relevant professional body to investigate the matter and report back with its findings in the matter. The benefit for the member of the public raising the complaint against the lawyer is that it is free of charge, although many lawyers understandably do not feel the same way about this! The Legal Complaints Commission is funded by way of an annual levy paid by individual members of the legal profession.

Public inquiries

The government will often choose to set up an independent public inquiry regarding a problem over which the public has expressed concern and, more importantly, where there may be serious legal consequences if nothing is done. There are no general rules governing these inquiries and they will differ very much in shape and form depending on the situation. In October 2003, Lord Fraser of Carmyllie QC, a former Lord Advocate, began an investigation into the spiralling costs of the new building for the Scottish Parliament at Holyrood. Lord Fraser is being assisted by Mr John Campbell QC and Professor Robert Black, the Auditor General for Scotland. This investigation was launched by the Scottish Executive as a direct result of mounting public anger over the cost of the project which was originally estimated at £40 million. The cost of the project in September 2003 was a staggering £400 million. The inquiry reported its findings in September 2004.

The ICL or Stockline Enquiry commenced proceedings in July 2008 and sat for some 12 weeks in Maryhill Community Hall. The Enquiry was headed by Lord Gill, the Lord Justice Clerk (Scotland's second most senior judge in the College of Justice), and it examined the circumstances surrounding the explosion at a factory in the Maryhill district of Glasgow in May 2004 where nine people were killed and 33 individuals also sustained injuries. Liquefied petroleum, which is highly flammable, had escaped from a pipe at the factory and this was the cause of the explosion. Two companies which had responsibility for operating the factory were fined £200,000 for breach of health and safety laws. In July 2009, the Enquiry made public its primary conclusion that the explosion at the factory was an avoidable disaster.

In July 2009, the Government of the United Kingdom announced that it would hold a Public Enquiry which would review the decision of the then Prime Minister Tony Blair to commit British armed forces to participate in the American-led invasion of Iraq in March 2003. The invasion, which led to the overthrow of Saddam Hussein, the former Iraqi dictator, was hugely controversial and was opposed by many people in Britain and across the world. It has long been alleged that the Blair Government knew all along that Iraq did not possess weapons of mass destruction and, therefore, that the basis of the invasion was fundamentally flawed and against international law. Sir John Chilcott, the current Chair of the B&CE (building and Civil Engineering) Group heads the enquiry.

 Key point: Public inquiries are set up by the Government on a temporary basis to investigate particular problems or important issues, for example, the Hutton and Fraser inquiries 2003–2004.

Arbitration, mediation and conciliation procedures

Parties to a legal dispute may not wish to go to court or a tribunal for a variety of different reasons. Instead, as an effective alternative, they may wish to use the services of a neutral third party to help them resolve the disputes. In these situations, the parties often make the choice of taking responsibility for dispute resolution upon themselves rather than relying upon a court which will impose its own judgement.

In a commercial dispute, the parties may wish to use an arbitration procedure to come to some sort of agreement. Arbitration allows the parties to appoint a neutral person, known as an arbiter in Scotland, who will hear both sides of the argument and who will then suggest a solution which hopefully will be broadly acceptable to both sides. The mechanism for appointing an arbiter is simple. The parties may have anticipated a dispute occurring and they have taken steps to address this by inserting an arbitration clause in the contract that they have formed with one another.

Here is an example of an arbitration clause:

ARBITRATION CLAUSE

Any dispute or difference arising out of or relating to this contract, its interpretation or the breach thereof, shall be settled by arbitration before an Arbiter selected and appointed by the President or Vice-President for the time being of the Law Society of Scotland from the panel of Arbiters maintained by the Law Society of Scotland and conducted in accordance with the Arbitration Rules of the Law Society of Scotland current at the date of the appointment of the Arbiter; and we consent to registration hereof for preservation and execution.

The Scottish Mediation Network can be found at: www.scottishmediation.org.uk. ACAS can be found at: www.acas.org.uk.

The Chartered Institute of Arbitrators (Scottish Branch) is located at: www.scottish-arbitrators.org

Alternatively, when a dispute first arises, the parties may agree to use arbitration instead of the courts. Once the parties have chosen arbitration over the courts, they are committed to this procedure and they cannot withdraw unless the arbitration process is seriously flawed. Arbitration is not permitted, however, in criminal matters or in family law (divorce, separation or custody of children). Arbitration is often preferred in business as it is private (as opposed to public court hearings), it is usually faster than the courts, it may be less expensive than court and the parties can decide the most appropriate procedures that will be used.

The Advisory, Conciliation and Arbitration Service (ACAS) is a publicly-funded body established in 1974 which attempts mainly to resolve disputes in the workplace. During industrial action or strikes, ACAS can be used by both employers and Trade Unions as a neutral referee to help resolve the dispute. The input of ACAS may simply amount to the provision of a neutral meeting place for the parties in the presence of neutral conciliators who will try to bring the parties towards a solution. The parties to an industrial dispute can even approach ACAS having agreed to submit to its binding arbitration procedures.

When parties have taken a dispute to an Employment Tribunal, ACAS has a statutory duty to act as a conciliator between the parties. Both parties will attempt to solve the dispute that they now find themselves in and ACAS will suggest possible ways in which the parties can achieve this outcome. In Employment Tribunal disputes, it is very common for both parties or their solicitors to use the services of ACAS in order to negotiate an out-of-court settlement. This is often a very successful process and it can avoid the necessity of the parties going to an Employment Tribunal. ACAS now provides a voluntary arbitration scheme whereby parties to a straightforward unfair dismissal claim can use this as an alternative to proceeding to an Employment Tribunal.

 Key point: Arbitration, mediation and conciliation are procedures that can be used by parties who do not wish to go court and, as an alternative, a neutral third party can be appointed to help reach an out-of-court settlement.

Arbitration Case Law

 In **Hickman _v_ Kent or Romney Marsh Sheep Breeders' Association (1915)** Hickman, a member of the Association, attempted to raise a legal action on the basis that the Association had refused to register some of the sheep that he owned. The membership rules of the Association's (its articles of association) stated that such disputes had to be resolved by an arbitration procedure. Hickman had broken the rules by raising a legal action against the Association.

Held: the court action was halted and Hickman was forced to use the internal arbitration procedure to resolve his dispute with the Association.

 In **Roxburgh _v_ Dinardo (1981)**, the partners had included an arbitration clause in their agreement which would be used in the event of any disputes arising between them in relation to the running of the business of the firm. The firm was later dissolved and some of the partners attempted to use this clause to deal with all matters in respect of the winding-up of the business. This would have meant that any partners who wished to challenge the decision of the arbiter would not be permitted to lodge a legal challenge before the courts.

Held: an arbitration clause in a partnership agreement cannot be used to oust the legitimate jurisdiction of the Scottish civil courts in matters relating to the winding up or dissolution of the firm as this would deny some of the partners the right to an effective legal remedy before a properly constituted court of law. Arbitration is a perfectly valid method for resolving disputes between the members **during** the term of the partnership agreement, but it may not be valid to resolve disputes which arise **after** the partnership agreement has been terminated.

Arbitration can even be used when a legal dispute has gone to court. In a small claims hearing in the Sheriff Court, the Sheriff will ask the parties in the dispute whether they wish to have the matter referred to an independent expert (an arbiter) whose decision in the matter is final. The Sheriff will give the litigants this choice when they meet formally for the first time in court. Once the litigants have decided that they wish to have the matter decided by an independent expert, they cannot later choose to ask the Sheriff to become involved in the case.

Arbitration reform

In June 2008, the Scottish Government introduced an Arbitration (Scotland) Bill to the Scottish Parliament. The provisions of the Bill are the result of discussions that the Scottish Parliament has had with various bodies such as the Scottish Council for International Arbitration and the Chartered Institute of Arbitrators (Scottish branch). The Bill was also greatly influenced by the work of the Scottish Advisory Committee on Arbitration Law which sat in session throughout the 1990s.

The main aim of the Bill is to attempt to have a single Act of the Scottish Parliament regulating the practice of arbitration in Scotland. Anyone in the future wishing to have a legal dispute settled by arbitration will find all the rules governing the procedure contained in a single piece of legislation. One of the criticisms of the way in which arbitration operates at the moment is that the rules are fragmented and outdated. It is hoped by modernising the law that arbitration will come to be regarded as more attractive way of resolving a variety of consumer and commercial disputes. The theory is that if more people were willing to use arbitration procedures to resolve disputes, it would be more cost effective than having the matter dealt with by a court or a tribunal and it would also remove pressure from the legal system which is currently overburdened as a result of the sheer number of cases with which it has to deal on a year in year out basis. The Scottish Government has also publicly gone on the record that it wishes to make Scotland a centre for international arbitration in the hope that individuals and businesses from overseas will make use of the proposed new rules. The business of arbitration can be very lucrative for the economy as arbitration practitioners in London would no doubt already attest.

Summary

- Since the introduction of devolution as a result of the Scotland Act 1998, Scotland now has its own Parliament in Edinburgh which has law-making powers.

- The Scottish Parliament's powers are restricted to devolved matters.

- Scots law has many influences and has evolved through the centuries through a combination of judge-made law, Parliamentary laws, European law, customs and practices and historical sources.

- The Westminster Parliament is still the supreme law-making body in the UK, despite the introduction of devolution.

- There are two types of lawyers who appear in court in Scotland; solicitors and advocates. Commercial Attorneys may also appear in Sheriff Courts for small and summary claims from 2009.

- The civil justice system mainly exists to resolve disputes between private individuals.

- The three main civil courts in increasing order of importance are the Sheriff Court, the Court of Session and the Supreme Court of the United Kingdom.

- Since 1 October 2009, the Supreme Court of the United Kingdom has replaced the House of Lords as the highest civil appeal court in Scotland.

- The criminal justice system exists to uphold law and order and to punish those individuals who commit criminal acts.

- In Scotland, there is a public system of prosecution and private prosecutions are extremely rare.

- The three main criminal courts in increasing order of importance are the Justice of the Peace Court, the Sheriff Court and the High Court of Justiciary.

- The Supreme Court of the United Kingdom can hear criminal appeals from the High Court of Justiciary when such cases involve human rights and devolution issues.

- There are a variety of alternatives to going to court in order to solve legal disputes: arbitration, conciliation, mediation.

- There are numerous alternative courts: the Employment Tribunal, the Scottish Land Court, Courts Martial, the Lands Tribunal for Scotland.

- Owing to the fact of the UK's membership of the European Union, European law is now a major source of Scots law.

- If there is a conflict between European law and Scots law, the European legal rule will be preferred.

Test your knowledge

Short answer questions, examination standard essay questions and case-studies.

1 List two sources of Scots law.

2 What is meant by the common law? Give at least two examples.

3 What is an Act of Parliament? Give five examples.

4 Describe in detail how the British Parliament makes new laws.

5 Explain the following:
 • A Government Bill
 • A Private Member's Bill

6 How is the Court of Justice organised?

7 How is the Court of First Instance organised?

8 Name the main institutions of the European Community.

9 Regarding European Law, what is meant by:
 • Primary Legislation
 • Secondary Legislation

10 Describe in detail each of the following:
 • A regulation
 • A directive
 • A decision
 • A recommendation

11 How is the European Parliament organised?

12 How is the European Commission organised?

13 How is the Council of Ministers organised?

14 List the three courts which form part of the Scottish civil court structure.

15 List the civil courts in order of importance.

16 How many Sheriffdoms are there in Scotland? Name them.

17 What is meant by the term 'jurisdiction'?

18 Describe in detail the main features of the Small Claims Procedure in the Sheriff Court.

19 How is the Sheriff Court under the civil law system organised?

20 How is the Court of Session organised?

21 What is the burden of proof required by a Scottish civil court?

22 If a Scottish criminal court seeks to punish a convicted offender, what does a Scottish civil court seek to do?

23 Name the two parties involved in a dispute before a civil court.

24 What do we call people who go to court?

25 Which judges would sit in the following courts:
 • The Sheriff Court
 • The Court of Session
 • The House of Lords

26 What type of lawyer would you need to represent you in the following courts:
 • The Sheriff Court
 • The Court of Session
 • The House of Lords

27 Who is responsible for running the Sheriff Court system?

28 Where would the following cases be dealt with?
 • A divorce
 • Tenor of a lost document
 • An appeal from a summary cause

29 Why might a pursuer choose the Sheriff Court in preference to the Outer House of the Court of Session?

30 Consider the following civil disputes. Advise the aggrieved party (the victim) about the following two issues:
 • Which civil courts have jurisdiction over the action

 • To which courts they can appeal if dissatisfied with the decision of the court of first instance

 a) John Willis is owed £10,000 by Janice Long for computer equipment delivered ten weeks ago. The agreed credit period has now expired and, despite repeated reminders, Janice Long still refuses to pay this outstanding invoice. John feels that he must now go to a court of law to resolve this dispute.

b) Agnes Pratt purchased a tumble dryer from Shockz Electrical Goods Ltd for £350. One day, two weeks later, the tumble dryer caught fire causing £150 worth of damage to her kitchen and destroyed clothes worth £200. The tumble dryer was faulty but Shockz Electrical Goods Ltd is refusing to compensate Agnes in any way. She is now considering suing them for £700.

c) As a result of a breach of contract by Jack MacDonald, Dougie Fisher has suffered a loss of £4,500. Jack has offered £500 compensation which Dougie thinks is unacceptable. Dougie has now decided to sue Jack for the full £1,000.

d) Frank bought a new television costing £799. However, after a few days, Frank discovers that his advanced flatscreen, LCD television does not work. Clearly unhappy, he takes the television back to Livewire Electric but they refuse to change it. Frank is very angry and decides to sue the shop.

e) A company called Fly-by-Night PLC has made some very stupid business decisions. As a result of this, the company has run out of money and is about to be wound-up. The company had a share capital of £5 million pounds. Jim is owed a very substantial sum of money by the company and he wishes to know which court will deal with winding up Fly-by-Night PLC.

31 Name the three Scottish Criminal Courts.

32 What is a crime?

33 What is the level of proof required by the Scottish Criminal Courts?

34 What is the difference between summary and solemn proceedings?

35 Which judges sit in the following Courts:
- The Justice of the Peace Court
- The Sheriff Court
- The High Court

36 In a criminal case, to which Court would you appeal if you had first appeared in the following Courts:
- The Justice of the Peace Court
- The Sheriff Court
- The High Court

37 List the powers of the Justice of the Peace Court.

38 List the powers of the Sheriff Summary Court.

39 List the powers of the High Court.

40 Name the Courts in which the following prosecutors will appear:
- the Procurator Fiscal
- the Advocate Depute

41 What is the name of the Government Department in Edinburgh which has responsibility for the Scottish system of public prosecution?

42 Name the three possible verdicts/decisions in a criminal court.

43 Name the Sovereign's three law officers in Scotland.

44 What punishments might a Scottish criminal judge consider imposing on someone who has been convicted of a crime as an alternative to a term of imprisonment?

45 a) What is the difference between a Police Officer's powers of arrest and detention?

b) Last week, Lyn was detained by the Police on suspicion of being in possession of Ecstasy, the Class A drug. Although Lynn was later released without charge, she wishes to know in what circumstances the Police are permitted to exercise their powers of detention. Explain these to her.

46 Jordan was charged with theft and, on the advice of his solicitor, he decided to plead not guilty to the charge. The solicitor has informed Jordan that his trial will take place under summary procedure in the Sheriff Court and there are two important stages in such trial: the intermediate diet and the trial diet. What is the purpose of the intermediate and trial diets in summary criminal proceedings?

CHAPTER 2

THE LAW OF CONTRACT

Introduction

The law of contract is one of the most important foundations of commercial and business law. The influence of contract can be found in almost every aspect of the business world, for example, employment contracts, contracts of sale, contracts of agency, contracts of partnership, company law. It is, therefore, vital that people in business have a sound grasp of basic rules of contract law.

> ### This chapter covers the following areas:
> - The definition of a contract •
> - The composition and formation of a contract •
> - The factors which affect the validity of a contract •
> - Exclusion clauses and other unfair terms •
> - The remedies available for breach of contract •
> - The ways in which a contract can be terminated •

The definition of a contract?

Basically, a contract is a legally enforceable agreement i.e. an agreement which the courts will enforce. This is an important definition because it is worth bearing in mind that there are many types of agreements that the courts will have nothing to do with. In effect, a court will wash its hands of an arrangement which it considers not to be a proper contractual agreement.

 Key point: A contract is a legally enforceable agreement between two or more legally distinct parties.

A contract centres around important matters, certainly not issues which are of a trivial nature. A number of individuals living in shared accommodation may have established a rota which sets out whose turn it is to do the cleaning, the cooking and the washing-up. On a very simple level, this rota is an agreement, but it is not a contract. If a dispute arose between the parties to this rota they most definitely could not threaten one another with legal action to enforce it. The individuals involved must sort things out for themselves. Where contracts are concerned, the courts must be convinced that a failure to comply with an agreement will very often lead to one of the parties suffering prejudice or real harm. If this is so, then it is right and proper that the courts should step in to protect the innocent party to the agreement by granting a decree in his favour.

At least two legally distinct persons must be party to a contract, for example, a buyer and a seller in a contract for the sale of goods (a bilateral agreement/contract). However, it is possible for more than two individuals to be involved in a contract, for example, partners in a firm or shareholders in a limited company (a multilateral agreement/contract).

 Key point: The law of contract relates to every sort of business activity imaginable.

The law of contract relates to everything you buy or sell. It would be a mistake to assume that the study of contracts always involves an examination of very complex documents. It is only in a number of limited situations that the law will demand that contracts should be in writing or that some sort of written evidence be produced. Admittedly, businesses will often prefer to have some sort of written contract or agreement in place, but this preference usually reflects the fact that a lot of money is at stake and businesses feel more secure if the main terms of the contract are written down. In the event of a dispute occurring in relation to the agreement, it is obviously a lot easier to prove something if you can refer to some written evidence rather than by attempting to remember what someone said six months or a year ago and even what they meant by their statements.

The composition and formation of a contract

It is often surprising to learn that forming a contract is usually a very straightforward task. In fact, people enter into many different contracts every day. You make a contract when you pay for your bus or train ticket; when you buy a newspaper or a magazine; when you buy your lunch; or when you purchase an item of clothing. A contract can be written, verbal or implied and can be proved by the production of any relevant, competent evidence including witnesses or documents in the event of dispute. A legally enforceable agreement or a contract has two basic elements – an offer and an acceptance of that offer. This can be expressed in a simple formula as:

Offer + Acceptance = Contract

 Key point: Contracts are entered into everyday and are much more common than you would expect.

However, this can be a deceptively simple formula. As we will learn later, it is absolutely crucial to be able to identify a genuine offer and to see whether this is matched by an unqualified acceptance. It is only when the offer and the acceptance are in place that we can say that a contract has been formed. However, an offer and an acceptance do not miraculously appear on the table leading automatically to a contract. In most cases, contracts will be formed only after a series of negotiations between the parties have been completed.

The formation of a contract should be regarded as more of a process rather than a one-off event. Contractual negotiations will involve the parties wheeling and dealing before one individual places a definite offer on the table which the other person may or may not want to accept.

 Key point: The main elements of a contract are the offer and the acceptance.

However, it should be re-emphasised that not all agreements are contracts. In other words, there are certain types of agreements that the Scottish courts will refuse to enforce. It is important to remember that a contract in Scots law is an agreement that the courts will enforce. Most commercial agreements, which involve the sale of goods and services, will be regarded as legally enforceable.

Unenforceable agreements

So, what are these types of agreements which the courts will refuse to enforce? They fall into several categories:

◆ Social agreements
◆ Domestic agreements
◆ Agreements binding in honour only

Let us look at each of these types of agreement in turn.

Social agreements

A social agreement would cover arrangements such as dinner invitations, an invitation to meet friends in the pub for a drink or if you were asked out on a date by someone. Should you choose to break such an arrangement, the consequences will be no more serious than upsetting or disappointing your friends. There is no way that the disappointed individual could raise a legal action against you in an attempt to recover damages for a new outfit that she had bought in anticipation of the social occasion or to pay for travel expenses which she has incurred. Simply put, social arrangements are not something with which the courts have either the inclination or the time to get involved.

Domestic agreements

Domestic agreements, on the other hand, involve arrangements that people put in place to regulate their private lives. Examples of this type of arrangement would include the way in which a married/cohabiting couple or a group of young people (students) run their household affairs. These types of agreements would cover various run-of-the-mill tasks like whose turn it was to prepare meals, to clean the dishes, to clean the house or to put the bins out the night before the weekly refuse collection. It is up to the individuals involved to determine responsibility for these tasks and certainly not the job of the courts. However, it should be stressed that married or cohabiting couples can enter into legally binding contracts with one another, but not usually where household tasks are concerned.

 An interesting example of a domestic agreement coming before the courts occurred in **Spellman v Spellman (1961)**. In this case, a husband bought a car for his wife. The marriage had been under strain and the husband's purpose in buying the car was to try and save the marriage. Unfortunately, this was a doomed gesture and the couple later split up and went their separate ways. However, the husband took the car – his argument being that as he had paid for the car he had every right to it now that the marriage was over. The wife argued that the husband was bound by his agreement to let her use the car. The court disagreed stating that the husband and wife had made a domestic agreement not a contract. Therefore, the wife could not enforce the agreement before the courts.

Agreements binding in honour only

Agreements binding in honour only involve situations where the parties clearly intend that they will not be bound by any agreement that they might choose to enter into. If one person decided to withdraw from such an arrangement, his honour or integrity might well be called into question, but the individual concerned could probably live with this knowing full well that he would not be facing any legal consequences.

 An example of an agreement binding in honour only can be seen in the case of **Rose & Frank Co _v_ J R Crompton & Bros Ltd (1924)**. Rose & Frank had the exclusive right to distribute the products of J R Crompton & Bros in the United States of America. In 1913, both parties entered into a new distribution agreement which contained the following clause:

'This arrangement is not entered into, nor is this memorandum written, as a formal or legal agreement and shall not be subject to legal jurisdiction in the law courts . . . but it is only a definite expression and record of the purpose and intention of the three parties concerned to which they each honourably pledge themselves with the fullest confidence, based upon past business with each other, that it will be carried through by each of the three parties with mutual loyalty and friendly co-operation.'

A dispute later arose when Crompton refused to supply Rose & Frank with certain of its carbon paper products for distribution in America. Rose & Frank brought a legal action against Crompton in an attempt to have the distribution agreement enforced.

Held: by the House of Lords that the agreement was not a legally binding contract and, therefore it could not be enforced in a court of law. Their Lordships were in agreement with the original trial judge (Mr Justice Bailhache) that the agreement should be viewed as an example of a gentlemen's agreement i.e. an agreement binding in honour only and that the parties had, from the outset, not intended to be bound legally by its provisions.

Gambling agreements (_sponsione ludicrae_)

Gambling agreements or _sponsione ludicrae_ (ludicrous promises) are contracts which people enter into usually by way of placing a bet on a variety of sporting events or other frivolous activities, for example, who will be the latest evictee from Channel 4's Big Brother or who will win this year's X Factor. Historically, it was often remarked that the British State was quite hypocritical in its treatment of gambling activities in that it was happy to impose a tax on punters, yet the Scottish and English courts refused to act as a referee in relation to disputes which arose out of these very same agreements. Typically, the courts regarded gambling agreements as below their dignity and not worth the waste of valuable time. In the past, those reluctant punters who refused to settle outstanding debts with a bookie often found themselves having to run from hired 'muscle' who had been engaged by the bookie to persuade them to pay up.

The hostility of the Scottish (and English) courts over the centuries to the enforcement of gambling contracts stems from the time when Christianity was a much more powerful force in society. Gambling was seen as a social evil and, in no circumstances should such activities be tolerated or promoted. By denying gamblers an effective means of enforcing these kinds of agreement, the courts were warning people that they indulged in these activities at their peril.

Two examples of the way in which gambling agreements were dealt with by the Scottish courts in the past can be seen below:

 Ferguson v Littlewoods Pools Ltd (1997), the members of a pools syndicate had won several million pounds on a football coupon – or so they thought. The syndicate was completely unaware of the fact that the agent for Littlewoods Pools had not forwarded the stake money because he had stolen it. When the theft was discovered, the syndicate members not unnaturally demanded that Littlewoods should honour the winning ticket. Littlewoods claimed that it had never received the winning ticket. In response, the syndicate members argued that Littlewoods was responsible for the actions of its dishonest agent.

Held: by Lord Coulsfield in the Outer House of the Court of Session that the contract between the syndicate and Littlewoods was an example of a gambling or gaming contract and it was, therefore, unenforceable. Lord Coulsfield refused to order Littlewoods to pay out the sum owed to the syndicate.

 Robertson v Balfour (1938) Robertson had entered into gambling agreements with Balfour, a bookie, to place bets on two horses, 'Swift and True' and 'Scotch Horse'. Both horses won their respective races, but Robertson received a mere £10 in winnings from Balfour. In fact, Balfour owed Robertson another £33 in winnings. Robertson had agreed that he would give Balfour extra time to pay him the balance.

Held: Robertson could not enforce the agreement against Balfour to pay out the additional £33. This was a gambling debt and the courts would not enforce such an agreement.

 Key point: Historically, the Scottish courts refused to enforce gambling agreements which effectively left the parties to the dispute without a remedy.

The Gambling Act 2005

As a result of Section 335 of the UK Gambling Act 2005, which came into force on 1 September 2007, the doctrine of *sponsiones ludicrae* or ludicrous promises in relation to gambling contracts has been repealed.

Section 335(1) of the Gambling Act simply states that:

'The fact that a contract relates to gambling shall not prevent its enforcement.'

This important legal reform now means that the Scottish courts will have to deal with disputes between parties to a gambling agreement and provide them with a remedy.

Section 335 of the Gambling Act is a very significant legal development which sweeps away the doctrine of *sponsiones ludicrae*. This doctrine had long been an important and well established part of the Scots Law of Contract and ensured that those individuals who become involved in gambling agreements had no effective legal remedy should a dispute arise (see, for example, **Ferguson v Littlewoods Pools (1996)** discussed above). This important reform effectively consigns cases about gambling contracts to the history books and means that such agreements will, in the future, be legally binding upon the parties.

It is little surprise that the UK Parliament introduced the Gambling Act given the current British Government's enthusiasm for Super Casinos and a greater toleration shown towards gambling activities by members of the general public.

 Key point: The UK Gambling Act 2005 now means that gambling agreements are enforceable in the Scottish courts and this important legislative reform effectively sweeps away hundreds of years of Scottish legal practice.

Gambling syndicates

Despite the previous unwillingness of the Scottish courts to provide a remedy to a party seeking to enforce a gambling agreement, agreements to split winnings between members of a gambling syndicate could be legally enforceable. This will remain the legal position in Scotland and, in many ways, the provisions of the Gambling Act 2005 will actually make it easier for members of gambling syndicates to enforce their agreements against one another should the need arise.

The Inner House of the Court of Session courts re-emphasised the legal position relating to agreements between members of a gambling syndicate in the following case:

 Robertson v Anderson (2002) both women were friends who regularly attended Bingo sessions together. On one occasion, the women travelled to the Mecca Bingo Hall in Drumchapel from their homes in Dunoon. That particular evening, Anderson enjoyed a huge win of over £100,000 (three prizes of £390, £8000 and £100,000 approximately). Robertson claimed that she was owed half of the National Prize of £100,000 – a claim that Anderson disputed. Evidence was heard which established that Robertson and Anderson had an agreement that they would share equally any money that they might win during a game of Bingo. As this case occurred before the introduction of the Gambling Act 2005, the Inner House accepted that if one of the parties had attempted to sue Mecca for payment of the winnings this action would have been unsuccessful. The question then centred around whether the agreement between Robertson and Anderson was a collateral contract and, therefore, enforceable despite the fact that it was slightly tainted by association with the main gambling contract between Anderson and Mecca.

Held: by the Inner House that Robertson could enforce the collateral contract that she had with Anderson. Collateral contracts are linked to another contract and they often give rise to a completely separate set of rights and duties. Their contract related to gaming, but it was not itself a gaming contract. The issue before the court – whether Anderson was under an obligation to share with Robertson the winnings which she received did not involve the enforcement of a gaming contract. This was the crucial difference between this case and **Ferguson *v* Littlewoods Pools Ltd** (above). In any event, the Gambling Act 2005 will mean that, in the future, members of syndicates should simply be able to have their agreements enforced without having to rely on overly technical, legal arguments about collateral contracts.

 Key point: Agreements between members of gambling syndicates regarding the sharing of any winnings are legally enforceable before the Scottish courts.

Unilateral promises or gratuitous obligations

We have already described a contract as a legally enforceable agreement between two or more legally distinct parties. The traditional model of contract in both Scotland and England anticipates that the parties will bring some form of consideration to the bargain. Consideration is best understood as meaning that in order to get the benefit of an agreement a party must do something in return or more, colloquially, 'if you scratch my back, I'll scratch yours'. The parties have rights, but they also have duties. In a contract for the sale of goods, the seller's consideration would be to deliver goods to the buyer which comply with the contract, but the reverse side of the coin is that the buyer will also have to provide consideration by paying the contract price for these goods. Admittedly, the vast majority of contracts in Scotland will be supported by some form of consideration. However, unlike the situation in England, consideration is not an essential requirement of contractual formation in Scotland.

In fact, it is possible in Scotland for one party to make a unilateral promise and be legally bound by its consequences. We might begin to understand this type of obligation by turning to the old tried and trusted saying 'my word is my bond'. The *promisor* is under a legal obligation to make good on his promise, but in contrast to the traditional model of contract the beneficiary of the promise need do nothing in return. Examples of unilateral promises would include unconditional gifts, rewards, donations and promises to keep an offer open for a specified period of time. The terms of the promise must be definite and sufficiently certain, there can be nothing vague about them as this will be fatal to a beneficiary's claim.

 Key point: In Scotland, the phrase 'my word is my bond' could apply to unilateral promises.

At first glance, a unilateral promise may have many similarities to a contract. There are clear differences:

◆ A contractual offer is not legally binding until it is accepted by the other party.

◆ A unilateral promise binds the promisor as soon as it is made – even if the promise will only be performed under certain conditions, for example, the promisor will give the beneficiary £10,000 when she completes her university education securing an upper second class Honours degree in law.

◆ Written evidence supporting the existence of unilateral promises should be provided. An exception is a unilateral promise made in the course of business where a verbal promise will be more than adequate for enforcement in the courts. Additionally, unilateral promises can be enforced where the beneficiary can prove that he acted on the strength of the promise, the promisor was aware of this and if the promise is not enforced, the beneficiary will suffer severe harm or hardship. Generally speaking, the existence of contracts can be proved without having to rely on written evidence.

◆ In many cases, the beneficiary will not even have to communicate his acceptance of the promise to the promisor. Scots law makes the assumption that no reasonable person would want to turn down the benefits of a promise, for example, the offer of a gift or a donation. A beneficiary can, of course, always reject a promise and this will mean that the promisor is no longer under a legal obligation. A beneficiary can even sue the promisor in order to compel him to make good on his promise, but Scots law does not permit the promisor to enforce a promise against the beneficiary.

 Key point: A contract consists of bilateral obligations in sense that the parties owe duties to one another, but where unilateral promises are concerned, only one person (the promisor) is duty bound to do something for the other party (the beneficiary).

Although there are clear differences between contracts and unilateral promises they are related. A unilateral promise can often be used in business by an individual in the hope that this will encourage the beneficiary to enter a contract with the promisor. If, for example, a seller of goods is attempting to encourage a potential buyer (the beneficiary) to enter a contract he might promise the interested party that he will not sell the goods to a third party for a specified period of time – until the end of business on Friday afternoon. Effectively, the beneficiary is being offered first refusal for a specified period of time. If the seller later sold the goods before the deadline has passed and the beneficiary returned before the end of business on Friday with the intention of purchasing the goods, the seller could be liable to pay compensation to the beneficiary. This will most certainly be the case, if the beneficiary can show that he has suffered a loss owing to the breach of promise; for example, he has had to go to another seller in order to buy the goods and he has had to pay more for them. As we shall see, a promise can be quite costly in Scotland.

Evidence for the proposition that the Scottish courts recognise the concept of binding unilateral promises can be found in the following cases:

 Petrie *v* Earl of Airlie (1834) in 1831, a political meeting had been held in Forfarshire to debate the Reform Bill which was currently progressing through Parliament. The Reform Bill, if given the Royal Assent, would extend the franchise in Westminster parliamentary elections to many individuals who were currently denied the right to vote (the following year the Bill was passed into law becoming the Reform Act 1832). The Earl of Airlie was in the Chair at the meeting and a vote was taken whereby the assembly was asked to approve or disapprove the Bill. The Earl was in a group that voted against the Bill, although the majority of those present voted in its favour. Some time after this meeting, notices appeared around several districts in the county which appeared to defame the Earl by suggesting that his actions at the meeting had somehow been disloyal to the King, his Government and his people. The Earl issued a proclamation stating that he would pay a reward of 100 guineas to anyone who came forward with information to reveal the identities of the people who had written and printed the notice. Such a reward would be payable on the conviction of those (as yet unknown) persons. Alexander Petrie came forward with information to say that his brother and another individual were responsible for the notice. The Earl attempted to have the two prosecuted but the Crown's law officers refused to take this matter further because no indictable offence had been committed. They informed the Earl that he had two options: he could begin a criminal action himself or he could raise a civil action for damages. The Earl chose not to prosecute the two suspects.

Held: by the Inner House of the Court of Session (affirming the judgement of the Lord Ordinary) that the Earl must pay the reward to Alexander Petrie. The Earl had obtained everything that he had asked for in his offer of the reward and he was not entitled to evade making the payment to Petrie.

 Morton's Trustee *v* Aged Christian Friend Society of Scotland (1899)
Morton had written to the Society agreeing to pay the pensions of 50 individuals selected by the Society for the remainder of their lives. Unfortunately, Morton died and the executors of his estate were unwilling to continue paying out the pensions to the 50 individuals. The Society claimed that Morton's promise had bound his estate, even in death.

Held: Morton had made an enforceable unilateral promise which continued to have legal effect after his death. His executors would have to continue to pay the life pensions until every one of the 50 individuals died. This, of course, could mean that a considerable period of time might pass before the consequences of the promise were fulfilled.

 Littlejohn *v* Hawden (1882) Lord Fraser (in the Outer House of the Court of Session) made the point that, if an offeror made a unilateral promise to keep an offer open for a certain period of time, for example, ten days from the date of the original offer, he cannot withdraw it until this period of time has passed. If he does so, he will run the risk of the offeree raising an action against him for breach of promise. Clearly, in such a situation, there will be no contract as the offeror has taken steps to withdraw the offer before the offeree has had an opportunity to accept it. Should the offeror honour his promise, the offer will lapse when the period for acceptance has passed and the offeror has failed to take advantage of this opportunity.

A & G Paterson *v* Highland Railway Co 1927 Viscount Dunedin, speaking obiter in the House of Lords, expressly approved Lord Fraser's approach to the question of unilateral promises in Scots law:

'... *if I offer my property to a certain person at a certain price, and go on to say: 'This offer is to be open up to a certain date,' I cannot withdraw that offer before that date, if the person to whom I made the offer chooses to accept it. It would be different in England, for ... there would be no consideration for the promise to keep the offer open.'*

 Key point: Unilateral promises in Scotland are capable of being legally enforced.

The offer

An offer must be a precise and definite proposal. Anything that lacks certainty or specifics cannot be regarded as an offer. An offer must be capable of being accepted by the person to whom it is properly addressed or communicated. An area of difficulty often arises when it comes to determining whether a definite offer exists which is capable of being accepted. An offer demonstrates that the *offeror* intends to be legally bound by the consequences of his/her undertaking if it is accepted in an unqualified fashion as the following example demonstrates:

Brian: 'I will sell my stereo to you for £700.'

Valerie: 'It's a deal!'

An offer must be sufficiently definite in its terms.

 Harvela Investments Ltd *v* Royal Trust Company of Canada Ltd [1985] the House of Lords refused to permit the practice of referential bidding by an offeror. This practice would have allowed an offeror to contact the offeree and submit a bid say of £10,000, but he could then add the following proviso: 'or £5,000 over and above any other offer that you receive.' In **Harvela Investments**, Harvela and Sir Leonard Outerbridge were locked in a battle to take control of Harvey & Co Ltd. Harvela offered to purchase shares in Harvey for 2,175,000 Canadian dollars, whereas Sir Leonard Outerbridge made an offer to purchase shares in Harvey in the following terms: '2,100,000 Canadian dollars or 100,000 Canadian dollars in excess of any other offer'.

Held: by the House of Lords that Sir Leonard Outerbridge had not submitted a valid offer because its terms were not definite enough.

 Key point: An offer must be a precise and definite proposal.

An offer can be made to one person, a group of persons or to the world at large (for example, an automatic vending machine).

An invitation to treat

It can often be problematic when it becomes necessary to be able to tell the difference between an offer and an invitation to treat. It is important to distinguish between an offer and other representations or statements that, at first glance, appear to resemble offers. However, invitations to treat can be refused therefore resulting in a binding contract not being formed. A statement which merely suggests a willingness to negotiate or to consider offers is referred to as an invitation to treat. An invitation to treat can most effectively be explained with reference to the phrase 'make me an offer which I may or may not accept'. An alleged offer may be little more than a mere price indication.

 Key point: It is important to distinguish between an offer and other representations or statements made by someone which amount to an invitation to treat i.e. 'make me an offer'.

Examples of invitations to treat include the following situations:

◆ Goods or services which are advertised in newspapers, trade journals, catalogues and on the Internet
◆ Goods displayed in shop windows and on the shelves
◆ Price lists
◆ Goods at auctions
◆ Company prospectuses/adverts in connection with sale of securities

If you make an offer to someone, you are indicating by words, writing or by your actions that you are willing to be bound on certain terms and should these terms be accepted by another person, both of you will be locked into a legally enforceable agreement. Therefore, once your offer has been accepted and an agreement has been formed, the consequences of withdrawing from a contract can be potentially serious. If, for example, after having had your offer accepted by another individual, you wished to withdraw from it, it is highly likely that you would face a legal action for breach of contract. In most cases, this would mean that you would have to pay damages or compensation to the innocent party as a direct result of your breach of contract. In other situations, the court may force you to comply with the original terms of your offer.

 Key point: If a person makes a definite offer which is subsequently accepted by another person, a legally enforceable contract now exists between these two parties.

The acceptance of an offer will only result in a binding contract if it corresponds exactly to the essential terms of the offer. The terms of the acceptance must be identical to the original offer. Any attempt by the offeree to change the terms of the offer will mean that no contract is formed. Even simple misunderstandings between the parties can mean that no contract is formed. The parties must show that they have achieved a meeting of minds or, as expressed in the old Latin phrase, *consensus in idem*.

 Key point: The offeree is the person or party to whom the offeror makes an offer.

A good illustration of a failure to achieve a meeting of minds can be seen in the following case:

 Mathieson Gee (Ayrshire) Ltd *v* Quigley (1952) Mathieson Gee wrote to Quigley stating that they could supply mechanical equipment for the purpose of removing mould which was deposited at the bottom of Quigley's pond. Quigley responded in writing by saying that he was confirming his verbal acceptance of Mathieson Gee's offer to remove the silt and deposit from his pond. However, had both parties actually managed to conclude a contract? In other words was there a meeting of minds or agreement? Mathieson Gee had made an offer to supply equipment to Quigley to carry out the job in question – they had not offered to supply the equipment and carry out the job. Quigley had mistakenly assumed that Mathieson Gee were offering to supply both the equipment and remove the silt from his pond. The parties were, therefore, completely at cross-purposes.

Held: By the House of Lords that there was no contract between them because they were not in agreement about the same things i.e. the offer and acceptance did not mirror one another.

An offer may be communicated to an individual, a group of people or to the world at large.

Carlill *v* Carbolic Smokeball Co (1893) demonstrates an offer being made to the world at large, which Mrs Carlill impliedly accepted by purchasing the product and following the instructions to the letter. The manufacturers of the carbolic smokeball were so confident of its properties that they stated in advertisements (in various newspapers) that they would pay £100 to anyone who bought the smokeball, used it according to the strict instructions and still caught flu. They added that they had deposited £1000 in the Alliance bank to show sincerity in the matter. Mrs Carlill bought the product, followed the instructions, but still caught flu. It was held that the wording of the advert was such that it amounted to an offer. There was a clear intention that the company intended to be bound by the offer. Mrs Carlill accepted the offer by performing the actions required by the advert. Mrs Carlill was therefore entitled to the money. This case illustrates that there can be implied acceptance of an offer. It also emphasises the importance of communication of the offer. If Mrs Carlill merely chanced to buy a smokeball without having seen the advert, she would not have been entitled to the £100. Her actions constituted implied acceptance of the offer because it was in response to the offer. Offers must be definite, capable of being accepted and the offeror must intend to be bound by the consequences of it being accepted.

Hunter *v* General Accident Fire and Life Assurance Corporation Ltd (1909) Mr Hunter responded to an advertisement in a Lett's diary on 25 December 1905. The advertisement was offering up to £1,000 in insurance cover for those individuals who were killed in a train accident. A condition of the advertisement was that all applicants had to ensure that their names were registered at the company's head office. A further condition of the advertisement was that any claim made under the policy must relate to a fatal accident which occurred within one year of each applicant's registration. On the event of death, £1,000 would be paid to the deceased's executor. Hunter received a letter from the insurers dated 3 January 1906 which contained an official confirmation of his registration dated 29 December

1905. On 28 December 1906, Hunter was seriously injured in a rail accident and he died of his injuries the next day. His wife, who was executrix, lodged a claim for £1,000 in accordance with the terms of the policy on 2 January 1907. The company refused to pay this sum to her. It claimed that Hunter had been accepted for the policy on 27 December 1905. If this was the case, then Mrs Hunter's claim was several days too late as it fell outside the period of one year in which any claim should have been lodged.

Held: by the House of Lords that the company could not prove with any certainty when it had actually registered the deceased. The date of 3 January 1906 was to be regarded as the date upon which registration became effective and this meant that Hunter's wife had brought the claim within one year of his registration. The company failed to prove when registration had actually taken place and it, if anyone, should have been able to pinpoint this date exactly. Mrs Hunter was, therefore, entitled to enforce the policy. Lord Loreburn, the Lord Chancellor, made the point that every judge who had considered the case thought that the advertisement was an offer which had been accepted by every individual, including Hunter, who managed to comply with its conditions. During consideration of the case in the Court of Session, Lord Kinnear stated:

'It is suggested that this is making a contract by an advertisement, but it is none the worse for being an advertisement if it is a distinct and definite offer capable of acceptance.'

 Key point: Offers can be communicated either to a single person, to a group of people or to the world at large.

The offer and an invitation to treat contrasted

The contrast between invitations to treat and offers can clearly be seen in:

 Harvey *v* Facey (1893) The legal issue in this case centred around whether the parties had concluded a contract of sale for an estate in Jamaica or whether they were still in a state of negotiation. Events began with the pursuer contacting the defender by telegram and posed the following question: "Will you sell us Bumper Hall Pen? Telegraph lowest cash price." Bumper Hall Pen was the name of the estate in Jamaica that the pursuer was interested in purchasing. The defender duly obliged the pursuer's request for information by sending a telegram in reply which stated: "Lowest price for Bumper Hall Pen £900." The pursuer thought that this reply was a definite offer from the defender and sent an 'acceptance' in the following terms: "We agree to buy Bumper Hall Pen for £900 asked by you. Please send us your title deeds in order that we get early possession." Rather ominously the defender did not respond to this 'acceptance' by the pursuer and it soon became apparent that the defender was disputing the existence of a contract of sale. As far as the defender was concerned its response to the pursuer's first telegram was a mere invitation to treat and not a definite offer. In other words, if the pursuer wished to be regarded as a serious contender to buy the property, an offer greater than £900 would have to be made. All that the defender was indicating was the lowest cash price that it would consider selling the property for. The Supreme Court of Jamaica, however, decided the case in favour of the pursuers. The defender then appealed to the Privy Council in London.

Held: by the Privy Council that the parties had failed to conclude a binding contract. The defender's response to the pursuer's original enquiry was merely a response providing the desired information about the estate. The defender had made an invitation to treat i.e. make me an offer which must be at least £900 or above if you want to be regarded as a having a serious chance of purchasing the estate. As far the defender was concerned, their telegram was alerting the pursuer to the fact that they would not even consider offers under £900. The Privy Council stated that the pursuer had made an offer to buy the estate for £900 which the defender had quite clearly refused to consider.

Another situation where it is important to know the difference between an offer and an invitation to treat is where goods are sold at auction:

 Fenwick v Macdonald, Fraser & Co Ltd (1904) the pursuer made a bid for a bull that was part of a herd of cattle being sold at auction. In the auctioneer's catalogue, the cattle were described as being "offered for unreserved sale". The pursuer, in common with the other bidders, thought that this phrase meant that the owners had not placed a reserve price on the bull. There was certainly no mention made of any reserve price in relation to the sale of the animal. If a reserve price has been placed on goods by the owner, the auctioneer has absolutely no authority to sell for anything less than this. The owners of the bull decided to withdraw the animal from the auction on the grounds that a reserve price of 150 guineas had not been met by any of the bidders, including the pursuer. The pursuer sued for breach of contract.

Held: by the Inner House of the Court of Session that there was no contract. Lord MacDonald, the Lord Justice Clerk, stated that:

'Whatever might have been the law formerly, the law of Scotland is now that a sale by auction is complete when the auctioneer announces its completion by the fall of the hammer or in other customary manner. Until such announcement is made, any bidder may retract his bid.'

The judges of the Second Division then went on to consider whether a seller could withdraw his property for sale before the fall of the auctioneer's hammer. The seller, by putting goods up for auction, was making an invitation to treat and, by withdrawing the bull from auction, he was indicating that none of the offers was acceptable to him. Interestingly, the Court of Session did appear to suggest that the law of Scotland, before the introduction of the Sale of Goods Act 1893, would not always have permitted the seller to withdraw from the auction in similar circumstances.

 Jaeger Brothers Ltd *v* J & A McMorland (1902) the pursuers were in the market to purchase a quantity of iron which they intended to ship to Australia. They contacted the defenders and made enquiries regarding the prices of 500-600 tons of iron of various specifications. They stressed the urgency of a response from the defenders to their enquiries. The pursuers were anxious to confirm to their Australian business associates that they had managed to secure the iron and they wished to send notification of this by telegram to Australia the following day. The defenders replied the next day by telegram stating:

"Offer 600 tons half one, half three, Govan, Leith, 75s 9d; c.i.f. Hamburg 80s 9d."

The terms "half one" and "half three" referred to the specification of the goods and the amount i.e. the consignment was to consist of two different types of goods. The term c.i.f. meant the defenders would bear responsibility for all aspects of shipping the goods Hamburg i.e. the cost, insurance and freight to – obviously for an increased price. If the pursuers were not interested in this arrangement, a lower price was payable.

The pursuers replied accepting the "offer" to supply 500 tons of the iron (half one and half three) for shipment from Govan on c.i.f. terms to Hamburg. A disagreement emerged later between the parties as to the date of delivery. The defenders stated that no contract had actually been formed as their response to the pursuers' original enquiry was a mere quote expressed in general terms and could not be considered as an offer capable of acceptance.

Held: by the Inner House of the Court of Session that the pursuers' original letter addressed to the defenders was in the manner of an invitation to treat i.e. make us an offer. Unfortunately, the defenders had responded to this enquiry in a very precise fashion and they had conveyed an offer to the pursuers by telegram. They had offered the pursuers two options: either delivery of a specific quantity of iron placed aboard a ship of the pursuers' choice at Govan or Leith for a specific price or delivery of a specific quantity of iron to Hamburg at a specific price. The pursuers, of course, had accepted the second offer. The pursuers' acceptance of the defenders' offer had resulted in the formation of a contract.

Contrary to popular opinion, advertisements displayed in newspapers, magazines, trade journals and on the internet are not offers, but are regarded as invitations to treat. The offer is to be made by the consumer in response to the advertisement. The advertiser is at liberty to accept or decline any offers potential customers might choose to make. An invitation to treat can take the following forms: goods in a shop window display, on a shop shelf or in a catalogue, goods exposed for sale at an auction. The offer can be made by taking goods to the cash desk or requesting them from the shop assistant, it is then up to the advertiser or the shop assistant to decide whether to accept or refuse the offer. A shop assistant does not have to give a customer a reason for refusing to accept an offer and is not bound by the marked price on the goods. If, for instance, you happen to be under 18 years of age and you attempt to purchase alcohol from your local supermarket, the assistant will be well within her rights to refuse to accept your offer to purchase the goods.

 Pharmaceutical Society of Great Britain *v* Boots Cash Chemists (1953) the judges helpfully distinguished between an invitation to treat and an offer. The case arose as a result of a provision of the Pharmacy and Poisons Act 1933, which stipulated that the sale of certain medicines must take place within the presence of a registered pharmacist. Boots operated a self-service system whereby customers were able to place medicines that they wished to purchase in their shopping baskets. The customers would then take the medicines to the cash register in order to pay for them. The essence of the case centred around the issue of when the sale actually took place. Was the display of goods an 'offer' in the legal sense or merely an invitation to treat? If it was an offer then, on the selection of goods (articles are put in a basket) a contract would be formed and the sale would be unlawful under the Act because a pharmacist was not present at that time. However, if the display of goods was merely an invitation to treat, customers would have to make an offer to buy at the cash desk, at which point the pharmacist would accept the offer or would be present to supervise the salesperson, a contract would be formed and the sale would therefore be properly supervised and, thus, comply with the provisions of the Act.

This case established that placing goods on display in shops does not constitute an offer to sell those goods – it is merely an invitation to treat. This is why an advance indication of the price of goods or services, by notice, labelling or price tickets, is a non-binding estimate. Such advance notifications are quotations or simply an expression of a willingness to negotiate.

This may seem like a clever legal distinction which is more apparent than real, but the outcome of some cases has turned on whether a trader has been making an invitation to treat or an offer. We can see how this distinction operates in the following English High Court case:

 Fisher *v* Bell (1961) a flick-knife with a price label on it was displayed in a shop window. The shopkeeper was charged with the offence of offering such a knife for sale. He was found not guilty. Lord Parker CJ said:

'It is clear that, according to the ordinary law of contract, the display of an article with a price on it in a shop window is merely an invitation to treat. It is in no sense an offer for sale, the acceptance of which constitutes a contract.'

 Key point: An invitation to treat could take the from of an advertisement, catalogue, brochure, price list or quotation and is a means by which sellers alert potential buyers to the existence of certain goods services. It will then be up to these buyers to make an offer to purchase these goods and services which the seller may or may not accept.

Under the criminal law, a shop which has wrongly or mistakenly displayed misleading prices would fall foul of the provision of the Consumer Protection from Unfair Trading Regulations 2008 (see Chapter 4). However, the aggrieved consumer will still not be entitled to receive the goods at the (wrongly) marked price because it is the consumer who is making the offer to the shop – an offer which the shop has rejected and it follows that there can be no contract.

Other situations

What about vending machines? We could take the view that the machine is making an implied offer to the world and when an individual places his/her money in the machine s/he has accepted that offer. Therefore, we have a contract.

In **Thornton *v* Shoe Lane Parking (1971)** the Court of Appeal stated that the ticket machine at the entrance to the car park represented an offer to the world at large which was capable of being accepted by members of the public. Acceptance of this offer became a reality when an individual approached the machine and took the issued ticket. Lord Denning said:

'The customer pays his money and gets a ticket. He cannot refuse it. He cannot get his money back. He may protest to the machine, even swear at it; but it will remain unmoved. He is committed beyond recall... The contract was concluded at that time. It can be translated into offer and acceptance in this way. The offer is made when the proprietor of the machine holds it out as being ready to receive money. The acceptance takes place when the customer puts his money into the slot. The terms of the offer are contained in the notice placed on or near the machine stating what is offered for the money. The customer is bound by those terms if they are sufficiently brought to his notice beforehand, but not otherwise. He is not bound by the terms printed on the ticket if they differ from the notice, because the ticket comes too late.'

Withdrawal or revocation of offer

An offer can be cancelled at any time *before* it is accepted. In Scotland, the exception to this rule would cover a situation whereby the offeror has made a unilateral promise to potential offerees to the effect that he will keep the offer open for a specified period of time, for example, that the offer will remain valid until noon on Friday. If no one has accepted the offer by noon on the Friday, the offeror is quite free to withdraw it, but not before this (self-imposed) deadline. Once it has been accepted, an offer cannot be withdrawn and this will be the case even if the offeror has made a mistake in the terms of the offer as can be seen in the following case:

 Centrovincial Estates PLC *v* Merchant Investors Assurance (1983) a firm of solicitors, acting for a property letting company, had communicated a definite offer to the effect that their clients were willing to rent offices to potential tenants for the sum of £65,000 per year. The offerees promptly accepted this offer of the tenancy at the stated rent. However, in what turned out to be an extremely costly mistake, the solicitors realised that the landlord wished to charge the tenants a sum of £126,000 for the yearly rent. The solicitors then telephoned the tenants and invited them to regard the terms of the original offer as changed to reflect the true position of their clients. Understandably quite happy with the outcome of the negotiations, the tenants refused to take this request seriously. The landlord then attempted to have the contract with their new tenants cancelled by reason of the unilateral mistake contained in the original letter of offer.

Held: by the English Court of Appeal that a binding contract had been formed. The tenants would get the benefit of the tenancy for a very favourable price. Unfortunately for the landlord, it had learned a very harsh lesson in the sense that the law did not protect it from the consequences of its own stupidity when it made an exceptionally bad bargain with the new tenants. It should be stressed that the tenants were completely unaware of the landlord's error and that they had acted in good faith when accepting what they regarded as a very favourable offer. Had the tenants known that the landlord had made such a serious error then the case would have had a very different outcome. As something of a consolation, the landlord would have a claim for damages against the solicitors as a result of their negligence.

If the offeree knows that the offeror is mistaken, the contract may be void on the grounds of unilateral mistake.

 The Scottish case of **Krupp v John Menzies Ltd (1907 SC 903)** stands in stark contrast to the decision of the English Court of Appeal in **Centrovincial Estates** (above). In **Krupp**, the parties had already made a verbal agreement that the employee, the manageress of the Mallaig Station Hotel, would receive a salary representing 5% of the profits of the business. When this agreement was formalised, the written contract contained a clerical error which stated that the employee's salary was to be 20% of the profits of the business. This, of course, was a considerably more attractive salary than the employee had originally anticipated. The employee knew that this calculation in the written contract was completely in error, but it did not prevent her from attempting to enforce this much more favourable agreement in preference to the original, verbal agreement.

Held: the Court of Session permitted the employer to have the written contract changed to reflect the true contractual position which the original verbal agreement represented. The difference between this case and the **Centrovincial Estates** decision was that the hotel manageress was not acting in good faith – she was fully aware of the clerical error in the written document. As we shall see later in this chapter, the Contract (Scotland) Act 1997 allows additional external sources of information (for example, verbal statements or documentary evidence) to be used in court in order to give true expression to the parties' intentions in a written contract. Generally speaking, of course, the 1997 Act takes the position that a written document will contain all the main terms of the agreement.

 Key point: Generally, an offer can be withdrawn at any time by the offeror (unless he has promised to keep it open for a specified time) before it can be accepted by the offeree.

How can the offeror effectively cancel any offer that he has made?

Such an intention on the part of the offeror must be communicated to the offeree before the offer can be accepted. Effective communication of a change in the offeror's intention to be bound by the offeror merely implies that the offeree has some knowledge that the offer is no longer valid. Presumably, the offeree cannot turn a blind eye to facts which strongly suggest that the offeror has had second thoughts and now intends to cancel the offer such as failure by the offeree to open a letter with the offeror's name and address stamped on the rear of the envelope.

Communication of an intention to withdraw the offer may be made to the offeree by the offeror or via some other reliable source, for example, the offeror's agent (a solicitor).

 Key point: When the offeror decides to withdraw or cancel his offer, he must communicate this decision effectively to the offeree or his agent.

The effect of the death of one of the parties

Does the death of one of the parties affect the creation of a contract or, perhaps more ghoulishly, is it possible to contract with the dead? The answer to this question would seem to depend on whether the death occurred before or after acceptance of the offer.

Death of the offeror before acceptance

The Scottish position, according to Viscount Stair and Professor Bell, concerning the death of the offeror is very clear. Generally speaking, if the offeree has not accepted the offer at the time of the death of the offeror, then no contract is formed. In other words, the offer terminates automatically upon the death of the offeror. Interestingly, the position in England is slightly less clear and it has been argued that an offer does not automatically lapse on the event of the offeror's death. English law seems to take the view that, when a contract does not require a high degree of personal involvement of the offeror, for example, when it is not an employment contract or a contract for services, death may not necessarily be a barrier to the creation of a legally enforceable agreement. If we follow this logic, then it would be possible for the estate of the deceased to be bound in contract to the offeree for the sale of land. However, this theory sits very much at odds with statements made by an English Court of Appeal judge, Lord Justice Mellish, in **Dickinson v Dodds (1876)**. His Lordship was overwhelmingly hostile to the idea that that an offer does not necessarily cease to be capable of acceptance when the offeror dies. The obiter statement of Lord Justice Mellish reflects Scots law: the offer cannot be accepted after the offeror's death.

Death of an offeree before acceptance

If the offeree has not accepted the offer prior to his death, the parties have clearly failed to enter into a contractual relationship. It is very important to stress that an executor of the deceased offeree does not have the authority to accept the offer. The operation of this rule is not dependant upon the nature of the proposed contract. Quite simply, the offeree failed to accept the offer when he was alive, there is no chance of him accepting it now that he is dead. In the English decision of **Reynolds v Atherton (1922)**, Lord Justice Warrington in the Court of Appeal stated that the death of the offeree terminates the offer and not even his executor will have the authority to accept it on his behalf.

Interestingly, a case from Canada determined by the Appellate Division of the Supreme Court of Ontario considered the issue of the effect of the offeree's death before any acceptance of any offer had been made.

 Re Irvine (1928), it was held that a son had no authority to accept an offer on behalf of his deceased father. Apparently, the deceased had written a letter of acceptance in response to a offer. He asked his son to post this letter, but before the son was able to do this, the father died. Nevertheless, the son decided to post the letter despite the fact of his father's death.

Held: Sensibly, the Supreme Court of Ontario stated that no contract had been created. The offer had been personally addressed to the deceased and it ceased to have any legal effect upon his death. The offer could not be accepted by anyone other than the deceased.

There may, however, be an exception to this rule that the death of the offeree means that the offer is no longer capable of acceptance. There may be an enforceable contract in circumstances, where an agent has concluded a contract with a third party and who is completely unaware that his principal has died before the conclusion of this agreement. Such a rule was deemed to be sensible in the absence of modern and instantaneous methods of communications (see **Campbell v Anderson (1829) in Chapter 5**). It was not unusual for the principal to die in Scotland and it might take many months before this news reached his agent in, for example, Australia. It will, of course, be appreciated that, as the personal representative of the principal, the agent may have accepted many offers on the principal's behalf before news of the death reached him. Even with the advent of modern communications, this exception to the general rule may still have its uses.

 Key point: In Scots law, it would appear that the death of either the offeror or the offeree before the offer can be accepted will mean that no contract is formed as the offer lapses automatically.

Death of the parties after acceptance

Obviously, if an offer has been accepted prior to the death of one of the parties, this is a completely different situation. As Viscount Stair, one of Scotland's institutional writers, remarked: 'An offer accepted is a contract.' From this statement it is possible to find support for the notion that the death of either the offeror or the offeree would have no effect unless, of course, the contract involved the provision of personal services, for example, an employment contract or a contract of agency. What about the sale of heritable or moveable property? Such a contract should still be enforceable in Scotland. As we have seen in the case of **Mortons Trustees v Aged Christian Friend Society of Scotland (1899)** (above), a unilateral promise to provide 50 life pensions continued to be binding and the death of the promisor mattered not one bit.

Lapse of an offer

An offer will no longer be capable of acceptance in the following circumstances:

◆ If it is rejected
◆ If the other party makes a counter-offer
◆ If a time limit for acceptance fixed by the offeror expires
◆ If the subject-matter of the contract is destroyed or materially altered
◆ If the proposed contract becomes illegal or otherwise becomes impossible to perform
◆ If either party dies or the offeror becomes insane or pronounced bankrupt
◆ If the offer is not accepted within a reasonable time

 Key point: An offer will be deemed to be no longer capable of acceptance in the following circumstances – if it is rejected, if it is the subject of a counter-offer, expiry of the time-limit for acceptance, if the subject matter of the contract is destroyed or materially altered, if the proposed contract becomes illegal, if either party dies, becomes insane or is declared bankrupt or if it is not accepted within a reasonable time.

The offer is not accepted within a reasonable time

An offer which is not accepted within a reasonable time is presumed to lapse. Simply put, offers have a limited shelf-life. They do not last forever. It would be quite absurd, if the offeror was placed in a position whereby he could be bound by the consequences of an offer which he made ten years previously which the offeree now wishes to accept. This, of course, is an extreme example and some offers will have an extremely short life. A reasonable time may vary on the circumstances of the case, the nature of the transaction and the nature of the market which the parties are operating in. The phrase 'a reasonable time' means different things in different situations and, therefore, it will be a matter for the court to determine what constitutes a reasonable time.

Offers involving perishable goods or commodities, for example, agricultural produce, oil and precious metals that tend to suffer fluctuating market prices will clearly leave the offeree with a shorter time to decide whether to accept such an offer than offers for goods or services which tend to experience less volatile price movements. An example of this situation can be seen in the following two cases:

 Wylie and Lochhead *v* McElroy and Sons (1873) an offer to carry out work which involved fitting iron decorative work on stables was not accepted for five weeks. During this time the price of iron increased significantly. By this time, the offeree had decided to accept the original offer at the much lower price. The offeror argued that the original offer was no longer capable of being accepted. A dispute ensued. It was held that because there had been no acceptance within a reasonable time the offer had been impliedly withdrawn and no contract was formed. The court took the view that where such a commodity as iron was concerned with its tendency to experience price fluctuations 'hours must suffice for a decision, not weeks or months'.

 Glasgow Steam Shipping Company *v* Watson (1873) Watson, the defender, had made an offer to the Glasgow Shipping Company, the pursuers, to supply coal to them for the period of a year and the price was to be based on seven shillings per ton. The defender made this offer on 5 August, but the pursuers did not accept it until 13 October. By this point, the price of coal had risen considerably to nine shillings per ton. The defender refused to supply the coal at the price stated on 5 August claiming that a reasonable time for acceptance of that offer had passed. If the pursuers wished to purchase the coal, they would have to do so at the higher price. The pursuers raised an action for breach of contract. The dispute arose because the defender had not laid down a time-limit for acceptance of the offer and this situation made it possible for the pursuers to argue that they were acting well within a reasonable time-limit when they eventually communicated their acceptance in response to the offer of 5 August.

Held: there was no contract as the defenders had failed to accept the offer within a reasonable time frame. Lord Deas made a memorable statement in the following terms:

'But as regards such an offer as this, to supply an article which at all times fluctuates in price, and which at the time in question was rapidly

rising in price, it is altogether out of the question to hold it to have been a continuing offer for so long a period as is here contended for. . .'

The above cases of **Wylie and Lochhead** and **Glasgow Steam Shipping Company** clearly demonstrate that an offeree will not be permitted to keep the offeror hanging on until the last possible moment when he finally decides whether or not to accept the offer. If this situation was tolerated by the courts, an offeree would have an unfair advantage whereby he could watch price movements in the relevant market. If the price increases in value substantially, the offeree would be able to hold the offeror to the contract price which was originally quoted. On the other hand, if the value of the goods decreases significantly, the offeree could demand that the price be completely renegotiated. There is, of course, a very simple way in which the offeror could avoid disputes surrounding the issue of what is a reasonable time for acceptance of his offer. He could state a time for acceptance of the offer, for example, 'Your acceptance of this offer must be in our hands by 5 p.m. on Friday 16 January'.

 Key point: Where the offer does not state a time-limit for acceptance, the offeree must accept it within a reasonable time and what is a reasonable time will depend on the circumstances of each case.

Acceptance

Acceptance of the offer means that a contract has been formed. Once an offer is said to exist, the court must be satisfied that it has actually been accepted, otherwise no contract has been created. Acceptance of an offer is an expression by the offeree of his willingness to bind himself legally to a contract with the offeror with the conditions stated in the offer.

 Key point: Acceptance of an offer means that a contract has been formed.

For an acceptance to result in a legally binding contract it must correspond exactly to the essential terms of the offer. *Consensus in idem* or 'a meeting of minds' must be said to have been achieved. Therefore to achieve *consensus in idem*, acceptance by the offeree must be of a completely unconditional nature. An acceptance will not be deemed to be valid if it does not mirror all the essential terms of the offer. If an acceptance includes terms which are not contained in the offer, it is said to be a conditional acceptance. This is viewed as a completely new offer which must subsequently be accepted in order for a contract to come into existence.

 Key point: The acceptance of an offer must be a mirror image of the terms of the offer.

Such a qualified acceptance will not bind the offeror and, thus, form a contract. Any response to an offer which seeks to adapt in any way or add to the conditions of the original offer, must be regarded as a counteroffer. A counteroffer cancels the original offer and no subsequent acceptance of the original terms will be effective. An acceptance is only valid when it has been effectively communicated to the offeror.

 Key point: Acceptance is only valid when it has been effectively communicated to the offeror.

Communication of an acceptance

This could take the form of writing, verbal acceptance or by implication (for example, the fall of an auctioneer's hammer). The acceptance must comply with any requirements of the offer as to the mode of acceptance, for example, the offer may state that acceptance should be made in writing or telephone. Accepting a sum of money in response to an offer to buy, dispatching goods, issuing a ticket or putting a coin in a slot machine are all actions which are regarded as acceptance by performance. In Scots law, if the offeror fails to stipulate a particular method of communication, then the manner of acceptance must be effective and usually follows the same manner as the offer.

The offer can then only be accepted by a person to whom it is addressed. Acceptance must be communicated by a person generally authorised to do this.

 Powell *v* Lee (1908) Powell applied for the post of Head Master of The Cranford School. The managers of the school considered Powell's offer and decided to appoint him by three votes to two. Powell successfully beat off competition for the post from two other candidates. In what proved to be an important decision, the managers chose not to communicate their acceptance of the offer immediately to Powell. In fact, no decision had been taken as to how the results of the selection process were to be communicated to the successful applicant. Dismore, one of the managers, informed Powell that his application had been successful – this statement was, of course, completely truthful. However, Dismore, had no actual or ostensible authority to release this information to Powell (**see Chapter 5 for an explanation of an agent's authority**). The managers later changed their earlier decision to select Powell as Head Master and decided to appoint one of the previously unsuccessful candidates in his place. Powell sued the managers for breach of contract.

Held: by the King's Bench Division of the English High Court that Powell's claim for breach of contract should be dismissed. At no time had Dismore been given authority to inform Powell of the managment's decision. The statement that Powell had been accepted for the position of Head Master was, therefore, completely unauthorised and did not bind the managers into a contract with him.

 Burr *v* Commissioners of Bo'ness (1896) an employee received information through unofficial sources that his employer had decided to increase his annual salary from £10 to £20. This increase was never officially communicated to the employee. About a month after making the initial decision to increase the employee's salary, the employer decided not to proceed with this. The employee sued for the increased salary.

Held: by the Inner House of the Court of Session that the employee was not entitled to the increase because his employers had not communicated this decision to him.

 Key point: An offer must be accepted by the offeree, the person to whom it is addressed, or someone who is authorised to act on his behalf (an agent) for this purpose.

An offer may, however, be addressed to the world at large or to members of the public (see **Carlill _v_ Carbolic Smokeball Company (1893)** or **Thornton _v_ Shoe Lane Parking (1971)**).

The offer cannot state that silence shall be taken as an acceptance. It is unacceptable that the offeree should have to go to the effort of expressly refusing an offer. Silence on the part of the offeree, therefore, cannot usually be regarded as a valid means of communicating acceptance.

 Felthouse _v_ Bindley (1862) the pursuer had been negotiating to purchase his nephew's horse and there had been problems regarding the price to be paid. Eventually, the pursuer wrote to his nephew stating that if he did not hear anything from him then the pursuer would consider the horse as his for the price specified in the letter. The nephew did not reply, but he wished to sell the horse to his uncle and for this purpose he instructed his auctioneer not to sell the horse. The auctioneer, however, inadvertently sold the horse. The uncle sued the auctioneer basing his claim on the fact that his nephew had sold the horse to him and, therefore, the auctioneer had wrongly sold his property.

Held: the action failed because although the nephew wished to sell to his uncle he had not communicated this fact. There was no contract between uncle and nephew.

Admittedly, in the case of **Carlill _v_ Carbolic Smokeball Company (1893)** (above), Mrs Carlill did not reply to the Smokeball Company personally and communicate her intention to accept the offer, but her actions in responding to the advert by buying the product and using it according to the instructions were taken by the court as implied acceptance of the Company's offer.

The common law rule in **Felthouse _v_ Bindley** provides an element of protection against the practice of inertia selling where goods are delivered to potential customers who have not requested delivery.

 Key point: An offeror cannot insist that the offeree's silence can indicate that he has accepted the offer as acceptance must consist of either positive words or behaviour.

Previously, the Unsolicited Goods and Services Acts 1971 and 1975 went a long way to prevent these kinds of trade practices. The Acts put in place a system of fines which were imposed on unscrupulous traders who made demands for payment of goods which were unsolicited i.e. they had not been requested by the people who received the goods. If a demand for payment for the unsolicited goods/services was accompanied by threats, a higher scale of fines would apply.

Section 1 of the 1971 Act stated that unsolicited goods may be kept by a recipient without payment after a period of 30 days providing that the recipient gave notice to the sender asking that they be collected or after six months regardless of any such notice. These Acts protected consumers **not** businesses.

Consumers are now protected by Regulation 24 of the Consumer Protection (Distance Selling) Regulations 2000 which permits the recipient to treat the unsolicited as an unconditional gift or give the sender 14 days in which to retrieve it at their expense (see Chapter 4).

 Key point: The Unsolicited Goods and Services Acts 1971 and 1975 previously protected consumer buyers against the dangers of so-called inertia selling by businesses. The relevant legal provisions are now contained in the Consumer Protection (Distance Selling) Regulations 2000.

Instantaneous communications

A contract will not have been concluded unless the acceptance is effectively communicated and the offeror has notice of this intention. When using so-called instantaneous methods of communication such as facsimiles, telexes, e-mails and text messages to send an acceptance, it is vital that the offeree ensures that the acceptance has been properly received by the offeror.

If, for example, the offeree left a message on the offeror's voicemail answering service stating that he had decided to accept the offer, this message must reach the offeror. If the message was accidentally erased by the offeror before he had listened to his messages, then no contract would have been formed because the offeree's acceptance could not be said to have been effective.

It does not take a stretch of the imagination to realise that such messages can be misdirected or even rendered unreadable when received by the offeror. The responsibility will very often be on the offeree's shoulders to ensure that the acceptance was received and actually understood. The dangers of using instantaneous communications are all too obvious from a brief examination of the following Scottish decision:

 Verdin Brothers *v* Robertson (1871) Robertson sent a telegram from Peterhead to Verdin in Liverpool. Robertson's telegram stated:

"Send on immediately fifteen twenty tons salt invoice in my name cash terms."

Owing to the fault of the clerks in the telegraph office, Verdin received the telegram in a completely different format:

"Send on rail immediately fifteen twenty tons salt Morice in morning name cash terms."

Needless to say, this led to a great deal of confusion because Verdin dispatched the goods to "Morice, Peterhead" and sent invoices to the same address. The invoices were later returned to Verdin by reason of the fact that no one of that name and address could be found. When the confusion was cleared up, Robertson refused to take delivery of the goods because he no longer required them.

Held: Lords Cowan, Benholme and Neaves (in the Inner House of the Court Session) all agreed that there was no contract because there was no true agreement i.e. the parties had failed to achieve consensus in idem. The parties had not properly communicated with one another. Lttle real sense could be made of the true intentions of the parties at a time when this was of vital importance.

 Key point: When using so-called instantaneous methods in order to communicate an acceptance, the offeree must ensure that the acceptance reaches the offeror in the form that he intended to send it.

The following cases demonstrate that acceptances sent by instantaneous methods of communication will conclude a contract when they have been received by the offeror.

Entores Ltd v Miles Far Eastern Corporation [1955] the pursuers who carried on a business in London sent an offer to the defender's agent in Amsterdam using their telex machine. The defender's agent in Amsterdam responded to the pursuers' offer by sending an acceptance via a telex machine. This acceptance was received by the pursuers on their telex machine in London. Some time later, the pursuers were attempting to serve a writ on the defender for breach of contract. The English courts would only grant them authority to commence the action against the defender if it could be proved that the contract had been concluded in England. If this was the case, the English courts would have the necessary jurisdiction to hear the pursuers' action for breach of contract. The case, therefore, centred around two issues: when and where the defender had accepted the pursuers' offer. The defender claimed that proper acceptance of the offer had taken place in Amsterdam at the time when the message of acceptance was typed into the telex machine. The pursuers, on the other hand, argued that the acceptance only became valid when it was received on their machine in London and printed out.

Held: by the English Court of Appeal that a contract had been concluded between the parties. Lord Denning stated that when the parties use instantaneous methods of communication, for example, telex machines, the acceptance is only valid when it is actually received by the offeror and the contract is made at the place where acceptance is received. The acceptance had, therefore, become valid when it was received on the pursuers' telex machine in London. The contract had been concluded in England and was subject to the jurisdiction of the English courts. Lord Denning also highlighted the dangers of using so called instantaneous methods of communication. What if, for example, a telephone line goes dead just as the offeree has made his acceptance? Did the offeror hear the vital words of acceptance? If not, then there can be no contract. Similarly, a clerk who sends an acceptance by telex must ensure that the message actually reached its destination and in the proper form. To be on the safe side, it may be advisable for the clerk to send a second communication (and a third and a fourth . . .) to ensure that the acceptance has been received and understood by the offeror. Until he receives verification from the offeree that the acceptance has been received, he cannot be certain that the contract has been successfully concluded. All sorts of accidents can and do happen with these types of communications. Better to be safe than sorry.

 Key point: When the parties use instantaneous methods of communication, for example, telex machines, e-mail, faxes and telephones, the acceptance is only valid when it is actually received by the offeror and the contract is made at the place where acceptance is received.

 The House of Lords approved the decision of the Court of Appeal in **Entores Ltd v Miles Far Eastern Corporation** in the later case of **Brinkibon v Stahag Stahl [1982]**. The facts of **Brinkibon v Stahag Stahl** were quite similar in that the offeree had sent a message of acceptance by telex. This case also involved an attempt by the English buyers to sue the sellers, who were based in Vienna, for breach of contract. The English courts would only allow a writ for breach of contract to be issued if they had jurisdiction to hear the case. The question once again arose as to where and when the contract had been formed. This time the offeree had sent the acceptance from London to Vienna. Following the decision in **Entores**, the House of Lords held that the contract had been formed in Vienna not London. In other words, the acceptance became valid when it was received by the offeror on the telex machine in Vienna. The summons could not be served because the contract had been made in Vienna and not in London and, therefore, the English courts had no jurisdiction regarding the contract.

 Key point: When using so-called instantaneous methods in order to communicate an acceptance, the offeree must ensure that the acceptance reaches the offeror in the form that he intended to send it.

Counteroffers or qualified acceptances

A counteroffer is a qualified acceptance, which contains additional or contradictory terms/conditions. A counteroffer cancels the original offer; the original offer disappears and is no longer capable of acceptance.

 This is shown in the case of **Wolf & Wolf v Forfar Potato Co Ltd (1984)** where a Scottish company sent a telex to a Dutch company offering to sell a quantity of potatoes. It was a condition of the offer that it had to be accepted by 5 p.m. the next day. The following morning the Dutch company sent a telex which appeared to be an acceptance of the offer but which contained new conditions. The Scottish company advised by telephone that these conditions were unacceptable and the Dutch company sent another telex, still within the time limit, which 'accepted' the original offer. The Scottish company ignored the second telex and the Dutch company raised an action for damages for breach of contract. The court held that no contract had been formed. The first telex was a counteroffer, which had the effect of causing the original offer to be cancelled. Therefore when the second 'acceptance' was sent there was no offer to accept.

 A similar case, **Hyde v Wrench (1840)**, also establishes a counteroffer; Hyde offered to sell his farm for £1000, Wrench offered £950. On rejection of Wrench's offer, he later advised Hyde that he would pay the original offer of £1000. Wrench's offer of £950, constituted a counteroffer, which cancelled out Hyde's original offer. Accordingly, Hyde's original offer was no longer open for acceptance.

 Key point: Qualified acceptance of the offer does not result in the creation of a contract, because the offeree has, in fact, rejected the original offer and replaced it with a new offer of his own which the offeror may or may not choose to accept.

Requests for additional information by the offeree are not necessarily counteroffers as can be seen in the following case:

 Stevenson v McLean (1880) on Saturday, the defender addressed a definite offer to the pursuers to sell them a specified quantity of iron at a specific price. The pursuers were given until the close of business on Monday to communicate their acceptance of this offer to the defender. The pursuers wished clarification of certain aspects of the defender's offer and, to this end, they addressed some questions to the defender. The pursuers primarily wished to know how long the defender was prepared to supply them with the goods at the quoted price, whether the goods could be delivered by instalment as and when required, and the terms of payment. The pursuers sent a telegram requesting this information on Monday morning, but the defender did not reply to this communication. In the early afternoon, the pursuers decided to accept the offer and sent off a second telegram to this effect. Shortly before, the defender had sent a telegram of his own withdrawing his offer, but this communication did not reach the pursuers until after they had sent their acceptance. The defender claimed that there was no contract because the pursuers' first telegram should be regarded as counter-offer. In response, the pursuers claimed that this telegram was merely a request for further information to clarify the terms of the offer.

Held: that the pursuers' first telegram should be viewed as an inquiry for further information. It was not a counter-offer. The original offer had not been rejected and the pursuers had accepted it in good time before the defender could effectively withdraw it. A legally enforceable contract had been created.

 Key point: Request for additional information in order to clarify the terms of the offer are not necessarily counter-offers, but great care will have to be taken by the offeree that his request for clarification should not be viewed as a rejection of the offer.

'The Battle of Forms'

In this electronic age, it is increasingly likely that businesses will use their own pre-printed forms (usually stored as a template on a computer's hard drive) to make an offer or to conclude an acceptance of an offer. These forms will no doubt contain terms and conditions which are peculiar to each party. Such terms might cover such issues as the law which will govern the contract, for example, Scottish or English law; which party has to bear the cost of insurance for the goods; which party has to organise delivery of the goods; or when property in the goods passes from seller to buyer.

It is highly unlikely that both parties' pre-printed forms will contain conditions which match exactly. It is probable that if the offeree responds to an offer contained in a pre-printed form by using his own paperwork or invoice he may well have unwittingly made a counteroffer which, of course, results in a rejection of the original offer. Therefore, no contract would be formed. In these situations, the courts have attempted to take a more flexible approach and this can be demonstrated in the following case.

 Butler Machine Tool Co Ltd *v* Ex-Cell-O Corpn (England) Ltd (1979)
Butler quoted a price for a machine tool of £75,535, delivery to be within ten months of order. The quotation gave terms and conditions which were stated expressly to prevail over any other conditions contained in the buyer's order. One of the terms was a price variation clause which operated if costs increased before delivery. Ex-Cell-O ordered the machine, their order stating that the contract was to be governed by Ex-Cell-O's terms and conditions as set out in the order. These terms did not include a price variation clause, but did contain

additional items to the Butler quotation, including the fact that Ex-Cell-O wanted installation of the machine for £3100 and the date of delivery was changed from ten to eleven months. Ex-Cell-O's form had a slip attached to it which Butler filled in and returned. The slip stated that Butler had to accept Ex-Cell-O's contractual terms. The machine was ready for delivery, but owing to a delay on Ex-Cell-O's part, the costs rose and Butler insisted that Ex-Cell-O compensate them. The Court of Appeal employed a traditional counteroffer analysis. Butler's original quotation was an offer, Ex-Cell-O's reply was a counteroffer which Butler had accepted by filling in the form and returning it. Ex-Cell-O did not have to pay the extra costs. If Butler had wanted the price variation clause to be enforceable, it should not have filled in the slip and returned it – this was tantamount to acceptance of Ex-Cell-O's terms.

 Key point: Great care will have to be taken by the parties when they use standard forms to communicate with each other which contain very different terms.

The postal rule

There is a special rule which will affect the creation of contracts where the offer and acceptance are sent using the Royal Mail. We first hear of the postal rule being established in the English case of **Adams v Lindsell (1818)** and, shortly afterwards, the rule was introduced into Scots law as a matter of convenience. Obviously, a great deal of trade was conducted between Scotland and England and it would have caused great inconvenience to have radically different rules governing the formation of postal contracts in both countries.

On the face of things, the effect of the rule is problematic and appears to fly in the face of common sense. Most people would assume that a letter of acceptance, sent in response to a letter containing an offer would only be valid when the acceptance actually reached the offeror or his agents.

When the offeror posts his letter containing the offer to the offeree, a contract will be formed as soon as the offeree responds to the offer by placing his letter of acceptance in the postbox or by handing the letter to a Royal Mail employee such as a counterclerk who is authorised to forward the letter for posting. This is in spite of the fact that it could take anything from a day to a couple of days for the letter of acceptance to reach the offeror who will be completely in ignorance of the offeree's decision. A contract will nevertheless have been formed. If an acceptance is sent by post, a contract is immediately formed.

 Key point: As soon as a letter of acceptance in response to a postal offer is posted a valid contract will have been formed.

 A very good illustration of the postal rule can be found in **Jacobsen v Underwood (1894)**. On 2 March, Underwood sent a letter containing an offer to Jacobsen using the Royal Mail. Underwood's letter stated that the offer must be accepted by 6 March. On 6 March, Jacobsen posted a letter of acceptance to Underwood. This letter of acceptance did not reach Underwood until 7 March. It was held that the postal rule applied and that the offer had been accepted on time i.e. by being posted on 6 March. In order to protect himself, Underwood should have insisted that acceptance would not be valid until the acceptance had physically reached him. In other words, he could have expressly excluded the postal rule.

There are two potentially problematic situations when the Royal Mail is used by the parties to communicate with one another:

◆ What if the offeror has second thoughts and decides to withdraw the original offer that he has made to the offeree?
◆ What if, on the other hand, the offeree decides to cancel the acceptance after having posted it?

We will look at these situations in turn.

 Key point: The postal rule can be problematic when a) the offeror decides to withdraw his offer or b) the offeree decides to cancel his acceptance.

Withdrawal of a postal offer

What if the offeror had second thoughts and wished to withdraw his offer? In order to ensure that any withdrawal was effective, the offeror would have to cancel the offer and communicate this new development to the offeree before the offeree was able to put his letter of acceptance in the post box and thus form a contract. So there is a real incentive on the part of the offeror to cancel his offer before the offeree accepts it by placing his letter of acceptance in the post box.

 Thomson v James (1855) James contacted Thomson by letter on 26 November offering to sell him a piece of land. Thomson sent a letter of acceptance to James on 1 December. In the meantime, James had had second thoughts about his original offer of 26 November and on 1 December he sent a letter to Thomson which contained a withdrawal of his earlier offer. James' withdrawal letter and Thomson's letter of acceptance crossed in the post. Both letters arrived on 2 December. Did James have a contract with Thomson?

Held: in order for James' letter of withdrawal to be effective, it would have to have reached Thomson before Thomson posted his letter of acceptance. Unfortunately for James, his withdrawal arrived (on 2 December) after Thomson had posted his acceptance (on 1 December) and, therefore, a contract had been formed.

 Key point: In order to make his cancellation of the offer effective, the offeror must ensure that his letter of cancellation reaches the offeree before a letter of acceptance can be posted.

The Scottish courts have not addressed directly the problem of what will happen if an acceptance goes missing in the post. It has been suggested that so long as the offeree has a receipt of posting, the acceptance will be valid and the contract will stand. Such a proposition, as we shall see, is not without significant problems and some clarity on this issue would be very welcome. Such a situation occurred in the following English case and the court ruled that the offeror was bound in contract to the offeree.

 Household Fire Insurance Company v Grant (1879), the defender handed a written application (the offer) to purchase shares in an insurance company to the company's agent. The application contained a declaration to the effect that the defender had paid a deposit to the company's bankers so that he could be certain of acquiring the shares. Under the terms of the proposed contract, the defender also agreed to pay an additional sum to the company within twelve months of the shares being allotted to him. The agent posted the defender's offer to the company. Upon receipt of the defender's offer, the company secretary wrote a letter to the defender informing him that he was now a member of the company. This letter (which was the acceptance of the defender's offer) was posted to him using the Royal Mail. For some unexplained reason, the letter was never received by the defender. The defender assumed that his offer to purchase shares in the company had been unsuccessful. Completely unknown to the defender, the company listed his name on the share register and credited him with the proceeds of dividends. The company later experienced severe financial difficulties and, eventually, it was forced to go into liquidation. The liquidators began to sue those members of the company who either had not paid for their shares or who still owed the balance of their shares. This group of individuals included the defender. The defender not unnaturally objected to this unexpected development and he argued that his attempt to purchase shares in the company had been unsuccessful.

Held: by the English Court of Appeal that the defender was liable to pay for the shares. A contract had been successfully concluded when the company secretary had posted the letter of acceptance. The Royal Mail was the common agent of the parties and delivery to it of the letter of acceptance meant that the defender's agent had effectively received this acceptance. This view did not find favour amongst all the judges of the Court of Appeal. Lord Justice Bramwell issued a strongly dissenting judgement. His Lordship was of the opinion that the acceptance of the offer had to be properly communicated to the defender. If a letter fails to arrive at its destination, this can place the offeror at a significant and serious disadvantage as this case only too well demonstrates.

 Key point: The offeree's letter of acceptance forms a valid acceptance as soon as it is posted and this is despite the fact that the letter could go missing in the post or be destroyed.

Withdrawal of a postal acceptance

The better view in English law is that an acceptance cannot be withdrawn once it has been posted, even though it has not yet reached the offeror. This approach seems very sensible since the offeror is bound by contract as soon as the acceptance is posted. The Countess of Dunmore, however, demonstrates that the situation is radically different in Scotland. Normally, of course, an acceptance cannot be withdrawn once made unless the offeree wishes to face the possibility of an action for breach of contract.

 Countess of Dunmore *v* Alexander (1830) Lady Agnew's servant, Betty Alexander was seeking new employment. The Countess of Dunmore was sufficiently interested in the possibility of engaging Betty as her new servant that she took the trouble to write to Lady Agnew asking for a reference and she stated that she would pay Betty an annual salary of £12 and 12 shillings. This was regarded as an invitation to treat from the Countess. Lady Agnew replied on Betty's behalf with a reference recommending Betty for the position and stating that the wages the Countess was prepared to pay were acceptable to her. Betty Alexander, like many servants of the time, could not read or write, and this is why Lady Agnew wrote the letter on her behalf. This letter from Lady Agnew was, therefore, an offer from Betty to the Countess. The Countess sent her acceptance by post on 5 November in response to Betty's offer. However, for some reason, she changed her mind about employing Betty and the next day she posted a second letter withdrawing her original acceptance. Betty received both the letters of acceptance and withdrawal at the same time. Betty then sued the Countess for breach of contract and the loss of wages for the six month period that she was without work.

Held: by the Court of Session that there was no contract between Betty and the Countess. This, of course, was a blatantly biased decision against Betty Alexander, a mere servant, who had dared to bring a claim for damages against an aristocratic lady such as the Countess. This case did establish an important legal principle in Scotland regarding the formation of postal contracts. A withdrawal of an acceptance will be effective if it reaches the offeror before, or at the same time as, the original letter of acceptance. For those with overly analytical minds, it does not matter which letter goes through the letterbox first or which letter the offeror opens first – as long as both letters arrive together. Clearly, if the letters arrived a post apart, this would make a difference to the question of whether a contract had been cancelled or not, which was a point forcefully made by Lord Balgray. In **Thomson v James (1855)**, Lord M'Neill, the Lord President referred to this decision as 'a very peculiar case', whereas Lord Deas would have gone further and abandoned the principle that it established.

This case can be criticised for a number of reasons, but it is worth bearing in mind that the Scottish courts have never overruled the decision and it remains very much in force. The case has been justified (on the rather unconvincing ground) that the second letter from the Countess should be treated as an addition to the first letter and reading the two letters together it became obvious that the Countess was totally hostile to the idea of employing Betty Alexander.

 Key point: The offeree can withdraw his letter of acceptance by sending a second letter cancelling his acceptance but, in order to be effective, this second letter must reach the offeror before or at the same time as the original letter of acceptance.

Repeal of the postal rule

The repeal of the rule was last considered in 1992 by the Scottish Law Commission, but as yet no concrete steps have been taken to change the law. Particularly astute lawyers will opt out of the rule by, for example, inserting an express term in the letter of offer to the effect that the postal rule does not apply.

 Key point: It is possible for the parties to exclude the postal rule by simply stating that it does not apply to their dealings.

When the offer and acceptance will have to be implied by the courts

So far, we have approached the formation of a legally enforceable agreement using a tried and tested formula i.e. offer + acceptance = contract. It follows from an application of this formula, that it is important to be able to identify when a definite offer is on the table and, in response to this willingness to be bound on the part of the offeror, we can say that an unqualified acceptance has been made by the offeree. When we have these two elements in place, we can say with some satisfaction that the parties are bound together in contract.

There are a number of situations where the formation of a contract will be not immediately apparent to the casual or inexperienced observer. Applying the above formula (offer + acceptance = contract) will perhaps only lead to a great deal of frustration. In these kinds of circumstances, the casual observer may well seek in vain for the more traditional and familiar features which herald the creation of a legally enforceable agreement. There may not even be a semblance of contractual negotiations between the parties indicating that a bargain is about to be concluded. The absence of these familiar contractual features, however, has not proved an insurmountable obstacle to the Scottish courts.

A court may be perfectly happy to imply or presume the existence of contractual obligations from the actions of the parties. Admittedly, the individuals concerned may not have used the words 'offer' and 'acceptance' in the course of their dealings with one another and perhaps they are completely oblivious to the fact that they have become subject to a range of legally binding obligations. In a number of situations, Scots law recognises the concept of collateral contracts that are linked to another contract and this relationship often gives rise to a completely separate range of rights and duties and to ignore these obligations is to act perilously. An example of a collateral contract can be found in the decision of the Inner House of the Court of Session in **Robertson v Anderson 2002** (above). In **Robertson**, it will be recalled that two friends who attended bingo together on a regular basis had an informal agreement to share their winnings. The informal agreement between the friends was linked or was collateral to the main gambling contract between the winner of the National Prize that evening and Mecca Bingo and the Inner House of the Court of Session stated that it was capable of enforcement by Robertson against Anderson.

The creation and enforcement of collateral contracts has been recognised in some of the older cases:

 Clarke v Earl of Dunraven [1897] the owners of two yachts named *Satanita* and *Valkyrie* respectively entered them in the Mudhook Yacht Club Regatta which was to be held on the River Clyde. As a condition of entry to the event, all participants had to sign a written undertaking to obey the rules of the Club. The rules imposed a duty of responsibility upon all yacht owners for any damage that they caused to other vessels competing in the Regatta. Whilst heading for the starting line, *Satanita* collided with *Valkyrie* and, consequently, *Valkyrie* sunk. The owner of *Valkyrie* sued the owner of *Satanita* for damages. *Satanita*'s owner claimed that he was only his liable in terms of statute which, in any case, permitted him to limit any sum of compensation to £8 per ton. He argued that he was in no way legally bound by the rules of the Mudhook Yacht Club. This limited sum payable under statute would in no way have adequately compensated the losses of the owner of the sunken *Valkyrie*.

Held: by the House of Lords that the participants in the Regatta had bound themselves in contract to the Club and to one another. They had no choice but to obey the rules of the event. This meant that the yacht owner who was responsible for the damage to the *Valkyrie* had to compensate its owner fully for the losses that he had suffered.

 Key point: Collateral contracts are linked to another contract and they often give rise to a completely separate set of rights and duties.

Certainty of the terms of an agreement

Contracts will not be enforced unless both parties have expressed themselves with a sufficient amount of clarity regarding the essential terms of their agreement. Sometimes, aspects of the contract are not at all clear and are very confusing. Does this situation affect the status of the contract? Indeed, can a contract even be said to exist? Courts will not go out of their way to label a contract unenforceable, but sometimes the parties do not help matters when they fail to express themselves clearly enough and it is little wonder that the validity of the contract is subject to question.

There are a variety of devices that the courts can rely upon in an attempt to salvage an agreement. Many trades and professions have well-established customs and practices of which the courts are perfectly aware and are only too happy to enforce on behalf of the parties if this means that the survival of the agreement can be ensured. As we shall see in Chapter 5, in a contract of agency, the agent is entitled to be paid at the customary rate (whatever that is) when the agreement fails to address the issue of a salary or commission. Alternatively, the agent can be paid on a *quantum meruit* basis i.e. as much as he has earned or at a reasonable rate (**see Kennedy v Glass (1890)** in Chapter 5). In many situations, the parties themselves may have foreseen the possibility of a dispute arising in relation to particular terms of the contract. To this end, they may have put in place the machinery for resolving such a dispute, for example, an arbitration clause. Furthermore, as we shall see in **Hillas & Company Ltd v Arcos [1932]** and **Foley v Classique Coaches Ltd [1934] (discussed below)**, a previous course of business dealings by the parties can greatly assist the courts to flesh out the terms of the contract. Very often, disputes will arise concerning the certainty of contractual terms because one party (sometimes both) now wishes to cancel the agreement or to change radically the terms of the contract.

Reference to an Act of Parliament may be helpful where the price of goods is disputed or the parties have failed to address this issue. Sections 8 and 9 of the Sale of Goods Act 1979 can be very useful in this regard. Section 8 states that the parties can leave the price of goods to be fixed by the contract or by reference to a method laid down by the contract. Alternatively, the parties may have had previous dealings that can be referred to in order to calculate the price. If the contract is silent on the issue of the price or there have been no previous dealings between the parties, the buyer must pay a reasonable price for the goods and what is reasonable will depend on the facts of each situation. Section 9 permits the parties to a contract of sale to fix a price by appointing a third party to carry out a valuation of the goods. Sections

12–15 of the Sale of Goods Act also address some of the most important terms in a contract of sale (title, description of the goods, quality and fitness for purpose and sales by sample) and these can be used to determine and clarify the rights and duties of the parties (**see Chapter 4 for a fuller explanation**).

However, if such avenues do not exist, or if all these options have been exhausted without success, the court will be unable to enforce the agreement. The contract is said to suffer from uncertainty.

If a term turns out to be unworkable by reason of a lack of certainty, the courts may have no option but to remove or sever it from the contract. The risk of such an action could mean, of course, that the rest of the contract is fatally undermined. It should go without saying that the parties go to great pains to express themselves clearly and effectively.

 Key point: Contracts will not be enforced unless both parties have expressed themselves with a sufficient clarity as to the essential terms.

 Hillas & Company Ltd _v_ Arcos (1932) the contract centred around an order for a quantity of a Russian soft wood of fair specification to be supplied over the season 1930. The contract contained an option which allowed the pursuers to order a further quantity of wood the following year. The contract was performed during 1930 without problems despite the vague wording of the contract to do with the specification of the wood. The pursuers tried to take advantage of the option for 1931, but the defenders refused to supply the wood owing to the vague wording. Where they were concerned, the contract was inchoate.

Held: by the House of Lords that this option was valid despite its vagueness. There had been a previous course of dealings between the parties which the court could use to overcome any difficulties. Indeed, the parties had not previously experienced any major difficulties in carrying out the contract.

 Foley _v_ Classique Coaches Ltd [1934] Foley had supplied Classique with petrol at an agreed price for a period of three years. Classique had agreed to purchase petrol from Foley in return for Foley agreeing to sell it land of which he was the owner. The agreement operated perfectly well and the parties had agreed that any disputes could be settled by arbitration. Eventually, Classique gave notice of its intention to withdraw from the contract simply because it could purchase petrol more cheaply from an alternative supplier. Classique argued that it was entitled to take this unilateral action since there was no agreement in writing addressing the price of petrol.

Held: by the English Court of Appeal that there was a perfectly enforceable contract between the parties which had had been in existence for 3 years and which was concerned with the supply of petrol at a reasonable price and of a reasonable quality. It did not undermine the agreement that the parties had failed to agree a price beyond the initial 3 year period of the contract. Future prices could be negotiated by the parties and, if disagreements did arise, they could be resolved by a reference to arbitration.

Key point: A lack of clarity as to the material terms of the contract may mean that the agreement cannot be enforced.

Contractual terms

It is important that the parties understand the extent of their rights and duties under the contract. Unless the parties have taken the step of writing down the main terms of their agreement, how can they identify with any certainty what the main contractual terms are? 'With a great deal of difficulty' may be the most honest answer! It is highly likely that the need to identify the main terms of the agreement will only really become a matter of some urgency when the parties are heading towards a dispute.

It will be important to establish whether, by behaving in a particular way, one of the parties has breached the terms of the agreement. Clearly, if a party breaks his side of the bargain certain consequences flow from this. If someone commits a breach of contract this leaves the other party with an option to sue for damages. Where a material breach of contract has been committed, this may give a party the right to cancel the agreement in addition to the remedy of damages.

If a lack of clarity surrounds the contractual main terms this can be a recipe for disaster. By failing to communicate with one another properly, the parties may have made it impossible for an agreement to work effectively.

In the event of a dispute, courts are often left with the thankless task of trying to make sense of what the parties have said and done in the course of their dealings with one another. As a starting point, a court could examine any written evidence surrounding the contract. If this resource is not available or is, more likely, inconclusive, the court will scrutinise verbal statements that the parties have made leading up to formation of a contract. Written documents and verbal statements are known as the *express terms of a contract*. The rights and duties of the parties could also be implied from their behaviour. Additionally, various Acts of Parliament, for example, the Sale of Goods Act 1979 (as amended) automatically include certain terms into a contract of sale which address the seller's right to sell the goods, the description of the goods, the quality of the goods and their fitness for purpose and sales by sample (**see Chapter 4**). Such terms whether in reference to the parties' behaviour or to statute are referred to as the *implied terms of a contract*. As a general rule, express terms will be preferred over implied terms. However, under the Unfair Contract Terms Act 1977, an express term which attempts to exclude the seller's liability to a consumer buyer in relation to the implied terms of the Sale of Goods Act 1979 will be automatically void.

The common law also implies various rights and duties into particular contracts. In an agency relationship, the courts have gone to great pains to develop the rights and duties of the parties. An agent, for example, has the right to be paid, the right to be indemnified and the right to be compensated by his principal. The agent is also said to have a right of lien. By comparison, the agent must not delegate his functions, must render true accounts and must put the interests of his principal above his own.

 Key point: Statute and the common law can imply the existence of rights and duties in relation to the contract that the parties have entered.

Before the introduction of the Contract (Scotland) Act 1997, the courts tended not to accept verbal evidence which would contradict a contract which is entirely in written form. Following on from this, courts were also less than willing to accept previous communications between the parties as evidence, whether written or not, once the agreement had finally been committed to writing. As we shall see, in the discussion about contractual formality, the courts are now more relaxed about the range of external sources of evidence that can be used to clarify the terms of a written contract. Generally speaking, the parties are free to make up their own minds as to what form the contract will be in. However, the courts tend to prefer a written document which embodies all the rights and duties of the parties. Obviously, the courts will not have to refer to additional or external sources of evidence where the written contract is clear and precise and contains all the terms by which the terms have agreed to be bound.

When examining words or phrases that the parties have used, the court must give these their plain ordinary meaning. Words which are commonly used in a particular trade, business or profession may appear in the contract and the court may be totally unfamiliar with these. Where there is any doubt in relation to words that imply a technical meaning or where the words are not commonly used in the English language because they are foreign, the court may call upon expert assistance to determine their true meaning.

If the meaning of a word is ambiguous, the court will do its best to give it a meaning which will aid the operation of the contract. This is often expressed as the giving of business efficacy to the contract, the judge regarding himself as doing merely what the parties themselves would in fact have done in order to cover the situation if they had addressed themselves to it. This, of course, is easier said than done and frequently the careless use of certain words or phrases by the parties can make it all but impossible for the court to determine their true meaning. Ultimately, of course, the parties have no one to blame but themselves.

 Key point: Generally, the courts prefer written evidence of a contract, but there is nothing to stop the parties from relying on verbal testimony or their own actions.

 The Moorcock (1889) the contract stated that the pursuers' steamship known as *The Moorcock* was to come alongside the defenders' wharf and jetty on the River Thames in order to unload her cargo and for the purpose of having a new cargo placed aboard the vessel. These activities were supposed to be carried out at low tide on the Thames. Both parties were well aware that it was dangerous for any vessel to approach the wharf at low tide as there was real chance that it would be exposed to the risk of running aground. Neither party had bothered to address explicitly in their contract, the issue of the vessel's safety. The vessel was brought alongside the wharf, but she sustained serious damage when she came to rest on hard ground when the tide went out and left her stranded. The English Court of Appeal implied a term (that it was safe for *The Moorcock* to come alongside the wharf at low tide) to give the contract the business efficacy which the parties surely must have intended because no reasonable person would have wished to expose the vessel to the risk of serious damage. The defenders had not been asked to give any assurances about the vessel's safety, but they should have given such an undertaking to the pursuers. The defenders were, therefore, liable to pay compensation to the pursuers for the damage sustained to *The Moorcock*.

A court (according to Lord Justice Bowen in **The Moorcock**) cannot imply a term into a contract simply because it is reasonable to do so. If the parties have concluded an agreement that is simply unworkable, then this must have been their intention! It is very unusual for a court to intervene as the Court of Appeal did in **The Moorcock**. When judges do act in this way, they are often referred to as officious bystanders who are saying to the parties: 'Look, you forgot to add that term to make the agreement work,' and the parties respond: 'Yes, of course, we completely overlooked that term because it was so obvious. We both assumed that it would form part of the final contract between us.' The court takes this particular course of action so that the contract may be given business efficacy.

To paraphrase Lord McClaren, in **Morton (William) & Co v Muir Brothers (1907)**, the concept of an implied term relates to contracts of every description. However, the approach to this area of law shows that they are either enforced because they rely on a universal custom or the nature of the contract itself. If a reasonable person wished to include such an obvious term in an agreement for his own protection and the other party, also being a reasonable person, could have no possible objections, surely such a term should be regarded as part of the contract? The problem arises in the first place because the term is so obvious that the parties merely forgot to include it. The courts have implied terms into contracts on a number of occasions (**Robb v Green (1895)** and **Lister v Romford Ice and Cold Storage (1957)** where a duty to act in good faith and show fidelity to the employer was implied into employment contracts).

Lord Denning, the famous English judge, wanted to go further than this, admittedly, limited approach demonstrated in **The Moorcock**. In **Liverpool City Council v Irwin [1977]**, his Lordship opened himself to severe criticism when he attempted to imply certain terms into contracts by virtue of the fact that it was reasonable for a court to do so. The implied term did not have to be of vital commercial importance in order to give the contract business efficacy, it was merely reasonable to include it in the agreement. On appeal to the House of Lords, Lord Denning's approach to the incorporation of implied terms attracted little support from their Lordships. The Scottish and the English courts pointedly refused to follow Lord Denning's lead, preferring a much more limited approach.

 Key point: Generally speaking, courts will only imply a term into the contract in situations where it is commercially vital in order to make the contract effective.

Courts can also use certain rules of construction when it comes to the interpretation of contracts. The *ejusdem generis rule* allows a judge to group certain words or phrases together so that they form a particular group or subset which have characteristics in common. If a reference in a contract contained the words 'dogs, cats and other animals', the phrase 'and other animals' would be understand to mean animals of a domestic type. This would exclude animals such as lions, tigers and elephants which are most definitely not domestic in nature. Additionally, the *contra proferentum rule* arises in situations where one of the parties wishes to rely on a contractual term which they themselves have drafted and which is vague or ambiguous, for example, an exclusion clause. The court will not allow the party relying on this clause to reap full advantage of the clause if it is in any way vague or ambiguous.

 Key point: The courts can also rely on the *ejusdem generis* and *contra proferentum* rules to make sense of the contractual terms.

Contractual terms which impose duties upon the parties can be classified in various ways:

◆ Those which have immediate effect or those which have to be performed within a reasonable time after the formation of the agreement
◆ Those which are dependent upon some future, specified event
◆ Those which are contingent or rely upon the fulfilment of some condition

Title to sue and third party rights

Generally speaking, third parties or outsiders have absolutely no rights in relation to a contract. To put things rather bluntly, it is not their agreement having had no involvement in its creation. Consequently, they do not enjoy any rights and they are not under a duty to do something for any other person. It follows from this general rule, that third parties do not have the right to bring a court action relating to a contract in which they do not have a legal interest.

There are certain situations, however, where third parties may be able to enforce terms of a contractual agreement that relate specifically to them or where they are entitled to claim some sort of benefit. Usually the contract will either name a specific individual or a specific class of persons who are entitled to benefit from the agreement. Such third parties are entitled to enforce either a *jus quaesitum tertio* or a *jus quaesitum*. In **Carmichael v Carmichael's Executrix (1920)**, Lord Dunedin explained the difference between a *jus quaesitum tertio* and *jus quaesitum*. A *jus quaesitum tertio* would arise where A and B have made a contract and C, who is entitled to benefit from the agreement, is forced to sue because A refuses to recognise C's rights. A *jus quaesitum*, on the other hand, would occur where A and B have a contract but, this time, it is B who objects to C enforcing his third party rights.

Insurance policies are good example of this where a parent insures the life of his child. Obviously, the contract is between the insurer and the parent, but the child may become entitled to any dividends payable under the policy when he becomes an adult.

 Carmichael v Carmichael's Executrix (1920) where a father had taken out a policy for his son who was aged 9. When the son reached adulthood, he became entitled to claim the benefits of the policy. Tragically, the son died soon after becoming an adult and, according to the terms of is will, his aunt Miss McColl was to benefit from his estate. As part of the son's estate, Miss McColl claimed a dividend that was payable under the insurance policy. The father objected to this by claiming that he was entitled to the money having paid the premium over many years.

Held: by the House of Lords that Miss McColl was entitled to enforce the third party rights (*jus quaesitum*) that she had inherited from her nephew. The money payable under the terms of the policy was rightfully hers.

Similarly, in **Morton's Trustee v Aged Christian Friend Society of Scotland (1899)** (discussed above), the 50 beneficiaries were able to enforce their rights to a life pension despite the fact that they were not parties to the original agreement between Morton and the Society. Morton's trustee did not wish to continue paying the pensions following Morton's death, but the pensioners benefited from this *jus quaestium tertio*.

Factors which affect the validity of a contract

In many situations, individuals will emerge from contractual negotiations in the belief that they have managed to form a binding contract. However, these individuals should avoid giving themselves a pat on the back just yet because there is still plenty of room for things to go wrong.

By becoming exposed to a variety of factors or situations, a potential agreement can be rendered *void* or *voidable* because in the eyes of the law there is a lack of consensus *in idem* or insufficient agreement. Furthermore, the so-called 'contract' (note the inverted commas) may be affected by such varying factors as error, misrepresentation, lack of formality, illegality, duress and undue influence.

If such situations do arise it is absolutely essential to be able to predict how any potential agreement will be affected. The main issue to consider here is whether the 'contract' will be rendered void or whether it will be merely voidable.

 Key point: A seemingly valid contract may be rendered void or voidable after it has been negotiated and this will have serious consequences for the parties.

Void contracts? This phrase is actually something of a contradiction in terms because if an agreement is said to be void this will mean that no contract actually exists. In fact, there never was a contract. The parties may have been involved in negotiations and will probably believe that they have concluded a 'contract', but this will be of little consequence since the courts will declare that there is no contract. It follows that, if there is no contract, neither party can have any rights or duties.

This situation has extremely serious consequences for third parties who may purchase property which forms the subject matter of a void contract. Unfortunately for these third parties they will be unable to enforce any legal rights to such property and any items will have to be returned to their original owners. Any such 'contract' which the courts consider to be void will, therefore, be completely unenforceable.

Examples of void contracts arise in the following situations:

◆ Where the contract is illegal
◆ Where one of the parties has been forced into the agreement by the use of force and fear
◆ Where there is substantial error
◆ Where one of the parties suffers from insanity
◆ Where the contract is with a child under the age of 16

 Key point: When a contract is declared void, the court is making a statement to the effect that a contract has never existed, despite what the parties may believe, and, therefore, no party can be said to have rights or duties.

Voidable contracts

This is a slightly more problematic area of the law. At one point, the parties have managed to conclude a legally binding contract. However, because of certain factors at play, one or both of the parties may have the option of cancelling the contract. Unlike the situation with void contracts, however, third parties can become the legal owners of property which forms the subject matter of voidable contracts. This is why it is essential for the party which has the right to cancel the agreement to act swiftly. Any hesitation on their part may mean that the other party may have transferred ownership of goods to a third party. If this turns out to be the case, it is highly unlikely that such property will be returned to its original owner. Examples of voidable contracts arise in the following situations:

◆ Where one of the parties has made a misrepresentation of fact
◆ Where there is a lack of formality
◆ Where one of the parties was intoxicated as a result of alcohol and/or drugs (whether prescription medicines or illegal drugs)
◆ Where the one of the parties was 16 or 17 years of age
◆ Where there has been facility and circumvention
◆ Where there has been undue influence

 Key point: In complete contrast to a void contract, a voidable contract remains valid until one of the parties takes steps to have it cancelled. In practical terms, this parties will continue to have rights and duties under the agreement until such time as it is cancelled.

Error

When a party to a contract is influenced by some sort of error, they have a mistaken or distorted view of the facts surrounding the agreement.

When we speak about error or mistake in relation to contracts, we are entering an area which is particularly complex. There are different categories of error in Scots law which may or may not undermine the validity of a contract. Clearly, we are particularly interested in those categories of error which undermine the formation of a contract. It is important to determine whether the error in question renders the contract void or voidable.

There are three key questions which must be asked when dealing with the issue of error in relation to contracts:

◆ Did the error or mistake directly influence the party to enter the contract?
◆ Was the error caused by the ignorance of one of the parties?
◆ Did one of the parties, knowing the other party to be in error, actively encourage this mistaken belief as to the facts?

It may seem a very harsh rule, but the law will not protect people from the consequences of their own stupidity or ignorance. It is only where the error or the mistake has been actively encouraged by one of the parties, who is fully aware of the true factual situation, that the courts will show a willingness to intervene. Such a situation may lead to the cancellation of the contract.

 Key point: It is particularly important to distinguish between mistake and misrepresentation because a contract affected by mistake is void, whereas a contract affected by misrepresentation is voidable. In void contracts, third parties cannot acquire good title to contractual goods, whereas in voidable contracts third parties can enforce their right to property acquired.

Induced or uninduced error

Uninduced error arises in situations where a person has entered a contract owing to their ignorance of the true facts. Such a person has not been influenced or encouraged by statements or representations of another party. Usually, the contract has been formed as a result of stupidity or ignorance. It is unlikely that the courts will intervene to remedy such a situation.

Induced error means that you have been encouraged to enter a contract because of something that the other party has told you whether by accident or design on their part. This piece of (false) information has directly influenced you to enter the contract. Perhaps you asked a seller of goods a direct question and his answer has encouraged you to make a contract with him. In these situations, the court is much more likely to provide some sort remedy to the innocent party, for example, cancellation of the contract and/or financial compensation.

 Key point: Induced error means that the other party has actively encouraged your mistaken view of the facts, whereas uninduced error relates to situations when the mistaken view as to the factual situation is entirely of your own making.

It must be stressed that the law does absolutely nothing to protect people from making a bad bargain which will leave them at a disadvantage, for example, making a financial loss if this is a result of their own stupidity or lack of business experience. The law will only provide assistance where someone has entered into a bad bargain where there has been some flaw in the agreement or, upon further investigation, it becomes obvious that there really is no agreement between the parties. Such types of agreement are usually void or voidable.

Mistakes which affect the status of the contract must relate to factual situations and not mistakes about the law. Furthermore, 'mistake' has a technical meaning and does not cover, for example, errors as to value. When a person makes a mistake due to his own stupidity or negligence, the rule expressed as *caveat emptor* (let the buyer beware) normally applies.

 Key point: The law does not usually protect people from the consequences of their own stupidity or negligence which, in turn, influences them to make a bad bargain.

Types of error

There are three types of error which can, potentially, undermine a contract:

◆ Common bilateral error
◆ Mutual bilateral error
◆ Unilateral error

 Key point: Errors may be common bilateral, mutual bilateral or unilateral.

We will examine each of these in turn.

Common bilateral error

Such a situation will occur when both contracting parties make an identical mistake. Where common bilateral error is present, it cannot be said that the parties lack agreement. The only exception to this may be a situation where the error affects the *substantials* of the contract. In fact, a contract affected by common bilateral error will be rendered void if the error relates to the existence of the subject matter of the contract. We can see the effects of this type of error in the following cases:

 Dawson v Muir (1851) the contracting parties had concluded the sale of sunken vats being sold by Dawson to Muir. Both parties believed that the vats were empty. This was not the case and later it was discovered that the vats contained white lead, a very valuable substance.

Held: that the contract was valid and the seller was not entitled to have the goods returned and certainly not the contents of the vats.

 Couturier v Hastie (1856) Hastie placed a cargo of corn aboard a ship in the Greek port of Thessalonikki. The documents of title to the goods were sent in advance to his London agents so that contracts of sale for the goods could be negotiated with buyers in advance of the ship's arrival at London. The London agents engaged Couturier to approach prospective buyers, one of whom entered a contract for the goods. At this point, the parties were unaware that the cargo had started to overheat while the ship was sailing through the Mediterranean. The Master, seeing that this was an emergency, put the ship in at the port of Tunis in North Africa and sold the remaining goods. In this way, the Master was acting as an agent of necessity (**see Chapter 5**) This meant that when the contract of sale had been concluded in London, the subject matter had ceased to exist. When this situation became common knowledge, the buyer communicated his intention to cancel the contract. Hastie sued Couturier because as a *del credere* agent he had given an undertaking to his principal that he would compensate him for any losses if the contract failed to go ahead.

Held: by the House of Lords that the action against Couturier should be dismissed because the contract with the buyer was totally dependent upon the continued existence of the goods.

 Key point: Common bilateral error occurs when both contracting parties make an identical mistake, but a contract is still said to have been formed despite the parties' error. The contract may be set aside if the error affects the material terms of the agreement.

Mutual bilateral error

This is a more serious situation because there are real grounds for questioning the very existence of any agreement. It should be remembered that, if there is no agreement, there is no contract. The courts will have to be very careful here and any vagueness surrounding the parties' intentions could fatally undermine any agreement. The parties must have expressed a certain level of clarity with regard to all the important terms of the contract. If this is not the case, then the agreement will be void on the grounds of uncertainty. If, for example, X offers to sell his desktop PC and Y agrees to buy thinking that X means to sell his laptop computer, there is a bilateral mistake which is non-identical or, in other words, a mutual misunderstanding. It will be remembered that in the previous category the mistake of error was bilateral but both parties had made an identical mistake. Confusion of this non-identical bilateral kind generally exists in the mind of one party only and may, therefore, have no effect on the contract.

 Key point: Mutual bilateral error is a much more serious situation because there are real grounds for questioning the very existence of any agreement.

Unilateral error

With this type of error, one of the parties will have a mistaken view of the contract. The quality of this error will determine whether the contract is ultimately rendered unenforceable. The law can be quite strict here because, generally, people are supposed to be able to look out for their own interests and the courts cannot be expected to offer protection to those who suffer the consequences of their own stupidity. If, however, the other party misrepresented certain facts and this misrepresentation encouraged an individual to enter the contract then the agreement could be voidable. In other words, the innocent party would be able to petition the court and request that the contract be cancelled, but he would have to act extremely quickly before the property could be transferred to an innocent third party.

 Macleod v Kerr (1965) a rogue named Galloway approached Kerr and offered to purchase his Vauxhall Cresta car which had been advertised in the *Edinburgh Evening News*. Both parties agreed terms and, in return for a cheque signed in the name of L. Craig, Kerr permitted Galloway to take away the car and its registration book. Kerr then discovered that the cheque had been stolen. Galloway, in the meantime, had been busy selling the car to an innocent third party named Gibson. Kerr attempted to have his property returned to him from Gibson.

Held: by the Inner House of the Court of Session that property in the goods had passed to Gibson. The contract between Kerr and Galloway was voidable on the grounds of Galloway's fraud. Kerr had acted too slowly to recover his property by cancelling the contract with Galloway and Gibson was now the owner of the vehicle. The question of Galloway's identity was not an issue in the sense that it did not influence the creation of the contract. Kerr was not the slightest bit interested in the Galloway's identity – only his ability to pay for the car.

 Phillips v Brooks [1919] Phillips, the pursuer, carried on a business as a jeweller. On April 15 1918, a well-dressed man had entered Phillip's premises and stated that he was interested in purchasing some pearls and a ring. Phillips offered this individual some items in his stock for inspection. The customer entered a contract with Phillips to purchase pearls costing £2550 and a ring costing £450. The customer paid for these items by cheque. Normally, Phillips would not have permitted a customer paying by cheque to take items purchased from the shop until confirmation had been received by him that the customer had adequate funds in his bank account to pay for the goods. While the customer was writing the cheque, he had claimed to be Sir George Bullough of St James' Square. Phillips consulted a telephone directory and his enquiries confirmed that there was such an individual living at that particular address. On the strength of the stranger's claim, Phillips allowed him to take the ring away. The customer had claimed that it was his wife's birthday the following day and he was particularly anxious to take the ring home to her.

Unfortunately for Phillips, his customer turned out to be a fraudster called North and the cheque was subsequently dishonoured. Phillips then took steps to retrieve the ring. The fraudster, however, had wasted little time because on 16 April, he had pledged the ring to Brooks, who was a pawnbroker, to secure a loan of £350. Phillips attempted to force the pawnbroker to return the ring to him. The pawnbroker replied that he had acted in good faith and he refused to return the ring or pay over its value to Phillips.

Held: the issue of North's identity was not a material factor in relation to the formation of the contract of sale. Phillips was not the slightest bit interested in North's identity until the issue of payment for the jewellery arose. Until this point, Phillips would have entered a contract with anyone who wished to purchase the jewellery. In other words, ownership of the ring had passed to North, the fraudster, when the sale had been concluded. The problem, as Phillips was to discover later, was that North was not in a position and had no intention of paying for the goods. The only solution open to Phillips was to sue North for the price of the goods and he could not force Brooks, the pawnbroker, to return the goods to him. This was an example of a voidable contract and the attempts by Phillips to cancel the contract for the sale of the ring were too little, too late.

The difference between the outcomes in **Macleod v Kerr** and **Phillips v Brooks** compared with that of **Morrisson v Robertson (1908) (discussed below)** was the fact that the identity of the buyer in **Morrisson** was a crucial factor right from the outset which determined the seller's decision to form a contract with the buyer (a rogue called Telford). The legal issue in **Macleod v Kerr** and **Phillips v Brooks** is, therefore, identical to the case of **Lewis v Averay [1972] (see Chapter 4 for the details of this case**). In **Lewis**, the identity of the buyer only became an important issue where the seller was concerned *after* a contract of sale had been formed and the question of the buyer's ability to pay for the goods arose.

 King's Norton v Edridge Merret (1897) Wallis, a rogue set up a company called Hallam & Company. He had stationery printed in such a way that it made the company appear very creditworthy. Using this stationery, he wrote ordering goods on credit from King's Norton. King's Norton supplied the goods.

Held: by the English Court of Appeal that the contract should not be rendered void on the grounds of unilateral mistake. The mistake in question concerned a minor term only i.e. the creditworthiness of one of the parties – a 'mere attribute.'

 Cundy v Lindsay (1878) a rogue called Blenkarn, based at 37 Wood Street, wrote to Lindsay ordering goods on credit. He made his order look as though it had come from a creditworthy firm called Blenkiron & Company, based at 123 Wood Street. Lindsay supplied the goods.

Held: by the House of Lords that the unilateral mistake concerned a material term of the contract i.e. the true identity of one of the parties to the contract.

In both the above cases, the rogues (Wallis and Blenkarn) sold the goods to innocent third parties (Edridge Merret and Lindsay). When the frauds were discovered, the sellers attempted to recover the goods from the third parties on the grounds that the identity of both rogues was absolutely central to the formation of the contracts.

The difference in outcomes between **King's Norton** and **Cundy** is that, in the first case, the pursuers intended to deal with the person who had written the letter offering to purchase goods. Wallis, the rogue, had set up a front company trading as Hallam & Co and he had used the front company's headed notepaper on which to write to the pursuers to place an order for goods. The pursuers only became concerned about his identity when it became obvious that he was not going to pay for the goods. In **Cundy**, on the other hand, the pursuers had always clearly intended to deal with a particular party (Blenkiron) and the issue of identity was, therefore, vitally important to the formation of this contract. The pursuers would not have entered the contract had they known the true identity of the rogue, Blenkarn.

 Key point: To render a contract void, a unilateral mistake must be related to a crucial term and not a minor term; the very fundamentals/material terms of the contract.

To summarise, if a situation indicates that there has been a unilateral mistake, a court will not consider declaring the contract void *ab initio* i.e. from the very beginning, unless all the following conditions are met:

1   The mistake must be about a crucial term of the contract, not a minor term

2   The mistaken party must have established that s/he was in no way to blame for the mistake

3   It must be shown that the other party knew (or, perhaps, ought to have known) of the mistake

The effect of these three preconditions, taken together, is that it is a rare event for a contract to be held void at common law for unilateral mistake. One reason for this judicial reluctance is that, if a contract is declared void *ab initio*, third parties may lose rights to property that they acquired innocently and in good faith.

 Key point: It is very difficult for a party to convince a court that a court should be declared void *ab initio* on the grounds of unilateral mistake.

Error in the substantials

When we talk about an error we usually mean that someone is labouring under a mistaken view of the facts. Substantial error, however, is an extremely serious problem because it usually means that the mistaken belief goes to the very roots of the contract and, therefore, completely undermines any potential agreement. In such situations, the mistaken beliefs of the parties do not centre around trivial matters which can easily be resolved. Error in the substantials concerns one or more of the important aspects of the agreement. In situations where an agreement is affected by substantial error there can be no true consensus *in idem* or agreement. In fact, the actual contract is radically different from the one that the parties originally intended to create.

Any 'contract' will be considered null and void from the beginning. In other words, there never was a contract despite what the parties might otherwise believe in their own minds. Practically speaking, this will mean that any property or money that has been transferred to the other party under the 'contract' must be returned to the original owner. Neither party can be said to acquire any rights or duties in such instances.

 Key point: Substantial error is a mistake that is so serious that it strikes at the very heart of the contract i.e. the material terms to the effect that there can be no real agreement between the parties thus rendering the contract void.

Professor Bell, one of the institutional writers, identified four types of substantial error in respect of the following issues which the House of Lords affirmed in **Stewart v Kennedy (1890)**.

Identity of one of the contracting parties

This will usually occur where one person is operating under a mistaken belief as to the identity of the other party with whom they are attempting to form a contract. However, the issue of mistaken identity must be fundamental to the formation of a contract. In order to convince a court that mistaken identity should render the agreement void, a person would have to demonstrate that he intended to enter into a contract with a particular person and no other.

 Morrisson v Robertson (1908) Robertson, a farmer, was approached by an individual (later discovered to be named Telford) who wished to buy two cattle from him. This individual wished to buy the cattle on credit. Morrisson was unhappy about this, but Telford stated that he was the son of a man called Wilson with whom Morrisson had dealt with previously. Morrisson knew Wilson to be a man of good credit. Morrisson gave the cattle to Telford who promptly sold the cattle to an innocent third party, Robertson who was ignorant of the fraud. Telford disappeared and Morrisson, who was still awaiting payment, sued for the return of the cattle.

Morrisson thought that he was contracting with Wilson's son, but unknown to him he was in fact contracting with Telford. In a credit transaction like this, Telford's identity was absolutely vital to the formation of a contract. Morrisson would never have contracted with Telford had he known Telford's true identity. Telford, therefore, did not have good title (i.e. ownership) to the cattle.

Held: the cattle had to be returned to Morrisson, the true owner.

Generally, in cases of mistaken identity as in **Phillips v Brookes (1919)** above, the court starts from the presumption that the claimed identity of each party is a crucial factor where the contracting parties are at a distance from one another. Where the parties are face-to-face, the court presumes that the each party intended to contract with the person present and therefore, the claimed identity is only a minor term and will, therefore, not affect the formation of a contract. Although in **Morrisson v Robertson (1908)** the parties were dealing face to face, the nature of the contract (a credit transaction) made Telford's statements about his identity an essential or material term of the contract.

 Key point: In **Morrisson v Robertson**, Telford's identity was an absolutely material term of the contract because Morrisson would not have entered the agreement had he been aware of the deception.

207

The subject matter of the contract

Such a situation is likely to arise where the parties are completely confused and mistaken as to the subject matter of the agreement. One party (the potential buyer) believes that a particular item is being offered for sale whereas the other party (the potential seller) believes that she has made an offer to sell a completely different item. Both parties are completely at cross purposes. There can be no real agreement between them and, therefore, no contract.

 Raffles *v* Wichelhaus (1864) the case involved two ships named Peerless both sailing from Mumbai in India carrying a cargo of cotton. This situation was the subject of much confusion as it will doubtless be appreciated. To complicate matters further, the ships were sailing from Mumbai two months apart. The defenders thought that they were purchasing the cotton aboard the first Peerless, whereas the pursuer thought that they were selling the cotton on the second Peerless. The defenders refused to take delivery of the second cargo when it arrived and were sued for breach of contract.

Held: that since there was a mistake as to the subject matter of the contract, there was in effect no contract or at least no contract which corresponded with the so-called agreement that both parties had supposedly concluded. Consequently, the pursuer's action failed.

 Key point: In **Raffles *v* Wichelhaus**, there was complete confusion in respect of the subject-matter of the contract and this totally undermined the agreement.

The price

The price that one party expects to pay and the price that the other party expects to receive will, obviously, be a very important term of the contract. Any confusion surrounding the price will render the contract void. Admittedly, it is possible for the parties not to fix a price and still have a valid contract as long as some mutually agreed system or mechanism exists for determining the price (Sale of Goods Act 1979 (as amended)).

 Wilson *v* Marquis of Breadalbane (1859) both Wilson and Breadalbane had intended to enter into a contract for the sale of cattle. However, both men had misunderstood at what the price the cattle were to be sold. Breadalbane took delivery of the cattle and paid what he assumed to be the correct price of £13 per head. Wilson informed Breadalbane that £13 per head was not the correct price and he later sued for the alleged balance. Clearly, both individuals had failed to conclude a mutually satisfactory price and, therefore, they had failed to form a contract.

An important matter to consider in this case is that it was not physically possible for the Marquis of Breadalbane to return the cattle to Wilson as they had been slaughtered and the carcasses eaten. Therefore, the court had to do the next best thing which was to order the payment of compensation to Wilson. This sum was fixed at an appropriate amount to reflect the loss suffered by Wilson.

 Key point: Wilson *v* Marquis of Breadalbane demonstrates that the price is a material term of the contract.

The type or nature of contract

This may occur where both parties misunderstand the nature of the contract. They may both be in agreement as regards the identity of the contracting parties and the subject matter of the contract. However, a mistaken belief as to how the contract will operate may completely undermine matters. An individual may believe that he will have use of an item under a contract of hire (or rental agreement) whereas the owner of the goods may well believe that she is agreeing to sell the goods. Clearly, a contract of hire and a contract of sale are legally distinct and have very different consequences.

 Foster v Mackinnon (1869) Foster, an old man of feeble sight was induced to sign a document which he thought was a guarantee for £3000. In fact, the document was a bill of exchange for £3000. A guarantee was a completely different type of agreement from a bill of exchange. The bill of exchange became immediately payable whereas the guarantee only became payable upon the event of someone becoming insolvent – an event which might not happen. The old man would not have signed the bill of exchange had it known its true nature. The document was, therefore, void.

 Key point: In **Foster v Mackinnon**, the old man thought he was entering a completely different type of contract than the one which was presented to him for signing.

 Key point: Substantial error occurs when there is error as to the identity of the contracting parties, error as to the subject matter of the contract, error as to the price and error as to the type of contract the parties are entering.

Force and fear

A contract will seldom be formed as a result of actual violence but threats of violence are more probable. Violence or the threat of violence must be such that they are enough to overwhelm a mind of ordinary firmness. Force and fear will have the effect of making the contract void. Threats to take legitimate legal action against someone do not fall into the category of force and fear. The following case gives a particularly vivid example of the effect of force and fear on a contract.

 Earl of Orkney v Vinfra (1606) the Earl summoned Vinfra to his castle and presented him with a written contract which he was to sign. The effect of this agreement was that Vinfra would have to pay the Earl a sum of money. Vinfra refused and the Earl turned nasty. The Earl started to curse and laying his hand on the hilt of his dagger threatened to kill Vinfra if he did not sign the document. Vinfra had no reason to believe that the Earl was anything but serious in his intentions and he wisely signed the document in order to save his life. Later, Vinfra refused to pay the money that he supposedly owed to the Earl claiming that he had only entered the agreement because he had feared for his life. The Earl claimed that he had been joking and that Vinfra's fears were misplaced.

Held: Vinfra's fears were all too real and the contract was, therefore, declared void.

Key point: Violence or very real threats of violence that are used to pressurise a party to enter an agreement will have the effect of rendering the contract void.

Contractual capacity

A valid contract requires that the parties must have capacity. A person of full capacity is capable of taking on duties which the law recognises and will force them to comply with. Additionally, the law will recognise any rights that these individuals are entitled to and will enforce these rights on their behalf. Most *natural legal persons* i.e. human beings, have full capacity.

Certain groups have no capacity or limits are placed on their ability to enter contracts. These are:

◆ Young people under the age of 18
◆ Adults with incapacity
◆ Intoxicated persons
◆ Enemy aliens

 Key point: In order to enter a contract that the law will recognise, a person must have the power or ability to do this. This power or ability is known as contractual capacity.

Children and young persons

The law relating to young people and children was changed by the Age of Legal Capacity (Scotland) Act 1991. By young people and children, we mean those individuals who have not yet reached the age of 18 (the age of their majority). When a person reaches his eighteenth birthday, he will be regarded as an adult with powers of full capacity in the eyes of the law.

The 1991 Act draws a distinction between children aged under 16 and those who are 16 and over (young persons).

Children under 16

The general rule is that a child under 16 has no capacity to enter into any legal transaction. Technically, this means that any transaction entered into by an individual under the age of 16 will be void. However, the law in this area is capable of flexibility and there are exceptions to this rule. The contract that an under 16 has entered into will be enforceable if it satisfies two tests. The contract must be:

1 Of a kind usually entered into by persons of his age and circumstances

2 On terms which are not unreasonable

 Key point: The general rule is that a child under 16 has no capacity to enter into any legal transaction.

We are really talking about everyday types of contracts that a child would be a party to such as buying sweets. Obviously, as the child becomes older, the range of goods and services that he can purchase will increase dramatically. However, any doubts about the child's capacity should be referred to the child's guardian.

Young persons aged 16 and 17

These individuals are regarded as having full legal capacity in much the same way as an adult would. However, the 1991 Act does explicitly recognise that this group of young people will perhaps require some protection. It should be remembered that young people will have less experience of life and could be taken advantage of by unscrupulous older people. The courts will, therefore, cancel a contract that a young person has entered into if it can be shown that the agreement was harmful/prejudicial to the young person's interests. Potentially, a contract made with a young person aged 16 or 17 could be declared voidable by the courts.

 Key point: Contracts involving young persons are capable of being enforced, but they could be declared voidable by the courts.

However, the young person must satisfy two conditions if he is to demonstrate that the agreement was prejudicial/harmful to his interests. These two conditions are that:

1   It is highly unlikely that a sensible/reasonable adult would have entered into the contract under the same circumstances

2   The contract is likely to cause substantial prejudice/harm to the young person

Only the young person can use the protection that the 1991 Act provides. Other people (usually older persons) cannot use it to get out of the contract.

However, the protection offered to young persons under the 1991 Act has limitations. The young person must use this defence before he reaches the age of 21. Furthermore, the young person cannot use this defence to get out of a contract he has made in the course of his business or to which he has now agreed (ratified) after reaching the age of 18. It is also important to bear in mind that the young person will have no protection under the 1991 Act if he pretended to be 18.

Given the problems surrounding contracts and young persons, businesses may be very reluctant to enter contracts if they think the young person will use this defence. If there are doubts about the agreement's fairness, it may be worth approaching the Sheriff Court and requesting a Sheriff to decide whether the proposed contract could be harmful to the young person's interests. The Sheriff's decision cannot be challenged later.

 Key point: A young person may be able to have a contract cancelled if he can show that no sensible or reasonable adult would have entered the agreement and, furthermore, the agreement will cause him real harm if it is allowed to stand.

Some of the older cases concerning the capacity of young people can still provide useful guidance.

 Wilkie v Dunlop (1834) Wilkie, a young man who was just short of becoming an adult, ran up a bill when he stayed at an inn for three weeks. Wilkie was accompanied by an adult friend who had promptly paid his bill. Wilkie, however, failed to pay his part of the bill. His guardians also refused to pay the bill arguing that they had not authorised Wilkie's contract with the innkeeper. Part of their refusal to pay stemmed from the fact that his guardians were claiming that Wilkie was already adequately supported by them. The court was extremely unsympathetic towards Wilkie and his guardians stating that the amount of the bill was reasonable and that it would be unreasonable for someone to stay at an inn for three weeks and not pay for his board and lodging.

Held: Wilkie may not have been adult, but the contract that he had entered into was in way harmful or prejudicial to his interests.

 In the English case of **Chaplin *v* Leslie Frewin (Publishers) [1965]** the pursuer, who was the son of the silent film star Charlie Chaplin, entered a contract with the defender for the purpose of publishing a book that was to be written on his behalf and which would recount his life story. The book was entitled *I Couldn't Smoke the Grass on My Father's Lawn*. At the time the contract was made, Chaplin junior was not yet an adult and, therefore did not have full contractual capacity. He later sought to have the contract cancelled on the grounds that the book had caused him to suffer prejudice or severe harm. In the book, he had been portrayed in a very unflattering light and he felt that his reputation had suffered as a result.

Held: Chaplin failed to have contract cancelled. The book had actually benefited him at the time he had signed the contract because it had helped to establish his career as a writer. It is worth pointing out that the dispute between Chaplin and the publishers was not about money. In fact, Chaplin had made rather a lot of money from the publication of the book. In terms of the Age of Legal Capacity (Scotland) Act 1991, Chaplin's contract with the publishers would be regarded as a business contract and, as a young person, the defence that he had suffered prejudice because he had proceeded with it would not be available to him.

 Key point: Any adult entering into a contractual agreement with a child or a young person will have to be particularly careful.

Adults with incapacity

This category of people would include, for example, the insane, people with dementia and people who suffer from some sort of mental disability such as Downs Syndrome and are, therefore, incapable of entering into contracts which would be recognised by the courts. The Adults With Incapacity (Scotland) Act 2000 allows a guardianship to be declared where someone can act for a person who lacks capacity. The guardian may act for the incapable person in one transaction only, in a series of transactions or in relation to all the incapable person's affairs. The 2000 Act recognises various means by which a guardianship can be established.

 Key point: The Adults With Incapacity (Scotland) Act 2000 permits a guardian to be appointed to act for an individual who has been declared mentally incapacitated.

Insanity

Many of the older court cases involving an individual's mental incapacity deal with the issue of insanity. Insane persons have no capacity. A contract entered into by an insane person is, therefore, void. However, there could be an exception during a 'lucid interval' i.e. when the insane person regains sanity for a short period.

Someone who supplies essential items or necessaries to an insane person is entitled to be paid for these items (Section 3(3): Sale of Goods Act 1979). Clearly, the courts would be unlikely to view luxury sports cars as an essential item. By necessaries we mean, for example, food and clothing or the basic items necessary for a person's survival.

Someone can be appointed to a guardianship to act for an insane person. There are different levels of guardianship depending on the severity of the illness. A guardian can, of course, make contracts and enter into agreements on the insane person's behalf. This is particularly useful where the insane person has business or financial interests. A guardian can be appointed in a variety of different ways. Before the introduction of the Adults With Incapacity (Scotland) Act 2000, a guardian was known as a *curator bonis*.

 Loudon *v* Elder's Curator Bonis (1923) on 23 and 28 March, Elder, a wholesale meat merchant, placed orders with Loudon & Co for supplies of frozen meat. On 31 March, Elder was certified insane. The meat had not yet been delivered by Loudon to Elder. On 1 April, Thomas Hunter, Elder's legal guardian or *curator bonis* informed Loudon that the contracts were void on the grounds of Elder's insanity. Loudon refused to accept this situation and sued for breach of contract. Hunter in turn argued that, although the contracts had been made before Elder's insanity became public knowledge, medical evidence would prove that Elder was insane when he entered into the contracts with Loudon.

Held: the contracts were void on the grounds of Elder's insanity and, consequently, no damages for breach of contract were payable.

 Key point: Contracts entered into with an insane person will generally be declared void.

Intoxicated persons

This category would include people under the influence of drink, drugs or medication. However, the individual must be so intoxicated that s/he does not know what they are doing and cannot give true consent. Viscount Stair, the institutional writer, remarked that those who through fear, drunkenness or disease have not for a time the use of reason do not legally contract.

The intoxicated individual would have to take immediate steps to get out of the contract and the level of intoxication will matter, for example, a few after-dinner drinks which put a person in a good mood will rarely affect the validity of an agreement. A contract which has been formed as a result of one of the parties being under the influence of alcohol or drugs may be voidable.

 Taylor *v* Provan (1864) Provan offered to buy cattle from Taylor at £14 per head. Taylor, however, demanded that Provan pay a price of £15 per head for the cattle. No contract, therefore, was formed. Later that evening, Provan returned and offered Taylor £15 per head and Taylor accepted this offer. Provan later attempted to have the contract declared voidable on the grounds that he had been drunk when he had made the second offer to Taylor. Provan argued that his drunken state had prevented him from realising what he was doing when he made the second offer.

Pollock v Burns 1875

Held: Provan had failed to provide evidence that he was so drunk that he had lost his reason and was, therefore, completely unaware of the consequences of his actions. The mere fact that he had been under the influence of alcohol when he entered the agreement was not sufficient to have it cancelled.

Key point: A contract with a drunken person must in effect always be voidable by him because presumably the fact that he is drunk will be known to the other party. This is not so in cases of unsoundness of mind which might not be known to the other party. However, a drunk person will have to take immediate steps to cancel the contract because delay may give the impression that he has agreed to stand by the agreement.

Enemy aliens

Those citizens of countries that the United Kingdom is at war with are known as enemy aliens. Such individuals continue to live in territory controlled by the United Kingdom during hostilities. It is, therefore, illegal for British citizens to enter into contracts with enemy aliens or with businesses controlled by them. Any contract with enemy aliens is generally regarded as being void. Interestingly, however, the contract becomes enforceable in the British courts when hostilities cease upon conclusion of a peace treaty or armistice and it is possible for the former enemy aliens to assert any rights that they have or may have had under the contract with British citizens and businesses. During the First and Second World Wars, German citizens and businesses controlled by them would have been regarded as enemy aliens. More recently, Iraqi citizens and businesses would have been regarded as enemy aliens. Sometimes the British government takes a hostile stance towards various countries and imposes sanctions on those states. Countries such as Libya, the former Yugoslavia and Iraq have all been the subject of international sanctions and it would have been illegal for any British citizen to do business with any of the citizens of these countries. An example of a contract with enemy aliens can be seen in the following case:

 Cantiere San Rocco SA *v* Clyde Shipbuilding and Engineering Co Ltd (1923) a Scottish shipyard had entered into a contract with an Austrian business just before the First World War began. Austria entered the First World War as an ally of Germany and declared War on the United Kingdom. This meant that Austrian citizens and businesses were now to be regarded as enemy aliens and any contracts that had been entered into were null and void and, consequently, unenforceable. After the War had ended, the House of Lords stated that the contract between the Scottish shipyard and the Austrians was capable of being enforced.

See also **Stevenson and Sons Ltd *v* AG Für Cartonnagen Industrie (1918)** discussed later in this Chapter.

Corporate bodies

Registered companies and local authorities fall into this category and are known as *artificial legal persons*.

Local authorities are governed by the Local Government (Scotland) Act 1994. They enjoy powers given to them by this Act and other pieces of legislation. They must not act outside these powers (*ultra vires*). Any contract which is not within their powers will be void.

Registered companies are now governed by the Companies Act 2006 which allows a company to carry on business as a general commercial company in any trade or business whatsoever. No act done by a company may be questioned by the fact that it was beyond its legal capacity as stated in its memorandum of association.

A person dealing with a company does not have to check to see whether there are any limits on the company's capacity. Practically speaking, all contracts are enforceable against the company. The abolition of the *ultra vires* rule does not allow directors to escape personal liability to shareholders in situations where they have acted beyond the authority given to them by the company's Articles of Association (see Chapter 5). The harshness of the *ultra vires* rule can be seen in the following case:

 Ashbury Railway Carriage & Iron Co v Riche (1875) According to its Memorandum of Association (i.e. its constitution) the company had been set up in order to manufacture and sell railway wagons, other railway equipment and to carry on the business of mechanical engineers and general contractors. The company took on a project to build an entire railway system in Belgium and it sub-contracted the building of the actual railway line to Riche. Riche began work and the company paid him for this. Problems arose when the company experienced a number of financial problems and the shareholders made it clear that the company should cease to play a further role in the construction of the railway. The directors then informed Riche that the company was withdrawing from the project. Riche promptly raised an action for breach of contract.

Held: by the House of Lords that the company could withdraw from the contract because the directors had acted *ultra vires* i.e. beyond their powers when they took over responsibility for constructing the railway. According to the company's objects clause in the Memorandum of Association, the contract with Riche was void. The objects clause, which listed *all* the business activities of the company, did not permit the company to construct an entire railway. The company was only permitted to supply materials for railway construction, but had no power to take on overall responsibility for a major project like the one in Belgium. Riche was deemed to have notice of this limitation on the company's powers because the Memorandum of Association was a publicly available document. It did not matter if he had not actually bothered to read this document.

The *ultra vires* rule was a Victorian device which allowed members of a company to restrict the powers of the company and the directors. This meant that directors would be prevented from acting in an unauthorised way so that they could not enter a transaction which was not included in the objects clause of the Memorandum of Association. This was a device to protect present and future members of the company by ensuring that the directors could only enter contracts which had been pre-approved by the members. An added protection of the rule was that it prevented a company from approving the unauthorised acts of its agents after the fact by passing a special resolution. Nowadays, of course, *ultra vires* has been relegated to the status of an internal company matter.

 Key point: Certain bodies such as local authorities must act strictly within their powers otherwise any transaction entered into which goes beyond these powers will be declared void.

Formality

Many people believe that it is a legal requirement that all contracts must be in writing and witnessed. Under Scots Law, many contracts do not require formalities i.e. the need to have written terms and conditions. The majority of contracts will be verbal agreements or their existence can be proved by looking at the parties' behaviour or by implication (see **Carlill *v* Carbolic Smokeball Company (1893)** or **Thornton *v* Shoe Lane Parking (1971)**). The existence of contracts can be usually proved by any type of evidence (statements from parties' testimony and their witnesses). Some contracts, however do need to be in written form.

 Key point: Many people believe that it is a legal requirement that all contracts must be in writing and witnessed. Under Scots Law, many contracts do not require formalities i.e. the need to have written terms and conditions to prove the existence of the contract.

The Requirements of Writing (Scotland) Act 1995

In modern Scots law, contracts involving land and buildings (heritable property) are covered by the Requirements of Writing (Scotland) Act 1995. A contract for the sale of land has to be in writing and must contain all the terms expressly agreed by the parties and each of those terms must be set out in the written document. The Act does allow terms of the agreement to be incorporated in the document where it refers to some other document or documents containing the terms. Failure to draw up a written contract has the effect of making such an agreement voidable. In other words, one or both of the parties could withdraw by justifying their actions on the basis that there was no written agreement. Both parties may have a verbal agreement and, normally, in many other situations this would be enough, but not if the contract concerns land or buildings.

 Key point: Land and buildings and things attached to land and buildings are referred to as heritable property. Leases and rents are also classified as heritable property.

The Requirements of Writing (Scotland) Act 1995, which came into force on 1 August 1995 changed the law here with regard to the evidence required to prove the existence of gratuitous obligations and bilateral contracts.

As previously discussed in this chapter, it is still the general rule that contracts or unilateral promises do not have to be in written form. However, certain types of legal obligations must be in written form. These include the following:

◆ Contracts or unilateral promises which involve transactions in relation to heritable property i.e. land and buildings and anything which is attached to or forms part of land

◆ Unilateral promises except those which are made in the course of business

◆ A trust where a person declares himself to be the sole trustee of his own property or property that he acquires
◆ Where a person makes a will

It should also be noted that if parties to an Employment Tribunal dispute (e.g. a claim for unfair dismissal) wish to settle the matter out of court before the case proceeds to a full Hearing, the parties must draw up a written document by virtue of Section 203 of the Employment Rights Act 1996. Solicitors or legal advisers acting for the parties may wish to draw up a Compromise Agreement whereby the Claimant who lodged the Employment Tribunal proceedings agrees to withdraw the claim usually (but not always) in return for receiving a financial settlement from the Respondent. Alternatively, the parties may wish to settle the claim with the assistance of Conciliation Officers working for the Advisory, Conciliation and Arbitration Service (ACAS) by way of a COT3 Agreement. Examples of a Compromise Agreement and a COT3 Agreement can be seen on the Introductory Scots Law website.

www

The Consumer Credit Act 1974 insists that all the main terms of a regulated credit agreement must be in writing, otherwise the creditor will only be able to enforce the agreement with a court order. An example of such an agreement can also be seen on the website. Furthermore, the Bills of Exchange Act 1882 insists that all negotiable instruments, for example, a bank cheque or promissory note must be in written form.

 Key point: In situations where the law demands that the parties draw up a written contract, an informal agreement will regarded as voidable.

In terms of the Requirements of Writing (Scotland) 1995, what type of evidence is required to prove the existence of a contract?

All that is necessary is that the document is signed by the relevant persons (i.e. the parties or their agents). Only one witness is required under the 1995 Act and the document will be perfectly valid. Unless the court has any reason to be suspicious about the validity of the document, it will take the witness's signature at face value. Should the parties to the written document fail to get it witnessed, the court will demand evidence from the parties that the agreement is, in fact, an accurate statement of their intentions. Such evidence will be in the form of sworn affidavits (statements). A court can also issue a certificate which authenticates the validity of a document. The Contract (Scotland) Act 1997 clarified the law in this area and additional external sources of information whether consisting of verbal statements or documentary evidence can be used in court to flesh out additional express terms in relation to a written contract. Otherwise, the 1997 Act assumes that a written document will contain all the main terms of the agreement.

 Key point: The Requirements of Writing (Scotland) Act 1995 states that the signature of one witness will be all that is required to validate a written contract and the Contract (Scotland) Act 1997 now allows external evidence to clarify the terms of the written agreement.

Electronic signatures

Section 7 of the Electronic Communications Act 2000 states that electronic signatures incorporated in electronic documents will now be admissible as evidence in a court.

Failure to draw up a written agreement

What if the parties fail to provide a written agreement or document when the 1995 Act places a duty on them to do so?

It might be thought that if the parties have a purely verbal contract involving heritable property, the courts would refuse to enforce it. However, this is not the case. Despite the fact that the 1995 Act states that all contracts involving heritable property should be in writing, there are situations where the courts will enforce unwritten contracts. A contract (and for that matter a unilateral promise) can be enforced where there have been 'significant actings'.

If one party attempted to withdraw from an informal contract involving heritable property on the grounds that there was nothing in writing, they might be in for something of a shock. It will not be possible to use the argument that as there is no written contract then the agreement can be cancelled if:

1 The other party has relied on the contract

2 The other party knew of their actions and agreed to them

3 The actions of the party wishing to honour the contract were material (not trivial) so that they would be prejudiced or severely disadvantaged if the other party pulled out

 Key point: In situations where the law imposes a duty on the parties to have a written contract and they have failed to draw one up, an unwritten agreement may still be enforced if one or both of the parties can demonstrate that there have been significant actings.

 The importance of concluding a written contract for the sale or purchase of heritable property has been re-emphasised in the decision of the Outer House of the Court of Session in **Thomas Park and Another, Petitioner (2009)**. In this case, it was decided that missives concluded by fax were not legally binding on the parties to the potential agreement. In other words, it would appear that a faxed offer and a faxed acceptance in contracts for heritable property (i.e. land and buildings) do not comply with the provisions of the Requirements of Writing (Scotland) Act 1995. This means that the original documents (presumably signed by the parties' solicitors and witnessed) will have to be exchanged before a binding legal contract is said to exist.

Standard Missives

Moves towards greater use of standard term contracts in conveyancing have continued apace and many firms of solicitors appear to be adopting these types of arrangements which will hopefully mean that the sale and purchase of heritable property will be greatly speeded up.

Examples of standard missives and the accompanying documentation for the various areas of can be viewed by accessing the website of the Law Society of Scotland, the regulatory body for Scottish solicitors (www.lawscot.co.uk).

From 1 October 2009, solicitors in both Edinburgh and Glasgow will be able to use a standard set of missives in conveyancing transactions (see examples of written contracts for heritable property on the Introductory Scots Law website).

Effect of undue influence on the parties to the contract

Undue influence renders the contract voidable so that it may be rescinded or cancelled. However, if rescission is being sought by one of the parties to the contract as a remedy, there must be no delay in claiming relief after the influence has ceased to have an effect. Delay in claiming relief in these circumstances may bar the claim since delay is evidence of affirmation or agreement.

Undue influence can perhaps occur in the following relationships: parent and child and husband and wife. There will, of course, be other relationships where a stronger party may exert a particularly negative influence on the weaker party, for example, members of a religious cult who unquestionably obey the orders of their spiritual leader.

 Key point: Undue influence renders the contract voidable so that it may be rescinded or cancelled.

 Allcard v Skinner (1887) in 1868, Allcard, the pursuer, became a novice in an all female religious order called St Mary at the Cross, which had a particular emphasis on works of charity. In 1871, Allcard became a full member of the order. All members of the order had to take a vow of obedience to Skinner, the Superior (head) of the order. The order was run along very oppressive lines and in the modern age might be regarded as something of a religious cult. The Superior was to be regarded as one of God's personal representatives on earth and this person's word was effectively law. Furthermore, all issues and problems affecting the members had to be discussed with the Superior and members were absolutely forbidden to seek counsel or advice from outsiders. Shortly after becoming a full member of the order, Allcard drew up a will leaving all of her possessions to the group. Allcard was a wealthy young woman and, over the next few years, she came into possession of large sums of money and shares in various companies. She transferred large amounts of her wealth to the order. In May, 1879, Allcard decided to leave the order and she took immediate steps to change her will to reflect the fact that she no longer wished the order to be her beneficiary. Unfortunately, Allcard failed to raise an action to recover the money and shares that she had transferred to the order until 1885. Allcard alleged that she had only handed over her property to the order, without taking independent advice, because of the Superior's undue influence.

Held: by the English Court of Appeal that Allcard's action to recover her property should be dismissed. The Court of Appeal was strongly of the opinion that the pursuer's claim was time-barred by the fact that she did not bring a claim against the order until nearly six years after she ceased to be a member. Clearly, the pursuer's claim against the order may have succeeded if only she had commenced legal action much sooner.

 Anderson v The Beacon Fellowship (1992), Lord McCluskey (in the Outer House of the Court of Session) considered whether the defenders, a religious group, had used undue influence in relation to the pursuer to procure donations of money from him. Representatives of the Fellowship regularly visited the pursuer and exerted a very strong influence over him.

The pursuer suffered from a number of psychiatric illnesses and had been taking medication from time to time to control his various ailments. He was, therefore, somewhat vulnerable to the overtures of the Fellowship i.e. that money was worthless and that it should be given away. The pursuer eventually raised an action to recover the various donations that he had made to the Fellowship. Lord McCluskey felt that there was sufficient evidence to suggest that there had been undue influence and allowed the case to proceed to a proof.

Husbands and wives: a presumption of undue influence?

In Scotland, the issue of undue influence has been reconsidered in connection with the relationship of husband and wife. During the 1990s, several cases were brought before the Scottish and English courts regarding the issue of undue influence. All these cases had remarkably similar facts, whereby the pursuers, a number of wives, alleged that they had agreed to re-mortgage the marital home so that a bank would lend money to their husbands (usually, but not always, for business purposes). These wives claimed that they had not been given sufficient information by their husbands when they had agreed to approve what later turned out to be very risky transactions. Some of the pursuers had not sought independent legal advice before agreeing to take out the second mortgage.

The House of Lords, in **Barclays Bank plc v O'Brien [1993]**, stated that a married woman (or cohabitee) must be regarded as a special, protected class of guarantor when agreeing to guarantee her husband's (or partner's) debts because of the nature of the relationship. The bank should be on alert for signs of undue influence which would undermine the validity of the transaction. The bank is under a duty to ensure that the wife or the cohabitee has the benefit of independent advice. Their Lordships, however, did make a distinction in these types of cases. In **CIBC Mortgages v Pitt [1994]** a wife was not allowed to succeed in her claim of undue influence because the mortgage was in the names of both husband and wife and, therefore, she was benefiting from it.

However, the decision of their Lordships in **Barclays Bank plc v O'Brien** was not followed by the Inner House of the Court of Session in **Mumford v Bank of Scotland (1996)** where it was held that banks are not under a general duty to explain all the material circumstances of a loan to someone who has guaranteed it. In **Smith v Bank of Scotland (1997)**, the House of Lords attempted to bring Scots law into line with English law. Lord Clyde stated that there were a number of sound reasons for attempting to harmonise the laws of Scotland and England:

"I am not persuaded that there are any social or economic considerations which would justify a difference in the law between the two jurisdictions in the particular point here under consideration. Indeed when similar transactions with similar institutions or indeed branches of the same institutions may be taking place in both countries there is a clear practical advantage in the preservation of corresponding legal provisions."

In a further English case, **Royal Bank of Scotland PLC v Ettridge (No. 2) (2001)** the House of Lords appeared to retreat from the position that it had originally laid out in **Barclays Bank v O'Brien (1993)** whereby that married women or cohabitees should be regarded as a special, protected class of guarantor. The House of Lords in Ettridge has stated that undue influence will not be automatically presumed merely because the parties to a transaction are husband and wife.

In a series of cases **(Forsyth v Royal Bank of Scotland PLC (2000), Clydesdale Bank Ltd v Black (2002)** and **Royal Bank of Scotland PLC v Wilson & Ors (2003))**, the Inner House of the Court of Session had refused to accept that wives were unduly influenced by their husbands. Misrepresentations by the husband were more likely to have induced the wives to agree to become guarantors rather than any hint of undue influence.

In **Mumford v Bank of Scotland (1996)**, Lord Hope made the following statement which sums up the approach taken by the Scottish courts in these types of cases between husbands and wives:

"There is no indication in this passage that a presumption of undue influence can arise merely from the nature of the transaction and the fact of the relationship. What is important is the effect of that relationship in the particular case, *with the result that each case must be examined upon its own facts.*" [our italics]

Facility and circumvention

An individual may be able to withdraw from what appears to be a perfectly valid contract if he can later prove that at the time of entering the agreement, the other party took advantage of some personal weakness such as old age or physical weakness. This leaves the individual in a vulnerable position in the sense that he is more open to persuasion, advice or intimidation usually coming from the other party. The affected individual is not suffering from some form of mental incapacity, but his condition will have been taken advantage of by the other party.

 Cairns v Marianski (1852) a father had two daughters. One of the daughters was married to Marianski, the other to Cairns. The father had lived with the Marianskis from just after their wedding until his death at the age of 90. The Marianskis had looked after the old man and he felt under an obligation to them which they were later to exploit. Upon the father's death, it emerged that certain documents signed by the father conferred benefits on Marianski. Cairns was convinced that the Marianskis had taken advantage of the old man's frail health and their close personal relationship in order to persuade him to give them certain rights over his estate when he died.

Held: by the House of Lords that there had been facility and circumvention and that the documents drawn up in Marianski's favour were to be cancelled.

 Key point: Facility and circumvention involves situations where someone's weakness of will or ill-health is used by another person to gain advantage in relation to property or contracts.

Misrepresentation

A misrepresentation occurs when one party, during negotiations leading to the formation of a contract, makes a materially false statement of fact which has the effect of encouraging or inducing the other party to enter the agreement. It is usually after the contract has been formed that the party who relied on the statement will discover that it factually false. The innocent party must be able to prove that, if he had been aware that the statement was in fact false, he would never have entered the contract in the first place. In the course of making a misrepresentation, a party does not have to be aware that the statement was false. A misrepresentation is not necessarily a deceitful or dishonest statement.

The nature of the misrepresentation

Since the decision of the House of Lords in **Hedley Byrne & Co Ltd *v* Heller & Partners Ltd (1963)**, three categories of misrepresentation are recognised by the Scottish Courts:

1 Innocent

2 Fraudulent

3 Negligent

With an innocent misrepresentation, the party who made the statement genuinely believes what he is saying to be the truth. There is no intention to deceive, but the statement is still factually incorrect and it may have encouraged another individual to enter the contract.

Fraudulent misrepresentation, on the other hand, is a deliberate attempt by the party making the statement to deceive another person and, therefore, influence the innocent party to enter the contract. The party who made the fraudulent statement is fully aware of the falseness of his statement. In other words, he is being consciously dishonest when he makes the misrepresentation to the other party.

Lord Herschell, a former Lord Chancellor, described fraudulent misrepresentation in **Derry *v* Peek (1889)** as:

'A false representation of fact, made with a knowledge of its falseness or in utter disregard if it be true or false, with the intention that it should be acted upon and actually inducing the other party to act upon it.'

The facts of **Derry *v* Peek (1889)** are as follows:

 A special Act of Parliament permitted a tramway company to be created. The Act stated that the new company's carriages might be moved by animal power, for example, by using horses and mules. If the company wished to use steam power to move the carriages using steam power, it had to obtain the consent of the Board of Trade (a British government department). The company directors issued a prospectus containing a statement claiming (falsely as it later turned out) that the special Act of Parliament permitted the company to use steam power instead of horses. There was no mention that the consent of the Board of Trade was required to authorise this activity. The pursuer, however, decided to invest in the new company on the basis of this statement in the prospectus. The Board of Trade afterwards refused to give its consent authorising the use of steam power and the company was wound up. The pursuer claimed that the directors had made a fraudulent misrepresentation that had encouraged him to enter the contract and he sued for damages.

Held: by the House of Lords, reversing the decision of the English Court of Appeal and restoring the decision of the trial judge, that the directors were not liable. They had included the statement regarding steam power in the honest belief that it was true. They had made an innocent misrepresentation and no damages were payable.

It can be difficult for an innocent party to prove that someone has made a fraudulent misrepresentation. Conscious dishonesty must be proved according to the criminal standard i.e. beyond a reasonable doubt, and not according to the civil standard of proof i.e. on the balance of probabilities.

Negligent misrepresentation is a relatively recent concept. Prior to the **Hedley Byrne** decision, a misrepresentation was either of an innocent or fraudulent nature. This position meant that there was no middle ground for the innocent party. The party making the statement may not have been dishonest, but he may have been reckless. Fraud, as we have seen, can be difficult to prove and, in many cases, the courts found that the misrepresentation was of the innocent variety. This approach by the courts did not always favour the victim because damages were not payable for innocent misrepresentation in Scotland and the parties could not always be returned to their original pre-contractual positions. As a result, a finding of even innocent misrepresentation did not necessarily leave the innocent party any better off. As we shall see when we come to a discussion of the remedies available for misrepresentation, the decision in **Hedley Byrne** strengthens the position of the innocent party.

A negligent misrepresentation is very different from innocent and fraudulent misrepresentation. Someone who makes a negligent statement does not intend to deceive the other party but, at the same time, he cannot prove that he had reasonable grounds for believing the truth of his statement. In other words, he has made the statement recklessly without verifying its accuracy. Generally, negligent misrepresentation will occur in situations where the parties have a special relationship and the party making the statement will owe the other party a duty of care. Negligent misrepresentation is also very much part of the law of the delict and is discussed in detail in Chapter 3. Clearly, where a contract is concerned, the parties have a special, legal relationship and they will owe duties (of care) to one another.

Types of misrepresentation

We shall examine the three types of misrepresentation, by reference to case law.

Innocent misrepresentation

 Boyd & Forrest *v* Glasgow & South-Western Railway Co (1912) the railway company had invited tenders from various contractors for the purpose of building part of a railway line. All the contractors had been shown the findings from various studies which indicated the type of soil that would have to be dug up along the proposed stretch of line. On the basis of the information supplied by the railway, Boyd & Forrest submitted a successful bid to carry out the work for $243,000. The work commenced, but Boyd & Forrest discovered that the ground contained a much larger quantity of rocky subsoil than the original studies had indicated. Instead of stopping the work and querying the findings studies, Boyd & Forrest pressed ahead with the work and completed it at a total cost of £379,000 (£136,000 more than had been originally anticipated – a truly colossal figure). It later emerged that one of the railway engineers, Melville, had altered the findings of the studies because he honestly believed that they were mistaken. Boyd & Forrest attempted to recover the extra figure of £136,000 from the railway alleging that Melville had fraudulently altered the information. Boyd & Forrest claimed that Melville's alleged fraud had encouraged them to enter the contract.

Held: by the House of Lords that Melville's actions had been completely honest – there was no attempt on his part to make a fraudulent misrepresentation. He had made an innocent misrepresentation. The action by Boyd & Forrest, therefore, failed.

Fraudulent misrepresentation

 Edgington *v* Fitzmaurice (1885) the directors of a company issued a prospectus inviting investors to take out debentures in the company. A debenture is effectively a loan made to the company. The prospectus stated that the proceeds raised from the debentures would be used to expand and develop the company's business. The real object of the loan was to enable the directors to pay off financial debts that had been run up and which the company's creditors were now demanding should be paid. The pursuer advanced money on some of the debentures under the mistaken belief that the prospectus offered a security over the property of the company, and stated in his evidence that he would not have advanced his money but for such belief. Furthermore, he also relied upon the statements contained in the prospectus. The company became insolvent.

Held: by the English Court of Appeal (affirming the decree of Denman J), that the directors had made a fraudulent misrepresentation in the prospectus which had partly influenced the pursuer to advance loans to the company. However, this partial reliance on the misrepresentation was enough to allow the innocent party to raise a claim for damages.

Negligent misrepresentation

 The leading case is **Hedley Byrne & Co Ltd *v* Heller & Partners Ltd (1963)** and is discussed in greater detail in Chapter 3. An advertising agency had relied on statements made by a bank about the financial solvency of a mutual client. The bank had assured the agency that the client had enough money in a bank account to pay for advertising contracts that the agency had entered into on the client's behalf. The bank, however, had made this statement negligently. The client did not have sufficient funds in the bank account to pay the advertising costs. Consequently, the agency lost £17,000 as a result of the bank's negligent misrepresentation. The agency sued the bank for the losses it had suffered. The bank argued that it had excluded its liability for negligence by issuing a statement to the effect that the information provided should not be relied upon by the agency. The bank's disclaimer was issued together at the same time as it had provided the financial advice in respect of the client.

Held: that in the present case, the presence of the disclaimer excluded a duty of care owed by the bank to the agency. However, if the bank had failed to issue the disclaimer, it would have been liable to the agency for the losses caused by its negligence for making a false statement. This was in spite of the fact that the bank did not have a fiduciary relationship (relationship of trust) or a contract with the agency. The House of Lords effectively introduced a new type of misrepresentation into the law i.e. negligent misrepresentation as a result of this case.

The House of Lords stated that the duty of care arose where there was a special relationship requiring care. It has been argued that a duty of care will be owed by the parties in a contractual relationship. The boundaries of **Hedley Byrne**, even to this day, are still not firmly settled, but the existence of a special relationship between the parties is a useful starting point. Lord Devlin said that when one party pays for information or advice this strongly indicates that the party requesting the information will be using it to make important decisions and the adviser will not to be able to argue, convincingly, that he did not know this. Furthermore, the fact that the information was not paid for by the person who requested it does not mean that an adviser can be reckless or negligent when issuing it. If the existence of a special relationship between the parties can be proved between the parties, the adviser will still have to take care if he is aware that the other party will be relying on this information regardless of whether he received payment or not.

There is a more detailed discussion in Chapter 3 concerning the types of special relationship that the courts have recognised give rise to a duty of care in respect of negligent misrepresentation.

Did the misrepresentation influence the innocent party?

In order to be able to raise an action against the party who made the misrepresentation, the innocent party must prove that the false statement influenced his decision to proceed with the contract. If the innocent party fails to show that the misrepresentation had no influence on his decision and that he would have entered the contract in any case, his claim will fail.

 Smith *v* Chadwick (1884) an action was brought by Smith, a steel manufacturer, against Messrs Chadwick, Adamson and Collier who were accountants and promoters of a company. Smith claimed an amount of money as losses caused as a result of his decision to buy shares in the company which were worth much less than the price he had paid for them because of certain misrepresentations contained in the company prospectus issued by the defenders. Among the misrepresentations alleged by Smith was the statement that a certain Member of Parliament was a director of the company. In fact, this Member of Parliament had withdrawn from the company on the day before the prospectus was issued.

Held: the statement about the Member of Parliament was false but not material, because Smith had never heard of him and his decision to buy shares in the company had not been influenced by this piece of information. Smith's action for damages was, therefore, unsuccessful.

Attwood _v_ Small (1838) during negotiations for the sale of a mine, the defender made false statements to the pursuer about the mine's potential. The pursuer, however, appointed his own surveyor who broadly confirmed what the defender had said about the mine's potential. On the strength of the surveyor's report, the pursuer then proceeded to purchase the mine.

Held: the pursuer's reliance on his own survey clearly demonstrated that he had not been influenced in respect of his decision to purchase the mine by the original misrepresentation of the defender.

The effect of misrepresentation

Generally, misrepresentation has the effect of making a contract voidable. In other words, it will be up to the party who is the victim of the misrepresentation to take effective steps within a reasonable period of time to have the contract set aside or cancelled (the remedy of rescission). If the victim of the misrepresentation fails to cancel the contract within a reasonable time, the courts will treat this failure as evidence that he has decided to ratify or approve the agreement and he will have lost his right to cancel.

In order to cancel the contract, the court must be able to return the parties to their pre-contractual positions (_restitutio in integrum_). As shall become apparent, this remedy is not always available to the courts because of the impossibility of returning the parties to their original positions. Returning the parties to their original positions, for all practical purposes, means that any money or property that has been transferred must be returned to the original owners.

We can contrast the approach taken by the courts towards the remedy of rescission in two cases: **Boyd & Forrest _v_ Glasgow & South-Western Railway Co (1915)** and **Erlanger _v_ New Sombrero Phosphate Co (1878)**.

 Boyd & Forrest, a misrepresentation (innocently made) by the Glasgow & South-Western Railway's engineer as to the hardness of a section of subsoil, which was to be removed for the purpose of building a railway, cost the contractors £136,000 in additional costs. The House of Lords refused to return the parties to their original positions. What could be realistically achieved by ordering the parties to be returned to their pre-contractual positions? Tear down the brand new railway and replace all the rock and soil which had been extracted? This was a ridiculous suggestion on the part of the contractors and the court rightly refused to order this course of action. When the contractors realised that the information that they had received from the Railway was wrong, they should have stopped work immediately and informed the Railway of this problem. Instead, the contractors foolishly decided to proceed with the work.

 Erlanger, the pursuer was induced to buy an island containing mines on the basis of representations made by the other party as to their production capacity. It was held that although the mines had been substantially worked by the pursuer, he was entitled to rescind (cancel) the contract on condition that both the mines and all the profits received from working it were returned to the other party. The pursuer, of course, would be entitled to reclaim the price that he had paid for the island and the mines.

It is also worth appreciating that the remedy of damages may not available to the victim who has suffered loss as result of the misrepresentation. Where the misrepresentation is of an entirely innocent nature, the Scottish courts will not award damages and the only course of action (which may not provide much of a consolation) would be to attempt to have the contract rescinded or cancelled – if indeed this is a realistic possibility. In **Boyd & Forrest**, the misrepresentation was of an innocent nature and, consequently, the contractors were not awarded damages.

In situations involving negligent and fraudulent misrepresentation, there are a number of options available to the victim. The following remedies or combination of remedies is available to the victim:

1 Rescission or cancellation of the contract

2 Rescission or cancellation of the contract and an award of damages

3 Retention of the contract and an award of damages

In England, as a result of the Misrepresentation Act 1967, it is possible for the victim of an innocent misrepresentation to obtain damages.

Silence as a misrepresentation

By contrast, in the face of silence, the court normally applies the maxim *caveat emptor* – let the buyer beware. During contractual negotiations, the parties are allowed to keep their cards close to their chests in an attempt to obtain the best bargain for themselves. Obviously, when a party is asked a direct question during negotiations which concerns some aspect of the future contract, that question should receive an honest answer. As a matter of policy in these cases, the onus is placed on a party to discover the truth by means of interrogation, inquiry and examination. The law does not protect a party from the consequences of his own stupidity and which will lead him to make a bad bargain with the other party.

 This approach can be seen most clearly in the case of **Gillespie *v* Russel (1856)** where an individual who had taken out a lease on a gold mine discovered that the mine also contained a very valuable seam of coal. This fact was not communicated to the owner. The owner of the mine was completely unaware that the property also contained coal. Upon this discovery, the owner attempted to have the contract cancelled.

Held: the contract had already been concluded and it was up to the owner to keep a proper record of his assets.

If a party uses half-truths to conceal material facts, this may be regarded as a misrepresentation.

 Couston *v* Miller (1862) Miller had read out the contents of a deed that Couston intended to sign – Couston did not read the document. What Miller failed to do was to read out the most important part of the deed which, if he had done so, would have prevented Couston from going ahead and signing it. Miller had not told any lies, but his conduct was dishonest and amounted to a misrepresentation (see also **Chemical Cleaning and Dyeing Co (1951)** in relation to exclusion clauses below).

See also the issue of concealed fraud discussed below.

The difference between an opinion and a misrepresentation

An opinion is just an opinion and everyone is entitled to his opinion for what it may be worth. This may sound very democratic, but in practice the person who voices his opinion may be viewed as an expert or someone who possesses specialist knowledge. If this is the case, it may be that the person who got the benefit of the opinion may attach greater significance to it if it came from an expert. Sometimes, the dividing line between an opinion and a misrepresentation will be a very fine one.

 Hamilton *v* Duke of Montrose (1906) an advertisement in a newspaper of 'hill grazing capable of keeping about 2000 black faced sheep and summering 100 cattle' was not a misrepresentation. It was held to be a statement of opinion.

 Bisset *v* Wilkinson (1927) the buyer had purchased land in New Zealand, but he later wished to cancel the contract because he claimed that the seller had made a false statement as to how many sheep the land could accommodate.

Held: by the Privy Council, on the evidence, that the statement made by the seller of land was merely an opinion that he honestly held and, consequently, the buyer's action to have the contract cancelled or rescinded failed.

Requirements of disclosure

Sometimes the law imposes a duty on one or both of the parties to disclose all material facts that may have an effect on a contractual relationship.

Fiduciary relationships

A fiduciary relationship is a relationship of confidence that imposes a special duty of care on one or both of the parties. Examples of such relationships include those of solicitor/client, principal/agent, doctor/patient, parent/child and the partners in a firm. If a party owes a fiduciary duty to someone else this means that he must disclose all material facts to the other person. The duty arising from these types of fiduciary relationships are different from the duties that arise under contracts *uberrimae fidei* i.e. of the utmost good faith. In contracts *uberrimae fidei*, it is the nature of the contract, for example, an insurance contract which requires disclosure in spite of the relationship between the parties. In the fiduciary situation it is the relationship of the parties and not the particular contract which gives rise to the need to disclose. Fiduciary duties are discussed in relation to the law of agency in Chapter 5.

 McPherson's Trustees *v* Watt (1877) Watt, a solicitor or law agent who represented the interests of the trustees, had been given instructions to sell four houses for the trustees. Watt entered into an arrangement with his brother that he would sell the properties to his brother. Watt did not disclose this arrangement to the trustees. This arrangement was to operate on the condition that Watt's brother would later sell two of the houses to him at half the purchase price. The trustees discovered this arrangement between Watt and his brother and, before they could carry out the contract, the trustees obtained an interdict or court order to prevent it going ahead.

Held: the contract for the sale of the houses was invalid. A solicitor, as a law agent, has a duty to act in good faith and there must be no conflict of duty and interest.

 Pillans Brothers *v* Pillans (1908) the three Pillans brothers carried on a partnership business as rivet, bolt and nut manufacturers mainly in the Motherwell area. Richard Pillans, one of the brothers, later bought a business at Greenfield, four miles outside Motherwell, in which was involved in the same line of trade as the business that he ran with his brothers and which had directly competed against the family firm. Richard did not disclose to his brothers the fact that he was now the owner of a rival business. His brothers discovered this fact and raised a legal action against him.

Held: Richard had to disclose to his brothers all the profits that his rival business had made and, furthermore, he had to give them a share of these profits. Effectively, Richard had to surrender control of his business at Greenfield to the family firm.

Contracts *uberrimae fidei*

In a small number of situations, the law demands that, during pre-contractual negotiations, a party must act with the utmost good faith (*uberrimae fidei*). The example of insurance contracts are often used to demonstrate how this duty to act with the utmost good faith works in practice. The proposer (the person intending to take out the policy) is under a positive duty to bring all material facts to the insurer at the time of making the contract of insurance. If the proposer is in any doubt about the importance of a fact, for safety's sake and to protect his own position, he should bring it to the attention of the insurer. Failure by the proposer to do so may allow the insurer to treat the contract as voidable and refuse to pay out under the policy as the House of Lords made it quite clear in **Pan Atlantic Insurance *v* Pine Top Insurance (1994)**.

 The Spathari (1925) the owners of a ship deliberately concealed from the insurance company that the vessel was Greek owned. The ship later sank and the owners attempted to make a claim under the insurance policy. The insurance company at that time, in common with many other insurers, was refusing even to consider insuring Greek ships because they were regarded as such a bad risk. The insurance company later discovered the true facts concerning the vessel's ownership and informed the proposer that it would not honour the contract.

Held: by the House of Lords that the contract was voidable because the proposer had not disclosed all material facts as he was duty bound to do. The insurance company was entitled not to honour the contract.

The law is very strict with regard to insurance contracts because the proposer is could quite easily conceal material facts and the insurance company would be none the wiser. This would result in the insurers agreeing to take on a risk, without full knowledge on their part. However, if the insurance company decides to treat the contract as voidable, it must return the premiums paid to the proposer (**Banque Keyser Ullmann SA *v* Skandia (UK) Insurance Co (1989)**). In other words, the contract is rescinded or cancelled and the parties must be returned to their pre-contractual positions. Admittedly, most proposals for insurance require a proposer to sign a declaration in which he is stating for the record that the information he has provided is, to the best of his knowledge, truthful and accurate. This declaration by the proposer becomes part of the contract and, later if the proposer's failure to reveal all material facts is discovered, the insurers can treat the contract as void.

 Dawsons Ltd *v* Bonin (1922) the pursuers insured a lorry against loss by fire and stated on the proposal form that the lorry would be garaged at their business address. However, there was no garage at this address and the lorry had to kept elsewhere. The insurance company had insisted that the pursuers sign a declaration that all information provided was factually correct. The pursuers' secretary, who signed the proposal form on behalf of the company, knew that this statement was a mistake, but she failed to bring it to the attention of the insurers. The lorry was destroyed by fire and the pursuers tried to enforce the policy.

Held: by the House of Lords that by signing a declaration stating that all information provided to the insurers was accurate, the false statement regarding the lorry's whereabouts rendered the insurance contract null and void.

Where statute requires disclosure

When a company has a full listing on the London Stock Exchange, the **Financial Services and Markets Act 2002** imposes a requirement that certain types of information must be disclosed in an advert or prospectus issued by a company which is for the purpose of inviting members of the public to subscribe for shares or debentures. This advert or prospectus must be detailed enough so that essential information is given to investors and professional advisers so that they can make a reasonably informed decision about purchasing the shares or taking up the debentures. The provisions of the **Financial Services and Markets Act** apply to businesses who are engaged in a wide variety of investment activities. Offering shares to the public without an approved prospectus is a criminal offence punishable by up to two years in prison and/or a fine.

Clearly, a false statement in a company prospectus may amount to a misrepresentation of some variety or other which may the give the innocent party a right of action against the person who was responsible for it (but see **Smith *v* Chadwick (1884)** above).

Concealed fraud

Silence can amount to misrepresentation in the case of concealed fraud.

 Gibson *v* National Cash Register Co Ltd (1925) the seller of cash registers had work carried out on the goods to make them appear as if they were brand new items. The goods were, in fact, second hand, but the buyer was not aware of this and the basis of the appearance of the goods he entered a contract with the seller thinking that he was purchasing brand new goods. The seller, of course, did not inform the buyer of the true facts. The buyer later discovered the truth about the goods and sued the seller for damages on the grounds of fraudulent concealment.

 Gordon *v* Selico Co Ltd (1986) a block of flats which had recently been converted by a developer was leased to the pursuer for 99 years. Not long after the pursuer had moved into the property, dry rot was discovered.

Held: by the English Court of Appeal that deliberate concealment of dry rot by the developer could be regarded as fraudulent misrepresentation and damages were awarded to the pursuer.

Failure to disclose a change in circumstances

Parties have a duty to disclose any change in circumstances.

 Shankland *v* Robinson (1920) the seller of a traction engine reassured a potential buyer that the item was not going to be requisitioned by the Government. It later emerged that the Government now intended to requisition the machine.

Held: by the House of Lords that, if the seller had definitely been aware that the machine was going to be requisitioned, and had attempted to conceal this from the prospective buyer this would have amounted to fraudulent concealment. A seller in these circumstances was under a duty to reveal a change in circumstances to a buyer as soon as he became aware of the relevant facts.

 With *v* O'Flanagan (1936) the seller of a medical practice informed the prospective purchaser that the practice was a profitable business. This statement was quite true when it was originally made. Time passed and the practice ceased to be profitable, but the seller chose not to inform the purchaser of this change in circumstances before the sale took place. The sale went ahead and the purchaser discovered the true state of the business.

Held: by the English Court of Appeal that the seller's failure to notify the change in the circumstances of the business amounted to a misrepresentation.

Illegality

When we talk about illegal contracts, it is worth emphasising as Lord Wheatley did in the case of **Dowling & Rutter and Others *v* Abacus Frozen Foods Limited (2000)** (Outer House of the Court of Session) that a distinction should be made as to the illegal creation of a contract and the illegal performance of a contract. If performance of a perfectly legal contract is carried out in a way which involves a breach of statute, the courts may be prepared to overlook this by taking the view that it involved such a minor degree of illegality as to be irrelevant to the main purpose of the contract; or that the breach was outwith the scope of the statute in question. In such cases, it would be extremely harsh if the courts prevented one or both of the parties from enforcing the contract as a result of a very minor breach of statute. The parties to an agreement which breaches statute may not escape completely. They may find that breaches of the statutory provisions result in fines or some other punishment being imposed.

Lord Wheatley made it very clear, however, that if the creation of a contract is forbidden by statute it would be very difficult, impossible even, for the courts to enforce it. It would be ridiculous if a party attempted to form a contract to do something which was forbidden by statute law and then turned to the courts for assistance in order to enforce the illegal agreement.

As a general rule, the doctrine of illegality penalises those parties who create particular contracts that are regarded as illegal (sometimes referred to as *pacta illicita*). The greatest sanction that the court has is to refuse to enforce the agreement if its creation breaches the common law or statute. Such an agreement is void from its creation. This means that, in the event of a dispute, the parties will not have any rights or duties under the agreement – the courts will simply not recognise its validity. The general rule regarding illegal contracts is often expressed as *ex turpi causa non oritur actio* i.e. a party can have no right of action when the dispute involves an immoral or illegal situation.

 Key point: The creation of a contract may be illegal either at common law or as a result of statute.

What would be the situation if, for example, a man hired a contract killer to murder to his wife, he paid the killer in advance to go ahead and carry out the murder, but at the last the killer decided to pocket the money and not carry out the job? Firstly, the husband would be unable to sue for the return of his money and, secondly, he could not sue the contract killer for breach of the agreement and even begin to convince a judge that he should be awarded damages as compensation. If the husband brought this agreement to the attention of the courts, it would mean exposing the whole scheme to the criminal authorities. This example of illegal contracts is a particularly dramatic one, but not all illegal contracts will involve breaking the criminal law.

 Key point: An illegal contract will not necessarily involve breaches of the criminal law but such contracts often breach civil law.

An example of an illegal contract and the attitude of the courts can be seen in the following case:

Cowan v Milbourn (1867) a person hired a hall for lectures which were illegal under the blasphemy laws. When the purpose of the lectures was revealed, he was then refused possession of the hall. His action claiming possession was refused on the grounds that the court could not enforce the contract when its purpose was illegal.

If the parties have exchanged property or money under such an illegal agreement, there is very little chance of it being returned to the original owners. Any contract which is illegal will be null and void.

 Key point: Neither party can enforce an illegal contract as it has no legal force whatsoever i.e. it is completely void.

In situations where a pursuer can argue that he is not equally to blame or in the wrong (*in pari delicto*), he may be able to recover damages or money paid under the contract. Where the contract is unlawful on the face of it, equal guilt is presumed but this may be disproved if the pursuer can show that the defender is to blame and that he is an innocent party.

 Cuthbertson v Lowes (1870) the contract involved the sale of potatoes and the price had been calculated using Scottish measurements. On the face of it, there was nothing wrong with this agreement, but the Weights and Measures Acts prohibited the use of Scottish measurements – the imperial measure should have been used to calculate the price of the goods. The Weights and Measures Acts stated that if parties used a measure other than the imperial measure, the contract would be void. The seller delivered the goods, but the buyer refused to pay for them. The seller raised an action for the price, but the statutes had declared the contract void.

Held: if the seller was prevented from suing for the price of the goods this would result in a totally unjust situation as the buyer would get the goods for nothing. The buyer had to pay the value of the goods at the time of their delivery.

 Key point: In exceptional circumstances, the courts may enforce an agreement tainted by illegality if one of the parties can show that he was an innocent party and, therefore, unaware of the illegal nature of the agreement.

Illegality in terms of statute

Parliament (either Westminster or the Scottish Parliament) will have passed legislation (statute law) in order to make certain types of contracts illegal. In situations where the creation of some contracts are forbidden by statute with the effect that they are rendered illegal, the word 'unlawful' will appear in the statute to describe these types of agreement. Statute includes orders, rules and regulations that ministers of the Crown and other persons authorised by Parliament can issue. Statutory prohibitions may be expressed or implied.

Under the Consumer Credit Act 1974, for example, it would be illegal for an individual to operate a consumer credit business without having first secured a licence from the Office of Fair Trading. Any transactions entered into with consumers by the creditor would, therefore, be tainted with illegality. The aim of the

Consumer Credit Act 1974 is to protect debtors and to ensure that those who engage in a credit business are fit and proper people. This is primarily achieved through the operation of the Act's licensing system (see Chapter 4).

 Bigos v Bousted (1951) a contract to supply lire in Italy in exchange for payment in sterling in the UK contravened the Exchange Control Act 1947. One of the parties refused to supply the Italian currency and the other party sued for breach of contract. This was a deliberate attempt by both parties to circumvent United Kingdom currency regulations and, since both parties were equally to blame, neither could enforce the contract.

Implied statutory prohibition

The statute, in such a situation, may not provide a great deal of detail as to the types of conduct it considers to be illegal. The courts will have to make sense of Parliament's intention regarding this matter i.e. whether there is an intention to prohibit certain types of behaviour or whether the statute is designed to achieve some other purpose. The statute may have an indirect effect on a contract thus rendering it illegal in some way.

Illegality at common law

Some agreements will be illegal because judges have developed common law rules over the years which have forbid the formation of such agreements.

Examples of illegal contracts at common law include the following:

◆ Contracts to commit crimes or civil wrongs
◆ Contracts promoting sexual immorality
◆ Contracts harmful to good foreign relations between the United Kingdom and friendly states
◆ Contracts harmful to the administration of justice
◆ Contracts promoting corruption in public life
◆ Contracts entered into with enemy aliens
◆ Contracts to avoid (by illegal means) the payment of taxes
◆ Contracts in restraint of trade or restrictive covenants

Contracts promoting sexual immoral behaviour

 Pearce v Brooks (1866) the pursuers hired a carriage to the defender for a period of 12 months. The defender was to pay the price by instalments. The defender was a prostitute and the carriage was of a very attractive design in order to attract customers. It was established that one of the pursuers knew what use the carriage was to be put to and that, consequently, their claim for sums owed under the contract of hire failed due to the illegal nature of the contract. The contract would have been valid had the pursuers not known how the carriage was going to be used.

Contracts which harm good foreign relations

 Regazzoni v Sethia (1958) a contract to supply jute to Apartheid-era South Africa which was legal under English law, was not enforceable in the English courts because it was in breach of anti-Apartheid regulations in India, the country where the contract was to be performed. India was a country that the United Kingdom had friendly relations with and it is not usually the practice of the British courts to enforce contracts which break the laws of friendly countries. The jute was to be shipped from India to Italy and then on to South Africa. The defenders had failed to deliver the jute bags as agreed and this is why the action was brought before the courts.

Contracts which promote corruption in public life

 Parkinson _v_ College of Ambulance (1925) Parkinson donated a large sum to the College on the understanding that by doing so he would be given a knighthood. However, Parkinson did not receive his knighthood and he demanded that the donation be returned to him. The College refused to return the donation and Parkinson sued for its return.

Held: Parkinson's action failed because the court felt that the buying and selling of knighthoods and other honours was clearly corrupt. The court did not wish to enforce an agreement that would clearly lead to greater levels of corruption in public life. The agreement was void and Parkinson did not get his money back.

Contracts involving trading with the enemy

 Cantiere San Rocco SA _v_ Clyde Shipbuilding and Engineering Co Ltd (1923) the pursuers were an Austrian firm which had entered into a contract with a Scottish company, the defenders. When the First World War began on 4 August 1914, the Austrian firm became an enemy alien owing to the fact that Austria and her ally, Germany, were now at war with the United Kingdom.

Held: by the House of Lords that the contract was to be regarded as void and unenforceable during the course of the War, but when hostilities ended the contract would be capable of enforcement. The defenders could not continue to have a contractual relationship with the Austrians during wartime because this would have amounted to trading with the enemy.

Restrictive covenants or contracts in restraint of trade

1. Anthony v Rennie 1981
2. Dallas, McMillen and Sinclair
   Simpson 1989
3.

A restrictive covenant is used by one party in a contractual relationship to protect his legitimate business interests from unjustified exploitation or interference by another person, for example, ex-employees who are now employed by business rivals and former owners of a business who are now attempting to set up rival businesses. Legitimate business interests might include the following:

- Trade secrets
- Designs for new products
- Manufacturing processes
- Business expansion plans
- Investments
- Customers and other business connections

These types of contractual terms are restrictive in the sense that they limit the freedom of one of the parties to the contract to do certain things. They are particularly common in contracts of employment and are often inserted at the employer's insistence. By using them, the employer is attempting to prevent an employee from working for a business rival after his current employment has ended. However, such contractual terms are potentially abusive and they are usually scrutinised very strictly by the Scottish courts. Scottish judges will tend to display an almost instinctively suspicious attitude when asked to consider contracts in restraint of trade. After all, they are first and foremost anti-competitive agreements. Why should employees be prevented from taking up an offer of alternative employment which is more lucrative and satisfying if they so choose? If an employer cannot retain the services of a valuable employee then perhaps, as a consequence, he deserves his business to suffer. Similarly, why should a person who has just sold a business at a large profit be prevented from establishing a new business in the same trade or profession?

 Key point: A restrictive covenant may be used to protect legitimate business interests such as trade secrets, designs for new products, manufacturing processes, business expansion plans, investments and customers and other business connections.

Restrictive covenants or contracts in restraint of trade, as they are alternatively known, are contractual terms commonly found in the following types of agreement:

◆ Employment contracts

◆ Contracts involving the sale of a business

◆ Solus (exclusive supply) and franchise agreements

◆ Agreements between trade associations and their members

 Key point: Restrictive covenants are commonly found in employment contracts, sales of businesses, solus and franchise agreements and trade association agreements.

Free and fair competition

The statement that free and fair competition makes for a healthy economy is a self-evident truth. This statement begs the question as to whether restrictive covenants should be tolerated in a free market economy. Surely, employees have an absolute right to work and businesses have an absolute right to trade on terms which promote their interests? However, competition must be fair if it is to be effective. The former employer of a particularly competent employee may have legitimate business reasons for wanting to restrict the employment opportunities of the individual in question. On a similar theme, the new owner of a business may be less than delighted to discover that the person, from whom he has just purchased the concern, has set up a new establishment in the same trade or profession a few hundred yards down the street. Although the motives of those individuals seeking to rely on these types of contractual arrangements may be entirely understandable, it is worth bearing in mind that anti-competitive agreements (no matter how well intentioned) may actually breach the provisions of the Competition Act 1998 and European Union competition policy (**Articles 101 and 102: Treaty on the Functioning of the European Union**).

A useful rule of thumb for an individual wishing to enforce a restrictive covenant is to remember not to impose unduly excessive terms on a weaker party and to do nothing more than is absolutely necessary to protect legitimate business interests. Ultimately, however, the Scottish courts will determine what is reasonable by carefully examining all the circumstances of the case.

 Key point: Anti-competitive agreements (no matter how well intentioned) may actually breach the provisions of the Competition Act 1998 and European Union competition policy (Articles 101 and 102: Treaty on the Functioning of the European Union).

The judicial approach to contracts in restraint of trade

The role of the courts in all of this is to weigh up the competing interests of the parties and determine whether the party who wishes to rely on the contract in restraint of trade has a legitimate interest which should be protected. If such an interest is deemed worthy of protection, then the court will issue an interdict to prevent a former employee from taking up alternative employment with a business rival or the new owner of a business may win an interdict which prevents the former owner setting up in competition just down the road (or even next door as has occurred on occasion). When relying upon a restriction in the contract, an individual must show that he is taking legitimate measures to protect his position. After all, these restrictions are anti-competitive and the courts are right to treat them with suspicion. Employees should have the right to seek alternative employment and businesses should have the right to compete against one another. The courts are, therefore, placed in a position where they will have to perform a delicate balancing act, weighing up, for example, the employer's right to protect legitimate business interests such as trade secrets and, on the other hand, the employee's right to seek profitable work wherever he can find it.

A contractual restriction may be challenged in a number of ways:

◆ The restraint is unreasonable between the parties i.e. it is an illegitimate attempt to limit a person's freedom. The restriction may not be an honest attempt by the party relying on it to protect his legitimate business interests. In short, the clause may be nothing more than a blatant attempt to stifle competition by preventing an employee from seeking alternative employment.

◆ The length of the restraint is unreasonable i.e. it lasts for a period of time which is longer than is absolutely necessary. The new owner of business may attempt to prevent his predecessor from starting a rival business for a period of ten years. This could be excessive in a situation where a two year restriction would have been more than adequate.

◆ The geographical area of the restraint is unreasonable i.e. United Kingdom, European or global restrictions may immediately excite suspicion and may be viewed as excessively wide. Excessively wide local restrictions can also be struck down by the courts. It would not be reasonable for someone to impose a term in a contract for the sale of a business which stated that the previous owner could not establish a similar business anywhere within a twenty-five mile radius of

Hamilton. If the business was purely local in nature and confined largely to the Hamilton area, the new owner has no right to prevent the previous owner from setting up another business in Edinburgh.

◆ The restraint is not in the public interest – restrictive business practices clearly do not benefit the public and can restrict consumer choice.

A court, when reaching its decision, may also take into account any other relevant factors such as trade customs and practices, the ease with which an employee will be able to secure new employment and the employee's need to continue working in order to gain valuable experience and to keep his skills updated. It will be appreciated that trade customs and practices must be reasonable and must be essential for the protection of legitimate business interests.

 Key point: A restrictive covenant must be reasonable between the parties, in terms of its duration, its geographical area and its enforcement must be in the public interest.

The consequences of an unreasonable restraint of trade

A party who wishes to enforce a restraint of trade must realise that if the court regards it as anti-competitive and abusive, it will be struck down. In other words, such a contractual term will be regarded as automatically null and void. The offending clause will be removed or severed from the contract. Furthermore, the Scottish courts will not redraft the clause in more reasonable terms. This means that the party who sought to enforce the restraint is now left completely unprotected and there is nothing to stop the other party doing pretty much what he pleases (**see Dumbarton Steamboat Co v MacFarlane (1899) discussed below**). It is worth bearing in mind that a judge's decision to render a restraint void and unenforceable will not affect the functioning of the other terms of the contract. The court will usually delete only as much of the invalid part of the clause as is strictly necessary, for example, a line or a word. It is not usual judicial practice to treat the whole clause as void unless it has no other option (**see Nordenfelt v Maxim Nordenfelt Guns and Ammunition Co [1894] discussed below**). The remaining contractual terms are very much capable of enforcement by both parties. It is only in very unusual circumstances, that the removal of the offensive term from the agreement will completely undermine the operation of the remainder of the contract.

 Key point: If a restrictive covenant is found to be excessive and completely unreasonable in the sense that it goes beyond what is adequate to protect legitimate business interests, it will be automatically void and the party relying on it will be left completely vulnerable as the courts will refuse to replace it with something more reasonable.

Employment contracts and restraints of trade

One of the greatest fears that many employers have is that a high-flying or extremely competent employee might be tempted to go and work for a business rival or set up in business on his own account. Generally speaking, however, a court will not prevent an individual from using skills or information gained in the course of previous employment (**see Centre for Maritime Industrial Safety Technology Ltd v Crute [2003] below**). The dangers for an employer of failing to insert some sort of restraint in the employment contract becomes all too obvious upon an examination of the following case:

 Faccenda Chicken Ltd v Fowler [1986] Fowler was employed in the position of sales manager with Faccenda Chicken Ltd. He had worked for the company for seven years and had played a very prominent role in the creation and expansion of the company's refrigerated poultry selling operations. The company operated a fleet of refrigerated vans which travelled around various retailers and wholesellers in the local area selling products directly to these individuals. Fowler eventually decided to leave his employment with Faccenda. He set up his own business which competed directly with his ex-employer. Fowler had also persuaded some of his former colleagues at Faccenda to come and work for him at his new business. Not surprisingly, Faccenda was extremely alarmed at this development and attempted to obtain damages from Fowler alleging that he had breached his contractual duty not to use confidential information in a way that harmed the interests of his former employer.

Held: by the English Court of Appeal that Faccenda's attempt to sue Fowler for damages should be dismissed. The information that the company claimed was confidential (names of customers, delivery routes, times of deliveries) was widely known. By no stretch of the imagination could this information be described as a trade secret. Faccenda had no one to blame but itself for its failure to include restraints in the employment contracts of Fowler and other former employees.

A business rival will obviously be eager to recruit such an individual because of the kind of information that they will possess: knowledge of trade secrets, designs, business expansion plans, lists of customers and other investments. The ex-employee will doubtless have gained invaluable skills and experience in his last job and, furthermore, he may have benefited from a range of training and educational opportunities which were all provided to him courtesy of his ex-employer. All these features, which made the employee so valuable, are now, potentially, at the service of the new employer. It is not uncommon for a business rival to attempt to headhunt highly rated employees from their current employers by offering them much better terms and conditions (and various other incentives). It is not stretching the imagination to suggest that an ex-employee will be only too eager to get off to a flying start in his new job by divulging confidential information, gained in his previous employment, to his new employer and that the ex-employer will have real concerns about this.

 Key point: An employer would be well advised to insert a restrictive covenant in an employee's contract of employment in order to protect legitimate business interests as failure to do so can often be catastrophic.

In certain trades or professions, for example, information technology, the law and banking and financial services, the defection of valuable employees is always a very real threat. Faced with the realisation that they are not able to retain the services of such individuals, many employers will have made sure that a damage limitation mechanism is in place. Employers will, therefore, attempt to restrict the immediate and future employment opportunities of their ex-employees – albeit for a fairly limited period of time. The theory goes that, by the time the ex-employee is ready to take up a position with a new employer, most of the knowledge gained may be outdated or even redundant. This would clearly make the employee less attractive to prospective employers. There is also the question of how a restraint may harm the ex-employee's skills – he may work in an industry or profession where continued updating of skills and experience is both necessary and expected. Effectively forcing the ex-employee to pursue an alternative career (even for a relatively short period of time) may do irreparable harm to his long-term career prospects. The age of the employee may also be an important factor for the courts to consider when deciding whether or not to enforce the restraint.

 Key point: Restrictive covenants are basically anti-competitive devices and may actually do irreparable harm to an ex-employee's long-term career prospects so the courts will have to be particularly careful when deciding whether or not to enforce such a term of the contract.

 Bluebell Apparel v Dickinson [1978] Dickinson was a management trainee who worked for a subsidiary of an American company that was involved in the production of "Wrangler" jeans. As a management trainee, Dickinson had access to trade secrets and information about business connections and customers. There was a term in Dickinson's employment contract that, if he left the company's employment, he would not seek employment with any business rival of his employer anywhere in the world for a period of two years. Later, Dickinson left his employment and, in breach of this restriction, he accepted an offer of employment with Levi Strauss & Co who were also involved in the global business of manufacturing denim jeans. Dickinson's former employers sought an interdict to prevent him from continuing to work for Levi Strauss.

Held: the restriction was reasonable in terms of time and geography and that Dickinson's former employer was taking reasonable steps to protect its legitimate business interests. The court granted an interdict to Dickinson's former employers and he had to give up his new job with Levi Strauss.

 Centre for Maritime Industrial Safety Technology Ltd v Crute [2003] Clive Crute, the defender, had worked as a manager for the pursuer, Centre Maritime Industrial Safety Technology (known as C-MIST). He had commenced employment with the pursuer on 4 April 2002. Crute had previously been employed as a Master Mariner for over 30 years. C-MIST was involved in the provision of a wide range of services relating to health and safety issues in connection with the operation of marine terminals and jetties. Crute was offered new employment with Briggs Marine Contractors Ltd, a client of C-MIST's on 11 November 2002 (with 1 February 2003 envisaged as a starting date). Briggs operated the Coryton Terminal in Essex for British

Petroleum. The new post with Briggs was described as Contractors Manager for jetty operations at the Coryton Terminal. On 25 November 2002, Crute submitted a letter of resignation to C-MIST and he explained that he was going to work for Briggs. He was informed by a one of C-MIST's directors that he was prevented from working for Briggs due to a restrictive covenant and confidentiality clause in his contract. The restrictive covenant stated that Crute could not provide services (whether paid or unpaid) to clients of C-MIST for a period of 18 months after the termination of his contract. The confidentiality clause stated that Crute was prevented from using skills in his new employment that he had acquired while working for C-MIST. C-MIST was fearful that if Crute was allowed to take up employment with Briggs it would mean that he would be in a position to establish in-house health and safety training courses so that Briggs would eventually dispense with their services.

Held: by Lord Mackay of Drumadoon (in the Outer House of the Court of Session) that the restrictive covenant of 18 months was excessive and went far beyond what was required to protect C-MIST's legitimate business interests. His Lordship balanced C-MIST's interests against those of Crute and was strongly of the opinion that the employee would be harmed if the restriction was enforced. A number of factors were taken into account: Crute was 57 and, at his time of life, his future employment prospects might be harmed if he was restrained from working for Briggs or any other prospective employer covered by the restriction in his contract. Furthermore, C-MIST's fears that Crute would be able to provide in-house health and safety training for Briggs at its expense was completely unfounded. C-MIST and Briggs still had the better part of two years of a three year contract remaining in relation to the provision of consultancy services. As for the confidentiality clause in Crute's contract, an employee is permitted to use skills that he has acquired in the service of a new employer. As we shall see, an employee will commit a breach of his implied duty of good faith and fidelity if he divulges confidential information, gained in the course of his previous employment, to his new employer.

An employer would argue very strongly that he has a right to protect his business and very few people would take issue with such an argument. What the courts will not tolerate is a blatant attempt by the employer to ruin the future employment prospects of an ex-employee. Employees, after all, have the right to seek better employment opportunities. This is particularly the case when we remember that the modern United Kingdom labour market is characterised in the main by the high dependency shown by employers on short-term, temporary employment contracts. It is little wonder that today many employees have no concept of company loyalty. Given the short-term nature of many employment contracts, it may now be even more unreasonable for an employer to attempt to impose a lengthy time restriction on the employee. As we have seen in **Centre for Maritime Industrial Safety Technology *v* Crute [2003]**, Lord Mackay of Drumadoon was strongly of the view that an eighteen month restriction went much further than was strictly necessary to protect the interests of the employer.

Key point: The decisions in Bluebell Apparel and Centre for Maritime Industrial Safety Technology demonstrate very clearly that the courts examine the time limit in the restrictive covenant very much on its individual merits and what is a reasonable time in one situation may be completely unreasonable in other circumstances.

Restrictive covenants and junior employees

It would be a mistake to assume that these restrictions appear only in the employment contracts of senior executives and highly skilled professionals. In **Scottish Dairy Farmers Company (Glasgow) Ltd v McGhee (1933)** and **Home Counties Dairies v Skilton [1970]** the employees in question were both milkmen who were successfully restrained from approaching the customers of their former employers. McGhee and Skilton had left their previous employers to go and work for rival dairies. It should be understood that both employees were, therefore, in a very strong position to approach their ex-employers' customers and persuade them to use the services of their new employers. This practice is often simply referred to as poaching customers. McGhee and Skilton had both set out to commit a deliberate breach of contract by approaching the customers of their former employers in complete defiance of the restriction to which they had voluntarily agreed. The Inner House of the Court of Session in **McGhee** and the English Court of Appeal in **Skilton** found in favour of the employers. Neither restriction was excessive in terms of the time limit (both lasted for a year after termination of the employment), the employers were protecting legitimate business interests (their customer base) and the geographical area of the restrictions was not unreasonable (both milkmen were forbidden from approaching customers that they had previously dealt with who lived in the area of their former rounds). Furthermore, in **Skilton**, the English Court of Appeal did not think that the phrase 'dairy produce' as it appeared in the milkman's contract applied to an excessively wide range of products. Dairy produce covered all the items that that a milkman ordinarily sold to customers as part of his rounds. There was something of a crumb of comfort for the employee in **Skilton**, as the Court of Appeal did concede that he would be allowed to approach those individuals who had ceased to be customers of his ex-employer in the 6 month period prior to the termination of his employment contract. It had been a condition of the restrictive covenant that he could not approach those individuals who had been customers of his ex-employer during the six months before his contract had ended.

Key point: Although restrictive covenants will often be found in the contracts of high-flying and more senior employees, many employers may wish to seek the protection of such a term in relation to more junior employees.

The consequences of divulging confidential information to a new employer

In **PSM International and McKechnie v Whitehouse and Willenhall Automation [1992]** the English Court of Appeal has stated that any attempt by a former employee to divulge confidential information acquired in the course of his previous employment should be regarded as a material or extremely serious breach of that contract. The previous employer may even be able to obtain an interdict in order to prevent the new employer from capitalising on this information if he can show that the ex-employee's breach of contract has caused him to suffer loss. The effect of this interdict would mean that the new employer would be unable to derive any benefit from the information given to him by his new employee. However, the burden of proof will clearly be placed upon the ex-employer to demonstrate that there is a direct link between the breach of confidence and the losses that he has sustained.

Individuals will not be permitted to use trade secrets or confidential information acquired during the course of their employment for their own benefit. Therefore, a deliberate attempt by an individual to use trade secrets or confidential information in this way can be subject to legal challenge. It does not matter whether the contract of employment contained a restraint or not.

 In **Robb v Green [1895]**, a manager quite deliberately, and in an extremely calculated fashion, copied the names of his employer's customers. The manager's intention was to canvas these customers at a later date with a view to persuading them to use the services of the business that he was setting up.

Held: by the English Court of Appeal that, although there was no restrictive covenant in the manager's contract of employment, he owed an implied duty of good faith and fidelity. By acting deliberately in a way that harmed his employer's interest, the ex-employee had breached an important term of his contract and he was not permitted to approach this group of customers.

It will be recalled in **Faccenda Chicken Ltd v Fowler (above)**, that the employer attempted to argue (unsuccessfully) that Fowler, its former manager, had breached his duty of confidentiality which he continued to owe to the company despite leaving its employment. Information may be regarded as confidential if it can be regarded as a trade secret and the employer has continually stressed its confidential nature. The information will not be treated as confidential if it was readily available to members of the employer's staff in the course of their ordinary duties.

There is always the danger for an employer that the employee will build up personal relationships with customers who may wish to follow the employee if he leaves his current employment for a new position in a competing business undertaking. An added danger may be that the ex-employee may approach these customers directly in a brazen attempt to secure their business. This is why it is vital for an employer to include a restrictive covenant in the employee's contract of employment.

 Key point: Any attempt by a former employee to divulge confidential information acquired in the course of his previous employment should be regarded as a serious breach of that contract. The previous employer may even be able to obtain an interdict in order to prevent the new employer from capitalising on this information.

Extended notice periods ('garden leave' clause)

An employer can always use an alternative approach to the problem of protecting trade secrets and business connections. Some employers, rather than including a restrictive covenant in the employment contract – which can always be challenged on the grounds that it is unreasonable, will insist that an employee has to give an extended period of notice if he wishes to terminate his employment. Eighteen-month notice periods are not unknown in some trades and professions where the employee is in a very senior position within the organisation. This gives the employer time to prepare for the employee's departure by taking precautions to protect trade secrets or business connections. Furthermore, the current employer may actually state that it is not necessary for the employee to turn up for work – he may as well tend his garden (hence the phrase 'garden leave'). The beauty of these contractual notice periods is that the employee cannot work for any other employer who is competing against his current employer.

This arrangement effectively prevents the employee from gaining access to any trade secrets or having any dealings with customers of the employer. By the time that the extended notice period is at an end, the employee will represent less of a threat to his former employer if he goes to work for a rival business. These extended notice periods will not escape examination by the courts. These arrangements can stifle or prevent genuine competition and employers would be well advised to act reasonably when incorporating these types of terms in employment contracts. They can be used to get round some of the problems that restrictive covenants pose, but they are not without their problems. Employees who are affected by these 'garden leave' clauses can challenge them by putting forward the argument that it is important that they are allowed to continue to work in their chosen profession in order to keep vital skills updated and current. A software engineer could argue that an 18-month 'garden leave' clause was excessive in that it prevented him from developing his skills and gaining valuable work experience in an industry which is notoriously susceptible to rapid changes in technology.

In **William Hill Organisation Ltd v Tucker (1998)** (discussed below), the English Court of Appeal criticised the growing use by employers of garden leave clauses in employment contracts. The Court was particularly concerned that this was little more than an attempt to get round the strict rules governing the use of restrictive covenants in employment contracts. It was felt that garden leave clauses should be scrutinised carefully and, furthermore, the rules surrounding these types of clauses should be considerably tightened to prevent abuse by employers.

 William Hill Organisation Ltd v Tucker (1998) William Hill, the pursuers and appellants, attempted to prevent Tucker, the defender, from going to work for a business rival, City Index Ltd, during his notice period. The contractual notice period was for six months. The notice period had originally been for one month, but the defender had later agreed to extend it to six months. The defender worked for a subsidiary of the pursuers called William Hill Index Ltd which operated a gambling business known as 'spread betting'. This type of gambling activity is regulated by the Securities and Futures Authority (SFA) and William Hill Index Ltd was one of only five companies authorised by the SFA to carry on such a business. One of the other four was City Index Ltd. The defender commenced employment with the pursuers in 1995 as the senior dealer. There was a term in the defender's employment contract that stated:

'Whilst in employment, you must not undertake any other employment, or hold office, which creates a conflict of interest with the Company, or any company within the Group. You should declare to your Manager any interests/connections with existing/potential suppliers or customers of the Company. If so directed, you will sever the interest/connection immediately or render yourself liable to disciplinary action.'

On 2 February 1998, the defender decided to leave his employment with the pursuers and go to work for City Index Ltd – a rival of the pursuers. The defender gave one month's notice despite the fact that he had agreed to extend it to six months in return for an enhancement to his conditions of employment. The defender argued that the pursuers had not made good on the promises made to him and that they should not stand in the way of his attempt to further his career with another employer. The pursuers attempted to obtain an interdict to prevent the defender from doing this, claiming that they were concerned that the defender would divulge confidential information to his new employer. It was also confirmed by the pursuers that the defender did not have to turn up to work during his extended notice period and that he would continue to enjoy his salary and other benefits during this period. The defender argued that he wanted to continue working in order to develop his skills and, in any case, he longer possessed confidential information to pass on to his new employer.

Held: by the English Court of Appeal that the defender's post of senior dealer was a special and unique one. It was important that the defender continued to develop his skills in this area by being permitted to continue to work in the specialised field of spread betting. The interdicts were, therefore refused.

 Key point: Very often it will be better for the employer to insist on an extremely long notice period (a garden leave clause) whereby the employee is paid but does not have to turn up to work and, during this period, the employer knows that the employee has no access to trade secrets or dealings with customers.

Informal arrangements between employers

In certain situations, a group of employers may enter into informal arrangements with the aim of preventing their employees from seeking alternative employment.

 Kores Manufacturing Co Ltd *v* Kolok Manufacturing Co Ltd (1958)
the premises of the two companies were located next to one another and they were both in a similar line of business. They had an informal agreement whereby Kores would refuse to offer employment to an individual who had worked for Kolok in the last five years and vice versa. A former employee of Kores sought employment with Kolok and Kores took steps to prevent this.

Held: by the Court of Appeal that the attempt by Kores to obtain an interdict to prevent its former employee from taking up employment with Kolok should fail. Kores and Kolok were operating a completely unreasonable agreement which was not in their employees' interests nor in the wider public interest. If Kores and Kolok wished to take proper steps to protect their interests, it would have been more approriate and more reasonable to include a restrictive covenant in the contracts of their employees.

Restraints imposed on the seller of a business

Such a restraint would be void, unless it is necessary to protect the goodwill of the business sold and not to stifle competition. Sometimes, the sale of a business can involve a global restraint. However, these global restraints will be very strictly examined by the courts and, more often than not, they will be unsuccessful.

 Nordenfelt *v* Maxim Nordenfelt Guns and Ammunition Co (1894)
Nordenfelt was the manufacturer of machine guns and other armaments. When he sold the business to a company he agreed to a restriction that would severely restrict the scope of his business interests. Nordenfelt had, in fact, agreed that he would not set up another business in any part of the world for the purpose of producing armaments for a period of 25 years and, furthermore, that he would not compete with the new venture in any trade or business whatsoever that it was involved in.

Held: by the House of Lords that the global restriction lasting 25 years regarding the sale of the armaments business was valid and enforceable, even though it was very wide. The armaments industry was highly specialised and the pool of potential customers was very small. The new company needed the time to build up a relationship with Nordenfelt's former customers in order to establish itself in this particular market. However, the court was able to remove the other part of the clause which attempted to prevent Nordenfelt from competing against the new company in any other trade or business whatsoever. This part of the agreement was void because it was plainly anti-competitive and was completely unnecessary to protect the business interests of the new company.

 British Reinforced Concrete Co *v* Schelff (1921) the seller of a local business producing 'loop' road reinforcements, at the insistence of the buyer, promised not to manufacture or sell any road reinforcements as part of any other business that he might establish at a later date. The buyer was a large manufacturer and seller of all types of road reinforcements who sold these products on a United Kingdom-wide basis. The clause that the seller had agreed to prevented him from competing against the buyer in the manufacture or sale of such products anywhere in the United Kingdom.

Held: the new owner of the business could not enforce the clause in the contract of sale because it went further than was necessary to protect legitimate business interests. The buyer had manufactured and sold just one type of product. The clause attempted to prevent the buyer from manufacturing other types of products. This clause was, therefore, unreasonable and anti-competitive.

Dumbarton Steamboat Co *v* MacFarlane (1899) MacFarlane had operated a carrier business on the River Clyde running between Glasgow, Greenock and Dumbarton. He later decided to sell the business and the buyer insisted upon the inclusion of a clause in the contract sale that effectively prevented MacFarlane from establishing a similar business anywhere in the United Kingdom for a period of ten years. MacFarlane's business operations were of a purely local nature being confined to the River Clyde. Some three years later, after selling the business, MacFarlane set up another carrier business operating between Glasgow and Dumbarton. The buyers applied for an interdict to prevent MacFarlane from carrying on his new business.

Held: the restriction in the contract of sale was totally excessive and the court refused to replace it with a more reasonable alternative. This meant that MacFarlane was totally free to run his new business with complete impunity much to the buyers' anger and frustration.

Restrictions on shareholder-employees

The courts will generally allow wider restraints on the sellers of businesses than in the case of employees. An interesting question for the courts to deal arises in situations where the person affected by the restrictive covenant is both an employee and a shareholder i.e. a part-owner of the business.

 Systems Reliability Holdings plc *v* Smith (1990) Smith, the defender, was employed as a computer engineer and he developed his skills to an extremely high level. It was Smith's involvement in the business that greatly contributed to its expansion. However, Smith's employer was taken over by another company and his contract was terminated. Smith also held a small amount of shares in his former employer, but the new owner of the company paid Smith a very large sum of money for these shares. The new owner of the company attempted to rely on a clause in contract of sale that restrained Smith from working for a period of 17 months for any business rival or involvement in a business competing against the company. Smith was also expected not to divulge any confidential information or trade secrets that he had gained access to during the course of his employment. Smith decided to set up a business which competed against his old company. The new owners of the company sought an interdict to prevent him doing this.

Held: by the English High Court that the restraint satisfied the requirement of reasonableness and it could be used to prevent Smith from running a rival business. Seventeen months was not an unreasonable length of time for a restraint of this nature to run. The restraint was more in line with what would normally appear in a contract for the sale of a business rather than an employment contract. The High Court was, therefore, prepared to be more flexible in allowing the new owner of the business to enforce it. Admittedly, Smith had not been a major shareholder in his old company, but the new owner had been very generous when they bought out his shares.

Solus or exclusive supply agreements

This type of agreement is known as a *solus* or exclusive supply agreement whereby an individual, for example, a pub landlord is 'tied' to a brewery or someone who runs a petrol station has to stock the products of a particular petrol company. In other words, the pub is not a 'Free House' because the landlord will have to sell the brewery's products and the person who runs the petrol station will have to sell the petrol company's products. These types of agreements are void if they are unreasonable. Where a garage owner is concerned, the cases which have involved challenges to *solus* agreements have centred around mortgages that a petrol company has granted to the garage owner. One of the terms of the mortgage is that the owner promises not to stock the products of the company's business rivals. The rules about *solus* agreements do not apply where the garage and the land upon which it is situated are owned by the petrol company. In this situation, a tenant will have no choice but to supply the company's products.

 Esso Petroleum Co Ltd *v* Harper's Garage Ltd (1967) two solus agreements were involved preventing Harper, a petrol station owner, from stocking the products of any competitor of Esso. Harper had agreed to this arrangement because Esso were prepared to lend him money in order to modernise his property. The owner had to grant Esso a mortgage in relation to his two filling stations in order to secure the loan. The first *solus* agreement was to last for four years and five months and the second was to last for 21 years. Harper attempted to pay off the second mortgage of 21 years early, but this course of action was not permitted by reason of a clause in the mortgage which stated that the agreement had to run for the specified period. Harper broke his agreement with Esso when he began to sell another petrol company's products. Esso tried to prevent Harper from doing this and, therefore, tried to obtain an interdict.

Held: by the House of Lords that the rule of public policy against unreasonable restraints also applied to the *solus* agreements and the mortgage. The shorter period of four years and five months was reasonable, but the longer period of 21 years was totally unreasonable and unenforceable.

 Texaco *v* Mulberry Filling Station (1972) the owner of a garage under a *solus* agreement for the exclusive supply of Texaco petrol broke the agreement during a tanker drivers' strike by obtaining and supplying Jet petrol. Since the duration and the extent of the restraint were reasonable, Texaco were entitled to enforce the agreement. The court would not accept that the agreement was contrary to the public interest.

Trade associations

A trade association or professional body may decide to impose certain practices or restraints on its members without their prior consent. Such restraints would be void if they are unreasonable. Many members of trade associations or professional bodies will have little choice but to accept the rules because this is the price of membership. In many trades or professions, an individual will have to be approved by the relevant body if he is to be regarded as a fully practising member. This puts the relevant professional body in a very powerful position and abuses of this power have been known to occur.

 Pharmaceutical Society of Great Britain *v* Dickson (1968) the Society passed a resolution that any new pharmacies that were opened by its members would be required to provide a very narrow range of predetermined services. This would mean that new pharmacies were not free to decide for themselves which services they wished to develop. Furthermore, members who ran existing pharmacies would have to obtain the prior approval of the Society's Council if they wished to expand the range of services that they were currently offering to members of the public. Dickson brought an action against the Society on the grounds that the proposed new rule was *ultra vires* i.e. beyond or outwith its powers as an unreasonable restraint of trade. A declaration was made by the court to this effect and the Society appealed to the House of Lords. The appeal was dismissed.

The House of Lords made a number of observations about this type of restrictive agreement:

◆ If a professional association passes a resolution, even if binding in honour only, its validity is a matter for the courts since failure to observe it is likely to be seen as misconduct and disciplinary action will follow.

◆ A professional association's resolution is *ultra vires* if it is outwith the main objects (aims) of the organisation. The resolution in this case was quite clearly *ultra vires*.

◆ A professional association's resolution regulating the conduct of its members will be void if it is an unreasonable restraint of trade.

The consequences of an illegal restraint of trade

The offending clause will be removed or severed from the contract. Crucially, the courts will not substitute it with a more reasonable alternative. It is not for the courts to do a party's job for him in this regard (see **Dumbarton Steamboat Co *v* MacFarlane (1899)**). It is important to note that the court will usually delete only the invalid part of the clause, for example, a line or a word. The court will not generally treat the whole clause as void unless it has no other option (see **Nordenfelt *v* Maxim Nordenfelt Guns and Ammunition Co (1894)**).

Exclusion clauses and other unfair terms

Parties to a contract have rights under the agreement, but they also are under a duty to do something for the other party. If a party fails to honour a duty i.e. commits a breach of contract or performs the duty in a negligent fashion this may cause the innocent party to suffer loss, damage or injury. Naturally enough, the innocent party would wish to raise an action for damages against the other party who was in breach or who had been negligent in some way. In certain situations, however, this course of action by the innocent party may become problematic because there are ways in which the offending party can limit or exclude his liability. The offending party may have insisted, before or at the formation of the contract, that a term should be included in the agreement which allows him to limit or exclude his liability for contractual breaches or acts of negligence on his part. Such contractual terms are popularly referred to as exclusion and limitation clauses. Exclusion and limitation clauses are, admittedly, very narrow definitions. Other examples of potentially unfair terms include exemption/exception clauses and indemnity clauses. The former category of term is used by a party to escape liability in certain situations. An indemnity clause, on the other hand, (**see British Crane Hire Corporation v Ipswich Plant Hire Ltd [1975]**) is used by one party to claim compensation from another individual for losses sustained while performing the contract

Exclusion and limitation clauses are widely used in pre-printed or standard form contracts and they are also found on tickets such as train, plane and bus tickets. However, it is possible for one party to insist upon an inclusion of a term in a verbal contract that would allow him to limit or exclude his liability. Exclusion and limitation clauses can also be found in non-contractual notices, for example, a notice in a park that states the local authority will not be liable for any injuries suffered by persons using the park. It is important to note that the individual who has suffered an injury will not have a contractual relationship with the local authority and, prior to 1 April 1990, would not have been able to raise an action under the Unfair Contract Terms Act 1977. Such notices are now covered by the Unfair Contract Terms Act 1977 as a result of Section 68 of the Law Reform (Miscellaneous Provisions) (Scotland) Act 1990.

If the offending party was able to rely on some term of the contract which allowed them to walk away from the consequences of their breach of contract or negligence, this would clearly give them an unfair advantage. We might like to think of exclusion and limitation clauses as a 'get out of jail card'. As discussed above, in such situations where the contract has been breached, the innocent or aggrieved party would wish to sue the person who broke the agreement. However, the existence of a limitation or exclusion clause in the contract might make this action impossible or much less effective than might otherwise have been the case.

 Key point: The common law of contract permits a party to exclude or limit his liability for loss, damage, personal injury and even death caused by his negligence or breach of contract.

An example of an exclusion clause is:

'All cars are parked at the owners' risk. Crossan and Wylie Car Parks Ltd accept no liability whatsoever for any loss, damage or injury caused to vehicles, property or persons that occurred on our premises.'

The courts can often take a very tough line towards exclusion clauses because realistically it is an attempt by one party (usually the stronger one) to escape liability completely.

An example of a limitation clause, on the other hand, is:

'Our liability for loss or damage in relation to passengers' luggage and personal belongings carried by us or by our agents shall in no circumstances exceed the sum of £100.'

Limitation clauses come in a wide variety of shapes, in that they restrict rather than totally exclude liability. The person who relies on a limitation clause is admitting his responsibility for the breach of contract or for negligence, he just wishes to reduce that liability to a very small amount of compensation which in no way reflects the losses suffered by the innocent party.

 Key point: An exclusion clause attempts to exclude a party's liability for loss, injury, damage or death caused by his negligence or contractual breach, whereas a limitation clause attempts to restrict liability, for example, by restricting the compensation payable to the innocent party to a very small sum of money.

The law here is complex and there are three areas of it which apply to exclusion and limitation clauses:

◆ Unfair Contract Terms Act 1977
◆ Unfair Terms in Consumer Contract Regulations 1999
◆ Enterprise Act 2002

The situation before the Unfair Contract Terms Act 1977

Before the Unfair Contract Terms Act 1977, it was possible for a person to exclude his liability for negligent performance and non-performance of the contract as long as he gave the other party adequate notice of the existence of an exclusion clause. The law before 1977 meant that it was possible for someone to exclude his liability for death and personal injury caused by his negligence or by failing to perform the contract. Now, the case law before 1977 will largely be of historic interest. However, if an exclusion clause survives the tests laid down by both the Unfair Contract Terms Act 1977 and the Unfair Terms in Consumer Contract Regulations 1999, the old case law could still be relevant. In other words, the parties would have to argue whether adequate notice of the existence of the clause had been given by the party who wishes to rely upon it to escape or limit his liability.

Clearly the old common law was very unsatisfactory because exclusion clauses tended to encourage people not to perform their contractual duties properly. The common law positively encouraged abuses of the contract. You might have a situation where someone had put their car into a garage to have the brakes tested by a mechanic. What if the mechanic insisted that the car owner sign a document which stated that the garage would not be responsible for death or personal injury caused by the mechanic's failure to carry out the job properly? This would be an outrageous situation, but the mechanic might yet escape liability for the death of the owner if he drew such a clause to the attention of the car owner. The owner would be regarded as having accepted this clause if he signed the document or went ahead and put his car into the garage without bothering to raise a protest.

The widespread use of exclusion clauses, therefore, encouraged people to be lazy, complacent and careless. Why bother to go the extra mile when you always had the protection of an exclusion clause to fall back on? However, Parliament had other ideas and decided that this situation could no longer be tolerated. The Unfair Contract Terms Act 1977 was an attempt by Parliament to prevent the worst abuses which had been encouraged by the use of exclusion clauses.

 Key point: Before the introduction of the Unfair Contract Terms Act 1977, it was possible for a party to exclude his liability completely for loss, injury, damage or even death.

An example of the worst type of exclusion clause before 1977 can be found below:

'Crossan and Wylie Ltd accepts no responsibility for the death or any personal injury, damage, loss, delay or accident wheresoever and howsoever caused and whether by the negligence of our employees or otherwise.'

The Unfair Contract Terms Act 1977

Part II of the Unfair Contract Terms Act 1977 applies to Scotland only and Part III of the Act applies throughout the United Kingdom generally (Part I of the Act has application to England, Wales and Northern Ireland only). The strongest possible protection is given by the Unfair Contract Terms Act 1977 to those individuals who are classed as consumers. However, there are situations where it may still be possible for those individuals who are not consumers to claim the protection of the Act. It will be much more difficult for businesses, but by no means impossible for them, to use the Act in order to strike down exclusion and limitation clauses.

Section 17 of the Act describes a consumer contract as consisting of one party who is dealing in the course of his business and another party is who *not* dealing in the course of business (a consumer). Such a contract must involve the sale or the hire of goods and these goods are usually supplied for the private use and consumption of the non-business party to the contract.

Section 25(1) of the Unfair Contract Terms 1977 Act states that a consumer contract is where 'one party to the contract deals and the other party to the contract (the consumer) does not deal or hold himself out as dealing in the course of business'.

In **Chapman v Aberdeen Construction Group Limited (1991)** Lord Caplan made the following remarks in relation to the distinction between consumer and non-consumer contracts:

'The word "business" is notoriously difficult to define precisely but in my view in its ordinary sense it implies not only activity for gain but a degree of organisation of activity for gain.'

It will, therefore, be possible for a business to act outwith its ordinary trade or profession and enter into contracts with other parties. Merely because this contract involves, at first glance, two businesses does not mean that the transaction should be treated as a non-consumer sale.

R & B Customs Brokers Co Ltd *v* United Dominions Trust (1988)
R & B Customs Brokers bought a car so that one of its directors could use it. The contract of sale contained an exclusion clause whereby the seller of the car, United Dominions Trust, attempted to escape liability in relation to Section 14(3) of the Sale of Goods Act 1979. Section 14(3) imposes a duty on the seller to supply goods that must be fit for their purpose. An exclusion clause like this would have been automatically void and ineffective in a consumer transaction in terms of Section 20 of the Unfair Contract Terms Act 1977 in Scotland. The key question was whether this contract, which undoubtedly involved two business parties, could be regarded as a consumer contract for the purposes of the Unfair Contract Terms Act 1977?

Held: by the English Court of Appeal that when a business buys goods from another business, the transaction will not always be a straightforward non-consumer contract. The business buyer in certain situations may actually find that it may have the protection of consumer law in common with ordinary members of the public if the transaction is not a regular business contract. In this particular case, R & B Customs Brokers must be regarded as a consumer. The purchase of the car was not a frequent business transaction and unless United Dominions Trust could prove anything to the contrary, R & B Customs Brokers should have the benefit of the law protecting consumers in relation to exclusion clauses. The clause was, therefore, void and ineffective.

As should now be apparent, the vast majority of exclusion and limitation clauses will be contained in standardised contracts. Unfortunately, there is no definition of 'written, standard terms' or 'standard form contracts' in the 1977 Act, but these definitions would obviously cover cases in which the seller insists that all (or nearly all) of his customers buy or hire goods on the same terms with no change from one contract to another.

It is worth emphasising that a private transaction between a private seller and a private buyer is not to be regarded as a consumer transaction.

 Key point: The Unfair Contract Terms Act 1977 gives the strongest possible protection to consumers in relation to the use and abuse of exclusion and limitation clauses.

What types of contract does the Unfair Contract Terms Act cover?

Section 15 lists the types of contract which the Act covers. These include:

- Contracts for the sale of goods
- Contracts of hire
- Contracts of hire purchase
- Contracts of employment or apprenticeship
- Contracts for the provision of services
- Contracts relating to occupier's liability (where the occupier is a business, for example, a cinema, pub, theatre or fairground)
- Contracts which grant a right to enter or to use land

The Unfair Contract Terms Act does not apply to the following types of agreement:

- ◆ Insurance contracts
- ◆ Contracts for the transfer of an interest in land
- ◆ Auction sale contracts
- ◆ Contracts for the sale of goods on an international basis
- ◆ Contracts involving the creation, membership and termination of partnerships and companies

House purchases will not be covered by the Act, although liability for misrepresentations made in the course of a sale of a house by a surveyor, where he has been employed by a bank or building society, cannot be excluded unless such a term can pass the test of reasonableness. Nor does the Act apply to certain contracts for the sale of goods on an international basis because these are covered by international conventions, for example, the Vienna Convention 1980. Furthermore, it should be noted that a written arbitration agreement will not be treated as excluding liability or restricting liability for the purposes of the Unfair Contract Terms Act and such an agreement is valid.

 Key point: There are certain types of contracts that are not covered by the Act: insurance contracts, contracts transferring an interest in land, auction sales, international sales of goods, the creation, membership and termination of partnerships and companies.

Void exclusion and limitation clauses under the Unfair Contract Terms Act 1977

The Act has the effect of rendering some types of exclusion and limitation clauses void and ineffective. It will not matter whether adequate notice of the existence of the clause was given by the party relying on it to the other party. Any attempt to include the clause in the contract will quite simply fail.

Under section 16 of the Act, any clause where a party attempts to escape or limit his responsibility for having caused death or personal injury to another as a result of his actions will be automatically void. The clause cannot be relied upon and will not be enforced by the courts.

 Key point: As a result of the Unfair Contract Terms Act 1977, any attempt to exclude liability for personal injury or death will be automatically void.

In terms of Section 19 of the Act, a manufacturer's guarantee cannot exclude or restrict his liability for loss or damage arising from defects in goods used by a consumer which was caused by negligence in the manufacturing or distribution process. Any such attempt by the manufacturer will be void and ineffective.

 Key point: Attempts by manufacturers to exclude or limit their liability to consumers in relation to defective goods will be void and ineffective.

Very often, a business seller will attempt to exclude or limit his liability to a consumer buyer in a sale of goods transaction. Sections 12 to 15 of the Sale of Goods Act 1979 gives a consumer buyer extensive protection in respect of the following:

◆ The buyer is entitled to assume that the seller will have the right to sell the goods at the time of the sale (Section 12)
◆ If the seller uses a description in relation to the goods, this description must comply with the goods actually supplied (Section 13)
◆ The goods supplied by the seller must be of satisfactory quality and fit for their purpose (Section 14)
◆ If the transaction is a sale by sample, the goods supplied must comply with the sample in terms quality and fitness for purpose (Section 15)

Sections 12 to 15 of the Sale of Goods Act 1979 are referred to as the *implied terms* which form part of every contract involving the sale of goods. They are material terms of the contract i.e. they are at the very heart of the agreement and, obviously, any attempt to exclude or limit their operation should be treated with extreme suspicion by the courts.

Section 20 of the Unfair Contract Terms Act 1977 states that any attempt to exclude or limit the implied terms of the Sale of Goods Act in a consumer sale will be automatically void. In a non-consumer sale, Section 20 of the Unfair Contract Terms Act makes it clear that any attempt by a seller to limit his liability in terms of Section 12 of the Sale of Goods Act, will be automatically void.

In a non-consumer sale, a seller may be able to exclude or limit his liability in relation to Sections 13 to 15 of the Sale of Goods Act, but Section 20 of the Unfair Contract Terms Act states that this will only be permitted if this is fair and reasonable.

 Key point: Any attempt by a seller to exclude or limit his liability in terms of Section 12 of the Sale of Goods Act 1979 regardless of whether it is a consumer contract or a non-consumer contract will be automatically void. In a consumer sale, a business seller will not be permitted to exclude or limit his liability in relation to Sections 13 to 15 of the Sale of Goods Act 1979.

A manufacturer's guarantee cannot exclude or restrict his liability for loss or damage arising from defects in goods used by a consumer which was caused by negligence in the manufacturing or distribution process. Any such attempt by the manufacturer will be void and ineffective.

The enforcement of exclusion and limitation clauses

Under Section 16 of the Unfair Contract Terms Act, exclusion or limitation clauses will now only be capable of enforcement in situations involving liability for loss or damage caused to another person's property and this clause is regarded as fair and reasonable.

However, determining when a clause will be fair and reasonable has caused a fair amount of legal debate and argument.

Section 17 of the Act addresses a number of situations regarding any term in either a consumer contract or a standard form contract which would allow the party relying on such a clause to do any of the following:

1 To exclude or limit his liability for breach of contract

2   To avoid performance of his contractual obligations completely

3   To perform the contract in a totally different way from that which was reasonably anticipated by the other party

Section 17 goes on to state that any term falling into the three categories listed above will be completely ineffective unless the party who wishes to rely on it can demonstrate that it was fair and reasonable to insist that it should form part of the contract. Although consumers receive the maximum amount of protection under the Act, Section 17 leaves it open to a business to argue that its attempt to escape or limit liability in relation to consumer contracts should be regarded as fair and reasonable.

It should be remembered that some exclusion and limitation clauses will be automatically void in relation to death and injury generally and in respect of Sections 12 to 15 of the Sale of Goods Act 1979 in a consumer transaction (and Section 12 in a non-consumer sale). Any other type of exclusion or limitation clause will have to pass the test of reasonableness. Obviously, an attempt by the seller to exclude or limit liability will only be really worth attempting in respect of some of the less important terms of the consumer contract.

Furthermore, in terms of Section 18, an indemnity clause in a consumer contract will be ineffective if it fails the test of reasonableness. Such clauses are used where a business may agree to perform work for a consumer, but only if the consumer will indemnify (compensate) the business in relation to any liability which it may incur during the performance of the contract. An employee of the business, for example, may injure a third party as a result of his negligence and the business will turn to the consumer for compensation when it is sued by the victim. Generally, a business should take responsibility for its negligence and this exposure to risk can always be reduced by means of an insurance policy. Such indemnity clauses in consumer contracts will, therefore, be treated with suspicion by the courts.

 Key point: In terms of the Unfair Contract Terms Act 1977, a person relying on an exclusion or limitation clause in order to escape or limit his liability for damage caused to another person's property must demonstrate that the clause is fair and reasonable.

The reasonableness of exclusion and limitation clauses

One of the key questions that the Unfair Contract Terms Act poses is whether an exclusion or limitation clause can be regarded as reasonable. Although the matter of reasonableness is primarily a question for the courts to answer, there are guidelines which appear in Section 24 and Schedule 2 of the Act.

Section 24 states that the matter of reasonableness must be decided by referring to the circumstances surrounding the contract when it was made and exactly what facts the parties were aware of or should have been made aware of. Where a clause limits the amount of compensation payable, the courts should examine the resources of the person who is relying upon the clause and whether he could have reduced the risks that he was exposed to by taking out an insurance policy. The purpose of this rule is to encourage businesses to take out insurance wherever possible in order to safeguard themselves against liability. A failure to do so would doubtless play very badly with the court. However, the court will be well aware that there are some risks that insurers will simply not entertain.

Where the contract is for the supply of goods i.e. under a contract of sale, hire-purchase, hiring or work and materials, Schedule 2 of the Act states that the following factors must be examined:

a) The strength of the bargaining position of the parties i.e. a stronger party may not be allowed to rely upon the exclusion or limitation clause where it is quite obvious that this would permit an abuse of power. This, of course, depends upon the circumstances of the situation.

b) The availability of alternative supplies. If a seller who holds a dominant position in the marketplace and attempts to use a clause he may well be prevented from doing so because the opportunity for the buyer to secure the goods from another source is severely restricted.

c) Inducements that encourage the buyer to accept the inclusion of the clause in the contract. This would occur for example, if the buyer benefits from lower prices or where he was offered a gift from the seller which persuades him to agree to the clause. Behaviour like this on the part of the buyer may persuade the court that the seller has attempted to be reasonable as regards the clause.

d) The buyer's knowledge of the extent of the clause. Has adequate notice of the clause's existence been given? Is the buyer fully aware that his rights have been reduced under it? If these conditions are satisfied, the court may hold the clause reasonable.

e) Customs of trade and previous dealings. It seems to be the position that previous dealings in consumer contracts do not appear to be relevant, unless they occur on a frequent basis.

f) Whether the goods have been made, processed or adapted to the order of the buyer. Obviously, if the seller has been required by the buyer to produce goods to order, then it may be fair and reasonable for the seller to exclude liability which might arise because of faults in the buyer's design which he insisted should be followed. In such a business transaction, it is probably the case that the seller would be acting in a completely reasonable way if he insisted upon excluding the implied term (contained in Section 14 of the Sale of Goods Act 1979) that the goods should be of satisfactory quality or fit for purpose.

 Key point: The issue of whether an exclusion or limitation clause is reasonable will be primarily a matter for the courts based on the evidence presented to them by the parties.

We can see below how the courts have developed the test of reasonableness:

 Woodman v Photo Trade Processing Ltd (1981) Woodman had been the only photographer present at the wedding of his friends. It was his intention to have these photographs developed and have them included in an album which he would then give to his friends as his wedding gift to them. He put his roll of film in to be developed by the defenders. The film quite obviously had a unique value, but, unfortunately, due to the defenders' negligence the film was lost and it was never recovered. Woodman sued the defenders for the loss of the film. They attempted to limit their liability to the cost of a replacement roll of film. The defenders claimed that they were merely relying upon a standard limitation clause which was widely used in their particular line of business. Furthermore, the defenders argued that Woodman had been given adequate notice of the existence of such a clause and there could no dispute that it formed part of the contract. The defenders did concede that customers were taking a risk when they entrusted their films to them – accidents can and do happen. However, the defenders were able to offer customers a very valuable and efficient service at highly competitive prices. They would not be able to do this if they were forced to operate their business without the protection of such limitation clauses. Expensive legal action, the likes of which Woodman had commenced, would eventually be passed on to the consumer in the shape of much higher prices. Woodman argued that, although he had been given adequate notice of the clause, it was not fair and reasonable in the circumstances. The developers were only too well aware that customers attached an extremely high value to their films which were records of important events in their lives. The clause read as follows:

'All photographic materials are accepted on the basis that their value does not exceed the loss of the material itself. Responsibility is limited to the replacement of film. No liability will be accepted consequently or otherwise, however caused.'

Held: by Judge Clarke QC in the English County Court that the customer had no means of challenging such a clause. He had to take it or leave it. Practically speaking, there was no real alternative as most, if not all, businesses in this particular line would have operated according to similar or identical conditions. Woodman, being a consumer, was the much weaker party in the contractual relationship and the developers were in a much stronger position in that they could impose highly unfavourable terms. The film clearly had a unique or sentimental value (it was irreplaceable) and the defenders were only too aware of this fact. The clause placed an unacceptably high degree of risk on the weaker party i.e. the consumer. The clause was unfair and unreasonable and Woodman was awarded damages of £75.

 Smith *v* Eric S Bush (1990) a surveyor attempted to rely on an exclusion clause which effectively allowed him to escape liability for any negligence on his part. The surveyor had been instructed by a building society to carry out an inspection of the property in order to have it valued. The cost of the survey was to be paid by the prospective buyer. The surveyor was aware that the prospective buyer would rely on this report and it was highly unlikely that the buyer would consult another surveyor for the purpose of obtaining a second opinion in relation to the property. The sale of the house went ahead, but it soon became apparent that the property suffered from serious defects and, consequently, it was not suitable for habitation. The buyers raised an action against the surveyor who attempted to rely on the exclusion clause in order to escape liability.

Held: by the House of Lords that, in terms of the Unfair Contract Terms Act, it was unreasonable to allow the surveyor to rely on such a clause. The building society and the surveyor could not be permitted to pass on the risk of loss due to their incompetence or carelessness when the high cost of houses and the high cost of interest rates were taken into account.

 St Albans City and District Council *v* International Computers Ltd (1996) the pursuers, the Council, had entered into a contract with the defenders, International Computers, for the purchase and installation of a software package. The software package would permit the Council to set up a database of eligible poll tax payers. The software package contained some sort of error which led to the pursuers to over-estimate the number of eligible tax payers. This meant that the pursuers received a less generous grant from central government. The pursuers sued the defenders for damages for the losses suffered. The defenders attempted to rely on a limitation clause which reduced their liability to a sum of £100,000.

Held: by the English High Court that reliance by the defenders on such a clause was unreasonable in terms of the Unfair Contract Terms Act. The defenders were a very large business concern being part of a multinational company which had a great deal of financial resources. The defenders had taken out insurance in relation to their products and this policy covered them for up to £50 million. Finally, the defenders were one of a very limited number of businesses who could meet the pursuers' requirements and all of these rival businesses used very similar clauses in their standard terms and conditions. This put the defenders in a very strong position in comparison to the pursuers. The defenders appealed, but the English Court of Appeal ruled against them.

Unfair Terms in Consumer Contract Regulations 1999

These Regulations replace the Unfair Terms in Consumer Contracts Regulations 1994. The original Regulations of 1994 implement the EC Directive on Unfair Terms in Consumer Contracts. The 1999 Regulations (like their predecessor) are entirely separate from the Unfair Contract Terms Act 1977 and, therefore, it is possible to challenge an exclusion clause under both pieces of legislation. As the title of the Regulations suggests, the law in this area applies only to consumer contracts. They create an entirely separate regime from the Unfair Contract Terms Act 1977.

 Key point: The Unfair Terms in Consumer Contracts Regulations 1999 as the title suggests provide protection to consumers not businesses and, furthermore, the Regulations are completely separate from the Unfair Contract Terms Act 1977.

There is a clear difference in approach between the Regulations and the Unfair Contract Terms Act 1977. The Unfair Contract Terms Act deals with exclusion and limitation clauses rather than unfair terms generally. The Regulations will, therefore, have a much wider application than the Act. The Act does, however, have a major strength in the sense that some contractual terms are considered to be automatically void in all situations (death or personal injury generally and Sections 12 to 15 of the Sale of Goods Act in relation to consumer contracts specifically). The Regulations, on the other hand, apply a test of fairness before an exclusion or limitation clause can be regarded as void and unenforceable. With regard to the issue of excluding or limiting liability for death or personal injury, the Regulations state that such terms may be unfair whereas the Act makes these automatically void.

When dealing with the question of unfair terms, it is important to realise that the Unfair Contract Terms Act and the Unfair Terms in Consumer Contracts Regulations do not always cover the same types of contracts. This means that particular care will have to be taken when dealing with unfair terms and it will be sensible to keep a copy of both the Act and the Regulations at hand.

 Key point: The Unfair Contract Terms Act 1977 applies only to exclusion and limitation clauses in consumer and business contracts whereas the Unfair Terms in Consumer Contracts Regulations 1999 applies generally to unfair terms in consumer contracts.

Unfair terms

Schedule 3 of the Regulations provides 17 examples of terms in consumer contracts that *may* be unfair. These examples cover the following issues:

a) An attempt by the seller or the supplier to rely on a clause that excludes or limits his liability for death and/or personal injury to a consumer resulting from the seller or supplier's negligence.

b) An attempt by the seller or the supplier to force a consumer to pay an unfair penalty as compensation if the consumer breached the contract in some way. This would cover situations involving non-refundable deposits.

c) An attempt by the seller or the supplier to change the terms of the contract without first having sought the consumer's consent.

d) An attempt by the seller or the supplier to limit the range of actions available to the consumer in the event of the business not being able to perform its duties under the contract or where there is partial performance by the business.

 Key point: One of the features of the Regulations is that they apply a test of fairness to a term in a consumer contract rather than render the term automatically void as is the case with the Unfair Contract Terms Act 1977.

What types of contractual terms do the Regulations cover?

Regulation 3(1) makes it clear that the Regulations apply to all contracts concluded between a seller or a supplier *acting in the course of business* and a consumer where terms are not individually negotiated. This, of course, means that the terms are standardised or uniform and the buyer will have to take them or leave them. These types of standard or uniform terms will most often be found in pre-printed documents, but standard terms can be found in contracts of a purely verbal nature.

A court is unlikely to be impressed by a seller or supplier's argument that the term must be fair because token negotiations have taken place with the buyer if it soon becomes apparent that the seller or supplier has managed to impose most of his standard conditions on the buyer. The burden of proof will be on the seller to prove that the term, which is at the centre of the dispute, was individually negotiated and not imposed on the buyer by way of a standard condition.

 Key point: The Regulations apply to standard terms in written or verbal contracts used by a business seller or supplier, these terms are imposed on a consumer buyer and, generally, the buyer will not be in a position to negotiate with the seller or the supplier.

Generally, the Regulations do not apply to terms which address the price to be paid by the consumer for goods and services or those terms which describe the subject-matter of the contract. It must be remembered, however, that the Regulations impose a general requirement that every standard term of a consumer contract must be written in plain and intelligible language so that they can be easily understood by the buyer. Traders could be challenged by a consumer if the meaning of a term is difficult to understand and, if this situation does arise, the meaning most favourable to the consumer will be the one favoured by the court (Regulation 6).

Regulation 3 states that a number of contracts will not be covered by the Regulations:

◆ Contracts of employment
◆ Business contracts
◆ Contracts between private individuals
◆ Contracts relating to succession rights
◆ Contracts relating to rights under family law
◆ Contracts relating to the incorporation of companies or partnerships
◆ Any contractual term incorporated in order to meet United Kingdom statutory or regulatory provisions or international conventions
◆ Contracts made before 1995

Despite these exclusions the Regulations are still wider than the Unfair Contract Terms Act 1977 because they include contracts for the transfer of interests in land, contracts involving the transfer of securities, auction sales and contracts of insurance.

 Key point: Despite the fact that the Unfair Terms in Consumer Contracts Regulations will not apply in every situation, their application is potentially wider than the Unfair Contract Terms Act.

The test of fairness

Regulation 4 contains a test of fairness which will be applied to contractual terms. A term will be considered to be unfair if it can be demonstrated that a business has not acted in good faith and it causes a significant imbalance in the parties' rights and obligations under the contract and, as a result, a consumer is placed at a serious disadvantage.

The requirement of good faith means that traders must deal fairly and openly with consumers. Although traders may have very good reasons for using standard terms and conditions in contracts, any provision that exploits or harms the consumer could be potentially unfair.

Regulation 4 also states that an examination of the unfair nature of the term should take into account the following:

a) The nature of the goods or services for which the contract is concluded

b) The circumstances surrounding the conclusion of the contract

c) Other terms of the contract or of another contract on which it is dependent

Schedule 2 of the Regulations lists the kinds of factors that a court will consider when deciding whether a clause is unfair:

a) The relative bargaining positions of the parties (did a business impose unfavourable terms on the consumer, the weaker party?)

b) Whether the consumer has an inducement to agree the term (did the consumer accept a discount or a gift or some other benefit in exchange for agreeing to include certain terms in the contract?)

c) Whether the goods or services where sold or supplied to the special order of the consumer (was the seller or supplier contractually bound to provide custom-made goods in order to comply with requirements laid down by the consumer?)

d) The extent to which the seller or supplier has dealt fairly and equitably with the consumer (did the seller or the supplier attempt to take advantage of the consumer's inexperience, naivety or age?)

 Key point: When relying on exclusion clauses in its dealings with consumers, a business must act in good faith and such a clause will be probably be unfair if it causes consumers to be placed at a serious disadvantage.

The consequences of including unfair terms in a contract

According to Regulation 5, an unfair term will not be capable of enforcement against the consumer – it is not binding. This does not mean that the consumer can refuse to honour all of his duties as the contract will continue to be in force provided that the unfair term does not undermine the whole contract.

Additionally, the Regulations do not apply to contractual terms which determine the price or define the product or service i.e. the subject-matter of the contract. Terms in consumer contracts that set the price or define the product or service being supplied are the material terms of the contract and are exempt from the test of fairness as long as they are expressed in plain language.

 Key point: The Unfair Terms in Consumer Contracts Regulations 1999 do not apply to the following agreements – contracts made before 1995, private contracts, business contracts, non-consumer contracts, where the contract is the result of genuine negotiation between the parties and where the law imposes a duty to include particular terms in the contract.

Enforcement of the Regulations (Regulation 8)

A number of organistions or 'qualifying bodies' have been given enforcement powers under the Regulations, including the Office of Fair Trading, the utilities regulators (gas, telecommunications, water and electricity), the Information Commissioner, the Consumers' Association, the Department of Enterprise, Trade and Investment in Northern Ireland, the Financial Services Authority, and all trading standards services.

It is not up to the various bodies that have been given powers under the Regulations to decide whether a term is or is not unfair or whether any individual consumer is entitled to compensation. It is their duty to consider any complaints about the unfairness of a contract term and if they believe that a term is unfair, the courts can be approached and asked to issue an interdict to prevent the term being used or recommended for use. However, only the courts can finally decide whether a term is or is not unfair.

Alternatively, it may be acceptable on the part of the trader to give a promise not to use the term and, therefore, court action will be unnecessary.

 Key point: The Regulations give powers to certain agencies, for example, the Office of Fair Trading in order to take action against sellers or suppliers who use unfair terms in their contractual dealings with consumers.

The Enterprise Act 2002

This Act gives the Office of Fair Trading the power to investigate the use of exclusion clauses and other unfair terms being used in consumer transactions. The Office of Fair Trading is supposed to investigate consumer trade practices and, in particular, terms and conditions on which or subject to which goods or services are supplied. If after the investigation, the Office of Fair Trading feels that a particular practice in terms of exemption clauses should cease it can make a report to the Minister who may introduce a statutory instrument to stop the practice, for example, the **Consumer Transactions (Restrictions on Statements) Order 1976** makes it a criminal offence to sell or supply goods and purport that the implied terms in sale of goods and hire-purchase legislation can be excluded in a consumer sale since this might suggest to the consumer that he has no rights so that he will not bother to enforce them.

 Key point: The Enterprise Act 2002 gives power to the Office of Fair Trading to investigate and challenge the use of exclusion clauses and other unfair terms by businesses.

263

The Unfair Terms in Consumer Contracts Regulations 1999 has been used successfully to challenge the widespread practice whereby banks and credit companies impose hefty charges on consumers who either fail to make monthly payments on time or who exceed the terms of an overdraft agreement.

Previously, it was not uncommon for a bank or credit card company to impose penalties of anything between £25 and £35 on those consumers who were late making their monthly repayments. For several years now, consumers are being actively encouraged by organisations like the Office of Fair Trading to reclaim many of the extortionate charges imposed on them in the past and compensation could run into thousands of pounds.

There is no problem in theory with the concept that a creditor can impose a penalty on a debtor who fails to fulfil a contractual duty when required to do so. There is a problem, however, if the penalty imposed is unfair and disproportionate (Schedule 2 of the Unfair Terms in Consumer Contracts Regulations 1999).

The same types of arguments outlined above have also been used by consumers to challenge the practice by lenders to charge very high redemption penalties when individuals switch mortgages between various lenders in order to get a better deal or rate of interest. Previously, many consumers have been put off switching their current mortgage to another lender because their existing lender will charge them an excessively high charge (effectively a penalty). As a result of a combination of investigations by the Financial Services Authority and the Office of Fair Trading and the threat of legal action, many lenders have stopped this dubious practice.

In the case of **Murray v Leisureplay (2005)**, the English Court of Appeal stated that clauses which impose a penalty upon the contract breaker will not be capable of enforcement if it can be demonstrated that the sum payable on breach is 'extravagant or unconscionable'. Although this case involved a penalty clause in an employment contract, the underlying rationale of the court's decision that an excessive penalty charge will not be capable of enforcement against someone who breaches a contract has been used successfully to attack exorbitant banking charges.

Attempts by customers of the banks and building societies to reclaim charges which were levied on them as a result of exceeding their overdraft facilities were dealt a major blow by a recent decision of the Supreme Court of the United Kingdom. Many lenders have been criticised for imposing charges of £35 or more in situations where an overdraft facility has been exceed by a lender by as little as a penny. The lenders, in turn, argued that borrowers had been fully informed about these charges prior to the overdraft facility being set up. The lenders also argued that borrowers were in breach of contract by exceeding the agreed overdraft limit and it was only fair that they should have some sort of penalty imposed.

Office of Fair Trading v Abbey National plc and others (2009) the Office of Fair Trading had attempted to force lenders to curtail their practice of imposing excessive charges on those borrowers who had exceeded their agreed overdraft facilities. The case was brought under the Unfair Terms in Consumer Contracts Regulations 1999 and, in a largely technical judgement, the Supreme Court ruled that the Office of Fair Trading had no jurisdiction to challenge lenders. The Supreme Court, however, did leave the door open to challenge bank charges by another route.

In the meantime the hopes of thousands of borrowers that they would be able to reclaim hundreds (if not thousands) of pounds in compensation for paying unfair banking charges has been dashed.

The attitude of the courts to exclusion and limitation clauses

One of the ways that the courts have dealt with the use of such clauses in contracts is by examining the type of contract. Over the years, the courts have tended to take a much tougher approach to the use of these clauses in consumer contracts. A consumer contract is one where the seller is selling in the course of a business and the buyer is purchasing the goods or services for his own personal use. Normally, a consumer will not have the bargaining power to impose contractual conditions on the seller. Very often, a business seller will be in the position of being able to impose his standard conditions on the buyer. In other words, the buyer will have to like or lump the seller's conditions. In a consumer contract, there will be little prospect of the buyer entering into complex negotiations with the seller. Here lies the danger because an unscrupulous seller, who is perfectly aware that the buyer is in a much weaker position may seek to take advantage. Ultimately, this will mean that the seller could impose all sorts of negative conditions on a consumer and there is very little that the consumer can do.

 Key point: The common law could still be used to attack an unfair term in a contract in situations where the term satisfies the tests laid down by the Unfair Contract Terms Act and the Unfair Terms in Consumer Contracts Regulations 1999.

Lord Diplock, in **Schroeder v Macaulay (1974)**, made a powerful argument when he highlighted the weakness of consumer buyers in comparison with business buyers. The seller is effectively saying to the consumer buyer 'if you want these goods or services at all, these are the only terms on which they are obtainable. Take it or leave it.'

It is true to say, however, that the courts have taken a less sympathetic attitude towards those individuals who have fallen foul of such clauses in commercial or business contracts. The courts often expect business parties to a contract to have conducted serious negotiations, where both of them have had a real chance to determine the shape of the final agreement and where both parties will be fully aware of the consequences of each individual term.

In a business, the theory (rather than the practice) suggests that both parties will have had a fair chance to insist that contractual terms which are favourable to them are included in the final deal. If, later on, one of the parties discovers or realises that negative terms have been imposed on him, the courts may take the view that this individual had ample opportunity to object to these being included in the contract and, ultimately, he could have refused to enter the contract if the offensive terms were not removed. Therefore, any losses suffered by a party who is the victim of an exclusion clause will have to be offset by an insurance policy (if he has one which covers this situation) or it may have to come out of that party's own pocket.

The concept of equal bargaining power

The approach that the judges have taken towards exclusion clauses in business contracts, however, is very much based on an assumption that both parties are coming to negotiations with equal bargaining power. Just as the consumer is often the weaker party in a consumer contract, it is perfectly possible that one business will be stronger than another and this situation will lead the stronger party to impose all sorts of unfavourable conditions on the weaker party. Very often the concept of equal bargaining power in business negotiations is nothing less than an illusion.

 Key point: The courts tend to treat parties to a business contract less sympathetically when they have fallen foul of an exclusion clause.

The courts have protected consumers of goods in two ways by:

◆ Deciding that the exclusion clause was never part of the contract
◆ Examining the wording and the likely impact of the clause in such a way as to prevent its use

Was the clause part of the contract?

The court will demand that the person wishing to rely upon the clause bring evidence to show that the other party agreed to include the term in the contract, otherwise it will not form part of the agreement. A number of issues will arise:

1 What if an agreement is formed by the parties signing a written contract containing potentially unfair terms?

The party who signs such an agreement will, generally, be bound by all the terms which the document contains. This will be the case even if he has not read the contract properly, unless he was encouraged to enter the contract as a result of a misrepresentation made by the other party as to the legal effect of the document and its terms.

 Curtis *v* Chemical Cleaning and Dyeing Co [1951] the pursuer took a white satin wedding dress with beads and sequins to the defender's shop for cleaning. She was asked to sign a receipt which contained the following clause:

'This article is accepted on condition that the company is not liable for any damage howsoever arising.'

The pursuer claimed in evidence that she had asked why she had to sign the document and the assistant said that the clause excluded the company's liability for damage that occurred to beads and sequins only. The clause did not, therefore, apply to damage caused to the dress itself. She did not read all of the receipt before she signed it. The dress was returned with a stain and the pursuer sued for damages. The company relied on the clause.

Held: by the English Court of Appeal that the company could not enforce the exclusion clause because the assistant had innocently misrepresented the legal consequences of the document. As a result of the assistant's response to her query, the pursuer was entitled to believe that damage to the beads and sequins was covered by the exclusion clause, but not damage to the dress itself.

 Key point: Generally, the courts take the attitude that those individuals who voluntarily enter contracts which contain an exclusion clause, for example, by signing a document will be bound by the consequences of this action on their part.

2 What is the legal effect of potentially unfair terms contained in documents like tickets, receipts or vouchers?

If the primary purpose of such a document is merely to provide basic evidence that the parties have a contract, it can hardly be argued that it should be treated as an important contractual document containing all the terms of the agreement. The person seeking to rely on the clause must prove that the other party should have realised that the document would contain the essential terms of the agreement. If this can be proved, the clause will apply even though the other party was not aware of its existence because he failed to read the document properly.

 L'Estrange Ltd *v* Gracoub (1934) the pursuer, a café owner, purchased a cigarette slot machine from the defender. The defender had presented a written contract for the pursuer to sign. Unknown to the pursuer, the defender had included a clause which stated:

'Any express or implied condition, statement or warranty, statutory or otherwise, is hereby excluded.'

The pursuer did not bother to read the part of the contract which contained the exclusion clause and went ahead and placed her signature on the written contract. The machine was later found to be defective and unsatisfactory and the pursuer sued the defender for damages in respect of the now unusable machine.

Held: the exclusion was enforceable against the pursuer and her arguments that she had not read the written contract because she thought it was merely an order form did not impress the court. Furthermore, despite the fact that the defender had not drawn the pursuer's attention to the clause nor had he read it to her, no misrepresentation or fraud had been committed.

 Chapelton *v* Barry UDC [1940] Chapelton wished to hire deck chairs and went to a stack of chairs owned by the defenders, behind which was a notice stating:

'Hire of chairs 2d per session of three hours.'

The pile of deck chairs was regarded as a general offer to members of the public that Chapelton had accepted when he selected two chairs. He paid for them and received two tickets which he put into his pocket after merely glancing at them. One of the chairs collapsed and he was injured. A notice on the reverse of the ticket stated that:

'The Council will not be liable for any accident or damage arising from the hire of the chairs.'

Chapelton sued for damages and the Council attempted to rely on the clause.

Held: by the English court of Appeal that the clause could not be relied on by the Council to escape its liability towards Chapelton for his injuries. The board by the chairs made no attempt to limit the Council's liability because it did not alert the pursuer to the existence of the exclusion clause. In any case, Chapelton had accepted the offer by selecting the deck chairs and it could be argued that the attempt to rely on the exclusion clause was an attempt to introduce new terms into the contract. However, the ticket was a mere voucher and not a document that an ordinary member of the public would suspect contained all the terms of the contract.

 Taylor *v* Glasgow Corporation (1952) Mrs Taylor, the pursuer, had suffered injury when she fell down a staircase inside Glasgow Woodside Public Baths and she brought a subsequent action for damages against Glasgow Corporation. She alleged that the accident had been caused by the negligence of the Corporation's employees. When Mrs Taylor had paid the entrance fee to the Baths, she had been given a ticket. On the front of the ticket there was the following statement: 'For conditions see other side.' The statement on the back of the ticket said the following:

'The Corporation of Glasgow are NOT responsible for any loss, injury or damage sustained by persons entering or using this establishment or its equipment '

Mrs Taylor admitted that she had seen the printing on the ticket, but she had not bothered to stop and read the statements.

Held: by the Court of Session that the ticket was a voucher and not an important contractual document containing all the terms of the agreement of which a person in Mrs Taylor's position should have been made aware. Lord Thomson, the Lord Justice Clerk, stated:

'My view of the evidence is that this voucher aspect of this 'ticket' was the significant aspect, and that the purchaser regarded it as a pass or voucher or as a receipt for sixpence which entitled her to be given a hot bath, she was entitled so to regard it . . .'

The exclusion clauses in **Chapelton and Taylor** would now fall foul of both the Unfair Contract Terms Act 1977 and the Unfair Terms in Consumer Contracts Regulations 1999.

Lord Denning in **Spurling *v* Bradshaw [1956]** did make a very interesting comment regarding the incorporation of exclusion clauses into contracts. He said that they would 'need to be in red ink with a red hand pointing to it – or something equally startling.' Lord Denning expressed this view again in **Thornton *v* Shoe Lane Parking [1971]** a case which demonstrates very clearly the attitude of the courts towards attempts by individuals to incorporate exclusion clauses after an agreement has been concluded between the parties.

Thornton _v_ Shoe Lane Parking (1971) demonstrates that the requirement of adequate notice will be strictly enforced by the courts. In the English Court of Appeal, Lord Denning remarked that such a clause would 'need to be in red ink with a red hand pointing to it – or something equally startling.'

 Key point: If additional documents contain exclusion clauses such as tickets, it is a sensible precaution for the party relying on the clause to bring it to the other party's attention so that it can be said to be fully incorporated into the contract.

3   What if the parties have dealt with one another previously and on a regular basis and the pursuer, being a reasonable person, would know that the defender always contracts on identical or very similar terms?

 Hardwick Game Farm _v_ Suffolk Agricultural Poultry Producers Association [1969] a farmer was in the habit of purchasing feeding stuff for his poultry from the same supplier. On the first occasion that the farmer had done business with the supplier, the goods, when they were delivered, were accompanied by a sold note which contained an exclusion clause. This exclusion clause had no legal effect, of course, because the supplier had not drawn it to the farmer's attention before the contract had been formed. It was, therefore, an attempt to introduce a new term after the original agreement had been formed. Over the next few years, the farmer entered into a regular series of contracts of sale with the supplier (on average 3 or 4 a month). Every consignment of goods was accompanied by a sold note which contained the same exclusion clause – there was never any variation. In total, the farmer received over 100 of these sold notes as a result of his dealings with the supplier. Problems occurred when the supplier attempted to rely on the exclusion clause in the sold note. A consignment of the goods had been contaminated and this had resulted in much of farmer's livestock being poisoned.

Held: by the House of Lords that the seller was permitted to enforce the clause because a consistent course of dealings between the parties had incorporated the clause into the contract. The farmer's protests that he had never bothered to read the sold note and was, therefore, completely unaware of the consequences of the exclusion clause were irrelevant. The parties had now established a regular and consistent course of dealing. The farmer was well aware by now that every delivery was accompanied by a sold note which contained an identical exclusion clause. In other words, the supplier always contracted on the same terms. The farmer was under a duty to discover what these terms were and to raise objections if they were not to his liking. The farmer had never bothered to do this and, by implication, it was the supplier's terms (including the exclusion clause) which governed the contract.

The person relying on the incorporation of the exclusion clause must demonstrate that the clause was always included in the contract if there has been a course of dealing between the parties. In other words, there must be a consistent pattern whereby the clause is always included in the contract – not most of the time or some of the time, but all of the time. The party against whom the clause will be enforced against must be left in no doubt whatsoever that the clause forms part of the standard terms of the contract.

 In the leading Scottish case of **McCutcheon v David MacBrayne Ltd [1964]**, the House of Lords was asked to consider whether or not there had been a consistent course of dealings between MacBrayne, a ferry operator, and an individual who had used the ferry service to transport a relative's car from Islay, one of the Western Isles, to the Scottish mainland.

The car owner (McCutcheon) had asked his brother-in-law, McSporran, to arrange to have the vehicle placed aboard the ferry, *Lochiel*. McSporran had previously used the services of the ferry operator to transport goods. On several of these previous occasions (but not on every occasion as it turned out), McSporran had been asked to sign what MacBrayne described as a 'risk note'. This 'risk note' contained a statement that goods were shipped at the owner's risk. Due to the negligence of MacBrayne's employees the ferry hit a rock during the crossing and sank. Nothing of value could be salvaged from the wreck. The owner sued MacBrayne for damages for the loss of the car. MacBrayne then attempted to escape liability by relying upon an exclusion clause. The ferry operators claimed that the exclusion had been incorporated into this particular contract of carriage. On this occasion, however, McSporran had not been asked to sign any 'risk note'. As Lord Reid pointed out:

'This time he (McSporran) was offered an oral contract without any reference to conditions, and he accepted the offer in good faith . . .'

A particularly significant fact of this case was that, in the course of previous dealings, MacBrayne had sometimes failed to insist that McSporran sign such a 'risk note' when he used the ferry service. On some occasions he might be asked to sign it and on other occasions the 'risk note' was not even mentioned. There was no consistency on MacBrayne's part. In his evidence, furthermore, it was stated by McSporran that, on those occasions when he signed the document, he had never bothered to read it.

Held: by the House of Lords that MacBrayne had failed to demonstrate that there was a consistent business practice which would have allowed the incorporation of this clause into this particular contract. If anything, the ferry company's approach to the incorporation of exclusion clauses was extremely haphazard and the fact that McSporran sometimes signed a 'risk note' owed more to luck than the application of a consistent policy.

 Hollier v Rambler Motors (AMC) Ltd [1972] Hollier's car had an oil leak and he left the vehicle to be repaired at a garage owned by the defenders, Rambler Motors. While the car was at the garage, it was destroyed in a fire caused by the negligence of the defenders. Rambler Motors attempted to escape liability by relying on an exclusion clause which allegedly formed part of its contract with Hollier. The clause excluded liability, amongst other things, for damage caused by fire to cars left at the garage by their owners. As part of its argument to have the clause enforced, Rambler Motors claimed that Hollier had previously dealt with them on 3 or 4 occasions over a five year period and that, consequently, he was perfectly aware that the exclusion clause was part of the garage's standard business conditions. Every time that Hollier had booked his car into the garage, he had been asked to sign a form containing the exclusion clause and he had not raised any objections. The problem for Rambler Motors was that, on this occasion, it had failed to ask Hollier to sign the form containing the clause. Unfazed by this problem, Rambler Motors argued that it should still be permitted to enforce the clause against Hollier because there was an established custom and practice on its part with regard to the incorporation of the exclusion clause in its contracts with this particular customer. In other words, there was a consistent course of dealings between the parties.

Held: the defenders were not entitled to enforce the clause against Hollier. The English Court of Appeal was unconvinced that Hollier's previous dealings with Rambler Motors represented a regular and consistent course of dealing. Lord Denning MR (speaking in the later case of **British Crane Hire Corporation *v* Ipswich Plant Hire Ltd [1975]**) also stressed the fact that this was a consumer transaction and that the parties did not have equal bargaining power i.e. the garage was clearly the stronger party in the contract and was, therefore, in a position to impose unfavourable terms (exclusion clauses) upon Hollier.

A point worth noting is that in certain trades or professions, the incorporation of potentially unfair clauses into contracts will be a well-established and well-publicised business practice. Any member of that trade or profession dealing with a colleague will, therefore, be presumed to possess knowledge of the existence of terms peculiar to their area of industry or commerce.

 British Crane Hire Corporation *v* Ipswich Plant Hire Ltd [1975], both parties were in the business of hiring out heavy earth moving equipment. The defenders had hired special equipment from the pursuers, which they urgently required. After the contract had been formed, the pursuers had asked that the defenders sign a printed form containing their conditions of hire. One of the conditions was that the defenders would compensate or indemnify the pursuers for all expenses incurred while using the equipment. The defenders failed to sign this form but, in meantime, the equipment had sunk into marshy ground suffering damage as a result. The pursuers attempted to enforce the clause claiming that any reasonable person involved in this particular area of business would have been aware of the existence of such a clause in the contract and, furthermore, the defenders would have been only too aware of the fact that the pursuers would have absolutely refused to hire the equipment out if this term had not been included in the agreement.

Held: by the English Court of Appeal that the clause had been incorporated into the contract because the defenders were well aware that their particular line of business operated on standard conditions which were, according to Lord Denning MR: 'habitually imposed by the supplier of the machines and both parties knew the substance of those conditions.' The defenders, in fact, admitted that variations of a form containing similar terms and conditions of business (known as the Contractors' Plant Association Form) were widely used in their business. Lord Denning also made the point that facts in this case were quite different from **Hollier v Rambler Motors (AMC) Ltd [1972]** because in this case the parties enjoyed equal bargaining power.

 Key point: If the parties deal with one another on a regular basis, the party relying upon the exclusion clause must be able to show that it has consistently formed part of the contract and the other party is either aware of this or should have been aware of this fact.

4 Any attempt to introduce an exclusion clause after the contract has been made will be ineffective because it is an attempt to introduce additional terms to the agreement.

 Olley v Marlborough Court Ltd [1949] Mr and Mrs Olley arrived at a hotel where they had pre-booked a room. At the reception desk, they finalised their booking and were given the keys to their room. On one of the walls of the room was the following exclusion notice:

'The proprietors will not hold themselves responsible for articles lost or stolen unless handed to the manageress for safe custody.'

The wife locked the room and took the key down to leave it at the reception desk. An unidentified third party stole the key from behind the reception desk, used it to gain access to the Olleys' room and stole some of the wife's furs. This theft should have come as no surprise because the hotel staff had not taken reasonable precautions to prevent unauthorised third parties from having access to the room keys held behind reception. The hotel now sought to escape liability by arguing that the exclusion notice in the bedroom had been successfully incorporated into the contract with the Olleys.

Held: by the English Court of Appeal that the contract was completed at the reception desk and the attempt by the hotel to rely on the exclusion clause was nothing less than a blatant attempt to incorporate new (and unfavourable) terms into the contract. The exclusion clause should have been prominently displayed at reception if the hotel wished it to form part of the contract with guests. The guests, on seeing such a notice, would have received adequate warning of the existence of the clause.

In **Spurling v Bradshaw [1956]**, the Court of Appeal did suggest that if the Olleys had been previous visitors to the hotel, the exclusion may well have been enforceable against them because it would have been possible to argue that they now had adequate notice of its existence. This suggestion has been criticised and, has indeed to a certain extent, been contradicted by the Court of Appeal's later decision in **Hollier v Rambler Motors [1972]** (the facts of which are discussed above) where a garage's attempt to rely on a exclusion clause against a customer who was private individual failed. It had been argued in **Hollier** by the garage that the exclusion clause had been successfully incorporated into the contract because the customer had used the garage on 3 or 4 occasions over a 5 year period.

 Thornton v Shoe Lane Parking (1971), the Court of Appeal decided that the conditions releasing the company from certain liabilities on a ticket issued by an automatic barrier at the entrance to the car park were communicated too late. The contract was made in the following way: the ticket machine at the entrance to the car park was to be regarded as an offer to provide services to members of the general public. This offer was accepted when the pursuer drove his car to the ticket machine which issued him with a ticket and then the barrier rose and the pursuer was given access. The exclusion clause was on the back of the ticket, but this was too late because the physical act of driving up to the machine and taking the ticket implied acceptance of the offer. This had all happened before the pursuer had even read the conditions on the back of the ticket. In any case, most drivers would have regarded the ticket as a mere voucher and not an important contractual document. If the defender had wanted to incorporate the exclusion into the contract, it should have displayed a large notice at the front of the car park that clearly informed customers about the existence of the exclusion clause. This would have given drivers the opportunity to decide whether or not to enter into a contract with the car park owners.

 Key point: As a general rule, new terms (including exclusion clauses) cannot be introduced by one party after the contract has been finalised.

5 A party may be prevented (personally barred) from claiming the protection of an exclusion clause where he has made a verbal promise that is in direct contradiction to the clause.

 Evans (J) & Son (Portsmouth) Ltd _v_ Andrea Merzario Ltd (1976) the parties had contracted with one another since 1959. In 1967, the defenders, who were forwarding agents, gave certain assurances to the pursuers that machines which had to be transported by ship would be carried below deck. This had been standard practice on the previous occasions when the pursuers had used the defenders' services. From 1967 there had been a change in the way that the contract was performed in that containers were used to transport the goods as opposed to storing them in crates. The standard conditions used by the defenders contained a condition that the goods could be stored on the deck of the ship. This was clearly inconsistent with the practice on board the ship and contrary to the promise given by the defenders to the pursuers. Some of the pursuer's machines (precision equipment) were carried on deck and were lost when the container in which they were stored went overboard during bad weather.

Held: the court found that the defenders' statement that the goods would be carried below deck was a term of the contract. This contractual term had been breached by the defenders' decision to store the goods on the deck. The defenders' actions were in direct contradiction to the promise given to the pursuers and the standard practice that had been followed over many years. This verbal promise was part of the contract and any attempt by the defenders to rely on inconsistent exclusion clause had to fail.

 Key point: If the party relying on the exclusion makes a statement to the other party to the effect that the exclusion clause is not part of the contract, he will be prevented form enforcing the clause in his favour.

Judicial control of exclusion and limitation clauses

It should be obvious from the previous discussions that, from the 1970s onwards, potentially unfair terms have generally become subject to a range of statutory controls with the introduction of the Unfair Contract Terms Act 1977, the Unfair Terms in Consumers Contracts 1994 and 1999 and the Enterprise Act 2002. It would be misleading to suggest, however, that prior to more effective Parliamentary regulation in this area, there was a complete absence of control regarding the use (and abuse) of such clauses. Over many years, the Scottish courts, together with their English counterparts, had developed a number of mechanisms or rules of interpretation that sought to control some of the blatant injustices and abuses that the use of unfair terms appeared to encourage. The two major control mechanisms or rules of interpretation developed by the courts are:

◆ The *contra proferentum* rule
◆ The doctrine of fundamental breach

It must be stressed, however, that the above control mechanisms are merely guidelines to assist the courts to determine whether such clauses are capable of being enforced. They are not rules of law.

The *contra proferentum* rule

This rule is based on a very simple principle. A party who wishes to rely upon potentially unfair term in a contract must be able to demonstrate that such a provision clearly and unequivocally allows him to escape or reduce his liability in respect of breaches of contract or acts of negligence committed by him (or by his servants or employees). If the wording of the clause creates confusion or ambiguity, this may be absolutely fatal to a party's attempt to escape or limit his liability. In situations, where a clause lacks sufficient clarity, the court will punish the party relying on it by refusing to enforce it.

 Smith *v* South Wales Switchgear; UBM Chrysler (Scotland) Ltd [1978], in a decision of the House of Lords, Lord Keith singled out for approval remarks made by Lord Justice Sellers in **Walters *v* Whessoe [1968]** that attempts to limit or exclude liability must use 'adequate or clear words' or such a contractual term 'could have no reasonable meaning or application unless so applied.' Lord Keith went on to say that when applying the contra proferentum rule:

'the matter is essentially one of the ascertaining the intention of the contracting parties from the language they have used, considered in the light of surrounding circumstances which must be taken to have been within their knowledge.'

An example of the contra proferentum rule in operation can be seen from the following case:

 Houghton *v* Trafalgar Insurance Co Ltd [1954] This involved an attempt by an insurance company to escape its liability under an insurance policy. A car had been involved in a crash and its owner submitted a claim to the insurers. The insurance company discovered that, at the time of the accident, the car was carrying six people (the driver and five passengers). Strictly speaking, the car had a maximum seating capacity for a driver and four passengers at any one time. Armed with this information, the insurers argued that a term in the policy relieved them of any liability when the driver was carrying more than four passengers. The relevant clause stated that the insurers were entitled to exclude liability for damage:

'caused or arising whilst the car is conveying any load in excess of that for which it was constructed.'

The dispute, therefore, boiled down to the meaning of word 'load' in the above clause and whether it could be interpreted to cover the transport of passengers.

Held: by the English Court of Appeal that the word 'load' did not apply to passengers travelling in the car. Lord Justice Romer stated that he 'had not the least idea' what the word 'load' meant 'if applied to a private motor car'. The insurers had failed to use sufficiently clear and precise language when they drew up the policy and, unfortunately for them, they were liable to the assured.

Hopefully, it should now be obvious that attempts to construct overly elaborate clauses will often end in disaster for the party seeking to rely upon them.

The doctrine of fundamental breach and consumer contracts

The courts (in particular the English courts) have also developed the doctrine of fundamental breach as an aid to the interpretation of exclusion and limitation clauses. The doctrine is particularly useful where one of the parties has committed a material breach of contract. The party in breach will then attempt to rely upon a clause in the agreement in order to escape or limit his liability. The problem with this is that the material breach contract has effectively destroyed the whole agreement as originally concluded by the parties (including the exclusion or limitation clause). Following on from this, the innocent party will argue that enforcement of the clause would result in a grave injustice being suffered by him. Such a result would clearly be in direct contradiction to the original purpose of the contract. As we shall see, it is possible for these types of clauses to be enforced, but very precise words must be used. Clauses written in very general terms which attempt to exclude or limit liability for material breaches of contract will also certainly not be enforced by the courts. Clearly, the courts do not wish to encourage widespread use of terms that allow people to escape or limit their liability for what are extremely serious breaches of contract.

 The decision of the House of Lords in **Pollock & Co v Macrae [1922]** encouraged a mistaken view (promoted especially by Lord Denning) that the courts would not enforce a clause allowing a party who had committed a material breach of contract to escape or limit his liability. The facts of **Pollock** are as follows:

The defenders were in the business of building and supplying marine engines. They entered into a contract to supply engines for use in the pursuer's fishing vessels. The defenders had included an exclusion clause in the contract which permitted them to defeat any claims by the pursuer if the engines did not meet the required standard of quality owing to defective materials and workmanship. The pursuer was supplied with engines that were so defective as to be entirely useless.

Held: by the House of Lords that the exclusion clause was so repugnant that it was in direct contradiction to the essence of the contract i.e. that the defenders were under a duty to manufacture and to supply working engines. In this case, the defenders had committed a material or fundamental breach of contract. Lord Dunedin did concede that it was possible for a party to exclude his liability for material breach. However, he went on to say that such conditions to be effective 'will be most clearly and unambiguously expressed.' Following a thorough examination of the exclusion clause, the House of Lords was of the opinion that it was not sufficient to exclude liability for a material breach of contract. The pursuer's claim for damages was allowed to proceed.

In the following two cases, the House of Lords decided that the defenders were able to exclude their liability for material breaches of contract because the clauses that they were relying upon happened to be clearly and unambiguously expressed.

 Photo Production Ltd *v* Securicor Transport Ltd (1980) the pursuer's premises were burned down when the night security guard provided by Securicor deliberately started a fire on the premises. Securicor had no reason to suspect that its employee would have behaved in such a fashion – the guard's actions could not have been predicted i.e. they were not reasonably foreseeable. Furthermore, the guard had come to Securicor with good references. Securicor had an exclusion clause in the contract which permitted it to escape liability for all deliberate acts and negligence which were not reasonably foreseeable. The House of Lords found that the terms of the contract were wide enough and sufficiently precise to exclude deliberate acts as well as negligence.

 Ailsa Craig Fishing Co Ltd *v* Malvern Fishing Co Ltd (1983) where the negligence of another Securicor employee caused two vessels in Aberdeen harbour to collide with another and one of the ships sank to the bottom of the harbour. One of the ships had slipped from its moorings and drifted off. The employee in question had left his post and gone off to join the New Year celebrations. The employee's actions, which led to the accident, were quite clearly a fundamental i.e. material breach of contract, but Securicor attempted to limit its liability to £1000.

Held: by the House of Lords that the clause had been drawn up in wide enough terms to include events such as this. Securicor was, therefore, able to limit its liability to £1000 by relying on the exclusion contract. The trial judge had awarded damages of £55,000, but this of course was overturned.

As we have seen, it will be consumers who benefit most from the provisions of the Unfair Contract Terms Act 1977 and the Unfair Terms in Consumer Contracts Regulations 1999. Attempts by businesses to exclude or limit their liability for fundamental breaches of contract in relation to consumer transactions will almost certainly fail.

Remedies for breach of contract and limitation of actions

By breach of contract, we mean that one of the parties has broken the agreement in some way. In other words, someone has failed to carry out their side of the bargain. The innocent party – the victim of the other party's breach – will then have to approach the courts and request a remedy. A remedy for breach of contract should hopefully be capable of putting the victim in the position that he would have been in had the breach not taken place.

 Key point: A breach of contract means that one of the parties has broken the agreement in some way.

Examples of breaches of contract would include a seller supplying goods which were not of satisfactory quality; a buyer wrongfully refusing to accept goods; the buyer failing to pay for goods on the agreed date for payment; or the seller failing to deliver goods on the agreed delivery date.

It should also be remembered that breaches of contract have different consequences. Some breaches will be regarded as material which means that they are so serious that they strike at the very heart of the agreement and completely destroy it. Other breaches will not be as serious and the consequences will be less severe. Late delivery of goods by the seller, for example, may or may not be a material breach of contract. The courts will look at the circumstances of the case and draw the appropriate conclusions. Having done so, the courts will then decide the most appropriate remedy to award to the pursuer. We can see an example of how the courts decide whether a breach is material or not in the following case:

 Simpson *v* London & North Western Rail Co (1876) the pursuer had entered into a contract of carriage with the defenders for the purpose of transporting product samples to an agricultural exhibition which was taking place at Newcastle. The pursuer expressly communicated his wishes to the defenders by writing on the packages containing the goods: 'Must be at Newcastle on Monday certain.' The defenders failed to deliver the goods to Newcastle in accordance with the pursuer's strict instructions and were, therefore, liable in damages for the potential loss of profits. The defenders were fully aware of the pursuer's special instructions and they had agreed to be bound by them when they accepted the goods for transport to Newcastle.

In the Scots law of contract, there are four possible remedies available to a party who has suffered a breach of contract. These are:

◆ Damages
◆ Specific implement

◆ Retention and lien
◆ Rescission

 Key point: The main remedies for breach of contract are damages, specific implement, retention and lien and rescission.

Damages

Damages will usually be the most common type of remedy which an aggrieved party will seek. Generally, damages are awarded to compensate the pursuer for his loss and not to punish the defender. In situations where the pursuer has not suffered loss, for example, the seller fails to deliver goods on time but the buyer is able to purchase the goods elsewhere at no extra cost, the court will award nominal damages. Nominal damages is an award of a small sum of money, for example, £75, to reflect the view that the issue of loss or damages is of a purely technical nature.

 Key point: In situations where one of the parties has not suffered a loss due to the other party's breach of contract, the courts will often award nominal damages i.e. a very small sum of money which emphasises that the breach is of a minor nature.

General and special damages

General damages are awarded to the pursuer when the loss he has suffered is a reasonably foreseeable and direct result of the defender's breach of contract. The amount of damages will ensure that the pursuer is placed in the position that he would have been had it not been for the defender's actions. General damages, therefore, compensate the pursuer for loss caused in the ordinary way of things.

Special damages, on the other hand, are awarded to the pursuer when the defender's breach of contract causes abnormal loss or loss which was not reasonably foreseeable. In these situations, the pursuer will have to take steps to inform the defender that there are special circumstances that would cause him to suffer losses far in excess of what might ordinarily be the case. If the pursuer fails to inform the defender about these special circumstances, there can be no award of special damages.

 Victoria Laundry v Newman Industries (1949) the pursuers, a laundry, had ordered a new boiler for the purposes of taking on more business. The boiler was delivered some 20 weeks late – a clear breach of contract by the defenders. The defenders were perfectly aware that delivery of the new boiler was a matter of urgency because, at the time, there was an extremely high demand for laundry services. The pursuers had hoped to benefit from this demand by being able to use the new boiler. The loss of this business (£16 per week) was reasonably foreseeable in the ordinary course of things and the pursuers were awarded general damages on this basis. The pursuers, however, also claimed special damages for the loss of special government contracts which would have made them £262 per week. The pursuers lost their claim for special damages because from the defenders point of view, it was not reasonably foreseeable that their breach of contract would result in the loss of these special government contracts. The pursuers had never taken steps to warn the defenders that their breach of contract would cause them to suffer abnormal losses. The defenders were in complete ignorance of the existence of these special contracts and, therefore, were not in a position to predict fully the consequences of their breach of contract. The pursuers' loss in relation to the special contracts was simply too remote and not something that would have entered the defenders' consciousness.

Hadley *v* Baxendale (1854), which is discussed below, is another good example of the judicial approach to awards of general and special damages.

What can be claimed as damages?

When the pursuer raises a claim for damages, the compensation awarded will normally cover personal injuries, damage to property and financial losses suffered by him. It is only in exceptional circumstances, however, that damages will include an element for disappointment and mental distress experienced by the pursuer as a result of the defender's breach of contract.

 In **Jarvis *v* Swans Tours Ltd (1973)** Swans promised Jarvis a 'Houseparty holiday in Switzerland'. All sorts of things were promised as part of the holiday package (good food, entertainment and companions) and the hotelier was said to speak English – this was untrue. During, the first week of the holiday there were 13 people at the hotel, but the during the second week Jarvis was left on his own. The food and entertainment were, however, seriously substandard.

Held: by the English Court of Appeal that the pursuer was entitled to an award of £125 in damages (the holiday had cost £63).

The Jarvis case is exceptional because, generally speaking, damages for disappointment, inconvenience or loss of enjoyment are not awarded. The nature of the contract was different from ordinary commercial contracts in that the pursuer's pleasure had been ruined and his expectations had not been met.

The issue of damages for disappointment, anxiety and vexation has been examined, once again, in a number of cases before the House of Lords. In **Johnson *v* Gore Wood & Co [2001]**, Lord Cooke of Thorndon stated the familiar rule that:

'Contract-breaking is treated as an incident of commercial life which players in the game are expected to meet with mental fortitude.'

However, this general rule may be ignored where the contract is concerned with or connected to the provision of pleasure, relaxation or peace of mind.

 Farley *v* Skinner [2001] the pursuer had engaged the surveyor to investigate a property, Riverside House, situated in the Sussex village of Blackboys, which he was interested in purchasing. The property lay some 15 miles from Gatwick Airport and the pursuer was understandably concerned with potentially unacceptable levels of noise from aircraft flying over the property. The pursuer specifically asked the surveyor to investigate the possibility of unacceptable levels of noise pollution. He did not want to purchase a property on a flight-path. In that sense, the contract was, according to Lord Clyde, not an 'ordinary surveyor's contract'. The request for the report on aircraft noise was an additional requirement above and beyond what was usually asked of a surveyor. No doubt the surveyor could have charged an extra fee if he had bothered to spend the extra time researching the issue of aircraft noise. The surveyor informed the pursuer that the noise levels were not particularly bad. The pursuer proceeded to purchase the property which he considered to be a dream home to be used, primarily, for the purposes of relaxation. Unfortunately, the property was situated close to a navigation beacon where, during busy times at Gatwick Airport, aircraft would circle before they were permitted to land. Obviously, there were times when significant numbers of aircraft were circling the beacon. This fact completely ruined the character of the property and the pursuer's enjoyment of it. He could not raise an action against the Airport authorities because the Civil Aviation Act 1982 authorised these activities. The pursuer raised an action for damages against the surveyor for failing to alert him to the huge levels of noise generated by aircraft circling the navigation beacon.

Held: the House of Lords awarded damages of £10,000 to the pursuer in relation to disappointment and anxiety caused by the negligent report of a surveyor. Lord Clyde stated that:

'. . .*it is possible to approach the case as one of the exceptional kind in which the claim would be for damages for disappointment. If that approach was adopted so as to seek damages for disappointment, I consider that it should also succeed.*'

It was the specific provision in relation to the peacefulness of the property in respect of aircraft noise which made this an exceptional case.

 Key point: Generally, damages for disappointment, inconvenience or loss of enjoyment are not awarded to the victim of a breach of contract.

The calculation of damages

The courts use two tests when comes it to calculating the amount of damages that the aggrieved party will receive. These tests are remoteness of damage and minimisation of loss.

Remoteness of damage

The effects of a breach of contract may be far ranging but, as a matter of public policy, the courts must draw a line and say that the damages incurred beyond a certain limit are too remote to be recovered. The proximate cause of the loss will, therefore, be uppermost in the minds of the judges.

Remoteness of damage means that damages in a contract will not be recovered by the pursuer unless they are proved to be a direct and natural consequence of the defender's breach i.e. the losses caused to the pursuer occurred because of the defender's actions. If the losses have not occurred directly owing to the defender's fault, then it is likely that the defender, as a reasonable man, did not realise that such an outcome was likely to occur. Damage which does not arise naturally and which is not in the contemplation of a reasonable man can only be recovered if the defender was made aware of it and agreed to accept the risk of the loss.

We can see how this test operates in the following case:

 Hadley v Baxendale (1854) the pursuer owned a flour mill. The crank shaft of the pursuer's mill had been broken and was completely useless. The pursuer had asked a manufacturer in Greenwich to make him a new piece of machinery. The broken shaft had to be taken Greenwich so that it could be examined by the manufacturer in order to make the new piece of machinery. The pursuer hired the defender, a carrier, to take the shaft to Greenwich. The delivery of the machinery to the manufacturer was subject to unreasonable delay caused by the negligence of the carrier. This meant that operations at the flour mill literally ground to a halt and the pursuer began to suffer financial losses. The pursuer raised an action against the carrier for the loss of profits during the unexpected period of delay.

Held: the pursuer's claim for damages for loss of profits for the entire period that his mill was forced to stop operating was dismissed. The pursuer had failed to notify the carrier that he did not possess a spare crank shaft and that he was utterly dependent on the new piece of machinery being manufactured and dispatched to him as quickly as possible. The carrier was entitled to assume that most mill operators would have had a spare crank shaft for just such emergencies. There was no explanation by the pursuer of his predicament. Clearly, the carrier had committed a breach of contract because he would know that his failure to deliver the crank shaft to the manufacturers would cause the pursuer some inconvenience i.e. the mill would have been prevented from operating until a spare crank shaft was fitted – even if this was for a short period only. Unfortunately, as we have seen, the pursuer did not have a substitute item of machinery, but how was the defender to know this when the pursuer failed to inform him?

Mitigation of loss

The injured party has a duty to mitigate or to minimise his loss i.e. he must take all reasonable steps to cut his losses. Thus, a seller whose goods are rejected must attempt to get the best price for them elsewhere and the buyer of the goods which are not delivered must attempt to buy as cheaply as possible elsewhere. Should the parties in both these situations fail to cut their losses, they cannot rely upon the courts to award them full damages in respect of their losses. However, a pursuer only has to show the courts that he has taken reasonable steps to cut his losses. Superhuman efforts on the part of the pursuer are unnecessary.

 Gunter & Co v Lauritzen (1894) the pursuer had entered into a contract to purchase a consignment of hay. The pursuer intended to sell these goods at a profit. However, this was not possible because the defender delivered goods which did not meet the requirements of the contract and the pursuer rightfully rejected them. The pursuer then raised an action for damages against the defender. The defender claimed that the pursuer had failed to mitigate its losses. The defender stated that it had been possible for the pursuer to obtain substitute goods and this the pursuer had failed to do. The pursuer in turn pointed out that this would have meant approaching three different sellers from different parts of Scotland and negotiating with each of them in turn for the sale of the goods. The original contract was to have been performed in Aberdeen.

Held: it would have been completely unreasonable to force the pursuer to negotiate the sale of three separate consignments of goods from three different sellers throughout Scotland. The pursuer was awarded the damages for loss of profit.

 Key point: When it comes to the calculation of damages, the innocent party must show that he has taken reasonable steps to reduce (mitigate) his losses and that the losses suffered are not too remote.

Liquidated damages or penalty clauses

The parties to an agreement may actually be far-sighted enough to insert a remedy into their contract which addresses the issue of the amount of damages payable should one of them break the contract. These damages are known as liquidated damages and sometimes such a clause is known as a penalty clause. The phrase penalty clause can be misleading because the courts will not enforce the provision for liquidated damages if the amount is not a genuine pre-estimate of loss. The courts, in other words, will not allow one party to punish the other – even if one of the parties is in breach. The courts will then award damages in the usual way i.e. by applying the tests of remoteness of damage and mitigation of loss.

Hugely extravagant sums in penalty clauses will usually invite judicial suspicion and may be not be enforceable. Very often, damages can be accurately assessed and the party hoping to take advantage of the extravagant penalty clause will be left exposed. If the sum provided for in the contract is payable on the occurrence of any one of several events, it is probably a penalty for it is highly unlikely that each event can produce the same level of losses. Penalty clauses will not be enforced by the courts in the pursuer's favour if the breach of contract was the pursuer's fault.

 One of the leading cases illustrating the approach of the Scottish courts to the enforcement of penalty clauses is **Clydebank Engineering & Shipbuilding Co *v* Yzquierdo y Castaneda (1904)**. The House of Lords was asked to determine whether a clause in a contract fixing damages at £500 per week for every week of late delivery of 4 torpedo boats was a penalty or if the sum was liquidate damages capable of enforcement.

The contract involved the construction of four torpedo boats for the Spanish navy. The Scottish shipyard was unable to complete the vessels in accordance with the completion date set down by the contract. In the interim, the Spanish-American War had occurred in which Spanish forces were decisively defeated on land and at sea. Especially galling for the Spaniards was the loss of the Island of Cuba (the richest province in its Empire) and the Philippine Islands. The Spanish Government alleged that the Scottish shipbuilders' failure to perform their obligations, as demanded by the contract, had contributed directly to the huge losses suffered by Spanish forces at the hands of the Americans during hostilities in the Cuban theatre of operations (the entire Spanish fleet had been sunk off Cuba). The Spaniards argued that they would not have lost the War had the shipyard delivered the four torpedo boats on the due date in accordance with the terms of the contract. The Spaniards sued for £75,000 to which they claimed that they were entitled in terms of the penalty clause. The shipyard argued that this was not a genuine pre-estimate of loss and that compensation should be calculated according to the ordinary rules of damages i.e. minimisation of loss and remoteness of loss.

Held: by the House of Lords that the Spaniards' demand for £75,000 did not represent a genuine pre-estimate of loss and that this sum should be instead regarded as liquidate damages. Clearly, no one could have calculated the extent of the losses suffered by the Spaniards before the war and, therefore, it would have been impossible to make a genuine pre-estimate of loss. However, the shipyard had committed a breach of contract and would, therefore, have to pay compensation. The House of Lords set a figure of £67,000 as the compensation payable to the Spanish government.

The Scottish courts will enforce penalty clauses if the party relying on it can prove that the clause is a genuine pre-estimate of loss as can be seen in the following case:

 Cameron-Head *v* Cameron & Co (1919) in April 1919, the pursuer, the owner of the Inverailort estate in Inverness-shire, brought a claim against the defenders who were timber merchants. The contract involved the sale of a forest which was to be cut down and the timber removed by the defenders. Failure by the defenders to perform their part of the contract by 1 April 1918 would result in them being liable to pay a daily penalty of 10 shillings for as long as they were in breach of contract. By the following April of 1919, the defenders had not yet managed to cut down all of the forest and clear the timber away. The claim brought by the pursuer was, therefore, for one year's penalty at the daily rate of 10 shillings.

Held: by the Court of Session that the penalty accrued on a daily basis from 1 April 1918 onwards and that the pursuer could bring an action to claim this at any time, despite the fact that full contractual performance by the defenders had not yet been achieved. Upon examination of the daily sum of 10 shillings, it was decided that this was a genuine pre-estimate of loss. The pursuer had not dreamt up this figure and it accurately reflected her losses on a day-to-day basis.

Reforming the law on penalty clauses

In 1999, the Scottish Law Commission published a Report on Penalty Clauses (**Scot Law Com No 171**). The main reform to this area of law proposed by the Commission is that a judge should be permitted to modify an excessively high penalty clause in order to make it enforceable. Currently, if the penalty clause is not a genuine pre-estimate of loss, a judge will have no option but to assess compensation in accordance with the ordinary rules of damages. The current test, centring on the concept of a genuine pre-estimate of loss, should be replaced. The proposed reforms would allow a judge to enforce a clause which was 'not manifestly excessive' even if the sum claimed is not a genuine pre-estimate of loss. The burden of proof will be on the party against whom the clause is being enforced to demonstrate that the clause is 'manifestly excessive'. Whether or not a clause is 'manifestly excessive' should be the new test applied to penalty clauses.

Specific implement (or a decree *ad factum praestandum*)

This is a very limited remedy in the sense that it will only be granted to the pursuer if the court thinks that it is appropriate. Basically, the pursuer is asking the court to make an order (a decree) which will force the defender to carry out his contractual obligations. In a small claims action in the Sheriff Court, for example, a pursuer could ask the court to force a builder who has only half-completed a patio to finish the job.

An example of the remedy of specific implement being granted to a pursuer by the Scottish courts can be seen in the following example:

 John Anderson *v* Pringle of Scotland (1998) the employer attempted to ignore parts of its redundancy policy which formed part of a collective agreement that had been incorporated into the employees' contracts. One of the employees raised an action for specific implement in order to force the employer to obey the terms of its own redundancy policy.

Held: by the Court of Session that the employer must follow the provisions of its redundancy policy. This was something of a hollow victory for the employee because, subsequently, he was made redundant by the employer who used the proper redundancy procedures this time.

The remedy of specific implement will not be appropriate in the following circumstances:

◆ Where the court is of the opinion that an award of damages is a more than adequate remedy.

◆ Where the defender owes the pursuer money, the court will not grant specific implement because the appropriate action on the pursuer's part is to sue for damages. On a technical point, a decree of specific implement is a court order and failure to comply with it would mean that the defender was in contempt of court. This means that the defender would face imprisonment, but being sent to prison for a civil debt is no longer available to the courts in Scotland.

◆ Where the pursuer can obtain goods or services from a variety of alternative sources and there is no great inconvenience caused. If the pursuer had to pay a greater price than the contract price for these goods and services, he could sue the defender in damages for the difference. It is only where the goods or services have some unique value that the courts will grant an order for specific implement.

◆ Where the grant of an order would cause injustice or harm to someone.

◆ Where the contract in question involves a high degree of personal contact, for example, an employer cannot be compelled by an Employment Tribunal to reinstate or re-engage an employee that has been dismissed. Even if the employee wins his unfair dismissal claim and the Employment Tribunal grants a Reinstatement Order, the employer cannot be forced to take him back.

◆ Where the defender is outwith the jurisdiction of the Scottish courts.

◆ Where the granting of an order would, in effect, be ordering the defender to do something which was impossible to carry out.

Key point: Specific implement is an order from the court that forces the party in breach of contract to carry out his duties under the agreement, but it is not always an appropriate remedy and, therefore, the courts will not always grant it.

Retention and lien

The right of retention (or lien as it is known as in England) allows an innocent party to suspend his contractual duties as a result of a breach of contract by the other party to the agreement. This does not mean that the innocent party is freed from his contractual duties. Retention simply allows the innocent party to retain property, goods or money that belong to the contract-breaker until such time as the other party carries out his side of the agreement. However, it should be noted that the innocent party can only use this remedy in relation to property, goods or money of the contract-breaker that he rightfully possesses at the time of the breach. A solicitor, for example, could refuse to hand over documents that she holds for a client until the client pays her legal bill. A hotel can also exercise its right of retention by refusing to release a guest's luggage until the guest pays his hotel bill.

The innocent party is under a duty of care to the contract-breaker, however, to ensure that any property, goods or money which is subject to the right of retention is properly safeguarded. The right of retention is a very useful remedy because it is likely that the contract-breaker will need to use his property, sell the goods on to a third party or have need of the money to meet all sorts of bills. To say that the innocent exercising his right of retention will cause the contract-breaker all sorts of inconvenience is something of an understatement. There is a very real incentive for the contract-breaker to carry out his side of the bargain.

 Haig-Boswell *v* Preston (1915) a tenant refused to pay rent to his landlord until such time as the landlord completed repairs to the tenant's roof which was letting in substantial quantities of rainwater. It was the duty of the landlord to ensure that the tenant had a suitable property which was windproof and watertight. Clearly, the landlord was in breach of contract and the tenant decided to suspend his duty to pay rent on a temporary basis until the repairs were carried out.

Held: the tenant was entitled to take this action against the landlord.

 Key point: Where one party is in breach of the agency contract, the innocent party is entitled to exercise his right of lien which allows him to retain possession of property or money that he holds in trust for the party in breach.

Rescission

This remedy will be sought by the pursuer when the defender has committed a material breach of contract. A material breach of contract is such a serious breach that it goes to the very roots of the agreement and completely undermines the contract. The practical effect of rescission is that the pursuer wishes the court to cancel the contract.

Minor breaches of contract will rarely allow the pursuer to cancel the contract and very often the court will grant damages to the pursuer as an alternative. The parties to a contract could state, however, that certain breaches of the agreement will be regarded as material and this will allow the innocent party to apply to the courts for rescission.

 Shaw, Macfarlane & Co. *v* Waddell & Sons (1890) the buyers were supposed to send a ship to pick up a cargo of coal during the period 12 to 16 April. Unfortunately, due to the fault of the buyers, the ship was delayed and could not uplift the cargo on the dates specified. In fact, there was a delay of almost eleven days. The sellers were caused great inconvenience by this delay caused by the buyers that they decided to cancel the contract.

Held: the sellers were entitled to cancel the agreement because the time for loading the ship was a material term of the contract and the buyers had committed a material breach by failing to load the cargo between 12 and 16 April.

According to Section 15B(2)(a) of the Sale of Goods Act 1979, in a consumer contract, any breach by the seller of an express or implied term as to the quality of the goods or their fitness for purpose, for example, shall be regarded as a material breach. Consequently, Section 15B(1)(b) of the 1979 Act allows the buyer to reject any goods delivered under the contract and to treat the contract as cancelled (or repudiated).

 Key point: The remedy of rescission allows the innocent party to have the contract cancelled where the breach committed by the other party amounts to a material breach of contract.

Termination of contract

Obviously, contracts and the rights and duties established by them do not exist forever. With this thought in mind it is now time to examine the various ways in which a contract is discharged or terminated.

Performance and payment

Most contracts will come to an end simply by the parties performing their duties under the agreement, for example, a supplier of goods will deliver the goods conforming to the contract to the buyer and the buyer will, in turn, make payment to the seller for this property.

Acceptilation and discharge

An individual will effectively waive or give up his rights under the agreement which means that the other party is released from his contractual duties. One party could choose to inform the other party that payment of his debt of £10,000 is no longer required.

Delegation

An individual agrees that the other party can be released from his contractual duties and be replaced by another party. All the parties to the agreement must consent to this new arrangement. This type of arrangement is very common where the original debtor is released from his obligation to pay a debt to a lender or creditor because a new debtor has agreed to take responsibility for payment of the debt. The benefit of this kind of arrangement from the creditor or lender's point of view is that he is far more likely to see the debt repaid than if he insisted on payment by the original debtor.

Novation

A new agreement is formed with the mutual consent of the parties and this new contract replaces any previous agreement that the parties may have had.

Compensation

This allows one of the parties to a contract to make a counter-claim against the other party which has the effect of reducing his overall liability. If, for example, A owes B £10,000 and B lodges a counter-claim against A for £8000, B's overall liability will be reduced to £2000 (assuming that his counter-claim is valid). This is often a very common situation in wrongful dismissal claims where an employee sues the employer for compensation in respect of breach of contract, the employer can launch a counter-claim for compensation. If the employee is found liable to the employer in terms of the counter-claim, he may find that his compensation for wrongful dismissal is reduced dramatically.

Confusion

This situation arises when someone owes to a debt to himself. This seems a rather ridiculous situation, but it could easily arise. If, for example, a person had borrowed £10,000 from her mother and her mother later died making the daughter beneficiary of her estate, the daughter would inherit the debt of £10,000 owed by herself to her mother. Clearly, any court action raised by the daughter to sue herself for £10,000 is would result in a farcical situation. The daughter's debt is now cleared.

Material breach of contract

A material breach it will be remembered is an extremely serious breach of contract which leaves the aggrieved party with the option of using the remedy of rescission. Rescission effectively allows the aggrieved party to cancel the contract. If the contract is cancelled, all rights and duties under the original agreement are wiped out.

Lapse of time – prescription

The Prescription and Limitation (Scotland) Act 1973 has the effect of ensuring that contractual rights and duties must be exercised within certain periods of time. Failure to enforce rights or duties by the parties to the agreement within these periods has the effect of terminating the agreement. If someone owes you a debt and you do not take legal action to enforce the debtor's obligation within five years, you will lose your rights to any money owed. If a pursuer does not bring a legal action against the defender within a time laid down by the Prescription and Limitation (Scotland) Act 1973, he may find that his claim is time-barred i.e. he has had enough time to raise an action and he has failed to do so.

 Key point: Contracts do not last forever and can be terminated in a variety of ways. In the vast majority of situations, a contract will come to an end when the parties perform their obligations under the agreement.

Impossibility, frustration and illegality

Since the formation of the contract, the circumstances surrounding the agreement may have changed dramatically. The contract may now be impossible to perform or the contract may have been rendered illegal by changes in the law.

Physical destruction of the subject-matter of the contract operates to frustrate the agreement.

 Taylor v Caldwell (1863) the Surrey Gardens and Music Hall was hired by the pursuers from the defenders for the purpose of holding four grand concerts and fêtes. Before the first concert on 17 June 1862 could took place, the hall was completely destroyed by fire. Neither party was responsible for this incident. The pursuers, however, brought an action for damages against the defenders for wasted advertising costs.

Held: By the English High Court that it was clearly impossible for the contract to be performed because it relied on the continuing existence of the venue. The pursuers claim for damages was dismissed on the grounds that the purpose of the contract had been frustrated.

 Vitol SA v Esso Australia 1988 a contract for the sale of petroleum was discharged on the grounds of frustration when both the ship and its cargo of petroleum were completely destroyed in a missile attack in the Persian Gulf during the Iran-Iraq War of the 1980s. The sellers had attempted to sue the buyers for the price of the goods, but this claim was dismissed.

 Key point: If the subject matter of the contract is destroyed, the contract will be considered to have been frustrated.

Does the cancellation of an event result in frustration of contract?

In **Krell v Henry [1903]**, Lord Justice Vaughn-Williams was of the opinion that frustration of contract was not limited to either the destruction or non-existence of the subject matter of the contract. It will be important to identify the substance or the purpose of the agreement. The cancellation of an event can frustrate the performance of a contract where that event is an absolutely material term of the agreement.

 Krell v Henry [1903] the pursuer was the owner of a flat in the central London district of Pall Mall. The pursuer's flat was on the route of the proposed coronation procession of the new King, Edward VII, which was scheduled to take place on 26 and 27 June 1902. The pursuer had advertised his flat for rent during the daytime on 26 and 27 June for the purpose of viewing the procession. The defender, who was anxious to view the procession, responded to the advertisement and entered into an agreement to hire the flat on the days specified. An announcement was made on 24 June stating that the procession was to be cancelled owing to the King's illness. The defender refused to pay the balance of the rent for the flat by reason that events had frustrated performance of the contract. The pursuer brought an action against the defender for payment of the balance of the rent.

Held: by the English Court of Appeal that the cancellation of the event frustrated the contract and discharged the parties from their obligations under it. The clinching argument in the defender's favour was that both parties clearly entered into the contract with the same intention. The reason behind the hire of the flat was, therefore, a material term of the contract. Had the defender failed to communicate his motivation for hiring the flat, then the contract would have remained capable of enforcement by the pursuer. Lord Justice Vaughn-Williams was of the opinion that frustration of contract was not limited to either the destruction or non-existence of the subject matter of the contract. It was also important to identify the substance or the purpose of the agreement. In other words, did the parties share the same intentions?

The illness of King Edward resulted in a second legal action. This time, however, the English Court of Appeal took a completely different approach to the issue of frustration of contract.

The decision in **Krell *v* Henry** can be contrasted with the decision below:

 Herne Bay Steamboat Co *v* Hutton [1903] the pursuers had entered into a contract to hire a steamship to the defender for two days. The Royal Navy was assembling at Spithead to take part in a naval review to celebrate King Edward's coronation. The King was to review the fleet personally. The defender wished to transport paying guests from Herne Bay to Spithead to see the naval review. Due to the King's illness, an official announcement was made cancelling the review. It would still have been perfectly possible for the defender to take his passengers on a cruise to see the assembled fleet. The defender, however, refused to use the vessel claiming that the contract had been frustrated. The pursuers brought an action against the defender for the balance of the fee of £250 owed by the defender who was refusing to pay for the hire of the boat.

Held: the contract was not discharged by reason of frustration. The main purpose of the contract could still be achieved i.e. to take paying guests for a cruise around the fleet.

The difference in approach taken by the Court of Appeal in both cases is sometimes difficult to understand. In **Krell *v* Henry**, both parties had clearly intended that the purpose of the contract was to view the procession. Reinforcing this fact, was the fact that the defender was only entitled to use the flat during the daytime. In **Herne Bay Steamboat Co *v* Hutton**, the purpose of the defender in hiring the steamship was to see the naval review, but this was not the purpose of the owners who were not the slightest bit interested why the vessel had been hired. Lord Justice Vaughn-Williams compared the situation to someone who hires a carriage to go and see the

Epsom Derby, but the outbreak of some unforeseen epidemic means that the races are cancelled. This makes no difference to the owner of the carriage who will still expect to be paid for the hire of his vehicle.

 Key point: Cancellation of an event may mean that the contract could be regarded as frustrated, but it will be important to examine the terms of the agreement.

Frustration can only be used to have the contract discharged in situations where neither party is to blame. When one party is to blame for the failure to perform his obligations under the agreement, this represents a breach of contract and the innocent party can raise the appropriate action.

 Tsakiroglou v Noblee Thorl GmbH [1961] the sellers had agreed to transport Sudanese ground nuts from Port Sudan in the Red Sea to Hamburg in Germany. The ship was to take the fastest route to Europe through the Suez Canal. This proved to be impossible because the Canal was closed as a result of military hostilities following the Anglo-French-Israeli invasion of Egypt causing the Suez Crisis in late 1956. The sellers would have to ship the goods around the alternative route of the Cape of Good Hope in South Africa. This meant that the distance the ship had to travel from Port Sudan to Hamburg was greatly increased and this would also mean a dramatic increase in the costs of carriage in respect of the goods.

Held: by the House of Lords that a party will still have a duty to perform a contract even if this means that performance is more difficult or expensive than was originally intended by the parties. The closure of the Suez Canal did not mean that the sellers' duties were discharged by reason of frustration of contract.

 Key point: Merely because the contract becomes more difficult or more expensive to perform does not mean that the contract is to be regarded as frustrated.

Contracts for personal services

Such a contract is discharged by the death of the person who was to perform it. The incapacity of a person who is to perform a contract may discharge it. However, temporary incapacity is not enough unless it affects the performance of the contract in a really serious way. If an employee is killed or permanently incapacitated, it will be very difficult to argue that the employment contract should be allowed to continue.

The purpose of the contract becomes impossible to perform

As we have seen, a situation involving the physical destruction of the subject-matter of the contract will discharge the parties from performance of their duties by reason of frustration. However, frustration can also occur in situations where physical destruction of the subject-matter of the contract may not be the issue.

 In **Jackson v Union Marine Insurance Co (1874)** the pursuer owned a ship which had been chartered to go with all possible speed from Liverpool to Newport for the purpose of loading a cargo bound for San Francisco. The pursuer had insurance with the defenders to protect himself in the event that the charter might be prevented from being carried out. The vessel was stranded whilst on its way to Newport. It was not refloated for over a month and could not be properly repaired for some time. The charterers hired another ship and the pursuer turned to the insurers. They suggested that the pursuer should sue the charterer for breach.

Held: the fact that the ship was stranded effectively frustrated the agreement's commercial purpose and, therefore, the charterers were free to go elsewhere. The pursuer had no remedy against the charterers and was in turn entitled to seek compensation under the insurance policy.

 Key point: A contract may be impossible to perform or its essential commercial aim becomes impossible to achieve and, therefore, it has to be regarded as discharged due to frustration.

Illegality

 Stevenson & Sons Ltd *v* AG für Cartonnagen Industrie (1918) an English company, Stevenson, was in partnership with a German company acting as a sole agent to sell the German company's goods. By continuing to carry on business with an enemy during wartime, Stevenson would be committing a criminal act and there was no alternative but to have the partnership dissolved. (See also **Cantiere San Rocco SA *v* Clyde Shipbuilding & Engineering Co Ltd (1923)**.)

In other situations, contracts can become illegal because Parliament introduces legislation to this effect. After the murder of schoolchildren and a teacher at Dunblane Primary School in 1996 by Thomas Hamilton, the British government made it illegal to own particular models of firearms. Therefore, anyone who entered a contract to purchase firearms shortly before the legislation was introduced could not force the supplier to perform the contract. If the buyer insisted on performance of the contract by the seller, the seller would be complying with his contractual duty, but he would also be breaking the law as the contract would be illegal.

 Key point: If a contract later becomes illegal, it will be regarded as void and the parties will not be able to enforce it.

Termination of the contract as a result of breach

Breach of contract can arise in a number of situations:

- ◆ Failure to perform the contract
- ◆ Express repudiation of the contract
- ◆ Unsatisfactory performance of the contract

It is worth re-emphasising at this stage that a breach of contract does not automatically give the innocent party the right to terminate the agreement. The seriousness of the breach will largely determine this question. The only remedy available to the innocent party may be to raise an action for damages. The innocent party may find this rather galling, but a failure by him to perform his duties in response to an earlier breach by the other party will mean that he is now in breach of contract.

Anticipatory breach

This situation will arise when one party gives advance warning (either by express communication or by his behaviour) that he has decided not to comply with his duties under the contract when performance is due. This means that the breach of contract will be anticipated by the innocent party and will, therefore, be far less of a shock. The innocent party has one of two possible courses of action open to him: he is entitled to raise an action for damages immediately therefore anticipating the breach or he may choose to wait and see what the other party will actually do when the time for performance actually arrives. Clearly, which of the two options is chosen may be influenced by personal circumstances. The concept of anticipatory breach where it involves the defender expressly communicating his intention to repudiate or cancel the contract has been criticised as illogical. After all, this individual could change his mind regarding his refusal to perform the contract. Furthermore, the innocent party can still insist on performing his obligations even in the face of overwhelming evidence that the other person has no intention of performing his side of the agreement.

In **White and Carter (Councils) Ltd *v* McGregor [1961]**, a decision of the House of Lords discussed below, Lord Reid used the example of someone who has been commissioned to go to Hong Kong for the purpose of compiling a report. This individual has agreed to pay his own expenses, but he expects to be paid £10,000 in exchange for the report when he returns to the United Kingdom. Prior to his departure to Hong Kong, the person is given notice that his report is no longer required. Owing to the concept of anticipatory breach, this individual would be entitled to go Hong Kong and compile the report (even when it is clearly no longer required). There is something highly illogical and unsatisfactory about this result. Lord Hodson drew attention to the fact that an anticipatory breach does not mean that the contract should be regarded as automatically terminated. He went on to state that either the innocent party can sue for damages immediately (as a consequence of the anticipatory breach) or he can await performance of the other party's duties. When it becomes clear that the other party will not perform his duties, the innocent party can then take action and this delay will not be regarded as fatal to his claim. In **White**, the House of Lords appeared to place limits on the concept of anticipatory breach. These limits were best summed up by Lord Reid's remarks:

'It may well be that if it can be shown that a person has no legitimate interest, financial or otherwise, in performing the contract rather than claiming damages, he ought not to be allowed to saddle the other party with an additional burden with no benefit to himself.'

This statement would appear to suggest that an innocent party may have no option but to raise a claim for damages when the other party has indicated that he has no real intention of performing his obligations.

An important point worth noting is that when an anticipatory breach of contract occurs, the innocent party will only have the right to treat the agreement as terminated when the breach is material in nature.

 Hochster *v* De la Tour (1853) the defender agreed to engage the pursuer as a courier for European travel, his duties to commence two months later. Three weeks before the pursuer was due to begin the job, the defender wrote to him stating that his services were no longer required. The pursuer commenced an action for breach of contract a week before his starting date and the defence claimed that there was no cause of action until the date due for performance.

Held: the defender's express repudiation enabled the innocent party to raise a claim for breach of contract before the date for the performance of the contract.

 White and Carter (Councils) Ltd *v* McGregor (1961) the respondent had entered into a contract for advertising services. However, the respondent quickly repudiated the contract, writing to the appellants asking them to cancel the contract and, at this stage, the appellants had not carried out any work. The appellants, however, refused to cancel the agreement and prepared the advertisements. The advertisements were publicly displayed several months later. These adverts were continually displayed for the next three years. Eventually, the appellants demanded payment, the respondents refused to pay. The appellants sued for sums owed under the contract.

Held: by the House of Lords that the appellants were entitled to recover the contract price. Even though the respondents had repudiated the contract, the appellants were not bound to accept this. The contract survived and the appellants had completed it. There was no duty to minimise loss until there was a breach which the appellants had accepted and they had not accepted this one. This decision has been criticised because it appears to allow the innocent party to continue to perform the contract when it is quite clear that the other side has no intention of performing their contractual duties.

More recently, the Inner House of the Court of Session re-examined the right of the innocent party to treat the contract as discharged or repudiated by reason of the other party's breach of the agreement.

 Macari *v* Celtic Football and Athletic Company Ltd (1999) Macari, the pursuer, had been appointed as the manager of Celtic Football Club. There was an express term in his employment contract to the effect that Macari would have to reside within a 45-mile radius of George Square in Glasgow. Furthermore, it was expected that Macari would attend regularly at Celtic Park and provide the Chief Executive with weekly reports on the progress of the Celtic team. When Macari accepted the appointment he was currently living in England and his contract envisaged that he would move to Glasgow with his family by Easter 1994. By June 1994, Macari had still not moved to Glasgow and, on 10 June, Celtic's Chief Executive ordered him to comply with his contract and move to Glasgow. Macari responded by sending an undated fax to the Chief Executive in which he stated that he had no intention of complying with this part of his contract at the present time owing to personal circumstances. Together with a subsequent telephone conversation with the Chief Executive, Macari made it quite clear that he was opposing his employer's lawful authority and he was perfectly aware that he was flouting his employer's instructions in respect of the residency requirement, regular attendance at Celtic Park and his duty to provide weekly reports. In response to Macari's refusal to abide by the terms of the contract, Celtic dismissed him from his employment. Macari claimed that he had been wrongfully dismissed in that he had not been given the proper notice period by Celtic in accordance with the terms of his contract.

Held: in June 1994, the pursuer was in material breach of contract by reason of his failure to comply with the residence clause, by reason of his failure to comply with the instruction to attend more regularly at Celtic Park and by reason of his failure to comply with his undertaking to report to the Chief Executive on a weekly basis. Quite simply, the pursuer's behaviour indicated that he was repudiating his contract with Celtic and, as a result, his employer was entitled to treat the contract as discharged. The pursuer was, therefore, not entitled to treat himself as having been wrongfully dismissed and he was not entitled to receive a compensation payment.

 Key point: Discharge of a contract owing to a breach by one of the parties can occur where the party in breach fails to perform it lawfully by breaking one or more terms of the contract or by expressly repudiating the agreement or by making it impossible to perform.

Summary

- A contract is a legally enforceable agreement, which consists of an offer and an acceptance.

- Without both an offer and an acceptance, a contract is not formed.

- Before the contract is formed, both the offer and acceptance must reach *consensus in idem.*

- A contract is formed by a definite offer and an unqualified acceptance, thus achieving *consensus in idem* or a legally enforceable agreement.

- If a counter-offer is made, it cancels out the original offer, which is then no longer capable of acceptance.

- Offers and acceptances can be either express or implied.

- A clear distinction must be identified in the contrast between an offer and an invitation to treat.

- An offer is capable of acceptance and therefore able to form a contract, whereas an invitation to treat cannot be accepted and is merely an indication of a willingness to negotiate.

- Communication of offers, acceptances and revocations are also particularly important and can be crucial to whether or not a contract is actually formed.

- Contracts can be invalidated in a variety of ways: substantial error, lack of capacity, lack of formality, misrepresentation, error, facility and circumvention, force and fear and illegality.

- The parties can attempt to exclude or limit their liability under the contract but the Unfair Contract Terms Act 1977 and the Unfair Terms in Consumer Contracts Regulations 1999 will often determine how successful these attempts are.

- Contractual obligations do not last forever; all contracts come to an end sooner or later.

Short answer questions, examination standard essay questions and case studies.

1 'A contract is an agreement, but not every agreement is a contract.' Explain this statement.

2 Examine the advertisement below:

> The latest innovation from Crossan & Wylie Beauty Products
>
> Ladies!
>
> What is your trouble? Is it unseemly facial wrinkles? Do you despair about your rapidly ageing looks? Fear not! Help is at hand.
>
> In no time at all, not a wrinkle in sight and that's a promise!
>
> Thanks to our new, revolutionary facial gel, Plastere de Paris, wrinkles can be a thing of the past. All you have to do is apply the cream regularly each day.
>
> Many of our clients who have already used this epoch-breaking product have been truly amazed by its qualities.
>
> Catriona Campbell of Tobermory, Isle of Mull (aged 29) says: 'Plastere de Paris has completely changed my life. Thanks to Wylie & Crossan Beauty Products I now feel that I can face the day with renewed confidence. I no longer feel that I have to wear a head scarf and dark glasses when I'm out tending the sheep. I've definitely rediscovered my zest for life!'
>
> So ladies, try Plastere de Paris today – what have you got to lose but your wrinkles?
>
> Because you shouldn't have to suffer alone!
>
> This product is available from all good retailers of beauty treatments.

3 a) In order to form a contract, the parties must achieve consensus *in idem*. What is 'consensus *in idem*'?

b) Sandeep has offered to sell her mobile phone to her friend, Balinder, for £50. Balinder quickly responds to this offer and sends her acceptance to Sandeep by e-mail. Sandeep replies and promises to bring the phone into work the following day. However, when Sandeep brings the phone into the office Balinder is not best pleased. She informs Sandeep that she thought she was purchasing a phone with a camera not just an ordinary mobile phone. Sandeep informs her that she had no intention of selling a mobile phone with a camera as she does not own one. Sandeep and Balinder are totally at cross-purposes.

What is the legal position?

4 In order for an acceptance to be valid, the offeree must ensure that she communicates it effectively to the offeror.

Assess the accuracy of this statement.

5 On 6 June, Suhail Ahmed posted an application form offering to buy shares in a highly successful company called McCannell Ltd. Suhail, a keen investor, knows that the company's shares are likely to be highly sought after. McCannell Ltd received Suhail's application on 8 June and the company's Chief Executive drafted a letter of acceptance which was posted on 20 June to Suhail. Suhail never received the letter of acceptance from McCannell Ltd. Some months later, Suhail is reading the financial section of his newspaper and he discovers that McCannell Ltd has gone into liquidation leaving a huge trail of debts behind. Suhail feels that he has had a lucky escape. Unfortunately, McCannell Ltd entered Suhail's name on the share register and credited him with dividends from the shares after it had issued the letter of acceptance. The liquidator is intent on bringing an action for the balance of £50,000 against Suhail for payment of the shares allotted by the company.

What are the legal consequences of this situation?

6 Creative Designs Ltd offered to design and supply Asma with business stationery for £8000. Asma is very keen to accept this offer and, to this end, she faxes a letter of acceptance to Creative Designs Ltd. There was a problem with Creative Designs' fax machine and Asma's letter of acceptance was never received.

Does Asma have a contract with Creative Designs Ltd?

7 In situations where the offeror has either forgotten or declined to impose a time limit for acceptance of his offer, the offeree will have to communicate his acceptance within a reasonable time if he wishes to form a contract with the offeror.

In relation to the acceptance of an offer, what is a reasonable time?

8 McCracken, a self-employed builder, offers to build Anne-Louise, a patio, a garden wall and conservatory for £15,000. Anne-Louise has been thinking about making these improvements to her home for some time. She thinks that McCracken's offer is just a bit on the pricey side and she accepts the offer on the condition that McCracken carries out the work for £13,500. McCracken is not prepared to do this and, in any case, he has managed to line up another lucrative building job with Anne-Louise's neighbour, Marion. Anne-Louise then says that she will accept McCracken's original offer and that she expects him to turn up to start work at her house early on Monday morning. McCracken is starting work for Marion on Monday morning.

Can Anne-Louise sue McCracken for breach of contract if he refuses to start work for her on Monday morning?

9 a) In Scotland, the law recognises the class of obligations known as gratuitous or unilateral promises.

What is this type of obligation and does the Scots law differ from English law?

b) Craig phones Katy offering to sell her a second hand Volkswagen Lupo 1.4, Special Edition, registration number SO52 BBX. Craig has promised that he will keep this offer open for ten days. Katy is not sure whether she wishes to accept this offer and she decides to take time to think about this. Five days later, Katy contacts Craig to inform him that she has decided to accept his offer, but Craig has sold the car to someone else. Katy has to spend at least £600 more on a similar type of car as Craig's offer was an exceptionally favourable one.

Advise Katy.

10 Gavin is walking down Sauchiehall Street one Friday afternoon when he stops to look at plasma televisions in the window of White Lightning, a well-known Glasgow electrical retail outlet. Gavin notices that one of the televisions is priced at £200. He is astonished at the low price marked on the television and he immediately rushes into to the shop where he heads straight for the cash desk so that he can purchase the goods. On reaching the cash desk, Gavin is incredibly annoyed to be told by the cashier that the goods have been incorrectly priced and that he must pay £2000 for the television. Gavin insists that White Lightning has made him a definite offer and that he has accepted that offer – there is a legally enforceable contract between him and the store. The cashier is not sure about this. She knows that it is store policy to give customers goods at the price on the ticket when the shop has made an error, but she is pretty certain that, in this situation, her supervisor would be most unhappy if Gavin was able to obtain the goods for £200. Gavin begins to rant and rave and the other customers in the store are beginning to look ill at ease and some are even heading for the doors. However, the cashier still refuses to sell the television to Gavin for £200.

Do you think that Gavin is correct?

11 Netta and Annie are regulars at the local bingo hall. Both women are in the habit of sharing their winnings on a equal basis. One night, Netta wins £120,000 while playing the National Game. The bingo hall manager comes over to congratulate Netta on her win and to present her with flowers and a bottle of champagne. He asks Netta what she intends to do with the money. Netta replies that she will give some of the money to her family and close friends, but first of all she is going to write a cheque for £60,000 made out to Annie. Netta goes on to explain that she and Annie always go halves on anything that they win at bingo. The manager is deeply impressed by this attitude. Some weeks later, however, Netta has second thoughts about writing Annie a cheque for £60,000 – after all it's her money. As an alternative, she gives Annie a cheque for £1000. Annie is not best pleased and she decides to sue Netta for the remaining £59,000 that she feels is hers by right.

What are Annie's chances of success?

12 a) In order to have an enforceable contract, there are certain situations where Scots law demands that the parties have put their agreement in writing.

Is this statement correct?

b) Lisa made a verbal offer to purchase a piece of land on South Uist that belongs to Suzanne. The plot of land is just the ideal size for building a holiday home. Lisa has put forward a very fair price for the land and Suzanne telephones Lisa to accept the offer. Suzanne states that there is no need to put anything in writing because it would mean having to pay ridiculous fees to lawyers and, quite simply, it would cause them too much trouble. This is an agreement between friends and they are both perfectly capable of taking care of things. Lisa has given Suzanne the money for the land and the builders are currently on the land to start work on the new house. To begin with, Lisa had some problems with the local council over planning permission, but Suzanne asked her cousin, a prominent solicitor, to attend the council's planning sub-committee meeting in order to argue Lisa's case. The solicitor was successful and the council has given Lisa permission to proceed with the building work which is now at an advanced stage. However, just when Lisa thinks everything is going well, Suzanne contacts Lisa to inform her that she will have to give back the land. Lisa protests, but Suzanne says there is nothing in writing and, therefore, a legally enforceable contract was never concluded. In any case, Suzanne will return the money that was paid for the land. Lisa later finds out that Suzanne has received a much better offer for the land.

Evaluate the situation.

c) What is the effect of the Contracts (Scotland) Act 1997?

13 a) What is contractual capacity?

⚖ **b)** Simon is a record producer with a history of signing young unknowns who later go on to enjoy a high degree of success in the pop charts. Simon was having a drink in a local nightclub one evening when a young singer called Hugh (age 16) appeared on stage and performed a terrific vocal set for the regulars at the club. Simon thinks that Hugh has got a great future in pop music and is determined to sign him to his record label. Hugh seems very keen to develop his career with Simon's label and signs a contract on the spot. Just before signing the agreement, Hugh asked Simon if it would be a good idea if he sought some legal advice in order to clarify a couple of issues. Simon, however, brushes these concerns aside and tells Hugh that he has nothing to worry about. The contract entitles Simon to 60 per cent of Hugh's future earnings, ten albums over the next ten years and touring twice a year. Furthermore, Simon is entitled to claim back all expenses incurred by him in relation to promoting Hugh's career. Hugh feels that this is a once in a lifetime opportunity

and, carried away by a rush of excitement (or could that be the after effects of the ecstasy tablet that he took before going on stage?), he decides to sign the contract. Some months later, Hugh starts to have second thoughts about his business relationship with Simon.

What legal options should Hugh explore?

c) How does the Adults with Incapacity (Scotland) Act 2000 affect the Scots law of contract?

14 Explain the terms void and voidable in relation to contracts. Provide one example of a void contract and one example of a voidable contract.

15 a) Some contracts are unenforceable because they contravene public policy in a variety of ways.

Explain this statement with examples of *pacta illicita*.

⚖ **b)** Henry hates his wife, Julie. He has hired a very shady individual whom he met in the local pub to kill Julie. Henry overheard this individual bragging to a friend about the number of murders he had committed. Henry has paid the killer £60,000 to carry out the murder, but after accepting this sum of money, the killer dupes Henry and runs off with the cash leaving Julie very much alive. Henry is very bitter and £60,000 poorer – after all he had a legally enforceable contract with the killer didn't he?

Can Henry enforce his agreement with the contract killer?

16 Explain the meaning of the term error in the substantials.

17 Ruaridh is a local farmer and recently he has encountered a number of problems and he seeks your advice.

⚖ **a)** Ruaridh entered into an agreement with Gary who runs a local brewery to sell hops and barley to be used in the brewing process. Gary, however, thinks that he is paying a price of £50 per ton for the goods. Ruaridh swears blind that the price is £60 per ton. However, the goods have already been delivered to Gary and he has used them in the brewing process.

⚖ **b)** Ruaridh was approached by an individual who made him an offer to buy his flock of prize sheep for £100 per head. The individual had asked Ruaridh to sell him the sheep on credit, but Ruaridh was not keen to do this. This individual claimed to be the son of another local farmer, David Campbell, who Ruaridh has had previous business dealings with and knows to be a man of good credit. Swayed by this knowledge, Ruaridh enters a contract with Campbell's son and lets him take the sheep away with him. It later turns out that the individual is a well known fraudster called O'Donnell who sold the sheep to an innocent third party called McDonald who is refusing to return the sheep.

⚖️ c) Ruaridh remortgaged a house that he owns for the purpose of raising money to invest in the expansion of his organic produce business. The bank has recently contacted Ruaridh to inform that his endowment mortgage will not raise enough money to pay off the mortgage. Ruaridh is puzzled because he stated explicitly that he wished to take out a capital and interest mortgage to repay the bank. Ruaridh would not have taken out an endowment policy because they have an extremely poor reputation.

⚖️ d) Ruaridh entered a contract to sell potatoes to FreshFields, a local food store that specialises in organic produce. Ruaridh is under the impression that an agent of FreshFields would pick the goods up at the end of the month. Freshfields have sent an agent along to the farm to pick up the goods. The agent is convinced that a consignment of potatoes currently lying in Ruaridh's warehouse are the goods that Freshfields contracted for. It is not yet the middle of the month. Ruaridh informs Freshfields that the potatoes have not yet been harvested.

Advise Ruaridh.

18 a) Explain the effects of misrepresentation upon a contract. Your answer should distinguish between innocent, fraudulent and negligent misrepresentation.

⚖️ **b)** Robin, an antique dealer, says to Alasdair who is interested in buying a painting which is unsigned: 'I've had this item looked over by a leading art expert who assures me that it is the work of the up and coming Scottish artist, John Mitchell. Mitchell's work is now highly sought after by collectors and is fetching very favourable prices at auction. The painting is an absolute steal at just £3000.' Alasdair is completely swayed by Robin's statements and he proceeds to write a cheque for £3000. Robin has never bothered to have the painting examined by an expert. One evening, Alasdair has a friend over for dinner. This friend is acquainted with the work of John Mitchell and he asks to see the painting. The friend informs Alasdair that the painting is not by Mitchell, but by one of Mitchell's pupils, Stuart Findlay.

What steps should Alasdair take?

19 Provide examples of the following:

   a) A contract *uberimae fidei*

   b) A fiduciary relationship.

20 a) What is meant by a contract in restraint of trade?

⚖️ **b)** Iain is a highly skilled computer engineer who has been responsible for expanding the business of his employer, Global Communications Networks PLC, over the last five years. The company is based in Glasgow, but it has a strong, international profile. Iain's area of work is highly specialist and he is one of only five computer engineers in the UK who possesses the kind of skills vital to the continuing success of his employer. Iain is becoming somewhat disenchanted with his job at Global Communications Networks. He has recently had an offer to take up a new post with a rival company. This offer is very tempting because it means that Iain will effectively double his current salary. However, there is a term in Iain's contract of employment to the effect that he must not divulge any information about trade secrets or customers to rivals of is current employer. Furthermore, Iain cannot take up employment with a business rival of his current employer for a period of 12 months. This restriction applies to business rivals who operate anywhere in the world.

Will Iain be able to accept the offer of new employment with the rival business?

   c) What is a 'garden leave' clause and where would you be most likely to encounter it?

21 ⚖️ Susan is a young, impressionable woman who also happens to be extremely wealthy. At University, she became deeply involved with a fanatical religious cult. Over a number of years, Susan got more deeply involved with the group to the extent that she had no contact with her family. The rules of cult demanded that members must hand over all of their possessions to the cult's leader, a mysterious individual who styles himself 'The Enlightened One'. The cult's leader is later convicted on charges of tax evasion and he is imprisoned for five years. Consequently, the cult breaks up and the members go their separate ways. Unfortunately, Susan suffers a breakdown and she is placed in psychiatric care. It is only after successful course of treatment that the full extent of her experiences with the group is revealed. Susan is now anxious to reclaim the money and the property that she donated to the group.

What is the likelihood of Susan succeeding in her claim?

22 Look carefully at the following notice which is prominently displayed at the cash desk of a store:

IMPORTANT NOTICE

THE STORE EXCLUDES ALL LIABILITY IN RELATION TO ANY UNSATISFACTORY GOODS PURCHASED BY CUSTOMERS. FURTHERMORE, WE REFUSE TO ACCEPT ANY RESPONSIBILITY WHATSOEVER FOR LOSS, DAMAGE OR INJURY CAUSED BY DANGEROUS OR DEFECTIVE GOODS PURCHASED AT THIS STORE BY CUSTOMERS.

How effective is this notice?

23 How does the law regulate the use of exclusion and limitation and unfair terms generally in contracts?

24 What are the main remedies for breach of contract?

25 **a)** Explain fully why the Scottish courts will not always grant the remedy of specific implement to a pursuer in a breach of contract claim.

b) Mary owes Chapelhill Housing Association £735 in unpaid rent. The Association has taken Mary to the Sheriff Court and requested that the Sheriff grant it the remedy of specific implement.

Will the Sheriff grant the Housing Association the remedy of specific implement in this case?

26 Explain the following terms:

a) Minimisation of loss

b) Remoteness of loss

27 **a)** What is a penalty clause and how does it function?

b) Davinder and Tommy had entered into an agreement whereby Tommy's construction company was to build a set of smart new offices for Davinder's graphic design business. The offices should have taken 18 months to build. However, Tommy is now six months behind with the project and it will take a further six months at this rate to complete the contract. Davinder is not best pleased and he points to a clause in the contract to the effect that Tommy will have to pay £10,000 per month to Davinder representing every month that completion of the building project is overdue. This figure of £10,000 is based on Davinder's calculation of how much business he is likely to lose if the offices are not completed on time. Tommy finds out, however, that Davinder's monthly losses are more in the region of £2000 to £3000. Davinder is demanding that Tommy pay out £120,000 in total which he claims will represent his final, overall losses.

How realistic are Davinder's chances of being able to enforce the penalty clause against Tommy?

28 Explain the difference between general and special damages.

29 Some breaches of contract will be much more serious than others.

With the above statement in mind, what is a material breach of contract?

30 Contracts do not last forever and they will all come to an end sooner rather than later.

Discuss the ways in which a contract can be terminated.

situations, the defender is said to have been negligent or careless. The law, therefore, imposes a duty on each of us not to cause harm to others. Each of us has interests which the law protects, for instance, the right to personal security and the right to enjoy a good reputation.

Harmful conduct may be intentional, for example:

◆ Assault
◆ Dangerous driving
◆ Defamation of character
◆ Fraud
◆ Intimidation
◆ Conspiracy
◆ Inducing a breach of contract
◆ Trespass
◆ Unlawful imprisonment
◆ Wrongful arrest
◆ Passing off
◆ Nuisance
◆ Enticement
◆ Seduction
◆ Non-natural use of land and water

Remedies

The civil remedies that are available to the injured party are:

◆ Reparation
◆ Interdict

Reparation

This covers the issue of compensation or damages for the harm caused. Damages for personal injury can address a number of different issues such as the pain and suffering which the pursuer has experienced (*solatium*) and financial loss suffered by the pursuer caused as a result of the injury (patrimonial loss). Financial losses, including loss of wages and reasonable expenses, could cover the period between the time of the accident and when the pursuer's civil action is finally heard in court. The pursuer could even receive damages for future losses such as ongoing medical treatment and future earnings. It is also possible that the pursuer can receive interest in addition to the damages that he receives from the defender. If the defender's negligence results in the death of the pursuer, the pursuer's family or executor of his estate are entitled to maintain a claim for damages against the defender.

Interdict

The pursuer applies for a court order which should stop the wrong recurring where it is likely to be repeated.

 Key point: The main remedies in a delictual action sought by the pursuer are reparation and interdict.

The Criminal Injuries Compensation Scheme

The Criminal Injuries Compensation Act 1995 is for compensating victims of crimes of violence. Its object was to put qualifying victims in the same position financially as they would have been in had they not been injured but not to make them better off. A Scottish criminal court can make a compensation order making the offender pay a sum compensating the victim of the crime as well as a fine or sentence which may also be imposed. This would only occur in the case where the injuries are minor and compensation orders cannot be made in the case of motor accident cases. If the offender cannot be traced or is not worth suing, a claim can be made instead to the Criminal Injuries Compensation Board.

Motor Insurance Bureau

Situations may arise where an innocent driver has been involved in a motor collision caused by the negligent or dangerous acts or omissions of another driver who happens not to have a valid policy of insurance in place. In such circumstances, it may be possible for the innocent driver to submit a claim for a compensatory payment to be made by the Motor Insurance Bureau (which operates a statutory scheme) to deal with such eventualities. It is now increasingly common for many drivers in Scotland not to have motor insurance (which is a criminal offence in itself) and many innocent drivers would be left high and dry were it not for the existence of the Motor Insurance Bureau and its ability to make compensation payments.

The pursuer must show that there is a direct connection between the wrongful actions of the defender and the harm that was caused. It is important to stress that the defender's actions must cause the pursuer to suffer loss, injury or damage. If this is not the case, then the pursuer does not have a claim in terms of the law of delict. If, for example, a person attempted to punch you, but missed and as a result you suffered no harm, you have would no claim for compensation. If, however, the person managed to assault you physically and caused you to suffer injury this would be a completely different matter.

In many situations, people will suffer loss but this does not necessarily mean that they will have a bring a claim under the law of delict. If, for example, an individual invests money in companies listed on the London Stock Exchange, there is always a possibility that the value of the investment can go down as well as go up. The companies in which the investor choose to invest may hit a rough patch through no fault of their directors and may suffer losses which affects their value.

 Key point: The main aim of the law of delict is to compensate the pursuer/victim for loss, injury or damage caused by a wrongful act committed by the defender.

The voluntary pre-action protocols in Scotland

It should be noted that many delctual claims do not proceed to a court hearing in Scotland. Those individuals who are contemplating the idea of pursuing a personal injury claim have three years from the date of the incident to lodge such an action before either the Sheriff Court or the Court of Session. In many situations, lawyers acting for the pursuer are often able to negotiate an out of court settlement of the claim with the defender's insurance company.

Making this task somewhat easier in Scotland has been the establishment of agreements between the Law Society of Scotland (the regulatory body for solicitors) and many British insurance companies. These agreements are known as the Voluntary Pre-Action Protocols. The Protocols establish a common and simple procedure for dealing with personal injury claims with a value of up to £10,000, professional negligence claims (up to £20,000 in value) and disease claims (up to £10,000 in value). As the name suggests, they are entirely voluntary. There is nothing to stop parties using the protocols to deal with cases which have a greater value than the limits set out in the various agreements.

The main advantage to be gained by parties using the Protocols is the speedy resolution of the claim and, for solicitors, there is added advantage that a mechanism exists which means that their legal fees will be agreed in advance should the pursuer's claim be successful. For examples of the Voluntary Pre-Action Protocols see the Introductory Scots Law website.

Culpa/fault

For a delictual liability to exist, there must be harm, loss or injury which is caused by fault on the part of the wrongdoer. The pursuer must establish that the wrongdoer was to blame for what happened. The fault is called *culpa* and, generally, there can be no liability without *culpa*. The general rule in Scotland is that there can be no delictual liability without fault. Quite simply, this means that the pursuer must prove, on the balance of probabilities that the defender's actions caused him to suffer loss, injury or damage. If the pursuer cannot prove to the court that the defender was responsible for his loss or injury, then the pursuer's case will collapse. Very often, all the defender has to show is that he has taken reasonable care to prevent the harm from occurring (see **Bolton v Stone (1951)** and **Paris v Stepney Borough Council (1951)** both discussed below) and if the court is satisfied that all reasonable precautions were taken, the defender will escape liability. *Culpa* or fault is very different from intentional wrongdoing (*dolus*) where the defender has set out deliberately to cause loss or injury to the pursuer.

Key point: The general rule in Scots law is that there can be no liability without fault (*culpa*) in Scotland.

Strict liability

Admittedly, there are situations where the pursuer does not have to show that the defender was to blame for the injuries or the losses caused. In certain situations, the defender's liability is said to be strict. In other words, the law automatically presumes that the defender is to blame for the harm caused to the pursuer. This means that the defender will have to bring evidence to show, on the balance of probablities, that he was not responsible for the injuries or losses caused to the pursuer. A defender will be strictly liable for injuries or losses caused to the pursuer for dangerous products (Part 1 of the Consumer Protection Act 1987) and where animals that he is responsible for cause loss or injury to the pursuer (Animals (Scotland) Act 1987). Situations of strict liability favour the pursuer as the burden of proof is on the defender to show that he is not liable for the harm that occurred.

Key point: In situations of strict liability, for example, the keeper's responsibility for animals, the pursuer does not have to prove fault, it is the defender who will have to show that he is not at fault.

Duty of care and negligence

Negligence is harm caused unintentionally and is, by far and away, the most likely type of delictual action that the Scottish courts will have to deal with. Negligence claims arise because the defender owes what is known as a duty of care to the pursuer and, unfortunately, a breach of this duty occurs and, as a result, the defender suffers loss, injury or damage. The leading case for negligence claims is **Donoghue v Stevenson (1932)**. The facts of **Donoghue** are as follows:

 Mrs Donoghue and her friend went into a Paisley café owned by Mr Minchella. Mrs Donoghue's friend ordered two ice creams and two bottles of ginger beer. The bottles of ginger beer were not of the clear glass type where it was possible to see the contents. Mrs Donoghue poured the contents of her bottle of ginger beer over ice cream. To her horror, the remains of a decomposed snail slid out from the ginger beer bottle. Mrs Donoghue later claimed that she had suffered gastro-enteritis as a result of consuming parts of the snail. Mrs Donoghue also claimed that she had suffered a psychiatric injury as a direct result of her experience. The question then arose as to whom Mrs Donoghue could bring a civil action for damages against. She did not have a contract with Mr Minchella, the café owner, as her friend had purchased the ginger beer. Furthermore, Mr Minchella was not aware of any impurities contained in the bottle as it had been sealed from the time that it had left the manufacturer's factory and it was not a clear glass bottle. Mr Minchella could hardly be blamed for Mrs Donoghue's unpleasant experience. Who then could Mrs Donoghue sue? The manufacturer of the product was the most obvious target. Mrs Donoghue argued that a manufacturer of goods owed to a duty of care to anyone who might use the products.

Held: manufacturers owed a duty of care to anyone who might use their product and suffer loss, injury or damage as a direct result. Manufacturers must make sure that their products are safe when they left the factory. The ginger beer manufacturers did not have to predict that Mrs Donoghue personally would use their product, but they knew that someone would use the product and be harmed if it contained impurities like the remains of a decomposed snail.

In order to succeed when bringing a negligence claim before the courts, the pursuer must show that the defender owed him a duty of care, that the defender was in a position to cause harm and that the defender failed to prevent this foreseeable kind of harm from occurring. Additionally, the pursuer must show that the defender's breach of duty was the effective cause of the loss or harm suffered by him.

 Haley v London Electricity Board (1965) workmen employed by the Electricity Board had dug up part of the street. The pursuer, a blind man, fell into the hole and was injured because it had not been properly fenced off. The Electricity Board claimed that it could not foresee or predict that a blind person would be walking about on his own along the street. In any case, the vast majority of people who could see the hole would walk round it and, therefore, avoid any injury being suffered to themselves.

Held: the Electricity Board was liable for the pursuer's injuries. It was not beyond the realms of possibility that a blind person would come walking along the pavement without being accompanied by a fully sighted person. It was not uncommon to see blind people walking along the street and the appropriate safety measures should have been taken to protect people such as the pursuer from suffering injury as result of the failure of the Electricity Board to take proper precautions.

 Bourhill *v* Young (1942) Young was speeding along Collinton Road in Edinburgh on a motorcycle when he collided with a car and was killed. The occupants of the car were injured as a result of the crash. Mrs Bourhill, a pregnant fishwife, was getting off a tramcar which Young had passed just minutes before he hit the car further up Collinton Road. Mrs Bourhill did not personally witness the accident happening. However, rather foolishly, after hearing the noise from the crash, Mrs Bourhill made her way up the road to see what had happened. Mrs Bourhill saw the wreckage from the crash and bloodstains on the road. She claimed this sight and the noise had caused her to suffer a psychiatric injury (post traumatic stress disorder) which resulted in her miscarrying her pregnancy.

Held: Young did not owe a duty of care to Mrs Bourhill. Young was certainly negligent the way in which he drove his motorcycle at a dangerous speed along Collinton Road. Any reasonable person ought to have known that if Young lost control of his vehicle there was a very great risk of him colliding with other road users who were nearby. Furthermore, there was every chance that these road users who were in the path of the collision would suffer injury or, at the very least, suffer damage to their property as a result of Young's failure to drive his vehicle safely. Mrs Bourhill was nowhere near the scene of the accident and was, therefore, not placed in immediate danger by Young's behaviour. A person as sensitive as Mrs Bourhill claimed to be should not have rushed up the road to see the aftermath of the accident. This was asking for trouble and, arguably, Mrs Bourhill had placed herself in a dangerous position as a direct result of her own actions and not those of Young.

 Key point: The leading case in respect of negligence actions in Scotland is **Donoghue *v* Stevenson (1932)**.

The neighbourhood principle

Lord Atkin who gave the leading speech in **Donoghue *v* Stevenson (1932)** went to great pains to stress a concept which has since become known as the neighbourhood principle:

The rule that you are to love your neighbour becomes, in law, you must not injure your neighbour; and the lawyer's question, 'who is my neighbour?' receives a restricted reply, 'you must take reasonable care to avoid acts or omissions which you can reasonably foresee would be likely to injure your neighbour'. Who then, in law, is my neighbour? The answer seems to be persons who are so closely and directly affected by my act that I ought reasonably to have them in my contemplation as being so affected when I am directing my mind to the acts or omissions which are called into question.

Lord Atkin's statement is initially misleading in that he deliberately uses the language of the Christian Gospels by referring to your neighbour. When Jesus Christ was asked the question by one of his followers: 'Lord, who is my neighbour?' the fairly daunting reply that the disciple received is that 'Everyone is your neighbour'. To lawyers, however, the above question receives a much more restricted answer. The defender does not owe a duty of care to the whole wide world, but only to those individuals whom the defender, if he were a reasonable person, would realise that his actions might cause them to suffer loss, injury or damage. Basically, the defender should have realised that his actions or failure to act will result in certain negative consequences being suffered by the pursuer.

 Key point: The rule in **Donoghue v Stevenson** states that the defender owes a duty of care to those individuals whom the defender, if he were a reasonable person, would realise that his actions might cause to suffer loss, injury or damage.

The extent of the duty of care

There is no legal requirement in Scotland to go to someone's aid or assistance or to intervene to prevent a harm from occurring. In **Donoghue v Stevenson (1932)**, Lord Atkin deliberately drew upon the Christian parable of the Good Samaritan when he formulated the neighbourhood principle. For those unfamiliar with the parable, the Jewish man (who had been attacked and robbed by brigands and left for dead on the road to Jericho) was rescued by a Samaritan (an individual who belonged to a group detested by the Jews for their failure to adhere to the more rigorous rules of Judaism). Before the Samaritan came down the road, a Priest and a Levite stumbled upon the aftermath of the robbery, decided not to intervene and passed by on the other side of the road. Lord Diplock in **Dorset Yacht Co. Ltd v Home Office (1970)** famously stated that despite the questionable morality of their decision not to help the injured man, the Priest and the Levite would have incurred absolutely no civil liability in English law for their actions and, indeed, in Scotland the position would have been exactly the same.

 The House of Lords recently re-examined the scope of the duty of care in **Mitchell & Another v Glasgow City Council (2009)**. Mitchell and his family lived in the Bellahouston area of Glasgow and had a long running dispute with their anti-social neighbour, Drummond. The Mitchell family and Drummond were tenants of Glasgow City Council. Drummond had a history of anti-social behaviour and he had attacked several neighbours with a tyre lever at his previous Council residence. Indeed, the Council had been forced to move

Drummond to the Bellahouston area after this incident. Needless to say, Drummond embarked upon a reign of terror where he threatened to kill Mr Mitchell after the Mitchell family had complained to the Police and the Council about his anti-social behaviour (he had attacked the Mitchell home one night with an iron bar causing extensive damage after they had complained about the level of noise coming from his home). This threatening type of behaviour was repeated by Drummond on several occasions. Eventually, the Council called Drummond to a meeting to try to resolve the issue and to inform him that, if the situation did not improve, he faced the very real threat of eviction from his home. At the meeting, Drummond verbally abused the Council staff in attendance, but he appeared to calm down and apologised for his behaviour. After the meeting, Drummond returned home whereupon he confronted Mitchell and assaulted him to his severe injury. Tragically, Mr Mitchell later died as a result of the injuries inflicted on him by Drummond. Mr Mitchell's wife and daughter subsequently brought an action against the Council on the basis that it had been negligent, amongst other things, in not warning Mr Mitchell that a meeting with Drummond had been set up, that he had behaved abusively at the meeting and by its failure to not contact the Police to inform them about the situation.

Held: by the House of Lords that the Council was not under any duty of care towards Mr Mitchell and his family to inform them about the circumstances of the meeting. In other words, the Council had in no way been negligent and foreseeability of harm does not mean that a duty of care has been imposed. Lord Hope of Craighead mentioned the case of **Yuen Kun Yeu *v* Attorney General of Hong Kong (1988)**, where Lord Keith of Kinkel stated that, if the law did indeed impose a positive duty to protect people from the consequences of foreseeable harm, then there would be liability in negligence on the part of an individual who sees another person about to walk over a cliff with his head in the air, and fails to shout a warning. The Mitchell decision also reaffirms Lord Diplock's statement that the Priest and the Levite would have incurred no civil liability whatsoever as a result of their decision not to intervene in the aftermath of the incident on the road to Jericho. Clearly, of course, if someone puts someone in harm's way, they have a duty to take steps to protect the person from that danger.

The standard of reasonable care

If the pursuer can show that he is owed a duty of care, the defender can escape liability in many situations by demonstrating that he took the appropriate standard of care which the law expects of him in order to reduce the risk of loss or injury being suffered by the pursuer. The standard of care which is expected of the defender is one of reasonable care. Reasonable care is the standard of care expected of the 'hypothetical' reasonable man or woman who is a person of ordinary care and prudence and who is neither overcautious nor overconfident. This is an objective test and is not based on the defender's personal characteristics. Very often, a reasonable person will foresee or predict that there are particular individuals who are especially vulnerable in some way and this means that they may suffer a greater degree of harm if the defender fails to take reasonable care.

Paris *v* Stepney Borough Council (1951) a mechanic was blind in one eye as a result of active service during the Second World War. His employer was not aware of this disability. Later, however, one of the Council's doctors discovered the disability during a medical examination. Incredibly, the employee was not given protective goggles by his employer to protect his one good eye. During the course of his work, the employee was hammering on a piece of metal and a splinter broke off and lodged itself in his remaining good eye. This accident meant that the employee was blind in both eyes. The court heard evidence that it was not normal practice in the industry to supply protective goggles to employees. The question then arose as to whether or not the Council had been negligent by failing to protect someone it knew to be particularly vulnerable.

Held: by the House of Lords that the employer had been negligent in that it had fallen far short of the standard of reasonable care which would be expected of a reasonable man or woman.

If the defender is a child, the standard of care expected of this person is that of an ordinarily careful and reasonable child of the same age.

 Mullin *v* Richards (1998) the pursuer and the defender were both 15-year-old school girls. They were playing around during a school lesson by hitting one another with plastic rulers. One of the rulers snapped and a piece of plastic lodged itself in the pursuer's eye. The pursuer was effectively blind in this eye as a result of the injury that she had suffered.

Held: by the English Court of Appeal that the correct test was whether an ordinarily careful and reasonable 15-year-old could have predicted or foreseen that the behaviour in question might result in someone suffering an injury. The Court considered the fact that fencing with rulers was not an activity that had been banned by the school, it was a very common activity and the girls had received no warnings from the teachers that the activity was in any way dangerous. The injury was, therefore, not foreseeable and the defender was not liable to the pursuer for the injuries that she had suffered.

The correctness of the approach in **Mullin *v* Richards** to the standard of reasonable care expected of children was affirmed in the following case:

 Orchard *v* Lee (2009) a 13 year old school boy had collided with a lunchtime supervisor and caused her to suffer injury while playing a game of tag in the school playground. The supervisor subsequently brought a claim for damages in respect of her injuries.

Held: by the English Court of Appeal that the child had been involved in an activity which was fairly typical behaviour of a 13 year old, he was not breaking any school rules when playing the game of tag and he could not have reasonably foreseen that his conduct was careless and potentially harmful. The child was, therefore, not negligent and he should be judged according to the standard of reasonable care normally expected from a 13 year old boy.

What if the defender has some special skill, knowledge or expertise? In such cases, the courts will judge the defender according to the standard that is expected of a member of that particular trade or profession. So, in a medical negligence case, the standard of care expected of a doctor would be that of an ordinary skilled member of the medical profession who is performing his duties properly in relation to his patients. However, particularly in the area of medicine, the courts have accepted that members of the profession may have different opinions about how best to treat patients. One doctor may apply a particular procedure in order to treat a patient, whereas another doctor may rely on a completely different course of treatment.

 Bolam *v* Friern Barnet Hospital Management Committee (1957) a patient with psychiatric problems had been undergoing electric shock treatment and, as a result, of being given relaxant drugs before the treatment, had suffered from broken bones. It was not always the practice of every doctor to give patients these drugs before electric shock treatment. Some doctors felt that by giving patients these drugs, the risk of damage to bones was greatly increased. Other doctors, however, felt that the drugs benefited the patients. So, which group of doctors was correct and how was the court to decide whether the doctor in this case had failed to meet the standard of care expected of a reasonable doctor?

Held: the court decided to give doctors and by extension other professions a certain amount of leeway to determine their own professional rules. A doctor would not be negligent if he used a medical procedure which was accepted as being a proper procedure by a responsible body of doctors who are skilled in a particular field of medicine.

 In **Bolitho *v* City & Hackney Health Authority (1997)** admittedly, the above decision in **Bolam** was criticised because it seemed to give too much power to the medical profession and other professions to set their own standards. In **Bolitho**, the House of Lords looked at the issue of professional negligence once again. A two-year-old boy was admitted to hospital suffering from breathing difficulties. He had not been examined by a doctor. Shortly after being admitted to hospital, the boy suffered a further breathing problems which caused him to stop breathing completely whereupon he had a heart attack and died. The boy's mother sued claiming that he should have been examined by a doctor and that a tube should have been inserted into the boy's throat to assist him with his breathing. The hospital had failed to do any of these things and was, therefore, responsible for the boy's death. It was claimed that even if the boy had been examined by a doctor, she would not necessarily have gone ahead and had a tube inserted into his throat to assist him with his breathing. The doctor was able to produce one expert witness who backed her claim, whereas the mother produced another expert witness who stated that the doctor should have carried out the procedure.

Held: the pursuer's claim failed. Lord Wilberforce stated that the **Bolam** test was still the correct one to apply. However, doctors could not expect to escape liability for negligence by pointing out that their decision was backed by accepted medical procedures. A court would have to be certain that these procedures and the opinions of medical experts were reasonable. However, the fact that many medical experts backed a particular procedure would often be taken to mean that the doctor had behaved reasonably by relying on the procedure in the question. Only rarely would a court be entitled to reject the views of a body of medical experts.

The test in **Bolam** also establishes the fact that if a defender is exercising a skill in the course of his profession, he will be judged according to the standard expected of a reasonably competent member of that profession. His actual experience will not be taken into account by the courts. Admittedly, a recently qualified doctor will not have the same level of skill that would be expected of a consultant. However, the public has a right to expect that the new doctor is trained to a level which allows him to treat patients safely.

 Djemal v Bexley Health Authority (1995) the standard of care expected was that of a senior houseman. The defender who was employed in the Accident and Emergency Department was a senior houseman and was judged according to the standards of this post and the issue of how long the defender had been employed in this position was not a matter for debate.

When deciding whether a defender has failed to meet the necessary standard of care, it is important not to use hindsight. After all, since the mid-1990s, we now know that the condition BSE (popularly known as Mad Cow Disease) found in animals can affect humans through the food chain who then might go on to show signs of Creutzfeld Jakob Disease (CJD). During the 1980s, the risks from eating animals infected by BSE could not be predicted. Should farmers, therefore, be held liable when it became apparent that the risks from BSE infected animals had extremely serious consequences for humans? Defenders can only be judged according to the knowledge that they actually possessed or could have gained access to at the time when the pursuer suffered loss or injury.

 Roe v Ministry of Health (1954) a patient had undergone surgery under anaesthetic. The anaesthetic had been stored in such way that meant that it had become contaminated. The capsules containing the anaesthetic were stored in disinfectant. The disinfectant leaked through microscopic cracks in the glass containers containing the anaesthetic which caused the contamination. The anaesthetic had been injected into the patient's spine and, as a result, it caused permanent paralysis. Expert medical evidence was heard that the method of storage for the anaesthetic was a standard one and there was no way that it could be considered dangerous – at the time of the injuries to the pursuer. The injuries suffered by the pursuer had revealed the risks caused by this method of storage.

Held: the pursuer's personal injury claim failed. Lord Denning stated that 'we must not look at the 1947 accident with 1954 spectacles'.

 Key point: In many situations, a defender will be able to escape delictual liability by proving that he took reasonable care to avoid causing loss or injury to the pursuer.

Hall & Co v Simmons (2000) until the decision of the House of Lords in this case, advocates and barristers enjoyed immunity from legal action in relation to anything negligent done by them in the conduct of legal work carried out by them e.g. conducting pleadings in court or providing legal opinions. The House of Lords decided that this immunity could no longer be justified and that advocates and barristers should be subject to the normal rules of negligence governing other groups of professional persons. In other words, any lawyer falling below the objective standard of the legal profession will be potentially opening him/herself to the possibility of an action in negligence.

Reasonable foreseeability

An important question that the court will have to look at when it is deciding whether the defender is liable for loss or injury that the pursuer has suffered is whether or not the harm was reasonably foreseeable. In other words, if the defender is judged according to the standard expected of a reasonable person, it should have occurred to him that his actions or failure to act in a particular situation are likely to cause the pursuer to be harmed in some way.

 Hughes *v* Lord Advocate (1963) the defenders had statutory authority to open a manhole in an Edinburgh street for the purpose of carrying out repairs to telephone cables located below the street. The defenders' workers placed a brightly coloured tent over the manhole and surrounded it with paraffin warning lamps. The workers left the manhole unattended at approximately 5 p.m. on a winter's evening. The pursuer, who was aged 8 years old, and his uncle, who was 10, decided to enter the tent and go down the manhole. They took one of the paraffin lamps to light their way. When they re-emerged from underground, one of the boys knocked the lamp into the hole which caused a huge explosion (it was reported that flames had shot some 30 feet into the air). The force of the explosion caused the pursuer to fall back into the hole and, as a result, he suffered several serious injuries. Both the Court of Session at first instance and on appeal dismissed the pursuer's claim for damages. The pursuer appealed to the House of Lords.

Held: by the House of Lords that the defenders were liable to the pursuer as the accident was completely foreseeable and reasonable precautions had not been taken to guard against the harm which had occurred. Lord Pearce referred to the tent and the paraffin lamps as a 'dangerous allurement' which had been 'left unguarded in a public highway in the heart of Edinburgh. It was for the defenders to show that, although this was a public street, the presence of children there was so little to be expected that a reasonable man might leave the allurement unguarded. But in my opinion, their evidence fell short of that …' Lord Pearce went to say that although the exact shape of the disaster was hard to predict, all the elements were present: a partially closed tent, the lamps, the ladder, a cavernous hole – 'a setting well fitted to inspire some juvenile adventure that might end in calamity.'

 Home Office *v* Dorset Yacht Co Ltd (1970) a group of borstal boys (who would be known as young offenders today) were camping on an island. The boys were accompanied on the island by their guards. A chain of events then unfolded with the end result being entirely foreseeable or predictable. The guards went to their beds and soon fell asleep leaving the boys completely unsupervised. The boys decided to escape from the island. They couldn't swim from the island because it is too far to the mainland, so they had to steal a yacht. None of the boys had ever sailed a yacht before. The yacht that the boys were attempting to sail from the island ended up colliding with another yacht owned by Dorset Yacht and a substantial amount of damage was caused as a result.

Held: by the House of Lords that the guards had failed in their duty of care to supervise the boys properly. This failure resulted in damage to property which was entirely foreseeable.

 Key point: Reasonable foreseeability is a test that the courts apply to assess whether a reasonable person in a similar position to the defender would have realised that his actions or failure to act in a particular situation were likely to cause the pursuer to be harmed in some way.

The seriousness of the risk

This issue deals with the likelihood of damage occurring and, if so, how serious the damage will be that the pursuer suffers.

 Bolton *v* Stone (1951) the pursuer was standing outside her house which was situated in a quiet street which lay next to a cricket ground. The pursuer was struck by a cricket ball that had been hit out of the cricket ground and over the fence. The pursuer suffered injuries as a result of being hit by the cricket ball and she brought an action against the ground authorities. The pursuer claimed that the cricket ground authorities had not taken adequate steps to protect members of the public from being struck by cricket balls. It was reasonably foreseeable that some cricket balls would be hit out of the ground and that these might end up striking people and thus cause injury. In fact, cricket balls had been hit out of the ground some six times in the last 30 years, but no one had ever been hurt as a result. The cricket ground authorities had erected a 17-foot fence, there was a considerable distance from the cricket oval to the edge of the ground and the ground sloped upwards in the direction that the ball had travelled.

Held: by the House of Lords that the chance of anyone being injured where the pursuer was standing was extremely unlikely. The cricket ground authorities had not been negligent in allowing the game to be played. They had taken proper precautions and, therefore, demonstrated the fact that they had taken reasonable care to avoid loss or injury from occurring. Was the pursuer seriously suggesting that an extremely high fence should be erected or that a roof should be constructed over the cricket ground? Clearly, these types of safety measures would have been extremely expensive for the cricket ground authorities and, realistically, they would have been completely over the top in order to safeguard individuals from what was a relatively low risk activity.

As we have seen, the cost and trouble of reducing the likelihood of the risk of loss or injury which the defender must bear is an issue which the courts take into consideration.

 Latimer *v* AEC (1952) a factory had been flooded as a result of heavier than usual rainfall. The excess water combined with oil and grease on the factory floor which made walking on the floor extremely treacherous. The defenders, the factory owners, attempted to reduce accidents from occurring by putting sawdust down. However, the defenders did not have enough

313

sawdust to cover the whole floor. One of the workers slipped on an untreated part of the floor and suffered injury as a result. The injured party brought an action against the defenders for damages claiming that they should have shut down the factory in order to prevent any accidents from happening.

Held: the House of Lords stated that closing the factory would certainly have prevented any accidents. However, the dangerous patches which had been left uncovered were clearly visible and could be avoided. Closing the factory would be a solution that was out of proportion to the actual risks involved of continuing to work there.

 Key point: In assessing whether the defender has taken reasonable care to prevent loss or injury to the pursuer, the seriousness of the risk of the defender's actions will be examined by the courts.

Causation

Where there is an alleged breach of a duty of care, the actual breach must be the *causa causans* (the direct cause) of the harm to the pursuer. This means that the pursuer must be able to show, on the balance of probabilities, that the defender's negligence caused him to suffer loss or injury. The defender will be able to escape liability if he can show that his negligence should be regarded as the *causa sine qua non*. This means that the defender may have behaved negligently, but his actions should not be regarded as the direct cause of the loss or injury suffered by the pursuer. The *causa sine qua non* should be seen as part of the background and not a primary cause of harm to the pursuer. As the following cases demonstrate, it is not always obvious whether the defender's actions caused the pursuer to suffer loss or injury.

 Kay's Tutor *v* Ayrshire & Arran Health Board (1987) a child was admitted to hospital suffering from meningitis and was given an overdose of penicillin from which he recovered as a result of quick medical intervention. The child did, however, become deaf. Clearly the doctor had been negligent by giving the child an overdose of penicillin and this was admitted by the hospital. However, the hospital refused to take responsibility for the child's deafness. It was the hospital's belief that the overdose of penicillin had not caused the child to suffer from deafness. There was no known medical case of a patient developing deafness as a result of a penicillin overdose. There were, however, plenty of cases where patients had developed deafness as a result of suffering from meningitis.

Held: it was probably the case that the meningitis had caused the child's deafness. The child's illness was, therefore, the *causa causans* or the main reason for the child's deafness.

 Barnett *v* Chelsea & Kensington Hospital (1969) the pursuer's husband drank a cup of tea. He began to vomit and was rushed to hospital. The hospital doctor who dealt with the husband told him to go home and make an appointment to see his own doctor in the morning. The husband, however, died as the result of poison having been administered to him. The doctor had no doubt been negligent in the way that he had treated the pursuer's husband. If the doctor had given the victim a proper medical examination this would not have prevented the victim's death. The poison was fast acting and there was no antidote.

Held: the defender may have been negligent, but this in itself did not cause the victim's death. It was the nature of the poison that was the cause of death. Medical attempts to save the victim's life would have been utterly futile.

 Mount *v* Barker Austin (1998) the pursuer had entered a contract to which a bank was one of the parties. The pursuer made an allegation that the bank had breached its duty towards him and he raised an action for damages against it. The pursuer appointed solicitors to represent him in this action. The solicitors, however, failed to raise the action within the proper time limits. The pursuer then appointed a second firm of solicitors to pursue a claim against the first firm of solicitors. Unbelievably, the second firm of solicitors also failed to raise the action in time and the pursuer brought an action against them. The pursuer's claim was based on the argument that he would have won the original action against the bank and that he had suffered loss as a result of the negligence of the two firms of solicitors. The trial judge was deeply unimpressed by the pursuer's claim and he found that the action against the bank would have failed. There was not even an outside chance that the action would have succeeded. All the pursuer was entitled to were the costs of the actions against the bank and the first firm of solicitors. The pursuer appealed.

Held: by the English Court of Appeal that the pursuer would never have won the action against the bank and, consequently, the bank's alleged negligence had not caused the pursuer any loss. The pursuer could always bring evidence to show that he had a realistic chance of success against the bank, but he had not been able to do this.

 Key point: Where there is an alleged breach of a duty of care, the actual breach must be the causa causans (the direct cause) of the harm to the pursuer and not the causa sine qua non i.e. a factor which is merely superfluous to the direct cause of the harm.

Multiple causes of harm

Sometimes there will be many possible reasons to explain why the pursuer suffered loss, injury and damage and the defender's behaviour may only be one of the possible reasons. The explanations that the courts have used to make their decisions have not always helped matters.

 McGhee *v* National Coal Board (1972) the pursuer had developed an allergy in relation to brick dust that he was exposed to at his place of work. The pursuer normally finished his shift covered in the dust and he did not have an opportunity to wash it off until he got home. This allergy caused the pursuer to suffer from dermatitis. It was known that people who carried out the type of work that the pursuer was employed to do could develop dermatitis. The pursuer argued that the defender's failure to provide showering facilities for workers at the end of the shift had increased the likelihood of him developing dermatitis. The defender, in turn, argued that the pursuer might have developed his allergy even if the showers had been installed. Had the employer's negligence, therefore, caused the pursuer's condition?

Held: by the House of Lords stated that where a defender's negligence had made a substantial contribution to the pursuer's injuries, the defender could be liable. It was not essential to prove that the defender's negligence was the only cause of the pursuer's loss or injury.

The House of Lords took a different and contradictory approach in the following case:

 Wilsher v Essex Area Health Authority (1988) the pursuer, Martin Wilsher, had been born three months prematurely. His premature birth had caused him to suffer from all sorts of health problems. The pursuer had to be helped with his breathing and, to this end, he received oxygen. On two occasions, however, the pursuer was given too much oxygen which caused him to go blind permanently. The doctor in question admitted that the oxygen had been administered negligently. The hospital then faced a legal action raised by the pursuer's family. Medical evidence showed that the pursuer's blindness could have been caused by him receiving too much oxygen, but his situation could also have been caused by the five separate medical conditions that he was currently suffering from.

Held: by the House of Lords that the pursuer would have to prove that the defender's breach of its duty care would have to be a material cause of the harm suffered by the pursuer. It was not enough for the pursuer to show that the defender's actions had increased the risk of harm occurring. The defender's actions was only one possible cause of the pursuer's condition and this was not enough to prove that the defender had caused the pursuer to suffer loss or injury.

McGhee is obviously a case which favours the pursuer, whereas **Wilsher** is much more restrictive in its scope. Lately, however, the test in **McGhee** seems to be making something of a comeback.

 Key point: In cases involving multiple causes of harm, the pursuer may be successful if he can demonstrate that the defender's breach of a duty of care substantially contributed to his loss or injury.

Intervening events (*novus actus interveniens*)

On certain occasions, the courts will have to consider situations where the defender has breached his duty of care, but after this event some new factor is introduced into the picture which can also cause harm to the pursuer. This new cause of loss or injury will not have been the defender's fault. The introduction of this new factor can have effect of breaking the chain of causation. This means that the defender will only be liable for the harm that he has caused and he will not be liable for any harm caused to the pursuer by the introduction of the new factor to the equation.

Rouse _v_ Squires (1973) Allen was driving his lorry along a three-lane motorway. He lost control of the lorry with the result that it ended up blocking two of the motorway lanes. The driver of a car crashed into Allen's lorry. Rouse who was driving another lorry witnessed the accident and brought his vehicle to a halt on the motorway just in front of Allen's lorry. It was Rouse's intention to help the victims of the accident. Another driver, Franklin, appeared on the scene and parked behind Rouse's lorry. Franklin thought that by training his headlights on the scene of the original crash that this would assist Rouse. However, by this time, another driver, Squires, appeared on the scene. Squires did not realise that there had been an accident and he decided to move from the inside lane to the outside lane in order to get round the obstructions which he thought were slow moving traffic. Unfortunately, it was too late by the time that Squires discovered that he was in the middle of a serious accident. He hit both the car and Allen's lorry which had been involved in the original collision. The lorry moved forward and killed Rouse who had been standing in front of it.

Held: the trial court decided that Squires was fully to blame for the death of Rouse. Squires should have been alerted to the accident by the fact that Franklin's headlights were pointed towards the scene. The English Court of Appeal was unhappy with this decision. After all, this let Allen, the lorry driver who had caused the accident in the first place as a result of his negligent driving, completely off the hook. Undoubtedly, Squires had been negligent, but should he be held totally responsible for Rouse's death? Allen, therefore, was partly responsible for the death because his actions were partly to blame for the dangerous conditions encountered by Squires. Squires could not be blamed totally for the death. The chain of causation from the original accident to Rouse's death had not been broken by Squires' actions and Allen was one-quarter to blame for the death.

Section 4 of the Law Reform (Miscellaneous Provisions) (Scotland) Act 1940 allows a court or jury to divide the responsibility between a number of defenders for acts or omissions that cause loss or injury. The court or jury are given considerable discretionary power to determine what sum the defenders will have to pay to the pursuer when deciding the question of damages. The 1940 Act, therefore, allows two or more defenders to be found jointly or severally liable. This means that the defenders can be sued as a group by the pursuer or they may be sued individually. In these situations, if one defender has had to pay all the damages to the pursuer, he is entitled to approach other individuals who could have been sued by the pursuer and demand that they also contribute to the damages.

 Reeves _v_ Commissioner of Police for the Metropolis (1999) a prisoner hanged himself whilst being held in custody in his police cell. The police were only too well aware that this particular prisoner was a suicide risk, although he had not been diagnosed as suffering from a specific psychiatric illness. The police admitted that they owed the prisoner a duty of care, but they went on to argue that they should be allowed to escape liability because the suicide should be considered as an intervening act that broke the chain of causation. In other words, it was the prisoner's actions that caused him to die, not the police's breach of their duty of care towards the prisoner.

Held: the House of Lords stated that the suicide was not a new intervening factor which broke the chain of causation. This was precisely the sort of act on the part of the prisoner that the police were supposed to guard against and prevent. The police owed the prisoner a duty of care to make sure that he was not given an opportunity to commit suicide. The police had, obviously, failed to perform this duty.

 MacFarlane *v* Tayside Health Board (1999) the pursuer had become pregnant after her partner had undergone an operation to be sterilised. The pursuer refused to have an abortion and later gave birth to a perfectly healthy baby girl. The parents sued the Health Board on the grounds that the botched sterilisation procedure had resulted in an unwanted pregnancy which meant that the couple were put to the not inconsiderable expense of bringing up a child.

Held: by the House of Lords that the refusal by the mother to have an abortion was not unreasonable on her part and could not be regarded as an intervening factor which broke the chain of causation. The parents were not entitled to claim damages for the expenses involved in bringing up the child, but the mother was entitled to sue for damages for the pain and discomfort that she had suffered as a result of her unexpected and unwanted pregnancy.

 Sabri-Tabrizi *v* Lothian Health Board (1999) the facts of the case were very different from **MacFarlane**. The pursuer had undergone a sterilisation procedure that she knew had been a failure – she was still able to become pregnant. The pursuer had sexual relations but she did not use any contraception to prevent her from becoming pregnant. She later discovered that she was expecting a child. The pursuer sued the Health Board for breach of its duty of care to carry out the sterilisation procedure properly.

Held: the pursuer's knowledge that the operation had failed and her decision to have sex without taking the appropriate contraceptive precautions were intervening factors which broke the chain of causation. The Health Board's negligence had not caused her to conceive an unwanted pregnancy.

 Key point: The introduction of a new factor can have the effect of breaking the chain of causation meaning that the defender will only be liable for the harm that he has caused and that he will not be liable for any harm caused to the pursuer by the introduction of the new factor.

The facts speak for themselves (*res ipsa loquitur*)

There are situations where the only possible explanation for the harm suffered by the pursuer is that the defender's actions or failure to act caused it. There is no other credible explanation – the defender's negligent actions or omissions must have caused harm to the pursuer. The defender is then forced to bring evidence before the court to show why he is not liable to the pursuer. If the defender can show that there is a plausible explanation that demonstrates that he is not to blame, then the pursuer's claim will fail. However, the defender's explanation must be a plausible one and not one which is only theoretically possible. It should be remembered that the principle of the facts speaking for themselves does not remove the burden of proof from the pursuer to show that the defender was at fault. The pursuer must show that the facts are credible and that they do speak for themselves.

The pursuer can only make use of this legal rule in the following circumstances:

1 The events which led to the pursuer suffering harm must have been controlled by the defender or his employees.

2 Loss or injury does not usually happen when reasonable care is taken by a responsible person.

3 The defender must not be able to provide an alternative and credible explanation for the harm suffered by the pursuer which effectively gets him off the hook.

 Scott v London and St Katherine's Docks (1865) the pursuer was walking by the defender's warehouse when a six sacks of sugar fell out of an open door above him. The sacks landed on the pursuer and, as a result, he suffered injury. The defender had had been in the process of lowering the sacks to the ground through the use of a crane. There were no warning signs and the area in front of the warehouse had not been blocked off to prevent pedestrians from passing directly beneath the open door from where the sacks had fallen into the street.

Held: by the English Court of Appeal stated that although there was no actual evidence of negligence, this could be implied because sacks of sugar do not fall out of open doors by themselves.

 Gee v Metropolitan Railway (1873) the pursuer was injured as a result of falling out through the door of a railway carriage just after the train had pulled out of the station. The pursuer had been standing against the door when it somehow opened. The staff at the station had a duty to make sure that railway carriage doors were properly shut before the train left the station.

Held: the court implied that because the accident had happened so soon after the train had left the station that the staff had been negligent by not checking to make sure that the door had been shut properly.

 Cassidy v Minister of Health (1951) the pursuer was admitted to hospital so that two of his fingers could undergo a surgical procedure. After the surgery was completed, it was discovered that the pursuer could not use four of his fingers on the hand that had been operated upon. The trial judge dismissed the pursuer's claim stating that negligence on the part of the hospital staff had not been proved. The pursuer appealed.

Held: by the English Court of Appeal that the only plausible explanation for the pursuer's injuries was that the hospital staff had been negligent when they performed the surgical procedure on the pursuer.

 Radcliffe v Plymouth and Torbay Health Authority (1998) the pursuer had been admitted to hospital for the purpose of an operation to his ankle.

While in hospital he developed a serious neurological condition which it was agreed had occurred as result of an injected spinal anaesthetic that the pursuer had been given before the operation. The pursuer argued that the injection must have been administered negligently and that this had caused him to suffer an injury. The Health Authority relied on expert evidence to show that the pursuer had a susceptibility to spinal cord damage and although the injection may have caused this condition to occur there had been nothing negligent about the way in which it was administered.

Held: by the English Court of Appeal that the defender had provided a plausible explanation as to why it had not been negligent. The pursuer could not come up with an explanation to prove that the defender had been negligent and, therefore, his claim failed.

 Key point: *Res ipsa loquiter* works on the presumption that the only possible explanation for the harm suffered by the pursuer is that the defender's actions or failure to act caused it.

Remoteness of damage

If the court decides that the defender has breached his duty of care towards the pursuer there still remains the issue of the extent of the defender's liability for the loss or injury caused. The defender's negligence can unleash a chain of events which can very quickly have all sorts of unintended consequences. Should the defender be liable for all the harm that has been caused by his acts or omissions even if this is not reasonably foreseeable or should the extent of the defender's liability be restricted to those consequences that he ought to have realised were likely to occur? There are two opposing viewpoints: either the defender should be liable for all the consequences of his negligence even if this is not reasonably foreseeable or the defender's liability should be limited to those consequences that were reasonably foreseeable. Unfortunately, until recently, the case law was somewhat contradictory and confusing in this area of delictual liability. The following two cases provide dramatic examples of the serious consequences of the defender's initial negligence and show very different approaches as to how the courts may decide the extent of the defender's liability.

 Re Polemis and Furness, Withy and Co Ltd (1921) a ship had substantial quantities of petrol stored in its hold. The ship had docked at Casablanca where it suffered a most unfortunate and dramatic accident. The dockworkers negligently dropped a wooden plank into the ship's hold. It was reasonably foreseeable that damage to the ship or some of the goods stored in the hold would have occurred. The consequences, however, were much more serious than this and far less foreseeable. When the plank hit the bottom of the hold and it caused sparks. These sparks ignited petrol vapour causing a fire and the ship was destroyed as a result. Should the dockworkers be held responsible for all the consequences of the accident? Clearly, the dockworkers had been negligent by allowing the plank to fall into the hold, but should they be held liable for everything that followed as a result?

Held: the English Court of Appeal awarded full damages to the pursuer. The key question to ask was whether the harm caused to the pursuer was a direct result or consequence of the defender's negligence.

 Overseas Tankship (UK) Ltd *v* Morts Dock & Engineering Co (the **Wagon Mound No. 1**) **(1961)** a ship was being loaded with oil at a dock in Sydney. As a result of carelessness of Overseas Tankship, some of the oil ended up spilling into the harbour. While this spillage was occurring, some employees of Morts Dock, who were welders, were carrying out repairs on another ship at a neighbouring dock. This job was stopped for a while in order to make sure that the oil floating in the harbour could not be ignited by stray sparks from the welders' blowtorches. The oil did cause some damage to a slipway. Several days later, when the danger appeared to have passed, the welders started their job again. There was still oil floating in the harbour and sparks from the welding equipment ignited it causing a very serious fire which spread to the dock which was burned down.

Held: by the Privy Council that the damage to the slipway was reasonably foreseeable, but the damage caused by the fire was not. In order to catch fire, the oil had to be heated to a very high temperature. The Privy Council overruled the trial judge who had followed the reasoning laid down in **Re Polemis (1921)** and awarded damages for both the damage to the slipway and the fire damage to the dock. Interestingly, Viscount Simonds, one of the judges of the Privy Council, wrongly stated that the Scottish courts had rejected outright the reasoning laid down in **Re Polemis (1921)**.

In a much quoted statement from **Allan *v* Barclay (1864)**, Lord Kinloch suggested that the extent of the defender's liability should be based on the consequences which arise directly and naturally from his breach of duty to the pursuer and that the harm caused should be reasonably foreseeable. Arguably, this reasoning would seem to favour **Overseas Tankship** over **Re Polemis**. Despite Lord Kinloch's statement (which did not form part of the actual judgement in **Allan *v* Barclay**), the tension between **Re Polemis** and **Overseas Tankship** lay unresolved in Scotland for many years. This has led to a considerable amount of confusion. In England, however, the courts have favoured the reasoning laid out in **Overseas Tankship** and this led to this case being established as the standard test for remoteness of damage in negligence cases.

In 2002 the House of Lords reconsidered the issue of remoteness of damage in relation to the Scots law of delict. In **Simmons v British Steel PLC [2004]**, an appeal from the Inner House of the Court of Session, Lord Hope of Craighead stated that:

'I would not accept the Second Division's observation that the principles governing remoteness of damage are still not finally resolved in Scots Law. In my opinion the basic principles are well settled.'

Lord Rodger of Earlsferry stated that the reasoning of the Privy Council in **The Wagon Mound No 1** '... was entirely consistent with the trend of Scottish authority, including **Allan *v* Barclay** as interpreted in subsequent cases.' His Lordship went on to say that:

'The English courts quickly adopted the new test in **The Wagon Mound**. Since the Scottish courts had not subscribed to the rule in **Re Polemis**, they might have been expected to welcome the repentance of the Privy Council and the English courts and to make common cause with them in applying the approach in **The Wagon Mound**. It was not to be ... there is a line of Scottish authority, stretching back to **Allan v Barclay**, that is consistent with **The Wagon Mound** in that it limits a defender's liability to damage that was reasonably foreseeable."

It would now appear that this decision of the House of Lords has brought Scots and English law into line as regards the question of remoteness of damage. This means that **The Wagon Mound No 1** is the standard test for remoteness of damage in the Scotland.

 Key point: It is now the case that the defender's liability should be restricted to those consequences that he ought to have realised were likely to occur.

The thin skull rule

The thin skull rule comes into operation when the pursuer has proved that the defender has been negligent and this negligence has caused the pursuer to suffer a personal injury i.e. physical and mental injuries. It should be noted that this rule does not apply to situations where the harm suffered by the pursuer merely amounts to damage to property or pure economic loss (**Liesbosch Dredger v SS Edison (1933)**). The thin skull rule has potentially serious consequences for the defender in the sense that he will be responsible for the pursuer's injuries even if these were not reasonably foreseeable. If, for example, the defender delivered a blow to the pursuer's head, some physical damage would surely be expected to occur. What if, however, the pursuer collapsed and died as a result of the defender's assault because of some physical condition that he suffered from which caused a massive haemorrhage? According to the thin skull rule, the defender should be held responsible for the pursuer's death. This may seem an extremely harsh situation, but the law expects the defender to take his victim as he finds him.

 Smith v Leech Brain & Co (1962) the pursuer was splashed with molten metal as a result of the defender's negligence and he suffered a serious burn to his lip. The pursuer had a pre-cancerous condition which the burn triggered off and he went on to develop cancer. The pursuer later died as a result of the cancer and his widow raised an action against the defender for negligence.

Held: the defender was held liable for all the consequences of his negligence to the pursuer.

 In **Page v Smith (1995)** the pursuer had been injured in a car crash due the defender's negligence. The pursuer claimed that he had also suffered psychiatric injuries as a result of the crash which had caused the condition known as ME (myalgic encephalomyelitis) to reappear. The pursuer had suffered from ME for approximately 20 years, but when the accident had occurred it appeared that he was making a recovery.

Held: the House of Lords decided in favour of the pursuer's claim.

Simmons v British Steel PLC [2004] the pursuer, Christopher Simmons, was employed as a burner at the defender's Clydebridge Works at Cambuslang. While using a hand-held burning torch, the pursuer's legs became entangled in the equipment's fuel cables. This accident caused the pursuer to fall heavily and he struck a metal stanchion, shattering the visor of his protective headgear in the process. The pursuer sustained a number of injuries. The defender was aware that the cables represented a health and safety hazard and, at two other work stations, reasonable precautions had been put in place to minimise the risks to employees. In fact, the pursuer and his colleagues had often complained about these dangers, but the defender had failed to introduce appropriate safety measures to the workstation at which the pursuer suffered injury. In the immediate aftermath of the accident, the pursuer was dazed, sweating profusely and he developed swelling at the top right-hand side of his head and above his right ear. Later, the pursuer complained of severe headaches and his vision deteriorated badly. The pursuer took a successful action for damages to the Court of Session in relation to his physical injuries. This was not the end of the matter. The pursuer went on to develop the severe skin condition known as psoriasis and also began to suffer from a serious depressive illness. Admittedly, he had suffered from psoriasis in the past, but he was now alleging that his accident had, in fact, made things much worse. As a result of his additional injuries, Simmons was unable to return to work (in fact he did not return to work at all). The pursuer raised a second action for damages in relation to his skin condition and the depressive mental illness. The defender countered by arguing that these conditions had been brought on by the anger that the pursuer felt because he was the victim of an avoidable accident and the subsequent (negative) treatment that he had received from his employer. The defender should not, therefore, be held liable for the severe skin condition and the mental illness which the pursuer had developed.

Held: by the House of Lords that the aggravated skin condition and mental illness suffered by the pursuer had been caused by the defender's negligence. Applying the thin skull rule, the defender must take the victim as he finds him. It made no difference to the result that the pursuer had a predisposition to psoriasis. The defender was liable to pay compensation of £498,221.77 to the pursuer. Their Lordships also pointed out, in situations where it is reasonably foreseeable that a working practice would result in an employee suffering physical injury, the pursuer is entitled to bring a claim for damages for psychiatric injury even if the employer could not reasonably foresee that the pursuer would develop such an illness.

 Key point: The thin skull rule has potentially serious consequences for the defender in the sense that he will be responsible for the pursuer's injuries even if these were not reasonably foreseeable.

Pure economic loss

It is important to stress that, generally speaking, the courts tend to award damages to a pursuer who has suffered some sort of harm in the shape of personal injuries (whether physical or psychiatric) or for damage to property which has been caused by the defender where the defender has been negligent. The courts do not have a problem with awarding damages for pure economic loss where the defender has acted in a deliberately harmful fashion. We have to be very clear when we talk about damage in terms of delictual liability. Where the pursuer has suffered financial or pure economic loss as a result of the defender's negligent actions, the courts are much more reluctant to grant compensation. Defects in property will not be regarded as providing a pursuer with an opportunity to sue the defender for damages. The defects in the property must actually cause damage to other property or cause injuries to other people. The courts have not always been consistent on this point as can be seen in the case discussed below:

 Anns *v* Merton London Borough (1978) large cracks in the walls of pursuer's house started to develop because the house had been badly built. Were the cracks in the wall to be treated as property damage or merely as pure economic loss because they would cause the house to lose value? However, it should be remembered that property damage must be able to cause harm to the pursuer.

Held: by the House of Lords that the cracks in the walls should be regarded as property damage and, therefore, the pursuer could be receive compensation. This approach by the House of Lords went against long established legal principles.

In **Murphy *v* Brentwood District Council (1991)** the House of Lords overruled **Anns *v* Merton London Borough (1978)**. The case also involved defects that had developed in a building and the same question arose as to whether the pursuer could claim compensation. As a result of **Murphy**, defects in products are not to be classified as damage to property and should be treated by the courts as an issue of pure economic loss.

Traditionally, the courts attempt to restrict the number of cases which can be brought before them and they are very wary of opening the floodgates which would mean them being overwhelmed by large numbers of new cases being brought before them. In cases where the pursuer has suffered pure economic loss, the courts will often state that an insurance policy should be used to make good the losses (assuming, of course, that the pursuer has one). Alternatively, the parties may have a contractual relationship. If so, a breach of a duty of care by the defender may be more appropriately dealt with under a contractual claim for damages rather than by raising a delictual action.

It should be stressed, of course, that the courts will award damages for pure economic loss to a pursuer when the defender has intentionally committed a wrongful act.

 Key point: The courts will award damages for pure economic loss to a pursuer when the defender has intentionally committed a wrongful act.

The following case shows the correct judicial approach to the issue of pure economic loss:

 Spartan Steel & Alloys Ltd *v* Martin & Co (Contractors) (1972) the defenders who were contractors negligently cut the power cable that supplied the pursuers' factory. The resulting power cut lasted for 14 hours. The pursuers' furnace, which was used to produce molten metal, could not be operated without electrical power. Consequently, the metal which was already in the furnace when the power cut occurred solidified and had to be completely written off. The pursuers were forced to shut down their factory while the power cut lasted and this, of course, meant that they were not able to carry out any of its scheduled industrial processes. The pursuers based their claim for damages on the following three factors:

1   Damage caused to the metal in the furnace when the power cut occurred i.e. physical damage to property.

2   Loss of the profit that would have been made if they had sold the metal had it not been damaged (economic loss as a result of damage to property).

3   Loss of profit in relation to the metal which would have been put into the furnace but for the power cut (pure economic loss).

Held: by the English Court of Appeal that the pursuer could be awarded damages for the first two claims for compensation, but the third claim was to be regarded as pure economic loss and, therefore, no damages were payable.

 Simaan General Contracting Co *v* Pilkington Glass (1987) the pursuers were involved in a building project in Abu Dhabi. The building owner stated to the pursuers that he wanted the windows to be a particular shade of green. Green is the colour which represents the Muslim religion. The pursuers entered a contract with a firm who would purchase the glass for the windows and fit it. This firm entered into a contract with the defenders who were to manufacture the glass and supply it. The glass turned out to be the wrong colour and it was rejected and new glass had to be manufactured. This resulted in the building project being delayed which caused the pursuers to suffer economic loss. Normally, the pursuers would have sued the firm who supplied and fitted the glass. Unfortunately, for the pursuers this firm had gone into liquidation, so the pursuers sued the glass manufacturers for damages.

Held: the pursuers' claim for damages failed because the case centred around pure economic loss. The glass to be used in the windows was not defective, it was simply not fit for its purpose. Furthermore, there was no contract between the pursuer and the defender.

 Macdonald *v* FIFA & SFA (1999) Macdonald attempted to sue FIFA and the Scottish Football Association for financial losses after an international football match involving the Scotland Football Team was cancelled at the last minute. The financial losses allegedly suffered by Macdonald amounted to the cost of the ticket for entry to the stadium and the cost of travelling to the game.

Held: the pursuer's claim for damages amounted to pure economic loss and, consequently, the action was dismissed.

Key point: Generally speaking, the courts tend to award damages to a pursuer who has suffered some sort of harm in the shape of personal injuries (whether physical or psychiatric) or for damage to property which has been caused by the defender where the defender has been negligent.

Junior Books: a unique case?

Junior Books *v* Veitchi Co (1982) is a most unusual case and therefore the courts do not generally tend to rely upon it. It goes against the generally accepted rules that govern pure economic loss. Later cases have tended not to rely upon this decision.

The facts of the case were as follows:

The pursuers had entered a contract with builders who were engaged to build a new factory. The floor of the new factory had to be of a special construction because it was required to support the type of machinery that the pursuers would be using in the factory. The builders recommended a specialist flooring company to the pursuers who they said could carry out this task. The pursuers relied upon this recommendation and used the flooring company. After the new floor had been laid down, however, it was found to be defective, although it was not dangerous. The pursuers had to spend money in order to repair the defective floor. This, of course, meant that they had suffered a pure economic loss as a result of the builder's negligence in recommending the flooring company.

Held: by the House of Lords that despite the fact that the loss was a pure economic one, the pursuers could recover damages from the builders because the builders owed a duty of care to the pursuers.

Junior Books appears to suggest that a defender could be liable for causing pure economic loss if the pursuer relied on negligent advice supplied by the defender. It has been argued that courts will still continue to refuse to grant compensation where a negligent act committed by the defender causes pure economic loss to the pursuer. If this reasoning is correct, it would make **Junior Books** much more closely related to the line of cases which started with **Hedley Byrne & Co Ltd *v* Heller & Partners Ltd (1963)** (see below).

Key point: The decision in **Junior Books** seems very much to go against the rule that damages for pure economic loss caused by the defender's negligence will not be recoverable by the pursuer.

Liability for negligent statements or negligent advice

The parties to a contract will owe one another a duty of care not to make negligent statements which could result in one of them suffering financial loss. It was previously thought that the courts would not grant damages to a party who suffered financial losses as a result of relying on a negligent statement in the absence of a contractual agreement. This position has been altered by the decision of the House of Lords in **Hedley Byrne & Co Ltd *v* Heller & Partners Ltd (1963)**. The facts of the case were as follows:

Hedley Byrne were advertising agents and Heller were merchant bankers. Hedley Byrne had a client, Easipower who was a customer of Heller. Hedley Byrne had contracted with Easipower to run an expensive advertising campaign and they wished to know if Easipower had funds in the bank to meet the advertising bill. Hedley Byrne approached Heller, as Easipower's bankers, to confirm that it had the money to pay the bill in its bank account. Heller confirmed that Easipower was solvent. Admittedly, Heller did say that the value of the work that Hedley Byrne was proposing to carry out on Easipower's behalf was bigger than anything it had ever seen in the account. Heller also said that the reference was given without any liability. Relying on the reference, Hedley Byrne went ahead with the campaign and assumed personal liability for the advertising costs. Later, Easipower became insolvent leaving £17,000 in advertising costs still owed to Hedley Byrne. Heller was sued by Hedley Byrne for issuing negligent advice.

Held: luckily for Heller, the disclaimer excluded the duty of care that it would normally have owed to Hedley Byrne. However, if Heller had failed to issue the disclaimer it would have been liable to Hedley Byrne despite the fact that there was no contract or fiduciary relationship between them.

The House of Lords in **Hedley Byrne v Heller & Partners Ltd** stated that the duty of care resulted from the existence of a special relationship between the parties. Obviously, a duty of care will be owed by the parties to a contractual relationship, but it is worth emphasising that Hedley Byrne and Heller were not parties to a contract. How far **Hedley Byrne** goes is still an open question, but the presence of a special relationship between the parties is useful guide. Lord Devlin said that payment for information or advice is very good evidence that one of the parties is relying upon the statement. In situations where there is no consideration, it will be necessary to exercise greater care.

In a number of situations, the pursuer has been able to show that he has a special relationship with the defender who made the negligent statement and that he relied upon the information supplied by the defender. As a result of satisfying these conditions, the courts have awarded damages to the pursuer for pure economic loss caused by the defender's negligent statement.

 Key point: Until the House of Lords' decision in **Hedley Byrne**, it was previously thought that the courts would not grant damages to a party who suffered financial losses as a result of relying on a negligent statement in the absence of a contractual agreement.

Applying the **Hedley Byrne** principle to claims for pure economic loss

Reliance upon the legal principle in **Hedley Byrne** has arisen in a number of relationships where negligent advice or the negligent provision of services has been an issue.

Solicitors and beneficiaries of a will

 White v Jones (1995) a father had initially fallen out with his daughters and changed the terms of his will in order to prevent them from inheriting any of his property. The father later changed his mind about this action and instructed his firm of solicitors to rewrite his will to include the daughters once more. The solicitors failed to draft a new will according to the father's instructions – despite the fact that he told them to do this on a second occasion. At the time of the father's death, the new will had not been drawn up and the daughters got nothing. The daughters sued the solicitors for breach of their duty of care towards them.

Held: by the House of Lords that the solicitors owed the daughters a duty of care because they had given assurances to the father that his will would be rewritten to include his daughters.

Surveyors who issue negligent survey reports

 Smith *v* Eric S Bush (1990) it was held that it was unreasonable to allow a surveyor to rely on a general disclaimer to exclude the consequences of his negligence where he had been asked by a building society to carry out a reasonably careful visual inspection of the property for valuation purposes (to be paid for by the prospective buyer) The surveyor knew that the buyer would rely on this report and was not likely to get another one. The house was purchased, but because of the defects, turned out to be unfit for habitation. The surveyors when sued by the buyers attempted to rely on the disclaimer to escape liability.

Held: by the House of Lords that it would not be fair and reasonable to allow the surveyor to exclude his liability in terms of the Unfair Contract Terms Act 1977. The case suggests that in so far as disclaimers are used by professional persons they may not be effective, at least as regards ordinary consumers of professional services.

Employers who provide references to third parties regarding ex-employees

 Spring *v* Guardian Royal Assurance PLC (1994) the pursuer, an ex-employee of Guardian Royal Assurance, was prevented from gaining new employment in the insurance industry because Guardian Royal provided a prospective employer of the pursuer with a negligent employment reference. The reference claimed that the pursuer had committed fraud while he had been working for Guardian Royal. This was not true, the pursuer had merely been incompetent in carrying out his duties for Guardian Royal.

Held: by the House of Lords that Guardian Royal owed the pursuer a duty of care and it was foreseeable that he would suffer harm as a result of the negligent reference. Clearly, the pursuer and Guardian Royal had a special relationship – that of employer and employee.

Accountants and auditors who draw up accounts for shareholders in a company

 Caparo Industries PLC *v* Dickman (1990) Caparo owned a large number of shares in a company called Fidelity. Caparo wished to take over Fidelity and bought more shares in the company. When the takeover bid had succeeded, Caparo discovered that Fidelity was practically a failed company. Caparo claimed that it only launched the takeover bid because it relied on figures provided by Fidelity's auditors in their annual report which, by law, has to be carried out. This report claimed that Fidelity had made a good profit, but this was, in fact, not the case. Caparo sued the auditors for not exercising reasonable care when drawing up their report.

Held: by the House of Lords that the auditors' report was drawn up as requirement of law to provide existing shareholders with important information about the company. The report was not for the benefit of outsiders who wished to invest in the company, nor those existing shareholders who wished to increase their holding in the company. Lord Bridge stated that there was no special relationship between Caparo and the auditors. The auditors did not know that their report was being relied upon by Caparo to guide it in its decision to buy more shares in Fidelity. Lord Bridge admitted, however, that there may be situations where the defender knows the information that he has provided will reach the pursuer and that the pursuer will rely upon it for a specific purpose and that it will be reasonably foreseeable that reliance upon this information will cause loss to the pursuer.

 Key point: In order to bring a successful claim for pure economic loss, the pursuer must show that he has a special relationship with the defender who made the negligent statement and that he relied upon the information supplied by the defender.

The defender's liability for psychiatric injuries

The vast majority of claims that involve personal injuries will centre around the issue of whether the defender's negligence caused the pursuer to suffer physical harm. In contrast to this, there will be occasions when the defender's negligence causes the pursuer to suffer from physical *and* psychiatric injuries. It is even possible that the pursuer's injuries may be purely of a psychiatric nature. In the past, such a medical condition was unhelpfully referred to as 'nervous shock'. The term nervous shock did not really convey the seriousness of the pursuer's psychiatric injuries. In modern times, the term post-traumatic stress disorder (commonly referred to by the initials PTSD) may be a more useful label to describe the pursuer's medical condition.

In Scotland, it is always possible for the pursuer to bring an action against the defender who has been negligent if this results in psychiatric injuries being suffered by the pursuer. In **Bourhill v Young (1942)**, the House of Lords did recognise that a defender's negligent actions could cause a pursuer to suffer psychiatric injury. Unfortunately, for Mrs Bourhill it will be remembered that her claim did not succeed.

A recognised medical condition

Before proceeding further, it should be stressed that we speak of psychiatric injury the pursuer must show that he is suffering from a medically recognised condition. It is true to say that the pursuer will be able to show that he has suffered from fear, stress, grief or a range of other emotional conditions of varying levels of intensity caused by the defender's negligence. This is not enough to sustain a claim for psychiatric injury against the defender. The defender's negligence must result in the pursuer developing a medically recognised psychiatric condition.

Simpson *v* ICI (1983) a large explosion occurred at the pursuer's place of employment. The pursuer was present when the incident took place and it was fair to say that he certainly got a fright as a result. The defenders admitted that their negligence was the cause of the explosion. The pursuer attempted to claim damages for psychiatric injury as a result.

Held: the pursuer had experienced a state of fear as a result of being within the vicinity of the explosion, but he had not gone on to develop a medically recognised condition where it could be said that he was suffering from psychiatric injuries as a result of the defender's negligence.

The pursuer must also be someone who will possess a reasonable level of mental or psychological strength that would not normally be undermined or overcome by exposure to the often shocking, even horrific, consequences of the defender's negligence. In **Bourhill *v* Young**, the pursuer admitted that she had a naturally nervous disposition, yet she still went up the road to view the scene of the accident where the defender had been killed. Obviously, someone of the pursuer's temperament should not have placed herself in a position where she might later suffer psychiatric injuries.

However, if the pursuer is an ordinary person who possesses a reasonable level of emotional and psychological strength it is perfectly possible for him to go on and develop a more serious medical condition than the defender might have expected. In these situations, the defender will have to take the pursuer as he finds him.

 An interesting illustration of the 'thin skull rule' in operation can be found in the case of **Page *v* Smith (1995)** where the pursuer was involved in a car crash caused by the defender's negligence. The pursuer did not suffer from any physical injury as a result of his involvement in the car accident. However, he went on to develop psychiatric injuries. Admittedly, the pursuer had suffered from psychiatric problems in the past, but it had been many years since his last illness.

Held: by the House of Lords that the defender was liable for the psychiatric injuries suffered by the pursuer – he had to take his victim as he found him.

 Key point: Psychiatric injuries are a recognised medical condition, for example, post-traumatic stress disorder – fear, stress and anxiety are emotions which may fall outside this category.

A sudden and unexpected shock

It is also important to appreciate that the pursuer must prove to the court that his psychiatric injuries were caused as the result of suffering a sudden and unexpected shock. When a relative or friend dies after an illness, a pursuer will not be able to bring a successful action for the grief and distress caused by this bereavement.

 In **Sion *v* Hampstead Health Authority (1994)** the pursuer had witnessed his son slowly dying in an intensive care ward. The boy had been the victim of medical negligence. The strain was too much for the father and he developed psychiatric injuries.

Held: the pursuer's psychiatric injuries had not been caused by him experiencing a sudden and unexpected shock. Therefore, his claim for compensation failed.

 Key point: The pursuer must prove to the court that his psychiatric injuries were caused as the result of suffering a sudden and unexpected shock.

Who can be affected by psychiatric injuries?

The law recognises two kinds of victim who can develop psychiatric injuries as a result of the defender's negligence:

◆ Primary victims
◆ Secondary victims

Primary victims are those individuals who have been directly involved in an accident caused by the defender's negligence. They may have suffered both physical and psychiatric injuries or their injuries may be limited purely to psychiatric damage.

Secondary victims, on the other hand, are not directly involved in the initial accident that occurred as a result of the defender's negligence. In fact, they may not have witnessed the occurrence of the accident at all. This category of victim often appears on the scene during the aftermath of the accident as in **Bourhill v Young (1942)** when the important events had already taken place. Alternatively, secondary victims are related or connected to the primary victims and as such it would be reasonably foreseeable that they would suffer some sort of distress. Whether or not secondary victims can claim compensation for their psychiatric injuries is another matter altogether.

Primary victims have always had an easier task when it comes to convincing the courts that they should be awarded damages for the psychiatric injuries that they have suffered. However, as we shall see, strict rules are now in place that will determine whether a secondary victim should succeed in his claim for damages against the defender.

 Key point: The law recognises two kinds of victim who can develop psychiatric injuries as a result of the defender's negligence – primary victims and secondary victims.

Secondary victims

 McLoughlin v O'Brian (1983) the pursuer's husband and three children were all victims of a serious car accident which had been caused as a result of the defender's negligence. One of the pursuer's daughters was killed in the accident and the surviving family members were all seriously injured. It is important to realise that the pursuer was not physically present at the scene of the accident and she was not informed about the accident until several hours after it had occurred. When the pursuer reached the hospital she saw for herself the graphic and serious nature of the injuries that her family had suffered. This all proved too much for the pursuer to deal with and she developed a long-running and serious psychiatric condition which she claimed had been caused by the defender's negligence. The difficulty for the pursuer was that she was clearly a secondary victim and the law relating to psychiatric injuries was quite clear – only primary victims could be granted compensation for the psychiatric injuries that they had suffered as a result of the defender's negligence. The House of Lords, therefore, had to consider the issue of whether the pursuer was someone that the defender could reasonably foresee would suffer harm as a result of his negligence. Furthermore, some of the Law Lords felt reasonable foreseeability of harm was not enough and the strength of the pursuer's relationship with the primary victims had to be examined.

Held: the psychiatric injuries suffered by the pursuer were reasonably foreseeable. The ties of love and affection were clearly a crucial feature of her relationship with the primary victims. She was, therefore, entitled to compensation from the defender.

McLoughlin *v* O'Brian is not without its critics and it did not entirely settle the question of whether secondary victims were entitled to sue for psychiatric injury. Lord Bridge suggested that reasonable foreseeability of the pursuer suffering harm should be enough to establish liability. Lords Wilberforce and Edmund-Davies felt that reasonable foreseeability was only one part of the story. The strength of the pursuer's relationship with the primary victims was a very important factor in determining whether any claim for psychiatric injury should be allowed.

 McFarlane *v* E E Caledonia Ltd (1994) the pursuer had witnessed the fire that swept and destroyed the Piper Alpha oil rig in the North Sea in 1987. The fire had started as result of the rig operator's failure to take proper fire safety precautions. The pursuer was a painter who had been working on the rig, but when the fire occurred he was on board a rig support vessel. The support vessel was very near to the rig for the purposes of rescue and fire fighting activities. As a result of witnessing the fire, the pursuer claimed that he had developed psychiatric injuries.

Held: by the English Court of Appeal that the pursuer could not be regarded as a primary victim. He was a secondary victim who could not prove that he had close ties of love and affection with those individuals who were directly affected by the tragedy. It was not reasonably foreseeable that a man in the pursuer's position would go on to develop psychiatric injuries. The pursuer, therefore, had to be treated as a mere bystander who was not in any immediate danger and had no expectation of being placed in such a position.

 Robertson and Rough *v* Forth Road Bridge Joint Board (1995) the pursuers were workmen who had been carrying out work on the Forth Road Bridge when one of their colleagues had been blown off the Bridge during a heavy gale. The pursuers had witnessed this tragedy and they had both seen their colleague's dead body minutes after the accident took place. The pursuers brought claims for psychiatric injuries.

Held: the actions failed because neither pursuer had sufficiently close ties of love and affection with the deceased. Furthermore, it was not reasonably foreseeable that both pursuers would suffer psychiatric injuries as a result of witnessing the victim falling to his death.

Key point: Some of the most difficult cases involving liability for psychiatric injuries have involved so-called secondary victims.

Important developments relating to secondary victims

It was not until the decision of **Alcock and Others _v_ Chief Constable of the Yorkshire Police (1992)** that the approach that Lords Wilberforce and Edmund-Davies had taken in **McLoughlin** was confirmed as correct. **Alcock** was regarded as a special case because the pursuers represented a group of individuals who had a broad range of relationships with the primary victims. The pursuers included parents, children, siblings, grandparents, in-laws, fiancés and friends. All these individuals were claiming that they had suffered psychiatric shock as a result of the harm that had been suffered by the primary victims to whom they were connected. The House of Lords was left with the task of deciding which of these secondary victims was entitled to claim compensation for psychiatric injuries.

The facts of **Alcock and Others _v_ Chief Constable of the Yorkshire Police (1992)** are detailed below:

 The events surrounding this case relate to the English FA Cup semi-final which was being contested by Liverpool and Nottingham Forest. The match was being played at the neutral venue of Hillsborough (the Sheffield Wednesday ground) and it was a sellout. The game was also being televised live on the BBC – although individuals who were caught up in the crush could not be identified from the live television pictures. The South Yorkshire Police force which was responsible for policing the match was accused of negligence for the way in which it operated its crowd control procedures. The game had to be stopped after six minutes of play because too many fans had been allowed into a section of the terraces and many of these individuals were crushed against the fencing which prevented access to the pitch. Ninety-five people died as a result of the incident and at least another 400 had to be treated in hospital for the injuries that they received. The police paid compensation to the primary victims of the incident i.e. those had suffered physical and psychiatric injuries as a result of being directly involved in the accident. This compensation payment, however, did not settle the claims of a group of secondary victims, consisting mainly of relatives of the primary victims. These secondary victims, of course, had not been directly caught up in the incident. Many had, admittedly, been present at Hillsborough and had witnessed the terrible scenes from a distance. Others in the group of secondary victims had witnessed the incident on live television, had been told about the incident by third parties or had gone directly to the ground after hearing the information in order to search for family and friends who were missing presumed injured or dead.

The pursuers attempted to rely upon Lord Bridge's test in **McLoughlin _v_ O'Brian** that their psychiatric injuries were reasonably foreseeable and, therefore, they could claim compensation. The House of Lords felt that although the secondary victims had suffered as a result of the incident at Hillsborough, stricter rules had to apply to their claims than was the case with the primary victims. The starting point of any secondary victim's claim for damages the psychiatric injuries must be reasonably foreseeable. This is only the first hurdle placed in the pursuer's way. There are a further three tests that the pursuer must satisfy:

◆ Do they belong to a group of individuals that the courts should recognise are capable of suffering psychiatric injury as a result of the defender's negligence?
◆ How close to the accident was the pursuer in terms of time and space?
◆ How was the psychiatric injury caused?

The pursuer will find the above tests very difficult to satisfy in order to succeed in his claim.

Held: all the pursuers failed to meet one of the three tests listed above.

 White and Others *v* Chief Constable of the South Yorkshire Police (1998) also arose out of the events which took place at Hillsborough. The pursuers in this case were police officers who had been on duty that day at the Hillsborough ground and who had been involved in attempts to rescue people from the crush on the terraces. The pursuers claimed that their employer, the South Yorkshire Police force, owed them a duty of care for the psychiatric injuries that they had suffered in the line of carrying out their duties and in their role as rescuers. Undoubtedly, these officers had been exposed to horrific scenes where they had pulled the dead and the severely injured from the crush. They could not fail to have been affected in some way by what they had experienced. The pursuers argued that because they had been directly involved in the incident they should not be looked upon as secondary victims. They should be treated as primary victims. Should these officers, therefore, be allowed to claim compensation?

Held: the English Court of Appeal agreed that the pursuers should not be regarded as secondary victims and their claims succeeded. On appeal to the House of Lords, however, all the claims failed. A primary victim was a person caught up in a dangerous incident and who was either in danger of suffering a serious physical injury or reasonably believed that he would suffer serious physical harm. Anyone not in this situation was, therefore, a secondary victim and had to satisfy the tests laid down in **Alcock**. The House of Lords stressed the fact that the pursuers lacked a close relationship with the primary victims (often expressed as the ties of love and affection). Their Lordships were at great pains to stress the fact that rescuers should not expect to receive preferential treatment when claiming compensation for psychiatric injuries that they had suffered.

 Key point: Secondary victims claiming damages for psychiatric injury will have to show that the injury was reasonably foreseeable and also satisfy the tests laid down in **Alcock** – membership of a group of individuals capable of suffering psychiatric injury due to the defender's negligence; closeness to the accident in terms of time and space; and the manner in which the injury was caused.

Rescuers

It is now clear from the judgement of the House of Lords in **White and Others *v* Chief Constable of the South Yorkshire Police** that rescuers are not to be treated more favourably than other individuals when the issue of psychiatric injury arises. Rescuers can be primary victims if, by placing themselves in a dangerous situation, they suffer serious physical harm or they have a reasonable belief that by being exposed to the danger they may suffer physical harm. Later on, these rescuers may develop psychiatric injuries as a result of their physical injuries. Where rescuers are involved in dangerous situations where they are very unlikely to suffer physical harm, they will be regarded as secondary victims if they claim that they suffered psychiatric injuries.

White clearly overrules the earlier case of **Chadwick v British Railways Board (1967)** where the pursuer was involved for more than 12 hours helping the victims of a horrific train crash where over 90 people had been killed The accident had occurred near to where the pursuer lived and he had gone to the scene to offer assistance. The pursuer won damages for the psychiatric injuries that he had suffered as a result of his involvement in the aftermath of the accident.

 Key point: It is now the case that rescuers will not receive more favourable treatment by the courts when they bring claims involving psychiatric injuries.

Psychiatric injuries caused by damage to the pursuer's property

Two cases suggest that a pursuer may be able to sue the defender for psychiatric injuries suffered where the defender's negligence has caused damage to the pursuer's property.

 Attia v British Gas PLC (1987) the pursuer developed psychiatric injuries as a result of witnessing her home being burned down. This incident had been caused by the defender's negligence.

Held: the pursuer was entitled to compensation for the injuries that she had suffered.

 Clark v Scottish Power PLC (1994) employees of the defender had forced their way into the pursuer's home unjustifiably in order to switch off the power supply. The pursuer developed psychiatric injuries caused by the unexpected and sudden shock that she received when she was confronted by the damage caused by the defender's actions.

Held: the pursuer was entitled to damages from the defender in respect of her psychiatric injuries.

 Key point: A pursuer may be able to sue the defender for psychiatric injuries suffered where the defender's negligence has caused damage to the pursuer's property.

An employer's liability for psychiatric injuries

An employer owes a duty to his employees not only to take reasonable care for their physical, but also their mental well-being. In modern times, more stressful working environments and practices have led to a dramatic increase in the number of employees suffering from psychiatric injuries. An employer will usually start off from the understanding that the employee should be able to handle the normal pressures of the job unless he has knowledge that the employee has a particular problem or weakness that makes it much more likely that this person is more susceptible to the risk of developing psychiatric injuries as a result of a stressful working environment. Clearly, it is easier for an employee to put into place safety measures in the workplace that protect an employee's physical well-being. Reducing the risk of psychiatric injuries to employees caused by work-related stress is much more of a challenge for employers. Very often, employers can only take what an employee tells them about their emotional and mental health at face value. To go further, would be perhaps a breach of the employee's right to privacy.

 In **Walker v Northumberland County Council (1995)** the pursuer worked in a particularly stressful social work post for the Council. He had already suffered a breakdown due to overwork and a lack of support from his employers. His employer gave assurances that safeguards would be put in place upon his return from sick leave in order to reduce the risks of stress. The pursuer returned to work, but suffered a second breakdown because the Council had failed to take reasonable care to prevent him suffering from psychiatric injuries. The pursuer brought a claim for damages against the Council.

Held: by the House of Lords that the pursuer should be treated as a primary victim who was entitled to claim damages as a result of the Council's negligence. The Council had returned him to his previous (stressful) post and it was, therefore, reasonably foreseeable that if the pursuer was exposed to these stressful conditions it was likely that this would cause him to suffer psychiatric injury. If an employee is regarded as a secondary victim, he must satisfy the tests laid down in **White and Others v Chief Constable of South Yorkshire Police (1998)** which was discussed above.

 The English Court of Appeal in **Hatton v Sutherland (2002)** stressed that the key question to be asked in situations where an employee raised an action for damages for work-related psychiatric injuries was whether the harm suffered by the pursuer was reasonably foreseeable. The pursuer had to prove that he had suffered an injury to his health which is quite different from occupational stress and this injury had been caused by stress at work and not other factors that could affect the pursuer's health. Very importantly, the Court of Appeal stated that it was wrong to assume that some jobs are more dangerous than others. All jobs should be judged according to the same test.

Hatton involved four claims in total against different employers: Mrs Hatton and Mr Barber were teachers in public sector secondary schools, Mrs Jones was an administrative assistant at a local authority training centre and Mr Bishop was a raw materials operative in a factory. All four pursuers won their cases in the County Court. However, the Court of Appeal dismissed three of the employees' claims and only narrowly approved the Mrs Jones' claim.

It will still be very important for employers to show that they take reasonable care to prevent their employees from developing psychiatric injuries, especially if the employer is aware that the employee is particularly vulnerable in this regard. The approach taken by the Court of Appeal in **Hatton** was affirmed by the House of Lords in **Barber v Somerset County**

Council (2004). However, employers should be mindful of stress suffered by employees and they should regularly update their knowledge of the effects of stress in the workplace.

An example of a questionnaire produced by the Health and Safety Executive which employees can use to measure stress levels of employees in the workplace can be seen on the Introductory Scots Law website.

 Key point: The most important question to ask in situations where an employee raised an action for damages for work-related psychiatric injuries is whether the harm suffered by the pursuer was reasonably foreseeable.

Defences to a negligence action

The two most common defences that are used by the defender in an action of delict are:

1   Contributory negligence

2   *Volenti non fit injuria* (to one who is willing a wrongful act cannot be done)

Contributory negligence

This defence is used where the defender is claiming that the pursuer failed to take reasonable care for his safety. In other words, the defender is claiming that the pursuer was partly to blame for his own injury. The aim of this defence is to, hopefully, reduce the amount of damages awarded against the defender to reflect the pursuer's responsibility for the damage or injury sustained.

The Law Reform (Contributory Negligence) Act 1945 states that 'if a person (the pursuer) is injured, partly because of his own fault and partly due to the fault of another (the defender), damages will be reduced to the extent that the court thinks fit, having regard to the pursuer's share in the responsibility for the harm.'

 Hanlon *v* Cuthbertson (1981) this involved a claim by a female passenger in a taxi who was injured as a result of an accident and the taxi driver's negligence. The taxi driver argued contributory negligence because she was not wearing a seat belt which would otherwise have protected her in the accident.

Held: that as a result of contributory negligence, the pursuer should have her damages reduced by ten per cent. Despite this reduction, she was still awarded compensation of £14,584 plus interest.

 McLellan *v* Dundee City Council (2009) Rodney McLellan, the pursuer, was employed as a gardener by the Council. He suffered an injury in the course of his employment while trying to clear a blockage caused by a build-up of grass in the blades of his lawnmower. The lawnmower (a Ransomes Jacobsen Highway 2130 triple mower) was switched off when McLellan attempted to clear the blockage. McLellan lost part of his finger when stored power in the machine caused the blades to rotate suddenly and without warning. He had attempted to clear the blockage by using a crowbar, but unfortunately while doing so he held it in such way that he dropped it and his finger became caught in the blades. The Council had failed to warn

337

McLellan and other gardeners about the potential dangers of stored energy in the lawnmower's hydraulic system which caused the blades to rotate in this way. Significantly, however, the Council had warned its employees to ensure that they kept their hands away from the blades of the lawnmower at all times and McLellan admitted, during the course of his evidence, that his action in attempting to clear the machine was irresponsible and that he was fully aware of the Council's warning in this regard.

Held: Lord Hodge in the Outer House of the Court of Session found that the Court had breached its duty of care by exposing McLellan to a far greater level of risk than was reasonably foreseeable. At the same time, however, McLellan had contributed to his injuries as a result of his actions and his initial award of £16,430 was reduced by 20% to £13,144.

Volenti non fit injuria

The main point of this defence is that the pursuer has, with full knowledge of the facts, voluntarily assumed and accepted the risk of injury and, in this way, has absolved the defender of the consequences of the defender's breach of duty. The defender still owes a duty of care but the chain of causation has been broken by the pursuer voluntarily undertaking the risk.

 ICI *v* Shatwell (1965) the pursuer and his brother were explosives experts who, contrary to instructions issued by their employer, agreed to test their detonators before returning to a safety shelter. There was an explosion and one man was injured while his brother was killed. It was held that the employer could successfully plead *volenti* as the pursuer and his brother had agreed to run the risk of injury by not returning to the safety shelter.

Besides contributory negligence and *volenti non fit injuria*, there are several other defences which are available to the defender.

Prescription and limitation

In terms of the Prescription and Limitation (Scotland) Act 1973, most delictual claims must be brought within five years of damage being suffered. Personal injury claims must usually be lodged within three years (the triennium date).

Compliance with statutory authority

Authority to do something which would otherwise be actionable can be conferred by statute. This is the only defence which can be used when the defender is accused of committing behaviour which amounts to a nuisance.

 Lord Advocate *v* North British Railways (1894) waste which was being disposed of under statutory authority was left near an army barracks. Compliance with the statute could been achieved by disposing of the waste not at the army barracks, but at another, more suitable location. As a result, North British Railways could not use the defence against the accusation that it was causing nuisance.

The Consumer Protection Act 1987 also provides the defence of compliance with a statutory provision which the defender can use in order to escape liability for dangerous products.

Necessity

This may not be a terribly effective defence when used by the defender to escape liability for negligence, but may excuse a deliberate act on his part, for example, he acted in order to prevent an accident from occurring.

Damnum fatale

The defender could not have prevented an accident from occurring because it was completely unforeseeable. The incident which led to the harm being suffered by the pursuer amounts to an Act of God, for example, a tidal wave engulfing part of the City of Glasgow. In **Caledonian Railway Co *v* Greenock Corporation (1917)** the defender's argument that freakishly heavy rainfall in Greenock, but not for the rest of Scotland, should be considered as an act of God failed to impress the House of Lords and the defender was found liable for causing damage to the pursuer's property.

Criminality

The pursuer will be unable to claim damages if he and the defender were involved in criminal activity.

 In **Pitts *v* Hunt (1990)** the pursuer was injured while he was a passenger on a motorcycle being driven by the defender. The defender was not covered by insurance and he had been drinking. The pursuer was perfectly aware of these facts, but he still encouraged the defender to break the law by driving the motorcycle. The English Court of Appeal refused to award damages to the pursuer.

 Furthermore, in **Ashton *v* Turner (1981)** the pursuer and the defender had been involved in a plan to break into a house. The defender was to drive the getaway car, but he drove the car dangerously and the pursuer was injured as a result. The pursuer sued the defender for damages. The court refused to award damages to the pursuer because he had been involved in a criminal activity when he had suffered the injury caused by the defender's dangerous driving.

The Sovereign

Any delictual action commenced against Her Majesty Queen Elizabeth II would fail. The Queen enjoys personal immunity from suit meaning that such a court action would be incompetent.

Foreign Heads of State and Ambassadors and their diplomatic staff

Foreign Heads of State and members of their households generally enjoy immunity from suit and any delictual action commenced against them in the Scottish courts would be incompetent. Ambassadors and members of diplomatic staff present in the United Kingdom will also enjoy immunity, but in a more limited sense. The wrongful act must have occurred in connection with the carrying out of their diplomatic duties by the Ambassador and his staff.

 Key point: The most common defences that are used by the defender in an action of delict are contributory negligence, *volenti non fit injuria*, prescription and limitation, compliance with statutory authority, necessity, *damnum fatale* and criminality.

Landownership

A landowner may be entitled to exercise a broad range of rights in relation to his property thus allowing him to enjoy it to the fullest extent. A landowner is not entitled, however, to do whatever he wishes on his property and he should always display sensitivity towards his neighbours. A landowner who carries on dangerous activities on his property, or who subjected his neighbours to behaviour that could be classified as a nuisance, should made be aware of the serious penalties that may be imposed upon him. This will be especially the case if his conduct causes loss or injury to an innocent third party.

Restrictions imposed on land

A landowner's rights may be restricted in the following ways:

◆ by statute
◆ by common law and
◆ by agreement or by contract.

However, we are, of course, primarily concerned with the law of delict in relation to landownership.

We will first examine the liability of landowners for the escape of dangerous things from their property which cause loss or injury to neighbours. We will then consider the liability of a landowner or an occupier of property for loss or injury suffered by third parties who have entered the property in question.

The escape of dangerous things from property

It has been stated that Scots law takes a completely different approach from England as regards the burden of liability imposed on a landowner in relation to loss or injury caused by non-natural use of property. In England, the landowner's liability is said to be strict in relation to the escape of dangerous things from his property. English legal doctrine in this area stems from the decision of the House of Lords in **Rylands v Fletcher (1868)**. In several important Scottish decisions, such as **Kerr v Earl of Orkney (1857)** and **Caledonian Railway Company v Greenock Corporation (1917)**, there is a clear willingness on the part of Scottish courts to impose strict liability on the landowner who uses his property in a dangerous fashion. It should be emphasised that the burden of strict liability is confined to a small number of situations and is the exception rather than the rule in Scotland. Scottish judges have a distinct tendency to become almost apoplectic with rage in relation to any suggestion that a **Rylands v Fletcher** liability exists in Scotland. Lord Fraser of Tullybelton, in **RHM Bakeries (Scotland) Ltd v Strathclyde Regional Council (1985)**, was particularly opposed to any extension of the general rule of strict liability in **Rylands** becoming part of the law of Scotland.

Activities by a landowner that are considered to fall into the category of non-natural use of property by a landowner would include any of the following:

◆ Toxic chemicals used in industrial processes contaminating the environment
◆ The escape of fire from the premises
◆ Water accumulated in a dam which later bursts
◆ The escape of armaments or explosives stored on the property

It should go without saying that all of the above examples can expose a landowner's neighbours to terrible dangers. It is important to note that a landowner may bring something on to his property that is perfectly safe if proper precautions are taken. The issue of danger occurs (and so too, inevitably, the question of delictual liability) when the thing in question escapes from the property and causes loss or injury to a neighbour.

 Rylands *v* Fletcher (1868) the defender was a mill owner who had instructed independent contractors to build a dam on his property. The dam would be used to supply the defender's mill with water. While the dam was being built, the contractors discovered old mine shafts and passageways on the defender's property which extended into the mine of a neighbouring property owner. The contractors chose not to block up the passageways and shafts. The dam was filled with water and it burst into the neighbour's property via the old mine works causing substantial damage.

Held: by the House of Lords that a property owner who brings something onto his land for his own purposes, and the thing in question is likely to cause harm if it escapes, does so at his own peril and he will be responsible for any harm caused as a natural consequence of the thing's escape. In other words, the defender was strictly liable for the harm caused to his neighbour's property.

The House of Lords has considered the escape of dangerous things from land in the more recent case of **Cambridge Water *v* Eastern Counties Leather (1994)**. This case involved the escape of dangerous chemicals from the defender's property over a fairly lengthy period of time. The House of Lords held that the pursuer's claim should fail because the damage suffered was too remote. The really interesting aspect of this decision is that Lord Goff emphasised the fact that storage of chemicals on property (even if it is used for industrial purposes) is a classic case of a non-natural use of property. The defender will receive short shrift from the courts if he attempts to justify his non-natural use of the property by pointing to the benefits that the community receives – in this case, the employment opportunities afforded to the local community.

 Key point: Scots law often reflects the English rule which stipulates that a landowner is strictly liable for all damage caused by the escape of dangerous things as a consequence of his non-natural use of the property, for example, fire escaping, water accumulated in a dam which later bursts and stored explosives which later explode unintentionally. However, Scottish judges have made clear that the rule in **Rylands *v* Fletcher** is very much against Scottish legal practice.

Dangerous and harmful acts committed on the property of a landowner

What if dangerous or harmful acts were carried out on the property of an owner or an occupier by a third party with the result that neighbours suffer loss or injury? What if the harm or damage was reasonably foreseeable?

In what way might the Scottish courts impose liability on a landowner who abandons his property or fails to secure it properly thus affording an opportunity to third parties to enter the property and, while present there, carry out a range of dangerous or harmful activities? Situations involving vandals, squatters, trespassers or housebreakers who use property in a way that not only threatens the immediate interests of the landowner, but also the safety and security of his neighbours spring immediately to mind.

 The House of Lords clarified many of these issues in **Smith v Littlewoods; Maloco v Littlewoods (1987)**. Trespassers had entered an abandoned cinema owned by the defenders. The defenders were intending to clear the land in order to build a supermarket. The trespassers were using the premises to light fires amongst other things. One such fire got out of control and spread to a neighbouring building causing substantial damage.

Held: by the House of Lords that the defenders were not liable for the consequences of the dangerous activities carried out on their premises by the unauthorised third parties. The defenders were able to demonstrate that they had been unaware that their property constituted a danger to their neighbours i.e. that it had become a fire hazard. If the defenders had possessed knowledge that trespassers were in the habit of lighting fires, they would have owed a duty to take reasonable care in order to prevent the trespassers from entering the property and behaving in a dangerous manner that clearly threatened the interests of neighbouring owners and occupiers.

The consequences of Smith v Littlewoods; Maloco v Littlewoods (1987)

What does the above decision of their Lordships actually mean? What are its consequences for landowners and their neighbours?

Their Lordships stated that an owner or occupier of property owed important responsibilities to neighbouring owners or occupiers of properties.

The relevant standard imposed on the property owner is a duty to take reasonable care of his property so that his neighbours do not suffer physical injury or experience damage to their property. The House of Lords limited the extent of liability of an owner or occupier for physical injuries or damage caused to neighbours as a result of the dangerous or harmful activities of unauthorised third parties while on the property. A duty of care may be imposed on an owner or an occupier of property if it was highly probable (*not* reasonably foreseeable) that negligence on his part might provide an opportunity to a third party to cause physical injury or damage to a neighbouring owner or occupier of property.

An owner or occupier will not be liable to his neighbours for the consequences of the dangerous or harmful activities of unauthorised third parties merely because such consequences are reasonably foreseeable. If, for example, a person leaves the door of his flat unlocked and a thief enters the premises to gain access to the adjoining property, the owner of the flat is not under a duty of care to take reasonable care to prevent this situation. The owner or occupier of the flat will have to seek a remedy against the thief. The situation may have a radically different outcome, however, if the owner of the flat was well aware that a high number of burglaries had taken place in the area recently. However, as we shall from an examination of **Canmore Housing Association v Bairnfather (t/a B R Autos) [2004]** (below), the fact that the risk of harm must be highly probable can represent a significant obstacle to a pursuer's claim.

The decision reached by the House of Lords in **Smith v Littlewoods; Maloco v Littlewoods (1987)** sits very awkwardly with the decision of the Inner House of the Court of Session in **Squires v Perth and Kinross District Council (1986)** and it must be respectfully submitted (with the benefit of hindsight) that the earlier case was wrongly decided. In this case, the pursuer owned a jewellery business which had been successfully burgled by a thief. Apparently, the thief was able to gain access to the jeweller's premises because contractors for the District Council, who happened to be carrying out building work on a flat situated above the shop, had failed to take proper security precautions to prevent any unauthorised parties from gaining access to the flat. The Inner House allowed the pursuer to succeed in the action for damages against the building contractors.

 The Court of Session recently had to reconsider the impact of **Smith *v* Littlewoods; Maloco *v* Littlewoods in Canmore Housing Association *v* Bairnfather (t/a B R Autos) [2004]**. The case involved a dispute between a Housing Association (Canmore) and a garage (owned by Bruce Bairnsfather t/a B R Autos). Bairnsfather was in the habit of leaving a variety of derelict and unroadworthy vehicles situated in a lane of which he was the owner. He claimed that the vehicles were used by him as a source of spare parts in his business. The lane bordered a block of flats owned by Canmore and both parties used the lane to gain access to their respective properties. The vehicles were placed nose to tail against one another and their presence often hindered access to Canmore's property. Canmore made an allegation that the vehicles were an eyesore, a danger to children, an invitation to vandals to come on to the property, constituted a nuisance and, furthermore, that they represented a potential risk to neighbouring property. Nuisance is harmful conduct or behaviour which is not a one-off event, but rather an ongoing series of incidents which harm a neighbour's enjoyment of his property.

One of the abandoned vehicles had been set on fire by vandals and Canmore's property had sustained damage in the region of £3,000. Canmore was so fearful that vandals might attempt to set fire to the other vehicles in the lane, that it had refused to allow 22 potential tenants to move in to the block of flats. Canmore was also concerned it might be denied fire insurance if the alleged nuisance was allowed to continue. Bairnsfather had attempted to defuse the situation by offering to remove one of the vehicles and by clearing up the rubbish which had accumulated around the remaining vehicles. This offer did nothing to pacify Canmore which brought a petition for an interdict on the basis that it was highly probable that the continuing presence of the vehicles would cause further acts of vandalism. It was accepted by Bairnsfather that risk of an event which would cause damage might be enough to prove nuisance on his part. Lord Brodie weighed up the risks represented by the presence of the vehicles: they could be potentially attractive to vandals because of their derelict condition, they could be potentially a fire hazard as they were filled with rubbish of a flammable nature and, within the immediate vicinity of the lane, there was a piece of waste ground where vandals were known to gather.

Held: by the Court of Session that Canmore's petition for interdict should be dismissed. Taking all the elements together, it was not highly probable that there was a real risk of further fires threatening Canmore's property. Lord Brodie made the following statement:

'*... even having regard to the additional circumstances which favour the petitioners' [Canmore] contention that I should find there to be a material risk of fire damage to their property due to vandals setting the respondent's vehicles on fire, I am not persuaded, on the basis of one incident, that the necessary degree of risk has been established. On what has been put before me, therefore, I do not find the respondent's use of his property has been shown to be,* prima facie, *a nuisance.*'

In other words, following the test laid down in **Maloco v Littlewoods (1987)**, it was not highly probable that there was a real risk of fire damage to Canmore's property.

Tenant's liability

An occupier of property, for example, a tenant will often become liable to the owner for any loss or damage caused to the property as a result of his acts or omissions (whether deliberate or otherwise). Usually, but not always, an occupier of property will have a contractual relationship with the owner of the property and this agreement will specifically address the issue of liability for any damage caused. Where there is no contractual relationship, the occupier of property owes a duty care to the owner to behave in a way that does not cause loss or injury during the period of his occupation.

 Fry's Metals v Durastic Ltd (1991) the defenders were found liable for failure to ensure that a burglar alarm continued to operate properly. The defenders argued that their responsibility for the property had come to an end after their tenancy agreement with the pursuer had expired. However, the court said that it was an extremely significant fact that the defenders had failed to return the only set of keys to the property to the pursuer. Consequently, the defenders were liable for damage caused to the property by vandals who had broken into the pursuer's property. The likelihood of such an event occurring was made highly probable due to the fact that the defenders had failed to take adequate steps to ensure that the property was effectively protected by a functioning burglar alarm.

 Key point: A duty of care may be imposed on an owner or an occupier of property if it was highly probable (not reasonably foreseeable) that these individuals' negligence might allow a third party to cause real harm to a neighbouring owner or occupier of property.

Occupier's liability

An owner or occupier of property may well become liable if the derelict state of the property causes injury, loss or damage to another person or his property. The main piece of legislation in this area is the Occupiers' Liability (Scotland) Act 1960 which establishes the rule that the occupier of property must take reasonable care to minimise the risks that any visitors to the property (whether invited or not) might encounter. The term occupier is given a broad definition in terms of Section 1(1) of the Act of 1960 and means any person or corporate body in actual possession, physical control or occupation of the premises. The occupier of premises is not necessarily the owner of the premises. Premises could be any fixed or moveable structure and could include aircraft or ships.

In **Telfer v Glasgow District Council (1974)** it was held that the occupier was the person who could control or exclude others from entering the premises. In the case of **Fry's Metals v Durastic Ltd (1991)** examined above, the tenant of the property in question would be the occupier under the 1960 Act because he had retained the only set of keys and, therefore, controlled legitimate access to the building. Not even the landlord could gain access to the building while the tenant had the keys in his possession.

To stand any chance of success in such delictual actions, the pursuer must prove that the defender (i.e. the occupier) was at fault.

We can see an example of this test of reasonable care in relation to occupiers in **Glasgow Corporation v Taylor (1922)** where the Corporation had failed to put up fences or warning signs around the bush from which poisonous berries were growing. A very young child died as a result of eating the berries. The court stated that the Corporation as occupiers were liable for the child's death. It had failed in its duty to take reasonable care.

 In the House of Lords decision of **McGlone v British Railways Board (1966)**, a 12-year old boy climbed up an electricity transformer which was the property of British Railways Board and which was situated on its land. The boy had sustained an electric shock and, consequently, he had suffered severe burns. The Board had placed high fencing around the transformer on three sides. Access to the transformer could still, therefore, be gained by unauthorised individuals who simply entered by the unfenced side. The Board had also put up a danger sign in an attempt to deter members of the public from going anywhere near the transformer. The House of Lords felt that the Board had taken reasonable measures to implement its duty of care. All the circumstances were examined when reaching this decision such as the existence of high fencing, the danger sign and the age of the boy. A 12-year old boy should have been fully aware that he was taking part in a dangerous activity by climbing the transformer. After all, the strong element of danger probably explained his desire to climb the transformer in the first place.

 Titchener v British Railways Board (1984) the pursuer, a 15-year old girl, was hit by a train while she was attempting to cross a busy railway line in the company of her boyfriend. The couple were using railway property as a shortcut. The girl was perfectly aware of the dangers involved in taking such a shortcut and she was normally in the habit of taking the precaution of looking in both directions when crossing the line. In the couple's haste to get to the other side, they threw caution to the wind and did not bother to take this most basic precaution. Tragically, the girl's boyfriend was killed as a result of the accident. In her claim, the girl argued that the Board had been negligent as a result of its failure to repair holes in the railway fence – she alleged that the Board was fully aware of the dilapidated condition of the fence. The girl, however, was forced to make a fairly damning admission that she had pulled down a section of fencing in order to make the task of entering the Board's property that much easier.

Held: by the House of Lords that the existence of a duty of care owed by the occupier (the Board) hinged on the circumstances of the incident, the age and the intelligence of the particular person who entered the premises.

In this case, the Board did not owe the girl a duty of care when the facts of her claim were scrutinised. Quite simply, the girl was of an age and possessed of an ordinary degree of intelligence where it should have been obvious that she was endangering her safety.

It will, of course, be appreciated that in both **McGlone** and **Titchener**, the pursuers failed precisely because they were aware or should have been aware that their activities were dangerous. British Railways Board was able to escape liability by relying on the defence of *volenti non fit injuria* i.e. a pursuer who knowingly and recklessly exposes himself to danger will not have a claim should he suffer injury. The outcome in both cases would have been very different if both pursuers had been young children who were unaware of the dangers of entering the Board's property. Clearly, the Board would have failed to exhibit the necessary level of care had this been the case.

 Murray v Edinburgh District Council (1981) a home help employed by the Council was working in the home of an elderly client. A ventilator came away from the wall and landed on the home help injuring her wrist. She subsequently brought a claim for damages against her employer in terms of the Occupier's Liability (Scotland) Act 1960.

Held: the pursuer's claim failed because the Council was not in control of the premises where the accident had occurred and was, therefore, not liable in terms of the Act.

 Key point: In terms of the Occupiers' Liability (Scotland) Act 1960, a pursuer must demonstrate that the occupier has failed to take reasonable care to ensure that a person entering his premises will not suffer injury or damage by reason of any danger due to the state of the premises or of anything done or omitted to be done on them.

The occupier's liability for obvious dangers on the property

An occupier cannot be held liable as a result of their failure to provide protection against an obvious danger on their land arising from a natural feature such as a lake or a cliff as the following cases amply demonstrate.

 Fegan v Highland Council (2007) the pursuer fell from a cliff top path (known as Victoria Walk near Thurso) and sustained serious injuries. While sitting on a bench, she dropped her personal stereo which she attempted to retrieve but, as she did so, she slipped and fell over the cliff edge to the beach below.

Held: the pursuer's claim for damages under the Occupiers' Liability (Scotland) Act 1960 failed. Lord Johnston, delivering the decision of the Extra Division of the Court of Session, stated:

"I do not consider that there is a duty on the defenders to protect the pursuer against natural and obvious dangers. I consider it self evident that the cliffs at Victoria Walk are a natural and obvious danger... you cannot 'expect an occupier to provide protection against an obvious danger on his land arising from a natural feature such as a lake or a cliff and to impose a duty on him to do so..."

The decision in **Fegan v Highland Council (2007)** confirms the approach taken in an unreported decision of the Sheriff Court in the case of **Strachan v Highland Council (1999)** where the pursuer fell off a cliff after accessing a pathway at the top of the cliff in the early hours of the morning. The pursuer had gained access to the path by stepping over a damaged section of fencing which separated the path from the car park.

Held: the pursuer's claim to have the Council held liable as the occupier failed because the cliff was such an obviously dangerous place and it was extremely foolish for the pursuer to attempt to gain access to the path at that time of the morning.

 Duff v East Dumbartonshire Council and others (2002) an occupier of property will be under no legal duty to take safety precautions where the risk of danger was so obvious that any reasonable person should have been put on a state of alert and thus would have been able to avoid injury to themselves. Duff had sustained injuries as a result of falling down a steep embankment. He sought damages from the Council and other parties for the failure to fence off the embankment.

Held: by the House of Lords that the danger was obvious so that Duff and any other reasonable person should have been aware of the risk of walking too close to the embankment. The occupiers were not liable for Duff's injuries and they were not under a duty to fence off the area where the accident occurred. It should be noted, however, that the outcome might have been very different if the accident had involved a very young child (see **Taylor v Glasgow Corporation (1922)** discussed above).

 Key point: An occupier cannot be expected to provide protection against an obvious danger on his land arising from a natural feature such as a lake or a cliff and to impose a duty on him to do so.

 Struthers-Wright v Nevis Range Development Company Ltd (2006) a ski range where the pursuer had suffered an injury was deemed to be premises in terms of the Occupier's Liability Act 1960, although the occupier does not owe a special duty of care to users of the premises in respect of natural and obvious features of the premises which may constitute a danger.

The *actio de effusis dejectis* and the *actio de positis vel suspensis*

It has been (unsuccessfully) argued that an owner or an occupier of property could be strictly liable where something was poured or thrown out of a building (the *actio de effusis dejectis*) causing harm to the victim.

Similarly, where something was placed on the building or attached to the building fell, causing harm to the victim (the *actio de positis vel suspensis*) it has been argued (again unsuccessfully) that the owner or the occupier would be under strict liability.

It has even been suggested that these delicts are not a proper part of Scots law. Bankton, one of the Institutional Writers, argued, however, that Scots law had adopted these two actions from Roman law (*Institute* 1.4.31 and 32). Baron Hume, another Institutional Writer discussed both actions in his *Lectures* Vol. 3, Chapter 16. Hume, however, spoke about these actions in terms of negligence and fault as opposed to examples of strict liability. The position has now been clarified somewhat by the Court of Session's decision in **McDyer v Celtic Football and Athletic Company Ltd and Others (3 March 2000)**.

The facts of the case were as follows:

 McDyer, the pursuer, was attending the opening ceremony of the European Special Olympics at Celtic Park in Glasgow on 21 July 1990. The pursuer and his family made their way to the West Terrace of the ground and sat with other spectators on a perimeter wall surrounding the park. While the pursuer was sitting on the wall, a block of wood fell and landed on his hand causing him to suffer injury. The wood had been used as a temporary measure to secure a banner which was hanging from the stadium canopy. The day was calm and a securely attached piece of wood was unlikely to have been dislodged in any case. Furthermore, the stadium canopy was not accessible to the public. The pursuer sued Celtic Football Club (the occupiers of the stadium), European Summer Special Olympic Games 1990 (Strathclyde) Limited (which had control of the stadium had the time of the incident) and Zurich Insurance.

In addition to Celtic Football Club's potential liability under Section 2 of the Occupiers' Liability (Scotland) Act 1960 and the legal principle of *res ipsa loquiter* (the facts speak for themselves), the pursuer also alleged that Celtic Football Club was

'*strictly liable in terms of the* actio de positis vel suspensis *for causing or allowing a piece of timber to be placed or suspended from the said stadium canopy where it could fall upon the pursuer who was in a part of the stadium where the public were likely to pass or congregate.*'

Their Lordships examined the influence of Roman law on Scots law and pointed out that many of the older cases supposedly involving the *actio de positis vel suspensis* were really concerned with the liability of occupiers and owners of buildings for injury and damage caused to those outside the premises, whether in the streets or in open spaces or on neighbouring properties. The issue as the Court of Session saw it could be dealt with purely in terms of the Occupiers' Liability (Scotland) Act 1960. It will be remembered, of course, that the occupier has to demonstrate he has taken reasonable care to ensure that a person entering his premises will not suffer injury or damage by reason of any danger due to the state of the premises or of anything done or omitted to be done on them. The pursuer's claim based on the *actio de positis vel suspensis* implying strict liability was, therefore, largely irrelevant and unnecessary. The Court of Session acknowledged that in Scotland, generally speaking, there can be no liability without fault (or *culpa*).

The Court of Session's reasoning in **McDyer** largely confirms the approach taken in two previous Sheriff Court decisions in which reliance by pursuers on the Roman legal principles was defeated:

 Gray v Dunlop (1954) the pursuer's son was passing a hostel run for homeless people when an unnamed individual poured a pot of urine from one of the upper floors of the building. The contents landed on the young boy and, consequently, his father (the pursuer) brought an action against the occupier of the building. The pursuer's claim proceeded on the basis that an occupier should be strictly liable for anything poured or thrown out of the property which resulted in injury to anyone in the vicinity. The pursuer's claim was based on the *actio de effusis dejectis*.

Held: by the Sheriff that the pursuer had failed to prove that the occupier (the defender) was at fault. In Scotland, generally speaking, there can be no liability without fault. The pursuer's argument that the defender's liability should be strict was dismissed.

 MacColl v Hoo (1983) high winds dislodged a slate from the defender's roof. The slate landed on the pursuer's car causing damage. The pursuer raised a claim against the defender basing the action on the *actio de positis vel suspensis*. The pursuer argued that the defender should be held strictly liable for any objects that were attached to his property which came loose and caused damage to property or injury to persons.

Held: by the Sheriff that the pursuer had failed to prove that the defender was at fault and that the claim must be dismissed. The argument that the pursuer's claim should be allowed to succeed on the basis of strict liability failed.

 Key point: A property occupier or owner will not be strictly liable for any object or thing that is poured out or thrown or falls from his premises – the pursuer will have to show that the owner did not take reasonable care to prevent loss or injury.

Delicts traditionally associated with landownership

The law of Scotland regards a landowner as owning his property 'from the heavens to the centre of the earth' (*a coelo usque ad centrum*). This means that the landowner's property rights extend to the skies (i.e. the airspace) above the land and the earth below. This important principle of landownership, however, can always be limited by law or by agreement or by the nature of the property i.e. a tenement building or block of flats where the owners of flats in the lower storeys will not benefit from the application of this principle. It is not an absolute right and Section 76 of the Civil Aviation Act 1982, for example, continues to allow the passage of aircraft over property. Furthermore, in **Farley v Skinner [2001]**, a decision of the House of Lords, Lord Steyn noted that:

'Noise from aircraft is exempted from the statutory nuisance system and in general no action lies in common law nuisance by reason only of the flight of aircraft over a property (see Section 6(1): Civil Aviation Act 1982)'

 The case of **Brown v Lee Constructions Ltd (1977)** provides an extremely interesting example of how this principle operates in practice. The pursuer, a house owner, objected to the intrusive behaviour of a construction firm in relation to his property. The defender, a construction company, was involved in a building project on neighbouring land and, as part of the its activities, the defender's crane operator was in the habit of sweeping the crane over the pursuer's property. The pursuer raised an action to obtain an interdict in order to prevent what was effectively an act of trespass by the defender.

Held: that the defender, by allowing the crane to sweep over the pursuer's property was committing an act of trespass i.e. committing an act of intrusion – albeit of a temporary nature. The court granted an interdict to the pursuer in order to prevent the defender from continuing to commit the act of trespass in the future.

 Key point: An owner of property is said, subject to certain restrictions, to own the land from the heavens to the centre of the earth.

Trespass

This is an issue which will concern many landowners. Trespass is defined as a temporary intrusion upon land or property. A landowner's primary remedy will amount to the right to have trespassers ejected from his land. However, the means used in the ejection of an individual from the property should be reasonable. The courts would not treat a landowner sympathetically if he was shown to have used force to eject a person from his property.

The most common way that the Scottish courts will deal with an act of trespass is to grant an interdict or court order against the defender which prevents him from repeating the temporary intrusion on the pursuer's property. If the trespass is of a more serious nature i.e. where the defender's intrusive behaviour has caused loss or injury, the landowner always has the option of pursuing a claim for damages.

 The Scottish courts are not in the habit of granting the remedy of interdict where an incident of trespass is of a truly trivial nature. In **Winans v Macrae (1885)**, the court felt that the pursuer could have solved the problem of an alleged incident of trespass without having to approach it and request that the remedy of interdict be granted. The trespasser in question was the defender's lamb (kept as a pet) which was in the habit of straying on to the pursuer's land and eating the occasional blade of grass. Needless to say, the lamb did not cause any damage to the pursuer's property and, if the pursuer really found the animal's presence on his property so objectionable, he was perfectly at liberty to build a fence which would have kept the animal out.

In Scotland, an act of trespass is generally viewed as a breach of civil law. It is possible, however, for a trespasser to commit a crime in terms of the Trespass (Scotland) Act 1865. This will occur where a trespasser enters property with the deliberate intention of dispossessing the true owner and this state of affairs lasts for an unspecified period of time. Such a criminal offence will tend to be committed mainly by squatters.

In terms of the civil law, squatters should always be aware that they may fall foul of the delictual remedy of violent profits whereby the Scottish courts will award the dispossessed owner of property the greatest profits that he potentially could have made had it not been for the fact that he was prevented from occupying and using it. In addition, the owner may be entitled to claim damages for any loss or damage caused as a result of the illegal occupation of the property.

Key point: Trespass is a temporary intrusion upon a person's land and the customary judicial remedy is that of interdict. Compensation may be payable by the trespasser if this causes damage to the property.

Statutory restrictions

Over the years, many statutes and secondary legislation have prevented or limited the uses to which a landowner can make in relation his property. Examples of statutes that impose a wide range of restrictions upon a landowner include:

◆ Housing (Scotland) Acts 1987, 1988, 2001 and 2006
◆ Water Act 1989
◆ Environmental Protection Act 1990
◆ Crofters (Scotland) Act 1993
◆ Town and Country Planning (Scotland) Act 1997
◆ Abolition of Feudal Tenure (Scotland) Act 2000
◆ Water Industry (Scotland) Act 2002
◆ Agricultural Holdings (Scotland) Act 2003
◆ Land Reform (Scotland) Act 2003
◆ Salmon and Freshwater Fisheries (Consolidation) Act 2003
◆ Title Conditions (Scotland) Act 2003
◆ Anti-social Behaviour (Scotland) Act 2004
◆ Tenements (Scotland) Act 2004

Common Law Restrictions imposed on a landowner

This area of law is primarily concerned with the 'law of the neighbourhood'. Very simply, a landowner is not permitted to use his property in a way that causes harm to his neighbours or their property (*sic utere tuo ut alienum non laedas*). This area of the law is very much part of the law of delict. A delict is a civil wrong causing loss or damage to another person. A landowner's liability for harmful conduct can arise under two headings:

◆ Nuisance and
◆ Spiteful use of property rights.

 Key point: A landowner must use his property in a reasonable and responsible manner so that he does no harm to his neighbours.

Nuisance

As has previously been stated, a landowner must behave in a considerate fashion towards his neighbours. A landowner who uses his property in a manner that causes harm or interference to a neighbour's property may find that the neighbour decides to take legal action against him on the grounds that his inconsiderate behaviour should be regarded as a nuisance. It is important to state from the outset that the courts will make a finding of nuisance against a landowner if the harmful behaviour is part of a regular and ongoing pattern. The neighbour who, once in a blue moon, plays music a little too loudly during the early hours of the morning will not generally fall foul of the laws regulating nuisance behaviour. Examples of nuisance include unacceptable levels of noise, neighbour's animals (especially dogs) which foul communal areas or cause damage to property, illegal dumping of rubbish or toxic chemicals/substances, carrying on commercial or industrial activities in a residential area and anti-social behaviour generally. Harmful occurrences which are caused by nature are not usually regarded as a nuisance.

Anti-Social Behaviour

Since 30 April 2006, all private landlords in Scotland have had to be registered. In order to complete the registration process successfully, private landlords have to be vetted to ensure that they are 'fit and proper persons'. In practice, people with certain types of criminal convictions e.g. violence or dishonesty who are seeking landlord registration may find that they are not permitted to register. This, of course, means that they will not be able to let their properties to prospective tenants.

This major reform was introduced as a result of the Anti-Social Behaviour (Scotland) Act 2004 and is a deliberate attempt to target irresponsible private landlords who fail to regulate the behaviour of their tenants. It is also about driving up standards and forcing private landlords to take their duties to their tenants and the wider community seriously. Feckless or irresponsible landlords can cause all sorts of harm and an anti-social tenant can be the cause of misery for owners and residents of neighbouring properties. Landlords are now being encouraged to stipulate in a contract of lease what kinds of behaviour are acceptable by tenants and what is not acceptable so that there can be no room for doubt if and when a complaint arises in connection with a tenant's use of the property.

It was thought that by making private landlords directly responsible for anti-social tenants, that many problems could be sorted out quickly and effectively. Landlords who refuse to take seriously complaints about tenants could find themselves at the sharp end of various legal penalties. The local council may eventually feel that enough is enough and wrest control of the property from the landlord. This would mean that the council would be responsible for administering the property and could withhold rental income from the landlord.

Landlords owning properties in several local council areas will be expected to register their interests, but registration does last for three years and then will have to be renewed. On a positive note, the fee for registration is not particularly high and will be within the means of most private landlords.

 Key point: The Anti-Social Behaviour (Scotland) Act 2004 now means that private landlords could be held directly responsible for those of its tenants who behave in an anti-social fashion by indulging in a range of activities which are regulated by the Scots Law of Nuisance.

Remedies for nuisance behaviour and limitation of actions

The remedies of damages and/or interdict (a court order that prevents the defender from repeating the harmful behaviour) are available to the neighbour of a landowner who is causing a nuisance.

In terms of the Prescription and Limitation (Scotland) Act 1973, a pursuer may lose the right to raise an action if he has consented to or tolerated a neighbour's nuisance activities for over twenty years (the negative prescription period). A pursuer who belatedly decides to complain after twenty years have passed will be regarded as having acquiesced (i.e. given in) to the nuisance. Twenty years, after all, is more than an adequate period of time in which to raise a complaint. However, should someone new move to the neighbourhood and rightly raise objections to the nuisance, the person causing the nuisance cannot rely on the fact that previous or existing neighbours fell foul of the negative prescription period. The new neighbour will have every right to take legal action against the individual causing the nuisance.

If the remedy of interdict is sought by the pursuer, there is no need to prove or imply fault on the part of the defender. The defender's liability is said to be strict. If the nuisance has caused loss or damage to the property and the pursuer is seeking compensation he must prove fault on the part of the defender.

Judicial attitudes towards nuisance actions

 A particularly interesting example of nuisance arose in **Webster v Lord Advocate (1984)**. Miss Webster had purchased a flat within the vicinity of Edinburgh Castle. Miss Webster's enjoyment of her property, however, was spoiled by preparations for the annual Edinburgh Military Tattoo. The Tattoo was (and still is) a cultural and social event of international importance in the life of the City of Edinburgh. Deafening levels of noise were caused by workmen who were involved in the construction of a grandstand for spectators of the Tattoo. The grandstand was being raised on the Castle Esplanade and, consequently, was very close to Miss Webster's flat.

Miss Webster objected to the level of noise caused by the construction of the grandstand and, consequently, she raised an action against the organisers of the Tattoo claiming that their activities in preparation for the event should be regarded as a nuisance. The court found itself agreeing with Miss Webster that the noise caused by the preparations was a nuisance. The defender's argument that Miss Webster could reduce the level of noise suffered by her by shutting her windows or by installing double-glazing did not impress the court. Miss Webster stated, not unreasonably, that: 'One of the nice things about summer is that you are able to open your windows.'

Clearly, the court was faced with the conflicting interests in this case – Miss Webster's completely reasonable expectation that she be allowed to enjoy her property, and the fact that the Tattoo played a very important role in relation to Edinburgh's tourist industry. Lord Stott was only too aware of this when he remarked: 'I was left in no doubt that the Tattoo is a spectacle appreciated by the public and a valuable publicity and commercial asset to the city.'

The noise generated from the construction of the grandstand was a nuisance that no reasonable person should have to tolerate. Miss Webster was being prevented from enjoying her property to the fullest extent. Significantly, however, the court was not saying that the Tattoo should be banned, but the preparations for this important event in the cultural life of the City of Edinburgh could be achieved without an unacceptable level of noise being caused. The authorities responsible for the organisation of the Tattoo would have to be much more considerate of the rights of those people who lived within the vicinity of the Castle Esplanade and who would be directly affected by the noise.

 Miller v Jackson (1977) the pursuers moved into a house which was located next to a cricket ground. It was very common for a large number of cricket balls to be hit into the pursuers' garden. This was such a common event that the pursuers applied for an interdict in order to stop the cricket club from holding any further games. The cricket club stated that the pursuers had known about the existence of the cricket ground before they had moved into their house. The pursuers, therefore, had come to the nuisance of their own free will.

Held: by the English Court of Appeal that the cricket club's attempt to argue that the pursuers had come to the nuisance of their own free will must fail. However, the cricket ground went on to win the case using a different argument. The point is well made by this decision that, an attempt to justify the continuation of a nuisance activity, will not meet a sympathetic response if the defender argues that he was there first and is, therefore, justified in acting in a harmful way.

 In the House of Lords decision **RHM Bakeries (Scotland) Ltd v Strathclyde Regional Council (1985)**, it was held that a pursuer will only be successful in a claim for damages in relation to a harm caused by nuisance if he can successfully demonstrate that the nuisance was caused as a result of the defender's acts or omissions. In other words, the pursuer must prove that the defender was at fault. In this case, a bakery was flooded owing to the collapse of a sewer. The flooding caused damage to food and packaging materials which were stored in the bakery. The responsibility for maintaining the sewer lay with the Regional Council. The pursuer's action was dismissed by the House of Lords because it failed to prove that the defender (the Regional Council) had been negligent as regards its responsibility for maintaining the sewer.

The RHM Bakeries case appeared to depart from the reasoning of the House of Lords in **Caledonian Railway Company v Greenock Corporation (1917)**. However, the House of Lords was at pains to stress that the legal issues in **Caledonian Railway Company** were quite different. The defenders, in the earlier House of Lords' decision, were strictly liable because they had deliberately diverted the natural direction of a stream. The **RHM Bakeries** case, on the other hand, was not concerned with damage caused by unnatural use of property and the issue centred around whether the defender had failed to take reasonable care to maintain the sewer.

 The judicial reasoning underpinning the **RHM Bakeries** decision was followed in **Argyll and Clyde Health Board v Strathclyde Regional Council (1988)**. The pursuer sought compensation for flood damage caused to a field that it owned. The flood damage had occurred when a water-pipe owned by the defender burst. The water-pipe in question was buried below the surface of the field.

Held: the pursuer's action for damages was dismissed because it had failed to prove that the defender's negligence had caused the water-pipe to burst.

The claim might have been treated more sympathetically if the pursuer had been able to show that the damage to the property had been caused by a failure on the part of the defender to inspect and maintain the pipe on a regular basis.

 Hunter v Canary Wharf Ltd and London Docklands Development Corporation Ltd [1997] is one of the most recent and high profile actions dealing with nuisance to come before the House of Lords. In this case, hundreds of residents of an area in London sued for damages in relation to the huge amounts of dust generated from construction activity at the massive Canary Wharf site and the interference that the construction work caused to television signals. The House of Lords essentially stated that dust was a feature of urban life and that the builders could not have known that the construction work would affect television signals. All the claims for damages were dismissed. Furthermore, their Lordships stated that someone bringing a claim for damages in a nuisance action must have an interest in the land. All the pursuers in this case lacked an interest in the land and, therefore, they did not have the right to bring an action. This case also considered the issue of a defence to nuisance on the grounds of compliance with statutory authority. The Canary Wharf project had received fast-track planning permission by virtue of statutory regulations which had established the London Docklands Development Agency, the body created for the purpose of regenerating that particular area of the City. Their Lordships, however, rejected the argument that Parliament had conferred immunity on certain buildings in relation to actions for nuisance.

For a recent consideration of the approach by the Court of Session to alleged nuisance activities see **Canmore Housing Association v Bairnsfather (t/a BR Autos) [2004]** (above).

 Key point: Nuisance is harmful conduct or behaviour which is not a one-off event, but rather an ongoing series of incidents which harm a neighbour's enjoyment of his property.

Possible defences to a nuisance action

An individual causing a nuisance cannot make use the following arguments as defences if he is responsible for causing a nuisance. They will usually end in failure for the defender.

◆ A neighbour should not have purchased the property if he had known of the existence of the nuisance (see **Miller v Jackson (1977)** and **Webster v Lord Advocate (1984)**)
◆ The nuisance benefits the public in some way (see **Webster v Lord Advocate (1984)**)
◆ The complainer has contributed to the nuisance
◆ The nuisance is merely the net result of the owner's ordinary use of his property

Statutory authority

A defender will really only be able to justify a nuisance if he can prove that the nuisance occurred as a result of his compliance with statutory authority (see **Hunter *v* Canary Wharf Ltd and London Docklands Development Corporation Ltd [1997]** above).

 Lord Advocate *v* North British Railways (1894) waste which was being disposed of under statutory authority was deposited close to an army barracks. The aim of this particular statute could have been complied with by the defender disposing of the waste at another more suitable location. Accordingly, the court was not impressed by the railway company's attempt to use this defence.

 Allen *v* Gulf Oil Refining (1981) local residents attempted to bring an action alleging nuisance against the operators of an oil refinery. The operators' defence was that the nuisance was a natural result of running the refinery and they had a statutory right to do so. The particular Act had given the operators the right to purchase compulsorily the land on which the refinery was to be built, but it did not appear to give the operators immunity from being sued in a nuisance action by the local residents.

Held: by the House of Lords that a power could be implied into the Act which prevented the operators from being sued in a nuisance action for the way in which they ran the refinery.

Whether an activity will be classed as a nuisance will very much depend on the location of the property. Activities which may be tolerated in the countryside may well meet condemnation in an urban or residential area.

 Key point: The only competent defence to a nuisance action is for the defender to show that the action complained of has been authorised by statute.

Aemulationem vicini or spiteful use of property rights

This delict reinforces the fact that a landowner will have to act in a responsible and reasonable way when he exercises his property rights in relation to his neighbours. *Aemulationem vicini* deals with situations where a landowner has certain, legally recognised property rights but he chooses to exercise these rights in a completely unjustified way with the deliberate intention of causing distress or inconvenience to a neighbour. The landowner's reason for behaving in this fashion is usually motivated by a sense of spite or malice towards his neighbours. In order for a pursuer to have any chance of success with this type of action, he will have to show that the landowner has used his legitimate rights in a way that is malicious. The spiteful behaviour is intended to prevent the neighbour making full use of his own property rights. A pursuer would be quite justified in raising a claim of *aemulationem vicini* in relation to spiteful behaviour that has occurred just once. There is no need for the pursuer to demonstrate that the behaviour complained of is part of an ongoing series of occurrences. The pursuer is entitled to ask the courts to grant an interdict and a claim for damages may also be competent.

An example of *aemulationem vicini* arose in **Campbell v Muir (1908)**. In this case, the defender conducted himself in a totally malicious fashion whereby he brought his boat as close to the river bank as possible in an attempt to stop anglers who were situated on the bank from casting out their fishing lines into the river. The defender was perfectly entitled to exercise his right to fish from the river using his boat, but he was not permitted to do this in a manner that blatantly interfered with the rights of other anglers. The defender's actions were motivated by spite and the court granted an interdict to stop this behaviour from reoccurring.

The House of Lords has stated in **Bradford v Pickles [1895]** that *aemulationem vicini* was not a concept recognised by the law of England. This statement stands somewhat at odds with some English decisions (**Christie v Davey (1893)** and **Hollywood Silver Fox Farm Ltd v Emmett (1936)**) which were most certainly concerned with spiteful use of property rights (or malice as the English would say).

 Christie v Davey (1893) Christie was a piano teacher and she and Davey, her neighbour did not get along. Christie's music students came to her house for piano lessons. Davey was aware of this and when the students were present in his neighbour's house, he made as much noise as possible to disrupt lessons. Christie also held musical social events in her house and Davey attempted to disrupt these too.

Held: although Davey was on his own property, he was behaving in a spiteful and malicious fashion which could not be permitted to continue.

 Hollywood Silver Fox Farm Ltd v Emmett (1936) Emmett had the right to shoot game on his land. He was in dispute with his neighbour who bred silver foxes so that they could later be killed for their fur to make clothing. The foxes were very sensitive to things like loud noises and were easily frightened. Their sensitivity to noise and other stimuli was at its height during the breeding season. Vixens who were put into such a state of fear and alarm by loud noises often killed their offspring. Emmett was aware of these facts and he went to the edge of his property and fired a gun into the air. He wanted to create as much noise as possible in order to frighten the creatures and, in turn, harm his neighbour's business. The neighbour later took legal action against Emmett for using his property in a malicious or spiteful fashion and causing a nuisance. Emmett countered by stating that he was legally entitled to use a gun for hunting purposes anywhere on his property.

Held: although Emmett was carrying on an activity which was perfectly legal, he was going about his business in a spiteful manner. He was ordered to pay £250 in compensation and he was prevented from behaving this way in the future.

In **Bradford v Pickles**, Lord Watson, the Scottish Lord of Appeal in Ordinary, stated:

'No use of property, which would be legal if due to a proper motive, can become illegal because it is prompted by a motive which is improper or even malicious.'

Lord Watson's statement has been challenged by some leading Scottish lawyers and academics. Professor Joseph Thomson has argued that Lord Watson's confident assertion flew in the face of accepted Scottish legal practice. Lord Watson's statement of Scots law seems to have had little influence on the outcome of the decisions in **Campbell v Muir (1908)** and in **More v Boyle (1967)** (a later decision of the Sheriff Court). In any case, it should be remembered that, strictly speaking, Lord Watson was speaking *obiter* and his remarks did not form part of the *ratio decidendi* of the actual judgement in **Bradford v Pickles**.

Lord Brodie briefly addressed the issue of spiteful use of property rights and its application to Scots law in **Canmore Housing Association v Bairnsfather (t/a BR Autos) [2004] (above)**. His Lordship did concede that there was general acceptance that Lord Watson's *obiter* statement in **Bradford v Pickles** 'is far too widely stated,' but he refused to be drawn any further. Somewhat regrettably, an opportunity to clarify the law relating to *aemulationem vicini* was lost.

 Key point: Merely because a landowner has property rights does not mean that he can exercise them in a deliberately spiteful fashion which causes loss or injury to other property owners.

Agreements imposing restrictions on land use

A property owner drew up an agreement with a neighbour which imposed conditions or burdens upon the land. This agreement may prevent the landowner from using his property in a particular way or it may grant the neighbour certain (real) rights over the property. A servitude is an example of a burden imposed on land e.g. a right to use a footpath across someone's land.

An important issue for us to think about is that these agreements often survive changes in ownership of the property. They are said to run with the land and these agreements will legally bind past, present and future owners of the property. Landowners can have many restrictions removed from property by appealing to the Lands Tribunal for Scotland (see Chapter 1). However, many of the outdated feudal conditions imposed on land were abolished when the Abolition of Feudal Tenure (Scotland) Act 2000 was brought into force in November 2004. The feudal system of landownership should not be viewed in entirely negative terms. Some feudal charters were useful in that they prevented landowners from carrying on certain types of activities that would be classified as nuisance. Many of these burdens contained in the old feudal charters may actually be preserved under the new system of land ownership which will operate from November 2004 onwards and which will be recognised by the Title Conditions (Scotland) Act 2003.

 Key point: Landowners can agree not to carry on activities which would be regarded as causing a nuisance, but these agreements will often survive changes of ownership of the land.

Interference with the natural course of a river or burn or non-natural use of water

Very often, rivers or burns will flow through a landowner's property. A landowner will have to be particularly sensitive to the rights of third parties where such a river or burn is concerned, especially if the water flows out of his property and into neighbouring properties. A landowner most certainly would not be allowed to alter or change the course of a water-channel (a river or burn) for irrigation and manufacturing purposes if this action interfered with the rights of his neighbours. These neighbours may also rely on the water from the river or burn in question for their own legitimate purposes. A landowner will be allowed to divert the course of a burn or a stream as long as this does not reduce the flow of water to his neighbours downriver. Diverting the course of a river or a burn landowner is, after all, interfering with the natural order of things and the dangers of flooding and pollution should always be uppermost in the mind of the landowner. The important question that the landowner should ask is: how will these activities affect my neighbours? A landowner will clearly incur delictual liability if his activities cause loss or damage to his neighbours, but he might like also to recall the provisions of the Water Act 1989 which make it an criminal offence for an individual to pollute a river or a burn.

In situations where a landowner takes it upon himself to alter or divert the course of a stream, the Scottish courts impose the burden of strict liability. This means that, where another landowner who has suffered loss or injury as a result of the defender's interference with the natural course of the stream or river, he will not be inconvenienced by the small matter of having to prove fault. This area of delict is commonly referred to as non-natural use of water. The dangers for a landowner when he decides to alter or interfere with the course of streams or rivers are all too obvious as **Kerr v Earl of Orkney (1857)** and **Caledonian Railway Company v Greenock Corporation (1917)** demonstrate.

 In **Kerr v Earl of Orkney (1857)**, the defender went ahead with plans to construct a dam on his property which had the effect of reducing the flow of water to his downstream neighbours. Four months later, after several days of heavy rain, the dam burst and a torrent of water was released which swept downstream and completely destroyed the pursuer's property. The pursuer's argument centred around the fact that the defender's decision to build the dam had interfered with the natural flow of the burn which created the conditions which led, ultimately, to the destruction of his property (his mill and houses were completely swept away by the torrent). The defender attempted to escape liability by claiming that the unfortunate incident was an act of God (*damnum fatale*). This defence, the only possible one that the defender could plead, did not find favour with the court. The defender was strictly liable for his actions in relation to diverting the natural flow of the burn for the purpose of building the dam. If the defender had not interfered with nature in the first place, the horrific damage to the pursuer's property would not have occurred.

When the defender puts forward a defence of *damnum fatale*, he is effectively arguing that an event has occurred which was not reasonably foreseeable and that no amount of precautions or safety measures put in place by a reasonable person would have prevented the harm from occurring. A huge tidal wave engulfing the City of Aberdeen might properly be regarded as an act of God or an example of *damnum fatale*, but heavy rainfall in Scotland is very unlikely to qualify for admission to the league of truly catastrophic disasters outwith human control and foresight.

 Caledonian Railway Company *v* Greenock Corporation (1917)
Greenock Corporation diverted the course of a burn in order to fill a paddling pool. Later, heavy rainfall occurred which was unusual for Greenock at the time, but not for the rest of Scotland which habitually experienced very heavy rainfall. Subsequently, the paddling pool could not cope with the excess water and, as a result, it overflowed causing flood damage to the pursuer's property. The House of Lords awarded damages to the pursuer on the basis that Greenock Corporation should be held strictly liable for its decision to interfere with the course of the burn to create the paddling pool. This decision follows **Kerr** and emphasises the fact that a landowner will act at his peril if he alters or diverts the course of a water-channel.

The House of Lords, in a number of modern cases, has reaffirmed the burden of strict liability as illustrated by **Kerr** and **Caledonian Railway Company**. In **RHM Bakeries (Scotland) Ltd *v* Strathclyde Regional Council (1985)**, the House of Lords was at pains to point out that a landowner who diverts the course of a stream which causes damage to another person's property will continue to be held strictly liable.

 Key point: In such cases where the individual diverts the course of a stream or a river, he will find himself strictly liable for his actions i.e. another landowner who has suffered loss as a result of the individual's actions has no need to prove fault.

Strict liability

So far in relation to the defender's liability for wrongful acts which cause harm, negligence has to be proved by the pursuer and this can be difficult to establish in many cases. The defender must owe a duty of care to the pursuer and, furthermore, it must be shown that he has failed to take reasonable care. In many cases, the defender is able to escape liability where he can satisfy the court that he has taken reasonable care.

Strict liability is different because there is no defence available to the defender to claim that he had taken all reasonable care to prevent the harm. Where there is strict liability, reasonable care is not enough. In other words, the pursuer is not under an obligation to prove negligence by the defender and this puts the pursuer in an immediately stronger position. We have already discussed the concept of strict liability in relation to non-natural use of water (above).

Strict liability as laid down by statute covers two important areas:

◆ Liability for animals
◆ Product liability

 Key point: In situations where the defender is said to be strictly liable, the pursuer does not have to prove fault and it will do the defender no good if he claims that he took reasonable care to avoid causing loss or injury to the pursuer.

Liability for animals

This area is now governed by the Animals (Scotland) Act 1987. Section 1 of the 1987 Act states that:

'if an animal belongs to a species whose members generally are, by virtue of their physical attributes or habits, likely (unless controlled or restrained) to injure severely or kill persons or animals, or damage property to a material extent, the keeper of the animal is (strictly) liable for any injury or damage caused by the animal and directly referable to these physical attributes or habits.'

This means that if you are the keeper of any animal that is covered by Section 1 of the Act and the animal causes injury or death to other persons or animals then you will be strictly liable for the harm caused. Liability cannot be escaped by showing that you took reasonable care and negligence does not have to be shown by the pursuer. Strict liability means that you must have taken effective precautions to stop the injury occurring in the first instance.

 Burton *v* Moorhead (1881) an extremely aggressive dog attacked the pursuer and injured him. The keeper of the animal tried to defend himself by stating that a strong chain was used for restraining purposes and that this chain normally did the trick. Unfortunately, the keeper's defence that he thought the chain was more than adequate to restrain the dog was simply not good enough. The keeper was fully aware of the dog's nature and, with this knowledge, he should have taken special precautions (not reasonable care) to make sure that the dog was prevented from harming passers-by.

 Behrens *v* Bertram Mills Circus (1957) the pursuer, a circus performer was injured by a circus elephant and he sued the circus. The circus claimed that the animal was extremely well trained, but the court felt that the circus should be judged according to the burden of strict liability. The circus should have taken special precautions to prevent the elephant from causing harm. The fact that the animal had not previously injured anyone was not enough to allow the circus to escape liability to the pursuer.

 Welsh *v* Brady (2009) Welsh (the pursuer) was out walking her Golden Retriever, Cava, in an open field at her home in the village of Wellbank near Dundee. Brady (the defender) accompanied by his four year old daughter was also present in the field with his dog, a black Labrador, called Ebony. Both dogs were running around the field together quite happily. Eventually, Welsh decided to leave the field and she called on her dog to return to her side which the animal did. Unfortunately, Brady's Labrador also ran towards Welsh and collided with her thus causing Welsh to suffer serious injury to her right knee (the Labrador weighed about 25 kilograms and struck Welsh with 'considerable force'). Welsh sought damages of £160,000 from Brady on the basis that he was strictly liable as the keeper of the dog in terms of Section 1 of the Animals (Scotland) Act 1987 and under the common law of negligence.

Held: by the Extra Division of the Inner House of the Court of Session that the defender should be absolved of any guilt or liability both in terms of the statute or the common law. In particular, the judges were of the opinion that the conditions for strict liability found in Section 1 of the Animals (Scotland) Act 1987 had not been satisfied. These conditions are:

> A person shall be liable for any injury or damage caused by an animal if:
> (a) at the time of the injury or damage complained of, he was a keeper of the animal;
> (b) the animal belongs to a species whose members generally are by virtue of their physical attributes or habits likely (unless controlled or restrained) to injure severely or kill persons or animals, or damage property to a material extent; and
> (c) the injury or damage complained of is directly referable to such physical attributes or habits.

There was no doubt that the defender was the keeper of the Labrador, so the key question simply revolved around whether he should be held strictly liable for the animal's actions. In other words, were black Labradors likely (unless controlled or restrained) to injure severely or kill a person and could such an injury be directly referable to such physical attributes or habits? Despite the pursuer relying on the testimony of an expert in dogs and dog-handling, the judges of the Extra Division stated that:

> 'It went no distance at all towards demonstrating that black Labradors (or any sub-division of the breed, whether by reference to age, sex or any other criterion) are, by virtue of their physical attributes or habits, likely to injure severely or kill persons or animals.'

According to Section 5 of the Animals (Scotland) Act 1987, the keeper of the animal is deemed to be the person who:

◆ Is the owner

or

◆ Has possession of the animal at the time

or

◆ Has actual care or control of a child under 16 who is the owner or has possession of the animal

The keeper of an animal will remain strictly liable for injuries or damage caused by an animal for which he has responsibility, even where it has managed to escape from his custody or in situations where has abandoned it. A third party who finds such an animal and takes it into his custody will not become liable for it. However, if this third party adopted the animal as his own, then the burden of strict liability would now apply to him.

Defences available to the owner are the following:

◆ If the injury or damage was due wholly to the fault of the pursuer, for example, where the pursuer goaded a docile animal which then attacked the pursuer in defence

◆ Where the pursuer has voluntarily accepted the risk i.e. *volenti non fit injuria*

 Key point: A keeper of an animal will be strictly liable for any loss or injury that the animal has caused to the pursuer's person or property.

Product liability

The Sale of Goods Act 1979 (as amended) incorporates implied terms into a contract of sale to protect the buyer. In particular, Section 14 of the Act provides remedies to the buyer where the goods in question are dangerous and their use results in personal injury or property damage being suffered by the buyer. This piece of legislation is, however, designed only to protect the buyer of goods i.e. someone who has a contractual relationship with the seller. In **Donoghue v Stevenson (1932)** it was Mrs Donoghue's friend who had bought the defective product from Mr Minchella, the Paisley café owner. As a result, Mrs Donoghue had to sue the manufacturer of the ginger beer bottle that contained the decomposing snail because she did not have a contract with the seller and, furthermore, the seller could not be expected to open every sealed bottle of ginger beer in order to make sure that they were completely safe. It will also be recalled that bottles were not made of clear glass or clear plastic which might have assisted the seller in an examination to ensure that the products were safe.

In other situations, for example, where the product was given as a gift or if the pursuer was a bystander who was injured by the product, there would be no legal remedy under the Sale of Goods Act 1979 (as amended). There are a number of legal options that are available to someone who has suffered damage to property or a personal injury as a result of using a dangerous product or coming into contact with such a product. We are already well aware of the existence of the standard test for negligence as laid down in **Donoghue v Stevenson (1932)**. This case established the rule that a manufacturer owes a duty of care to anyone who may use his products or come into close contact with these products. Alternatively, however, a pursuer who has suffered harm as a result of a dangerous product can now make use of Part 1 of the Consumer Protection Act 1987. Unlike the test for negligence in **Donoghue v Stevenson (1932)**, the Consumer Protection Act 1987 imposes a burden of strict liability on the producer of the goods. We shall discuss the Consumer Protection Act 1987 and its regime of strict liability in respect of dangerous and defective products more fully in Chapter 4.

The Consumer Protection Act 1987

This Act brought into force the European Community Directive on Product Liability (Directive 85/374/EEC). Part 1 of the Act establishes a regime of strict liability in relation to defective products which cause damage to other property and/or injuries to people who were injured as a result of using the product or coming into close contact with the product. Strict liability, it is important to remember, means that the pursuer does not have to prove fault. In other words, strict liability automatically presumes that the defect in the product must be the fault of the producer of the goods – there is no other reasonable explanation for the defect. The producer must come up with a credible explanation to show why he is not to blame for the injuries or loss that the pursuer has suffered. Part 1 of the Act provides a civil remedy for those individuals who have suffered injury, loss or damage caused by a defective product. Part 1 of the Act is, therefore, not concerned with criminal liability in relation to the supply of defective and dangerous products.

A pursuer will be prevented from raising an action under the Act if the defective product was supplied before 1 March 1988. Furthermore, a producer cannot be held liable after ten years have passed since the date of supply of the product and any claims involving claims of personal injury or death must be brought within a three-year period. Under Section 7 of the Act, a producer cannot exclude or limit his liability for defective goods by means of exclusion or limitation clauses.

Parts 2 and 3 of the Act deal with criminal offences. The Act is admittedly complicated as it operates within both the civil and the criminal law.

 Key point: Part 1 of the Consumer Protection Act 1987 establishes a regime of strict liability where goods that are dangerous cause loss or injury to the pursuer.

Summary

- The law of delict is concerned with the defender's wrongful behaviour.

- Wrongful behaviour can have both criminal and civil consequences, but the law of delict is only concerned with the civil consequences of a wrongful act or omission.

- Delict is a very different area of law from contractual obligations. With contracts, the parties enter the agreement of their own free will – they are not forced to contract with one another. The law of delict is not about personal choice – we all owe a duty of care to other people and we are expected to comply with this duty.

- Delicts which are committed unintentionally by the defender resulting in loss, injury or damage to the pursuer are the most common type of civil wrong. In these situations, the defender is said to have been negligent or careless.

- Damages in a delictual action are awarded for personal injuries (whether physical or psychiatric) and for damage to property.

- Where the pursuer has suffered financial or pure economic loss as a result of the defender's negligent actions, the courts are much more reluctant to grant compensation.

- The courts will sometimes award damages for pure economic loss, but there must be evidence to show that the parties had a special relationship with one another.

- The leading case for negligence claims is **Donoghue v Stevenson (1932)**.

- The rule in **Donoghue v Stevenson** is that you must take reasonable care to avoid acts or omissions which you can reasonably foresee would be likely to injure your neighbour.

- The standard of care which is expected of the defender is one of reasonable care. Reasonable care is the standard of care expected of the 'hypothetical' reasonable man or woman who is a person of ordinary care and prudence and who is neither overcautious nor overconfident.

- Harmful conduct may be intentional, for example, assault or fraud.

- The civil remedies that are available to the injured party in a delictual are reparation and interdict.

- The general rule in Scotland is that there can be no delictual liability without fault. Quite simply, this means that the pursuer must prove, on the balance of probabilities that the defender's actions caused him to suffer loss, injury or damage.

- In certain situations, the defender's liability is said to be strict. In other words, the law automatically presumes that the defender is to blame for the harm caused to the pursuer.

- The most common defences that are used by the defender in an action of delict are:

  a) Contributory negligence

  b) *Volenti non fit injuria* (to one who is willing a wrongful act cannot be done)

  c) Prescription and limitation

  d) Compliance with statutory authority

  e) Necessity

  f) *Damnum fatale*

  g) Criminality

Test your knowledge

Short answer questions, exam standard essay style questions and case-studies.

1 The starting point for a pursuer in a negligence action is that he will have to prove that the defender owed him a duty care and that the defender's subsequent actions have breached that duty of care causing him to suffer loss or injury.

What is a duty of care?

2 a) Aggie, Mahmoud, Tom and Paul are neighbours who live in a shared property which has a communal back garden. There appears to be a problem with the property's water and sewerage system which has caused the back garden to be flooded on a number of occasions. The four property owners hold a meeting to discuss the best way of tackling the problem. Paul is friendly with a plumber and he suggests that they call the plumber in to carry out some basic exploratory work in order to trace the source of the problem. The other three think that Paul's suggestion is an excellent one and they tell him to go ahead and contact the plumber. The following week, Harry, the plumber, comes along to look at the water and sewerage system. Harry is under strict instructions from Paul to carry out a survey, but he is not authorised to dig up the garden. Harry carries out the survey and informs Paul that the local water company will have to be informed as the water and sewerage system appears to be in a serious state of disrepair. A week later, Paul receives a letter from Aggie's solicitor informing him that Aggie intends to sue him for £10,000 in an ordinary action at the local Sheriff Court. Apparently, Aggie is claiming that she broke her ankle when she fell into a twenty-two foot trench in the back garden. Aggie states that Paul and Harry dug this trench during the survey. Furthermore, Paul and Harry were negligent in that they did nothing to warn people about the existence of the trench.

What will Aggie have to prove in order to win her case?

b) Following on from the above incident involving Aggie, Paul and Harry, consider the following issues:

i) Paul and Harry deny digging a trench. Paul was away in London on business the day that the trench was allegedly dug and George claims that he merely carried out a survey.

ii) Paul's solicitor has a witness, Phil a window cleaner, who states that no trench was ever dug. Phil is a willing witness and he has absolutely nothing to gain by coming forward and offering to give evidence on Paul and Harry's behalf.

iii) Aggie produces one witness to back up her story, but under cross-examination by Paul's solicitor, she is forced to admit that she only saw Harry carrying out a survey in the back garden.

iv) During her evidence, Aggie begins to change her story and speak about a hole rather than a trench.

In the light of the above information, assess Aggie's chances of success at the trial.

3 a) In certain situations, a defender will be able to escape delictual liability by proving that he took all reasonable care to avoid causing loss or harm to the pursuer.

What is meant by reasonable care?

b) Graham is a keen golfer. One day when he was out on the course he was hit in the face by a golf ball. Due to this accident, Graham lost the sight in one eye. He successfully sued Lorne who hit the golf ball which caused the injury. Lorne is now claiming that the golf club should also take part of the blame for Graham's injuries. Lorne is arguing that the golf club should have put up a fence or a screen to protect golfers at the first hole from being hit by golfers teeing off at the second hole. The golf club did put up a sign which asked golfers on the second hole not to tee off until those golfers at the first tee had already done so, but this rule is hardly ever obeyed in practice. The golf club claims that it consulted an expert who advised them not to erect a fence or a screen between these two holes as it would do nothing to prevent the likelihood of accidents. Furthermore, over a million rounds of golf have been played on the course and only one accident at that particular spot has occurred (and it was by no means a serious accident).

Do you think that the golf club has taken reasonable care to prevent accidents from occurring?

4 A group of teenage boys who are currently serving sentences in a young offenders institution are taken on an adventure holiday. They are staying at a centre near Loch Lomond which caters towards the rehabilitation of young offenders. None of the boys is considered a threat to members of the public. On the last evening of the holiday, the staff who have accompanied the boys are so pleased with the success of the holiday that they decide to leave the boys unsupervised and head for a celebratory drink in the local pub. The boys are soon bored with nothing to do. Seeing an opportunity to liven things up, one of the older boys persuades some of the younger members of the group that it would be a good idea to go for a drive as it is a lovely summer's evening. In any case, they will all be back before the pub's closing time and no one will miss them for a few hours. They decide to borrow the centre's minibus and they decide to go on a tour up the western side of the Loch. None of the boys is a qualified driver. On the way up the road, the boy driving the minibus is forced off the road in order to avoid a sheep that was blocking the way. Although no one was injured in the accident, the minibus is a complete write-off and a farmer's wall has been extensively damaged. As a result, the farmer's sheep managed to escape from the field. It is only later that the farmer discovers that some of his lambs have drowned in the loch.

Evaluate the above situation.

5 a) As a general rule, the Scottish courts do not award damages to a pursuer in situations where the defender's behaviour causes the pursuer to suffer pure economic loss.

Evaluate this statement.

b) McBurney Leisure Services PLC has just entered a contract with builders who have been hired to build a new, luxury hotel. Each bathroom in the hotel will be fully tiled using only the best materials. In order to complete this task, the builders have recommended that McBurney use a particular firm of specialist subcontractors with which the builders have had extensive dealings. McBurney relied upon this recommendation and allowed the builders to use the subcontractors. After the completion of the bathrooms, however, it was discovered that many of the tiles had not been properly secured to the walls. The tiles in no way pose a danger to guests and staff, but this is a luxury hotel and the guests are likely to be unimpressed by the poor quality of the decor in their bathrooms. McBurney has

had to spend a lot of money in order to repair the defective tiling. McBurney now wishes to take action against the builders claiming that it was negligent when it recommended the specialist subcontractors.

Should the builders be liable in negligence to McBurney for recommending the subcontractors?

6 Write short notes on the following matters:
a) The *causa causans* and the *causa sine qua non*
b) A *novus actus interveniens*.

7 a) In Scots law, who will have primary responsibility for animals that cause damage to property or cause harm or injury to other animals or humans?

b) Jan is driving her car along the promenade at Ayr Beach. Drivers are expected to observe a 20-mile-an-hour speed limit on this promenade because the road is next to a large grassy area where lots of children play. Jan is a very careful and experienced driver and she is observing the speed limit. Suddenly, Jan has to brake very hard in order to avoid a dog that has run out into the middle of the road. Unfortunately, Jan is unable to stop her car from hitting the dog. The dog is badly injured, but it will survive the accident if it receives immediate medical attention from a vet. The collision has also caused several hundred pounds worth of damage to Jan's car. It turns out that a 15-year-old boy (the owner's son) had responsibility for the dog. The boy had the dog on a leash but he was busy having a conversation on his mobile phone when the dog broke free and ran out into the path of Jan's car. This fact does not prevent the dog's owner from sending Jan a solicitor's letter demanding payment of the vet's bill. Jan is understandably enraged about this turn of events. After all, she took the boy with the injured dog straight to the vet in order that the animal would receive prompt medical treatment.

What is the legal position?

8 When a pursuer raises a delictual action in the Scottish courts, he must always be able to demonstrate that his loss or injuries were caused by the fault of the defender in order for his claim to have any chance of success.

Assess the accuracy of this statement.

9 a) The Occupiers' Liability (Scotland) Act 1960 uses the term 'occupier' rather than the owner of a property.

What is the difference legally between an occupier and an owner?

b) Examine the following notice carefully:

> **WARNING NOTICE**
>
> DEMOLITION OF DANGEROUS STRUCTURE IN PROGRESS.
>
> UNDER NO CIRCUMSTANCES SHOULD MEMBERS OF THE PUBLIC ATTEMPT TO ENTER THESE PREMISES WITHOUT THE EXPRESS PERMISSION OF LYNCH DEMOLITION SERVICES LTD.
>
> MEMBERS OF THE PUBLIC RUN THE RISK OF SERIOUS INJURY OR EVEN DEATH IF THEY ENTER THE PREMISES UNACCOMPANIED BY KEY SITE PERSONNEL.
>
> VISITORS SHOULD REPORT TO DESMOND LYNCH, SITE MANAGER, IMMEDIATELY UPON ARRIVAL.
>
> LYNCH DEMOLITION SERVICES LTD, 190 WEST REGENT STREET, GLASGOW G2 1PR, T: 0141-242 0999

Lynch Demolition Services Ltd is currently in the process of demolishing a dangerous structure. As the job is a matter of urgency, the demolition team has not had time to put proper fencing around the site which would ensure that trespassers are kept out and other curious members of the public are kept at a safe distance. However, the demolition team has placed the above notice at a numerous points around the site and it has hired the services of a security firm to provide security guards who work a nine to five shift, Monday to Friday. Patrick Lynch, a Director of the demolition company, felt that it was unnecessary to retain the services of the security firm at the weekends. This decision was all part of a cost-cutting exercise. On Sunday afternoon, Desmond Lynch, the site manager and a Director of the company, receives some bad news from one of his foremen. It would seem that a four-year-old child has managed to gain access to the site and, while there, was badly injured as a result of part of a wall falling on him. The child's parents are threatening to sue Lynch Demolition Services Ltd.

Advise Lynch Demolition Services.

10 **a)** What are the main defences to a delictual action in Scotland?

b) Michael was visiting Paisley Zoo when he accidentally dropped his mobile phone into the lions' enclosure. The phone is very expensive and Michael is desperate to retrieve it. He looks about to see if any of the keepers are around, but he does not see anyone. Michael is a very impatient person and the only lion that appears to be in the cage is sound asleep. Michael decides to take a chance and he climbs over the wall and drops into the enclosure. He quickly picks up the phone and heads back to the wall without disturbing the lion. At that moment, however, his phone begins to ring (it is a very loud ring tone) and the lion awakens. It sees Michael standing below the wall and promptly gives chase. Five minutes later, Michael is dragged from the enclosure by the keepers, more dead than alive, after having received a savaging from a very angry lion that was awakened from a sound sleep. He is very lucky, a member of the public alerted the keepers and one of them managed to shoot the lion with a fast-acting tranquilliser dart. On his way to the ambulance, a delirious Michael was heard to mumble that the Zoo would be hearing from his lawyers.

Assuming that Michael survives his experience, would he be advised to raise an action against the Zoo?

11 **a)** In certain situations, the defender's negligence will be the only obvious explanation for the loss or injury suffered by the pursuer.

Explain the phrase *res ipsa loquiter* and use examples from previously decided cases to illustrate your answer.

b) Brian went in to use the toilets at his local supermarket before he began his weekly shopping. The toilet floors were very slippery because one of the supermarket's employees had just finished cleaning them. Thinking that the supermarket was quiet, the employee decided to nip up to the staff room for an unofficial cigarette break. The employee did not think it was worth putting up signs to warn customers that the toilet floor was dangerous. It was during the employee's absence that Brian came in to use the toilets. He slipped and fell heavily breaking his arm in the process. He was totally unaware that the floor was slippery and he did not see any warning signs.

How strong a claim does Brian have against the supermarket?

12 **a)** The decisions of the House of Lords in both **Alcock and Others *v* Chief Constable of the Yorkshire Police (1992)** and **White and Others *v* Chief Constable of the South Yorkshire Police (1998)** have clarified the law of delict in relation to claims involving nervous shock or psychiatric injury.

Explain the guidelines in relation to cases involving psychiatric injuries as laid down by the House of Lords in **Alcock** and **White**.

b) Pamela was driving along the motorway when she fell asleep at the wheel of her car. She collided with a school bus and both vehicles skidded out of control before stopping in such a position that three lanes of the motorway were completely blocked off. As a result of this accident, the driver and several school children were killed. Many of the school children were also seriously injured in the accident. Pamela's legs were broken as a result of the crash and she was not able to escape from the wreckage of her car. To make matters worse, visibility was dreadful that day and ten cars were not able to stop in time to avoid the wreckage of the first accident and a multiple pile-up occurred on the motorway. The emergency services are called out and have to deal with a truly horrific road accident. The accident also receives extensive media coverage and images of the crash are shown on the lunchtime, evening and late television news bulletins. The school is also named on these television programmes. Quite apart from the physical injuries that the victims have suffered in the accident, many are now claiming that they have gone on to experience psychiatric injury. Many relatives of the dead and injured have developed psychiatric illnesses which they claim were caused by the accident. Finally, several police officers, paramedics and fire personnel are bringing a legal action on the grounds that, since the accident, they have gone on to suffer from a variety of psychiatric conditions.

Using the legal principles laid down by the House of Lords in relation to claims involving psychiatric injury advise the pursuers.

c) Consider the following situation:

Tracy has just been released from the psychiatric unit of the local hospital. Tracy suffers terribly from a nervous condition for which she has to take medication in order to control it. Her home is situated not far from the motorway and she heard the crash involving Pamela and the school bus. Immediately afterwards, Tracy heard the sound of more cars being involved in a crash. Being in possession of a very curious nature, Tracy rushed to the side of the motorway and saw the immediate aftermath of the accident. She is absolutely horrified and she promptly suffers nervous shock. When Tracy regains consciousness, she realises that she has been admitted to the acute ward of the psychiatric unit. Tracy now wishes to sue the person who caused the accident on the motorway.

What are the chances of Tracy's claim succeeding?

13   Write explanatory notes on the following topics:
a) Trespass
b) Nuisance
c) Spiteful use of property rights
d) The *actio de effusis dejectis* and the *actio de positis vel suspensis*
e) Non-natural use of water

CHAPTER
4

CONSUMER LAW

Introduction

This chapter will focus on the rights of consumers. Consumer law is now a huge area as it covers sales of goods, the provision of consumer credit, product liability, the provision of services and unfair commercial practices by traders. As we shall see, this area of the law has been increasingly underpinned by statutory intervention in an attempt by Parliament to strengthen the rights of individual consumers

This chapter covers the following areas:

- Introduction to the Sale of Goods Act 1979 (as amended) •
- The classification of goods •
- Transfer of title •
- Implied terms •
- Delivery of goods •
- Remedies for breach of contract •
- The Consumer Protection Act 1987 •
- The Consumer Credit Act 1974 (as amended) •
- Unfair commercial practices by traders •
- Distance selling contracts •
- E-commerce contracts •
- The law governing services •

Introduction to the Sale of Goods Act 1979 (as amended)

The rules which govern sale of goods transactions are contained in the Sale of Goods Act 1979 (as amended). The original Act of 1893 codified many of the common law provisions regulating contracts for the sale of goods. The Act contains detailed rules governing contracts for the sale of goods. The Act applies to those contracts formed after 1 January 1894. Despite amendments, it can be argued that Sir MacKenzie Chalmers, who was responsible for drafting the original Act of 1893, would have little difficulty recognising many of the major provisions of the modern Sale of Goods

Act. This is why many of the cases used in this Chapter were decided by the courts before the introduction of the current version of the Sale of Goods Act. In other words, the rules relating to sale of goods transactions have survived in a remarkably consistent fashion over a long period of time.

 Key point: The rules which govern sale of goods transactions are contained in the Sale of Goods Act 1979 (as amended).

A genuine sale

Section 2 of the Sale of Goods Act 1979 defines a contract for the sale of goods as one where the seller transfers or agrees to transfer the property (ownership) of the goods for a money consideration called the price.

The provisions of the Act only apply to transactions that operate by way of a sale of goods contract. The Act does not apply to arrangements which operate by way of a mortgage, pledge, charge or other security arrangement (Section 62(4)). A security arrangement, for example, a mortgage arrangement is where a debtor grants security over an item of his property to a creditor in exchange for a loan. Under such an arrangement, the creditor hands over a sum of money to the debtor who, in turn, hands over his property. To the casual observer, this may look like a sale. However, the arrangement is merely a device whereby the creditor is protecting himself by insisting upon possession of the debtor's goods. Should the debtor fail to repay the loan, the creditor will refuse to hand over the goods and, in this way, he has managed to cut his losses to some extent. Sometimes, however, for reasons best known to the parties, it is not always simple to decide whether a transaction is a genuine sale and, therefore, covered by the 1979 Act, or some sort of security transaction which is outside the scope of the Act. This area of the law has often caused confusion for the Scottish courts (see **Aluminium Industrie Vaassen B V v Romalpa Aluminium Ltd (1976)** and **Armour and Another v Thyssen Edelstahlwerke AG (1990)**).

Furthermore, the courts have not always consistently distinguished between a contract for the sale of goods and a contract for services. Services would be classed as 'incorporeal moveable property' in terms of Scots law and would, therefore, fall outside the definition of goods under the Sale of Goods Act. Unfortunately, the courts have not always been consistent when it comes to being able to distinguish between a genuine sale of goods which is covered by the provisions of the Act and a contract for services which is outwith scope of the Act.

 Robinson v Graves (1935) the parties had entered into a contract for the purpose of painting a portrait.

Held: by the English Court of Appeal that this contract was not a sale of goods, but rather a contract for the provision of work (services) and materials.

 However, in **Philip Head & Sons v Showfronts Ltd (1970)** the parties into entered into a contract for the supply and the fitting of a carpet.

Held: this was a contract for a sale of goods.

This definition would seem to insist that in order to become the owner of the goods, the buyer must pay cash (or a cheque etc.) for them. This would seem to rule out transactions where the parties exchange goods and no money changes hands.

However, contracts which work as part exchanges of goods will be covered by the Act because the buyer makes a cash payment, for example, the buyer trades in his old car when he goes to buy a newer model from a dealership. It would seem that as long as some money is exchanged the conditions laid down in Section 2 are met.

 Key point: A sale of goods is where the buyer pays money to the seller or his agent in order to acquire ownership of the goods and the transaction does not operate by way of a mortgage, charge, pledge or other similar arrangement.

Corporeal, moveable goods

According to Section 61(1), the Act only applies to a particular class of goods – all corporeal, moveable property with the exception of money.

Moveable goods are all goods which are by their very nature able to be physically transferred from seller to buyer in a contract of sale. Corporeal means that the goods are tangible (they have a physical shape). Thus, corporeal moveable property covers all goods which are tangible and can be moved, for example, a chair, a table, a stereo system, a video and a television – the list is endless.

The major types of property which are not covered by the Act include heritable property, money and incorporeal moveable property. Incorporeal property would include shares in a company, patents, trade marks and copyrights. Furthermore, the Act does not apply to the contracts for the sale of services.

 Key point: The Act applies to corporeal, moveable goods i.e. goods that have a physical shape and which can be moved from seller to buyer.

Rules about capacity, formality, the price and stipulations as to time

Many rules of contract are recognised by the Act in relation to capacity, formality, the price and stipulations as to time. A number of significant examples are briefly discussed below.

The parties to a contract must have contractual capacity (Section 3), but there is no need for a sale of goods contract to be in writing (Section 4).

Sections 8 and 9 deal with the important issue of the price that is to be paid by the buyer for the goods in question. Section 8 makes it clear that a sale will only really be a sale if the buyer exchanges a money consideration called the price for the goods. According to Section 8, the parties can leave the price to be fixed by the contract or by reference to a method laid down by the contract. Alternatively, the parties may have had previous dealings that can be referred to in order to calculate the price. If the contract is silent on the issue of the price or there have been no previous dealings between the parties, the buyer must pay a reasonable price for the goods and what is reasonable will depend on the facts of each situation.

Section 9 does allow the parties to fix a price by appointing a third party to carry out a valuation of the goods. If such a valuation cannot or is not carried out, the contract is rendered voidable. If one of the parties to the contract of sale prevented the valuation from being carried out, the innocent party could bring an action for damages.

Section 10 makes it clear that, unless the parties agree differently, statements about time in relation to the sale of goods transaction are not to be regarded as a material term of the contract. In order to determine whether a contractual term about time is material, the content of the contract and the intentions of the parties will have to be examined. Late delivery of goods by the seller, for example, will not necessarily mean that the buyer has the right to treat the contract as cancelled. The most appropriate remedy for the seller's breach may be to lodge an action for damages. Additionally, Section 59 states that where references are made to a reasonable time, the question of what is a reasonable time is a question of fact.

 Shaw, Macfarlane & Co *v* Waddell & Sons (1890) there was an express stipulation in the contract that the goods should be delivered at Grangemouth for shipment by the buyer's vessel L'Avenir between April 12 and 16. The buyer failed to honour this contractual term which was considered to be a material part of the agreement and the sellers were, therefore, justified in cancelling (rescinding) the contract.

 Key point: Stipulations as to time in the contract of sale are not necessarily material terms of the contract.

Property in the goods

Quite simply, property in the goods means that the person has now become the owner of the goods. An owner of goods is said to have real rights in the property or goods. By real rights we are talking about an exercise of power i.e. the owner of the goods can effectively say to the world at large 'get your hands off my property'. The owner can do anything he likes with the goods as long as he does not break the law.

It is worth remembering that it is not necessary to have possession of the goods to be the owner of the property. Ownership and possession are not the same thing. If I lend you my mobile phone for the day, you have possession of the item but I will still remain the owner. An agent and an employee will often have possession of their principal's or employer's property in the course of their duties, but they are most certainly not the owners of these items – the principal or the employer will continue to exercise ownership civil possession of the property through them.

We should, therefore, not place too much reliance on the old saying that possession is nine-tenths of the law. Even delivery of moveable goods in a contract of sale is not definite proof of the transfer of property from seller to buyer. Transfer of ownership of the goods can occur before or after delivery has taken place.

The general rule is that the parties to a contract will decide when property in the goods is transferred from seller to buyer. The parties to a contract of sale are said to have freedom of contract in the sense that they decide what arrangements best suit themselves. It is important to appreciate that the Sale of Goods Act 1979 provides a set of very detailed rules which govern the transfer of ownership, but at the end of the day, the parties are often free to use these rules or reject them entirely.

 Key point: Someone who has property in the goods or who has good title to them is regarded as having rights of ownership.

The importance of identifying when ownership is transferred

The main rules dealing with the transfer of ownership of corporeal moveable goods are contained in sections 16 to 19 of the Act. Determining when ownership will be transferred is important for a variety of reasons:

1   If the seller has not yet passed property in the goods, the buyer only has personal rights (i.e. the right to sue) in relation to the seller and this means that the seller can still exercise his rights of ownership over the goods.

2   If the seller has remained the owner of the goods, theoretically he can sell the goods to another buyer and this second buyer can gain good title to the goods.

3   The owner of the goods will have to suffer the risk of loss, damage or theft in relation to the property.

4   If the seller of the goods has not yet transferred ownership and becomes insolvent after the buyer has paid for the property, the buyer will not have a right to demand the goods. In this situation, the buyer will have to attempt to reclaim his money – which as an unsecured creditor may be a very remote possibility.

5   If the seller of the goods has transferred ownership and the buyer becomes insolvent before he has paid for the property, the seller no longer has ownership rights over the goods. In this situation, the seller is not in a position to demand any goods that he has delivered to the buyer. The seller will have to place a claim for payment of the goods – which as an unsecured creditor may well be an unsuccessful course of action.

6   The owner of goods is said to have real rights in the property which means that he has the power to determine who will use the goods, how the goods will be used and what they will be used for. Ownership is, therefore, an exercise of power. If a person is not the owner of the goods, they merely have personal rights in relation to the goods which usually amounts to the right to raise a claim for damages as a part of a breach of contract claim. Personal rights may give the party the right to sue, but this will not him the right to own or control the goods.

 Key point: Ownership is important because it is the owner of goods who will be able to exercise control over them (real rights) but, on the downside, the owner will have to suffer the risk of loss, damage or theft in respect of the goods.

The passing of ownership

The point at which ownership passes to the buyer depends on whether the contract is said to be a sale or an agreement to sell.

Section 2(4) states that if the property in the goods is transferred from the seller to the buyer the contract is called a sale.

So, upon the conclusion of a sale, ownership usually passes to the buyer immediately because the goods are identified and agreed upon. Imagine a situation where the buyer selects a particular shirt from the shelves and tries the item on for size, comfort and style. Once he has satisfied with the shirt, the buyer then makes an offer to buy the item which the seller accepts. The buyer now has a contract of sale with the seller and, more importantly, he has become the new owner of the shirt.

Section 2(5) states that if the transfer of property in the goods is to take place at a future time or upon the fulfilment of some condition, the contract is called an agreement to sell.

Therefore, in an agreement to sell, the passing of ownership is postponed until some time in the future, either by the mutual consent of the parties or after the fulfilment of some condition. What if the goods you have ordered have yet to be manufactured or acquired by the seller – a three-piece leather suite. Does the buyer wish to become the owner of the furniture before it is even made? In this situation, it is only when the suite has been manufactured and the buyer informed of this that ownership passes to the buyer. The agreement to sell has now become a sale regardless of whether the suite has been delivered or paid for.

 Key point: The point at which ownership passes to the buyer depends on whether the contract is said to be a sale or an agreement to sell.

Classification of goods

In deciding whether ownership of goods has been transferred from seller to buyer, Section 5 of the Act distinguishes between certain types of goods.

Existing goods are owned or possessed by the seller and can be specific or unascertained.

- Specific goods can be identified at the time of the contracting, for example, the painting entitled 'The Mona Lisa' by the artist Leonardo da Vinci. In this case, ownership usually passes immediately.

- Unascertained goods cannot be identified because they are part of a larger quantity, for example, 30 tonnes of cotton in a storeroom containing 100 tonnes of cotton. In this case, there can only be an agreement to sell.

Future goods are yet to be acquired or manufactured by the seller, for example, handmade jewellery. In this case, there can only be an agreement to sell. Ownership cannot pass until the goods are manufactured or acquired and the seller has notified the buyer of this fact.

 Key point: Existing goods are owned or possessed by the seller and future goods are goods that will have to be acquired or manufactured by the seller.

Specific goods and generic goods

Section 61(1) of the 1979 Act describes specific goods as goods identified or agreed upon when the contract of sale is formed. Specific goods include an undivided share, specified as a fraction or a percentage of goods that have been identified and agreed upon by the seller and the buyer.

Generic goods, on the other hand, can be obtained from a variety of sources. The buyer will often merely state that he wishes to purchase a particular quantity of these goods and he has absolutely no interest in the seller's source of supply. It has been remarked that generic goods can never really perish or be destroyed because the seller can easily replace them. Consequently, contracts involving generic goods which have perished or which have been destroyed cannot be made void, unlike contracts involving specific goods (see Sections 6 and 7).

Critically, section 17 of the Act states that in a contract for the sale of specific or ascertained goods, ownership passes when the buyer and the seller intend that it should pass. In this situation, the courts will examine the intentions and the conduct of the parties carefully. Usually but not always, in a contract for ascertained goods, ownership will be transferred as soon as the contract is formed i.e. offer + acceptance. The seller, for instance, may choose to delay the passing of property until he has been paid for the goods (this very issue will be examined later).

An example of specific goods can be seen in the following situation:

An individual wishes to purchase a leather jacket from a retailer. She chooses the product in question from a display and makes an offer for it at the cashpoint which is accepted by the sales assistant (offer + acceptance = contract: see **Pharmaceutical Society of Great Britain v Boots Cash Chemists (1953)**). The leather jacket is an example of ascertained goods because it is that very jacket with which the customer will be leaving the store and not a similar item picked out by the sales assistant or ordered for the customer from the retailer's warehouse.

 Key point: Specific goods are the very goods that the buyer will physically receive from the seller – not a copy or a similar item.

Unascertained goods

The Sale of Goods Act does not define unascertained goods. These are goods which are not identified and agreed upon at the time when the contract was formed.

The customer has selected a widescreen television that she wishes to purchase. She approaches the cashpoint and makes an offer to buy the goods which the sales assistant accepts. However, the customer does not yet have a contract of sale with the seller. The sales assistant informs the customer that the store will have to contact its warehouse and arrange delivery of the product to the customer. Ownership of the television set has not yet passed to the customer and it will not do so until such time as the seller singles out the very item and puts the goods in a deliverable state and informs the buyer of this fact. Section 61(5) states that goods will be in a deliverable state when they are in such a state that the buyer under the contract would be bound to take delivery of them.

 Key point: Unascertained goods are goods that form part of a larger quantity held by the seller and the buyer cannot single out the goods that he will receive – the seller will have to do this and place the goods in a deliverable state.

There are two types of unascertained goods, those which:

◆ Form an unsevered (undivided) portion of a particular quantity of goods such as 20 tons of cotton taken from 100 tons of cotton lying in the hold of a ship named 'Peerless'

◆ Are generic goods i.e. a quantity of goods which can be acquired almost anywhere such as 1000 tons of cane sugar. The buyer is not the slightest bit interested where the seller will get his supplies.

Section 16 states that where unascertained goods are concerned, there can only be an agreement to sell and property will not pass to the buyer until the goods become ascertained i.e. until they become unconditionally appropriated to the contract by the seller. This will usually occur when the seller puts the goods in a deliverable state and informs the buyer of this development. Goods in a deliverable state means that the buyer must accept the goods.

The harsh reality of the rule in section 16 can be seen in **Hayman & Son v McLintock (1907)**.

The **Hayman** case concerned a contract for the sale of unascertained goods which fell into the first category above (i.e. a portion of a larger quantity of goods). McNairn, a flour merchant, sold and was paid for some sacks of flour. The merchant's flour was stored in a warehouse owned by Hayman. McNairn sent word to Hayman that two buyers had purchased 100 and 250 sacks of flour respectively. Hayman let the buyers know that he had the sacks at his warehouse and that he was awaiting their orders. In his records, Hayman kept a note of the number of sacks to which the buyers were entitled. However, he did nothing to separate these sacks from the other sacks belonging to the merchant. He did not even put the buyers' names on the sacks.

McNairn became bankrupt and a trustee in bankruptcy was appointed to seize all the merchant's property in order to sell it to pay his debts. The trustee, however, attempted to seize all the merchant's sacks in the warehouse. The buyers, understandably, objected to this course of action. The trustee in bankruptcy was held by the court to be entitled to keep all the sacks and use them to pay off the merchant's debts. The goods were unascertained, therefore, property in them could not pass to the buyer. Nothing had been done to make the goods ascertained, for example, by labelling them and thereby ensuring the transfer of ownership from seller to buyer.

 Key point: In contract involving unascertained goods, there can only be an agreement to sell – ownership will not pass to the buyer until the goods become ascertained.

The Sale of Goods (Amendment) Act 1995

The effects of the Hayman case have been reduced with the introduction of the Sale of Goods (Amendment) Act 1995. This legislation addresses the question of unascertained goods which form part of an identifiable bulk and undivided shares in goods. The 1995 Act only applies to contracts formed on or after 19 September 1995. The 1995 Act inserts a new Section 20A into the Sale of Goods Act 1979.

Now, on payment of either some or all of the price, property in goods which form an undivided share in an identified bulk will immediately pass to the buyer. This means that the buyer becomes a common owner of bulk goods. This would cover a situation where the buyer has contracted to buy 30 sacks of flour and the goods in question are still lying in a warehouse. In other words, no attempt has yet been made to separate the buyer's property from all the other sacks of flour in the warehouse.

As a result of Section 20A, the Hayman case would be decided differently. The buyers would have become the owners in common of the bulk when the warehouse owner communicated to the buyers that he was holding the sacks for them. The buyers' claims would, therefore, rank ahead of that of the trustee in bankruptcy.

The parties to the contract, however, can still agree to opt out of this new provision. Such a term in the contract would have the effect of retaining the Hayman rule. Section 20B of the Sale of Goods Act (1979) (also inserted by the 1995 Act) ensures that co-owners in bulk goods have the necessary authority to transact in these goods.

 Key point: It is now possible to become the owner in common of bulk goods (unascertained goods) in situations where they form an undivided portion of particular goods, for example, 500 bottles of New Zealand cabernet sauvignon forming part of a quantity of 10,000 identical bottles in Smith's warehouse.

Future goods

Future goods are goods that the seller must either manufacture or acquire from a third party. There can only be an agreement to sell and ownership of the goods will not pass to the buyer until the seller manufactures the goods or obtains them from a third party and the buyer is given notice of this fact. An example of future goods can be seen in the following case:

 Stark's Trustees v Stark (1948) an uncle had left instructions in his will that his nephew was to inherit any motor car that the uncle possessed upon the event of his death. When the uncle died, he had a car on order but it had not yet been supplied to him. The nephew failed in his action to be given possession of the car because the goods were held to be future goods. Ownership of the car had never passed to the uncle and, therefore, it did not form part of his estate.

 Key point: Future goods are goods that do not yet exist when the contract is formed and the seller must acquire or manufacture them and, therefore, there can only be an agreement to sell.

Transfer of the title in goods

Property in the goods can only pass and the title be transferred if the goods are ascertained. If the goods are unascertained, the property in them passes to the buyer only when they become ascertained (see **Hayman & Son v McLintock (1907)** above). Section 17 of the Sale of Goods Act 1979 states that the property in specific or ascertained goods passes when the parties intend that it should pass. This may be expressly stated in the contract, but if it is not, the intention will have to be implied.

 Re Blyth Shipbuilding & Dry Docks Co Ltd (1926) involved a shipbuilding contract i.e. a contract for future goods. The parties had agreed that the buyer would make payment by instalments. However, a term of the contract was that, on payment of the first instalment, ownership of the uncompleted ship would pass to the buyer. Normally, of course, ownership would not have passed to the buyer until the ship's completion and the ship was in a deliverable condition and the seller had given the buyer notice of this.

As we shall see in the Romalpa cases (see **Aluminium Industrie Vaassen BV** *v* **Romalpa Aluminium Ltd (1976)** and **Armour and Another** *v* **Thyssen Edelstahlwerke AG (1990)**), the parties are quite free to decide at what point ownership of the goods will pass from buyer to seller.

 Key point: Generally, ownership of the goods will pass from the seller to the buyer when they are ascertained, but the parties to the contract are always free to decide when ownership will be transferred.

Identifying the parties' intentions

Section 18 of the Sale of Goods Act 1979 provides five rules from which the parties' intentions can be presumed.

Rule 1

Where there is an unconditional order for the sale of specific goods in a deliverable state, the property in the goods passes when the contract is made and it is immaterial that the time of payment or delivery is postponed.

 We see how this rule operates by looking at the case of **Tarling** *v* **Baxter (1827)**. The facts were as follows: the contract involved the sale of a haystack. The contract was formed on 6 January, the price was to be paid on 4 February and the haystack was to be removed on 1 May. The haystack, however, was burned down in a fire on 20 January. As a result of the formation of the contract, ownership of the haystack had been transferred to the buyer. The buyer not the seller, therefore, had to suffer the loss.

Rule 2

Where there is a contract for the sale of specific goods and the seller is bound to do something to put them into a deliverable state, ownership will not pass until this is done and the buyer has notice.

The case of **Underwood** *v* **Burgh Castle Brick & Cement Syndicate (1922)** provides a demonstration of Rule 2:

 The sellers agreed to sell a condensing machine to the buyers. At the time the contract was made, the engine was at the seller's premises and was fixed to a bed of concrete by bolts. It was, therefore, necessary to detach the machine before it could be delivered. The machine was damaged whilst preparing it for dispatch and, when delivered, the buyers refused to accept it. The sellers naturally argued that the property in the goods had passed to the buyers when the contract was made – the buyers must accept the machine.

Held: that the property in the goods had not passed to the buyers because the goods were not in a deliverable state.

Rule 3

Where the contract is for the sale of goods in a deliverable state, but the seller is bound to weigh, measure or test, or do anything else to calculate the price, the property in the goods does not pass until this is done and the buyer has notice.

 Nanka-Bruce *v* Commonwealth Trust Ltd (1926) involved a contract to sell a consignment of cocoa at an agreed price for a certain weight. The parties were unsure about the total weight of the cocoa. The buyer was going to resell the cocoa to another individual and it was agreed that this party would weigh the cocoa and this would allow the price to be calculated. The Privy Council decided that because, technically, the seller would not be weighing the cocoa, Rule 3 did not apply and ownership of the goods would pass to the buyer either under Rule 1 or 2.

Rule 4

Where the goods are delivered to the buyer on approval or a sale or return basis, the property in the goods passes to the buyer when the buyer does one of the following:

◆ Signifies his acceptance
◆ Adopts the goods as his own (by using them)
◆ Retains them without giving notice of rejection (in this situation, property passes after a reasonable time has expired or after the time stated in the contract)

 Kirkham *v* Attenborough (1897) the seller had provided the buyer with jewellery on a sale or return basis. The buyer, however, used the jewellery as a security for a debt that he owed to a third party. The seller attempted to reclaim the goods arguing that they were still his property.

Held: the seller's claim failed because the buyer had done something inconsistent with the seller's ownership. He had used the goods as security for a debt and he, therefore, no longer had control over the goods so that he was unable to return them to the seller when this was demanded.

 Elphick *v* Barnes (1880) the seller supplied a horse to the buyer on an eight-day trial. The horse subsequently became ill on the third day and died. The horse's death was the fault of neither party. However, the question arose as to who owned the horse.

Held: this was a sale on approval and, therefore, property in the goods remained with the seller who would have to bear the loss.

Rule 5

Where there is a contract for the sale of unascertained or future goods by description, ownership is transferred to the buyer when such goods, complying with the contractual description, are unconditionally appropriated to the contract in a deliverable state. Appropriation of the goods may be achieved either by the seller with the buyer's consent, or by the buyer with the seller's consent. Such consent may be express or implied, and may be given either before or after appropriation.

 Wardars *v* Norwood (1968) the sale of 600 frozen kidneys was a contract of sale of unascertained goods. At the time the contract was made, the buyers could not specify which 600 items they would receive from the other thousands of kidneys which made up the seller's stock. The sellers sent the buyers a delivery note for 600 kidneys which the buyers gave to a firm of carriers in order to have the goods delivered. The carriers, acting as the buyers' agents, picked up the goods and received a receipt with them. Unfortunately, the carriers forgot to switch on the refrigeration system in the truck and, as a result, the kidneys perished.

The vital question was: whose property were the kidneys?

Held: that the property in the goods belonged to the buyers and the sellers would have to be paid for the kidneys. The buyers would have to sue the carriers for their negligence. The act of handing over the goods by the sellers to the carriers was legally the same thing as handing the goods to the buyers personally.

This has the effect of making the formula of ascertainment by exhaustion part of the Sale of Goods Act 1979. This means in certain situations where the buyer's goods form part of a larger consignment, it may be possible to identify them eventually when other individuals have removed their goods from the consignment.

In other words, there can be no doubt that the remaining goods belong to the buyer, for example, an individual has contracted to buy 200 barrels of beer which form part of a larger consignment of 2000 barrels at the seller's warehouse. All the other buyers have long since taken possession of their barrels of beer leaving only 200 barrels. These must belong to the buyer.

Rule 5 is an addition to the Sale of Goods Act 1979 and was introduced as a result of the Sale of Goods (Amendment) Act 1995.

 Key point: Section 18 contains five rules that the courts can use to determine when ownership of the goods was transferred to the buyer from the seller, but these rules are subject to the terms of the parties' contracts which will often take priority.

The issue of risk (loss or damage) to the goods

One crucial issue that we have already considered is that of risk. The issue of risk relates to any harm or damage caused to the goods and, more importantly, who will have to bear the loss should this happen i.e. the buyer or the seller.

 We can see how risk operates in the following case. In **Philip Head & Sons v Showfronts Ltd (1970)** the sellers agreed to supply and to fit carpets in various rooms in an office block. A carpet for one of the largest rooms had to be made from several lengths of material that would be stitched together by the sellers. It would take six men to lift this carpet. The carpet was put together and left in the room on the Friday afternoon – although it was not fitted, the intention being to do so after the weekend. Some time during the weekend, the carpet was stolen. The question then arose as to who was to bear the risk – the seller or the buyer?

Held: this was a contract for the sale of unascertained goods to be put into a deliverable state by the sellers. Unfortunately, the sellers had not yet put the goods into a deliverable state. Had the sellers laid the carpet the property in the goods would have passed from them to the buyers. The carpet remained the sellers' property and, consequently, they would have to bear the loss caused by the theft.

Sometimes the terms of the contract will determine whether the buyer or the seller has to bear the risk in respect of the goods.

Leigh and Sillavan Ltd _v_ Aliakmon Shipping Co Ltd (the _Aliakmon_) (1986) Leigh and Sillivan had entered into a contract with a Korean seller for the purchase of a consignment of steel coils. The goods were to be shipped from Korea to England on the defenders' vessel, the _Aliakmon_. The contract of sale stipulated that the buyers were responsible for the risk to the goods. This was despite the fact that the buyers would not become the legal owners until the goods had been paid for. The goods were damaged while on board the _Aliakmon_ due to the defenders' negligence. The buyers sued the defenders for damages caused by the their negligence.

Held: by the House of Lords that the buyers had not yet become the owners of the goods, despite the fact that they were responsible for the risk. The buyers' only possible claim was for damages for economic loss and the defenders owed them no duty of care in this respect.

Key point: Risk refers to loss, damage or theft in respect of the goods and it is usually the owner (subject to the contractual terms) who will have to bear the risk in situations where the goods are lost, damaged or stolen.

Situations where the goods perish

Sections 6 and 7 of the Sale of Goods Act address situations where the goods are said to have perished and, in this way, they are closely related to the issue of risk. These provisions relate to specific goods – not generic goods which are considered not to be capable of perishing or being destroyed.

Section 6 states that where there is a contract for the sale of specific goods, and the goods have perished at the time that the contract was formed, such a contract will be declared void.

Couturier _v_ Hastie (1856) Hastie had placed a cargo of corn on a ship sailing from Greece. The documents of title were forwarded to London agents in order that the corn might be sold. The London agents employed Couturier to find someone to sell the goods to – which he duly did. Unknown to the parties, the cargo had overheated aboard the ship and had been landed at the nearest port and sold, so that when Couturier entered the contract the corn did not really exist.

Held: by House of Lords that the contract was void because the cargo (ascertained goods) did not exist when the contract of sale was formed.

Barrow, Lane & Ballard Ltd _v_ Phillip Phillips & Co Ltd (1929) the buyer entered a contract with the sellers for the sale of a specific lot of goods which consisted of 700 bags of Chinese ground nuts still in their shells. The lot was stored in the warehouse of a wharf company. Both the sellers and the buyer were completely ignorant of the fact that 109 bags had been stolen before the contract had been formed. Some 150 bags were delivered to the buyer after the original theft had taken place, but after this initial delivery, the remaining bags were also stolen.

Held: Section 6 applied since the original theft had caused the specific lot of 700 bags to perish. It was said that to force the buyer to accept delivery of the smaller quantity would be to make him accept something that he had not contracted to take would be an injustice.

Section 7 applies to situations where the seller and the buyer have an agreement to sell specific goods and the goods subsequently perish before the risk passes to the buyer. In such situations, the contract would be regarded as voidable.

 Key point: Sections 6 and 7 of the Act apply to specific goods – not generic goods.

The Sale and Supply of Goods to Consumers Regulations 2002

The Regulations introduce a new rule which governs the operation of risk. It will now make a difference whether the transaction is classified as a consumer contract or a non-consumer (i.e. business) contract.

Where business contracts are concerned, Section 20 of the Sale of Goods Act 1979 states that, unless the parties agree differently, the owner of the goods will have to bear the risk of any loss or damage to the property. The general rule is that risk passes with ownership. The seller will have to bear the risk to the goods until he transfers the ownership in them to the buyer. Transfer of ownership will usually (but not always) occur when a sale is formed between buyer and seller. Obviously, in an agreement to sell, ownership will not pass to the buyer until a later date or on the completion of some condition.

However, in certain situations the rule in Section 20 could be made redundant. In a non-consumer contract if delivery of the goods was delayed and, as a result, they were damaged lost or stolen, the party responsible for the delay (the seller or the buyer) would have to bear responsibility for the loss. So, if the seller failed to deliver the goods on time to the buyer and after this the goods were damaged, lost or stolen, the seller would have to bear responsibility for this even if the buyer was now the owner and, therefore, potentially the one who has to bear the risk.

The new Regulations mean that Section 20 deals differently with consumer contracts. It will now be the case that risk will not pass to a consumer buyer until the goods are delivered by the seller to him. The seller could hand the goods to the buyer personally or to the buyer's agent. Once these conditions have been met, the buyer will be responsible for the goods.

Interestingly, both parties owe one another a common law duty as custodians to take care of each other's property. If the goods were lost or damaged as a result of one party's negligence or carelessness, the owner may very well consider raising a delictual action for breach of a duty of care.

 Key point: In a consumer sale, but not a business or non-consumer sale, risk will not pass to the buyer until such time as the goods are delivered by the seller to him.

Nemo dat quod no habet

The general rule regarding the transfer of title to corporeal moveable property from seller to buyer is that only the true owner of the goods (or her authorised agents) can pass ownership of the goods. A thief, for example, can almost never pass good title to a third party if the goods were stolen by him or the contract was induced by fraud (see **Morrison v Robertson (1908)** discussed in Chapter 2 and below).

This general rule is often expressed as follows: **NEMO DAT QUOD NON HABET** i.e. you cannot pass that which you do not have (i.e. ownership). The practical effect of this rule is that stolen property will almost always be returned to its true owner. As we shall see, however, the *nemo dat quod no habet* rule is not an absolute legal principle and there will be situations under both the common law and statute where the true owner will not be able to force the return of the property to her.

 Key point: Only the true owner of corporeal moveable goods (or her authorised agents) can transfer title to the buyer.

Section 12(1) of the Sale of Goods Act 1979 offers protection to a buyer who purchases corporeal moveable property in good faith from most of the negative consequences of the *nemo dat quod non habet* rule. It states that in a contract of sale . . . there is an **implied condition** on the part of the seller that in the case of a sale, he has a right to sell the goods and, in the case of an agreement to sell, he will have a right to sell the goods at the time when the property is to pass. This means that the buyer will be able to sue for the return of the price of the goods from the seller (who had no right to sell them in the first place). This applies even where the buyer has used the goods.

It will not always be possible, however, to return the stolen property to the true owner when the goods have been converted into other goods and cannot be retrieved e.g. when cattle have been stolen, slaughtered and eaten. In such situations, the true owner will have to be content with an award of damages based on the value of the property now lost to her forever.

Furthermore, **Section 21** of the Sale of Goods Act 1979 states that a buyer will not acquire good title to goods in a situation where the person selling them is not the owner and lacks the authority to sell them. In other words, the buyer cannot become the owner of the goods and the true owner will be able to reclaim the goods even from a person who bought the property in good faith.

 Key point: Section 12(1) offers protection to a buyer who purchases corporeal moveable property in good faith from most of the negative consequences of the nemo dat quod non habet rule meaning that he will be able to sue for the return of the price of the goods from the seller.

 Morrisson v Robertson (1908) Morrisson, a farmer, was approached by an individual (later discovered to be named Telford) who wished to buy two cattle from him. This individual wished to buy the cattle on credit. Morrison was unhappy about this, but Telford stated that he was the son of a man called Wilson with whom Morrison had dealt with previously. Morrison knew Wilson to be a man of good credit and someone he could trust to pay for the goods at an agreed date in the future. Morrison gave the cattle to Telford who promptly sold the cattle to an innocent third party, Robertson who was completely ignorant of Telford's fraudulent activities. After selling the cattle to Robertson, Telford promptly disappeared and Morrison, who by now had discovered the deception (and he had not received payment for the cattle) decided to take action to recover possession of the goods. Robertson resisted this attempt by Morrisson to recover the goods. He had purchased the cattle in good faith from Telford and felt that he had become the true owner of the property.

Held: the cattle had to be returned to Morrisson who had always been the true owner despite what Robertson may have believed. The contract between Morrisson and Telford was void from the very beginning because Morrisson would never have handed over the cattle had he been aware of the fraudster's true identity. In a credit bargain, such as this one, the true identity of the debtor (Telford) was absolutely vital to the creditor (Morrisson). It should be appreciated, of course, that Robertson was a completely innocent party in all of this and he did have the right to bring legal action against Telford to recover the money paid for the cattle – provided that he could actually find the fraudster and get him into court. Obviously, fraudsters do not make life easy for the Robertsons of this world having a tendency to leave the scene of the crime very swiftly when the dirty deed has been done.

See also **Rowland *v* Divall [1923]** which is discussed later in the chapter where a stolen car had to be returned to its true owner. This was despite the fact that possession of this vehicle had been transferred to several different individuals after it had originally been stolen from its true owner.

More recently, Jewish groups have successfully threatened international auction houses with legal action to force the return of paintings which were stolen by the Nazis from their true owners. Many of the true owners of these items subsequently perished in the Holocaust in the 1940s, but their descendants (their grandchildren and great grandchildren) have tenaciously pursued legal actions to recover this property. This, of course, demonstrates the fact that property stolen some sixty years ago remains stolen property and anyone thinking of purchasing such items should be cautious as they may fall foul of legal action brought by the true owners who are intent on wresting back possession.

 Key point: A thief, for example, can almost never pass good title to a third party if the goods were stolen by him or the contract was induced by fraud as in **Morrison *v* Robertson (1908)**.

Exceptions to the nemo dat quod non habet *rule*

The *nemo dat quod non habet rule* is only a general rule. Like most general rules in the law, however, there are a number of exceptions under both the common law and statute which might mean that someone who is not the true owner of the goods can pass good title to a third party. The practical effect of this is that the third party will often become the lawful owner of the goods despite the original owner's protests.

The main exceptions to the general rule will occur in the following situations:

The doctrine of personal bar

This will arise in situations where an owner has put the seller in possession of the goods (the seller may be the owner's agent or employee) and the act of giving possession in relation to the property creates the strong impression in the mind of a buyer that the seller had fully intended a sale to go ahead. In such circumstances, Section 21(1): Sale of Goods Act 1979 actively prevents the owner from attempting to claim that the property in the goods has not passed to the buyer. In other words, the circumstances of the transaction prevent or personally bar the seller from claiming that a transfer of ownership to the buyer has not taken place. As we shall see in Chapter 5, which discusses the law of Agency, any third party dealing with the seller's agent may be entitled to claim that they had every right to assume that the sale was authorised by the seller. Why else would the seller have given the goods to the agent?

Sales under a voidable title

It is important to remember that a sale under a *voidable* title means that the contract is flawed in some way to a greater or less extent. The practical effect of a voidable contract in a sale of goods transaction is that the seller can exercise a right to have the agreement cancelled. Such a right of cancellation or rescission must, however, be exercised rapidly by the seller. Very often, an attempt to cancel the contract will be worthless with the result that the property in the goods can be transferred to third parties by the buyer. When a contract is merely voidable, the legal position is starkly different from cases such as **Morrisson v Robertson (1908) (discussed in Chapter 2** and above) where the contract is void (i.e. there never was a contract) from the very beginning owing to the buyer's fraud. In situations where a contract is said to be *voidable*, there is a legally enforceable agreement from the outset, but certain circumstances permit the seller to cancel the contract. In circumstances where the contract is said to be voidable, Section 23: Sale of Goods Act 1979 permits the seller to exercise his option to have the contract cancelled (i.e. made void). Sellers of goods, as we shall see, will have to be especially wary in these types of situations as the following case demonstrates only too well:

 Lewis *v* Averay (1972) Lewis, a student, was the owner of a car that he wished to sell. He entered into a contract of sale for the car with a buyer who wanted to pay for the goods by cheque. Lewis would much have preferred to receive cash in return for the car and he was not keen to hand over the vehicle to the buyer. The buyer then claimed to be none other than the famous British actor, Richard Greene. Greene had achieved fame playing a variety of swashbuckling roles in films and television during the 1950s. He became particularly well known for his portrayal on British television as Robin Hood). This individual bore a very strong resemblance to Richard Greene and, as proof of his identity, he presented a Pinewood Studio ID card to Lewis. On the basis of this evidence, Lewis permitted the buyer to take possession of the car in return for the cheque. Unfortunately, this story does not have a happy ending and, when Lewis cashed the cheque, the bank in question refused honour it. Lewis discovered rather belatedly that he was the victim of a fraudster. Sadly, his buyer was clearly an imposter. Lewis then took steps to recover possession of the goods, but the car had been very swiftly sold by the fraudster to an innocent third party, Averay.

Held: by the English Court of Appeal that the fraudster had managed to pass good title to Averay. Unfortunately, Lewis would have to raise an action against the fraudster to recover the price of the car – provided of course that he could find him, which he never did.

It is important to distinguish the abve decision in **Lewis** from **Morrisson v Robertson 1908** to which it bears superficial resemblances. However, it will be remembered that the decision reached in **Morrisson** was quite different. In Lewis, the identity of the fraudster was never a central issue regarding the formation of the contract. The identity of the buyer only became an important issue when the matter of payment for the car arose. Until methods of payment were discussed by the parties, Lewis could not have cared who the buyer was – he would have entered into a contract of sale with anyone willing to pay the price for the car. In **Morrisson**, the formation of the contract hinged on the identity of the buyer (albeit a false identity) and this factor clearly influenced the seller from the very beginning as to whether he should enter an agreement. The decision reached by the Court of Appeal in **Lewis** follows a line of cases where the identity of the buyer was not regarded as a material term of the contract (**see Kings Norton v Edridge Merret (1897); Phillips v Brooks [1919]; and Macleod v Kerr 1965 in Chapter 2**).

Mercantile Agents

Section 61(1) of the Sale of Goods Act 1979 continues to recognise the right of a category of agents known as mercantile agents to pass title to goods. Agents such as auctioneers, del credere agents, factors, brokers, commercial agents and warehousemen are regarded as mercantile agents. The rights of mercantile agents in this area were originally recognised by the Factors Act 1889 and the Factors (Scotland) Act 1890. Mercantile agents operate by possessing the goods of their principal i.e. the seller and this possession has been fully consented to by the seller. The mercantile agent will then enter into a contract with a third party, on his principal's behalf, for the sale of the goods. Such a sale must have taken place in the ordinary course of the mercantile agent's business and the buyer must not be aware of any problems with the agent's authority. Clearly, the very fact that the agent possesses the goods with his principal's consent would tend to allay any fears that a third party might have regarding the issue of a lack of authority on the part of the agent. It is important not to confuse an agent known as a factor in Scotland who acts as an estate manager because this type of agent is not a mercantile agent.

Pawnbrokers

Very often, a person will have to borrow money. In order to raise the sum required, this individual may approach someone who runs a pawn-broking business. A pawn-broking business operates on a simple principle: the pawnbroker will lend money on the understanding that the debtor pledges some item of property as security for the loan. The debtor is given a certain period of time in which to pay back the loan whereupon he can redeem his property. If, however, the debtor does not return within the specified period to pay back the loan, the pawnbroker is legally entitled to sell the goods to a third party. The third party who purchases goods from a pawnbroker will acquire good title to the property in question.

The seller remains in possession of the goods after the sale

As we should now be aware, it is perfectly possible for someone to be the owner of goods without necessarily having possession of them. Section 24 of the Sale of Goods Act 1979 comes into operation in circumstances where the seller remains the possessor of the goods, but the buyer has become the legal owner of the property. Before the buyer can acquire possession of the goods, however, the seller mistakenly sells the goods to an innocent third party. The Sale of Goods Act chooses to resolve this problem by deciding the question of ownership in favour of the innocent third party i.e. the second buyer. The only solution open to the first buyer is to sue the seller for damages for breach of contract.

The buyer is in possession of the goods with the seller's consent

According to Section 25 of the Sale of Goods Act 1979, a buyer who has entered into a sale or an agreement to sell and who obtains possession of the goods or documents of title to the goods *with the seller's agreement* can transfer good title in the property to an innocent third party. The buyer can enter into the sale with the innocent party personally or he may have appointed a mercantile agent to act for him in this second transaction or sub-sale. This innocent third party will be unaware of any lack of title to the goods on the buyer's part (i.e. he will have acted in good faith and will be unaware of the terms of the contract between the seller and the buyer). Consequently, the innocent third party will become the legal owner of the goods. Section 25 provides useful protection to an innocent third party especially in situations where the buyer's insolvency becomes an issue. Provided that the innocent third party is able to satisfy the conditions laid down in Section 25, it would seem that he will be able to defeat any claims that the seller may advance to repossess the goods under a retention of title clause.

 Archivent Sales & Development Ltd _v_ Strathclyde Regional Council 1985 demonstrates such a situation where ownership of the goods became a very important issue on the event of the buyer's insolvency. In Archivent, it should be understood that the first buyer had been given possession of the goods with the seller's full consent. According to the terms of the contract, however, ownership of the goods had not yet transferred to the first buyer when the sale was concluded. Archivent had entered into a contract of sale for building materials with R Ltd, a firm of building contractors. Archivent had insisted that an enforceable price only retention of title clause should form part of its contract with R Ltd. It should be recalled that such clause operates to delay the transfer of ownership from seller to buyer until such time as the buyer pays in full for the goods *in relation to that particular transaction only*. This type of clause is not as powerful as a Romalpa clause.

Before the goods had been delivered, R Ltd entered into a further contract with Strathclyde Regional Council (a sub-sale with a third party). This second contract or sub-sale involved a building project for which R Ltd was one of the contractors and the building materials acquired from Archivent were going to be used for this work. Under this second contract, R Ltd and the Regional Council agreed that the Council would become the owners of the materials when they were delivered to the building site. The

Council was completely unaware of any problems or restrictions relating to R Ltd's title to the goods. The Council had no reason to be suspicious that R Ltd may have lacked title to the goods since Archivent delivered them to R Ltd at the Council's building site. R Ltd later went into liquidation and a dispute between Archivent and the Council concerning the ownership of the building materials inevitably occurred. Archivent, not surprisingly, attempted to rely on the retention of title clause which formed part of the original contract of sale with R Ltd. The Regional Council, on the other hand, argued that it had become the owner of the goods by virtue of fulfilling the conditions laid down by Section 25 of the 1979 Act.

Held: by the Court of Session that R Ltd had come into possession of the goods with the full agreement of Archivent, the seller. The Regional Council had been unaware of any defect in R Ltd's title and had it had acted completely in good faith when it entered the sub-sale to purchase the building materials. By virtue of Section 25, the Council had acquired ownership of the goods.

 Key point: The Sale of Goods Act recognises a number of exceptions to the rule in Section 12 which means that the buyer could acquire good title to goods even where the seller's title is defective in some way.

Retention of title/ownership

Section 19 of the Sale of Goods Act 1979 permits the seller to retain title or ownership of the goods. Sometimes, the seller will have delivered the goods to the buyer, but he will be anxious to ensure that, although he has surrendered possession of the goods to the buyer, he continues to be the owner of the goods. The seller can insert a term in the contract which means that the goods continue to be owned by him despite the fact that the buyer has possession of the goods. Such a contractual arrangement may occur in situations where the seller has a very real fear that the buyer could become insolvent. If the seller has transferred ownership of the goods and the buyer becomes insolvent, the goods could be used as assets to pay off the buyer's creditors. Obviously, this is something that the seller will want to avoid as much as possible. One way of doing this is to delay the transfer of ownership of the goods until such time as the buyer can pay for the goods or until such time as the buyer as paid all debts that he owes to the seller. The buyer can, by all means, have possession of the goods, but he is not the owner. This arrangement means that, should the buyer become insolvent before paying for the goods, the seller can reclaim possession of his property. More significantly, the goods cannot be used to pay off the buyer's creditors.

If the buyer pays for the goods or pays all debts to the seller, then ownership of the goods will pass to him and the seller will quite happily surrender any of his rights over the goods to the buyer. Contractual arrangements whereby the seller retains title or ownership of the goods until the buyer fulfils some condition are often referred to as Romalpa clauses. Romalpa clauses are so named after the decision of the English Court of Appeal in 1976 that first permitted their use (at least in England and Wales). As we shall see, the Scottish courts had serious problems with Romalpa clauses and it was not until 1990 that Scots law and English law were brought into line with respect to this type of contractual term.

 Key point: Ownership of the goods will pass to the buyer when he complies with some condition laid down by the seller.

The English Court of Appeal decision which first permitted the use of Romalpa clauses was **Aluminium Industrie Vaassen B.V. *v* Romalpa Aluminium Ltd [1976]**.

 The contract involved the sale of aluminium foil. The seller was a Dutch company (**Aluminium Industrie Vaassen**) and the buyer was an English company (**Romalpa Aluminium Ltd**). The seller's standard terms of sale governed the contract of sale. Critically, one of the standard terms addressed the issue of the transfer of ownership of the aluminium foil from seller to buyer. According to this term, ownership would pass to the buyer when it had paid all debts owed to the seller. Until such time as the buyer had paid all debts to the seller, there were a number of conditions with which it had to comply:

1 The goods had to be labelled to indicate to third parties dealing with the buyer that they remained the property of the seller.

2 The buyer was free to sell the goods to third parties, but the proceeds from such sales were to be paid into a seperate bank account by the buyer and held on trust for the seller.

3 If any of these third parties had yet to pay the buyer for the aluminium foil, the Dutch seller could exercise its right to pursue these individuals for payment. This right, of course, effectively meant that the Dutch seller could step into the English buyer's shoes and prevent it from receiving payment from third parties.

4 Finally, the standard term imposed a duty on the buyer to the effect that any products which it manufactured using the aluminium foil and remained in its possession were to be treated as a guarantee for full payment of all monies owed to the seller.

A dispute arose concerning the legality of the standard term when the buyer went into receivership as a result of insolvency. The receiver put forward the argument that the aluminium foil and any proceeds of the sale of these goods to third parties should be regarded as assets of the buyer. If the receiver's argument was correct, these assets could be used to pay off the buyer's debts to its various creditors. The seller strongly objected to the receiver's argument claiming that, although possession of the goods had been transferred to the buyer, this did not mean that any rights of ownership had automatically transferred to the buyer. The standard term that the seller relied on stated that ownership of the goods would pass to the buyer when all debts owed to the seller had been paid. The buyer still owed debts to the seller and, therefore, under the terms of the contract of sale, ownership remained with the seller.

Held: by the English Court of Appeal that the seller had retained ownership of the goods and the receiver had no right to treat them as the property of the buyer which could be used to pay debts to creditors. The seller was entitled to reclaim possession of any foil that was still stored at the buyer's premises and it had the right to pursue third parties who had purchased the foil from the buyer. This meant that the receiver was barred from pursuing those third parties who still owed money to the buyer in relation to sub-sales of the foil. Furthermore, the receiver had to turn over any money to the seller that had been obtained from sub-sales of the foil by the buyer to third parties.

 Key point: The decision by the English Court of Appeal in Aluminium Industrie Vaassen B.V. v Romalpa Aluminium Ltd [1976] permitted the seller to give possession of the goods to the buyer, but not ownership. Ownership would pass when the buyer had paid for the goods and settled all other debts owing to the seller.

The Scottish approach to Romalpa clauses

In Scotland, there has been a huge amount of argument concerning the validity of such contractual clauses. The Scottish Courts appeared to tolerate clauses which allowed a seller to withhold the transfer of title to goods until he had been paid for that particular transaction only. These clauses were referred to as price-only retention clauses.

More powerful clauses, known as all-sums retention clauses, which allowed the seller to delay the passing of ownership until the buyer paid over all monies owed to the seller – regardless of whether they were part of one particular transaction or not – were unenforceable in Scotland. In three Scottish decisions: **Clark Taylor & Co. Ltd *v* Quality Site Development (Edinburgh) Ltd 1981, Emerald Stainless Steel Ltd *v* South Side Distribution Ltd 1982** and **Deutz Engines *v* Terex Ltd 1984**, it was held that Romalpa clauses were attempting to create a security situation without the need for the creditor to possess the goods. This situation was totally contrary to Scottish practice. In Scotland, therefore, the use of Romalpa clauses was forbidden. Lord Ross, who was particularly hostile towards Romalpa clauses, took the view, wrongly it has to be said and with the benefit of hindsight, that such arrangements were not really sales at all and, therefore, were not covered by the Sale of Goods Act (**Section 62(4)**). This view of Lord Ross ignored the fact that the seller had every intention of transferring the property in the goods to the buyer *at some time in the future to be decided by the parties*. Lord Ross's hostility towards such contractual terms also ignored the fact that the buyer had never owned the goods – the seller remained the owner of the goods until such time as the buyer paid all debts owed to the seller. In a security situation, the debtor who pledges goods must actually own the property – he cannot pledge goods as security that belong to someone else. The fact that the seller had surrendered possession of the goods to the buyer did not mean that he had also surrendered his rights of ownership.

 Key point: The Scottish courts, for many years, chose not to follow the English court of Appeal's decision in Aluminium Industrie Vaassen B.V. v Romalpa Aluminium Ltd [1976].

We can see the position that the Scottish courts adopted in relation to Romalpa clauses by examining the following example:

A wishes to borrow money from B. B wishes to minimise the risk which is involved in lending money to A. In order to lessen this exposure to risk, B demands that A pledges some item of moveable property in order to secure the loan. A writes a letter to B, which states that if he is unable to repay the loan, B can take the Van Gogh painting that he owns. This letter, however, does not create a valid security situation in Scotland. In order for B to have security which he can enforce, A would have had to hand the painting over physically to B. Therefore, under Scots law, there can be no security without possession.

There was one exception (to the former rule) in Scots law: a registered company may create a security over its corporeal moveable and heritable property (i.e. its assets) by way of a floating charge. This would allow a creditor to have security over the company's assets without having possession of them. Floating charges must, however, be registered in the register of charges.

 Key point: The traditional Scottish legal approach to security situations is that there can be no effective security without possession.

Armour and Another v Thyssen Edelstahlwerke AG (1990)

This was the view held by the Scottish courts concerning Romalpa clauses until November 1990. In the important decision of **Armour and Another *v* Thyssen Edelstahlwerke AG**, however, the House of Lords ruled that Romalpa clauses were valid under Scots law.

The facts of the Armour case were as follows:

 A German company, Thyssen, had entered into a series of contracts with a Scottish manufacturing company, Carron Co. Ltd., which was based at Falkirk. The contracts involved the sale of steel strip by the Germans to the Scots. A dispute arose between the Germans and the Scots because Carron had been declared bankrupt. The heart of the dispute concerned the ownership of £71,769 worth of steel supplied by Thyssen to Carron. Thyssen put forward the argument that the contracts of sale were governed by its own "General Conditions of Delivery and Payment". These conditions contained a very important term to the effect that all goods delivered by Thyssen were to be regarded as its property until all debts owed by Carron to the Germans had been paid. Basically, the Germans were arguing that, although they had given Carron possession of the goods, this did not mean that they had surrendered any rights of ownership in relation to the goods.

The two receivers who had been appointed by some of Carron's creditors took a completely different view and claimed that the property in the goods had passed to the buyers. They saw the steel as a valuable asset which could be used to pay off Carron's debts. The receivers conveniently ignored the fact that the German company had not yet received any payment for the steel. Thyssen claimed, referring to the terms of its contract with Carron, that the steel clearly remained its property. The receivers, on the other hand, continued to argue that property in the goods had passed to the buyers.

When the case was heard by the Court of Session it followed the line of reasoning laid down in the earlier Scottish cases of **Clark Taylor & Co. Ltd *v* Quality Site Development (Edinburgh) Ltd 1981, Emerald Stainless Steel Ltd *v* South Side Distribution Ltd 1982** and **Deutz Engines *v* Terex Ltd 1984**. The term in Thyssen's "General Conditions of Delivery and Payment" should be viewed as a Romalpa clause and, therefore, had no legal force in Scotland. The sellers had transferred ownership of the steel to the buyers and this meant that the receivers were entitled to use these goods as an asset to pay of the buyer's debts. The sellers appealed against this judgement to the House of Lords.

The House of Lords completely disagreed with the judgement of the Court of Session which had favoured the receivers. The House of Lords explained the operation of a Romalpa clause. Under a Romalpa clause, the seller remains the owner of the goods until the buyer either pays for them or pays all debts that he may owe to the seller whether connected to this particular transaction or not. The seller had intended to transfer ownership of the goods the buyer, but only upon the fulfilment of certain conditions which may or may not occur. The transfer of ownership in this particular situation hinged upon the buyer's ability to pay for the goods until all debts owed by it to the German sellers had been paid. If the buyer could not pay these debts, then quite simply it would not become the owner of the goods. To create a security over the property, the debtor must be the owner of any goods that he is pledging. The problem with the reasoning of the Court of Session was that Carron had never owned the steel strip because Thyssen, although surrendering possession of the goods, had never allowed the Scottish company to acquire title to the goods.

 Key point: The law relating to Romalpa clauses would now appear to be in harmony in both Scotland and England.

The limits of Romalpa clauses

The usefulness of Romalpa clauses should not be overestimated. The seller will lose the protection of such a clause if the goods are sold by the buyer to third parties who then convert them into other products by making them undergo some form of manufacturing process.

 Borden (UK) Ltd *v* Scottish Timber Products Ltd [1981] The sellers sold resin to the buyers. The contract contained an express term which stated that ownership of the goods would not pass to the buyers until all debts owed to the sellers by the buyers had been paid. The resin was used in an industrial process to make chipboard. This was an irreversible process meaning that the resin was effectively destroyed to make a completely new product. The sellers were owed £300,000 by the buyers, but the buyers became insolvent and the receivers were called in. The sellers attempted to claim rights of ownership over the chipboard and a share of the profits made as a result of its sale.

Held: the resin had effectively ceased to exist when it became part of the new product and, therefore, the sellers could not be owners of a product that no longer existed.

Key point: Although Romalpa clauses can offer the seller valuable protection, they will not be effective where the character of the goods undergoes some drastic change or where the goods are destroyed in order to make other products, for example, a quantity of hops is converted into beer.

The Implied Terms in a contract for the sale of goods

Under the Sale of Goods Act 1979, consumer and business buyers entering into a sale of goods transaction benefit from the protection of **FOUR** key legal rights. These legal rights are automatically incorporated into every contract of sale i.e. they are assumed to form part of the terms and conditions of every sale. These rights are known as the implied terms and are outlined below:

(a) The seller's **TITLE** to the goods (**Section 12**)

(b) Sale by **DESCRIPTION** (**Section 13**)

(c) **QUALITY** and **FITNESS** (**Section 14**)

(d) Sale by **SAMPLE** (**Section 15**)

Admittedly, a seller can attempt to limit or exclude his/her liability in a business sale or non-consumer transaction, but such attempts are subject to the Unfair Contract Terms Act 1977. In a consumer sale, any attempt by the seller to limit or exclude liability in relation to the implied terms will be automatically void in terms of the 1977 Act – even if such an attempt was expressly made known to the buyer or the buyer ought to have been aware of the seller's intentions in this regard.

Although this section of the book concentrates on the existence of the implied terms in a contract of sale, other transactions, for example, a hire purchase agreement or a contract of lease or a contract for services involving the provision of corporeal moveable property benefit from very similar (if not identical terms). Such legal protection has been extended to these individuals courtesy of legislation like the Hire Purchase Act 1973 and the Sale and Supply of Goods Act 1982.

 Key point: The implied terms of the Sale of Goods Act 1979 cover the sellers title, description of the goods, quality and fitness for purpose of the goods and sales by sample.

Title (Section 12)

Section 12 of the Sale of Goods Act 1979 provides the rules which govern a seller's title to the goods or his right to sell them. In terms of Section 12(1), the seller must have the right to sell the goods at the time of the actual sale or, if the contract is an agreement to sell, he will have the right to sell the goods at the time when the property is to pass to the buyer. Problems usually arise in this area when the buyer later discovers that the seller has supplied him with stolen goods. Alternatively, the buyer's use of the goods may infringe a copyright or a trade mark.

Section 12(2)(a) also imposes a duty on the seller that the goods will continue to remain free from any undisclosed encumbrances after the sale has taken place.

Encumbrances are anything that would interfere with the buyer's property rights in the goods. For example, an encumbrance would occur if the seller fails to disclose that he is only a part-owner of the goods and, that consequently, the buyer will only be entitled to a part-share in the goods. Furthermore, Section 12(2)(b) states that the buyer has the right to enjoy quiet possession of the goods and any disturbance of this right by third parties will mean that a potential claim lies against the seller.

Section 12(3) addresses situations where the seller can only give the buyer a limited title to the goods. If such a situation applies to the sale of goods, the seller is duty bound to inform the buyer that he only enjoys limited rights in the property and, therefore, it will be entirely the buyer's choice if he wishes to proceed with the sale. However, at least the buyer will have made an informed choice.

The main protection that Section 12 gives to a buyer is that the seller is promising that he has the right to sell the goods to the buyer. So, if the goods were stolen, then the seller would be in breach of the duty imposed by this Section and the buyer would be entitled to reclaim the whole of the purchase price from the seller.

 Rowland *v* Divall [1923] In April 1922, Divall bought an 'Albert' motor car from a man who had stolen it from the true owner. One month later, Divall sold the car to a dealer named Rowland for £334. Rowland repainted the car and sold it to a Colonel Railsden for £400. In September, the police seized the car from Railsden.

Held: by the English Court of Appeal that the car had to be returned to its true owner. Railsden brought a successful action to recover the price of £400 that he had paid to Rowland. Rowland, in turn, successfully sued Divall for £334. Poor Divall, however, was not so fortunate. As he had purchased the car from the person who had originally committed the theft, he would have to have brought a claim against this person. Thieves, by their very nature, tend not to hang around waiting to be caught and they have a nasty habit of vanishing into thin air. Rowland, the pursuer in this case, had contracted for the ownership of the car and not just the right to possess it. A fairer result might have been for the court to reduce the amount of money awarded to Rowland because he had enjoyed the use of the car.

 McDonald *v* Provan (of Scotland Street) Ltd (1960) the buyer was unfortunate enough to purchase a vehicle from the dealers which was later found to consist of two different Ford cars that had been welded together. One half of the car turned out to have been part of a stolen vehicle. The buyer was informed of this fact some three months after the sale when Police officers turned up to confiscate the whole car on the grounds that it partly consisted of stolen property. The buyer raised an action under Section 12 of the Sale of Goods Act 1893 on the grounds that the seller did not have the right to sell the goods at the time of sale as they partly consisted of stolen property.

Held: by the Outer House of the Court of Session that the sellers would be liable under Section 12 if the buyer could prove the facts.

 Key point: In terms of Section 12(1), the seller is promising that he has the right to sell the goods to the buyer.

Another important protection for the buyer contained in Section 12(2)(b) is that he has the right to enjoy quiet possession of the goods after the sale has taken place. Effectively, the seller promises that no third party can dispute the buyer's right to own the goods or disturb his enjoyment of them. This implied term can, however, operate very harshly against seller who has acted in good faith.

 Microbeads AC _v_ Vinhurst Road Markings Ltd [1975] the buyer had purchased road-marking machines from Vinhurst. Some two years after this sale had taken place, a third party became the patent owner in relation to the machines. The net effect of this development was that if the buyer continued to use the machines this would represent an infringement of the third party's patent rights. The third party had made it clear to the buyer that an action for damages would follow if the machines continued to be used. The buyer was understandably furious and refused to pay the seller for the machines. The seller raised an action against the buyers for payment. As a defence, the buyers claimed that the seller had committed various breaches of Section 12. The alleged breaches amounted to the following: that, at the time of the sale, the seller did not have the right to sell the goods (**Section 12(1)**) and that the buyer's right to enjoy quiet possession of the goods had been disturbed (**Section 12(2)(b)**)

Held: by the English Court of Appeal that the buyer's quiet possession of the goods had indeed been disturbed after the sale had taken place. The seller was in breach of Section 12(2)(b) in this regard and the buyer was entitled to claim damages. However, the buyer was not entitled to claim damages under Section 12(1) on the grounds that when the sale had taken place, the seller had the right to sell the goods. There was nothing defective about the seller's title when the sale originally took place. At that point, the third party was not yet the patent owner and there was no way that seller could have predicted that the buyer's quiet possession would have been disturbed at some point in the future.

McDonald _v_ Provan (of Scotland Street) Ltd (1960) it was held by the Court of Session that the buyers would have a potential claim under Section 12(2)(b) if the facts of the case could be proved. It will be recalled that Police officers confiscated a car which the buyer had purchased from the sellers on the grounds that it partly consisted of stolen property. This might be construed as interference with the buyer's right of quiet possession.

 Niblett Ltd _v_ Confectioners' Materials Co Ltd [1921] The defenders sold 3,000 cases of condensed milk to the pursuers. About 1,000 of these cases had labels with the name 'Nissly' attached to them. The Nestlé Company raised objections saying that this name infringed its trade mark. The use of the name 'Nissly' was an unauthorised attempt to trade on the goodwill of Nestlé which, understandably, may have created confusion in the minds of consumers. The pursuers accepted this claim by Nestlé and agreed to stop using the labels. Unfortunately, by removing the labels, the goods lost some of their value.

Held: by the English Court of Appeal that, at the time of the sale, the sellers had no right to sell the goods as this could only be achieved by infringing a third party's trade mark rights. Lord Justice Atkin also stated that the sellers had committed a breach of Section 12(2) because the buyer had not enjoyed quiet possession of the goods.

 Key point: Section 12(2(b)) guarantees that the buyer has the right to enjoy quiet possession of the goods.

However, as Section 12(3) recognises, there will be situations where the buyer purchases goods where his rights of ownership will be limited in some way. Provided that the seller honestly alerts the buyer to these limitations, the seller will be entirely in the clear. Such a situation may arise where the seller is a landlord and seizes goods from a tenant who has failed to pay the rent. The seller would have to point out to the buyer the precise circumstances relating to the goods. It may be that the tenant was not the owner of the goods e.g. he bought a stereo on hire purchase and the true owner (the retailer or the finance company i.e. the creditor) may appear at a later date to attempt to reclaim his property from the buyer.

 Key point: Section 12(3) does recognise situations where the buyer will gain only a limited title to the goods, but the seller would have to make this abundantly clear to the buyer.

Sale by description (Section 13)

In terms of Section 13 of the Sale of Goods Act 1979, if the seller describes the contract goods in a certain way e.g. a black leather jacket, the buyer is entitled to receive goods which conform to this description. So, if the seller supplied a brown leather jacket to the buyer, she would be in breach of her obligation under Section 13. It should be appreciated, of course, that there is nothing wrong with a brown leather jacket (it is not defective in any way), but it is not what the buyer asked the seller to supply to him under the terms of their contract and, therefore, the seller has committed a material breach of the agreement. As we shall see, Section 13 does not address the issue of damaged or defective goods or goods which are not fit for their purpose – such issues are properly treated as a breach of Section 14 of the Act of 1979.

 Beale v Taylor (1967) The defender advertised a second hand car for sale in a newspaper. The car was described as a 1961 Triumph Herald 1200 and the seller was acting in good faith when he applied this description to the goods. In response to the advert, the pursuer went to view the vehicle. During his examination, the pursuer saw a metal badge on the rear of the car with the figures 1200. The pursuer decided to go ahead and buy the car. However, it was later discovered that only rear of the car was 1961 Triumph Herald 1200. The front of the vehicle was actually a Triumph Herald 948 which someone had welded to the rear. The welding was unsatisfactory and, consequently, the car was dangerous and completely unroadworthy.
Held: The pursuer's claim for damages, based on Section 13 of the Sale of Goods Act 1979 was successful. The pursuer had relied upon the description contained in the advert and on the metal badge on the rear of the car. The sale was one of description and it made no difference that the buyer had

actually seen and examined the vehicle before entering the contract of sale with the seller.

 Nichol *v* Godt (1854) the buyer had entered a written contract with the seller to purchase 33 tonnes of what was described by the seller as 'foreign refined rape oil'. The seller had permitted the buyer to examine a sample of the goods. After the bulk of the goods had been delivered, the buyer discovered that they were a mixture of rape and hemp oil. As it turned out, the sample which the seller had allowed the buyer to examine was also a mixture of rape and hemp oil.

Held: the seller had committed a breach of description despite the fact that the buyer had examined the sample and, furthermore, that the bulk corresponded to this sample. The seller had applied a description to the goods which the buyer had relied on. The buyer thought that he was purchasing foreign refined rape oil not the mixture of rape and hemp oil which had been delivered to him. The bulk goods were clearly an inferior product in all respects. It will be recalled that the buyer in **Beale *v* Taylor [1967]** (above) had also examined the goods, but this did not prevent the transaction from being a sale by description.

Reliance on the seller's description

An important point to note is that for the buyer to succeed in any claim under Section 13, she must be able to show that she relied on the seller's description of the goods. It will not be enough for the buyer to say that the seller uttered a misleading statement when describing the goods, this statement **must** influence the buyer. If the seller can prove that the buyer did not rely or was not influenced by the description of the goods, then there is no breach of Section 13. So, if the buyer decided to commission his own expert to verify the authenticity of an antique to which the seller had applied a description ("I believe that the vase is from the late Ming Dynasty period"), by doing so it is perfectly obvious that he is not prepared to accept the seller's statement or description at face value. In other words, he has not relied upon or been influenced by the seller's description of the goods. If the expert (wrongly) states that the vase is from the late Ming Dynasty period and the buyer proceeds to purchase the item, it was not the seller's description which swayed him, but rather the appraisal of the expert appointed by him to verify the authenticity of the goods. The buyer should, therefore, pursue the expert for damages **not** the seller based on a contractual duty of care owed by the expert to the buyer. Such a scenario can be seen in the following case.

 Harlingdon *v* Hull Fine Art Ltd [1990] Hull, an art dealer, was asked to sell two paintings described as being painted by Gabriele Münter, a German Expressionist artist. Hull was completely ignorant of the work of the German Expressionists and he contacted Harlingdon, also art dealers, who possessed expert knowledge of this particular School. Hull stated to Harlingdon that he believed that the two paintings were by Münter, but he admitted to Harlingdon that he could not be certain of this because he was not an expert in this field. Harlingdon sent one of its experts, named Runkel, to conduct an inspection of the paintings. On the strength of this examination, Runkel bought one of the paintings on behalf of Harlingdon paying £6,000 for the privilege. It later emerged that this painting was a forgery and its actual value was probably only between £50 and £100. Harlingdon raised an action against Hull for breach of description in terms of Section 13.

Held: by the English Court of Appeal that the action against Hull should be dismissed. Harlingdon had not relied totally on Hull's description of the painting. They had taken steps to verify the authenticity of the painting by subjecting it to an expert examination (one of their own experts no less) and his decision to purchase the goods was based very much on the strength of his own judgement. The description had not, therefore, influenced Harlingdon to enter the contract with Hull for the painting.

In other situations, the seller may make it perfectly clear to the buyer that he is not prepared to provide a description in connection with the goods which should be relied upon in anyway or should be used by the buyer as a basis for legal action under Section 13 at a later date.

 In **Cavendish-Woodhouse *v* Manley (1984)** a seller was able to demonstrate that the buyer was not entitled to claim that the description of the goods was a term of the contract of sale. A seller will be entitled to claim that the duty in Section 13 does not apply when certain phrases are applied to the goods, for example, 'sold as seen' or 'bought as seen'. Such phrases, however, will not protect the seller when he has breached the requirements of fitness and satisfactory quality in terms of Section 14 of the Sale of Goods Act 1979 because these phrases do not operate as general exclusion clauses. The effect of these phrases indicate is that they indicate to the buyer that the seller does not regard the transaction as a sale by description.

The key to Section 13 is the identity of the goods

Unfortunately, in the past, the courts have had a tendency to confuse the respective remits of Sections 13 and 14, but Lord Diplock in **Ashington Piggeries Ltd *v* Christopher Hill Ltd (1972)** (discussed below) did much to clarify the law here. To paraphrase his Lordship, the key to understanding Section 13 is to realise that description is intimately connected with the identity of the goods.

If, for example, a car dealer says to a prospective buyer: "Yes, we do have one silver coloured Volkswagen Passat 1.9 TDi (59 licence plate) in the car lot which you can purchase if you are interested", it is not asking too much of most buyers to go out onto the lot and find this car. The dealer's statement is a description which clearly identifies the goods. We would expect the buyer to be able to tell the difference between a silver Volkswagen Passat and a similar model which was in black in colour. It should be noted that the dealer's description of the car has nothing to do with the quality or the fitness for purpose of the goods, it is merely a statement which identifies the goods.

Another statement by the dealer that one of the cars on the lot has a defective power steering system is not a description. If the dealer was talking in reference to three identical red Ford Fiestas sitting on the lot, it is unlikely that the buyer would be able to go out and identify the model which had the defect by simply looking. Rather it should be treated as a statement about the quality of the goods i.e. that they suffer from a defect.

In both **Ashington Piggeries** and **Border Harvesters**, the pursuers claimed that the sellers had committed a breach of description in terms of Section 13. In fact, in both cases, the sellers had supplied goods that were either not fit for their purpose or did not comply with the required standard of quality. The sellers had, therefore, committed breaches of Section 14.

 Ashington Piggeries Ltd *v* Christopher Hill (1972), foodstuff, which had been specially prepared, was supplied for mink that the buyer was breeding. Both the seller and the buyer were completely ignorant of the fact that a small quantity of the goods contained a chemical which would cause serious harm and even death if consumed by the mink. Apparently, the mink had a much lower tolerance to the chemical contained in the food preservative in comparison with other animals. The goods supplied under the contract were neither fit for their purpose nor did they meet the expected standard of quality. The seller had, therefore, committed a breach of Section 14 rather than Section 13 of the Sale of Goods Act 1893 (as it then was).

 Border Harvesters *v* Edwards Engineering (1985), the contract was for agricultural machinery, but its performance was unsatisfactory. Again, the sellers had committed a breach of the Sale of Goods Act 1979 in connection with the implied term relating to quality in Section 14 and not a breach of description relating to Section 13. As can be seen in both cases, the buyers' claims that there was a breach of description failed. Both buyers had received the item that they had contracted for so there was no breach of description. The goods were either unsatisfactory or unfit for their purpose and this raised a completely different legal issue which is addressed by Section 14, not Section 13.

Cases such as Ashington Piggeries and Border Harvesters may appear to be unduly technical. It is worth pointing out, however, that if a buyer wrongly pursues an action under Section 13 of the Sale of Goods Act 1979 rather than Section 14, she will not only have gone to considerable expense on a wild goose chase, but more seriously she may have lost the right to raise a fresh action under the legal doctrine of *res judicata* which literally means the matter has already been judged. This doctrine prevents litigants from raising multiple claims about issues which the courts have already determined. So, if you raised an action under Section 13 when the matter should have been raised under Section 14, you have had your day in court and that is it!

Quality and fitness of the goods (Section 14)

Section 14 is the implied term in the contract of sale of which most sellers are likely to fall foul. A seller of goods may breach Section 14 in a number of ways. The buyer may bring a claim against the seller if the goods supplied are not of satisfactory quality or they were not fit for the buyer's purposes.

The protection extended to buyers by Section 14 will only apply if the seller is selling the goods in the course of his business. Therefore, a buyer purchasing goods from a private seller will not be protected by Section 14. Consequently, in private sales, the general rule is best summed up by referring to the old Latin expression *caveat emptor* – let the buyer beware. In other words, the law does not exist to protect a buyer in a private sale from the consequences of making a bad bargain as a result of his own stupidity or his failure to ask the seller important questions about the condition or the suitability of the goods.

 Key point: There are two heads of liability in Section 14: the goods may not meet the requirement of satisfactory quality or they are not fit for their purpose.

Who will be covered by Section 14?

Realistically speaking, only manufacturers, wholesalers, retailers and dealers in new or second hand goods will be caught out by the implied conditions contained in Section 14. Furthermore, a business seller will not be able to escape the provisions of Section 14 by claiming that he does not usually supply or deal in such goods. Therefore, if the buyer ordered a particular brand of goods from a business seller who previously had never sold these, he would have a claim against the seller under Section 14 if the goods were not fit for their purpose or defective in some way. The seller's protests that the goods supplied were not in the normal course of his business would cut little ice with the courts.

 Stevenson v Rogers (1999) the English Court of Appeal considered the meaning of the phrase 'a seller selling goods in the course of a business' in Section 14. The seller, a fisherman who had been in the business for than 20 years, put his trawler, *Jelle*, on the market because he was replacing it with a brand new vessel. *Jelle* turned out not to comply with the requirement of satisfactory quality and the buyer sued in terms of Section 14(2) of the Sale of Goods Act 1979. The seller argued that Section 14(2) did not apply to this case because it was a private sale. He was not in the business of selling second hand trawlers. The Court of Appeal disagreed stating that this sale was closely connected with the seller's commercial activities and should, therefore, be treated as a business sale which was governed by Section 14(2). The buyer had a right to challenge the seller in terms of Section 14 as it appeared that there had been a breach of the requirement of satisfactory quality.

 Key point: Section 14 has the effect of ensuring that in all sales of goods, with the exception of private sales, that the goods supplied must comply with the requirements of satisfactory quality and fitness for purpose.

The two heads of liability in Section 14: satisfactory quality and fitness for purpose

It is absolutely vital that the two heads of liability in Section 14 are distinguished. Goods will fail to comply with the implied term of satisfactory quality (**Section 14(2)**) if they suffered from some sort of manufacturing defect or because they were faulty to a greater or lesser degree. To put it another way, if the seller had supplied a similar or identical product in perfect working order there would have been no cause for complaint from the buyer. In stark contrast, goods may not be fit for their purpose because of their design or mode of construction (**Section 14(3)**). By no stretch of the imagination could the goods be regarded as defective or faulty in any way – they are simply unsuitable for the buyer's intended purpose. If the seller attempted to repair or to modify such a product this would a totally inappropriate response to the buyer's problem. The goods are in perfect working order, but to all intents and purposes they are of absolutely no practical use to the buyer. A racing bicycle, for example, is not fit for the purpose of off-road racing – only a mountain bike in such circumstances would be adequate. Clearly, if the seller supplied the buyer with a racing bicycle in place of a mountain bike, the item would not be not fit for its purpose.

Baldry v Marshall (1925) is a particularly instructive case in that it goes a long way to dispel the confusion which often surrounds the two heads of liability in Section 14 i.e. satisfactory quality and fitness for purpose respectively. The facts of **Baldry** are as follows:

The pursuer owned a Talbot racing car. He made enquiries about the possibility of exchanging the Talbot for a touring car as a result of pressure from his wife who had bluntly informed her husband that she did not wish be driven about in a racing car. The pursuer contacted the defenders by letter requesting details of a model of car known as a Bugatti, for which they were agents and suppliers. The pursuer did not know anything about this type of vehicle, but he made quite clear to the defenders that he was relying on their skill and expertise when he stated that he required a car that was suitable and comfortable for the purpose of touring. The pursuer was, therefore, quite clearly communicating to the defenders that he required a particular type of car for a very specific purpose. In response to the pursuer's stated requirements, the defenders made a recommendation that he should purchase a Bugatti. Relying on this recommendation from the defenders, the pursuer decided to purchase the Bugatti. Admittedly, the pursuer had inspected the chassis of a Bugatti at the invitation of the defenders before he had entered the contract. Critically, the pursuer had not seen a completed vehicle. When the car was delivered to the pursuer, it was quite obvious that the defenders had supplied him with a racing car, not a vehicle suitable for touring as he had explicitly stipulated. The pursuer raised a claim to recover the purchase price of £1,000 on the grounds that the defenders had supplied him with a car that was not fit for its purpose.

Held: by the English Court of Appeal that the pursuer had clearly relied on the defenders' skill and expertise when he had entered into a contract with them to supply him with a suitable car. The pursuer had made known the particular purpose for which the goods were required. This reliance by the pursuer on the seller's skill and expertise could not be said to be in any way unreasonable because the defenders' business involved the sale of motor cars. The Bugatti, of course, was in perfect working order and the issue of whether it complied with the standard of quality that a buyer was entitled to expect was completely irrelevant in this case. The defenders had committed a breach of Section 14(1) of the Sale of Goods Act 1893 (now Section 14(3) of the 1979 Act) when they supplied the pursuer with an unsuitable vehicle.

Key point: Goods which are not of satisfactory quality are defective in some way whereas goods which are not fit for purpose are in perfect working order but they are totally unsuitable for a specific purpose or requirement that the buyer has made known either expressly or impliedly to the seller.

Satisfactory quality

Section 14(2) of the Sale of Goods Act 1979 expressly states that a seller selling goods in the course of business will be under a duty to ensure that the goods are of 'satisfactory quality'.

Section 1 of the Sale and Supply of Goods Act 1994 changed the standard of quality which a buyer has a right to expect in terms of Section 14 of the Sale of Goods Act 1979. Prior to the Act of 1994, the standard of quality that the buyer could expect was that of *merchantable quality*. This was often a problematic concept. Goods that were slightly defective did not always mean that the seller had failed to comply with the requirement of merchantable quality. The concept of merchantable quality, therefore, could be a difficult one to understand, especially for consumers, and it has to be said that the courts did not always apply it consistently.

 In **Millars of Falkirk v Turpie (1976)** – perhaps one of the best known Scottish cases dealing with the problematic nature of merchantable quality – it was held that a new car a minor defect which afflicted could be easily remedied and, consequently, the seller had not failed to supply goods of merchantable quality (the power steering had a slight oil leak). Since the introduction of the reforms to the Sale of Goods Act 1979, it is highly likely that **Millars of Falkirk** would be decided in the buyer's favour. It is still permissible to use the older cases, which were decided prior to the reforms introduced by the Sale and Supply of Goods Act 1994, by bearing in mind that the older requirement of merchantable quality roughly corresponds to the current requirement that the goods are of satisfactory quality.

 Key point: In terms of Section 14(2) of the Sale of Goods Act 1979, when a seller sells goods in the course of business, the buyer is entitled to receive goods which are of satisfactory quality.

The judicial reasoning behind the decision in **Millars of Falkirk** has since been comprehensively rejected as a result of the judgement of the Inner House of the Court of Session in **Lamarra v Capital Bank plc & Shields Automative Ltd t/a Shields Landrover (2006)**. We can now be certain that the purchaser of the defective vehicle in **Millars of Falkirk** would be successful if that case was now brought before the Scottish courts.

Although the legal action in **Lamarra** involved goods which were supplied under a hire purchase agreement (not a sale of goods transaction), such contracts are governed by an implied term relating to satisfactory quality which has absolutely the same legal effect as the provision contained in Section 14 of the Sale of Goods Act 1979.

 Lamarra v Capital Bank plc & Shields Automative Ltd t/a Shields Landrover (2006) Lamarra had entered a hire purchase agreement for the supply of a brand new, top of the range Land Rover vehicle from the Shields garage in Glasgow. The vehicle was sold to Capital Bank plc by Shields and the total cash price for the goods was £51,550. Under the terms of the hire purchase agreement, property in the goods would pass to Lamarra when the final payment had been made by him to Capital Bank. Initially, Lamarra had paid a deposit of nearly £7,000 to Capital Bank and he was to make a further

36 monthly payments under the hire purchase agreement. Lamarra, however, paid the deposit and just two of the monthly payments which came to a total of just under £10,000. He refused to make any further payments to Capital Bank. His reason for refusal to make further payments under the agreements was his belief that the vehicle supplied to him was not of satisfactory quality particularly having regard to the price paid for it. The defects which allegedly affected the vehicle included:

◆ It pulled to the right when being driven causing undue tyre wear
◆ The layout of the pedals was very poor – on one occasion, Lamarra's foot had become trapped under the brake pedal
◆ The engine made an extremely loud noise through its transmission system
◆ Deep scratches could be found on the ashtray
◆ The glovebox had not been fitted correctly.

It was Lamarra's contention that no reasonable person would have been satisfied with the condition of the vehicle. In other words, it did not meet the statutory requirement that it be of satisfactory quality. By letter dated 30 March 2001, Lamarra rejected the vehicle (this was within two weeks of the vehicle being supplied to him). The vehicle itself was not uplifted by Capital Bank from Lamarra until sometime early in June 2001 and, by this time, it had been driven approximately 6,000 miles.

Consequently, Lamarra raised an action at Hamilton Sheriff Court to have his contract with Capital Bank cancelled and to recover all monies (including interest) that he had paid so far under the hire purchase agreement. The Sheriff at Hamilton was of the view that Lamarra had not validly rejected the vehicle on the grounds of a failure to meet the requirement of satisfactory quality. The vehicle was not unsafe and it appeared to the Sheriff that Lamarra had exaggerated many of his complaints. The Sheriff appeared to have been influenced by the fact that many of the defects which formed the basis of the action could be easily fixed and, therefore, the vehicle was of satisfactory quality. Consequently, the Sheriff dismissed Lamarra's attempt to have the contract cancelled. Lamarra then sought leave to appeal to the Sheriff Principal who overruled the decision of the Sheriff. Capital Bank then appealed to the Inner House of the Court of Session.

Held: by the Inner House of the Court of Session which approved the decision of the Sheriff Principal in that that Lamarra had been supplied with goods which were not of satisfactory quality. The Inner House appeared to criticise the attitude of the Sheriff for failing to take into account that the vehicle was a brand new, luxury car. The Sheriff was also criticised for being apparently swayed by the willingness of the garage (Shields) to make all sorts of repairs to the car. Quite simply, Lamarra was entitled to reject the goods and he was entitled to the return of any monies and interest paid by him under the terms of the hire purchase agreement.

 Key point: The decision in **Lamarra v Capital Bank Plc** and **Shields Automotive Ltd t/a Shields Landrover (2006)** comprehensively rejects the older case of **Millars of Falkirk v Turpie (1976)**.

According to Section 14(2A), goods are of satisfactory quality if they meet the standard that a *reasonable person* would regard as satisfactory, taking account of any description of the goods, the price (if relevant) and all the other relevant circumstances. A point worth noting in relation to the operation of Section 14(2A), and one that will be discussed further in connection with partially defective goods and minor defects, is that satisfactory quality critically depends on the expectations of a reasonable person. The reference to a reasonable person in Section 14(2A) goes some way to providing sellers with protection from buyers who have impossibly high standards that can never be satisfied.

Section 14(2B) contains a list of five examples of quality that buyers can use to help them decide whether the goods supplied by the seller are in any way unsatisfactory:

- fitness for all the purposes for which goods of the kind in question are commonly supplied
- appearance and finish
- freedom from minor defects
- safety and
- durability.

 Key point: Section 14(2B) of the Sale of Goods Act 1979 lists five possible aspects of quality: fitness for purpose, appearance and finish, freedom from minor defects, safety and durability.

If a buyer felt that the seller had failed to provide goods which did not live up to just one of these aspects of quality, then the buyer would have a potential claim under Section 14(2). Buyers do not have to demonstrate that the seller has failed to meet all five aspects of quality in order to have a claim. Clearly, such a situation would only apply to the most dangerous, useless and unsatisfactory goods, as can be seen in the following case:

 Grant *v* Australian Knitting Mills Ltd [1936] The buyer purchased a pair of long woollen underpants. The manufacturer had failed to remove sulphite, a dangerous chemical, used in the manufacture of the goods. The buyer wore the underwear next to his skin for a few days, when he broke out in a rash which spread over his body. The buyer was taken into hospital and, in fact, very nearly died as a result of his condition. The buyer raised a claim against the seller under the South Australian Sale of Goods Act 1895 which used the same terminology (i.e. merchantable quality and fitness for purpose) as the United Kingdom Sale of Goods legislation.

Held: by the Privy Council that the goods were not of merchantable quality in the sense that they were not fit for their purpose, that they were defective in the sense that they had not been properly finished and, most seriously of all, they were very clearly dangerous.

Obviously, if a case like **Grant** came before the Scottish courts today, the seller would continue to fall far short of the duty in Section 14(2) that goods supplied should be of satisfactory quality. If we use the five aspects of quality in Section 14(2B) and apply them to the facts of **Grant**, the goods were clearly not fit for their common purpose, their finish was unsatisfactory, they were unsafe and they were not durable (i.e. they suffered from a latent defect). The underwear would, therefore, fail to comply with four of the five aspects of quality outlined in Section 14(2B).

Unreasonable reliance by the buyer on the requirement of satisfactory quality

The seller's duty to supply goods to the buyer that are of satisfactory quality has its limits as Section 14(2C) makes abundantly clear. According to Section 14(2C), buyers will lose the statutory protection contained in Section 14(2) in the following circumstances:

◆ Defects which were specifically drawn to the buyer's attention before the contract of sale was concluded.
◆ Where the buyer examines the goods before the contract is made and this examination ought to have revealed defects.
◆ In a sale by sample, the buyer may lose his right to claim that the goods are not of satisfactory quality if a reasonable examination of the sample by him ought to have revealed any defects.

More generally, the buyer's claim that he was sold goods that were not of satisfactory quality will meet with little success in the following circumstances:

◆ Deterioration in the goods due to wear and tear caused by the buyer's use
◆ Misuse or accidental damage caused to the goods by the buyer and
◆ Where the buyer simply takes a dislike to the goods.

 Key point: Section 14(2C) lists a number of situations where the buyer will not be permitted to rely on the presumption that the goods supplied to him meet the requirement of satisfactory quality.

Does the buyer have to examine the goods?

The buyer is not under a duty to examine the goods before the contract is made. If, however, he chooses to examine the goods he will not be permitted to bring a claim under Section 14(2) if he fails to notice obvious defects e.g. the climate control system in a car only works on an intermittent basis during a test drive.

What about defects specifically drawn to the buyer's attention by the seller?

It is possible for the buyer to lose his right to bring a claim under Section 14(2) in situations where the seller has specifically drawn defects in the goods to the buyer's attention as can be seen in the following case:

 Bartlett v Sidney Marcus Ltd (1965) the buyer purchased a second hand car from the seller, a car dealer. The car had a defective clutch, but the seller alerted the buyer to this fact before the contract of sale was concluded. The seller reduced the price to be paid by the buyer to take account of the defective state of the car. The problem with the clutch turned out to be much more serious and more costly to repair than the buyer had anticipated. The buyer attempted to reject the car on the ground that it did not comply with the standard of quality that he was entitled to expect.

Held: the buyer's claim must fail because the seller had been at pains to alert him to the fact that the clutch was defective

Key point: The buyer does not have to examine the goods in order to gain the protection of Section 14, but obvious defects should be noticed and he will have no claim in relation to defects specifically drawn to his attention by the seller.

Factors which may be used to determine whether goods are of satisfactory quality

It should be recalled that Section 14(2A) states that the certain factors should be taken into account when determining whether the goods meet the requirement of satisfactory quality that a reasonable person is entitled to expect. These factors, which may or may not be relevant, are:

◆ Any description applied to the goods by the seller
◆ The price paid by the buyer
◆ All other relevant circumstances.

We will now examine each of these factors in turn and their relationship to satisfactory quality.

How did the seller describe the goods?

Descriptions that the seller attaches to goods may very well have an impact on the buyer's perceptions as to their quality. Several years ago, one Glasgow fashion retailer had prominent notices displayed in the store that alerted customers to the fact that the clothes had been exposed to high levels of smoke which had been the direct result of a fire in a neighbouring building. These notices explained why the goods were being sold much more cheaply than usual. Therefore, any buyer who purchased clothing from this retail outlet would not have been able to bring a complaint under Section 14(2) on the grounds that the goods suffered from smoke damage. Similarly, in situations where the seller applies descriptions to the goods such as 'Seconds', 'Slightly soiled goods', or 'Second hand goods', the buyer would be completely unreasonable if he expected very high standards of quality. As previously discussed in relation to Section 13, the decision in **Cavendish-Woodhouse v Manley (1984)** demonstrates that phrases such as 'bought as seen' or 'sold as seen' simply indicate that the buyer has actually seen the goods and this is all that such a phrase means. An attempt by the seller to claim that he had successfully excluded or limited his liability in relation to the implied term of quality by using these phrases would almost certainly be bound to fail.

 Key point: The buyer will not be able to claim a breach of satisfactory quality where descriptions of the goods used by the seller clearly convey that the goods are not of satisfactory quality, for example, seconds or smoke-damaged goods.

What price did the buyer pay for the goods?

If the buyer intends to resell the goods after he has purchased them from the seller, he may find that the price he is able to get is less than the original price that he paid. In terms of Section 14(2A), it will be a question of fact for the courts to decide whether differences in the original price and the resale price indicate that the goods were not of satisfactory quality when they were originally supplied by the seller. If the goods are not defective it is highly unlikely that the difference in price could be used by the buyer to sustain a claim against the seller that the goods supplied were somehow of unsatisfactory quality. After all, it is no shock to learn that some goods lose value very quickly e.g. brand new cars can start to lose value as soon as they are driven away from the dealership! However, the buyer's suspicions may be aroused if the difference in purchase and resale price is substantial. The following case is an interesting example of a situation where the buyer claimed that a difference between the original price and the resale price clearly indicated that when the seller had supplied the goods they did not meet the required standard of quality.

 BS Brown & Son Ltd v Craiks Ltd (1970) Brown bought a quantity of cloth from Craiks. The cloth was for making dresses, but Brown failed to tell Craiks, who thought the cloth was for industrial use. The price paid was higher than the normal price for industrial cloth, but not to the extent that this should have excited the buyer's suspicions. The cloth was unsuitable for dresses and Brown cancelled the contract and claimed damages. Both parties were left with substantial quantities of cloth but Craiks managed to sell some of its stock at a lower (but not a catastrophic) price. Perhaps fatally for Brown, he had not relied on the seller's expertise and an action on these grounds was, therefore, not competent. Brown was left with no option but to sue for damages under Section 14(2) claiming that the goods supplied were not of merchantable quality.

Held: by the House of Lords that Brown's claim that the seller had supplied goods that were not of merchantable quality (thus committing a breach of Section 14(2)) should be dismissed. The cloth was perfectly adequate for industrial purposes and it had not been difficult to find third parties who were perfectly willing to purchase the goods, albeit at a slightly lower price than the original price paid for the goods. The slight difference between the purchase and resale prices was not conclusive evidence that the goods had failed to meet the requirement of merchantable quality when they were originally supplied to Brown. It should be borne in mind that, if there is a significant difference between the original price and the resale value, it is always open to the buyer to lead evidence that the goods were not of satisfactory quality.

 Key point: A sharp or significant drop in the price of goods, especially in situations where the buyer intends to make subsequent sale shortly after his purchase, may indicate that the goods were not of satisfactory quality.

All other relevant circumstances

The description applied to the goods by the seller, and the price paid by the buyer for the goods, can obviously help to determine whether there has been a breach of quality in terms of Section 14(2). Other relevant circumstances that may assist a buyer to prove that the goods were not of satisfactory quality might include the following:

◆ Partially defective goods
◆ A lack of durability
◆ Manufacturer's guarantees supplied with the goods.

What if the buyer is supplied with goods that are partly defective?

When part of the goods is unsatisfactory, a buyer's position would seem to depend on the extent to which the goods are defective. However, even minor defects in the goods can represent a material breach of contract and the fact that only some of the goods are affected may be an argument that is unlikely to impress the buyer. It will also be recalled that since the reforms introduced by the Sale and Supply of Goods Act 1994, it is now much easier for a buyer to reject goods that are partially defective or where they suffer from minor defects. When address the issue of partially defective goods, it is always wise to bear in mind that the requirement of satisfactory quality is judged according to the standards of a reasonable person. Buyers who are overly fussy or those hard-to-please individuals may have a difficult task persuading a court that the goods were not of satisfactory quality.

 Jackson _v_ Rotax Motor and Cycle Co [1910] the pursuers had sold a large quantity of car horns to the defenders. A particular consignment of goods was rejected by the defenders who stated that they did not meet the standard of merchantable (now satisfactory) quality that they were entitled to expect. Over half the goods were dented and scratched because the pursuers had not properly packed them when they were making them ready for delivery to the defenders. The pursuers offered to repair the defective car horns, but the defenders considered this offer to be totally unacceptable.

Held: by the English Court of Appeal that the buyers were entitled to reject the whole consignment on the grounds that the goods supplied were not of merchantable quality.

In **Jackson**, the fact that half the consignment was defective seemed to exert a particularly strong influence on the reasoning of the Court of Appeal. The situation outlined above does not represent a slight breach of the standard of satisfactory quality and the case would still be decided emphatically in the buyer's favour, even with the seller's right to offer to repair the goods for the buyer (see now the **provisions of the Sale and Supply of Goods to Consumers Regulations 2002**). No reasonable person would have accepted goods in the type of condition that were supplied to the pursuers in **Jackson**. Undoubtedly, the Court of Appeal was quite correct in its treatment of this case – the goods were simply not of merchantable quality.

 Key point: When part of the goods is unsatisfactory, a buyer's position would seem to depend on how much of the consignment is defective.

Duration of satisfactory quality

Before the introduction of the Sale and Supply of Goods to Consumers Regulations 2002, the law was very unclear as to the length of time during which goods must meet the standard of satisfactory quality. Admittedly, Section 14(2B) of the Sale of Goods explicitly stated that the durability of the goods was an important aspect of satisfactory quality. What the Sale of Goods Act most certainly did not attempt, however, was to state the length of time that goods should comply with the requirement of satisfactory quality. Disputes between the seller and the buyer involving the issue of durability would turn on their own facts. In any case, the seller is liable for any defects which were not obvious to the buyer when the goods were originally supplied and which may emerge to cause the buyer problems at some point in the future. As we have seen in **Grant v Australian Knitting Mills Ltd (1936)**, the buyer could not have been aware when he purchased the underwear that they contained a latent defect i.e. an excess of the chemical sulphite which should have been removed as part of the manufacturing process. It was only some time after the goods had been delivered and used by the buyer that their unsatisfactory nature became all too apparent.

As a result of Section 48A(3) of the Sale of Goods Act (a provision introduced the Sale and Supply of Goods to Consumers Regulations 2002), there will now be a strong presumption operating against the seller that, if the goods suffer from or develop defects within six months of delivery to the buyer, then they will probably have failed to meet the requirement of satisfactory quality. The seller is, of course, perfectly at liberty to challenge this presumption. It should be appreciated, however, that the new Regulations do not confer upon buyers a general right to wait six months after the goods have been delivered before deciding whether or not to bring an action against the seller for supplying unsatisfactory goods. The buyer is still under a duty to take reasonably swift steps to bring a claim against the seller when he discovers that the goods are not of satisfactory quality. The six month time period laid down by the Regulations merely recognises that some defects (particularly those of a latent nature) may take longer to appear. A seller who attempts to limit drastically the period of time in which defective goods can be returned by the buyer (e.g. '*Faulty or defective goods must be returned within 28 days of purchase*') will not be treated sympathetically under the Regulations. Generally speaking, buyers must accept that the goods will not always meet the requirement of satisfactory quality as time marches on – deterioration of the goods through normal use, accidental damage and even misuse by the buyer ensure that the goods will not always remain free from defects for long. In such circumstances, the seller is not responsible for the fact that the goods no longer comply with the requirement of satisfactory quality.

 Key point: In situations, where goods become defective within six months of delivery to the buyer, there will be a strong presumption operating against the seller that, when originally supplied to the buyer, the goods were not of satisfactory quality.

In **Lamarra v Capital Bank plc & Shields Automotive Ltd t/a Shields Landrover (2006)** (discussed above), a consumer who had been supplied with a luxury vehicle, which turned out to suffer from all sorts of defects, was entitled to reject the goods on the ground that it did not satisfy the requirement of satisfactory quality. The consumer's argument to be permitted to reject the goods was greatly strengthened by the fact that he had taken swift steps to inform the supplier of the goods that he intended to exercise his right of rejection (i.e. within two weeks the vehicle being supplied to him). The fact that the supplier did not reclaim the vehicle until some months later and that it had driven nearly 6,000 miles by this point in no way undermined the consumer's right to have the contract cancelled.

It would seem, therefore, that any indecision or delay on the part of the consumer in rejecting goods which are not of satisfactory quality could be absolutely fatal to any subsequent legal action raised by him. Failure to reject defective goods speedily could be used as evidence by the seller or the supplier to demonstrate that the consumer has acquiesced (accepted) to the situation and, accordingly, he has lost the right to insist that the contract be cancelled. The simple moral of the story is that if you don't complain about being supplied with defective goods quickly and vociferously, you will lose the right to reject these goods and demand a refund from the seller or supplier.

 Mash and Murrell *v* Joseph I Emmanuel (1961), (1962) provides an interesting example regarding the issue of durability in relation to perishable goods. The goods (potatoes) were loaded aboard the *SS Ionian* in Cyprus for transport to the buyer in England. When the ship arrived at its destination in Liverpool, it was discovered that the goods had become rotten. In this case, two facts were important:

1   The potatoes were in good condition when placed aboard the vessel before it departed from the Port of Limassol in Cyprus.

2   The ship had not been seriously delayed during its voyage from Cyprus to Liverpool.

Held: by Diplock J at first instance that the sellers were liable in terms of Section 14(2). The sellers should have taken reasonable precautions to ensure that perishable goods, such as potatoes, reach their destination so that they comply with the statutory requirement of quality. The length of the voyage and the nature of the goods did not reduce the duty imposed by Section 14(2) upon the sellers. These were factors that the seller was only too aware of and which had to be taken into consideration. On appeal to the English Court of Appeal, the sellers were able to demonstrate that the potatoes perished owing to a combination of excessive heat (not entirely unexpected in the Mediterranean) which was made far worse by a lack of ventilation in the hold of the vessel. Simply put, it was not the fault of the sellers that the goods had perished while in transit. Although the decision of Diplock J in favour of the buyers was reversed on the facts in the Court of Appeal, his statement of the law regarding the sellers' duty in relation to perishable goods continues to be correct.

 Key point: Buyers are entitled to presume that the goods will continue to comply with the requirement of satisfactory quality for a reasonable time after they have been supplied by the seller.

Manufacturer's guarantees

Manufacturing guarantees may also give an indication as to the length of time that a buyer can reasonably expect the goods to meet the appropriate standard of quality. If, for example, a television broke down in the first five months following its purchase, when it was guaranteed for three years, this might be a strong indication that the product contained a major defect. Regulation 15 of the Sale and Supply of Goods to Consumers Regulations 2002 states that a manufacturer's guarantee is directly enforceable against both the manufacturer and any person who uses the guarantee in connection with goods that are for sale to a consumer. Sellers will have to be extremely careful in these circumstances as they often use guarantees to market the goods to potential buyers. Buyers may well be swayed by the seller placing a great deal of emphasis on the manufacture's guarantee and this may encourage them to purchase the goods. All guarantees must be in intelligible English and they must be made available in writing to consumers, if so requested, within a reasonable time. The provisions in the Regulations relating to guarantees can be found in Sections 14(2D), (2E) and (2F) of the Sale of Goods Act 1979.

 Key point: A guarantee is now directly enforceable against the person who issued it and against any other person who uses it as part of his marketing operations to sell goods.

How helpful is the requirement of satisfactory quality?

In theory, the reforms introduced by the Sale and Supply of Goods Act 1994 make it much easier for buyers to reject goods even when the defect is not particularly serious e.g. the occasional leaking of oil from a car's power steering system. In such situations, buyers should be able to rescind the contract and receive a refund from the seller. In addition, the buyer may also be entitled to claim damages where appropriate. This important reform affecting the standard of quality, which clearly favours the buyer, has meant that the seller has had to raise his game in order to ensure that he supplies goods which meet the standard of satisfactory quality.

The modern statutory requirement of satisfactory quality is a much easier concept to understand than the older requirement of merchantable quality. It will, of course, remain fatal to any claim brought by the buyer if he fails to take reasonably swift steps to cancel the contract upon the discovery of a defect in relation to the goods. However, the changes introduced by the Sale and Supply of Goods Act provide protection to buyers in one important respect. They will only be deemed to have accepted the goods when they have had a reasonable opportunity to satisfy themselves that the article in question conforms to the contract. The question of what is a reasonable opportunity will, of course, be a factual one for the courts to decide.

 Key point: In theory, the requirement of satisfactory quality makes it much easier for a buyer to reject defective goods than was previously the case.

Fitness for purpose

Section 14(3) is concerned with a situation where the buyer relies expressly or impliedly on the seller's expert knowledge in relation to the goods. Where the seller sells goods in the course of a business and the buyer makes known to the seller any *particular purpose* for which the goods are being bought, there is an implied condition that the goods supplied under the contract are reasonably fit for that purpose whether or not that is one of the usual purposes for which those goods are commonly supplied. Section 14(3) would not apply if it was obvious from the circumstances of the contract that the buyer had chosen not to rely, or that it was unreasonable for the buyer to rely on the skill or judgement of the seller. In certain situations, the buyer may be more of an expert than the seller or the buyer will have given the seller very specific instructions concerning the type of goods that are to be supplied under the contract of sale.

There is no need for the buyer to spell out to the seller the particular purpose for which the goods are bought when they have, in the ordinary way of things, only one particular purpose e.g. a hot water bottle or a pair of woollen underpants. If ordinary goods in everyday use are required for a particular or unusual purpose this must be made known to the seller if the buyer is to have any chance of bringing a successful claim under Section 14(3) at some point in the future.

 Key point: Where the seller sells goods in the course of a business and the buyer makes known to the seller any particular purpose for which the goods are being bought, there is an implied condition that the goods supplied under the contract are reasonably fit for that purpose.

 Priest *v* Last (1903) An india rubber hot-water bottle burst open severely scalding the pursuer's wife in the process. The pursuer wife was suffering from cramp and she been had advised to apply a hot water bottle to those areas of her body that were particularly painful in order to ease her discomfort. The pursuer had asked the chemist if the hot water bottle could be filled with boiling water. The chemist told him only to use hot water to fill the bottle. The pursuer followed this advice, but unfortunately the bottle was not fit for its purpose (in terms of the old Section 14(1) of the Sale of Goods Act 1893) and the bottle burst open causing the pursuer's wife to sustain serious injuries when she was scalded by the hot water. The chemist was liable for the injuries caused.

 Griffiths *v* Peter Conway Ltd (1939) The pursuer bought a Harris tweed coat from the seller which had been made to order in accordance with the buyer's specific instructions. Unfortunately, the garment's material inflamed the pursuer's skin and, consequently, she developed serious dermatitis. The pursuer brought a claim for damages alleging that the goods were not fit for their purpose in terms of Section 14(1) of the Sale of Goods Act 1893 (now Section 14(3)).

Held: The pursuer failed in her claim under Section 14(1) because she had not taken steps to inform the seller that she was highly allergic to a material like Harris tweed. A very important aspect of this case was that the seller had acted in accordance with the buyer's instructions and, at no time, had the seller's skill and expertise been relied on by the buyer. Furthermore, the buyer's discomfort was a direct cause of her unusually sensitive skin and not a failure by the seller to supply goods that were fit for their purpose.

 Key point: If ordinary goods in everyday use are required for a particular or unusual purpose this must be made known to the seller if the buyer is to have any chance of bringing a successful claim under Section 14(3) at some point in the future.

Relying on the seller's skill and expertise

It is now a good question as to what extent buyers will rely on the seller's alleged skill and expertise in relation to the fitness of the goods for a particular purpose. Many retail outlets stock brand goods and, arguably, it is the manufacturer's reputation that will be a major influence on whether the buyer decides to enter the contract of sale. Volkswagen cars, for example, are considered to be very reliable products and have an excellent reputation. Will the buyer then be relying on the seller's skill and expertise when he purchases a Volkswagen car?

Clearly, however, there are many situations where the buyer will be relying on the expert knowledge of the seller. Basically, this means that the buyer expects the seller to select his stock with the necessary degree of care. The buyer, in turn, must show that he has made known the particular purpose for which the goods are being bought. Reliance will then be presumed and it will be up to the seller to show that this was not the case or that the buyer had unreasonable expectations.

Grant v Australian Knitting Mills Ltd (1936) the buyer was held to have relied on the seller's skill and judgement in the sense that there was an implied duty imposed upon the seller that he will take reasonable care when selecting goods to be sold in his shop, retail outlet or as part of his general business activity The goods (long woollen underpants) were not fit for their purpose and, as previously discussed, they were not of merchantable (now satisfactory) quality.

The difference in treatment of the buyers in both **Grant v Australian Knitting Mills Ltd and Griffiths v Peter Conway Ltd** can be explained by the fact that the buyer in Grant had perfectly normal skin and his injuries were caused by the seller supplying goods that were not fit for their purpose.

Situations where the buyer's reliance on the seller's skill and expertise will be unreasonable

Slater v Finning Ltd (1997) the House of Lords decided that the buyers had not relied on the seller's skill and expertise. The sale involved the supply of a replacement camshaft that was to be fitted to a marine diesel engine. The camshaft was known to operate perfectly in many types of engines. Unfortunately, when it was fitted to the buyer's engine it caused a huge amount of noise and it was prone to a great deal of wear and tear. These problems, however, appeared to be caused by the design of the boat to which the engine was fitted. The buyer had failed to inform the seller that the boat had an unusual feature which made that particular camshaft unfit for the buyer's purposes. The seller had not committed a breach of Section 14(3) when the goods were supplied to the buyer.

Wren v Holt (1903) The defender held the tenancy of a public house. The pub was tied to a brewery and the defender was obliged to sell a particular type of beer supplied by the brewery. The pursuer was a regular customer and knew that the pub was a tied house, and that only one type of beer was sold. The pursuer became ill and it was proved that he had suffered arsenic poisoning as a result of the beer that he had consumed. The pursuer sued the defender.

Held: that there was no claim under Section 14(1) of the 1893 Act because the pursuer could not be said to have relied upon the defender's skill and judgement when it came to the selection of the stock, because the defender was bound to supply these products. However, Section 14(2) of the Act applied and since the beer was not of merchantable (satisfactory) quality, the pursuer was entitled to compensation.

B S Brown & Sons Ltd v Craiks Ltd (1970) the buyers brought a claim against the sellers for breach of Section 14(1) of the Sale of Goods Act 1893 on the grounds that the sellers had supplied goods that were not fit for their purpose. The buyers failed to communicate to the sellers that the goods were required to make dresses. The sellers supplied cloth that was perfectly suitable for a variety of industrial uses.

Held: by the House of Lords that it was totally unreasonable for the buyers to insist that they had relied on the sellers' skill and expertise in terms of Section 14(1).

 Key point: The buyer must demonstrate that he relied on the seller's skill and expertise and that it was reasonable for him to so in order to be protected by Section 14(3).

Quality and fitness for purpose: an unfortunate overlap?

We have already noted that there is a distinction between the two heads of liability in Section 14: quality and fitness for purpose (**see Baldry v Marshall (1925)**). This distinction, however, is perhaps not quite as clear as it should be and there is certainly a relationship between the two heads of liability. The phrase fitness for purpose appears in both Section 14(2B) and Section 14(3). It would be a mistake to assume that the phrase, as it appears in both sub-sections, has the same meaning. In terms of Section 14(2B), fitness for purpose appears as an aspect of satisfactory quality. In relation to the requirement of satisfactory quality, fitness for all the purposes that goods of that type are commonly supplied refers to the common or general purpose of the goods. In clear contrast, the phrase fitness for purpose as it appears in Section 14(3) refers to situations where the goods are supplied for a very specific or particular purpose. Furthermore, Section 14(3) operates on the basis that the buyer has expressly or impliedly communicated the purpose for which he requires the goods and the seller is aware of this purpose. It is very unfortunate that Parliament, by introducing the modern standard of satisfactory quality, which goes a long way in greatly improving the law, has confused matters by using similar phrases which mean different things depending upon which sub-section is relevant.

Fitness for purpose distinguished?

A useful way of distinguishing between fitness for purpose in Section 14(2B) and Section 14(3) is to examine the decision of the House of Lords in **Slater v Finning Ltd (1997)**. It should be recalled that the camshaft supplied for use in the buyer's engine was of satisfactory quality in the sense that it was perfectly fit for all its common purposes (or general uses) in terms of Section 14(2B). The camshaft was not fit for a specific purpose i.e. it was not suitable for use in the buyers' boat because a peculiarity of this vessel. However, the buyer failed to bring a successful claim against the seller on the grounds that the goods were not fit for their purpose in terms of Section 14(3). The reason for the failure of the buyer's action was the fact that the vessel suffered from a peculiarity of movement that was never communicated to the sellers.

A useful distinction can also be made here by applying the facts of **Griffiths v Peter Conway Ltd (1939)** to the modern Sale of Goods Act. Had the buyer taken steps to communicate to the seller the fact that she had hyper-sensitive skin, the seller would have been duty bound to supply a Harris Tweed coat that was fit for its purpose i.e. a garment that would not cause the buyer to develop dermatitis. In other words, the goods would be able to cope with any of the buyer's special needs or peculiarities. The buyer in **Griffiths**, of course, failed to alert the seller that she had hyper-sensitive skin condition. On the other hand, the coat was fit for all of its common purposes and would, therefore, comply quite easily with the modern requirement of satisfactory quality. It should be appreciated that most buyers who purchased such a coat would have experienced no problems and the item in question would have been perfectly suitable.

Does Section 14 apply to sale or discounted goods?

Where ordinary consumers are concerned, there appears to be something of an urban legend which suggests that buyers are not entitled to raise complaints with the seller in connection with the requirements of quality and fitness if the goods were purchased in the course of a sale or where the goods were discounted. Section 14 undoubtedly applies to situations where the goods are sold in a sale. Very often, the whole point of the seller holding the sale in the first place is in order to clear unwanted or out of season stock. It will hopefully be appreciated that there is nothing wrong with these sale goods and they should fully comply with the requirements of fitness for purpose and satisfactory quality. In any case, the seller will continue to be able to escape liability in a sale for defects which were drawn to the buyer's attention or defects which should have been obvious to a buyer who has carried out a reasonable examination of the goods before the contract was formed. Furthermore, the seller can also escape if he is able to prove that the buyer did not rely on his skill or expertise when the goods were sold during the sale. Should a seller even attempt to exclude the possibility of refunds in relation to sale goods this would be unlawful and such a disreputable practice is treated as automatically void in terms of the Consumer Transactions (Restrictions on Statements) Order 1976.

 Key point: Sale goods will be covered by Section 14, unless the seller makes it clear that the reduction in price relates to the fact that the goods are not of satisfactory quality or they are not fit for their purpose.

Packaging, instructions and other items supplied with the goods

The implied terms in Section 14 covering fitness and satisfactory quality also apply to any additional items supplied with the goods as part of the contract of sale – even if such items are returnable to the seller e.g. a glass bottle. Such items might include packaging, boxes, bottles, containers, batteries, tools and instructions detailing the various uses of the product. All these items must satisfy the requirements of fitness and quality.

 Geddling *v* Marsh (1920) The defenders were manufacturers of mineral water and they supplied these products to the pursuer who ran a small general store. The bottles were returned to the store when the mineral water had been drunk by the consumers. One of the bottles was defective, and while the pursuer was packing it away in a crate, it shattered and she sustained injuries as a result.

Held: that even though the bottles were returnable, they were supplied in connection a contract of sale and, therefore, Section 14(3) of the Sale of

Goods Act applied. The court was of the opinion that, although the bottles had been supplied to the pursuer on a loan basis, the manufacturers were still subject to the implied term that items such as bottles must meet the requirement of fitness for purpose. Consequently, the defenders were liable in damages to the pursuer for the injuries that she had suffered.

 Wormell v RHM Agriculture (East) Ltd (1987) The English Court of Appeal was at pains to point out that instructions supplied with goods must meet the requirements of Section 14 of the Sale of Goods Act 1979. If instructions were supplied to the buyer that were either wrong or seriously confusing, this could mean that the buyer has a potential claim under Section 14(2) (satisfactory quality) and/or Section 14(3) (fitness for purpose). Happily for the seller in this case, the Court of Appeal held that the instructions complied with the requirements of Section 14 and the buyer's argument that the instructions supplied with the goods were completely inadequate was dismissed.

 Key point: Packaging and instructions supplied with the goods must also meet the standards of fitness and satisfactory quality as required by Section 14.

Goods in their natural state

If the sale involves goods which are still in their natural state i.e. they have not undergone some sort of manufacturing process, the buyer is still entitled to presume the goods meet the requirement of satisfactory quality in relation to Section 14(2) and he can rely on the seller's skill and expertise in selecting such items in terms of Section 14(3). Producers and sellers of organic food products will have, therefore, have to be particularly careful.

An extremely good example that goods in their natural state must comply with the requirement of fitness for purpose in Section 14(3) of the Sale of Goods Act 1979 can be seen in the following case:

 Frost v Aylesbury Dairy Co Ltd (1905) The pursuer was able to demonstrate that it was not unreasonable for him to rely on the seller's skill and expertise. The defenders had sold milk to the pursuer, but the milk had become contaminated with an extremely virulent germ that was the cause of the death of the pursuer's wife from typhoid fever. Despite the fact that the goods had not undergone a manufacturing process, the seller had a duty to select his stock with the necessary level of skill and care and it was not unreasonable for the buyer to rely on the presumption that the goods were fit for their purpose.

Held: by the English Court of Appeal that the sellers must have been aware that the milk had been purchased for a particular purpose which the buyer had no need to communicate to the seller i.e. the goods were to be drunk by someone. The defenders were in breach of Section 14(1) of the Sale of Goods Act 1893 for failing to supply goods that were fit for their purpose. It should be noted that the seller's liability in this case was deemed to be strict.

Key point: A seller will be strictly liable for any breaches of the implied terms regarding quality or fitness in terms of Section 14 which have occurred in relation to the supply of goods in their natural state.

Second hand goods

It would obviously be unrealistic for buyers to presume that second hand goods comply with extremely high standards of quality or that they are fit for their purpose. Merely, however, because goods are second hand does not mean that the seller can escape liability for breaches of Section 14 in relation to the issues of quality and fitness for purpose. The buyer will be entitled to presume that the seller has demonstrated the necessary level of skill and care demanded by Section 14 of the Sale of Goods Act when it comes to selecting items of his stock.

 Crowther v Shannon Motor Company (1975) The pursuer had purchased an eight year old Jaguar car which had 85,000 miles on the odometer from the defenders. He claimed that he had relied on the skill and judgement of the defenders when selecting the vehicle for purchase. For a period of three weeks after purchasing the car, the pursuer's total mileage was approximately in the region of 2,000 miles. However, problems with the car began to occur and, soon afterwards, the engine seized up meaning that it had to be completely replaced. During evidence at the trial, given by the previous owner of the car, it emerged that the defenders were fully aware that the engine was not fit for its purpose.

Held: the defenders had committed a breach Section 14(1) of the Sale of Goods Act 1893 by supplying a vehicle to the pursuer that was not fit for its purpose. The buyer had quite clearly relied on the seller's recommendation and he had the right to expect that the seller's selected items of their stock with the necessary degree of skill and care. It made no difference whether the goods were second hand or not. It will also be appreciated that the car was not of merchantable quality in terms of Section 14(2) of the Sale of Goods Act 1893.

As a result of the introduction of the Sale and Supply of Goods to Consumers Regulations 2002, the buyer in the above case would now have an even stronger claim. The Regulations provide that if defects in goods emerge or they are not fit for their purpose within six months of the date of the contract of sale, there is a strong presumption in the buyer's favour that the seller has committed a breach of Section 14(2) and (3) of the Sale of Goods Act 1979.

 Key point: The implied terms in Section 14 relating to quality and the fitness also apply to second hand goods sold by the seller in the course of business.

Trade customs and practices

Section 14(4) provides that an implied term relating to quality or fitness for a particular purpose may be incorporated into a contract by sale by reference to particular trade customs or practices. Certain trades and professions have their own rules or customs which permit a court to imply certain terms concerning fitness and quality into the agreement.

Using an agent to sell goods

If a private seller uses an agent to sell the goods, it is absolutely vital that the agent takes all necessary steps to alert potential buyers to the seller's status. The statutory protection afforded by Section 14 to a buyer will only apply if the seller is selling in the course of business. However, if the agent of a private seller fails to communicate the seller's status to the buyer, the seller may be liable under Section 14(5) if the goods do not comply with the requirements of quality and fitness in Section 14(2) and 14(3) respectively.

As the following case demonstrates, an auctioneer acting for a private seller will have take to special care to publicise the status of his principal:

 Boyter v Thomson (1995) an auctioneer, failed to alert potential buyers to the fact that the principal, the owner of a cabin cruiser, was selling the goods in his capacity as a private seller. The buyer later discovered that the vessel was unfit for its purpose (it was unseaworthy) and he sued the seller. The seller argued that Section 14 did not apply to him because he had not been selling the goods in the course of business. The buyer, in turn, argued that Section 14(5) applied since at no time had the auctioneer alerted him to the seller's private status.

Held: by the House of Lords that Section 14(5) applied and the buyer was entitled to damages for breach of the implied term as to fitness. The seller became liable to the buyer under Section 14 when the agent failed to communicate the information about his private status. It would, of course, be an option for the seller to sue the auctioneer for breach of his duty of care.

 Key point: Private sellers who use agents to sell the goods will have to be careful that they are not caught out by provisions of the Sale of Goods Act.

Strict liability

The seller is liable for all breaches of the implied terms in Section 14 even though he is merely marketing the goods as a wholesaler or a retailer. This means that the seller is also liable for any defects that were not apparent when the goods were originally sold, but which later emerge within six months of the goods being supplied to the buyer (**Sale and Supply of Goods to Consumers Regulations 2002**). The seller cannot use the fact that the goods have a manufacturing defect in order to escape his liability to the buyer. The buyer's contract is with the seller and it is irrelevant to the buyer whether the defect has been caused by a manufacturing fault or not. All the buyer is concerned with is that the seller has supplied him with faulty goods. In this way, the seller's liability is said to be strict in the sense that the buyer does not have to prove fault or blame on the seller's part. A seller can in turn sue the manufacturer for supplying him with defective goods if the buyer has successfully sued him for defects in the goods. In **Grant v Australian Knitting Mills Ltd (1936)**, the retailer was strictly liable to Grant for the sale of dangerous and defective goods which caused injury. Clearly, the injuries were caused as a direct result of the manufacturer's negligence i.e. the failure to remove the dangerous chemical from the underwear. However, the buyer had a contract of sale with the retailer and it was the retailer who remained strictly liable for the defective goods and for the buyer's injuries. The retailer would, of course, have a contractual claim for damages against the manufacturer.

It is important to appreciate that the seller is not just potentially liable to the buyer for the price of the goods. The buyer may have suffered a personal injury (as in **Grant *v* Australian Knitting Mills Ltd (1936)**) or his property may have been damaged as a result of using the defective goods. The seller will, therefore, have to compensate the buyer for any injuries suffered or any damage caused as a result of using the goods.

The seller's liability is also said to be strict if he breaches any of the other implied terms in relation to Sections 12, 13 and 15. In these situations, the buyer does not need to prove fault on the seller's part.

 Key point: When strict liability applies, the seller is responsible for all defects in the goods even though he may not be the manufacturer of the goods and he will do him no good if he states to the buyer that he is not responsible for the defects.

The seller's liability in respect of injuries to third parties

It is important for the seller to be aware of the following situation. Should he sell goods to the buyer which cause injury to third parties or damage to the property of these individuals as a direct consequence of the buyer using the goods, he must compensate a buyer who has been successfully sued by a third party. The seller, however, will escape liability if the buyer has continued to use the goods in the full knowledge that they have become defective and dangerous.

 Lambert *v* Lewis (1981) a trailer that was being towed behind a Land Rover owned by Lewis broke loose from the vehicle and crashed into a car coming in the opposite direction. Two of the occupants of the second vehicle (a father and son) were killed in the accident and the remaining two passengers (the mother and daughter) were badly injured. It later emerged that the trailer had been defective i.e. its towing hitch had been badly designed so that it was only a matter of time before the trailer broke free from any car to which it had been attached. The survivors of the accident brought an action for damages against Lewis who in turn claimed that the seller of the trailer should be liable for breach of the implied terms in Section 14 (i.e. the goods were not fit for their purpose nor were they of merchantable (satisfactory) quality).

Held: by the House of Lords that the victims' claims against Lewis should be allowed to succeed. However, the claim by Lewis against the retailer was rejected because he had been fully aware for some time that the trailer was defective and, indeed, dangerous. It is important to realise that if a buyer continues to use goods that he has become fully aware are dangerous, his claim for a compensation payment from the seller will be rejected.

Sale by sample (Section 15)

Section 15(1) states that a contract of sale is a contract of sale by sample where there is a term in the contract, express or implied, to that effect. The mere fact that the seller provides a sample to the buyer is not enough. There must be an express provision in the contract to that effect, or there must be evidence that the parties intended the sale to be by sample.

There are three implied conditions in a sale by sample:

◆ That the bulk will correspond with the sample in quality (Section 15(2)(a))
◆ The buyer shall have a reasonable opportunity of comparing the bulk with the sample (Section 15(2)(b))
◆ That the goods will be free from any defect, making their quality unsatisfactory, which would not be apparent on reasonable examination of the sample (Section 15(2)(c))

The buyer will not have accepted the goods until he has had an opportunity to compare the bulk with the sample, and will be able, therefore, to reject the goods, even though they have been delivered, if the bulk does not correspond with the sample.

The seller is entitled to assume that the buyer will examine the sample. This means that the buyer will lose any protection guaranteed by the implied condition of satisfactory quality if the defect could have been discovered by reasonable examination of the sample. This will be the case whether or not there has in fact been an examination of the sample. A reasonable examination for the purpose of a sale by sample is the type of examination which is usually carried out in the trade concerned.

 Key point: The mere fact that the seller provides a sample is not enough for the transaction to be regarded as sale by sample – there must be clear evidence that the parties intended the transaction to operate in this way.

 Steels & Busks Ltd v Bleecker Bik & Co Ltd (1956) the buyers purchased five tons of pale, crepe rubber 'quality as previously delivered'. This phrase was understood to mean that the transaction was intended to be a sale by sample, the sample being the goods previously delivered. The goods were intended to be used in the manufacture of corsets, but unlike the previous deliveries the goods contained an invisible chemical which stained the corset fabric.

Held: the sample corresponded with the bulk in quality in terms of any visual examination and the goods were of merchantable (satisfactory) quality in that the stains could be easily washed out or neutralised. There was no breach of the implied term.

 This is in contrast to **Ruben v Faire (1949)** where the buyers had seen a sample of the goods which consisted of soft rubber. The bulk goods, however, were crinkly, but the sellers claimed that this problem could easily be solved by heating the goods to make them soft in order to comply with the sample that had been presented to the buyers. When the sample was compared with the bulk goods it was obvious, after a visual inspection, that the sample and the bulk did not correspond with one another.

Held: this was a breach of the implied term in Section 15.

 Key point: In a sale by sample, the actual goods must correspond with the sample in quality, the buyer must have a reasonable chance to compare the sample and the goods and the goods must not have any defects that would not have been apparent when the sample was first examined.

Exclusion or limitation of the implied terms by the seller of goods

In theory, the seller could attempt to exclude the implied duties of the Sale of Goods Act 1979 (Section 55). As was previously discussed in Chapter 2, the introduction of the Unfair Contract Terms Act 1977 and the Unfair Terms in Consumer Contracts Regulations 1999 has meant that a seller's ability to use such clauses has been considerably weakened. Section 20 of the Unfair Contract Terms Act states that the seller cannot attempt to exclude his liability for breaches of Section 12 in either a consumer or a non-consumer sale. Such an attempt by the seller would be automatically void. Breaches of Sections 13, 14 and 15 of the Sale of Goods Act will also be governed by Section 20 of the Unfair Contract Terms Act 1977. However, Section 17 of the Unfair Contract Terms Act classifies sales as either a consumer transaction or a non-consumer transaction. Any attempt by a seller to exclude or limit his liability in relation to Sections 13, 14 and 15 will be automatically void in terms of Section 20 of the Unfair Contract Terms Act. A seller in a non-consumer sale may be able to exclude or limit his liability in terms of Sections 13, 14 and 15 if he can show that this attempt is reasonable. Furthermore, Section 61(5A) of the Sale of Goods Act 1979 firmly places the burden of proof on the seller to show that the buyer is not acting as a consumer. The additional rights granted to consumers under the Sale and Supply of Goods to Consumers Regulations similarly cannot be excluded by the seller. It should be recalled from the discussion in Chapter 2, that the Unfair Contract Terms Act does not prevent a business seller from excluding or limiting his liability in a consumer transaction. The implied terms are sacred, of course, but the seller may be able to try his luck with some of the less important terms of the contract and this may be viewed as not an entirely unreasonable attempt. In terms of the test of reasonableness, useful guidelines are to be found in Section 24 and Schedule 2 of the Unfair Contract Terms Act (see Chapter 2 for a fuller discussion).

As for the Unfair Terms in Consumer Contracts Regulations 1999, any standard term in consumer contract for the sale of goods (whether written or verbal) can be subjected to a test of fairness. Many, blatantly unfair terms will fall foul of the Regulations. Schedule 3 of the Regulations, it will be recalled, provides 17 examples of clauses that may be regarded as unfair.

An example of an unreasonable clause in a non-consumer contract can be seen in the following case:

 Knight Machinery (Holdings) Ltd v Rennie (1995) the contract of sale imposed a term whereby the buyer of a printing machine had to give a written notice of rejection of the goods within seven days of delivery. The installation of the machine took several days and any defects would probably not be discovered by the buyer until a considerable period of time had passed. The clause limiting liability was completely unreasonable.

The decision of the House of Lords in **Smith v Eric S Bush (1990)** and the decision of the English Court of Appeal in **St Albans City and District Council v International Computers Ltd (1996)** are both interesting examples of the judicial approach to the test of reasonableness under the Unfair Contract Terms Act 1977. Both cases were reviewed in Chapter 2.

Key point: There is a far greater chance that the implied terms could be excluded by the seller in a contract of sale, but this is subject to the Unfair Contract Terms Act 1977. Consumers, on the other hand, are very well protected in terms of the 1977 Act and the Unfair Terms in Consumer Contract Regulations 1999.

The supply of goods – implied terms

It should perhaps be drawn to the reader's attention that not all contracts for the supply of corporeal, moveable goods will satisfy the definition of a sale contained in Section 2 of the Sale of Goods Act 1979 (as amended). Some goods will be supplied to a consumer under a hire purchase agreement whereby the property in the goods remains with the supplier even though the consumer will have possession and the use of the goods during the currency of the agreement. Admittedly, the consumer in a hire purchase agreement does have an option to become the owner of the goods, but only when the last instalment payable under the agreement has been made or upon payment of a final, nominal sum to the supplier.

As a hire purchase agreement is a transaction which cannot be classified as a sale in terms of Section 2 of the Sale of Goods Act 1979 and as such the consumer simply does not benefit from the protection offered by the implied terms (in Sections 12–15 of the 1979 Act) which a buyer of goods enjoys.

Where does this situation leave the consumer in a hire purchase agreement should a problem arise in relation to disputes about the supplier's title; the description of the goods, the quality and fitness of the goods; and sample goods?

Thankfully, consumers in a hire purchase agreement already enjoy many of the rights taken for granted by buyers of goods courtesy of provisions to be found in the Supply of Goods (Implied Terms) Act 1973. This Act contains provisions which are almost identical in scope and effect to the implied terms found in the Sale of Goods Act 1979. In **Lamarra v Capital Bank plc & Shields Automative Ltd t/a Shields Landrover (2006)**, a consumer who had been supplied with a vehicle under a hire purchase agreement which was not of satisfactory quality brought a successful action in the Court of Session to have the goods rejected.

The relevant provisions of the Supply of Goods (Implied Terms) Act 1973 can be seen below:

Section 8 – Implied terms as to title
Section 9 – Bailing or hiring by description
Section 10 – Implied undertakings as to quality and fitness
Section 11 – Samples

Consumers in hire purchase agreements and transactions where goods were redeemed in exchange for trading stamps, however, were the only individuals to benefit from the protection of these types of implied terms. Individuals who perhaps leased or hired goods from a supplier did not enjoy the protection of the implied terms. Similarly, those individuals who sold goods e.g. plant and equipment to a person in order to raise funds and then leased these goods back to use them in their business activities (with a view to re-purchasing these items at a later date) were not covered by the protection of any implied terms.

Since the passage of the Sale and Supply of Goods Act 1994, which inserted Part

1A into the Supply of Goods and Services Act 1982, many more individuals who enter into contracts for the supply of corporeal, moveable goods (for short or long term use) will now enjoy the automatic protection of the implied terms. Such contracts include not only hire purchase agreements and goods supplied in exchange for trading stamps, but also the following types of transactions:

◆ general contracts of hire and lease
◆ contracts for which there is no consideration (i.e. no money consideration called the price) e.g. barter or exchange contracts
◆ contracts which operate by way of mortgage, charge or pledge

Part 1A of the Supply of Goods and Services Act 1982 came into force on 1 January 1995 and applies to contracts entered into after this date. As we shall see, this legislation is particularly relevant to goods supplied in contracts for services.

 Key point: Not all corporeal moveable goods supplied under a contract will satisfy the definition of a sale as contained in the Sale of Goods Act 1979.

Delivery of corporeal moveable goods

The Sale of Goods Act 1979 provides a set of rules (Sections 27 to 37) which govern delivery of the goods. According to Section 61(1) delivery is defined as the voluntary transfer of possession from one person to another. Goods, therefore, are considered to be delivered if the seller delivers them physically to the buyer or his agent. In many situations, symbolic delivery of the goods will be enough, for example, where the seller hands over the only set of keys to the buyer granting him access to the warehouse where the goods are stored. Where bulk goods owned commonly are concerned (Sections 20A and 20B) delivery can occur when the goods are appropriated to the contract with the result that the ownership transfers from seller to buyer.

It is worth emphasising that the delivery of the goods does not mean that the seller has necessarily transferred the ownership of the goods to the buyer (see **Aluminium Industrie Vaassen BV v Romalpa Aluminium Ltd (1976)** and **Armour and Another v Thyssen Edelstahlwerke AG 1990)**. Delivery is about the transfer of possession as Section 61(1) makes abundantly clear.

 Key point: Delivery is the voluntary transfer of possession of the goods to the buyer by the seller.

We shall now examine the rules relating to delivery in turn.

Section 27

The seller is under a duty to deliver the goods and the buyer has a duty to accept the goods and to pay for them, in accordance with the contract.

Section 28

Unless otherwise agreed by the parties, the seller does not have to deliver the goods unless the buyer is ready to pay for them. On the other hand, the buyer does not have to pay for the goods until the seller is willing to deliver them.

Section 29

Some general rules concerning delivery are provided by this section:

1   The contract may indicate if the seller is to send the goods to the buyer or whether the buyer will have to pick the goods up. If the contract does not address the issue of delivery, the place of delivery is taken to be the seller's place of business, if he has one, and if not, the seller's residence.

In a sale of specific goods and both parties know that the goods are located in another location, then this location will be the place of delivery.

Where goods are held by a third party, there can be no delivery until this individual acknowledges to the buyer that he is holding the goods on the buyer's behalf.

2   Where the contract stipulates that the seller must deliver the goods to the buyer but no time period for this has been agreed by the parties, delivery must take place within a reasonable time. Delivery must take place at a reasonable hour of the day.

3   Unless the parties agree otherwise, the seller must bear the cost of putting the goods into a deliverable state.

Section 30

This section deals with situations where a quantity of goods delivered is wrong. If fewer goods are delivered, the buyer may reject the goods only if the shortfall is material (i.e. a serious breach of contract). The buyer could choose to accept the smaller amount of goods, but he must pay for this at the contract rate.

 Robertson v Stewart (1928) shipbreakers sold to Stewart the wreck of the SS Sheila and all the property that had been salvaged from her by them. Stewart claimed that he was entitled to cancel the contract for material breach on the ground that the shipbreakers had not delivered all the subjects sold but had disposed of some property salvaged by sale or donation to others.
Held: the buyer was entitled to rescind the contract with the seller and was not forced to accept the seller's proposals for a reduction in the price.

Where a larger quantity of goods is delivered, the buyer may accept the amount and pay for the contract amount and reject the remainder. The buyer could accept all the goods if he so wishes, but he must pay for the extra goods. The buyer can only reject the whole of the goods if the surplus is a material breach of contract.

 Shipton, Anderson & Co v Weil Bros & Co (1912) the seller contracted to deliver 4950 tons of wheat. He actually delivered 55 pounds too much, an excess in the goods representing an extra 20 pence in value. The contract between the parties was worth in the region of £40,000.
Held: the excess for which the buyer was not being charged was so slight that it was of no effect.

Section 31

Unless the parties agree otherwise, the buyer should not have to accept delivery of the goods by instalments.

The parties may agree that delivery of the goods can be made by instalments and each instalment will be paid for separately. However, a situation may arise where either the seller makes defective deliveries or the buyer refuses to accept or pay for one or more consignments of the goods. Depending on the circumstances, the breach of contract by either party may amount to a complete rejection of the contract. Alternatively, the contract may still be viable and any claim that a party has would be for damages.

 Maple Flock Co Ltd *v* Universal Furniture Products (Wembley) Ltd (1934) Maple had agreed to sell to Universal 100 tons of a particular product to be delivered in three loads per week as required. The weekly deliveries would be separately paid for. Eighteen loads had been delivered by the sellers each one weighing 1½ tons. The buyers, however, wrote to the sellers informing them that they wished to cancel the contract on the grounds that the sixteenth load was unsatisfactory.

Held: a single breach of contract did not justify the cancellation of the contract, the buyers' remedy was to seek damages.

Section 32

This covers delivery of goods to a carrier.

This Section has been altered by the Sale and Supply of Goods to Consumers Regulations 2002. A distinction will now be made between a consumer buyer and a buyer who purchases goods in relation to his trade, business or profession. We will deal first with the law as it stands for business buyers.

If the contract states that the seller must deliver the goods to the buyer, delivery to a carrier by the seller will discharge this duty. A seller must enter a contract of carriage on terms which are beneficial/reasonable to the buyer. In these circumstances, the seller should have regard to the type of goods and all the circumstances when he enters a contract with the carrier. If the seller does not take reasonable care and the goods are damaged in carriage, the buyer may reject the goods and sue the seller for damages.

 Young *v* Hobson & Partner (1949) the seller arranged a contract with the carrier where the goods were at the 'owner's risk'. The seller could have arranged a contract where the goods were at the carrier's risk at no extra cost to the buyer. The goods were damaged in transit.

Held: the buyer could reject the goods because the seller was in breach of his duty to make the best possible contract with the carrier.

If the buyer is a consumer, delivery of the goods to a carrier by the seller is not to be regarded as delivery to the buyer. This will be the case where the seller is authorised or required to send the goods to the buyer. However, if the buyer arranges for the seller to deliver goods to a carrier who is acting as his agent, this will mean that the goods have been delivered to the buyer. After all, by appointing a carrier to act as his agent, the buyer is sending this person to uplift the goods on his behalf.

Section 33

Goods delivered to a distant place. If the seller agrees to deliver goods at his own risk, the risk of damage to or destruction of the goods remains with the seller until delivery is accomplished. This is regardless of whether ownership has passed to the buyer. Crucially, however, the buyer must accept any deterioration in the goods which normally occurs in the course of transit.

Section 34

Unless otherwise agreed the buyer must accept goods which are delivered and which conform to the contract. If the buyer has not yet had an opportunity to examine the goods which have been delivered, he is considered not to have accepted them until he has had a reasonable chance to examine them. The buyer, of course, will wish to examine the goods in order to ensure that they comply with the contract.

Section 35

The buyer is considered to have accepted the goods:

◆ When he communicates his acceptance to the seller.

◆ When he does anything in relation to the goods which is inconsistent with the seller still being the owner (for example, by using them).

◆ When he has held on to the goods and he has not informed the seller that he intends to reject them. The buyer must inform the seller within a reasonable time that he intends to reject the goods. After the passage of a reasonable time, the buyer loses his right to cancel the contract.

 Mechans Ltd *v* Highland Marine Charters Ltd (1964) the buyers agreed to purchase two steel water buses, the Lomond Lass and the Lomond Princess, from the sellers. The buses were delivered and, after inspection by Ministry of Transport inspectors as provided for in the contract, acceptance certificates were signed by the buyers. After the buses had been used for a few weeks, the buyers took steps to reject them on the grounds of major defects.

Held: that the buyers had expressly accepted the goods and were, therefore, no longer entitled to reject the goods.

Section 35A

The buyer may reject the goods owing to a breach of contract on the part of the seller which affects some or all of the goods. In this situation, the buyer will have the right of partial rejection. The buyer may even accept some of the goods i.e. those which are not affected by the breach and reject the remainder.

Section 36

Unless the parties agree otherwise, if the buyer rightfully refuses to accept goods which have been delivered, he is not obliged to return them to the seller. All the buyer must do is inform the seller about his refusal to accept the goods.

Section 37

If the buyer wrongfully neglects or refuses to take delivery of the goods, he will be liable in damages to the seller.

Shaw, Macfarlane & Co *v* Waddell & Sons (1890) the buyers had entered into a contract to purchase a cargo of coal at a fixed price per ton. There was an express stipulation in the contract that the goods should be delivered at Grangemouth for shipment by the buyer's vessel L'Avenir between April 12 and 16. At the time when the contract was made, a strike by Welsh miners was threatening and the price of Scottish coal was rising rapidly. The L'Avenir sailed late from Belgium and did not arrive at her destination until April 19. The cargo could not be loaded on board the ship until April 23. This delay meant that the sellers were caused great inconvenience because their railway sidings had become completely blocked by the wagons containing the coal intended for the L'Avenir. The sellers rescinded the contract.

Held: the time of delivery was of a material term of the contract, so the sellers were justified in rescinding the contract, and so the buyers were not entitled to damages for the sellers' failure to implement the contract.

 Key point: The rules governing delivery of goods are contained in Sections 27 to 37 of the Sale of Goods Act 1979.

Breach of contract

We are already familiar with the main remedies for breach of contract which form part of the common law of contract from our discussions on the subject in Chapter 2.

The Act provides the buyer and the seller with a number of remedies should they find themselves victims of a breach of contract by the other party.

The seller's remedies

The remedies that a seller can take action under can be divided into two groups and are outlined in Section 38:

◆ Personal remedies i.e. suing the buyer for the price of the goods and/or raising a claim for damages against the buyer.

◆ Remedies against the goods i.e. lien, stoppage in transit and resale.

The seller will wish to rely on these remedies usually when the buyer refuses to pay or cannot pay for the goods. Section 39 states that a seller is to be regarded as an unpaid seller in the following circumstances:

◆ If the whole price of the goods has not been paid or tendered by the buyer.

◆ If the buyer chooses to pay for the goods by cheque, for example, this is to be regarded as a conditional payment.

◆ If the buyer's cheque bounced, then the seller would not have been paid.

◆ If the buyer pays by credit or charge card and there are problems with this payment, then this is the responsibility of the card issuer and not the buyer. The seller would have to raise an action against the card issuer.

Key point: The seller's personal remedies in the event of a breach of contract consist of suing the buyer for the price of the goods and/or raising a claim for damages against the buyer. Additionally, the seller has remedies against the goods consisting of lien, stoppage in transit and resale.

Section 49 – an action for the price

The seller would be able to pursue the buyer for the price of the goods in either of the following circumstances:

◆ The buyer, having now become the owner of the goods, has wrongfully refused or neglected to pay for them as demanded by the contract.

◆ If the contract states that the price was to be paid by the buyer on a certain date and the buyer has wrongfully neglected or refused to do this. It will not matter whether the goods have been delivered or whether ownership of the goods has passed from seller to buyer.

In Scotland, there is nothing to prevent the seller from seeking interest on the price from the date of delivery or from the date of payment.

Section 50 – Damages for non-acceptance

In any of the situations outlined in Section 49 above where the buyer has committed a breach of contract, the seller is entitled to pursue a claim for damages against him.

Usually, the courts presume that the seller will attempt to find another buyer for the goods from the moment that the first buyer breached the contract. In other words, the seller is expected to minimise his losses (see **Gunter & Co v Lauritzen (1894)** in Chapter 2). The courts will calculate the amount of damages by comparing the difference between the contract price and the market price on the date that the buyer was bound to accept the goods. It may be that substantial losses could be suffered by the seller. Alternatively, the market price may have risen and the seller will suffer no real losses and, in that case, the court may merely award nominal damages. The seller will also have to demonstrate to the court that the loss suffered by him is not too remote (see **Hadley v Baxendale (1854)** in Chapter 2).

If the seller fails to take immediate action to find a replacement buyer, he will have to bear the consequences of this decision. He may be fortunate in that a buyer may be willing to pay a higher price for the goods. However, the price may have fallen dramatically causing the seller to make substantial losses. This is a risk that the seller will have to bear. Generally, if the seller does not suffer a loss as a result of the buyer's breach of contract, he will be awarded nominal damages only.

 Key point: A seller will be able to seek damages against the buyer, but he must minimise his loss and the loss claimed must not be too remote.

Sections 39 to 43 – Lien

A right of retention allows the unpaid seller to withhold possession of the goods from the buyer until the price is paid. A right of retention will arise where the buyer has become the owner of the goods but where he still does not enjoy possession of them.

An unpaid seller will have a right of lien where the buyer has not yet become the owner of the goods and where the seller has still not delivered them to him.

The rights of retention or lien are useful remedies for depriving the buyer of the use of his property. Very often the exercise of these rights by the seller will be enough to bring the buyer to his senses and offer payment for the goods to the seller.

 Key point: A right of retention is a very effective remedy in that it allows the unpaid seller to withhold possession of the goods from the buyer until the price is paid.

These rights are only useful where the seller lawfully has possession of the goods. If the seller surrenders possession of the goods then he effectively has given up his right of retention or lien. The seller cannot keep possession if he has given it up.

The seller will be able to use his rights of retention and lien in the following situations:

◆ The seller has not granted the buyer a period of credit in order to pay for the goods.
◆ The goods were sold on credit, but the time for repayment of the credit has expired.
◆ The buyer's insolvency.

Section 44 – Stoppage in transit

An unpaid seller can prevent delivery of the goods to the buyer as long as the goods are in the possession of an independent carrier. An independent carrier is an individual who is not an agent of the buyer. Delivery of the goods to the buyer's agent would, legally, just be the same as handing over possession of the goods to the buyer himself. It is important to note that this right can only be used by the seller in the event of the buyer's insolvency.

 Key point: Stoppage in transit of the goods is only effective in the event of the buyer's insolvency and as long as the goods have not been handed over to the buyer's agent for delivery.

Section 45 defines the duration of transit. Transit will usually begin when the goods are forwarded to a carrier for delivery to the buyer. Transit is regarded as having ended if any of the following apply:

◆ The buyer obtained possession of the goods before delivery.

◆ The goods arrive at their destination and the carrier informs the buyer that he is holding the goods for him.

◆ The goods are delivered to a ship chartered by the buyer and the ship's captain is the buyer's agent.

◆ The carrier has wrongfully refused to deliver the goods to the buyer.

◆ Part delivery of the goods has been made to the buyer and under the contract this indicates an agreement by the seller to give up possession of all of the goods.

Transit will not have ended:

◆ If the goods are rejected by the buyer and the carrier still possesses them. This is even the case if the seller refuses to take the goods back.

- ◆ If the goods are delivered to a ship's captain who commands a ship which has not been chartered by the buyer and the goods are on this vessel.

- ◆ Where part delivery of the goods has been made to the buyer, the remainder of the goods may be stopped in transit.

In terms of Section 46, the seller will issue orders to the carrier to the effect that the goods must be returned to him or he will take possession of the goods personally.

 Key point: The seller can only exercise his right of stoppage if the goods are deemed to be in transit and nothing has been done that gives the buyer possession of them.

Section 48 – Resale

Where the unpaid seller has used his right of lien or has exercised his right to stop the goods in transit, the right to resell the goods may be an attractive option. The right of resale can be used in situations where the goods are perishable (such as foodstuffs). The seller will have informed the buyer that he intends to resell the goods to someone else if the buyer fails to make payment for the goods within a reasonable time.

Alternatively, the contract of sale may contain an express term allowing the seller to resell the goods in these circumstances. If the seller enjoys such a power under the contract, he can sell the goods to alternative buyers and give them good title to the property. If the seller makes a larger profit then he is entitled to this. The only duty imposed on the seller in these circumstances is where the buyer has already made a part payment for the goods and the seller will have to refund this. However, if a refund to the buyer resulted in the seller suffering a loss, the return of the part payment would not be necessary.

There is always the possibility that the seller could make a loss if he chooses to resell the goods to another buyer. An action for damages against the original buyer is, therefore, a viable possibility.

In addition to his right of resale under Section 48, the seller will be able to resell the goods if the buyer has informed the seller that he intends to withdraw from the contract without justification and the seller has accepted this situation.

 Key point: The seller's right of resale can only be exercised by him if the goods are of a perishable nature.

The buyer's remedies

The buyer has three main remedies:

- ◆ Rejection of the goods
- ◆ Damages
- ◆ Specific implement

Section 15B – Rejection of the goods (Rescission)

This remedy will only be available to the buyer if the seller has committed a material breach of contract i.e. a breach of one of the implied terms in sections 12, 13, 14 and 15. If the buyer chooses to reject the goods, he will be able to claim back part or all of the price that he may have paid. Additionally, he may also sue the seller for damages.

In **Clegg v Olle Andersson t/a Nordic Marine (2003)**, Lady Justice Hale (sitting in the English Court of Appeal) made the following remarks about the buyer's right to reject goods which are most illuminating:

In English Law [*and in Scotland*], however, the customer has a right to reject goods which are not of satisfactory quality. He does not have to act reasonably in choosing rejection rather than damages or cure. He can reject for whatever reason he chooses. The only question is whether he has lost that right by accepting the goods... Once again, amendments [*were*] made in... 1994... to strengthen the buyer's right to reject by restricting the circumstances in which he might be held to have lost it...

Lady Justice Hale then went on to clarify the circumstances when the buyer will lose the right to reject the goods:

◆ If he informs the seller that he has accepted the goods
◆ If he acts inconsistently with the seller's interest in the goods (by using them or adopting them as his own)
◆ If he leaves it too long (i.e. the passage of a reasonable time) before telling the seller that he wishes to reject them.

All of the above circumstances (to a greater or lesser extent) depend upon the buyer having a reasonable opportunity of examining the goods to determine whether they conform to the contract (including the implied terms in Sections 12–15).

Significantly, a buyer is not to be regarded as having accepted the goods merely because he asks for or agrees to their repair and he still retains his right of rejection.

Section 51 – Damages for non-delivery

The buyer has a right to sue for damages in situations where the seller wrongfully refuses or neglects to deliver the goods. The buyer may or may not go out and immediately seek a replacement supplier for the goods. If the buyer delays finding replacement goods, he will have to bear the consequences of this decision; he may be fortunate and the price of the goods has gone down in value. However, the price may have risen steeply causing the buyer to pay out more than the original contract price. This is a risk that the buyer will have to consider. Generally, if the buyer does not suffer a loss as a result of the seller's breach of contract, he will be awarded nominal damages only. The amount of damages (as already discussed in relation to the seller's remedies) is subject to the buyer mitigating or minimising his loss and being able to show the court that the loss is not too remote.

Section 52 – Specific implement

It will be remembered from the law of contract that a court can force the party who has broken the contract to carry out his duties under the agreement. In a contract of sale, this would mean that the seller is ordered to deliver the goods. However, this is a very limited remedy and will only be available if the goods are specific or ascertained. Furthermore, the goods must have a unique value, for example, a valuable painting or an antique.

Section 53A – The amount of the buyer's damages

This provision addresses the issue of the amount of damages payable to the buyer as a result of the seller's breach of contract. This amount will be decided by reference to the losses suffered by the buyer which are reasonably foreseeable and are a direct result of the seller's breach. Additionally, if the seller delivers goods to the buyer which are not of the quality required under the contract, the buyer may retain the goods. The amount of damages would be the difference in value of the goods at the time of delivery to the buyer and the value that they would have had if the goods had complied with the contract.

 Key point: The buyer has three main remedies in respect of the seller's breach of contract – specific implement, damages and rejection of the goods.

Additional remedies

Additional remedies available to the consumer buyer are:

◆ Repair
◆ Replacement
◆ Reduction in price
◆ Rescission

If the seller supplies goods which breach Section 13 (sale by description) or Section 14 (implied terms about quality or fitness), then the goods do not conform to the contract of sale.

Under the Sale and Supply of Goods to Consumers Regulations 2002, additional provisions are introduced to the Sale of Goods Act 1979 in the shape of Sections 48A to 48D. The aim of these new Sections is to give consumers more remedies in situations where the goods do not conform to the contract at the time when the buyer becomes the owner of the goods.

Goods which do not conform to the contract of sale within six months of the date of delivery to the consumer will be presumed not to have been in conformity with the contract at the time of delivery (Section 48A(3).

In certain circumstances, the buyer may ask the seller to repair the goods or replace them (Section 48B). The seller will be under a duty to give effect to the buyer's wishes within a reasonable time. The seller must not cause significant inconvenience to the buyer and the seller has responsibility for paying any necessary costs which arise as a result of the buyer's choice of remedy (labour, material or postage). However, the buyer's rights are limited in the sense that it may be impossible for the seller to provide the buyer with his preferred remedy. Furthermore, the buyer's choice of remedy may either place the seller under a completely unreasonable burden or it may be simply more appropriate for the seller to give the buyer a reduction in the price of the goods (Section 48C) or, as a last resort, cancellation of the contract (rescission) may be the only reasonable solution (Section 48C). Although the Regulations use the language of consumer choice, the seller will still have a great deal of say as to whether the goods are repaired or replaced.

If the seller fails to comply with the buyer's wishes within a reasonable time, the buyer will, in any case, be able to demand a reduction in price or rescission of the contract. The courts have power under the Regulations to award an appropriate remedy to a consumer – although it may not be the one originally requested.

However, the remedy of rescission must still be exercised speedily in Scotland and the new Regulations most certainly do not give a consumer a six-month period in which to make up his mind whether to accept or reject the goods. The Regulations also establish a very peculiar legal position. The Regulations give the consumer a right of rescission in respect of the contract, but the seller may be able to side-step this by repairing or replacing the goods. However, many consumers may not realise that the Sale of Goods Act continues to give them a right of rescission which is completely independent of the new Regulations. Consumers who are aware of their legal rights will be able to push for rescission of the contract despite the Regulations.

 Key point: The Sale and Supply of Goods to Consumers Regulations 2002 give consumers additional remedies of repair, replacement, reduction and rescission in situations where the seller breaches Sections 13, 14 and 15.

The Consumer Protection Act 1987

This legislation implements the European Community Directive on Product Liability. **Part 1** of the Act establishes a regime of strict liability in relation to defective products. Part 1 provides **a civil remedy** for those individuals who have suffered injury, loss or damage caused by a defective product. Although liability is said to be strict, a claimant or pursuer must demonstrate that the dangerous product caused loss or injury (see **Kay's Tutor v Ayrshire and Arran Health Board (1987)** in Chapter 3).

Under the Act, an individual does not have to prove that s/he has a contract of sale with the seller of the goods. Remember, this was one of the drawbacks with the Sale of Goods Act 1979 and why Mrs Donoghue in **Donoghue v Stevenson [1932]** could not raise a civil claim against Mr Minchella, the Paisley Café owner who sold the dangerous and defective goods to her companion.

A person who was injured whilst using a defective product will be able to use the Act and also those individuals who were injured as a result of being in close proximity to the product. The injured party will not have to show that someone in the chain of supply has been negligent. Under the Act, the individual need only show that **(a)** loss, injury or damage has been caused; **(b)** that the product suffers from a dangerous defect and **(c)** that this defect caused the loss, injury or damage.

Part 2 of the Act establishes enforcement mechanisms, especially, in relation to the general safety requirement. As we shall see, important amendments have been made to Part 2 of the Act by the introduction of the General Product Safety Regulations 2005.

Part 3 of the Act previously governed misleading price indications, but these sections of the legislation have been all but repealed as a result of the introduction of the Consumer Protection from Unfair Trading Regulations 2008.

The Act is admittedly complicated as it operates within both the civil and the criminal law.

The **General Product Safety Regulations 2005** introduce a general product safety requirement of which distributors and manufacturers will have to be aware.

Breach of the general product safety requirement by a manufacturer or distributor may constitute a criminal offence.

The weakness of the common law on product liability

It should be remembered that the general rule in Scotland where delictual liability is concerned that the pursuer will fail to win his case if he cannot prove that the defender was at fault. The common law which governs product liability cases is no exception to this rule. **Evans v Triplex Safety Glass Co Ltd (1936)** is often used to demonstrate why Part 1 of the Consumer Protection Act 1987 is an improvement on the legal principle which established a manufacturer's liability for dangerous products as laid down in **Donoghue v Stevenson (1932)**. Although most product liability cases will now be brought under the Consumer Protection Act 1987, some cases will still continue to be brought under **Donoghue** and it is important to appreciate that the liability of a defender under the common law and under statute are quite different. The facts of **Evans** are as follows:

 A windscreen was fitted to a car. The windscreen later shattered and it showered the driver and the passengers of the car with glass causing them to suffer injuries. The pursuer brought a claim against the manufacturer for supplying a defective and dangerous product that had caused him to suffer injury.

Held: the pursuer's claim failed because he could not prove that the manufacturer was to blame for supplying a defective product. The windscreen might have been defective and dangerous, but the way in which the windscreen was installed may have made it a dangerous product. The pursuer could not prove with certainty which of these two possibilities was the more likely explanation.

 However, the English decision of **Carroll v Fearon (1999)** now makes it clear that the pursuer in negligence action does not have to pinpoint exactly which part of the manufacturing process caused the dangerous defect in the product. In this case, a car crash resulted in the death of a young girl, a woman lost her sight and six others were injured or harmed in a variety of ways. The cause of the crash was faulty tyres manufactured by Dunlop and the evidence presented at the trial very strongly suggested that Dunlop's manufacturing process had caused the defect. It also emerged at the trial that Dunlop was aware of these defects because there had been other accidents involving Dunlop tyres. The company, however, decided not to go public about these defects. If Dunlop had publicised the defects, the tyres could have been recalled thus preventing more accidents from happening in the future. The trial judge found that Dunlop had been negligent, but Dunlop decided to appeal on the grounds that the judge had not been able to specify where precisely in the manufacturing process Dunlop had been negligent.

Held: by the English Court of Appeal that it was not necessary for the pursuers to pinpoint where exactly in the manufacturing process the defender had been negligent. The pursuers had already presented very strong evidence to show that the tyres were defective and that Dunlop was only too well aware of this.

Key point: The common law rules concerning product liability put the pursuer at a disadvantage because it had to be proved that the manufacturer had been fault by supplying a dangerous product that caused loss or injury to the pursuer.

What types of products are covered by the Consumer Protection Act 1987?

We first of all have to ask ourselves the question what is a product? This question is addressed in Section 1. A product includes any goods (including components and raw materials) as well as gas, water and electricity. This definition would, of course, cover most consumer goods i.e. goods supplied for private use from a business seller/supplier. Heritable property i.e. land and buildings would not be covered by the Act, but the items used to construct buildings would be covered – so building contractors will fall within the scope of the Act. Agricultural produce is also covered by the Act. It used to be the case that agricultural produce had to have undergone some sort of an industrial process in order for Part 1 of the Act to apply. Agricultural produce is 'any produce of the soil, of stockfarming or fisheries'.

Key point: Section 1 of the Consumer Protection Act 1987 states that a product includes any goods (including components and raw materials) as well as gas, water and electricity.

To whom does the Act apply?

The Act really applies to the producer of the defective and dangerous goods. We have to ask ourselves, however, who exactly is the producer? Section 2 of the Act provides us with some helpful answers. The producer can be any one of the following people:

◆ The manufacturer
◆ The abstracter of the product, for example, quarrying or mining activities
◆ The processor of the product (who must have altered the product's essential features)
◆ An own-brander (where someone else manufactures the product but another individual puts his own label on the product)
◆ The individual who imported the product into the European Union

Key point: The Consumer Protection Act 1987 mainly applies to producers and manufacturers of dangerous and defective products.

Who will be regarded as a supplier of goods?

A supplier in the chain of supply could also find himself being sued by the pursuer under the Act. It is essential that a supplier responds as honestly as he can to any enquiries that the pursuer makes regarding the identity of the producer. The pursuer's efforts to identify the producer may not be successful and he will have no option but to rely on the supplier's assistance. If the supplier is unwilling to provide this information, the pursuer will suffer considerable inconvenience which may actually result in him being prevented from pursuing his claim against the producer. The pursuer must address a query to the supplier within a reasonable time and the supplier must respond to the pursuer with the information concerning the producer's identity within a reasonable time. A supplier includes any individual who supplies goods to the pursuer. Section 45 states that the act of supplying goods will include such activities as selling, hiring, lending or supplying them under a hire purchase contract. Furthermore, the goods need not be exchanged for money. Goods supplied as a prize would be covered by the Act.

 Key point: Part 1 of the Consumer Protection Act applies to the following individuals – the manufacturer, the abstracter of the product, the processor of the product, an own-brander and an individual who imported the product into the European Union.

What do we mean when we talk about defective and dangerous goods?

We are really concerned with the product's safety. It must be a dangerous product capable of causing damage to the pursuer's property or capable of causing the pursuer to suffer some sort of personal injury. The fact that the product is not working properly will not give a pursuer the right to raise an action against the defender. Many products are defective without being dangerous in any way. Section 3 deals with this issue and the standard of safety will depend on what individuals 'generally are entitled to expect'. The design of the product, the reasons why it was placed on the market, any warnings or instructions provided and when the product was supplied will all be issues which must be taken into account. To protect himself, a producer should take special precautions in order to reduce any danger that the product might cause. People, amateur DIY enthusiasts, teenagers and children especially, have a tendency to misuse products.

 Key point: A dangerous product is one that is capable of causing damage to the pursuer's property or capable of causing the pursuer to suffer some sort of personal injury – the fact that the product is not working properly will not give a pursuer the right to raise an action against the defender

In terms of damages, what will the pursuer be entitled to claim?

Section 5 addresses the question of damages that the pursuer is entitled to claim from the defender. The Act covers damage which includes death, personal injury or any loss or damage to any property. Liability cannot arise in situations of pure economic loss. When we talk about damage caused by defective products, we have to bear in mind the following issues:

◆ The Act only covers damage to private and not business property.

◆ The Act only applies to claims valued at over £275. The limit of £275 does not apply to cases involving death and personal injuries.

◆ The producer is not liable for damage caused to the defective product itself or any of the product's component parts. In such situations, the pursuer will have to continue to bring an action under the Sale of Goods Act 1979 or the law of delict. The defective product or component must cause injury to persons or damage to other property before the producer will be liable under the Act.

 Key point: Damages will be awarded for loss or injury caused by dangerous products, but economic loss is not recoverable.

Does the Consumer Protection Act give the producer any defences?

Section 4 provides the producer with several defences which he may use to try and escape liability for dangerous products. A pursuer will be fail in his action in the following circumstances:

- The defect was as a result of the defender complying with a statutory provision which relates to the product.

- The producer did not supply the product at any time to another person, for example, this would cover stolen products or products which the producer only intended for his personal use.

- The product's supply was not made in the course of business or for profit.

- The defect did not exist in the product at the time when it was supplied. This would cover wear and tear or tampering.

- The 'development risks' defence which allows the defender to escape liability because scientific or technical knowledge would not be able to pinpoint defects in the product at the time that it was supplied. In order to escape liability, the defender will have to show that no other producer of the goods could have discovered dangers lurking in the product. Manufacturers of mobile phones will no doubt be relieved to discover that they can rely on this defence if ten years from now scientists do manage to prove that these products cause cancer. The development risks defence is the only exception to the standard of strict liability in the Act. This defence is the statutory equivalent of Lord Denning's statement in **Roe v Ministry of Health (1954)** that 'we must not look at the 1947 accident with 1954 spectacles'.

- Contributory negligence i.e. the defect was partly caused by the producer's negligence and partly by the actions of the claimant. Accordingly, the amount of the pursuer's damages may be reduced by the court.

- *Volenti non fit injuria* i.e. the pursuer knowingly and recklessly continued to use the product in a dangerous fashion despite the apparent risks in such a course of action. This is a complete defence and the pursuer will receive no damages.

The defences available to a producer amount to the following:

- The product is not covered by the Act. As we have already seen, Section 1 provides a list of products that are covered by the Act.

- The pursuer cannot prove or identify that the defender is the producer or supplier of the product. Section 2 provides a list of individuals who can be regarded as the producer of the goods.

- The defect in the product is not covered by section 3. In other words, the product has not caused the pursuer to suffer property damage or personal injury.

- The damage is not covered by Section 5. This would cover situations where the product is causes the pursuer to suffer pure economic loss only.

- The defect in the product did not cause the damage.

Key point: Although a defender is said to be strictly liable in relation to dangerous products, there are a number of defences that he can plead in order to escape liability, for example, contributory negligence, *volenti no fit injuria* and the development risks defence.

Part 2 of the Consumer Protection Act 1987 – a short history

Prior to the introduction of the General Product Safety Regulations 2005, Part 2 of the Act established a **general safety requirement (section 10)** in relation to consumer goods and failure to comply with could potentially result in a criminal offence being committed. The general safety requirement applied to all consumer goods i.e. all goods intended for private use or consumption. Some goods such as **growing crops, food, water, feeding stuffs, fertilisers, gas, aircraft, motor vehicles, drugs, tobacco, second-hand goods** and **goods for export** were not covered by this part of the Act. These goods were governed by other areas of the law.

Section 10(1) previously stated that a person will be guilty of a criminal offence if he:

(a) supplies any consumer goods which fail to comply with the general safety requirement;

(b) offers or agrees to supply such goods; or

(c) exposes or possesses any such goods for supply.

Manufacturers and retailers, therefore, had to pay particular attention to the general safety requirement because failure to do so by them could have resulted in a criminal prosecution.

Very simply, consumer goods had to be reasonably safe i.e. the risk of death or personal injury had to be reduced to a minimum having regard to all the circumstances.

However, as we shall see, Section 10 of the Act has now been repealed and replaced with a new general safety requirement which is contained in the General Product Safety Regulations 2005.

How is Part 2 of the Act enforced?

The local council's trading standards officer will be the Act's first line of defence. Under Section 14, they can issue **suspension notices** which effectively prevents suppliers from selling goods which appear to breach the general safety requirement. Under the Act, an aggrieved supplier has the right to challenge the imposition of a suspension notice and they may even be given compensation if it can be proved that the trading standards officer acted wrongly. The trading standards officer also has the power to apply to the procurator fiscal for a **forfeiture order** which would allow them to confiscate the dangerous goods.

Furthermore, Section 13 of the Act gives powers to the Secretary of State at the Department of Business Enterprise and Regulatory Reform (formerly the DTi) and s/he can issue a **prohibition notice** which has the effect of preventing suppliers continuing to sell goods without his consent. The Secretary of State has the additional power under Section 13 of being able to force a trader to publish, at his/her own expense, a **warning notice** about goods which are considered to be dangerous. The worst situation, however, that a manufacturer or retailer could face is a criminal prosecution for breach of the general safety requirement in terms of the General Product Safety Regulations 2005 or for failure to comply with an order or a notice issued under the Act.

Under Section 11(2), the Secretary of State is also given powers to make regulations relating to the safety of products.

Which defences could a manufacturer or a retailer use under the Act?

(a) the manufacturer or retailer took all reasonable precautions and exercised all due diligence to avoid committing a crime;

(b) the offence was caused by another person or due to the fact that the manufacturer/retailer relied on information supplied by another person (this other person **must** be identified); and

(c) the retailer (but not the manufacturer) could show that s/he did not know or had no reason to suspect that the goods were not in compliance with the general safety requirement.

The General Product Safety Regulations 2005

These regulations became effective on 1 October 2005 and implement the EC General Product Safety Directive 2001/95/EC. They repeal the **General Product Safety Regulations 2005 and Section 10 of the Consumer Protection Act 1987 (Part 2)**. The remainder of Part 2 of 1987 Act remains very much in force.

Arguably, the regulations are supposed to reinforce Part 2 of 1987 Act. Considerable criticism has been levelled at Parliament over the continuing practice of having primary legislation (the 1987 Act) and secondary legislation (the 2005 Regulations) which govern the same area. Why not just have one Act which addresses the issue of liability for dangerous and defective goods rather than several different pieces of legislation?

What kinds of things goods the regulations cover?

They cover **new and second hand goods**, but not antiques (**Regulation 30**). Furthermore, a product which is already covered by a specific European Union law which deals with safety will fall outwith the scope of the Regulations. There will, of course, be a presumption (unless the contrary is proven) that products are safe if they comply with certain UK and European rules concerning the safety of the product e.g. the British Safety Institute's kite mark.

The Regulations do make use of the enforcement mechanism which is part and parcel of Part 2 of the 1987 Act and reference must be made to both pieces of legislation. Generally speaking, the Regulations will cover items such as clothing, medicines, agricultural and horticultural products, DIY tools and equipment, food and drink, household goods, nursery goods and motor vehicles.

What do the Regulations have to say about product safety of products?

The regulations are primarily concerned with ensuring the safety of products which consumers will use or are very likely to use. Producers and distributors of goods will now have to be very careful when they supply goods. The regulations apply to second hand goods. The regulations cannot be made use of where the products have been supplied for repair or reconditioning before use. This is, of course, as long as the supplier clearly informs the person with whom he is doing business that the product may not be safe (**Regulation 4**).

Who will be covered by the Regulations?

Producers and distributors will fall within this legislation. According to Regulation 2, a producer of goods can either be a manufacturer or an own-brander. If the manufacturer does not have a place of business or a representative within the European Union, then the person who imported the goods into the European Economic Area (a wider grouping of countries than just the 27 members of the EU) shall be regarded as the producer. Producers can also be any other professionals in the supply chain whose actions can affect the safety of the product. A distributor is any professional whose activity does not affect the safety qualities of a product.

What is a safe product?

The answer to the question can be found in **Regulation 2** which states that a safe product:

> means a product which, under normal or reasonably foreseeable conditions of use including duration and, where applicable, putting into service, installation and maintenance requirements, does not present any risk or only the minimum risks compatible with the product's use, considered to be acceptable and consistent with a high level of protection for the safety and health of persons.

What is the general safety requirement?

This is contained in regulation 5(1) which states that 'no producer shall place a product on the market unless the product is a safe product. A safe product is one which does not present any risk or only the minimum risks when the product is used normally or under reasonably foreseeable conditions, including duration. Regard must be had to whether or not the use of the product was acceptable and consistent with a high level of protection for the health and safety of people. A number of issues **must** be directly addressed:

(a) the characteristics of the product, including its composition, packaging, instructions for assembly and, where applicable, instructions for installation and maintenance,

(b) the effect of the product on other products, where it is reasonably foreseeable that it will be used with other products,

(c) the presentation of the product, the labelling, any warnings and instructions for its use and disposal and any other indication or information regarding the product, and

(d) the categories of consumers at risk when using the product, in particular children and the elderly.

Regulation 7 places a duty on producers to supply consumers with the relevant information regarding the product so all the risks of using the product are readily transparent. The producer should safeguard him/herself against any risks which the product may present and, if the worst comes to the worst, s/he may even have to recall or withdraw the product from the market.

Regulation 8 imposes a duty on a distributor to 'act with due care in order to help ensure compliance with the applicable safety'.

Regulation 9 places a duty on a distributor or a producer with the effect that s/he **must** act with due care in order to ensure compliance with the general safety requirement in regulation 5. A distributor should on no account supply goods which s/he knows to breach the general safety requirement. Furthermore, a distributor should monitor the safety of products, notify enforcement agencies if they placed a dangerous product and pass on information to his/her customers regarding any risks.

NB: A producer or a distributor shall commit a criminal offence if (i) s/he offers or agrees to place on the market any dangerous product or (ii) exposes any such product for placing on the market or (iii) offers or agrees to supply any such product or (iv) exposes or possesses any such product for supply.

Defences

Under Regulation 29, the defence of due diligence is available i.e. the accused took all reasonable steps and exercised all due diligence to avoid committing the offence. The accused could allege (the defence of incrimination) that someone else committed the offence or that s/he relied on information supplied by another. This other person **must** be identified.

Regulation 30 also provides a defence in respect of the supply of antiques. As previously remarked, the supply of antiques is not covered by the Regulations and it will, therefore, not be competent to bring a prosecution under the Regulations in respect of this matter.

Enforcement of the Regulations

Local authority trading standard departments have responsibility for the enforcement of the Regulations (see **Part 2 of the Consumer Protection Act 1987**).

Penalties for contravention of the Regulations

A producer or distributor who places a dangerous product on the market for supply to consumers potentially commits a criminal offence which could be punishable by a maximum fine of £5,000 and/or a prison sentence of up to three months.

The Consumer Credit Act 1974

The credit industry has seen a dramatic expansion since the 1960s onwards in the United Kingdom. There are many new financial products being introduced every month. It is true to say that large numbers of people would not even consider entering a contract of sale for goods and/or services if the supplier was either unwilling to give them credit or allow them to use credit. If, for example, you were thinking about buying a new television from a store and the assistant informed you that the store did not accept credit cards it is highly likely that you would decide to go and shop elsewhere at an outlet where your card was accepted. Similarly, many consumers will often frequent retail outlets where generous credit terms are available, for example, 12-months interest-free credit on any leather suite purchased. Furthermore, retailers are well aware of this growing sophistication on the part of shoppers. Suppliers of goods and services advertise the fact that credit is available in order to tempt consumers to enter into contracts with them. The credit industry provides a valuable service because how many of us would be in a position to purchase the goods and services at the drop of a hat? The reality is that for a vast majority of people a range of goods and services would be out of their reach – perhaps even permanently – if it were not for the availability of credit.

Credit clearly makes the world go round, but it is an industry where strict controls must be applied. For all those individuals who use credit wisely there are many more who incur serious levels of debt which means they face a variety of legal and social problems. The Consumer Credit Act 1974 (as amended) was largely a result of the recommendations of the Crowther Committee. In 1968, the Committee, under the chairmanship of Lord Crowther, had been given a remit by the Labour Government of Harold Wilson to investigate the possibility of introducing a new and unified regulatory system for the consumer credit industry in the United Kingdom. The Committee also had as one of its aims the need to protect ordinary consumers who very often found themselves being taken advantage of by unscrupulous creditors. The poor were often particularly vulnerable and many of these individuals found themselves in the clutches of illegal moneylenders with no realistic hope of paying off the debts that they had run up.

The 1974 Act swept away the old fragmented system of controls on the consumer credit industry. One of the major disadvantages of the law before 1974 was that there were several pieces of legislation which contained different rules governing different areas of the industry. This made the law very confusing for ordinary consumers. There were four major pieces of legislation before 1974:

◆ Pawnbrokers Acts 1872 and 1960
◆ Moneylenders Act 1900
◆ Hire Purchase (Scotland) Act 1965

It was hoped that, by introducing a single, unified regulatory system for the industry, widespread abuses would be stamped out. One of the most distinctive features of the 1974 Act is the fact that those businesses or individuals wishing to provide credit facilities to members of the public must be in possession of a licence. Failure to obtain a licence means the imposition of a number of civil and criminal penalties. As we shall see, licences are not just given to anyone.

It should also be noted that the 1974 Act established a licensing system which covers all activities related to the provision of credit.

On 6 April 2007, the Consumer Credit Act 2006 came into force and considerably amended the Consumer Credit Act 1974. The 2006 Act, which does not replace the Act of 1974, amends the older legislation and greatly strengthens the ability of the Office of Fair Trading to acquire information from credit businesses which currently hold a consumer credit licence.

The new Act introduced an Alternative Dispute Resolution (ADR) procedure run by the Financial Services Ombudsman which was set up for the benefit of debtors to ensure that they incur little or no costs when they decide to challenge an unfair practice of a creditor. It should be noted that debtors who had a dispute with a creditor prior to 6 April 2007 will not be permitted to make use of this procedure.

Furthermore, the procedure cannot be used if the creditor was not actually licensed to conduct a credit business at the time when the dispute arose.

Any debtor who wishes to use the ADR procedure must first submit a complaint in writing to the creditor setting out the background to their grievance. In this way, the creditor is being given an opportunity to resolve the dispute informally. Once the creditor has responded formally to the complaint, the debtor can use the Ombudsman if such a response is deemed to be unsatisfactory.

If, however, the debtor has failed to receive a response from the creditor within 8 weeks of the submission of the complaint then s/he is perfectly at liberty to contact the Ombudsman.

Lastly, reforms will be made to the provisions of the Consumer Credit Act 1974 which govern what were previously referred to as extortionate credit agreements with the aim of providing a more effective means of challenging such agreements in the courts.

 Key point: The Consumer Credit Act 2006 introduces significant changes to the Consumer Credit Act 1974. The 1974 Act continues to be the major piece of legislation which governs the provision of consumer credit in the United Kingdom.

The Annual Percentage Rate (APR)

The Consumer Credit Act 1974 also makes it easier for debtors to compare rates of interest that different creditors charge for providing credit. All creditors must use a standard measure for calculating the interest that they will charge debtors on the sum that they have borrowed. This standard measure is known as the Annual Percentage Rate or the APR. A creditor who charges 9.9% APR on credit card loans for the next six months is a more attractive option that another creditor who charges 17.4% APR for the same period. In this way, the APR can be used by debtors to identify loans with a lower rate of interest payable on them. Previously, creditors could use very different methods to calculate the interest payable on credit and this, obviously, put the debtor at an immediate disadvantage who very often had little idea of how the interest had been calculated and even less of an idea how to make comparisons between different lenders.

The **Credit (Total Charge for Credit) Regulations 1980 (as amended)** and now **Schedule 1 of the Consumer Credit (Advertisements) Regulations 2004** will be used to determine the amount of the total charge for credit (TCC) and specify how to calculate the APR, which takes into account many of the additional charges that are required to be paid by the debtor. The 1980 Regulations also provide guidance in respect of the relevant APR to be paid when a debtor makes early payment of the sums due under a credit agreement.

The 2004 Regulations brought in new rules about the calculation of the APR for running account credit agreements when these details are to be used in advertisements. These Regulations now ensure that at least 66% of credit agreements entered into by the creditor and debtor will be at the typical APR which appears in the advertisement in question. This should mean that the creditor will have to be more transparent and more honest about the typical APR which is relevant to any one of their credit agreements. Previously, a creditor would often use a headline grabbing APR to attract debtors who would then enter an agreement only to be told that they would not benefit from the rate publicised in the advertisement in question.

Finally, the **Consumer Credit (Agreements) (Amendment) Regulations 2004** introduced new rules regarding the calculation of the APR which is to be used in a running account credit agreement.

 Key point: All creditors must use a standard measure for calculating the interest that they will charge debtors on the sum that they have borrowed. This standard measure is known as the Annual Percentage Rate or the APR.

Consumer Credit Agreements

Before 6 April 2008, a consumer credit agreement was principally understood to include an arrangement whereby a creditor provided a debtor with an amount of credit not exceeding £25,000. Reforms introduced by the Consumer Credit Act 2006 have abolished this limit although those credit agreements exceeding £25,000 which were made before 6 April 2008 will not be subject to the provisions of the Consumer Credit Act 1974.

Section 8 of the 1974 Act lays down a definition of a regulated consumer credit agreement i.e. one to which the rules contained in the Act will apply. Such an agreement is an agreement between an individual ('the debtor') and any other person ('the creditor') by which the creditor provides the debtor with credit of any amount.

According to Section 9, the provision of credit would include a cash loan or any other financial arrangement, for instance, a period of time given to the debtor in order to make payment such as six months interest free period on goods purchased.

 Key point: The Consumer Credit Act 1974 now applies to credit bargains valued at more than £25,000 (with no upper limit).

What is consumer credit?

There are two types of credit agreement to which the Consumer Credit Act 1974 applies:

- consumer credit agreements
- consumer hire agreements

As we shall see, certain categories of credit agreements are exempt from the provisions of the legislation, but will be regulated by other laws.

A consumer credit agreement is a contract and, according to Section 189 of the Act, there are two parties to this type of agreement:

- The creditor who is supplying the finance
- The debtor who borrows the money

 Key point: The Consumer Credit Act 1974 applies to consumer credit agreements and consumer hire agreements.

Creditors

Creditors can include any type of business organisation from the individual operating as a sole trader to a major limited company.

Debtors

A debtor is generally regarded as a private person who is seeking to borrow credit. Business organisations such as a company, a limited partnership or a limited liability partnership will not be regarded as a debtor within the meaning of the 1974 Act. Unincorporated business organisations, for example, sole traders and partnerships may be regarded as debtors and may enjoy protection under the Act. Under provisions contained in the Consumer Credit Act 2006, a partnership must consist of 2 or 3 persons not all of whom are bodies corporate.

 Key point: The parties to a consumer credit bargain are known as the creditor (who supplies the credit) and the debtor (who borrows the credit).

Consumer hire agreements

According to Section 15 of the Consumer Credit Act 1974, a consumer hire agreement is one where goods are hired by the owner to an individual ("the hirer"). The agreement is not a hire purchase agreement in that the hirer is not given an option to purchase the goods at the end of the agreement. A consumer hire agreement usually lasts for more than three months.

Hire purchase agreements

In a hire purchase agreement, the hirer of the goods has an expectation that ownership of the goods will pass to him when he either pays the final instalment of the credit loan or makes a final nominal payment for the goods.

A consumer credit agreement can be further classified in the following ways: Running account credit where the debtor can borrow money up to an agreed limit. This category would cover bank overdrafts, credit cards and store cards (Section 11).

Fixed-term credit where the sum borrowed by the debtor is fixed at the beginning of the agreement. This category includes bank loans and hire purchase agreements (Section 11).

Restricted use credit where the sum borrowed by the debtor is for an agreed purpose, for example, a car loan from a bank. This category includes bank loans and hire purchase.

Unrestricted use credit where the debtor is completely free to spend the credit provided on whatever he wishes. This category would include credit cards, store cards and bank overdrafts.

Small agreements are fixed sum credit or running account credit agreements where the value of the credit advanced to the debtor is less than £50 (Section 17). Small agreements tend to be exempt from many of the rules contained in the Act.

Debtor-creditor agreements where the debtor simply borrows money from the creditor. The creditor is not involved in any further transaction which the debtor may enter with a supplier of goods. The creditor lends the money to the debtor and this credit will be used to pay for the goods from the supplier. This is the traditional type of credit agreement and would cover such activities as bank loans.

Debtor-creditor-supplier agreements where the creditor and the supplier of goods may be the same person or where the supplier has links to a creditor who will provide credit to the supplier's customers (the debtors). This is a very common arrangement where car dealerships are concerned in that customers will buy a car from the dealer and then be offered credit to pay for their purchase through a finance house or a bank associated with the dealer (Section 12).

 Key point: Consumer credit agreements can also be classified in the following ways – running account credit, fixed-term credit, restricted use credit, unrestricted use, small agreements, debtor-creditor agreements and debtor-creditor-supplier agreements.

Debtor-creditor-supplier agreements

Debtor-creditor-supplier agreements where the creditor and the supplier of goods may be the same person or where the supplier has links to a creditor who will provide credit to the supplier's customers (the debtors). This is a very common arrangement where car dealerships are concerned in that customers will buy a car from the dealer and then be offered credit to pay for their purchase through a finance house or a bank associated with the dealer (Section 12). This was the kind of relationship which formed the background to the supply of the Land Rover in the case of **Lamarra *v* Capital Bank plc & Shields Automotive Ltd t/a Shields Land Rover (2006)** previously discussed in this chapter.

In terms of Section 56 of the Consumer Credit Act 1974, the supplier in a debtor-creditor-supplier agreement is the agent of the finance house or the bank. When the debtor deals with the supplier during the discussions leading up to his purchase of the goods, the supplier is acting as an agent for the finance house or bank. This kind of arrangement benefits all three parties. The debtor is given access to a source of credit; the supplier can be confident of selling more goods because he is in a position to offer credit to potential customers and the finance house/bank gets someone else (the supplier) to generate custom on its behalf.

Admittedly, however, a creditor could still be liable for any false statements or misrepresentations made by a retailer which influenced the debtor's decision to enter a contract in terms of Section 56 of the Consumer Credit Act 1974. In such situations, the retailer would be regarded as the agent of the creditor.

 Key point: Consumer credit agreements can also be classified in the following ways – running account credit, fixed-term credit, restricted use credit, unrestricted use, small agreements, debtor-creditor agreements and debtor-creditor-supplier agreements.

Debtor-creditor-supplier agreements, however, have certain legal consequences for the finance house or bank if the goods purchased are worth more than £100 in value. Section 75 of the Act allows a debtor to sue either the creditor or the supplier in the above arrangement for a breach of contract committed by the supplier. Section 75 makes the creditor and supplier jointly and severally liable to the debtor for any misrepresentations or breaches of contract committed by the supplier. If the supplier, for example, provides a car which is not of satisfactory quality under Section 14 of the Sale of Goods Act 1979, the debtor could sue either the supplier or the creditor. This may be an attractive option because the supplier may have become insolvent, the debtor may have bought the goods from a foreign supplier, the supplier may be refusing to accept responsibility or the supplier may be difficult to trace.

It should be noted that the cash price of the item purchased by the debtor must be over £100 but must not exceed £30,000.

 Key point: In a debtor-creditor-supplier agreement, the creditor and supplier are jointly and severally liable to the debtor for any misrepresentations or breaches of contract committed by the supplier.

It should be appreciated, however, that these types of agreements do **not** include situations where, for example, a retailer transfers ownership of goods to a creditor in exchange for payment of the purchase price. The goods are then supplied to the debtor and it is to the creditor that the debtor then makes regular repayments in respect of the sum borrowed. The debtor has a contractual relationship with the creditor, not the supplier of the goods.

Loans and credit cards are not always necessarily examples of debtor-creditor-supplier agreements. A loan made by a bank to one of its customers is unlikely to be an example of such an arrangement because the bank is only providing credit and it is not the slightest bit interested where the customer buys the goods. The bank does not have an arrangement with the supplier of goods. However, a company that supplies fitted kitchens may make a loan to a customer so that the customer can have the work carried out. This would be an example of a loan being a debtor-creditor-supplier agreement. The use of credit cards by debtors might also be an example of a debtor-creditor-supplier agreement. If the debtor is not under a duty to pay off the credit owed in one payment, but can make a series of repayments then this will be a debtor-creditor-supplier agreement.

Exempt agreements

Some credit agreements are exempt from UK consumer credit legislation in terms of the following provisions:

◆ Sections 16A, 16B and 16C of the 1974 Act
◆ The Consumer Credit (Exempt Agreements) Order 2007
◆ The Legislative Reform (Consumer Credit) Order 2008

Exempt agreements include the following:

First charge mortgages
The vast majority of mortgage lending in relation to domestic or residential heritable property will be exempt. Such loans can be provided by a local authority, a named bank, building society or insurance company for the purpose of the debtor purchasing the property. These types of arrangements will, in the main, be regulated by the Financial Services Authority rather than the Office of Fair Trading.

Second charge mortgages

Certain second charge mortgages which are secured on heritable property (any exemption will depend on the type of the agreement and the indentity of the mortgage lender). These arrangements are often entered by debtors to raise additional finance (often with the permission of the primary mortgage lender) by means of a 'second mortgage' over the property. Such an arrangement will be ranked lower than the primary or first charge mortgage which the property owner has granted to a bank.

Certain credit agreements involving goods and services

Agreements involving the provision of goods or services in which the debtor has to repay the sum borrowed within one year and the payments must not exceed 4 instalments will benefit from an exemption.

Charge cards

Charge cards and other credit agreements which oblige the debtor to repay fully any balance at the end of the relevant period e.g. per month.

Agreements with credit unions

Agreements entered into with credit unions in situations where the APR does not more than 26.9%.

Low cost debtor-creditor agreements

This is an agreement where the cost of the credit does not exceed a predetermined rate of interest or a rate of interest that is one per cent above the highest of lenders' base rates in the twenty-eight days leading up to the formation of the contract.

Credit to be used in international trade transactions

Credit provided in connection with an international trade contract i.e. where the parties to the contract are based in different states, for example, the United Kingdom and the United States.

Credit to 'high net worth' individuals

This exemption has been inserted by Section 3 of the Consumer Credit Act 2006 (new Section 16A of the Consumer Credit Act 1974). Loans to persons who are deemed to be 'high net worth' individuals i.e. such individuals will have a net income greater than £150,000 or net assets greater than £500,000 and they will have to provide evidence of their income and/or assets.

Loans greater than £25,000 to business organisations

Finance to businesses where the value of this loan is greater than £25,000 **and** this arrangement is primarily for commercial purposes.

With reference to business loans, It should be appreciated that any business organisation which borrows a sum less than £25,000 will remain fully regulated by the consumer credit legislation

Buy-to-let loans

Buy-to-let loans where the debtor borrows a sum to purchase heritable property. To qualify for exemption, such loans cannot be secured on the debtor's main residence (i.e. where s/he is domiciled) and the debtor (or a family member) is not permitted to use or occupy at least 40% (by reference to the land area) of the heritable property.

Key point: Some credit agreements are exempt from UK consumer credit legislation.

The Office of Fair Trading (www.oft.gov.uk)

The Consumer Credit Act 1974 originally gave authority to a Director-General of Fair Trading assisted by the Office of Fair Trading to oversee the regulation of the consumer credit industry in the United Kingdom. The post of Director-General of Trading had been established by the Fair Trading Act 1973. However, the introduction of the Enterprise Act 2002 has resulted in the Office of Fair Trading being given legal status as a corporate body. The post of Director-General of Fair Trading has been abolished.

The Office of Fair Trading is headed by an individual simply known as the Chairman and a Chief Executive (in early 2010 these posts were held respectively by Philip Collins and John Fingleton). The Chairman, is appointed by the Secretary of State at the Department of Business Enterprise and Regulatory Reform (formerly the Department of Trade and Industry) and is aided in his tasks by a Board of two executive directors and seven non-executive members. The Chairman, Chief Executive and the Board are appointed for a period of office not exceeding five years.

The Office of Fair Trading is fully accountable to the UK Parliament and the various devolved administrations such as the Scottish Parliament and it must publish an Annual Report detailing its past activities and its plans for the forthcoming year.

The Office of Fair Trading has a major role to play in promoting free and fair competition amongst businesses and consumer protection. It will continue to be the major enforcement body in the United Kingdom for the law relating to consumer credit.

 Key point: The Office of Fair Trading oversees the regulation of the consumer credit industry in the United Kingdom.

Local authorities and their Trading Standards Departments will also have a role to play as enforcement bodies under the Consumer Credit Act 1974. These bodies will often assist the Office of Fair Trading to carry out investigations of those businesses and individuals suspected of breaking the rules under the Act. If a breach of the Act results in a criminal offence, the local procurator fiscal will commence criminal proceedings against the accused.

Officials of the various enforcement bodies can gain access to premises for the purposes of examining goods and documentation related to credit business activities. These items may even be seized by enforcement officers and used in evidence in later civil or criminal proceedings. Often, the enforcement officers may be refused entry to premises in which they wish to carry out an investigation. If this is the case, it will be necessary to obtain a search warrant from a Sheriff, Stipendiary Magistrate or a Justice of the Peace. It is a criminal offence to hinder or to prevent an enforcement officer from carrying out his duties.

The Office of Fair Trading has primary responsibility for the granting of credit licences under the 1974 Act and the associated secondary legislation. Any individual or business wishing to provide credit facilities must obtain a licence. The licensing system is the main way in which the Office of Fair Trading regulates the credit industry. Activities for which a licence is required include:

1   Consumer credit

2   Consumer hire

3   Credit brokerage

4   Debt adjusting and debt counselling

5   Debt collecting

6   Credit reference agencies

7   Debt administration

8   Credit information services

Activities 3, 4, 5, 6, 7 and 8 are classed as ancillary credit businesses i.e. they are **not** primarily about the creditor requiring regular payments from the debtor.

Failure to obtain a licence when carrying out any of these ancillary credit activities is regarded as unlicensed trading. Creditors will have to be particularly careful that they do not carry out any activities which are forbidden by their licences or which fall outside the scope of their licences.

Furthermore, those creditors who are involved in other financial activities, for example, first charge mortgages and payment protection insurance will also have to ensure that they have obtained the necessary authorisation from the UK Financial Services Authority (FSA).

It is possible for a business to give credit to customers if this is regarded as an occasional transaction. Sometimes, businesses will give particularly good customers credit in order to pay for goods or services. As long as this does not happen very often, the business will not need a licence from the Office of Fair Trading. However, businesses will have to be particularly careful here because if giving credit to various customers becomes a common practice, they may very well be breaking the law if they fail to get a licence. The moral of the story is that if granting credit to customers becomes more frequent, it is better to apply for a licence.

 Key point: In order to carry on a consumer credit business in the United Kingdom it is necessary to obtain a licence from the Office of Fair Trading.

Failure to obtain a licence has certain consequences:

1   It will be a criminal offence to provide credit without a licence (Section 39).

2   The unlicensed trader may be unable to enforce a regulated agreement against the debtor (Section 40).

3   An ancillary credit agreement will be unenforceable if the creditor had failed to obtain a licence when it was made (Section 148).

4   A regulated credit agreement will be unenforceable, if the credit broker who set it up did not possess a licence (Section 149).

However, a creditor who has broken the rules in relation to the licensing requirements of the Act can always apply to the Office of Fair Trading for what is known as a validating order. A validating order allows the creditor to enforce agreements which would otherwise fall foul of the licensing requirements in the Act.

Key point: Failure to obtain a licence when carrying out any of these ancillary credit activities is regarded as unlicensed trading.

Types of consumer credit licence

There are two types of licence recognised by Section 22 of the Consumer Credit Act 1974:

◆ Standard
◆ Group

From 6 April 2008, standard licences are granted to individuals for an indefinite period as a result of reforms introduced by the Consumer Credit Act 2006.

Previously, under Section 22 of the Consumer Credit Act 1974, individuals had to renew such licences every five years.

A group licence is now issued for a period of five years after which it will have to be renewed by the Office of Fair Trading.

Those individuals who are seeking to apply for a licence or to renew an existing one will have to pay a fee to the Office of Fair Trading (Section 6A of the Consumer Credit Act 1974).

 Key point: There are two types of licence recognised by Section 22 of the Consumer Credit Act 1974: standard and group licences.

The Office of Fair Trading can take any information about a creditor's circumstances into account when considering whether to grant or renew a credit licence. Creditors must be fit to carry on commercial activities regulated by the Consumer Credit Act 1974 and they must adhere to these standards of fitness while they hold a licence.

As a result of the Consumer Credit Act 2006, all creditors applying for a licence from 6 April 2008 onwards must satisfy more stringent requirements than was previously the case under the older licensing system. The Office of Fair Trading will now scrutinise an applicant's credit competence and will focus on skills, knowledge and experience which are deemed absolutely necessary to the type of credit activity which the applicant wishes to carry on. The applicant must also provide information to the Office of Fair Trading about its business practices and procedures which it either currently has in place or intends to introduce in order that fully complies with consumer credit legislation.

Individuals who wish to carry on debt collection activities must complete a Credit Competence Plan (CCP1 form) which requires evidence of credit competence and those individuals who wish to be involved in activities deemed to be high risk lending, broking and administration will need to submit a Credit Risk Profile (CRP1 form). Credit reference agencies will also have to submit this form before initiating any activities.

Section 36 imposes a duty on a licence holder to inform the Office of Fair Trading of particular changes which affect the credit business within a period of 28 days. A business would have to inform the Office of Fair Trading if there were changes in personnel to the company's officers or changes affecting the membership of partners in a firm. If the changes in a partnership meant that a firm had a new name, the licence would no longer have any legal effect.

Under Section 37, the following events will cause a licence to become null and void:

◆ If the licence holder dies
◆ If the licence holder is bankrupt and has his estate seized by creditors
◆ If the licence holder becomes mentally incapacitated

Failure by a creditor to inform the Office of Fair Trading of any changes affecting its licence could result in the imposition of a maximum fine of £50,000 (Section 39A).

In any case, the reforms introduced by the Consumer Credit Act 2006 give the Office of Fair Trading far greater powers to demand information from creditors to ensure compliance with the licensing rules.

 Key point: Failure by a creditor to inform the Office of Fair Trading of any changes affecting its licence could result in the imposition of a maximum fine of £50,000.

Under the previous licensing regime (prior to 6 April 2008), the Office of Fair Trading was really restricted in that it could only request documents and information from a creditor in advance of a licence application being considered. Now, a creditor can be asked to supply any document or information requested by the Office of Fair Trading at any time during the duration of the licence. If the creditor is slow to respond to such requests, representatives of the regulator have the power to enter premises in order to inspect any documentation which they are seeking or to obtain any relevant information. In extreme circumstances, warrants can be issued by the courts which allow searches of a creditor's premises to be carried and for documents to be seized.

The Office of Fair Trading has wide-ranging powers in relation to the issue of a creditor's non-compliance with the rules governing licences. Some of these powers include the following actions:

◆ The licence could be suspended
◆ The current terms of the licence could be changed
◆ The licence could be cancelled
◆ A new licence application could be refused
◆ A current or new licence could have obligations or restrictions imposed on it with which the creditor must comply

It is worth noting that failure by a creditor to meet any requirements or conditions imposed on a licence by the Office of Fair Trading could result in the creditor incurring a maximum fine of £50,000 (Section 39A).

In terms of Section 39B of the Consumer Credit Act 1974, the Office of Fair Trading should issue an official notice to a creditor that warning it is in breach of its licence conditions and this notice should detail what steps must be taken by the creditor to remedy the breach(es).

If the applicant is refused a licence by the Office of Fair Trading, the reasons for this decision must be set out in writing. It will then be up to the applicant whether he wishes to challenge such a decision. An appeal against the decision to refuse to grant a licence by the Office of Fair Trading should be submitted to the Consumer Credit Appeals Tribunal. If the Tribunal agrees with the decision of the Office of Fair Trading, the applicant could always appeal further on a point of a law to the Court of Session. In the Court of Session, the judges will scrutinise the grounds upon which the application for a licence were refused. Any earlier decisions by the Office of Fair Trading and the Consumer Credit Appeals Tribunal could be overturned.

 Key point: The Office of Fair Trading has wide-ranging powers in relation to the issue of a creditor's non-compliance with the rules governing licences such as suspension of the licence, changing the terms of the current licence or cancelling the licence.

The Consumer Credit Appeals Tribunal

Since 6 April 2008, an appeal against a refusal by the Office of Fair Trading to grant a licence should be lodged with the new Consumer Credit Appeals Tribunal. A further appeal against the decision of the Tribunal can be submitted to the Inner House of the Court of Session in Edinburgh.

The Consumer Credit Appeals Tribunal was established as a result of the introduction of the Consumer Credit Act 2006. This development is part of growing trend necessitated in part by the Human Rights Act 1998 which aims to remove quasi-judicial powers from Ministers of the Crown. As we have seen in Chapter 1, the UK Secretary State for Justice and the Lord Chancellor no longer sits as a judge in the House of Lords. Ministers of the Crown who are responsible for the formulation of laws and their implementation should not be seen to be sitting in judgement if such rules are challenged as there is an obvious conflict of interest and, therefore, a completely independent review body is required for this purpose.

Previously, an appeal had to be lodged with the Secretary of State at the Department of Business Enterprise and Regulatory Reform (BERR) and before that the Department of Trade and Industry (DTI). An independent panel operating on behalf of the Secretary of State will hear appeals against decisions of the Office of Fair Trading to issue a licence if the complaint relates to an application which was submitted before 6th April 2008. There is a right of further appeal to the Inner House of the Court of Session on a point of law if the creditor disagrees with a decision of the panel and this route of appeal existed under the previous licensing arrangements.

 Key point: An appeal by a creditor against the decision to refuse to grant him a licence by the Office of Fair Trading should be submitted to the Consumer Credit Appeals Tribunal.

Advertising

The Consumer Credit (Advertisements) Regulations 2004 (which replace the previous 1989 Regulations) and they cover advertising relating to the provision of consumer credit in any form which would include print, radio, television, film, video, DVD, notices, goods, circular letters or price lists.

Consumer credit advertising covering consumer hire activities is now covered by the general legal principles contained in the Consumer Protection from Unfair Trading Regulations 2008. Part 8 of the Enterprise Act 2002 also applies to consumer credit activities.

 Key point: The Consumer Credit (Advertisements) Regulations 2004 and they cover advertising relating to the provision of consumer credit in any form which would include print, radio, television, film, video, DVD, notices, goods, circular letters or price lists.

The Consumer Credit (Advertisements) Regulations 2004 apply to the following types of agreements:

◆ Consumer credit
◆ Consumer brokerage

The Regulations 3 and 4 provide strict guidelines as to how an advertisement is to be presented (*its form*) and what sort of information will appear in it (*its content*). Advertisements should be clearly understood by debtors. In all advertisements, the creditor's name must be included and, if certain financial information is used, the creditor's business address must also be included.

In the booklet entitled '**Credit Advertising**' (published in August 2008), the Office of Fair Trading provides the following guidelines in respect of advertisements:

When a credit advertisement includes:	It must include:
Any one or more of the following: ◆ Amount of credit ◆ Deposit on account ◆ Cash price ◆ Advance payment	The name of the advertiser (this is required in all credit advertisements)
Any one or more of the following: ◆ Frequency of repayments ◆ Number of repayments ◆ Description (not amount) of any other payment or charge	◆ The name of the advertiser ◆ Typical APR
Any one or more of the following: ◆ Amount of any repayment ◆ Amount of any other payment or charge ◆ Total amount payable	◆ The name of the advertiser ◆ A postal address (in most cases) ◆ Typical APR ◆ Amount of credit ◆ Any deposit on account ◆ Cash price of goods or services ◆ Any advance payment ◆ Frequency, number and amounts of repayments ◆ Description and amount of any other payment or charge ◆ Total amount payable

In terms of Regulation 7, the creditor must state whether the debtor has to pledge a security for the loan and, if so, the nature of this security.

The Regulations also impose a duty on a creditor to include warnings in an advertisement to potential debtors which clearly highlight the consequences of debtors breaching any agreement.

Regulation 7 provides the following examples of the kinds of warnings which should be used by the creditor depending, of course, on the nature or type of agreement:

Example 1

YOUR HOME MAY BE REPOSSESSED IF YOU DO NOT KEEP UP REPAYMENTS ON A MORTGAGE OR ANY OTHER DEBT SECURED ON IT.

Example 2

THINK CAREFULLY BEFORE SECURING OTHER DEBTS AGAINST YOUR HOME.

Example 3

CHECK THAT THIS MORTGAGE WILL MEET YOUR NEEDS IF YOU WANT TO MOVE OR SELL YOUR HOME OR YOU WANT YOUR FAMILY TO INHERIT IT. IF YOU ARE IN ANY DOUBT, SEEK INDEPENDENT ADVICE.

Example 4

CHANGES IN THE EXCHANGE RATE MAY INCREASE THE STERLING EQUIVALENT OF YOUR DEBT.

Example 5

YOUR HOME MAY BE REPOSSESSED IF YOU DO NOT KEEP UP REPAYMENTS ON A HIRE AGREEMENT SECURED BY A MORTGAGE OR OTHER SECURITY ON YOUR HOME.

Regulation 8 imposes a duty on creditors to ensure that any mention of the APR is transparent and can be easily understood by potential debtors. If, for example, the APR is a variable rate of interest i.e. it is not a fixed rate and, therefore, subject to change, the advertisement must clearly state this.

The Regulations do not apply to consumer hire agreements (as was previously the case under the 1989 Regulations), but it is worth bearing in mind that the Consumer Protection from Unfair Trading Regulations 2008 will apply to these kinds of agreement. The 2008 Regulations will provide debtors with remedies if the information in a credit advertisement is regarded as misleading or if the advertiser omits to include certain information which could have an important bearing on the decision of the debtor to enter a credit agreement or not.

Furthermore, in terms of Part 8 of the Enterprise Act 2002, the Office of Fair Trading and other enforcement bodies may take legal action against a credit advertiser if they are of the opinion that the advertisement breaches the collective interests of consumers.

Any advertiser who breaches the Advertising Regulations will be liable to criminal prosecution.

Key point: Any advertiser who breaches the Advertising Regulations will be liable to criminal prosecution.

Quotations

Since 10 March 1997, creditors are given discretion as to how they respond to requests for a written quotations. Previously, under the Consumer Credit (Quotations) Regulations 1989, there were strict rules for providing a written quotation to a member of the public. These 1989 Regulations no longer have legal force and it would seem that the main duty that a creditor has is to ensure that a quote is not misleading.

If the creditor issues a misleading quote, it could face legal action in terms of civil and criminal remedies available under the Consumer Protection from Unfair Trading Regulations 2008.

Creditors will also have to be aware of the provisions of general contract law relating to misrepresentation when issuing quotations to potential customers.

 Key point: Creditors must ensure that any quotations that they provide to potential customers are not misleading and, if this is the case, a creditor could commit a criminal and/or civil offence in terms of Consumer Protection from Unfair Trading Regulations 2008 and they could commit a misrepresentation in respect of the common law of contract.

The Consumer Credit (Disclosure of Information) Regulations 2004

From 31 May 2005, these Regulations impose a duty on creditors to provide information to potential debtors so that they are in a position to make an informed choice about whether to enter a credit agreement or not. The Regulations, in theory, ensure that the debtor is given a durable document by the creditor i.e. a paper copy or an e-mail which they can take away to study before making an informed decision whether s/he wishes to enter the agreement. The information supplied to the debtor will be legible and the key terms will all be given equal prominence. Such a document may be entitled 'Pre-contract Information' and will be completely separate from the proposed credit agreement.

The Regulations do not prescribe a particular order for setting out the key information to be given to debtors, but key terms should all be equally prominent to assist the debtor to make a decision whether or not to enter a contract with the creditor.

 Key point: The Consumer Credit (Disclosure of Information) Regulations 2004 impose a duty on creditors to provide information to potential debtors so that they are in a position to make an informed choice about whether to enter a credit agreement or not.

We can see an example of a quotation (below) which has been provided to a customer who is considering whether to take out an interest free credit agreement with a retailer.

Crossan & Wylie
Since 1989

**1050 Cathedral Street
Glasgow G4 0NB
Tel: 0141 224 0011**

**VAT No: 900000100
INTEREST FREE BREAKDOWN**

KEY FINANCIAL INFORMATION

Amount of credit	£860.00
Minimum duration of the agreement	09 months

Under this agreement you will pay 9 consecutive monthly payments of £95.55 commencing one month after either the date of this agreement, or if later, the date of each following month unless there is no such date or it is not a day on which banks are open, in which event, the payment will be due on the next day banks are open.

Monthly payments will continue until the amounts you owe under this agreement have been paid.

OTHER FINANCIAL INFORMATION

	Cash Price
Goods	£1060.00
Total Cash Price	£1060.00
Advance Payment (Deposit)	£200.00
Total Charge for Credit (Interest)	£0.00

Interest Rate 0% per annum variable unless the interest rate is 0% in which case it is not variable.

If you exercise your right to settle this agreement under section 94 of the Consumer Credit Act 1974 to repay the loan early on the date:

When a quarter of the term has elapsed you will pay	£573.33
When half of the term has elapsed you will pay	£382.22
When three quarters of the term has elapsed you will pay	£191.11

DATE: 09/06/09   TIME: 19:40:11

The content of the agreement

Section 60 of the Consumer Credit Act 1974 governs the content of a regulated agreement. The agreement must include the following:

- The amount of credit that the debtor has borrowed or the credit limit
- The amount of each repayment by the debtor and the times when these are to be made
- The total charge for the credit
- The annual percentage rate (APR)
- Details of any security that the debtor has had to provide to the creditor
- The debtor's rights in relation to cancellation of the agreement, termination of the agreement and repossession of the goods

An example of a consumer credit agreement can be seen on the Introductory Scots Law website.

 Key point: Section 60 of the Consumer Credit Act 1974 governs the content of a regulated agreement and certain information must be included in the agreement.

Section 61 of the Act imposes a duty on the creditor to make sure that the agreement presented to the debtor is legible and, additionally, all the main terms must be contained in it. The Consumer Credit (Agreements) (Amendment) Regulations 2004 make it compulsory for the agreement to have a heading which describes what type of agreement it is that the creditor and the debtor have entered into e.g. "This is a Consumer Credit Agreement regulated by the Consumer Credit Act 1974". The agreement must have a signature box where both the creditor and the debtor will be able to sign the agreement.

An agreement will only be considered to form a binding contract between the parties when both of them sign it. The agreement will then be known as an executed agreement. The debtor must be given a copy of the agreement when his signature forms the contract (Section 62). If the debtor has signed the agreement, but the creditor has not yet done so, there is no binding agreement. In these circumstances, the creditor must provide the debtor with a copy of the unexecuted agreement and then a second copy within seven days of the agreement being signed by the creditor (Section 63).

Failure to comply with any of the documentation rules will mean that it may only be possible for a creditor to enforce the agreement by means of a court order (Section 65). The courts may not always grant an enforcement order where the agreement is improperly executed. A court, for example, may well decide not to enforce an agreement if it is a cancellable one and the creditor has failed to notify the debtor of his right to cancel the agreement.

Sometimes the creditor will demand that the debtor provide some sort of security or collateral for the loan e.g. an item of the debtor's property like shares in a company. In other words, the debtor could lose ownership of this item pledged as security if he fails to repay the loan to the creditor. The beauty of this arrangement for the creditor is that he will be able to cut his losses if the debtor either refuses to pay the loan completely or only pays back part of it. At the very least, the creditor will be able to put his hands on something of value belonging to the debtor.

However, the creditor will not be able to enforce the security against the debtor if the documentation requirements listed above are not complied with. According to Section 105, the creditor must get a court order to enforce the security and, ultimately, the court has the final say as to whether it will allow the creditor to enforce the security (Section 127).

The Consumer Credit (Agreements) (Amendment) Regulations 2004

In a consumer credit agreement, the creditor has a very strict legal obligation to ensure that all the key financial information affecting the transaction is grouped together and not hidden away in the small print. The Regulations now go further by stating that an agreement will have to have the following three sections:

1   Key financial information

2   Other financial information

3   Key information

The Consumer Credit (Miscellaneous Provisions) Regulations 2004

These Regulations also stress that the key information about an agreement must be presented together on the first page to ensure that the debtor is fully aware of his/her rights and obligations. These key terms must be given equal prominence and nothing should be concealed away in the small print of the agreement. The Explanatory Memorandum to the Regulations issued by the UK Government in October 2004 expressly states that:

'If optional products, such as payment protection insurance, are incorporated in the credit agreement, a second signature will be required.'

 Key point: The content of the consumer credit agreement is very strictly regulated and the creditor must ensure that certain key information is included for the debtor's benefit.

Consumer Credit Act 1974 (Electronic Communications) Order 2004

From December 2004 onwards, the above Order came into force which now permits e-mail to be used to conclude consumer credit agreements and for important information affecting such agreements to be used by the debtor and creditor.

Before the Consumer Credit Act 2006 was introduced, it was absolutely essential that the credit agreement was properly executed i.e. complied with all the necessary formalities because failure by the creditor to ensure this meant that the agreement with a debtor was automatically unenforceable. This penalty has now been removed as a result of the repeal of Sections 127(3) to 127(5) of the Consumer Credit Act 1974 meaning that courts have much wider scope in deciding whether or not to enforce an improperly executed agreement.

Provision of information by the creditor

Since 1 October 2008, Section 77A of the Consumer Credit Act 1974 imposes a duty on creditors in a fixed sum credit agreement to supply debtors with an annual statement detailing the amount of the loan paid and the amount still outstanding. Debtors have the right to receive these annual statements throughout the duration of the credit agreement. The first statement should be supplied to the debtor one year after the agreement was entered into with the creditor. An example of such a statement can be seen on the Introductory Scots Law website.

In any case, Sections 77 and 78 of the Act impose a general duty on creditors to supply debtors with information as to how much has already been repaid and how much is still outstanding under the agreement. Should a debtor wish to make early repayment of a debt due under a credit agreement, the creditor is legally obligated under Section 97 to provide accurate information of the amount still outstanding. Section 79 confers a similar right on debtors in a consumer hire agreement and even individuals who have agreed to act as guarantors for a debt are entitled to this kind of information upon payment of the appropriate fee to the creditor (Sections 107–109).

 Key point: Section 77A of the Consumer Credit Act 1974 imposes a duty on creditors in a fixed sum credit agreement to supply debtors with an annual statement detailing the amount of the loan paid and the amount still outstanding.

Default by the debtor

One of the most common ways in which the agreement can be brought to an end is where the debtor breaks the agreement e.g. by not making the agreed repayments to the creditor. If the agreement is broken by the debtor this is often referred to as the debtor defaulting on the agreement.

If the debtor defaults on the agreement, the creditor, in terms of Section 87, must serve an arrears or a default notice on the debtor. Without serving this default notice, the creditor is not entitled to use any of the following remedies for breach of contract:

1 To end the agreement

2 To demand earlier repayment of any money owed by the debtor under the agreement

3 To recover possession of any goods that the debtor holds

4 To behave as if any of the debtor's rights under the agreement have been suspended, limited or even terminated

5 To enforce any security.

It should be noted that the terms of the credit agreement will often state what action the creditor will be able to take against the debtor if he defaults. Only some of the options listed in 1–5 may be available to the creditor. The agreement will, therefore, determine what the creditor can and cannot do. The important thing to remember is that any of the actions open to the creditor under the agreement will be useless if a default notice was not served on the debtor.

As a result of changes introduced by the Consumer Credit Act 2006, creditors are now placed under additional duties when dealing with a debtor who is in default in terms of the agreement.

An example of an information sheet published by the Office of Fair Trading for people who have received an arrears notice can be seen on the Introductory Scots Law website.

Key point: If the debtor defaults on the agreement, the creditor must serve a default notice on the debtor in order to be entitled to use any of the available remedies for breach of contract under the Consumer Credit Act.

Sections 86B and 86C of the Consumer Credit Act 1974 now mean that a creditor is legally obliged to inform a debtor that s/he has breached the agreement. The debtor will be informed of the breach by means of a written notice issued by the creditor. These notices should be sent to the debtor within 14 days where the debtor has either failed to make four weekly repayments or two monthly repayments depending on the repayment schedule contained in the credit agreement.

Section 86B regulates fixed sum credit and hire agreements whereas Section 86C regulates running account credit agreements.

The consequences for failure to comply with Sections 86B and 86C are particularly serious for creditors:

1　The agreement is incapable of being enforced during the time when the creditor failed to give notice to the debtor of the default

2　The creditor will be enable to obtain interest on arrears owed by the debtor during the period of default when a notice was not issued

In circumstances, where a debtor is in arrears the creditor must provide a notice of arrears (to be issued every six months) until the outstanding amount is paid off. This information must be accompanied by a circular (an example can be seen below) from the Office of Fair Trading which provides useful information to debtors who find themselves in arrears to their creditors.

Despite the changes in the law relating to default notices, credit card companies can still prevent debtors from using a card if the credit limit has been reached and, obviously, a default notice is not required for this type of action.

 Key point: Sections 86B and 86C of the Consumer Credit Act 1974 now mean that a creditor is legally obliged to inform a debtor that they have breached the agreement. The debtor will be informed of the breach by means of a written notice issued by the creditor.

Simple interest on arrears

Section 86F also includes a new provision which significantly improves the position of debtors who find themselves in default in that the creditor is entitled to charge simple interest only in respect of any outstanding sums of money owed. Previously, the spectre of compound interest was something of which debtors had to be acutely aware of if they were unfortunate enough to fall behind with their contractual repayments to creditors.

 An information sheet on arrears can be found on the Introductory Scots Law website.

 Key point: A debtor who finds himself in default is entitled to be charged simple interest only in respect of any outstanding sums of money owed under the credit agreement.

Default Notices

In the event of a debtor breaching an agreement, creditors must issue a default notice if they wish to take the following actions:

1   End the agreement

2   Enforce any collateral or security pledged by the debtor

3   Secure early repayment of any sums owed

4   Repossess any moveable or heritable property which is the subject matter of the agreement

5   Restrict, cancel or impede any rights which the debtor currently enjoys

Under Section 88, the default notice must contain the following information:

- It must inform the debtor in what way he has broken the agreement
- Whether it is possible for the debtor to take action to resolve the situation and what this action is
- If the breach cannot be resolved, the creditor must state the amount which the debtor must pay in compensation
- The date by which the action to resolve the breach must be taken or the date by which compensation must be paid

The debtor will be given at least seven days by the creditor to resolve the breach or pay compensation. If the debtor takes steps to comply with the default notice, Section 89 states that the breach of the agreement cannot be referred to by the creditor in the future. It will be as if the breach of the agreement committed by the debtor never occurred.

 Key point: In order for the creditor to take any action against a debtor, a default notice must first be served on the debtor.

Time Orders

The debtor, however, may not comply with the creditor's default notice. There are still options available to the debtor in that he could apply to the court for a Time Order under Section 129. In these kinds of situations, the court can either allow the creditor to use one of the remedies under the agreement or the debtor can be given the protection of a time order.

A time order basically gives the debtor more time to pay the money owed to the creditor under the agreement. Obviously, the court will have to look at the debtor's financial circumstances and the likelihood of his being able to pay back the money before a time order was granted. The court has wide discretion in this area and it is permitted to take such steps which are just and reasonable in the circumstances of each case.

 Key point: A Time Order basically gives the debtor more time to pay the money owed to the creditor under the agreement.

In **Cedar Holdings Limited v Begum 2002** the debtor had borrowed money from Cedar Holdings and this loan had been secured over the debtor's home. The debtor later got into financial difficulties and was finding very difficult to meet the monthly contractual payment of £129. The creditor had taken the debtor to court and been given the right to eject the debtor from her home. Eventually, however, the debtor sought the protection of a time order under Section 129 whereby she would be permitted to pay £50 per month to the creditor (who argued unsuccessfully for this sum to be set at £100 per month).

Held: Sheriff McIver at Glasgow Sheriff Court granted the time order and the debtor had to pay the loan back at £50 per month. The Sheriff, however, made a provision that this arrangement was to be reviewed within eight months in order to reassess the debtor's financial situation which was expected to have improved somewhat when she paid back a social fund loan to the Department of Social Security.

In **Director General of Fair Trading v First National Bank plc (2001)**, Lord Bingham, who gave the leading judgement in the House of Lords, referred to Section 129 of the Consumer Credit Act 1974 stating that:

'I would in general agree that time orders extending over very long periods of time are usually better avoided.'

Lord Bingham agreed with the reasoning of the English Court of Appeal in **Southern District Finance plc v Barnes (1996)** which took the view that the power to make a time order under Section 129 of the Act was to assist a debtor to overcome a temporary financial difficulty. If it became apparent to the court that the debtor would never be in a position to resume making repayments at the contractual rate, no time order should be issued and the creditor should be permitted to enforce the terms of the agreement.

According to Lord Bingham 'the court should be ready to include in a time order any provision amending the agreement which it considers *just to both parties* [our italics]'.

Key point: Time orders extending over very long periods of time are usually not granted by the courts.

Protection Orders

Section 131 does potentially provide the creditor with some peace of mind. The creditor can apply to court for what is called a protection order. This order effectively means that the court can restrict or prohibit the use of the creditor's property which the debtor currently has in his possession. These orders are very useful while the creditor is awaiting the outcome of the court's decision mainly in relation to disputes that centre around the debtor's alleged default.

Key point: A Protection Order effectively means that the court can restrict or prohibit the use of the creditor's property which the debtor currently has in his possession.

Varying the terms of the credit agreement

As a result of Section 136 of the Act, the courts are given power to vary or amend the terms of an agreement in order to provide the debtor with some relief.

In Scotland, as a result of the Sheriff's decision in **Murie McDougall Limited v Sinclair (1994)**, there is considerable doubt as to whether the Sheriff Court would be entitled to vary or amend the interest rate which governs the credit agreement. Had Sheriff Fitzsimmons in this case taken the view that he had the power to vary the interest rate (from the contractual rate of 27.1% to the debtor's preferred rate of 10.95%), repayment of the loan would have taken 13 years to achieve rather than the 4 years originally agreed by the parties to the credit agreement.

In **Southern District Finance plc v Barnes (1996)**, a completely different decision was arrived at by the English Court of Appeal which approved the County Court's decision to amend or vary the rate of interest in order to give the debtor some relief. Lord Bingham in **Director General of Fair Trading v First National Bank plc (2001)** expressly approved the decision of the Court of Appeal in **Southern District Finance plc** not to permit the creditor to gain any additional interest payable on the loan other than that amount which had already accrued.

 Key point: Under the Consumer Credit Act, the courts are given power to vary or amend the terms of an agreement in order to provide the debtor with some relief.

Termination clauses

This type of contractual term is commonly found in hire purchase and conditional sale agreements and is relevant when the debtor defaults on the contract. Such a clause means that, theoretically, a debtor will be forced to return the goods to the creditor. The debtor will not become the owner of the goods. The debtor is not entitled to the return of any payments that he has already made under the agreement and will also have to pay any arrears. There is even the possibility that the goods may be damaged or may have lost value during the time that they were in the debtor's possession and the creditor may receive compensation to reflect this. Finally, the debtor will have to pay any interest charges due under the agreement, but this must not exceed the APR payable under the agreement.

 Key point: Termination clauses are commonly found in hire purchase and conditional sale agreements and will become effective upon the event of the debtor's default meaning that the debtor will have to return the goods to the creditor.

Accelerated payments clauses

An agreement may contain an accelerated payments clause. The clause comes into operation when the debtor defaults on the agreement. The debtor will have to pay all of the instalments due under the agreement even if these were to be made some time in the distant future i.e. months and years from now. The immediate effect of such a clause is that the debtor will become the owner of the goods if the agreement is hire purchase or a conditional sale. In all other types of credit agreement, the debtor is entitled to keep the goods. The debtor may be charged interest on any payments that he has fallen into arrears with, but the interest rate will not exceed the APR payable under the agreement. The debtor may even be entitled to a rebate of charges for the early payment of the loan.

There is always the situation that the debtor could face severe financial difficulties if he was forced to make all payments under the agreement immediately to the creditor. This may be a very real pressure that the debtor could face if he has fallen into arrears of payment. The debtor could, therefore, ask the court to make a time order under Section 129 which gives him extra time to make the repayments to the debtor.

 Key point: Accelerated payments clauses become effective when the debtor defaults on the agreement meaning that all sums due under the contract become payable to the creditor, but the debtor will either become the owner of the goods or will be able to retain possession of them.

Early settlement

Some debtors may wish to pay off or settle their debt in advance and may, therefore, be entitled to a rebate from the creditor. The amount of the rebate to which debtors are entitled to receive is governed by legal provisions which are examined below.

Indeed, Section 94 of the Consumer Credit Act 1974 gives debtors the right to make early repayment of any amount borrowed (plus any interest due) by giving the creditor notice of this intention. Section 95 of the Act envisages a situation whereby the debtor may be entitled to receive a rebate as a result of the decision to repay the loan early.

As we have seen, Sections 79, 97, 107–109 of the Act impose a duty on creditors to provide accurate information to debtors and guarantors about any outstanding sums owed if early settlement of the agreement is contemplated.

 Key point: Debtors are not entitled to pay off debts early by giving proper notice of this intention to the creditor.

The Consumer Credit (Early Settlement) Regulations 2004

These Regulations introduce new rules in respect of rebates to be paid to debtors who settle credit agreements early.

Some creditors were not be bound by these provisions until 31 May 2007 (if their current credit agreement was to run for 10 years or less) or 31 May 2010 (if the credit agreement is to run for 10 years or more) and the older Regulations of 1983 will be applicable.

The principal change which the new Regulations introduce is the way which creditors are obliged to calculate the amount of the rebate to be paid to those debtors who decide to settle their credit agreements before the due date. Actuarial formulae has been laid down by the UK Government which creditors must follow when working out the size of the rebate.

The Regulations contain worked examples of the ways in which rebates are worked out according to the actuarial formulae employed by the UK Government.

The new provisions replace the previous Consumer Credit (Rebate on Early Settlement) Regulations 1983.

Key point: The Consumer Credit (Early Settlement) Regulations 2004 introduce new rules in respect of rebates to be paid to debtors who settle credit agreements early.

Unfair Credit Agreements or Relationships

Previously, a debtor could bring a legal action to challenge the terms of a credit agreement which s/he regarded as extortionate i.e. unfair or unduly harsh or oppressive under Sections 137-140 of the Consumer Credit Act 1974.

The Consumer Credit Act 2006 now updates the terminology used by the Consumer Credit Act 1974 and debtors will be able to challenge the terms of an agreement on the basis that it is unfair. The reason for changing the terminology from an extortionate credit agreement to one that is deemed to be unfair seems to be motivated by the fact that this complements other legislation which aim to protect and promote consumer rights, for example, the Unfair Contract Terms Act 1977 and the Unfair Terms in Consumer Contract Regulations 1999.

Interestingly, a debtor can still bring a legal action under Sections 137 to 140 of the Consumer Credit Act 1974 if the agreement was completed i.e. the sum borrowed was paid back before 6 April 2007.

The new remedies can be found in Sections 140A to Section 140B of the Consumer Credit Act 1974 and give courts additional powers to tackle unfair credit agreements.

In terms of Section 140A, a court will consider the following issues in deciding whether a consumer credit agreement is unfair to a debtor:

1   The actual terms of the agreement

2   Any way in which the creditor has chosen to enforce the terms of the agreement or exercise any rights thereunder

3   Any other act or omission by the creditor in relation to the agreement

If the relevant court is of the opinion that the credit agreement is unfair, the following remedies are available:

1   The terms of the agreement can be effectively rewritten to make it fairer to the debtor

2   The amount which the debtor has to repay under the agreement can be lowered

3   The creditor could be ordered to repay a sum of money to the debtor

4   The debtor could be freed from certain duties which were imposed on him or her under the agreement

5   The creditor could have certain duties imposed on it or any of its associates

 Key point: The Consumer Credit Act 2006 now updates the terminology used by the Consumer Credit Act 1974 and debtors will be able to challenge the terms of an agreement in the courts on the basis that it is unfair.

The Office of Fair Trading and other enforcement bodies such as Trading Standards Departments of local councils also have a role to play in challenging unfair credit agreements in terms of Part 8 of the Enterprise Act 2002 if such agreements are

deemed to be harmful to the broader interests of consumers or if the actions of a creditor represent a breach of European Union laws.

Generally speaking, the Office of Fair Trading and other enforcement bodies will attempt to take action against a creditor only when necessary and such actions should always be proportionate i.e. do no more than is strictly necessary to achieve the desired result. In many situations, the creditor will be given a period of time to redress the breach of the law. It is only in situations where it is absolutely necessary that enforcement bodies will resort to raising a court action against the creditor. To prevent multiple enforcement actions against a creditor, the Office of Fair Trading and other relevant bodies are expected to co-ordinate their activities and a Co-ordination Unit has been established to monitor any actual or proposed enforcement activities in terms of Part 8 of the Enterprise Act 2002.

Part 8 of the Enterprise Act 2002 does not permit individual debtors to pursue actions or complaints against creditors.

 Key point: In addition to the courts, the Office of Fair Trading and other enforcement bodies such as Trading Standards Departments of local councils also have a role to play in challenging unfair credit agreements.

Credit reference agencies

It is no secret that creditors will want to look hard at the previous credit records of potential customers before making a decision as to whether or not to provide them with finance. One of the ways in which a creditor can obtain this information is by approaching a credit reference agency. Section 145 defines a credit reference agency as a person who carries on a business with the purpose of providing other persons with information about a particular individual's financial status. Credit reference agencies will, therefore, collect this information with the express purpose of supplying it to creditors.

The result of this particular activity is that creditors may refuse to supply finance to those individuals who have a bad history of making repayments or failing to repay money under previous credit agreements. If debtors have a poor credit history they are effectively blacklisted and this means that they will find it very hard to secure credit at all or on favourable terms in the future.

Unfortunately, a lot of information that the credit reference agency holds on various debtors may be inaccurate and completely misleading. It would not be the first time that debtors with impeccable credit records were wrongly listed as having a poor or atrocious credit history. It is vital, therefore, that the agency's records are kept as accurate as possible.

 Key point: A credit reference agency is an organisation that provides information to creditors about the individual credit histories of a debtor and once the creditor has studied this information he will decide whether or not to lend credit to the debtor.

Debtors, whether they have been wrongly blacklisted or not, have certain rights:

1   The creditor will have to provide the debtor with details of the credit reference agency which he used in order to make a decision.

2   After making a written request, the debtor has a right to obtain a copy of his file from the agency within seven days.

3   The debtor has a right to demand that any wrong or inaccurate information that the agency holds on file is corrected within 28 days.

The debtor's right to a copy of his file held by the agency is guaranteed by Section 158 and a failure to comply is a criminal offence. If the debtor is dissatisfied with the agency's response, he can apply to the Office of Fair Trading which will take the appropriate action on his behalf.

 Key point: Credit reference agencies will have to be particularly careful that the information that they hold is in no way misleading or inaccurate and debtors will have the right of access to their files and can force the agency to correct any mistakes.

Consumer Protection from Unfair Trading Regulations 2008

These Regulations introduce major changes to the field of consumer law and, at the same time, supersede several earlier pieces of legislation which had previously governed retail practices. Part 3 of the Consumer Protection Act 1987 (Misleading Price Indications) is repealed in its entirety and large parts of the Trade Descriptions Act 1968 have been replaced as a result of the new laws. The law, however, relating to unfair terms in contracts i.e. the Unfair Contract Terms Act 1977 and the Unfair Terms in Consumer Contracts Regulations 1999 remains unchanged and unaffected by the new legislation.

Implementation of the Regulations

The Regulations came into force on 26 May 2008 and were implemented into UK law as a result of the European Union's Unfair Commercial Practices Directive. The new laws are further evidence of the European Union's desire to standardise or harmonise consumer law across the member states and to ensure that consumers in the Single European Market and the european Economic Area benefit from tougher legislation which aims to tackle disreputable trading and retailing practices by businesses.

 Key point: The Consumer Protection from Unfair Trading Regulations 2008 came into force on 26 May 2008 and introduce major changes to the field of consumer law.

The purpose of the Regulations

The most important feature of the Regulations is that they impose a general duty on retailers and traders to act fairly and honestly in their dealings with consumers. More specifically, the new laws target particular trading practices which are deemed to be aggressive or misleading where consumers are concerned and certain practices will be banned altogether.

As the title of the Regulations suggests it will be consumers i.e. individuals who purchase products for their own private use who will benefit the most from the protection offered by the new legislation. For the most part, business or non-consumer contracts will not be affected, but there may be situations where such contracts can have an impact on consumers and, therefore, the Regulations might apply. A trader may sell products mainly to other businesses, but if there is a possibility that consumers might purchase these items then the Regulations will almost certainly apply to the transaction. Wholesalers or suppliers dealing with supermarkets, for example, will have to ensure that they meet the requirements of the Regulations because such transactions have a direct impact on the consumers who will go on to purchase these products.

Obviously, it will be up to the British courts to provide guidance as to the scope and the effect of the Regulations.

In theory, the Regulations should provide protection to consumers before they enter a contract, during the currency of the contract and even after the conclusion of the contract.

Traders or retailers who are involved in the promotion, sale or supply of products to or from consumers will have to aware of the provisions of the new laws. Any act or omission by a trader or retailer which prejudices or harms the rights of consumers may fall foul of the Regulations. It is important to note that transactions which involve the trader or retailer purchasing a product from a consumer are also covered by the Regulations. This would include a situation where a motor dealer purchases a used car from a customer as part of a trade-in deal for a new motor vehicle and where the sales person acting for the dealership deliberately under-estimates the value of the second hand vehicle.

 Key point: The most important feature of the Regulations is that they impose a general duty on retailers and traders to act fairly and honestly in their dealings with consumers.

The general prohibition (Regulation 3)

Regulation 3 prohibits, in a general sense, unfair commercial practices. A commercial practice will be regarded as unfair if the retailer or trader has behaved in a way which is not **professionally diligent** and if it materially distorts or is likely to **materially distort** the behaviour of the **average consumer**. The essential thing to focus on here is that the behaviour of the retailer or trader (whether by act or omission) has caused the consumer to make a decision which has left him/her materially disadvantaged. In other words, the consumer has made a decision which s/he would probably not have made if the retailer or trader had acted with honesty and integrity. The UK Office of Fair Trading has suggested that such a situation could arise if consumers proceed to purchase a product that they would not normally have purchased or if they failed to exercise their cancellation rights under the contract as a direct result of the retailer's or trader's conduct.

 Key point: The Regulations prohibit, in a general sense, unfair commercial practices by a retailer or trader which is to the detriment of the average consumer.

Professional diligence?

Regulation 2(2) states that professional diligence is

*'the standard of special skill and care which a trader may reasonably be expected to exercise towards consumers which is commensurate with either —
(a) honest market practice in the trader's field of activity, or (b) the general principle of good faith in the trader's field of activity'.*

Professional diligence is an objective test and will be determined by the standard of service or conduct that a consumer is entitled to expect from a reasonably competent trader.

 Key point: Professional diligence is the standard of service or conduct that a consumer is entitled to expect from a reasonably competent trader.

A material distortion?

Regulation 2 also explains what is meant by the term material distortion. A material distortion might occur in situations where a trader behaves in such a way towards a consumer which could cause the consumer to make a decision which would significantly alter his or her behaviour and thus prevent him or her from being able to make an informed decision about the product.

 Key point: A material distortion could arise where a trader behaves in a way which prevents the consumer from being able to make an informed decision about the product.

The average consumer?

The Court of Justice has defined an average consumer as someone who is reasonably well informed and reasonably observant and circumspect; taking into account social, cultural and linguistic factors. This, of course, reflects the fact that the Regulations are part of a European Union initiative to deal with unfair commercial practices. The use of the word average in the Regulations does not refer to some statistical value.

 Key point: The average consumer as someone who is reasonably well informed and reasonably observant and circumspect; taking into account social, cultural and linguistic factors.

Misleading commercial practices (Regulations 5–7)

Regulations 5–7 ban commercial practices by a trader which are deemed to be misleading (whether such practices involve an act or omission) or aggressive and again where the average consumer is influenced to such an extent whereby they make a different decision which, in the short or long term, could be harmful or detrimental to his or her interests. It will be necessary for the courts to consider evidence as to what is an aggressive or misleading commercial practice by a trader or retailer and the likely effect of such conduct on consumers. If a consumer can demonstrate that a trader behaved in a dishonest or unreasonable way and this led him or her to suffer real harm as a result there will surely be a strong case to answer.

Regulation 5 covers situations where the trader or retailer commits a misleading action. The trader or retailer could commit such an action by giving the consumer false information or presenting information in such a way that it creates a completely false impression in the mind of a consumer. Regulation 5 would apply where the trader or retailer has been careless about the information provided to consumers or where there has been a deliberate intention to deceive.

Misleading actions can include:

1 The provision of misleading information generally;

2 Attempts to cause confusion in the minds of consumers between the trader's products and those of competitors; and

3 The failure by traders or retailers to abide by duties imposed on them by professional Codes of Conduct to which they are a party.

 Key point: Regulations 5–7 ban commercial practices by a trader which are deemed to be misleading or aggressive and where the average consumer's interests could be harmed as a result of these practices.

Regulation 6 deals with the consequences of misleading omissions by a trader or retailer and would include situations where the trader has failed to provide the consumer with sufficient material information (whether by accident or design) about a product. Material information is the kind of information which a consumer must possess in order to make fully informed decisions about whether or not to purchase a product. The context or the background to the commercial transaction will clearly be very important and there will be many circumstances where a trader or retailer will not be obliged to provide all that much information about a product, for example, on a sweet wrapper where it would not be possible to display all the information about the product.

Clearly, however, when the product is more complex in nature, for example an LCD television, there will be a duty on the retailer or trader to provide sufficient information for the consumer to make an informed decision as to whether or not it would be beneficial to purchase such an item.

Traders or retailers who are involved in the promotion, sale or supply of products to or from consumers will have to aware of the provisions of the new laws. Any act or omission by a trader or retailer which prejudices or harms the rights of consumers may fall foul of the Regulations.

The omission of material information by a trader in such a situation will obviously be very important.

Regulation 6(4) specifically addresses commercial practices referred to as 'invitations to purchase' products which a trader might use as a means of communicating with consumers in order to promote the sale of products. Importantly, the 'invitation to purchase' must identify the product's price and characteristics.

Such 'invitations to purchase' products might include any or all of the following:

◆ Advertisements which contains an order form which the consumer can complete to purchase a product
◆ Interactive television channels i.e. shopping channels where the consumer can order and pay for the products featured
◆ Websites where consumers can place an order to purchase a product from the trader
◆ A menu in a restaurant
◆ Price indication/ticket on a product
◆ Text message promotion to which consumers can reply in order to complete their purchase of the product
◆ An advertisement on the radio which is promoting mobile telephone ringtones and details are provided (a code and a number) to consumers whereby they can purchase the ringtone and pay for this via their telephone bill.

It is important to note that an 'invitation to purchase' a product must include the price, the item's characteristics and an opportunity for the consumer to purchase the item in question. General advertisements which merely promote a trader's brand rather than a specific product will not usually be regarded as an 'invitation to purchase'.

 Key point: An 'invitation to purchase' a product must include the price, the item's characteristics and an opportunity for the consumer to purchase the item in question. General advertisements which merely promote a trader's brand rather than a specific product will not usually be regarded as an 'invitation to purchase'.

When making an 'invitation to purchase' a product, traders must be aware that Regulation 6 imposes a duty on them to provide material information to consumers about the item. Material information could include any of the following factors:

◆ The principal characteristics of the product i.e. what it is and what it does
◆ The trader's identity which would include things like the business's trading name and details of any other trader which the trader dealing with the consumer is acting for
◆ The trader's physical business address
◆ The price of the product (including any relevant taxes) and, in situations where the price cannot be quoted, the mechanism for calculating the price at a later date
◆ Any additional charges such as postal or delivery costs or, if these cannot be provided, an indication from the trader that consumers will have to pay these costs in addition to payment of the price of the product
◆ Any arrangements for payment, delivery and contractual performance which differ significantly from the usual professional standards expected of traders dealing with the product

 Key point: When making an 'invitation to purchase' a product, traders must be aware that Regulation 6 imposes a duty on them to provide material information to consumers about the item.

Regulation 7 deals with the problem of aggressive practices by traders in their dealings with consumers. The Office of Fair Trading describes such practices as behaviour which, in certain circumstances, would be regarded as intimidation and exploitation which may restrict consumers from making a free or informed choice about the product in question. Critically, however, an aggressive commercial practice must cause the average consumer to make a different choice if it such a practice is to be regarded as unfair.

Aggressive practices by a trader could constitute any of the following types of behaviour:

◆ Harassment, coercion (including physical force) or undue influence
◆ Practices which significantly impair or are likely to impair signifcantly the average consumer's freedom of choice or conduct in relation to a product

Critically, however, an aggressive commercial practice must cause the average consumer to make a different choice if it such a practice is to be regarded as unfair.

The Regulations do not provide an explanation of what constitutes harassment and coercion, but the Office of Fair Trading has stated that such behaviour would include physical and non-physical behaviour i.e. the use of psychological pressure.

Regulation 7(3)(b) does, however, provide a definition of undue influence. Such behaviour is described in the following terms:

'exploiting a position of power in relation to the consumer so as to apply pressure, even without using or threatening to use physical force, in a way which significantly limits the consumer's ability to make an informed decision'.

Undue influence by a trader could, therefore, involve that individual taking advantage of the consumer's ignorance of a particular product and turning this ignorance to his or her benefit.

The Regulations also attempt to deal with situations where traders who are a party to a Code of Practice where the use of such a Code promotes unfair commercial practices. Most of the time, enforcement agencies will attempt to encourage traders and trade associations to alter the Code of Practice in order to promote fairer commercial practices. Consumers who feel that they have been penalised as a result of an unfair commercial practice permitted by a Code of Practice can pursue a civil action using Part 8 of the Enterprise Act 2002.

 Key point: Regulation 7 deals with the problem of aggressive practices by traders in their dealings with consumers which amount to intimidation and exploitation which may restrict consumers from making a free or informed choice about the product in question.

Automatically unfair commercial practices

Schedule 1 to the Regulations goes further and pinpoints **31 commercial practices** which are to be regarded as automatically unfair and, therefore, unlawful. These practices are listed below as they appear in Schedule 1 of the Regulations:

1   Claiming to be a signatory to a code of conduct when the trader is not.

2   Displaying a trust mark, quality mark or equivalent without having obtained the necessary authorisation.

3   Claiming that a code of conduct has an endorsement from a public or other body which it does not have.

4   Claiming that a trader (including his commercial practices) or a product has been approved, endorsed or authorised by a public or private body when the trader, the commercial practices or the product have not or making such a claim without complying with the terms of the approval, endorsement or authorisation.

5   Making an invitation to purchase products at a specified price without disclosing the existence of any reasonable grounds the trader may have for believing that he will not be able to offer for supply, or to procure another trader to supply, those products or equivalent products at that price for a period that is, and in quantities that are, reasonable having regard to the product, the scale of advertising of the product and the price offered (bait advertising).

6 Making an invitation to purchase products at a specified price and then

  (a) refusing to show the advertised item to consumers,

  (b) refusing to take orders for it or deliver it within a reasonable time, or

  (c) demonstrating a defective sample of it, with the intention of promoting a different product (bait and switch).

7 Falsely stating that a product will only be available for a very limited time, or that it will only be available on particular terms for a very limited time, in order to elicit an immediate decision and deprive consumers of sufficient opportunity or time to make an informed choice.

8 Undertaking to provide after-sales service to consumers with whom the trader has communicated prior to a transaction in a language which is not an official language of the European Economic Area (EEA) State where the trader is located and then making such service available only in another language without clearly disclosing this to the consumer before the consumer is committed to the transaction.

9 Stating or otherwise creating the impression that a product can legally be sold when it cannot.

10 Presenting rights given to consumers in law as a distinctive feature of the trader's offer.

11 Using editorial content in the media to promote a product where a trader has paid for the promotion without making that clear in the content or by images or sounds clearly identifiable by the consumer (advertorial).

12 Making a materially inaccurate claim concerning the nature and extent of the risk to the personal security of the consumer or his family if the consumer does not purchase the product.

13 Promoting a product similar to a product made by a particular manufacturer in such a manner as deliberately to mislead the consumer into believing that the product is made by that same manufacturer when it is not.

14 Establishing, operating or promoting a pyramid promotional scheme where a consumer gives consideration for the opportunity to receive compensation that is derived primarily from the introduction of other consumers into the scheme rather than from the sale or consumption of products.

15 Claiming that the trader is about to cease trading or move premises when he is not.

16 Claiming that products are able to facilitate winning in games of chance.

17 Falsely claiming that a product is able to cure illnesses, dysfunction or malformations.

18 Passing on materially inaccurate information on market conditions or on the possibility of finding the product with the intention of inducing the consumer to acquire the product at conditions less favourable than normal market conditions.

19 Claiming in a commercial practice to offer a competition or prize promotion without awarding the prizes described or a reasonable equivalent.

20 Describing a product as 'gratis', 'free', 'without charge' or similar if the consumer has to pay anything other than the unavoidable cost of responding to the commercial practice and collecting or paying for delivery of the item.

21 Including in marketing material an invoice or similar document seeking payment which gives the consumer the impression that he has already ordered the marketed product when he has not.

22 Falsely claiming or creating the impression that the trader is not acting for purposes relating to his trade, business, craft or profession, or falsely representing oneself as a consumer.

23 Creating the false impression that after-sales service in relation to a product is available in an EEA State other than the one in which the product is sold.

24 Creating the impression that the consumer cannot leave the premises until a contract is formed.

25 Conducting personal visits to the consumer's home ignoring the consumer's request to leave or not to return, except in circumstances and to the extent justified to enforce a contractual obligation.

26 Making persistent and unwanted solicitations by telephone, fax, e-mail or other remote media except in circumstances and to the extent justified to enforce a contractual obligation.

27 Requiring a consumer who wishes to claim on an insurance policy to produce documents which could not reasonably be considered relevant as to whether the claim was valid, or failing systematically to respond to pertinent correspondence, in order to dissuade a consumer from exercising his contractual rights.

28 Including in an advertisement a direct exhortation to children to buy advertised products or persuade their parents or other adults to buy advertised products for them.

29 Demanding immediate or deferred payment for or the return or safekeeping of products supplied by the trader, but not solicited by the consumer, except where the product is a substitute supplied in accordance with regulation 19(7) of the Consumer Protection (Distance Selling) Regulations 2000 (inertia selling)(**11**).

30 Explicitly informing a consumer that if he does not buy the product or service, the trader's job or livelihood will be in jeopardy.

31 Creating the false impression that the consumer has already won, will win, or will on doing a particular act win, a prize or other equivalent benefit, when in fact either—

(a) there is no prize or other equivalent benefit, or

(b) taking any action in relation to claiming the prize or other equivalent benefit is subject to the consumer paying money or incurring a cost.

Key point: Schedule 1 to the Regulations goes further and pinpoints 31 commercial practices which are to be regarded as automatically unfair and, therefore, unlawful.

Legal consequences of the above commercial practices

As previously stated, if the trader or the retailer is involved in one of the 31 practices listed above, they will find themselves subject to the full force of the law. There is no need for the consumer to bring evidence that such a practice caused him or her to suffer harm. Such practices are unfair and, therefore, simply illegal.

Enforcement of the Regulations

At local level in Scotland, the Regulations can be enforced by a local council's trading standards department whereas, at national level, the Office of Fair Trading will have responsibility for their enforcement.

Enforcement of the Regulations might mean that a council or the Office of Fair Trading could use civil and criminal sanctions against traders who break the law in the ways already discussed, but this will not always be the case. Enforcement agencies could promote compliance with the law by providing education, guidance and advice in respect of the scope and content of the Regulations. Another alternative to legal action could be the publication of Codes of Conduct which can be used to assist traders and which has the effect of making them absolutely aware of their legal obligations towards consumers. The Office of Fair Trading currently operates a Consumer Codes Approval Scheme for this very purpose.

A further alternative which Enforcement Agencies may wish to consider is whether certain traders are already regulated by established bodies such as the Advertising Standards Agency, the Office of Electricity and Gas or the Office of Communications. It may be the case that such bodies already have the necessary powers to deal with traders who are found to be committing unfair commercial practices and makes perfect sense for these regulators to deal with the problem directly.

In most cases, the Enforcement Agency will attempt to persuade the trader to discontinue the unfair commercial practices and if the trader gives an undertaking to this effect that should really be the end of the matter.

If, however, an Enforcement Agency does wish to take legal action against a trader for an alleged breach (or a continuing breach) of the Regulations, they could apply to the Sheriff Court for an enforcement order (a civil remedy) in terms of Part 8 of the Enterprise Act 2002. Such an order, if granted by the court, must be obeyed by the trader. If the trader is unwise enough to infringe the enforcement order, s/he could then face the prospect of criminal sanctions for contempt of court i.e. up two years in prison and/or unlimited fine.

It is important to note that Enforcement Agencies have the power to deal with breaches of the Regulations which have an impact on consumers across the European Economic Area – not just the domestic market of the United Kingdom. It should be recalled that the Regulations are a European initiative with the aim of protecting consumers across Europe. Generally speaking, the Enforcement Agencies in the relevant European Union and European Economic Area member state will deal with their own 'rogue' traders, but the EC Regulation on Consumer Protection Co-operation (2006/2004) permits agencies to share information with similar bodies in other European countries about traders in order to maximise consumer protection.

 Key point: At local level in Scotland, the Regulations can be enforced by a local council's trading standards department whereas, at national level, the Office of Fair Trading will have responsibility for their enforcement.

Investigative powers

The various Enforcement Agencies have been given wide investigatory powers under the Regulations in order to achieve the aim of greater consumer protection.

Such powers include the following:

1   Test products to ensure that they comply with the Regulations. This may mean purchasing certain products from traders under investigation in order to determine whether the product complies with the law (Regulation 20).

2   Enter the premises of traders to further an investigation. Enforcement officers do not require a warrant if they enter a trader's premises during reasonable hours (Regulation 21).

Officers are permitted to inspect the suspect products, demand documentation and, in the most serious cases, seize and detain products. In certain situations, the officers may be entitled to break open products in order to further an investigation. These powers of seizure and detention can be exercised by the officers without the need for them to obtain a warrant.

If, however, the officers do obtain a warrant from a Justice of Peace, this would permit them to enter a premises which was also a dwelling house for the purpose of furthering their investigations (Regulation 22).

Any attempt by a member to public to impede or hamper an investigation by the Enforcement Agencies e.g. by making false statements or preventing access to a premises shall be regarded as a criminal offence (Regulation 23).

It is worth bearing in mind, however, that the officers will have to notify traders of the outcome of any investigatory action that they have taken (Regulation 24).

Where there is found to have been no breach of the Regulations, compensation for damage or loss caused by testing or seizure and detention of the products can be claimed by the trader (Regulation 25).

 Key point: The various Enforcement Agencies have been given wide investigatory powers under the Regulations in order to achieve the aim of greater consumer protection.

Penalties for breach of the Regulations

More seriously, in terms of Regulation 13, traders could face criminal penalties if they are found to be committing an unfair commercial practice. If the trader is convicted of a summary offence, s/he could be fined up to a maximum sum of £5,000. If however, the offence is an indictable one, the guilty party could be facing a maximum prison sentence of two years and/or a £5,000 maximum fine. Some of the criminal offences will be strict liability offences and all that is required is for the prosecution to show that the trader committed the prohibited act. Other types of offences will rely on the Scottish prosecution authorities being able to prove that not only did the prohibited act occur (the actus reus), but that the trader intended to commit this offence (the mens rea).

 Key point: In terms of Regulation 13, traders could face criminal penalties if they are found to be committing an unfair commercial practice.

Defences to prosecutions under the Regulations

Due diligence (Regulation 17)

If a trader is accused of committing a breach of Regulation 9 (misleading actions), Regulation 10 (misleading omissions), Regulation 11 (aggressive commercial practices) and Regulation 12 (specific unfair commercial practices), they can plead the defence of due diligence. This defence will be successful if the trader can demonstrate that the prohibited act occurred by reason of any of the following:

◆ It was caused by another person's mistake
◆ It was caused accidentally
◆ It was caused by reliance on information provided by another individual
◆ It was caused by the act or default of another individual or another cause beyond the trader's control

Critically, however, the second part of the defence entails the accused being able to demonstrate to the criminal that they exercised all due diligence to avoid committing an offence personally or to avoid someone under their control i.e. an employee or an agent from committing the prohibited act in question.

Innocent publication of advertisement (Regulation 18)

A second defence also exists that of innocent publication of advertisements. Advertisements can, of course, contain all sorts of misleading information which can have a direct influence on the decisions which consumers make about a product i.e. primarily the decision centres around whether or not to buy the product. An accused person will be able to plead this defence if they are able to show that had no control over the content of advertisements which breach the Regulations. In order for this defence to be successful, the accused must show that s/he accepted advertisement in the ordinary course of business i.e. it is the ordinary business of the accused to accept or arrange advertisements for publication and, when the material was accepted by the accused, s/he was not aware that the material breached the Regulations.

Offences committed by bodies of persons (Regulation 15)

This covers offences prohibited by the Regulations which are committed by corporate bodies and partnerships. This would mean that not only would the corporate body or partnership be punished on conviction, but an officer of such a body (whether a director, partner, member, manager, secretary or other designated officer) could also be prosecuted and, if found guilty, punished in terms of the Regulations.

Offence due to the default of another person (Regulation 16)

In situations where a trader (person X) has successfully defended a prosecution by under Regulations 9, 10, 11 or 12 by relying on Regulations 17 and 18, it is possible for another individual (person Y) to be successfully convicted of an offence under the legislation. Basically, person X will able to incriminate person Y by stating that the commission of the offence was Y's fault. This may well result in person Y being convicted of a criminal offence. It may be the case that person is not a trader, his/her conduct does not amount to a commercial practice and no criminal proceedings are taken against person X.

 Key point: The defences of due diligence, innocent publication of an advertisement and incrimination are available to a trader or a retailer who has been charged with an offence under the Regulations.

Time limit for prosecution (Regulation 14)

Generally speaking, prosecutions cannot be commenced against an accused after a period of three years from the date of the commission of the offence; or after the period of one year from the date of discovery of the commission of the offence.

Distance Selling

Over the last few years, the overwhelming popularity of the internet and digital home television shopping channels as places to buy and sell goods and services have resulted in the Consumer Protection (Distance Selling) Regulations 2000 (which were amended in 2005).

The Regulations bring into force European Directive 97/7/EC which has its aim the promotion of consumer confidence when purchasing goods and services at a distance from the seller. The Directive guarantees basic rights for consumers throughout the European Union.

In 2008, internet sales in the United Kingdom were worth approximately £43.8 billion – roughly 15% of the country's retail spending. (Source: 'On-line sales hit new high', *The Independent*, 15 January 2009).

As the name of the Regulations suggests, they give protection to consumers not business buyers who purchase goods and services at a distance from the seller i.e. consumers who have **not** entered into a face to face transaction with the seller.

 Key point: The Consumer Protection (Distance Selling) Regulations 2000 for consumers purchasing goods and services in situations where they will not have a face to face relationship with the retailer.

Typically, distance selling will involve the following methods:

- ◆ Telephone sales including mobile phones
- ◆ Text messaging
- ◆ Sales over the internet
- ◆ Digital TV shopping channels/interactive TV
- ◆ Facsimilies
- ◆ E-mail
- ◆ Catalogues
- ◆ Catalogues advertising in the media e.g. supplements in newspapers

Furthermore, the seller must have in place a sales structure or, to use the language of the Regulations, an "**organised scheme**" which administers the sales. Those businesses which generate much of their sales by the practice of 'cold-calling' i.e.

unsolicited telephone calls to the private residences of potential customers will have to comply with the Regulations if this part and parcel of an 'organised scheme' on its part.

 Key point: Distance selling methods typically include telephone sales, text messaging, internet sales, digital shopping channels/interactive TV, facsimilies, e-mail, catalogues (including supplements in media sources such as newspapers) and the distance seller must operate an organised scheme utilising these methods.

In terms of Regulation 3, the legislation does not apply to the following types of transactions:

◆ Financial services contracts
◆ Contracts heritable property i.e. land and buildings
◆ Goods purchased from vending machines
◆ Contracts concluded with a telecommunications operator through the use of a public pay-phone
◆ Goods bought at auction (including goods sold on interactive TV channels)

According to Regulation 6, many of the provisions in the Regulations will not have any legal effect in relation to the following types of transactions or will apply on a partial basis only:

◆ Services contacted with leisure, accommodation, catering and transport whereby the service provider agrees to provide the service on a specific date or within a specific period;
◆ Contracts for food, drink or other goods for normal, daily consumption which are delivered to a consumer's home or work-place by a regular roundsman (however, supermarket home deliveries which are the result of a distance selling contract will be covered by the provisions of the Regulations)
◆ Package holidays and time share contracts.

 Key point: Many types of transactions will not be covered by the Distance Selling Regulations.

The provision of information to consumers

Regulation 7 states that businesses must provide the following important information to consumers in respect of the following issues:

◆ The name and the address of the business
◆ The consumer's right to cancel the contract (the actual right)
◆ The goods and services that consumers can expect to receive
◆ Payment arrangements
◆ Delivery arrangements and costs
◆ The period for which the offer or the price remains valid
◆ Cancellation rights (the details of these)
◆ Procedures for returning the goods to suppliers in the event of cancellation of the contract and the costs
◆ After sales services and guarantees

The information provided to consumers must be set out in a clear and comprehensible manner appropriate to the means of distance communication used, with due regard in particular to the principles of good faith in commercial transactions and the principles governing the protection of those who are unable to give their consent such as children and young persons.

Regulation 8 stipulates that the supplier of the goods must provide consumers with a durable record of the transaction which must meet the requirements of Regulation 7 above (i.e. the important information about the contract which must be provided to the consumer).

Such a durable record should be in the form of a letter, fax or e-mail. Generally speaking, such a durable record of the details of the contract must be sent to the consumer prior to the performance of the transaction.

 Key point: The Regulations impose a legal obligation on distance sellers to provide consumers with certain types of information.

Performance of the contract by the supplier

Regulation 19 stipulates time limits for the performance of a distance selling contract by the supplier.

Unless the supplier and the consumer agree otherwise, the supplier shall perform the contract within a maximum of 30 days beginning with the day after the day the consumer sent his order to the supplier.

Should performance of the contract within this time period be impossible or unrealistic due to the goods or services being unavailable, the supplier has a duty to inform the consumer or reimburse any sum paid by or on behalf of the consumer under or in relation to the contract to the person by whom it was made.

 Key point: The Regulations impose certain time limits on distance sellers to perform their contractual duties towards consumers.

Cancellation of a distance selling contract

Regulations 10–13 contain the detailed provisions outlining the consumer's right to cancel a distance selling contract.

Regulation 10 – the general right to cancel a distance selling contract

A significant right that consumers enjoy under the Regulations is the right to cancel the contract (a cooling-off period). This is an unconditional right and it cannot be excluded or limited by terms in the contract. Obviously, the practice of distance selling will mean that a consumer does not enjoy the same opportunities for testing the goods or services as would be the case in an ordinary face to face transaction between the parties hence the importance of including such a right of cancellation.

The time limits for cancellation are slightly different depending upon whether the subject matter of the contract relates to goods or services.

However, businesses will have to be particularly careful that they provide consumers with proper notice of the cancellation periods (by means of a durable record). Failure to do so may mean that the cancellation period for goods is extended to three months and seven working days running from the day after the day the consumer receives the goods and the period for services is extended to three months and seven working days running from the day after the contract is agreed.

Consumers must communicate their intention to cancel the contract by creating a durable record. A telephone call to the seller would not be an adequate way of cancelling the contract effectively.

Regulation 11 – the cancellation period in the case of contracts for the supply of goods

Generally, a buyer of goods will have seven working days in which to exercise the right of cancellation commencing on the day following the delivery of the goods.

Regulation 12 – the cancellation period in the case of contracts for the supply of services starts on the day the contract is agreed.

The cancellation period will end in the following circumstances:

◆ seven working days commencing on the day after the contract was agreed provided the supplier issues written/durable information on or before the day the contract is concluded;

◆ when performance starts, if by that time the supplier has supplied the written/durable information and the consumer has agreed to the service commencing before the expiry of the cancellation period;

◆ seven working days after the day the consumer receives the written/durable information, if the consumer has agreed to the service commencing before the expiry of the cancellation period and the supplier issues the durable information in good time during performance of the service;

◆ when performance is completed, if the consumer has agreed to the service commencing before the expiry of the cancellation period and the supplier issues the written/durable information in good time during performance of the service and performance is completed within seven clear working days of the consumer having received the written/durable information;

◆ three months and seven working days from the day following the day the contract was agreed, if none of the above applies.

For those individuals who entered into a contract for services, the cancellation period of seven working days generally runs on or before the day that the contract is agreed.

Regulation 13 – exceptions to the right to cancel

Consumers should be aware, however, that where certain types of goods or services are concerned, they will not be permitted to cancel the contract. These include:

◆ Those products made to the special order of the consumer
◆ Goods which by their nature cannot be returned
◆ DVDs, CDs, software, audio or video tapes which have been opened
◆ Newspapers, magazines or journals
◆ Perishable goods
◆ Betting and lottery services

 Key point: Consumers have an unconditional legal right to cancel a distance selling contract.

The consequences of cancellation

Cancellation of a distance selling contract by the consumer has a number of consequences as outlined below:

- Regulation 14 imposes a duty on the supplier to repay to the consumer any sums which have been paid or to release or return any security which has been tendered by the consumer.
- Regulation 15 cancellation of the distance selling contract by the consumer also means that any related credit agreement is automatically cancelled.
- Regulation 16 guarantees that, in the event of cancellation of the contract, the consumer has a right to be repaid any interest that they have incurred under a related credit agreement.
- Regulation 17 states that the consumer remains under a duty of care to look after goods which remain in his/her possession until such time as they are returned to the seller following any decision to cancel the contract.
- Regulation 18 places a duty on the supplier to return goods to the consumer which were given in part-exchange under the terms of the contract.

E-commerce Regulations

Another important area for businesses to be aware of are activities covered by the Electronic Commerce (EC Directive) Regulations 2002.

Regulation 7 states that any business using electronic communications to promote the sale or supply of goods or services must clearly indicate to potential customers that these are commercial communications coming from a business

Regulation 7 also places a duty on a business to identify any discounts, gifts, promotions or games that it may be promoting and any conditions which are attached to these should be made readily accessible to customers.

In terms of Regulation 8, businesses will have to be careful that, when they send unsolicited e-mails to potential customers, they clearly identify these as unsolicited commercial communications.

Regulations 6 and 9 impose a duty on businesses to provide the following information to customers:

- A full business name and (geographical) address including an e-mail contact address
- A proper explanation of the business's pricing policy including delivery costs and taxes
- A VAT number where applicable
- Details of membership of a trade or professional association where applicable
- Details of whether the finalised contract will be stored and how it can be accessed by the business
- Details of how a customer can check and correct any errors contained in the contract
- The language which will be used to make the contract
- Codes of conduct to which the business is a party
- The terms of the contract should be made readily to customers so that they can be saved by downloading onto the customers' own computer
- If the contract is being concluded electronically, the different technical steps for the consumer to follow to conclude the contract

In terms of Regulation 11, businesses will have to provide electronic acknowledgement of a customer order quickly and efficiently and there will have to be in place a facility which allows the customer to correct any errors relating to the order for which the business is responsible.

Failure on the part of the business to have such a facility in place may mean that the customer is entitled to cancel the contract (Regulation 15).

 Key point: The Electronic Commerce (EC Directive) Regulations 2002 impose strict legal duties on businesses which use electronic communications to sell and market products to consumers.

Enforcement of the Distance Selling and Electronic Commerce Regulations

Both the Distance Selling and E-Commerce Regulations can be enforced the Office of Fair Trading, local authority trading standards departments throughout the UK and the Department of Trade, Enterprise and Investment in Northern Ireland. All these organizations can enforce the Regulations by applying for the appropriate court order.

Services

One area of Scots law which has definitely been ignored by Parliament is that of the service sector or industry. This historic failure by the Westminster Parliament to legislate in Scotland is somewhat curious given the fact that the same cannot be said for England and Wales where legislation in the form of the Sale and Supply of Goods Services Act 1982 has been introduced over the last twenty-five years to govern the ever expanding services industry. Part I of the Act of 1982 governs the supply of goods in relation to contracts for work and materials whereas Part II governs the actual provision of the service by a contractor. Regrettably, Part II of the Act was never extended to Scotland denying Scottish consumers a valuable source of protection.

 Key point: The provision of services in Scotland is mainly based on common law principles.

What is a service?

- An act or performance offered by one party to another (*performances are intangible, but may involve use of physical products*)
- An economic activity that does not result in ownership, or
- A process that creates benefits by facilitating a desired change in customers themselves, physical possessions or intangible assets

As already discussed in this Chapter, considerable confusion can arise as to whether a transaction involves the provision of services or the sale of goods (see, for example, **Robinson v Graves (1935)** discussed earlier in the Chapter). Should, for example, a contract to commission a painting or a contract to prepare a meal be classified as a services transaction or a sale of goods? Currently, there is real debate going on as to whether downloaded music and film purchased from Internet suppliers are goods or services. Almost certainly, opinion would be sharply divided as to what is the correct classification. This, however, is not an arcane legal debate because depending on how such transactions are classified will determine what legal rules govern the transaction. If such transactions are to be regarded as sale of goods contracts, then the Sale of Goods Act 1979 will be the appropriate point of reference. If, on the other hand, the transactions in question are to be regarded as the provision of services, then in the absence of a legislative framework, the common law will be used to resolve any disputes.

Traditionally, services have been classified as invisible products or intangibles or incorporeal moveable products which are quite different in nature from corporeal moveable products (which in the main are governed by the provisions of the Sale of Goods Act 1979).

The supply of goods to consumers under contracts for services

In situations where service providers or contractors are supplying goods as part of the contract e.g. the mechanic at the local garage is replacing worn out brake pads on a privately owned motor vehicle, the consumer will benefit from significant legislative protection which is very similar in scope to the provisions contained in the Sale of Goods Act 1979. If the brake pads supplied by the garage later turned out to be defective for any reason, the consumer would be able to rely on very similar legislative protection to the kind enjoyed by buyers of goods under Section 14 of the Sale of Goods Act 1979. It should be stressed, however, that the supply of goods by a contractor is not a sale of those goods and this is why the provisions of the Sale of Goods Act do not apply. In such situations, the goods supplied are incidental to the contract for services.

The relevant legislation in this area is Part 1A of the Supply of Goods and Services Act 1982. As with contracts for the sale of corporeal moveable goods, Section 11A of the 1982 Act makes it very clear that certain terms are implied into contracts where the service provider or contractor has agreed to supply goods to a consumer. The consumer will, therefore, have the protection of the following provisions of the Supply of Goods and Services Act 1982 in relation to goods supplied under a service contract:

Section 11B – the supplier's title to goods which s/he provides
Section 11C – the description of the goods supplied
Section 11D – the quality and fitness for purpose of the goods supplied
Section 11E – the sample must correspond to the bulk of the goods

As we can see, Sections 11B–E provide consumers of services with very similar (if not identical) levels of protection to those enjoyed by consumer buyers under Sections 12–15 of the Sale of Goods Act 1979. We are, therefore, already familiar with the kind of protection enjoyed by consumers under the implied terms having discussed these in-depth earlier in the chapter on the section relating to the Sale of Goods Act 1979.

 Key point: Where goods are supplied by a business to consumers as part of a service contract, Sections 11A–11E of the Supply of Goods and Services Act 1982 provide almost identical levels of statutory protection as can be found in Sections 12–15 of the Sale of Goods Act 1979.

Duties of a service provider

There are certain rules governing the provision of services which the courts have developed over the years and to which service providers or contractors must pay more than just lip service. These rules can be summed up as follows:

1 Duty to perform the service with the requisite or appropriate degree expected of the contractor

2 The service must be performed by the contractor within a reasonable time-scale

3 Cost of the service

4 Duty of care to safeguard client's property

The duty of skill and care

The contractor must perform the service with the requisite degree of skill and care. That is to say that the contractor must take reasonable care when providing the service – the level of care that consumers would be entitled to expect from a reasonably competent member of a trade or profession e.g. a motor mechanic, a plumber, a solicitor or an accountant. Admittedly, many trades or professions will have highly detailed rules which spell out what constitutes the standard of professionalism that users of services are entitled to expect from contractors. In other situations, the customs and practices of the trade or profession under scrutiny may be so well established or widely accepted that the question of whether the contractor has failed to deliver a decent service will be largely a foregone conclusion.

As should be obvious to students of the law of delict, any individual who claims to possess special skills or experience (see **Chaudhry v Prabhakar (1989)** in Chapter 5) or who states that s/he is proficient when it comes to the delivery of a particular service must meet the standards of a reasonably competent member of the trade, profession or occupation which routines delivers such a service.

What if the contractor is acting on an unpaid basis for a member of the public i.e. undertaking a mandate or acting as a gratuitous agent?

In Scotland, the duty of skill and care expected of a particular contractor will not be any less stringent merely because that individual was acting on an unpaid basis (see both **Copland v Brogan (1916)** and **Chaudhry v Prabhakar (1989)** in Chapter 5). Contractors acting on an unpaid basis must, therefore, take the same sort of care that would be expected of them in the management of their own affairs.

In order to practise as a solicitor in Scotland, an individual must meet all the requirements laid down by the Law of Society of Scotland. It does not matter how long that individual has been practising law, in theory all members of the Law Society must satisfy a minimum requirement of basic competency before they are unleashed on unsuspecting members of the public. In fact, it could be argued that membership of the Law Society is the kitemark or guarantee by which solicitors will be judged.

Admittedly, some solicitors will be brilliant in the discharge of their duties whereas others will be good or merely mediocre. It does not matter as long as all carry out their duties to their clients competently. The standard of professionalism expected by the Law Society of its members is an objective one and is not based on a person's personal characteristics such as their age, personal experience, academic brilliance or otherwise. This objective standard of professionalism will be applied equally to the newly qualified solicitor and the practitioner of some thirty years' standing. It will not be a defence for a newly qualified solicitor to use the excuse that s/he is just in the door and therefore should benefit from leniency if mistakes or errors are made. The Law Society has admitted such individuals to its ranks because they have passed the necessary examinations and training which allow them to practise as solicitors. The same could be said of newly qualified doctors.

It therefore follows that individuals qualified or licensed to carry out a particular occupation, trade or profession satisfies certain minimum requirements and if they fall below the accepted standard then this would leave them open to a potential negligence action. Obviously the consequences of negligence in certain professions (the medical profession) may be more serious than other trades or occupations (accountants).

 In **McIntyre v Gallacher (1883)** Gallacher was a plumber who carried on his trade in Glasgow. He had received a commission to carry out plumbing work in several tenement buildings in the city. The legal action arose in relation to a job where Gallacher had been instructed to seal several pipes. Gallacher failed to seal one of these pipes properly and, consequently, water later leaked out from the pipe causing damage to lower floors of the tenement building. McIntyre, the landlord of the tenement building, was sued by his tenants who were affected by the water damage. Upon further investigation of the incident, it was found that Gallacher had failed to seal the water pipe effectively and it was his negligence that was the direct cause of the loss and damage suffered by McIntyre's tenants could be explained by Gallacher's negligence. Quite simply, Gallacher's workmanship did not meet the normal standards customarily expected of a reasonably competent plumber.

(See also **Bolam v Friern Management Committee (1957)** and other medical negligence cases in Chapter 3 for examples of medical practitioners following below the generally accepted and established standards of their profession).

Obviously, when the contractor belongs to a particular profession or trade, the member of the public will have selected this person because s/he has the perfectly reasonable belief that the contractor will have the necessary level of skill and care to complete transactions successfully.

 Key point: The person supplying a service must display the requisite level of skill and care which would reasonably be expected of him.

Performance of a service within a reasonable time period

What if the contractor cannot perform the service within a reasonable time period? It is highly probable that the contractor is potentially liable to the recipient of the service who, unsurprisingly, is unlikely to be happy with excessive delays. There is a potential problem here because the key question will centre around the issue of what is meant by the passage of a reasonable time? In one situation, the passage of a certain time period may be regarded as completely excessive whereas in another situation the passage of the same length of time could hardly be used as justification to raise a legal action. It follows from this line of reasoning that it will be absolutely impossible to lay down a universally accepted definition of what is a reasonable time for performance of a service. Consequently, it will be left largely to the courts to exercise their judgement in this matter. A reasonable time could, therefore, be little as a few hours, a few days, a few weeks or a few months. Clearly, the courts will have to determine the issue by looking closely at the intentions of the parties to the contract and the circumstances of the case. It is not unusual for a contractor to state the period in which the consumer can expect the service to be carried out.

 Charnock v Liverpool Corporation (1968) a car had been damaged in an accident and was taken to a garage in order to be repaired. An estimate for the repair work to the car was agreed between the parties, but it took more than eight weeks for the work on the car to be completed. Needless to say, the owner of the car was less than pleased with this turn of events and he sued the garage for the cost of hiring a replacement vehicle for a number of weeks. The owner argued that the length of time taken by the garage to repair his car was excessive and unreasonable. The owner accepted that he would be inconvenienced as a result of the accident to the car, but he was not prepared to accept a situation where he would be forced to be without the use of the vehicle for longer than he considered strictly necessary. The owner calculated that, after the passage of a particular period of time without the use of the car, the garage was in breach of its obligations to him. It was held by the court that there was an implied term in the owner's contract with the garage that the repair work should have been carried out fairly quickly. In fact, five weeks to have the work carried out on the car would have been reasonable, over eight weeks was not. The owner was, therefore, entitled to recover the costs of hiring the replacement vehicle for the additional three week period.

 Charles Rickards Ltd v Oppenhaim (1950) Mr Oppenhaim had instructed Rickards to build the body of a car onto a chassis which he owned. The work should have taken six or seven months to complete according to the garage. The garage failed to carry out the work within this time period. Oppenhaim kept having to ask the garage when the completed car would be delivered to him. Eventually, in June 1948, Oppenhaim wrote to the garage stating that he was not prepared to accept delivery of the completed article after 25 July. Despite this warning, the garage failed to complete the job by this date and, in fact, it did not finish the job until October 1948. Oppenhaim refused to accept delivery of the car. Held: by the English Court of Appeal that six or seven months for completing the job as stipulated in the contract was a reasonable time limit for completion. The time limit was therefore a material term of the contract and the garage had breached its obligation by its failure to complete the job in this time period. Oppenhaim was perfectly entitled to reject the finished article.

 Key point: A service must be performed within a reasonable time period.

Cost of the service

It will not be unusual for the contractor to give the consumer an estimate of the cost of the work to be performed. It might be thought very sensible for the parties to agree the cost of performance of the service in advance in order to avoid any future disputes. Parties to a contract are not always so far-sighted and sensible and it may be the case that working out the cost of the service will be dictated by trade custom or professional practice. In Scotland, for example, solicitors engaged in personal injury work on behalf of clients have negotiated an agreement with insurance companies called the Voluntary Pre-Action Protocol which provides a framework for the payment of legal expenses in cases where it is possible to obtain an out of court settlement. Other trades or professions have customary rates or the well established legal principle in agency i.e. that an agent should be paid on a quantum meruit basis (see **Kennedy v Glass (1890)** in Chapter 5) can always be called upon to determine how much the contractor should be paid upon satisfactory completion of the service.

 Kennedy v Glass (1890) Kennedy had put in a lot of time and effort on behalf of Glass in order to complete a contract for the purchase of machinery (although the contract was never concluded). Nonetheless, Kennedy had the right to receive commission from Glass. Kennedy was not, however, a professional agent and, therefore, he received a reasonable rate of commission of £50.

 Robert Allan & Partners v McKinstray (1975) a firm of architects met with a client who instructed them to prepare drawings of a house that the client was interested in building. The client wanted more detailed information about the proposed construction of the house in order to pass the details to a builder so that the cost of the project could be better determined. Later, the client refused to pay the architects' fees stating that the project had been of a speculative nature. The architects were forced to sue the client for the cost of the work performed by them. The Sheriff Principal (probably following older decisions such as **Kennedy v Glass**) ruled that the architects were entitled to be paid on a *quantum meruit* basis i.e. as much as they were entitled to.

It, therefore, follows that the parties should agree the cost of the provision of services in advance, but failure to do so will not represent a significant hurdle in any subsequent legal action. A court will have the power to make an estimate as regards any fee sought by the contractor by referring to trade or professional practices. Again, turning to solicitors, those individuals who take on clients under the various Legal Aid Schemes will have to be aware that the Scottish Legal Aid Board determines what the practitioner can charge for telephone calls, letters, the time spent in attendance at Tribunal or Court on behalf of the client. At the conclusion of the case, the solicitor simply submits a fee in accordance with the current guidelines laid down by the Board.

 Key point: The cost of a service will be determined by the contract between the parties or, in the absence of such an agreement, the price will be determined by trade practice or custom.

Duty of care to safeguard client's property

If the contractor is in a position where s/he has possession of a customer's goods, money or property a duty of care is imposed whereby it is imperative that reasonable care of the client's property etc. is guaranteed.

Sinclair v Junor (1952) a garage had agreed to repair the pursuer's car, but failed to carry out the necessary work. In the interim period, the car was destroyed by a fire while still at the garage. The garage owners could not provide any plausible or alternative explanation as to why they should not be held responsible for this turn of events. The common sense explanation for the damage caused to the car was the result of the negligence of the garage owners or their employees.

 Forbes v Aberdeen Motors Ltd (1965) the defenders failed to implement the duty of care expected of them when they left a car in a hotel car park which had no security measures in place. The keys to the vehicle were left in the ignition and, consequently, the car was stolen. To add insult to injury, the thief was a very poor driver and was under the influence of alcohol and these factors contributed to the vehicle being involved in a collision and sustaining serious damage. The owner of the car was able to sue the people who had responsibility for his car for failing to discharge their duty of care.

 Copland v Brogan (1916) a carriage driver had been asked by an acquaintance to cash cheques at the bank in the neighbouring town. The carriage driver did so, but he mislaid the money (there was no question of dishonesty) owing to carelessness on his part. Although the carriage driver was doing a favour and was not receiving payment, he was still liable for the loss suffered because he had failed to take reasonable care of property which he voluntarily agreed to take into his possession.

It follows from the above cases that, if individuals deposit property with contractors, they are entitled to expect that contractors will take reasonable care of the items deposited in their care.

 Key point: The service provider must safeguard the property of any client which has been entrusted to him under the contract.

Services involving the provision of materials or goods

This is one area where Parliament has had a positive input to the law governing services.

Part IA of the Supply of Goods and Services Act 1982 established rules which are very similar in scope and effect to the provisions of the Sale of Goods Act 1979 in relation to the seller's title to the materials or goods, how these goods and materials are described and the quality and fitness for purpose of the goods or materials supplied. The recipients of services will, therefore, enjoy very similar levels of protection which consumers of corporeal moveable goods take for granted courtesy of Sections 12-15 of the Sale of Goods Act 1979.

It should be appreciated that recipients of services must have a contractual relationship with the provider in order to gain the protection of Part IA of the Supply of Goods and Services Act 1982.

 Key point: In service contracts involving the provision of goods and materials, consumers will enjoy similar levels of protection as consumers in a sale of goods transaction.

The legal relationship between contractors and recipients of services

In the vast majority of cases, service providers will have entered into a contractual relationship with the person who benefits from the service. What if a solicitor, for example, has been approached by a client to provide employment law advice and wrongly advises the client about the time limits for submission of an unfair dismissal claim to an Employment Tribunal? The solicitor and client have entered a contractual relationship.

Following on from the advice given by the solicitor, the client later attempts to submit the claim to Tribunal but is informed by letter from the Office of Employment Tribunals that the potential action is time-barred. The claim should have been submitted within three months (less one day) from the date of the termination of the client's employment, but unfortunately the solicitor thought the relevant time-limit was six months. Clearly, the client will have suffered harm as a result of the solicitor's incompetence or negligence. Any claim for compensation pursued by the client against the solicitor will be based on the contractual relationship between the parties (see **McIntyre v Gallacher (1883)** above).

There will be situations, of course, when the service provider and the recipient will not have entered into a contractual relationship. Such a situation does not represent a huge problem as we have already seen. In **Copland v Brogan (1916)**, it should be recalled that the carriage driver acted on an unpaid basis when he agreed to cash cheques for an acquaintance at the bank in the neighbouring town. This did not prevent the carriage driver from being successfully sued for misplacing the proceeds of the cheques.

Therefore, it follows that a recipient of a service can sue the provider by raising an action for negligence in situations where accidental loss or damage or injury are an issue. The key question to ask is whether service providers owe a duty of care to members of the public who may be harmed as a result of their acts or omissions.

 Even solicitors can be liable to third parties for carrying out their duties negligently or carelessly. In **White v Jones (1995)**, a client instructed his solicitors to write a new will which would include his daughters as beneficiaries of the estate on the event of his death. The client had previously excluded his daughters from his will. Unfortunately, the solicitors failed to implement the client's instructions and the new will was never drafted. The client died and his daughters were not entitled to receive any portion of his estate. The daughters brought a successful action against the solicitors for negligence. The House of Lords stated that the solicitors owed the daughters a duty of care because they had given assurances to the father that his will would be rewritten to include his daughters.

The decision in **White v Jones (1995)** clearly has its roots in the earlier ruling by the House of Lords in the case of **Hedley Byrne & Co Ltd v Heller & Partners (1963)** which involved the provision of negligent advice by a bank to an advertising agency about the financial solvency of a mutual client. The bank provided the wrong information which the advertising agency relied upon. Later, the agency suffered serious financial losses as a result of relying upon the bank's information. The bank was able to escape liability to the agency only for the simple fact that it had included a disclaimer in the letter containing the information.

Nevertheless, the legal principle was established by the House of Lords that it was possible for someone to be sued for negligent advice even in situations where no contractual relationship existed between the person providing the advice and the recipient of that information.

As already noted in Chapter 3, we have examined situations whereby members of the public who have received medical treatment on the National Health Service (NHS) have suffered injury as a result of medical negligence. Obviously, the victims in such cases as **Cassidy v Ministry of Health (1951)** did not have a contract with the NHS in the normal sense, but this in no way proved to be a barrier to the victim bringing a successful claim in negligence against the medical practitioners concerned.

In many respects, this brings us back full circle to the duty of skill and care imposed by law on a service provider irrespective of whether that individual has a contractual relationship or not with the recipient.

The primary remedy which will be available to parties who have suffered loss, injury or damage as a result of the wrongful acts or omissions of service providers will be that of damages or financial compensation.

However, the decision by the House of Lords in **Farley v Skinner (2001)** (see Chapter 2) puts things into perspective somewhat. Their Lordships were of the view that sometimes situations will arise whereby the victims of poor service will have to take things on the chin and it will not be possible to recover compensation or damages for every loss experienced.

 Key point: The legal relationship between service providers and recipients of the service will mainly be based on a contractual agreement.

Summary

- The Sale of Goods Act 1979 establishes rules that govern the transfer of ownership of corporeal, moveable goods from seller to buyer.

- The Sale of Goods Act 1979 imposes certain implied duties upon a seller of goods with which he must comply.

- The implied terms (Sections 12 to 15) cover the following issues – the seller's title or his right to sell the goods, the way in which the goods are described, the quality and the fitness of the goods and those situations where the goods are sold using a sample.

- A material breach of contract in Scotland would include breaches of Sections 13, 14 and 15.

- The Sale and Supply of Goods to Consumers Regulations 2002, which came into force on 31 March 2003, make important changes to the Sale of Goods Act 1979. The Regulations provide consumer buyers with additional remedies – repair, replacement, reduction in the price and rescission.

- Since the introduction of the Unfair Contract Terms Act 1977 and the Unfair Terms in Consumer Contracts Regulations 1999, a seller's ability to use exclusion and limitation clauses in order to avoid the implied duties of the Sale of Goods Act has been considerably weakened. However, consumer buyers, as opposed to business buyers, will continue to enjoy much greater protection in relation to the use of exclusion and limitation clauses.

- The Sale of Goods Act 1979 also lays down important rules that govern the delivery of corporeal, moveable property (Sections 27 to 37).

- The Sale of Goods Act provides the buyer and the seller with a number of remedies should they find themselves victims of a breach of contract by the other party.

- One of the most distinctive features of the Consumer Credit Act 1974 is the fact that those businesses or individuals wishing to provide credit facilities to members of the public must be in obtain possession of a licence and failure to do so could mean the imposition of a number of civil and criminal penalties.

- The Consumer Credit Act 1974 contains rules which apply to two types of credit agreements. These agreements are consumer credit agreements and consumer hire agreements.

- A consumer credit agreement is a contract consisting of a debtor (the borrower) and a creditor (the lender).

- The Consumer Credit Act 1974 originally gave authority to a Director-General of Fair Trading assisted by the Office of Fair Trading to oversee the regulation of the consumer credit industry in the United Kingdom.

- The introduction of the Enterprise Act 2002 has resulted in the Office of Fair Trading being given legal status as a corporate body and the post of Director-General of Fair Trading has been abolished.

- The Office of Fair Trading has primary responsibility for the granting of credit licences under the Consumer Credit Act 1974.

- Under the Consumer Credit Act 1974, there are strict controls imposed on businesses which advertise credit facilities to members of the general public.

- Strict guidelines regulate how an advertisement is to be presented (its *form*), what sort of information will appear in it (its *content*) and that they should be easily understood by members of the public.

- According to the Consumer Credit Act 1974, all consumer credit agreements must be in writing.

- The Consumer Credit Act 1974 imposes a duty on the creditor to make sure that the agreement presented to the debtor for signing is legible and, additionally, all the main terms must be contained in it.

- Failure by the creditor to comply with any of the rules regulating the content and appearance of a regulated agreement will mean that it can only be enforced by a court order against the debtor.

- Under the Consumer Credit Act 1974, a debtor will have the right to cancel a credit agreement if two conditions are met – if you, the debtor, entered into face-to-face discussions with the creditor or the creditor's agents with the aim of entering a credit agreement; and the signing of the credit agreement by both parties did not take place on the creditor's business premises.

- Under the Consumer Credit Act 1974, a court may examine the terms of a credit agreement in order to establish whether it operates fairly between the parties and to ensure that it is not an unfair agreement.

- Creditors often use credit reference agencies in order to discover whether someone is creditworthy before giving that person a loan or some other from of credit.

- Credit reference agencies must ensure that the information that they hold in relation to actual debtors and potential debtors is up to date and accurate.

- The areas of distance selling and e-commerce are now regulated by the Consumer Protection (Distance Selling) Regulations 2000 and the Electronic Commerce (EC Directive) Regulations 2002 respectively and give consumers far greater legal rights in their dealings with businesses.

- The Consumer Protection from Unfair Trading Practices Regulations 2008 outlaw a number of commercial practices which could potentially harm the interests of consumers.

- Although the service industry is a hugely important area of economic activity in Scotland, it is regulated surprisingly by common law principles and not by legislation – unlike the situation in England and Wales.

Test your knowledge

Short answer questions, exam standard essay style questions and case-studies.

1 a) What do we mean by a sale of goods?
   b) Explain the following terms:
      i) A sale
      ii) An agreement to sell
      iii) Specific goods
      iv) Unascertained goods
      v) Future goods
   c) What kinds of goods have the various individuals purchased in the situations described below and does a sale or an agreement to sell exist?

   ⚖ i) Sarah has had her offer accepted to buy a second hand Volkswagen Polo (registration number: FA52 DKY; colour black) from Harold Marks Automobiles.

   ⚖ ii) Fred owns the local licensed grocer and he has just placed an order with the local wholesaler for 1000 bottles and cans of beer (lager and ale), 200 bottles of white wine, 150 bottles of red wine, 75 bottles of whisky, 60 bottles of vodka and 50 bottles of gin. To complicate matters, these goods are supplied by a variety of brewers, distillers, vineyards and manufacturers. It is normal practice for the wholesaler to confirm two days after Fred has placed his order that the goods are ready for delivery.

   ⚖ iii) Alan and Caroline have recently become engaged to be married. To mark the special occasion, Alan has asked the jeweler to supply an engagement ring according to his own design. The jeweler is quite happy to accommodate Alan, but it will take six weeks to make the ring.

2 a) In a contract of sale, a buyer may be able to acquire ownership rights to property in situations:
   • Where the seller lacked the authority to sell the goods
   • Where the seller was not the true owner of the goods

   Explain the above statement.

   ⚖ b) Laura is a student at Granton College of Further and Higher Education. Financially, she is finding it very tough as a full-time student. Although Laura has part-time employment and she has taken out the full student loan, this is not enough to make ends meet. Laura's parents gave her an expensive mobile phone for her Christmas present and she decides to take it along to the local pawnbrokers to see whether she can use it to secure a cash advance. The pawnbroker gives Laura £60 for the phone. She is also given a ticket which states that she has 30 days in which to repay the loan otherwise she will lose the right to reclaim her goods.

   What action can the pawnbrokers take if Laura fails to reclaim her property within the 30-day period?

3 a) It is important to remember that the Sale of Goods Act 1979 (as amended) applies to contracts of sale involving the transfer of ownership of corporeal, moveable goods.

   Define corporeal, moveable goods and provide ten examples of this type of property.

   ⚖ b) Derek has sold a house to Marina. A dispute has arisen in relation to the property because Derek is arguing that, under the contract, he has the right to remove an ornamental shrub from the front garden, but Marina is refusing to allow Derek to do this. Marina claims that the ornamental shrub is rightfully her property. In any case, removing the shrub would cause it to suffer irreparable damage.

   Will Marina or Derek be entitled to raise an action under the Sale of Goods Act 1979 (as amended) in order to resolve this dispute?

4 a) What are the implied terms in a sale of goods transaction?
   b) Consider the following transactions:

   ⚖ i) Kevin wishes to purchase a new leather jacket. He has a bit of money to spend and he decides to have the jacket specially made. Kevin goes to a local gents clothing store which has an excellent reputation for producing leather jackets made especially to the customer's order. Kevin is shown several styles of jacket. He particularly likes one style of jacket. All that remains is for him to choose the colour and the texture of the finished article from a range of leather samples shown to him by the sales assistant. Kevin decides to select a sample which is camel in colour and made from nubuck leather. The jacket will cost Kevin £400 and he makes it very clear to the assistant that he wants to get everything just right. He is particularly anxious that the sample shown to him accurately represents the colour and the texture of the finished article. The sales assistant is very quick to lay these anxieties to rest. A week later, Kevin receives a phone call from the gents store informing him that the jacket is ready to be picked up. When Kevin see the jacket, he is acutely aware that it is the wrong colour (it is a brown jacket, but it is a much darker brown than camel) and the appearance and texture of the jacket consists of glazed leather rather than the nubuck leather that he had anticipated.

ii) Tariq bought a brand new turbo diesel car at a cost of £16,000 from a reputable car dealer. Two weeks after the delivery of the car and with less than 200 miles on the odometer, the car experiences a catastrophic engine failure. This incident occurred when Tariq was driving along a road where the national speed limit of 60 miles per hour applied. He was not able to bring the vehicle under control quickly enough and it spun off the road ending up in a ditch. The car was extensively damaged and Tariq suffered severe whiplash and minor cuts and bruises. The car dealer is refusing to admit liability for the fault in the engine claiming that Tariq will have to take the matter up with the vehicle's manufacturer.

iii) Foundation Menswear has just received its new range of shirts for Spring/Summer. The contract stated that each box of clothing supplied would each contain 30 short-sleeved shirts. When the boxes are all opened, they each contain 25 shirts. This packaging method makes no difference whatsoever to the number of shirts supplied. However, when the plastic wrapping is removed, it becomes evident that a large number of the shirts have long-sleeves.

With reference to the Sale of Goods Act 1979 (as amended), how would you decide the three cases above?

5 a) Section 14(2) of the Sale of Goods Act 1979 (as amended) states that the seller must supply the buyer with goods which meet the standard of satisfactory quality and Section 14(3) of the Act stipulates that the seller must supply the buyer with goods which are fit for their purpose.

What is the difference between satisfactory quality and fitness for purpose?

b) Tartan Touring Services Ltd is a company which organises touring holidays throughout the UK and to far-flung destinations throughout Europe. Tartan needs to replace

seven buses which form part of the company fleet. To this end, Tartan has entered into a contract with Cameron Coachbuilders Ltd for the construction of seven buses. Tartan told Cameron that the buses should be suitable for long-distance travel and should have luxury seating. When the vehicles are delivered, Tartan discovers that they do not have toilets, entertainment systems (TV, DVD and video) and the buses are not sufficiently robust or comfortable enough for touring purposes. These vehicles would be more suitable for traveling short journeys around the local bus routes in Edinburgh and Glasgow.

Where does Tartan Touring Services stand legally?

6 a) The Sale and Supply of Goods to Consumers Regulations 2002 came into force on 31 March 2003 and they introduce important changes to the existing sale of goods legislation of the United Kingdom.

Would you agree that consumers are much better protected with the introduction of the Sale and Supply of Goods to Consumers Regulations 2002?

b) Ethsham bought a brand new LCD television from SHOCKZ, a well-known electrical retailer. The television was very expensive and Ethsham was unsure whether he wanted to spend such a large amount money on this item. The sales assistant was very keen to sell the television to Ethsham and he pointed out that the goods were covered by a three-year manufacturer's guarantee. Some four months later, however, the television broke down and Ethsham took it back to SHOCKZ. Ethsham demanded a refund, but the store informs him that the situation is not that simple. The store can either replace or repair the goods, but it does not have to refund the purchase price of the goods. Furthermore, the store cannot be held responsible for the manufacturer's guarantee which was issued independently. Ethsham is very confused and now seeks your advice.

Advise Ethsham.

7 a) Any attempt by a seller to exclude or limit his liability to a buyer in a sale of goods transaction will be automatically void.

Assess the accuracy of this statement.

b) Entertainment Services Ltd, an international supplier of DVDs, CDs, videos and books, has entered into a contract of sale with Specialist Software Solutions plc for the purchase and installation of a cutting edge software package. The software package would allow Entertainment Services to set up a database which would keep track of its distribution and supply operations. Customers would be automatically billed when a transaction was completed and this would stop the Entertainment Services from wasting a great deal of time going through the paper records and sending out a paper invoice to customers. As an alternative, customers would receive an invoice via e-mail. However, the software package contained some sort of error and a lot of important customer information was wiped from the database. This information included details of customers who had still not paid for goods. This meant that Entertainment Services could not account for a valuable source of revenue. Entertainment Services is now suing Specialist Software Solutions for substantial damages for the losses it has suffered. Specialist Software Solutions is attempting to rely on a clause in the contract of sale which reduces its liability to a sum of £10,000.

Will Specialist Software Solutions be able to enforce the contractual term against Entertainment Services?

8 a) Risk passes with property.

Is this statement true in light of the recent changes made to sale of goods transactions by the Sale and Supply of Goods to Consumers Regulations 2002?

b) i) Smith Solicitors have selected two new leather sofas from Luxury Leather Ltd to be used in their client waiting room. The goods in question were sale items and were the last two items in stock of that particular line of furniture. Luxury Leather had promised to deliver the sofas first thing on Monday morning, but on Sunday evening Luxury Leather was broken into by thieves and the sofas were stolen.

Who will be responsible for the risk to the goods in the above situation?

ii) Consider the following scenario:

What if Euan and Lynne had entered into a contract to purchase the two sofas from Luxury Leather for their sitting room which has just been redecorated and the sofas had been stolen from the storeroom. Luxury Leather had promised the couple that it would deliver the goods on Thursday.

What would have been the legal position in this situation?

9 Examine the following situations carefully:

a) Jasminder went shopping for some new clothes on Saturday morning. She is really pleased with her purchases having bought a couple of pairs of jeans and a pair of leather boots from her favourite designer store. Just as she is leaving the store to head back to her car, Jasminder runs into an old friend, Sadia, and they spend the next 20 minutes talking. When Jasminder eventually reaches the car park, she realises that she has left her bag containing all her new clothes in the store. She must have put the bag down while she was deep in conversation with Sadia. In a complete panic, Jasminder heads back into the store to see whether she can find the bag. Unfortunately, after searching everywhere with the help of the staff it becomes obvious that the bag is nowhere to be seen.

b) Steve has just entered into a contract with Reddie Motors for the purchase of a luxury second hand car. Before the contract was formed, Steve stated that he wanted Reddie to make a number of adjustments to the car:
1 Alloy wheels were to be fitted
2 The car was to be fitted with a multi-changer CD player
3 The glass in the car windows were to be tinted.

Reddie Motors have informed Steve that these modifications to the car will be carried out on Saturday and that he can pick the vehicle up on Monday morning. On Friday afternoon, the car was damaged when one of Reddie's employees was moving it into the workshop.

c) FreshFields Supermarket has agreed to purchase Farmer Giles' entire crop of potatoes which he just harvested. However, a term of the contract stipulates that Farmer Giles will have to weigh the potatoes in order to calculate the price to be paid by FreshFields. Before Farmer Giles can weigh the potatoes, he discovers that the some of the potatoes have been infected by blight.

d) Norma ordered an expensive new dress from the catalogue because she needed something to wear at Janice's wedding. The catalogue operates a policy whereby customers must return goods that they have no intention of keeping within a two-week period. The dress has now been in Norma's possession for three weeks and, furthermore, she wore the dress to the wedding where Ellen accidentally spilled a glass of wine over the dress and the stain is so bad that it cannot be removed.

e) Sweeney's Slaughterhouse has agreed to sell Bill, a butcher, 50 frozen lamb carcasses. Sweeney's Slaughterhouse is a huge business concern supplying meat to butchers all over Central Scotland. At any one time, it has hundreds of animal carcasses in stock. Bill sent two of his employees, Andy and Jamal, to pick up the goods. One of Sweeney's foremen had arranged for Andy and Jamal to uplift the goods from loading bay 9 of the slaughterhouse. When Andy and Jamal arrived at Sweeney's, the last crate is being piled up ready for them to put into their refrigerated lorry and all Jamal had to do was sign the invoice for the goods. It was nearly lunchtime and Andy suggested that he and Jamal should go over to the local café and have a quick bite to eat. Jamal was a bit dubious at first, but Andy said that they would be no more than half an hour at most and, in any case, there were plenty of people about the loading bay who would keep an eye out for the goods. When Andy and Jamal returned from lunch, the goods had been stolen.

Who is the owner of the goods in each of the five situations described above?

10 a) Romalpa clauses and other retention of title clauses can provide a seller of goods with valuable protection where there is a real danger that the buyer may become insolvent and will, therefore, become unable to pay the seller. These types of contractual terms, however, have their limitations and there may be situations where the seller's attempt to rely upon them will be utterly doomed to failure.

How effective are Romalpa and other retention of title clauses and are they worth the paper that they are written on?

b) Stuart owns the local timber merchants. On Friday, he was approached by Wylie Homes, which is currently building a new housing estate, and it wishes to purchase a large consignment of timber from him. Stuart has had previous dealings with Wylie, but lately he has become somewhat wary of doing business with the builder. Stuart has heard rumours that the builder has serious financial problems and, furthermore, Stuart is still owed a substantial amount of money from previous transactions. The proposed contract represents a very valuable piece of business that Stuart can ill afford to turn down. Stuart decides to supply the goods to Wylie but he insists that an all sums retention of title clause is inserted into the contract. Several months later, Stuart receives information that Wylie has become insolvent and he attempts to enforce the all sums retention of title clause.

Since the contract was formed, only a very small part of the timber that Stuart supplied is in its original state. Most of it has been used by Wylie to build the houses on the new estate.

What are the chances of Stuart being able to enforce the all sums retention of title clause?

11 a) What is the definition of delivery in terms of the Sale of Goods Act 1979 (as amended) and in what part of the Act would you find the rules relating to delivery?
b) What is the appropriate section of the Sale of Goods Act 1979 (as amended) in relation to each of the scenarios described below:
  i) The contract states that the seller must deliver the goods to the buyer, but there is nothing in the agreement which lays down a time period for delivery of the goods.
  ii) The seller has delivered a larger quantity of goods than the amount stated in the contract.
  iii) The seller is proposing to deliver the goods by instalments, but the buyer is totally opposed to this arrangement.
  iv) The seller has handed the goods over to a carrier in order to carry out delivery.
  v) The goods have been delivered to the buyer, but he has not yet had a reasonable opportunity to examine them.
  vi) The buyer has rightfully refused to accept the goods, but the seller is demanding that the buyer return the goods.
  vii) The buyer has wrongfully refused to take delivery of the goods from the seller.
  viii) The seller has breached the contract and the buyer wishes to exercise his right of partial rejection in relation to some of the goods.
  ix) The buyer has accepted the goods.
  x) Where the seller agrees to deliver the goods to a distant place.

12 When one of the parties commits a breach of contract, the innocent party will have access to a number of remedies.

Describe the remedies available for breach of contract to **a)** the buyer and **b)** the seller.

13 Write explanatory notes on the following topics:
a) The difference between a sale or security situation
b) Frustrated contracts
c) Calculating the price in sale of goods contracts
d) Capacity to enter into contracts
e) Stipulations as to time in a contract of sale

14 Morag has been running a shop which specialises in the sale of work by local artists. When Morag first started the business, she generally refused to give credit to customers. Very occasionally, she would make an exception and extend credit to close friends. As her business has grown, Morag finds that customers expect to be given six months credit (at the very least) when they make a purchase from her shop. Morag has had to move with the times and credit sales now represent the majority of her sales. However, Morag is now very concerned because one of her friends has told her that she has been breaking the law for some time. Morag does not possess the necessary legal documents which would permit her to provide credit facilities to her customers.

Is Morag's friend correct and, if so, what steps will she have to take in order to comply with the law?

15 Sheila and her husband are interested in having a conservatory built. The couple had received a telephone call from a company that specialises in building conservatories and they decided to allow a salesperson to come to their house to explain the various options which would be available to them. One Monday evening, the agent arrived at the couple's house at 7 p.m. and did not leave until 11 p.m. Against their better judgement, the couple decided to sign the contract allowing the company to build the conservatory. Sheila and her husband would have liked more time to think about things, but the salesperson was very persuasive and very determined to close the deal. The couple would now like to withdraw from the agreement, but they are bound in contract to the company aren't they?

Can Sheila and her husband cancel the consumer credit contract?

16 The Consumer Credit Act 1974 gives powers to a court permitting it to examine the terms of a credit agreement in order to establish whether it operates fairly between the parties and to ensure that it is not an extortionate agreement.

What is an extortionate credit agreement?

17 The Bank of the Firth of Clyde has been running a series of advertisements. The advertisements give the impression that if anyone applies for a loan with the Bank they will automatically be granted one. Asif applied for a loan, but was turned down on the grounds that he has been unemployed for six months. The advertisements did not say that loans were dependent upon an applicant's employment status.

Should the Bank have taken greater care when it used the above advertisement?

18 One of the most common ways in which a credit agreement can be brought to an end is where the debtor breaks that agreement. If the agreement is broken by the debtor this is often referred to as the debtor defaulting on the agreement.

What steps can the creditor take when the debtor breaches the credit agreement?

19 Write short, explanatory notes on the following:
a) Running account credit
b) Fixed term credit
c) Restricted use credit
d) Unrestricted use credit
e) Debtor-creditor agreements
f) Debtor-creditor-supplier agreements

20 Some agreements are not governed by the rules contained in the Consumer Credit Act 1974. Exempt agreements, however, do not escape sections 137 to 140 of the Act which deal with agreements that are considered to be extortionate.

What agreements are exempt from the provisions of the Consumer Credit Act 1974?

21 Manuel runs a herbal shop called Natural Highs. He has recently started to stock a product called Mexican Magic (chemical name: *salvia divinorum*), a drug made from the mint plant that was extensively used by Mexican shamans in a variety of religious rituals. People who use the product are said to experience an improved mood, calmness and an enhanced connection with nature. Manuel is under the impression that the product is perfectly safe and, to this effect, he has placed advertisements in a number of local papers and the product is prominently displayed on his website and in his shop window. Internet sales of the product look like they could be particularly strong as Manuel has already received 150 advance orders from potential customers. Manuel, however, is in for a shock. He receives a visit from trading standard officers at the local council who have received a complaint from Lyn who was given some Mexican Magic at a party. Lyn was hospitalised for ten days after ingesting a mild dose of the drug and will likely need psychiatric help to aid her recovery. The officers inform Manuel that he may be charged and prosecuted for exposing hallucinogenic drugs to the public.

Explain the potential criminal liability of Manuel's actions.

22 Hugh runs a very successful chain of clothing stores. He has recently become aware that major new legislation, the Consumer

Protection from Unfair Trading Regulations 2008 came into force last May which made important changes which could affect the running of his business.

Assess the importance of the reforms introduced by the Consumer Protection from Unfair Trading Regulations 2008.

23 ⚖ Bridget and Frances run a flower shop in the high street. They have recently developed a website which allows them to reach a larger group of potential customers with the result that there has been a marked increase in these types of sales. Bridget and Frances, however, are only vaguely aware of the legal rules governing these types of transactions and they have approached you, their solicitor, for a proper explanation of the law.

Draft a letter which is to be sent to Bridget and Frances which clearly sets out the legal rules governing these types of transactions.

24 ⚖ Lloyd put his expensive Swiss watch into an upmarket jewellers to have it properly serviced by a fully qualified technician. The assistant informed Lloyd that he should get the watch back within four weeks. Some ten weeks later, Lloyd has still not had the item returned to him despite repeated phone calls to the jewellers in order to chase things up. Lloyd is beginning to suspect something is badly amiss and the manager of the jewellers finally admits that the watch was irreparably damaged at the workshop. Apparently, the technician broke the watch when she tried to fit a component part which was completely unsuitable for that type of time piece.

What remedies, if any, does Lloyd have against the jewellers?

The importance of agents

Why appoint an agent in the first place? There are two reasons why the principal would wish to appoint an agent to represent him. First, it will not be physically possible for the principal to carry out every task which is necessary for the successful running of a business. There are only so many hours in the day and there are only so many tasks that even the most gifted person can get through in a day. Sometimes you just have to delegate tasks to another person in order to complete them. Second, an agent will often be appointed by the principal because he will have special skills or experience of which the principal wishes to take advantage. When it comes to selling a house, for example, many ordinary people would not even know how to go about this and would have even less knowledge of the legal rules that have to be complied with in order to complete the transaction successfully. It is no wonder in such a situation that they would choose to appoint a solicitor to act for them.

 Key point: Agents are often employed or hired as it is physically impossible for the principal to carry out every activity that relates to his business personally and the agent may have special skills or expertise from which the principal can benefit.

Agents crop up in many different areas of commercial life. A list of agents can be seen below:

- Solicitors
- Architects
- Accountants
- Auctioneers
- Commercial agents
- Partners in a firm
- Members of a limited liability partnership
- Company directors
- Managers
- Sales assistants
- Factors
- Stockbrokers
- Captain of a ship or an aircraft

 Key point: Agents are encountered in many different areas of commercial life.

Employees or independent contractors

An agent can either be an employee or an independent contractor. An agent who is an employee will carry out services for the principal under a contract *of* service, whereas an independent contractor carries out services for the principal under a contract *for* services. It may be useful to think of a contract of service as an employment contract and, by way of a comparison, a contract for services involves a situation where the agent will hire out his services on an as required basis to the principal. A solicitor may serve as a useful example. If a solicitor works permanently for the legal services department of a local council, he will be an agent *and* an employee of the council. If, however, a solicitor is a partner in a private law firm and hires out his services to private clients as and when they require his advice and assistance, he will be acting as an agent, but he is an independent contractor and not an employee of his private clients.

Not all employees, of course, can call themselves agents of their employer. It should be remembered that the most important function of an agent is to bind his principal into contracts with third parties. Many employees will simply not have the power to do this. It is highly unlikely that someone who works on a factory production line and has absolutely no dealings with third parties would be in a position to describe himself as his employer's agent.

 Key point: Agents can either be employees of the principal or independent contractors for services.

Mandatory and agent

An agent expects to receive some sort of reward for performing services for the principal. In Scotland, a person can act for someone very much like an agent, but this type of representative would not expect to receive a reward. Sometimes this type of relationship is referred to as gratuitous agency or unpaid agency. It is more properly called mandate and the person who acts in this way is known as a mandatory. Although acting on an unpaid basis, a mandatory will still owe a duty of care to the person for whom he is acting. This means that a mandatory will not be able to use the fact that he was acting unpaid as a defence to a claim of negligence. The following two cases provide interesting examples of the duty of care expected of a mandatory.

 Copland *v* Brogan (1916) a school teacher had asked a carriage driver to go to a bank in a nearby town in order to cash three cheques at the bank. The carriage driver had carried out various tasks for the school teacher in the past. The carriage driver was not expecting to be paid for carrying out this favour. However, after cashing the cheques at the bank, the carriage driver lost the school teacher's money. There was no question of dishonesty on the carriage driver's part. The school teacher sued on the grounds of the carriage driver's negligence. The carriage driver's defence was, that as he was acting on an unpaid basis, he could not be sued for negligence.

Held: by the Inner House of the Court of Session that a mandatory must take the same sort of care that would be expected of him in the management of his own affairs. Had the proceeds from the cheques belonged to the mandatory, it is likely that he would have made sure that they were kept safe. This he had failed to do and he had not taken reasonable care of the school teacher's property.

 Chaudhry *v* Prabhakar (1989) Chaudhry had recently passed her driving test and she asked a friend, Prabhakar, to advise her in relation to buying a second-hand car. Chaudhry made it clear to Prabhakar that she did not want to buy a car that had been involved in an accident. Prabhakar found a car for Chaudhry, but the car had a dent in its bonnet. Prabhakar noticed the dent, but he did not make any enquiries as to whether or not the car had been involved in an accident. Chaudhry specifically asked Prabhakar if the car had been involved in an accident and he replied that it had not. Relying on Prabhakar's statement, Chaudhry bought the car from the seller. Later, the car turned out to be unroadworthy as result of the accident. Chaudhry sued Prabhakar for negligence.

Held: the English Court of Appeal decided that Prabhakar had been negligent when he told Chaudhry that the car had not been involved in an accident in response to her very specific question. It made no difference that Prabhakar had acted for Chaudhry without payment. He should have exercised the type of care that would have been expected if he had been looking after his own interests. He had failed to take reasonable care and, therefore, he was liable.

 Key point: A mandatary or gratuitous agent does not expect to be paid by the principal for his services, but he must take reasonable care in the way that he performs his duties.

Del credere agents

A *del credere* agent is an agent who introduces third parties to his principal and, critically, he promises to indemnify or compensate the principal if the contract does not go as planned and the principal suffers losses as a result.

 Couturier v Hastie (1856) Hastie had placed a cargo of corn on a ship sailing from Greece. The documents of title were forwarded to London agents in order that the corn might be sold. The London agents employed Couturier to find someone to sell the goods to – which he duly did. Unknown to the parties, the cargo had overheated aboard the ship and had been landed at the nearest port and sold, so that when Couturier entered the contract the corn did not really exist. The buyer later cancelled the contract and Couturier was sued by Hastie on the grounds that he was a *del credere* agent.

Held: the claim against Couturier failed on an important technicality because the contract was based on the understanding that the goods were actually in existence when Couturier contracted to sell them to the third party.

 Key point: A *del credere* agent is an agent who introduces third parties to his principal and, critically, he promises to indemnify or compensate if the third party fails to honour the contract causing the principal to suffer loss as a result.

General and special agents

General agents act for the principal in connection with all of his interests in a particular line of business. One example of a general agent is a solicitor. General agents can possess both actual and ostensible authority.

Special agents, on the other hand, have extremely limited authority. They usually act for the principal in one type of transaction only. An example of a special agent would be an estate agent. Special agents possess actual authority only.

 Morrison v Statter (1885) Calder, the head shepherd on Statter's farm, bought sheep from Morrison without having received explicit instructions from Statter. Morrison attempted to obtain payment from Statter for the sheep, but Statter refused claiming that he had never authorised Calder to act in this way.

Held: Calder had no actual authority to bind Statter in this way. There had been no previous dealings between Morrison and Statter which might have led Morrison to believe that this type of transaction was within Calder's ostensible or apparent authority. Morrison knew that Statter had not given Calder authority to purchase the sheep.

 The Ocean Frost (1986) the third party was well aware that the agent, who held a senior position with the principal, had no general authority to enter into a particular contract on the principal's behalf. Both the English Court of Appeal and the House of Lords stated that the third party knowing full well that the agent had no authority to act could not rely on the agent's statement that he did have the necessary authority to bind his principal in contract with the third party.

 Key point: General agents act for the principal in connection with all of his interests in a particular line of business whereas special agents have extremely limited authority.

The capacity of the principal and the agent

Clearly, it is important that the law recognises the ability of the principal and the agent to enter into the agency agreement. Factors such as the mental incapacity of one of the parties, intoxication as a result of alcohol or drugs, or one of the parties being declared an enemy alien in times of war may undermine the agency agreement. Interestingly, however, it would appear that an agent lacking capacity will not undermine any agreement that he may have negotiated between the principal and the third party. However, the position would be very different if the principal lacked capacity. The principal cannot use an agent to get round the problem of his lack of contractual capacity if the law would prevent him from entering a contract with the third party personally. A young person under the age of 16, for example, will not be able to use an agent in this way to enter contracts which he would otherwise be prevented from entering.

An agent must also be acting for a principal who actually exists and who is recognised by the courts as being able to take on rights and duties under a contract. It is not possible to act as an agent for someone who has not yet been born or for someone who has since died.

 Tinnevelly Sugar Refining Co v Mirrlees, Watson & Yaryan Co Ltd (1894) Darley & Butler claimed to be acting on behalf of a company called Tinnevelly. They entered into a contract with Mirrlees to purchase new machinery for Tinnevelly. Unfortunately, at the time Darley & Butler entered the contract with Mirrlees, Tinnevelly did not exist. It had not yet been registered as a company and, therefore, it was not recognised as a legal person capable of being a party to a contractual agreement. The new machinery later broke down and Tinnevelly sued Mirrlees for breach of contract.

Held: Tinnevelly was not a party to the contract with Mirrlees because Darley & Butler could not have been acting as agents for a principal that did not yet exist. When the original contract had been entered into (11 July 1890), Tinnevelly did not exist as a person in the eyes of the law. In fact,

Tinnevelly only became a legal person on 29 July 1890 a number of weeks after the contract of sale had been entered into. It is not possible to act as an agent for a non-existent principal. In other words, the law must recognise the existence of the person who is supposedly the agent's principal.

 Key point: An agent cannot represent a non-existent principal.

The creation of an agency relationship

The relationship between the principal and the agent is based on the law of contract. In the diagram below, two contracts exist. The primary and most important contract is the one between the principal and the agent. The secondary contract is between the principal and the third party.

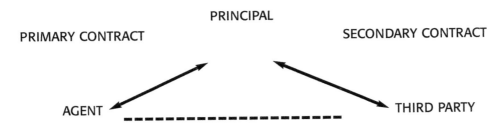

There are five ways in which an agency relationship can be created:

1 By express contract

2 Implied by the conduct of the parties or by law

3 By holding out

4 By ratification

5 By necessity

 Key point: The agency relationship can be created in the following ways – express contract, implied by the conduct of the parties or by law, holding out, ratification and necessity.

Express agency

The contract between principal and agent can either be of a verbal nature or it can be in writing. This is known as an express contract. A written agreement is obviously a more desirable option because if the parties have gone about things properly it will spell out clearly the agent's powers and duties. There is no legal requirement to have a written agency agreement, but generally speaking, courts tend to prefer dealing with documents because in the event of a dispute the rights and the duties of both parties are much easier to identify. Partners in a firm may well choose to have a written deed of partnership which names each partner and lays out very clearly the rights and duties of each partner. Similarly, members of a Limited Liability Partnership may also choose to draw up a members' agreement which will name each member and determine the extent of the members' ability to bind the business into contracts with third parties.

 Key point: An agent can be appointed expressly by way of a written contract or a verbal agreement.

Implied agency

Agency can be implied by law or by the actions and conduct of the parties. By law under Section 5 of the Partnership Act 1890, every partner is an agent of the firm and an agent of his fellow partners for the purpose of the business of the partnership. Furthermore, according to Section 6 of the Limited Liability Partnerships Act 2000, every member of such a business organisation is to be regarded as an agent. Very often, a person's occupation or job will indicate that they are entitled to be regarded as an agent. The director of an incorporated company is impliedly an agent for the company in all the matters usually entrusted to directors. It can also be implied that a pub manager who contracts on behalf of the pub owner with third-party suppliers of goods and services as part of his job is acting as an agent.

 Key point: Sometimes the law recognises that an individual who holds a particular position is to be regarded as an agent or, alternatively, it can be implied that someone is an agent because of the position that he holds.

Agency by holding out

Such a situation arises when the principal's actions allow or encourage third parties to believe that a person is acting as an agent on the principal's behalf. Problems will occur later when the principal tries to deny that he encouraged the third party to believe that someone was acting as his agent. However, if the third party can show that he relied on the principal's representations, the principal will be liable to the third party for any agreement that the agent has negotiated. The principal may have made statements to the effect that someone is to be regarded as his agent.

 Hayman v American Cotton Oil Co (1907) the American Cotton Oil Company had made statements in several newspaper advertisements and in letters to prospective customers that McNairn & Co, a Glasgow firm, were acting as its agent. Ferguson Shaw & Sons, a third party, bought a quantity of goods from McNairn and paid for them before delivery. McNairn became insolvent and its creditors attempted to claim the goods that Ferguson Shaw & Sons had bought. Ferguson Shaw & Sons then turned to the American Cotton Oil Company demanding that it honour the contract that McNairn had negotiated on its behalf. The American Cotton Oil Company now attempted to deny, conveniently, that McNairn had ever been its agent. Ferguson Shaw & Sons pointed out that they had always believed that McNairn was the American Cotton Oil Company's agent. The newspaper advertisements and the letters to potential customers had led to an understandable belief that McNairn was the agent of the American Cotton Oil Company.

Held: the American Cotton Oil Company by placing advertisements and sending out letters to potential customers had given the impression to third parties dealing with McNairn that the Glasgow firm was its agent. See also **Hosie v Waddell (1866)** discussed later in this Chapter in relation into partnership.

 Key point: Agency by holding out occurs when the principal's words or actions encourage a third party to believe that another individual is his agent.

Agency by ratification

This occurs when an agent does something which he has not been authorised to do by the principal. The principal however, chooses to ratify or approve the unauthorised actions of the agent. In other words, by ratifying the agent's unauthorised actions, the principal is prepared to forgive the fact that the agent has committed a breach of the agency agreement. It is not necessary for a relationship to have existed between the agent and the principal when the unauthorised actions occurred, but, usually there is some kind of existing contractual relationship. In order for the principal to be able to ratify an unauthorised transaction, a number of conditions must be satisfied:

◆ The agent must disclose all material facts surrounding the contract so that the principal is fully aware of all liabilities that he is taking on.

◆ The principal must ratify the contract within a reasonable time.

◆ The principal must have existed at the time the contract was entered into.

◆ The principal must have the power and capacity to ratify the act otherwise the contract will be void.

◆ The agent must act with an identifiable principal in mind and not contracting on his own with the hope that he will find someone who will later ratify the contract. It is important that the third party knows that the agent *is* acting as an agent and does not believe the agent to be in business on his own account.

◆ The principal will not be in a position to ratify any contract that is illegal.

 Keighley Maxsted & Co *v* Durant (1901) Roberts was an agent authorised to buy wheat at a certain price. Roberts made a contract with Durant for wheat at a higher price than the price his principal had originally authorised. Furthermore, Roberts made the contract in his own name without mentioning to the third party that he was acting for his principal, Keighley. Keighley originally agreed to ratify the contract which Roberts and Durant had entered into, but when Keighley failed to take delivery of the wheat at a later date, Durant sued for damages.

Held: the House of Lords stated that Roberts had not told Durant that he was working for Keighley and, as a result, Durant was not entitled to sue them on the contract.

 Kelner *v* Baxter (1866) the pursuer, Kelner, sold a quantity of wine to Baxter who claimed to be acting as an agent of a hotel company which had not been registered. This meant that the company did not yet exist in the eyes of the law and, therefore, was not capable of having rights and duties which would be recognised by the courts. The wine had been used, but Kelner had not been paid.

Held: Baxter was personally liable to Kelner for payment since a principal who does not exist at the time the contract was made cannot later ratify it.

 Key point: The process of ratification allows a principal to approve the actions of an agent who, strictly speaking, has gone beyond the limits of his authority.

Agency of necessity

In the event of an emergency, a person is deemed by law to have the authority to act as agent for another party. However, it must be impossible for the person acting as agent of necessity to contact the principal. Before the use of modern communications such as faxes, telephones, ship-to-shore radios and e-mail, this type of agency was extremely useful, but it is now highly unlikely that a principal would be unable to be contacted in an emergency situation. In saying that, however, this type of agency should not be written off completely and it may still have its uses. As long as the agent of necessity acts in good faith to protect the interests of the principal, he will not be held liable for any losses which his actions may have caused the principal.

 Couturier *v* Hastie (1856) the cargo had overheated aboard the ship and was beginning to rot. In order to prevent the cargo from being written off completely, it had been landed at the nearest port and sold. The captain of the ship was acting as an agent of necessity in an emergency situation in order to prevent further losses to his principal. It will be understood that in the 1850s when this case occurred, the captain was stuck on board a ship in the middle of the Mediterranean Sea. He did not have modern communications available to him in order to contact the principal for further instructions and he had to make a swift decision about the cargo.

 Great Northern Railway *v* Swaffield (1874) a horse was being transported to Swaffield who failed to collect it at the railway station. There was no accommodation at the station and the Railway company arranged for the horse to be put in a livery stable for the night. It was held that the Railway was entitled to claim reimbursement of the expenses involved because it had acted as an agent of necessity in an emergency situation where the principal could not be contacted and his instructions as regards the welfare of the horse established.

In order to be able to show that someone acted as an agent of necessity, it is necessary to prove that the principal could not be contacted.

 Springer *v* Great Western Railway (1921) Springer was the owner of tomatoes delayed in a railway strike. The railway company's traffic agent sold the tomatoes locally as he believed they would not have made it to Covent Garden in a saleable condition. Springer argued that if the agent had contacted him he could have transported them by road and still got the same high price.

Held: the claim that the railway's traffic agent had acted as agent of necessity should fail because the principal could have been contacted.

 Key point: In the event of an emergency, a person is deemed by law to have the authority to act as agent for another party.

Duties of an agent

The relationship between an agent and his principal is known as a fiduciary relationship i.e. a relationship of trust. At all times, the agent is expected to act in the best interests of the principal. This means that the principal's interests must

Tyler v Logan (1904) Tyler owned a number of shops which specialised in selling boots. Tyler had appointed Logan as a branch manager of one of his shops in Dundee. At a stocktaking carried out by Tyler, it was discovered there was a shortfall of about £62 at the Dundee branch. No one could explain this loss and Logan was not suspected of any dishonesty or negligence. Tyler, however, brought an action against Logan for the payment of the missing amount of money.

Held: Logan had to pay Tyler the missing £62.

If the agent acts for several principals, he must ensure that he keeps proper and separate accounts for each of his clients. Many trades and professions will have their own rules which affect client accounts. The Law Society of Scotland which regulates the conduct of solicitors has very strict rules about how client accounts should be kept and solicitors who fall foul of these rules can find themselves in very serious trouble.

 Key point: The agent must keep proper accounts and allow the principal access to these as and when required.

To act in good faith

Agency is a fiduciary relationship and this means that the agent must show that he can be trusted by the principal and he must do this by always acting in good faith. The agent must not allow his personal interests and those of his principal to conflict with one another. It is often the case that a dishonest agent will be able to profit personally from the agency because of his position or because third parties may offer him a benefit or bribe if the agent introduces them to his principal. It is worth emphasising that an agent who sees the opportunity to make a fast buck or take advantage of some benefit which comes his way will not have the principal's best interests at heart. The agent may view these benefits as perks of the job, but such behaviour could result in disastrous consequences for the principal. The agent may not have properly scrutinised the deal proposed by the third party and this could cause the principal some serious losses in the future.

The Companies Act 2006 now imposes a specific duties on company directors to avoid conflicts of interest, to declare benefits received from third parties dealing with the company and they must make a public declaration if they have a personal interest in any transaction which the company is proposing to enter with a third party (Sections 175–177).

 Guinness plc v Saunders and Another (1990) is a very good example of a director (Thomas Ward) obtaining a secret profit (a payment of £5.2 million) which had not been expressly approved by the full Board of Directors as was legally required by the company's articles of association. Guinness sued the director for repayment of this sum. Ward tried to defend his acceptance of the payment by claiming that he had a defence that he had acted honestly and reasonably in terms of Section 727 of the Companies Act 1985.

Held: by the House of Lords that the director was entitled to repay the sum to Guinness because the payment had only been authorised by a small committee of directors (the so called Guinness War Cabinet) and not by the full Board.

The law governing breach of an agent's fiduciary duty can be very strict as can be seen in the following case:

 Industrial Development Consultants Ltd _v_ Cooley (1972) Cooley was an architect who also acted as the managing director of Industrial Development Consultants. The company had previously attempted to bid for a contract to perform work for the Eastern Gas Board. The Gas Board had planned to build a new depot at Letchworth, but difficulties arose and the project looked as if it would be abandoned entirely. Cooley later obtained intelligence that the project was going ahead, but he did not inform his company about this. The Eastern Gas Board was very interested in commissioning Cooley to carry out much of the design work for the depot, but it made clear to him that it did not wish to deal with his company. In order to be released from his contract with Industrial Development Consultants, Cooley pretended to be suffering from a serious health problem and the company reluctantly agreed to release him from his post. Cooley received a generous severance package from the company when he resigned from his post as managing director. He was then free to perform the work for the Eastern Gas Board – or so he thought. Unfortunately for Cooley, his former company had learned of his deceit and brought a legal action against him to force him to account for his secret profit. Cooley argued that the Eastern Gas Board would not have awarded the contract to the company and it was him alone that they wished to deal with.

Held: Cooley had been a fiduciary position as a director of the company and he had abused this by pursuing his own interest. He was liable to account for the extent of his profit to Industrial Development Consultants Ltd. Mr Justice Roskill acknowledged the fact that Industrial Development Consultants never had a realistic chance of securing the contract from the Eastern Gas Board, but this was irrelevant as Cooley had used and exploited his position with the company to obtain a benefit which was in clear breach of his fiduciary duty. Cooley's argument that he had engaged in discussions with the Gas Board in his private capacity was unconvincing because, at the relevant time, he was a director of Industrial Development Consultants and he should have kept it fully informed of what was going on.

 Key point: The agent is regarded as a fiduciary and must act in the best interests of the principal at all times.

Conflict of interests

There does not need to be an actual conflict between the agent's and the principal's interests. It is very often enough for there to be a potential conflict. If the agent sees an opportunity to make a profit, the principal should always be informed of this. It will then be completely up to the principal whether or not to allow the agent to receive the benefit. It is often forgotten that the only reason that the agent is in a position to receive a benefit is because the principal appointed him in the first place.

The extent of the agent's fiduciary duty is limited to how it affects the agency agreement. It is still entirely possible for an agent to promote his own interests when he is not acting for the principal. The agent may even act for a number of different principals. If a principal wished to prevent his agent from pursuing his own interests outside the agency agreement or from working on behalf of other principals, there would have to be an express term in the agency agreement to this end. Such a condition could never be implied into all agency agreements. However, such a restraint of trade might be declared illegal if it was in any way excessive or anti-competitive.

 McPherson's Trustees *v* Watt (1877) Watt, a solicitor acting for the trustees, had to sell four houses for them but he arranged to sell them to his brother, on the understanding that the brother would then sell two of the houses to Watt for half the purchase price. The 'contract' was formed but the trustees discovered the secret contract and raised an action to stop it going ahead.

Held: by the House of Lords that the contract for the sale of the houses that Watt and his brother had negotiated was cancelled. A solicitor, as a law agent, has a duty to act in good faith and there must be no conflict between the principal's interests and those of the agent.

 Lothian *v* Jenolite Ltd (1969) Jenolite Ltd, an English company, entered into an agreement with Lothian, under which Lothian was instructed to sell some of Jenolite's products in Scotland and receive a commission on sales. The contract was to last for four years from July 1964, but in November 1965, Jenolite ended the agency agreement. Lothian claimed damages for breach of contract. Jenolite claimed that the reason that the agreement had been ended in this way was because Lothian had bought and resold a rival business's products. It was claimed by Jenolite that Lothian had even ordered his staff to sell the rival business's products in preference to Jenolite's products. Jenolite considered this to be a material breach of contract.

Held: there was no implied condition in the agency agreement which meant that Lothian had to have secured Jenolite's permission in order to sell the products of a business rival.

The agent must not divulge any confidential information in relation to the principal's business that he obtains in the course of his agency.

 Liverpool Victoria Legal Friendly Society *v* Houston (1900) as an agent of the insurance company, Houston had access to lists of customers and their details. Houston was later dismissed by the insurance company whereupon he decided to pass these customer details to another insurance company which was competing against his former principal.

Held: the details of customers were strictly confidential and by divulging them to business rivals of his former principal, Houston was in breach of his fiduciary duty. Furthermore, Houston would have to compensate his former principal for the loss of any custom that his breach of duty had caused.

 Key point: The agent must not allow his personal interests and those of his principal to conflict with one another – the agent's interests must take second place to the principal's.

Secret profits

The agent must not accept bribes from the third party or keep the benefit of any transaction to himself which he knows would result in him breaching his fiduciary duty to his principal. In such cases, the principal could sue the agent in order to recover the bribe or the benefit that the agent had gained.

Islamic Republic of Iran Shipping Lines *v* Denby (1987) a solicitor accepted a sum of $200,000 from a third party in order to settle a legal dispute which the solicitor's client had brought against the third party.

Held: the sum of $200,000 was quite simply a bribe and the solicitor had to pay this to his client.

 Attorney-General for Hong Kong *v* Reid (1994) Reid had been the acting Director of Public Prosecutions in Hong Kong. He accepted bribes in order to prevent the prosecution of a number of criminals.

Held: the Privy Council stated that Reid, as an agent of the British Crown, had to account for all the bribes that he had accepted. Consequently, the British Crown could recover all these sums. See also **Reading *v* Attorney-General (1951)** discussed in Chapter 6.

There are a number of serious consequences which arise as a result of an agent making a secret profit:

◆ The agent has committed a material breach of the agency agreement and the principal is, therefore entitled to terminate the contract with immediate effect.

◆ The agent cannot claim payment for that particular transaction.

◆ The agent can be sued by the principal with the intention of recovering the secret profit that the agent has made.

◆ The third party may find that the principal refuses to honour the contract that the agent negotiated.

◆ The third party himself may be sued by the principal if he bribed or encouraged the agent to breach his fiduciary duty to the principal.

◆ If the third party refuses to pay the bribe or the commission to the agent, the agent cannot take legal action against the third party because their agreement is illegal and, therefore, unenforceable.

◆ Bribery is a criminal offence in terms of the Prevention of Corruption Acts 1906 and 1916.

 Key point: An agent who makes secret profits on his own account will be in breach of his fiduciary duty to the principal and, if discovered, will have to face the potentially criminal and civil consequences of his actions.

The Bribery Bill was introduced by the UK Government on 25 March 2009 and, originally, its provisions did not extend to Scotland (the Scottish Government later published its own version of a draft Bribery Bill in July 2009). Subsequently, after discussions between the two Governments on this matter, the Scottish Government has agreed that the provisions of the UK Bribery Bill should be extended to Scotland. If the Bill receives the Royal Assent it will consolidate and update the law governing bribery and, theoretically, it should make it easier for law enforcement agencies to combat corrupt practices in both the public and private sectors.

Rights of an agent

The agent enjoys the following rights in relation to his principal under the agency agreement:

Barry, Ostlere & Shepherd Ltd *v* Edinburgh Cork Importing Co (1909) a third party had negotiated with an agent, the manager of cork merchants, to buy goods and to have them delivered. The agent failed to deliver the goods and the third party had to find goods from an alternative supplier at a higher price. The third party sued the agent's principal for damages claiming that it had failed to honour the contract negotiated on its behalf by the agent. The principal argued that the agent had not been given authority to enter into a contract with the third party.

Held: a contract had been formed between the third party and the principal since the third party had every right to assume that, because of the agent's position as a manager in the principal's company, entering into a contract for these goods was well within his authority.

 Key point: Ostensible authority is the authority which a third party (wrongly) assumes that an agent possesses and it is the actions of the principal that creates this false impression in the third party's mind. Therefore, the principal will be bound in contract to the third party.

Liability when agents act outwith actual and ostensible authority

If an agent acts outwith both his actual and ostensible authority then he will bring personal liability upon himself. There will be no contract between the principal and the third party, but the third party can sue the agent for breach of warranty of authority.

 Anderson *v* Croall & Sons (1903) an auctioneer had been given instructions to sell the winning horse at a race meeting. The auctioneer, however, carelessly sold the horse that had come in second at the race. The horse's owner had no intention of selling it. The horse had to be returned to its true owner.

Held: the auctioneer was liable in damages to the third party who had bought the horse for acting completely outwith his authority.

Key point: When the agent acts outwith his authority and the third party is fully aware of this fact, the principal will not be bound into contract with the third party.

Summary of an agent's authority

Actual authority (Real authority)	Principal is bound into contract with third Party. (Agent incurs no liability.)
Ostensible authority (Presumed, fictitious authority)	Principal is bound into contract with third Party. The third Party genuinely believes the agent has authority and has no reason to be suspicious. (Agent is liable to principal for breach of agency agreement.)
Agent has no authority	Principal is not bound in contract to third Party. The third Party cannot claim that he believed the agent had actual or ostensible authority. The agent can be sued by third Party for breach of warranty of authority.

A disclosed and undisclosed principal

Where the third party is aware of the existence of the agent's principal, such a person is referred to as a disclosed principal. It does not matter whether the third party can name the principal personally.

 The Santa Carina (1977) the defenders were agents who acted as brokers on the Baltic Exchange. The defenders had telephoned the pursuers, also brokers on the Baltic Exchange, and asked them to supply bunkers to the ship called the *Santa Carina*. The bunkers were supplied to the ship, but the defenders' principal failed to pay the pursuers. The pursuers sued the defenders for breach of contract. The defenders claimed that they were acting as agents and although they had not disclosed the name of their principal the pursuers were perfectly aware of this situation.

Held: the English Court of Appeal stated that the principal was a disclosed principal and in this situation the defenders should have sued the principal.

However, there may be situations where the third party is completely unaware that the agent is, in fact, acting for a principal. In such a case, the principal would be described as an undisclosed principal.

It is important to determine whether the agent is acting for a disclosed or an undisclosed principal. Generally, an agent who acts for a disclosed principal plays no further part in proceedings when an agreement is eventually completed between the principal and the third party. Should a dispute arise in relation to the agreement, the agent – as long as he acted properly – will not be liable to the third party for the principal's failure to honour the agreement.

The position is more complicated where the agent has not revealed to the third party that he is acting for a principal. Should the principal fail to honour the agreement, the third party will, naturally enough, sue the agent. At this moment, the agent may then reveal the fact that he was acting as an a agent. It will be up to the third party whether he wishes to sue the principal or the agent for breach of contract. Once the third party makes this choice, such a decision will be final.

It is usually a sensible precaution on the agent's part to indicate to third parties that he is acting as an agent in order to avoid any potential liability in the future. It is widely understood that the abbreviation pp (*per pro*) at the end of a letter indicates that the signatory is acting as an agent and not acting in his personal capacity:

Yours sincerely
Alistair B Wylie
pp The Business Law Consultancy

Therefore, Alistair B Wylie is clearly indicating to anyone who receives this letter that he has signed the letter in his capacity as an agent of The Business Law Consultancy.

 Stewart *v* Shannessy (1900) Shannessy acted as an agent for two companies that sold bicycles. He decided to employ Stewart to act as a representative of one of the companies. Stewart's appointment and his terms and conditions of employment were confirmed in a letter that Shannessy sent him. Shannessy's letter was written on company headed notepaper, but when Shannessy signed the letter it seemed to suggest that *he* was employing Stewart and not the company. The letter contained indication that Shannessy was, in fact, acting for the company in his capacity as an agent. Stewart received all of his instructions from Shannessy, all payments from Shannessy and was dismissed by Shannessy. Stewart then sued Shannessy for arrears of pay that he claimed that he was still owed.

Held: Shannessy was personally liable to Stewart since he had signed the letter and had not given any indication that he was acting as an agent for the company.

 Key point: Very often it may not be obvious to a third party whether the agent is acting as an agent when the identity of the principal is undisclosed.

The Commercial Agents (Council Directive) Regulations 1993

The Commercial Agents (Council Directive) Regulations 1993 give effect to the EEC Directive 86/653 on self-employed commercial agents. The Regulations came into force on 1 January 1994 and were slightly amended in 1998. Commercial agency contracts created or amended after 1994 will be primarily affected by these rules. The Regulations are unusual because, unlike the common law rules, they single out a particular group of agents for protection. Furthermore, the Regulations emphasise the fact that a commercial agency agreement is almost a partnership of equals where the principal and the agent should cooperate with one another in order to benefit from the relationship.

The overall purpose of the European Council Directive was not only to achieve harmonisation of the legal relationship between commercial agents and principals throughout the European Union but also to deal with the insecurity that commercial agents experienced especially when principals decided to terminate the agreement. It might take many years of hard work on the agent's part to turn a profit. If the principal then ended agreement the commercial agent would lose his livelihood with very little to show for all of his efforts. The principal, on the other hand, will often continue to profit from the agent's efforts on his behalf.

 Key point: The Commercial Agency Regulations are unusual because, unlike the common law rules of agency, they single out a particular group of agents for protection.

Commercial agents

Regulation 2(1) states that a commercial agent is a self-employed intermediary who has continuing authority to negotiate the sale or the purchase of goods on behalf of the principal or to negotiate and conclude the sale or purchase of goods on behalf of or in the name of the principal.

As we have seen, the agency relationship at common law lists the rights and the duties of both the agent and the principal. The Regulations very much build on this situation and Part II lists the duties of both parties.

 King *v* T Tunnock Ltd (2000) the agents were father and son who had entered into a verbal agreement with Tunnock that ran for many years. The contract stated that the father and son were to act as Tunnock's agents in order to sell its cakes and biscuits. The agents sold Tunnock's products only and were paid commission on the products that they sold. The agents had no freedom to fix the prices of the products as Tunnock determined this. All monies received from customers were made payable to Tunnock. The agents were even provided with a van for their business activities which Tunnock maintained. The agents were also required to wear Tunnock's uniforms. However, despite the close relationship with the principal, the agents were self-employed. According to Sheriff Reeves, who decided the case at first instance, the definition of a commercial agent in Regulation 2(1) was an exact description of the activities of the agents in this case.

 Key point: A commercial agent is a self-employed intermediary who has continuing authority to negotiate the sale or the purchase of goods on behalf of the principal or to negotiate and conclude the sale or purchase of goods on behalf of or in the name of the principal.

The scope of the Regulations

The 1994 Regulations, however, only apply to a very small number of agents, so their impact will be limited. They only apply to commercial agents who trade in goods. The Regulations do not cover the following types of agents:

◆ Commercial agents who provide services
◆ Commercial agents working on commodity exchanges in the commodity market
◆ Unpaid or gratuitous agents
◆ Persons who act as commercial agents but this is regarded as a secondary activity and not part of their main business

The Regulations will also not apply to agreements where the parties have decided that their agency agreement will be governed by the law of another European member state. However, since the decision of **Ingmar GB Ltd v Eaton Leonard Technologies Inc (2001)**, the Regulations will apply even if the parties have attempted to exclude them by stating in their agreement that the agreement is governed by the law of a state which is *not* a member of the European Union.

 In **Ingmar**, an English agent carried on business activities in the United Kingdom on behalf of a Californian principal. Both the agent and principal had agreed that the contract was to be governed by Californian law. This would have appeared to exclude the Regulations. However, the English Court of Appeal referred the matter to the European Court of Justice which made it clear that the Regulations applied to situations even where the parties themselves had chosen the law by which they wished to be bound.

The Regulations do not apply to Northern Ireland.

 Key point: The Regulations apply to a very small group of agents only.

The agent's duties (Regulation 3)

◆ The agent must protect the principal's interests by acting dutifully and in good faith at all times.

◆ The agent must make proper efforts to negotiate and, where appropriate, conclude the transactions that he has responsibility for.

◆ The agent must provide the principal with all the information that he has at his disposal.

◆ The agent must obey all reasonable instructions given to him by the principal.

The principal's duties (Regulation 4)

◆ The principal must pay or remunerate the agent for carrying out his duties under the agency agreement.

◆ The principal must reimburse the agent for any expenses that the agent has incurred in the line of duty.

◆ The principal must provide the agent with the necessary documents and the necessary information relating to the goods in order for the agent to carry out his duties.

◆ The principal must tell the agent within a reasonable time whether he intends to honour or refuse to honour the contract that the agent has set up with a third party.

◆ The principal must inform the agent within a reasonable time of any breach of the contract with the third party that the principal is responsible for.

According to Regulation 5(1), the rights and duties contained in Regulations 3 and 4 are not negotiable and both parties are bound by them whether they like them or not.

 Key point: The Regulations outline the agent's duties and the principal's duties in Regulations 3 and 4 respectively.

The agent's right to be paid or to be remunerated (Regulations 6 to 12)

Part III of the Regulations deal with the issue of the agent's right to be paid or remunerated.

The agent has a right to receive payment for carrying out his duties under the agency agreement even where the parties have failed to address the issue directly. If there is no term about payment in the agency agreement, the agent is entitled to be paid at the customary rate which agents of his type and background would normally or customarily receive. If there is no customary or normal practice that exists to help the principal decide how much the agent should be paid, then the agent should be paid a reasonable remuneration. What is a reasonable rate of remuneration or pay will, obviously, depend on the circumstances.

The agent has a right to receive commission and this commission will become payable when the agent concludes a contract with a third party on the principal's behalf.

An important right that an agent will enjoy under the Regulations is where he has acted as the principal's sole agent in relation to a specific geographical area or a specific group of customers. Even after the agency agreement has ended, the agent will continue to be entitled to receive commission from the principal. This is only fair because the principal may continue to enjoy the fruits of the agent's work for a long time after the agency agreement has ended. It is worth bearing in mind that, very often, it is the efforts of a determined and successful agent which will ensure that the principal enjoys a loyal customer base or strong business links in a particular area.

As a result of Regulation 10, there are strict time limits for the payment of commission. Commission will, therefore, become payable to the agent from the time that the agreement between the principal and the third party should have come into force. However, should the agreement fail to come into effect and this is through no fault of the principal, the agent is not entitled to receive commission. In fact, if any commission has been paid to the agent in these circumstances, the agent will have to return his part payment to the principal.

Regulation 12 now means that the agent has a right to receive a statement from the principal detailing the amount of commission owed to him. This statement must be received by the agent no later than the last day of the month following the quarter in which the commission was earned. The statement must give a breakdown detailing how the amount of the commission was arrived at and the agent will be able to demand information from the principal which allows him to check the principal's calculations.

 Key point: Regulations 6 to 12 deal with the agent's right to be paid by the principal.

The termination of the commercial agency agreement (Regulations 14 to 16)

Like all contracts, a commercial agency agreement will come to an end sooner rather than later and the rules which apply to this event will be found mainly in Part IV of the Regulations.

Regulation 13 establishes beyond any doubt that either party has the right to request a signed copy of the agency agreement which lays out the main terms of the commercial agency agreement. The terms of the agreement will, of course, address how the commercial agency will come to an end. It should be noted that the parties are not allowed to opt out of this requirement to provide a signed copy of the agreement.

Regulation 14 applies to contracts that are to last for a fixed period of time, for example, five years. In many situations, the parties will continue to keep the agreement running without feeling the need to renegotiate the terms. In cases like this, the parties will continue to have the same rights and duties as before, the only major difference being that the agreement is now considered to last for an indefinite period of time.

Regulation 15 establishes compulsory minimum notice periods which the parties have to obey if they wish to end the agreement. The basic periods of notice are as follows:

◆ One month's notice during the first year of the agreement
◆ Two months' notice during the second year of the agreement
◆ Three months' notice during the third year or any subsequent year of the agreement

All notice periods end on the last day of the month, unless the parties have agreed a different arrangement. The parties to the commercial agency agreement are, of course, free to negotiate longer notice periods if they so wish. They are just prevented from shortening the minimum notice periods as outlined above. If the agreement was originally to last for a fixed term but has since become one of an indefinite duration, the minimum notice periods also apply.

However, Regulation 16 makes it perfectly clear that both parties can end the agency agreement immediately where one of the parties has failed to carry out all or part of his duties under the contract. The contract can also be ended in exceptional circumstances.

 Key point: Regulation 15 establishes compulsory minimum notice periods which the parties have to obey if they wish to end the agreement.

The Agent's right to an indemnity or compensation (Regulations 17 to 19)

The Agent's right to an indemnity or compensation is a completely new development in both Scottish and English law. This right reflects the fact that the principal benefits from the agent's efforts to build up a customer base. If the principal ends the agreement, the agent is the party who tends to suffer financially from this decision. The principal, on the other hand, will often continue to enjoy the fruits of the agent's labours for a very long time to come. It is important to stress that the agent has a right to receive a fair and equitable payment for services rendered to the principal, not a windfall.

It is important to distinguish between the agent's right to compensation and his right to an indemnity because they are not the same thing. Lord MacFadyen in **Hardie Polymer Ltd _v_ Polymerland Ltd (2001)** stated that:

'Compensation and indemnity are distinct concepts. It is not surprising that there are elements of similarity between them, since they are alternative ways of making provision for the same situation, namely the termination of the agency contract.'

Usually, according to Regulation 17(2), the agent shall be entitled to be compensated rather than indemnified, unless the commercial agency agreement specifies that he is entitled to receive an indemnity.

 Key point: Under the Regulations, compensation and indemnity are two different rights.

The European Court of Justice in **Case C-465/04 Honeyvem Informazioni Commerciali Srl _v_ Mariella De Zotti (2006)** has made it very clear that there is no European-wide procedure, to be used across all the Member States, for determining the amount of an indemnity or compensation payment. It will be up to the courts of each Member State to determine this issue.

In **King _v_ T Tunnock Ltd (2000)** the Court of Session made a distinction between compensation and indemnity:

'on any view indemnity and compensation, as set out by both Directive and Regulations, have different features . . . The agent is entitled to compensation for damage he suffers as a result of the termination of his relationship with the principal. The word "suffers" is in the present tense, which suggests that the point of time defining damage is the termination of the agency. Moreover, what *is compensated is "the termination of his relations with his principal". The emphasis is not on his future loss but on the impact of the severance of his agency relationship with the principal. An agency generally has commercial value.'*

In the leading judgment given during the determination of **Lonsdale (t/a Lonsdale Agencies) v Howard & Hallam Limited (2007)**, Lord Hoffman remarked that:

'It is clear that the agent is entitled to compensation for 'the damage he suffers as a result of the termination of his relations with the principal' and that the method by which that damage should be calculated is a discretionary matter for the domestic laws of the Member States. It is the way in which our domestic law should implement that discretion which has been uncertain and the resolution of that uncertainty is the task of this House and not the European Court of Justice.'

According to Regulation 17, therefore, the agent will be entitled to be compensated by the principal where he has suffered loss as a result of the principal terminating the commercial agency agreement.

In the English High Court decision **Moore v Piretta PT Ltd (1998)** Deputy Judge John Mitting QC described the agent's claim to an indemnity in the following terms:

'The purpose of the indemnity seems to me to be to award a share of the goodwill built up by the efforts of the agent to him on the termination of the agency. Otherwise the whole benefit of that goodwill will remain with his former principal.'

Deputy Judge Mitting QC then went to say that according to Regulation 17, there are three stages involved in assessing an agent's right to an indemnity:

◆ Where the agent has increased the number of the principal's customers or where the agent has dramatically increased the amount of the principal's business with existing customers.

◆ The payment of the indemnity must be fair and equitable taking into account all of the circumstances surrounding the agreement. The commission lost by the commercial agent on the business carried out with such customers will be a factor to which the court will have to pay particular attention.

◆ The calculation of the indemnity itself, but this is subject to limits provided for in Regulation 17(4).

 Key point: An agent will be entitled to be compensated by the principal where he has suffered loss as a result of the principal terminating his agency agreement and he will be entitled to an indemnity where he has increased the number of the principal's customers or where he has dramatically increased the amount of the principal's business with existing customers.

The amount of the indemnity

In terms of Regulation 17(4), the amount of the indemnity awarded to the agent shall not be greater than a figure equivalent to an indemnity for one year calculated from the commercial agent's average annual remuneration over the previous five years and, if the contract goes back less than five years, the indemnity shall be calculated on the average for the period in question.

It is important to note that the payment of an indemnity does not prevent the agent from seeking compensation or damages from the principal.

Commercial agency case law

In **Moore v Piretta PT Ltd (1998)** it was said that the aim of Regulation 17 was to give British commercial agents the same rights and duties in relation to remuneration as was the case in France and Germany. Regulation 17 was held to apply to the whole of an agency agreement even if the agreement had come into force before the Regulations.

In **Moore**, the pursuer had acted as an agent for the defender under an unbroken series of contracts commencing in 1988. The last agency agreement had been in force in 1994. Although most of the agency agreements had been entered into before the Regulations came into force, the agent was still entitled to claim an indemnity from the principal which covered the period from 1988 to 1994. Significantly, of the 40 customers whom the principal had dealings with, only six or seven of these had not been acquired by the agent. Therefore, the agent was directly responsible for the success of the principal's business.

Regulation 17(6) states that the agent shall be entitled to compensation for damages that he has suffered as a result of the principal ending the commercial agency agreement. Regulation 17(7) strongly suggests that the agent will have suffered loss or damage in one or both of the following situations:

◆ Loss of future commission by the agent
◆ The agent has been unable to recover any expenses which he properly incurred on the principal's behalf

The agent's claim for compensation should be lodged, however, within one year of the end of the agreement. If the agent's death has caused the agreement to end, then the agent's estate will not be prevented from pursuing the principal for any compensation or expenses owed.

The agent must receive a fair amount. In **King v T. Tunnock Ltd (2000)** the Inner House of the Court of Session unanimously decided that the sum paid to an agent on termination of the agreement should be based on two years' gross commission which amounted to £27,144. The Court of Session controversially overruled the Sheriff who had decided that the value of the commercial agency was nothing. Lord Caplan, who headed the Extra Division in the Court of Session, remarked:

'In these circumstances we consider it likely that the pursuer [King] would have expected and required a relatively high level of compensation to surrender his successful and long-established agency. The compensation would, of course, require to be tied to the commission he was earning. Thus this is a case where we can conclude, even on the limited information that is available, that the agent would have expected to receive a capital sum representing at least the total for the last two years of his earnings to be paid before he would voluntarily have given up his agency.'

The reasoning behind the Court of Session's decision in **King** does not appear to have found universal acceptance in the English courts.

In **Ingmar GB Ltd v Eaton Leonard Technologies Inc (2001)** (see below), Mr Justice Morland in the English High Court stated that the Court of Session in King had laid down guidelines, not binding rules of law. The English judge preferred to calculate compensation by looking at three years' gross commission in order to determine the level of compensation payable to the agent. It should be noted that the courts have been given a great deal of freedom to decide what is a fair amount in each case.

In **Barrett McKenzie v Escada (UK) Ltd (2001)**, Judge Bowers, sitting in the English High Court, did not favour the approach taken by the Court of Session. In **King v T. Tunnock Ltd (2000)** Judge Bowers did agree with the Court of Session in one respect:

'... *one is valuing the agency and its connections that have been established by the agent at the time at or immediately before termination, and it is really a question of compensating for the notional value of that agency in the open market* ...'

However, Lord Hoffman in **Lonsdale (t/a Lonsdale Agencies) v Howard & Hallam Limited (2007)** has explicitly criticised the reasoning of the Extra Division of the Court of Session (given by Lord Caplan) in **King v T. Tunnock Ltd (2000)** which was used to determine the amount of compensation payable to the agent. The Court of Session had expressly overruled the decision of the Sheriff at first instance who was strongly of the opinion that the value of the commercial agency was worth nothing. Lord Hoffman stressed that the notional value of a commercial agency must be determined by '... circumstances as they existed in the real world at the time: what the earnings prospects of the agency were and what people would have been willing to pay for similar businesses at the time.'

Following the decision of the Court of Session in **King,** it is standard practice for a commercial agent claiming compensation to provide evidence as to the value of the commercial agency and what the financial consequences of the termination of the relationship with the principal will be. With the benefit of hindsight (admittedly), the approach taken by the Court of Session towards the issue of the amount of compensation appears to have disproportionately favoured the commercial agent. Since the decision in **Lonsdale**, it would appear that a much more rigorous approach to this issue will have to be taken by the courts when determining either the amount of compensation or indemnity to be paid to the agent.

 Tigana Ltd v Decoro (2003) Mr Justice Davis, sitting in the English High Court, was prepared to estimate the amount of compensation to be paid to the commercial agent upon the termination of the relationship of the principal by reference to the amount of commission earned (minus expenses) during a fourteen to fifteen month period when the agency had been in existence. The judge justified his decision by pinpointing fourteen different factors in the relationship as a justification for the size of the payment made to the agent. Lord Hoffman in **Lonsdale** was critical of this approach in that Mr Justice Davis had failed to justify the importance of each factor when arriving at his decision and, furthermore, the judge appears not to have heard evidence which would have demonstrated that someone would have paid such a figure for a comparable business.

In **Smith, Bailey Palmer *v* Howard & Hallam Ltd (2006)** the English High Court estimated that 42% of the sales and distribution expenses incurred by Howard & Hallam (the principal) over a three year period prior to the sale of the brand to another company had consisted of the agent's commission. On this basis, the agent's commission was calculated on this basis. Lord Hoffman in **Lonsdale** was, again, critical of this approach ('a flawed method of calculation') in that the agent's efforts were taken as the dominant factor in generating sales of the product and very little credit was given to the idea that sales may have been generated because the company sold good shoes. Furthermore, the High Court had failed to enquire what value someone would have paid for the agency (or a comparable business) and no evidence was led to show how much the agent was actually receiving for the services performed on behalf of the principal.

 Lonsdale (t/a Lonsdale Agencies) *v* Howard & Hallam Limited (2007) the House of Lords was asked to determine the issue of how the amount of compensation owed to a commercial agent should be calculated upon the termination of the contractual relationship with the principal. In the United Kingdom, a commercial agent can claim either an indemnity (if the contract provides for this) or compensation upon termination of the relationship with the principal. As we have seen, indemnity and compensation are not the same thing – although they both arise from the termination of the commercial agency relationship and the consequences of such an event for the agent.

Lonsdale was a commercial agent who travelled around his territory on behalf of the various principals. His task was to secure orders for shoes manufactured by his principals and, to facilitate this, he carried catalogues and samples when visiting actual or potential customers. During the 1990s, Lonsdale was appointed to act, firstly, for an English shoe manufacturer based in Leicester (Howard & Hallam Limited) and then, secondly, for a German shoe manufacturer. By 2000, the sale of the German company's products represented two-thirds of Lonsdale's business activities. Sales of Howard & Hallam's products had declined markedly over the period and, consequently, this had a direct impact on the amount of commission paid to Lonsdale (the commission paid to him had more than halved). In 2003, Howard & Hallam had stopped trading altogether due to insolvency of the company, but not before selling the product which Lonsdale had been responsible for to another business. Lonsdale and Howard & Hallam had never put the commercial agency agreement between them in writing so there was no formal mechanism for ending their relationship. The relationship should, therefore, have been terminated by reasonable notice and, to this end, Howard & Hallam had given Lonsdale six months' notice. This was regarded as a reasonable period by the parties and, furthermore, the outstanding commission owed to Lonsdale had been paid by his principal. Lonsdale, however, claimed that he was also owed compensation in the region of £30,000 for the termination of his contract with Howard & Hallam. This figure had been arrived at following on from advice that Lonsdale had received from his accountant. The last completed year of the agency had generated £12,239.34 in commission which was then multiplied by two and half to give the compensation figure of over £30,000. Lonsdale, of course, was not permitted to claim an indemnity because his contract with the principal did not address this issue.

Judge Harris QC, sitting in the County Court at Oxford, was strongly influenced by the fact that Lonsdale's agency had produced:

'... *a modest and falling income in a steadily deteriorating environment. There is no evidence that anyone would have paid anything to buy it... I am strongly tempted to find that no damage has been established...But perhaps that conclusion, though I regard it as logical, is a little over rigorous given that the defendant [Howard & Hallam] has already made a payment. Doing the best I can, I find that the appropriate figure for compensation is one of £5,000.*'

Lonsdale appealed to the Court of Appeal which approved the decision of the County Court, whereupon he was given leave to appeal to the House of Lords.

Held: by the House of Lords that the analysis of Judge Harris QC had been correct and Lonsdale's appeal was dismissed. The value of this commercial agency had depreciated badly, commission had already been paid to Lonsdale by Howard & Hallam and the figure of £30,000 that the agent was claiming in compensation was totally unrealistic given the fact that the principal's business had failed. Lord Hoffman expressly approved the statement made by Judge Harris that he had been strongly tempted to find that no damage had actually been suffered by the agent as a result of the contractual relationship with the principal having come to an end. Lord Hoffman also stated that, in a situation where an agent acts for more than one principal the costs of each agency must be fairly attributed to each principal when attempting to determine the amount of compensation payable.

 Graham Page *v* Combined Shipping and Trading Co Ltd (1997) the pursuer had been appointed as a commercial agent on a fixed-term basis by the defender. The defender's South African parent company had ended all business links with the defender not long after the agent had been appointed. The pursuers treated this turn of events as a repudiation of the agency contract. The pursuer decided to freeze the defender's goods which had a value of £300,000 on the grounds that they were entitled to compensation under Regulation 17(6). The defender argued that he was not obliged to use the services of the pursuer for every transaction in order to sell his goods. The defender argued that, in this situation, the pursuer would have made a profit of precisely zero and, therefore, no compensation was payable.

Held: The English Court of Appeal overturned the decision of the lower court. The pursuer had an arguable case that this claim for compensation owed by the principal in terms of Regulation 17(6) might well be successful. The central issue in the case was the amount of commission that the pursuer would have earned if the contract had continued to be performed in the normal manner intended by both parties during its fixed-term period.

Duffen *v* FRABO SpA (2000) it was held that the agent's right to claim damages for loss of future commission because the principal had ended the agreement was very much dependent on whether the agent could prove that the principal was still reaping the benefits of his efforts. In this case, the agent failed to secure new customers for the principal during the agency agreement and his attempts to retain those existing customers of the principal were extremely unsuccessful. His claim for compensation under the Regulations was, therefore unsuccessful. However, owing to the express provisions of his contract, the agent was still entitled to claim some compensation from the principal.

 Hardie Polymer Ltd *v* Polymerland Ltd (2001) the meaning of Article 10 of the commercial agency agreement was in doubt as to whether the agent was entitled to compensation or an indemnity. Much of the confusion in this case stemmed around the fact that the parties had failed to use clear language when the agreement was originally drawn up. Admittedly, the heading of Article 10 – 'Compensation after Termination' was not helpful to the principal's claim that the agent was only entitled to an indemnity and not compensation in the sum of £120,000 as claimed. Lord MacFadyen in the Court of Session took the view, however, that despite this heading, all that Article 10 of the agreement entitled the agent to claim was an indemnity for the termination of the agreement. The agreement, therefore, prevented the agent from claiming compensation. Lord MacFadyen expressly approved the remarks of Deputy Judge Mitting QC in **Piretta**:

> 'I agree with the view expressed by the Deputy Judge . . . that the purpose of indemnity . . . is to award to the agent a share of the goodwill built up by his efforts. That being so, the use of the phrase "the goodwill payment" in article 10.2 [of the commercial agency agreement] is in my view confirmation that the parties did indeed intend to elect for indemnity.'

 Ingmar GB Ltd *v* Eaton Leonard Technologies Inc (2001) the principals were the manufacturers of sophisticated products including specialist equipment costing up to and beyond £100,000 designed for a limited but high quality market in the aircraft and automotive industries. An agent selling such products had to have engineering training and experience and expert knowledge of the qualities and performance of the principals' products so as to be able to sell them to the limited potential customer base which would also be expert and knowledgeable.

Held: that the pursuer had the right to receive compensation of £183,600 under Regulation 17.

The loss of a right to claim compensation or an indemnity

Regulation 18 describes certain situations where the agent will forfeit any rights to compensation or an indemnity under Regulation 17:

◆ Where the principal ends the agency agreement because the agent has committed a repudiatory breach of the agreement.

◆ If the agent ended the agreement, he may not be entitled to receive compensation unless the reason involved the agent's age, infirmity or illness.

♦ If the agent transfers or assigns his rights and duties under the agreement with the principal's consent.

A repudiatory breach by the agent would cover extremely serious breaches of the agency agreement, for example, where the agent has made secret profits on his own behalf or where the agent has pursued his own interests at the expense of the principal's.

It will, of course, be appreciated that the agent will be allowed to terminate the agreement if the principal behaves in a totally unreasonable way by, for example, committing a material breach of the contract.

According to Regulation 19, the rules about compensation and indemnity may not be excluded or limited by contract.

 Key point: Regulation 18 outlines situations where an agent will lose the right to claim compensation or an indemnity from the principal.

Restraint of trade or restrictive covenants (Regulation 20)

It will often be the case that the principal will want to protect his business interests by limiting the agent's ability to work for a competitor after the agency agreement has ended. The agent will have had access to all sorts of sensitive information about the principal's business, for example, customer lists, designs, products, business development plans and marketing strategies. Obviously, the principal will not want to see a business rival benefiting from this information to which the agent has been given access as a result of the agency agreement. Therefore, can the principal prevent the agent from taking up new employment with a new principal and, if so, for how long?

Regulation 20 provides the answers to these important questions. First, in order for a restraint of trade clause to be valid, it must be in writing and it must cover the group of customers and goods to which the agent's work was connected. Second, the maximum amount of time that such clause can last for is two years after the end of the agency agreement.

 Key point: A restraint of trade clause in an agency agreement must be in writing, must cover the agent's customers or goods and cannot last longer than two years after the agency has ended.

Termination of the agency relationship

The agency relationship, like any contract, can be terminated in a number of different ways by:

♦ Mutual agreement
♦ The principal withdrawing the agent's authority
♦ The agent withdrawing from the relationship
♦ Insolvency of the principal
♦ Death or insanity
♦ The expiry of a fixed term contract

Mutual agreement

This will occur when the parties have both agreed that the agency agreement will end on a particular date or after the completion of a particular transaction by the agent.

Galbraith & Moorhead *v* The Arethusa Ship Co Ltd (1896) Galbraith offered to buy £500 worth of shares in The Arethusa Ship Company on the basis that they were appointed sole chartering brokers. The offer was accepted by Arethusa and an agency relationship between the company and Galbraith lasted for several years. Arethusa later experienced a change of management which attempted to end the arrangement as it currently stood with Galbraith. The company no longer wished Galbraith to act as its sole agent. Galbraith brought an action against Arethusa claiming £600 in damages for breach of contract.

Held: the agency agreement, in the particular circumstances of this case, could not be ended simply by the decision of one of the parties.

Withdrawal of the agent's authority

The agent is the principal's representative and has been given authority to bind the principal into contracts with third parties. If the principal decides to withdraw the agent's powers or authority, then quite simply, the agent can no longer carry out his tasks. In these circumstances, the relationship between the principal and the agent is as good as over.

The agent's withdrawal

The agent may withdraw from the agency agreement at any time as long as it is not in the middle of a transaction. If the agent failed to complete a transaction this may cause loss to the principal.

The principal's insolvency or the ending of the principal's business

The agency agreement may also come to an end if the business of the principal is coming to an end or if the principal is declared insolvent. The principal may no longer wish to carry on a particular business or he may be forced to end his operations in a particular line of business. This would, of course, mean that the agent may no longer have a role to play as the principal's representative in a particular business activity.

 Patmore & Co *v* Cannon & Co Ltd (1892) Patmore & Co, warehousemen, agents and merchants of Glasgow and Leith, agreed with Cannon to act as Cannon's agent in Scotland for sales of goods manufactured by Cannon for a fixed period of five years from October 1891. In January 1892 Cannon communicated to Patmore, its intention to give up its fancy leather trade.

Held: Patmore was unsuccessful in its claim for damages for breach of contract. Cannon should not be forced to carry on a business against its will for five years or for any other period of time in order to keep Patmore in work as an agent.

The death of the principal or the agent

The death of either party has the effect of ending an agency relationship. There may be rare occasions, however, when an agent will not be aware of the principal's death and contracts with third parties may have been entered into after this event. Before the invention of modern communications, it may have been difficult to contact an agent to inform him of the principal's death and much of the case law in this area is quite old. In situations where the agent is unaware of the principal's death, the contract with a third party will be enforceable against the principal's estate and the agent is in no way personally liable.

 Campbell *v* Anderson (1829) the agent believed that his principal was alive when he negotiated the contract on the principal's behalf. It was only after the contract had been entered into with the third party that the agent heard the news that his principal was dead and, as a result, the agency agreement was at an end.

Held: the principal's estate was bound to honour the agreement with the third party and the agent was not personally liable to the third party.

Expiry of a fixed contract

Both the principal and the agent may have negotiated an agency agreement which is to last for a fixed period of time, for example, two years. Once the period of time has passed, the agency relationship comes to an end.

 Brenan *v* Campbells Trustees (1898) Brenan was employed in 1890 as a factor by the Trustees, the appointment to last for four years. Brenan claimed that he was entitled to six months' notice and sued for six months' pay.

Held: Brenan was not entitled to notice as he was well aware that his contract was of a fixed period of four years.

 Key point: The agency relationship can be terminated in a number of different ways – mutual agreement, principal withdrawing the agent's authority, the agent withdrawing from the relationship, principal's bankruptcy, death or insanity or the expiry of a fixed term contract.

Business organisations

To say that someone runs a business is to make a very vague statement. What kind of business does that person run? This is an important question because there are different rules which govern the creation of the various types of businesses that Scots law recognises. If, for example, someone wished to set up *business* as a sole trader, there are not that many legal rules covering this type of business. A sole trader does not even have to register the fact that he has set up a business. On the other hand, however, someone who wished to set up a *company* would have to be aware of the many different legal requirements that they would have to satisfy before they were allowed to do this. A new company must be registered with the Registrar of Companies and its directors must ensure that all sorts of information about the company's business activities are available to interested members of the public.

 Key point: In order to set up a business, certain legal requirements will have to be followed whereas in other situations there may be no rules about setting up a business.

Another important factor in setting up a business is the kind of liability that those individuals who are responsible for running it will face should the business fail. Some businesses like sole traders and partnerships operate under unlimited liability. This means that a sole trader or partners in a firm could lose everything if the business collapses. Alternatively, other businesses like limited liability partnerships and corporate bodies enjoy limited liability. Should the business fail, the members will only be liable for business debts up to a limit which they have already agreed amongst themselves. Clearly, this type of arrangement is much better than being chased by the creditors of the business for your last penny.

 Key point: The extent of a person's liability for business debts will often determine the type of business to be set up.

There are a number of different business organisations which exist under Scots Law:

◆ Sole trader
◆ Partnerships
◆ Limited partnerships
◆ Limited liability partnerships
◆ Corporate bodies

We will examine each of these in turn.

Sole traders

A sole trader is the simplest form of business organisation recognised by Scots law. In many respects, the law regards someone operating as a sole trader as a self-employed person. There are no legal requirements imposed on a person who wishes to operate as a sole trader except for the submission of income tax returns to the Inland Revenue and the disclosure requirements of Sections 1200–1208 of the Companies Act 2006 which partly repeals Section 1 of the old Business Names Act 1985. In law, no difference is made between the sole trader and his business; they are indistinguishable.

A sole trader will have total control over his business and will not have to take into account the opinions of any shareholders, members or partners. However, should the business fail, the sole trader is said to have unlimited liability for any debts or obligations owed to third parties. In practical terms, this means that a sole trader can be pursued through the courts for his last penny – in other words he could lose everything. Additionally, a sole trader may find it difficult to fund an expansion of the business because he cannot offer shares to other parties in order to raise funds. If he wished to do this, he would lose the control that he has over the business. Furthermore, he would be forced to change the nature of his business operation by converting it into a partnership or a corporate body.

 Key point: A sole trader is the simplest form of business organisation recognised by Scots law.

Partnership

A partnership is special type of business organisation which is often referred to as a firm. The name under which the partners collectively carry on business is referred to as the 'firm name'. The partners can, within limits, choose whatever name they want. However, the firm name will be subject to disclosure requirements of Sections 1200–1208 of the Companies Act 2006 if the partnership uses a name other than the surnames of each partner. A partnership calling itself The Business Law Consultancy will have to disclose the fact that its two partners are Alistair B Wylie and Seán J Crossan and the location of the firm's principal place of business. The official stationery of The Business Law Consultancy should contain these details so as to provide important information about the firm to third parties. These details should also be displayed in a prominent place to which customers will have access at the firm's business premises. If the partners fail to comply with these rules, they will commit a criminal offence. A partnership must not, for example, use a firm name which suggests government or local authority connections. Other important restrictions in relation to the firm's name are that a partnership must not use 'limited', 'public limited company' or 'limited liability partnership' as the last words of its name.

 Key point: A partnership is often referred to as a firm.

A partnership can sometimes be referred to as a joint adventure and the word 'adventure' denotes some sort of risk taken by the participants. The element of risk in a partnership business is, of course, the fact that the participants in the venture could lose money or become prey to the spectre of unlimited liability. A joint adventure, although undoubtedly a type of partnership, tends to be characterised by its short-term, temporary nature and usually has a single goal in its sights.

An example of a joint adventure can be seen in the following case:

 Mair v Wood (1948) there were five partners in a joint adventure. One of the partners provided the fishing boat and equipment and the remaining four partners provided their labour as members of the crew of the vessel. Once the outgoings had been dealt with, any profits from the venture were to be divided equally between the five partners. This was a classic example of a short-term temporary partnership created by its members to make a profit.

Lord President Cooper stated:

'A joint adventure is simply a species of the genus partnership, differentiated by its limited purpose and duration (which necessarily affect the extent of the rights and liabilities flowing from the relationship), but in all other essential aspects indistinguishable from any other partnership.'

The creation of a partnership

When a partnership is set up, the members do not have to comply with any formal legal requirements. In other words, unlike companies, limited partnerships and limited liability partnerships, a partnership does not have to be registered with the Registrar of Companies. The contract of partnership can be a verbal agreement, a written agreement or it can even be implied from the behaviour of the members. Obviously, a written agreement between the partners which clearly sets out their rights and duties will make good business sense because it will give the courts something to work with in the event of a dispute. If the partners have failed to put anything in writing, the courts can use the rules contained in the Partnership Act 1890 to resolve any problems or disputes that the partners may currently be experiencing in relation to one another. It should be stressed from the beginning, however, that the Partnership Act 1890 only provides guidelines which the partners are free to ignore if they so wish. In theory, the partners are largely left to run their business as they see fit. If the partners have chosen to depart from any of the rules contained in the Partnership Act 1890, the courts will have to respect this decision.

evidence proving the issue either way, was happy to accept testimony given on oath that the firm was, in fact, the owner of the property.

The Abolition of Feudal Tenure etc. (Scotland) Act 2000, which came into force on 28 November 2004, was notable for the introduction of important reforms affecting land ownership in Scotland. Section 70 of the Act made a significant change to legal rights of partnerships. It is now the case that a firm will be able to hold heritable property in its own name as if it were a completely separate legal person in its own right. Previously, the claim that a firm had separate personality was undermined by restrictions which prevented it from holding property in its own name.

The firm can also raise a legal action in its own name and it can be sued by a third party in the event of a legal dispute occurring.

 Key point: In Scotland, a firm is legally distinct from its partners.

Liability of the partners

Creditors of the firm must first sue the business for any debts that are owed, but if a firm lacks assets or funds to meet the payment of the debt, the creditors are entitled to raise an action against individual partners or the partners as a group. In this way, the partners are to be regarded as jointly and severally liable for the firm's debts. Normally, partners operate under the burden of unlimited liability which, practically speaking, will mean that every partner can be pursued to his last penny by the firm's creditors. In theory, a partner in a failed business could be forced to use all of his personal assets to pay off the debts of the firm. Should any partner have to pay a debt, he has the right to demand that his fellow partners compensate him. So, if there are five partners in a firm and they are all equally liable for the firm's debts, they must each pay one-fifth towards the debt owed to the creditors. The partnership agreement, however, may state that different partners are expected to pay different levels of contributions towards partnership debts. The assumption that the Partnership Act makes about the partners contributing equally towards the firm's debts cannot always be taken for granted.

 Key point: Creditors must first sue the firm for any business debts owed and, after having exhausted this source, then the partners who are said to be jointly and severally liable for all the firm's liabilities.

The vicarious liability of the firm

Sections 10, 11 and 12 of the Partnership Act impose the burden of vicarious liability on the firm for any delicts or negligent acts which are committed by the partners. This means that the firm will be liable to a third party if a partner injures the third party or if damage is caused to the third party's property while the partner is acting in the course of the firm's business. It is important to stress that the firm will not be liable where one partner causes loss or injury to a fellow partner while acting in the course of the partnership business. In such a situation, the injured partner would have to sue the partner who had committed the wrongful act in his personal capacity.

 Kirkintilloch Equitable Co-operative Society Ltd *v* Livingstone (1972) the Society had hired the services of a firm of chartered accountants to audit its accounts for a period of approximately 15 years from 1952 until 1967. The Society later sued the firm for professional negligence on the basis that the partner who had acted as the principal auditor of its accounts had failed to display the requisite level of care expected of a reasonably competent member of the accounting profession. In particular, the Society claimed that the partner had made a number of mistakes when auditing the accounts.

Held: the firm was liable to the Society for any acts of professional negligence committed by the partner responsible for auditing the accounts.

 Mair *v* Wood (1948) the five partners had entered into a joint adventure whereby one of them would provide a fishing vessel and the other four would provide their services as the crew. The agreement between the partners was that any catch would be sold and the proceeds split equally between all the participants in this enterprise. While at sea, the vessel ran into difficulties because the propeller was not working properly. In order to fix the problem, the captain of the vessel ordered that the wooden planks making up the engine room floor were to be removed to gain access to the damaged propeller. Unfortunately, Mair, one of the crew, sustained a serious injury when his foot plunged into the space which had been left exposed when the planks were removed. Subsequently, Mair raised an action for damages against the partnership.

Held: that Mair's action for damages should fail because he should have sued the captain of the fishing vessel in his personal capacity and not as partner of the joint adventure or enterprise.

 Key point: A firm can be responsible to third parties for the negligent actions of the partners which cause loss or injury.

The delict of fraud

If a third party accuses one or several partners in a firm of acting fraudulently, it is important that the alleged wrongdoers are named individually in any summons submitted as part of a civil action for damages. The firm is, of course, vicariously liable for the fraudulent actions of its partners, but this type of situation departs from the normal legal principle of joint and several liability. Fraud is considered to be a delict of a personal nature and that is why the alleged wrongdoers in the firm must be identified individually from the other partners who are completely blameless (**Thomson & Co *v* Pattison, Elder & Co (1895)**).

The balance of proof required in a civil action for fraud is also much higher than the normal standard in that the pursuer must prove conscious dishonesty on the part of the individual accused of acting fraudulently which is in line with the criminal standard of proof i.e. beyond a reasonable doubt. Clearly, in such a situation, blanket accusations of wrongdoing levelled against all the partners will not be particularly effective.

Partnership by holding out

It will be remembered from the study of agency, that a principal can create an agency relationship by holding out someone as an agent. This means that the actions or words of the principal can give third parties the impression that someone is acting as his agent. Third parties will often take the principal's words or actions at face value and deal with an individual as the principal's agent. The principal can then find himself being bound into contracts with third parties due to the actions of 'his agent'. Section 14 of the Partnership Act addresses situations where an individual could become liable for the debts and wrongful acts of the firm by holding himself out to be a partner or where the firm itself has held him out to be a partner. If an individual claims to be a partner in a firm or where he allows third parties to believe that he is a partner, such a person will be liable to any creditor who has loaned the firm money on the strength of these claims. Clearly, the individual who has allowed himself to be represented as a partner is not really a member of the firm, but the important point to consider here is that third parties believe that he is a partner. If the partnership has led third parties dealing with the firm to believe that someone is a partner, the partnership will be liable for any debts incurred or wrongful acts committed by the false partner. If the third party is aware that an individual's claims to be a partner in a firm are false, there is no liability.

 Hosie *v* Waddell (1866) Hosie raised an action for the recovery of a business debt owed to him by Waddell. Waddell countered this claim by stating that he had already paid the debt to Hosie's partner and, therefore, the matter was now at an end. Hosie responded that he did not have a partner and, upon further investigation, it emerged that Waddell had paid the money to Hosie's office manager whom he believed was a partner in the business. In fact, there was a common assumption prevailing amongst many people in the district that Hosie was in partnership with his office manager. Indeed, Hosie had done nothing to counter this belief and had previously gone so far as to say on numerous occasions to a range of individuals that he intended to make the office manager a partner in his business. This intention was never actually carried out, but nonetheless the belief was that the office manager had become Hosie's business partner and, therefore, had the necessary authority to bind the business into contracts with third parties.

Held: Hosie's statements, made over the years, about his manager's status in the business and his intention to make him a partner had actively contributed to the impression prevailing locally that this individual was a partner and therefore had all the necessary authority which such a position entails. This was an example of the creation of partnership by holding out. When Waddell had paid his debt to the office manager, he genuinely believed that he was dealing with Hosie's partner and thus he had fulfilled his duty to the business.

 Key point: If the firm encourages third parties to believe (wrongly) that an individual is a partner, the firm will be liable for the debts or wrongful acts of the false partner.

The liability of an incoming partner for debts or wrongful acts

Under Section 17 of the Partnership Act, new partners joining the firm will not be responsible for any partnership debts or wrongful acts committed by the business that were run up or occurred before their involvement in the firm. Similarly, a partner who has left the firm will cease to have any responsibility for business liabilities after his departure. A former partner in order to escape liability will have to publicise his departure from the firm in the *Edinburgh Gazette* and this is regarded as giving proper notice to third parties of his changed role in relation to the business. It is worth pointing out that former partners continue to be liable for business debts or for wrongful acts committed by the partnership which occurred during their involvement with the firm.

 Thomson *v* Balfour, Boag & Son (1936) an individual who was in business as a carpenter decided to enter a partnership agreement with his foreman. The foreman contributed a substantial amount of capital to the business and both partners agreed that any past debts or liabilities of the business were not to be the responsibility of the newly created partner. However, any debts or liabilities created by the business after the entry of the foreman to the firm would be the responsibility of both partners.

Held: all debts owed by the carpenter before the entry to the business of his foreman were his responsibility and the new partner was under no duty whatsoever to contribute towards the payment of these pre-existing liabilities.

 Key point: A notice in the *Edinburgh Gazette* informs outsiders and third parties that a partner has left the firm and that he has no further responsibility for debts incurred by the firm after the publication of this notice.

The liability of a retired partner for debts or wrongful acts

 Tower Cabinet Co Ltd *v* Ingram (1949) Ingram and Christmas had established a partnership which had the business name 'Merry's'. The firm was in the business of selling furniture. Both partners later decided to dissolve their business association by mutual agreement. Ingram had communicated the fact that the partnership was being terminated to the firm's bank and it was agreed by Christmas that he would take upon himself to inform all third parties dealing with the firm that Ingram was no longer a partner. It was agreed by the former partners that Christmas would continue to trade under the name of Merry's. Unfortunately, both individuals failed to place an advertisement in the *London Gazette*, which they were required to do by the Partnership Act 1890, which would have had the effect of making public the fact that their partnership had ended. Furthermore, new headed notepaper for Merrys was ordered with Ingram's name removed to take into account the changed situation of the business. Some nine months later, Merry's entered into a contract to supply furniture to Tower Cabinet. Problematically, Christmas used Merry's previous headed notepaper (which still listed Ingram as his partner) to communicate with Tower Cabinet. A dispute arose between Merry's and Tower Cabinet, which went to court, and Tower Cabinet obtained a decree against Merry's which it attempted to enforce against both Ingram and Christmas.

Held: Ingram was not liable to Tower Cabinet for anything done by his former partner, Christmas. He had no previous business dealings with Tower Cabinet before the termination of his partnership with Christmas and was, therefore, completely unknown to them. He could not be regarded as an apparent partner in the firm. Furthermore, at no point, had Ingram held himself out or represented himself to be a partner in Merry's during any dealings with Tower Cabinet.

The relationship between the partners in a firm

Partnership is a contract *uberrimae fidei* – a relationship of the utmost good faith. The partners have a special relationship with one another and, as a result, they are expected to be completely honest and above board in their dealings. In other words, they owe fiduciary duties towards one another because they are regarded as being in a relationship of trust. Partners must not do anything which undermines the firm, for example, by competing against it by running another business. A partner must not make secret profits at the expense of his fellow partners (see **Pillans Brothers v Pillans (1908)** in Chapter 2).

The Partnership Act 1890 spells out the fiduciary duties of a partner in the following ways:

1   Every partner must keep proper accounts when handling and receiving partnership funds on behalf of his fellow partners. A partner is also under a duty to inform his fellow partners about any matter which may affect the firm **(Section 28)**.

2   Every partner must inform his fellow partners of any profit made or benefit received as a result of his position as a partner or as a result of using the firm's property or assets **(Section 29)**.

3   Any partner who competes against the firm by running another business without having been given permission by his fellow partners will have to hand over all profits made in the course of the competing business to the firm **(Section 30)**.

 Key point: Partnership is a contract *uberrimae fidei* i.e. of the utmost good faith.

The rights of the partners

Section 24 of the Partnership Act 1890 provides some important guidelines which illustrate the rights and duties of each partner in the firm (unless the partners have come to a different agreement among themselves):

◆ All partners can expect to share equally in the profits that a partnership makes. On the other hand, of course, all partners are expected to contribute equally towards any losses that the firm may suffer.
◆ All partners are expected to share equally the partnership funds or capital.
◆ All partners have the right to be relieved of any liabilities or expenses that they have incurred as a result of acting properly in the course of the partnership business.
◆ All partners who have advanced money to the partnership over and above their agreed contribution to partnership funds are entitled to receive interest on the money loaned at the rate of five per cent per annum from the date on which the loan was made.
◆ All partners have the right to participate in the running of the partnership.
◆ All partners are entitled to receive a share of the profits and this means that individual partners are not entitled to be paid for participating in the business.
◆ All the partners must first agree before any new partner can join the partnership.
◆ The partners can reach a decision by majority vote. However, any changes to the nature of the partnership agreement must be agreed by all of the partners.

◆ The partnership books are to be kept at the partnership's head office where all the partners are entitled to have access to them so that they can be consulted at any time.

 Key point: Section 24 of the Partnership Act lists the rights and duties of a partner in the absence of any agreement to the contrary.

Expulsion of a partner from a firm

Section 25 of the Partnership Act 1890 prevents a majority of partners from expelling a fellow partner from the firm, unless this power is part of the contract of partnership. If such a power of expulsion exists, the partners who wish to make use of it must be seen to be acting in good faith.

It must be emphasised again that the above rules governing the rights and duties of the partners in a firm are merely guidelines which the members of a partnership are free to exclude if they so wish. Many partnerships will be run along very different lines from the model that is described in Section 24 of the Partnership Act 1890.

 Key point: Generally, majority partners are not permitted to expel one of their number from the firm unless such a general power exists in the partnership agreement.

Determining the existence of a partnership

The question as to whether or not a partnership exists may arise either between the alleged partners or between the alleged partners and a third party. According to Section 2 of the Partnership Act 1890 if an individual is entitled to a share of the profits of the business, this may be used in evidence to prove that he is a partner in a firm. It is obviously open to the individual concerned to dispute this allegation made by a third party.

The Partnership Act 1890 provides rules for determining whether a partnership does or does not exist. These are a re-enactment of rules originally contained in 'Bovill's Act', which was passed in 1865 to regulate the liabilities of persons sharing profits.

The first rule is that owning property jointly or in common does not of itself create a partnership, even where profits from its use are shared.

 Sharpe v Carswell (1910) Sharpe had a small shareholding in respect of the ownership of a schooner named *Dolphin*. He was also employed as the master of this vessel receiving a fixed salary for his services. Sharpe was involved in an accident which had occurred, within the course of his employment, on board the vessel and he suffered serious injuries which later caused his death. His widow attempted to claim compensation for his death in terms of the Workmen's Compensation Act 1906. The Act operated a scheme whereby victims of industrial accidents who were classified as 'workmen' received compensation in respect of injury and death. The vital question here was whether Sharpe's shareholding in the vessel meant that he was a partner in the business and not a workman (i.e. an employee of the venture). If Sharpe had been a partner in the business his widow would be disqualified from claiming compensation for his death in terms of the Act.

Held: the fact that Sharpe had owned some shares in the vessel did not mean that he ought to be classified as a partner in the business. His widow was, therefore, entitled to receive compensation under the Act in respect of his work-related death.

 Davis v Davis (1894) a father left his two sons his business and a number of freehold houses. Both sons had equal shares as tenants in common in the freehold property. The sons let one of the houses and used the rent obtained to enlarge the workshops attached to the remaining two houses. The sons continued to carry on the business. They each drew out from it a weekly sum, but no accounts were kept. The proceeds from rent for the third house were divided between them.

Held: the sons were carrying on a partnership in relation to the business, but not in relation to the freehold houses.

 Key point: Owning property jointly or in common does not necessarily confirm the existence of a firm.

The second rule is that the sharing of gross returns does not of itself create a partnership. It does not matter whether the persons sharing the returns have or have not a joint or common right or interest in any property from which the returns are derived. This rule can be seen in the case of **Cox v Coulson (1916)**.

 The defender, Coulson, was the manager of a theatre and he had entered into an agreement with a Mr Mill to provide the use of the theatre, pay for the lighting and promotional materials for plays. He was to receive 60 per cent of the gross takings, whilst Mr Mill was to secure the services and pay for a theatrical company. Mr Mill was also to provide the scenery and he had the right to receive the remaining 40 per cent of the takings. The pursuer was injured by a shot fired by an actor during the performance of a play at the theatre. The pursuer claimed that the defender was liable on the ground that he was a partner of Mr Mill.

Held: by the English Court of Appeal that the defender could not be made liable because he was not a partner, for by Section 2(2) of the Partnership Act 1890 the sharing of gross returns did not by itself create a partnership.

 Key point: The sharing of gross returns does not necessarily indicate the existence of a firm.

The third rule relates to the sharing of profits, as opposed to gross returns. The word 'profits' means net profits, i.e. the amount remaining after the expenses of the business have been deducted from the gross returns.

It will be remembered that Section 2 of the Partnership Act 1890 states that, if a person receives a share of the profits of a business, this will strongly suggest that such an individual is a partner in the business. However, the sharing of profits is by no means conclusive proof that someone is a partner in a business. Before the case of **Cox v Hickman (1860)**, the sharing of profits was regarded as conclusive evidence of a partnership. However, this case changed the common law and it established the rule that parties may share profits without necessarily being partners.

In accordance with the decision in **Cox v Hickman**, the Partnership Act describes certain situations where the sharing of profits does not of itself make the recipient a partner in the business. These situations are as follows:

◆ If a person is owed a debt by the partnership and this debt is paid by instalments from partnership profits.

◆ Where an individual is an employee of the partnership and his wages are paid from partnership profits.

◆ A deceased partner's widow or child who receives a pension or an annuity from partnership funds.

◆ Where money is loaned to a person engaged in a business where the contract states that the lender is to receive a rate of interest varying with the profits or is to receive a share of the profits, the lender is not a partner in the business. However, so close is the relationship to partnership in this instance that the contract must be in writing and signed by or on behalf of all the parties to it. Otherwise the lender would be held to be a partner.

◆ A person who has sold the goodwill of a business and receives as payment a portion of the profits or a pension or annuity from partnership profits is not a partner.

 Key point: A person who is entitled to a share of the profits of a business may be regarded as a partner unless he can bring evidence to defeat this presumption.

Proving the existence of partnership

This is a very much a factual question and will be determined by the evidence presented to the court. Clearly, creditors of a failing partnership business will have a very real incentive to demonstrate that individuals involved in the business are partners because of the legal principle of joint and several liability which operates in this area of business.

 Stewart *v* Buchanan (1903) Buchanan had leased property to Saunders for the purpose of carrying on a business at 16 and 20 Springfield Court, Queen Street in Glasgow. Both parties had even entered into a formal legal agreement which stated that Buchanan was not a partner in Saunder's business and therefore could not be called upon by any creditors of the business to pay anything towards debts run up by Saunders in the course of his commercial activities. Crucially, however, Buchanan contributed money and equipment to Saunders which were to be used for running the business. An individual called Stewart later brought a legal action against both Buchanan and Saunders for payment of an unpaid business debt which he alleged that, as partners, both individuals were responsible. Buchanan denied a partner of Saunders and attempted to rely on the formal legal agreement which had previously entered into.

Held: despite the contents of the legal agreement between Buchanan and Saunders, the court was swayed by the fact that both individuals had acted as if they were, in fact, business partners. Particularly compelling in evidential terms was the fact that Buchanan had contributed money and equipment to the running of the business. Buchanan and Saunders were partners and, consequently, jointly and severally liable for the debts of the business.

Clark v G R & W Jamieson (1909) Clark had been drowned at sea off the Shetland Isles while working on a small vessel which ferried cargo. He was paid for his services directly from the gross earnings of the business and the court had to consider whether or not this fact made him a partner in the venture. This issue arose because Clark's surviving family wished to pursue a claim under the Workmen's Compensation Act 1906 which had been passed by the Liberal Government to ensure that families of employees injured or killed at work received some sort of compensation. This was a particularly important piece of social legislation passed at the beginning of the twentieth century when men were considered to be the breadwinners for families and, if they sustained injury or suffered death in the line of work, this could lead to destitution for their families. If Clark was indeed a partner in the business, he could not be considered a workman or an employee and, therefore, his family would not be eligible to receive compensation under the Act.

Held: Clark was a workman or employee in terms of the Act and his family was entitled to claim compensation for his death while at work.

In **Protectacoat Firthglow Ltd v Szilagyi (2009)**, the English Court of Appeal held that an attempt by Protectacoat Firthglow to rely on documentary evidence apparently showing that Mr Szilagyi had entered a partnership with certain other individuals was little more than a sham. Mr Szilagyi was not acting as an independent sub-contractor (heading his own firm) in order to provide services to Protectacoat Firthglow. The real legal relationship between the parties (Szilagyi and Protectacoat Firthglow) was that of employee and employer (see Chapter 6 for a full description of this case).

 Key point: The existence (or not) of a firm is very much a factual matter to be determined by the courts.

Termination of a partnership

According to provisions contained in Sections 32 to 35 of the Partnership Act 1890, a partnership may be dissolved in the following ways:

End of fixed period

If a partnership was created for a fixed period of time, the business comes to an end when this period expires. The members of a firm may set up a business which is to operate for, say, ten years (Section 32). Once this ten-year period has passed, the business is at an end. However, there is nothing to stop the partners continuing in business together after the expiry of the ten-year period if they are so minded. This would be known as partnership at will or tacit relocation and the firm will continue to trade for the indefinite future.

 Neilson v Mossend Iron Co (1886) the agreement between the partners contained a clause which permitted any of its members to leave the firm in the last three months prior to the expiry of the full partnership term (which was for a seven year period). The members, however, decided to remain in partnership after the expiry of the original term of seven years. One of the members subsequently wished to exercise the three month notice period in order to leave the business. The other members of the firm objected to this on the grounds that this clause in the original partnership agreement had been overtaken by events.

Held: by the House of Lords that this clause no longer had any legal validity and, therefore, could not be enforced. Lord Watson remarked that such arrangements were suitable for partnerships of a fixed duration, but not in situations where the partners had clearly decided to continue their association for an indefinite period.

 Key point: A partnership could last for a fixed time period.

Goal accomplished

If the firm was set up to achieve a particular goal, it will come to an end when this purpose is accomplished (Section 32).

 Winsor v Schroeder (1979) Schroeder and Winsor contributed equal amounts of money in order to buy a house, modernise it and then sell it on at a profit – the profit to be divided equally between the partners.

Held: the partnership would come to an end when the land was sold and the profit, if any, was divided between Winsor and Schroeder.

 Key point: A firm may be set up to achieve a particular goal and, once this has been achieved, the partnership will be at an end.

Notice given

One of the partners could give notice to the other members that he wishes the firm to cease trading. So long as a partnership has not been formed for a particular period of time or for a particular purpose, it can be dissolved by notice given by any partner. The notice must be in writing if the partnership agreement is in the form of a deed. If not, then a partner can notify the other members verbally of his desire to dissolve the business. This notice will take effect when all partners have knowledge of it. No particular period of notice is required.

 Peyton v Mindham (1972) it was held that a court could and would declare a dissolution notice to be ineffective if it was given in bad faith as where A and B dissolve a partnership with C by notice, in order to exclude C from sharing in valuable, future contracts. Dissolution by notice may be prevented by the provisions of the partnership agreement.

 Moss v Elphick (1910) the partnership agreement stated that dissolution could only occur if all the partners were in agreement (Section 32).

 Key point: A partner may be entitled to terminate the partnership by giving notice of this intention to the other partners.

Death of a partner

The death of a partner dissolves the firm. The share of the partner who has died goes to his personal representatives who are usually appointed by his will. They have the rights of a partner in a dissolution. Partnership agreements usually provide that the firm shall continue after the death of a partner so that the dissolution is

parties which were entered into before the partners decided to dissolve the business. It will also be necessary for the partners to continue to have authority to deal with matters which are related to the termination of the partnership agreement. However, the partners are most definitely prevented from drumming up new business on behalf of the firm.

The partners will usually manage to dissolve the business themselves without having to rely on outside help. There may be situations, however, where the intervention of the courts will be necessary to achieve the termination of the partnership agreement. Under Section 39, partnership property and assets must first be used to pay off the firm's debts and liabilities. If anything is left after the debts and liabilities of the firm have been paid off, any partner who has loaned the firm money is entitled to be repaid. Next, the partners will effectively be repaid their contribution towards the firm's capital. If anything remains of the firm's capital or assets after this, then the partners share what is left according to the rules by which they share profits.

 Thomson, Petitioner (1893) the Court of Session agreed to grant the petition of a partner to have the firm dissolved following on from a series of material breaches of the partnership agreement committed by his fellow partner. The net effect of these breaches of the agreement contributed to a complete breakdown in the relationship between the partners and, therefore, it was impossible for the innocent party to continue in business with an individual in whom he had clearly lost all trust and confidence (an absolute prerequisite for a fiduciary relationship such as partnership). It should be noted that a petition for dissolution of a firm should be lodged by the aggrieved partner and not by the partner who has consistently undermined the fiduciary relationship as result of his behaviour.

 Key point: In certain situations the courts may grant an order to dissolve the firm.

The appointment of a judicial factor

In situations where it becomes clear to a court that the partners cannot agree on the practicalities or mechanics of dissolution, a judicial factor may have to be appointed to oversee this task.

 Dickie v Mitchell (1874) both partners lacked the necessary legal capacity to manage the dissolution of the partnership and it was considered necessary to appoint a judicial factor to deal with the management of the firm's affairs during the period of the dissolution.

In this case, Lord Inglis, sitting in the Court of Session, provided a number of useful guidelines which should be considered before a court finds it necessary to appoint a judicial factor to oversee the dissolution of a partnership. A judicial factor can be appointed in the following situations:

1   In the event of the death of all the partners in the firm; or

2   In the event that there is only one partner who has survived and s/he is clearly not able to deal with the dissolution of the firm owing to the fact of some infirmity or lack of capacity.

Generally speaking, a court will operate on the presumption that there is no need to appoint a judicial factor if, following on from the death of a partner, the remaining members of the firm are more than fit and able enough to deal with the dissolution of the business.

 Key point: In some situations, a judicial factor may be appointed by the courts to assist in the dissolution of the firm.

Rescission

A partnership can also come to an end where the contract is rescinded. Rescission involves the setting aside of the contract usually on the grounds of misrepresentation or fraud.

 In **Ferguson v Wilson (1904)** a partnership agreement was rescinded on the grounds of innocent misrepresentation. Wilson, an engineer in Aberdeen, had advertised for a partner. Ferguson replied to the advertisement and, during the contractual negotiations that followed, Wilson innocently misrepresented the profitability of his business. On the basis of these figures, Ferguson agreed to enter a partnership with Wilson.

Held: Ferguson was entitled to rescind or cancel the partnership agreement owing to the fact of Wilson's innocent misrepresentation.

 Key point: The rules concerning termination of partnership are contained in Sections 32 to 35 of the Partnership Act 1890.

The authority of the partners after the termination of a partnership

After a partnership has been terminated or the decision to dissolve a firm has been made, the authority of the partners to enter into new contracts with third parties dealing with the business comes to an end. This is a common sense position and it is an explicit recognition of the fact that the business has reached the end of its life.

There may, however, be situations which arise when a partnership is ending or has ended where it is sensible for one or some of the partners to continue to have some sort of residual authority in order to conclude the affairs of the firm. It should be said from the outset that any such authority will be of an extremely limited nature and it would not be legitimate for a partner who has been given this type of authority to enter into a wide-ranging series of new contractual entanglements. Any such authority simply exists to bring partnership business to a close.

 Dickson v National Bank of Scotland Ltd (1917) a solicitor who had been a partner in a law firm which had been dissolved some eight years previously, withdrew money from the bank account of a trust fund and promptly used this sum for his own private purposes. The solicitor, together with his other partners in the firm, had authority to withdraw money from the account due to their position as trustees. All that the bank required for any money to be withdrawn from the account was the signature of one of the trustees. The bank had no reason to suspect that the solicitor was acting dishonestly when he withdrew the money from the trust account. The beneficiaries of the trust later brought a claim against the bank alleging that it had not discharged its duty of care to them when it had released the funds to the solicitor.

Held: the solicitor had the necessary authority to withdraw money from the account, but he did not have the right to use this sum for his own private purposes – a clear breach of his fiduciary duty as a trustee of the beneficiaries of the trust fund.

 Key point: After dissolution of the firm, the partners no longer have authority to enter new contracts with third parties dealing with the business.

The goodwill of the partnership

Following on from any dissolution or termination of the partnership agreement, it may be necessary to determine whether some of the former partners are entitled to benefit from the goodwill of the firm. In **Tower Cabinet Co Ltd *v* Ingram (1949)**, Christmas would clearly have benefited from being able to retain the existing business name ('Merry's') after the dissolution of his partnership with Ingram. Such an arrangement would have, in all likelihood, permitted Christmas to retain his association with the customers of the business, as well as benefiting from any good reputation that he and Ingram had managed to establish while in partnership together.

In the English decision of **Cruttwell *v* Lye (1810)**, Lord Eldon was of the opinion that the goodwill of a business should be regarded as 'nothing more than the probability that the old customers will resort to the old place'. This statement was criticised by Lord Herschell, in **Trego *v* Hunt** (1896), a decision of the House of Lords, who stated that:

'If the language of Lord Eldon is to be taken as a definition of general application, I think it is far too narrow, and I am not satisfied that it was intended by Lord Eldon as an exhaustive examination.'

In a Scottish decision, **Hughes *v* Assessor for Stirling (1892)**, Lord Wellwood was of the opinion that the goodwill of business was 'an elastic term of which it is not easy, if it is possible, to give an exhaustive definition'.

Complicating matters further in Scotland is the fact that the goodwill of a business can be classified as either moveable or heritable property. Goodwill will be classified as moveable property if it is closely associated with the partners who comprise the firm. On the other hand, the goodwill of a business will be regarded as heritable in nature if it is connected to the location of the premises of the firm e.g. a dental surgery in a busy high street or a fashion retail outlet in an exclusive shopping mall.

 Smith *v* McBride (1888) Smith and McBride had previously been partners who had since decided to dissolve their business association. It was agreed by them that Smith, for an agreed sum, could purchase the business and its assets (including equipment and good will). One condition of sale imposed on Smith by McBride was that he was not permitted to use the business name of the firm. Later, McBride formed a new partnership with Smith's brother and they (imaginatively) used the same business name, Smith & McBride, as the previous partnership. Smith alleged that this was an attempt to misappropriate the goodwill of the business and applied to the court for an interdict to prevent the new partnership using this name.

Held: McBride's attempt to use the name of his previous firm should not be allowed and interdict was granted to Smith. This was an attempt to benefit from the goodwill of the previously named firm of Smith & McBride which was in clear breach of the contract of sale which McBride had entered into with his former partner. This contract of sale, of course, explicitly included the goodwill of the former partnership and McBride's attempt to appropriate the name of his former business association with Smith was a blatant violation of this agreement.

 Key point: After the dissolution of a firm, some or all the partners may dispute which of them is entitled to benefit from the goodwill of the business.

Right of outgoing partner in certain cases to share profits made after the dissolution of the firm

Section 42 of the Partnership Act 1890 extends a right to an outgoing partner i.e. an individual who has died or who has since left the firm to claim a share of any profits after the firm has been dissolved. Such a right will arise in situations where the surviving partners have continued to trade using the assets or the capital of the business and where they have failed to make a final settlement of the accounts. The outgoing partner or his representative will have the right to receive a share of any profits which can be directly attributed to his partnership share or, alternatively if this cannot be achieved, to receive interest at the annual rate of 5% in respect of his share.

 Clark *v* Watson (1982) a partnership consisting of two dentists came to an end on the death of one of the partners. Unfortunately, the partnership agreement lacked clarity as to how the capital of the firm was to be divided between the surviving partner and the estate of the deceased partner.

Held: the surviving partner had continuing authority to draw up a list of all the assets of the firm in order that they could be properly valued so that the estate of the deceased partner could receive its proper entitlement to a share of the capital.

 Key point: In some situations an outgoing partner may have the right to share in the profits of the firm after dissolution.

The Scottish and English Law Commissions' Joint Report on Partnership Law

On 18 November 2003, the Scottish and English Law Commissions (Scot Law Com No 192 and Law Com No 283) published a Joint Report on Partnership Law. This Report has not yet been formally adopted by Parliament.

The Commissions wish to see the introduction of a new Partnership Act to replace the existing 1890 Act. If these proposals were formally adopted by the Westminster Parliament, it would mean that, for the first time, the law in relation to partnership in Scotland, England and Wales would largely be the same. Partnerships in England and Wales would become legal entities as is already the case in Scotland in order to reflect commercial reality. Partnerships in England and Wales would, therefore, be able to enter contracts and hold property in their own right as is already the case in Scotland. Partners would still be personally responsible for obligations of the firm and they would continue to stand in a fiduciary relationship to one another. This means that partners will still have to labour under the burden of unlimited liability.

As we have seen, Parliament has adopted the Commissions' recommendation that the previous restriction on partnerships being limited to a mere 20 members be removed. Perhaps one of the most significant changes that the proposed new law would make is that partnerships would not automatically be wound up when there is a change of partner as is presently the case. Where partnerships, which are solvent, are going to be wound up, the Report proposes that, in both jurisdictions, the law allows the partners to decide by majority vote how this will be achieved. Currently, the courts in England and Wales or a judicial factor become involved when a partnership is wound up. Insolvent partnerships could be wound up under the Insolvency Act 1986.

 Key point: In November 2003, the Scottish and English Law Commissions published a joint report on partnership which proposed having the same general rules governing this type of business in Scotland and England and Wales.

Limited partnerships

This type of business is governed by the Limited Partnerships Act 1907. Unlike a traditional partnership, this type of business must be registered with the Registrar of Companies in Edinburgh. The following information must be supplied to the Registrar:

◆ The name of the limited partnership.
◆ A brief description of the type of business that it carries on.
◆ The location of its main office.
◆ The full names of each of the partners.
◆ A statement, if appropriate, of how long the partnership is to last and the date upon which the business began.
◆ A statement that the partnership is limited and who the limited partners are.
◆ The amount of each limited partner's contribution to the business.

The Act allows at least one general partner and one limited partner to form a business. However, there must always be at least one general partner at any time. The limited partner is effectively a silent or a sleeping partner and plays no part in the day-to-day running of the business. In an ordinary partnership, all the partners operate under the burden of unlimited liability where they will all be responsible for the firm's debts. This is not the case in a limited partnership, where the limited partner will lose only the amount of money that he advanced to the firm. If the limited partner becomes involved in the daily management of the business, his liability for business debts or delicts which were the responsibility of the business would become unlimited. Limited partners see their role as that of an investor wishing to make a profit. They do not want to be bogged down with the responsibilities of management. The 1907 Act makes it quite clear that a majority of the general partners will decide the aims and the policies of the business. A limited partner will not even be able to oppose the introduction of a new general partner if the existing general partners have made up their minds on this matter.

Even the death, lunacy or bankruptcy of a limited partner will not mean that the partnership has to be ended as with an ordinary firm. It will be the general partners who will decide when the business is to be ended. The major disadvantage of being a limited partner is that it will not be possible for such a person to withdraw his investment while the partnership is still trading. The general partners may allow a limited partner to transfer or assign his investment in the business to a third party, the public must be notified by the placing of an advertisement to this effect in the *Edinburgh Gazette*. These types of businesses tend to be encountered rarely because private limited companies are seen as a more popular means of investing money.

The relationship between the general partners is governed by the Partnership Act 1890 and the associated case law in mostly the same way as would be found in an ordinary firm.

 Key point: A limited partnership allows the firm to have silent or limited partners who take no part in the day-to-day running of the firm's business and, furthermore, these individuals enjoy limited liability. However, limited partnerships must register with the Registrar of Companies.

Limited liability partnerships

The Limited Liability Partnerships Act 2000 came into force on 6 April 2001. The Act introduces a new type of business vehicle in addition to companies, traditional partnerships, limited partnerships and sole traders.

According to Section 1 of the Act, a limited liability partnership or LLP is a corporate body which has completely separate legal personality from that of its members. Section 1 also makes it very clear that the law of partnership does not apply to LLPs.

A business trading as a limited liability partnership will be immediately recognisable by the use of the initials LLP after its name.

It was originally thought that LLPs would be attractive business organisations for existing professional partnerships such as law firms, surveyors and accountants. In many situations, though they are exceptions, such businesses have faced difficulties in trying to run limited companies because of the rules laid down by their professional associations. The major advantage of setting up an LLP for existing partnerships is that the members can limit their liability. In a traditional-style partnership, it will be remembered that should the business fail and run up huge debts, the members will face the burden of unlimited liability. This effectively means that creditors of the partnership can and will pursue the members to their last penny. The partner's personal assets, for example, a home, savings, a car and other valuables will be eyed up by creditors.

 Key point: Limited liability partnerships (LLPs) are corporate bodies and the members can limit their liability in respect of the business's creditors.

People involved in setting up new businesses may also wish to form LLPs. Previously, the individuals involved in this type of venture would have probably chosen to run the business as a limited company. Existing limited companies, however, are prevented from re-registering as LLPs.

The creation of limited liability partnerships

Section 2 of the Act contains the rules for establishing an LLP:

◆ The LLP must have at least two members who have signed an incorporation document.
◆ The founding members of the LLP must register this incorporation document and other necessary documentation with the Registrar of Companies.
◆ A fee of £95 is also payable by the proposed members of the LLP to the Registrar.

If an LLP operates with just one member for more than six months, the business loses the protection of limited liability and the remaining member will have complete responsibility for any business debts or liabilities.

The incorporation document

An incorporation document must contain the following details:

◆ The name of the limited liability partnership (which must comply with Sections 1200–1208 of the Companies Act 2006).
◆ The country in which the registered office of the limited liability partnership is to be situated i.e. England and Wales, in Wales or in Scotland.
◆ The address of that registered office.
◆ The name and address of each of the persons who are to be members of the limited liability partnership on its incorporation (The Companies Act 2006 allows members to apply for an exemption if they have a real fear about revealing their address e.g. they may have good reason to fear for their personal safety or that of their family).
◆ Details of those persons who are to be designated members or details of every person who from time to time will be a member of the limited liability partnership and who is to be a designated member.

If a person deliberately makes a false statement to the Registrar in the incorporation document, he commits a criminal offence.

In terms of Section 3, when the Registrar is satisfied that all legal requirements have been complied with, he will then issue a certificate of incorporation which allows the new business to begin trading. The certificate of incorporation is conclusive proof that the members of the LLP have complied with all the necessary legal requirements.

 Key point: An LLP must be registered with the Registrar of Companies who will issue a certificate of incorporation signifying that the business has complied with all necessary legal requirements.

The members of an LLP

It is very important that those people who are involved in running an LLP should not be called partners. The proper term for these individuals is members.

Section 4 states that the first members of the LLP are those individuals whose names appear on the incorporation document which is delivered to the Registrar. At least two members must be 'designated members' and their names must be given to the Registrar as such. Designated members have additional responsibilities in comparison to the general members of an LLP. The designated members will be responsible for administrative and filing duties which would normally be carried out by a director or a company secretary in a company. Some of the tasks that a designated member is responsible for include the following:

◆ Signing the annual accounts
◆ Filing the annual accounts and annual returns with Companies House
◆ In the event of insolvency proceedings, providing any statement setting out the affairs of the business i.e. assets, debts and liabilities

There is nothing to stop a person becoming a member of the business at a later date either with the agreement of the existing members or under the terms of a membership agreement (if one exists). A person may no longer be regarded as a member as long as this is with the agreement of the other members or in accordance with the membership agreement (again if one exists). The death of a member (if the LLP was not thereby dissolved) means that membership of the business will come to an end. Generally speaking, members are not regarded as employees of the business.

 Key point: The designated members of an LLP have additional responsibilities that would normally be carried out by a director or a company secretary in a company.

A membership agreement

Corporate bodies must register a memorandum and articles of association with the Registrar and these documents provide important information about the way in which the business is run. Although there is no legal requirement for LLP members to commit anything to paper, Section 5 of the Act makes it clear that it would be a very sensible practice for the LLP members to draw up a detailed members' agreement (currently known as a partnership agreement). This agreement would deal with all the important issues that the business will face, for example:

◆ The authority of the members to bind the LLP
◆ Each member's financial contribution to the LLP
◆ Shares of profits and losses
◆ The circumstances in which the LLP agreement will come to an end
◆ The appointment of new members
◆ Special classes of members with different rights and duties
◆ The expulsion of existing members
◆ How disputes between the members are to be resolved
◆ Whether changes to the members' agreement are to be made unanimously or by majority

 Key point: There is no legal requirement for the members of an LLP to have a written agreement, but it will be sensible to have one in order to determine how the business is to be run.

The authority and liability of LLP members (Sections 6 and 7)

According to Section 6, the members of an LLP are to be regarded as the agents of the business. However, an LLP will not be bound in contract to a third party by the actions of one of its members if the member in question lacked authority to act on behalf of the business and the third party dealing the LLP member in question is fully aware that the member lacks authority. Where the third party does not know or believe a person to be a member of the LLP, the business will not be bound in contract to the third party.

If an individual ceases to be an LLP member, this fact must be communicated to third parties dealing with the business and, additionally, there is a legal requirement to inform the Registrar of Companies. Failure to inform third parties dealing with the business that someone is no longer an LLP member means that the former member will continue to be regarded as being involved in the business.

An LLP is classed as a completely separate legal entity from its members. In a partnership, the partners are jointly and severally liable for the firm's debts and any delicts committed by the partners in the course of partnership business. Members of an LLP are not jointly liable for contracts entered into by the LLP and they are not jointly and severally liable for any delicts committed by the LLP. However, members will be liable for their own acts of negligence or wrong-doing in a very similar way to company directors. It would be a sensible precaution for members to take out professional liability insurance which would offer them protection if a third party decided to bring an action against one of them.

The main benefit of an LLP in relation to a traditional partnership is that the members of the LLP enjoy limited liability if something goes wrong with the business, in much the same way as shareholders in a company do. It will often, however, continue to be the usual practice where anyone who lends money to the LLP, for example, a bank will demand personal guarantees from the members, as is the current practice when dealing with shareholders in a company.

Section 7 describes a number of situations where an individual will lose the right to be involved in the affairs of the LLP as a member. Such individuals would include:

◆ Those persons who have left the LLP
◆ Those members who have died
◆ Those members who have become insolvent or who have had their estate sequestrated by creditors
◆ Those members who have granted a trust deed for the benefit of their creditors
◆ Those members who have transferred all or part of their share in the business to provide security for a debt

However, these individuals may be entitled to continue to receive a share of any profits that the business makes. It is important to stress that they are prevented from being involved in the day-to-day running of the business. Furthermore, the representatives, creditors, trustees in bankruptcy of individuals, trustees under a trust deed for the creditors or assignees of those members or ex-members of an LLP who are affected by Section 7 are forbidden to interfere in the management of the business.

 Key point: Every member of an LLP is to be regarded as an agent of the business and of the his fellow members and each member has a right to participate in the running of the LLP.

Changes in the membership of an LLP (Section 9)

Any changes in the membership of an LLP must be notified to the Registrar of Companies within 14 days. When there is any change in the name or residential address of a member, notice of this fact must be given to the registrar within 28 days. The Registrar does not require notice where individuals either become or cease to be designated members of the LLP. Failure to comply with these notice requirements is a criminal offence.

Taxation and National Insurance (Sections 10 to 13)

Where business owners have wanted to limit their personal liability in the past, they have normally set up companies and any profits made by those companies are subject to corporation tax. Dividends paid by the companies can then be taken as income of the shareholders. LLPs are taxed quite differently in that any profits are treated as the personal income of the members as if they had run their business as a partnership. There are no such things as shares in an LLP as would be the case with a company.

LLPs are required to produce and publish financial accounts which contain a level of detail equivalent to a similar sized limited company and they will have to submit accounts and an annual return to the Registrar of Companies each year. This legal requirement is far stricter than the rules which apply to traditional style partnerships.

Existing partnerships which wish to convert to an LLP will not necessarily be negatively affected in relation to their tax burden. This is likely to be the case provided there are no changes in membership or in the way in which the partnership operates. Obviously, the members of an existing partnership would be advised to seek advice on taxation matters before making any final decision to convert their business into an LLP.

 Key point: LLPs will have to publish financial accounts containing the same sorts of detail as a similarly sized limited company and these accounts and an annual return will have to be submitted to the Registrar of Companies.

Corporate bodies

The vast amount of corporate bodies or companies are business organisations where the members have agreed to limit their liability to an agreed amount of money. This money will either a) have already been paid to the company or b) will be paid to the creditors of the company should the business fail. Most limited companies are limited by shares, although on some occasions the company may be limited by guarantee. Even more rarely, the members of a company may be under the burden of unlimited liability as in sole trader businesses and partnerships. Limited companies may be either private or public in nature. The main legal provisions relating to limited companies are now to be found in the Companies Act 2006 which superseded the previous Acts of 1985 and 1989. It is possible for some companies to be founded by earlier legislation such as the Companies Act 1948 or the Industrial and Provident Societies Acts 1965 and 2002 (i.e. for the establishment of housing associations in Scotland). In other cases, companies or corporate bodies were founded by Royal Charter, for example, the University of Strathclyde in 1964, or even by Papal Bull, for example, the University of Glasgow in 1451. In modern times, however, the most common way of forming a company will be to meet the requirements of the Companies Act 2006. This is the single, biggest piece of legislation ever to be passed by the Westminster Parliament and runs to a staggering 1400 sections. A company is the most complicated type of business organisation recognised by Scots law. Unlike sole traders or partnerships, certain legal requirements have to be met before a company can be formed. The main legal requirement consists of registering the company with the Registrar of Companies. Until the new business has been registered, it is not regarded as a person recognised by law and, therefore, it cannot enter into contracts with third parties.

 Key point: A modern company is a business which has been incorporated in terms of the Companies Acts and has been registered with the Registrar of Companies.

Limited liability

The term 'limited' relates to the fact that the members of the company enjoy 'limited liability' status. This means that a member's individual liability is confined solely to the amount unpaid, if any, on their shareholding in the business. If, for example, a member has agreed to purchase £30,000 worth of shares in a company, should the company fail the creditors can only pursue the individual member for any money that he still owes for the shares. So, if the member still owed £15,000 for his shares he would have to pay this sum over to the company's creditors. Once this sum has been paid, however, the member cannot be held liable for any more of the company's debts – he has met all his obligations. If, on the other hand, the member has paid for all of his shares his liability is at an end and he cannot be forced to pay out over and above the sum that he agreed to pay for his shares. In companies limited by guarantee, the members agree to be liable to the company's creditors for an agreed sum should the business fail. Companies limited by guarantee are run as private companies. Clearly, no member of a company will want to have to pay money to the business's creditors, but limited liability is a very effective way by which the members can protect themselves. With unlimited liability, it will be remembered that the members of a business can be pursued to their last penny – in other words, they can lose everything. Companies where the members are under the burden of unlimited liability can only be set up as private companies. The members of a public company are spared the worry of unlimited liability. The huge advantage of limited liability is that it allows members of a company to at least reduce their losses to an agreed sum.

 Key point: Generally speaking, subject to a few exceptions, members of a company enjoy limited liability.

The separate legal personality of companies

All limited companies, whether private or public, must be registered under the Companies Act. This means that the company becomes an independent legal person in its own right, legally separate from its members and officers, a person recognised by the law, a person capable of having rights and taking on duties which the courts will recognise and enforce.

When a company with limited liability becomes a separate legal person this process is referred to as 'the veil of incorporation'.

It is worth remembering that separate corporate personality means that:

◆ The company can raise legal actions in its own right and be the subject of legal actions against it.
◆ The company has legal capacity and becomes a party to the contracts which it enters into.
◆ The company can exercise ownership over its property.
◆ The company continues to exist despite changes in its membership.
◆ The company's members enjoy limited liability.

The concept of separate corporate personality was forcefully recognised in the following case:

 Salomon v Salomon & Co Ltd (1897) Salomon owned a boot business which he sold to a company which he had formed, called Salomon & Co Ltd. There were seven members in the business: his wife, daughter and four sons who took one share each and Salomon himself who took 20,000 shares. The price paid by the company to Salomon was £30,000 but instead of giving him cash, the business gave him 20,000 fully paid £1 shares and £10,000 in secured debentures i.e. he lent the company £10,000. As a result of strikes within the boot trade, the company was wound up. The assets of the business amounted to just £6000 out of which £10,000 was owed to Salomon and £7000 to unsecured creditors. The unsecured creditors claimed that as Salomon & Co Ltd and Salomon were really the same person, he could not owe money to himself and that they should be paid their £7000 first.

Held: the House of Lords stated that Salomon was entitled to the £6000 and the unsecured creditors got nothing. The reason for this decision was that the company was to be regarded as a completely separate person in the eyes of the law from its members and its officers. The House of Lords thought it a completely irrelevant argument that Salomon was the leading shareholder in the company and that he could effectively control the destiny of the business.

The Salomon decision has been followed in other court cases described below:

 MacAura v Northern Assurance Co Ltd (1925) MacAura controlled a company where he was the majority shareholder. He was the owner of a forest and he decided to transfer ownership of this property to his company. MacAura had insured the forest against possible damage or loss, but when the company became its owner MacAura failed to transfer responsibility for insuring the property to the company. Unfortunately for MacAura, the forest later burned down and he tried to enforce the insurance policy. However, the insurance company argued that MacAura was no longer the owner of the forest and that he did not have an insurable interest. The person who did have an insurable interest in the forest and who should have protected it against loss or damage was the company, its new owner.

Held: although MacAura remained the majority shareholder in the company he had transferred ownership of the forest to the company. Therefore, the company should have insured the forest. It had not and the insurance company did not have to pay out. MacAura and the company were completely separate persons in the eyes of the law and should be treated as such.

 Lee v Lee's Air Farming Ltd (1961) Lee had set up a company where he was the owner of all but one of the shares. Lee was the company's only director and he had appointed himself as the company's chief pilot. Tragically, Lee was killed in an air accident while on company business and his wife later sued the company for compensation for his death.

Held: Mrs Lee was entitled to compensation from the company. Again, Lee and the company were to be regarded as completely separate people in the eyes of the law. One person (Lee) an employee of another person (the company) had been killed in the course of his employment and under current rules his widow was entitled to receive compensation from the company.

 Key point: A company is treated as a completely separate legal person in relation to its members.

The Salomon rule will be ignored in the following situations:

1   In a public company, there must be at least two members. If, for a period of more than six months, the company operates with a single member this individual becomes personally responsible for all debts of the business.

2   If a company was set up so that the members can carry out an illegal activity, they will not be allowed to benefit from the Salomon rule.

3   In times of war, a company that is controlled by citizens of an enemy state will not be allowed to continue trading for the duration of hostilities. Normally, the law is not interested in the nationalities of individual members, but in times of war this becomes a very important issue.

4   Company officers, for example directors and company secretaries, will have to be especially careful when signing cheques in their personal capacity and where third parties will not be aware that they are doing so on behalf of the company. Additionally, the company officer can make an error when he writes the name of the company on a cheque that will be given to the third party. In both situations, the company officer will be personally responsible to the third party if the company does not meet the debt that the cheque represents.

 Key point: The concept of separate corporate personality will sometimes be ignored and this is known as 'lifting the veil of incorporation'.

Types of companies

Four types of company can be incorporated in the United Kingdom. These are:

1   Private companies limited by shares – this type of business issues shares and its members are said to enjoy limited liability in the event of the company's insolvency. The company's shares, however, are not permitted to be offered for sale to the public. Volkswagen Group United Kingdom Limited is an example of a famous private company limited by shares which is currently operating in the UK.

2   Private companies limited by guarantee – no share capital can be issued by this type of business **(Section 5 of the Companies Act 2006)**. The members agree the extent of their liability when they first join the company and such liability is said to be limited because when they pay the agreed sum to the company's creditors in the event of the business becoming insolvent that is the end of the matter for them. Companies which operate with these kinds of arrangements are often incorporated to pursue a range of charitable or social objectives e.g. Oxfam or university student unions or they can simply be not for profit organisations e.g. Network Rail.

3   Private companies which are unlimited – this type of corporate body is quite rare in practice and is often compared to partnership. It can issue shares to its members if it wishes, but there is no obligation on its part to do so. The members operate under the burden of unlimited liability in the event of the company's insolvency. The benefits of this type of business organisation are secrecy in its financial affairs (there is no need to file annual accounts) and there is a very small risk of insolvency. In the United Kingdom, the Equitable Life Assurance Society was incorporated as an unlimited company and so was the clothing store C&A before it closed its British stores in 2000.

4   Public companies limited by shares – like private limited companies, these types of corporate body issue share capital owned by its members who enjoy limited liability. Unlike private companies, however, a public limited company may offer its shares for sale to the public and its shares can be publicly traded on the stock exchange. Celtic and Rangers Football Clubs are both examples of prominent Scottish public limited companies.

In practice, it is much more common to encounter private companies limited by shares and public limited companies in the business world and we shall, therefore, concentrate on these two types of corporate body.

The main characteristics of private and public limited companies

The main characteristics of a private limited company are:

1   Company name must end in 'limited' or 'ltd'

2   The articles of association of a private limited company may provide for a right of pre-emption so that when a member wishes to sell or to transfer ownership of his shares he must first offer them to existing members

3   There is no minimum capital requirement

4   The shares in a private limited company cannot be traded or listed on the stock exchange

5   Only one director is required, but this individual must be at least 16 years of age

6   A private company limited by shares or by guarantee need only have one member

7   There is no upper age limit for directors

8   No requirement to hold an Annual General Meeting of the members unless the Articles of Association insist on this event being held. In any case, the Articles of Association can always be changed by the members via a special resolution

9 There is no longer any need to have a Company Secretary

10 Audited accounts must be produced within nine months of the year end

11 Trading can start as soon as a Certificate of Incorporation is obtained

A private company limited by shares and an unlimited company with a share capital may re-register as a public limited company (PLC). A private company must pass a special resolution to allow it to become registered as a public limited company. A copy of the members' special resolution and the appropriate application form must be lodged with the Registrar of Companies in order to give legal effect to this change.

The main characteristics of a public limited company are:

1 The company name must end in 'public limited company' or 'plc'

2 Members must be free to transfer their shares as they please

3 A public company must have minimum issued share capital of at least £50,000 or 65,600 Euros (previously the minimum share capital had to be in Sterling)

4 Shares can be listed on the stock exchange and can be traded

5 There must be at least two directors

6 There is a continuing requirement to have a Company Secretary

7 There must be at least two members

8 Directors are no longer required to retire when they reach the age of 70 (under the previous Companies Act of 1985 this was the case), but there is now a minimum age requirement of 16

9 An Annual General Meeting of the shareholders must be held

10 Audited accounts must be produced within seven months of the year end

11 After incorporation, a 'trading certificate' issued by the Registrar of Companies no longer has to be in the form of a statutory declaration

The members of public limited company can agree (by passing a special resolution) to convert the business into a private limited company. A copy of this resolution and the appropriate application form must be sent to the Registrar of Companies so that the change in the legal status of the business can be publicly registered at Companies House.

 Key point: Limited companies and public limited companies have different characteristics.

Formation of a company

To incorporate a company in the United Kingdom, the following documents, together with the current registration fee, must be sent to the Registrar of Companies:

◆ Forms 10 and 12
◆ The articles of association
◆ The memorandum of association

The articles of association

The articles of association regulate the internal management of the company and deal with issues such as the appointment and removal of directors, the conduct of meetings of the members and new share issues. Companies do not have to go to the expense of hiring a company lawyer to draw up personalised articles of association. In terms of Section 18 of the Companies Act 2006, a company **must** have articles of association.

A company's articles, which are delivered or intimated to the Registrar of Companies, must be signed by each subscriber in front of a witness who must attest the signature.

From 1 October 2009, the articles of association will be the sole constitutional document for companies (Section 17: Companies Act 2006) – there will be no need for a separate memorandum of association. Under the previous legislation (Companies Act 1985), there were model articles of association known as Tables A to F.

The Companies (Tables A–F) Regulations 1985 (as amended) provided model articles of association. In other words, members of the company did not have to go to the expense and trouble of drawing up a memorandum because the 1985 Regulations already provided completed examples ready for immediate use. The members would simply select the most appropriate Memorandum of Association depending on the type of company, for example, a public limited company or a company limited by guarantee. The old Table A contained a memorandum of association which was suitable for both a public limited company and a private company. Many companies which have been set up prior to the Companies Act 2006 will continue to the use the old model memoranda in Tables A–F.

From 1 October 2009, the older Tables A–F will no longer be applicable for new companies being incorporated in the United Kingdom and will be replaced by three sets of model articles of association. These are:

- Model articles for companies limited by shares
- Model articles for companies limited by guarantee
- Model articles for public companies

Examples of all three model articles of association can be found on the Introductory **www** Scots Law website.

Typical clauses which appear in the articles of association include:

- The process by which changes can be made to the articles of association
- Rules about share capital and changes which affect shareholders' rights
- Alteration of share capital
- Notice of general meetings and procedure at these meetings
- Voting powers of members
- Number, remuneration, qualifications, duties, rotation and removal of directors
- Appointment of directors
- Use of the company seal
- Declaration and payment of dividends
- Keeping of accounts and auditing procedures
- Borrowing powers

 Key point: According to Section 18 of the Companies Act 2006, a company must register articles of association.

The Memorandum of Association

In terms of Section 8 of the Companies Act 2006, the **memorandum of association** is now simply a statement (in the prescribed form) that the signatories (or subscribers) wish to form a company in terms of the Act and such individuals agree to become members of the company and, in the case of a company that is to have a share capital, to take at least one share each.

Previously, the memorandum of association contained the name of the company, the location of the registered office and the company's objectives. The memorandum was regarded as the principal source of information for third parties dealing with the company and was, therefore, a document of considerable legal importance.

This information will now be contained in an application for registration of the company (known as a Form 10) which is submitted to the Registrar together with the memorandum (Section 9 of the Companies Act 2006). There is now no requirement for a company to state its objects or aims as was previously the case.

The memorandum, which is delivered to the Registrar of Companies, must be signed by each subscriber in front of a witness who must attest the signature.

 Key point: A memorandum of association now simply states that the signatories wish to form a company.

Form 10

Form 10 provides details of the first directors, the first secretary and the address of the registered office. Each director must give his or her name, address, date of birth, occupation and details of other directorships held within the last five years. Each officer appointed and each subscriber (or their agent) must sign and date the form.

Form 10 will contain the following information:

1 The company name – Any name can be chosen for the business as long as the last word is "limited", "ltd" or "plc". A register of names is maintained by the Registrar of Companies at Companies House and names of companies must comply with the requirements of Sections 1200–1208 of the Companies Act 2006 (these rules supersede the rules previously contained in the Business Names Act 1985).

In **Exxon v Exxon Insurance Consultants (1972)** an insurance company attempted to use the name Exxon. The Standard Oil Company which traded under the internationally recognised name of Exxon objected to this because it would suggest to many people that the insurance company was connected to Standard Oil when this was not the case. The oil company raised a successful legal action which prevented the insurance company from using the name Exxon.

As a result of Section 69 of the Companies Act 2006, a third party can object to the attempted use of a new company name on the ground of 'opportunistic registration'. An individual can raise an allegation of 'opportunistic registration' against a new company in the following circumstances:

◆ if the new company's name is identical to that of an existing company in which the individual who has made the complaint enjoys goodwill in the older, established business

◆ if the new company's name is so similar that its continued use in the United Kingdom would cause a belief to arise that there is a connection between the new business and the older, established business.

In terms of Sections 70–73 of the Companies Act 2006, the Secretary of State has appointed a number of Adjudicators who sit on the Company Names Tribunal (which operates under the jurisdiction of the UK Intellectual Property Office) and these individuals will hear and decide any challenges to the continued use of a particular name by a new company. Section 73 gives the adjudicators the right to order the company to change its name.

2   The location of the registered office – every company must have a registered office as soon as it commences trading or within 14 days of its incorporation, whichever is earlier. The memorandum must state whether the registered office is in Scotland; England and Wales (the office can be either country) or just Wales.

3   The limitation of liability statement (appropriate to PLCs and companies limited by shares) – this is a statement to confirm that the liability of the members is limited.

4   The capital of the company – this information states the amount of nominal or authorised share capital and its division into shares of a fixed amount.

5   A public limited company statement – if the company is to be a PLC, this is a statement by the members to this effect.

Since the earlier reforms introduced by the Companies Act 1989 and the most recent reforms contained in the Companies Act 2006, there is no longer any need for a company to have a detailed and exhaustive objects clause. In any case, as a result of the reforms contained in the Companies Act 2006, from 1 October 2009, there will no longer be any need for a company to state publicly what its objects are. It will simply be assumed that a company incorporated in the United Kingdom after 1 October 2009 is a general commercial company involved in trade or business whatsoever.

Form 12 is a statutory declaration of compliance with all the legal requirements relating to the incorporation of a company. It must be signed by a solicitor who is forming the company, or by one of the people named as a director or company secretary on Form 10. It must be signed in the presence of a commissioner for oaths, a notary public, a justice of the peace or a solicitor.

The Certificate of Incorporation

If the Registrar of Companies is satisfied with the documents provided for incorporating a company, they will register these documents at Companies House (Section 14: Companies Act 2006).

Under Section 15 of the Companies Act 2006, the certificate of incorporation is issued by the Registrar of Companies. According to Section 16 of the Act, this is conclusive proof that the company has met the statutory requirements and the date on the certificate indicates the point at which the company became a corporate body with separate legal personality.

Until the company is incorporated, it is not a legally recognised person (see **Kelner v Baxter (1866)** and **Tinnevelly Sugar Refining Co v Mirrlees, Watson & Yaryan Co Ltd (1894)** discussed earlier in the Chapter) and it, therefore, cannot assume any rights or duties.

Key point: A company does not have legal status until the certificate of incorporation is issued by the registrar.

The objects of a company

The old style of objects clause (widely used from Victorian times onwards) was used to define the purposes for which the company had been incorporated or established. The presence of such a clause in a company's memorandum of association was previously a strict requirement of law. Prior to the Companies Act 1989, if a company was engaged in any activities or contracts not covered by the objects clause then these contracts were considered *ultra vires* i.e. outwith the powers of the company and could not be enforced by either the third party or the company. The *ultra vires* rule was originally established to protect potential and existing members of a company. Companies were forced to list all of their business activities and they were not allowed to become involved in any business transaction which was not on the list. This meant that members could control the directors and prevent them from entering into contracts which might be regarded as risky in some way. More basically, all the members knew exactly what line of business the company was in and as long as the company confined itself to these activities everyone in theory was happy. The 1989 Act, permitted companies to state that its objects were to carry on a business as a 'general commercial company' meaning that it can be involved in any trade or business whatsoever. This means that *ultra vires* has become an internal matter for most companies. Directors and officers of the company can still be sued in their personal capacity if they carry out any act or enter into any transaction which strictly speaking would be forbidden by the company's objects clause. Third parties, however, dealing with the company need not worry that the contract is in any way unauthorised. Such a contract can be enforced against the company by the third party and now the third party cannot use the ultra vires rule to escape a contract with the company.

 Key point: The contents of a company's object clause is no longer particularly important for outsiders dealing with the company.

The legal consequences of the *ultra vires* rule

The harshness of the old *ultra vires* rule can be seen in the following case:

 Ashbury Railway Carriage & Iron Co *v* Riche (1875) the company was founded for the purposes (stated in the memorandum of association) of making and selling railway wagons and other railway plant and carrying on the business of mechanical engineers and general contractors. The company bought a concession for the construction of a railway system in Belgium and entered into an agreement whereby Messrs Riche were to construct the railway line. Riche began the work and the company paid over certain sums of money in connection with the work. The Ashbury company later ran into financial difficulties and the shareholders wished the directors to take over responsibility for the project in their personal capacities. The shareholders no longer wished to become personally liable for the project. The directors thereupon repudiated the contract on behalf of the company and Riche sued for breach of contract.

Held: the directors were entitled to do this because according to the company's objects clause the contract to construct a railway was ultra vires and therefore void. On examination of the objects clause, the company had power to supply materials for the building of railways, but had no power to engage in the actual construction of them. Furthermore, in those days, the law did not allow a company to approve the ultra vires acts of its agents. Nowadays, the company would pass a special resolution of the members to approve an action which was, strictly speaking, *ultra vires.*

Reform of the *ultra vires* rule

From the late 1980s to the present day, successive UK Parliaments have introduced legislative provisions with the specific intention of reforming and severely limiting the operation of the *ultra vires rule.*

1. The Companies Act 1989

Section 3A of the previous Companies Act of 1985 permitted a company to carry on business as a general commercial company in any trade or business whatsoever. This change came about due to provisions in the Companies Act 1989. From 1991 onwards (when the reforms came into force), no act done by a company could be questioned due to the fact that it was beyond its legal capacity as stated in its memorandum of association. This meant that a person dealing with a company did not have to check to see whether there are any limits on the company's capacity. Practically speaking, all contracts were enforceable against the company. This effective abolition of the *ultra vires rule* did not allow directors to escape liability in situations where they have acted beyond the authority given to them by the company.

2. The Companies Act 2006

The Companies Act 2006 has gone further and removes the need to have an objects clause in the company's memorandum. Any limits on the powers of the directors or other agents of the company will now be addressed in the Articles of Association. This means that any director or company officer breaching their authority will be potentially answerable and liable to the members of the company, but critically such an unauthorised act cannot be challenged in terms of the old *ultra vires* rule.

 Key point: To all intents and purposes, the old *ultra vires* rule has become an irrelevance for outsiders dealing with the company.

The legal effect of a company's constitution

Previously, the legal effect of the memorandum of association and the articles of association (a company's constitutional documents) was spelt out in Section 14 of the Companies Act 1985. These two documents (taken together) represented two binding contractual agreements:

1 between the individual members of the company as a general body; and

2 between all members and the company.

A company's constitution is now to be found in the articles of association (**Section 17: Companies Act 2006**).

According to **Section 33** of the Companies Act 2006, the provisions of a company's constitution bind the company and its members as if it were a covenant i.e. a contract and the members must observe these provisions. In other words, the members and the company are legally bound to each other as much as the parties would be in any normal contractual relationship. Furthermore, any money owed to the company by a member in terms of the Constitution is to be treated as a debt owed by that member to the company.

Section 33 of the Companies Act 2006 has, therefore, a number of consequences for members of a company:

1 If a member feels that one of his membership rights that he enjoys under the Constitution has been ignored or abused by the company, he can raise a legal action against the company and force it to recognise these rights.

 Wood v Odessa Waterworks Co (1889) the Articles stated that all dividends payable to shareholders of the company must be paid in cash. The company tried to get round this rule by passing a resolution which would have prevented the shareholders from receiving the dividend in cash.

Held: the shareholders were entitled to use the Articles to force the company to pay the dividend in cash.

2 On the other hand, however, the company can raise a legal action against members of the company who breach the rules regulating membership as laid out in the Constitution.

 Hickman v Kent or Romney Marsh Sheep Breeders' Association (1915) a member took his dispute with the company to the courts. Under the rules contained in the Articles, the members had all agreed to resolve any dispute with the company under an internal arbitration procedure.

Held: the court action was halted and the member was forced to use the internal arbitration procedure to resolve his dispute with the company.

3 The members can sue one another for breach of the Constitution.

 Rayfield v Hands (1960) company members were obliged under the Articles to offer their shares to the directors if they wished to sell or transfer ownership of their shares. The directors were supposed to give members wishing to sell their shares a fair price for them. However, this rule in the Articles meant that members were prevented from selling their shares to outsiders. The directors refused to buy the member's shares thus making it impossible for him to leave the company. He raised a legal action against the directors.

Held: as a result of the Articles, the directors had no choice but to buy the shares from the member at a fair price determined by the court.

4 The rights given to members under the Constitution cannot be enforced by non-members or where the member is effectively acting as an outsider.

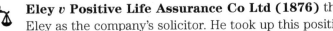 **Eley v Positive Life Assurance Co Ltd (1876)** the Articles appointed Eley as the company's solicitor. He took up this position and he bought

shares in the company. Some time later, the company decided to dispense with his services as solicitor. Eley claimed that his rights as a member had been abused as a result of his dismissal.

Held: Eley's dismissal did not affect his rights as a member of the company. He would continue to enjoy his rights and any benefits which membership of the company involved. The contract of employment between Eley and the company was in no way connected to his role as a member of the company.

Key point: A company's constitution has the legal status of a covenant between the company and its members and between the members themselves.

The Board of Directors and the members of the company

The Board of Directors is the primary management organ of the company and, therefore, it will have responsibility for the day to day running of the company's affairs. Not all of the directors (some of whom will be classed as non-executive members of the Board) will exercise management powers as this will be the preserve of the company's Chief Executive and executive directors e.g. the Finance Director.

It is important to note that directors are agents of the company itself and they are not present on the Board to represent individual members of the company or groups within the organisation. Like any other agents, directors must have regard to the powers or authority conferred upon them by the company. Such authority will now be derived from the company's Articles of Association. An interesting example of directors exceeding the authority conferred upon them by the company can be seen in the following case:

 Guinness plc v Saunders & Another (1990) Thomas Ward, an American lawyer, was a director of Guinness plc during its successful attempt to launch a friendly takeover of the Edinburgh based company, United Distillers plc. This was a very lucrative takeover and would have huge financial benefits for Guinness plc. For services rendered to Guinness plc during this time, Ward received a payment of £5.2 million from the company. This secret or undisclosed payment to Ward was approved by a small committee of directors drawn from the Guinness Board (chaired by Ernest Saunders). The committee (which was referred to as the Guinness War Cabinet) had not sought approval for this payment from the full Board of Directors. The company's Articles of Association, however, quite clearly stated that payments of this type had to receive authorisation from the Board of Directors of Guinness plc, not a mere committee. The company sought legal action to recover the payment from Ward. He, in turn, attempted to rely upon Section 727 of the Companies Act 1985 which provided a defence to directors and officers of a company that they had acted honestly and reasonably in their dealings. Successful reliance on this defence would have permitted Ward to retain the sum of £5.2 million and he would have avoided any liability to Guinness plc.

Held: by the House of Lords that the committee of Guiness plc directors had no authority to make such a payment to Ward and he would have to repay this sum to the company. In 1993, Ward was finally exonerated of all criminal charges that he had stolen the money from Guinness plc. This, of course, did not effect his civil liability to the company and his obligation to account for the money that he had received.

Although, as we shall see the consequences of a director exceeding his or her authority are not now nearly so dire for the company (see **Ashbury Railway Carriage & Iron Co v Riche (1875)** discussed above), any individual director guilty of a breach of authority will be personally liable to the company in damages.

The membership of the company (whether the ordinary rank and file shareholders or the big institutional shareholders) can make its views known to the Board through the medium of the general meeting of the company (whether these are scheduled meetings or whether they are called in extraordinary circumstances within the required notice periods laid down by law). Company policy or procedures can be changed by a vote or a resolution of the membership in a general meeting. It is not necessary for members to attend the general meeting of the company in person and there was the option of casting a vote by proxy. In theory, the directors are answerable to the members of the company for decisions made by them through the medium of the general meeting.

The members can pass the following resolutions:

1   Ordinary resolutions (which require a simple majority of those attending a meeting or participating in a vote) and tend to involve less contentious issues;

2   Special resolutions e.g. for changes to the articles of association which depend on securing 75% of the votes of the members attending a general meeting or participating in such a vote; and

3   Extraordinary resolutions e.g. to wind up a company voluntarily in the event of its insolvency, again, requires the securing of 75% of the votes of the members attending a general meeting or participating in such a vote

It should be emphasised, however, that the articles of association will determine who has the right to participate in important decisions affecting the company. It may indeed be the case that all the members may be given a right to vote in certain matters, but in other situations, the right to vote may be restricted to certain classes of members e.g. preference shareholders.

 Key point: The Board of Directors and the members are supposed to act in concert in order to run the company.

A shareholder democracy?

Although the Companies Act 2006 has removed the former requirement for a private company to hold an Annual General Meeting, the aim of the new legislation (theoretically) is to improve the participation of the members in the affairs of the company. Nowadays, modern communications have made it much easier for the members to communicate with the directors and these methods are much more effective than gathering for the annual general meeting of the company in some

Edinburgh or London hotel. In the past, lip service was always paid to the notion that the members of a company were participating in a shareholder democracy. This may have been a noble idea, but the reality was always different in that big institutional shareholders (banks) and individual shareholders with large stakes in the business were able to thwart the designs of the smaller members of the company. Sections 459–461 of the Companies Act 1985 did provide some protection for minority groups in that any decision taken by the majority had to be for the benefit of the company as a whole.

The unwillingness of the ordinary rank and file membership to challenge decisions of the Board was also a major impediment to the establishment of the utopian ideal of a shareholder democracy and it remains to be seen whether the reforms introduced by the Companies Act 2006 will have the desired effect.

Directors' Duties

Generally speaking, the Companies Act 2006 should ensure that the regulation of directors is, in theory, much tougher. In the past, the conduct of directors (except in cases of blatant fraud) was not strictly regulated. Admittedly, the courts did develop general rules that such individuals had to act in good faith and exercise skill and care when they were dealing with the company's business. However, this regulatory regime proved to be unsatisfactory and piecemeal. Basically, anyone could be a company director and there was no requirement for such individuals to hold professional qualifications in the way that a solicitor or an accountant would be required to possess.

General duties of directors

There are several general duties imposed on directors by the Companies Act 2006. These are:

- ◆ Duty to act within the powers conferred upon them (Section 171)
- ◆ Duty to promote the success of the company (Section 172)
- ◆ Duty to exercise independent judgment (Section 173)
- ◆ Duty to exercise reasonable care, skill and diligence (Section 174)
- ◆ Duty to avoid conflicts of interest (Section 175)
- ◆ Duty not to accept benefits from third parties (Section 176)
- ◆ Duty to declare interest in proposed transaction or arrangement (177)

A very good example of the historical weakness of the law in this area is the decision in the **Marquis of Bute's Case (1892)**. The Marquis of Bute became the President of the Cardiff Savings Bank when his father, the previous holder of the office, died. The striking thing about this appointment was that the Marquis was then a mere six months old. He was not a particularly diligent or active officer of the company and this was evidenced by the fact that he attended just one board meeting in 38 years of his having held the office of President. Later, the bank got into legal difficulties owing to a lack of proper control in relation to certain loans which had been approved. Despite the fact that the Marquis was President of the bank and should have been aware of what was going on, Mr Justice Stirling held that he was not liable for certain irregular lending practices that were common within the company. In today's more rigorous climate of regulation, the Marquis would doubtless be in breach of Sections 172, 173 and 174 of the Companies Act 2006.

We have also seen the serious legal consequences when a small group of directors operates outwith the control of the main Board of Directors as in **Guinness plc v Saunders and Another (1990)**. Such a decision of the so called War Cabinet of Guinness plc to remunerate Thomas Ward to the tune of £5.2 million would now arguably constitute breaches of Sections 171 and 175 of the Companies Act 2006.

 Key point: The Companies Act 2006 has tightened the law regulating director's duties.

The avoidance of conflicts of interest by directors

Section 175 of the Companies Act 2006 imposes a general duty on directors to avoid conflicts of interest. Clearly, a director's first loyalty should be to the company which s/he serves and they should not be using their office to seek personal advantage or benefit as Thomas Ward arguably did when accepting a payment of £5.2 million from Guinness plc which had not been authorised by the company's full Board of Directors as required by the Articles of Association (see **Guinness plc v Saunders and Another (1990)**).

 In **Industrial Development Consultants Limited v Cooley (1972)**, Cooley, the managing director of the company, obtained a benefit deceitfully. Cooley had to account for this benefit and, although the company itself would not have gained from the contract which Cooley had entered into with the Eastern Gas Board, he was still in breach of his fiduciary duty as a director. In terms of the Companies Act 2006, Cooley would potentially be in breach of Sections 172, 175, 176 and 177.

Sections 176 and 177 consolidate the general duty of a director to avoid conflicts of interest. Directors must not accept benefits e.g. gifts or hospitality from a third party (Section 176) and they are duty bound to declare any interest relating to a proposed transaction or arrangement which the company is about to enter with a third party (Section 177).

Even after directors have disclosed any interest in a potential transaction which the company is going to enter with a third party, the members must give their consent to such an arrangement before it can proceed (Section 180(1) to (3) and (4)(b)).

Hopefully, the new controls on directors will mean that such individuals will be held more easily to account by the company and its members which they are supposed to be serving.

Company donations for political purposes and activities

An area of controversy in company law over many years has been the practice whereby corporate bodies have used money to fund the activities of certain political parties or organisations. In the United Kingdom, it was often claimed by those (mainly) on the left of the political spectrum that the British Conservative and Unionist Party was a net beneficiary of donations from a host of domestic and foreign corporations. Critics have often argued that these corporations were pursuing a policy of naked self-interest in making regular donations to Conservative Party coffers given the overwhelmingly pro-business nature of the free market reforms enthusiastically introduced by the Thatcher and Major Governments (1979-

97). In the interests of political balance, however, it be must be remarked that the Labour Government, which came to power in May 1997, has also benefited from generous donations from corporate donors since it ditched its commitment to old style socialism in the 1990s and embraced more business friendly policies.

In any case, it was often pointed out that criticism from the left was rather rich because the Labour Party could not function without the financial support of the Trade Unions (admittedly, ordinary members of a union could, by law, opt out of paying the political levy which was included in their membership dues).

One valid criticism that can be levelled against the practice of donations to political parties is that the rank and file of company members were often never asked if they were in favour. Part 14 of the Companies Act 2006 now attempts to address this issue.

Sections 362–379 of the Act place an obligation on a company that it must seek authorisation from its members before it can make a donation to a political party, organisation or candidate which is greater than the sum of £5,000 in any given year. This rule equally applies to candidates who are supported by political parties or organisations and those candidates who are standing for public office independently of any party political affiliation. Public office would cover members of the Westminster, Scottish and European Parliaments, the London, Northern Irish and Welsh Assemblies and local and regional authority councillors.

Furthermore, a company must also obtain authority from its members before it uses funds in relation to political activities, for example, paying for advertisements supporting political parties or organisations or candidates prior to and during an election.

The rules relating to the regulation of political donations were introduced in two stages:

♦ In the mainland United Kingdom, the reforms relating to funding and donations in respect political parties, organisations and candidates were brought in on 1 October 2007 (in Northern Ireland, these reforms were introduced on 1 November 2007); and

♦ Across the United Kingdom and Northern Ireland as a whole, the reforms were introduced to cover independent candidates from 1 October 2008.

 Key point: The law governing donations to political parties by companies has, in theory, been tightened by the Companies Act 2006.

Promoters of companies

Someone or a group of people will often be required to set up a company and comply with all the necessary registration procedures. Practical steps will have to be taken by such an individual or individuals such as buying or leasing property in order to have premises for a registered office, entering into contracts with third parties in order to buy or lease equipment that will be used by the new company or entering into contracts of employment with prospective employees of the new business. Clearly, it would not make good business sense to wait until all the legal requirements of the registration process had been complied with before attending to these important matters. The sooner everything is in place, the sooner the new business can begin to trade and, hopefully, begin to make profits for its members.

A person who takes care of these matters before the company is formed is referred to as a promoter. In **Twycross v Grant (1877)**, a promoter was defined as someone who undertakes to form a company with reference to a given project, and to set it going, and who takes the necessary steps to accomplish that purpose. A promoter of the company is not an agent of the company. In **Tinnevelly Sugar Refining Co v Mirrlees, Watson & Yaryan Co Ltd (1894)** Darley & Butler claimed to be acting on behalf of a company called Tinnevelly. Tinnevelly, however, did not exist when Darley & Butler entered into the contract for machinery supposedly on its behalf. Therefore, Tinnevelly was not a party to the contract with Mirrlees because Darley & Butler could not have been acting as agents for a principal that did not yet exist. Darley & Butler had the right to sue Mirrlees, but Tinnevelly had no such right.

'A contract that purports to be made by or on behalf of a company at a time when the company has not been formed has effect, subject to any agreement to the contrary, as one made with the person purporting to act for the company or as agent for it, and he is personally liable on the contract accordingly.'

 Key point: A promoter is someone who undertakes to form a company with reference to a given project and takes the necessary steps to achieve this aim.

A contract that purports to be made by or on behalf of a company at a time when the company has not been formed has effect, subect to any agreement to the contrary, as one made with the person purporting to act for the company or as agent for it, and he is personally liable on the contract accordingly.

Promoters are not to be regarded as agents of the as yet to be formed company and will be personally liable in relation to any pre-incorporation contracts which they have entered. As a promoter is not an agent of the new company, he has no right to be paid for his services. In reality, many promoters are likely to be directors or members of the new company and, therefore, they have an interest in setting the company up. In any case, the new board of directors may have powers in the Articles of Association to pay the promoter or reimburse him for his expenses.

The downside of being a promoter is that they are personally responsible for any contracts that they enter into with third parties. The company cannot sue or be sued in relation to contracts that were formed before it was registered. This is a dangerous situation for the promoter because it means that the company need not reimburse him for any expenses which result from entering into contracts with third parties. A promoter is regarded as having a fiduciary relationship with the as yet non-existent company. This means that the promoter cannot use his position to make a profit unless the directors or members of the new company are aware of this and are comfortable with this situation. This means that a promoter will have to account for everything that he has done in his role. It is not beyond the realms of possibility that the new board of directors or members might sue a promoter to regain any secret profit that he has made from his activities.

A promoter can always try to escape personal liability for contracts with third parties by insisting that third parties agree not to sue him in the event that the company fails to honour the contract once it has been registered. Alternatively, a promoter may insist that the contracts will only take effect when the new company is legally recognised and that such a contract will be between the new company and the third party.

 Key point: A promoter is not an agent but they still own fiduciary duties to the new business of the company.

Summary

- No business organisation, no matter its shape or size, can operate without the assistance of agents.

- An agent is the legal representative of someone called the principal and the principal authorises the agent to act on his behalf in dealings with third parties.

- The agent, therefore, negotiates and enters contractual agreements on behalf of the principal with third parties. When the third party deals with the agent it is as if he is dealing directly with the principal.

- The agent is not a party to the contract between the principal and the third party – he merely makes this business transaction occur.

- An agent is appointed in the first place because it is either physically impossible for the principal to carry out all the tasks demanded by his business or he possesses skills and expertise to carry out a particular job.

- The agency relationship is a contractual agreement.

- Both the principal and the agent have rights as well as duties under the agreement.

- One of the most important features of agency is that an agent expects to be paid for carrying out tasks on the principal's behalf.

- The agency relationship can be created in a number of ways – by express contract, implied by the conduct of the parties or by law, by holding out, by ratification or by necessity.

- Agency is a fiduciary relationship and this means that the agent must show that he can be trusted by the principal and he must do this by always acting in good faith.

- The agent's ability to bind his principal into a contract with a third party depends on the extent of his authority.

- There are two types of authority that an agent can possess – actual or ostensible.

- Actual authority is the authority which the agent really possesses whether expressly or impliedly. If he stays within his actual authority, the agent will bind the principal into a contract with the third party.

- Ostensible authority is the authority which a third party mistakenly assumes that the agent possesses. This mistaken belief is caused by the principal and, because of this, the third party will be able to enforce the contract against the him.

- Where the agent has no authority and the third party either knows this or should be aware of this, the principal will not be bound in contract.

- The Commercial Agents (Council Directive) Regulations 1993 are unusual because, unlike the common law rules, they single out a particular group of agents for protection and codify the rights and duties of the parties.

- The agency relationship, like any contract, can be terminated in a number of different ways. This can be done by mutual agreement, the principal withdrawing the agent's authority, the agent withdrawing from the relationship, the bankruptcy of the principal, the death or insanity or the expiry of a fixed term contract.

- Scots law recognises a variety of business organisations, for example, sole traders, partnerships, limited partnerships, limited liability partnerships, private limited companies, public limited companies and unlimited companies.

- It is very important to be able to differentiate between types of business because they are all governed by different rules.

- Another important factor in setting up a business is the kind of liability that those individuals who are responsible for running it will face should the business fail.

- Some businesses like sole traders and partnerships operate under unlimited liability. This means that a sole trader or partners in a firm could lose everything if the business collapses.

- Alternatively, other businesses like limited liability partnerships and corporate bodies enjoy limited liability. Should the business fail, the members will only be liable for business debts up to a limit which they have already agreed amongst themselves.

- Some types of business organisation are relatively informal, for example, sole traders and partnerships can be set up immediately – there are no formal requirements.

- Other types of business organisations, however, do have to be registered, for example, companies, limited liability partnerships and limited partnerships.

- Some businesses have a completely separate legal personality from that of their members, for example, partnerships, companies, limited liability partnerships and limited partnerships.

Test your knowledge

Short answer questions, exam standard essay-style questions and case-studies.

1 a) Describe the various ways in which an agency relationship can be established.

Examine both case studies carefully:

⚖ **b) i)** Katrina has written to several of her customers informing them that Beverley is acting as her agent. Katrina also publicises this information about Beverley in a number of newspaper adverts. Jocelyn entered into a contract with Beverley in order to purchase some goods. Jocelyn had always believed that Beverley was acting as Katrina's agent. Before the goods were delivered to Jocelyn, Beverley is declared bankrupt and her creditors seize all the goods that are currently stored in her warehouse. Jocelyn now turns to Katrina and demands that she honour the contract. Katrina is now denying that she ever appointed Beverley to act for her.

⚖ **ii)** Jonathan appointed Robert to act as his agent in relation to the purchase of a house. The owners of the house are also selling an adjoining piece of land, but Jonathan has not given Robert any instructions to purchase this land. However, Robert goes ahead in any case and purchases both the house and the land. When informed about this turn of events by the seller's agent, Jonathan makes the following statement: 'He is my agent after all and I'll just have to accept everything that he has done on my behalf.' Jonathan later attempts to withdraw from the sale involving the land.

Using previously decided cases and principles from the law of agency, advise the parties in each of the case studies outlined above.

2 a) The agency relationship is characterised by its contractual nature and, accordingly, both the principal and the agent have rights as well as duties.

Outline the rights and duties of the principal and the agent.

⚖ **b)** Mitchell owns a business which specialises in finding suitable tenants for residential properties in Glasgow and Edinburgh. One client has approached Mitchell and asked him to find a tenant to occupy her flat in Glasgow's West End. This client is being sent on a work placement by her employers to Canada and she will be out of the country for the next nine months. Mitchell has found a tenant for the property and the lease has been duly signed. A week later, however, Mitchell receives a telephone call from his client informing him that her work placement in Canada has fallen through and, consequently, she no longer wishes to lease the property out for the agreed nine-month period. Mitchell has to inform the tenant of this decision by his client and the tenant promptly sues Mitchell for breach of contract. To add insult to injury, Mitchell's client is now refusing to pay him for his efforts on her behalf.

What advice would you give Mitchell?

3 a) What is the difference between an agent's actual and ostensible authority?

⚖ **b)** Pamela, Laura and Lindsey-Anne are members of a partnership. According to the partnership agreement, Pamela and Laura have the authority to sign cheques on the firm's behalf. One day, Lindsey-Anne is purchasing a new computer and she uses a partnership cheque to pay for the goods. The firm does a great deal of business with the computer store and its manager is well aware that Lindsey-Anne is a partner in the firm. The bank later dishonours the cheque and the store sues the firm for payment.

What is the legal position?

4 a) What is the difference between an agent and a mandatary?

⚖ **b)** Michelle has just passed her driving test and she is looking for a suitably reliable second-hand car. Michelle does not feel confident enough to select a car without first consulting a more experienced driver. Michelle has a friend, Joe, who although not a qualified car mechanic does have some knowledge about cars. Joe is prepared to accompany her around various motor dealers and give her the benefit of his advice. After going round various dealerships, Michelle has seen a car that she really likes. Joe is also of the opinion that the vehicle is just right for Michelle and he encourages her to purchase it. Joe did notice that one of the car's doors had been repaired, but he did not think that this was an issue worth raising with the dealer. In fact,

Michelle specifically asked Joe whether he thought that the car had been ever been involved in an accident to which he replied no. Michelle went ahead and bought the car. Some weeks later, the car broke down and it turned out that the car was completely unroadworthy because it had been previously involved in a serious accident.

What can Michelle do?

5 a) The relationship of agency is said to be a fiduciary relationship.

Explain the concept of a fiduciary relationship and what are the consequences for the agent if he does anything to undermine this relationship?

b) Bob is a buyer for Jazz Clothing which runs a highly successful chain of gents clothing shops. Recently, Bob entered into contracts with a clothing manufacturer that Jazz has dealt with on numerous occasions. This manufacturer gave Jazz a ten per cent discount on all clothing purchased by Bob. Bob has not informed Jazz about these discounts and, with the aid of an accomplice in the finance office, he has managed to forge the invoices from the manufacturer. Bob now fully intends to keep the discounts given by the manufacturer to Jazz. Bob is also in the habit of accepting bribes from other clothes manufacturers who are keen to enter contracts with Jazz. Many of the products supplied by these manufacturers do not meet the highest standards of quality that customers of Jazz have come to expect and, recently, Jazz has experienced less than healthy sales figures. The Chief Executive decides to hold an investigation and Bob's misdeeds are uncovered in the process.

What are the legal consequences of Bob's actions?

6 Rapid changes in communications and technology have meant that agency of necessity is a concept that is no longer relevant in the modern world.

Do you agree with this statement?

7 a) In terms of Regulations 3 and 4 of the Commercial Agency Regulations 1993, describe the duties of an agent and his principal.

b) Lesley-Anne is a commercial agent for a Californian company which specialises in the production of sophisticated software packages. Lesley-Anne has customers in France, Germany, Italy and Spain. The principal's software packages are designed for a limited but high quality market in the banking and financial services sector. An agent selling such products must have the proper training, experience and expert knowledge of the qualities and performance of the principals' products so as to be able to sell them to potential customers. Lesley-Anne has acted for her principal for the last seven years. Over the last three years, her activities have resulted in profits of £20 million pounds. The commercial agency agreement states that Lesley-Anne is entitled to receive five per cent commission on all sales directly achieved as a result of her efforts. Lesley-Anne has managed to secure a number of new customers for her principal and, furthermore, she has increased the volume of business with the principal's existing customers. Recently, however, it has become obvious that the principal has decided to terminate the agency agreement. Lesley-Anne, therefore, seeks your advice in connection with the following matters:

i) Is the principal legally obliged to give her any notice if he decides to terminate the agreement?
ii) Will she be entitled to receive some sort of indemnity or compensation package from the principal which takes into account the fact that the she managed to increase the volume of business with existing customers and, furthermore, the new customers that she managed to acquire?
iii) What if the principal insists on enforcing the restrictive covenant in the agency agreement that prevents Lesley-Anne from accepting work with any business rival for a period of five years?
iv) What if the principal attempts to rely on a term in the agreement that states that Californian law will govern the contract and not Scots law?

Explain to Lesley-Anne where she stands legally.

8 Write brief notes on the following topics:
a) General and special agents
b) Disclosed and undisclosed principals
c) *Del credere* agents
d) independent contractors and employees

9 Describe the ways in which an agency relationship can be terminated.

10 To say that someone runs or is involved in a business in some way is not a particularly precise statement as Scots law recognises the existence of a variety of different business organisations.

What are the main the main types of business organisations recognised by Scots law?

11 Cameron, Howard and Iain have decided to form a partnership trading under the name of the League of Highland Gentlemen. They have recently purchased a hotel in the Highlands and they intend to offer guests traditional Highland hospitality and outdoor pursuits (hunting, shooting and fishing). The three partners are in complete ignorance of the legal requirements for setting up this kind of business. They do not wish to leave anything important out of their partnership agreement. Fortunately, Cameron, Howard and Iain are in agreement about the most important aspects of the business. Each of the three will have to contribute the same amount of capital to the firm's account. Furthermore, they have agreed that each partner will take part in the day-to-day running of the firm's affairs. They are all agreed that the death or insanity of a member of the firm would not necessarily mean that the partnership should be dissolved. They also have stated that the firm should continue to trade if one of the partners chooses to leave. Finally, all three partners are agreed that the business should run for an initial period of five years on the condition that the agreement will be reviewed at the end of this period.

Cameron, Howard and Iain have appointed you as the firm's solicitor and they wish your guidance in respect of the following issues:

a) the personal liability of each partner to the firm's creditors should the business run up debts or should it fail completely;

b) the ability of each partner to bind the firm into contracts with third parties;

c) the introduction of new partners to the firm;

d) the ability of the partners to participate in other business ventures;

e) the firm's liability for delicts committed by one of the partners;

f) the termination of the partnership agreement; and

g) the way in which the partners make decisions.

Advise Cameron, Howard and Iain.

12 Eileen, John and Barry are members of a partnership. They wish to secure an injection of capital to expand the business. They are not keen, however, to admit another partner to the firm as they are perfectly happy with the current set-up. They are perfectly aware that, unlike a company limited by shares, their investment opportunities are somewhat restricted. Barry is vaguely aware that the law permits a partnership to have silent or sleeping partners, but he is unsure what this actually means in practice.

What are silent or sleeping partners and how does this arrangement work in practice?

13 On 6 April 2001, the Limited Liability Partnerships Act 2000 came into force in the United Kingdom.

As a result of this legislation, a new type of corporate body is recognised by Scots law.

What is a limited liability partnership and what would be the point of setting one up?

14 Aaron is engaged in the promotion of a new company (to be incorporated on 31 December) and he seeks your advice in relation to a number of issues, namely, his legal status, his rights and his duties as a promoter.

What advice would you give Aaron?

15 The concept of separate corporate personality is a very important legal rule, but situations will arise when the courts are prepared to ignore it.

Outline the situations where a court will refuse to recognise the separate legal personality of a company.

16 a) What does the Companies Act 2006 have to say about the legal relationship between the various company members *and* the relationship between the members and the company itself?

b) Look at the following situations carefully:

i) Stephanie is a large shareholder in a newly formed company. The company's Articles of Association appointed Stephanie to the first Board of Directors. Stephanie, however, does not attend regularly Board meetings regularly and a majority of her fellow Directors decide to remove her from her position as a Director. Stephanie decides to sue the company.

ii) Emma is a member of a plc. The company has recently updated its previous paper records containing all shareholder details to a computerised system. During the data transfer, the company's employees wrongly entered details about the extent of Emma's shareholding. The effect of this mistake is that Emma is credited with a much smaller shareholding than is actually the case. Emma is not best pleased about this and, with a group of her fellow disgruntled shareholders who are also affected by this error, they lodge a class action at the Court of Session. However, there is a provision in the company's Articles of Association which states that all disputes between members and the company must be referred to independent arbitration.

iii) Gillian is a shareholder in a small, privately owned family company. Recently, she has not been getting on with her two uncles, who are the other shareholders in the company. Gillian now wishes to sell her shareholding in the company and move on. She is prevented, however, from selling her shares to an outsider by reason of the company's Articles of Association. The Articles state that, if a member wishes to leave the company, he or she must offer the shares to the existing shareholders who will then give the seller a fair price for the shares. Gillian's uncles are refusing to purchase her shares and things have become so unpleasant that she is at a loss what to do next.

 iv) Fiona is the Chief Executive of what has been a very successful company. Over the years, shareholders in the company have been paid regular dividends. This year, however, Fiona will have to address the shareholders at the company's Annual General Meeting and inform them that they will be receiving debentures as an alternative to the payment of dividends. The company has made some bad financial decisions and it is necessary to take drastic steps to get the business back on even keel – even if this means upsetting the shareholders. Predictably, the shareholders are furious about this decision and they decide to take legal action against the company.

Advise the parties.

17 a) When a new company submits Form 10 to the Registrar of Companies as part of its incorporation procedure, what information will this document contain?

b) Donna is the Chief Executive and a member of the Board of Directors of a

company called Ashbury Engineering Services plc. The company specialises in building hulls to be used in the construction of on-off passenger and car ferries. One of Ashbury's major customers, Tartan Transport Ltd, is a ferry operator which runs services between the various Hebridean Islands. Tartan Transport has approached Ashbury with a request to build four new ferries. Ashbury has never built a complete ferry before but this is a very valuable project. Donna persuades her fellow Directors, despite a few reservations on their part, to enter into a contract with Tartan Transport. Problems begin to emerge for Ashbury when it turns out the design of the ferries is substandard. Tartan Transport has raised an action for substantial damages against Ashbury because one of the ferries sank off the island of Lewis during its maiden voyage and it was only a miracle that no one was killed. Donna and her fellow Directors now attempt to avoid any potential liability on the part of Ashbury to Tartan Transport by arguing that this is not the type of contract that they would have normally undertaken.

Answer the following questions:
i) Will Ashbury be able to escape its liability to Tartan Transport?
ii) What are the consequences for Donna and her fellow Directors?

18 What are the major differences between a company with the word 'limited' after its name and a company with the words 'public limited company' in its title?

CHAPTER
6

INTRODUCTION TO THE LAW OF EMPLOYMENT PART 1

Introduction

During the nineteenth century, the terms and conditions which made up the contract of employment were almost wholly determined by negotiations carried out between the employer and the employee. In theory, therefore, it was up to the parties to the agreement to decide which terms and conditions would form part and parcel of the contract. Very often, employment contracts were not even in writing and it is still a common misconception that such contracts have to be in writing and witnessed. Historically, the employer was often in the stronger position and he could dictate the terms of the employment contract to the employee. It was for this reason that the employment relationship was often characterised in terms of master and servant.

> **This chapter will cover the following areas:**
> - The contract of employment -
> - Dismissal -

The contract of employment

From the beginning of the twentieth century onwards, however the terms of the contract of employment became increasingly subject to parliamentary intervention and employers now have to be aware of the effects of such major pieces of legislation as the:

- Equal Pay Act 1970
- Health and Safety at Work Act 1974
- Sex Discrimination Act 1975
- Race Relations Act 1976
- Disability Discrimination Act 1995
- National Minimum Wage Act 1998
- Working Time Regulations 1998
- Employment Relations Act 1999
- Employment Act 2002
- Employment Relations Act 2004
- Equality Act 2006
- Work and Families Act 2006

Parliament has also introduced laws in respect of the contract of employment, banning discrimination in employment on the grounds of age, religion and belief and sexual orientation. All of this legislation has a major impact on the relationship between the employer and the employee.

The European Union is also a very important source of contractual terms and conditions. As we shall see in Chapter 7, some of the Articles of the Treaty of Rome (Article 141) and Directives (the Equal Treatment Directive 76/207/EEC) have been used to imply terms relating to equal pay directly into the employee's contract. Admittedly, European Union law will be mostly implemented by the Westminster Parliament, but nonetheless an employer will have to be aware of the numerous, ongoing developments in employment policy at the European level.

The contract of employment can also be influenced by the following sources:

◆ The common law rights and duties of the parties
◆ Collective agreements
◆ The written statement of terms and particulars of employment issued by the employer
◆ Handbooks, codes of practice and other documents issued by the employer

 Key point: During the twentieth century, it became increasingly common for the Westminster parliament to pass legislation that had a direct influence on the main terms and conditions of the employment contract, although statute law is not the only source of the rules that govern the employment relationship.

Contract of service or contract for services

Section 230(1) of the Employment Rights Act 1996 provides a definition of who can be classified as an employee. In this Act 'employee' means an individual who has entered into or works under (or, where the employment has ceased, worked under) a contract of employment.

Section 230(2) of the Act provides a definition of a contract of employment. In this Act 'contract of employment' means a contract of service or apprenticeship, whether express or implied, and (if it is express) whether oral or in writing.

At face value, both these definitions seem relatively straightforward, but who is an employee and what is a contract of employment can be two of the most litigated issues in this area of law. On the positive side, it has been remarked that a court or tribunal recognises an employee and a contract of employment when they come across these.

The old chestnut as to whether a person works under a contract of service or a contract for services continues to be an important issue in a number of recent cases.

If you are an employee i.e. you have a contract of service you are theoretically in a much better position than someone who has a contract for services i.e. an independent contractor or someone who is a casual or atypical worker. This is an absolutely critical distinction in UK employment law and one that we shall return to time and time again in this particular area.

Why should this distinction matter?

If you are an employee the law gives you greater protection and more benefits that you would not receive if you were merely an independent contractor for services. The rights that an employee is entitled to claim can be highly significant:

◆ Statutory protection against unfair dismissal (as long as they can show that they have the appropriate length of service or meet certain requirements)

◆ Entitlement to compensation if they are made redundant if certain conditions are met

◆ A statutory right to a minimum period of notice of termination of their employment contracts

◆ Rights to maternity pay and leave

◆ Rights to paid paternity

◆ The right to time-off for public duties

◆ The right to statutory sick pay

◆ Access to important social security and welfare benefits

◆ The right to be consulted about changes affecting the employer

 Key point: An individual who has a contract of service (i.e. is an employee) will enjoy greater employment rights than someone who has a contract for services (i.e. is an independent contractor).

It is worth emphasising that those individuals who work as independent contractors (under a contract for services) are highly unlikely to receive any of these benefits. So, it follows that if a particular contract comes to an end, an independent contractor, for example, will not be entitled to a redundancy payment. However, employers should be aware that other classes of people in the workforce, known by the catch-all term 'worker', who have been given rights under a variety of statutes. Workers, therefore, benefit from and are protected by provisions in the major anti-discrimination laws such as the Sex Discrimination Act 1975 and in more recent legislation such as the Working Time Regulations 1998, the Part-time Workers Regulations 2000, the Employment Equality (Sexual Orientation) Regulations 2003 and the Employment Equality (Religion or Belief) Regulations 2003.

Workers can be but are not necessarily employees and the term will include a person who undertakes to perform personally any work or services for another party to the contract. Some lawyers have gone as far as to argue that the traditional distinction between employees and independent contractors is becomingly increasingly irrelevant. This is an oversimplification and many of the key employment rights recognised by United Kingdom employment law are really only available to employees. However, it is not always easy to distinguish between employees and independent contractors and workers so employers will have to tread particularly carefully in this area.

 Key point: The concept of a worker does not merely include those individuals who would be traditionally regarded as employees – it also covers individuals who would normally be classified as independent contractors for services.

Who is an employee?

In the real world, the honest answer to this question can only be answered with some difficulty! The legal system has developed a number of different tests in an attempt to determine whether someone works under a contract of service or a contract for services. However, British courts and tribunals have not always applied these tests in a way that makes sense to the lay person and even lawyers.

range of fees that he will charge clients for his services. Although this test can be very useful, it does not replace either the control test or the economic reality test.

 Hall v Lorimer (1992) there was a tax dispute surrounding the employment status of the defender who worked as a freelance television technician. If the defender was classified as an employee for taxation purposes, he would be liable to pay more to the Inland Revenue. In order to prove that the defender was an employee, the Inland Revenue relied on the control test by arguing that this particular individual had to follow the orders of the television companies for whom he worked.

Held: by the English Court of Appeal that the defender was not in business on his own account and should, therefore, be regarded as an employee. The mere fact that someone carries out a job where a higher level of skill or technical expertise is required does not mean that he should automatically be regarded as an independent contractor for services. The Court of Appeal also made the point that the labels used by the parties to a contract will not always be decisive.

 Key point: The courts have developed a number of different tests in an attempt to determine whether someone works under a contract of service or a contract for services, for example, the control test, the economic reality test and the organisation test.

Recent case law determining an individual's employment status

 In **Rodger v C & J Contracts Ltd 30 March 2005**, Lord Elmslie in the Outer House of the Court of Session had to examine the employment status of a pursuer who was bringing a damages action against a company run by his son.

The pursuer, Henry Rodger, had been working on a building as part of construction project run by his son's company, C & J Contracts Ltd. The pursuer had fallen through a roof and landed on a concrete floor causing him to suffer severe injury and permanent disability. The accident had occurred because the company had failed to put in place proper safety precautions. The company's insurers disputed the pursuer's employment status arguing that he was a casual worker who, consequently, was not covered by the company's employer liability insurance scheme. The insurers asserted that the pursuer's action was an attempt to defraud them. In reliance of this assertion, the insurers pointed to the fact that the pursuer and his son had conveniently entered into a contract of employment a few days before the accident whereby the pursuer had been appointed to the position of General Manager with the company. Surely the timing of this contract was suspicious to say the least?

Held: by Lord Elmslie that the pursuer was an employee of C & J Contracts Ltd (which had subsequently become insolvent) and that he was entitled to claim £251,000 in damages from the company's insurers. His Lordship, although unhappy with certain aspects of the pursuer's testimony, was satisfied that there was no attempt to defraud the insurers and that the pursuer was employed under a contract of service.

In **Younis *v* Trans Global Projects Ltd and Charnock 6 January 2006**, the Employment Appeal Tribunal (EAT) examined the definition of an employee and that of a worker. The EAT has stated in this case that 'mutuality of obligation' between the parties is a crucial feature of a contract of service – a statement which powerfully echoes the decision of the House of Lords in **Carmichael *v* National Power plc (2000)** the facts of which are discussed later in this chapter.

Younis had been hired to carry out consultancy services for Trans Global Projects between April 2002 and October 2004. He had received payment for these services. Later, Trans Global decided to dispense with Younis' services. Subsequently, Younis lodged a number of claims at the Employment Tribunal, namely, unfair dismissal, failure to provide written reasons for the dismissal, unauthorised deductions from wages, breach of contract, non-payment of accrued holiday pay and race discrimination. The EAT held that Younis was not an employee of Trans Global and, therefore, it was not competent for him to bring claims of unfair dismissal, failure to provide written reasons for the dismissal and breach of contract under the Employment Rights Act 1996. The EAT was strongly of the view that the claim by Younis that he was an employee of Trans Global 'foundered on the rock of absence of mutuality'.

Furthermore, the relationship between Younis and the company 'did not feature the minimum level of control in the employer necessary for a contract of employment. There was a co-operative relationship but not one which entailed any authority in the Company whatsoever'. An unfair dismissal claim under the Employment Rights Act 1996 can only be brought before a Tribunal by an employee.

However, as a worker (a much broader legal category than that of employee) i.e. an individual engaged under a contract for personal services, Younis was entitled to proceed with his claims before the Employment Tribunal for unauthorised deductions from wages, holiday pay and race discrimination.

 Protectacoat Firthglow Ltd *v* Szilagyi (2009) EWCA Civ 98 Szilagyi claimed that he had been unfairly dismissed by Protectacoat because he refused to work in dangerous conditions. Protectacoat argued that Szilagyi had no right to bring a claim for unfair dismissal in terms of the Employment Rights Act 1996 because he was an independent contractor working in partnership with another individual supplying services to the company. According to Protectacoat, Szilagyi could not an employee as defined by Section 230(1) of the Employment Rights Act 1996 which states:

◆ In this Act 'employee' means an individual who has entered into or works under (or, where the employment has ceased, worked under) a contract of employment.

Documents, signed by Szilagyi, were produced as evidence by Protectacoat in an attempt to demonstrate that he was fully aware of the nature of his relationship with the company. The first document was entitled 'Partnership Agreement' which set up a business called M & G Coatings whereby Szilagyi and Glen Nesbitt, another individual, on the face of things became business

'The nature of many professionals' duties these days is such that they must serve higher principles and values than those determined by their employers. But usually there is no conflict between them, because their employers have engaged them in order that they should serve those very principles and values. I find it difficult to discern any difference in principle between the duties of the clergy appointed to minister to our spiritual needs, of the doctors appointed to minister to our bodily needs, and of the judges appointed to administer the law, in this respect.'

In any event, Miss Percy was clearly not a statutory office-holder and I also doubt whether her particular post fell within the classic common law definition of an office, for example in **Great Western Railway Co v Bater (1920)**:

'a subsisting, permanent, substantive position, which had an existence independently of the person who filled it, and which went on and was filled in succession by successive holders.'

 In **Sylvester v New Testament Church of God (2007)**, the English Court of Appeal held that the Employment Appeal Tribunal and the Watford Employment Tribunal had been correct in finding that Sylvester was an employee of the Church in terms of Section 230 of the Employment Rights Act 1996. Sylvester had been dismissed when his post with the Church came to an end and he had the right to bring a claim for unfair dismissal.

It is important to note, however, that courts or tribunals will have to determine whether a minister of religion is an employee by a careful examination of the facts in each case which may lead to a different conclusion depending on the evidence presented by the parties to the dispute. Various religions will treat their ministers or priests differently and due consideration will have to be given to these differences in treatment.

 Key point: It is a purely factual question for the courts or tribunals to decide whether an individual is an employee or not.

Casual and atypical workers

One area of the law that causes particular difficulty for employers are contracts involving the use of casual and atypical workers. Casual and atypical workers are being increasingly used by employers and one of the main concerns here is whether these individuals should be given the benefit of employment rights. Usually, the employment status of such workers is resolved by asking a relatively simple question i.e. when the employer offers such an individual work is s/he bound to carry out the work for the employer? If the answer is in the positive, then the worker is likely to be an employee and not an independent contractor for services.

In more recent times, the courts have also tended to stress the importance of a mutuality of obligation between an employer and employee. In other words, the employee is under a duty to accept work when the employer requires his services.

 Carmichael v National Power plc (2000) two women, Carmichael and Leese, were employed by National Power for the purpose of taking visitors on a guided tour around a power station. National Power made it quite clear that the work was on a casual basis and the women would be employed as and when their services were required. There was no fixed pattern of working hours and the women could be called upon at any time during the day to come into work in order to conduct the guided tours for National Power. When they were first appointed, both women were more than happy to be employed on a casual basis. They did receive some training in how to conduct the tours and they were expected to wear a uniform when working and to follow National Power's first aid policy. Problems arose, however, when both women claimed that National Power was in breach of its obligation to provide them with a written statement of terms and particulars of employment as required under Section 1 of the Employment Rights Act 1996. It should be remembered that only individuals who have a contract of service (employees) are entitled to receive a written statement from the employer. National Power denied that both women were employees. One of the compelling arguments that the House of Lords considered was that Carmichael and Leese were not obliged to accept work when it was offered to them. On quite a number of occasions, both had turned down offers of work because they were either unavailable or simply not interested. There was never any question of National Power taking disciplinary action against the women on these occasions when they failed to turn up to work. There was no mutuality of obligation between the parties.

Held: by the House of Lords that the parties had never intended to create a contract of employment. Carmichael and Leese both performed work for National Power under a contract for services. They were, therefore, not entitled to a written statement as they were not employees of National Power.

The point has been well made in **McMeechan v Secretary State for Employment (1997)** that the label placed on a relationship between the parties is not always decisive. After analysing the content of the contract at the centre of the case, the English Court of Appeal came to the view that its title 'Conditions of Service' (Temporary Self-Employed Workers) was not a true reflection of the nature of the contractual relationship. Upon closer examination, it became apparent that, despite the label, this agreement was not a contract for services at all, it ought to be regarded as an employment contract.

 Key point: Casual or atypical workers can be problematic category when it comes to distinguishing between those individuals who have a contract of service and those who have a contract for services.

Agency workers

A number of cases have demonstrated the dangers for employers who use agency workers. It was previously thought that such workers were either employed by the Recruitment Agency which supplied them to various organisations or that these individuals had self-employed status.

In **Bunce v Postworth Ltd t/a Skyblue (2005)** (before the English Court of Appeal); **Royal National Lifeboat Institution v Bushaway (2005)** and **Astbury v Gist Ltd (2006)** (both the latter cases before the Employment Appeal Tribunal), it was held that any business which uses workers supplied by an agency may be regarded as the employer of these individuals. Clearly, these decisions indicate that businesses which are in the habit of using agency workers will have to be very careful in this regard.

 Key point: A business which hires agency workers may be regarded as the employer of these individuals.

Vicarious liability

Vicarious liability can arise where there is a contract of service meaning that the employer may be vicariously liable for the delicts or negligence of an employee. This means that the employer can be liable for harm that he did not directly cause. An employer can only be liable for the negligent acts of an employee not an independent contractor. Vicarious liability of the employer is another area where it is very important to distinguish between an employee and an independent contractor.

For an employer to be vicariously liable, the harm must have been caused by the employee while within the scope of his employment. The courts will often look to see whether or not the employee was acting within the scope of his employment and this can be a difficult point to establish.

Generally, if the employee was acting for the purpose, protection or enhancement of the employer's business and was not using his employer's time for his own purposes then the employer would be held vicariously liable if the employee committed a delict.

Furthermore, an employer may be vicariously liable for the acts of an employee even if the employee:

◆ Did what he was employed to do but carrried out these functions in a negligent or unauthorised way
◆ Was negligent whilst doing something he was not authorised to do
◆ Committed the act outwith working hours
◆ Commits an assault in the course of the employment but only with a contract of service

 Century Insurance Co *v* Northern Ireland Transport Board (1942)
the driver of a petrol tanker negligently discarded a lighted match that he had used to light a cigarette. This act was carried out while he was standing in a petrol station just as the petrol from the tanker was being unloaded. The match landed on flammable material and this caused a fire to start which spread to the tanker. The driver attempted to drive the burning vehicle from the petrol station into the street. Unfortunately, the vehicle exploded causing damage to other vehicles and houses in the street. The driver's employers attempted to make their losses by claiming their insurance policy, but the insurers argued that the driver was not actually working at the time when his negligence caused the accident. It was agreed that the driver had struck the match for his own purposes. The driver, however, had been standing by while the petrol was being unloaded from his vehicle and, during this process, he was not actually being called upon to drive. Therefore, the insurers stated he was not within the scope of his employment.

Held: by the House of Lords that the driver was within the scope of his employment and, consequently, his employers were vicariously liable for his actions. The driver was expected to supervise the unloading of his vehicle and this meant that he was still acting within his employment. The insurers had to pay out to the driver's employers. The Lord Chancellor made a very strong statement to the effect that 'they also serve who only stand and wait.' This statement can be taken to mean that there will be periods in any job where the individual employee may not actually be working strictly speaking, but he will still be considered to be within the scope of his employment. In this particular case, the employee may not have been driving, but he was still supposed to be acting in his own employers' interests.

 Conway *v* George Wimpey & Co (1951) a driver, against the express orders of his employer, gave a lift to an individual who was not a fellow employee. An accident occurred and the passenger was injured as a result of this. The passenger sued the employer for damages.

Held: the employer was not vicariously liable to the victim because the driver could not be said to be promoting his employer's interests by giving this individual a lift. The employer was not benefiting from the driver's decision to give a lift to a third party.

 Rose *v* Plenty (1976) the employers had a very clear policy whereby children were not allowed to travel on milk floats. One of the milkmen, in clear defiance of this policy, allowed a young boy to travel on his milk float in order to help him with his rounds. Due to the milkman's negligent driving, the boy was injured.

Held: this case differed from **Conway *v* George Wimpey & Co** in that the employers were benefiting from the assistance that the victim had provided to the milkman. There was no question that the milkman was doing anything other than acting within his employment.

 Williams *v* Hemphill (1966) a lorry driver had been instructed by his employer to pick up a group of Boys Brigade members who were camping at Benderloch near Oban. The driver was supposed to take the boys directly back to Glasgow. He was persuaded by some of the boys, however, to make a detour on the way home to Glasgow. The boys wanted him to stop at a camp for Girl Guides. An accident occurred due to the driver's negligence and some of the boys were injured. The father of one of the boys who had not asked the driver to make the detour raised an action on the grounds of the driver's negligence.

Held: by the House of Lords that the driver, although acting in defiance of his orders, was still within the scope of his employment and, consequently, his employer was vicariously liable for his negligent actions. The House of Lords chose not to answer the question of what would have happened if the parents of the boys who had asked the driver to make the detour had tried to sue the employer.

 Key point: Vicarious liability means that an employer can be liable to third parties for the negligent acts that were committed by one of his employees, as long as the act complained of was committed within the scope of employment.

Joint and several liability

If an employer falls foul of vicarious liability, he can sue the employee who committed the delict and, in this way, he may be able to get back some or all of the damages that he has had to pay out to the victim. Vicarious liability means that an employer and an employee are both jointly and severally liable for the negligent acts or omissions of the employee that result in harm being caused to third parties. The negligence of the employee may also provide the employer with a good reason to dismiss him summarily on the ground of gross misconduct.

 Lister *v* Romford Ice and Cold Storage (1957) a lorry driver drove his vehicle negligently and injured his father who was also a fellow employee. The father sued his employer on the grounds of vicarious liability and was awarded damages. These damages were paid to the father by the employer's insurers. At the insistence of the insurers, the employer then sued the lorry driver for failing to drive safely (an implied term of his employment contract).

Held: by the House of Lords that the employer was entitled to regain the damages from the lorry driver that it had paid to his father.

In practice, insurers tend not to insist that the employer use **Lister** in order to sue negligent employees. **Lister** has been criticised because employers find it much easier to obtain insurance to cover themselves against the negligent acts or omissions of their employees.

 Key point: When vicarious liability is established, both the employer and the employee will be jointly and severally liable to the innocent third party.

Independent contractors (or employment *pro hac vice*)

Vicarious liability only becomes an issue when a contract of service exists. Generally speaking, individuals are not responsible for the negligent actions of an independent contractor (an individual acting under a contract for services).

 Mersey Docks and Harbour Board *v* Coggins & Griffith (Liverpool) Ltd (1947) A, a mobile crane driver, was employed by B who sent him out to do a job for C. The contract between B and C contained a term which stated that A was to be regarded as C's employee for the duration of the job. Despite this contractual term, B, however, would continue to pay A's wages and had the power to dismiss him. A was negligent whilst operating the crane and someone was injured. The question then arose as to which party – either B or C – should be sued by the victim of A's negligence?

Held: by the House of Lords that B was to be regarded as A's employer. At no time could C be regarded as having control over A's activities. It was quite clear from the evidence, that A would have resented and resisted any attempt by C to tell him how to do his job.

The House of Lords laid down three rules to resolve similar issues that might arise in future cases:

1   The reality behind the contractual terms agreed between two potential employers will have to be investigated. These terms should not necessarily be taken at face value.

2 The permanent employer will usually be presumed to bear responsibility for any of his employee's negligent acts, unless he can show that this should not be the case.

3 In situations where employees are hired out, it will often be presumed that the hirer is the employer. If a skilled employee brings equipment to the job, the situation becomes more complex because the hirer may not be in a position to dictate how the job should be carried out. In other words, the employee will enjoy considerable freedom from interference and he will basically decide how the job is to be carried out. A hirer can become vicariously liable if it was proved that he told the employee how to carry out the job.

The hirer will, however, become responsible for the activities of an independent contractor if he is aware that this individual is not a reasonably competent member of his trade or profession. In other words, it is likely that the contractor will act negligently.

 Key point: Usually, employers are not liable to third parties for the negligent actions of an independent contractor.

Recent developments in case law

A number of interesting cases have come before the courts in recent years in relation to the issue of an employer's vicarious liability for the negligence or wrongful acts of employees.

 Trotman v North Yorkshire County Council (1998) was a somewhat controversial decision by the English Court of Appeal. The Court decided that a local authority was not vicariously liable for the wrongful actions of a deputy head master who had sexually abused a vulnerable pupil during a holiday camp.

The Court of Appeal stated that the teacher's employment had merely afforded him an opportunity to commit the wrongful acts, but this ignored the fact that the County Council was responsible for the care and the protection of vulnerable children. In other words, the Court of Appeal was taking the view that the teacher's employment was merely background to the incidents and, consequently, that the wrongful acts had not been committed in the scope of his employment with the County Council.

 This reasoning behind the decision in **Trotman** was challenged before the House of Lords in **Lister v Hesley Hall (2001)**. In this case, a warden employed by a boarding school had abused vulnerable and disturbed children who were under his control. The school had entrusted the children to the warden's care and the question centred around the issue of whether the wrongful acts were so closely associated with his employment that it would be fair and just to hold the employers vicariously liable. In this particular case, the answer to this issue was in the affirmative. The school was, therefore, vicariously liable for the wrongful acts of the employee. In consequence of this decision, the House of Lords stated that **Trotman** had been wrongly decided by the Court of Appeal.

In **Viasystems (Tyneside) Ltd *v* Thermal Transfer (Northern) Ltd and others (2005)**, the English Court of Appeal applied the legal principle of dual vicarious liability. In this case, Darren Strang, a young fitter's mate, who was employed by a sub-contractor (CAT Metalwork Services), had negligently switched on a sprinkler system while working on a factory's air conditioning system. The main contractor, Thermal Transfer had sub-contracted work to S & P Darwell who subsequently contracted work out to CAT Metalwork Services for the hire of fitters and fitters' mates with a view to completing the sub-contract.

Both the second sub-contractor (Darwell) and the third sub-contractor (CAT Metalwork Services) were held to be vicariously liable for the damage caused by the negligent actions of Strang. What is particularly interesting about this case is the fact that, while for many years legal scholars (Professor Atiyah especially) had suggested that situations of dual vicarious liability could arise, the courts were not prepared to accept this. Obviously, this case will necessitate a reappraisal of this area of the law.

 In **Majrowski *v* Guy's and St. Thomas' Hospital NHS Trust (2006)**, the House of Lords ruled that an employer can be vicariously liable when an employee bullies or harasses a fellow employee.

In the above case, Mr Majrowski was subjected to bullying and harassment by his manager, Sandra Freeman. Subsequently, Mr Majrowski brought a claim against the Hospital Trust, but this was rejected at first instance because the employer was not deemed to have been negligent. On appeal, however, Mr Majrowski was able to use the Protection from Harassment Act 1997 (legislation which mainly applies to England and Wales) to argue his case. The House of Lords agreed with him and it would now appear, in England and Wales at least, that employers can be liable for acts of bullying and harassment committed by their employees even when there is no evidence of negligence on an employer's part.

 Green *v* DB Group Services (UK) Ltd (2006) Helen Green was employed by Deutsche Bank as a Company Secretary Assistant in the secretariat department from 6 October1997. While working at the Bank, Green experienced very hostile treatment from several of her colleagues which amounted to harassment and which, over time, had an extremely detrimental effect on her mental health. The treatment manifested itself in derogatory comments (which were sometimes lewd in nature) and being ignored or isolated. Much of the treatment came from four female colleagues and thus it could not be regarded as less favourable treatment on the grounds of Green's gender. The employer became aware of the problems that Green was experiencing and even sent her to attend stress counselling and assertiveness training for which it paid.

On 7 November 2000, Green was taken into hospital suffering from a very serious bout of depression. After receiving treatment for this illness, Green returned to her work on the 13 March 2001. It had been agreed with her employer that she would work part-time to begin with. Unfortunately, in October 2001, Green experienced further bouts of depression, which were so bad, that she was forced to take sick leave. In fact, Green did not resume

working for her employer and she was dismissed from employment in 2003 by a notice issued by her employer. Green then decided to pursue a personal injury claim against her employer alleging that her depressive illness had been caused by the bullying and harassment that she had experienced at the hands of her colleagues and that her employer was vicariously liable and negligent for failing to deal with this matter properly. Green's claim also relied in part on the Prevention from Harassment Act 1997 (as in the case of **Majrowski v Guy's and St. Thomas' Hospital NHS Trust (2006)**).

Held: by the English High Court that Green had been subjected to bullying and harassment by her colleagues and that her employer was vicariously liable for this treatment. Green was awarded over $800,000 in damages which included $35,000 for pain and suffering, $25,000 for disadvantage in the labour market, $128,000 for lost earnings and $640,000 for future loss of earnings including loss of pension rights.

It has been suggested that the net effect of cases like **Majrowski v Guy's and St. Thomas' Hospital NHS Trust (2006)** and **Green v DB Group Services (UK) Ltd (2006)** is that, in the future, all bullying and harassment in the work-place will be unlawful. Whether such a claim is merited will depend on the results of future litigation in this field by employees.

 Key point: In recent years, various decisions of UK courts tend to suggest that the extent of an employer's vicarious liability has widened.

The nature of the contract of employment

Generally speaking, in Scotland, employment contracts do not have to be in written form and witnessed. It is quite legitimate to have an employment contract which is completely verbal in nature. Employment contracts may even be implied from the behaviour of the parties i.e. it is perfectly obvious to all and sundry that an employment relationship exists between two individuals. However, it is probably advisable to have some written proof concerning employment contracts as this can be used to determine the extent of the rights and the duties of the parties to the agreement in the event of a dispute.

The ordinary rules about offer and acceptance which govern the law of contract which were discussed in Chapter 2 are particularly relevant in this area of the law.

However, under Section 1 of the Employment Rights Act 1996, employees must be issued with a written statement of the terms and particulars of their contract of employment. It should be noted that this statement is not the contract of employment. Merely, it provides general information about the nature of the relationship and the extent of the main provisions of the agreement. Such a statement must be issued to the employee within two months of the start of the employment contract. If the employer does not give the employee a copy of a written statement of terms and particulars, the employee can take him to an Employment Tribunal as part of an unfair dismissal claim for failure to issue such a statement. However, this is generally an unusual course of action on the part of the employee.

Key point: The employer with more than 50 employees has a general legal duty to consult employees about proposed redundancies, changes in terms of employment and transfers of business under TUPE as a result of the ICE Regulations 2004.

The Working Time Regulations 1998

The Working Time Regulations 1998 guarantees most workers (there are exceptions) the right not to be forced to work more than 48 hours per week. The Regulations also force the employer to give workers regular breaks and they also regulate the amount of hours that the worker can be forced to work in any one day. There is special protection for younger workers regarding breaks and the maximum daily hours that they are permitted to work. The basic rights and protections that the Regulations provide are:

◆ a limit of an average of 48 hours a week which a worker can be required to work (though workers can choose to work more if they wish)
◆ a limit of an average of 8 hours work in each 24 hour period which night workers can be required to work
◆ a right for night workers to receive free health assessments
◆ a right to 11 hours rest a day
◆ a right to a day off each week
◆ a right to an in-work rest break if the working day is longer than 6 hours
◆ a right to 5.6 weeks paid leave per year

It is normal practice, for many employers to have a collective or work-place agreement which governs the length of in-work rest breaks if the working day is longer than six hours. If there is no such agreement, adult workers are entitled to a 20 minute uninterrupted break which should be spent away from the work-station and such a break should not be scheduled at the end of a shift. Younger workers are entitled to a longer, uninterrupted break of 30 minutes if their working day is longer than four and a half hours and, similarly, this break should be spent away from a person's workstation.

Working time
Working time may cover travelling time where it is part of the job, working lunches and job-related training. Working time, however, does not include travelling between the worker's home and the work-place, lunch breaks, evening classes or day-release courses. 'On-call' time would be regarded as working time when an employee is required to be at his or her place of work. When a worker is permitted to be away from the workplace when 'on-call' and, therefore, perfectly at liberty to pursue leisure activities, on-call time is not to be regarded as 'working time'.

The average weekly working time is normally calculated over 17 weeks (the **reference period**) or however long a worker has been working for the Employer if this is less than 17 weeks. Sometimes the reference period can be longer (26 weeks) or it can be extended by means of a collective or workforce agreement (52 weeks).

In respect of workers' rights under the Working Time Regulations, they are required to advise the employer of any other remunerated work which they undertake and which may take their total average working hours to more than 48 per week.

Young workers

Under the Working Time Regulations, special rules apply to young workers i.e. those individuals above the minimum school leaving age, but are under 18 years of age. Young workers may not ordinarily work more than:

◆ **8 hours a day**
◆ **40 hours a week**

The hours of young workers cannot be averaged out and such individuals are not permitted to opt out from the rules regulating working time. Young workers may, however, work longer hours where this is necessary to either:

◆ **maintain continuity of service or production, or**
◆ **respond to a surge in demand for a service or product**

and provided that:

1 there is no adult available to perform the task

2 the training needs of the young worker are not adversely affected

Night workers

According to the Working Time Regulations, a night worker is an individual who normally works at least three hours at night and who works between the hours of 11pm and 6am (night time) although workers and employers may agree to vary this. If workers and employers do agree to vary this period, night time must be at least seven hours in length and include the period from midnight to 5 am. The Regulations anticipate a situation whereby night workers will work no more than eight hours daily on average and this will include overtime where such an arrangement is part of a night worker's normal hours of work. The relevant reference period for averaging out a night worker's hours is 17 weeks – although this period can be longer in certain situations (up to 52 weeks as a result of a collective agreement or workforce agreement). A night worker will not be permitted to opt-out of the night work limit.

Young workers and night work

Young workers may not ordinarily work at night between 10pm and 6am or between 11pm and 7am if the contract of employment provides for work after 10pm. However, exceptions apply in particular circumstances in the case of certain kinds of employment, as set out below. Young workers may work throughout the night if they are employed in hospitals or similar establishments.

The circumstances in which young workers may work are that the work they are required to do is necessary to either:

◆ **maintain continuity of service or production, or**
◆ **respond to a surge in demand for service or product**

and

◆ **there is no adult available to perform the task**
◆ **the employer ensures that the training needs of the young worker are not adversely affected**
◆ **the young worker is allowed an equivalent period of compensatory rest**

Young workers should be properly supervised at all times to ensure their protection.

Health assessments for night workers

The employer is obligated to ensure that the health of night workers is in no way adversely affected as a result of performing their duties. Consequently, the employer should offer free, regular health assessments to night workers. To facilitate this process, the employer should keep a record of:

- The name of the night worker;
- When an assessment was offered (or when he or she had the assessment if there was one); and
- The result of any assessment.

By law, the employer is required to retain such records for a period of two years.

 Key point: Young workers and night workers enjoy special protection under the regulations.

Opt-outs from 48 hour week

It is possible for employees or workers to agree to work longer than the 48-hour limit. Any such agreement must be in writing and signed by the affected employee. This is generally referred to as an opt-out. The employer is required to maintain proper records in respect of those individuals who have chosen to work over and above the 48 hour weekly limit and such records must be retained for a period of two years.

It can be for a specified period or an indefinite period. Workers can cancel the opt-out agreement whenever they want, although they must give their employer at least seven days' notice, or longer (up to three months) if this has been agreed with the employer. An example of an opt-out can be seen below:

OPT-OUT AGREEMENT

I, Katherine Bennett, agree that I may work for more than an average of 48 hours a week. If I change my mind, I will give my employer seven days' notice in writing to end this agreement.

Signed ....

Dated ....

 Key point: By mutual agreement the employer and the employee or worker can opt out of the 48 hour working week.

The National Minimum Wage

The National Minimum Wage Act 1998 now means that workers must receive a basic hourly wage depending on their age.

One of the most important changes to the National Minimum Wage Scheme since February 2005 is the inclusion of young workers i.e. young persons aged 16 and 17 years old. Previously, these individuals were not covered by the National Minimum Wage Act 1998. The British Government, however, finally accepted the recommendation of the Low Pay Commission that the Scheme should be extended to young workers.

From 1 October 2009, the Minimum Wage will be as follows: the **Adult Rate** (for workers aged 22 and over) is projected to increase from the present hourly rate of £5.73 to £5.80; the **Development Rate** (for workers aged 18–21 inclusive) is scheduled to increase from the present hourly rate of £4.77 to £4.83; the **16–17 Year Old Rate** will increase from the rate of £3.53 to £3.57 an hour.

October 2006
- ◆ Main rate for adults – £5.35
- ◆ Development rate for 18–21 year olds – £4.45
- ◆ The rate for 16–17 year olds – £3.30

October 2007
- ◆ Main rate for adults aged 22 and over – £5.52
- ◆ Development rate for 18–21 year olds – £4.60
- ◆ The rate for 16–17 year olds – £3.40

October 2008
- ◆ £5.73 per hour for workers aged 22 years and older
- ◆ A development rate of £4.77 per hour for workers aged 18–21 inclusive
- ◆ £3.53 per hour for all workers under the age of 18, who are no longer of compulsory school age

October 2009
- ◆ £5.80 per hour for workers aged 22 years and older
- ◆ A development rate of £4.83 per hour for workers aged 18–21 inclusive
- ◆ £3.57 per hour for all workers under the age of 18, who are no longer of compulsory school age

---

 Key point: Under the National Minimum Wage Act 1998, employees and workers must receive a basic hourly rate.

Maternity and Paternity Rights

Time-off to attend ante natal care (Sections 55–57: Employment Rights Act 1996)

Section 55 of the Employment Rights Act 1996 gives female employees who are pregnant the right to take time off work to attend an ante natal care appointment and such an appointment will have been arranged by a registered nurse or a doctor. Furthermore Section 56 of the Act, gives pregnant employees the right to be paid while taking time off in working hours to attend an ante natal care appointment. If the employer refuses to permit a female employee to attend such an appointment during working hours or refuses to pay the employee for the time spent at the appointment, the employee has the right to lodge a complaint to the Employment Tribunal (within the normal three month time limit) in terms of Section 57 of the Act.

Maternity rights

Female workers who give birth to a child after 6 April 2009 are entitled to take 26 weeks' paid ordinary maternity leave and a further 26 weeks' additional maternity leave provided they give their employers the appropriate notification. A female employee must notify the employer no later than the end of the 15th week before the week the baby is due (or as soon as is reasonably practicable) that she is expecting a child; when the expected week of childbirth is; and when she wishes her maternity leave to start. The employer is then obligated to inform the employee (within a period of 28 days) when her maternity leave will commence and when it will end.

The entitlement to maternity leave applies to all female employees who wish to take maternity leave regardless of their length of service. The minimum length of maternity leave which a female employee must take is two weeks (four weeks for those working in factories) and this period of maternity leave will begin as soon as the child has been born.

During the period of maternity leave, the employer and the employee can stay in touch with one another (the level of contact should be reasonable) in order to discuss a variety of issues such as the employee's return to work, changes in the work-place and promotion opportunities. An employee is also entitled to work up to a maximum of ten days for the employer during the period of her maternity leave (this is known as 'keeping in touch days'). The employer and the employee must reach agreement on the type of work which is to be performed and the rate of pay for this work.

The employer cannot penalise a female worker who takes maternity leave by refusing to allow her to return to work when the period of leave is at an end and the employer cannot treat a female employee less favourably for exercising her statutory maternity rights. An employee can choose to change the date of her return from maternity leave as long as she gives her employer at least eight weeks' notice (or whatever the contractual period of notice may be) in advance of the new return date.

 Key point: Female employees who are pregnant are entitled to time off for ante-natal treatment and they can take a year's maternity leave.

Statutory Maternity Pay

Statutory maternity pay is paid by the Employer. All employees, whether full or part time, who are pregnant or who have just given birth are entitled to 39 weeks' statutory maternity pay.

If your average gross earnings are above £97 a week or £421 per month before tax i.e. the current lower earnings limit for national insurance contributions, Statutory Maternity Pay is payable for 39 weeks.

To qualify for Statutory Maternity Pay you must have been employed by the same employer without a break for at least 26 weeks by the end of the 15th week before the week the child is due to be born.

The rates of Statutory Maternity Pay in 2010–2011 are:

◆ 90% of your salary (with no upper limit) for the first six weeks of your maternity leave
◆ either £124.88 or 90% of the employee's average earnings (whichever is the lower figure) for the remaining 33 weeks

By April 2010, the Government has indicated that it intends to introduce legislation to increase the period of Statutory Maternity Pay from 39 weeks to 52 weeks.

Statutory Maternity Allowance

Those employees who do not qualify for Statutory Maternity Pay may be entitled to claim Statutory Maternity Allowance. The Allowance is payable to those individuals who have stopped work to give birth to a child, who have been employed or self-employed for a minimum period of 26 weeks in the 66 weeks (the test period) before the birth of the child is expected to take place and their average gross weekly earnings are at least £30 per week (which is averaged over a 13 week period in the 66 week test period).

The rates of Statutory Maternity Allowance in 2010–11 are either £124.88 or 90% of the employee's average earnings (whichever is the lower figure) and is payable for 39 weeks. The earliest Maternity Allowance can be paid to an individual is from the 11th week before the week of the child's birth and the latest it can be paid to the employee is from the day after the child's birth. By April 2010, the Government has indicated that it intends to introduce legislation to increase the period of Statutory Maternity Allowance from 39 weeks to 52 weeks.

The rules governing maternity rights are governed by the following legislation:

- The Maternity and Parental Leave etc. and the Paternity and Adoption Leave (Amendment) Regulations 2006
- The Employment Act 2002
- The Maternity and Parental Leave (Amendment) Regulations 2002
- The Maternity and Parental Leave (Amendment) Regulations 2001
- The Maternity and Parental Leave etc Regulations 1999
- The Employment Rights Act 1996
- The Employment Relations Act 1999
- The Statutory Maternity Pay, Social Security (Maternity Allowance) and Social Security (overlapping Benefits) (Amendment) Regulations 2006
- The Social Security, Statutory Maternity Pay and Statutory Sick Pay (Miscellaneous Amendments) Regulations 2002
- The Social Security Contributions and Benefits Act 1992
- The Statutory Maternity Pay (General) Regulations 1986/1987/1994
- The Sex Discrimination Act 1975

 Key point: Female employees on maternity leave are entitled to receive either Statutory Maternity Pay or Statutory Maternity Allowance.

Paternity Rights

Rules about paternity rights have been in force since 6 April 2003. The latest rules apply to those individuals who are to become fathers or adopters of a child on or after 6 April 2009.

New fathers or adopters of a child who qualify under the rules of the scheme are entitled to take two weeks' paid paternity leave. Paternity leave must be taken at least 56 days after the birth or the adoption of the child. The leave period cannot be split into individual days and must be taken in either a one or a two week block. If the employee chooses to exercise his full entitlement to paternity leave, the two weeks must be taken together. To qualify for paternity leave, an employee must have worked for a continuous period of 26 weeks with the employer up to and including the 15th week before the child is to be born or adopted. Furthermore, the employee must remain in employment with his employer until the date of the child's birth or adoption.

By April 2010, the Government has indicated that it intends to introduce legislation to permit fathers to take 26 weeks of Additional Paternity Leave with entitlement to pay during this period if the mother has returned to work and has not taken her full entitlement to maternity leave.

 Key point: New fathers or adopters of a child are entitled to take Statutory Paternity Leave.

Statutory Paternity Pay

The rates of Statutory Paternity Pay in 2010–11 are either £124.88 or 90% of the employee's average earnings (whichever is the lower figure) and is payable during the leave period (whether one week or two weeks). The employee must earn at least £97 per week (the lower earnings limit) or £421 per month to qualify for Statutory Paternity Pay.

The rules governing paternity rights can be found in the following legislation:

◆ The Employment Rights Act 1996
◆ The Employment Act 2002
◆ The Paternity and Adoption Leave Regulations 2002
◆ The Maternity and Parental Leave etc. and the Paternity and Adoption Leave (Amendment) Regulations 2006
◆ The Statutory Adoption Pay and Statutory Paternity Pay (General) Regulations 2002
◆ The Statutory Paternity Pay and Statutory Adoption Pay (General) and the Statutory Paternity Pay and Statutory Adoption Pay (Weekly Rates) (Amendment) Regulations 2006

 Key point: New fathers or adopters of a child who take paternity leave are entitled to be pad Statutory Paternity Pay.

Additional paternity rights

From April 2011, fathers will have the right to take additional paternity leave. Currently, fathers are entitled to take two weeks' paternity leave. The draft Additional Paternity Leave Regulations, recently published by the British Government, will allow a mother to transfer the remaining six months of her 12 months' maternity leave to the father of her child. These new rules are expected to apply to children whose expected week of birth (or adoption) begins on or after 3 April 2011. The right to transfer the remaining six months of the mother's maternity leave are subject to certain conditions:

1   The father must have 26 weeks' continuous service with the employer.

2   The father must (apart from the mother) be mainly responsible for raising the child.

3   The father must provide specified information to his employer some eight weeks prior to the birth of the child clarifying certain matters.

In relation to point 3 above, the information which an employee must supply to his employer includes a written declaration from the mother that he is the biological father of the child (or he is her spouse or her civil partner if he is not the biological father of the child) and that, as far as she is aware, he is the only person taking advantage of the right to additional paternity leave in respect of the child.

It is worth pointing out that, from 6 April 2010 onwards, those parents wishing to take advantage of the new Regulations will have the right to take legal action should they be subjected to less favourable treatment by their employer or be unfairly dismissed from employment.

The draft Regulations apply to all employers and there is no exemption for small businesses.

Adoption Leave

In order to qualify for adoption leave, employees must satisfy certain criteria:

- they must be matched with a child for adoption by a recognised adoption agency
- they have worked 26 weeks continuous service by the week in which they are notified of being matched for adoption (this also applies to an employee who adopts a child from overseas)
- the employee must earn at least £97 per week (the lower earnings limit) or £421 per month to qualify for Statutory Paternity Pay

Adoption leave can be taken for 26 weeks (Ordinary Adoption Leave) and for a further 26 weeks (Additional Adoption Leave). The leave period normally begins when the child is placed with the parents or it can begin earlier as long as it is at least 14 days before the child's placement. Employees who are couples and who adopt a child must choose who takes adoption leave and who takes paternity leave as only one parent is entitled to adoption leave.

Statutory adoption leave or pay is not normally available to employees if they intend to take on a role as a special guardian, if they intend to adopt a stepchild or have a child through surrogacy or a private adoption agreement.

 Key point: For those employees who qualify, a total period of one year's Statutory Adoption Leave may be taken.

Statutory Adoption Pay

The rates of Statutory Adoption Pay in 2010–2011 are either £124.88 or 90% of the employee's average earnings (whichever is the lower figure) and is payable for 39 weeks. For those individuals who do not qualify for Adoption Pay, they will still be entitled to take unpaid leave and they may also qualify for Income Support. Statutory Adoption Pay is payable for a period of 39 weeks. By April 2010, the Government has indicated that it intends to introduce legislation to increase the period of Statutory Adoption Pay from 39 weeks to 52 weeks.

The principal rules governing adoption leave and pay are contained in the following pieces of legislation:

- The Employment Rights Act 1996
- Employment Rights Act 2002
- The Paternity and Adoption Leave Regulations 2002
- The Maternity and Parental Leave etc. and the Paternity and Adoption Leave (Amendment) Regulations 2006
- The Employment Rights Act 1996 (Application of Section 80B to Adoptions from Overseas) Regulations 2003

◆ The Paternity and Adoption Leave (Adoption from Overseas) Regulations 2003
◆ The Statutory Adoption Pay and Statutory Paternity Pay (General) Regulations 2002
◆ The Statutory Paternity Pay and Statutory Adoption Pay (General) and the Statutory Paternity Pay and Statutory Adoption Pay (Weekly Rates) (Amendment) Regulations 2006
◆ The Social Security Contributions and Benefits Act 1992 (Application of Parts 12ZA and 12ZB to Adoptions from Overseas) Regulations 2003

 Key point: Those employees taking Statutory Adoption Leave are entitled to receive Statutory Adoption Pay.

Parental leave

Parental leave can be taken by either of the parents or the adoptive parents of a child. It is an individual right and it cannot be shared or transferred between the parents. Foster parents do not have the right to take parental leave.

The rules relating to parental leave (made under powers contained in the Employment Rights Act 1996) are found in the following legislation:

◆ The Maternity and Parental Leave etc. and the Paternity and Adoption Leave Regulations 1999
◆ The Maternity and Parental Leave etc. and the Paternity and Adoption Leave (Amendment) Regulations 2006

An employee is entitled to take 13 weeks' unpaid leave in the following situations:

◆ Any time up until a child's fifth birthday, and
◆ If the child was adopted, any time before the 5th anniversary of his/her placement or up until his/her 18th birthday (whichever is sooner), and
◆ If the child is disabled i.e. receiving Disability Living Allowance, the employee is entitled to 18 weeks' parental leave until the child's 18th birthday.

In order to qualify for the right to take parental leave, an individual must satisfy the following criteria:

1 Have been continuously employed for a year more by the same employer

2 Is an employee working under a contract of employment (as defined by Section 230 of the Employment Rights Act 1996)

3 Is the parent named on the child's birth certificate

4 Has adopted a child under the age of 18

5 Has acquired formal parental responsibility for a child who is under five years old or, if the child is disabled, under 18 years old)

6 Employees who take parental leave of four weeks or less are entitled to return to the job in which they were employed before the absence. Employees must notify the employer and provide 21 days' notice of their intention to take leave

In addition, employees must be mindful of the following requirements governing parental leave:

1   They must usually take leave in blocks of one week upwards (this does not apply in relation to child with disabilities) and parents of disabled children born on or after are able to use their leave allowance over a longer period (i.e. they can take days off rather weeks at a time), up until the date of the child's 18th birthday

2   Not take more than four weeks' leave in respect of any individual child during a particular leave year

Employers can postpone leave for a maximum of six months e.g. for business reasons. Should such a situation arise, the employer will discuss this with the employee and give notice in writing, which should include the reason(s) for the postponement and set out the new dates for parental leave. If employees have applied to take parental leave immediately after the birth of their children or, in the case of adoption, the placement of a child, then the employer cannot postpone the leave.

In late 2009, the Swedish Presidency of the European Council, proposed the adoption of a new Directive on Parental Leave. If the Directive is implemented, the law governing parental leave could be subject to the following changes:

This included the adoption of a political agreement on the Commission's proposal for a new Directive on parental leave which would lead to the following changes:

◆ The period of leave should increase from three to four months per parent.
◆ Employees who return from parental leave should be permitted to submit a request to their employer that they be permitted to work (for a limited period only) more flexible working patterns and the employer will be legally obliged to take these requests seriously.
◆ Any employee who asserts his/her right to take parental leave will be protected from victimisation or harassment or other less favourable treatment by the employer which is motivated by the fact that the employee asserted a statutory right.

Entitlement to time-off for dependants

An employee is entitled to take reasonable time off in relation to the following situations:

◆ To assist in the organisation of care arrangements when a dependant falls ill, gives birth or is injured or assaulted
◆ To make arrangements following the death of a dependant because of a disruption to termination of care arrangements
◆ To deal with an incident involving a dependant child during school hours or on a school trip or in circumstances when the school has responsibility for the child

This right to take reasonable time off for dependants applies to the following persons:

◆ A spouse or partner
◆ A child
◆ A parent or in-law

◆ Someone who lives in the same household as a member of the family (other than employee, tenant, lodger, boarder)
◆ An elderly neighbour who relies upon an employee in an emergency situation

The employer must be notified as soon as reasonably practicable of the reason and how long the employee expects to be absent unless this is impossible to verify until the employee returns to work. No qualifying period of service with the employer is necessary and there is no age limitation governing this entitlement.

It should be emphasised that the employer is under no obligation to pay an employee for the time that they take off from work in order to care for a dependant.

 Key point: An employee may be entitled to take reasonable time off from work to care for dependants.

Employees and flexible working

Flexible working includes working patterns such as annualised hours, flexi-time, job sharing, shift working and term time working. Employers will now have to consider seriously any such requests for flexible working patterns.

The major rules relating to the right to request flexible working are contained in several pieces of legislation:

◆ The Employment Act 2002
◆ The Flexible Working (Procedural Requirement) Regulations 2002
◆ The Flexible Working (Eligibility, Complaints and Remedies) Regulations 2002

An employee to be given who is the parent of a child or children under the age of 16 or who is the parent of a disabled child aged under 18 who receives Disability Living Allowance or cares for certain categories of adults who require care may request flexible working patterns.

In general, these rights to flexible working apply to employees who:

◆ have 26 weeks continuous service with the employer at the date that the application is made
◆ are not agency workers or members of the Armed Forces
◆ have not made a previous application under the new rights during the past 12 months
◆ have a child aged under 16 or a disabled child aged under 18 who receives Disability Living Allowance; have, or expect to have, responsibility for the upbringing of the child
◆ if the flexible working request involves a child, such a request must be made before the child is 17 or, if the child is disabled, before the age of 18 is attained
◆ are the parent/guardian/special guardian/foster parent/private foster carer or as the holder of a residence order or the spouse, partner or civil partner of one of these and are applying to care for the child
◆ are a carer who has responsibility, or expects to be responsible, for an adult who is a spouse, partner, civil partner or relative; or who although not related to the employee, resides at the same address as the employee

Upon receiving a flexible working request, the employer should meet with the employee within 28 days to discuss the request and should provide a written decision within 14 days of this meeting. Employees have a right of appeal within 14 days of receiving the employer's decision regarding the flexible working request if they disagree with it. The employer should notify the employee in writing of any decision regarding the appeal meeting within 14 days after the date of the appeal meeting.

This notification will either:

1   uphold the appeal; specify the agreed variation and start date, or

2   dismiss the appeal, state the grounds for the decision and contain a sufficient explanation of the refusal.

 Key point: Flexible working includes working patterns such as annualised hours, flexi-time, job sharing, shift working and term time working.

Time-off for domestic incidents

Section 57A of the Employment Rights Act 1996 provides employees with a statutory right to take a reasonable amount of unpaid time off work to deal with a domestic incident. This right shall allow employees to take necessary time off to deal with an urgent, short-term problem which occurs during their working hours. There is no length of service requirement to exercise this right. If an employer refuses to allow the employee to take a reasonable amount of time off to deal with a domestic incident, the employee may lodge a complaint to an Employment Tribunal (subject to the normal three month time limit) in terms of Section 57B of the Employment Rights Act 1996.

These provisions were inserted into the Employment Rights 1996 by the Employment Relations Act 1999. The type of domestic incidents which this right covers may include the following situations:

◆ The death of an employee's parent, partner, child, sibling or a parent-in-law
◆ The death of a person close to the employee
◆ Sudden illness or accident involving an employee's immediate family or other dependant
◆ A crisis requiring the employee's immediate attendance e.g. being called to attend a child's school as a result of an incident involving that child
◆ A domestic crisis such as a burglary or severe damage to property
◆ Making arrangements for the care of children due to the illness of the normal carer
◆ Dealing with the impact of domestic abuse

 Key point: Employees have a statutory right to take reasonable time off from work to deal with domestic incidents.

The rights and duties of the parties to a contract of employment

As with any contract of employment, the parties have rights, but they also have duties. One party's duties should, of course, be viewed as the other party's rights under the contract. We will begin by looking at the employer's duties under the contract of employment. These include:

◆ To pay wages
◆ To provide work
◆ To indemnify his employees
◆ To treat employees with trust and respect
◆ To take reasonable care for the safety of employees

The employer's duty to pay wages and to provide work

In return for performing his duties under the employment contract, the employee is entitled to be paid by the employer. It is highly debatable whether the employer has a duty to provide work for the employee. Implying a general duty that the employer must provide work would cause all sorts of practical and economic difficulties. In **Turner v Sawdon & Co (1901)** it was stated that an employer is under a duty to pay wages in return for the employee's services. The employee, however, will be in no position to complain in situations where the employer pays wages, but does not provide any work for the employee to carry out.

This point was re-emphasised in **Collier v Sunday Referee Publishing Co Ltd (1940)** with the remark that 'provided I pay my cook her wages regularly, she cannot complain if I take any or all of my meals out'.

Failure by the employer to pay the agreed wages is a material breach of the contract of employment. The Employment Rights Act 1996 states that the employer must not make any unauthorised deductions from the wages of any worker employed by him or receive any payments unless:

◆ The deduction is authorised by a statutory provision, for example, PAYE
◆ The deduction is authorised in the employee's contract, for example, pensions contributions
◆ The worker has agreed to the deduction in writing in advance

 Key point: The employer may have a duty to pay wages, but it is doubtful whether the employer has a duty to provide work.

The employer's duty to indemnify his employees

An employer will have a duty to indemnify or compensate an employee who has incurred expenses while properly carrying out his duties under the employment contract.

The employer's duty to treat his employees with trust and respect

This is a duty which has taken on more importance in recent years. If the employer fails to treat an employee with trust and respect and this may lead to the complete breakdown of the employment relationship. In such a situation, an employee may feel that he can no longer remain in employment and the only option is to resign. An employee who is forced to resign in such circumstances may be able to argue that he was constructively dismissed by the employer's conduct and this would give rise ⌐ claim for unfair dismissal.

 TSB Bank PLC v Harris (2000) Harris was employed by TSB. She was looking for new employment with another employer and she put down on her application form that TSB were her current employers. TSB informed Harris'

prospective employers that a large number of customers had made complaints about her conduct. The prospective employers naturally refused to go further with Harris' application. Significantly, TSB had completely failed to bring these complaints to the attention of Harris. Harris later discovered that she had been the subject of customer complaints and this had led to her failing to secure new employment. Harris, of course, had been denied the right of natural justice to defend herself against these customer complaints. Given the present circumstances, Harris felt that her employer had lost all trust and confidence in her. In response, Harris, therefore, resigned and brought a claim of constructive dismissal against her employer.

Held: by the Employment Tribunal and the Employment Appeal Tribunal that the employer had failed in its duty to demonstrate trust and confidence in Harris as an employee. Harris had been constructively dismissed and, even more damaging from Harris' point of view, the employer's conduct had made it impossible or very difficult for her to pursue a career in the financial services industry where personal integrity is vitally important.

An employer who breaches the duty of trust and confidence by running his business in a corrupt and dishonest manner and this conduct later destroys or seriously damages an employee's future career prospects may have to pay stigma damages to the employee.

 Malik *v* BCCI SA (1997) the House of Lords awarded stigma damages to an employee who found it impossible to secure employment because the bank (BCCI) that he had previously worked for had become internationally notorious for its corrupt and dishonest business practices.

Generally, the employer owes a duty of care not to damage the employee's future career prospects.

 Spring *v* Guardian Royal Assurance PLC (1994) Guardian Royal Assurance provided a negligent reference for an ex-employee to his new employer. The reference claimed that the ex-employee had been in the habit of behaving fraudulently while in the course of his employment. The ex-employee failed to secure the post with the new employer. However, the reference was negligent – the ex-employee had been incompetent, but not fraudulent. The ex-employee sued Guardian Royal for breach of its duty of care.

Held: by the House of Lords that Guardian Royal owed the pursuer a duty of care and it was foreseeable that he would suffer harm as a result of the negligent reference.

The importance of the employer providing an honest, but accurate and fair reference for the employee as part of the duty of trust and confidence was re-emphasised by the English Court of Appeal in **Bartholomew *v* London Borough of Hackney (1999)**.

 Key point: A failure by the employer to treat an employee with trust and confidence may lead to the complete breakdown of the employment relationship.

To take reasonable care for the safety of employees

The employer's contractual duties as regards the safety of employees were spelled out in the following decision by the House of Lords:

 Wilson's and Clyde Coal Ltd v English (1938) English had been employed as a miner. He was injured as a result of an accident at work. An action was raised against the employer for the injuries sustained by English. The employer attempted to avoid liability for the injuries by blaming it on the negligence of one of his normally competent mining managers.

Held: by the House of Lords that an employer owed an employee a personal duty of care. In this situation, the employer had failed to take reasonable care for the safety of the employee and, therefore, it was liable for his injuries.

As a result of **Wilson's and Clyde Coal Ltd v English (1938)**, the House of Lords imposed three common law duties on the employer in respect of his employees.

These include:

◆ The appointment of reasonably competent fellow employees
◆ The provision of safe equipment and materials
◆ To put in place reasonably safe working systems

A fourth common law duty was later added to the previous three:

◆ The provision of a reasonably safe place of work

Competent fellow employees

An employee must act in responsible manner at all times to ensure that he does not place his colleagues in a position where they would suffer harm as a result of his actions or failure to act properly. The negligent and dangerous behaviour of such an employee must cause a fellow employee to suffer harm and must be reasonably foreseeable in order to make the employer liable in delict. Two interesting examples from case law are described below:

 Smith v Crossley Brothers (1951) two apprentice motor mechanics seriously injured a fellow apprentice because they subjected him to a bizarre and demeaning initiation ritual. The two employees in question had forcibly inserted a piece of hose-pipe into the victim's rectum. Pressurised air was then pumped through the hose-pipe causing serious injury to the victim. The victim sued his employer for breach of his duty in subjecting him to the dangerous actions of his employees.

Held: the employer escaped liability because the actions of the two apprentices were not reasonably foreseeable. Such an initiation ritual had never occurred before in that particular workplace. There was no way that the employer could have taken reasonable care to protect fellow employees from a danger that could not have been foreseen.

 Waters v Commissioner of Police for the Metropolis (2000) Waters, a female police constable, had accused a male colleague of subjecting her to a sexual assault. The alleged assault had taken place outside working hours.

The police force had conducted an enquiry into Waters' allegations, but there was not enough evidence to prove that she had been sexually assaulted. Consequently, no further action was taken against her male colleague. Waters then claimed that she had been victimised by her colleagues for making the allegation in the first place. She believed that this victimisation had caused her to suffer psychiatric injuries.

Held: by the House of Lords that her delictual claim against her employer should be allowed to proceed. An employer may be in breach of his personal duty of care if either he knew that fellow employees were behaving in such a way as to cause the employee in question to suffer physical or psychiatric injury or if it was reasonably foreseeable that such actions would cause harm and that he failed to put reasonable safeguards to prevent the employee suffering harm.

 Key point: An employer must appoint reasonably competent employees.

Adequate equipment and materials

 Paris *v* Stepney Borough Council (1951) the employer was aware that the employee was blind in one eye, but safety goggles were not provided to protect the sight in the other eye. The employee was involved in a workplace accident and lost the sight in his remaining good eye.

Held: the employer had failed to take reasonable care for the safety of this employee by providing adequate equipment. The House of Lords that the employer had been negligent in that it had fallen far short of the standard of reasonable care which would be expected of a reasonable employer.

 Bux *v* Slough Metals (1973) the pursuer worked in a foundry and, whilst at work, he was splashed with molten metal and was made blind in one of his eyes. The employer had a statutory duty to provide the pursuer with safety goggles and had done so.

Held: the common law duty of providing adequate went much further than the statutory duty. The common law imposed a duty upon the employer to encourage or even enforce the use of safety equipment. The employer had failed to take reasonable steps to do this and was, therefore, liable.

 Smith *v* Northamptonshire County Council (2009) Smith was employed as care assistant and a driver by the Council. Her duties consisted in the main of going to the homes of elderly people and driving them in a Council minibus to a day centre. She suffered injury at an elderly person's home (a Mrs Cotter) while walking down a ramp at these premises. Smith had been pushing Mrs Cotter, who was in a wheelchair at the timer, down the wooden ramp when the edge of the ramp crumbled, causing Smith to lose her footing and sustain an injury. Smith had used the ramp many times before without being exposed to any danger. The ramp had been installed at Mrs Cotter's home in the past 10 years by the NHS **not** by the Council. Smith lodged a personal injury claim against the Council at the local County Court on the basis that the Council had breached the Provision and Use of Work

Equipment Regulations 1998, SI 1998/2306, the Manual Handling Operations Regulations 1992, SI 1992/2793 and in terms of common law negligence. Eventually, Smith abandoned her claims under the Manual Handling Regulations and the common law, but she continued to pursue the Council for breach of the Provision and Use of Work Equipment Regulations 1998.

At first instance, in the County Court, Smith won her claim against the Council which then immediately appealed to the English Court of Appeal. The County Court judge had decided that the ramp could be regarded as work equipment as defined by the 1998 Regulations. The Court of Appeal, however, found in the Council's favour whereupon Smith lodged an appeal to the House of Lords.

Held: by the House of Lords that Smith's appeal should fail. Although the ramp could be regarded as work equipment, critically in this case it had not been equipment provided to her with her employer's consent. Furthermore, the employer did not have sufficient control over the ramp. The Council had no right to maintain the ramp, which was a fixture at Mrs Cotter's home, and was used by a large number of people who were not Council employees.

The interesting aspect of this decision is that, had Smith's appeal been successful, all employers would have been placed under an even higher duty of care to ensure the safety of their employees. There are many situations where employees may have to use equipment to carry out their jobs, but this equipment has not been provided to them by their employers. It would, therefore, be something of an impossible task for employers to be able to monitor the safety of such equipment located on premises outwith their control. Perhaps Smith would have been more successful had she sued the NHS (which had installed the ramp) or Mrs Cotter (as the occupier of the premises).

 Key point: An employer must supply employees with adequate equipment and materials.

Safe working systems

An employer must take reasonable care to ensure that the work is properly and safely organised, that adequate numbers of workers are on site to carry out the job and that there are competent supervisors and managers in place to oversee the workers, especially if the work involves inexperienced and new employees.

 Walker *v* Northumberland County Council (1995) the pursuer worked in a particularly stressful social work post for the Council. As a result of the Council's failure to provide proper safeguards, the pursuer had developed a psychiatric injury.

The pursuer was eventually dismissed by the Council on the grounds of his poor health. The pursuer's injury was reasonably foreseeable as the Council knew that the he was vulnerable and had not taken proper steps to protect him. See also **Hatton *v* Sutherland (2002)** and **Barber *v* Somerset County Council (2004)** discussed in Chapter 3. An example of a questionnaire produced by the Health and Safety Executive (HSE) which employers can use to monitor stress levels of employees can be seen on the Introductory Scots Law webiste.

 Withers *v* Perry Chain (1961) the employee had, in the past, suffered from dermatitis. The dermatitis was appeared to be triggered when the employee came into contact with grease. In order to reduce the risk of her suffering from this condition in the future, the employer gave her work where she would not come into contact with grease. Despite this, the employee developed dermatitis again. The employee sued her employer on the ground that a duty of care was owed to her to eliminate or reduce all risks to her health.

Held: the English Court of Appeal stated that the employer had put in place a reasonably safe system of working for this particular employee which was aimed at protecting her health.

 Key point: An employer must take reasonable care to ensure that a safe working system is in place.

A safe place of work

An employer must take reasonable care to provide a safe working environment, but this does not mean that he has to ensure that employees are protected from all possible risks.

 Latimer *v* AEC (1952) an employee who had been injured at work when he slipped and fell on the factory floor which had been heavily flooded. The employer had taken great care to put down sawdust on the floor to minimise the risk of accidents. The employee argued that the factory should have been shut down until the water was cleared.

Held: the House of Lords stated that closing the factory would be a solution that was out of proportion to the actual risks involved of continuing to work there.

Key point: An employer must take reasonable care to provide employees with a safe working environment.

Defences

An employer may use two defences if a delictual claim is brought by an employee that he is in breach of one of his common law duties:

◆ Contributory negligence
◆ *Volenti non fit injuria* (those who wish an injury cannot be injured)

These defences were, of course, discussed in some detail in Chapter 3.

Health and Safety at Work Act 1974

It is worth noting that the employer's common duties which aim to protect the health and safety of employees establishes a regime of civil liability. In other words, should the employer breach these duties, he will most likely face a civil action by the injured employee who will be attempting to recover compensation.

The Health and Safety at Work Act 1974, on the other hand, makes an employer criminally liable if he fails to take reasonably practicable steps to protect the health and safety of his employees. An employer will, therefore, face criminal penalties in a criminal court for breaches of the Act. This means that an employer could face both a criminal action and a civil action for damages where he has neglected to obey the criminal law and the common law regulating the employees' health and safety.

The Health and Safety Executive and Commission are primarily charged with the enforcement of health and safety. Given the very small numbers of Health and Safety inspectors in relation to the huge number of workplaces in the United Kingdom, the Health and Safety Inspectorate cannot give every employer a clean bill of health. The Act, therefore, places a duty on employers and employees to cooperate fully with one another to promote health and safety within the workplace. Usually, a workplace will establish a health and safety committee, which will include trade union or employee representatives, with the express purpose of advising the employer on what steps or procedures are reasonably practicable to ensure that the health and safety of employees and visitors to the workplace is protected.

The Health and Safety at Work Act 1974 is a parent Act from which the appropriate British government minister is authorised to bring secondary legislation into force in order to make the Act work. Much of the law relating to health and safety is not actually contained in the original Act itself, but in a vast array of Regulations that it has spawned.

 Key point: The Health and Safety at Work Act 1974 imposes criminal penalties on an employer who fails to take reasonably practicable steps to ensure the health and safety of his employees.

The Health and Safety Offences Act 2008

The provisions of this Act came into force on 16 January 2009 and apply to offences committed after this date by employers. Scottish criminal courts will now have the power to impose maximum fines of £20,000 on employers who breach health and safety rules. In the most serious cases where health and safety rules have been breached or ignored, the courts may also have the right to imprison those responsible.

 Key point: Employers could face fines of up to £20,000 for health and safety breaches in terms of the Health and Safety Offences Act 2008.

The employee's duties

The common law duties of an employee are:

- ◆ To provide personal service
- ◆ To provide loyal service
- ◆ There must be no inconsistency with the duty of fidelity
- ◆ The employee must not make secret profits
- ◆ Act with honesty and integrity
- ◆ Do not disclose confidential information
- ◆ To obey lawful and reasonable orders
- ◆ To take reasonable care in the exercise of your employment

The employee's duty to provide personal service

An important characteristic of the employment relationship is that the employer expects the employee to carry out his job personally. It is not usually acceptable for an employee to delegate some of his functions under the employment contract to a third party. This was one of the reasons why the Court of Appeal in **Ready Mixed Concrete (South East) Ltd *v* Minister of Pensions (1968)** stated that the contract was one for services because the driver could appoint a substitute to cover for him when he wished to take time off from driving.

The employee's duty to provide loyal service

An employee is expected to serve his employer loyally which means that he must not do anything that would harm his employer's business by carrying out work for business rivals. Even work that the employee carries out in his own time may actually interfere with the employer's interests – especially if these activities could be viewed as harming the employer's business. The employee should not divulge any trade secrets or business secrets to his employer's rivals that he has acquired in the course of his employment.

 Forster & Sons Ltd *v* Suggett (1918) the defender, an ex-employee of the pursuers, had learnt secret production methods during the course of his employment. The defender had agreed that, for five years after his employment with the pursuers ended, he would not compete against them by setting up a rival business in the United Kingdom. In breach of his contract, the defender set up a business in direct competition against his ex-employer.

Held: the pursuers were entitled to enforce this perfectly reasonable contractual restraint in order to protect important business secrets.

In order to safeguard his business secrets, an employer should really insist that an express restrictive covenant be included in the employment contract. Such a restrictive covenant must, of course, be reasonable.

According to **Briggs *v* Oates (1991)** if a contract containing an employee restraint is repudiated by the employer, all contractual duties no longer have legal force and the restraint is completely worthless. In situations where an employer's conduct, for example, bullying or harassment results in an employee treating himself as constructively dismissed, the contract can no longer be enforced against the employee. The decision in **Briggs** will not apply if the employee resigns and is not dismissed.

 Faccenda Chicken Ltd *v* Fowler (1986) Fowler worked as a sales manager for Faccenda for seven years. During his employment, he was responsible for establishing operations where the company sent out vans containing its products with the purpose of approaching and selling these products directly to local retailers and suppliers. Later on, Fowler left his employment and set up his own business which was directly in competition with that of his ex-employer. A number of his fellow employees joined his business in order to work for him. All Fowler's fellow employees had in-depth knowledge of their ex-employer's business operations. Fowler's ex-employer was unsuccessful in its attempt to sue him for damages.

Held: by the English Court of Appeal a former employee will be entitled to use information in his new job if this information does not fall into the category of trade or business secrets. Very significantly, however, the Court of Appeal stated that the outcome of the case would have been different if the ex-employer had been able to prove that the employees had deliberately written down the information to use in their future employment. This would have been a clear breach of an employee's duty of confidentiality.

 Robb v Green (1895) the employee in question wrote down the names of his employer's customers before he left his employment. It was his intention to approach these individuals personally, after his employment had ended, in order to persuade them to use the services of the business that he had since set up and which was now competing directly against his that of his ex-employer.

Held: the employee was prevented from approaching his ex-employer's customers in order to poach them for his own business.

 Key point: An employer will be able to use a restrictive covenant in an employment contract in order to protect genuine trade secrets to which the employee has gained access.

The employee's duty to obey lawful and reasonable orders

An employee is under a duty to obey any lawful and reasonable orders that an employer may issue to him. Clearly orders to commit crimes or that would endanger safety should not be followed.

 Ottoman Bank v Chakarian (1930) Chakarian, who worked for the Ottoman Bank in Greece, was ordered to relocate to Istanbul in Turkey. Chakarian was not willing to go to Istanbul because he was an Armenian and the Turkish authorities had already sentenced him to death. Chakarian had no doubt that this was a sentence that the Turks would only be too happy to carry out if he ever set foot in Turkey again. He refused to obey his employer's order to relocate his employment to Turkey.

Held: by the Privy Council that the Ottoman Bank's order to Chakarian was unreasonable. He was entitled to refuse to obey the order given the extreme circumstances that his life would be placed in if he went to Turkey.

The following case is in complete contrast to **Chakarian** and also involved an Armenian employee:

 Bouzourou v Ottoman Bank (1930) the employee was an Armenian Christian who was ordered to work at a bank branch in Turkey. The employee was only too aware of the Turkish Government's aggressive attitude towards his race and religion and he refused to obey his employer's order.

Held: the employee had wrongfully refused to obey a lawful and reasonable order from his employer. It will, of course, be appreciated that the employee in this case did not face a death sentence, unlike the employee in the previous case.

 Morrish v Henleys (Folkestone) Ltd (1973) an employee was ordered by his employer to falsify the business accounts in order to aid and abet a tax fraud. He refused to carry out this order and was subsequently dismissed.

Held: the employee's refusal to carry out what was an illegal order was reasonable and, therefore, not in breach of his contract. He had been wrongfully dismissed by his employer.

See also **Macari *v* Celtic Football and Athletic Company Ltd (1999)** the facts of which are discussed in Chapter 2.

Key point: The employee is obliged to follow the employer's lawful and reasonable orders.

The employee's duty to act with honesty and integrity

An employee must not attempt to cheat his employer or to behave in a dishonest fashion towards his employer.

Reading *v* Attorney-General (1951) Reading was a British Army Sergeant who was based in Egypt. The smugglers had paid Reading substantial bribes to accompany their lorries to certain destinations. The smugglers had calculated quite correctly that the presence of a uniformed British Army Sergeant in their lorries would prevent the vehicles being searched by the police for illegal cargos. Eventually, Reading's illegal activities were discovered and he was arrested by the Military Police, but not before he had been paid almost £20,000 by the smugglers for his services. This huge sum of money was confiscated by the British authorities. Reading later attempted to recover this money.

Held: by the House of Lords that Reading had behaved in a totally dishonest fashion and that he had used his position as a servant of the Crown to obtain an unauthorised benefit. He failed to recover the confiscated sum.

An employee must act in good faith and must cooperate with his employer. However, employees do not owe fiduciary duties to their employers. If this were the case, employees would be labouring under an extremely heavy burden.

Nottingham University *v* Fishel (2000) Dr Fishel was employed by a University clinic that specialised in invitro-fertilisation (IVF) techniques. In addition to his work for the clinic, Fishel also performed a large amount of private work overseas in the area of IVF. He was also in the habit of sending the clinic's junior staff abroad to perform private work in order to gain valuable experience. Fishel's employment with the University was later terminated and it sought compensation for the work that he had carried out privately. The University claimed that this private work had been unauthorised and was, therefore, in breach of his employment contract.

Held: by Elias J in the English High Court that although Fishel had failed to gain prior approval for his private work, he was not in breach of any fiduciary duty to the University. The private clients would not have come to the United Kingdom for treatment, so the University had suffered no financial loss. Furthermore, the clinic may have benefited from Fishel's experience gained during his private work. However, Fishel had broken his contract by not seeking permission to continue his private work and, as a result, the University was entitled to damages for breach of contract.

Key point: The employee must act with integrity and do nothing which undermines the interests of his employer.

The employee's duty of care

There is an implied duty that the employee will take reasonable care in the discharge of his duties. Breach of the duty of care may arise in situations where the employer is held liable to an innocent third party for the negligent actions of his employee. The employer (or more likely his insurance company) can always exercise the right to sue the employee for breach of his duty of care. Insurance companies appear to have an informal agreement that they will not pursue the employee for breach of his duty should they have to pay out to his employer under an insurance policy. This has meant in practice, that these types of cases tend to be few and far between, but not unheard of.

Lister v Romford Ice and Cold Storage (1957) at the insistence of the insurers, the employer sued his employee, a lorry driver, for failing to drive safely (an implied term of his employment contract) and causing a fellow employee to suffer a personal injury as a result of the negligent driving.

Janata Bank v Ahmed (1981) Ahmed was employed as bank manager. His employer sued him for damages for overdrafts that he had negligently authorised in respect of certain customers. Unfortunately, Ahmed had failed to investigate whether these customers were in a financial position to pay back the overdrafts. They were not and the debts owed to the bank amounted to a considerable sum.

Held: by the English Court of Appeal that Ahmed was liable in damages (£34,640) to his employers for the losses caused by his negligence.

Key point: The employee owes his employer a duty of care when he carries out his functions under his employment contract.

Termination of the contract of employment

The contract of employment can be terminated like any other contractual agreement. It is normal practice for the contract to state the required notice period which binds both employer and employee. In the absence of such a contractual term, the common law states that either of the parties must give a reasonable amount of notice to the other party of their wish to terminate the contract. What is a reasonable amount of notice will clearly differ from situation to situation.

Statutory minimum notice periods

Section 86 of the Employment Rights Act 1996, however, lays down statutory minimum periods of notice. These statutory minimum periods of notice, which affect employees who have been continuously employed for four weeks or more, are detailed below:

◆ One week's notice is required to be given to those individuals who have been employed for more than four weeks but under two years
◆ If the employee has between two and 12 years' continuous service, s/he is entitled to a week's notice for every year of service

◆ If an employee has more than 12 years' continuous employment, the maximum notice period is 12 weeks

It is important to note that these are statutory minimum periods of notice and that contracts of employment may actually lay down a requirement for longer periods of notice.

Material breach of contract

A contract of employment can also be terminated in situations where one of the parties commits a material breach of contract.

 Gannon and Others v J C Firth Ltd (1976) 18 employees who walked off the job in order to take part in strike action committed a breach of their contracts by failing to provide their employer with services. The striking employees had also committed another breach of contract by failing to turn off a high pressure steam system. As a result of this failure, severe damage was caused to the employer's factory.

Held: by the Employment Appeal Tribunal that the 18 employees had automatically terminated their contracts by reason of them committing a material breach.

At common law, an employer can terminate the contract of employment summarily i.e. without giving notice, but legislation regulating unfair dismissal and redundancy make this a less useful right for the employer to exercise. Summary dismissal has been held to be an appropriate course of action where the employee has been found guilty of misconduct or wilful disobedience.

 Blyth v The Scottish Liberal Club (1983) an employee deliberately disobeyed his employer's instructions to attend certain meetings.

Held: that the employer was entitled to dismiss the employee summarily i.e. without notice on the grounds of his disobedience.

Termination by mutual agreement

A termination of contract can also occur where both parties agree either to end the agreement or that it will end on the occurrence or non-occurrence of some specified event. If there is genuine agreement between the parties that the contract should be ended, there is no dismissal of the employee at either common law or in terms of statute.

 Brown v Knowsley Borough Council (1986) Brown was employed as a temporary lecturer. Her contract came to an end because the course that she was teaching on did not receive further funding. The contract of employment contained a term which stated that 'the appointment will last only as long as sufficient funds are provided either by the Manpower Services Commission or by other firms/sponsors to fund it.' Brown brought an action against her employer claiming that she had been dismissed.

Held: by the Employment Appeal Tribunal that Brown had not been dismissed. Her contract had terminated on the failure of her employer to secure new funding for the course on which she was employed. Brown knew that her continued employment depended on securing additional funding and

she had accepted the employment on these terms. Therefore, the failure to secure the funding resulted in mutual termination of the contract.

Frustration

Further performance of a contract may be frustrated i.e. the contract becomes impossible to perform or further performance becomes radically different from the agreement that was originally contemplated by the parties (Lord Radcliffe: **Davis Contractors Ltd v Fareham UDC (1956)**). The Employment Appeal Tribunal sitting in England has stated that frustration of contract in employment cases means that the employee loses his entitlement either to notice or to a payment in lieu of notice (**G F Sharp & Co Ltd v McMillan (1998)**).

In situations, where the employee's sickness may result in the contract of employment being frustrated, certain guidelines were laid down in **Marshall v Harland & Wolff (1972)** Sir John Donaldson asked whether the employee's inability to work was of such a nature that further performance of his duty to provide services to the employer would either be impossible or radically different from that originally contemplated by the parties. Factors such as the employee's entitlement to sick pay, the likelihood of the relationship surviving the period of absence, the nature of the employment, the nature of the employee's ill-health and the employee's past employment with the employer should all closely examined before deciding whether the contract is indeed frustrated. All of these factors are related and should be taken into account, but there may be other factors to consider in different situations.

Performance of the contract

It may be the case that the employment contract will end upon completion of some task and it is this event that is said to terminate the agreement.

By operation of law

The contract may terminate automatically by operation of law without the intervention of either the employer or the employee. Such a situation may arise where the employer is compulsorily wound up under the insolvency legislation.

Fixed-term contracts

If a fixed-term contract is not renewed, the employer is regarded as having dismissed the employee and the employee may thus claim that the employer acted unfairly in not renewing the contract. If the employer attempts to dismiss an employee during the performance of a fixed-term contract, there is a very strong argument that the employee will be able to claim payment for the remainder of the period of the contract.

 Key point: Like all contracts, an employment contract can be terminated in a variety of ways – by giving notice, mutual agreement, material breach, frustration, completion of a task, operation of law, the expiry of a fixed-term contract and by reason of redundancy.

Redundancy

A contract may come to an end by reason of redundancy. This topic is discussed at length later in the Chapter.

Key point: An employee whose contract is terminated by reason of redundancy may be entitled to a statutory redundancy payment if he has two years' continuous service with his employer.

Dismissal

A dismissal of the employee by the employer will result in the termination of the contract of employment. It is important to ask what kind of dismissal terminated the contract – fair, wrongful, unfair or constructive dismissal. It is important to distinguish between these types of dismissal because there are different legal rights available to the dismissed employee. We have to be quite clear that there was, in fact, a dismissal and not a resignation by the employee or mutual agreement between the employer and the employee to terminate the contract.

The statutory definitions of dismissal

Section 95 of the Employment Rights Act 1996 states that an employee shall be treated as dismissed by his employer if, and only if:

- The employer terminates the contract of employment with or without notice
- The employee terminates the contract of employment with or without notice because of the employer's conduct (this is known as constructive dismissal)
- The employee is on a fixed-term contract which expires without being renewed by the employer

Section 136(1) of the Employment Rights Act 1996 contains an identical definition of dismissal in respect of situations where the dismissal is on the grounds of the employee's redundancy.

It must be appreciated that protection against unfair dismissal covers those individuals who have a contract of employment with their employer. In any claim for unfair dismissal, an Employment Tribunal must discover what was the employer's main reason for dismissing the employee *and* whether this reason actually justifies the dismissal. Section 94 of the Employment Rights Act 1996 makes it clear that an employee has the right not to be unfairly dismissed.

Wrongful dismissal

Wrongful dismissal arises in situations where an employer dismisses the employee in breach of his contract. In order to claim that he has been wrongfully dismissed, the employee does not have to show that he has had continuous service with his employer for at least one year. Employees with under a year's continuous service can also claim wrongful dismissal. Claims for wrongful dismissal should be lodged with the Office of Employment Tribunals within three months (less one day) of the date of the employee's dismissal. So, if the employee was dismissed on 10 February, a claim should be lodged by 9 May at the very latest. Time limits are very strictly adhered to and failure to submit the claim by the appropriate date will cause it to be time-barred.

When making an application to an Employment Tribunal, wrongful dismissal is referred to as 'breach of contract'. A note of caution, however, should be sounded. If the employee decides to pursue a wrongful dismissal claim, the employer can counter-claim for any losses caused by the employee's conduct. So, for example, an employee who broke a computer screen accidentally may find themselves being sued by the employer for compensation because he decided to pursue a wrongful dismissal claim against the employer.

The employer could dismiss an employee wrongfully by failing to give either the contractually agreed period of notice or the minimum period of notice laid down by Section 86 of the Employment Rights Act 1996. Very often, an employer will include a term in the contract which permits him to pay the dismissed employee a payment in lieu of notice. This payment is regarded as compensation to the employee for breach of his contract. In such situations, the employer will not force the employee to work either his contractual or statutory notice period. Wrongful dismissal may also arise where the employer breaches or ignores the disciplinary procedure, which must be followed under the terms of the employment contract, and dismisses the employee with unseemly haste.

 Morran v Glasgow Council of Tenants (1998) the employer dismissed Morran, but it failed to give him the necessary contractual notice period of four weeks to which he was entitled. The employer also failed to make a payment to Morran in lieu of the contractual notice period. Morran argued that, had he been allowed to work his contractual notice period of four weeks, he would have had enough continuous service to claim unfair dismissal against his employer. Morran raised an action for damages against the employer for wrongful dismissal and for the loss of his right to claim unfair dismissal.

Held: Morran was entitled to claim damages for wrongful dismissal. He was, however, not entitled to claim damages for the loss of his right to claim unfair dismissal. The point was well made that the employer had an option under the contract of employment to terminate the contract and make a compensatory payment to Morran which would effectively have freed him from the duty to work his contractual notice period of four weeks. Morran did not have a right to work his notice period – this arrangement was very much at the employer's discretion. The net effect of this contractual term would have been that Morran was still four weeks short of the necessary qualifying period required in order to claim protection against unfair dismissal. He had not lost his right to claim unfair dismissal because he never had this right in the first place.

It may, of course, be the case that an employer dismisses an employee in strict accordance with the terms of the contract of employment, for example, the employee receives his proper contractual notice period or receives a payment in lieu of this entitlement. In these circumstances, it would be premature to assume that the dismissal was fair. Employees with over a year's continuous service can challenge the decision on the grounds that it was unfair in terms of the Employment Rights Act 1996. Furthermore, there may be other employees who belong to protected categories, for example, dismissals for pregnancy and childbirth-related reasons who will have the right to claim unfair dismissal.

 Key point: Wrongful dismissal occurs in situations where the employee is dismissed in a manner that breaches the terms of his contract.

Remedies for wrongful dismissal

The main remedy that an employee who has been wrongfully dismissed may claim would be that of damages. The remedy of damages ensures that the employee will receive compensation from his employer which will usually be measured by reference to the wages that he would have earned had he been allowed to work his period of notice. The remedy of specific implement is not generally available to a dismissed employee. Specific implement, of course, is where the court forces the party who has breached the contract to perform his duties which he has failed to carry out properly. In an employment situation, this would mean that the employer would be forced to take back the dismissed employee. In Scotland, an employment contract is a contract which is highly dependent on the personalities of the contracting parties and the promotion of goodwill between them. It is, therefore, not appropriate for the courts to force the parties together where personal relationships have broken down completely with the result that there is little or no goodwill between them. So damages will be the preferred remedy for breach of an employment contract. Admittedly, Scottish courts have allowed interim relief (by way of interdict) in wrongful dismissal cases whereby the dismissal is effectively frozen until the contractual notice period has passed (**John Anderson v Pringle of Scotland (1998)**). It should be noted that the granting of interim relief will not prevent the employer from dismissing the employee eventually. The interim relief merely forces the employer to comply with the employment contract for a temporary period which could be very short. So, in **John Anderson v Pringle**, all the employee could do was force the employer to follow the contractual redundancy procedure that ultimately led to his dismissal.

Section 236 of the Trade Union and Labour Relations (Consolidation) Act 1992 reinforces the common law rule that no court shall issue an order for specific implement or an interdict which effectively forces both parties to continue to perform the employment contract.

Dismissal – overseas employment

Generally speaking an employee is not permitted to bring an unfair dismissal claim under the Employment Rights 1996 if his/her employment takes place outside the United Kingdom.

However, in **Lawson v Serco (2006)**, the House of Lords ruled that where the overseas employment has such a strong connection with the United Kingdom, it may be possible for the dismissed employee to bring an unfair dismissal claim. An example of a strong employment connection with the United Kingdom could occur where an employee of a UK based concern is transferred from the UK to take up a work placement overseas.

 Hughes v Alan Dick & Co Ltd (2009) the English Court of Appeal refused to permit Mr Hughes to bring a claim for unfair dismissal because his employment had a substantial connection with Nigeria (he was employed at Port Harcourt in Nigeria for over two years). Hughes had originally submitted a claim to the Office of Employment Tribunals, but it had ruled that it did not have jurisdiction to deal with his case. Admittedly, Mr Hughes' employment did have some connections with the United Kingdom i.e. his employer was a British company, he was paid in Sterling through a British bank account and his dismissal was issued from England. Despite all these factors, the Court of Appeal refused to allow Mr Hughes' claim to proceed to a hearing on the basis that the Employment Tribunal had been correct to state that it had no jurisdiction to hear the case. Quite simply, Hughes had never been employed in the United Kingdom by his employer. The Court of Appeal followed the reasoning of the House of Lords in **Lawson v Serco (2006)** to arrive at its decision in this case.

 Key point: The employer with more than 50 employees has a general legal duty to consult employees about proposed redundancies, changes in terms of employment and transfers of business under TUPE as a result of the ICE Regulations 2004.

Unfair dismissal

Generally, an employee who has less than one year's continuous employment cannot lodge a claim for unfair dismissal with the Office of Employment Tribunals (Section 92: Employment Rights Act 1996). Furthermore, people over the age of 65 are, generally speaking, not entitled to bring unfair dismissal claims. There are, however, many exceptions to these qualifications. As we shall see, dismissals on the grounds of the employee's sex, race, disability, sexual orientation and religious beliefs will be regarded as automatically unfair. Dismissals for health and safety reasons or the fact that the employee is a whistleblower will also be treated as automatically unfair. Unfair dismissal should be seen as a dismissal which contravenes statute and Section 94(1) of the Employment Rights Acts 1996 which states that an employee has the right not to be unfairly dismissed. If the employee qualifies for protection against unfair dismissal he can request that the employer provide a written reason for the dismissal. Failure by an employer to issue a written response would be highly suspect and an Employment Tribunal would be entitled to imply that the employer had not acted fairly when he dismissed the employee.

As with claims for wrongful dismissal, an application to the Office of Employment Tribunals alleging unfair dismissal should be lodged within three months (less one day) of the date of the original dismissal. Very often in unfair dismissal cases, the affected employee will submit an appeal against the employer's decision to dismiss. It is often mistakenly assumed that the three-month time limit for submitting an Employment Tribunal application begins to run from the date when the employer's decision in respect of the appeal is communicated to the employee. To reiterate, it is the date of the original decision to dismiss that matters, not any later decision which forms part of the appeals process. An employee aged 65 or over will not be able to claim unfair dismissal. An example of the documents submitted to the Office of Employment Tribunals in a dismissal claim (the ET1 and the ET3) can be seen on

 the Introductory Scots Law website.

 Key point: Unfair dismissal is a dismissal which is contrary to statute.

The employer's pre-dismissal procedures

Over the last twenty years or so, the employer's pre-dismissal procedures have come under greater scrutiny as a result of the decision of the House of Lords in **Polkey v**

A E Dayton Services Ltd (1987). Polkey had been made redundant by his employer without warning. He argued that this was breach of the employer's pre-dismissal procedures. His employer countered this argument by stating that he would have been made redundant in any case whether or not the pre-dismissal procedure had been followed. In other words, Polkey's dismissal on the grounds of redundancy was inevitable. The House of Lords stressed that an Employment Tribunal must take into consideration all the circumstances as to whether the employer has acted reasonably or not as the case may be by failing to follow procedure. It is no longer enough for the employer to rely on the fact that consultation with the employee is pointless because a dismissal will happen in any case. A pre-dismissal procedure which the employer fails to apply in a reasonable manner could lead a Tribunal to find that the employee has been dismissed unfairly. A tribunal must examine what the actions the employer took leading up to the dismissal and not what actions he might have taken.

Polkey remains a very important case because the House of Lords overruled the decision of the Employment Appeal Tribunal in **British Labour Pump v Byrne (1979)**. **Byrne** was often used by employers to justify flaws in their disciplinary procedures especially if such a procedure led to the dismissal of the employee. In effect, an employer could argue that the employee's dismissal was inevitable and that the employee's fate would have been exactly the same even if the procedure had been followed to the letter.

 The importance of granting a right of appeal to an employee who is threatened with dismissal on the grounds of misconduct was confirmed in the case of **West Midlands Co-operative Society v Tipton (1986)**. In this case, the employee was prevented from exercising his right of appeal against dismissal where such a right was guaranteed under the employer's disciplinary code. The House of Lords was of the opinion that such a refusal to allow an employee to appeal could make a dismissal unreasonable and, therefore, unfair. An employer can often rescue himself from having committed earlier defects in the way that he applies the disciplinary procedure by ensuring that the employee is given full access to an impartial appeal hearing.

Section 10 of the Employment Relations Act 1999 states that a worker has the right to be accompanied by a companion to disciplinary or grievance hearings. This companion can be a trade union official who is employed by the union or who has experience of attending grievance and disciplinary hearing or someone who received training in this respect. Alternatively, the worker could request that a colleague accompany him to the disciplinary or grievance meeting.

Many disciplinary and grievance procedures operated by employers do not, however, permit an employee to be represented at such hearings by a solicitor, advocate or barrister. There have been cases where employees have been able to force the employer to accept that they are entitled to be legally represented at disciplinary hearings.

Where public sector employees are concerned, employers will have to be very careful that disciplinary procedures are applied in way that does not breach a person's right to a fair hearing guaranteed by Article 6 of the European Convention on Human Rights. This means that a refusal by an employer to permit an employee to be legally represented at a disciplinary or grievance hearing could have very problematic consequences for the employer. The European Convention was, of course, implemented into Scots law by way of the Scotland Act 1998 and the Human Rights Act 1998.

Two cases which deal with an employer's refusal to permit an employee to be legally represented at a disciplinary hearing are discussed below:

R (on the application of 'G') *v* Governors of 'X' School & Ors (2010)

G was employed at the school as a part-time music assistant in order to gain work experience. He was accused of committing sexual acts with a 15 year old male pupil at the school. If the accusations proved to be correct, G would be placed on the Sex Offenders' Register and would, consequently, be prevented from working with children and young people in the future. The school informed G that he had the right to be accompanied to the disciplinary hearing by a colleague or a trade union representative. As G was employed by the school on a part-time, casual as required basis, he was not position to ask another member of staff to accompany him to the disciplinary hearing. Furthermore, G was not a member of a trade union and, therefore, he was not entitled to be represented by the officers of such a body. G asked his lawyers to write to the school to request that he be permitted to have a legal representative accompany him to the hearing and stressed the fact that he would face very serious career and legal consequences if the accusations against him were proved. Following advice from the local authority, the school refused to permit G to be legally represented at the hearing or the subsequent appeal hearing. G's lawyers submitted an application to the English High Court for a judicial review of the school's refusal to permit G to be legally represented during the disciplinary proceedings against him.

Held: by the English High Court that the school's actions in this case constituted a breach of G's human rights in terms of Article 6 of the European Convention on Human Rights (i.e. the right to a fair trial/hearing). The High Court was clearly influenced by the very serious consequences which G would face if the charges against him were proved i.e. possible criminal action, exclusion from the teaching profession and being placed on the Sex Offenders' Register. The Court was not convinced by the school's arguments that G's human rights were adequately protected in that he could always take a claim to an Employment Tribunal or instruct his lawyers to challenge his name being placed on the Sex Offenders' Register. The school governers appealed against the decision of the High Court to the Court of Appeal. The Court of Appeal affirmed the decision of the High Court that the music assistant should have been permitted to have legal representation at his disciplinary meeting given the gravity of the charges and the long-term consequences to his career.

Kulkarni *v* Milton Keynes Hospital NHS Foundation Trust (2009)

Kulkarni was employed as a doctor by the NHS Trust. He was accused of touching a patient in an inappropriate way. The patient lodged a formal complaint against Kulkarni who was subsequently suspended on full pay to await the outcome of an investigation into the allegations made against him. At the disciplinary hearing, the employer refused to permit Kulkarni to be legally represented. Kulkarni claimed that his right to a fair hearing in terms of Article 6 of the European Convention on Human Rights had been breached by his employer and he decided to challenge the decision of his employer not to permit him to be legally represented before the English High Court. Kulkarni lost his case on the grounds that his rights under the European Convention were guaranteed by his reason of his right to appeal to the General Medical Council against any disciplinary sanction imposed on him by his employer and he also had the right to pursue a potential legal action before an Employment Tribunal. Following on from the failure of his action for judicial review in the High Court, Kulkarni sought leave to appeal to the English Court of Appeal.

Held: by the Court of Appeal (overruling the judgement of the High Court) that the decision of the NHS Trust to refuse Kulkarni legal representation at his disciplinary hearing could breach his human rights. Again, the situation which Kulkarni was facing was so potentially calamitous if the allegations against him were proved that he should have been permitted to have a lawyer represent him during the disciplinary process operated by his employer.

 Key point: Employers would be well advised to ensure that their pre-dismissal procedures comply with current law.

Disciplinary and grievance procedures in the work-place: the ACAS Code or Practice 2009

From 1 April 2009, the ACAS statutory Code of Practice on discipline and grievance in the work-place is something that employers will have to be acutely aware. Although the Code is not compulsory, in relevant cases, Employment Tribunals may view a failure by an employer to use its provisions when dealing with a grievance or disciplinary matter in a negative light. If the failure by an employer to implement the Code is regarded as unreasonable, an Employment Tribunal may add up to a 25% uplift to the award granted to a disgruntled employee who has pursued a successful legal action. Such an award could be very significant in claims for discrimination where an Employment Tribunal can make an award for injury to feelings.

The ACAS Code of Practice does not apply to dismissals by reason of redundancy or the failure by an employer to renew a fixed-term contract of employment.

The ACAS Code of Practice stresses the following principles which should apply to the way in which an employer handles a disciplinary or grievance matter involving an employee:

◆ Employers and employees should raise and deal with issues promptly and should not unreasonably delay meetings, decisions or confirmation of those decisions
◆ Employers and employees should act consistently
◆ Employers should carry out any necessary investigations, to establish the facts of the case
◆ Employers should inform employees of the basis of the problem and give them an opportunity to put their case in response before any decisions are made

- ◆ Employers should allow employees to be accompanied at any formal disciplinary or grievance meeting
- ◆ Employers should allow an employee to appeal against any formal decision made

It is important to stress that many disciplinary and grievance issues can be dealt with informally in the workplace and it will not be necessary to use a formal mechanism to deal with such matters. A quiet word in someone's ear or a verbal warning can often achieve wonders. Being realistic, however, there are issues which will have to be dealt with by the employer by way of a formal procedure. Examples of disciplinary and grievance procedures can be seen on the Introductory Scots Law webiste. We shall now examine the main elements of such a procedure.

Essentially, there are three stages which should be part of most disciplinary or grievance procedures operated by an employer:

Stage 1: The investigation of the alleged disciplinary offence or grievance

Stage 2: The formal meeting where any evidence can be presented and the affected employee has a right to present his or her case

Stage 3: The appeal hearing if the outcome of the formal meeting is to be challenged by the affected employee

The investigation of the alleged disciplinary offence or the employee grievance should take no longer to complete than is absolutely necessary. If an employee is suspended during the course of the investigation, the employer should ensure that the affected individual is on full pay and that the period of suspension should be for a short while only. It should also be explained to the employee that a suspension from the workplace is not a punishment and that it is merely a way of facilitating the investigation.

The members of the employer's management who chair the formal meetings and the appeal should not be personally involved in the alleged breach of the disciplinary code or be the subject of an employee grievance. This may represent something a difficulty for smaller organisations which have a limited number of people on the management team.

It should go without saying that those members of the management team who participated in the initial formal meeting should not be involved in the conduct of the appeal hearing.

When a manager at the initial hearing or the appeal hearing has heard and reviewed the evidence presented, the affected employee should be made aware of the outcome of that meeting as soon as is reasonably practicable. There should be no unnecessary delays in the communication of a decision to the affected employee.

Key point: Prudent employers should ensure that their disciplinary and grievance procedures comply with the current ACAS Code of Practice.

Summary dismissals

A summary dismissal is a dismissal of an employee by the employer without notice. As we have seen, the Employment Rights Act 1996, lays down minimum notice requirements which employers have to comply with when contemplating dismissal of an employee. Failure to abide by these statutory notice requirements could mean that the dismissed employee has the right to bring a breach of contract claim against the employer. In situations, where the employee has over a years' continuous employment, a summary dismissal may also result in the employer facing a claim for unfair dismissal.

Popular culture, mainly through the medium of television soap operas, has a tendency to portray summary dismissals in the work-place as a fairly common event. The landlords or landladies of The Tall Ship, the Rover's Return or the Queen Vic public houses may be quick to use summary dismissal to resolve problems in the work-place (and who can doubt its dramatic effect?), but employers in the real world may fall foul when exercising this option too quickly and without due consideration of the potential legal consequences.

Most employment lawyers, currently plying their trade, would doubtless advise employers not to be too hasty in dismissing employee summarily, but rather to use a formal procedure (which is compliant with the ACAS Code of Practice) in order to deal with the matter properly. It may be time-consuming; it may even be frustrating for the employer – especially if the employee is caught red-handed committing an act of potential gross misconduct – but if the dismissal of an employee later results in an Employment Tribunal action, the employer will have little to reproach themselves about. In other words, it is often better for the employer to play safe in the beginning rather than to be sorry at a later date.

Admittedly, there will be situations where an immediate or summary dismissal of the employee is justified. If the employee had committed a very serious act of violence and there were real concerns that such an incident could be repeated in the work-place, few employers could be criticised for dismissing the guilty employee on the spot.

In any case, for many years now, employers have been expected to follow proper procedures before dismissing employees (**see British Home Stores _v_ Burchell (1980)**). It was often a brave employer (not to say a foolhardy one) who chose to dismiss an employee on the spot.

Alternatively, an employee accused of a very serious disciplinary offence where the ultimate sanction or penalty is dismissal could be suspended with pay from the work-place pending the outcome of an investigation and the conclusion of the disciplinary procedure. As discussed previously, if an Employment Tribunal concludes that an employer has acted unreasonably in the way that it dealt with a disciplinary matter, a 25% uplift could be added to any award obtained by an employee.

 Key point: A summary dismissal is where the employee is dismissed without notice and will only be utilised in a minority of situations.

Dismissal by letter

What if an employer decides to communicate a decision to dismiss an employee by letter? What is the effective date of termination of the employment? Is it the date of the letter or when the letter is opened and read by the employee?

 The English Court of Appeal in **Gisda Cyf _v_ Barratt (2009)** considered this issue when it had to look at a situation where the employer sent a dismissal letter by recorded delivery on 29th November 2006, the letter was delivered on 30th November 2006 to the employee's home address and the employee read the letter informing her that she had been summarily dismissed on 4th December 2006. The employee later submitted a claim for unfair dismissal on 2 March 2007. The employer argued that the employee's application was time-barred and therefore should not be permitted to proceed to a Hearing. The termination of the employment had occurred on 29 November 2006 according to the employer. The employee countered that the effective date was 4 December 2006.

Held: by the Court of Appeal that the effective date of termination of the employment was the day on which the employee opened the letter. Therefore, the claim was submitted within the three month time period and could proceed to a Hearing. The Court of Appeal made the following statement:

'Where a decision to dismiss is communicated by a letter sent to the employee at home, and the employee has neither gone away deliberately to avoid receiving the letter nor avoided opening and reading it, the effective date of termination is when the letter is read by the employee, not when it arrives in the post.'

 Key point: If an employee is dismissed by letter, the effective date of termination is when they open the letter.

Automatically unfair dismissals

 In a variety of situations, a dismissal by the employer will be automatically unfair and the employee does not need to have one year's continuous service in order to lodge a claim with the Office of Employment Tribunals. An example of an application submitted by a dismissed employee to an Employment Tribunal and the employer's response can be seen on the Introductory Scots Law website.

Dismissal on the grounds of pregnancy (Section 99: ERA 1996)

It will be automatically unfair, in terms of Section 99 of the Employment Rights Act 1996, to dismiss a woman from employment because she is pregnant, for a reason connected with her pregnancy or childbirth or for enforcing her rights under statutory maternity provisions. There is no need for a woman to have one year's continuous service with her employer in order to be protected under Section 99.

O'Neill v Governors of St Thomas More (1996) O'Neill was employed as a school teacher at a Roman Catholic school. She began a sexual relationship with a Roman Catholic priest and, subsequently, she discovered that she was pregnant. The Board of Governors decided to dismiss O'Neill on the grounds that she had failed to meet the strict moral standards expected of a teacher in a Roman Catholic school. O'Neill lodged a claim for unfair dismissal and sex discrimination on the grounds of her pregnancy.

Held: by the Employment Appeal Tribunal that the dismissal was automatically unfair. The Governors' argument that O'Neill had been dismissed due to the circumstances of her pregnancy (i.e. that her conduct amounted to immorality) rather than the pregnancy itself was rejected by the Employment Appeal Tribunal.

Dismissal on the grounds of race (Section 4: Race Relations Act 1976)

If an employer dismisses an employee on the grounds of his colour, nationality, racial, ethnic or national origin such a dismissal would be automatically unfair. The dismissal would also be an example of direct discrimination. (See Chapter 7 for a lengthier discussion of this subject).

Dismissal on the grounds of disability (Section 4: Disability Discrimination Act 1995)

If an employer dismisses an employee on the grounds of his disability such a dismissal would be automatically unfair. The dismissal would also be an example of less favourable treatment. (See Chapter 7 for a lengthier discussion of this subject).

Health and safety dismissals (Section 100: ERA 1996)

 Hynes *v* D E Bliss (Builders) ET Case No 12874/96 on a number of occasions, Hynes, a carpenter, had expressed fears about the safety of scaffolding used by the employers. Hynes eventually threatened to report his employer to the health and safety authorities unless something concrete was done to tackle the concerns that he had raised. The employer's response was to do nothing. In reaction to the employer's response, Hynes decided to resign from his employment and claim constructive dismissal.

Held: Hynes was entitled to claim constructive dismissal under Section 100 of the Employment Rights Act 1996. The employer owed a duty to the employees to provide a reasonably safe system of work and by failing to do this it had committed a material breach of contract. Hynes had, therefore, been dismissed on health and safety grounds.

 Harvest Press Ltd *v* McCaffrey (1999) McCaffrey was employed by the company to work the night shift with one other fellow employee. He had reason to make a complaint about his fellow employee's behaviour to the company management. Unfortunately, for McCaffrey, his fellow employee discovered who made the complaint against him. From then on, McCaffrey was subjected to abuse by his colleague. This abuse was extremely threatening and McCaffrey, fearing for his safety, left his place of employment one night after experiencing a particularly abusive exchange from his colleague. McCaffrey told his employer that he would return to work if his colleague was moved to another post within the organisation. The employer refused to do this and took the attitude that McCaffrey had actually resigned from his post. McCaffrey then claimed that he had been constructively dismissed.

Held: by the Employment Appeal Tribunal that McCaffrey had been constructively dismissed in terms of Section 100(d) of the Employment Rights Act 1996. Section 100(d) permits an employee to leave his workplace if to stay there would place him in risk of danger. Risks to an employee's health and safety could also include dangers caused by an employee's colleagues.

 Key point: A dismissal by reason of health and safety will be automatically unfair.

Dismissal for refusal to work on a Sunday (Section 101: ERA 1996)

In terms of Section 101 of the Employment Rights Act 1996, some workers, known as protected workers, have the right to refuse to work on a Sunday. If such a refusal results in their dismissal by an employer, the employee will have the right to claim unfair dismissal. The employee does not have to have a year's continuous service before they are entitled to the protection of Section 101. Generally speaking, employees who were not required to work on Sundays before the Sunday trading laws were liberalised are entitled to refuse to work on a Sunday. Employees who commenced employment after the newer, more liberal laws can give their employers three months written notice of their intention to opt out of Sunday work. After this notice period has expired, they cannot be forced to work on a Sunday.

Trustees of occupational pension funds (Section 102: ERA 1996)

A trustee of an occupational pension fund who is dismissed by his employer because he has carried out or proposes to carry out some task connected with his role will be regarded as having been unfairly dismissed.

Employee representatives (Section 103: ERA 1996)

According to Section 103 of the Employment Rights Act 1996, an employee who is classified as an employee representative or a candidate for such a position and who is dismissed by the employer because they have either carried out or propose to carry out the activities of such a representative will be regarded as having been unfairly dismissed. An employee representative will either be a member of a recognised and independent trade union or someone who has been elected to such a position by his fellow employees. These dismissals will either be connected to redundancies that the employer is proposing to make or to the transfer of an undertaking.

Whistle-blowing (Section 103A: ERA 1996)

The Public Interest Disclosure Act 1998 inserts a new provision, Section 103A, into the Employment Rights Act 1996.

The 1998 Act came into force on 2 July 1999 and gives employees additional protection against unfair dismissal by their employer. Since 1999, approximately 1200 cases involving the Act have arisen. The primary aim of the 1998 Act is to encourage employees to go public about their employer's criminal or fraudulent practices, for example, tax evasion, social security fraud or breaches of health and safety legislation. The Act also covers civil offences where the employer's conduct amounts to negligence or breach of contract where this could potentially cause harm or injury. As long as the employee (the whistle-blower) makes the disclosure in good faith, he will have the right to take a claim to an Employment Tribunal if he subsequently suffers victimisation or harassment by his employer. The conduct complained of may have occurred either here in the United Kingdom or abroad. It is not necessary for an employee to have one year's continuous service in order to claim the protection of the 1998 Act in situations where the employer has decided to punish the disclosure by dismissing the employee.

Where the employee experiences victimisation as a result of making a disclosure under the 1998 Act, he can lodge a claim with the Office of Employment Tribunals. Awards will be uncapped and based on the losses suffered. Furthermore, where an employee is dismissed, he may apply for an interim order to keep his job. An employer cannot rely on confidentiality clauses within the employee's contract where this would have the effect of preventing a disclosure under the Act.

In addition to employees, the Act also applies to trainees, agency staff, contractors, homeworkers, trainees and every professional in the NHS. Certain groups of people are not covered by theAct such as the genuinely self-employed, volunteers, the intelligence services, the army or police officers.

 Key point: The Public Interest Disclosure Act 1998 protects many employees who make a protected disclosure concerning their employer.

In the first instance, many employees will choose to address their concerns about malpractice in the organisation to a senior manager or representative of the employer. Many organisations will have an internal procedure for dealing with complaints by whistle-blowers. However, the existence of such a procedure is no guarantee that the employee's complaint or disclosure will be handled correctly.

In some situations, an employee may choose to make a disclosure to a prescribed regulator. In Scotland, some of the following bodies are recognised as prescribed regulators for the purposes of the 1998 Act:

- Accounts Commission for Scotland
- Audit Scotland
- Crown Office
- Customs and Excise
- Health and Safety Executive
- Inland Revenue
- Scottish Criminal Cases Review Commission
- Scottish Environment Protection Agency
- The Scottish Ministers
- Scottish Information Commissioner
- Scottish Social Services Council
- Secretary for Trade and Industry
- Standards Commission for Scotland and the Chief Investigating Officer
- Water Industry Commissioner for Scotland

In extreme cases, a failure by the employer to deal properly with a disclosure may result in the employee being forced to go outside the organisation by making a public disclosure to the media, the police, Members of the Westminster and Scottish Parliaments and non-prescribed regulators. A public disclosure will be permissible if it meets the following conditions:

- The disclosure has not been made for personal gain.
- The individual employee had a reasonable belief that he would suffer victimisation if he raised the matter internally or with a prescribed regulator.
- The individual employee had a reasonable belief that his employer would attempt to conceal malpractice and there was no prescribed regulator.
- The individual employee had already raised the matter internally or with a prescribed regulator.

In assessing how reasonably the person who made the disclosure has acted, an Employment Tribunal will wish to know to whom the disclosure was made, how serious were the concerns being raised by the disclosure, has the employer's conduct caused third parties to be exposed to danger, and has the disclosure breached a duty of confidence the employer owed a third party. If the disclosure was addressed to an employer or a prescribed regulator, the reasonableness of their response will be very important. Employment Tribunals will often examine an employer's internal whistle-blowing procedure (assuming, of course, that one exists) in order to assess if the employee's concerns or complaints were dealt with properly.

 Key point: An employee who wishes to make a protected disclosure can approach his employer or a prescribed regulator.

Case law under the Public Interest Disclosure Act 1998

 Miklaszewicz v Stolt Offshore (2002) Miklaszewicz had been dismissed in 1993 by Stolt Offshore after he had reported the company to the Inland Revenue for questionable taxation practices. Consequently, the company had been fined £3 million by the Inland Revenue. Miklaszewicz then obtained another job in the oil industry. In 1999 his current employers were taken over by Stolt Offshore. In 2000, Stolt Offshore made Miklaszewicz redundant and Miklaszewicz sued, claiming dismissal in breach of Public Interest Disclosure Act 1998 which had come into force in 1999.

Held: by the Employment Tribunal that Miklaszewicz's disclosure had been made before the Act came into force it could not, therefore, be regarded as a protected disclosure. On appeal, however, the Employment Appeal Tribunal overturned this decision because the important factor to consider was when the employee had suffered a detriment and not when he had made the original disclosure. Stolt Offshore continued to argue that the date of the disclosure was the crucial issue and appealed to the Court of Session. The Court of Session dismissed Stolt's appeal, stating that what the legislation affected was the dismissal, rather than the disclosure.

 El-Megrisi v Azad University (IR) in Oxford (2009) El-Megrisi was employed as an Academic Registrar and she had raised concerns about the immigration status of certain students and academic staff members at the Islamic Azad University. These concerns from El-Megrisi were first raised by her in November 2005 – some six months after commencing employment. In 2006, El-Megrisi went as far to put her concerns in writing which were addressed to the University's Pro-Vice Chancellor. In January 2007, El-Megrisi received four weeks' notice that she was being dismissed from her post on the grounds of redundancy. El-Megrisi then lodged a number of claims before the Employment Tribunal, namely, that her dismissal was unfair (she had not been dismissed legitimately on the grounds of redundancy) and that she had been subjected to harassment and victimisation for making a protected disclosure in terms of Section 47B of the Employment Rights Act 1996. The Employment Tribunal found that El-Megrisi had been unfairly dismissed and awarded her £16,000 in compensation. The Tribunal, however, failed to consider whether El-Megrisi had been also suffered a detriment by reason of her making a protected disclosure. The Employment Appeal Tribunal was then asked to consider whether the main reason for El-Megrisi's dismissal was due to the fact that she had made the protected disclosure which, in itself, would be a breach of Section 103A of the Employment Rights Act 1996.

Held: the Employment Appeal Tribunal decided that when determining whether someone has been dismissed for making a protected disclosure, the whole history of whistle-blowing should be considered and it is wrong merely to focus on one incident i.e. the final disclosure prior to the dismissal. The Employment Tribunal had failed to consider the whole history of El-Megrisi's concerns about the immigration status of staff and students at the University. These concerns had, of course, been voiced as early as 2005. Instead, the Tribunal had focused solely on the formal complaint that El-Megrisi had submitted to the Pro-Vice Chancellor in late 2006 and concluded that this public disclosure had not motivated the University to dismiss her. This reasoning was wrong and did not sufficiently take into account the past dealings of employee and employer. The dismissal had been by reason of El-Megrisi making the protected disclosure which was an unfair dismissal in terms of Section 103A of the Employment Rights Act 1996. Interestingly, El-Megrisi was not awarded any additional compensation and the Employment Appeal Tribunal's willingness to hear the case was doubtless driven by public interest concerns.

The President of the Employment Appeal Tribunal stated that:

'in a case where a claimant has made multiple disclosures section 103A does not require the contributions of each of them to the reason for the dismissal to be considered separately and in isolation. Where the Tribunal finds that they operated cumulatively, the question must be whether that cumulative impact was the principal reason for the dismissal.'

 Woodward *v* Abbey National plc (2006) the English Court of Appeal has stated that an employee could be subjected to post-employment victimisation by an employer in situations where a protected disclosure was made in the past. In this case, the ex-employee alleged that she had made a number of disclosures between 1991 and 1994 and, consequently, she suffered victimisation due to the fact that her ex-employer continually issued very negative references to prospective employers.

 Street *v* Derbyshire Unemployed Workers Centre (2004) the English Court of Appeal has emphasised the fact that, for any disclosure to be protected and thus benefit from the Public Interest Disclosure Act 1998, it must be made in good faith and not motivated by any animosity towards the employer.

 Key point: For a disclosure to be protected, it must be made in good faith by the employee.

Review of Employment Tribunal claims and the Public Interest Disclosure Act 1998

On 3 July 2009, the UK Department of Business, Innovation and Skills announced a review of the way in which Employment Tribunals deal with claims brought by people who are alleging that they have suffered a detriment by reason of the fact that they made a protected disclosure in terms of the Public Interest Disclosure Act

1998. The purpose of the review is to find the most appropriate way to involve the relevant regulatory authority where an allegation of wrongdoing or abuse has been raised by a claimant who has submitted a claim to an Employment Tribunal. Clearly, an Employment Tribunal does not possess the necessary expertise to deal with the disclosure by the claimant. The role of the Tribunal is merely to judge whether the claimant has suffered a detriment by reason of making the disclosure in the first place. In very serious cases of alleged wrongdoing or abuse, it will be right and proper to involve the appropriate regulator, but the key issues here are at what stage does the regulator become involved and how much information should the Tribunal exchange with the regulator? The Consultation period runs until 2 October 2009 and new Regulations will be introduced by the UK Government on 6 April 2010.

 Key point: In 2009, the UK Government announced a review of how employment tribunals deal with cases under the Public Interest Disclosure Act 1998.

Dismissal on the grounds of sexual orientation (Employment Equality (Sexual Orientation Regulations) 2003)

In terms of Regulation 6 of the Employment Equality Regulations, it is unlawful for an employer to dismiss an employee by reason of their sexual orientation. (This topic is treated to a lengthier discussion in Chapter 7).

Dismissal on the grounds of religion or belief (Regulation 6: Employment Equality (Religion or Belief Regulations) 2003)

It will be unlawful for an employer to dismiss someone by reason of their religion or belief. (This topic is treated to a lengthier discussion in Chapter 7).

Dismissal for asserting a statutory right (Section 104: ERA 1996)

 Mennell v Newell & Wright (Transport Contractors) Ltd (1997)
Mennell was employed as an HGV driver by Newell & Wright. The company wanted the employee to sign a contract which would have given it the right to make deductions from his wages when his contract ended in order to pay for training that it had provided. It was made quite clear to Mennell that he would be sacked if he continued to refuse the sign the contract. Mennell continued to refuse to sign the new contract. Mennell was eventually dismissed because of this refusal. Mennell lodged an unfair dismissal claim against his employer. At the Employment Tribunal, Mennell's action failed because he had not actually suffered unauthorised deductions from wages. His employer had only issued a potential threat that it intended to make unauthorised deductions from wages. It had not actually carried out this threat. Mennell appealed to the Employment Appeal Tribunal.

Held: by the Employment Appeal Tribunal that there was no requirement placed upon the employee to show that there had been an actual breach of one of his statutory rights. As long as the employee could demonstrate that he honestly believed that one of his statutory rights had been infringed and that his complaint had led to him being unfairly dismissed, a claim was competent. The case eventually went as far as the English Court of Appeal.

However, on the facts of the case Mennell failed to win his claim because he had failed to make an allegation that there had been an infringement of his statutory rights under Section 13 of the Employment Rights Act 1996. He could not say with any certainty where, when and to whom he had made the allegation of unauthorised deductions from wages. He had merely refused to sign the contract until the employer removed the contractual term that he found offensive.

 Key point: An employee who is dismissed for asserting a statutory right will be entitled to claim unfair dismissal.

Dismissals while the employee is taking part in industrial action (Section 16 & Schedule 5: Employment Relations Act 1999)

An employer cannot dismiss employees who are taking part in lawful, balloted industrial action for the first eight weeks of such action. This protection is absolute as long as the employee does not commit a further unlawful act over and above his initial breach of contract (i.e. by going on strike). A dismissal, regardless of the employee's age or length of service, will be automatically unfair as long as it is connected to the industrial action. This statutory protection could be extended beyond the first eight weeks if the employer has not taken reasonable steps to end the dispute.

After the initial period of eight weeks has ended, the employer cannot be selective as to which employees he decides to dismiss. All those employees engaged in the industrial action must be dismissed no matter what their motives for taking part might have been. If the employer decides to dismiss the employees who took part in industrial action, he cannot take back any of the dismissed employees for a period of at least three months.

If employees are taking part in unofficial industrial action, they will have no protection against dismissal. It is important to note that the employees who have been dismissed must be involved in unofficial action on the date of their dismissal. However, the employer cannot dismiss employees who have returned to work after taking part in an unofficial strike. A dismissal in those circumstances would not prevent these employees from lodging a claim for unfair dismissal with the Office of Employment Tribunals.

 Key point: It is unlawful for employers to dismiss employees who are taking part in legal, balloted industrial action for the first eight weeks of such action.

Dismissal on the grounds of trade union activity (Section 152: Trade Union and Labour Relations (Consolidation) Act 1992)

Dismissal for trade union membership and activity where the trade union is independent of the employer (i.e. not a staff association controlled by the employer), or a dismissal in connection with a refusal to join a trade union or a particular trade union whether it is independent or not will be regarded as unfair. Participation in trade union activities must take place at an appropriate time i.e. in the employee's own time or at time to which the employer has given his consent.

 O'Donovan v Central College of Commerce ET Case No 103652/2002
O'Donovan was employed as a lecturer at the College where he also acted as

the Branch Secretary of the Educational Institute of Scotland (Scotland's largest teaching union). O'Donovan was accused of the bullying and harassment of a support staff member who happened to be a member of the College's Board of Management. O'Donovan had put a question to this support staff member about possible lecturing staff redundancies in the event of a proposed restructuring exercise by College management. The support staff member had taken exception to this question and had made a formal complaint to the College's Principal. The College Principal, who had a very difficult relationship with O'Donovan owing to the latter's effectiveness as a trade union official, saw an opportunity to get rid of him. O'Donovan was accused of gross misconduct on very flimsy evidence. The College's disciplinary procedures were not followed correctly and O'Donovan was later dismissed. The College denied that O'Donovan had been dismissed on the grounds of trade union activity.

Held: by the Employment Tribunal that no reasonable employer would have concluded that O'Donovan's behaviour towards his colleague could have been interpreted as bullying or harassment. No rational person would have come to the conclusion that there had been gross misconduct on O'Donovan's part. In the absence of any other reasonable explanation, the Tribunal found that O'Donovan had been unfairly dismissed, in terms of Section 152 of the Trade Union and Labour Relations (Consolidation) Act 1992, for reason of his trade union activities.

 Key point: An employee who is dismissed on the grounds of participation in trade union activities will have the right to claim unfair dismissal.

Dismissal – transfer of undertakings (TUPE Regulations 2006)

The Transfer of Undertakings (Protection of Employment) Regulations 2006 (TUPE) came into force on 6th April 2006 and apply to transfers of undertakings which occur on or after this date. In many ways the updated Regulations are broadly similar to the previous Regulations of 1981, but there are significant differences.

One such difference is the duty placed upon the transferor (the previous employer) of the undertaking to provide all relevant 'employee liability information' to the transferee (the new employer). Failure to do so may mean that the transferor could be liable to pay compensation of £500 per employee. Theoretically, the new Regulations also make it easier to transfer businesses or undertakings which have become insolvent.

The 1981 TUPE Regulations continue to apply to transfers which took place prior to 6 April 2006.

The European Community Acquired Rights Directive of 1977 (as amended by Directive 98/50 EC and consolidated in 2001/23/EC) applies in situations where one employer is taken over (or transferred to) by another employer. The Directive ensures that when employees have been transferred to the new employer they will continue to enjoy the same contractual conditions that they had with their previous employer. The Directive states that the new employer will have to respect these contractual terms for a minimum of one year after the transfer has taken place. Unfortunately, this part of the Directive has never been implemented into United Kingdom law. The main provisions of the Directive were, originally brought into force by the Transfer of Undertakings (Protection of Employment) Regulations 1981 and can now be found in the 2006 version of the Regulations.

According to Regulation 3, the Regulations will apply to a relevant transfer in the following two situations:

(a) when a business or undertaking, or part of one, is transferred to a new employer; or

(b) when a 'service provision change' takes place (for example, where a contractor takes on a contract to provide a service for a client from another contractor).

Regulation 7(1) states that a dismissal of an employee that occurs either before or after a transfer will be automatically unfair if the reason for the dismissal was the transfer or a reason connected with it. It was previously the practice of many employers to dismiss the workforce either shortly before or after a transfer of a business had taken place and then offer the employees new terms and conditions of employment which were worse than those that they had previously enjoyed.

The Acquired Rights Directive 1977 and the 1981 Regulations apply in situations where a business (i.e. an undertaking) is taken over by another business. Furthermore, when a service is privatised or put out to contract, the directive and the Regulations will also apply. The Directive and the Regulations will not apply to situations where a business is taken over by someone buying up shares. Admittedly, transfers of undertakings can be a very difficult area of law to understand.

 Key point: The TUPE Regulations 2006 apply to transfers of undertakings which occur after 6 April 2006.

The European Court of Justice in **Allen _v_ Amalgamated Construction (2000)** made the following points about a relevant transfer:

'a change in the nature or legal person responsible for carrying on the business who by virtue of this acquires the obligations of an employer vis-à-vis employees of the undertaking, regardless of whether or not ownership is transferred.'

The European Court of Justice in **Allen** also stated that an entity or an undertaking is:

'an organised grouping of persons or assets facilitating the exercise of an economic activity which pursues a specific object.'

An undertaking could be, therefore, be identified by reference to its employees or workers, its management, the way in which it is organised, its operating procedures and its assets. An undertaking must be stable, identifiable and not confined to the performance of just one contract.

 Litster _v_ Forth Dry Dock and Engineering Co Ltd (1990) Forth Dry Dock went into receivership in September 1983. A company was formed in order to acquire the business of the dry dock. The transfer of the business to the new company was to take place at 4.30 p.m. on 6 February 1984. At 3.30 p.m. on that day, Forth Dry Dock dismissed the entire workforce with immediate effect. Within 48 hours, the new company began to recruit a similarly sized workforce, but at a lower rate of pay. Only 3 of the former dry dock workers obtained work with the new company. Litster, one of the employees who had failed to gain new employment with the new owner of the dock, lodged a claim for unfair dismissal in connection with a transfer of an undertaking.

Held: by the Industrial Tribunal found that Litster had been unfairly dismissed and that the Transfer of Undertakings (Protection of Employment) Regulations 1981 applied to his situation. Accordingly, the transferee, the new company had to pay him compensation. However, the Court of Session disagreed stating that even one hour before the transfer was enough to prevent the worker being employed immediately before the transfer. Litster appealed to the House of Lords. Here, the Court of Session's decision was overturned. The TUPE Regulations 1981 had to be interpreted on such a way as to give effect to the United Kingdom's duties under the Acquired Rights Directive 1977. The House of Lords effectively inserted new wording into the Regulations to cover instances of unfair dismissal. Litster could pursue an action for damages against the transferee because he would have been employed immediately before the transfer had he not been *unfairly dismissed*.

Regulation 8(2) states that paragraph (1) will not apply if the reason for the dismissal is an economic, technical or organisational reason involving changes in the workforce of either the transferor or transferee. If the employer can show that he has dismissed an employee for an economic, technical or organisational reason, the dismissal will not be classed as automatically unfair.

In **Katsikas *v* Konstantidis C132/91 (1993)**, the European Court of Justice ruled that an employee could not be transferred to the employment of a new employer against his will. If such an employee does object to his employment being transferred, the transfer effectively terminates his employment, but he will not be able to claim that he has been unfairly dismissed.

 Key point: A dismissal of an employee which takes place either before or after a transfer of an undertaking will be automatically unfair.

Dismissal in connection with spent convictions in relation to Section 4(3)(b) of the Rehabilitation of Offenders Act 1974

If the employee has previously been convicted of a criminal offence, he will, for certain periods of time laid down by the Rehabilitation of Offenders Act 1974, have to declare his conviction when applying for employment. However, there will come a point when many convictions are regarded as spent i.e. the individual will no longer have to declare them. If the employer decides to dismiss an employee for reason of a spent conviction, then the dismissal will be regarded as automatically unfair.

Other automatically unfair dismissals

An employee will be regarded as having been unfairly dismissed where he attempts to assert his rights to the national minimum wage (Section 104A: ERA 1996) and where he asserts his right to a tax credit (Section 104B: ERA 1996).

 Key point: When a dismissal is regarded as automatically unfair, an employee does not have to show that he or she has one year's continuous service with the employer in order to lodge a claim for unfair dismissal.

Constructive dismissal

Section 95(1)(c) of the Employment Rights Act 1996 recognises the concept of constructive dismissal. The employee's right to claim constructive dismissal arises in situations where the employer's conduct is to be regarded as a material breach of the employment contract and the employee is left with no alternative but to resign. However, the employee's resignation is not treated as the act which terminates the contract, rather it is the employer's conduct. The employer's conduct must be so serious in order to justify the employee's decision to resign. When an employee claims that he has been constructively dismissed, he is claiming that he was unfairly dismissed. The right of constructive dismissal would arise in situations where the employer made unauthorised deductions from wages, where the employer refused to follow the proper disciplinary or grievance procedures or where the employee was ordered to use equipment that was clearly dangerous.

 Sharp _v_ Western Excavating Ltd (1978) Sharp's contract of employment entitled him to claim time off in lieu if he worked overtime for his employer. Sharp played cards as part of a team and he wished to take some time off from work in order to play in a particular game. His request for time off was refused because the company had a lot of work on and could not spare him from his duties. Undeterred by his employer's refusal, Sharp decided to take the time off in any case. As a result of this conduct, the company's foreman decided to dismiss Sharp. He then appealed to the employer's Internal Disciplinary Board which overturned the dismissal and, in its place, he received a five-day suspension without pay. Sharp found himself short of funds and asked his employer for an advance on his accrued holiday pay. This request was refused by the employer. Sharp then asked his employer to lend him a sum of £40 which the employer again refused to advance. Sharp then decided to resign from his employment in order to force his employer to pay his accrued holiday pay. He also claimed that his employer had behaved unreasonably and that he had no option but to treat himself as having been constructively dismissed.

Held: by the English Court of Appeal that the employer's treatment of Sharp had been reasonable throughout and he could not treat himself as constructively dismissed. The employer's conduct could in no way be described as a repudiation of the contract which would have allowed Sharp to consider himself as having been constructively dismissed. In a very important passage from the Court of Appeal's judgement, Lord Denning laid down the essential conditions for constructive dismissal:

'An employee is entitled to treat himself as constructively dismissed if the employer is guilty of conduct which is a significant breach going to the root of the contract of employment, or which shows that the employer no longer intends to be bound by one or more of the essential terms of the contract, then the employee is entitled to treat himself as discharged from any further performance. If he does so, then he terminates the contract by reason of the employer's conduct. He is then constructively dismissed. The employee is then entitled in those circumstances to leave at that instant without giving any notice at all or, alternatively, he may give notice and say that he is leaving at *the end of the notice. But the conduct in either case must be sufficiently serious to entitle him to leave at once. .... the employee must make up his mind soon after the conduct of which he complains. If he continues for any length of time without leaving, he will be treated as having elected to affirm the contract and he will lose his right to treat himself as discharged.'*

 Sinclair v Fritz Companies (1999) Carole Sinclair received an invitation to go for lunch with her supervisors. During lunch, it became evident that this was not a purely social occasion as the supervisors began to discuss the possibility of imposing a disciplinary penalty on Sinclair. Sinclair had received absolutely no warning that the possibility of disciplinary action being taken against her would be discussed during lunch. Consequently, Sinclair felt that her trust and confidence in her employer had completely broken down and she resigned from her employment claiming that she had been constructively dismissed.

Held: by the Employment Appeal Tribunal that Sinclair's claim for constructive dismissal should succeed.

 Key point: An employee is entitled to treat himself as constructively dismissed if the employer is guilty of conduct which is a significant breach going to the root of the contract of employment, or which shows that the employer no longer intends to be bound by one or more of the essential terms of the contract.

Section 95(1)(c) of the Employment Rights Act 1996 recognises the concept of constructive dismissal whereby an employee may terminate his/her contract of employment in certain situations without the requirement to give the employer notice. Such a right arises when the employer breaches a material term of the contract and the employee feels that s/he has no alternative but to resign from employment (see Lord Denning's statement from **Sharp v Western Excavating Ltd (1978)**). This resignation is regarded in law as a dismissal owing to the employer's conduct. Successful constructive dismissal claims have arisen where the employee has been bullied or harassed by the employer, where the employer has made unauthorised deductions from wages or where the employee's trust and confidence in the employer has irretrievably broken down.

In **France v Westminster City Council (2003)**, the Employment Appeal Tribunal (EAT) gave the following definition of the concept of constructive dismissal:

'In relation to constructive dismissal, in broad terms, there have to be four elements. There has to be a breach of contract by the employer which can be either an actual breach or an anticipatory breach, and the breach must be sufficiently important to justify the employee resigning; or it can be one of the last of a series of incidents which justifies leaving. The two other conditions normally are that the employee must leave in response to the breach and not for some other unconnected reason, and, finally, the employee must not take too long about it.'

In **Wishaw & District Housing Association v Moncrieff (2009)** the Employment Appeal Tribunal in Scotland has more recently provided helpful guidelines for Employment Tribunals when dealing with claims for constructive dismissal.

 Moncrieff had taken a claim to the Employment Tribunal alleging constructive unfair dismissal against his employer, the Housing Association. Moncrieff had been absent from his employment as a property services officer due to ill health caused by stress. Prior to this sickness absence, his employer had alerted him to concerns about the way in which he was performing his job. Moncrieff claimed that the way in which his employer communicated these concerns to him caused him to suffer stress and anxiety. Furthermore, Moncrieff did not accept the allegations by his employer that he was failing to perform his job to the standard expected of him. The situation was also compounded by the fact that Moncrieff was apparently having to deal with problems in his private life which was causing him to suffer from stress and anxiety. In an attempt to get to the bottom of some of these issues, the employer had asked Moncrieff to attend an appointment with an occupational health professional. This did not resolve the situation and, eventually, Moncrieff instructed solicitors to act on his behalf regarding any dealings with his employer. Eventually, Moncrieff resigned from employment claiming that his employer had completely mishandled the situation and, therefore, this was the last straw which led to a complete breakdown in the trust and confidence which an employee should have in his or her employer. Moncrieff won his claim at the Employment Tribunal Hearing, but his employer appealed against this decision.

Held: by the Employment Appeal Tribunal that Moncrieff's claim for unfair constructive dismissal should not succeed. The Employment Tribunal had failed to carry out a proper analysis of the situation when deciding whether Moncrieff had been constructively dismissed by his employer. According to Lady Smith, the President of the Employment Appeal Tribunal, an Employment Tribunal dealing with unfair constructive dismissal must have regard to the following issues:

1   The specific incident which led the employee to resign from employment (the so called last straw) must be pinpointed;

2   Once this incident has been pinpointed, the Tribunal must carry out an objective assessment to judge whether it can contribute to a chain of events which taken together convey the overall impression that the employer has breached its implied duty of trust and confidence; and

3   If the incident has the potential to be viewed as breach of the duty of trust and confidence does it in fact constitute the last straw in a chain of events which would permit the affected employee to treat himself as constructively dismissed?

The Employment Tribunal had failed to pinpoint the specific incident which could be considered the last straw in a chain of events and it was quite obvious that it failed to approach the case in a systematic fashion. The Employment Appeal Tribunal then went on to consider two situations which might have been identified as the last straw i.e. two letters from the employer to Moncrieff – one about the employer's sickness procedures in the event of his further absence from work and the other suggesting that the Advisory Conciliation and Arbitration Service (ACAS) might become involved in order to aid a resolution of this employment law problem. Neither letter on objective analysis, however, had the potential to be considered as the last straw in a chain of events which would have led Moncrieff to conclude that he had the right to treat himself as constructively dismissed.

Unreasonable behaviour by an employer

The fact that an employer has behaved unreasonably towards an employee does not necessarily provide grounds for claiming constructive, unfair dismissal as the Employment Appeal Tribunal decided in a recent case.

 Nationwide Building Society *v* Niblett (2009) Niblett had held a senior post in IT with the Nationwide Building Society. He had resigned from his employment following an accusation by his manager that he had attempted to defraud the employer by falsely claiming payment for overtime for which he had not received authorisation. Niblett believed that, under the Nationwide's disciplinary procedure, his treatment had not been fair and he considered this to amount to a breakdown in the trust and confidence that he expected to be present in his relationship with his employer. Niblett claimed constructive, unfair dismissal and lodged a claim with the Employment Tribunal, which he won. Nationwide appealed.

Held: by the Employment Appeal Tribunal that Employment Tribunal had made an error in the way in which it had concluded that Niblett had been constructively dismissed. Admittedly, Nationwide had behaved unreasonably towards Niblett, but its conduct in the matter did not signify a deliberate intention to destroy the employment relationship which depends on the trust and confidence between employer and employee. The Employment Appeal Tribunal made the following statement:

'It is not the law that an employee can resign without notice merely because an employer has behaved unreasonably in some respect. In the context of the implied term of trust and confidence, the employer's conduct must be without proper and reasonable cause and must be calculated or likely to destroy or seriously damage the relationship of confidence and trust between employer and employee.'

In consequence, the Employment Appeal Tribunal ordered that the matter of whether Niblett had been constructively dismissed should now be heard by a different Employment Tribunal.

 Key point: Merely because an employer has behaved unreasonably will not give an employee the right to treat himself as constructively dismissed.

Remedies for unfair dismissal

Sections 111 to 132 of the Employment Rights Act 1996 contain much of the detail relating to remedies for unfair dismissal.

An Employment Tribunal, on finding that an employee has been dismissed unfairly, may issue an order addressed to the employer to the effect that the employee is to be re-employed. The problem with issuing these orders is that the Employment Tribunal cannot force the employer to re-employ the dismissed employee. This is because of the nature of employment contracts which depend, of course, on the personalities of the parties and a level of goodwill continuing to exist between these individuals. At common law and at statute, a court will not force an employer to take back a dismissed employee if re-employment means that the relationship between employer and employee was going to be characterised by conflict.

Many employers will choose not to comply with an order to re-employ the dismissed individual and will be quite happy to pay the increased compensation which follows as a result of this decision on their part. Section 117(4)(a) of the Employment Rights Act 1996 allows the employer to argue that it is not practical to re-employ the dismissed employee. An employer may wish to use this provision in situations where a considerable length of time has passed between the dismissal and the Employment Tribunal's decision. Very often, the employer will have appointed a new employee to take the dismissed employee's place and this individual may well have acquired employment rights i.e. protection against unfair dismissal so the employer cannot dismiss this person without risking further legal problems. Additionally, the dismissed employee's job may since have disappeared as a result of a reorganisation of the employer's business or because the post has become redundant.

The two orders that an Employment Tribunal can issue requesting that the employee be re-employed are:

1   Reinstatement orders

2   Re-engagement orders

Reinstatement order

This requires the employer to give the employee back the job that he previously held and to treat him as if the dismissal had never occurred. The employee is entitled to any benefits that he would have received, but for the termination of his contract. This would include pay rises or salary increments or any other benefits, for example, concessionary rail travel (Section 114(1) Employment Rights Act 1996).

Re-engagement order

This requires the employer to engage the employee on comparable employment to that from which he was dismissed or to be offered suitable, alternative employment. The Employment Tribunal will decide the terms upon which the employee is to be re-engaged. It should be noted that this type of Order differs from a Reinstatement Order in that the employee is not being given back his old job (Section 115(1) Employment Rights Act 1996).

Interim relief

In several situations, the Employment Tribunal can issue an interim order which means that the dismissed employee's contract will continue to have legal force until the outcome of the case is decided. An interim order can also be used to prevent the employee from being dismissed until the Employment Tribunal has made its decision. The employee, therefore, will continue to enjoy the benefits of his employment contract while his claim for unfair dismissal is being heard and ultimately decided upon. An interim order will only be granted in trade union dismissals, health and safety dismissals and dismissals where the employee has made a protected disclosure.

 Key point: An interim order can be very useful because it can prevent an employer from dismissing an employee until such time as the Employment Tribunal has made its decision.

Compensation

In most situations, an Employment Tribunal will award compensation to the dismissed employee. Compensation consists of two parts:

1 The basic award

2 The compensatory award

The basic award

Since 1 February 2009, the maximum amount for the basic award that any individual can receive upon winning a claim for unfair dismissal at an Employment Tribunal is £10,500. The basic award is calculated according to the following formula:

◆ The employee is entitled to one and a half weeks' pay for each year of service including and above the age of 41
◆ The employee is entitled to one week's pay for each year of service when the employee was aged between 22 and 40 inclusive
◆ The employee is entitled to half a week's pay for each year of service between the age 18 and 21 inclusive

However, this formula is subject to two further conditions:

◆ From 1 October 2009, the maximum weekly wage that can be claimed is £380 (from the previous figure of £350 which had been in force from 1 February 2009). Anything above the figure of £380 cannot be included in the calculation of the basic award
◆ The employee will only receive compensation for a maximum of 20 years' service – anything above 20 years will not be counted

In order to calculate the basic award, the employee should start with the effective date of the dismissal and count backwards. The following example can be quite useful:

Helen Smith, age 55, was employed continuously for a period of 30 years until dismissed on 1 October 2009. Helen received weekly wages of £350 at the time of her dismissal. To calculate her basic award Helen would count backwards from 1 October up to a maximum of 20 years. Therefore, ten years of her employment would not count towards the final total for the basic award and she could only claim £350 for her weekly wage not the maximum of £380. So, Helen has worked for 15 years between the ages of 55 and 41: (1½ × £350) = £525 × 15 = £7875. Helen has also worked for five years between the ages of 40 and 36: (1 × £350) = £350 × 5 = £1750. If the totals are added together (£5625 + £1250), Helen's basic award comes to £9625.

The basic award that the employee receives could be reduced for a number of reasons:

◆ Where the employee's conduct has contributed to the dismissal.
◆ Where the employer gave the employee a redundancy payment or ex-gratia payment.
◆ Where the employee has unreasonably refused an offer of reinstatement from the employer.

The compensatory award

The compensatory award for unfair dismissal from 1 February 2010 is subject to a limit of £65,300 (which is a reduction from the previous figure of £66,200). The award will cover immediate loss of wages, future loss, loss of pension rights and loss of statutory protection. The maximum award may be much greater in health safety dismissals, whistle-blowing cases and cases involving discrimination.

Future loss and loss of statutory rights

The Employment Tribunal will also consider a dismissed employee's future loss of wages and will estimate how long the individual is out of work. If, however, an individual bringing an unfair dismissal claim secures a new job fairly quickly, the Employment Tribunal will not give any consideration to this issue.

Another matter which the Employment Tribunal will have to consider when making an award to a dismissed employee is loss of statutory rights. An employee with more than one year's continuous service when dismissed loses the right to claim unfair dismissal until they complete a year's service with a new employer. This means that the employee has, for a period of his or service with the new employer, lost any protection that they previously enjoyed under the Employment Rights Act 1996 and the Employment Tribunal should take this situation into consideration when calculating the amount of compensation to be paid to the dismissed employee.

 Key point: An Employment Tribunal can issue Orders for Reinstatement or Re-engagement or, more commonly, an award of compensation will be made consisting of a basic award and a compensatory award.

Compensation for injury to feelings

In the House of Lords' decision **Johnson v Unisys Ltd (2001)**, Lord Hoffman suggested (in a remark which was *obiter* i.e. did not form part of the court's decision) that compensation can include an element for injury to the feelings of the dismissed employee. This, however, goes against the rule established in the much older case of **Norton Tool Co Ltd v Tewson (1972)**. In **Norton**, Sir John Donaldson was at pains to point out that compensation for dismissal only includes financial loss - not injury to feelings. These types of awards are, of course, available in discrimination cases. Strictly speaking, Lord Hoffman's remark about compensation for injury to feelings was not binding and did not overrule Sir John Donaldson's position in **Norton**. Lord Steyn, who was sitting as part of the same panel of judges that included Lord Hoffman in **Johnson**, did point out that, as the issue of mental stress and anxiety was not raised as part of the original action, it would be wrong for the House of Lords to comment.

However, **Johnson v Unisys Ltd (2001)** did at first suggest that there was going to be a significant development in this area of unfair dismissal law.

In **Dunnachie v Kingston upon Hull City Council (2004)**, the English Court of Appeal stated that a compensatory award for unfair dismissal could also include injury to an employee's feelings. The Court of Appeal was clearly relying upon an obiter remark made by Lord Hoffman during the decision of the House of Lords in **Johnson v Unisys (2001)**.

As far back as the decision by the National Industrial Relations Court in **Norton Tool Co Ltd v Tewson (1972)**, the position was quite clear: the compensatory award in unfair dismissal claims did not include injury to an employee's feelings in connection with the manner of the dismissal suffered by him or her. Lord Hoffman's obiter statement and the decision by the Court of Appeal in **Dunnachie** appeared to place this principle in considerable doubt and opened the door to what could have been a potentially significant, new development in unfair dismissal case law. Clearly, it would be advantageous for the House of Lords to provide a definitive ruling on this matter.

Subsequently, Kingston upon Hull City Council appealed against the judgement of the Court of Appeal to the House of Lords.

On 15 July 2004, the House of Lords delivered its judgement in this case. Their Lordships (Lord Hoffman amongst them) killed off any idea that an award for unfair dismissal could include injury to an employee's feelings for the manner of the dismissal. Compensation, therefore, in unfair dismissal claims will be concerned with the employee's economic losses only.

The decision of the House of Lords in **Dunnachie v Kingston upon Hull City Council (2004)** is a clear restatement of the orthodox position as set down by Sir John Donaldson all those years ago in **Norton Tool Co Ltd**.

As Lord Steyn remarked in **Dunnachie**:

*'On the other hand, the correctness of the **Norton Tool** decision was not an issue in **Johnson v Unisys**. It is true that there were references by both sides in the oral argument to **Norton Tool**. But the House heard no adversarial argument exploring the correctness or otherwise of that decision. In these circumstances a definitive overruling of a decision which had stood for nearly 30 years would have been a little surprising.'*

In fact, Lord Hoffman's observation (and it was nothing more than observation we are now assured) could in no way be interpreted as an attempt to overturn a long-standing and well-established legal principle. Lord Hoffman, in **Johnson v Unisys (2001)**, was not 'inviting the House to overrule a longstanding decision on a point of statutory construction that was not in issue and not explored in opposing arguments'. The statement by Lord Hoffman was clearly *obiter dictum* i.e. things said by the way which do not form part of the actual court's judgement and that was the end of the matter.

 Key point: Compensation for unfair dismissal does **not** include injury to feelings for the manner of the dissmisal.

 Many claims for unfair dismisssal do not proceed to tribunal and are settled out of court. Examples of COT3 and Compromise Agreements which settle claims can be seen on the Introductory Scots Law website.

Fair dismissal

Some dismissals by the employer will be automatically fair:

◆ On the grounds of national security
◆ During a strike or a lock-out

Section 98(2) of the Employment Rights Act 1996 details the reasons which an employer may rely upon to demonstrate that the dismissal was fair. The following reasons for dismissal are, therefore, potentially fair:

◆ Capability and qualifications of the employee for performing the work he was employed to do
◆ Sickness
◆ Conduct of the employee within and outwith employment
◆ Redundancy
◆ To avoid contravening statute
◆ Any other substantial reason

 Key point: Where an employee is claiming unfair dismissal, the employer may be able to counter this by relying on one of the potentially fair reasons for dismissal i.e. capability and qualifications, conduct, redundancy, contravention of statute or any other substantial reason.

Capability and qualifications

With respect to qualifications an employer may insist that, in order to be given employment, the employee must possess any relevant degree, diploma or other academic, technical or professional qualifications.

An employee may be said to lack qualifications if the employer states that he is required to pass any test after starting work which he then fails. In order to make this requirement legally binding upon the employee, there must be a term in the contract of employment which imposes a duty on the employee to gain the relevant qualifications.

Lack of qualifications

 Blackman *v* Post Office (1974) Blackman was appointed to the position of a post and telegraph officer. Blackman was appointed to the post on the strict understanding that he had to pass an aptitude test after he had he successfully completed his probationary period. Blackman failed the test three times (his third attempt was a very narrow fail). There had been no complaints about the quality of Blackman's work.

Held: the dismissal was fair because he had failed to secure the necessary qualification that his employer had made a condition of his continuing employment.

 Tayside Regional Council *v* McIntosh (1982) McIntosh was employed by the Regional Council as a motor mechanic. When the post was originally advertised, the Council had made it perfectly clear to all applicants that the successful candidate had to possess a clear, current driving licence. A potential problem later arose for the Council in that there was no term in McIntosh's contract that stated that he had to possess a clear, current driving licence. McIntosh had been disqualified from driving and the Council had dismissed him.

Held: by the Employment Appeal Tribunal that McIntosh's failure to retain a clear, current driving licence was a breach of a material and continuing condition of his employment with the Council.

Usually, the employer will have to include a term in the contract of employment stating that an employee's continued employment depends on him securing a particular qualification, for example, a welder's certificate or a teaching qualification. Obviously, failure to secure such a qualification will give the employer the option of dismissing the employee fairly.

However, there will be situations where the employer has failed to include such a term in the employee's contract. An argument open to the employer would be to state that his requirements have changed since the employee was first appointed and that he can no longer be kept fully employed. The employer must act reasonably in applying a unilateral change to the employee's contract.

 Rooney *v* Davies Engineering Ltd (1979) Rooney had passed the company's test and had successfully completed his probationary period. However, the company experienced a sharp decline in a particular area of work that Rooney was involved in. In fact, 90 to 95 per cent of the company's work was then carried out for one customer in particular. This customer demanded that those of the company's workers who were engaged in producing his goods had to possess a particular welding qualification. Rooney did not possess this qualification. He had, in fact, sat the test to obtain the qualification on three occasions and each attempt had ended in failure. The Company had warned Rooney of the potentially serious consequences of such a failure in respect of his continuing job security. After his third failure, Rooney was dismissed by the company because it did not have enough work to keep him fully employed. The customer had refused to allow the company to give Rooney a fourth opportunity to gain the necessary qualification.

Held: by the Employment Tribunal that the dismissal was fair because there had been a change in the employer's requirements and Rooney was fully aware of the consequences of a failure to gain the necessary qualification.

Incapability
Lord Denning MR in **Taylor *v* Alidair (1978)** stated:

'Whenever a man is dismissed for incapacity or incompetence it is sufficient that the employer honestly believes on reasonable grounds that the man is incapable or incompetent. It is not necessary for the employer to prove that he is in fact incapable or incompetent.'

A reasonable employer is in the best position to decide whether an employee is not up to the job on the ground of incapability. It is not the place of the Employment Tribunal to overrule the decision of a reasonable employer in this matter.

 Taylor *v* Alidair (1978), an airline pilot had landed the plane in a grossly negligent way that clearly endangered life and limb. The employer was quite clearly justified when it decided to dismiss this particular employee.

Clark *v* Airflow Streamlines PLC (1983) the employee was an experienced motor mechanic who had failed to carry out a job on a customer's car properly. Due to his negligence, the engine seized and the rear wheels locked while the customer was driving the vehicle. The employee was dismissed.

Held: the Employment Tribunal was influenced by the fact that the customer's safety could have been endangered and there was also the issue of the employer's good reputation being damaged by the employee's negligence. The dismissal was, therefore, regarded as fair.

 Steelprint Ltd *v* Haynes (1995) the company had introduced a new computer system. This meant that the employee's duties changed considerably. Her post had previously entailed proofreading. Her new duties meant that she was expected to input data into the new computer system. She was not able to carry out these duties to the standard required by the company. The employee had not received any training to help her cope with her new duties nor had she been offered alternative employment with the company that would have better suited her abilities. Nonetheless, the company decided to dismiss her for reason of incapability.

Held: by the Employment Appeal Tribunal that the dismissal was unfair. The lack of training and the failure to provide other opportunities was not the act of a reasonable employer.

Sickness

It is important that an employer investigate the background to the employee's sickness as fully as possible.

 Smith *v* Post Office ET Case No 7707/95 the Employment Tribunal found that it was highly unlikely that the employee in question who was suffering from clinical depression would be able to achieve a satisfactory level of attendance at his work in the future. The dismissal of the employee on the grounds of his ill-health was considered to be fair.

The Employment Appeal Tribunal stated in **Spencer *v* Paragon Wallpapers Ltd (1977)** that Tribunals must look at all the circumstances before weighing up the economic needs of the employer and the need to treat the sick employee decently. The question that should be asked is 'how long the employer must be kept waiting for the employee to return to work?'

Employment Tribunals, however, tend to take a more lenient approach where an employer has dismissed an employee for a series of short-term and unconnected absences from work which are usually justified on the grounds of illness. An Employment Tribunal will often be swayed by the hardship caused to smaller employers by these periodic absences.

 International Sports Co Ltd *v* Thomson (1980) in the last 18 months of employment leading to Thomson's dismissal, her absences from work reached a total of 25 per cent. All these absences could be explained by reference to medical certificates that Thomson had submitted. All of the illnesses were unconnected and there was no way that they could be independently verified by sending Thomson to a doctor for a medical examination. The employer, therefore, chose not to obtain a medical report before dismissing her. Thomson had been warned about her poor attendance on four previous occasions by the employer.

Held: by the Employment Appeal Tribunal that this dismissal was on the grounds of misconduct rather than the employee's sickness record and was, therefore, fair.

 Rolls-Royce v Walpole (1980) Walpole had just managed to achieve an attendance record at work of approximately 50 per cent during the last three years of his employment. The employer had warned Walpole about his failure to attend work and it had even sent him for counselling to identify the reasons behind his absences two years before he was dismissed. The employer, however, failed to obtain medical evidence before he decided to dismiss Walpole.

Held: by the Employment Appeal Tribunal that the dismissal was fair.

Even if the employee's absence from work is covered by a sick note, this should not be considered as conclusive proof that the employee is medically unfit for work.

 Hutchinson v Enfield Rolling Mills Ltd (1981) Hutchinson had submitted a sick note to cover his absence from work due to sciatica. He was later seen attending a trade union demonstration in Brighton during the period that the sick note covered. The employer did not follow any procedure and Hutchinson was dismissed.

Held: the dismissal was fair.

In **East Lindsey District Council v Daubney (1977)** the Employment Appeal Tribunal stated that before an employee decides to dismiss an employee on the grounds of ill-health, proper consultation must have taken place. Proper consultation will consist of the following factors:

♦ The employer must hold discussions with the employee at the outset of the illness and these should continue throughout the course of the illness. The employee should be alerted when his dismissal is a serious option.
♦ There should be personal contact between the employer and the employee.
♦ The employee should be asked for his opinion regarding his medical condition by the employer.
♦ The employer should consider alternative employment for the employee within the organisation.

In **Taylorplan Catering (Scotland) Ltd v McInally (1980)** the Employment Appeal Tribunal again stressed the importance of the employer holding consultations with a sick employee. Such a consultation exercise means that the employer's need to have the employee present at work can be weighed against the employee's need to be given time to regain his health and fitness which makes his return to work possible.

This area is now more complicated as a result of the Disability Discrimination Act 1995. When dealing with an employee who is absent from work due to ill-health, a reasonable employer should take steps to establish whether the individual in question is suffering from a disability. A disability will affect not only the individual's ability to perform his job, but also his ability to perform normal day-to-day activities. If this is the case, the employer will have to make reasonable adjustments in terms of Section 6 of the Disability Discrimination Act 1995 to the employee's working conditions in order to aid his return to work.

 Key point: When the employer decides to dismiss an employee on the grounds of his sickness record, he will have to tread carefully in order to avoid potential charges of disability discrimination.

Misconduct

This is a potentially fair reason that the employer can use to justify the employee's dismissal. However, dismissal for a single act of misconduct will normally be considered to be fair in cases of gross misconduct only. In many workplaces, the employer will have a disciplinary code. Where there are 20 or more employees, such a disciplinary code should form part of the written statement that each employee should receive within two months of commencing their employment.

Disciplinary codes should be well publicised and consistently applied. Consistent application of the disciplinary code does not mean, however, that the employer will achieve the same result in every situation. Sometimes a warning, whether written or verbal, may be a more appropriate method of disciplining an employee who has been found guilty of misconduct. Alternatively, more serious penalties such as demotion or dismissal may be considered to be the correct approach in dealing with the employee's misconduct. This range of options available to an employer in cases involving the employee's misconduct is known as the band of reasonable responses. A reasonable employer should be allowed to select the most appropriate punishment.

Dismissal is the harshest punishment that can be imposed on the employee for behaviour that the employer considers to be gross misconduct. If the employer has acted reasonably in making the decision to dismiss the employee, an Employment Tribunal has no right to overturn this by stating that it would have imposed a more lenient punishment. The Tribunal must accept a reasonable employer's decision **(Iceland Frozen Foods Ltd v Jones (1983))**.

An example of an employer failing to follow consistent disciplinary procedures is illustrated by the following case:

 Rankin v Compaq Computers ET Case No S 103023/2002 three computer plant workers were dismissed by the employer for sending and/or receiving e-mail messages with a sexual content. The three employees claimed that they were treated more harshly in that, previously, other workers had committed equivalent and, in some case, worse offences. The three went on to claim that the practice of sending offensive e-mails via the employer's network was widespread. Evidence was shown that at least 100 employees were investigated for alleged abuse of the network, but in many cases no further action was taken by the employer. In fact, one of the managers, who was supposed to monitor the network and prevent such abuses from occurring, was an active participant in these activities. The manager was not dismissed and the employer chose not to pursue disciplinary action against this individual.

Held: by the Employment Tribunal that the three employees who had been dismissed knew that their behaviour was inappropriate and furtive. The Tribunal found that the employer had failed to apply the disciplinary procedures consistently and that the three dismissals were unfair. Two of the workers received a year's salary in compensation, whereas the third employee was entitled to receive nine months' salary.

In **L B Harrow v Cunningham (1996)** the Employment Appeal Tribunal stated that factors such as an employee's record might justify an employer punishing different employees in different ways.

In **British Home Stores Ltd v Burchell (1980)** it was held that the employer does not have to prove beyond a reasonable doubt that the employee is guilty of misconduct. If the employer can show that, after a reasonable investigation has been carried out, he reasonably believes the employee to be guilty of misconduct, the dismissal will be fair.

If more than one employee is suspected of misconduct and it is not possible for the employer to discover who is in the wrong, the employer may be justified in dismissing all those employees who fall under suspicion.

 Monie v Coral Racing Ltd (1981), the employer suspected several employees of having committed theft by breaking into the company safe during the course of their employment. After an investigation by the employer, it was still not possible to identify beyond a reasonable doubt which of the two employees was to blame. However, of the two employees suspected, one of them had to have committed the crime. Both employees were, therefore, dismissed.

Held: by the English Court of Appeal that the dismissals were fair.

 Key point: In misconduct dismissals, the employer will have to show that he acted reasonably.

 In **Tesco Stores Ltd v Pryke (2006)**, the employee, a driver for Tesco, was driving a company lorry when the vehicle overturned at a roundabout. The driver was dismissed from employment by reason of misconduct despite having an exemplary safety record. Subsequently, the driver took a claim to the Office of Employment Tribunals where he won his claim and got the Tribunal to issue a Reinstatement Order. Tesco appealed against this judgement to the Employment Appeal Tribunal.

Held: the original Tribunal had committed an error in law by applying its opinion or view concerning how the employer should have handled the investigation which led, ultimately, to the employee's dismissal.

It should be remembered that employers should be given a certain amount of leeway by Tribunals as to how they handle situations such as this. By all means the employer's decision to dismiss an employee with an exemplary safety record may appear to be rather harsh, but it is still a reasonable response given the health and safety concerns raised by the incident. In other words, the Tribunal erred in law when it decided that the employer's decision to dismiss this employee was too harsh. Dismissal was just one of the band or range of reasonable responses that a reasonable employer was entitled to select in response to this particular situation.

Clearly, however, the reasonable employer will carry out a proper investigation to establish the facts and then, if necessary, commence the internal disciplinary procedure which should be fully compliant with the new ACAS Code of Practice on disciplinary and grievance which came into force on 6 April 2009.

Misconduct committed outside working hours

A popular misconception continues to circulate amongst employees that you cannot be dismissed from employment for misconduct committed outside of working hours or for other types of behaviour indulged in during your spare time.

Two fairly recent cases have highlighted the fact that an employer may be able to dismiss an employee for activities which take place outside employment but which have a negative impact on the employee's service.

In **Pay v Lancashire Probation Service (2003)** an employee was fairly dismissed by reason of activities that he participated in questionable activities which took place outside of working hours. It will be remembered that Pay, the employee in question, was a Probation Officer with special responsibility for sex offenders. Pay, in his spare time, performed as part of a circus act which had strong sexual overtones. His involvement in these types of activities was regarded as constituting gross misconduct by the Probation Service, his employer, which was extremely concerned how this would impact on his work with convicted sex offenders. Consequently, Pay was dismissed and the dismissal was held to be fair.

In a decision which at first seemed to sit at odds with **Pay** (above), an employee's outside activities were not deemed to be sufficient grounds for his dismissal by his employer.

In **Redfearn v Serco t/a West Yorkshire Transport Services (2005)** the employer dismissed Mr Redfearn on health and safety grounds because of his membership of the racist British National Party (BNP). The Employment Appeal Tribunal ruled that Redfearn's dismissal could be an example of racial discrimination. It is also worth considering that had this employee completed a year's continuous service with his employer then he would also have had the right to lodge a claim for unfair dismissal - whether or not such a claim would have been successful is purely a matter of speculation. The English Court of Appeal has now overruled the decision of the Employment Appeal Tribunal and reinstated the original decision made by the Employment Tribunal by ruling that Redfearn could be lawfully dismissed on health and safety grounds owing to his BNP membership which might lead to violence being caused in the workplace.

Redfearn's dismissal was **not** an example of unlawful, racial discrimination committed by the employer as previously stated by the Employment Appeal Tribunal.

Misuse of drugs and alcohol

Employment Tribunals have tended to take a much tougher approach to the issue of drug abuse by employees. The use of drugs is illegal in terms of the Misuse of Drugs Act 1971 and employers can also find themselves being convicted of a crime if they have knowledge that drugs have been consumed on the premises.

 Key point: Many Employment Tribunal decisions have explicitly recognised that there is a clear relationship between the act of misconduct committed outside working hours and the interests of the employer.

Dismissal in order to avoid contravening statute

In certain situations, the continued employment of the employee will cause the employer to breach a statute. Such situations are particularly common in relation to health and safety issues or where the employee holds a position as a driver and he has received a ban in terms of the road traffic legislation.

 Yarrow v QIS Ltd ET Case No. 1270/79 Yarrow was employed as a radiographer whose continued employment was covered by the Ionisation Radiation (Sealed Sources) Regulations of 1969. The Regulations made it illegal for an employer to continue to employee an individual who had developed a number of specified diseases. Yarrow developed psoriasis – a disease which the Regulations listed – and, as a result, the employer decided to dismiss him. The employer had thought about suspending Yarrow, but the trouble with psoriasis is that it is a disease that cannot be cured – it can only be controlled. There was no real likelihood that Yarrow would be able to return to his work and, therefore, he was regarded as being permanently unfit for work.

Held: there was no alternative work that Yarrow could have performed for the employer. The employer had been correct to dismiss Yarrow as to continue to have employed him would have meant breaking the Regulations.

 Appleyard v F M Smith (Hull) Ltd (1972) Appleyard was employed as a driver and maintenance fitter who was banned from driving for a period of 12 months. The employer decided to dismiss him when it learned about his driving ban. A condition of the contract of employment was that employees had to hold a current driving licence. As part of the job, Appleyard had to carry tools and spare parts which the employer argued could not be carried on public transport. Furthermore, Appleyard's colleagues could not be expected to drive him out to jobs. There was very little point in continuing to employ Appleyard if all he was doing was hanging about the workshop while his colleagues were forced to take on his duties.

Held: the dismissal was fair on the grounds of a statutory ban. The Employment Tribunal did make the point that a larger employer may have been a position to offer Appleyard alternative employment, but in the present case where there were only three employees in the department this was not possible.

Dismissal on the grounds of redundancy

Section 139(1) of the Employment Rights Act 1996 states that dismissal on the grounds of redundancy will occur if:

1 The employer has ceased or intends to cease carrying on the business

or

2 The requirements for employees to carry out work of a particular kind or to carry it out at the place in which they are employed have ceased or diminished

An employer can always manage redundancies by offering suitable, alternative employment to the affected individuals or the employment contract may contain a mobility clause which allows the employer to relocate employees to an alternative workplace.

If the employer makes an offer of suitable, alternative employment or the employment contract contains a mobility clause, an employee who either refuses the new post or refuses to move to a new work location may find that the refusal deprives him of the right to claim a redundancy payment.

When an employer is intending to terminate an employee's contract by reason of redundancy, he has a duty to consult with the appropriate representatives of the individuals who are affected by this decision (Section 188: Trade Union and Labour Relations (Consolidation) Act 1992).

Section 188 makes it very clear that an employer who fails to consult with the representatives of the affected employees could find himself taken before an Employment Tribunal by the appropriate representatives. This action could result in the Tribunal ordering the employer to pay compensation (a protective award) to the affected employees where it is proved that the employer failed to carry out proper consultation procedures.

Appropriate representatives of the affected employees will either be officials of a recognised and independent trade union or representatives whom the affected employees have elected for this purpose. Employers are under a duty to consult with representatives in situations where 20 or more redundancies will take effect at the one establishment within a 90-day period. Consultations must be commenced within good time and certain guidelines must be followed:

1   If at least 20 but less than 100 employees are to be affected by the redundancy situation within 90 days or less, the employer should begin consultations with their representatives at least 30 days before the first dismissal becomes effective.

2   If over 100 employees are to be made redundant within 90 days or less, consultation must take place 90 days before the first proposed dismissal.

If the above situations apply, an employer must notify the Secretary of State by putting his redundancy proposals in writing. The same time periods as outlined above must be observed and a failure to notify the Secretary of State at all or within the relevant time will mean that the employer has committed a criminal offence (Section 193: Trade Union and Labour Relations (Consolidation) Act 1992).

Employees who have two years' continuous service with the employer are entitled to statutory redundancy pay which is calculated according to the same rules for basic awards in unfair dismissal claims. From 1 October 2009, the maximum award for redundancy is £11,400 (20 years × 1½ × £380). This replaces the previous limit of £10,500 (20 × 1½ × £350) which had been in force from 1st February 2009.

An employer can use redundancy as a reason to justify the employee's dismissal. However, there will be situations where certain employees are selected for redundancy in circumstances where the employer will face accusations of unfair dismissal.

It is important to determine whether an employee has been dismissed on the grounds of redundancy or if the employee and the employer have both agreed to bring the contract to an end. Obviously, if both parties have agreed to a mutual termination of the contract of employment, no dismissal on the grounds of redundancy can be said to have taken place. It is vitally important to establish, therefore, who was responsible for bringing the employment to an end. If the employer was responsible, then potentially the employee has a claim for a redundancy payment and, if the procedures were not properly carried out, the employee may have a further claim for unfair dismissal.

 Caledonian Mining Ltd _v_ Bassett & Steel (1987) a number of the company's employees were faced with the prospect of redundancy. The company, which was part of a group, had given assurances to the affected employees that it would attempt to find them suitable alternative employment with an associated employer. Bassett and Steel received an offer of new employment from the National Coal Board. Both employees resigned from their employment with the company in order to take up the offer of new employment. Both Bassett and Steel later attempted to claim a redundancy payment from their former employer. Their old employer was disputing the fact that both men had been dismissed and argued that they had resigned from their employment in order to take up new employment with the National Coal Board. Therefore, both men were not entitled to a redundancy payment.

Held: by the Employment Appeal Tribunal that the employer's proposal to make these employees redundant had in effect terminated the contract. Bassett and Steel were entitled to receive a redundancy payment from their former employer.

 Murray _v_ Foyle Meats Ltd (1999) Murray had been employed in an abattoir as a meat plant operative. Murray's duties under his contract of employment were mainly concerned with working on the slaughter line. However, his contract did allow his employer to move him to other jobs within the abattoir and, from time to time, this had happened. Some of Murray's colleagues, who did not work on the slaughter line, had a similar term in their contracts that allowed the employer to move them to different jobs as and when required. The employer later experienced a fall in business and it was proposed that Murray and a group of his colleagues who worked on the slaughter line should be made redundant. The employer argued that there was now less demand for a particular type of work carried out by a particular group of employees to which Murray belonged. Murray argued that his dismissal was unfair by claiming that the employer had been wrong to select only those employees who worked on the slaughter line for redundancy. Those employees who could be asked to work on the slaughter line, but who usually did not, should also have been included in the redundancy pool. The employer had, therefore, unfairly selected Murray for redundancy.

Held: by the House of Lords that the requirements of the business for employees to work on the slaughter line had decreased and this state of affairs had led to Murray's dismissal on the grounds of redundancy. The fact that other employees were employed on similar conditions to Murray was not a relevant factor. The employer's dismissal of Murray had been carried out fairly. Murray's dismissal had been _attributable_ (the key word in Section 139(1)(b) of the Employment Rights Act 1996) to the fact that the employer's requirement for a particular type of work had decreased.

In **Lomond Motors Ltd v Clark (2009)** the Employment Appeal Tribunal sitting in Edinburgh has ruled that employers enjoy a very wide discretion when selecting a pool of candidates for possible redundancy. In this case, Clark had been employed as an accountant by Lomond Motors. The company employed three accountants at various garages which it owned and the decision was made to employ one accountant only in the future thus making two of the existing employees redundant. The company created a redundancy pool consisting of two of the accountants (Clark being one of the potential candidates). Clark was selected for redundancy on the ground of his shorter service with the company. He lodged a claim for unfair dismissal alleging that all three accountants should have been included in the selection pool. The Employment Tribunal agreed with him. His employer then appealed to the Employment Appeal Tribunal.

Held: by the Employment Appeal Tribunal (overruling the decision of the Employment Tribunal) that Clark's selection for redundancy was fair. The employer wished to make a redundancy at a particular location where it operated a business i.e. Clark's place of employment where there were two accountants (Clark and his colleague). The other location where the third accountant was employed was a completely separate business centre and there was no need for the employer to include the accountant working there as a candidate in the selection pool. Hence the employer was justified in including Clark and his colleague in the redundancy selection pool. Examples of matrices used by an employer to select individuals for redundancy can be viewed at the Introductory Scots Law website.

(**www**)

Dismissal on the grounds of redundancy will be automatically unfair if the employee was selected for redundancy in relation to any of the following:

1 Participation in trade union activities (Section 153: Trade Union and Labour Relations (Consolidation) Act 1992).

2 Pregnancy or for a reason connected with it (Section 99: Employment Rights Act 1996).

3 Making a protected disclosure in terms of the Public Interest Disclosure Act 1998 (Section 103A: Employment Rights Act 1996).

4 Raising or taking action on the grounds of health and safety (Section 100: Employment Rights Act 1996).

5 Involvement in activities related to his role as a trustee of an occupational pension scheme (Section 102: Employment Rights Act 1996).

6 Assertion of the right not to be forced to work on a Sunday because he was classified as a protected worker or a betting shop worker or because he has given an opting out notice to the employer (Section 101: Employment Rights Act 1996).

7 Assertion of certain statutory rights (Section 104: Employment Rights Act 1996).

8 Acting as an employee representative during consultations in relation to proposed redundancies or during the transfer of an undertaking (Section 103: Employment Rights Act 1996; and Regulations 10 and 11: Transfer of Undertakings (Protection of Employment) 1981).

Key point: In order to show that the dismissal is on the grounds of redundancy, it is important that the termination of the contract meets the statutory definition of redundancy in Section 139(1) of the Employment Rights Act 1996.

Dismissal for some other substantial reason

Section 98(1)(b) of the Employment Rights Act 1996 gives an employer the opportunity to argue that an employee has been dismissed for some other substantial reason. This is a potentially a very broad category, but it should be viewed as dealing only with a very small number of situations that are not covered by the other four named categories in Section 98(2) of the 1996 Act.

The employer must show that the substantial reason used to justify the employee's dismissal was potentially a fair one. Once this has been established, the employer must convince the Employment Tribunal that its actions leading to the dismissal of the employee have been reasonable. The substantial reason for dismissal must not be trivial or frivolous. The category of some other substantial reason has been used to justify dismissal in the following situations:

- Where the employer wishes to reorganise the business and it becomes necessary to change the terms and conditions of employment in respect of the employees.
- Where the employer tries to prevent the employee from divulging business secrets to competitors or where the employee is attempting to establish a rival business of his own.
- Where the employer has come under pressure from a customer who has threatened to break off business relations unless a particular employee is dismissed.
- Where a fixed-term contract has expired.
- Where a transfer of an undertaking has taken place and economic, technical or organisational reasons make it necessary to dismiss the employee.

 Hollister v National Farmers' Union (1979) Hollister was employed as an official by the NFU. The NFU wished to reorganise its activities and this meant that Hollister would be forced to accept new conditions of employment. Hollister had no intention of accepting the new contract and he made these feelings adequately clear to his employer. The employer was unimpressed and informed Hollister that, if he did not agree to the new contract, it would have no alternative but to dismiss him. Hollister continued to refuse to accept the new contract and the employer made good its threat to dismiss him.

Held: by the English Court of Appeal that the NFU had an urgent need to reorganise its activities. The only way in which this could be done was to end the contracts which employees like Hollister currently enjoyed and offer new contracts with reasonable terms and conditions in their place. Hollister had unreasonably refused to accept this situation and, therefore, his dismissal was fair for some other substantial reason.

 Abey v R & E Holdings (Yorkshire) Ltd t/a Quick Pass School of Motoring ET Case No 14985/82 Abey was employed as a receptionist by

Quick Pass, a driving school. She had a long-running personal relationship with one of the driving instructors. This driving instructor later left the company's employment and set up his own business which was directly in competition with Quick Pass. Quick Pass saw a substantial decline in its business. Given that Abey's position gave her access to customers and confidential information, her employer took the decision to dismiss her because there was a genuine commercial risk to the business if she remained in employment. It was felt that she would in a position to provide a serious competitor of Quick Pass with all sorts of confidential information and no reasonable employer could tolerate this situation.

Held: the dismissal was fair on the grounds of some other substantial reason.

In **Simmons *v* S D Graphics Ltd EAT 548/79** the Employment Appeal Tribunal pointed out that in situations where two employees with a close personal relationship both have access to confidential information, it is for the Tribunal to examine the facts in order to determine whether or not the decision of one of their employers to dismiss one of these individuals was for some other substantial reason.

 Meikle *v* McPhail (Charleston Arms) (1983) the previous employer (the transferor) who ran a public house had transferred the business to a new employer (the transferee). The new employer had to dismiss employees because he discovered that, by purchasing the business, he had financially over-extended himself. In order to remedy this situation, the new employer had to make cutbacks and this meant the loss of several jobs. Meikle claimed unfair dismissal in relation to the transfer of an undertaking.

Held: by the Employment Appeal Tribunal that Regulation 8(1) of the Transfer of Undertakings (Protection of Employment) Regulations 1981 states that a dismissal of an employee that occurs either before or after a transfer will be automatically unfair if the reason for the dismissal was the transfer or a reason connected with it. Regulation 8(2) states that paragraph (1) will not apply if the reason for the dismissal is an economic, technical or organisational reason involving changes in the workforce of either the transferor or transferee. If the employer can show that he has dismissed an employee for an economic, technical or organisational reason, the dismissal will not be classed as automatically unfair. In other words, the employer will able to rely on the defence of some other substantial reason for the dismissal, but he must show that the dismissal was reasonable. Meikle's dismissal was held to be fair for some other substantial reason because the new employer was now in financial difficulty as a result of buying the business and, therefore, cutbacks had to be made.

 Key point: Dismissal for some other substantial reason is not a broad category that allows the employer to dismiss an employee with impunity – it covers a limited number of situations that are not covered by the other four named categories in Section 98(2) of the Employment Rights Act 1996.

Summary

- During the nineteenth century, the terms and conditions which made up the contract of employment were almost wholly determined by negotiations carried out between the employer and the employee.

- From the beginning of the twentieth century, however, the terms of the contract of employment became increasingly subject to parliamentary intervention.

- The contract of employment can also be influenced by the following sources – the common law rights and duties of the parties, collective agreements, the written statement of terms and particulars of employment, handbooks, codes of practice and other documents issued by the employer.

- If you are an employee i.e. you have a contract of service you are theoretically in a much better position than someone who has a contract for services i.e. an independent contractor.

- This distinction matters because if you are an employee the law gives you greater protection and more benefits that you would not receive if you were merely an independent contractor for services.

- Admittedly, some pieces of legislation, for example, the Working Time Regulations 1998 protect the broader category of workers and not just employees.

- The courts have developed a number of different tests in an attempt to determine whether someone works under a contract of service or a contract for services, for example, the control test, the economic reality test and the organisation test.

- Vicarious liability can arise where there is a contract of service meaning that the employer may be vicariously liable for the delicts or negligence of an employee, but not those of independent contractors.

- In Scotland, employment contracts do not have to be in written form and witnessed and it is quite legitimate to have an employment contract which is completely verbal in nature or implied from the actions of the parties.

- Sources of the employment contract include legislation, the common law, collective agreements, written statement of terms and particulars and company handbooks and codes of practice.

- The employer's duties under the contract of employment include – the payment of wages, providing work, indemnifying employees, treating employees with trust and respect and to take reasonable care for the safety of employees.

- The Health and Safety at Work Act 1974 imposes criminal penalties on an employer who fails to take reasonably practicable steps to ensure the health and safety of his employees.

- The common law duties of an employee are to provide personal service, to provide loyal service, to obey lawful and reasonable orders and to take reasonable care in the exercise of the employment.

- The contract of employment can be terminated like any other contractual agreement, for example, material breach, mutual agreement, frustration, operation of law, completion of task and expiry of a fixed-term contract.

- Wrongful dismissal arises in situations where an employer dismisses the employee in breach of his contract.

- Unfair dismissal is a dismissal which is contrary to statute and usually the employee must have at least one year's continuous service with his employer to be able to claim protection under the Employment Rights Act 1996.

- An employee and not an independent contractor will enjoy protection against unfair dismissal.

- Where an employee is claiming unfair dismissal, the employer may be able to counter this by relying on one of the potentially fair reasons for dismissal i.e. capability and qualifications, conduct, redundancy, contravention of statute or any other substantial reason.

- In a variety of situations, a dismissal by the employer will be automatically unfair and the employee does not need to have one year's continuous service in order to lodge a claim with the Office of Employment Tribunals

- The employee's right to claim constructive dismissal arises in situations where the employer's conduct is to be regarded as a material breach of the employment contract and the employee is left with no alternative but to resign.

- When an employee claims that he has been constructively dismissed, he is claiming that he was unfairly dismissed.

- In relation to successful unfair dismissal claims, an Employment Tribunal can issue Orders for Reinstatement or Re-engagement or, more commonly, an award of compensation will be made consisting of a basic award and a compensatory award.

- Compensation in unfair dismissal cases does not include injury for hurt caused to feelings.

- An interim order can be very useful because it can prevent an employer from dismissing an employee until such time as the Employment Tribunal has made its decision.

Test your knowledge

1 a) What is the difference between a contract of service and a contract for services?

b) It has been said that a judge knows an employment contract when he or she sees one.

Explain this statement.

⚖ **c)** Leigh, Lloyd and Laurence are employed by the Metropolitan University of Aberdeen as guides in its Wilsonian Museum. The University made it quite clear that the work was on a casual basis and Leigh, Lloyd and Laurence would be employed as and when their services were required. There was no fixed pattern of working hours and the three individuals could be called upon at any time during the day to come into work in order to conduct the guided tours for the University. Lloyd, Leigh and Laurence are responsible for their own tax arrangements as the University does not deduct their tax at source. When they were first appointed to their present positions, all three were more than happy to be employed on a casual basis. On many occasions, all three turned down shifts at the Museum because it was not convenient. The University accepted this and, at no time, was the threat of disciplinary action raised for refusing to turn up to work. The three did receive some training in how to conduct the tours and they were expected to wear a uniform when working and they had received some instruction so that they could follow the University's first aid policy. In the last week, however, the University has informed Leigh, Lloyd and Laurence that it intends to terminate their contracts after the summer holiday has ended. All three have been working for the University for just over a year and are convinced that they will have the right to bring an unfair dismissal claim if the University goes ahead with its proposal to terminate their contracts.

What is the legal position?

2 a) There is no such thing as freedom of contract where the modern relationship between an employer and an employee is concerned.

Assess the accuracy of this statement.

⚖ **b)** Helen was offered a new job and she duly signed the contract. Her new employer had insisted that a number of terms be included in the contract of employment. Under the contract, Helen can be forced to work more than 48 hours per week, she will be paid less than the minimum wage and, should she become pregnant, she will not be entitled to take maternity leave or receive maternity pay.

Can the employer force Helen to accept these extremely poor terms of employment?

3 a) Examples of vicarious liability almost always arise in situations involving an employer and employee.

Explain the concept of vicarious liability.

⚖ **b)** Iain is employed as an electrician by Sparks Ltd. Sparks Ltd was awarded a contract by the local education authority to carry out extensive rewiring of the electrical circuits in one of the local schools. Iain was sent out by Sparks to complete this work. Unfortunately, Iain was not particularly careful when completing the job and, consequently, some of the teachers at the school have been the victims of particularly nasty electric shocks when they switched on their computers in the classrooms. The injuries were so serious that some of the victims were admitted to hospital and they will be absent from work for the foreseeable future. The victims, however, are unsure whether to sue the local authority or Sparks.

What course of action should the victims take?

4 a) What should the written statement of terms and conditions of employment contain?

b) What is the legal status of the written statement of terms and conditions of employment?

⚖ **c)** Jennifer, a student, works part-time as a waitress in a small, family-run restaurant. She has been employed in the restaurant for just over two months, but she has not been issued with any written contract or even a basic, written statement outlining the main terms of her employment. Jennifer has even approached the restaurant manager, Mark, and asked him to issue her with something in writing which she can keep for future reference. Mark replied that small businesses do not have to issue anything in writing to employees. Jennifer, however, is persistent and will not let the matter drop. A fortnight later, Mark asked to see Jennifer at the end of her shift. Mark told Jennifer that he had to let her go because the business had not been doing so well lately. Mark gave Jennifer a month's pay in lieu of her notice and he told her that she could be sure of a good reference. Jennifer knows that Mark is not being honest about the reason for her dismissal and she suspects that she was dismissed because she insisted on being issued with written terms and particulars of employment.

Where does Jennifer stand legally?

5 a) List the various sources of the contract of employment.

b) What is a collective agreement and in what way is it of benefit to both an employer and the employees?

c) United Scottish Airlines has witnessed a dramatic decline in business over the last year. It has now become obvious to the company's board of directors that the only way out of this crisis is to make redundancies amongst the cabin crew. Shirley, a stewardess, has been selected for redundancy by United Scottish Airlines. Shirley is extremely unhappy about this development because she feels that the company has ignored the collective agreement that contained a redundancy policy. This collective agreement, negotiated by the company and the employees' trade union, had been directly incorporated into Shirley's contract of employment. Under this redundancy policy, staff were allocated marks according to criteria such as educational qualifications, language skills, aptitude, work experience and length of service with the company. Those employees who scored the highest marks would retain their jobs, whereas those individuals with lower marks would be selected for redundancy. The company has now decided to use a single criterion to determine who will be made redundant. The company is now operating a redundancy policy of last in first out. Shirley is strongly of the opinion that United Scottish Airlines cannot simply change the terms of the collective agreement without consultation. Furthermore, Shirley's trade union did not agree to make any changes to the collective agreement.

Advise Shirley.

6 a) In a contract of employment, both the employer and the employee owe duties to one another.

Provide an outline of the main duties of the employer and the employee in an employment contract.

b) Examine the following situations carefully:

i) Samir worked for a very well-known firm of accountants. Some time ago, it became apparent that the partners in the firm were helping various criminals to launder money. The partners were all charged and convicted at the High Court of Justiciary in Edinburgh. The trials were widely covered by the newspapers and television. Consequently, the firm was dissolved and Samir found himself unemployed. Samir is a very honest person and he knew nothing of the illegal activities of his employers. He has found it very difficult to secure another job as an accountant because of his employment history. Samir is a young man who once had a very bright future in accountancy and he feels bitterly upset at the way things have turned out for him.

ii) William has his own firm of builders and, over the last few years, he has gathered together an excellent team of employees. During the winter months, work in the building trade tends to decrease significantly and many businesses have to lay off their workers. William, however, has always been in the habit of retaining his employees. It would be bad for the business if highly skilled and experienced members of the workforce were made redundant. These employees will continue to receive wages from William, but they will not necessarily be given any work to do until the Spring of the year when business picks up. Some employees have been complaining because they feel that William has a legal obligation to provide them with work.

iii) Shona is employed as a computer trainer by a training and education organisation. Part of Shona's job involves running computing courses for recovering drug addicts. These computing courses are held in local church and community halls as part of an outreach programme. Her employer has provided Shona with a van in order to transport the laptop computers to the various locations where each class is held. Usually 20 machines are required for each session. One day, when Shona was out at one of her classes, she received threats from some drug addicts, who were not members of her class, who wanted to steal the computers. Shona managed to get away without any of the equipment being stolen. Shona has reported this incident to her employer. She has asked her employer to improve security precautions at these classes. Her employer has refused to do anything and it informed Shona that she will have to continue to work alone at these classes. Shona is terrified that next time her personal safety could be seriously endangered.

iv) Norrie works as a barman in a pub in Stirling. His employer is determined to cut the costs involved in running the pub. Alcohol and tobacco products are considerably cheaper in countries such as France and Belgium in comparison to the United Kingdom. One day, Norrie's employer asks him to drive a truck to France and, while there, buy a large amount of alcohol and tobacco products which he is to bring back to the UK. Norrie can take two other members of staff so that if the Customs and Excise people stop the truck, he and his passengers can claim that their purchases are for personal use only and, therefore, the employer can avoid paying a substantial amount of duty. Norrie is deeply unhappy about this situation. His employer has told Norrie that if he does take the truck to France, he will be disobeying a lawful and reasonable order.

v) Gerry is a plumber who is employed by a large firm. Gerry feels that his employers could be paying him a much better salary in recognition of the amount of work that he does. Gerry is finding it very difficult to meet his mortgage repayments and he has a couple of bank loans to pay off. To make ends meet, Gerry approached some of his employer's customers and offered to do work for them at lower prices. Many of his employer's customers were very receptive to Gerry's proposal and took him up on his offer. The nature of Gerry's job means that he can work unsupervised and he fit these private jobs around his official work for his employer. Another bonus for Gerry was that he could use the tools, equipment and materials supplied by his employer to carry out jobs for his private clients. His employer is, of course, completely in the dark about Gerry's private clients. Eventually, Gerry is so successful in building up his private clients that he decides to quit his job and start up a business of his own which will be in direct competition with that of his former employer.

vi) David was employed as a driver by a florist. He was out delivering flowers when he decided to stop at a newsagents in order to buy a paper. When David drew up the van in front of the newsagents, he could see that the shop was empty. Thinking that he would not be in the shop for long, he left the keys in the ignition and he did not lock the van. When David came back out of the shop, the van had been stolen by some teenage joyriders. The van was later found abandoned and burnt out on a piece of waste ground and all the flowers which were in the van were completely destroyed in the fire.

With reference to the contract of employment, what is the legal position in relation to each of the scenarios described above?

7 a) Describe the ways in which a contract of employment can be terminated.

b) Hannah, a former solicitor, was sentenced to 18 months' imprisonment for embezzling money from her clients. Hannah had not been permitted to practise as a solicitor by the Law Society before her criminal trial, but she had managed to secure employment as an adviser to a local community group. Her employer has decided not to keep her job open for her during her prison sentence. The employer is arguing that the vacancy caused by Hannah's absence will have to be filled immediately and it would be totally unreasonable for Hannah to expect to walk back into her job 18 months down the line. The employer is also of the opinion that he does not have to give Hannah a period of notice or make her a payment in lieu of notice.

Do you think that Hannah's employer has behaved correctly?

8 a) What is the difference between wrongful dismissal and unfair dismissal?

b) Charlene has been dismissed by her employer. In terms of her contract, Charlene was entitled to receive four weeks' notice from her employer if he intended to terminate her employment. In fact, Charlene was given one hour to clear her desk and leave the premises. Her contract of employment also stated that the employer could make a payment in lieu of notice, but so far Charlene has not received a penny from her employer. Charlene's conduct during her employment has been absolutely impeccable and she is totally mystified at her employer's conduct. She has attempted to appeal against her employer's decision to terminate the contract, but she has been told that the decision has been made and will not be reversed.

What can Charlene do?

9 **a)** What is constructive dismissal and when are employees entitled to treat themselves as constructively dismissed by their employers?

b) Rose was employed as a sales assistant in a department store for a year and a half. She was subjected to bullying and harassment carried out by one of her supervisors. Rose took out a grievance against the supervisor and her employer promised to take appropriate action. In fact, the bullying got worse and Rose decided that she had had enough and resigned from her post.

Would Rose be entitled to bring a claim of constructive dismissal against her former employer?

10 In all of the situations described below, the employees have been dismissed from employment. Comment on the fairness of each dismissal.

a) Penny was the Branch Secretary of a trade union. She was very popular with her colleagues because she had successfully defended their terms and conditions of employment over many years. Penny was dismissed on the grounds of redundancy despite the fact that some of her colleagues with less experience and poorer qualifications retained their jobs. Penny is convinced that her employer's actions towards her are motivated by her trade union activities.

b) Colin was the Treasurer of his local golf club. He was convicted of stealing money from the cash register behind the club bar. Luckily for Colin, he received a fine and a suspended sentence because he had no previous criminal convictions. The criminal case, however, was widely reported in the local newspaper and Colin's employer decided to dismiss him from his employment. Colin had been a manager of a local building society.

c) Forth Council has decided to close some of the primary schools in the area because of falling numbers of pupils attending some of the schools. The Council has a redundancy procedure, agreed with the trade unions, which it has followed to the letter. Those individuals threatened with redundancy were offered suitable alternative employment where possible, but some redundancies were still unavoidable. Karen, a teacher with two years' teaching experience has been made redundant. She now wishes to challenge the fairness of her dismissal.

d) Monica worked for a butchers. She felt that her employer was not observing the appropriate food safety and hygiene rules.

Monica expressed her fears to the shop manager who promised to investigate matters. Several months later, it became obvious to Monica that her manager had no intention of following up the concerns that she had raised. Deciding that she had to take matters into her hands, Monica contacted the Council's Environmental Health Department and informed it of her fears. Monica's employer discovered that she had made the complaint to the Council and, consequently, she was dismissed from her employment.

e) Reza obtained employment as a trainee financial adviser. His contract stated that he would have to pass his financial planning certificate within three years of starting his employment. Reza has now been with his company for just over three years and he has not managed to obtain the appropriate qualification. He has attempted to pass his exams on the maximum number of opportunities permitted to him. His employer has now told him that it intends to terminate his contract.

f) The doctor has just confirmed that Susan is pregnant. She has informed her employer who has told her that he will have to dismiss her and employ someone in her place.

g) Arlene has a dreadful absence record. Every few weeks, she is absent from work due to ill health. There is no pattern to these illnesses and Arlene's employer asked her to attend a doctor's examination. The doctor can find nothing wrong with Arlene and her employer informs her that it will be monitoring her attendance at work for the foreseeable future. Several weeks later, Arlene sends in a sick-note from her doctor stating that she will be absent from work for the next eight weeks. Her employer has decided that enough is enough and informs Arlene that she is being dismissed from employment.

h) Ellie has been employed as a nurse in a psychiatric unit of a local hospital for the last six months. Some of the patients that Ellie has to work with can be dangerous and, on some shifts, not enough members of staff are present to supervise the patients adequately. On one occasion, a patient stabbed a nurse. Ellie, who is a health and safety representative, has consistently raised her concerns about the poor staffing levels in the psychiatric unit with the hospital management. Just before Ellie's temporary contract comes to an end, she is informed by one of the hospital managers that, regrettably, the hospital will have to let her go.

i) Sheelagh runs a business and many of her customers purchase goods on credit. The Consumer Credit Act 1974, of course, imposes a duty upon Sheelagh to apply for a licence from the Office of Fair Trading to be able to enter into consumer credit agreements with her customers. Recently some serious allegations about Sheelagh's her manager, Andrew, have come to her attention. It seems that in a previous job, Andrew had been successfully sued at the Employment Tribunal by individuals who claimed that he had discriminated against them on the grounds of their sex and race. Andrew is primarily responsible for deciding which customers are granted credit facilities by the business. Sheelagh's solicitor has informed her that by continuing to employ Andrew she may be endangering her credit licence because if the Office of Fair Trading hears about Andrew's previous history it will surely revoke the licence.

j) Workers at Boyle's factory have decided to go on strike for better pay and conditions as negotiations between the trade union and the management have completely broken down. The union has carried out the proper balloting procedure which the law demands, but two weeks into the strike the employer decides to dismiss Richard, Julie and Lorraine as they are considered to be the ringleaders behind this particular episode of industrial action.

k) Kevin is a senior manager with an IT company. He has just married Maureen, who is a director with a company which is a serious rival of his employer's. Upon his return to work from his honeymoon, Kevin is invited to a meeting by the Chief Executive of the company. The purpose of the meeting is to discuss Kevin's future employment with the company. The Chief Executive is extremely concerned that Kevin may divulge important business secrets to his wife. Unfortunately, his employer will now have to dispense with Kevin's services.

11 Describe the remedies that are available to a person who proves to an Employment Tribunal that he has been unfairly dismissed.

In relation to Chapter 7, readers should be aware that, since the initial publication of this book, the Equality Act 2010 has been introduced and is now in force. A full update detailing the relevant changes to this area of law can be found at **www.hoddereducation.co.uk/introscotslaw.**

INTRODUCTION TO THE LAW OF EMPLOYMENT PART 2

Introduction

Over the last thirty years, the Westminster Parliament has introduced a large amount of equality legislation aimed at combating discrimination experienced by people in a variety of situations. This chapter, however, is primarily concerned with discrimination in employment. Employees will suffer discrimination if they can demonstrate that their employers subjected them to less favourable treatment by reason of their gender, race, disability, sexuality, religion or even employment status.

> ### This chapter will cover the following areas:
> - Sexual and racial discrimination •
> - Equal pay •
> - Disability discrimination •
> - Part-time workers and fixed-term employees •
> - Discrimination on the grounds of age, sexual orientation, religion or belief •
> - The legal framework of employment law •

Discrimination in employment

British employment law now provides protection to a variety of individuals and groups of people who may suffer some form of discrimination. In the United Kingdom, discrimination is forbidden in the following circumstances:

◆ On the grounds of gender or sex (the Equal Pay Act 1970, the Sex Discrimination Act 1975 (as amended), Equal Pay Directive 75/117/EEC, the Equal Treatment Directive 76/207/EEC and the Sex Discrimination (Gender Reassignment) Regulations 1999).

◆ On the grounds of marital status (the Equal Pay Act 1970, the Sex Discrimination Act 1975 (as amended), Equal Pay Directive 75/117/EEC and the Equal Treatment Directive 76/207/EEC.

◆ On the grounds of colour, nationality, racial, ethnic or national origin (the Race Relations Act 1976 (as amended)).

◆ On the grounds of disability (the Disability Discrimination Act 1995).

◆ On the grounds of a person's age (the Employment Equality (Age) Regulations 2006)

◆ On the grounds of being a part-time worker (the Part-Time Workers (Prevention of Less Favourable Treatment) Regulations 2000).

◆ On the grounds of being a fixed-term worker (the Fixed-Term Employees (Prevention of Less Favourable Treatment) Regulations 2002).

◆ On the grounds of sexual orientation (the Employment Equality (Sexual Orientation) Regulations 2003).

◆ On the grounds of religious or philosophical beliefs (the Employment Equality (Religion or Belief) Regulations 2003).

After a brief examination of the above list, it should now be obvious that protection from discrimination in the field of employment has expanded greatly since the 1970s onwards.

 Key point: The United Kingdom's discrimination legislation protects a wide variety of individuals and groups.

What do we mean by discrimination?

Put simply, an individual or a group of individuals will suffer less favourable treatment by reason of gender or sex, transsexuality; colour, nationality, racial, national or ethnic origin, disability, their sexual orientation, religious or philosophical beliefs or employment status. In other words, someone will suffer some sort of detriment or harm which is related to one of their personal characteristics, for example, his race or her employment status, for example, the fact that she is a part-time worker. Detriments can come in all shapes and sizes:

◆ Lack of promotion and training opportunities
◆ Different pay scales and conditions of employment
◆ Unfairness in the recruitment process
◆ Dismissal from employment
◆ Failure to receive the same contractual benefits as fellow employees
◆ Different retirement ages
◆ Different dress codes
◆ Unilateral changes to an employee's contract of employment
◆ Age requirements in relation to certain posts
◆ Harassment and victimisation
◆ Selecting certain individuals for redundancy first
◆ Refusal to allow more flexible working patterns

 Key point: Discrimination means that an individual or a group of individuals will suffer less favourable treatment by reason of age, gender or sex, transsexuality, colour, nationality, racial, ethnic or national origin, disability, sexual orientation, religious or philosophical beliefs or employment status and this difference in treatment cannot be objectively justified.

The burden of proof in discrimination claims

Generally, an individual ("the Claimant") who makes an allegation of discrimination against his/her employer will have to bring evidence to an Employment Tribunal to support this claim.

In three conjoined appeals before the English Court of Appeal on 18 February 2005, new guidelines were established in relation to the operation of the burden of proof to be followed in all discrimination cases. The cases were:

◆ **Igen Ltd and others *v* Wong** (race discrimination)
◆ **Emokpae *v* Chamberlin Solicitors** (sex discrimination)
◆ **Webster *v* Brunel University** (race discrimination)

The appeals provide guidance to Tribunals when dealing with the issue of the burden of proof in discrimination cases. A number of things can be taken from the Court of Appeal's judgements. It is now apparent that, when an allegation of discrimination is brought to a Tribunal, a two-stage enquiry must be followed.

Firstly, the factual basis of the claim must be established and, if it appears at this stage that the employer has a case to answer, the burden of proof will transfer from the claimant to the employer. Once the claimant has succeeded in establishing that there is a case to answer, the second stage of the Tribunal's enquiry can proceed.

Here the claimant must be able to identify facts which demonstrate on the balance of probabilities that:

(a) they suffered an unlawful act of discrimination; and

(b) that the employer committed the act in question.

Following the conclusion of the second stage of the enquiry, if the Tribunal finds that the employer's explanation of the alleged discriminatory treatment is unsatisfactory it must find in favour of the claimant.

In the light of these appeals, employers will have to be aware that any unreasonable behaviour on their part towards an employee or a worker combined with factors such as gender, race, disability, sexual orientation etc., an Employment Tribunal may well reverse the burden of proof and find in favour of the claimant.

An interesting example of the operation of the new guidelines could be seen in the case of **Dattani *v* Chief Constable of West Mercia Police (7 February 2005)**. The Employment Appeal Tribunal found in favour of a claimant who was alleging race discrimination and who had brought proceedings against the employer. The employer had failed either to provide responses or had given evasive replies to a questionnaire served on it by the claimant in terms of section 65 of the Race Relations Act 1976. Such behaviour was enough to shift the burden of proof from the claimant to the employer and, in the absence of any adequate explanation from the employer, the Tribunal was entitled to arrive at the conclusion that there had been unlawful discrimination.

In **Madarassy v Nomura (2007)** the English Court of Appeal dismissed the claimant's case for alleged sex discrimination because she was not able to prove that the difference in treatment constituted less favourable treatment on the grounds of her gender. An employer can treat people differently, but this does not necessarily establish a prima facie case for discrimination. The employer may well be able to justify the difference in treatment on objective grounds.

Key point: The same burden of proof should be used by an Employment Tribunal in all discrimination claims as a result of the English Court of Appeal's decision in three conjoined appeals: **Igen Ltd and others *v* Wong** (race discrimination); **Emokpae *v* Chamberlin Solicitors** (sex discrimination); and **Webster *v* Brunel University** heard on 18 February 2005.

Sexual and racial discrimination

Sexual and racial discrimination are illegal in terms of the Sex Discrimination Act 1975 (as amended) and the Race Relations Act 1976 (as amended) respectively. Both pieces of legislation are very similar in that they use a common framework. However, the Race Relations Act has been amended twice since 2000 and very significant changes have been made to it. This is partly in response to the recommendations of the MacPherson Inquiry, published in 1999, in relation to the death of the black teenager, Stephen Lawrence, in 1993 and the European Race Directive (Council Directive 2000/43/EEC).

The Race Relations Act

The Race Relations Act 1976 outlaws racial discrimination in relation to terms of employment, trade union membership, education, the provision of goods and services, and in the disposal and management of housing and other premises. Section 4(2) provides that an employer may not commit an act of race discrimination in the same circumstances as outlined in Section 6 of the Sex Discrimination Act.

The Race Relations (Amendment) Act 2000 came into force on 2 April 2001 in England and Wales. The new Act came fully into force in Scotland on 30 November 2002. It strengthens and extends the scope of the Race Relations Act, but the new Act does not replace the 1976 Act. The amended Race Relations Act also imposes general duties on listed public authorities to promote racial equality. The general duty means that public authorities will have to eliminate unlawful discrimination and promote equality of opportunity and good race relations in carrying out their functions. The British government minister known as the Home Secretary can impose specific duties on listed public authorities (including non-devolved Scottish bodies) and Scottish Government Ministers can impose specific duties on devolved bodies in order to meet the general duty.

The phrase 'public authority' can be interpreted very widely and will most obviously include bodies such as the national government departments, devolved government in Scotland and Wales and local authorities across the United Kingdom. However, bodies such as the National Health Service, the Police, housing associations, schools, universities and further education colleges could all be classified as 'public authorities' in terms of the Race Relations Act.

The Race Relations Act makes it unlawful for any public authority to discriminate in the carrying out of all its functions. The definition of 'function' will include any action that a public authority takes in the course of its duties, and will cover law enforcement activities which were not covered previously by the Act. Public authorities will now have to draft a race equality scheme. This is a statement of how a listed public authority plans to meet both its general and specific duties to promote equality under the amended Race Relations Act. A listed public authority is one that is named in schedule 1A to the Race Relations Act.

The Race Relations Act also makes it illegal for private and voluntary sector bodies to discriminate in the carrying out of any function which is classed as a 'public function'. If a local council contracts work out to a private company, for example, to provide social work and care services to the elderly, the private company will be covered by the Act. In terms of employment law, public authorities with more than 150 full-time employees must pay particular attention to the following:

◆ Grievance procedures
◆ Disciplinary procedures
◆ Performance appraisals
◆ Training
◆ Dismissals

Furthermore, all public authority employers must take particular care must be able to provide information as to the numbers of individuals from the various ethnic groups who are currently employed, who have applied for positions, who have been promoted within the organisation and who have received training. This information must be published every year.

The Race Relations Act applies to all employers no matter how small or large these organisations may be. The Act also applies to employment agencies.

On 19 July 2003, the Race Relations Act 1976 (Amendment) Regulations 2003 ('the Race Regulations') were introduced to take account of the important changes introduced by the European Race Directive which, amongst other things, affects the definition of indirect discrimination. Significantly, the amended Race Relations Act now applies to police forces. Chief Constables will now be responsible for acts of race discrimination carried out by officers of their police forces.

 Key point: The Race Relations Act 1976 outlaws race discrimination in relation to terms of employment, trade union membership, education, the provision of goods and services, and in the disposal and management of housing and other premises.

Selecting a comparator in race discrimination claims

Section 3 of the Race Relations Act demands that a complainant alleging race discrimination must be able to carry out a like with like comparison with someone who is of a different colour or nationality or who is a member of a group that has different racial, ethnic or national origins. If the complainant cannot identify such a comparator, his case will fall at the first hurdle. The complainant can compare himself to an actual or hypothetical comparator. (See **Mandla v Dowell Lee (1983)** and **King v Great Britain-China Centre (1991)**, discussed later in the chapter.)

The Sex Discrimination Act

The Sex Discrimination Act 1975 outlaws sexual discrimination in relation to terms of employment, training, education, the provision of goods and services and the disposal of premises. Section 6 of the Act specifically applies to employment. An employer may commit an act of sex discrimination in the following circumstances:

◆ Making arrangements for the purpose of determining who should be offered employment, for example, discriminatory advertisements or sexist job titles.

◆ The terms on which employment is offered, for example, men enjoy more favourable treatment in respect of their conditions of employment in comparison with their female colleagues.

◆ A person is refused employment because of their sex or marital status.

◆ a person experiences discrimination or less favourable treatment in relation to opportunities for promotion, transfer or training or to other benefits, facilities or services by reason of his or her sex.

◆ A person is dismissed or experiences some other kind of detriment by reason of their sex.

Since November 1987, it is now unlawful, in terms of the Sex Discrimination Act 1986, for an employer to operate two different compulsory retirement ages – one for men and women. The European Court of Justice held that the practice of having different compulsory retirement ages where men retired at age 65 and women at age 60 was in breach of the Equal Treatment Directive (**Marshall South West Hants Area Health Authority (1986)**).

Extremely significant changes to the Sex Discrimination Act 1975 were introduced in October 2005 as a result of the Employment Equality (Sex Discrimination) Regulations 2005 and in April 2007 as a result of the Equality Act 2006. One of the most important effects of the reforms in the Equality Act 2006 is the introduction of the Gender Equality Duty. As with the reforms to the Race Relations legislation, public bodies or authorities must take positive action to promote equality between the sexes. This means that these bodies have a legal duty to establish a gender equality scheme which should eliminate unlawful discrimination on the grounds of a person's gender and to promote equality of opportunity between the sexes. Public organisations must publish detailed plans of how they intend to implement such policies which make the gender equality duty a reality and the Equality and Human Rights Commission can take action to ensure that these schemes and their objectives are fully implemented.

 Key point: The Sex Discrimination Act 1975 outlaws sexual discrimination in relation to terms of employment, training, education, the provision of goods and services and the disposal of premises.

Selecting a comparator in sex discrimination claims

Section 5 of the Sex Discrimination Act make it very clear that it is absolutely central to the success of a claim that the complainant can compare his or her allegedly less favourable treatment to an actual or hypothetical male/female comparator. If he or she cannot do this, the claim will fail. A woman claiming that she has suffered discrimination on the grounds of her sex must be able to carry out a like with like comparison. The woman's circumstances and those of her male comparator must be the same or they should not be materially different otherwise a meaningful comparison cannot be made. In cases where the alleged discrimination is connected to pregnancy, it is not necessary for a female complainant to identify an actual or hypothetical male comparator.

 Shamoon *v* Chief Constable of the Royal Ulster Constabulary (2003)
the Royal Ulster Constabulary removed one of its female Chief Inspectors from certain staff appraisal duties which formed part of her post. There had been a number of complaints made about the way in which she had handled these appraisals. Two of her male colleagues (also senior officers) were not

removed from these duties. Significantly, there had been no complaints made against these male officers concerning the way in which they operated procedures for staff appraisals. The female officer took lodged a claim with the Office of Employment Tribunals alleging unlawful sex discrimination.

Held: by the House of Lords that there was a genuine material factor which explained the difference in treatment. The male officers were not the subjects of complaints whereas the female officer was. Consequently, this justified the way that she had been treated. She could not compare herself to her male colleagues because their circumstances were materially different from her own. To have permitted her to make such a comparison would have been totally inappropriate i.e. she would not have been comparing like with like.

 Key point: The Sex Discrimination and Race Relations Acts employ a common framework, but the race legislation has been strengthened to take account of the recommendations of the MacPherson Report and the provisions of the European Race Directive.

Lodging sex and race discrimination claims

Sex and race discrimination claims must be lodged with the Office of Employment Tribunals within three months (less one day) of the discriminatory act complained of.

Once a claim has been lodged before an Employment Tribunal, the difficult issue of proving that the employer discriminated against the employee on the grounds of sex or race comes very much to the forefront. Many employers who are guilty of sex and race discrimination are unlikely to admit this publicly and even privately they will try to justify to themselves the less favourable treatment to which they subjected an employee.

 Key point: A claim for sex or race discrimination must be lodged with the Office of Employment Tribunals within three months (less one day) of the act complained of.

Jurisdiction of Employment Tribunals in relation to overseas employment

Generally speaking, British Employment Tribunals do not have the power to hear cases involving discrimination where the acts in question have been committed outside the United Kingdom (see **O'Connor v Contiki Travel (1976),** an unreported decision of the London Industrial Tribunal).

In **Saggar v Ministry of Defence (1985)**, the English Court of Appeal ruled that an Employment Tribunal can have jurisdiction to hear a claim for discrimination if the employee worked previously or subsequently for the same employer in the United Kingdom. The ruling stresses that the whole duration of the employee's employment should be looked at rather than by simply isolating when and where the discrimination took place.

Less favourable treatment

In terms of both the Sex Discrimination Act and the Race Relations Act, the less favourable treatment suffered by the complainant must have occurred by reason of

Key point: If the Equality Bill becomes law it will consolidate much of the current UK anti-discrimination law into a single Act of Parliament.

Positive discrimination

Generally speaking positive discrimination i.e. where an individual or a group are treated more favourably by an employer is not permitted. In **James v Eastleigh Borough Council (1990)** the House of Lords stated that although the Council was acting from motives of good faith, its policy in charging men entry to the swimming pool when women were admitted free was discriminatory. An employer can, however, under the Sex Discrimination and Race Relations Acts provide vocational training to existing employees of a particular sex, colour, nationality, race, ethnic or national origin on an extremely limited basis (SDA 1975: Sections 47 to 48 and RRA 1976: Sections 35 and 37 to 38)

It is, however, lawful for an employer to give preference to female candidates despite the fact that there is a suitably qualified male candidate. Such conduct by the employer is permitted where this forms part of an equality policy to try and do something about imbalances between men and women in the workplace (**Kalanke v Freie Hansestadt Bremen (1995)** and **Badeck and others (2000)**). The employer can claim, in terms of European law, that the positive discrimination is permitted by Article 2(4) of the Equal Treatment Directive which allows an employer to act to promote equal opportunity for men and women.

 Key point: The use of positive discrimination by an employer is strictly controlled.

Exceptions to the Sex Discrimination and Race Relations Acts

The rules promoting sexual equality may not be applicable in the following situations:

- ◆ Employment Overseas – persons working wholly or mainly outside the UK are not covered by the Act.

- ◆ Police – male and female officers may be treated differently in relation to requirements relating to height, uniform and equipment. Female Police officers may receive special treatment in connection with pregnancy and childbirth.

- ◆ Prison Officers – different height requirements may be applied to male and female prison officers.

- ◆ Ministers of Religion – particular faiths and denominations may require that their ministers be of the one gender, for example, the Roman Catholic priesthood is an all male institution and its members are not allowed to marry or be married.

- ◆ Provisions relating to death or retirement.

- ◆ Pregnancy or childbirth – special treatment may be given to women in connection with pregnancy or childbirth.

The rules promoting racial equality may not be applicable in the following situations:

- ◆ Employment Overseas – persons working wholly or mainly outside the UK are not covered by the Act.

- Employment on board ships – if a person making a complaint of racial discrimination was recruited abroad.

- The United Kingdom's immigration laws and nationality quotas for Civil Service posts.

- Employment in private homes.

- Judicial acts and decisions, as are decisions of the Lord Advocate and the Crown Office not to prosecute in criminal cases.

As a result of the Employment Equality (Sex Discrimination) Regulations 2005, more people will now be covered by the Sex Discrimination Act 1975. In terms of Section 10B, subject to a large number of exceptions, some office-holders, for example, those persons who are Crown appointees or who are appointed to an official position by a Minister of the Crown or who have to be approved or recommended by a Minister of the Crown before they can take up a particular office will now be entitled to receive the protection of the Sex Discrimination Act.

 Key point: The Sex Discrimination and Race Relations Acts will not always apply to every situation and will be subject to a number of exceptions.

Forms of discrimination

In terms of the equality legislation, discrimination can take a number of forms:

- Direct discrimination
- Indirect discrimination
- Harassment
- Victimisation

This equality legislation does, however, explicitly recognise that in some situations it may actually be right and proper to discriminate against someone by reason of that person's gender or race or nationality. Employers will be able to rely on genuine occupational qualifications when they are recruiting potential employees or when they are considering employees for promotion or for training opportunities. In some situations, for example, the post of rape counsellor it would probably be inappropriate to employ a man. Many victims of this appalling crime would doubtless prefer to be counselled by a female professional. Therefore, it would be perfectly legitimate for an employer to hire a female applicant for the post of counsellor in preference to a male counterpart.

 Key point: The main types of less favourable treatment are direct discrimination, indirect discrimination, harassment and victimisation.

Direct discrimination

The concept of direct discrimination is found in Sections 1 (relating to women) and 2 (relating to men) of the Sex Discrimination Act and Section 1(1)(a) of the Race Relations Act centres around the concept that someone, for example, a woman or a member of an ethnic minority has suffered discrimination in relation to their employment if the employer treats them less favourably than he treats or would treat other persons. The reason for this less favourable treatment is related to the person's gender or their membership of a racial group. Very often, an employer will be accused of direct discrimination because he has consciously made a decision to discriminate against someone by reason of a person's gender or race.

The House of Lords stated in **James v Eastleigh Borough Council (1990)** that the test that should be applied to cases of alleged direct discrimination is the 'but for' test. This test operates on the following principle: a person will have suffered direct discrimination if it can be demonstrated that a person would have been treated differently but for his or her sex or race. In **James**, men were forced to pay an entry fee for use of the Council's swimming pool whereas women were not forced to pay the entry fee. Mr James claimed that this was an example of direct sex discrimination because he would not have had to pay the entry fee, but for the fact that he was male. Interestingly, this case emphasises the fact that a man can use the Sex Discrimination Act to bring a claim of discrimination.

Direct discrimination will not be excused if an employer attempts to explain it by stating that he was motivated by good intentions. The less favourable treatment suffered by the employee will still be regarded as unlawful sex or race discrimination. So, in a situation where an employer refused to employ a woman because she would be the only female member of the team, his justification that he felt that the female employee would not be accepted by her male colleagues and that she may even have faced hostility cut little ice with the Employment Appeal Tribunal (**Greig v Community Industry (1979)**). This was an example of direct sex discrimination.

 Moyhing v Barts and London NHS (2006) Andrew Moyhing was training to be a nurse at Barts Hospital in London. He objected to the policy of having to be chaperoned by another nurse when he undertook intimate examinations of female patients. In particular, Moyhing alleged that he was prevented from carrying out and gaining vital experience in relation to such medical procedures as cervical smears or electrocardiogram tests where intimate parts of the patient's body would be exposed. Crucially, female student nurses were permitted to carry out procedures and examinations of an intimate nature in relation to male patients without them necessarily being accompanied by a chaperone. The Hospital argued in its defence that the chaperoning policy was designed to protect people like Moyhing, was not discriminatory and, therefore, could be justified on objective grounds. Moyhing stated that he had absolutely no issue or problem with a situation where a female patient expressed a preference to be treated by a female nurse. His contention was that often the patient was not given this choice and that he was simply not permitted to carry out treatment. Subsequently, Moyhing lodged an Employment Tribunal claim for sex discrimination against his employer. The Employment Tribunal however ruled in the employer's favour stating that the chaperoning policy could be viewed as an acceptable safeguard. Moyhing appealed against the judgement of the Tribunal.

Held: by the Employment Appeal Tribunal that the chaperoning policy used by the Hospital was unlawful and was an example of less favourable treatment by reason of Moyhing's gender. Moyhing had been the victim of direct discrimination. The Employment Appeal Tribunal awarded Moyhing £750 in compensation for injury to feelings which, interestingly, he refused to accept stating that he did not wish to divert resources from the NHS. The chaperoning policy it could be argued reinforced stereotypes about men being sexual predators and did nothing to encourage more men to enter the nursing profession. If an employer imposes a condition it must be imposed equally on male and female employees unless a difference in treatment can be objectively justified which in this case the employer failed to demonstrate.

 Switalski v F & C Asset Management plc & Ors (2009) Switalski, the claimant, was the Head of Legal Services at F & C Asset Management. She was also the mother of two young disabled boys and she had requested flexible working in order to care for them. This request was granted and Switalski was permitted to work part of her week from home. Problems began, however, when her employer was taken over by another company. Switalski's new manager constantly questioned her working arrangements despite the fact that a male colleague, who was the parent of children with special needs, was permitted to benefit from flexible working patterns. Switalski also claimed that she had her expenses claims questioned by her manager, that he had excluded her from various projects and that she was passed over for promotion opportunities. Eventually, this treatment had a detrimental effect on her health and she was absent from the company on sick leave. It was while on sick leave in September 2007 that Switalski resigned from employment. She subsequently lodged a claim for sex discrimination against her former employer.

Held; by the Employment Tribunal that Switalski had been the victim of direct discrimination on the grounds of her sex.

 Key point: Employers will not be able to justify direct discrimination on the grounds of sex or race by stating that the actions were motivated by good intentions.

Discrimination on grounds of pregnancy

 Dekker v Stichting Vormingscentrum voor Jonge Volwassen Plus (1991) was a Dutch case which came before the European Court of Justice. It was assumed to have clarified the law relating to sex discrimination claims where pregnancy is the issue. When Dekker went for a job interview, she informed the interviewing committee that she was pregnant. Dekker was undoubtedly the best candidate that the committee interviewed and, understandably, the committee selected her for appointment. Dekker's employers were less than happy about her pregnancy. They argued that it would be too expensive to pay her while she was on maternity leave and to pay the additional costs of hiring a replacement worker during this period. The employers refused to approve Dekker's appointment to the post.

Held: by the European Court of Justice that it is *always* direct discrimination to refuse to offer employment to a woman for reason of her pregnancy. The European Court of Justice made it clear that a pregnant woman does not have to compare herself to a man. The need for pregnant women to compare their situations with men was one of the major weaknesses of the Sex Discrimination Act as it was originally enacted. For the avoidance of doubt, men generally do not become pregnant and for a woman to look around for a pregnant man would be like looking for the proverbial needle in the haystack. A woman can also allege that she has suffered less favourable treatment which amounts to direct sex discrimination during the recruitment process when there are no male candidates for the job.

An employer will also commit an act of direct sex discrimination if a female employee is dismissed by reason of her pregnancy (see **O'Neill *v* Governors of St Thomas More (1996)** discussed in Chapter 6). The dismissal can also be challenged on the grounds that it is automatically unfair in terms of Section 99 of the Employment Rights Act 1996.

Dekker seems a fairly simple legal principle: employers must not discriminate against women on the grounds of their pregnancy. For some time after the decision in **Dekker**, an interesting question arose as to the legal position where a woman was appointed to a fixed-term temporary post and a short time later she discovered that she was pregnant. Employers were strongly of the opinion that it would obviously be impossible for the individual in question to perform her contractual duties as a result of her taking maternity leave. The European Court of Justice had to deal with the issue in the following case:

 In **Webb *v* EMO Air Cargo (UK) Ltd (1992)** the dismissal of a pregnant woman, recruited for an indefinite period, could not be justified merely because she would be prevented on a temporary basis from performing her work. The fact that Webb had initially been employed to cover another employee's maternity leave was irrelevant. Further, it was stressed that there should be no question of comparing Webb's position to that of a man similarly incapable for medical or other reasons. Although Webb won the legal argument in her case, a negative point of the decision was that many legal academics and practitioners were strongly of the view that she would not have won her case had she been employed on a fixed-term, temporary contract. Lord Keith of Kinkel was obviously influenced by the possibility that a woman on a fixed-term contract who goes on maternity leave may not be able to fulfill her contractual duties to her employer. This situation would have placed the employer at a clear disadvantage. The comparison was made with a female employee who enjoys all the benefits of an indefinite or permanent contract, and who would only be temporarily absent from work due to her pregnancy.

 Key point: A woman who is treated less favourably on the grounds of pregnancy or for pregnancy related reasons will have suffered direct sex discrimination.

Many of the perceived problems thrown up by the decision in **Webb** have now been dealt with as a result of the introduction of the Employment Equality (Sex Discrimination) Regulations 2005 on 1 October 2005. These regulations implement the provisions of the European Union's **Equal Treatment Directive (2002/73)**.

These Regulations insert into the Sex Discrimination Act 1975 stronger rules expressly forbidding discrimination on the grounds of pregnancy (**new Section 3A**) and maternity leave (**new Section 3B**). This should mean that pregnant women now receive much stronger legal protection in employment. Pregnant employees must, however, prove that the less favourable treatment suffered by them was by reason of their pregnancy.

 Madarassy *v* Nomura (2007) Madarassy was employed by Nomura, the international Japanese bank in the City of London as an equities banker. While on maternity leave, Madarassy was dismissed from her employment with the bank. She subsequently lodged Employment Tribunal claims for sex discrimination, victimisation and unfair dismissal (valued at £1 million) against her ex-employer. The Employment Tribunal concluded that Madarassy had been the victim of unlawful discrimination. Her ex-employer appealed to the Employment Appeal Tribunal where it won the appeal. Madarassy, in turn, appealed to the Court of Appeal.

Held: by the English Court of Appeal that Madarrasy had failed to achieve the necessary of burden of proof which would have established that she had suffered discrimination or less favourable treatment by reason of her gender. In discrimination cases, the balance of proof shifts between the parties in the sense that a claimant alleging sex discrimination must show that s/he has been treated differently by the employer and that the reason for this difference in treatment is motivated by gender. It will then be up to the employer to show that the different treatment was not discriminatory or less favourable.

Lord Justice Mummery stated in his judgement that:

'The bare facts of a difference in status and a difference in treatment only indicate a possibility of discrimination... They are not, without more, sufficient material from which a tribunal 'could conclude' that, on the balance of probabilities, the respondent [Nomura] had committed an unlawful act of discrimination.'

One thing is very clear from this judgement: a difference in treatment will not in itself be enough for a claimant to win a sex discrimination case (or any other type of alleged discrimination). The key flaw in Madarassy's allegations was that she could not prove that the difference in treatment was motivated by her gender.

 Key point: Female employees claiming discrimination on grounds of pregnancy must demonstrate that the less favourable treatment is limited to their pregnancy and not motivated by some other reason.

Discrimination on the grounds of marital status

Employers are not permitted to discriminate against people on the grounds of marital status (Section 3: Sex Discrimination Act). This means that a married person must be not less favourably treated in comparison to a single person of the same sex.

Direct discrimination on the grounds of race, colour, nationality or membership of an ethnic group or racial group

Racial discrimination will arise when a person suffers less favourable treatment by reason of colour, race, nationality or ethnic or national origin. Discrimination on the grounds of religion is covered indirectly by the Race Relations Act 1976 in that the religion in question must be one of the identifying characteristics of a racial, national or ethnic group. Jews and Sikhs are covered by the Race Relations Act, but Roman Catholics, Protestants and Muslims are not protected specifically by the legislation. Roman Catholics, Protestants and Muslims are found in many different racial, national and ethnic groups, so these religions cannot be said to be identified with any one particular group. Jews and Sikhs, for example, belong to distinct ethnic and racial groups where their religion is just one example of a shared identity.

Section 3 of the Race Relations Act defines 'racial grounds' as meaning a person's colour, race, nationality or ethnic or national origins. In other words, a person's membership of a specific racial group can be determined by reference to the criteria laid down in Section 3 above.

 Mandla *v* Dowell Lee (1983) a private school refused to give a Sikh boy a place at the school because he would not stop wearing his turban or have his hair cut. Sikhs, of course, belong to a religious group and the turban and long hair are symbols for male Sikhs. Obviously, the boy had suffered direct discrimination on the grounds of his religion, but the Race Relations Act 1976 does not forbid religious discrimination.

The House of Lords had to consider whether Sikhs were part of a racial group for the purposes of Section 3. It was held that Sikhs were not just a religious group, they were also an ethnic group who enjoyed protection under the Act.

 King *v* Great Britain-China Centre (1991) Ms King, who was ethnic Chinese, applied for a post with the Great Britain-China Centre. She had been born in China and was fluent in the Chinese languages. King believed that she was more than suitably qualified for the post, but she failed to gain an interview. The Industrial Tribunal noted that the Centre did not employ anyone from an ethnic Chinese background. Five ethnic Chinese candidates in total had applied for the post, but none had been interviewed.

Held: by the English Court of Appeal that the employer could offer no satisfactory explanation as to why King had not been given an interview for the position of Deputy Director of the Centre. King had suffered direct discrimination on the grounds of her race. In this case, the Employment Tribunal chose to make an inference (a presumption) that there had been discrimination on the grounds of race because King had presented strong evidence to support such a finding. Until recently, **King** was the standard burden of proof in race discrimination claims.

The cases of **Northern Joint Police Board *v* Power (1997)** and **BBC Scotland *v* Souster (2001)** demonstrate that the term 'racial group' can cover the Scots, English, Irish and Welsh people within the United Kingdom. It will be appreciated, of course, that the Scots, English, (Northern) Irish and Welsh share a common British nationality.

 Northern Joint Police Board *v* Power (1997) an applicant for the job of Chief Constable of the Northern Constabulary claimed that he had been discriminated against as he had been rejected for the post because he was English. There was no discrimination on the grounds of nationality because

Scots and English people are British, but there could be direct discrimination on the grounds of a person's racial origins.

Held: that the Scots and the English, although sharing the same nationality, were to be regarded as distinct racial groups who were protected by the Race Relations Act.

The term ethnic group has a much wider meaning than a racial group. It will be important to establish that the members of an ethnic group have a shared history and culture of which they are conscious and which sets them apart from other groups. Other important issues to consider are whether the group originates from the same geographical area or whether the members share a common ancestry. A common language may indicate membership of such a group, although it does not have to be peculiar to the members of this group. The group may also have a common literary tradition and religion. Finally, the group may, throughout its history, have experienced persecution and harsh treatment in its dealings with larger groups.

Under the above criteria, Jewish people have qualified as an ethnic group because being a Jew is not just about a person's religion it is also connected to notions of ethnic identity and national origin (**Seide *v* Gillette Industries Ltd (1980)**).

Certain racial groups who are predominantly Muslim in terms of their religion have been able to claim the protection of the Race Relations Act where indirect racial discrimination has been an issue. Generally, however, Muslims, like other religious groups, are not protected by the Act.

 J H Walker Ltd *v* Hussain & Ors (1996) the Employment Appeal Tribunal found that the employer's change of shift patterns resulted in fewer Asian employees being able to comply with a requirement of the employer that they work a particular day. The day that the employer wished the employees to work just happened to coincide with one of the holiest days in the Muslim calendar (the Feast of Eid). Many Asian employees simply refused to turn up to work on that day and were issued with final written warnings. They later claimed that they had suffered indirect racial discrimination. The employees had been discriminated against indirectly not because they were Muslims, but because as Asians a smaller number of them could comply with the employer's demand that they work a particular day in comparison with non-Asian employees.

 Key point: Discrimination on the grounds of a person's religion is not generally covered by the Race Relations Act 1976.

What it means to be a member of racial or ethnic group (as defined by the Race Relations Act 1976) has recently been examined in the following case. Although this case involved a legal challenge relating to the refusal by the Board of Governors to give a place at a school to a prospective pupil, it is instructive nonetheless for employment law purposes as it involves the issue of direct race discrimination.

 R (E) *v* Governing Body of JFS (2009) JFS, which was previously known as the Jewish Free School, was in the practice of giving preference to requests for places from pupils who were defined as Jewish under guidelines issued by the Chief Rabbi of the United Hebrew Congregation of the

Commonwealth (OCR). The school is very popular and has to turn down many placing requests. The child in this case, known as 'M', was refused a place at JFS on the grounds that he was not sufficiently Jewish because his mother, a convert to Judaism, had been instructed into the faith at a Progressive synagogue, a procedure not recognised by the Chief Rabbi.

In the main, a system of preferential treatment in education is permitted in England and Wales under the Equality Act 2006. This system allows religious institutions to treat people differently on the grounds of religion, **but not race**. So, in theory, it is permissible for Roman Catholic or Church of England schools to give priority to children whose parents profess or practise that particular religious faith.

In strict Jewish rabbinical tradition, a person born of a Jewish mother is a member of the faith and this definition, of course, excludes those individuals born of a Jewish father and a gentile (non-Jewish) mother. As a religious faith, Judaism does welcome converts, but such individuals have to be instructed into the faith by following strict guidelines issued by the Chief Rabbi. Upon achieving the criteria set down by the Chief Rabbi, these individuals can become full members of the Jewish faith.

Judaism, however, is not just a religion and to be Jewish is also to be a member of a racial or ethnic group. In other words, people who refer to themselves as Jewish may not necessarily be making a statement of religious belief, but rather a statement of racial or ethnic identity.

Held: by the English Court of Appeal that the priority given to Jewish pupils based on their ethnic background was unlawful direct discrimination on the grounds of race which was a breach of the Race Relations Act 1976. The Court of Appeal overruled the previous decision of the High Court which had ruled in favour of the admissions policy operated by JFS.

Lord Justice Sedley stated that:

'... *it appears to us clear (a) that Jews constitute a racial group defined principally by ethnic origin and additionally by conversion, and (b) that to discriminate against a person on the ground that he or someone else either is or is not Jewish is therefore to discriminate against him on racial grounds. The motive for the discrimination, whether benign or malign, theological or supremacist, makes it no less and no more unlawful. Nor does the factuality of the ground.* If for theological reasons a fully subscribed Christian faith school refused to admit a child on the ground that, albeit practising Christians, the child's family were of Jewish origin, it is hard to see what answer there could be to a claim for race discrimination. [our emphasis]'

Lord Justice Sedley went on to remark that he was not saying that it was impossible for Jewish schools to give preference to adherents of the Jewish faith; it was simply unlawful to operate a preference system based on racial or ethnic grounds and such decisions should depend on the practice of the faith i.e. individuals should be considered who profess to be practising Jews in spite of the fact that they may not quite meet strict, orthodox Jewish requirements. JFS appealed to the Supreme Court to have this decision overturned but the Supreme Court has confirmed the Court of Appeal's decision that the school was guilty of religious discrimination.

Examples of race discrimination cases

 Myers *v* Mark Two Distributors Ltd ET Case No. 3300482/04 Mr Myers, is black and of Afro-Caribbean origin, who was employed as a delivery driver. A Mr James, a white colleague, was sometimes sent to help Myers on certain deliveries. James would often use racist language to describe other road users. Myers made his objections clear to James concerning these comments, but his colleague showed his complete disregard for his feelings. Myers complained to his manager about the remarks and James' attitude towards him. The manager did absolutely nothing about the complaints that Myers had made. Feelings between the two colleagues became so bad that the two were eventually involved in a fight. Myers admitted that he had hit James first, but only after James had pushed him and racially abused him.

Both employees were suspended after the incident, but clear differences in the way that they were treated by the employer during the disciplinary process soon emerged. The letter that Myers received from the employer inviting him to attend a disciplinary meeting was entitled 'Assault on an employee (Paul James)' whereas the letter that James received was entitled 'Investigation into an incident'. The employer took James' account of the incident at face value without investigating the incident further. Following on from this, the employer decided to dismiss Myers, but no further action was taken against James. James, in fact, had a history of assaulting colleagues.

Held: by the Watford Employment Tribunal that Myers had suffered direct discrimination in breach of the Race Relations Act 1976.

 Bah *v* Dayat Food Ltd ET Case No. 3300481/04 Mr Bah, who is of black African race, was employed as a general warehouse assistant and forklift truck driver. Bah had a dispute with his manager, who was ethnic Chinese, when he discovered that a colleague's car which had been vandalised while situated on company premises had been repaired at the employer's expense. Bah's colleague was also ethnic Chinese. Bah's car had also been broken into while on company premises, but the employer had not offered to repair his vehicle. When Bah approached his manager for an explanation why his car had not been repaired at company expense, his enquiry was completely dismissed and Bah was subjected to racial abuse.

Both men then had a heated argument and, later that day Bah, told his manager that he would make a written complaint to the employer's managing director. The manager then informed Bah that he was being dismissed from employment with immediate effect. Following on from his dismissal, Bah received a letter from the managing director justifying the dismissal on the grounds of his misconduct.

Held: by the Watford Employment Tribunal that the racist comment made by the manager amounted to direct discrimination in breach of the Race Relations Act 1976. Bah's dismissal also amounted to discrimination by victimisation and was an unfair dismissal.

 Mitchell *v* Governing Body of Hayes School ET Case No. 1100812/04 Mr Mitchell, who is black, was employed by the school as a supply teacher. Mitchell was a very experienced and highly competent teacher of English.

The school was well aware of Mitchell's desire to secure a permanent teaching post and when he had originally taken up his job it was made known to him that certain permanent positions would eventually become available. The school's assistant head teacher informed Mitchell that he would be more than welcome to apply for any suitable post and he gave the impression that such vacancies would be advertised as part of a formal recruitment post. Subsequently, however, two white teachers (Mrs Beattie and Mr Steel) were appointed to permanent positions at the school without any formal recruitment process being followed. Needless to say Mitchell was not appointed to a permanent post and the school failed to offer a convincing explanation for this state of affairs. In fact, Mitchell was informed that he would have to apply formally for any job vacancies. Mitchell concluded that his failure to secure a permanent job was by reason of his race and he lodged a claim in terms of the Race Relations Act.

Held: by the Ashford Employment Tribunal that the school had failed to offer convincing explanations for the difference in treatment experienced by Mitchell when compared to his white colleagues. The Tribunal was influenced by the contradictory and confused evidence offered by representatives of the school and was, therefore, entitled to conclude that Mitchell had suffered less favourable treatment on the grounds of his race.

Khan *v* Direct Line Insurance plc ET Case No. 1400802/04 highlights an interesting example of indirect race discrimination (before the Bristol Employment Tribunal) brought in somewhat unusual circumstances.

Mr Khan, who is of Asian origin and a Muslim, was employed by Direct Line. Khan's departmental managers ran an incentive scheme for employees whereby certain individuals by complying with the rules of the scheme were entitled to win prizes. Various prizes were written down on pieces of paper which were then placed in a bucket containing a rather disgusting mixture of spaghetti, sausages and beans. Employees were then invited to pick out a piece of paper from the bucket in order to have an opportunity of winning a prize. Khan was initially reluctant to place his hand in the bucket, but after receiving verbal encouragement from his co-workers he did so. He was quite traumatised by this experience because, as a Muslim, he was forced to come into physical contact with pork sausages – an unclean food with which Muslims are forbidden to come into contact. Khan immediately raised a grievance against his employer and a number of hearings took place. After each hearing, Khan received a general apology from Direct Line. Khan considered these apologies to be unsatisfactory and he lodged a claim to the Office of Employment Tribunals on the grounds that he had suffered indirect race discrimination. His argument centred around the fact that a person of his ethnic origin (an Asian Muslim) had been subjected to a provision or a criterion which resulted in him experiencing less favourable treatment by reason of his race. It will, of course, be appreciated that British Asians are more likely to be Muslims than other members of the British population or members of an employer's work-force.

The employer first attempted to argue that the rules governing the incentive scheme were not a provision, a practice or a criterion which placed certain ethnic employees at a disadvantage. When this argument failed to impress the Tribunal, the employer put forward an alternative argument that such a scheme was necessary to motivate employees. Again, the Tribunal was not impressed stating that in order to be successful incentive schemes should not mean forcing employees (especially those of Khan's ethnic background) to handle pork sausages and other unclean foods. Finally, the employer was forced to state that it had never had any intention of causing offence to Khan.

Held: although Khan's claim had been lodged outside the three month time limit for submitting such an action to the Office of Employment Tribunals, the Tribunal felt that it was only fair that he should be permitted to proceed with what appeared to be a strong case. Khan would now, of course, be able to pursue such a claim via the Employment Equality (Religion or Belief) Regulations 2003 – a route closed to him since the incident at work took place before the Regulations were introduced in December 2003.

The Employment Appeal Tribunal has recently concluded in the case of **Edozie v Group 4 Securicor Plc & Anor (2009)** that discrimination on the grounds of a person's race, ethnic or national origins as defined by Section 54A of the Race Relations Act 1976 covers situations where a person has suffered less favourable treatment by reason of his or her skin colour. In its original form, Section 54A makes no mention of the word "colour" and doubt existed as to whether discrimination on grounds of person's skin colour was covered by this provision. The law has now been clarified as a result of this decision. Unfortunately for the Appellant (Edozie), he lost his appeal because he was not able to prove to the Employment Appeal Tribunal that the less favourable treatment he had experienced (i.e. being rejected for 7 job vacancies) was motivated by his skin colour.

The fact that religious discrimination is not covered by the Race Relations Act is no longer such a disadvantage with the introduction of the Employment Equality (Religion or Belief) Regulations 2003 on 2 December 2003. Interestingly, the provisions of the Race Relations Act were extended to combat religious discrimination in Northern Ireland, but not the rest of the UK. Both sets of Regulations are discussed in more detail later in the chapter.

Discriminatory adverts or job titles

Advertisements used in the recruitment process or the use of particular job titles in employment will be unlawful if they give the impression that a person from a particular gender or racial group will be given preferential treatment. If a public house placed an advertisement in the local paper stating that it required a barman, it would give a strong impression that women need not apply for the position as the employer obviously favours men over women. Such an advertisement would be unlawful. Similarly, glossy advertisements that give the impression of an all white workforce may deter people who belong to ethnic minorities from applying for a position with the organisation. However, a member of the public could not bring a claim under either the Sex Discrimination or Race Relations Acts in respect of a discriminatory advertisements or job title unless this person had actually applied for the job and had been refused employment on the grounds of sex or race. Generally speaking, either the Equal Opportunities Commission or the Commission for Racial Equality will take legal action against employers in respect of discriminatory

◆ The requirement or condition is to the affected person's detriment, because he or she cannot comply with it.

 Key point: The European Union's Equal Treatment Directive amends the definition of indirect sex discrimination in the Sex Discrimination Act 1975.

An updated definition of indirect racial discrimination

The Race Regulations 2003 provide a wider definition of indirect discrimination than arguably is the case under the Sex Discrimination Act 1975 and as was the case in terms of the Race Relations Act prior to 19 July 2003. However, it is important to note that the rules in the Regulations regarding indirect discrimination apply only to a person's **race** or **ethnic or national origin**. Discrimination on the basis of an individual's **colour** or **nationality** will still be covered by the older definition of indirect discrimination as laid down in Section 1(1)(b) of the Race Relations Act 1976. This means that are now two types of indirect discrimination in race discrimination cases.

According to Section 1A of the Race Relations Act, indirect discrimination will occur when an employer applies to another person:

◆ a provision, criterion or practice which the employer applies to everyone; and
◆ this provision, criterion or practice puts (or would put) people from the affected person's race or ethnic or national origin at a particular disadvantage; and
◆ the employer cannot show that the provision, criterion or practice is a proportionate means of achieving a legitimate aim

The words 'provision, criterion, or practice' have a broader meaning than the words 'requirement or condition' which still apply to claims brought under the Race Relations Act in respect of a person's colour or nationality. The new wording will, therefore, apply to an employer's informal as well as formal practices. Informal practices might include advertising posts or promotion opportunities by word of mouth as opposed to advertising these positions formally. It is hoped that this will mean that many more people will be placed in a position where claims of indirect discrimination may be brought against their employers.

There is another important difference between the older definition of indirect discrimination and the more modern approach. Previously, individuals making a complaint often had to base their claim on complex statistical evidence in order to show that people belonging to their particular group were placed at more of a disadvantage in comparison to another group of people.

 Key point: The newer definition of indirect discrimination introduced by the Race Regulations 2003 will apply when a person alleges that he has suffered less favourable treatment by reason of his racial, national or ethnic origin.

Indirect discrimination in practice

At first glance, the condition or the requirement that the employer imposes on everyone looks completely harmless. However, upon a closer inspection, it becomes obvious that more men than women can comply in practice with the employer's condition or requirement or that more white people can comply with the requirement or condition than can people from an Afro-Caribbean background. It is not just the fact that fewer people from a particular gender group or individuals of a particular colour or nationality can comply in practice with the requirement, they suffer an adverse impact because of it i.e. they suffer less favourable treatment.

What if, for example, the employer imposed a requirement that all job applicants had to be at least six feet in height? Admittedly, there are many tall women, but realistically there are many more tall men than tall women who can comply with this requirement in practice. More women would, therefore, be prevented from applying for this job. In other words, women are denied employment opportunities because the employer has imposed a height restriction.

In situations where an employer imposes 'desirable' and 'essential' criteria in a job advertisement, they may be examples of indirect discrimination (**Falkirk Council v Whyte (1997)**). In **Briggs v NE Education and Library Board (1990)**, a requirement of the employer that the successful applicant for a job be able to work full time was an example of indirect discrimination because fewer female applicants could comply in practice with this condition than their male counterparts.

Very often, a detailed statistical analysis will be carried out in order to calculate, for example, how many women or how many people of a particular colour, nationality, race, ethnic or national origin can comply in practice with the requirement imposed by the employer. If fewer Sikhs, for example, can comply with the requirement, it may be that the employer has indirectly discriminated against them.

Examples of the ways in which claims of indirect discrimination are dealt with can be seen in the following cases:

 London Underground v Edwards (No 2) (1998) a female lone parent, was employed as a train operator by London Underground. The employer decided to change the shift patterns. Such a change applied across the board to all drivers, whether male or female. The female employee complained about the new shift patterns claiming that fewer women than men could comply with them in practice.

She stated that as women had child-rearing responsibilities, the new shift patterns would make it much more difficult to organise child-care arrangements. The new shift patterns, therefore, indirectly discriminated against women. The employer carried out a statistical analysis comparing the percentages of men who could comply with the new patterns in practice with the percentage of women who were able to do so. The employer had to compare like with like, so male drivers were compared to female drivers. The results were as follows:

2023 male employees – 100% of them were able to comply with the new arrangements.

21 female employees – 95.2% of them were able to comply with the new arrangements.

In fact, only the complainant amongst all her female colleagues was unable to comply with the new pattern. This was, however, not the point. In practice, fewer women than men were capable of complying with the employer's requirement. The Tribunal found that the complainant had suffered less favourable treatment as a result of the employer's indirect discrimination.

Held: by the English Court of Appeal that the Tribunal was entitled to establish that Edwards had suffered indirect discrimination on the grounds of sex. Admittedly, the percentage difference between the two groups was small, but the Court of Appeal did not feel that this was an important factor in this case.

A refusal by an employer to grant an employee the right to have flexible working patterns, for example, to balance childcare responsibilities may constitute indirect discrimination:

 Network Rail Infrastructures Ltd *v* Gammie (2009) Gammie was employed as a railway signaller by Network Rail and she had been on maternity leave. On her return to work, Gammie requested that she be allowed to work part-time in terms the Regulations relating to flexible working. Network Rail refused to grant flexible working by stating that, when Gammie had submitted her request, there were not enough signallers to meet the needs of the organisation. Requests for flexible working from male and female employees were, therefore, being actively refused by Network Rail and, during this time, no signallers in Scotland worked part-time shifts. Gammie was of the opinion that this policy towards Network Rail's signallers had a significantly negative and disproportionate effect on female employees who were more likely to request flexible working arrangements in order to carry out childcare responsibilities. Upon being refused the right to flexible working patterns, Gammie resigned from her post claiming that she had been constructively dismissed on the grounds of sex discrimination. It should, of course, be appreciated that Network Rail's refusal to consider flexible working requests applied equally to both male and female employees. The key issue here, for the purpose of the sex discrimination legislation, is whether this provision criterion or practice has a disproportionately negative effect on one group of employees i.e. female signallers.

An Employment Tribunal found that Network Rail had indeed applied a provision criterion or practice which could not be 'strongly justified' and that Gammie had suffered indirect sex discrimination when her request for flexible working had been refused. Network Rail then appealed to the Employment Appeal Tribunal in Edinburgh.

Held: by the Employment Appeal Tribunal that the Tribunal had made an error in law when it stated that the provision criterion or practice imposed by Network Rail could not be 'strongly justified'. The Tribunal had indulged in too much speculation about the employer's refusal to grant flexible working by questioning the motives behind the decision. All the employer had to show in such circumstances was that the provision criterion or practice could be objectively justified i.e. that it is a 'proportionate means of achieving a legitimate aim'. The Tribunal had not given Network Rail a proper opportunity to justify its reasons for making the decision in the first place. Consequently, it was decided that the case should be heard by a new Employment Tribunal which could determine this issue once and for all.

An employer's change of shift patterns was also held to have be an example of indirect discrimination in **J H Walker Ltd *v* Hussain & Ors (1996)**. Here, the Employment Appeal Tribunal found that the employer's change of shift patterns resulted in fewer Asian employees being able to comply with a requirement of the employer that they turn up for work on a particular day.

 In **Singh *v* Rowntree MacKintosh (1979)** the employer imposed a requirement that male employees who were involved in the manufacture of products (sweets and chocolate) were not allowed to wear beards. This requirement indirectly discriminated against Sikh employees. It will be recalled that the Sikh religion insists that men wear their hair long and that they do not shave their beards.

Held: by the Employment Appeal Tribunal that such a condition, although it indirectly discriminated against Sikh employees, was justifiable on the grounds of hygiene in terms of Section 1(1)(b)(ii) of the Race Relations Act 1976. There is also a similar justification defence in terms of Section 1(1)(b)(ii) of the Sex Discrimination Act 1975.

 Key point: Employers will have to be particularly careful that they do not apply general conditions, requirements or criteria in relation to employees which may actually be examples of indirect discrimination.

Justification

In terms of Sections 1 of both the Sex Discrimination and Race Relations Acts, an employer will be permitted to discriminate on the grounds of sex or race in certain, appropriate circumstances. An employer can, therefore, justify discriminatory treatment by claiming that a candidate for a job, promotion, training or other benefit must be of a particular gender or be a member of a particular racial group.

Indirect discrimination on the grounds of hygiene has been justified in **Singh *v* Rowntree MacKintosh (1979)**, where the employer did not allow male employees who were involved in producing confectionary to wear beards. This rule indirectly discriminated against Sikh employees, but it was justifiable on hygiene grounds.

Genuine Occupational Qualifications (Sex Discrimination)

Section 7 of the Sex Discrimination Act lists seven situations where the person's sex may be regarded as a genuine occupational qualification:

1 For physiological reasons (not physical strength or stamina). The employer requires a candidate to be a member of a particular sex, for example, a local college running an art course may require a male model to pose for still life classes. This genuine occupational requirement would also cover situations where directors required male actors to appear in dramatic performances or other forms of entertainment.

2 To preserve decency and privacy because the job is likely to involve physical contact with members of a particular sex in situations where the presence of someone of the opposite sex might cause embarrassment or personal discomfort. The post might involve coming into contact with people who are in a state of undress or where individuals are using sanitary facilities. Clearly this would

cover situations where a woman applied for a job and that job involved working in a men's changing room at a sports centre or a swimming pool. The job involves the candidate working or living in a private home and this work entails a great deal of intimate contact with people of the opposite sex. This requirement would most obviously apply to nursing or care jobs.

3   The job requires that the candidate share sleeping accommodation with workers who are members of the same sex and the location of this accommodation makes it completely impracticable for the employer to provide separate sleeping accommodation and sanitary facilities for workers of the opposite sex. Furthermore, it would also be unreasonable to expect the employer to provide such accommodation and facilities for workers of the opposite sex.

4   The job is in a single sex institution, for example, a prison, a hospital, or other institution which provides its inmates with special care or supervision and it is reasonable that the job should be held by a person of a particular sex.

5   The holder of the job provides individuals with personal services aimed at promoting their welfare or educational services and where those services can be most effectively provided by a person of a particular sex. The best person for the post of a rape counsellor would probably be a female professional.

6   The job needs to be held by a person of a particular sex because performance of the employee's duties outside the United Kingdom will take place in a country whose laws or customs place considerable restrictions on the ability of a man or woman to carry out the job effectively. A company may refuse to appoint a woman to a senior position overseas if this job was based in Saudi Arabia where there are severe restrictions placed upon women generally.

7   The job is one of two to be held by a married couple.

Examples of attempts by employers to use gender as a genuine occupational qualification can be seen in the following cases:

 O'Connor *v* Kontiki Travel (1976) O'Connor, who was female, applied for a job as a coach driver on overseas tours. She was not given the job and the employer justified the refusal to hire her because she would have to drive through a number of Muslim countries where there restrictions placed on women which would effectively prevent her from carrying out her duties. On further investigation, it was discovered that the only Muslim country that the coach would be travelling through was Turkey. Although most Turks are Muslims, Turkey did not have particularly strict laws that prevented women from carrying out many jobs. In fact, Turkey was a liberal Muslim country and no objections would have been raised in relation to O'Connor being employed as a driver.

Held: the employer could not justify O'Connor's treatment on the grounds that being male was a genuine occupational requirement. O'Connor had been treated less favourably on the grounds of her sex and, consequently, she had suffered direct discrimination. However, O'Connor ultimately lost her case because the employment in question would be performed totally outside the UK and the Sex Discrimination Act did not, therefore, apply.

Wylie v Dee & Co (Menswear) Ltd (1978) Wylie, who was female, applied for a job in a menswear shop. The employers refused to hire her because she was female. The employers attempted to justify this discriminatory treatment on the grounds that being male was a genuine occupational requirement for the job. Evidence was led by the employers to show that the post involved a degree of intimate physical contact with male customers. From time to time, employees were required to take the inside-leg measurements of male customers who might be less than comfortable having their measurements taken by a female member of staff.

Held: by the Industrial Tribunal that the employers could not rely on a genuine occupational requirement to justify the refusal to employ Wylie. It was proved that the intimate physical contact with male customers did not occur on a regular basis and, furthermore, when male customers had to be measured in this way there were seven male employees who could take the measurements if so required. Wylie had suffered less favourable treatment as a result of her sex.

The Sex Discrimination (Gender Reassignment) Regulations 1999 also introduce additional genuine occupational qualifications which apply to transsexuals only. These are:

◆ The employment entails intimate body searches permitted by statute (Police and Customs officers).

◆ The employment is in a private home where there is social and physical contact with members of the household or where the employee gains knowledge of intimate details of house members' lives and distress may be caused if the employee is a transsexual.

◆ The employer has provided premises for the employee and it would be impractical for the employee to live elsewhere other than on these premises. Furthermore, it would offend decency and privacy if the employee was undergoing gender reassignment and it was not practical for the employer to provide separate facilities.

◆ The employee provides vulnerable individuals with personal services promoting their welfare.

Genuine Occupational Qualification (Race Discrimination)

Where the issue of race is concerned, there is less scope for an employer to justify discriminatory treatment. Section 5 of the Race Relations Act lists three very limited situations where the person's colour, nationality, race, ethnic or national origins may be regarded as a genuine occupational qualification:

1 Where a person of a particular race is required for authenticity to participate in a dramatic performance or other form of entertainment. Such a situation would apply to a director who casts a black actor as the Shakespearean character Othello in preference to a white colleague. For the avoidance of any confusion, Othello is black in William Shakespeare's play. This genuine occupational requirement would also apply where an artist's or photographic model is

required for the production of a work of art or visual image where members of particular racial groups are needed for reasons of authenticity.

2   Where a person is required to serve food and drink to the public in a place where members of a particular racial group are required to promote authenticity. It does not matter whether this work is carried out on a paid basis or not. This genuine occupational requirement allows Indian and Chinese restaurants to employ Indian and Chinese waiting and bar staff in order to provide customers with an authentic experience. However, it does not cover situations where staff do not have contact with the public, for example, kitchen staff. Being ethnic Chinese is not a genuine occupational requirement for working as a chef in the kitchen of a Chinese restaurant.

3   The holder of the job provides individuals with personal services aimed at promoting their welfare and where those services can be most effectively provided by a person of that particular racial group.

Special Occupational Requirements (Race Discrimination)

Section 4A of the Race Relations Act allows an employer to impose a genuine occupational requirement in respect of job applicants. Theoretically, this is much wider than the limited genuine occupational qualifications allowed by Section 5. It may be the case that certain jobs are best carried out by people belonging to particular race or who have particular ethnic or national origins. If this is indeed the case, an employer can legally discriminate in favour of certain races or people having certain ethnic backgrounds or national origins. However, an employer must show that imposing a genuine occupational requirement on the holder of a particular post is not disproportionate. Therefore, the employer must demonstrate that, having regard to the nature of the job or its context, it is best performed by a person who is a member of a particular race, ethnic or national group. Furthermore, by employing such a person the employer must be in a position to show that the benefits of discriminating in favour of particular applicants outweighs any disadvantages of such a policy.

Genuine occupational requirements do not apply to a job applicant's colour and nationality. An employer wishing to rely on a genuine occupational qualification in respect of an applicant's colour or nationality will have to continue to use the limited exceptions permitted by Section 5.

 Key point: Genuine occupational qualifications or special occupational requirements allow an employer to discriminate against certain individuals on the grounds of sex or race.

Sexual and racial harassment

To make offensive remarks of a sexually or racially motivated nature to a person will be regarded as direct sex or racial discrimination. Making discriminatory comments about a woman's body or racist comments in relation to a person's colour or race will amount to less favourable treatment. One sexually or racially motivated remark could amount to harassment.

On 6 April 2006, the Commission for Racial Equality's Race Discrimination Code of Practice came into force. This was the first update of the code since 1983 and provides useful information to employers and employees regarding the issue of racial discrimination.

Employment Tribunals have been greatly assisted by the publication of a European Commission Code of Practice on Measures to Combat Sexual Harassment. In **Wadman v Carpenter Farrer Partnership (1993)** the Employment Appeal Tribunal stated that Tribunals should use the Code to decide when sexual harassment has taken place.

 Institu Cleaning Co Ltd v Heads (1995) a male colleague had made a remark about the large breast size of a female colleague. This remark was unwelcome and the male colleague attempted to defend himself (unsuccessfully) by stating that he would not have made the remark if he had known it was going to cause offence.

Held: by the Employment Appeal Tribunal that this was a remark of a sexual nature that caused offence – it was totally unwanted and unsought – and, therefore, it was direct discrimination on the grounds of sex.

In **Reed and Bull Information Systems v Stedman (1999)** the Employment Appeal Tribunal laid down some guidelines as to what constitutes unwanted conduct in cases of sexual harassment. The test for sexual harassment is a subjective one in that it great stress will be placed on the feelings of the person who was subjected to the remark or the behaviour in question. Are the remarks or behviour unwelcome to the recipient and it is up to the recipient to decide what is welcome and what is offensive.

Obviously, racist remarks and racist behaviour should be treated completely differently in that they should not be tolerated at all. Racist remarks and behaviour will almost always be offensive in nature. The newly amended Race Relations Act now takes a much tougher approach to harassment. Section 3(A) states that harassment on the grounds of race or ethnic or national origin will be unlawful, if a person engages in unwanted conduct which has the purpose or effect of violating another person's dignity or creates an intimidating, hostile, offensive or disturbing environment. Section 3(A) makes it very clear that the perception or the opinion of the person claiming that they have suffered harassment will often be decisive in establishing that discrimination has occurred. Furthermore, Section 4(2A) states that it is unlawful for an employer to subject any employee or a person who has applied for employment to harassment on the grounds of race or ethnic or national origin.

 Key point: Harassment will occur when a person is subjected to unwanted conduct which has the purpose or effect of violating his or her dignity or creates an intimidating, hostile, offensive or disturbing environment.

It is not necessary for the person making the complaint to show that there has been a series of remarks. Similarly, direct discrimination will take place if an individual is subjected to a sustained campaign of sexual or racial harassment. It was wrongly thought by some commentators that women bringing claims of sexual harassment did not need to compare their treatment to that of a male comparator. It will be important to demonstrate that a woman would not have suffered sexual harassment but for the fact that she was female.

Porcelli v Strathclyde Regional Council (1986) Mrs Porcelli was employed by the Regional Council as a school lab technician. She worked with two male colleagues with whom she had a very poor working relationship. Both of these male colleagues went out of their way to subject her to a sustained campaign of harassment and bullying in order to force her to seek a transfer to another job or to leave her job altogether. Mrs Porcelli's colleagues had destroyed her work, slammed doors in her face and thrown her personal possessions into the bin. This was quite obviously appalling treatment, but it was gender neutral in the sense that Mrs Porcelli's colleagues would have subjected a man that they disliked to similar treatment. However, her colleagues' behaviour took a much nastier turn when the harassment and bullying started to take on sexual overtones. Both men used obscene language when they either spoke to or about Mrs Porcelli. They often used to compare her body (unfavourably) with nude pictures of women that appeared in newspapers and magazines. Mrs Porcelli was also subjected to suggestive remarks of a sexual nature and, on occasion, the men had brushed their bodies against Mrs Porcelli's body.

Held: by the Inner House of the Court of Session, affirming the decision of the Employment Appeal Tribunal, that Mrs Porcelli's treatment was an example of direct sex discrimination. Mrs Porcelli's colleagues had subjected her to a campaign of bullying and harassment that had sexual overtones. They would not have subjected a male colleague to the same kind of treatment. Mrs Porcelli had experienced this kind of treatment precisely because she was female. Lord Grieve remarked that: the treatment should be viewed as a 'sexual sword' which 'had been unsheathed and used because the victim was a woman'.

 Pearce v Governing body of Mayfield School (2003) Pearce's claim that she had suffered sexual harassment on the grounds that she was a lesbian failed because the employer was able to show that a male homosexual would also have been subjected to homophobic name calling by pupils at the school. Pearce, however, would now be able to bring a claim under the Employment Equality (Sexual Orientation) Regulations 2003 on the basis that she had suffered less favourable treatment (direct discrimination) on the grounds of her sexual orientation.

Held: by the House of Lords that although the treatment suffered by Pearce was extremely nasty, it was gender neutral. Pearce had suffered discrimination on the grounds of her sexual orientation, not her sex.

 Jones v Tower Boot (1997) a black employee was subjected to racist name calling over a period of time by a colleague. He was physically assaulted by his colleagues – his arm had been branded by a colleague who had attacked him with a hot screwdriver, metal bolts had been thrown at his head and his legs had been whipped.

Held: by the English Court of Appeal that this was harassment on the grounds of race and, therefore, direct discrimination. More significantly, the Court of Appeal stated that employers who failed to respond adequately in these situations to complaints were responsible for the racist bullying and harassment committed by other employees.

Key point: A person may subject another person to harassment by making a single sexist or racist remark or indulging in behaviour of this nature just once.

The European Union's Equal Treatment Directive

Changes to the Sex Discrimination Act 1975 were introduced by the Employment Equality (Sex Discrimination) Regulations 2005 on 1 October 2005 in response to the European Union's **Equal Treatment Directive (2002/73)**.

The most significant change which the Directive has made is the introduction of a new definition of sexual harassment. This means that both sex-based harassment and harassment generally will be expressly forbidden by the amended legislation.

A new **Section 4A** has been inserted into the Sex Discrimination Act 1975 which defines harassment and sexual harassment. Under the amended provisions, a person will have subjected a woman to harassment (including sexual harassment) on the ground of her sex if he engages in unwanted conduct which:

1 violates her dignity, or

2 creates an intimidating, hostile, degrading, humiliating or offensive environment for her

Furthermore, harassment will arise if a man has engaged in any form of unwanted verbal, non-verbal or physical conduct of a sexual nature that has the purpose or effect of:

1 violating her dignity, or

2 creating an intimidating, hostile, degrading, humiliating or offensive environment for her, or

3 subjecting her to less favourable treatment because of her rejection of or submission to unwanted conduct of a kind mentioned in 1 or 2 above.

Whether or not, the conduct complained of amounts to harassment will very much depend on the victim's perception of the treatment to which she has been subjected

Obviously, all the circumstances of the situation will have to be taken into account and the victim will have to demonstrate that she had a reasonable belief that she was being subjected to some sort of harassment.

It is worth noting that the provisions on harassment also apply to men and those individuals who are in the process of undergoing gender re-assignment (i.e. those who have decided to undergo a sex change operation).

 Key point: The European Union's Equal Treatment Directive significantly strengthens the law relating to protection from harassment.

Victimisation

Section 4 of the Sex Discrimination Act and Section 2 of the Race Relations Act provide an important range of safeguards and protection to individuals who have been involved in some way in sex and racial discrimination actions. Very often, the employer will subject an individual to less favourable treatment in the future because, at one time, they have had some involvement in a discrimination claim against the employer. It will be unlawful for an employer to victimise or harass such individuals in the following situations:

1   Where a person has brought an Employment Tribunal or a court action against the employer under the Equal Pay Act 1970, Sex Discrimination Act 1975 or the Race Relations Act 1976.

2   Where a person has given evidence in support of someone who has taken an Employment Tribunal or a court action under the above legislation.

3   Where a person has taken a legitimate course of action, for example, making a complaint against the employer in relation to the above legislation.

4   Where a person has made allegations against the employer that discrimination has occurred which is unlawful in terms of the above legislation.

 Waters *v* Commissioner of Police for the Metropolis (2000) Waters, a female police constable, had accused a male colleague of subjecting her to a sexual assault. The alleged assault had taken place outside working hours. The employee later claimed that she had suffered victimisation as a result of making the complaint of sexual assault against her colleague.

Held: by the House of Lords that her delictual claim against her employer should be allowed to proceed. An employer may be in breach of his personal duty of care if either he knew that fellow employees were behaving in such a way as to cause the employee in question to suffer physical or psychiatric injury or if it was reasonably foreseeable that such actions would cause harm and that he failed to put reasonable safeguards to prevent the employee suffering harm.

The issue of whether victimisation can continue after the employment relationship has ended has recently been decided by the House of Lords in a number of cases:

In **Relaxion Group plc *v* Rhys-Harper (FC)**; **D'Souza *v* London Borough of Lambeth**; and **Jones *v* 3M Healthcare Limited and Others (2003)** all the cases involved allegations of victimisation that had occurred after the employment of the individuals in question had ended. Claims were brought under the Sex Discrimination Act 1975, the Race Relations Act 1976 and the Disability Discrimination Act 1995.Their Lordships thought it would be illogical and completely arbitrary to give protection from victimisation up and until the contract of employment ended and, after this point, the employee could expect no further protection from victimisation. It was pointed out that an employee's duties towards his employer did not necessarily cease when the contract came to an end. An employee may be subject to obligations of confidentiality or restrictions on where he may work or for whom he may work. An employer may be subject to obligations regarding pension rights or bonus payments. The House of Lords used the following examples:

'... *the employee who asks for a reference before he retires from his employment is protected but the employee who asks for a reference the day after he left is not. It would mean that the employee who is dismissed with notice and whose appeal is heard before his notice expires is protected against discrimination in his recourse to the employer's appeal procedure, but the employee who is dismissed summarily and without notice is not. It would mean that retaliatory action taken by an employer before the contract of employment ends is within the scope of the legislation, but retaliatory action taken later, for instance, regarding bonus payments, is not.'*

Their Lordships concluded that it could not have been the intention of Parliament when it brought the equality legislation into force to deny protection to former employees who suffered victimisation after their employment had ended.

 Key point: It is important that those individuals who have been involved in discrimination claims either as a complainant or as a witness should be adequately protected against acts of victimisation by the employer during and after their employment.

The Equal Pay Act 1970

The Equal Pay Act 1970 did not come into force until 29 December 1975. Significantly, the Sex Discrimination Act 1975 was given legal force on the same day and there has been a close relationship between both pieces of legislation ever since. However, the Sex Discrimination Act is designed to provide protection against discrimination on the grounds of a person's sex in connection with the areas of recruitment, promotion and dismissal. The Equal Pay Act, on the other hand, is primarily concerned with discrimination in respect of employment terms and conditions. The Equal Pay Act is also more limited in its scope in that it does not cover discrimination on the grounds of marital status and it does it appear to deal with indirect discrimination. It is important to understand that the Act is not a charter for establishing fair pay in the labour market generally. There will continue to be many sectors of the labour market where low pay and poor conditions will be the norm and this will affect men as well as women. The Equal Pay Act attempts to eliminate inequalities as regards conditions of employment between men and women working for the same or an associated employer. There are exceptions, but generally women are not allowed to compare themselves with male workers who are employed by a different employer.

The phrase 'equal pay' in the title of the Act can be highly misleading. The Act does not just attempt to address inequality between men and women in relation to their pay. It would be unlawful, in terms of the Act, for an employer to give male employees all sorts of contractual benefits and not to extend these to female employees. Such benefits could include free or discounted membership of a gym, free or discounted rail travel, air-mile vouchers, gift vouchers, free or discounted PCs and mobile phones, access to subsidised mortgages and bank loans. However, many of the cases that are brought under the Act will be primarily concerned with the gap between the sexes in respect of what they earn.

In March 2009, Nicola Brewer, the former Chief Executive of the Equality and Human Rights Commission criticised the Equal Pay Act 1970 by stating that it should be subjected to radical reform in order to guarantee fair and transparent systems of pay.

Equal Pay – Class Actions

On 12 August 2009, www.emplaw.co.uk (a website specialising in British employment law), reported that the Law Society Gazette for England and Wales had obtained access to unpublished research commissioned by the UK Government that the best way to deal with the vast amount of equal pay claims before Employment Tribunals was to allow class actions to proceed. A class action is a legal case where numerous claimants have their claims co-joined in order to have the matter dealt with quickly and effectively by the legal system. In recent years, the UK courts and Tribunals have had to deal with a truly vast number of equal pay claims often brought against the same employer, for example, local authorities up and down the country. Class actions are particularly suited to situations where hundreds of employees (even thousands) wish to take action against the same employer and where the claims are very similar in nature. These types of legal action are particularly common in the United States and have been used by litigants to bring very successful claims for damages against tobacco companies.

 Key point: The Equal Pay Act can be used to combat inequalities in the terms and conditions of employment offered to men and women.

Pay

Pay has been defined as the ordinary basic or minimum wage or salary and any other consideration, whether in cash or in kind, which the worker receives, either directly or indirectly, in respect of his employment from his employer.

The above definition does not just include a person's salary. It also applies to pensions, employers' contributions to pensions, concessionary travel, social security benefits, maternity pay, sick pay, paid leave, contractual and statutory redundancy pay, paid leave, overtime pay and compensation for unfair dismissal.

According to the Equal Opportunities Commission in December 2003, it remains a shocking fact that, nearly 30 years after the Equal Pay Act made it unlawful to pay women less than men for doing the same job, statistically women working full-time are likely to be paid 18 per cent less than their male counterparts.

The European Union dimension

Article 141 of the Treaty of Rome 1957 and the Equal Pay Directive 75/117/EEC place a duty on Member States to ensure that men and women should receive equal pay for equal work. Furthermore, the Equal Treatment Directive 76/207/EEC makes it unlawful for an employer to discriminate in relation to conditions of employment. Very often, European Union legislation has been used to promote equality in order to overcome the shortcomings of the Equal Pay Act 1970. Article 141 can be directly applied and relied upon by litigants in the British courts – it is said to have direct effect (**Defrenne v Sabena (No 2) (1976)**). This means that individuals bringing equal pay cases will not be defeated by any deficiencies in United Kingdom legislation or where the British parliament has failed to bring equal pay rules into force which it is obliged to do so under European law. Individuals bringing a claim under Article 141 will able to rely on the principle of the supremacy of European Union law i.e. where there is a conflict between European law and United Kingdom law, the European rules are followed.

The Equal Pay Directive

In **Commission of the European Communities *v* UK (1982)** the Equal Pay Directive declared that the principle of equal pay for men and women was to be taken to include equal pay for work of equal value. This enables a woman to seek the same pay as a man doing an entirely different job where the woman believes her work is of equal value to his. The European Commission did not believe that the Equal Pay Act 1970, as originally introduced, gave protection to women in this situation. Enforcement proceedings were brought against the UK and the Commission's complaint was upheld. As a result, the UK government introduced secondary legislation (the Equal Pay (Amendment) Regulations 1983) which introduced the concept of equal pay for work of equal value.

Although the Equal Pay Act applies to direct discrimination only, Article 141 of the Treaty of Rome has been used to eliminate measures that would be regarded as examples of indirect discrimination.

R Secretary of State for Employment *ex parte* Equal Opportunities Commission (1994) the Employment Protection (Consolidation) Act 1978 contained a requirement that for an employee to be entitled to a statutory redundancy payment they had to work more than 16 hours per week. The employees in question worked less than eight hours per week.

Held: by the House of Lords that the Employment Protection (Consolidation) Act 1978 indirectly discriminated against women as fewer of them were able to comply in practice with the rules relating to entitlement to a redundancy payment. Many more men than women were employed in excess of 16 hours per week. Women tended to do more part-time work than men and they were less likely to meet the requirements of the 1978 Act.

Key point: European Union law has often been used to overcome the shortcomings of the United Kingdom's equal pay legislation.

Identifying a comparator

Under Section 1 of the Equal Pay Act, women must be able to compare themselves to man in the same employment otherwise their claim for equal pay will fail. It is, therefore, very important that a female worker is able to identify a male comparator (Section 1(2) and (6)). Unlike the Sex Discrimination Act 1975, where a woman can compare herself to a hypothetical male comparator, comparators in equal pay claims must be named.

In most cases, the male comparator will work for the same employer as the woman or for an associated employer. A male comparator employed by an associated employer will have common terms and conditions of employment. A female employee of the National Health Service who works for one Trust could compare her pay to that of a male comparator who is employed by another Trust under common conditions of employment. The woman must be employed at an establishment within the United Kingdom.

However, in some recent decisions, the courts have allowed women to compare themselves to men who, traditionally, would not be regarded as being in the same employment.

South Ayrshire Council *v* Morton (2001) a female teacher employed by South Ayrshire Council was permitted to compare herself with a male teacher employed by Highland Council as part of her equal pay claim. The reason behind this decision appears to centre around the fact that the terms and conditions that teachers are employed under in Scotland are so similar that the profession can be regarded as a national service.

On 17 September 2002, the European Court of Justice gave its ruling in **Lawrence *v* Regent Office Care Ltd (Case No C-320/00)**. The case centred around the choice of 'comparator' in a situation where the woman claimed that she was paid less than a man doing work of equal value. Until recently it was thought that the comparator had to be working for the same employer or an associated employer as the woman making the claim. However, this condition has not been regarded as being essential in a number of cases where the woman has been able to prove that the relationship between two different employers is sufficiently close. The European Court of Justice has held that for the relationship to be sufficiently close in order for European Union equal treatment rules to apply it is essential that the differences in pay must 'be attributed to a single source'. A single source would be where a Parliament or legislature makes the rules which govern the employment relationship or where the terms and conditions of employment come from a collective agreement or a policy laid down by the management of a corporate group.

This requirement for a single source of terms and conditions of employment is strictly interpreted by Tribunals as is clearly demonstrated in the following case:

 Department of Environment Food and Rural Affairs (DEFRA) *v* Robertson and Others (2003) Robertson and his co-applicants were employed as civil servants by DEFRA which is a UK Government Department. The six applicants brought a claim under the Equal Pay Act 1970. All six men sought to compare themselves with female civil servants working for the UK Department of Transport and the Regions (Central). On the face of it, every members of the UK civil service (as opposed to the devolved governments throughout the UK) is employed by the same employer and, theoretically, this meant the applicants should have faced little problem with their choice of comparators. However, there was no single source of terms and conditions of employment within the UK civil service because each Department was responsible for negotiating these with its own civil servants. Previously, the UK Treasury, as a central source, had set national terms and conditions of employment for the civil service, but this was now no longer the case.

Held: by the Employment Appeal Tribunal that the new arrangement meant that employment conditions varied significantly from department to department and the applicants were, therefore, not making a valid comparison when they selected their female colleagues in Department of Transport and the Regions (Central). The six applicants failed in their equal pay claim.

In **McCarthys Ltd *v* Smith (1979)** a woman discovered that she was being paid less as a manager than the man who held the post previously. The English Court of Appeal had held that the wording of the Equal Pay Act 1970 allowed comparisons only to be made with men employed at the same time as the woman. However, the European Court of Justice held that comparisons were not restricted to those individuals who were employed at the same time as the person seeking equal pay. The female applicant was entitled to compare herself with the man who had previously held her job.

Significantly, the Equal Pay Act does not prevent women from taking their employer to court in circumstances where a token man is employed on the same terms and conditions as they are (**Pickstone v Freemans PLC (1988)**). If this were allowed, the Equal Pay Act would be dealt a serious blow. As long as the women can demonstrate that they have been less favourably treated in comparison to a fellow male employee, they have the right to bring a claim.

In **Alabaster v Barclays PLC and DSS (2005)**, the English Court of Appeal has ruled that there is no need for a pregnant employee to identify a male comparator in an equal pay action. This brings the Equal Pay Act into line with the Sex Discrimination Act 1975 whereby pregnant women bringing claims of unlawful sex discrimination against their employers are not required to use a male comparator. Pregnancy, after all, is a uniquely female condition.

In **Degnan and others v Redcar and Cleveland Borough Council 7 April 2005**, the English Court of Appeal also made it very clear that women bringing a claim under the Equal Pay Act 1970 will not be able to 'cherry-pick' advantageous terms of pay enjoyed by several different male comparators if this results in a situation whereby the female workers would be better paid than their male colleagues.

The case was brought by a group of women against their employer, the Council. The Council accepted that all male comparators identified by the women were employed on work rated as equivalent. The male comparators in this case were gardeners, road workers, refuse workers and drivers. One of the women in this case, Mrs Johnston had been permitted to compare herself with gardeners employed by the Council for the purposes of a bonus payment as such a comparison was to her advantage. However, when claiming an improved attendance allowance, Mrs Johnston was permitted by the Employment Tribunal to compare herself to refuse workers employed by the Council. The end result was that Mrs Johnston's pay was greater than any of her male comparators. At the appeal, the Council accepted the Tribunal's decision regarding bonus payments, but it did not accept the approach taken in respect of the attendance allowance.

According to Lord Justice Kay, the purpose of the Equal Pay legislation is to achieve equalisation of women's pay rather than the upward movement of the women's rate of monetary pay to a level higher than that of any single male comparator. The women's appeals were, therefore, dismissed. The decision of the Court of Appeal confirms the correctness of the approach taken by the Employment Appeal Tribunal in this case.

 Key point: When bringing an equal pay claim, the Applicant must identify a suitable comparator who works for the same employer or an associated employer.

'Piggy-back' equal pay claims

The Employment Appeal Tribunal has, at last, given guidance on a difficult issue which has often plagued claims brought by male workers under the Equal Pay Act

1970 i.e. so called 'piggy back' claims. Previously, a problem existed as to whether male employees were entitled to bring claims for equal pay after their female colleagues have enjoyed success in their claims. Such an issue was likely to arise where a group of workers was predominantly female in character e.g. nursery nurses and catering staff employed by local authorities. Some men would be employed in these posts, but they would constitute a very small minority. Where did these men stand legally if their female colleagues brought successful equal pay claims against the employer? They were now in a position where they were less well paid than their female counter-parts. Could they use the Equal Pay Act to improve their position by piggy-backing onto the successful claims of their female colleagues. Some clarity has now been provided as a result of the following decision:

 South Tyneside Borough Council *v* McAvoy & Others (2009) Many local authorities in the North-East of England have been the subject of thousands of legal actions lodged by female employees who have sought to equalise their rates of pay by claiming that the work they carried out was of 'equal value' to the work being carried out in other areas which are dominated by men. However, some men (not many admittedly) worked alongside the women who were pursuing equal pay claims and the key question here was: if their female colleagues won the equal pay claims, could they in turn bring legal actions under the Act by using their colleagues as comparators in order to improve their situation?

Obviously, if female workers were successful in pursuing and winning equal pay claims, the male colleagues would be in a literally poorer position. The problem in these types of situations for men doing a poorly paid job with their female colleagues is that they cannot use the male comparator(s) which the women have selected as the basis of their claim. Therefore, are these male employees permitted to compare themselves to their (now) better paid female colleagues?

Held: the Employment Appeal Tribunal has now decided that male employees can use their female colleagues who have successfully pursued equal pay claims of their own as a comparator. These male employees will be able to claim that they should benefit from an equality clause in their contracts just as their female colleagues have benefited and this will also entitle them to claim arrears of pay (just as their female colleagues have been able to do so – the Employment Tribunal was specifically overruled on this point). One other important issue was also resolved: men will be able to lodge claims with the Office of Employment Tribunals for equal pay even if the claims of their female colleagues have not yet been resolved. These types of action by male employees are referred to as contingency claims in the sense that they are dependent on the success of their female colleagues' claims. The best way to deal with male contingency claims is to sist or freeze them until the actions by the female employees have been dealt with.

 Key point: In **South Tyneside Borough Council *v* McAvoy & Others (2009)** the Employment Appeal Tribunal has approved the practice of so-called 'piggy-back' equal pay claims.

Grounds for a claim

Section 1 of the Equal Pay Act ensures that each contract of employment contains an equality clause which means that it will be implied that men and women in the same employment should receive equal pay for equal work. The Equal Pay Act 1970 is not about establishing fair pay for everyone. Claims can only be brought under the Act if a person of a particular sex can show that she does not receive equal pay for equal work in comparison to a male colleague and the reason for this difference is related to her sex.

Section 1 of the Act states that women have the right to equal treatment in pay where they are employed on:

◆ Like work with a man
◆ Work rated to equivalent to that of a man
◆ Work of equal value compared to that of man

Like work

This applies in situations where a woman is the same or broadly similar work to a man. There may indeed be differences between the work carried out by the man and the women, but these are so slight or have little practical importance.

 Capper Pass v Lawton (1977) Lawton was employed as a cook in the kitchen from which prepared meals for the company directors and their guests. Lawton brought an equal pay action against her employer claiming that she was employed to perform like work in comparison with two male employees of the company. The two men, Brattan and Smith, were employed as assistant chefs in the kitchen which served food to the employees who worked in the company factory. Lawton worked alone and she prepared between ten and 20 meals a day approximately. Brattan and Smith, on the other hand, reported to a head chef, they had to prepare 350 meals per day in six sittings. Both men worked longer hours than Lawton.

Held: by the Employment Appeal Tribunal that although there were differences between the job that Lawton performed and the jobs performed by Brattan and Smith, it was work of a similar nature. The work was similar in that it required the employee to possess similar skills and expertise. Lawton was, therefore, employed to perform like work and she was entitled to equal pay.

Work rated as equivalent

Work rated as equivalent applies to situations where a job evaluation scheme is carried out. This category applies when a man and the woman are not be engaged in the same line of work. A woman who is employed as nursery nurse by a local council may be able to claim that she performs work rated as equivalent in comparison to a male clerical worker who receives a higher salary. Under the job evaluation scheme, both jobs must have an equal value in relation to the types of demands made upon a worker under such headings as effort, skill and decision-making. The jobs are broken down into their various functions and points will be awarded to each worker in relation to a function or heading. The scheme must be scrupulously fair in that it must be analytical and deploy objective (quantitative) criteria (**Eaton Ltd v**

Nuttall (1977)). Furthermore, the study should have been carried out at the organisation where the employee and her comparator are employed. Should the female worker's job receive a different score from that of her male comparator, she will not be in a position to claim that her work should be rated as equivalent. Job evaluation schemes can always be challenged on the basis that the employer did not use objective criteria when comparing a woman's job with that of a male comparator.

 Ryder and 113 Others *v* Warwickshire County Council and Others ET Case No 1301481/97 when a job evaluation study has been carried out, and the men's and the women's jobs had been rated as equivalent and the basic pay was the same, the employer had to justify why male staff received performance bonuses or other additional payments and female staff did not.

It is necessary to have regard to the full results of the job evaluation scheme, including the allocation of the claimant to the scale or grade at the end of the process:

 In **Springboard Sunderland Trust *v* Robson (1992)** a job evaluation scheme was carried out and two jobs were analysed. The woman received 410 points and her male comparator 428 points. Under the rules of the scheme they were placed on the same grade, but the employers refused to pay the woman properly for the grade that she had been allocated.

Held: by the Employment Appeal Tribunal that the two jobs were rated as equivalent within the meaning of Section 1(5) of the Equal Pay Act 1970.

Work of equal value

A woman may be able to claim that her work is equal value to that of a male comparator in situations where a job evaluation scheme has not been carried out. Again, the man and the woman are not engaged in like work, but this procedure allows the woman to compare herself to a man who is engaged in a completely different type of work. It is perfectly possible for the work carried out by a cleaning lady to be compared to that of a male solicitor who work for the same or associated employer. An Employment Tribunal can determine whether a woman is engaged in work of equal value in comparison to a male worker and the services of an independent expert are no longer required as used to be the case. When deciding whether a woman is employed in work of equal value, the Employment Tribunal will look at the demands made on the workers under such headings as effort, skill and decision-making.

 Ms White and Others *v* Alstons (Colchester) Ltd (1987) female employees who were sewing machinists wished to compare themselves to male colleagues who were employed as upholsterers and who were paid a higher wage. The women claimed that they were engaged on work of equal value to their male colleagues.

Held: the women were engaged on work of equal value and they were awarded equal pay.

 Key point: The Equal Pay Act ensures that each contract of employment contains an equality clause which means that it will be implied that men and women in the same employment should receive equal pay for equal work.

A genuine material difference

Section 1(3) of the Equal Pay Act allows an employer to justify the difference in pay by claiming that it is related to a genuine material difference and is not based on the grounds of the person's sex.

 Glasgow City Council v Marshall (2000) eight instructors, seven women and one man, working in special schools within the former local government area of Strathclyde region brought a claim for equal pay. Their employer had been previously been Strathclyde Regional Council before the local government reorganisation in the 1990s. That was the position when the applicants lodged their claims. After the local government reorganisation of 1996, the instructors were employed by the Regional Council's statutory successors. The instructors claimed that they were employed in like work to teaching colleagues at the schools in which they were employed. The staff at special schools included teachers as well as instructors. Admittedly, the teachers were more highly paid than the instructors. The teachers all possessed a teaching qualification, which the instructors did not. Some of the instructors were qualified, but the minimum qualifications demanded of teachers were much higher than those asked of qualified instructors. The seven female instructors claimed that, although they did not possess formal teaching qualifications, they were employed on like work with male teachers working in the same special schools. The only male instructor claimed that he was engaged on like work with female teachers. The instructors claimed that, accordingly, they were entitled to the same pay as their respective male and female teacher comparators. The Employment Tribunal and the Employment Appeal Tribunal ruled in favour of the instructors – they were employed on like work in comparison to their teaching colleagues. The education authorities appealed to the Inner House of the Court of Session which found in their favour. The instructors appealed to the House of Lords.

Held: by the House of Lords that the difference in the pay between the instructors and their teaching colleagues had nothing to do with discrimination on the grounds of sex. There was a genuine material difference between instructors and teachers. Teachers had to be more highly qualified than instructors and this justified the difference in pay.

 Key point: Employers will be able to justify a difference in the terms and conditions of employment offered to men and women if this is due to a material difference and is not based on the grounds of a person's sex.

Time limits for equal pay claims

In terms of Section 2(4) of the Equal Pay Act, a claim for equal pay must be lodged with the Office of Employment Tribunals either during a person's employment or within six months (less one day) of the termination of the employee's contract of employment.

According to Section 2(5), successful parties in an equal pay action were limited to claiming two years back pay from their employer which runs back from the date upon which legal proceedings were commenced. However, in **Levez v T H**

Jennings (Harlow Pools) Ltd (2000) the European Court of Justice has ruled that this two-year limit is unlawful in terms of Article 141 of the Treaty of Rome and the Equal Pay Directive 75/117/EEC. In **Levez**, the European Court of Justice allowed the successful party to claim six years' back pay.

The Equal Pay Act 1970 (Amendment) Regulations 2003 have now changed the law in this regard.

Equal pay questionnaires

From 6 April 2003, it is now possible for an employee to serve an equal pay questionnaire on the employer in terms of Section 7B of the Equal Pay Act 1970. Such a procedure should make the issues surrounding equal pay claims easier to understand and identify and reduce the delays which are often a feature of such cases. It is hoped that the use of questionnaires will also promote out of court settlements. By serving a questionnaire, it allows the employee to request important information from the employer which should help establish whether there is a potential equal pay claim. The questionnaire and the responses can be used in evidence at an Employment Tribunal hearing. It will be for the Employment Tribunal to decide whether discrimination has taken place. Employers are, therefore, encouraged to cooperate with such a questionnaire, but there may be some confidential information that they are entitled to withhold from the person bringing the complaint. If the employer fails or refuses to cooperate with the questionnaire procedure, this behaviour could be viewed very suspiciously by an Employment Tribunal where there is no justification on the employer's part. An example of an equal pay questionnaire can be seen on the Introductory Scots Law website.

Key point: Equal pay questionnaires are a useful tool for a claimant to gather evidence to use at an Employment Tribunal hearing.

The Equality Act 2006 and the Equality Bill

As a result of this legislation, the differences in pay between male and female employees working for public sector employers will come under far greater scrutiny than ever before. All public sector employers have a legal duty to promote gender equality in order to eliminate unlawful discrimination and this extends to the issue of pay. A public sector employer must now address how it intends to deal with the matter of gender pay gaps and, if it fails to meet these objectives, enforcement action could be taken against it by the Equality and Human Rights Commission or, ultimately, in a court or Employment Tribunal.

In any case, the Equality Bill currently proceeding through the Westminster Parliament, contains provisions which will force public sector employers to publish information detailing differences in pay between male and female workers in an attempt to put pressure on such organisations to take concrete steps to combat this type of discrimination in the work-place. The Equality Bill is expected to become law by 2010.

In **Newcastle upon Tyne Council v Allen & ors (2005)**, the Employment Appeal Tribunal has ruled that compensation for injury for hurt to feelings or other non financial losses **cannot** be awarded in terms of the Equal Pay Act 1970. It will be recalled, of course, that such types of awards can be made to a successful claimant who brings a discrimination action under the Sex Discrimination Act 1975 and other legislation which prohibits discrimination.

It is well established law that anyone taking out a claim under the Equal Pay Act 1970 e.g. a female employee must use an actual or hypothetical male comparator to demonstrate that they have suffered less favourable treatment.

 Key point: The provisions of the Equality Act 2006 and the Equality Bill impose tougher requirements on public sector employers to promote equal pay policies.

The Disability Discrimination Act 1995

The Disability Discrimination Act 1995 aims to promote equality of opportunity for disabled people in the following areas:

◆ Employment
◆ The provision of goods and services
◆ Buying or renting land or property
◆ Education

The Act should also be read together with a Code of Practice and Guidance. The Secretary of State, under powers contained in Section 3 of the Act, issued a document called Guidance which was to be used when questions relating to the meaning of disability arose in discrimination cases. The Employment Appeal Tribunal has stated in **Goodwin v The Patent Office (1999)** that Employment Tribunals must apply the Guidance in relation to disability discrimination claims. Part II of the Act relates specifically to employment and is accompanied by a Code of Practice that aims to introduce measures which will eliminate disability discrimination. The Code of Practice can be used as evidence in Employment Tribunal and other legal proceedings. Part III of the Act which deals with the rights of disabled people in respect of access to goods, facilities, services and premises should also be interpreted in line with the Code of Practice. These provisions were reinforced in 1999 when the Secretary of State for Education and Employment issued a Code of Practice regulating the conduct of trade associations in relation to disabled members and applicants.

The most recent Code of Practice (which exists in several versions for each part of the United Kingdom) came into force in December 2006 as a result of the provisions of the Disability Discrimination Act 2005. The Code places a duty on the 45,000 or so public bodies (e.g. schools, colleges, universities, NHS Trusts, councils and legislative bodies) across the United Kingdom to have regard to the Disability Equality Duty. This duty means that such bodies must pay 'due regard' to the promotion of equality for disabled people in every area of their work. This Code is used by Employment Tribunals as a yard stick when judging public bodies which find themselves being sued for alleged disability discrimination.

The Codes of Practice and Guidance are, therefore, extremely useful resources in that they provide important clarification of the law in relation to many of the issues in this area.

disabled employees, the Borough Council lost a high profile claim for nearly £1 million in damages for fraudulent or negligent misrepresentation which it brought against Christine Laird, its former Managing Director. The Council's claim was founded on the Local Government Act 1999 which applies to England and Wales and places a duty on local authorities to achieve best value in the discharge of their functions. Section 3(1) of the Act defines this duty in the following terms:

'*A best value authority must make arrangements to secure continuous improvement in the way in which its functions are exercised, having regard to a combination of economy, efficiency and effectiveness.*'

The Council alleged that Mrs Laird had had deliberately chosen not to reveal the fact that she had suffered from depression when completing a medical questionnaire issued to her by her employer when she commenced work in 2002. Subsequently, Mrs Laird was absent from her post due to her illness from June 2004 until her employment with the Council terminated in 2005. The basis of the Council's claim was that Mrs Laird had not been well enough to carry out the job when she was first offered the post and by failing to alert the Council to the full nature of her illness she had cost the employer a substantial amount of money in sickness pay, cover for a replacement and pension entitlements. The Council attempted to recover the cost of these expenses by suing Mrs Laird for misrepresentation.

Held: by the English High Court that Mrs Laird had not made false statements about her health in the medical questionnaire and the Council's claim for £1 million in damages was rejected. In point of fact, the Council was ordered by the High Court to pay 65% of Mrs Laird's legal costs. Although this case did not involve the Disability Discrimination Act 1995, it shows the very poor judgement of the Council in pursuing an action of this type against an employee who had a depressive illness. The ironic thing is Mrs Laird would have been in a better position, legally speaking, if she had indicated to her employer that she considered herself to suffer from a condition (a depressive illness) which is a recognised disability. Under the Disability Discrimination Act, a clear duty is placed on employers to make reasonable adjustments which allow disabled persons to continue in their employment and be supported by the employer.

 Key point: A disability is a physical or mental impairment which has a substantial and long term adverse effect on a person's ability to carry out normal day-to-day activities.

Normal day to day activities

Employers should not fall into trap of assuming that the phrase 'day to day activities' is confined to things like the employee being able to perform everyday tasks like being able to wash, prepare meals, clean the house and do shopping. Day to day activities can have a wide meaning as the Employment Appeal Tribunal has recently decided in **Dumfries and Galloway Constabulary *v* Adams (2009)**.

Adams commenced work as a probationary police officer in November 2005, but the following month he was diagnosed with symptoms that suggested the medical condition known as fibromyalgia. Sufferers tend to experience pain and stiffness in muscles, ligaments and tendons. Adams' working pattern comprised day and night shifts and it was during the night shifts (typically between 2am and 4am) that the condition was at its most acute. Between March and May 2006, Adams was working day shifts only as a result of his condition and his health had considerably improved. In May 2006, Adams began to work night shifts again and his health deteriorated in the sense that he experienced serious problems with his mobility. In February 2007, Adams was dismissed from his employment and he sued the Police for alleged disability discrimination. One of the issues which the Employment Tribunal had to deal was whether he was a disabled person in terms of the Disability Discrimination Act 1995 and this question was answered in the affirmative. The Chief Constable then decided to appeal against the decision of the Employment Tribunal on the grounds that, as Adams experienced these health problems at night, he could not be a regarded as carrying out normal day to day activities.

Held: the Employment Appeal Tribunal comprehensively rejected the Chief Constable's argument that night shift work should not be regarded as normal day to day activities. Many people are employed across the country to work at night, it is not unusual and, therefore, such work should be regarded as a normal day to day activity. This decision will have consequences in that it should prevent employers from arguing that night shift workers fall outside the scope of the Disability Discrimination Act.

Key point: The phrase day-to-day activities is given a very wide meaning.

An impairment or disability which is 'likely to recur'

The House of Lords has recently provided further clarification in respect of the definition of disability in terms of Section 1 and Schedule 1 of the Disability Discrimination Act 1995. This clarification is especially helpful to those individuals who have previously suffered from a disability or impairment and whether it can be said that such a condition is 'likely to recur' in terms of Schedule 1 of the Act.

SCA Packaging Limited *v* Boyle (2009) Boyle had worked for her employer since 1969 and she was made redundant in 2002. She alleged that her employer had made her redundant on the grounds of her disability. Her employer disputed the fact that she was disabled. In the past, Boyle had suffered from a medical condition which caused growths on her vocal chords. She had received an operation to remove these nodes and, following on from this, she was given intensive speech therapy which was aimed at preventing the recurrence of her condition. The therapy consisted of various techniques (e.g. speaking quietly) which attempted to ensure that Boyle's vocal chords were not subjected to any unnecessary stress. This approach seemed to work and, for about 7 or 8 years from 1992 onwards, the condition seemed to be dormant. In 2000, a change in Boyle's working conditions was made which led to increased levels of noise (a partition wall was removed). Consequently, Boyle was forced to speak much more loudly than she was accustomed to and in breach of the techniques that she had learned from her speech therapist. Boyle complained about this situation and asked her employer to make reasonable adjustments to her post to enable her to continue in employment. The employer argued that Boyle was not a disabled person within the meaning of the Disability Discrimination Act 1995. The Northern Ireland Industrial Tribunal and the Northern Ireland Court of Appeal were both of the opinion that Boyle was a disabled person and that the only thing preventing her disability from having a substantial adverse effect on her day to day activities were the speech therapy techniques that she had learned following on from her operation to remove the growths from vocal chords. Considering the balance or probabilities, it was likely that Boyle's condition would worsen if the employer did not make reasonable adjustments to her post. The employer appealed to the House of Lords.

Held: by the House of Lords that Boyle suffered from a disability where a recurrence 'could well happen' and this is the test which should be used when determining whether a disability is likely to have a substantial and long-term adverse effect on a person's ability to carry out normal day-to-day activities. Baroness Hale stated that the previous practice of using a 'more probable than not' test in respect of the issue of whether a disability was likely to recur or be ongoing was wrong.

Very often in disability discrimination cases, the employer may not be prepared to accept that an employee who is alleging less favourable treatment is actually a disabled person within the meaning of the 1995 Act. The Employment Appeal Tribunal has stated that, once an employer has accepted or conceded that an employee is a disabled person there is a duty to make reasonable adjustments to that individual's post and it is irrelevant whether the disability has a substantial and long term effect on that person's day to day activities (see **Bowers *v* William Hill Organisation Ltd (2009)**).

 Key point: Employers will have to treat employees sensitively if such individuals suffer from an impairment or disability which is likely to recur.

Establishing less favourable treatment of disabled employees

Previously, as a result of the English Court of Appeal's decision in **Clark *v* Novacold (1999)**, it was not necessary for an employee alleging disability discrimination in Employment Tribunal cases to identify a comparator. Disability discrimination cases were, therefore, treated quite differently from sex or racial discrimination claims before Employment Tribunals. The House of Lords has now completely overturned this approach by stressing that anyone wishing to bring a successful claim for disability discrimination will have to identify a comparator (see **London Borough of Lewisham *v* Malcolm (2008)**).

Although the claim in **London Borough of Lewisham *v* Malcolm (2008)** was not an employment dispute (it involved alleged disability discrimination in relation to the provision of services by a Council), it has consequences for anyone now contemplating taking such a claim to an Employment Tribunal.

The Employment Appeal Tribunal has followed the **Malcolm** decision in the case of **Stockton on Tees Borough Council *v* Aylott (2009)**.

 Aylott had brought a claim against the Council alleging that he had been dismissed by reason of his disability (he suffered from bi-polar disorder) and he had very high sickness absence. The Employment Tribunal found in Aylott's favour stating that he had been unfairly dismissed by reason of his disability. The Tribunal stated that another individual who did not suffer from bi-polar disorder would not have been treated in the same way as Aylott and, although no actual comparator had been identified, it was permissible to use a hypothetical comparator. Such a hypothetical comparator according to the Tribunal would be someone who was not suffering from bi-polar disorder and, from the evidence considered by the Tribunal, such an individual would not have been dismissed by the Council. The Council appealed to the Employment Appeal Tribunal claiming that the Employment Tribunal had used the wrong comparator when arriving at its decision.

Held: by the Employment Appeal Tribunal that the Employment Tribunal had made a crucial error when making its judgement. Following the decision of the House of Lords in **Malcolm,** the proper comparator was someone who had behaved in the same way as the person concerned (the disabled person), but did not suffer from that person's disability. In the essence, the Employment Tribunal had applied the wrong legal test and the case was remitted to the Office of Employment Tribunals for a fresh hearing.

As we shall see, however, there is no need for a disabled employee to specify or identify a comparator when the issue in dispute is the alleged failure by the employer to make or consider reasonable adjustments to his/her post (see **Fareham College Corporation *v* Walters (2009)**).

 Portman *v* Bromley Hospitals NHS Trust (1996) the employee had been absent from work for a long period. After her sick leave, the employee returned to work but her performance in her job was extremely poor. The employee claimed repeatedly, however, that her illness had nothing to do with her failure to cope with her job. The employer then gave her the choice of being demoted or being dismissed on the grounds of incompetent performance of her duties. The employee requested early retirement on the grounds of ill-health. She was examined by a doctor who diagnosed her as suffering from very serious depression and this meant that it was unlikely that she would ever be fit to work again. Her employer eventually dismissed her for incompetence, but the doctor's report was not brought to the attention of the appeal committee.

Held: the Employment Appeal Tribunal agreed with the Tribunal's decision that the employee had been fairly dismissed on the grounds of her incompetence. The employee had always stated that her inability to carry out her job had nothing to do with illness.

 Key point: A disabled person who alleges that they were treated less favourably will now have to identify a comparator when bringing a claim.

Failure of an employer to make reasonable adjustments

In terms of **Section 6**, an employee could experience discrimination where the employer either refuses or fails to make reasonable adjustments (see **SCA Packaging Limited v Boyle (2009)** discussed above where the employer failed to make reasonable adjustments to the employee's post).

Reasonable adjustments are measures which an employer will put in place in order to eliminate any physical features of the employer's premises or practices that would place a disabled person at a substantial (i.e. not trivial) disadvantage in comparison with a non-disabled person. When a disabled person brings a claim against an employer that he has failed to make reasonable adjustments, the Employment Tribunal must be satisfied that there is, in fact, a duty on the employer to make such adjustments. When such a duty has been established, the Employment Tribunal must then ask whether or not the employer has taken reasonable steps to put adjustments in place that will remove the substantial disadvantage in relation to the disabled person.

The Employment Tribunal can make use of **Section 6(3)** to decide whether the employer has failed to implement his duty. The following factors are reasonable adjustments that an employer might put in place:

1 Making adjustments to the employer's premises

2 Transferring some of his duties to another person

3 Giving him greater flexibility in his working hours

4 Transferring him to suitable, alternative employment

5 Changing his physical place of work

6 Permitting him to have time-off to attend medical treatment

7 Providing him with training opportunities

8 Modifying equipment for use by him

9 Modifying instructions and training or reference manuals

10 Modifying procedures for testing and assessment

11 Providing an interpreter or a scribe

12 Providing appropriate supervision

An employer may be able to argue that he is not under a duty to make reasonable adjustments if he either did not know or could have been reasonably expected to know that an employee or a job applicant is disabled (**Section 6(6)**). However, this argument will fail if it can be implied that any of the employer's agents or employees had knowledge of the disability. From October 2004, the employer has to take more active steps to discover whether any of his employees are, in fact, disabled and what reasonable adjustments can be put in place.

A failure by an employer to consider making reasonable adjustments to the post of a disabled person may well result in the dismissal of the employee which could be an unfair dismissal on the grounds of disability discrimination. The employee's case for disability discrimination will be greatly strengthened if the reasonable adjustments which the employer should have made to the post would have resulted in the disabled person remaining in employment.

 Fareham College Corporation v Walters (2009) Walters was employed as a college lecturer. She developed a medical condition which impaired her mobility. The likely impact of Walters' condition was assessed by doctors who were of the opinion that she would be absent from work for more than nine months. The College decided to rely upon a provision in its policy for managing employee absences which permitted it to dismiss members of staff who were likely to be absent on a long term basis. The College had spoken about the possibility of a phased return to work with Walters, but nothing had come of this. In fact, the College had already employed a new member of staff to take over Walters' post at the time of her dismissal.

Held: by the Employment Tribunal that the College had failed to make reasonable adjustments to Walters' post which would have permitted her to remain in employment. This failure by the College to make reasonable adjustments had resulted in Walters' dismissal and, consequently, she had experienced less favourable treatment by reason of her disability. The College then lodged an appeal to the Employment Appeal Tribunal on the grounds that Walters had failed to specify a comparator when she brought her claim to the Tribunal. The College's argument was based on the fact that non-disabled members of staff had been dismissed if their period of sickness absence lasted longer than nine months. The College lost the appeal. There is no need for a disabled person to specify or identify a comparator when the issue in dispute is the alleged failure by the employer to make or consider making reasonable adjustments to the disabled person's post.

Arguably, the decision of the Employment Appeal Tribunal in **Fareham College Corporation v Walters (2009)** will make it much easier for disabled employees to bring discrimination claims and will overcome some of the problems associated with the decision of the House of Lords in **London Borough of Lewisham v Malcolm (2008)**.

 Key point: Reasonable adjustments are measures or steps that an employer can take which should assist a disabled employee to carry out his job effectively.

Discriminatory advertisements

In its original form, the Disability Discrimination Act 1995 did not contain any rules that specifically prohibited the use of discriminatory advertisements. This omission was surprising given the fact that both the Sex Discrimination and Race Relations Acts contain rules forbidding the use by employers of discriminatory job advertisements.

Despite this potential weakness in the original Act, it would have been very foolish on the part of employers to think that they could have used such advertisements in respect of their recruitment activities and got away unscathed when dealing with disabled people. In terms of **Section 11**, an Employment Tribunal had the right to weigh up the impact of a potentially discriminatory advertisement if, for example, the employer subsequently refused to offer the disabled person employment or if the advertisement gave an indication that only a non-disabled person would be considered for the job. The Disability Discrimination Act 1995 (Amendment) Regulations 2003 which come into force on 1 October 2004 changed the law in this regard and employers have henceforth run the risk of incurring substantial legal penalties if they are found to have used discriminatory advertisements in recruitment.

 Key point: If an employer uses discriminatory adverts in recruitment campaigns which deter disabled people from applying for a position they could be sued under the Disability Discrimination Act 1995.

Transferred discrimination

In the past, one of the weaknesses of the Disability Discrimination Act 1995 was the fact that, unlike other equality legislation e.g. the Sex Discrimination and the Race Relations Acts, the issue of transferred discrimination was not recognised (see **Showboat Entertainment Centre Ltd v Owens (1984)**).

Under race relations legislation, for example, a white person who is married to an Afro-Caribbean person would potentially be able to claim that they had suffered discriminatory treatment if their employer was aware of this fact and treated him/her less favourably as a result.

Previously, no such protection existed for the carers or relatives of disabled people. To this end, questions were raised about the compatibility of the Disability Discrimination Act with European law (i.e. the Equal Treatment Framework Directive 2000/78/EC in particular).

In relation to disability cases, transferred or associative discrimination often occurs when a non-disabled person i.e. a parent or a carer of a disabled person experiences less favourable treatment from an employer because of his/her responsibility for that disabled person. An employer may refuse to grant flexible working arrangements to such a person which would permit him/her to look after the disabled person in question.

In July 2006, the Croydon Employment Tribunal referred the matter of transferred or associative discrimination in disability claims to the European Court of Justice as a result of the case of **Coleman v Attridge Law**. In particular, the Tribunal wished to know whether the Disability Discrimination Act should be interpreted in such a way as to comply with the European Directive which appeared to extend protection to the carers of disabled persons.

 Coleman v Attridge Law (2008) in 2001, Coleman was employed as a legal secretary at a firm of solicitors called Attridge Law. In 2002, Coleman gave birth to a son who was disabled (he suffered from bronchomalacia and congenital laryngomalacia) and she made overtures to her employers for the right to be granted flexible working arrangements in order to care for her son. Her request for flexible working arrangements was refused by her employer whereupon in 2005 she accepted voluntary redundancy from the firm. Subsequently, Coleman lodged a claim with the Employment Tribunal alleging that she been constructively dismissed and subjected to disability discrimination because of her association with her disabled son. At first, the orthodox or widely accepted legal position was that Coleman did not enjoy protection under the existing legislation, but she might be entitled to use the provisions of the European Directive to bring a claim for associative discrimination against her ex-employer. In other words, United Kingdom law should be interpreted in such a way as to give proper effect to the provisions of the Directive and thus extend protection to a large number of people who were both employees and carers for disabled persons.

Held: by the European Court of Justice that the European Union Equal Treatment Framework Directive could protect individuals who found themselves in Coleman's position i.e. non-disabled persons who were responsible for the care of disabled people and who could potentially suffer discrimination as a result such an association or relationship. Following on from this decision, it is now possible for people in Coleman's position to bring claims for disability discrimination under the Disability Discrimination Act 1995, although it is important to note that each case will turn on the factual evidence. Clearly, the existing UK legislation had failed to protect individuals like Coleman and this was a breach of European law.

This case has wider implications in the sense that the Equal Treatment Framework Directive is not just confined to disability, but it also covers discrimination on the grounds of age, religion and belief and sexual orientation.

 Key point: The European Court of Justice has ruled that non-disabled people can suffer less favourable treatment by reason of their association with a disabled person.

The Disability Discrimination Act 2005

The Disability Discrimination Act 2005 became law on 5 December 2005. As a result of this legislation, the definition of disability has been expanded to include conditions such as HIV and Aids, cancer and multiple sclerosis.

Employers will also have to be particularly careful when it comes to dealing with employees who suffer from a variety of mental illnesses. The 2005 Act changes the law by removing the previous requirement in the Disability Discrimination Act 1995 that such illnesses had to be clinically well-recognised.

The 2005 Act also tightens up the law in relation to discriminatory job advertisements.

In **Smith v Churchills Stairlift PLC 2005,** the English Court of Appeal has provided guidelines on the approach to be taken to the different legal tests which operate under the Disability Discrimination Act 1995.

In terms of Section 6 of the Disability Discrimination Act 1995, all employers have a legal duty to consider making reasonable adjustments to the work-place where disabled employees are concerned. The Court of Appeal has stated that an employer's behaviour in this regard should be judged according to objective standards i.e. the adjustments to the work-place that a reasonable employer would have made or considered in order to assist the disabled employee to carry out his or her duties effectively. An objective standard is an independently recognised standard which all reasonable employers are expected to achieve.

In situations where a disabled person is alleging that they have suffered less favourable treatment and where the employer attempts to justify the treatment in question, a subjective approach will be taken by the courts. Section 5 of the 1995 Act does permit an employer to discriminate against a disabled employee, but the reasons for this must not be minor or trivial. The employer must demonstrate that they acted within the range of reasonable responses from which an employer may have acted.

The difference in approach between the two legal tests is not an easy one to understand and employers would be very wise to take legal advice in relation to all of their dealings with a disabled employee. It is worth bearing in mind the serious consequences for employers who get things wrong when dealing with disability in the work-place. Under disability discrimination legislation, tribunals and courts can award unlimited compensation to an individual who has suffered less favourable treatment by reason of their disability (see **Mansoor _v_ Guest and Chrimes Ltd ET Case No. 2802060/97; A _v_ London Borough of Hounslow EAT 1155/98;** and **Callagan _v_ Glasgow City Council (2001)**).

 Key point: The Disability Discrimination Act 2005 expands the number of medical conditions which could be a disability to include HIV and AIDs, cancer and multiple sclerosis.

Disability discrimination in relation to the provision of goods and services

The Reading Employment Tribunal made a very significant decision by finding that an organisation with no presence in the United Kingdom could be in breach of the Disability Discrimination Act 1995 in the way that it provided services. Most people are, of course, aware that the Act penalises those employers who discriminate against disabled employees. The Act also protects disabled people if they experience discrimination in relation to the provision of services.

 In **Project Management Institute _v_ Latif (2007)** the Claimant (Latif), who worked as an IT Project Manager for a global company, had decided to undertake an internationally recognised professional course known as the Project Management Professional (PMP) qualification. The qualification is administered by a body called the Project Management Institute which is a not-for-profit organisation based in the United States. Candidates must pass a very demanding four hour, multiple choice examination which they sit at a variety of centres in their home country. Latif sat her examination in Edinburgh.

In preparation for the examination, the Institute recommends that candidates use its textbook known as the Project Management Body of Knowledge (the PMBOK Guide). Latif who is visually impaired attempted to find an electronic copy of the textbook for her exam preparation, but she was unsuccessful. The Institute attempted to send Latif electronic versions of the book, but she was either unable to open these files or could not read them. Latif found herself having to take a range of measures to cope with the demands of the examination e.g. by employing a student to prepare the materials in question for use by her. The Claimant sat the examination in Edinburgh and did pass it, but she faced considerable difficulties on her road to success which the Institute did very little to alleviate. The Employment Tribunal was very much of the view that just as employers are expected to put in place reasonable adjustments for disabled employees, the Institute was also under a similar duty in relation to exam arrangements. The Institute had not been reasonable where Latif's disability was concerned and, consequently, she had been placed at a significant disadvantage when preparing for the examination.

The Project Management Institute has appealed to the Employment Appeal

Tribunal, but companies or organisations without a physical presence in the United Kingdom will have to be very careful in the future how they provide services.

 Key point: Providers of goods and services could treat a disabled person less favourably and thus fall foul of the Disability Discrimination Act 1995.

Lodging a disability claim

An employee who believes that he has suffered less favourable treatment on the grounds of his disability must lodge a claim with the Office of Employment Tribunals within three months (less one day) of the discriminatory act complained of.

 Key point: Disability discrimination claims must be lodged at the Office of Employment Tribunals with three months (less one day) of the act complained of.

The employer's liability for the discriminatory acts of employees

Section 58(1) of the Disability Discrimination Act 1995 states that anything done by anyone in the course of his employment shall be treated . . . as also done by his employer, whether it was done with the employer's knowledge or approval. The question which an Employment Tribunal must pose is whether the employee was acting in the course of his employment when he committed the discriminatory act against the disabled employee. This is a much wider concept than the one used in cases involving an employer's vicarious liability for the acts of employees. Section 58(5) does, however, protect an employer who has taken reasonably practicable steps to prevent the discriminatory acts of his employees.

For an example of an Employment Tribunal claim which involves alleged disability discrimination see the Introductory Scots Law website.

www

The Disability Discrimination Act 1995 (Amendment) Regulations 2003

These Regulations came into force in October 2004. The Regulations make fundamental changes to the way in which the Disability Discrimination Act 1995 operates.

The original provisions of the Act did not apply to employers with less than 15 employees, but the Regulations abolished this exemption. A club with 25 or more members is also now covered by the amended Act and this will cover organisations such as political parties.

The Regulations will mean that certain professions or occupations which were not previously covered by the Act lose their exemption. These professions or occupations include advocates or barristers who operate from chambers, the police, prison officers and partners in a firm. The Regulations also place greater responsibility on employers to discover who amongst the workplace suffers from a disability. Employers will be expected to take more active steps to promote equal opportunities for disabled people within the workplace. Generally speaking, employers who are classified as public authorities (a concept which should be familiar from the amended race equality legislation) will be under a duty to promote equality of opportunity for disabled people.

Transport will also come under the remit of the Disability Discrimination Act. This was a major step forward since, previously, it was only the transport infrastructure which is covered by the Act rather than the provision of transport

Identifying a comparator

In order to bring a claim of less favourable treatment against her employer, Regulation 2(4) makes it very clear that a part-time worker must demonstrate the following:

◆ **She and her comparator are employed by the same employer under the same type of contract;**

and

◆ **She and her comparator are engaged in the same or broadly similar work.**

Furthermore, as Regulation 2(4) makes abundantly clear, the full-time comparator must work or be based at the same establishment as the part-time worker. However, Regulation 2(4) recognises that situations may arise where there is no full-time worker working or based in the same workplace who satisfies the requirements listed above. This situation would obviously be fatal to the part-time worker's claim. In order to deal with this problem, the part-time worker is, therefore, permitted to compare himself with a full-time worker who is based at a different establishment and satisfies the two requirements laid down by Regulation 2(4).

Regulation 2(3) lists various types of contracts which are considered to be very different in nature:

1   Employees employed under a contract that is not a contract of apprenticeship.

2   Employees employed under a contract of apprenticeship.

3   Workers who are not employees.

4   Any other description of worker that it is reasonable for the employer to treat differently from other workers on the ground that workers of that description have a different type of contract.

A part-time worker cannot compare herself to any full-time comparator. It would not be the correct legal approach for a part-time worker employed under an apprenticeship contract to compare her situation to full-time worker who is employed on a contract which is not an apprenticeship contract. A part-time apprentice alleging less favourable treatment must compare her situation with a worker employed under a full-time apprenticeship contract.

 Matthews and Others *v* Kent and Medway Towns Fire Authority and Others (2003) 12,000 part-time firefighters who alleged that they were being less favourably treated than full-time firefighters failed in their claim under the Part-Time Workers (Prevention of Less Favourable Treatment) Regulations 2000. The complaint mainly centred around the fact that part-timers were not permitted to take part in the very generous Fireman's Pension Scheme. A further complaint related to the fact that part-timers were less favourably treated under the service's sick pay scheme.

The Employment Appeal Tribunal ruled that the part-timers were not employed under the same type of contract as their full-time colleagues nor could they argue that they were employed in the same or broadly similar work. It is absolutely vital that in terms of Regulation 2(4), a part-time worker who alleges that s/he has received less favourable treatment owing to his/her part-time status must be able to identify a full-time comparator. This comparator must be employed by the same employer as the part-time worker and under the same type of contract. Furthermore, both part-timer and full-timer must be engaged in the same or broadly similar work.

The part-timers appealed to the English Court of Appeal (**Matthews and others v Kent and Medway Towns Fire Authority and ors (2004)**) which partially reversed the decision of the Employment Appeal Tribunal. The Court of Appeal held that the part-timers and the full-timers were employed under the same type of contract, but they were not engaged in the same or broadly similar work. Full-timers were expected to undertake all sorts of additional duties which part-timers were not.

There were also differences in entry, training standards and promotion opportunities between part-timers and full-timers. Therefore, the part-timers' claim ultimately failed under the Regulations. However, this issue has since been resolved by the House of Lords giving this area of law some much needed clarity at last.

The House of Lords, in a judgement, issued on 1 March 2006 clarified the law in relation to the dispute concerning the choice of comparator in **Matthews** by overruling the decisions of the Employment Tribunal, the Employment Appeal and the English Court of Appeal.

Retained (part-time) firefighters now have the right to join the Firemen's Pension Scheme (the original source of the dispute). This is recognition of the fact that, for contractual purposes, retained firefighters are to be regarded as equivalent to full-time firefighters.

For those part-timers wishing to bring a claim against an employer, choosing the correct comparator can be a major issue determining the success or failure of the action.

Wippel v Peek & Cloppenburg GmbH Co KG (2005) the European Court of Justice had to decide whether a part-time worker alleging less favourable treatment by an employer, had compared his/her situation with a comparable fulltime worker/employee.

The part-time worker in this case had no fixed working hours and worked as and when required for the employer. The part-timer was not allowed to proceed with a claim under the Part-time Workers Directive because there was no comparable full-time worker who was employed on an as required or on a demand only basis.

 Key point: A part-time worker alleging less favourable treatment by the employer must compare himself with an appropriate comparator.

Bringing a claim for discrimination by a part-time worker

A part-time worker can ask the employer to explain the difference in treatment. The employer has 21 days from the employee requesting an explanation to issue a written statement laying down the reasons for the difference in treatment between part-time and full-time workers (Regulation 6). It is open to the employer to deny that any discrimination has taken place. The employer's statement can be used in Employment Tribunal proceedings at a later date. If the employer fails to provide a statement on request or issues reasons for the treatment that could be considered evasive, it is up to the Employment Tribunal to draw its own conclusions. If the employee still wishes to take matters further, she is entitled to lodge an Employment Tribunal application within three months (less one day) of the conduct complained of (Regulation 8).

 Key point: A part-time worker is entitled to a written statement from his employer explaining any difference in treatment which should be issued within 21 days of the initial request for information.

Victimisation

Any part-time worker who makes a complaint or proceeds with an action under the Regulations has the right not to be victimised by the employer. Victimisation could take the form of dismissal or some other detriment, for example, harassment. If the employer dismisses a part-time worker for enforcing her rights under the Regulations, such a dismissal will be automatically unfair (Regulation 7). This protection is also extended to any other worker who agrees to be a witness or give evidence in respect of any complaint made against an employer under the Regulations.

An employer will be responsible for any breaches of the Regulations committed by an employee whether this act was done with or without the employer knowledge (Regulation 11).

 Key point: Part-time workers who bring a discrimination claim against their employers have the right to be protected against acts of victimisation, now and in the future.

Examples of case law dealing with part-time worker discrimination

 Clarke & Powell v Eley Kinoch Ltd (1982) the employer decided to make redundant 20 full-time male employees, 26 full-time female employees and all 60 of the part-time workers (all of whom were female). The company's policy was to make part-time staff redundant first, then to use the 'last in first out' principle in relation to all of the full-time workers. If the 'last in first out' principle had been applied to the whole workforce, Ms Clarke and Ms Powell would not have been made redundant.

Held: by the Employment Appeal Tribunal that the way in which the company had handled the procedures for redundancy was an example of indirect sex discrimination. The 'part-timers first' clause imposed a requirement or condition, which was to the detriment of the two women, and could not be objectively justified.

 Bilka-Kaufhaus v Weber Von Hartz (1986) part-time workers, who were employed by a German department store, were treated less favourably than their full-time colleagues in that they were not allowed to become members of the employer's occupational pension scheme. Some time later, the pension scheme was extended to part-timers as long as they had worked for at least 15 years out of a total of 20. Mrs Von Hartz did not receive a pension because she failed to meet this requirement. The European Court of Justice stated that this example of less favourable treatment could not be justified by the employer on objective grounds – there was no reason why part-timers could not be admitted to the pension scheme. Most of the part-time workers were, of course, female and the employer's refusal to admit them to the pension scheme amounted to indirect sex discrimination.

Re Secretary of State for Employment *ex parte* Equal Opportunities Commission (1994) the Employment Protection (Consolidation) Act 1978 contained a requirement that for an employee to be entitled to a statutory redundancy payment had to work more than 16 hours per week. Those employees who worked less than eight hours per week had no rights in terms of protection from unfair dismissal. The employees in question worked less than eight hours per week.

Held: by the House of Lords that the Employment Protection (Consolidation) Act 1978 indirectly discriminated against women as fewer of them were able to comply in practice with the rules relating to entitlement to a redundancy payment and rights against unfair dismissal. Women tended to do more part-time work than men and they were less likely to meet the requirements of the 1978 Act. Since this decision, all workers regardless of whether they are employed on a full-time or part-time basis have the same rights in respect of unfair dismissal and redundancy.

It is worth noting that these decisions were made before the introduction of the Part-time Workers (Prevention of Less Favourable Treatment) 2000 and they depend on the application of the principle of indirect sex discrimination. The Regulations now simply make it unlawful for employers to discriminate against part-timers (sex discrimination may be an issue, it may not be), unless the difference in treatment can be objectively justified.

The Fixed-term Employees (Prevention of Less Favourable Treatment) Regulations 2002

These Regulations came into force on 10 October 2002. Employees on a fixed-term contract should not receive less favourable treatment than comparable employees on the grounds of their contractual status unless this treatment by the employer can be objectively justified. Fixed-term employees will often experience less favourable treatment in comparison to their permanent colleagues. For the purposes of the Regulations, a permanent employee is someone who is not on a fixed-term contract. Permanent employees will, therefore, enjoy contracts for an indefinite or an indeterminate period of time.

The aim of the Regulations is to regularise as much as possible the position of fixed-term employees within the organisation. To this end, employees who have less than three months' service with the employer will be entitled to receive statutory sick pay, payments as a result of medical suspension and guarantee payments. In terms of notice requirements, fixed-term employees must receive from the employer at least one month's notice of his intention to terminate the employment contract. On the other hand, the employee must provide the employer with a similar notice of period if it is her intention to terminate the contract.

The widespread practice of employers continuing to employ fixed-term employees on a series of rolling contracts will be curtailed as a result of the Regulations (Regulation 8). In the past, it has not been unusual to see some employees working on temporary contracts for seven or eight years at a time – sometimes even longer. The Regulations aim to tackle this practice. Employers will now be able to keep an employee on a fixed-term contract for a maximum of four years only, unless the further use of such a contract can be objectively justified. The main impact of the Regulations will be that anyone who has been employed on a fixed-term contract from 10 July 2002 will automatically become a permanent member of staff in July 2006, providing of course that the contract with the employer has continued to be renewed over that four-year period. After four years, the employee can request and is entitled to receive a statement from the employer to the effect that his contract is now of an indefinite or indeterminate duration (i.e. she has become a permanent worker) (Regulation 9). The employer is under a duty to issue such a statement within 21 days of receiving the employee's request.

 In **Secretary of State for Children, Schools & Families *v* Fletcher (2009)**, the Employment Appeal Tribunal stated that an attempt by the Secretary of State to deny a school teacher the right to convert a temporary fixed term contract into a permanent contract could not be objectively justified. The teacher had been employed under a succession of fixed term temporary contracts which were renewed by his employer over a period of nine years. The teacher argued that he should have been made a permanent employee after four years' service by virtue of Regulation 8 of the Fixed Term Employees (Prevention of Less Favourable Treatment) Regulations 2002. The Employment Appeal Tribunal rejected the Secretary of State's arguments that the 2002 Regulations did not apply to this situation and found in favour of the teacher.

 Key point: Employers will now be able to keep an employee on a fixed-term contract for a maximum of four years only, unless the further use of such a contract can be objectively justified.

Fixed-term employees are also given additional rights in respect of redundancy and dismissal (Regulation 10). From 1 October 2002, the employer will no longer be able to include a term in the employment contract which effectively prevents the employee having a remedy against the employer in the event of redundancy. Such a term, amounting to a redundancy waiver, will be automatically void. Fixed-term employees who have more than two years' continuous service and who are dismissed by reason of redundancy will be entitled to a statutory redundancy payment in common with their permanent colleagues.

Furthermore, if an employer terminates a contract for a specified task once the task has been completed or if the contract comes to an end upon the occurrence or non-occurrence of a specific event, the employee will have been dismissed if the employer fails to renew the contract. Assuming that the dismissed employee has more than one year's continuous service, she can ask the employer to provide her with written reasons setting out the justification for the dismissal. Ultimately, the dismissal could be regarded as unfair and the employee will have the option of lodging a claim with the Office of Employment Tribunals.

Definition of a fixed-term employee

A fixed-term employee is defined, in terms of the Regulations, as someone who is employed on a contract that will last for a specified period of time or whose employment will end when a specified task has been completed or when a specified event either occurs or does not occur (Regulation 1).

Less favourable treatment

Less favourable treatment of a fixed-term employee could take many forms (Regulation 3). Such individuals could be denied access to the employer's sick-pay scheme, denied access to the employer's pension scheme, the employer may fail to notify them about permanent vacancies within the organisation, and they may be denied access to employment, promotion or training opportunities generally. There may be discrimination if a fixed-term employee's terms and conditions of employment were less favourable in comparison to their permanent colleagues with whom they would wish to make a comparison. Fixed-term employees now have a right to receive information from the employer about permanent vacancies in the organisation.

Justification of less favourable treatment

An employer will only be able to justify less favourable treatment of a fixed-term employee on objective grounds (Regulation 4). An employer may be able to justify the less favourable treatment by bringing evidence which demonstrates that a permanent worker has better qualifications and/or more experience than the person bringing the complaint.

Identifying a comparator

If a fixed-term employee decides to make an allegation of discrimination against the employer, it is important that they are able to compare themselves to a permanent employee (Regulation 2). The fixed-term employee cannot choose any permanent colleague with whom to compare himself. The comparator must be employed by the same employer and do the same or broadly similar work (the influence of the Equal Pay Act 1970 can undoubtedly be felt here). The employee must show that she has similar skills, qualifications and experience to her comparator. Like must be compared with like as much as possible. If the employee cannot point to a comparator in his workplace, he can always search for another permanent employee to make a comparison, as long as this individual is employed by the same employer the only difference being that he is employed at another workplace.

 Key point: A fixed-term term employee is someone who is employed for a specified period and should not be treated less favourably in comparison with a relevant permanent colleague.

Lodging a claim for discrimination by a temporary fixed term employee

The employee has a right to ask the employer to respond to his allegation of discrimination. The employer should respond by issuing a written statement, within 21 days of the employee's original request, setting out the reasons for the treatment that the employee has experienced (Regulation 5). The employer is perfectly at liberty to take issue with the employee's perception that he has somehow been discriminated against by reason of his status as a fixed-term employee. If the employee is still not satisfied with the employer's written response, she is entitled to lodge an Employment Tribunal application within three months (less one day) of the conduct complained of (Regulation 7).

An individual who claims that they have been discriminated against by an employer on the grounds that he is a part-time worker or a fixed-term employee must bring evidence to support such a claim. Once evidence of discrimination has been established, it will be up to the employer to rebut this. If the employer is unable to do this, the Employment Tribunal is entitled to make a finding of less favourable treatment.

 Key point: A claim for less favourable treatment under the Fixed Term Employees Regulations must be lodged within three months (less one day) of the discriminatory treatment.

Victimisation

Regulation 6 makes it very clear that employees who make complaints against the employer or who give evidence on behalf of a discriminated colleague have the right not to be victimised by the employer in respect of unfair dismissal or other detriments.

Employer's liability for breaches committed by an employee

An employer will be responsible for any breaches of the Regulations committed by an employee whether this act was done with or without the employer knowledge (Regulation 12).

 Key point: An employer must not victimise any employee who raises a claim under the Fixed Term Employees Regulations and employers could also be liable for an employee's discriminatory behaviour.

Discrimination on the grounds of sexual orientation, religion or belief

On 1 December 2003, owing to the introduction of the Employment Equality (Sexual Orientation) Regulations 2003, it became unlawful for an employer to discriminate against someone by reason of that person's sexual orientation.

Furthermore on 2 December 2003, in terms of the Employment Equality (Religion or Belief) Regulations 2003, it became unlawful for an employer to discriminate against someone on the grounds of religion or beliefs.

Both sets of Regulations, which implement the European Employment Directive (Council Directive 2000/78/EC), now provide protection to workers (not just employees, but also contract workers) who experience this kind of discrimination and harassment in the workplace. Employers and providers of vocational training are covered by both sets of Regulations. They cover all aspects of the employment relationship, including recruitment, pay, working conditions, training, promotion, dismissal and the provision of references. It does not matter whether the employer is a large or small organisation or whether it is in the public or private sector, the Regulations will apply. The police are also covered by the Regulations.

The Regulations apply to office holders appointed by the government and other office holders where they fall within the scope of the Directive (that is, if they are paid and are subject to some form of direction). This means that the regulations will cover clergy and judicial offices, for example, including magistrates and Employment Tribunal members. They do not cover people who hold elected office, or an office that cannot be regarded as a job, for example, a child's guardian.

Key point: Both sets of Employment Equality Regulations 2003 now make it unlawful to discriminate against a person on the grounds of sexual orientation and religion or belief.

The Employment Equality (Sexual Orientation) Regulations 2003 make it unlawful for employers to deny lesbian, gay and bisexual people employment and training opportunities. Obviously, lesbian, gay and bisexual people will benefit the most from the new law, but heterosexuals will also have a right to bring a claim against employers who discriminate against them on the grounds of their sexual orientation.

The Regulations will protect people from discrimination on the grounds of their sexual orientation, whether they are orientated towards people of the same-sex, the opposite-sex or both sexes.

Religion and belief discrimination cases

Since the Employment Equality (Religion or Belief) Regulations 2003 came into force on 2 December 2003, discrimination and harassment on grounds of religion or belief in large and small workplaces in England, Scotland and Wales, both in the private and public sectors, has been unlawful.

 Williams-Drabble v Pathway Care Solutions Ltd and another (ET Case No 2601718/04) the employee who was a practising Christian lodged a claim at the Leeds Tribunal alleging religious discrimination. The basis of the claim was that she had told her employer in no uncertain terms at her interview that she was not prepared to work on Sundays as this was against her religious beliefs. The employee was offered the post which she accepted. Later, the employer attempted to force her to work on Sundays and the employee naturally objected to this. The employer refused to back down and the employee felt that she was suffering discrimination because of her religion and that she had little choice but to resign from her post and claim constructive dismissal on the grounds that her trust and confidence in the employer had completely broken down.

Held: the employee's claim alleging religious discrimination and constructive dismissal was upheld by the Employment Tribunal.

 Khan v NIC Hygiene 14 January 2005 (Leeds Employment Tribunal) Mr Khan, who is a Muslim, took his 25 day annual leave period plus a further week of unpaid leave in order to complete the Haj Pilgrimage to the Islamic Holy Sites in Saudi Arabia. Every devout Muslim is expected to undertake the Pilgrimage at least once in their lives. Khan had requested time-off from his job as a bus cleaner with his employer, NIC Hygiene, but had received no response. His Union advised him to submit a written request for time-off – which he duly did – but his employer again failed to respond. One of Khan's managers then informed him that he could probably take the time-off since there had been no objection from the company. Khan went on the Pilgrimage, but on his return from Saudi Arabia, he was suspended without pay and later dismissed from his post. Khan then commenced an action against his ex-employer on the grounds that he suffered religious discrimination.

Held: by the Tribunal that Khan had experienced less favourable treatment on the grounds of his religious beliefs and he was awarded £10,000 in compensation.

Recent case developments

A number of cases have been brought under the Regulations:

 Glasgow City Council *v* McNab (2007). David McNab was employed as a Maths teacher at St. Paul's Roman Catholic High School in Glasgow. Mr McNab, who is an atheist, applied for the promoted post of Head of Pastoral Care (or Guidance) in the School. The Council decided not to proceed with Mr McNab's application and he was not given an interview for the post. The reason given by the Council was that certain holders of posts in Catholic schools e.g. Heads of Pastoral Care and Head Teachers had to obtain approval from the Roman Catholic Church authorities. Basically, the system of approval in Roman Catholic Schools in Scotland means that an employer will be able to insist that certain job applicants or an existing employee seeking promotion to a certain post (such as Mr McNab) must be prepared to support and promote the moral teachings of the Roman Catholic Church. Mr McNab claimed that he had suffered discrimination on the grounds of his atheism (his beliefs) when the Council refused to proceed with his application for the post and he brought an action against the Council under the Employment Equality (Religion or Belief) Regulations 2003. The City Council, in its defence, relied on Regulation 7 of the Employment Equality (Religion or Belief) Regulations which also allows organised religions, for example, the Church of Scotland or the Roman Catholic Church to apply genuine occupational requirements to employment where it is necessary to comply with religious doctrine or where it is appropriate to do so given the nature of the post.

Held: by the Glasgow Employment Tribunal that Mr McNab had suffered direct discrimination as a result of his philosophical beliefs and, consequently, he was entitled to receive £2,000 in compensation from his employer. The City Council subsequently appealed to the Employment Appeal Tribunal in order to have the Tribunal's judgement overturned. The Council, as part of its appeal claimed that there is a genuine need for posts such as Guidance Teachers to be approved by the Church. The City Council lost its appeal against the decision of the Employment Tribunal.

This case has caused much interest because it seemed to undermine the system of approval which operates in Roman Catholic Schools. This system ensures that certain teaching posts in Roman Catholic schools must be held a practising member of the Church and the post-holder's character in this regard will have been verified by a Roman Catholic priest. A certificate of approval is then issued by the local Bishop.

A number of points need to be clarified in respect of the **McNab** decision. Firstly, the Roman Catholic Church was not Mr McNab's employer – he was employed by the Council. Under the Education Acts and an Agreement (from 1991) between the Council and the local Roman Catholic Church authorities, however, the Council is obliged to make sure that certain post-holders in Catholic schools have been approved by the local Church authorities. The Head of Pastoral Care (or Guidance) is **not** such a post and the Council made an error in assuming that the Church would object to the appointment of an individual such as McNab. Secondly, it has been observed that the Council encountered difficulties in the first place because its system for approving job applicants and existing employees was allegedly not carried out in a consistent fashion. Those individuals predicting the imminent end of the system of approval in Catholic schools are likely to be disappointed as the case was more about the way in which appointments to promoted posts were handled by the Council rather than any policy of the Church authorities.

One of the important factors in dealing with claims for religious discrimination which an Employment Tribunal must ask itself is why the employer behaved in a particular way towards the employee in question and not to make an error in law by concentrating on the reasons why the employee has behaved in a particular fashion.

 Azmi v Kirklees Borough Council (2007) a school which employed a Muslim languages support teacher would not allow her to wear a hijab. In its very basic form, a hijab can simply consist of a head scarf worn by a woman, but more conservative Muslims may wear full body garments with only the wearer's eyes being visible. The literal translation of hijab from the Arabic is barrier or partition.

In this case, the school's main objection to the teacher's request to be permitted to wear the hijab was that her duties were carried out more effectively when the teacher's face was clearly visible to the pupils.

Held: by the Employment Tribunal that the school's prohibition on the wearing of the hijab was not an act of direct discrimination. The general prohibition on the wearing of the hijab could potentially be indirect discrimination, but it could be justified objectively given the necessity of teachers being able to communicate effectively with their students.

 McClintock v Department of Constitutional Affairs (2008)
McClintock, a magistrate, had refused to place children for adoption with gay and lesbian couples because this was in breach of his Christian beliefs. His employer, the Department of Constitutional Affairs informed him that it regarded his attitude as a breach of his judicial oath. McClintock then pursued a claim for religious discrimination to the Employment Tribunal.

Held: by the Employment Appeal Tribunal that McClintock was not being treated differently because of his religious beliefs. He was receiving the same treatment that anyone could expect if s/he refused to honour a judicial oath taken by him or her. In point of fact, McClintock experienced substantial difficulties in actually proving that his objections to the adoption of children by gay and lesbian couples were motivated by his religious beliefs.

 London Borough of Islington v Ladele (2008) Ladele, a Registrar with the Council, brought an action for religious discrimination against her employer because she was being forced to conduct civil partnership ceremonies for same sex couples in contravention of her Christian beliefs. The Council had disciplined Ladele for her refusal to participate in these types of ceremony and had, ultimately, threatened her with dismissal. The Employment Tribunal found to some extent in Ladele's favour that she had suffered religious discrimination. The Council appealed against this decision.

Held: by the Employment Appeal Tribunal that the original decision of the Tribunal had been made in error. Ladele had not been treated differently – she had been treated exactly the same as all her other colleagues. The English Court of Appeal subsequently confirmed that no religious discrimination had taken place.

As a result of an amendment made to the Employment Equality (Religion or Belief) Regulations 2003, it is now unlawful to subject individuals to less favourable treatment on the grounds of their philosophical beliefs and it is immaterial whether or not these beliefs are considered similar to a religious belief. This is a highly significant development which demonstrates quite clearly that the the Regulations are not just confined to the protection of religious beliefs.

 Grainger plc *v* Nicholson (2009) is a very important case for this reason. Tim Nicholson brought a claim under the Regulations against his employer, Grainger plc, a company involved in the development of residential property. Nicholson, who was Head of Sustainability at Grainger plc, alleged that he had been unfairly selected for redundancy by his employer because of his belief in the dangers of global warming and climate change. Nicholson was particularly vocal in his concerns that a company like Grainger had to promote environmental concerns as part of its business activities. The company had published environmentally friendly polices, but its alleged willingness to permit its executives to use certain types of vehicles which contributed to an increase in global warming suggested that there was contradiction between the company's statements about its commitment to environmental issues and their actual implementation. The beliefs of Nicholson and his willingness to state these openly appeared to clash with his employer's business objectives and this led Nicholson to conclude that he had been unfairly selected for redundancy.

Grainger plc attempted to have Mr Nicholson's claim struck out on the grounds that his belief in environmental concerns was not a philosophical belief which was protected by the Regulations.

Held: by the Central London Employment Tribunal at a Preliminary Hearing, that Mr Nicholson's belief in environmental issues did fall within the meaning of a philosophical belief as covered by the Regulations. This, however, was a procedural victory (albeit an important one) for Mr Nicholson who would still have to win his case at a full Hearing of the Employment Tribunal.

On 3 November 2009, the Employment Appeal Tribunal ruled that climate change could be capable of being a philosophical belief within the meaning of the Regulations. In order to succeed in his claim, Nicholson will still have to prove that his belief is *"a weighty and substantial aspect of human life and behaviour"*. A belief which demonstrates *"a certain level of cogency, seriousness, cohesion and importance"* and this belief is ultimately *"worthy of respect in a democratic society, [that it] be not incompatible with human dignity and not conflict with the fundamental rights of others"*.

An employer may have the right to dismiss an employee who engages in activities for the promotion of certain religious or philosophical beliefs at inappropriate times.

Chondol *v* Liverpool City Council (2009) Chondol (described as a committed Christian) was employed as a social worker by the City Council. He was dismissed from employment, amongst other things, because he was it was alleged that he had promoted his religious beliefs at inappropriate times i.e. when he was employed by the Council. Previously, Chondol had been reprimanded for "blurring" the boundaries between his profession and his religious faith when he had given a Bible to one of his clients or service users. He was further reprimanded for giving his clients his personal contact details and, one occasion, visiting a client on his own on a Saturday which contravened health and safety procedures concerning lone visits to clients. During one such lone visit, a client had assaulted Chondol, but this incident was not reported to his managers. At another meeting with a client, Chondol inappropriately promoted his Christian beliefs which led the client to make an official complaint to the Council in the following terms:

'... he [Chondol] was talking about God and church and crap like that.'

The client made it clear that he did not want to be visited by Chondol in the future.

There was also another incident on New Year's Day 2007, when Chondol visited a friend who was suffering from a psychiatric illness and who was living at a 'low support hostel'. Chondol took the friend away from the hostel for some four hours (albeit with the supervising nurse's permission). Chondol was supposedly visiting his friend in the hostel socially and not professionally. He had, however, signed in to the hostel as a social worker and he worn his identity badge when doing so. When Chondol returned with his friend to the hostel, the nurse asked him to record the details of his interaction with his friend in the patient notes. Chondol wrote in the notes that he did not consider his friend to be a risk or threat to other people and he highlighted his friend's wish to accompany him to church. When the psychiatrist reviewed the patient's notes, he strongly objected to Chondol's remarks.

Chondol was subsequently investigated by his employer and was accused of gross misconduct on two counts:

1   Not to work outside normal hours without prior agreement/notice

2   Not to promote Christianity

The Council found Chondol guilty of gross misconduct and dismissed him from employment. Chondol submitted a claim to the Employment Tribunal alleging that he had been discriminated against on the grounds of his religious beliefs.

Held: by the Employment Appeal Tribunal that Chondol had not been discriminated in terms of the Employment Equality (Religion or Belief) Regulations 2003. He had behaved inappropriately in the discharge of his duties as a social worker and the employer was entitled to treat such behaviour as gross misconduct which was punishable by dismissal. Chondol's claim for unfair dismissal on the grounds that he had been discriminated by reason of his religious beliefs was dismissed.

Two of the first cases to be brought under the Employment Equality (Sexual Orientation) Regulations 2003 were **Whitfield v Cleanaway UK (2005)** and **Phillips v Atherton (2005)**.

 Whitfield v Cleanaway UK (2005) (East Stratford Employment Tribunal). Rob Whitfield, who is gay, brought a successful claim against his employer, Cleanaway UK, after being subjected to a series of derogatory comments about his sexuality, for example, he was referred to as 'Sebastian' by some of his fellow workers – a clear reference to the gay character in the popular BBC series *Little Britain*. The Tribunal held that Mr Whitfield had suffered less favourable treatment in terms of the Regulations as a result of his sexual orientation and, consequently, he was awarded nearly £35,000 by the Tribunal.

 In **Phillips v Atherton (2005) (Croydon Employment Tribunal)** Mr Phillips worked as a researcher for the Labour MP for Falmouth & Cambourne, Candy Atherton. Phillips, who is gay, claimed that Atherton had put pressure on him to uncover any potential scandal in connection with the sexual orientation of a political opponent who was standing for the Conservative Party at the British General Election in 2005. He claimed that Atherton had asked him to use his gay contacts to find out whether her Conservative opponent frequented gay bars in order to meet potential partners.

Phillips objected to this request and he resigned from his post claiming discrimination on the grounds of his sexual orientation. He stated that Atherton's intention was to uncover information which could only be used to damage her political opponent. Phillips claimed that Atherton would not have asked a heterosexual employee to undertake these types of enquiries and, furthermore, this was kind of investigation was not properly within his job description as a researcher.

Subsequently, Phillips brought a claim against Atherton at the Croydon Employment Tribunal. Unfortunately for Phillips, the Tribunal preferred to believe the evidence of Atherton and his claim was dismissed.

 English v Thomas Sanderson Ltd (2008) this was a significant decision of the English Court of Appeal in that it answered a procedural question as to whether an individual (Stephen English) was able to use Regulation 5 of the Employment Equality (Sexual Orientation) Regulations 2003 to challenge harassment that he had received from a number of colleagues while engaged by Thomas Sanderson Ltd under a contract for personal services. The harassment consisted of homophobic taunts despite the fact that English was heterosexual and was, in fact, happily married with three teenage daughters. It was admitted by English that he knew that his detractors were perfectly aware that he was not gay. Eventually, the levels of harassment experienced by English forced him to resign from his position with Thomas Sanderson.

Held: the key question is whether the less favourable treatment (harassment in this case) suffered by an individual was motivated by sexual orientation and a person's actual sexual orientation is irrelevant and it does not matter whether an individual actually believes that another person is of a particular orientation. Lord Justice Lawrence Collins stated:

'In a case like the present, even if the claimant were homosexual, it was obviously not for him to show that he was homosexual, any more than a claimant in a racial discrimination case had to prove that he was Asian or a Jew.

There was nothing in the cases to require the court in the present type of case to inquire whether the maker of offensive homophobic statements actually thought that the victim was homosexual. The natural meaning of regulation 5 was sufficient to make such an inquiry irrelevant.'

This decision demonstrates that homophobic taunts or remarks (which are clearly offensive in themselves just as racist or sexist remarks would be) can be actionable even if the intended victim does not actually belong to the group (in this case gay people) which is being denigrated or targeted for less favourable treatment.

It is worth remembering, if a comparison is being made, that the earlier gender and racial equality legislation was primarily designed to protect women and ethnic minorities, but men and the majority white British population were also protected by these anti-discrimination laws. There is no reason to prevent heterosexuals and members of majority religious groups from using the appropriate set of Regulations to bring a claim if they feel that they have suffered discrimination as a result of their sexual orientation or religious beliefs.

Transferred discrimination

Transferred discrimination will also be illegal under the Regulations (see **Showboat Entertainment Centre Ltd *v* Owens (1984)** for an example of transferred race discrimination). Transferred discrimination occurs where person experiences less favourable treatment because of the sexual orientation or religious beliefs of the people with whom they associate, for example, their family and friends.

Perceptions about a person's sexual orientation or religious beliefs

The law also covers situations where an employer perception of a person's sexual orientation or religious beliefs will result in the employer treating that person less favourably. An employer may believe, wrongly, that an employee is gay and subject that person to discrimination, for example, by refusing to promote him. The fact that the employee is heterosexual does not prevent him from bringing a claim against his employer for discrimination on the grounds of sexual orientation. Similarly, an employer may wrongly believe that an employee is a Roman Catholic and, as a result, refuse to employ that person. (See **English *v* Thomas Sanderson Ltd (2008)** discussed above.)

 Key point: Both sets of Employment Equality Regulations 2003 make transferred discrimination and less favourable treatment arising from perceptions about a person's sexual orientation or religion unlawful.

Types of discrimination

The Employment Equality (Sexual Orientation) Regulations 2003 and the Employment Equality (Religion or Belief) Regulations 2003 take a common approach to the issue of discrimination:

Direct discrimination

Treating people less favourably than others because of religion, belief or sexual orientation (Regulation 3 of both Regulations).

Indirect discrimination

Applying a provision, criterion or practice which disadvantages people of a particular sexual orientation, religion or belief and which is not justified in objective terms (Regulation 3 of both Regulations).

Harassment

Unwanted conduct that violates people's dignity or creates an intimidating, hostile, degrading, humiliating or offensive environment (Regulation 4 of both Regulations).

Victimisation

Treating people less favourably because of action they have taken under or in connection with the new legislation – for example, made a formal complaint of discrimination or given evidence in an Employment Tribunal case (Regulation 5 of both Regulations).

The Regulations give protection to employees throughout the course of the employment relationship. Employees have the right not to be discriminated against during the recruitment process, in the workplace, on dismissal. In terms of Regulation 21 of both sets of Regulations, employees have the right not to be discriminated by way of victimisation in certain circumstances after the employment has ended (see **Relaxion Group plc v Rhys-Harper (FC)**; **D'Souza v London Borough of Lambeth**; **Jones v 3M Healthcare Limited and Others (2003)**).

 Key point: The Employment Equality Regulations 2003 make the following types of discrimination unlawful: direct discrimination, indirect discrimination, harassment and victimisation. In relation to less favourable treatment on the grounds of sexual orientation, religion or belief.

Genuine occupational requirements (Regulation 7 of both Regulations)

Regulation 7 of the Employment Equality (Sexual Orientation) Regulations states that an employer will be allowed to discriminate against people on the grounds of their sexual orientation where it is important that an applicant or an employee be of a particular sexual orientation. In situations such as these, a person's sexual orientation is a genuine and determining occupational requirement. The employer's insistence on applying such a requirement to an applicant or an employee must be proportionate (i.e. reasonable) in order to achieve a legitimate aim. The Arbitration, Conciliation and Advisory Service (ACAS) has used the example of a Gay Rights group (such as Stonewall) applying a genuine occupational requirement that its Chief Executive be a gay man or a lesbian or a bi-sexual in order for that person to enjoy credibility within the gay and bi-sexual community.

Regulation 7 of the Employment Equality (Religion or Belief) Regulations also allows organised religions, for example, the Church of Scotland or the Roman Catholic Church to apply genuine occupational requirements to employment where it is necessary to comply with religious doctrine, the nature of the post or the fact that by appointing a person who has a particular sexual orientation this may lead to conflict with a significant number of the religion's followers. Local authorities in Scotland will still be able to insist that being a practising Roman Catholic is a genuine occupational requirement for Head Teachers of Roman Catholic schools.

When applying genuine occupational requirements, both sets of Regulations state that the employer must either show that the individual to whom it is applied could not comply with the condition or the employer reasonably believed this to be the case.

 Key point: The Employment Equality Regulations 2003 permit employers, in limited situations, to discriminate against employees or applicants by reason of their sexual orientation or religion.

The burden of proof

Regulations 29 and 32 of the Employment Equality (Sexual Orientation) Regulations 2003 and of the Employment Equality (Religion or Belief) Regulations 2003 state that the burden of proof is on the person bringing the complaint who must show that he has suffered an act of discrimination on the grounds of his sexual orientation or religion or beliefs if the claim is brought before either the Employment Tribunal or the Sheriff Court. Once the Employment Tribunal or the Sheriff Court is satisfied from the circumstances of the case that an act of discrimination has taken place, the complaint must be upheld if the employer is unable to provide a satisfactory explanation for his conduct. This favours the employee and goes further than **King v Great Britain-China Centre (1991)** and **Zafar v Glasgow City Council (1998)** where Employment Tribunals and courts were permitted to infer discrimination, but they were not forced to make this finding.

Liability of employers

According to Regulation 22 of both the Employment Equality (Sexual Orientation) Regulations and the Employment Equality (Religion or Belief) Regulations, an employer will be liable for the discriminatory actions of any employee. Furthermore, Regulation 23 of both sets of Regulations makes it quite clear that it will be unlawful for any individual to aid someone to commit a discriminatory act.

 Key point: An employer will be vicariously liable for the discriminatory actions of an employee.

A significant improvement?

Both sets of Regulations represent significant progress in the sense that many more people will now enjoy protection from discrimination, victimisation and harassment than was previously the case. It should be recalled that discrimination on the grounds of a person's sexual orientation was not unlawful in terms of the Sex Discrimination Act 1975 (see **Macdonald v Advocate General for Scotland** and **Pearce v Governing Body of Mayfield School (2003)**). Similarly, the Race Relations Act 1976 did not prevent individuals suffering discrimination by reason of their religious beliefs, except in very narrowly defined circumstances (see **Mandla v Dowall Lee (1983); Seide v Gillette Industries Ltd (1980)** and **J H Walker Ltd v Hussain**

& Others (1996)). It is anticipated that the Regulations will now plug a very large and undesirable loop-hole in the United Kingdom's equality legislation.

The Regulations also use a wider definition of indirect discrimination which is very similar to that used in the amended Race Relations Act 1976. The words 'provision, criterion, or practice' have a broader meaning than the words 'requirement or condition' used in the older equality legislation from the 1970s. The new definition will apply to formal and informal practices of an employer where he imposes a provision, criterion or practice which disadvantages people of a particular sexual orientation or religion or belief. Furthermore, the more modern approach to indirect discrimination should mean that many more cases are brought before Employment Tribunals without having to rely on a complex statistical exercise in order to initiate them (see **London Underground v Edwards (No 2) (1998)**).

Genuine Occupational Requirements

Reaney v Hereford Diocesan Board of Finance (2007) the Anglican Diocese of Hereford attempted unsuccessfully to rely upon the defence or justification of a genuine occupational requirement in terms of Regulation 7 in order to explain why the job of Youth Development Officer was not given to Reaney, a gay man. The practice of homosexuality is regarded by many Christians (whether Anglican, Roman Catholic, Presbyterian or Evangelical) as being completely incompatible with traditional religious doctrine. Therefore, according to the Diocese, any applicant for the post of Youth Officer had to comply with traditional Christian beliefs and not be a practising homosexual. Reaney then took the Diocese to the Cardiff Employment Tribunal alleging direct discrimination on the grounds of his sexual orientation and won his claim. The Employment Tribunal was particularly swayed by the fact that Reaney had given an assurance to his prospective employer that he would not enter into a gay relationship during the five year tenure of the post and that it was not reasonable for the Diocese to have rejected this assurance by ultimately rejecting his application for the post. This was an expensive mistake for the Diocese in that it had to pay to Reaney over £47,000 in compensation, part of which included injury to feelings.

The **Civil Partnerships Act 2004** came into force on 5 December 2005. This legislation extends the same employment benefits that married couples already enjoy to same sex couples. However, same sex couples will have to make a legal commitment to one another by forming a civil partnership. In relation to the field of employment rights, the Act applies to employment and pension benefits e.g. a concessionary travel scheme and civil partners of an employee will be entitled to take advantage of these if existing provisions permit a heterosexual partner or spouse of an employee to claim these benefits.

 Key point: Both sets of the Employment Equality Regulations 2003 permit an employer to justify less favourable treatment in certain situations by relying on a special occupational requirement.

Age Discrimination

A very significant piece of legislation was introduced to the already crowded area of anti-discrimination law on 1 October 2006. The Employment Equality (Age) Regulations 2006 now ensure that it is unlawful for employers to discriminate against individuals on the grounds of a person's age.

The Regulations apply to recruitment policies and procedures, terms and conditions of employment, promotion and training opportunities and termination of the employment relationship.

Practically speaking, this will mean that employers will have to be especially careful when recruiting workers to their organisations. Any advertisements which seem to favour one age category over another should be discouraged. There has been much speculation in the popular press in relation to the Regulations about the legality and advisability of such tried and tested phrases like 'Mature person sought for post'; 'Dynamic individual preferred' or 'Youthful enthusiasm' (see **McCoy v James McGregor and Sons Limited and others 2007 discussed below**). Only time and litigation will tell whether such phrases are likely to be consigned to the dustbin of recruitment practice. One thing is certain, responsible employers should definitely err on the side of caution to avoid expensive and unnecessary law suits by emphasising the skills that a successful applicant should possess.

An employer will be entitled, however, to refuse to employ or hire an individual who is within six months of the organisation's normal retirement age or within six months of the person's 65th birthday if the organisation does not stipulate a normal retirement age.

The aim of the Regulations

An employer would be well advised to remember three important aspects of the Regulations:

◆ Any attempt to justify or defend behaviour which amounts to victimisation and harassment will simply be untenable;
◆ Vicarious liability applies here i.e. employers can be held responsible for the discriminatory behaviour of their employees; and
◆ There is no limit placed on the amount of compensation that an
◆ Employment Tribunal or court can award to a successful applicant who brings an age discrimination claim.

What kinds of individuals do the Regulations cover?

The Regulations cover a wide range of workers and they are not simply confined to the protection of employees. Agency workers, casual workers, independent contractors, job applicants and office holders (this category includes company directors) will receive protection under the legislation.

The Regulations specifically mention such organisations and individuals as the Police, Qualifications Authorities, the Serious Organised Crime Agency (SOCA), partnerships, staff who work for the House of Commons and the House of Lords, barristers and advocates, trade organisations, employment agencies, careers guidance bodies and higher and further education institutions.

The Regulations also apply to pension schemes (**Regulation 11**) and the provision of vocational training (**Regulation 20**). Thus, it is apparent that the Regulations are extremely wide-ranging in their scope and effect.

Regulation 10 defines the meaning of employment and contract work at an establishment in Great Britain.

According to Regulation 10(1), employment is to be regarded as being at an establishment in Great Britain if the employee does his work wholly or partly in

Great Britain or does his work wholly outside Great Britain subject to certain conditions. This means that workers employed outside the United Kingdom will be protected by the Regulations if they meet the following conditions:

(a) the employer has a place of business at an establishment in Great Britain;

(b) the work is for the purposes of the business carried on at that establishment; and

(c) the employee is ordinarily resident in Great Britain:

(i) at the time when he applies for or is offered the employment, or

(ii) at any time during the course of the employment (**Regulation 10(2)**).

What kind of protection do the Regulations offer?

The Regulations are very similar to older pieces of UK anti-discrimination legislation e.g. the Sex Discrimination Act 1975 and the Race Relations Act 1976 in the sense that they prohibit less favourable treatment by an employer on the grounds of a person's age which would amount to any of the following types of discrimination:

 Key point: Discrimination on the grounds of a person's age is now illegal under Scots Law.

◆ direct discrimination (**Regulation 3**)
◆ indirect discrimination (**Regulation 3**)
◆ harassment (**Regulation 4**)
◆ victimisation (**Regulation 6**)

 McCoy v McGregor and Sons Limited and others (2007), this case was brought under the version of the Employment Equality (Age) Regulations as they apply in Northern Ireland and was the first case of its type to be brought before an Employment Tribunal in the province. The Regulations which operate in Northern Ireland are very similar to the version operating within the UK mainland.

Mr McCoy, a 58 year old man applied for a job as a sales representative. His application was rejected despite having over thirty years of relevant employment experience. Critically, the advertisement for the job stated that the employer was looking for an applicant with "youthful enthusiasm". The employer eventually decided to hire two younger applicants (aged 42 and 43 respectively) who were not as experienced as Mr McCoy.

Held: the Tribunal found in Mr McCoy's favour that he had suffered direct discrimination on the grounds of his age and its decision was clearly influenced by the terminology used by the employer in the advertisement. Another factor which clearly influenced the Tribunal was the fact that the employer had placed a great deal of emphasis on the age of applicants and their levels of motivation, enthusiasm and energy. During the interview for the post, Mr McCoy had been asked questions such as 'Are you still hungry enough to succeed?' The younger candidates for the job were not asked these types of questions. Finally, the employer had used a scoring method to make differences between the candidates for the posts which was not transparent. Taken together and in the absence of any credible explanation offered by the employer, the Tribunal had no option to conclude that Mr McCoy had suffered discrimination by reason of his age.

 Key point: The Age Discrimination Regulations outlaw the following types of less favourable treatment: direct discrimination, indirect discrimination, harassment and victimisation.

The European Court of Justice has recently had to deal with the matter of age discrimination and should serve as warning to those employers who discriminate against workers on the grounds of age.

 Hutter _v_ Technische Universität Graz (2009) in this case from Austria, the European Court of Justice decided that an employer's decision to ignore an employee's work experience gained before reaching the age of 18 was unlawful direct discrimination on the grounds of age. Hutter was employed as an lab technician by the Technical University of Graz. He was paid a lower wage than a colleague who was nearly two years older than him. Both employees had originally begun their apprenticeships with the University at the same time, but Hutter was 16 and his colleague was 18. The University calculated that Hutter's colleague had accrued 28.5 months service since beginning work whereas he had accrued 6.5 months only after reaching the age of 18. Austrian national law permitted employers to make these kinds of distinctions. It was argued by the Austrian Government that the reason for this difference in treatment between age groups was to promote a legitimate and proportionate aim i.e. to ease the entry of younger apprentices into the work force and to ensure that general education was not treated unfavourably in comparison with vocational education. Nonetheless, Hutter brought a claim for age discrimination based on the Equal Treatment Directive 2000/78.

Held: by the European Court of Justice that Austrian law breaches the Equal Treatment Directive and that the policy of discounting job experience gained before the age of 18 was an example of direct discrimination on the ground of age. It should be noted that the European Court of Justice was at pains to point out that it can be legitimate from an employer to pay a higher salary to someone who has greater experience, but it is not legitimate to penalise an employee with identical work experience purely because he is younger.

 Key point: Discrimination on the grounds of age could breach the EU's Equal Treatment Directive.

Transferred discrimination

Regulation 5 also protects those individuals e.g. a fellow employee or a manager who are ordered by the employer to carry out some sort of discriminatory act and refuse to do so or raise an official complaint about this. If the employer takes some sort of punitive action against such an individual in these circumstances, it could lead to legal action being taken against the employer by the person who refused to follow the instructions in the first place. This type of detriment is known as transferred discrimination whereby an individual suffers some sort of less favourable treatment as a result of their association with another individual who is fully protected under the Regulations (**for an example of transferred discrimination see Showboat Entertainment Centre Ltd *v* Owens (1984) brought under the Race Relations Act 1976**).

This important protection against transferred discrimination is very similar to that which already exists under the Sex Discrimination and the Race Relations Acts whereby someone can suffer a detriment e.g. being subjected to disciplinary action which entails demotion or dismissal for refusing to follow an employer's instructions to carry out a discriminatory act against another individual.

According to Regulation 24, any discriminatory treatment by the employer which continues after an employment relationship has ended could still be actionable before the Sheriff Court or an Employment Tribunal. This would include situations where a former employer is asked to provide a reference for an employee who has since ceased to work for that employer. If the former employer deliberately provided a bad or a poor reference which would ensure that the employee failed to secure new employment, this may construed as discriminatory behaviour and a breach of the Regulations.

These concepts, of course, should be familiar from our previous studies of the UK Sex Discrimination and Race Relations Acts and other anti-discrimination laws.

 Key point: The Age Discrimination Regulations use similar legal concepts found in earlier UK anti-discrimination laws.

The prohibition in respect of discrimination on grounds of age

Regulation 7 provides various examples of situations where an employer will be absolutely prohibited from discriminating on the grounds of age against an employee or an applicant for a position in the organisation.

An existing employee could be subjected to discriminatory treatment as follows:

(a) in the terms of his/her employment;

(b) in the opportunities which exist for promotion, a transfer, training, or receiving any other benefit;

(c) a refusal by the employer to extend to an employee or a deliberate failure to extend any such opportunity; or

(d) by dismissing the employee, or subjecting the employee to any other detriment i.e. disadvantage.

Discriminatory treatment could affect a job applicant in the following ways:

(a) arrangements or procedures which are used for deciding who will be offered employment in the first place;

(b) the terms on which a person is offered employment;

(c) a refusal to offer or a deliberate decision not to offer someone employment.

 Key point: Regulation 7 of the Age Discrimination Regulations contains examples of less favourable treatment on grounds of a person's age.

Vicarious liability

An employer or principal can be vicariously liable for discriminatory acts or omissions carried out by an employee or an agent (see **Chapter 6**) Even if an employer or a principal did not personally commit a discriminatory act which is in breach of the Regulations, they may still be liable for the acts or omissions of their employees or agents which have resulted in someone suffering discrimination or a detriment on the grounds of age (**Regulation 25**). It does not matter whether the employer was aware that discriminatory acts or omissions were taking place.

It is defence for an employer to state that reasonable practicable steps were taken to prevent an employee from committing an act or an omission which results in discrimination being suffered by another employee.

 Key point: An employer could be vicariously liable for discriminatory acts committed by his employees.

Aiding unlawful acts

Regulation 26 prohibits situations where an individual may aid and abet another person in the carrying out of an act or omission which is unlawful. The individual aiding and abetting the unlawful act will be treated as if they themselves had committed the unlawful act or omission in question. It may be a defence for an individual accused of aiding and abetting unlawful treatment to state s/he relied on a statement or information from another person and it was reasonable for them to place reliance on such a statement. Any person who makes a statement which encourages another person to aid and abet an unlawful act may be guilty of a criminal offence and may be fined upon conviction.

 Key point: The Age Discrimination Regulations prohibit someone aiding and abnetting another person in the commission of an unlawful act.

Genuine Occupational Requirements (Regulation 8)

An employer may be able to justify less favourable treatment of an individual on the grounds if this can be objectively justified and is a proportionate way of achieving a legitimate aim. This type of justification which an employer may choose to use is known as a Genuine Occupational Requirement (GOR). In practice, however, an Employment Tribunal or a court will scrutinise very closely any arguments used by an employer that one of its policies, procedures or a criterion amounts to a GOR.

An advertising agency may wish to hire individuals of a certain age to appear in publicity material for television, press or magazine advertisements to promote authenticity. An advertisement which used young people in their twenties to promote insurance products for the over fifty age group would not be very effective and would almost certainly lack authenticity. Therefore, it would be justifiable and proportionate for the advertising agency to use older people to appear in the publicity material because this achieves a legitimate aim.

 Key point: An employer may be able to justify less favourable treatment on grounds of age if this behaviour can be objectively justified and it is a proportionate way of achieving a legitimate aim.

Other exceptions

There are also situations where the law will permit differences in treatment between different age groups. The National Minimum Wage Act 1998, for example, will continue to operate as before meaning that workers can be paid different minimum wage rates depending on their age (**Regulation 31**).

An employer can also use a person's length of service in order to calculate the payment of an award or benefit to certain employees e.g. a bonus award for long-service (**Regulation 32**) and enhanced redundancy payments (**Regulation 33**). In such situations, it is very likely that older workers may very well have longer service than their younger colleagues and will, therefore, be better off financially under the employer's arrangements.

Rolls-Royce PLC v UNITE the Union (2009) the English Court of Appeal assessed the legality of a situation whereby an employer had taken into consideration the length of service of workers who were in danger of being made redundant. The Court stated that favouring employees with longer service of service when considering redundancy could amount to age discrimination against younger members of staff. However, it may also be a proportionate and legitimate method of implementing compulsory redundancies in a peaceful way in order to avoid strife in the work-place. Interestingly, no redundancies had yet taken place and Rolls-Royce and UNITE, the Trade Union representing many of the employees, were attempting to establish the legality of procedures for dealing with an event in the future (admittedly something which would arise in the near future given the difficult economic situation in which the employer was having to operate). Normally, both the English High Court and the Court of Appeal would have been reluctant to hear such a case, but their involvement was justified on the grounds that there was a broader public interest at issue, namely, the operation and extent of the Employment Equality (Age) Regulations 2006. Certainly, an initial concern for the Court of Appeal was the fact that its decision in this case would almost certainly be used by either side to pursue their interests during any future Employment Tribunal claims in the event of Rolls-Royce making workers redundant.

There are also exceptions for compliance with statutory authority (**Regulation 27**), national security (**Regulation 28**), positive action (**Regulation 29**) which permits certain employment and training opportunities to be targeted at particular age groups and provision of life assurance cover to retired workers (**Regulation 34**).

Hampton v Ministry of Justice (2007) the claimant was a part-time Recorder (a type of judge found in the County or Crown Courts in England and Wales) who was being forced to retire at the age of 65 as per Ministry of Justice guidelines. He took his claim to the London South Employment Tribunal alleging age discrimination and won the case. The Ministry of Justice then raised the retirement age from 65 to 70 for a range of judicial appointments.

The following case was in complete contrast to the decision in **Hampton v Ministry of Justice (2007)**:

 Varcoe and Southgate v Ministry of Justice (2009) the two claimants were employed as immigration judges by the Ministry of Justice and brought a claim against their employer at the Reading Employment Tribunal for alleged discrimination on the grounds of age. Both individuals claimed that rules, which had been in force since the 1990s, which imposed a compulsory retirement age of 70 for immigration judges were discriminatory. The judges had applied for an extension of their employment beyond retirement age, but this had been refused. The Ministry of Justice can extend a judge's employment if it is in the public interest.

Held: by the Employment Tribunal that the compulsory retirement age had been imposed by statute and this was enough to defeat the actions by the claimants. The Ministry of Justice, furthermore, had been able to demonstrate that it no longer required the services of the judges.

 Key point: Some pieces of legislation e.g. the National Minimum Wage Act 1998 allow differences in treatment on grounds of a person's age.

Termination of the employment relationship

It should go without saying that any attempt to terminate a worker's contract with an employer on the grounds of age will be regarded as unlawful discrimination.

So, for example, a deliberate attempt by an employer to target all the younger workers for redundancy in order to retain the services of older workers would be a very dubious policy in terms of the Regulations and would probably be unlawful.

Speaking of redundancy, it is unlawful to cap redundancy benefits at the age of 65 and the practice of reducing redundancy payments for those aged over 64 has since been discontinued.

 Key point: Dismissing employees on the basis of their age would almost certainly be a discriminatory act.

Retirement (Regulation 30)

The first thing to say about retirement is that there is no automatic legal right conferred on workers to continue working beyond the age of 65. An employer who insists that an individual retire on their 65th birthday will not be breaking the law.

Admittedly, there is a requirement placed on the employer to consider seriously any requests by an individual to be permitted to work beyond the age of 65 (**Regulations 47** and **48**). There had been a suggestion that, with the introduction of the Regulations, employers should have abolished the compulsory retirement age of 65. This suggestion, as we shall see, was somewhat premature and the European Court of Justice has recently given cautious approval to the UK's current retirement age of 65.

 Incorporated Trustees of the National Council on Ageing (Age Concern England) *v* Secretary of State for Business, Enterprise and Regulatory Reform (2009) The National Council on Ageing (previously known as Heyday) made an application to the English High Court for a judicial review concerning certain aspects of the Employment Equality (Age) Regulations 2006. In particular, the Council wished the High Court to scrutinise the legality of the compulsory retirement age of 65 in the United Kingdom and whether this breached European law (the EC Equal Treatment Framework Directive (2000/78). The European Directive permits member states to justify different treatment of individuals on grounds of age if those differences 'are objectively and reasonably justified by a legitimate aim, including legitimate employment policy, labour market and vocational training objectives, and if the means of achieving that aim are appropriate and necessary.'

Given the complexity of the issue, the High Court decided to refer the matter to the European Court of Justice for a preliminary ruling under Article 234 of the Treaty of Rome 1957.

The European Court of Justice made a number of observations about the issues raised in this case:

1   The UK Regulations do not lay down a mandatory or compulsory scheme for an automatic age of retirement. Subject to certain conditions in the Regulations, employers do have the right to refuse to dismiss or to hire people who are aged 65 or over

2   It was argued by Age Concern that European law obliged all member states to draw up the same legislation in order to achieve the legal objectives in the EC Equal Treatment Framework Directive (2000/78). The European Court of Justice disagreed by stating that it was for the member states to decide on how best to implement legislation to combat age discrimination.

3   The issue was raised as to whether a different standard of proof should be used in legal proceedings depending upon whether the action involved direct or indirect discrimination. The European Court of Justice was of the opinion that the important matter was that a high standard of proof had to be demonstrated in legal actions involving age discrimination claims.

The conclusion of the judgement of the European Court of Justice in this case is that the UK's mandatory retirement age of 65 does not breach European law because it can be justified as a proportionate way of achieving a legitimate aim and the UK Regulations do not have to set explicitly a list of permissible legitimate aims.

It will now be up to British courts and Employment Tribunals how the guidance from the European Court of Justice is actually implemented. In April 2009, it was estimated that some 260 cases before UK Employment Tribunals involving age discrimination claims had been sisted or frozen pending the decision of the European Court of Justice. In any case, the UK Government initially indicated that it would review the retirement age of 65 in 2011.

On 14 July 2009, the UK Government stated that it would bring this review of the default retirement age of 65 forward by a year to 2010 and this may mean that much of the legal debate in this area becomes largely irrelevant and of historical interest only. Angela Eagle MP, the UK Pensions Minister justified bringing the review forward by claiming:

'As Britain's demographics change, it is sensible that we have the debate on what works for business and individuals. The retirement laws need to reflect modern social and economic circumstances.'

Also in July 2009, Lord Adair Turner, the Chair of the UK Pensions Commission, spoke out about the need for people to work until they reached 70 years of age. Previously, Lord Turner had recommended raising the UK retirement age to 68. He has since conceded that this proposal would not be adequate to deal with the looming pension crisis which the country is now facing.

Age UK, R (on the application of) v Attorney General [2009] the English High Court has now ruled that the UK compulsory age of retirement which is set at 65 does not breach the Employment Equality (Age) Regulations 2006 as it can be regarded as a proportionate way of achieving a legitimate social aim i.e. the regulation of the labour market in this country. Admittedly, the judge in this case, Blake J, did state that there were compelling reasons for reviewing the compulsory retirement age, but he noted that discussions in this area may be of historical interest only as recent comments from the British Government seem to indicate that the retirement age will be increased from age 65 to 67.

 Key point: No employee has the right to demand that they will be permitted to remain in employment after reaching their 65th birthday.

Continuing to work beyond 65

Schedule 6 of the Regulations sets out the procedure which employers should follow when dealing with situations where an employee may wish to work beyond the age of 65. The employer must inform the employee in writing of the date upon which it is expected that the employee will retire **and** the employee's right to request working beyond 65. Such notification must be given to the employee by the employer not more than one year and not less than six months before the proposed date of retirement. The duty to notify the employee arises irrespective of whether this information has already been previously communicated to the employee via the contract of employment or by any other method or means of communication.

If the employee decides to request working beyond retirement age, the employer must hold a meeting to discuss this matter. The employer should inform the employee of any decision reached about the request to work beyond retirement as soon as is reasonably practicable after the meeting has taken place. If the employer decides not to continue employment beyond retirement age, the affected employee has the legal right to appeal against this decision. If the affected employee decides to appeal against this decision, a meeting should be held to consider this matter. The employer should issue the employee with a decision as soon as is reasonably practicable. The employee is entitled to be accompanied by a trade union representative or a colleague to these meetings with the employer. The trade union representative or the colleague can address the meeting on behalf of the employee (but not answer questions) and s/he can confer with the employee during these meetings.

It should be stressed, however, that the employer has a duty to consider seriously those requests from employees to work beyond retirement age and there is absolutely no legal guarantee for people that their employment will continue beyond this age.

Early retirement

Earlier retirement ages, however, may well breach the Regulations and an employer will have to be able to justify on objective grounds a requirement that someone should be compelled to retire before their 65th birthday. In any case, an employer has a legal duty to give an individual six months' notice of their impending retirement and must inform the individual of the right to submit a request to be considered for continued employment with the organisation. In practice, the well-prepared employer will hold a meeting with the individual in question well before

Hospitals NHS Trust (2009) were able to demonstrate that they had both received less favourable treatment from their prospective employers when compared to the treatment given to younger job applicants. The difference in treatment could only be explained by the claimants' ages.

The burden of proof in age discrimination claims

Regulations 37 (Employment Tribunal claims) and 40 (Sheriff Court actions) address the question of the burden of proof in age discrimination cases.

The person bringing the action (the claimant or the pursuer) will win the claim for discrimination if s/he can prove facts from which the Tribunal or the Court is entitled to conclude that a discriminatory act has been committed and there is no adequate explanation from the employer (the respondent or the defender) to counter this allegation. The employer will, therefore, be obliged to bring evidence to prove that they did not, in fact, commit or be treated as having committed the discriminatory act in question.

This standard of proof clearly assists the employee in the sense that the employer will be forced to bring evidence to disprove the allegations of discriminatory behaviour.

Employees can also obtain evidence to assist their claims by serving a questionnaire which addresses certain issues to the employer (**Regulation 41**). These questionnaires can be used as evidence in any future legal proceedings which are contemplated by the employee.

If the employer refuses to complete the questionnaire or omits to answer certain questions contained in this document, Tribunals and Courts will be entitled to make interpret this unwillingness to cooperate with the employee's request for information in a negative way. In other words, the inference drawn by the Tribunal or the Court is that the employer did indeed commit a discriminatory act and has something to hide. Generally speaking, an employer has eight weeks in Tribunal proceedings and six months in sheriff Court actions to provide answers to the questions posed by the employer.

Samples of these questionnaires can be seen on the Introductory Scots Law website.

 Key point: An Employment Tribunal or the Sheriff Court will undertake a two-step enquiry as to whether a discriminatory act on the grounds of an employee's age was committed by the employer.

The legal framework of employment law

Many employment law cases, for example, dismissal, discrimination, working time disputes, paternity and maternity rights will be dealt with primarily by Employment Tribunals. There is, of course, a right of appeal from Employment Tribunals on a point of law to the Employment Appeal Tribunal with a possibility of further appeals to the Inner House of the Court of Session and, ultimately, the UK Supreme Court.

Employment law claims can also be brought before the civil courts in Scotland, for example, the Sheriff Court and the Court of Session. The institutions of employment law will, of course, be familiar from the descriptions contained in Chapter 1.

Summary

- The United Kingdom's discrimination legislation makes it unlawful to treat a person less favourably on the basis of gender, marital status, gender reassignment, pregnancy, colour, race, nationality, ethnic or national origin, sexual orientation and religion or belief and employment status (part-time workers and fixed-term employees).

- Someone will suffer discrimination when he or she is treated less favourably or experience some sort of detriment or harm which is related to one of their personal characteristics, for example, race or sexual orientation and this treatment cannot be objectively justified.

- Detriments can come in all shapes and sizes – lack of promotion and training opportunities, different pay scales and conditions of employment, unfairness in the recruitment process, dismissal from employment, failure to receive the same contractual benefits as fellow employees, harassment and victimisation, selecting certain individuals for redundancy first and refusal to allow more flexible working patterns.

- Sexual and racial discrimination are illegal in terms of the Sex Discrimination Act 1975 (as amended) and the Race Relations Act 1976 (as amended) respectively.

- The Sex Discrimination Act 1975 outlaws sexual discrimination in relation to terms of employment, training, education, the provision of goods and services and the disposal of premises with Section 6 applying specifically to employment.

- In sex discrimination claims, it will be for the employee to show the facts that prove less favourable treatment and if the employer is unable to come up with a satisfactory explanation which would disprove the complaint, the Tribunal must now decide in favour of the employee.

- The Race Relations Act 1976 outlaws racial discrimination in relation to terms of employment, trade union membership, education, the provision of goods and services, and in the disposal and management of housing and other premises with Section 4(2) applying specifically to employment.

- The amended Race Relations Act also imposes general duties on listed public authorities to promote racial equality. The general duty means that public authorities will have to eliminate unlawful discrimination and promote equality of opportunity and good race relations in carrying out their functions.

- The Equality and Human Rights Commission is a statutory body with wide powers of enforcement which has responsibility for ensuring that employers and other bodies implement their legal obligations under the various anti-discrimination laws now operating in the United Kingdom.

- The types of less favourable treatment which the Sex Discrimination Act and the Race Relations Act regard as unlawful are direct discrimination, indirect discrimination, harassment and victimisation.

- Direct discrimination occurs when a person experiences less favourable treatment by reason of their sex or race.

- Employers will have to be particularly careful that they do not apply general conditions, requirements or criteria in relation to employees which may actually be examples of indirect discrimination.

- Harassment on the grounds of sex or race will occur when a person is subjected to unwanted conduct which has the purpose or effect of violating his or her dignity or creates an intimidating, hostile, offensive or disturbing environment.

- It is important that those individuals who have been involved in discrimination claims either as a complainant or as a witness should be adequately protected against acts of victimisation by the employer during and after their employment.

- The Race Relations Act uses two definitions of indirect indiscrimination – a narrower one when the less favourable treatment involves colour and nationality and a broader one where a person experiences less favourable treatment on the grounds of racial, national or ethnic origin.

- Discrimination on the grounds of a person's sexual orientation is not covered by the Sex Discrimination Act, but the Employment Equality (Sexual Orientation) Regulations 2003 now make it unlawful to discriminate on these grounds.

- Discrimination on the grounds of a person's religion or beliefs is not generally covered by the Race Relations Act, but the Employment Equality (Religion or Belief) Regulations 2003 now make it unlawful to discriminate on these grounds.

- As a result of the Sex Discrimination (Gender Reassignment) Regulations 1999, transsexuals are protected against direct discrimination under Section 2A of the Sex Discrimination Act 1975.

- Genuine occupational qualifications or special occupational requirements allow an employer to discriminate against certain individuals on the grounds of sex or race.

- The Equal Pay Act 1970 can be used to combat inequalities in the terms and conditions of employment offered to men and women and not just pay as its title misleadingly suggests.

- European Union law has often been used to overcome the shortcomings of the United Kingdom's equal pay legislation.

- The Equal Pay Act ensures that each contract of employment contains an equality clause which means that it will be implied that men and women in the same employment should receive equal pay for equal work.

- Employers will be able to justify a difference in the terms and conditions of employment offered to men and women if this is due to a material difference and is not based on the grounds of a person's sex.

- A disability is a physical, sensory or mental impairment which has a substantial and long-term adverse effect on the ability of a person to carry out day-to-day activities.

- A disabled person will have been discriminated against if the reason for the less favourable treatment is related to his disability and a person to whom this reason does not apply would not have been treated less favourably.

- As a result of the Employment Equality (Age) Regulations 2006, workers who are treated less favourably by reason of their age will now be able to take a discrimination claim to an Employment Tribunal.

- Reasonable adjustments are measures or steps that an employer can take which should assist a disabled employee to carry out his job effectively.

- Less favourable treatment of a disabled employee can only be justified if, but only if, the reason for the less favourable treatment is material to the circumstances of the particular case and substantial.

- In disability discrimination claims where there is strong evidence of less favourable treatment, the Tribunal is entitled to infer discrimination in the absence of any reasonable explanation by the employer.

- As a result of the Part-Time Workers Regulations 2000, workers who are treated less favourably by reason of their part-time status will now be able to take a discrimination claim to an Employment Tribunal.

- Under the Fixed-Term Employees (Prevention of Less Favourable Treatment) Regulations 2002, a fixed-term term employee should not be treated less favourably than a comparable, permanent colleague.

Test your knowledge

1 What types of discrimination in employment does United Kingdom legislation prohibit?

2 In terms of the United Kingdom's equality legislation, list five ways in which an employee or a job applicant can experience discriminatory or less favourable treatment.

3 a) With reference to sex and race equality legislation, what is meant by the terms direct and indirect discrimination?

b) Examine the following advertisement carefully:

WANTED

BARMAN REQUIRED FOR BUSY CITY CENTRE BAR AND RESTAURANT.

THIS IS A FULL-TIME POSITION AND THE SUCCESSFUL APPLICANT WILL BE EXPECTED TO WORK 4–5 NIGHTS PER WEEK.

IDEALLY, THIS POSITION WOULD SUIT A SINGLE PERSON.

INTERESTED?

PHONE JASON ON 07967 43210 FOR FURTHER DETAILS.

Comment on the legality of the above advertisement.

c) McTavish Biscuits Ltd is currently recruiting production line workers for its factory in Dalry in Ayrshire. Dalry is a small village and is in a predominantly rural part of Ayrshire. McTavish has stated that the following criteria for prospective employees is highly desirable:
i) A high degree of fluency in spoken and written English
ii) Possession of educational qualifications from British schools and colleges
iii) Preference will be given to residents of Dalry and its surrounding area
McTavish is also insisting that every applicant selected for interview must sit and pass an aptitude test. McTavish has placed advertisements in attempt to recruit delivery drivers for its operation. Jutinder Singh, who is a Sikh, applied for a job and received an application form from the company. The form states that McTavish requires all male drivers to be clean shaven and have neat and tidy haircuts.

Do you think that McTavish acted properly in relation to its recruitment procedures?

4 a) In what situations will an employee be subjected to harassment in the workplace?

b) Sharon is a young graduate who is working as a trainee marketing executive. One day, Sharon logs on to her computer where she discovers that Tony, her manager, has sent pornographic images via the e-mail system. A colleague later informs Sharon that Tony has also been spreading stories about Sharon's sexual history. Tony had asked Sharon out on a date, but Sharon had politely, but very firmly turned him down. Sharon feels extremely angry and upset about Tony's offensive behaviour. Tony claims that he is merely indulging in a bit of harmless flirting and, if he had known that his behaviour would cause offence, he would never have sent the e-mails in the first place.

What are the consequences of Tony's behaviour?

5 a) When would less favourable treatment of employee by an employer be regarded as victimisation?

b) Shamaila has just left her old job. She saw a job advertised in the local paper and she has decided to apply for this post. The application form requires a reference from her former employer. Unfortunately, Shamaila had to leave her former job under something of a cloud. Shamaila had been forced to take a race discrimination claim to an Employment Tribunal against her former employer – which she won. To say that her former employer was not pleased about this outcome would be something of an understatement. Nevertheless, Shamaila decides to ask for a reference, but her former employer tells her that she must be joking to expect to be given a reference after the grief that she gave him by taking a claim to an Employment Tribunal. As a result of Shamaila failing to secure a reference, her application for new employment is rejected.

What can Shamaila do?

6 **a)** Until the introduction of the Employment Equality (Sexual Orientation) Regulations 2003, employees who were gay, lesbian or bisexual were not adequately protected by United Kingdom equality laws.

Discuss the accuracy of this statement.

b) Terry has been openly gay for many years. He has applied for a senior managerial position in the company for which he presently works. Terry was not given the job and a more junior colleague was appointed to the position in his place. Terry was considered to be the front-runner for the job and all the senior managers are shocked that he failed to secure the appointment. In the past, however, the Chief Executive of the company, who chaired the selection and interview panel, has made no secret of his intolerance of gay and lesbian people. The Chief Executive, who has strong religious views, is on the record as having said that he regards homosexuality as a grave moral disorder.

Advise Terry.

7 **a)** In terms of the Sex Discrimination Act 1975 and the Race Relations Act 1976, what is a genuine occupational qualification?
b) Examine the following situations carefully and decide whether the employer is entitled to claim that he is relying upon a genuine occupational qualification:

i) Joanne, a theatre director, is recruiting cast members for her latest play, a modern version of William Shakespeare's Romeo and Juliet. Joanne is refusing to consider male actors for the part of Juliet. Conrad, a struggling young actor who desperately wanted to play Juliet, is convinced that Joanne's decision not to audition male actors for this part is an example of less favourable treatment on the grounds of sex.

ii) Amanda applied for a job as a labourer on a building site. Kenny, the site manager, refused to employ her because he thought that Amanda would not be strong enough to carry some of the heavy lifting tasks involved in this type of work. Kenny feels that men are physically stronger than women and are, therefore, better suited for work on a building site.

iii) Rick and Debbie are trained counsellors. They have both applied for employment with Greenhill Men's Voluntary Association, an organisation, which amongst other things, provides counselling and support services, to men who have been the victims of serious sexual assaults. The Association also provides advice on matters relating to men's sexual health. Rick's application for employment with the Association is successful, but Debbie is not so fortunate. She feels that she has been discriminated against by the Association.

iv) Zura is from the former Soviet Republic Georgia and he has been resident in the United Kingdom for the last five years. The Georgian Cultural Society has just opened an office in Glasgow and it is looking to fill the post of development officer. The Society provides a range of cultural, support and welfare services to Georgians who are living in Scotland. Zura applied for this job and was accepted for the position after completing a successful interview. The successful applicant had to be fluent in the Georgian language and had to possess an in-depth knowledge of Georgian culture. Sandra, who had applied for the job but was not given an interview, feels that there was clear favouritism shown to certain candidates during the recruitment process for the job. Sandra has always been interested in Georgia and its people. She did complete a beginner's course in Georgian while she was at University back in 1989. The course was very basic and mainly dealt with everyday phrases that tourists would find useful when visiting Georgia.

v) Angus applied for a job as a chef in Mumbai Sunset, an Indian restaurant in Dundee. He was very surprised to be rejected for this job because he has extensive experience as a chef in relation to the preparation and cooking of Indian food. The restaurant owner, however, is keen to promote an authentic Indian experience for diners and he has decided to employ Rajiv, who is an ethnic Indian, in preference to Angus.

vi) The police service is currently running an advertising campaign in order to attract more recruits from ethnic minorities. As part of the campaign, black and Asian models will appear on posters which are to be displayed in public places such as train and bus stations. These posters will also appear in national and local newspapers. Fraser, who is white, applied to be a model in the poster campaign, but he was turned down by the advertising agency which is running the recruitment campaign on behalf of the police service.

8 In cases involving race discrimination, what is the difference between a genuine occupational requirement and a special occupational requirement?

9 **a)** The Equal Pay Act 1970 inserts an equality clause into every contract of employment.

What is an equality clause?

b) Give five examples of situations where an employer may breach the Equal Pay Act 1970.

c) With reference to the Equal Pay Act 1970, explain the following terms:
  i) Like work
  ii) Work rated equivalent
  iii) Work of equal value

d) Five female primary head teachers, supported by their trade union, decided to lodge a claim with the Office of Employment Tribunals alleging discrimination on the grounds of sex. These individuals are claiming that the local council pays them less for doing the same job as two male head teachers of local secondary schools. A major part of the council's defence to this Employment Tribunal claim is that the two secondary head teachers have far greater responsibilities than their female colleagues and this is why they are paid a higher salary.

Does the council have much chance of success in putting forward this particular defence?

10 In sex, equal pay and race claims, an employee who suspects that he or she is the victim of discriminatory treatment is permitted to serve an equality questionnaire on his or her employer.

Will an employee's case before an Employment Tribunal be helped in any way by serving an equality questionnaire on the employer?

11 **a)** How does the Disability Discrimination Act 1995 define less favourable treatment of disabled person?

b) In terms of the Disability Discrimination Act 1995, an employee could experience discrimination where the employer either refuses or fails to make reasonable adjustments.

What are reasonable adjustments and list five of them?

c) Matthew is registered blind and he has a guide dog to make his life much easier. Without his guide dog, Matthew would lose much of his independence and he would lack the confidence to leave his home. One day when Matthew was in the local shopping mall, he was refused entry to a particular store on the grounds that the management had banned pets. Matthew tried to explain to the store's security guards that his dog was not a pet. The security guards were completely unimpressed and continued to refuse Matthew entry to the store. Matthew was completely humiliated by his experience because it occurred on a Saturday afternoon when the shopping mall is at its busiest.

In terms of the Disability Discrimination Act 1995, what action can Matthew take against the store?

d) Simon is a technician who is employed at a local school. Simon suffers from schizophrenia, but for some time, he has been refusing to take his medication. Without the help of drugs to control his condition, Simon can become extremely violent and he is a serious threat to those around him. His employers have tried everything possible to encourage Simon to take his medication, but without success. Simon's job brings him into daily contact with staff and pupils at the school and there have already been complaints about some of his outbursts which are becoming much more frequent. Simon's employers decide that they have no alternative but to dismiss him.

Are Simon's employers justified in dismissing him?

12 Kathy has just returned to work on a part-time basis after her maternity leave. Kathy's employer had informed her that the only way that her request to work part-time could be accommodated if she agrees to accept a lower salary grade. Kathy is in a dilemma because she wants work part-time in order to spend more time with her new baby.

Advise Kathy.

13 Angela is employed in a temporary capacity. Recently, Angela was absent from her work for a week due to ill health. Her employer has informed Angela that, under the terms of her contract, she is not entitled to receive sick pay. Angela thinks that this unfair because all her permanent colleagues are contractually entitled to sick pay.

Do you think that Angela has been unfairly treated by her employer?

14 **a)** The introduction of the Employment Equality (Religion or Belief) Regulations 2003 now means that it will be unlawful for an employer to treat an individual less favourably as a result of that person's religion or beliefs.

Is this statement entirely accurate?

b) Heather, who is an atheist, applied for the post of Head Teacher of a Roman Catholic Secondary School. She was not even given an interview for the post despite the fact that she is currently employed as a Depute Head

Teacher at a non-denominational school within the same local authority area. Heather feels that she has been unfairly treated. The local authority has stated that the Head Teacher of a Roman Catholic school must be a practising member of the Roman Catholic Church.

Do you agree with the local authority's point of view?

15 **a)** In order to win a claim for discrimination at an Employment Tribunal Hearing, a Claimant must satisfy the necessary burden of proof. What is the necessary burden of proof in discrimination claims?

    i) A sex discrimination claim
    ii) A race discrimination claim
    iii) An equal pay claim
    iv) A disability discrimination claim
    v) A part-time worker discrimination claim
    vi) A fixed-term employee discrimination claim
    vii) A discrimination claim involving sexual orientation
    viii) A discrimination claim involving religion or belief.
    ix) A claim for discrimination on the grounds of a person's age

b) In each of the above discrimination claims, what are the relevant time-limits that an Applicant must observe in order to lodge a claim effectively with the Office of Employment Tribunals?

16 **a)** The laws of the United Kingdom offer absolutely no legal protection to people who suffer less favourable treatment or discrimination on the grounds of age.

Discuss the accuracy of this statement.

b) What are the legal consequences of the following situations:

    i) George, a 48 year old man applied for a job as a sales manager. His application was rejected despite having over fifteen years of relevant employment experience. The advertisement for the job stated that the employer was looking for an applicant with 'youthful enthusiasm'. The employer eventually decided to hire a younger applicant (aged 28) who was not as experienced as George.

    ii) Munro was employed as an IT technician by Townhead Council. He was paid a lower wage than a colleague who was nearly two years older than him. Both employees had originally begun their apprenticeships with the Council at the same time, the difference being that Munro was 16 and his colleague was 18. The Council calculated that Munro's colleague had accrued 27 months service since beginning work whereas he had accrued 6.5 months only after reaching the age of 18. Munro's service with the Council while he was under the age of 18 was completely discounted.

    iii) Carla is 64 years' old and she wishes to remain in employment beyond her 65th birthday. She believes that the employer's compulsory retirement age of 65 may be illegal.

Advise the above parties.

TABLE OF CASES

C

D

I

N

O

P

Table of Cases

TABLE OF STATUTES

Table of Statutes

International Treaties

Table of Statutes

ACKNOWLEDGEMENTS

This book would not have been completed without the support and assistance of a number of individuals.

A great debt of gratitude is owed to the members of the Law Cognate Group at Central College, Glasgow, in particular, George Cran, Jennifer Deegan, Jason Graham, Maureen Hastings, John McInarlin, Steven Murray (Course Leader), Kiran Patwal, Veronika Prag, Valerie Robertson and Ana Tuper – all of whom made helpful suggestions and alerted us to ongoing developments in Scots law. We would also like to thank Margaret Darroch and Munro McCannell, Head and Depute Head respectively of the School of Law and Social Sciences at Central College who have been particularly enthusiastic about this project and have supported it in numerous ways.

We would like to thank Dr Laurence Sullivan who provided assistance and information on the workings of devolved government in Scotland.

Katherine Bennett of Hodder Gibson deserves special praise for editing the text and carrying out her duties so professionally, patiently and conscientiously.

We would also like to thank the team at Hodder Gibson – John Mitchell, Jim Donnelly, Ian Maclean and Elizabeth Hayes for the wonderful support that they have given over the years to this project.

Finally, it should go without saying that any errors contained in this book are our responsibility alone.

Seán J Crossan and Alistair B Wylie

INDEX

Page numbers in *italics* refer to summaries.